The World *of* Psychology

The World *of* Psychology

Fifth Edition

Samuel E. Wood

Ellen Green Wood

Denise Boyd *Houston Community College System*

Boston | New York | San Francisco
Mexico City | Montreal | Toronto | London | Madrid | Munich | Paris
Hong Kong | Singapore | Tokyo | Cape Town | Sydney

Series Editor: Kelly May
Series Editorial Assistant: Adam Whitehurst
Development Editor: Sharon Geary
Executive Marketing Manager: Pamela Laskey
Production Supervisor: Michael Granger
Editorial Production Service: Lifland et al., Bookmakers
Composition Buyer: Linda Cox
Manufacturing Buyer: Megan Cochran
Cover Administrator: Linda Knowles
Electronic Composition: Monotype Composition Company, Inc.
Photo Research: Sarah Evertson, Image Quest
Text Design: Carol Somberg

For related titles and support materials, visit our online catalog at
www.ablongman.com

Library of Congress Cataloging-in-Publication Data

Wood, Samuel E.
The world of psychology / Samuel E. Wood, Ellen Green Wood, Denise Boyd.—5th ed.
p. cm.
Includes bibliographical references and index.
ISBN 0-205-36137-4
(Paperback 0-205-43932-2)
1. Psychology—Textbooks. I. Wood, Ellen R. Green. II. Boyd, Denise Roberts. III. Title.

BF121.W657 2004
15—dc20

2003070867

Printed in the United States of America

10 9 8 7 6 5 4 3 2 VHP 08 07 06 05 04

Sam and Evie dedicate this book with love to their grandchildren: Brittany, Danielle, Ashley, Hayley, Jesse, and Sarah.

Denise dedicates this book to the hundreds of introductory psychology students she has taught over the past 15 years. Their questions, comments, and concerns were the driving force behind her contributions to *The World of Psychology*.

Brief Contents

Contents

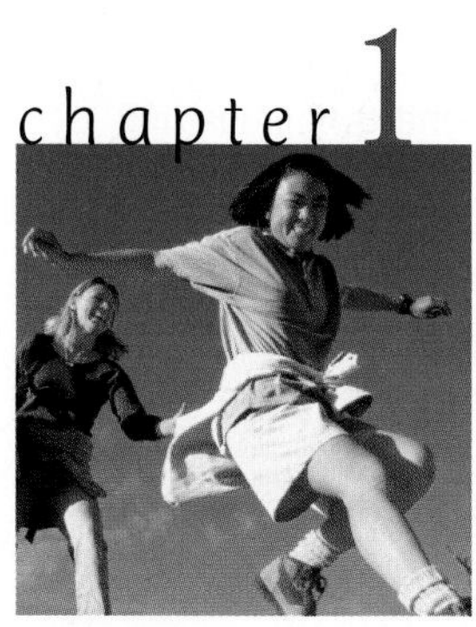

chapter 1

page 2

Introduction to Psychology

chapter 2

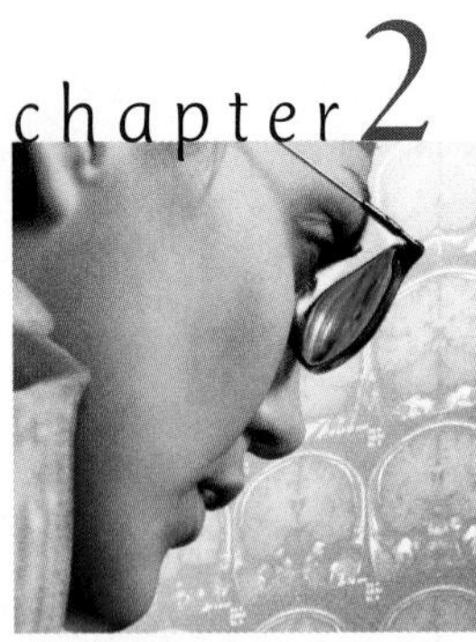

page 38

Biology and Behavior

chapter 3

page 78

Sensation and Perception

chapter 4

page 118

States of Consciousness

chapter 5

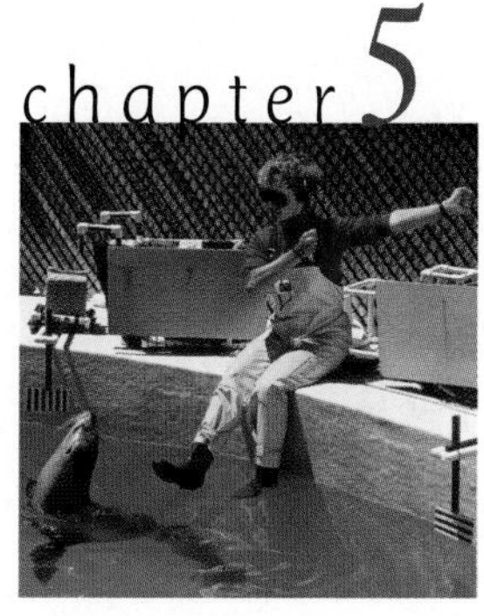

page 156

Learning

chapter 6

page 194

Memory

chapter 7

page 230

Cognition and Language

chapter 8

page 260

Intelligence and Creativity

chapter 9

page 298

Child Development

chapter 10

page 338

Adolescence and Adulthood

chapter 11

page 372

Motivation and Emotion

chapter 12

page 408

Human Sexuality and Gender

chapter 13

page 440

Health and Stress

chapter 14

page 468

Personality Theory and Assessment

chapter 15

page 502

Psychological Disorders

chapter 16

page 534

Therapies

chapter 17

page 560

Social Psychology

chapter 18

page 592

Psychology in the Workplace

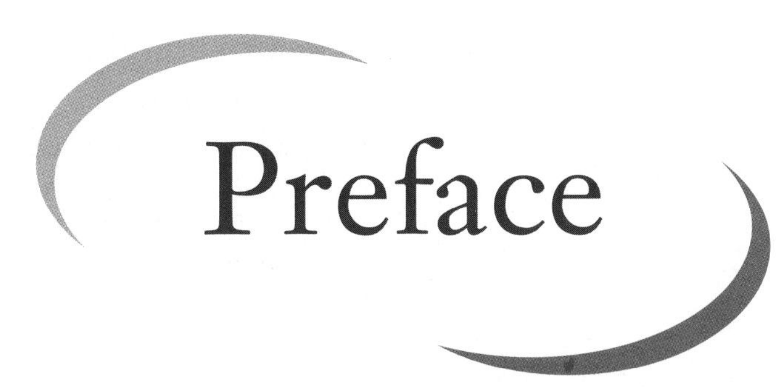

Preface

How This Textbook Can Help You Study

A Dedicated Focus on Learning and Application

The World of Psychology has a dedicated focus on learning and application. Like previous editions, the Fifth Edition provides superior pedagogical support while making the connection between the scientific principles of psychology and the everyday lives of today's diverse student audience. *The World of Psychology* introduces the field of psychology in an appealing way whether you are an accomplished student or a student developing your skills. For this new edition, the authors have re-examined all of the pedagogical features to ensure that this textbook continues to be the best learning tool for all students in introductory psychology.

Joining the Author Team: Denise Boyd, Ed.D.

Denise Boyd of the Houston Community College system joins Samuel Wood and Ellen Green Wood to author *The World of Psychology*. Dr. Boyd has taught introductory psychology courses at Houston Community College–Central for 17 years. Teaching in a community college system with a diverse student body has given Dr. Boyd extensive experience in working with students of different ages and from varied economic, educational, and cultural backgrounds. Along with her substantial teaching experience, Dr. Boyd brings to the author team an expertise in learning and development, which enhances an already student-friendly text. In addition, Dr. Boyd is the co-author (with Samuel E. Wood and Ellen Green Wood) of *Mastering the World of Psychology* (2004, Allyn and Bacon) and (with Helen Bee) of *Lifespan Development*, Third Edition (2002, Allyn and Bacon) and *The Developing Child*, Tenth Edition (2004, Allyn and Bacon).

Meeting the Needs of a Changing and Diverse Student Population

As today's college students, you and your peers are vastly different from the students who filled classrooms just a few years ago. Indeed, students are now more diverse, more mobile, and more technologically astute than ever before. This edition of *The World of Psychology* continues to evolve to meet the changing needs of all students. Extensive updates and new additions to content, research, pedagogy, and design combine with the accessible and engaging presentation for which the text is well known to make the study of psychology an enjoyable and meaningful experience for you.

Currency and Research

In this edition as in every other, the authors remain dedicated to citing current research and writing the most up-to-date text possible, while promoting an understanding of the foundation of psychology. To accomplish the goal of introducing the world of psychology accurately and clearly, the authors have gone back to original sources and have reread the basic works of the major figures in psychology and the classic studies in the field.

The authors have also ensured that all presentations are reflective of current thinking about the science of psychology. In all fields, the way people look at, examine, and conduct research in the subject area changes over time. This text reflects the most current approaches in the field of psychology. Also, expert reviewers examined all chapters for timeliness in approach and language. For example, Chapter 3, "Sensation and Perception," has been completely rewritten to reflect new approaches to everything from olfaction and Alzheimer's disease to attentional blindness. Chapter 4, "States of Consciousness," has also been completely rewritten to reflect new approaches to and research in circadian rhythms and neurological disorders, proactive properties of herbal supplements, and more.

Our Commitment to Learning

The Fifth Edition reflects the authors' continued commitment to learning. Based on instructor and student feedback, the authors re-examined and streamlined the pedagogical features and organization of each chapter to provide the best possible opportunities for learning.

The text's commitment to learning begins with the learning method called SQ3R. Made up of five steps—Survey, Question, Read, Recite, and Review—this method serves as the foundation for your success. Introduced in Chapter 1, the SQ3R method is integrated throughout the text to help you make the connection between psychology and life, while promoting a more efficient way to approach reading, studying, and test taking.

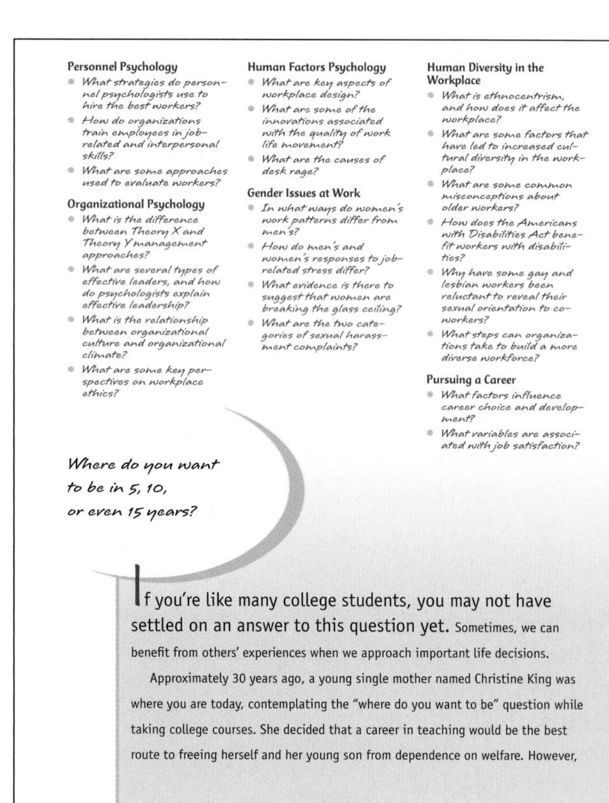

Personnel Psychology
- *What strategies do personnel psychologists use to hire the best workers?*
- *How do organizations train employees in job-related and interpersonal skills?*
- *What are some approaches used to evaluate workers?*

Organizational Psychology
- *What is the difference between Theory X and Theory Y management approaches?*
- *What are several types of effective leaders, and how do psychologists explain effective leadership?*
- *What is the relationship between organizational culture and organizational climate?*
- *What are some key perspectives on workplace ethics?*

Human Factors Psychology
- *What are key aspects of workplace design?*
- *What are some of the innovations associated with the quality of work life movement?*
- *What are the causes of desk rage?*

Gender Issues at Work
- *In what ways do women's work patterns differ from men's?*
- *How do men's and women's responses to job-related stress differ?*
- *What evidence is there to suggest that women are breaking the glass ceiling?*
- *What are the two categories of sexual harassment complaints?*

Human Diversity in the Workplace
- *What is ethnocentrism, and how does it affect the workplace?*
- *What are some factors that have led to increased cultural diversity in the workplace?*
- *What are some common misconceptions about older workers?*
- *How does the Americans with Disabilities Act benefit workers with disabilities?*
- *Why have some gay and lesbian workers been reluctant to reveal their sexual orientation to coworkers?*
- *What steps can organizations take to build a more diverse workforce?*

Pursuing a Career
- *What factors influence career choice and development?*
- *What variables are associated with job satisfaction?*

Where do you want to be in 5, 10, or even 15 years?

If you're like many college students, you may not have settled on an answer to this question yet. Sometimes, we can benefit from others' experiences when we approach important life decisions.

Approximately 30 years ago, a young single mother named Christine King was where you are today, contemplating the "where do you want to be" question while taking college courses. She decided that a career in teaching would be the best route to freeing herself and her young son from dependence on welfare. However,

Among the key learning features that promote use of the SQ3R method are the following:

Chapter-Opening Questions New to this edition, each chapter opens with a thought-provoking question that challenges you to think about the concept behind the opening vignette. This question attempts to draw the reader into the material in a more personal, inviting manner. These questions include:

- Have you ever wished there were 25 hours in a day? (Chapter 1, "Introduction to Psychology")
- How accurate is your memory? (Chapter 6, "Memory")
- How would you react to the news that you had a life-threatening disease? (Chapter 13, "Health and Stress")
- How much did your parents influence your personality? (Chapter 14, "Personality Theory and Assessment")
- Are there any circumstances under which you could be persuaded to deliberately harm another person? (Chapter 17, "Social Psychology")

Chapter-Opening Vignettes These stories, based on real-life events and people, offer an accessible and interesting introduction to the chapter material. Topics include the following:

- Student time management (Chapter 1, "Introduction to Psychology")
- Hypnosis—from Ben Franklin to *The Manchurian Candidate* (Chapter 4, "States of Consciousness")
- Controlling the movement of artificial limbs by brain activity (Chapter 7, "Cognition and Language")
- Lost Boys of the Sudan (Chapter 9, "Child Development")
- One path to career success: Christine King, CEO of AMI Semiconductor (Chapter 18, "Psychology in the Workplace")

Margin Learning Questions Margin learning questions challenge you to test your comprehension of the chapter coverage and help you identify key concepts. These questions have been completely revised to provide an opportunity for you to think more critically about your answers. Some examples of margin learning questions are

- How is biological psychology changing the field of psychology? (Chapter 1, "Introduction to Psychology")
- What patterns of inheritance are evident in the transmission of genetic traits? (Chapter 2, "Biology and Behavior")
- How does attending college affect adult development? (Chapter 10, "Adolescence and Adulthood")
- How do display rules for emotions differ across cultures? (Chapter 11, "Motivation and Emotion")
- What are some factors that have led to increased cultural diversity in the workplace? (Chapter 18, "Psychology in the Workplace")

Remember Its Appearing after all major text sections, these quick reviews reinforce comprehension by testing you on the section content. For the Fifth Edition, these questions have been rewritten to sharpen their focus on core concepts.

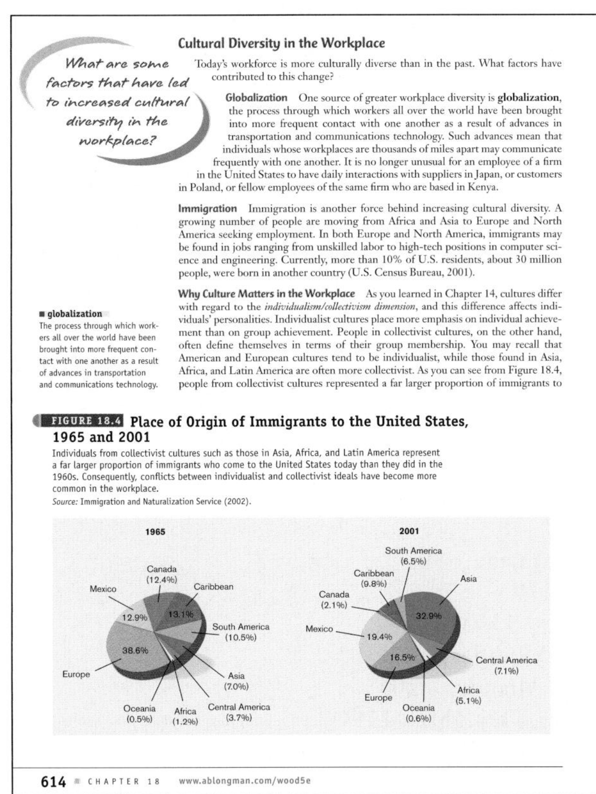

Cultural Diversity in the Workplace

What are some factors that have led to increased cultural diversity in the workplace?

Today's workforce is more culturally diverse than in the past. What factors have contributed to this change?

Globalization One source of greater workplace diversity is **globalization**, the process through which workers all over the world have been brought into more frequent contact with one another as a result of advances in transportation and communications technology. Such advances mean that individuals whose workplaces are thousands of miles apart may communicate frequently with one another. It is no longer unusual for an employee of a firm in the United States to have daily interactions with suppliers in Japan, or customers in Poland, or fellow employees of the same firm who are based in Kenya.

Immigration Immigration is another force behind increasing cultural diversity. A growing number of people are moving from Africa and Asia to Europe and North America seeking employment. In both Europe and North America, immigrants may be found in jobs ranging from unskilled labor to high-tech positions in computer science and engineering. Currently, more than 10% of U.S. residents, about 30 million people, were born in another country (U.S. Census Bureau, 2001).

Why Culture Matters in the Workplace As you learned in Chapter 14, cultures differ with regard to the *individualism/collectivism dimension*, and this difference affects individuals' personalities. Individualist cultures place more emphasis on individual achievement than on group achievement. People in collectivist cultures, on the other hand, often define themselves in terms of their group membership. You may recall that American and European cultures tend to be individualist, while those found in Asia, Africa, and Latin America are often more collectivist. As you can see from Figure 18.4, people from collectivist cultures represented a far larger proportion of immigrants to

globalization The process through which workers all over the world have been brought into more frequent contact with one another as a result of advances in transportation and communications technology.

FIGURE 18.4 Place of Origin of Immigrants to the United States, 1965 and 2001

Individuals from collectivist cultures such as those in Asia, Africa, and Latin America represent a far larger proportion of immigrants who come to the United States today than they did in the 1960s. Consequently, conflicts between individualist and collectivist ideals have become more common in the workplace.

Source: Immigration and Naturalization Service (2002).

614 ■ CHAPTER 18 www.ablongman.com/wood5e

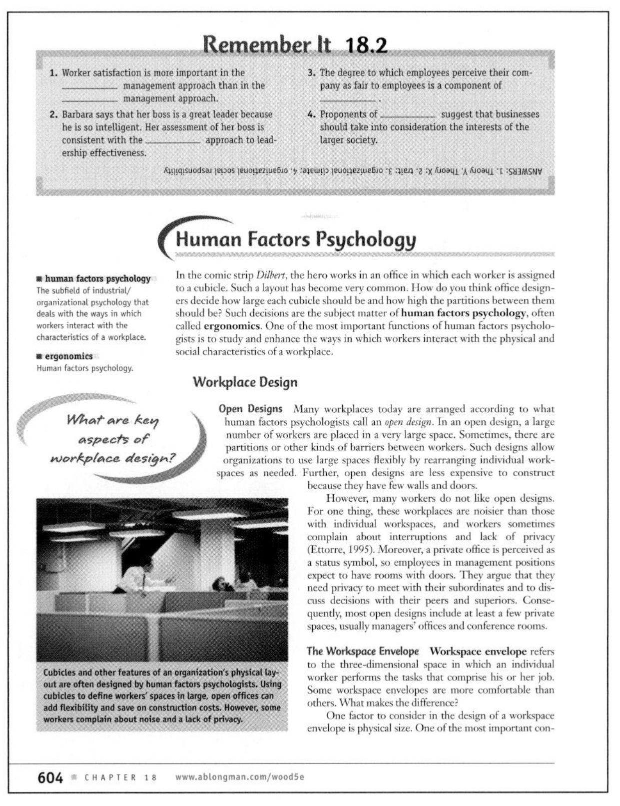

Remember It 18.2

1. Worker satisfaction is more important in the ________ management approach than in the ________ management approach.
2. Barbara says that her boss is a great leader because he is so intelligent. Her assessment of her boss is consistent with the ________ approach to leadership effectiveness.
3. The degree to which employees perceive their company as fair to employees is a component of ________ .
4. Proponents of ________ suggest that businesses should take into consideration the interests of the larger society.

ANSWERS: 1. Theory Y, Theory X; 2. trait; 3. organizational climate; 4. organizational social responsibility

Human Factors Psychology

In the comic strip *Dilbert*, the hero works in an office in which each worker is assigned to a cubicle. Such a layout has become very common. How do you think office designers decide how large each cubicle should be and how high the partitions between them should be? Such decisions are the subject matter of **human factors psychology**, often called **ergonomics**. One of the most important functions of human factors psychologists is to study and enhance the ways in which workers interact with the physical and social characteristics of a workplace.

human factors psychology The subfield of industrial/organizational psychology that deals with the ways in which workers interact with the characteristics of a workplace.

ergonomics Human factors psychology.

Workplace Design

What are key aspects of workplace design?

Open Designs Many workplaces today are arranged according to what human factors psychologists call an *open design*. In an open design, a large number of workers are placed in a very large space. Sometimes, there are partitions or other kinds of barriers between workers. Such designs allow organizations to use large spaces flexibly by rearranging individual workspaces as needed. Further, open designs are less expensive to construct because they have few walls and doors.

However, many workers do not like open designs. For one thing, these workplaces are noisier than those with individual workspaces, and workers sometimes complain about interruptions and lack of privacy (Ettorre, 1995). Moreover, a private office is perceived as a status symbol, so employees in management positions expect to have rooms with doors. They argue that they need privacy to meet with their subordinates and to discuss decisions with their peers and superiors. Consequently, most open designs include at least a few private spaces, usually managers' offices and conference rooms.

Cubicles and other features of an organization's physical layout are often designed by human factors psychologists. Using cubicles to define workers' spaces in large, open offices can add flexibility and save on construction costs. However, some workers complain about noise and a lack of privacy.

The Workspace Envelope **Workspace envelope** refers to the three-dimensional space in which an individual worker performs the tasks that comprise his or her job. Some workspace envelopes are more comfortable than others. What makes the difference?

One factor to consider in the design of a workspace envelope is physical size. One of the most important con-

604 ■ CHAPTER 18 www.ablongman.com/wood5e

Review and Reflect Tables These comprehensive summary tables help consolidate major concepts, their components, and their relationships to one another. The tables offer information in a visual form that provides a unique study tool.

Summary and Review Sections Organized around the margin learning questions, each end-of-chapter summary provides a comprehensive study tool as well as a quick reference to the chapter's key terms, listed alphabetically.

REVIEW *and* REFLECT 18.1

Three Types of Leaders

TYPE	CHARACTERISTIC
Charismatic	Lead by sheer force of personality
Transactional	Motivate followers to accomplish agreed-on goals
Transformational	Encourage followers to go beyond the status quo

Want to be sure you've fully absorbed the material in this chapter? Visit **www.ablongman.com/wood5e** for access to free practice tests, flashcards, interactive activities, and links developed specifically to help you succeed in psychology.

group or organization is best served by encouraging individual expression and personal growth. Business leaders exhibit individual consideration when they devise compensation schemes that allow all employees to share in a company's profits, based on their individual efforts.

Review and Reflect 18.1 summarizes the three types of leaders we've discussed.

Explaining Differences in Leaders' Effectiveness What makes leaders effective? One possible explanation, the **trait approach**, is that leaders possess intrinsic characteristics that help them influence others. In other words, the trait approach holds that some people are natural-born leaders. Cross-cultural studies showing that leaders in different societies demonstrate similar characteristics, such as problem-solving ability, support this view (Robie et al., 2001).

A different view of leadership is proposed by the **situational approach**. From this perspective, the effectiveness of a leader depends on the match between the leader's characteristics and the situations in which she or he is called upon to lead. For example, leadership researchers believe that the way in which U.S. President Franklin D. Roosevelt responded to the historical challenges that arose during his terms of office (the Great Depression and World War II) continue to shape positive perceptions of his leadership abilities. Similarly, prior to the terrorist attacks of September 11, 2001, many observers were critical of President George W. Bush's bluntness and rather direct way of expressing ideas. However, after the attacks, even his harshest critics acknowledged that these characteristics were assets that helped him build political support for changes in a variety of government policies.

But can leadership be taught? The **behavioral approach** to explaining leadership effectiveness holds that it can be taught and is, in fact, the result of specific behaviors exhibited by leaders. Many researchers classify leadership behaviors under two broad categories: consideration and initiating structure. *Consideration* includes behaviors that communicate the leader's interest in followers as individuals. By contrast, *initiating structure* encompasses behaviors that focus on a task and the means employed to accomplish it. To be most effective, a leader must know when and how to demonstrate both kinds of behaviors (Schermerhorn et al., 2000).

Effective leadership behaviors can be acquired through formal training (Tjosvold et al., 2003). However, some studies show that personality traits determine how well leaders do at learning both consideration and

■ trait approach A perspective on leadership that holds that leaders possess intrinsic characteristics that help them influence others.

■ situational approach A perspective that explains the effectiveness of leadership as depending on the match between a leader's characteristics and the situations in which she or he is called upon to lead.

■ behavioral approach A perspective that holds that leadership effectiveness can be taught and is the result of specific behaviors exhibited by leaders.

The situational approach to explaining differences in leadership claims that circumstances shape leaders' behavior and the perceptions their followers have of them. For example, even many of President George W. Bush's critics noted that he exhibited effective leadership behaviors after the terrorist attacks of September 11, 2001.

PSYCHOLOGY IN THE WORKPLACE ■ 601

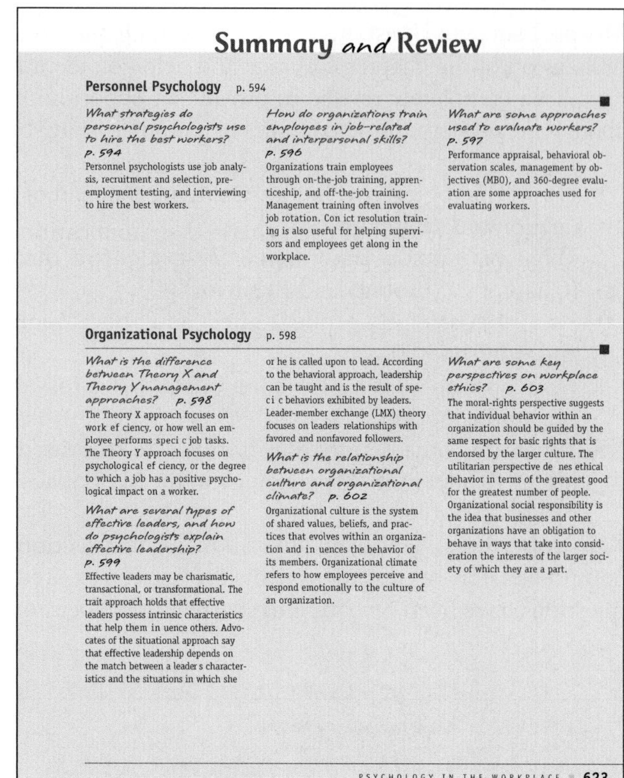
Summary *and* Review

Personnel Psychology p. 594

What strategies do personnel psychologists use to hire the best workers? p. 594
Personnel psychologists use job analysis, recruitment and selection, preemployment testing, and interviewing to hire the best workers.

How do organizations train employees in job-related and interpersonal skills? p. 596
Organizations train employees through on-the-job training, apprenticeship, and off-the-job training. Management training often involves job rotation. Con ict resolution training is also useful for helping supervisors and employees get along in the workplace.

What are some approaches used to evaluate workers? p. 597
Performance appraisal, behavioral observation scales, management by objectives (MBO), and 360-degree evaluation are some approaches used for evaluating workers.

Organizational Psychology p. 598

What is the difference between Theory X and Theory Y management approaches? p. 598
The Theory X approach focuses on work ef ciency, or how well an employee performs speci c job tasks. The Theory Y approach focuses on psychological ef ciency, or the degree to which a job has a positive psychological impact on a worker.

What are several types of effective leaders, and how do psychologists explain effective leadership? p. 599
Effective leaders may be charismatic, transactional, or transformational. The trait approach holds that effective leaders possess intrinsic characteristics that help them in uence others. Advocates of the situational approach say that effective leadership depends on the match between a leader s characteristics and the situations in which she or he is called upon to lead. According to the behavioral approach, leadership can be taught and is the result of speci c behaviors exhibited by leaders. Leader-member exchange (LMX) theory focuses on leaders relationships with favored and nonfavored followers.

What is the relationship between organizational culture and organizational climate? p. 602
Organizational culture is the system of shared values, beliefs, and practices that evolves within an organization and in uences the behavior of its members. Organizational climate refers to how employees perceive and respond emotionally to the culture of an organization.

What are some key perspectives on workplace ethics? p. 603
The moral-rights perspective suggests that individual behavior within an organization should be guided by the same respect for basic rights that is endorsed by the larger culture. The utilitarian perspective de nes ethical behavior in terms of the greatest good for the greatest number of people. Organizational social responsibility is the idea that businesses and other organizations have an obligation to behave in ways that take into consideration the interests of the larger society of which they are a part.

PSYCHOLOGY IN THE WORKPLACE ■ 623

Learning through Application

The authors recognize that your success lies not only in a strong learning pedagogy but in the ability to relate key psychological principles to your life and career choices. The Fifth Edition provides a variety of opportunities for you to make hands-on use of your studies.

Try Its This popular feature provides brief applied experiments, self-assessments, and hands-on activities, which help personalize psychology, making it simple for you to actively relate psychological principles to everyday life. The following Try Its appear in the text:

Apply Its At the end of each chapter, an application box combines scientific research with practical advice to show you how to handle difficult or challenging situations that may occur in your personal, academic, or professional life. These boxes cover the following topics:

New Chapter 18! Psychology in the Workplace

The Fifth Edition includes a new comprehensive chapter on psychology in the workplace (Chapter 18). This chapter balances theory and practical application to meet the needs of both students and instructors and to address the changing needs of both traditional and nontraditional students, who have become more career-driven, who often have work experience, and who want to better understand the dynamics of today's competitive work environment. Topics covered include personnel psychology, organizational psychology, human factors psychology, gender issues at work, and human diversity in the workplace.

Try It 18.1 Resolving Conflicts

How might a manager or supervisor implement the suggested conflict resolution strategy for each situation?

1. *Avoidance:* Two workers in a manufacturing facility disagree about where a trash can should be placed.
2. *Accommodation:* A new employee irritates co-workers by criticizing their actions and routines with the comment, "That's not the way we did it where I worked before."
3. *Compromise:* Cashiers in a busy retail store can't agree on which one of them should get to go on break first.
4. *Authoritative command:* An office employee is distressed because he is often asked to cover for a co-worker who is habitually tardy.
5. *Collaboration:* Teachers disagree about how to discipline disruptive students.

Evaluating Workers

What are some approaches used to evaluate workers?

Most organizations use a formal process to determine how well each employee is functioning in his or her job. This process is known as **performance appraisal.** In some cases, identifying an appropriate evaluation strategy is fairly straightforward. For example, an individual who is hired to sew shirts might be expected to produce a given number of shirts each day. If he produces fewer, he is judged as performing below expectations. If his production rate exceeds the target, he is judged as performing above expectations.

However, most jobs include performance expectations that are far less tangible than the number of shirts produced per day. To ensure that employee evaluations are as objective as possible, many organizations use **behavioral observation scales.** These instruments require respondents—the employee, co-workers, and/or the supervisor—to rate an employee's performance on observable behaviors. For instance, a supervisor might rate an employee on participation in meetings, which might be broken down into the behaviors of regular attendance and constructive responses.

Another approach to evaluation is known as **management by objectives (MBO).** With this strategy, subordinates and supervisors set performance goals together. In addition, they agree on how goal attainment will be measured and how much time will be allowed to reach each goal. Periodically, progress toward the goals is assessed. Employees' raises, bonuses, and promotions are often tied to this progress.

A relatively new evaluation strategy is **360-degree evaluation,** which combines worker performance ratings from supervisors, co-workers, subordinates, customers, and the workers themselves. Many people regard this approach as fairer and more meaningful than evaluations conducted exclusively by supervisors. However, research suggests that 360-degree evaluations have limited reliability and validity (Brett & Atwater, 2001; Hoffman et al., 2001; LeBreton et al., 2003). These limitations are largely due to discrepancies among ratings from various sources (Valle & Bozeman, 2002); self-ratings and supervisor ratings, for example, often vary considerably.

Who do you think is a better evaluator of a worker's performance—the worker or the supervisor? In one study that addressed this question, researchers collected job performance ratings from workers and from their supervisors, co-workers in similar positions, and subordinates (Atkins & Wood, 2002). These ratings were used to predict how well the workers would perform in a work-simulation test. They found that the most accurate predictions came from supervisors and subordinates. Workers tended to overestimate their own abilities and those of their co-workers. In fact, some of the poorest performers on the work-simulation test received the highest self- and peer-rating scores.

■ **performance appraisal** A formal process used to determine how well an employee is functioning in his or her job.

■ **behavioral observation scales** Instruments for employee evaluation that require respondents to rate an employee's performance on observable behaviors.

■ **management by objectives (MBO)** An evaluation approach in which subordinates and supervisors set performance goals together and agree on how goal attainment will be measured and how much time will be allotted to reach each goal.

■ **360-degree evaluation** An evaluation strategy that combines worker performance ratings from supervisors, peers, subordinates, customers, and the workers themselves.

PSYCHOLOGY IN THE WORKPLACE ■ 597

Apply It

Tips for Successful Interviewing

Do your skills and background look great on paper, but your job interviews usually go badly? Following several steps can help improve your chances of landing that elusive job.

Impression Management

Think of the interview as an opportunity to make a particular impression on a potential employer. Psychologists use the term *impression management* to refer to the process of deliberately controlling your behavior in ways that will create the impression you desire. For instance, dressing appropriately and using polite language are components of impression management. Researchers have found that interviewees who display these kinds of impression management behaviors are viewed more positively by interviewers (Bolino & Turnley, 2003). However, you should refrain from using strategies such as exaggerating your qualifications or experience. Experienced interviewers are skilled at recognizing such exaggerations and tend to look unfavorably upon interviewees who use them (Paulhus et al., 2003).

Educate Yourself

One of the most often overlooked keys to successful interviewing is learning about the job you're applying for. You should learn as much as you can about the business or industry you want to work in and about the particular firm to which you are applying. Many major corporations and organizations host Web sites that provide extensive information on their history, mission statement, products, employees, and job listings. These sites can be a great place to start researching potential employers. Study the job qualifications, both required and preferred, if they're available, and get a good idea of how your qualifications match up.

Prepare an Effective Resume

Even if the job you're applying for doesn't require a resume, it's a good idea to prepare one and take it—along with some extra copies—with you to the interview. For one thing, preparing a resume will provide an opportunity for you to rehearse your knowledge about your work history, job skills, and other qualifications. As a result, you'll be able to retrieve the information from your memory more rapidly when the interviewer questions you. A good resume is a quick source of information for the interviewer, who needs to know about your entire work history to create questions based on it. This preparation will leave more time for you to discuss more substantive issues with the interviewer. Most colleges and universities have career centers that provide advice on resume preparation and related services.

Practice

Practice answering interview questions with a friend. Many college career centers have lists of frequently asked interview questions, and you should always create your own list of questions that you think the interviewer might ask. Try to avoid saying negative things about yourself, even when answering such questions as "What are your strengths and weaknesses?" Remember, too, that consistent eye contact will show the interviewer that you have confidence.

Dress Professionally

When you are interviewing for a job, your clothing, visible adornments on your body (e.g., tattoos, jewelry), how well-groomed you are, and even the way you smell can be forms of artifactual communication (discussed earlier in this chapter). Thus, details are important. Male interviewees should consider the research finding that

both male and female interviewers respond more positively to clean-shaven applicants (de Souza et al., 2003).

Ideally, your appearance should communicate to the interviewer that you understand the environment in which you hope to be working. For example, if you are interviewing for a position as a construction worker, jeans and a t-shirt, along with a pair of sturdy shoes, are appropriate. When interviewing for an office job, a suit and dress shoes would be better choices. Keep in mind, too, that your appearance influences your own self-confidence. Researchers have found that the more formal interviewees' clothing is, the more positive are the remarks they make about themselves during the interview (Hannover & Kuehnen, 2002).

Be Punctual

Do you feel frustrated when others keep you waiting? Interviewers respond emotionally to tardiness, just as you do. Consequently, it's best to arrive early. And if you are unavoidably delayed, call and reschedule.

Greet the Interviewer Appropriately

Your greeting plays an important role in the interview process as well. In the United States, it's best to look your interviewer directly in the eyes, shake hands firmly, pronounce her or his name correctly, and have good posture.

Follow Up

After the interview, it's a good idea to send a thank-you note. If you met with more than one interviewer, send a note to each of them, mentioning some specific aspect of the discussion that you found interesting. This will indicate that you were fully engaged in the conversation, listening intently, and interested in the interviewer's knowledge about the open position and the organization. The note should also express your appreciation for the interviewer's time and your interest in the position.

622 ■ CHAPTER 18 www.ablongman.com/wood5e

Helping You Understand and Appreciate Human Diversity

The authors have remained dedicated to the goal of promoting and expanding the understanding of human diversity throughout the evolution of this text. You and your fellow students come from diverse backgrounds, cultures, and regions and have unprecedented opportunities for travel, careers, and communications, both in the United States and internationally. In recognition of this reality, the Fifth Edition embraces a fully global perspective in presenting issues of diversity concerning gender, ethnicity, sexuality, and age. Some examples of issues addressed are as follows:

Student Supplements

Grade Aid Study Guide Written by Arlene Lundquist and Lisa Bauer, both of Utica College, this comprehensive and interactive study guide is filled with in-depth activities. Each chapter includes "Before You Read," presenting a brief chapter summary and chapter learning objectives; "As You Read," offering a collection of demonstrations, activities, and exercises; "After You Read," containing three short practice quizzes and one comprehensive practice test; "When You Have Finished," presenting Web links for further information and a crossword puzzle using key terms from the text. An appendix includes answers to all practice tests and crossword puzzles.

Spanish Practice Tests New for this edition, practice tests from the Grade Aid study guide are now available in Spanish.

Companion Website This unique resource connects the textbook to the Internet. Each chapter includes learning objectives, chapter summaries, updated and annotated Web links for additional sources of information, flashcard glossary terms, a timeline, online practice tests, and psychology activities. Visit this site at **www.ablongman.com/wood5e**.

MyPsychLab This interactive and instructive multimedia resource can be used to supplement a traditional lecture course or to administer a course entirely online. It is an all-inclusive tool, a text-specific e-book plus multimedia tutorials, audio, video, simulations, animations, and controlled assessments to completely engage students and reinforce learning. Fully customizable and easy to use, MyPsychLab meets the individual teaching and learning needs of every instructor and every student. Visit the site at **www.mypsychlab.com**.

Research Navigator Guide: Psychology, with access to Research Navigator™ Allyn and Bacon's new Research Navigator™ is the easiest way to start a research assignment or research paper. Complete with extensive help on the research process and three exclusive databases of credible and reliable source material, including EBSCO's ContentSelect Academic Journal Database, New York Times Search by Subject Archive, and "Best of the Web" Link Library, Research Navigator™ helps you quickly and efficiently make the most of your research time. The booklet contains a practical and to-the-point discussion of search engines, detailed information on evaluating online sources, citation guidelines for Web resources, Web activities and links for psychology, and a complete guide to Research Navigator™.

Psych Tutor This service provides free tutoring via phone, fax, e-mail, and Internet during Tutor Center hours. Qualified college psychology instructors tutor on all material covered in the text, for students who have purchased a copy. Visit the site at **www.aw.com/tutorcenter/psych**.

Mind Matters II CD-ROM A unique tool that combines major concepts with interactivity, this CD-ROM offers a wide range of learning opportunities, including activities with immediate feedback, video clips of historic experiments and current research, animations, simulations, and an interactive glossary of key terms. New modules focus on development, personality, and social psychology. To see sample modules, visit **www.ablongman.com/mindmatters**.

Instructor Supplements

Instructor's Manual Written for the first time by text author Denise Boyd, Houston Community College system, this wonderful tool can be used by first-time or experienced teachers. It includes numerous handouts, a sample syllabus, lecture materials, chapter outlines, suggested reading and video sources, teaching objectives, and more. Also, Try Its from previous editions that are not included in the text are in the Instructor's Manual.

Test Bank Prepared by Daniel Houlihan, Minnesota State University, Mankato, the fully reviewed Test Bank contains over 100 questions, including multiple choice, true/false, short answer, and essay—each with an answer justification. Each question has a page reference, a difficulty rating, and a type designation. In addition, the appendix includes a sample open-book quiz. This product is also available in TestGen computerized version, for use in creating tests in the classroom.

Special thanks go to Leslie Minor-Evans of Central Oregon Community College, Jane Cirillo of Houston Community College, and Beth Barton of Coastal Carolina Community College for providing invaluable feedback.

Powerpoint Presentation Prepared by Larry D. Thomas, Blinn College, this multimedia resource contains key points covered in the textbook, images from the textbook, with demonstrations, a link to the companion Website for corresponding activities, and the electronic Instructor's Manual files.

Allyn and Bacon Transparencies for Introductory Psychology This set of approximately 200 revised, full-color acetates will enhance classroom lecture and discussion. It includes images from Allyn and Bacon's major introductory psychology texts.

Insights into Psychology, Volumes I and II This wonderful tool consists of two or three video clips on each of 16 topics, including animal research, parapsychology, health and stress, Alzheimer's disease, bilingual education, genetics and IQ, and many more. Critical thinking questions accompany each clip. In addition, the video guide provides further critical thinking questions and Internet resources for more information. *Also available on DVD.*

Allyn and Bacon Digital Media Archive for Psychology, 4.0 This comprehensive source for images includes charts, graphs, maps, tables, and figures, with audio clips and related Web links. Video clips include classic footage of psychology experiments.

CourseCompass Powered by Blackboard, this course management system uses a powerful suite of tools that allow instructors to create an online presence for any course.

MyPsychLab This interactive and instructive multimedia resource can be used to supplement a traditional lecture course or to administer a course entirely online. It is an all-inclusive tool, a text-specific e-book plus multimedia tutorials, audio, video, simulations, animations, and controlled assessments to completely engage students and reinforce learning. Fully customizable and easy to use, MyPsychLab meets the individual teaching and learning needs of every instructor and every student. Visit the site at **www.mypsychlab.com**.

Acknowledgments

We are thankful for the support of several people at Allyn and Bacon who helped bring our plans for the fifth edition of *The World of Psychology* to fruition. First, thanks to Carolyn Merrill for the idea of expanding the team to include a new author, Denise Boyd, who has many years of experience teaching introductory psychology. Carolyn earned kudos as well for adding Kelly May to the editorial team as Series Editor. Kelly deserves a great deal of the credit for monitoring the progress of the book and for ensuring that the final product is an introductory text that achieves the goal of being thorough while also being timely and accessible. We are also grateful for the assistance of developmental editors Kelly Perkins and Sharon Geary, whose suggestions and encouragement helped immeasurably in the pursuit of this goal. We would also like to acknowledge the fine work of Michael Granger, Production Supervisor, in overseeing the long and complex process of turning our manuscript into a book.

Copyeditors are indispensable to the production of any book, but we feel that the work of Jane Hoover of Lifland et al., Bookmakers, deserves special recognition. Jane and her team painstakingly scrutinized every word of this text. Moreover, thanks to Jane's careful work, each figure, photograph, table, Try It, Review and Reflect table, key term, and learning question is in the right place in the book, is clearly linked to the text, and is understandable to readers. Her suggestions improved our writing and helped us produce a text that is clear, concise, and well organized.

To Our Reviewers Numerous reviewers were invaluable to the development of the first four editions of *The World of Psychology*, and we thank them for their input and time.

Mark D. Agars, California State University, San Bernadino
Patricia Alexander, Long Beach City College
Beth A. Barton, The University of North Carolina at Wilmington
Shirley A. Bass-Wright, St. Philip's College

Kenneth Benson, Hinds Community College
John Brennecke, Mt. San Antonio College
Cari Cannon, Santiago Canyon College
Jane Marie Cirillo, Houston Community College
Maria G. Cisneros-Solis, Austin Community College
Betty L. Clark, University of Mary Hardin-Baylor
Dennis Cogan, Texas Technical University
Betty S. Deckard, California State University, Long Beach
Kimberly J. Duff, Cerritos College
Laura Duvall, Heartland Community College
Joy Easton, DeVry University Orlando
Leticia Y. Flores, Southwest Texas State University
James Francis, San Jacinto College
Alexander B. Genov, Heartland Community College
Colleen Gift, Highland Community College
Paula Goolkasian, University of North Carolina at Charlotte
Allen Gottfried, California State University, Fullerton
Barbara J. Hart, Arizona State University–West
Brett Heintz, Delgado Community College
Debra Hollister, Valencia Community College
Steven Isorio, Golden West College
Victoria A. Kazmerski, Penn State Erie, The Behrend College
Norman E. Kinney, Southeast Missouri State University
Callista Lee, Fullerton College
Elizabeth Levin, Laurentian University
Barbara Lusk, Collin County Community College
Laura Madson, New Mexico State University
Barbara B. Marcel, Regis College
Catherine J. Massey, Slippery Rock University
Wendy Mills, San Jacinto College North
George Mount, Mountain View College
Peggy Norwood, Metropolitan State College of Denver
Fernando Ortiz, Santa Ana College
Ginger Osborne, Santa Ana College
Jack A. Palmer, University of Lousiana at Monroe
Debra Parish, Tomball College—NHMCC
Janet R. Pascal, DeVry University
Dan Perkins, Richland College
Michelle Pilati, Rio Hondo College
Vicki Ritts, St. Louis Community College–Meramec
Kevin S. Salisbury, Community College of Rhode Island
H. R. Schliffman, Rutgers University
Mark S. Schmidt, Columbus State University
Susan Siaw, California Polytechnic University, Pomona
Nancy Simpson, Trident Technical College
Lynn M. Skaggs, Central Texas College
Donette A. Steele, Cerritos College
Genevieve D. Stevens, Houston Community College System—Central College
Chuck Strong, Northwest Mississippi Community College
Inger Thompson, Glendale Community College
M. Lisa Valentino, Seminole Community College
Fred Whitford, Montana State University
Sandra Wilcox, California State University, Dominguez Hills
Diane E. Wille, Indiana University Southeast
Jeana Wolfe, Fullerton College

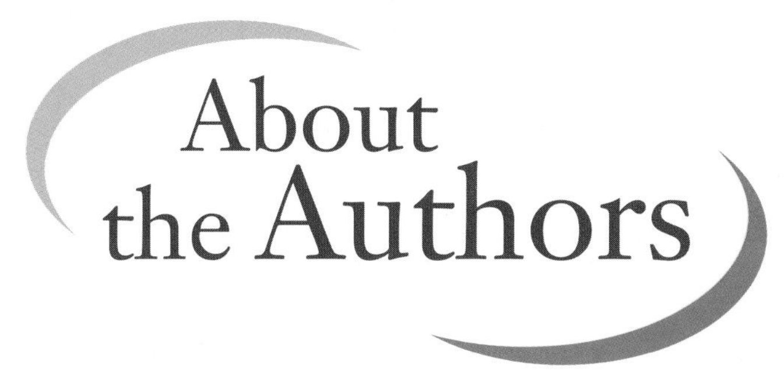

About the Authors

Samuel E. Wood received his doctorate from the University of Florida. He has taught at West Virginia University and the University of Missouri–St. Louis and was a member of the doctoral faculty at both universities. From 1984 to 1996, he served as president of the Higher Education Center, a consortium of 14 colleges and universities in the St. Louis area. He was a co-founder of the Higher Education Cable TV channel (HEC-TV) in St. Louis and served as its president and CEO from its founding in 1987 until 1996.

Ellen Green Wood received her doctorate in educational psychology from St. Louis University and was an adjunct professor of psychology at St. Louis Community College at Meramec. She has also taught in the clinical experiences program in education at Washington University and at the University of Missouri–St. Louis. In addition to her teaching, Dr. Wood has developed and taught seminars on critical thinking. She received the Telecourse Pioneer Award from 1982 through 1988 for her contributions to the field of distance learning.

Denise Boyd received her Ed.D. in educational psychology from the University of Houston and has been a psychology instructor in the Houston Community College system since 1988. From 1995 until 1998, she chaired the psychology, sociology, and anthropology department at Houston Community College–Central. She has co-authored three other Allyn and Bacon texts: with Helen Bee, *Lifespan Development* (Third Edition) and *The Developing Child* (Tenth Edition); and with Genevieve Stevens, *Current Readings in Lifespan Development.* A licensed psychologist, she has presented a number of papers at professional meetings, reporting research in child, adolescent, and adult development. She has also presented workshops for teachers whose students range from preschool to college.

Together, Sam, Evie, and Denise have more than 45 years of experience teaching introductory psychology to thousands of students of all ages, backgrounds, and abilities. *The World of Psychology* is the direct result of their teaching experience.

The World *of* Psychology

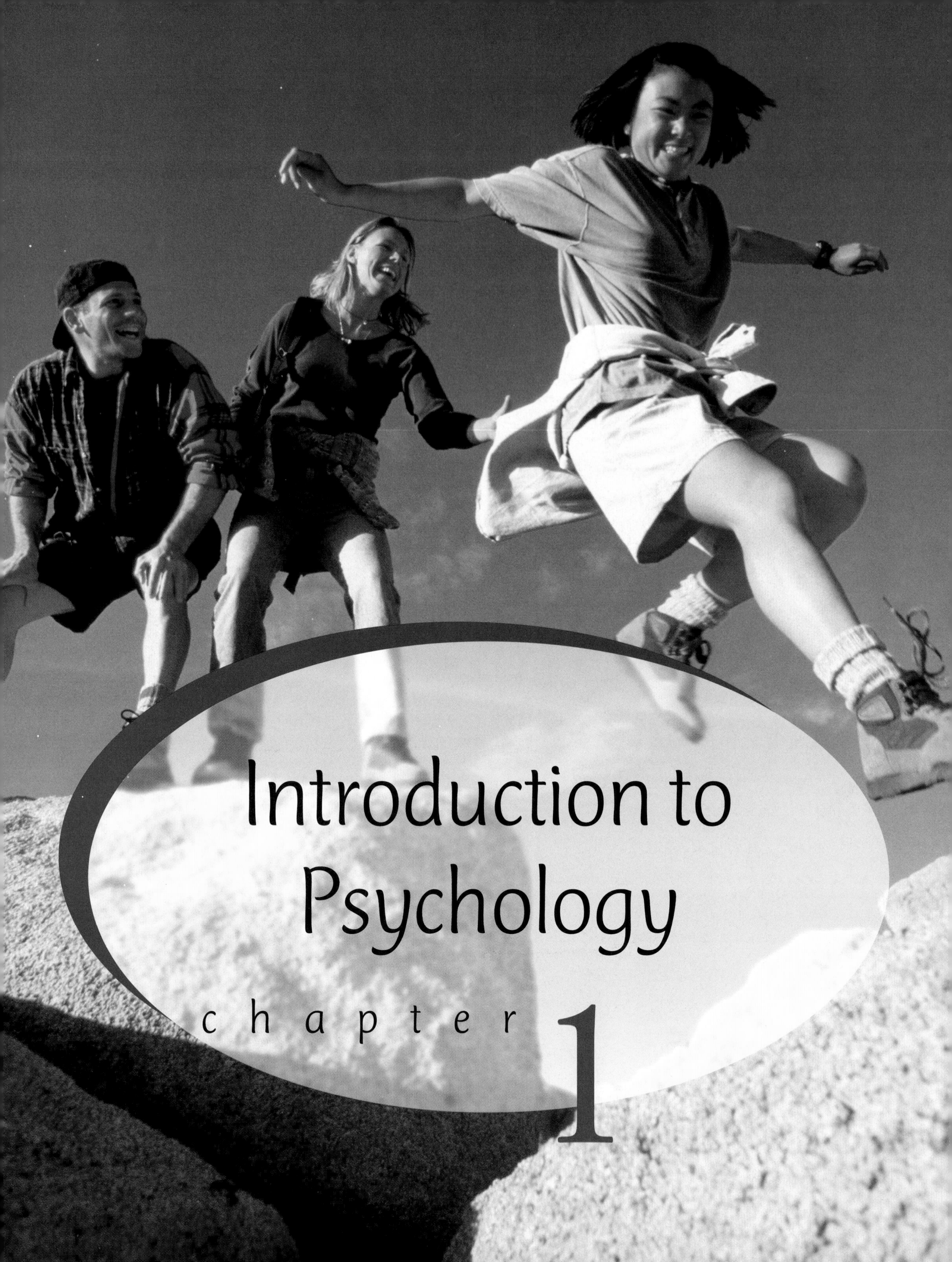

Introduction to Psychology

chapter 1

Psychology: An Introduction

- *What process do scientists use to answer questions about behavior and mental processes?*
- *What are the goals of psychology?*
- *How can you be a critical thinker?*

Descriptive Research Methods

- *How do psychological researchers use naturalistic and laboratory observation?*
- *What are the advantages and disadvantages of the case study?*
- *How do researchers ensure that survey results are useful?*

The Experimental Method

- *Why do researchers use experiments to test hypotheses about cause-effect relationships?*
- *How do independent and dependent variables differ?*
- *Why are experimental and control groups necessary?*
- *What kinds of factors introduce bias into experimental studies?*
- *What are the limitations of the experimental method?*

The Correlational Method

- *What is a correlation coefficient, and what does it mean?*
- *What are the strengths and weaknesses of the correlational method?*

Participants in Psychological Research

- *In what ways can participants bias research results?*
- *What ethical rules must researchers follow when humans are involved in studies?*
- *Why are animals used in research?*

Exploring Psychology's Roots

- *What roles did Wundt and Titchener play in the founding of psychology?*
- *Why is functionalism important in the history of psychology?*
- *In what ways have women and minorities shaped the field of psychology, both in the past and today?*

Schools of Thought in Psychology

- *How do behaviorists explain behavior and mental processes?*
- *What do psychoanalytic psychologists believe about the role of the unconscious?*
- *According to Maslow and Rogers, what motivates human behavior and mental processes?*
- *What is the focus of cognitive psychology?*

Current Trends in Psychology

- *What is the main idea behind evolutionary psychology?*
- *How is biological psychology changing the field of psychology?*
- *What kinds of variables interest psychologists who take a sociocultural approach?*
- *What are psychological perspectives, and how are they related to an eclectic position?*

Psychologists at Work

- *What are some of the specialists working within psychology?*
- *What kinds of employment opportunities are available for psychology majors?*

Have you ever wished there were 25 hours in a day?

If so, you're not alone. Time management is a challenge for most college students. And, by the way, there really is no such thing as a "typical" college student these days. Today's students face all kinds of demands on their time, many of which can interfere with studying. Which set of time management challenges described below is most like your own?

- A recent high school graduate, who lives on campus at a large state university, is involved in intramural athletics and several social organizations; he is having difficulty juggling social and academic demands.
- A first-generation college student, whose family has made substantial financial sacrifices to give her the opportunity to attend college, worries that she won't be able to live up to their expectations; she feels overwhelmed by the reading requirements of college classes.
- A young woman, who was recently discharged from military service, is attending college for the first time; she is having trouble adjusting to the change from the structure of military life to the self-discipline required for academic success.
- A young man is living, working, and studying in an English-speaking country for the first time; he must find time to practice and improve his language skills as well as fulfill the requirements of all his courses.
- A mother of two young children has returned to college after an absence of several years to pursue a career in teaching; she is finding that the demands of school and family often conflict.
- A middle-aged man is taking classes to upgrade his job skills after being laid off by the auto assembly plant where he had worked for 15 years; he is often distracted from his studies by the emotions associated with job loss and the feeling that he doesn't fit into the college environment.

Regardless of the kinds of time-management challenges you face, the study aids incorporated in *The World of Psychology* can help you manage your study time more effectively. By learning to manage your study time, you can gain a sense of control over your life, and feeling that you are in control can help you manage the negative emotions that sometimes accompany adjustment to college. You may not realize it, but when you incorporate time-management strategies into your daily routine, you are using psychological principles to improve your life. *The World of Psychology* is organized to help you maximize your learning by using a series of five learning strategies developed and tested by a psychologist: *Survey*, *Question*, *Read*, *Recite*, and *Review*. Together, these steps are known as the **SQ3R method.** You will learn and remember more if, instead of simply reading each chapter, you follow these steps. Here's how they work.

- *Survey.* First, scan the chapter. The chapter outline helps you preview the content and its organization. Read the section headings and the learning objective questions, which are designed to focus your attention on key information. Glance at the illustrations and tables, including the *Review and Reflect* tables, which organize, review, and summarize key concepts. Then read the *Summary and Review*, located at the end of each chapter. This survey process gives you an overview of the chapter.
- *Question.* You should approach each chapter by tackling one major section at a time. Before you actually read a section, reread its learning objective questions. But don't stop there; add a few questions of your own as you glance over the section's subheadings and key terms. For example, the first major section in this chapter is "Psychology: An Introduction." The first subheading is "The Scientific Method," and the associated question is "What process do scientists use to answer questions about behavior and mental processes?" As you look over the section, you might add this question: "What is the difference between common sense and science?" Asking such questions helps focus your reading.

SQ3R method
A study method involving the following five steps: (1) survey, (2) question, (3) read, (4) recite, and (5) review.

- *Read.* Read the section. As you read, try to answer the learning objective questions and your own questions. After reading the section, stop. If the section is very long or if the material seems especially difficult or complex, you should pause after reading only one or two paragraphs.
- *Recite.* To better grasp each topic in a section, write a short summary of the material. If you have trouble summarizing a topic or answering any learning objective question, scan or read the section once more before trying again. Compare your summaries to the question answers provided in the *Summary and Review* at the end of each chapter.
- *Review.* Each major section in the book ends with a *Remember It* feature that consists of a few questions about the preceding topics. Answer these questions, and then check your answers against those provided. If you make errors, quickly review the preceding material until you know the answers. When you have finished a chapter, revisit each *Remember It* and then turn to the *Summary and Review*. Review the key terms. If you don't know the meaning of a term, turn to the page where that term is defined in the margin. The marginal definitions provide a ready reference for the important terms that appear in **boldface** print in the text. All of these terms and definitions also appear in the *Glossary* at the end of the book.

Now that you know how to study this text effectively, let's consider in more detail how the work of psychologists impacts our everyday lives. Before we begin, think about all of the ways in which psychology—and the language of psychology—play an integral role in our lives.

Psychology: An Introduction

Just what is psychology? In the past, psychologists debated about the degree to which psychology ought to be restricted to the study of either behavior or mental processes. Today, the importance of both is recognized, and **psychology** is now defined as the scientific study of behavior and mental processes. Answer true or false for each statement in *Try It 1.1* to see how much you already know about some of the topics we will explore in *The World of Psychology*. (You'll find the answers in the text below.)

psychology The scientific study of behavior and mental processes.

Try It 1.1 Science or Common Sense?

Indicate whether each statement is true (T) or false (F).

1. Once damaged, brain cells never work again.
2. All people dream during a night of normal sleep.
3. As the number of bystanders at an emergency increases, the time it takes for the victim to get help decreases.
4. Humans do not have a maternal instinct.
5. It's impossible for human beings to hear a watch ticking 20 feet away.
6. Eyewitness testimony is often unreliable.
7. Chimpanzees have been taught to speak.
8. Creativity and high intelligence do not necessarily go together.
9. When it comes to close personal relationships, opposites attract.
10. The majority of teenagers have good relationships with their parents.

Can we make a valid claim that psychology is a science, or is it just common sense? In the *Try It*, common sense might have led you astray. All the odd-numbered items are false, and all the even-numbered items are true. So, common sense alone will not get you very far in your study of psychology.

The Scientific Method

What process do scientists use to answer questions about behavior and mental processes?

What makes a field of study a science? Many people believe that a field is a science because of the nature of its body of knowledge. Few people question whether physics, for example, is a true science. But a science isn't a science because of its subject matter. A field of study qualifies as a science if it uses the scientific method to acquire knowledge. The **scientific method** consists of the orderly, systematic procedures that researchers follow as they identify a research problem, design a study to investigate the problem, collect and analyze data, draw conclusions, and communicate their findings. The scientific method is the most objective method known for acquiring knowledge (Christensen, 2001). The knowledge gained is dependable because of the method used to obtain it.

Say, for example, a researcher finds that men consistently score higher than women on a test of map reading. If the researcher claims that the gender difference in map-reading scores is attributable to the effects of male and female hormones on the brain, she has moved beyond the domain of facts and into that of theory. A **theory** is a general principle or set of principles proposed to explain how a number of separate facts are related. Other researchers may not agree with the explanation. Still, any alternative theory proposed to explain this researcher's findings must be able to account for the fact that men outscore women on tests of map reading. Other psychologists might propose that the difference exists because society encourages men to learn to read maps but discourages women from doing so. They can't simply say that there is no such thing as a gender difference in map reading, especially if the researcher's results have been *replicated* by other scientists. (**Replication** is the process of repeating a study with different participants and preferably a different investigator to verify research findings.)

■ **scientific method**
The orderly, systematic procedures that researchers follow as they identify a research problem, design a study to investigate the problem, collect and analyze data, draw conclusions, and communicate their findings.

■ **theory**
A general principle or set of principles proposed to explain how a number of separate facts are related.

■ **replication**
The process of repeating a study with different participants and preferably a different investigator to verify research findings.

You might be thinking: Why bother with theories? Why not just report the facts and let people draw their own conclusions? Well, theories enable scientists to fit many separate pieces of data into meaningful frameworks. For example, in the hormone theory of gender differences in map reading, two facts are connected: (1) Men and women have different hormones, and (2) men and women score differently on map-reading tests. Connecting these two facts results in a theory of gender differences from which researchers can make predictions that can be tested.

Theories also stimulate debates that lead to advances in knowledge. The psychologist who thinks gender differences in map reading are due to learning may do a study in which male and female participants are trained in map reading. If the women read maps as well as the men do after training, then the researcher has support for her theory and has added a new fact to the knowledge base. Once the advocates of the hormone view modify their theory to include the new fact, they are likely to carry out new studies to test it. As a result of this back-and-forth process, knowledge about gender differences in map reading increases.

The Goals of Psychology

What are the goals of psychology?

What goals do psychological researchers pursue when they plan and conduct their studies? Briefly put, the goals of psychology are to describe, explain, predict, and influence behavior and mental processes. Let's look at each goal in a bit more detail.

Description is usually the first step in understanding any behavior or mental process and is therefore important in a very new area of research or in the early stages of research. To attain this goal, researchers describe the behavior or mental process of interest as accurately and completely as possible. A description tells *what* occurred.

The second goal, *explanation*, requires an understanding of the conditions under which a given behavior or mental process occurs. Such an understanding often enables researchers to state the causes of the behavior or mental process they are studying. But researchers do not reach the goal of explanation until their results have been tested, retested, and confirmed. The way researchers confirm an explanation is by eliminating or ruling out other explanations. An explanation tells *why* a given event or behavior occurred.

The goal of *prediction* is met when researchers can specify the conditions under which a behavior or event is likely to occur. Once researchers can identify all the antecedent (prior) conditions required for a behavior or event to occur, they can predict that behavior or event.

The goal of *influence* is accomplished when researchers know how to apply a principle or change a condition in order to prevent unwanted occurrences or bring about desired outcomes.

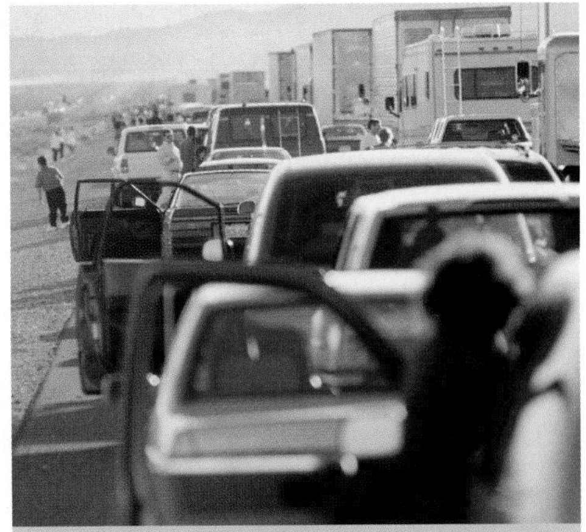

To achieve the goal of explaining road rage and the resulting violence—and perhaps eventually controlling it—psychological researchers might observe and describe the behavior of motorists under stressful conditions.

As an illustration of these goals, think back to the discussion of gender differences in map-reading skills. When a psychologist carries out a study in which male participants score higher than female participants on a map-reading test, she fulfills the description goal. Psychologists who theorize that the difference is due to the influences of male and female hormones on the brain are meeting the explanation goal. Formulating a hypothesis based on the hormone theory involves the prediction goal. Finally, researchers who devise and test training programs that help women learn to be better map readers are implementing the goal of influence.

Two types of research help psychologists accomplish the four goals just described: basic research and applied research. The purpose of **basic research** is to seek new knowledge and to explore and advance general scientific understanding. Basic research explores such topics as the nature of memory, brain function, motivation, and emotional expression. **Applied research** is conducted specifically for the purpose of solving practical problems and improving the quality of life. Applied research focuses on finding methods to improve memory or increase motivation, therapies to treat psychological disorders, ways to decrease stress, and so on. This type of research is primarily concerned with the fourth goal of psychology—influence—because it specifies ways and means of changing behavior.

■ **basic research**
Research conducted to seek new knowledge and to explore and advance general scientific understanding.

■ **applied research**
Research conducted specifically to solve practical problems and improve the quality of life.

How to Think Like a Scientist

How can you be a critical thinker?

When was the last time you heard or read about the results of a study? If you're like most people, you probably do so almost every day. Indeed, living in the Information Age, we are bombarded daily with information from the popular media on every conceivable subject. And, each day, we adopt the same thinking strategies used by scientists to help us sift through all this information. **Critical thinking,** the foundation of the scientific method, is the process of objectively evaluating claims, propositions, and conclusions to determine whether they follow logically from the evidence presented. When we engage in critical thinking, we exhibit the following characteristics:

- *Independent thinking.* When thinking critically, we do not automatically accept and believe what we read or hear.
- *Suspension of judgment.* Critical thinking requires gathering relevant and up-to-date information on all sides of an issue before taking a position.
- *Willingness to modify or abandon prior judgments.* Critical thinking involves evaluating new evidence, even when it contradicts pre-existing beliefs.

To think critically about information you encounter in this text and in the popular media, you need to (1) understand the various research methods psychologists use to achieve their goals, (2) know the advantages and limitations of these methods, and (3) be able to identify the elements that distinguish good research.

■ **critical thinking**
The process of objectively evaluating claims, propositions, and conclusions to determine whether they follow logically from the evidence presented.

Remember It 1.1

1. The orderly, systematic procedures scientists follow in acquiring a body of knowledge comprise the __________.
2. The four goals of psychology are __________, __________, __________, and __________.
3. __________ research is designed to solve practical problems.
4. The three characteristics of critical thinkers are __________, __________, and __________.

ANSWERS: 1. scientific method; 2. description, explanation, prediction, influence; 3. Basic; 4. independent thinking, suspension of judgment, willingness to change or abandon prior judgments

■ descriptive research methods
Research methods that yield descriptions of behavior.

■ naturalistic observation
A descriptive research method in which researchers observe and record behavior in its natural setting, without attempting to influence or control it.

Descriptive Research Methods

What is the simplest kind of research? Research that involves direct observation is usually easy to perform and often provides the clearest results. **Descriptive research methods** yield descriptions of behavior and include naturalistic and laboratory observation, the case study, and the survey.

Naturalistic and Laboratory Observation

How do psychological researchers use naturalistic and laboratory observation?

Have you ever sat in an airport or shopping mall and simply watched what people were doing? Such an activity is quite similar to **naturalistic observation,** a descriptive research method in which researchers observe and record behavior in its natural setting, without attempting to influence or control it. The major advantage of naturalistic observation is the opportunity to study behavior in normal settings, where it occurs more naturally and spontaneously than it does under artificial and contrived laboratory conditions. Sometimes, naturalistic observation is the only feasible way to study behavior—for example, there is no other way to study how people typically react during disasters such as earthquakes and fires.

Naturalistic observation has its limitations, however. Researchers must wait for events to occur; they cannot speed up or slow down the process. And because they have no control over the situation, researchers cannot reach conclusions about cause-effect relationships. Another potential problem with naturalistic observation is *observer bias*, which is a distortion in researchers' observations. Observer bias can result when researchers' expectations about a situation cause them to see what they expect to see or to make incorrect inferences about what they observe. Let's say, for example, that you're a psychologist studying aggression in preschool classrooms. You have decided to count every time a child hits or pushes another child as an aggressive act. Your decision to label this type of physical contact between children as "aggressive" may cause you to notice more such acts, and label them as "aggressive," than you would if you were casually watching a group of children play. The effects of observer bias can be reduced substantially when two or more observers view the same behavior. So, if you and another observer independently count, say, 23 aggressive acts in an hour of free play, the findings are considered unbiased. If, on the other hand, you see 30 such acts and the other observer records only 15, there is some kind of bias at work. In such situations, observers usually clarify the criteria for classifying behavior and repeat the observations. Using videotapes can also help eliminate observer bias because behavior can be reviewed several times prior to making classification decisions.

A kind of naturalistic observation occurs on a large scale in England; about a million closed-circuit TV cameras like this one monitor activity in streets and shopping centers.

Another method of studying behavior involves observation that takes place not in its natural setting, but in a laboratory. Researchers using **laboratory observation** can exert more control and use more precise equipment to measure responses. Much of what is known about sleep or the human sexual response, for example, has been learned through laboratory observation. However, like other research methods, laboratory observation has limitations. For one, laboratory behavior may not accurately reflect real-world behavior. For example, in sleep studies, some of the behavior people display while asleep in the laboratory may not occur in their homes. As a result, conclusions based on laboratory findings may not generalize beyond the walls of the laboratory itself. Another disadvantage is that building, staffing, equipping, and maintaining research laboratories can be expensive.

■ **laboratory observation**
A descriptive research method in which behavior is studied in a laboratory setting, where researchers can exert more control and use more precise equipment to measure responses.

The Case Study

What are the advantages and disadvantages of the case study?

The **case study,** or case history, is another descriptive research method used by psychologists. In a case study, a single individual or a small number of persons are studied in great depth, usually over an extended period of time. A case study involves the use of observations, interviews, and sometimes psychological testing. Exploratory in nature, the case study's purpose is to provide a detailed description of some behavior or disorder. This method is particularly appropriate for studying people who have uncommon psychological or physiological disorders or brain injuries. Many case studies are written about patients being treated for such problems. In some instances, the results of detailed case studies have provided the foundation for psychological theories. In particular, the theory of Sigmund Freud was based primarily on case studies of his patients.

Although the case study has proven useful in advancing knowledge in several areas of psychology, it has certain limitations. Researchers cannot establish the cause of behavior observed in a case study, and observer bias is a potential problem. Moreover, because so few individuals are studied, researchers do not know how applicable, or generalizable, their findings may be to larger groups or to different cultures.

■ **case study**
A descriptive research method in which a single individual or a small number of persons are studied in great depth, usually over an extended period of time.

■ **survey**
A descriptive research method in which researchers use interviews and/or questionnaires to gather information about the attitudes, beliefs, experiences, or behaviors of a group of people.

Survey Research

How do researchers ensure that survey results are useful?

Have you ever been questioned about your voting behavior or about the kind of toothpaste you prefer? If you have, chances are that you were a participant in another kind of research study. The **survey** is a descriptive research method in which researchers use interviews and/or questionnaires to gather information about the attitudes, beliefs, experiences, or behaviors of a group of people. The results of carefully conducted surveys have provided valuable information about drug use, sexual behavior, and the incidence of various mental disorders.

Selecting a Sample Researchers in psychology rarely conduct studies using all members of a group. For example, researchers interested in studying the sexual behavior of American women do not survey every woman in the United States. (Imagine trying to interview about 140 million people!) Instead of studying the whole **population** (the entire group of interest to researchers, to which they wish to apply their findings), researchers select a sample for study. A **sample** is a part of a population that is studied in order to reach conclusions about the entire population.

Perhaps you have seen a carton of ice cream that contains three separate flavors—chocolate, strawberry, and vanilla—packed side by side. To properly sample the carton, you would need a small amount of ice cream containing all three flavors in the same proportions as in the whole carton—a representative sample. A **representative sample** mirrors the population of interest—that is, it includes important subgroups in the same proportions as they are found in that population. A *biased sample*, on the other hand, does not adequately reflect the larger population.

The best method for obtaining a representative sample is to select a *random sample* from a list of all members of the population of interest. Individuals are selected in such a way that every member of the larger population has an equal chance of being included in the sample. Using random samples, polling organizations can accurately represent the views of the American public with responses from as few as 1,000 people (O'Brien, 1996).

Is the Osbourne family *representative* of the general population of families in the United States? Why or why not?

Internet surveys allow psychologists to gather lots of data from large numbers of respondents in a very short period of time. But how representative of the general population are people who respond to Internet surveys? How representative are they of Internet users in general? Questions such as these remain to be answered.

Interviews and Questionnaires Survey results can be affected by the questions' wording and the context for the survey (Schwartz, 1999). Also, the truthfulness of the responses can be affected by characteristics of the interviewers, such as their gender, age, race, ethnicity, religion, social class, and accent. In general, people are most inhibited when they give personal information to interviewers who are of the same age but the opposite sex. Survey researchers, therefore, must select interviewers who have personal characteristics that are appropriate for the intended respondents.

Questionnaires can be completed more quickly and less expensively than interviews, especially when respondents can fill them out in their homes or online. The Internet offers psychologists a fast and inexpensive way of soliciting participants and collecting questionnaire data, and Internet surveys often generate large numbers of responses (Azar, 2000). For example, an Internet survey posted by researchers who wanted to collect data about suicidal feelings attracted more than 38,000 respondents from all over the world (Mathy, 2002). However, such surveys have problems, including technical glitches that prevent respondents from completing a questionnaire. Moreover, the sample is often biased in that it represents only the population of Internet users who choose to participate in online research, *not* the general population or even the population of Internet users. The critical point to remember is that surveys in which respondents *choose* whether or not to participate, rather than being selected through some kind of random process, are not scientific.

■ **population**
The entire group of interest to researchers, to which they wish to generalize their findings; the group from which a sample is selected.

■ **sample**
A part of population that is studied in order to reach conclusions about the entire population.

■ **representative sample**
A sample that mirrors the population of interest; it includes important subgroups in the same proportions as they are found in that population.

Advantages and Disadvantages of Survey Research If conducted properly, surveys can provide highly accurate information. They can also track changes in attitudes or behavior over time. For example, Johnston and others (2001) have tracked drug use among high school students since 1975. However, large-scale surveys can be costly and time-consuming. Another important limitation of survey research is that respondents may provide inaccurate information. False information can result from a faulty memory or a desire to please the interviewer. Respondents may try to present themselves in a good light (a phenomenon called the *social desirability response*), or they may even deliberately mislead the interviewer. Finally, when respondents answer questions about sensitive subjects, such as sexual behavior, they are often less candid in face-to-face interviews than in self-administered or computerized questionnaires (Tourangeau et al., 1997).

Remember It 1.2

1. Which descriptive research method would be best for studying each of the following topics?

____ (1) attitudes toward racial profiling
____ (2) gender differences in how people position themselves and their belongings in the library
____ (3) physiological changes that occur during sleep
____ (4) the effects of oxygen deprivation during delivery on infant brain development

a. naturalistic observation
b. laboratory observation
c. case study
d. survey

2. One problem with the __________ is that it often does not generalize to individuals other than the subject of the study.

3. In order to be useful, a survey must be based on a __________ sample.

ANSWERS: 1. (1) d, (2) a, (3) b, (4) c; 2. case study; 3. representative

The Experimental Method

What comes to mind when you hear the word *experiment*? Many people use the word to refer to any kind of study. Among scientists, though, the term *experiment* refers only to one kind of study, the kind in which researchers seek to determine the causes of behavior.

Experiments and Hypothesis Testing

Why do researchers use experiments to test hypotheses about cause-effect relationships?

The **experimental method,** or the experiment, is the *only* research method that can be used to identify cause-effect relationships. An experiment is designed to test a **hypothesis**—a prediction about a cause-effect relationship between two or more variables. A *variable* is any condition or factor that can be manipulated, controlled, or measured. One variable of interest to you is the grade you will receive in this psychology course. Another variable that probably interests you is the amount of time you will spend studying for this course. Do you suppose there is a cause-effect relationship between the amount of time students spend studying and the grades they receive? Consider two other variables: alcohol consumption and aggression. Alcohol consumption and aggressive behavior are often observed occurring at the same time. But can we assume that alcohol consumption *causes* aggressive behavior?

Alan Lang and his colleagues (1975) conducted a classic experiment to determine if alcohol consumption itself increases aggression or if the beliefs or expectations about the effects of alcohol cause the aggressive behavior. The participants in the experiment were 96 male college students who were classified as heavy social drinkers. Half the students were given plain tonic to drink; the other half were given a vodka-and-tonic drink in amounts sufficient to raise their blood alcohol level to .10, which is higher than the .08 level that is the legal limit for intoxication in most states. Participants were assigned to four groups:

Group 1: Expected alcohol, received only tonic
Group 2: Expected alcohol, received alcohol mixed with tonic
Group 3: Expected tonic, received alcohol mixed with tonic
Group 4: Expected tonic, received only tonic

■ experimental method The only research method that can be used to identify cause-effect relationships between two or more conditions or variables.

■ hypothesis A prediction about a cause-effect relationship between two or more variables.

You might think that heavy social drinkers could detect the difference between plain tonic and a one-to-five mixture of vodka and tonic. But during a preliminary study, drinkers could distinguish between the two with no more than 50% accuracy (Marlatt & Rohsenow, 1981).

After the students had consumed the designated amount, the researchers had an accomplice, who posed as a participant, purposely provoke half the students by belittling their performance on a difficult task. All the students then participated in a learning experiment, in which the same accomplice posed as the learner. The subjects were told to administer an electric shock to the accomplice each time he made a mistake on a decoding task. Each participant was allowed to determine the intensity and duration of the "shock." (Although the students thought they were shocking the accomplice, no shocks were actually delivered.) The researchers measured the aggressiveness of the students in terms of the duration and the intensity of the shocks they chose to deliver.

Under what conditions might the happy, party mood of these young drinkers turn aggressive?

What were the results of the experiment? As you might imagine, the students who had been provoked gave the accomplice stronger shocks than those who

FIGURE 1.1 The Mean Shock Intensity Chosen by Provoked and Unprovoked Participants

In the Lang experiment, participants who thought they were drinking alcohol chose to give significantly stronger shocks, whether provoked or not, than those who believed they were drinking only tonic.

Source: Data from Lang et al. (1995).

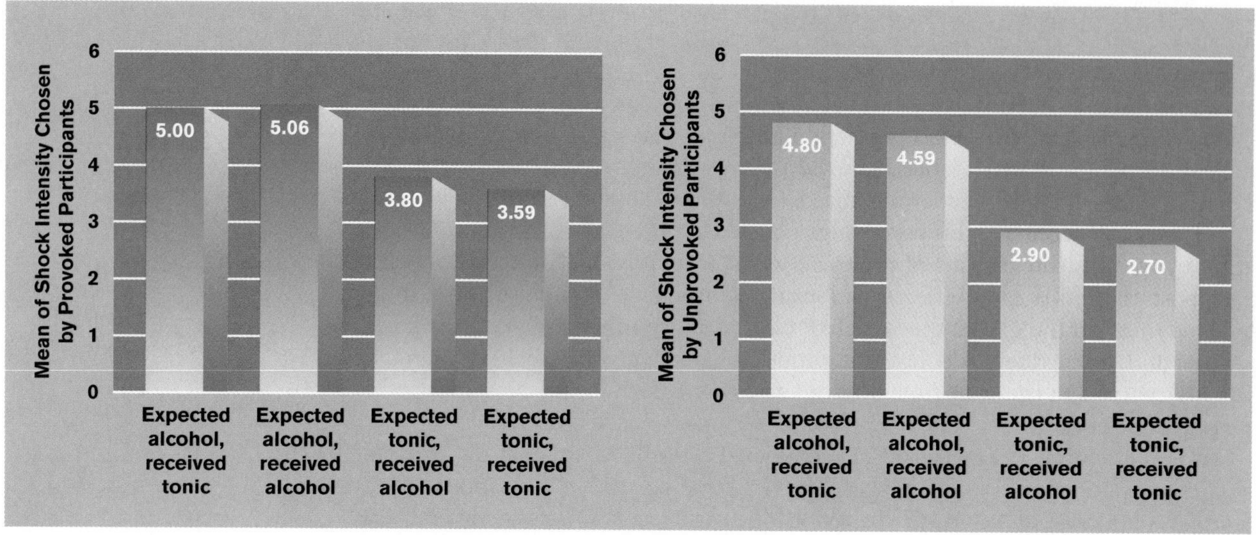

had not been provoked. But the students who drank the alcohol were not necessarily the most aggressive. Regardless of the actual content of their drinks, the participants who thought they were drinking alcohol gave significantly stronger shocks, whether provoked or not, than those who assumed they were drinking only tonic (see Figure 1.1). The researchers concluded that it was the *expectation* of drinking alcohol, not the alcohol itself, that caused the students to be more aggressive.

Independent and Dependent Variables

How do independent and dependent variables differ?

Recall that experiments test hypotheses about cause and effect. Examples of such hypotheses include "Studying causes good grades" and "Taking aspirin causes headaches to go away." Note that each hypothesis involves two variables: One is thought to be the cause (studying, taking aspirin), and the other is thought to be affected by the cause. These two kinds of variables are found in all experiments. An experiment has at least one **independent variable**—a variable that the researcher believes causes a change in some other variable. The researcher deliberately manipulates the independent variable (hypothesized cause) in order to determine whether it causes any change in another behavior or condition. Sometimes the independent variable is referred to as the *treatment*. The Lang experiment had two independent variables: the alcoholic content of the drink and the expectation of drinking alcohol.

The second type of variable found in all experiments, the one that the hypothesis states is affected by the independent variable, is the **dependent variable**. It is measured at the end of the experiment and is presumed to vary (increase or decrease) as a result of the manipulations of the independent variable(s). Researchers must provide operational definitions of all variables in an experiment—that is, they must specify precisely how the variables will be observed and measured. In the Lang study, the dependent variable—aggression—was operationally defined as the intensity and duration of the "shocks" the participants chose to deliver to the accomplice.

■ **independent variable**
In an experiment, a factor or condition that is deliberately manipulated in order to determine whether it causes any change in another behavior or condition.

■ **dependent variable**
The factor or condition that is measured at the end of an experiment and is presumed to vary as a result of the manipulations of the independent variable(s).

Experimental and Control Groups

Why are experimental and control groups necessary?

Most experiments are conducted using two or more groups of participants. There must always be at least one **experimental group**—a group of participants who are exposed to the independent variable, or the treatment. The Lang experiment used three experimental groups:

Group 1: Expected alcohol, received only tonic
Group 2: Expected alcohol, received alcohol mixed with tonic
Group 3: Expected tonic, received alcohol mixed with tonic

Most experiments also have a **control group**—a group that is similar to the experimental group and is also measured on the dependent variable at the end of the experiment, for purposes of comparison. The control group is exposed to the same experimental environment as the experimental group but is not given the treatment. The fourth group in the Lang study was exposed to neither of the two independent variables; that is, this group did not expect alcohol and did not receive alcohol. Because this group was similar to the experimental groups and was exposed to the same experimental environment, it served as a control group.

You may be wondering why a control group is necessary. Couldn't an experimenter just expose one group to the independent variable and see if there was a change? While this approach is sometimes used, it is usually preferable to have a control group because people and their behaviors often change without intervention. Having a control group reveals what kinds of changes happen "naturally" and provides a way of separating the effect of the independent variable from such changes. Say, for example, you want to find out if a certain medication relieves headaches. You could just find some people with headaches, give them the medication, and then find out how many still have headaches an hour later. But some headaches go away without treatment. So if the medication appears to work, it may only be because a number of headaches went away on their own. Having a control group allows you to know whether the medicine relieves headaches in addition to those that disappear without treatment.

■ **experimental group**
In an experiment, the group that is exposed to an independent variable.

■ **control group**
In an experiment, a group similar to the experimental group that is exposed to the same experimental environment but is not given the treatment; used for purposes of comparison.

■ **confounding variables**
Factors or conditions other than the independent variable(s) that are not equivalent across groups and could cause differences among the groups with respect to the dependent variable.

Sources of Bias in Experimental Research

What kinds of factors introduce bias into experimental studies?

Can the researcher always assume that the independent variable is the cause of some change in the dependent variable? Not necessarily. Sometimes an experiment is affected by **confounding variables**—factors or conditions other than the independent variable that are not equivalent across groups and that could cause differences among the groups with respect to the dependent variable. By conducting their experiment in a laboratory, Lang and his colleagues were able to control environmental conditions such as extreme noise or heat, which could have acted as confounding variables by increasing aggressive responses. Three additional sources of confounding variables that must be controlled in all experiments are selection bias, the placebo effect, and experimenter bias.

Selection Bias Why can't researchers allow participants to choose to be in either the experimental or control group? Such a procedure would introduce *selection bias* into a study. **Selection bias** occurs when participants are assigned to experimental or control groups in such a way that systematic differences among the groups are present at the beginning of the experiment. If selection bias occurs, then differences at the end of the experiment may not reflect the change in the independent variable but may be due to pre-existing differences in the groups. To control for selection bias, researchers must use **random assignment**. This process consists of selecting participants by using a chance procedure (such as drawing the names of participants out of a hat) to guarantee that each participant has an equal probability of being assigned to any of the groups.

■ **selection bias**
The assignment of participants to experimental or control groups in such a way that systematic differences among the groups are present at the beginning of the experiment.

■ **random assignment**
The process of selecting participants for experimental and control groups by using a chance procedure to guarantee that each participant has an equal probability of being assigned to any of the groups; a control for selection bias.

placebo effect The phenomenon that occurs in an experiment when a participant's response to a treatment is due to his or her expectations about the treatment rather than to the treatment itself.

placebo (pluh-SEE-bo) An inert or harmless substance given to the control group in an experiment as a control for the placebo effect.

experimenter bias A phenomenon that occurs when a researcher's preconceived notions or expectations in some way influence participants' behavior and/or the researcher's interpretation of experimental results.

double-blind technique A procedure in which neither the participants nor the experimenter knows who is in the experimental and control groups until after the data have been gathered; a control for experimenter bias.

Random assignment maximizes the likelihood that the groups will be as similar as possible at the beginning of the experiment. If there were pre-existing differences in students' levels of aggressiveness in the Lang experiment, random assignment would have spread those differences across all the groups.

The Placebo Effect Can participants' expectations influence an experiment's results? Yes. The **placebo effect** occurs when a participant's response to a treatment is due to his or her expectations about the treatment rather than to the treatment itself. Suppose a drug is prescribed for a patient and the patient reports improvement. The improvement could be a direct result of the drug, or it could be a result of the patient's expectation that the drug will work. Studies have shown that sometimes patients' remarkable improvement can be attributed solely to the power of suggestion—the placebo effect.

In drug experiments, the control group is usually given a **placebo**—an inert or harmless substance such as a sugar pill or an injection of saline solution. To control for the placebo effect, researchers do not let participants know whether they are in the experimental group (receiving the treatment) or in the control group (receiving the placebo). If participants getting the real drug or treatment show a significantly greater improvement than those receiving the placebo, then the improvement can be attributed to the drug rather than to the participants' expectations about the drug's effects. In the Lang experiment, some students who expected alcohol mixed with tonic were given only tonic. The tonic without alcohol functioned as a placebo, allowing researchers to measure the effect of the expectations alone in producing aggression.

Experimenter Bias What about the experimenter's expectations? **Experimenter bias** occurs when researchers' preconceived notions or expectations become a self-fulfilling prophecy and cause the researchers to find what they expect to find. A researcher's expectations can be communicated to participants, perhaps unintentionally, through tone of voice, gestures, or facial expressions. These communications can influence the participants' behavior. Expectations can also influence a researcher's interpretation of the experimental results, even if no influence occurred during the experiment. To control for experimenter bias, researchers must not know which participants are assigned to the experimental and control groups until after the research data are collected and recorded. (Obviously, someone assisting the researcher does know.) When neither the participants nor the researchers know which participants are getting the treatment and which are in the control group, the experiment is using the **double-blind technique**.

Limitations of the Experimental Method

What are the limitations of the experimental method?

You now know that experiments provide information about cause-effect relationships. But what are their limitations? For one thing, researchers who use the experimental method are able to exercise strict control over the setting, but the more control they exercise, the more unnatural and contrived the research setting becomes. And the more unnatural the setting becomes, the less generalizable findings may be to the real world. Another important limitation of the experimental method is that its use is either unethical or impossible for research in many areas of interest to psychologists. Some treatments cannot be given to human participants because their physical or psychological health would be endangered, or their constitutional rights violated.

What happens when we apply our knowledge about the problems associated with the experimental method to the results of Lang's study? Can we conclude that people in general tend to be more aggressive when they believe they are under the influence of alcohol? Before reaching such a conclusion, we must consider several factors: (1) All participants in this experiment were male college students. We cannot be sure that the same results would have occurred if females or males of other ages had been included. (2) The participants in this experiment were classified as heavy social drinkers. Would the same results have occurred if nondrinkers, moderate social drinkers, or alcoholics had been included? To apply this experiment's findings to other groups, researchers would have to replicate, or repeat, the experiment using different populations of subjects. (3) The amount of alcohol given to the students was just enough to bring their blood alcohol level to .10. We cannot be sure that the same results would have occurred if they had consumed more or less alcohol.

Remember It 1.3

1. The __________ is the only research method that can be used to identify cause-effect relationships between variables.
2. In an experiment, the __________ is manipulated by the researcher, and its effects on the __________ are measured at the end of the study.
3. The __________ group sometimes receives a placebo.
4. Random assignment is used to control for __________ bias.
5. __________ bias is controlled for when researchers do not know which participants are in the experimental and control grouops.

ANSWERS: 1. experimental method; 2. independent variable, dependent variable; 3. control; 4. selection; 5. Experimenter

The Correlational Method

Can you imagine a principal notifying parents that their son or daughter had been chosen to smoke marijuana for 2 years in order to further scientific knowledge? It is often illegal and always unethical to assign people randomly to experimental conditions that could be harmful. For example, to find out if smoking marijuana causes a decline in academic achievement, no researcher would randomly assign high school students to an experimental study that would require participants in the experimental group to smoke marijuana. When an experimental study cannot be performed to determine cause-effect relationships, the **correlational method** is usually used. This research method establishes the *correlation*, or degree of relationship, between two characteristics, events, or behaviors. A group is selected for study, and the variables of interest are measured for each participant. For example, the variables might be amount of marijuana previously used and grade-point average.

correlational method A research method used to establish the degree of relationship (correlation) between two characteristics, events, or behaviors.

The Correlation Coefficient

What is a correlation coefficient, and what does it mean?

What is the relationship between the price of a new car and the social status you gain from owning it? Isn't it true that as price goes up, status goes up as well? And isn't status one of the variables that many people take into account when buying a new car? As this example illustrates, correlations are part of our everyday lives, and we often use them in decision making.

When scientists study correlations, they apply a statistical formula to data representing two or more variables to obtain a *correlation coefficient*. A **correlation coefficient** is a numerical value that indicates the strength and direction of the relationship between two variables. A correlation coefficient ranges from +1.00 (a perfect positive correlation) to .00 (no relationship) to –1.00 (a perfect negative correlation). The number in a correlation coefficient indicates the relative strength of the relationship between two variables—the higher the number, the stronger the relationship. Therefore, a correlation of –.85 is stronger than a correlation of +.64.

correlation coefficient A numerical value that indicates the strength and direction of the relationship between two variables; ranges from +1.00 (a perfect positive correlation) to –1.00 (a perfect negative correlation).

The sign of a correlation coefficient (+ or –) indicates whether the two variables vary in the same or opposite directions. A positive correlation indicates that two variables vary in the same direction, like the price of a car and its associated social status. As another example, there is a positive though weak correlation between stress and illness. When stress increases, illness is likely to increase; when stress decreases, illness tends to decrease.

A negative correlation means that an increase in the value of one variable is associated with a decrease in the value of the other variable. For example, as mileage accumulates on a car's odometer, the less reliable it becomes. And there is a negative correlation between the number of cigarettes people smoke and the number of years they can expect to live.

Strengths and Weaknesses of Correlational Studies

What are the strengths and weaknesses of the correlational method?

Does the fact that there is a correlation between two variables indicate that one variable causes the other? Remember, only the experimental method can lead to conclusions about cause and effect. So, when two variables such as stress and illness are correlated, we cannot conclude that stress makes people sick. It might be that illness causes stress, or that a third factor such as poverty or poor general health causes people to be more susceptible to both illness and stress, as shown in Figure 1.2. For more information on the correlation coefficient, see the discussion of statistical methods in Appendix A, which follows Chapter 18.

So, you might be thinking, if a researcher can't draw cause-effect conclusions, why do correlational studies? There are three reasons. One reason is that it is sometimes impossible, for ethical reasons, to manipulate variables of interest. Scientists can't ethically ask pregnant women to drink alcohol just so they can find out whether it causes birth defects? The only option available in such cases is the correlational method. Researchers have to ask mothers about their drinking habits and note any association with birth defects in their babies. Knowing the correlation between prenatal alcohol consumption and the incidence of birth defects helps scientists make predictions about what may happen when pregnant women consume alcohol.

FIGURE 1.2 Correlation Does Not Prove Causation

A correlation between two variables does not prove that a cause-effect relationship exists between them. There is a correlation between stress and illness, but that does not mean that stress necessarily causes illness. Both stress and illness may result from another factor, such as poverty or poor general health.

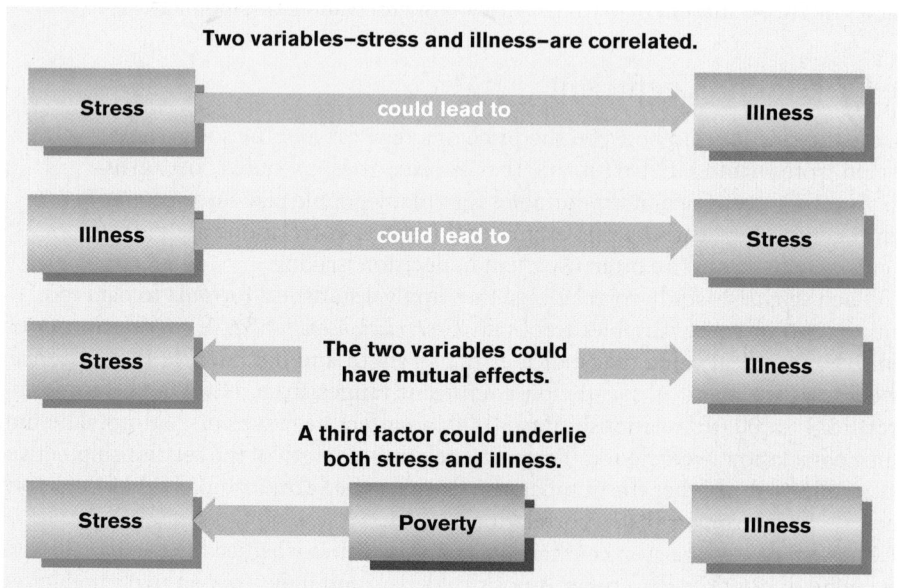

Another reason for using the correlational method is that many variables of interest to psychologists cannot be manipulated. Everyone wants to know whether biological sex (whether one is male or female) causes the differences we observe in men's and women's behavior. But we can't assign individuals to become male or female as we might ask them to take a drug or a placebo. Again, the only option is to study the correlations between biological sex and particular variables of interest, such as cognitive functioning and personality.

Finally, correlational studies can be done more quickly and cheaply than experiments. So, researchers sometimes choose to carry out correlational research even when an experiment would be ethically permissible and the variables could be experimentally controlled.

Review and Reflect 1.1 summarizes the different types of research methods we've discussed in this chapter.

Temperature is correlated with snow-cone sales. As temperature increases, so does the number of snow cones sold. Is this a positive or a negative correlation? What about the corresponding correlation between temperature and coffee sales? Is it positive or negative?

REVIEW *and* REFLECT 1.1

Research Methods in Psychology

METHOD	DESCRIPTION	ADVANTAGES	LIMITATIONS
DESCRIPTIVE METHODS			
Naturalistic and laboratory observation	Observation and recording of behavior in its natural setting or in a laboratory.	Behavior studied in everyday setting is more natural. A laboratory setting allows for precise measurement of variables. Can provide basis for hypotheses to be tested later.	Researchers' expectations can distort observations (observer bias). In natural setting, researcher has little or no control over conditions.
Case study	In-depth study of one or a few individuals using observation, interview, and/or psychological testing.	Source of information for rare or unusual conditions or events. Can provide basis for hypotheses to be tested later.	May not be generalizable. Time-consuming. Subject to misinterpretation by researcher.
Survey	Interviews and/or questionnaires used to gather information about attitudes, beliefs, experiences, or behaviors of a group of people.	Can provide accurate information about large numbers of people. Can track changes in attitudes and behavior over time.	Responses may be inaccurate. Sample may not be representative. Characteristics of interviewer may influence responses.
OTHER METHODS			
Experimental method	Random assignment of participants to groups. Manipulation of the independent variable(s) and measurement of the effect on the dependent variable.	Enables identification of cause-effect relationships.	Laboratory setting may inhibit natural behavior of participants. Findings may not be generalizable to the real world. In some cases, experiment is unethical or impossible.
Correlational method	Method used to determine the relationship (correlation) between two events, characteristics, or behaviors.	Can assess strength of relationship between variables. Provides basis for prediction.	Does not demonstrate cause and effect.

Want to be sure you've fully absorbed the material in this chapter? Visit **www.ablongman.com/wood5e** for access to free practice tests, flashcards, interactive activities, and links developed specifically to help you succeed in psychology.

Remember It 1.4

1. The __________ is a number describing the strength and direction of a relationship between two variables.
2. In positive correlations, two variables move in __________.
3. In negative correlations, two variables move in __________.
4. The closer a correlation coefficient is to +1.0 or −1.0, the __________ the relationship between two variables.

ANSWERS: 1. correlation coefficient; 2. the same direction; 3. opposite directions; 4. stronger

Participants in Psychological Research

Participant-Related Bias in Psychological Research

In what ways can participants bias research results?

Do you remember reading earlier about the importance of representative samples in survey research? With other methods, representativeness becomes an issue when psychologists want to generalize the findings of studies to individuals other than the studies' participants. For example, projections by the U.S. Bureau of the Census (2000) indicate that the percentage of non-Hispanic Whites in the U.S. population is expected to decrease from 71.5% in the year 2000 to 53% in 2050. Yet, Whites are often overrepresented in psychological studies because the majority of studies with human participants in the last 30 years have drawn from the college student population (Graham, 1992), which has a lower proportion of minorities than in the population in general. Moreover, college students, even those of minority ethnicity, are a relatively select group in terms of age, socioeconomic class, and educational level. Thus, they are not representative of the general population. This lack of representativeness in a research sample is a type of *participant-related bias.*

Gender bias is another type of participant-related bias. For example, Ader and Johnson (1994) found that, when conducting research in which all of the participants are of one sex, researchers typically specify the gender of the sample clearly when it is female, but not when the sample is exclusively male. Such a practice, according to Ader and Johnson, reveals a "tendency to consider male participants 'normative,' and results obtained from them generally applicable, whereas female participants are somehow 'different,' and results obtained from them are specific to female participants" (pp. 217–218). On a positive note, however, these researchers report that over the decades, gender bias in the sampling and selection of research subjects has been decreasing.

Another kind of bias happens when researchers, or consumers of research, overgeneralize the findings of a study to all members of a particular group. For example, Sandra Graham (1992) reported finding a methodological flaw—failure to include socioeconomic status—in much of the research literature comparing White Americans and African Americans. Graham pointed out that African Americans are overrepresented among the economically disadvantaged. She maintained that socioeconomic status should be incorporated into research designs "to disentangle race and social class effects" in studies that compare White and African Americans (p. 634).

Ageism is another continuing source of participant-related bias, especially apparent in the language used in psychological research (Schaie, 1993). For example, the titles of research studies on aging often include words such as *loss*, *deterioration*, *decline*, and *dependency*. Moreover, researchers are likely to understate the great diversity among the older adults they study. According to Schaie, "most research on adulthood shows that differences between those in their 60s and those in their 80s are far greater than those between 20- and 60-year-olds" (p. 50). Researchers should guard against using descriptions or reaching conclusions that imply that all members of a given age group are defined by negative characteristics.

Protecting Research Participants' Rights

Researchers are ethically obligated to protect the rights of all study participants. In 2002, the American Psychological Association (APA) adopted a new set of ethical standards governing research with human participants so as to safeguard their rights while supporting the goals of scientific inquiry. Following are some of the main provisions of the code:

What ethical rules must researchers follow when humans are involved in studies?

- *Legality*. All research must conform to applicable federal, state, and local laws and regulations.
- *Institutional approval*. Researchers must obtain approval from all institutions involved in a study. For example, a researcher cannot conduct a study in a school without the school's approval.
- *Informed consent*. Participants must be informed of the purpose of the study and its potential for harming them. Researchers can deviate from this standard of informed consent only when they have a justifiable reason for doing so. Typically, an institutional committee examines whether there is justification for deceiving participants in a study. Most such committees find, for instance, that the use of placebos doesn't violate this standard because a placebo control group enables experimenters to more effectively measure the effects of a treatment by controlling for participants' expectations.
- *Deception*. Deception of participants is ethical when it is necessary. However, the code of ethics cautions researchers against using deception if another means can be found to test the study's hypothesis.
- *Debriefing*. Whenever a researcher deceives participants, including through the use of placebo treatments, he or she must tell participants about the deception as soon as the study is complete.
- *Clients, patients, students, and subordinates*. When participants are under another's authority (for example, a therapist's client, a patient in a hospital, a student in a psychology class, or an employee), researchers must take steps to ensure that participation in a study, and the information obtained during participation, will not damage the participants in any way. Professors, for example, cannot reduce students' grades if the students refuse to participate in a research study.
- *Payment for participation*. Participants can be paid, but the code of ethics requires that they be fully informed about what is expected in return for payment. In addition, researchers are to refrain from offering excessive payments that may bias the study's participants in some way.
- *Publication*. Psychological researchers must report their findings in an appropriate forum, such as a scientific journal, and they must make their data available to others who want to verify their findings. Even when a study produces no findings, its results must still be reported; in such cases, the appropriate forum is the institution that sponsored the research, the organization in which the research was conducted, or the agency or foundation that funded it. Results must also be made available to participants.

Why are animals used in research?

The Use of Animals in Research

The new APA code of ethics also includes guidelines for using animals in psychological research. Here are a few of the important guidelines:

- *Legality.* Like research with human participants, animal research must follow all relevant federal, state, and local laws.
- *Supervision by experienced personnel.* The use of animals must be supervised by people who are trained in their care. These experienced personnel must teach all subordinates, such as research assistants, how to properly handle and feed the animals and to recognize signs of illness or distress.
- *Minimization of discomfort.* Researchers are ethically bound to minimize any discomfort to research animals. For example, it is unethical to perform surgery on research animals without appropriate anesthesia. And when researchers must terminate the lives of research animals, they must do so in a humane manner.

Even with these safeguards in place, the use of animals in research is controversial. Many animal rights advocates want all animal research stopped immediately. Books on animal rights devote an average of 63.3% of their content to the use of animals in research (Nicholl & Russell, 1990). Yet, of the approximately 6.3 million animals killed each year in the United States, only 0.3% are used in research and education, while 96.5% are used for food, 2.6% are killed by hunters, 0.4% are killed in animal shelters, and 0.2% are used for fur garments (Christensen, 1997).

In a survey of almost 4,000 randomly selected members of the APA, "80% of respondents expressed general support for psychological research on animals" (Plous, 1996, p. 1177). Among the general public, support for animal research is higher when the research is tied to human health and highest when the animals involved in such research are rats and mice rather than dogs, cats, or primates (Plous, 1996). Most agree that there are at least six reasons for using animals in research: (1) They provide a simpler model for studying processes that operate similarly in humans; (2) researchers can exercise far more control over animal subjects and thus be more certain of their conclusions; (3) a wider range of medical and other manipulations can be used with animals; (4) it is easier to study the entire life span and even multiple generations in some animal species; (5) animals are more economical to use as research subjects and are available at the researchers' convenience; and (6) some researchers simply want to learn more about the animals themselves.

Is animal research really necessary? Virtually all of the marvels of modern medicine are due at least in part to experimentation using animals. Animal research has yielded much knowledge about the brain and the physiology of vision, hearing, and the other senses (Domjan & Purdy, 1995). It has also increased knowledge in the areas of learning, motivation, stress, memory, and the effects on the unborn of various drugs ingested during pregnancy. Almost half of the research funded by the National Institutes of Health is conducted on animals (Cork et al., 1997).

Most psychologists recognize that many scientific advances would not have been possible without animal research. Where do you stand on this issue?

Overall, the animal rights controversy has had a positive effect on research ethics: It has served to increase concern for the treatment of animals as research subjects and to stimulate a search for alternative research methods that is reportedly resulting in a decrease in the numbers of animals needed (Mukerjee, 1997, p. 86).

Now that we've explored the process involved in psychological research and theory, let's look back at the beginnings of psychology and some of the individuals who helped shape the discipline.

Remember It 1.5

1. Psychologists are required to debrief participants thoroughly after a study involving __________.
2. __________, __________, and __________ have been overrepresented in many kinds of psychological studies.
3. By using __________ in research, researchers have learned a great deal about topics such as the effects of drugs ingested during pregnancy.

ANSWERS: 1. deception; 2. Whites, males, college students; 3. animals

Exploring Psychology's Roots

If you were to trace the development of psychology from the beginning, you would need to start before the earliest pages of recorded history, beyond even the early Greek philosophers, such as Aristotle and Plato. However, it was not until experimental methods were applied to the study of psychological processes that psychology became recognized as a formal academic discipline.

structuralism The first formal school of thought in psychology, aimed at analyzing the basic elements, or structure, of conscious mental experience.

The Founding of Psychology

What roles did Wundt and Titchener play in the founding of psychology?

Who were the "founders" of psychology? Historians acknowledge that three German scientists—Ernst Weber, Gustav Fechner, and Hermann von Helmholtz—were the first to systematically study behavior and mental processes. But it is Wilhelm Wundt (1832–1920) who is generally thought of as the "father" of psychology. Wundt's vision for the new discipline included studies of social and cultural influences on human thought (Benjafield, 1996).

Wundt established a psychological laboratory at the University of Leipzig in Germany in 1879, an event considered to mark the birth of psychology as a formal academic discipline. Using a method called *introspection*, Wundt and his associates studied the perception of a variety of visual, tactile, and auditory stimuli, including the rhythm patterns produced by metronomes set at different speeds. Introspection as a research method involves looking inward to examine one's own conscious experience and then reporting that experience.

Even though these children experience the same sensations (sweetness and coldness) as they enjoy eating their ice cream, their reported introspections of the experience would probably differ.

Structuralism

Wundt's most famous student, Englishman Edward Bradford Titchener (1867–1927), took the new field to the United States, where he set up a psychological laboratory at Cornell University. He gave the name **structuralism** to this first formal school of thought in psychology, which aimed at analyzing the basic elements, or the structure, of conscious mental experience. Like Wundt before him, Titchener thought that consciousness could be reduced to its basic elements, just as water (H_2O) can be broken down into its constituent elements—hydrogen (H) and oxygen (O). For Wundt, pure sensations—such as sweetness, coldness, or redness—were the basic elements of consciousness. And these pure sensations, he believed, combined to form perceptions.

The work of both Wundt and Titchener was criticized for its primary method, introspection. Introspection is not objective, even though it involves observation, measurement, and experimentation. When different introspectionists were exposed to the same stimulus, such as the click of a metronome, they frequently reported different experiences. Therefore, structuralism was not in favor for long. Later schools of thought in psychology were established, partly in a reaction against structuralism, which did not survive after the death of its most ardent spokesperson, Titchener. Nevertheless, the structuralists were responsible for establishing psychology as a science through their insistence that psychological processes could be measured and studied using methods similar to those employed by scientists in other fields.

Functionalism

Why is functionalism important in the history of psychology?

As structuralism was losing its influence in the United States in the early 20th century, a new school of psychology called functionalism was taking shape. **Functionalism** was concerned not with the structure of consciousness, but with how mental processes function—that is, how humans and animals use mental processes in adapting to their environment. The influential work of Charles Darwin (1809–1882), especially his ideas about evolution and the continuity of species, was largely responsible for an increasing use of animals in psychological experiments. Even though Darwin, who was British, contributed important seeds of thought that helped give birth to the new school of psychology, functionalism was primarily American in character and spirit.

■ **functionalism**
An early school of psychology that was concerned with how humans and animals use mental processes in adapting to their environment.

The famous American psychologist William James (1842–1910) was an advocate of functionalism, even though he did much of his writing before this school of psychology emerged. James's best-known work is his highly regarded and frequently quoted textbook *Principles of Psychology*, published more than a century ago (1890). James taught that mental processes are fluid and have continuity, rather than the rigid, or fixed, structure that the structuralists suggested. James spoke of the "stream of consciousness," which, he said, functions to help humans adapt to their environment.

How did functionalism change psychology? Functionalism broadened the scope of psychology to include the study of behavior as well as mental processes. It also allowed the study of children, animals, and the mentally impaired, groups that could not be studied by the structuralists because they could not be trained to use introspection. Functionalism also focused on an applied, more practical use of psychology by encouraging the study of educational practices, individual differences, and adaptation in the workplace (industrial psychology).

Women and Minorities in Psychology

In what ways have women and minorities shaped the field of psychology, both in the past and today?

From its beginning until the mid–20th century, the field of psychology was shaped and dominated largely by White European and American males. The reason for this was the thinking of the times. For centuries, conventional thought had held that higher education was exclusively for White males, that women should rear children and be homemakers, and that minorities were best suited for manual labor. And, as Thomas Paine observed in his influential pamphlet *Common Sense* (1776), "A long habit of not thinking a thing wrong, gives it a superficial appearance of being right." However, beginning in the late 19th century, women and minorities overcame these prejudices to make notable achievements in and contributions to the study of psychology.

Christine Ladd-Franklin (1847–1930) completed the requirements for a Ph.D. at Johns Hopkins University in the mid-1880s but had to wait over 40 years before receiving her degree in 1926, when the university first agreed to grant it to women. Ladd-Franklin formulated a well-regarded, evolutionary theory of color vision.

In 1895, Mary Whiton Calkins (1863–1930) completed the requirements for a doctorate at Harvard. And even though William James described her as one of his most capable students, Harvard refused to grant the degree to a woman (Dewsbury, 2000). Undeterred, Calkins established a psychology laboratory at Wellesley College and developed the paired-associates test, an important research technique for the study of memory. She became the first female president of the American Psychological Association in 1905.

Margaret Floy Washburn (1871–1939) received her Ph.D. in psychology from Cornell University and later taught at Vassar College (Dewsbury, 2000). She wrote several books, among them *The Animal Mind* (1908), an influential book on animal behavior, and *Movement and Mental Imagery* (1916).

Francis Cecil Sumner (1895–1954) was a self-taught scholar. In 1920, without benefit of a formal high school education, he became the first African American to earn a Ph.D. in psychology, from Clark University. This feat was accomplished "in spite of innumerable social and physical factors mitigating against such achievements by black people in America" (Guthrie, 1998, p. 177). Sumner translated more than 3,000 articles from German, French, and Spanish. He chaired the psychology department at Howard University and is known as the "father" of African American psychology.

Albert Sidney Beckham (1897–1964), another African American psychologist, conducted some impressive early studies on intelligence and showed how it is related to success in numerous occupational fields. Beckham also established the first psychological laboratory at a Black institution of higher learning—Howard University.

More recently, African American psychologist Kenneth Clark achieved national recognition for his writings on the harmful effects of racial segregation. His work affected the Supreme Court ruling that declared racial segregation in U.S. schools to be unconstitutional (Benjamin & Crouse, 2002). His wife, Mamie Phipps Clark, also achieved recognition when the couple published their works on racial identification and self-esteem, writings that have become classics in the field (Lal, 2002).

Hispanic American Jorge Sanchez conducted studies on bias in intelligence testing during the 1930s. He pointed out that both cultural differences and language differences work against Hispanic students when they take IQ tests.

Native American and Asian American psychologists have made important contributions to psychological research as well. Moreover, they are the fastest growing minority groups in the field of psychology. The percentage of doctorates awarded to individuals in both groups more than doubled from the mid-1970s to the mid-1990s (National Science Foundation, 2000). One contemporary Native American psychologist, Marigold Linton, is known for her research examining autobiographical memory. In 1999, Richard Suinn, an eminent researcher in behavioral psychology, became the first Asian American president of the American Psychological Association.

Today, more women than men obtain degrees in psychology, and minority group representation is growing. However, there continues to be a gap between the proportion of minorities in the U.S. population and their representation among professional psychologists. Indeed, although the proportion of minorities in the U.S. population is about 28%, only 16% of students pursuing graduate degrees in psychology are of minority ethnicity (APA, 2000). Consequently, the APA and other organizations have established programs to encourage minority enrollment in graduate programs in psychology.

Remember It 1.6

1. Classify each of the following people and concepts as being associated with (a) Wundt, (b) structuralism, and/or (c) functionalism. (Hint: Some items apply to more than one.)

____ (1) James

____ (2) based on Darwin's theory of evolution

____ (3) stream of consciousness

____ (4) elements of experience

____ (5) Titchener

____ (6) introspection

____ (7) became known in the 19th century

2. Match each of the following individuals with his or her contribution to psychology.

____ (1) Francis Cecil Sumner

____ (2) Mary Whiton Calkins

____ (3) Kenneth Clark

____ (4) Christine Ladd-Franklin

____ (5) Jorge Sanchez

a. first female president of the APA

b. conducted studies on cultural bias in intelligence testing

c. first African American to earn a Ph.D. in psychology

d. studied the harmful effects of racial segregation

e. had to wait 40 years to receive a Ph.D. in psychology after completing all the requirements

ANSWERS: 1. (1) c, (2) c, (3) c, (4) a, (5) b, (6) a, b, (7) a, b, c; 2. (1) c, (2) a, (3) d, (4) e, (5) b

Schools of Thought in Psychology

Why don't we hear about structuralism and functionalism today? In the early 20th century, the debate between the two points of view sparked a veritable explosion of theoretical discussion and research examining psychological processes. The result was the appearance of new theories that were better able to explain behavior and mental processes. The foundations of the major schools of thought in the field were established during that period and continue to be influential today.

Behaviorism

How do behaviorists explain behavior and mental processes?

Psychologist John B. Watson (1878–1958) looked at the study of psychology as defined by the structuralists and functionalists and disliked virtually everything he saw. In his article "Psychology as the Behaviorist Views It" (1913), Watson proposed a radically new approach to psychology, one that rejected the subjectivity of both structuralism and functionalism. This new school redefined psychology as the "science of behavior." Termed **behaviorism** by Watson, this school of psychology confines itself to the study of behavior because behavior is observable and measurable and, therefore, objective and scientific. Behaviorism also emphasizes that behavior is determined primarily by factors in the environment.

Behaviorism was the most influential school of thought in American psychology until the 1960s. It is still a major force in modern psychology, in large part because of the profound influence of B. F. Skinner (1904–1990). Skinner agreed with Watson that concepts such as mind, consciousness, and feelings are neither objective nor measurable and, therefore, not appropriate subject matter for psychology. Furthermore, Skinner argued that these concepts are not needed in order to explain behavior. One can explain behavior, he claimed, by analyzing the conditions that are present before a behavior occurs and by analyzing the consequences that follow the behavior.

■ **behaviorism**
The school of psychology founded by John B. Watson that views observable, measurable behavior as the appropriate subject matter for psychology and emphasizes the key role of environment as a determinant of behavior.

Skinner's research on operant conditioning emphasized the importance of reinforcement in learning and in shaping and maintaining behavior. He maintained that any behavior that is reinforced (followed by pleasant or rewarding consequences) is more likely to be performed again. Skinner's work has had a powerful influence on modern psychology. You will read more about operant conditioning in Chapter 5.

Psychoanalysis

What do psychoanalytic psychologists believe about the role of the unconscious?

Sigmund Freud (1856–1939), whose life and work you will study in Chapter 14, developed a theory of human behavior based largely on case studies of his patients. Freud's theory, **psychoanalysis,** maintains that human mental life is like an iceberg. The smallest, visible part of the iceberg represents the conscious mental experience of the individual. But underwater, hidden from view, floats a vast store of unconscious impulses, wishes, and desires. Freud insisted that individuals do not consciously control their thoughts, feelings, and behavior; these are instead determined by unconscious forces.

Freud believed that the unconscious is the storehouse for material that threatens the conscious life of the individual—disturbing sexual and aggressive impulses as well as traumatic experiences that have been repressed, or pushed down to the unconscious. Once there, rather than resting quietly (out of sight, out of mind), the unconscious material festers and seethes.

■ **psychoanalysis** (SY-ko-ah-NAL-ih-sis) The term Freud used for both his theory of personality and his therapy for the treatment of psychological disorders; the unconscious is the primary focus of psychoanalytic theory.

The overriding importance that Freud placed on sexual and aggressive impulses caused much controversy both inside and outside the field of psychology. The most notable of Freud's famous students—Carl Jung, Alfred Adler, and Karen Horney—broke away from their mentor and developed their own theories of personality. These three and their followers are often collectively referred to as *neo-Freudians.*

The general public has heard of such concepts as the unconscious, repression, rationalization, and the Freudian slip. Such familiarity has made Sigmund Freud a larger-than-life figure rather than an obscure Austrian doctor resting within the dusty pages of history. Although Freud continues to influence popular culture, the volume of research on psychoanalysis has continued to diminish steadily (Robins et al., 1999). Yet, the psychoanalytic approach continues to be influential, although in a form that has been modified considerably over the past several decades by the neo-Freudians.

Humanistic Psychology

According to Maslow and Rogers, what motivates human behavior and mental processes?

Humanistic psychologists reject with equal vigor (1) the behaviorist view that behavior is determined by factors in the environment and (2) the pessimistic view of the psychoanalytic approach, that human behavior is determined primarily by unconscious forces. **Humanistic psychology** focuses on the uniqueness of human beings and their capacity for choice, growth, and psychological health.

Abraham Maslow and other early humanists, such as Carl Rogers (1902–1987), pointed out that Freud based his theory primarily on data from his disturbed patients. By contrast, the humanists emphasize a much more positive view of human nature. They maintain that people are innately good and that they possess free will. The humanists believe that people are capable of making conscious, rational choices, which can lead to personal growth and psychological health.

As you will learn in Chapter 14, Maslow proposed a theory of motivation that consists of a hierarchy of needs. He considered the need for self-actualization (developing to one's fullest potential) to be the highest need on the hierarchy. Carl Rogers developed what he called *client-centered therapy,* an approach in which the client, or patient, directs a discussion focused on his or her own view of a problem rather than on the therapist's analysis. Rogers and other humanists also popularized group therapy as part of the human potential movement. Thus, the humanistic perspective

■ **humanistic psychology** The school of psychology that focuses on the uniqueness of human beings and their capacity for choice, growth, and psychological health.

continues to be important in research examining human motivation and in the practice of psychotherapy.

Cognitive Psychology

What is the focus of cognitive psychology?

Cognitive psychology grew and developed partly in response to strict behaviorism, especially in the United States (Robins et al., 1999). **Cognitive psychology** sees humans not as passive recipients who are pushed and pulled by environmental forces, but as active participants who seek out experiences, who alter and shape those experiences, and who use mental processes to transform information in the course of their own cognitive development. It studies mental processes such as memory, problem solving, reasoning, decision making, perception, language, and other forms of cognition. Historically, modern cognitive psychology is derived from two streams of thought: one that began with a small group of German scientists studying human perception in the early twentieth century, and another that grew up alongside the emerging field of computer science in the second half of the century.

■ cognitive psychology
The school of psychology that sees humans as active participants in their environment; studies mental processes such as memory, problem solving, reasoning, decision making, perception, language, and other forms of cognition.

■ Gestalt psychology
The school of psychology that emphasizes that individuals perceive objects and patterns as whole units and that the perceived whole is more than the sum of its parts.

■ information-processing theory
An approach to the study of mental structures and processes that uses the computer as a model for human thinking.

Gestalt Psychology **Gestalt psychology** made its appearance in Germany in 1912. The Gestalt psychologists, notably Max Wertheimer, Kurt Koffka, and Wolfgang Köhler, emphasized that individuals perceive objects and patterns as whole units and that the perceived whole is more than the sum of its parts. The German word *Gestalt* roughly means "whole, form, or pattern."

To support the Gestalt theory, Wertheimer, the leader of the Gestalt psychologists, performed his famous experiment demonstrating the *phi phenomenon.* In this experiment, two light bulbs are placed a short distance apart in a dark room. The first light is flashed on and then turned off just as the second light is flashed on. As this pattern of flashing the lights on and off continues, an observer sees what appears to be a single light moving back and forth from one position to another. Here, said the Gestaltists, is proof that people perceive wholes or patterns, rather than collections of separate sensations.

When the Nazis came to power in Germany in the 1930s, the Gestalt school disbanded, and its most prominent members emigrated to the United States. Today, the fundamental concept underlying Gestalt psychology—that the mind *interprets* experiences in predictable ways rather than simply reacts to them—is central to cognitive psychologists' ideas about learning, memory, problem solving, and even psychotherapy.

Is this person having a bad day? The perceptual processes described by the Gestalt psychologists are observable in everyday life. We often put frustrating events—such as getting up late and then having a flat tire—together to form a "whole" concept, such as "I'm having a bad day."

Information-Processing Theory The advent of the computer provided cognitive psychologists with a new way to conceptualize mental structures and processes, known as **information-processing theory**. According to this view, the brain processes information in sequential steps, in much the same way as a computer does serial processing—that is, one step at a time. But as modern technology has changed computers and computer programs, cognitive psychologists have changed their models. "Increasingly, parallel processing models [models in which several tasks are performed at once] are developed in addition to stage models of processing" (Haberlandt, 1997, p. 22).

A central idea of information-processing theory, one that it shares with Gestalt psychology, is that the brain interprets information rather than just responding to it. For example, consider this statement: *The old woman was sweeping the steps.* If information-processing researchers ask people who have read the sentence to recall whether it includes the word *broom,* a majority will say that it does. According to information-processing theorists, rules for handling information lead us to find associations between new input, such as the statement about a woman sweeping, and previously acquired knowledge, such as our understanding that brooms are used for sweeping. As a result, most of us construct a memory of the sentence that leads us to incorrectly recall that it includes the word *broom*.

Designing computer programs that can process human language in the same way as the human brain is one of the goals of research on *artificial intelligence*. Today, such research represents one of the most important applications of information-processing theory.

Cognitive Psychology Today Over the past 100 years or so, cognitive psychologists have carried out studies that have greatly increased our knowledge of the human memory system and the mental processes involved in problem solving. Moreover, the principles discovered in these experiments have been used to explain and study all kinds of psychological variables—from gender role development to individual differences in intelligence. As a result, cognitive psychology is currently recognized as one of the most prominent schools of psychological thought (Robins et al., 1999).

Remember It 1.7

1. Match the school of psychology with its major emphasis:

____ (1) the scientific study of behavior	a. Gestalt psychology
____ (2) the perception of whole units or patterns	b. humanistic psychology
____ (3) the study of the unconscious	c. cognitive psychology
____ (4) the use of the computer as a model for human cognition	d. behaviorism
____ (5) the uniqueness of human beings and their capacity for personal growth	e. information-processing theory
____ (6) the study of mental processes	f. psychoanalysis

2. Match the major figure with the appropriate school of psychology. (Options may be used more than once.)

____ (1) Freud	a. Gestalt psychology
____ (2) Skinner	b. humanistic psychology
____ (3) Maslow	c. behaviorism
____ (4) Wertheimer	d. psychoanalysis
____ (5) Watson	
____ (6) Rogers	

ANSWERS: 1. (1) d, (2) a, (3) f, (4) e, (5) b, (6) c; 2. (1) d, (2) c, (3) b, (4) a, (5) c, (6) b

Current Trends in Psychology

Do we know everything there is to know about psychology today? Absolutely not. Like the field of medicine, psychology is an evolving science in which new theories are being tested and more precise research is being conducted every day. Its ongoing advances will continue to illuminate our thinking and impact our behaviors. So, where is psychology headed today? In addition to the continuing influence of psychodynamic theory, behaviorism, humanistic psychology, and cognitive psychology, several other important trends in psychology have emerged in recent years.

Evolutionary Psychology

What is the main idea behind evolutionary psychology?

Why do you think all healthy babies form attachments to their primary caregivers? Why do you think most men prefer mates who are younger than they are? These are the kinds of questions that interest *evolutionary psychologists*. **Evolutionary psychology** focuses on how the human behaviors required for survival have adapted in the face of environmental pressures over the long course of evolution (Archer, 1996). Evolutionary psychology has been called, simply, a combination of evolutionary biology and cognitive psychology (Evans & Zarate, 2000). Two widely recognized proponents of evolutionary psychology, Leda Cosmides and John Tooby, hold that this perspective combines the forces of evolutionary biology, anthropology, cognitive psychology, and neuroscience. They explain that an evolutionary perspective can be applied to any topic within the field of psychology (Cosmides & Tooby, 2000). One of the most influential evolutionary psychologists, David Buss, and his colleagues have conducted a number of fascinating studies examining men's and women's patterns of behavior in romantic relationships (1999, 2000a, 2000b, 2001).

One of Buss's consistent findings is that men seem to experience more jealousy when faced with a partner's sexual infidelity than with her emotional infidelity (Buss, 1999; Buss et al., 1992; Shackelford et al., 2002). By contrast, the women in Buss's research appear to be more concerned about emotional than sexual unfaithfulness in a partner. Evolutionary psychologists claim that men's jealousy focuses on sexual infidelity because, in the evolutionary past, a man's certainty of his paternity was jeopardized if he learned that his mate had been sexually unfaithful. But the best chance a woman had to pass her genes on to future generations was to be able to rely on material resources, protection, and support from a mate that would help her offspring survive and reach sexual maturity. The man's emotional commitment to her, then, was of paramount importance. So, the presumably biological sex difference in reactions to infidelity favors the survival of offspring: Men's insistence on sexual fidelity ensures knowledge of paternity and, therefore, their willingness to commit to an investment in their children's upbringing. Women's insistence on emotional commitment promotes family harmony and continuity, which, in turn, provide a stable environment in which to bring up children.

■ **evolutionary psychology** The school of psychology that studies how humans have adapted the behaviors required for survival in the face of environmental pressures over the long course of evolution.

According to evolutionary psychology, this father is more likely to form a lasting emotional commitment to the baby if he is sure that the mother has been sexually faithful and, therefore, that the baby is genetically his own.

It's important to note, too, that Buss and his colleagues have gone beyond just asking men and women about jealousy. They tested participants of both sexes in the laboratory and asked them to imagine the two types of infidelity while connected to instruments for measuring heart or pulse rate, electrodermal response (sweating), and tensing of the brow muscles (frowning). The men showed high physiological distress at the thought of sexual infidelity, but far less when considering emotional infidelity. (Emotional infidelity is the creation of a bond with someone other than one's intimate partner that involves feelings, especially romantic love, that are assumed to have been promised only to that partner.) The women tended to exhibit high physiological distress when imagining emotional infidelity by their partner, but much less when confronting sexual infidelity. Apparently, men's and women's verbal reports in Buss's studies corresponded to what they were experiencing internally. As far as can be determined, these and similar findings appear to be universal. Results of a cross-cultural study in the United States, Germany, the Netherlands, and Korea are shown in Figure 1.3. By the way, as you might suspect, Buss's conclusions are controversial. Other psychologists (e.g., Eagly & Wood, 1999) explain his research results in terms of social and cultural variables. You'll read more about the controversy in Chapter 12.

FIGURE 1.3 **Gender Differences in Jealousy across Cultures**

Across all cultures, men experience greater distress in response to sexual infidelity than women do, while women experience greater distress in response to emotional infidelity than men do.

Source: From Buunk et al. (1996).

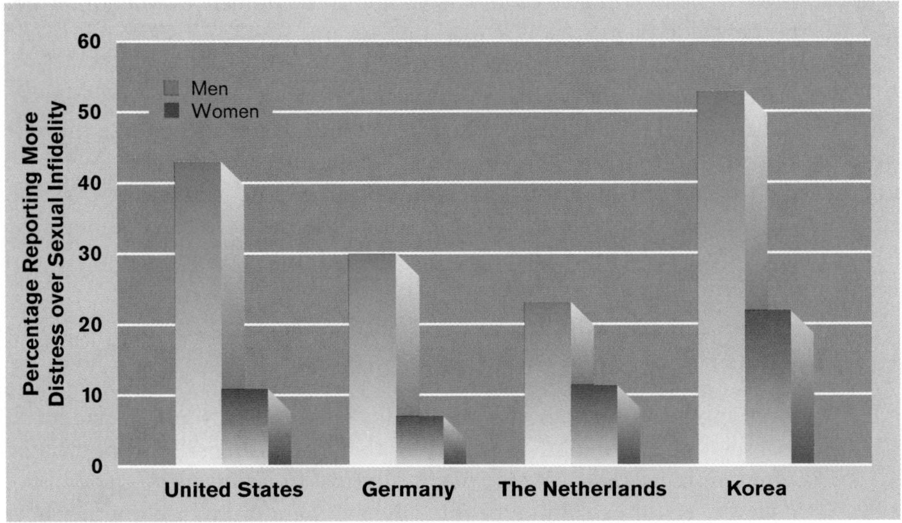

Biological (Physiological) Psychology

How is biological psychology changing the field of psychology?

Sometimes students are confused about the difference between evolutionary psychology and **biological psychology** (also referred to as *physiological psychology*). After all, many think, isn't evolution "biological" in nature? Yes, it is, but evolutionary psychology provides explanations of how certain biologically based behaviors came to be common in an entire species. Consequently, it focuses on *universals*, traits that exist in every member of a species. For instance, language is a human universal.

By contrast, biological psychologists look for links between specific behaviors and particular biological factors that often help explain *individual differences*. They study the structures of the brain and central nervous system, the functioning of neurons, the delicate balance of neurotransmitters and hormones, and the effects of heredity to look for links between these biological factors and behavior. For example, the number of ear infections children have in the first year of life (a *biological* individual difference) is correlated with learning disabilities in the elementary school years (a *behavioral* individual difference) (Spreen et al., 1995). (Remember, this finding doesn't mean that ear infections *cause* learning disabilities; most likely, some other factor links the two.)

Many biological psychologists work under the umbrella of an interdisciplinary field known as **neuroscience**. Neuroscience combines the work of psychologists, biologists, biochemists, medical researchers, and others in the study of the structure and function of the nervous system. Important findings in psychology have resulted from this work. For example, researchers have learned that defects in nerve cell membranes interfere with the cells' ability to make use of brain chemicals that help us control body movement (Kurup & Kurup, 2002). These findings shed light on the physiological processes underlying serious neurological disorders such as Parkinson's disease and help pharmacological researchers in their efforts to create more effective medications for these disorders. And the recently completed map of the human genome promises to provide new explanations for many mental illnesses (Plomin et al., 2003).

■ **biological psychology**
The school of psychology that looks for links between specific behaviors and equally specific biological processes that often help explain individual differences.

■ **neuroscience**
An interdisciplinary field that combines the work of psychologists, biologists, biochemists, medical researchers, and others in the study of the structure and function of the nervous system.

What kinds of variables interest psychologists who take a sociocultural approach?

The Sociocultural Approach

How do your background and cultural experiences affect your behavior and mental processing? Just as important as the current trend toward biological explanations is the growing realization among psychologists that social and cultural forces may be as powerful as evolutionary and physiological factors. The **sociocultural approach** emphasizes social and cultural influences on human behavior and stresses the importance of understanding those influences when interpreting the behavior of others. For example, several psychologists (e.g., Tweed & Lehman, 2002) have researched philosophical differences between Asian and Western cultures that may help explain cross-national achievement differences.

Just as someone can be quoted out of context and thus misunderstood, the actions or gestures of a person from another culture can be misinterpreted if the observer does not understand the cultural context in which they occur. Gergen and others (1996) have claimed that there is a "desperate need" for culturally sensitive research about people's behavior in such areas as health, "birth control, child abuse, drug addiction, ethnic and religious conflict, and the effects of technology on society" (p. 502).

What are psychological perspectives, and how are they related to an eclectic position?

Psychological Perspectives and Eclecticism

The views of modern psychologists are frequently difficult to categorize into traditional schools of thought. Thus, rather than discussing schools of thought, it is often more useful to refer to **psychological perspectives**—general points of view used for explaining people's behavior and thinking, whether normal or abnormal. So, for example, a psychologist may adopt a behavioral perspective without necessarily agreeing with all of Watson's or Skinner's ideas. What is important is that the psychologist taking such a view will explain behavior in terms of environmental forces.

The major perspectives in psychology today and the kinds of variables each emphasizes in explaning behavior are as follows:

- *Behavioral perspective*—environmental factors
- *Psychoanalytic perspective*—emotions, unconscious motivations, early childhood experiences
- *Humanistic perspective*—subjective experiences, intrinsic motivation to achieve self-actualization

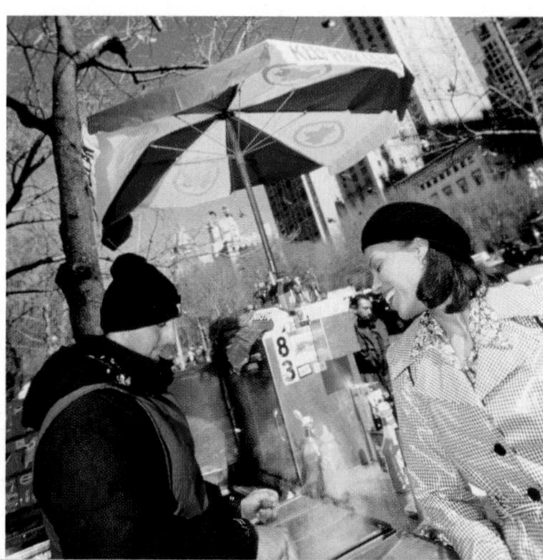

A sociocultural approach helps psychologists explain cross-cultural differences in behavior.

- *Cognitive perspective*—mental processes
- *Evolutionary perspective*—inherited traits that enhance adaptability
- *Biological perspective*—biological structures, processes, heredity
- *Sociocultural perspective*—social and cultural variables

Review and Reflect 1.2 lists these perspectives along with an illustration of how each might explain older adults' poor performance on researchers' memory tasks as compared to that of younger adults.

Psychologists need not limit themselves to only one perspective or approach. Many take an *eclectic position*, choosing a combination of approaches to explain a particular behavior. For example, a psychologist may explain a behavior in terms of both environmental factors and mental processes. A child's unruly behavior in school may be seen as maintained by teacher attention (a behavioral explanation) but as initially caused by an emotional reaction to a family event such as divorce (a psychoanalytic explanation). By adopting multiple perspectives, psychologists are able to devise more complex theories and research studies, resulting in improved treatment strategies. In this way, their theories and studies can more closely mirror the behavior of real people in real situations.

■ **sociocultural approach** The view that social and cultural factors may be just as powerful as evolutionary and physiological factors in affecting behavior and mental processing and that these factors must be understood when interpreting the behavior of others.

■ **psychological perspectives** General points of view used for explaining people's behavior and thinking, whether normal or abnormal.

REVIEW *and* REFLECT 1.2

Major Perspectives in Psychology

PERSPECTIVE	EMPHASIS	EXPLANATION OF OLDER ADULTS' POOR PERFORMANCE ON RESEARCHERS' MEMORY TASKS
Behavioral	The role of environment in shaping and controlling behavior	Older adults spend little or no time in environments such as school, where they would be reinforced for using their memories.
Psychoanalytic	The role of unconscious motivation and early childhood experiences in determining behavior and thought	Older adults' unconscious fear of impending death interferes with memory processes.
Humanistic	The importance of an individual's subjective experience as a key to understanding his or her behavior	Older adults are more concerned about finding meaning in their lives than about performing well on experimenters' memory tasks.
Cognitive	The role of mental processes—perception, thinking, and memory—that underlie behavior	Older adults fail to use effective memory strategies.
Evolutionary	The roles of inherited tendencies that have proven adaptive in humans	Declines in cognitive and biological functions are programmed into our genes so that younger, and presumably reproductively healthier, people will be more attractive as potential mates.
Biological	The role of biological processes and structures, as well as heredity, in explaining behavior	As the brain ages, connections between neurons break down, causing a decline in intellectual functions such as memory.
Sociocultural	The roles of social and cultural influences on behavior	Older people have internalized the ageist expectations of society and, as a result, expect themselves to perform poorly on memory tasks.

Want to be sure you've fully absorbed the material in this chapter? Visit **www.ablongman.com/wood5e** for access to free practice tests, flashcards, interactive activities, and links developed specifically to help you succeed in psychology.

Remember It 1.8

1. A(n) __________ psychologist would be interested in whether attachment is a universal feature of infant-caregiver relations.
2. A(n) __________ psychologist would be interested in the relationship between hormones and aggressive behavior.
3. A(n) __________ psychologist would be interested in whether members of minority groups have lower self-esteem than those who belong to a dominant group.
4. Which of the following statements represent an eclectic position?

a. Individual differences in aggression are genetic, but parents and teachers can teach highly aggressive children to be less so.

b. Children who are highly aggressive have not received enough punishment for their inappropriate behavior.

c. Aggressive children are probably using aggression to release pent-up feelings of frustration.

d. Going through a trauma like parental divorce may lead to increased aggression in children because they are feeling anxious.

ANSWERS: 1. evolutionary; 2. biological; 3. sociocultural; 4. a, d

Psychologists at Work

Specialties in Psychology

What are some of the specialists working within psychology?

Wherever you find human activity, you are very likely to encounter psychologists. These professionals work in a number of specialties, most of which require a master's or a doctoral degree.

Clinical psychologists specialize in the diagnosis and treatment of mental and behavioral disorders, such as anxiety, phobias, and schizophrenia. Some also conduct research in these areas. Most clinical psychologists work in clinics, hospitals, or private practices, but many hold professorships at colleges and universities.

Counseling psychologists help people who have adjustment problems (marital, social, or behavioral) that are generally less severe than those handled by clinical psychologists. Counseling psychologists may also provide academic or vocational counseling. Counselors usually work in a nonmedical setting such as a school or university, or they may have a private practice. Approximately 55% of all psychologists in the United States may be classified as either clinical or counseling psychologists (APA, 1995).

Physiological psychologists, also called *biological psychologists* or *neuropsychologists*, study the relationship between physiological processes and behavior. They study the structure and function of the brain and central nervous system, the role of neurotransmitters and hormones, and other aspects of body chemistry to determine how physical and chemical processes affect behavior in both people and animals.

Experimental psychologists specialize in the use of experimental research methods. They conduct experiments in most areas of psychology—learning, memory, sensation, perception, motivation, emotion, and others. Some experimental psychologists study the brain and nervous system and how they affect behavior; their work overlaps with that of physiological psychologists. Experimental psychologists usually work in a laboratory, where they can exert precise control over the humans or animals being studied. Many experimental psychologists teach and conduct their research as faculty members at colleges or universities. In most of their psychology laboratories, however, the array of laboratory fixtures of the past, such as specimen jars, "have been replaced largely by a single instrument, the computer" (Benjamin, 2000, p. 321).

Developmental psychologists study how people grow, develop, and change throughout the life span. Some developmental psychologists specialize in a particular age group, such as infants, children (child psychologists), adolescents, or the elderly (gerontologists). Others may concentrate on a specific aspect of human development, such as physical, language, cognitive, or moral development.

Educational psychologists specialize in the study of teaching and learning. They may help train teachers and other educational professionals or conduct research in teaching and classroom behavior. Some help prepare school curricula, develop achievement tests, or conduct evaluations of teaching and learning.

While most other psychologists are concerned with what makes the individual function, *social psychologists* investigate how the individual feels, thinks, and behaves in a social setting—in the presence of others.

Industry and business have found that expertise in psychology pays off in the workplace. *Industrial/organizational (I/O) psychologists* study the relationships between people and their work environments. You can read more about this subfield in Chapter 18.

Psychologists work in a wide range of settings.

Majoring in Psychology

What kinds of employment opportunities are available for psychology majors?

Have you considered majoring in psychology? Many students do. In fact, the number of undergraduate degrees awarded in psychology is second only to the number awarded in business administration (APA, 1995; Horn & Zahn, 2001).

As mentioned earlier, professional psychologists have graduate degrees. The American Psychological Association reports that it takes about 5 years of study beyond the bachelor's degree to obtain a doctoral degree in psychology (APA, 2000). However, there are many jobs open to those with a bachelor's degree in psychology. Figure 1.4 shows the variety of job settings in which individuals with undergraduate degrees in psychology are employed. And many men and women who intend to go on to postgraduate work in other fields—law, for example—major in psychology.

FIGURE 1.4 Jobs Held by Those with a Bachelor's Degree in Psychology

Even when undergraduate psychology majors don't pursue careers in the field, they find that the knowledge they gained is useful to them in their jobs, which represent a variety of settings.

Source: U.S. Department of Education, National Center for Education Statistics, 1991.

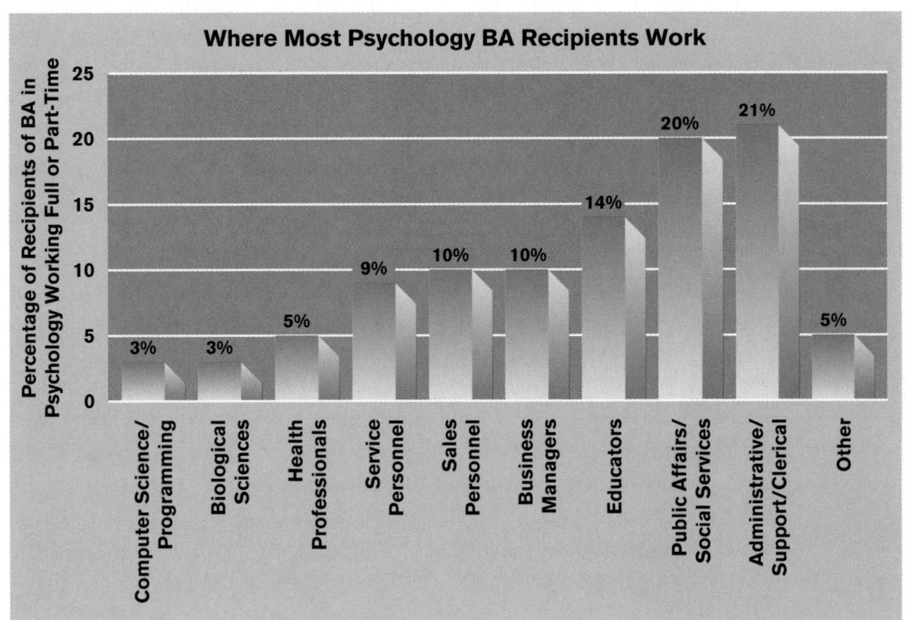

Remember It 1.9

1. The number of undergraduate degrees awarded in psychology is ____________ only to those awarded in business administration.

2. There are ____________ job opportunities for college graduates who major in psychology.

ANSWERS: 1. second; 2. many

Apply It

Best Practices for Effective Studying

Decades of research on learning and memory have uncovered a number of strategies that you can use, in addition to the SQ3R method, to make your study time more efficient and effective.

- Establish a quiet place, free of distractions, where you do nothing else but study. You can condition yourself to associate this environment with studying, so that entering the room or area will be your cue to begin work.
- Schedule your study time. Research on memory has proven that spaced learning is more effective than massed practice (cramming). Instead of studying for 5 hours straight, try five study sessions of 1 hour each.
- To be prepared for each class meeting, set specific goals for yourself each week and for individual study sessions. Your goals should be challenging but not overwhelming. If the task for an individual study session is manageable, it will be easier to sit down and face it. Completing the task you have set for yourself will give you a sense of accomplishment.
- The more active a role you play in the learning process, the more you will remember. Spend some of your study time reciting rather than rereading the material. One effective method is to use index cards as flash cards. Write a key term or study question on the front of each card. On the back, list pertinent information from the text and class lectures. Use these cards to help you prepare for tests.
- *Overlearning* means studying beyond the point at which you can just barely recite the information you are trying to memorize. Review the information again and again until it is firmly locked in memory. If you are subject to test anxiety, overlearning will help.
- Forgetting takes place most rapidly within the first 24 hours after you study. No matter how much you have studied for a test, always review shortly before you take it. Refreshing your memory will raise your grade.
- Sleeping immediately after you study will help you retain more of what you have learned. If you can't study before you go to sleep, at least review what you studied earlier in the day. This is also a good time to go through your index cards.

Once you've mastered these study strategies, use them to improve your comprehension and success in all of your courses.

Summary *and* Review

Psychology: An Introduction p. 5

What process do scientists use to answer questions about behavior and mental processes? p. 6

The scientific method consists of the orderly, systematic procedures researchers follow as they identify a research problem, design a study to investigate the problem, collect and analyze data, draw conclusions, and communicate their findings.

What are the goals of psychology? p. 6

The four goals of psychology are the description, explanation, prediction, and influence of behavior and mental processes. To describe means simply to tell what happened. Explanation involves telling why something happened. When an explanation leads to a hypothesis, the goal of prediction has been met. Research that is applied to some problem achieves the goal of influence.

How can you be a critical thinker? p. 7

To be a critical thinker, you must be independent, able to suspend judgment, and willing to change or abandon prior beliefs.

Descriptive Research Methods p. 8

How do psychological researchers use naturalistic and laboratory observation? p. 8

In naturalistic observation, researchers observe and record the behavior of human participants or animal subjects in a natural setting without attempting to influence or control it. In laboratory observation, researchers exert more control and use more precise equipment to measure responses.

What are the advantages and disadvantages of the case study? p. 9

As an in-depth study of one or several individuals through observation, interviewing, and sometimes psychological testing, the case study is particularly appropriate for studying people with rare psychological or physiological disorders or brain injuries. Disadvantages of this method include the time and expense involved in carrying out a thorough case study. In addition, the results of a single case study may not generalize to other individuals.

How do researchers ensure that survey results are useful? p. 9

In survey research, investigators use interviews and/or questionnaires to gather information about the attitudes, beliefs, experiences, or behaviors of a group of people. To be useful, surveys must involve a sample that is representative of the population to which the results will be applied.

The Experimental Method p. 11

Why do researchers use experiments to test hypotheses about cause-effect relationships? p. 11

The experimental method is the only research method that can identify cause-effect relationships.

How do independent and dependent variables differ? p. 12

In an experiment, an independent variable is a condition or factor manipulated by the researcher to determine its effect on the dependent variable. The dependent variable, measured at the end of the experiment, is presumed to vary as a result of the change in the independent variable(s).

Why are experimental and control groups necessary? p. 13

The experimental group is exposed to the independent variable. The control group is similar to the experimental group and experiences the same experimental environment but is not exposed to the independent variable. Comparing experimental and control groups allows researchers to judge the effects of the independent variable(s) compared to outcomes that occur naturally or in the presence of a placebo.

What kinds of factors introduce bias into experimental studies? p. 13

Environmental factors, such as heat or noise, can be a source of bias. Selection bias occurs when there are systematic differences among the groups before the experiment begins. The placebo effect occurs when a person's expectations influence the outcome of a treatment or experiment. Experimenter bias occurs when the researcher's expectations affect the outcome of the experiment.

What are the limitations of the experimental method? p. 14

Experiments are often conducted in unnatural settings, a factor that limits the generalizability of results. Also, this method may be unethical or impossible to use for some reseach.

The Correlational Method p. 15

What is a correlation coefficient, and what does it mean? p. 15

A correlation coefficient is a numerical value that indicates the strength and direction of the relationship between two variables. A positive correlation coefficient results when two variables move in the same direction; when two variables move in opposite directions, the correlation coefficient is negative. The closer a correlation coefficient is to +1 or −1, the stronger the relationship between the variables.

What are the strengths and weaknesses of the correlational method? p. 15

When the correlation between two variables is known, information about one variable can be used to predict the other. However, a correlation cannot be used to support the conclusion that either variable causes the other.

Participants in Psychological Research p. 18

In what ways can participants bias research results? p. 18

Participant-related bias happens when researchers fail to include underrepresented groups in their samples or when the research findings are generalized to groups not represented in researchers' samples.

What ethical rules must researchers follow when humans are involved in studies? p. 19

All research must conform to applicable laws and regulations. Researchers must obtain approval from all institutions involved in the study. Participants must give informed consent, may not be deceived unless necessary, and, if deceived, must be debriefed as soon as possible after they participate. Subordinates' participation in a study may not negatively affect them in any way. Participants may be paid after being fully informed about what is expected in return for payment. Researchers must report their findings in an appropriate forum, and results must be made available to participants.

Why are animals used in research? p. 20

Animals provide a simpler model for studying similar processes in humans; researchers can exercise more control over animals and use a wider range of medical and other manipulations; it is easier to study the entire life span and even several generations in some animals species; animals are readily available and more economical to study; and some researchers want to know more about the animals themselves.

Exploring Psychology's Roots p. 21

What roles did Wundt and Titchener play in the founding of psychology? p. 21

Wundt, who is considered the "father" of psychology, established the first psychological laboratory in 1879 and launched the study of psychology as a formal academic discipline. One of his students, Titchener, founded the school of thought called structuralism, an approach aimed at analyzing the basic elements of conscious mental experience through introspection.

Why is functionalism important in the history of psychology? p. 22

Functionalism, founded by William James, was the first American school of psychology and broadened the scope of the field to include examination of behavior as well as conscious mental processes. Its advocates were concerned with how humans and animals use mental processes to adapt to their environment.

In what ways have women and minorities shaped the field of psychology, both in the past and today? p. 22

Early female and minority psychologists had to overcome significant educational and professional barriers to work in the field. Still, many of these individuals made noteworthy contributions. Today, more women than men obtain degrees in psychology, and minority group representation in the field is growing.

Schools of Thought in Psychology p. 24

How do behaviorists explain behavior and mental processes? p. 24

Behaviorists, adherents of the school of psychology founded by John B. Watson, view observable, measurable behavior as the only appropriate subject matter for psychology. Behaviorism also emphasizes the environment as the key determinant of behavior.

What do psychoanalytic psychologists believe about the role of the unconscious? p. 25

According to Freud's theory of psychoanalysis, an individual's thoughts, feelings, and behavior are determined primarily by the unconscious—the part of the mind that one cannot see and cannot control.

According to Maslow and Rogers, what motivates human behavior and mental processes? p. 25

The humanistic theories of Maslow and Rogers focus on the uniqueness of human beings and their capacity for choice, personal growth, and psychological health. Humans are motivated by the need for self-actualization.

What is the focus of cognitive psychology? p. 26

Cognitive psychology is an influential school that focuses on mental processes such as memory, problem solving, concept formation, reasoning and decision making, language, and perception.

Current Trends in Psychology p. 27

What is the main idea behind evolutionary psychology? p. 28

Evolutionary psychology focuses on how human behaviors necessary for survival have adapted in the face of environmental pressures over the course of evolution.

How is biological psychology changing the field of psychology? p. 29

Biological psychologists look for connections between specific behaviors (such as aggression) and particular biological factors (such as hormone levels) to help explain individual differences. Using modern technology, biological psychologists have discovered relationships between biological and behavioral variables that have resulted in more effective medications for certain disorders and new insight into the genetic base of many mental illnesses.

What kinds of variables interest psychologists who take a sociocultural approach? p. 30

The sociocultural approach focuses on how factors such as cultural values affect people's behavior.

What are psychological perspectives, and how are they related to an eclectic position? p. 30

Psychological perspectives are general points of view used for explaining people's behavior and thinking. In taking an eclectic position, psychologists use a combination of two or more perspectives to explain a particular behavior.

Psychologists at Work p. 32

What are some of the specialists working within psychology? p. 32

There are clinical and counseling psychologists, physiological psychologists, experimental psychologists, developmental psychologists, educational psychologists, social psychologists, and industrial/organizational (I/O) psychologists.

What kinds of employment opportunities are available for psychology majors? p. 33

Individuals with bachelor's degrees in psychology are employed in many different settings—colleges and universities, elementary and secondary schools, medical settings, public affairs, sales, and business management. Majoring in psychology is also good preparation for postgraduate study in other fields (for example, law).

Key Terms

applied research, p. 7
basic research, p. 7
behaviorism, p. 24
biological psychology, p. 29
case study, p. 9
cognitive psychology, p. 26
confounding variables, p. 13
control group, p. 13
correlation coefficient, p. 15
correlational method, p. 15
critical thinking, p. 7
dependent variable, p. 12
descriptive research methods, p. 8
double-blind technique, p. 14
evolutionary psychology, p. 28
experimental group, p. 13
experimental method, p. 11
experimenter bias, p. 14
functionalism, p. 22
Gestalt psychology, p. 26
humanistic psychology, p. 25
hypothesis, p. 11
independent variable, p. 12
information-processing theory, p. 26
laboratory observation, p. 8
naturalistic observation, p. 8
neuroscience, p. 29
placebo, p. 14
placebo effect, p. 14
population, p. 9
psychoanalysis, p. 25
psychological perspectives, p. 30
psychology, p. 5
random assignment, p. 13
replication, p. 6
representative sample, p. 9
sample, p. 9
scientific method, p. 6
selection bias, p. 13
sociocultural approach, p. 30
SQ3R method, p. 4
structuralism, p. 21
survey, p. 9
theory, p. 6

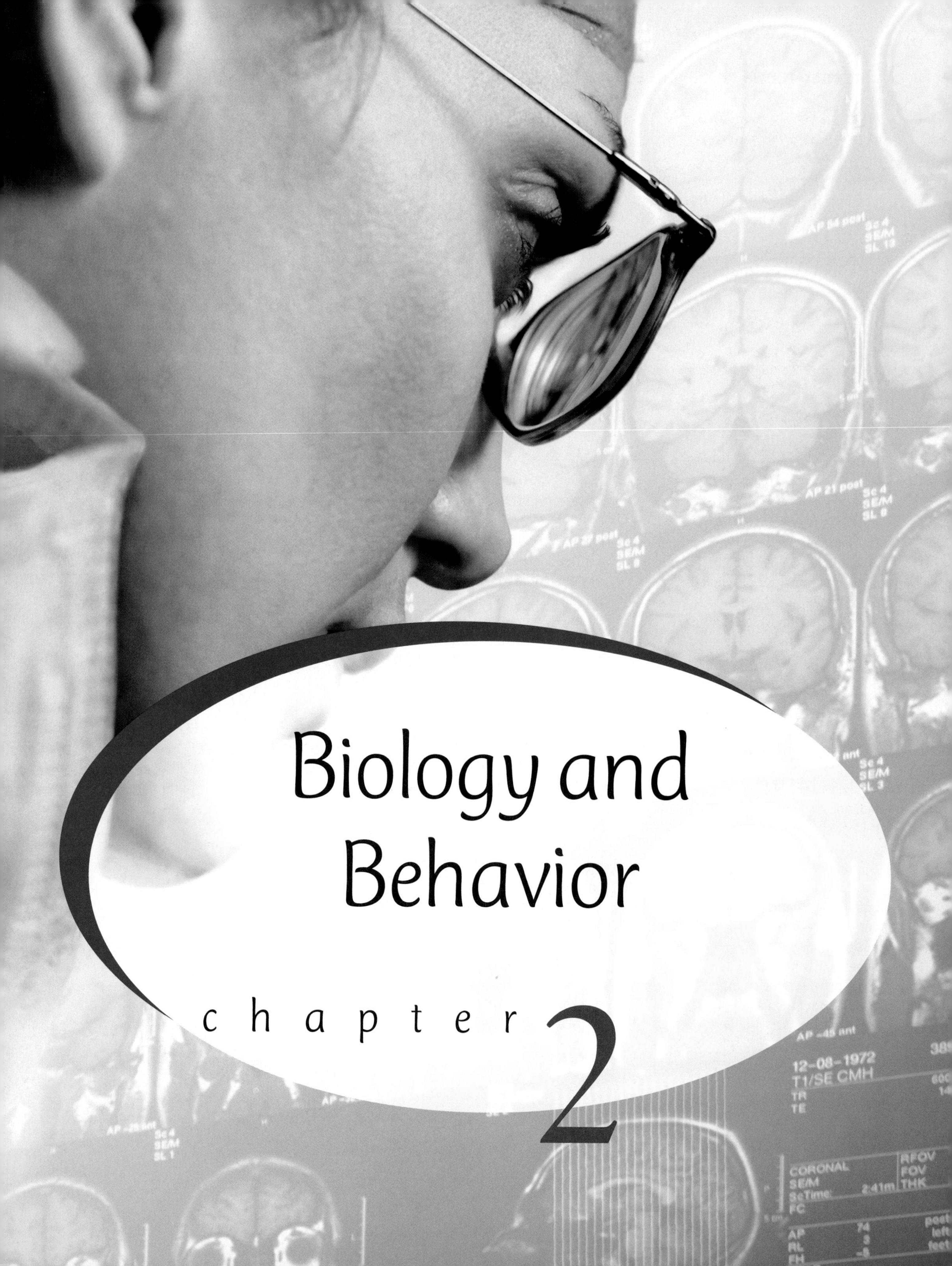

Biology and Behavior

chapter 2

The Neurons and the Neurotransmitters

- *How are messages transmitted through the nervous system?*
- *What are neurotransmitters, and what do they contribute to nervous system functioning?*
- *What are the functions of some of the major neurotransmitters?*

The Central Nervous System

- *Why is an intact spinal cord important to normal functioning?*
- *What are the crucial functions handled by the brainstem?*
- *What are the primary functions of the cerebellum?*
- *What important structure is located in the midbrain?*
- *What are the functions of the thalamus and the hypothalamus?*
- *How does the limbic system influence mental processes and behavior?*

The Cerebrum

- *What are the components of the cerebrum?*
- *Which psychological functions are associated with the frontal lobes?*
- *What is the somatosensory cortex, and what does it do?*
- *Why are the occipital lobes critical to vision?*
- *What are the major areas within the temporal lobes, and what are their functions?*

The Cerebral Hemispheres

- *What are the specialized functions of the left hemisphere?*
- *What are the specialized functions of the right hemisphere?*
- *What do researchers mean by the term "split brain"?*
- *How are handedness and brain function related?*

Discovering the Brain's Mysteries

- *What does the electroencephalogram (EEG) reveal about the brain?*
- *How are the CT scan and MRI helpful in the study of brain structure?*
- *How are the PET scan and newer imaging techniques used to study the brain?*

The Brain across the Lifespan

- *In what ways does the brain change across the lifespan?*
- *How do aging, learning, and stroke-related damage affect the brain?*

The Peripheral Nervous System

- *What is the difference between the sympathetic and parasympathetic nervous systems?*

The Endocrine System

- *What functions are associated with the various glands of the endocrine system?*

Genes and Behavioral Genetics

- *What patterns of inheritance are evident in the transmission of genetic traits?*
- *What kinds of studies are done by behavioral geneticists?*

Is it possible that a head injury could completely change your behavior and personality?

On September 13, 1848, Phineas Gage, a 25-year-old foreman on a Vermont railroad construction crew, was using dynamite to blast away rock and dirt. Suddenly, an unplanned explosion almost took Gage's head off, sending a 3½-foot-long, 13-pound metal rod under his left cheekbone and out through the top of his skull.

Much of the brain tissue in Gage's frontal lobe was torn away, along with flesh, pieces of his skull, and other bone fragments. This should have been the end of Phineas Gage, but it wasn't. He regained consciousness within a few minutes and was loaded onto a cart and wheeled to his hotel nearly a mile away. He got out of the cart with a little help, walked up the stairs, entered his room, and walked to his bed. He was still conscious when the doctor arrived nearly 2 hours later.

Although Gage recovered in about 5 weeks, he was not the same man. Before the accident, he was described as a hard worker who was polite, dependable, and well liked. But the new Phineas Gage, without part of his frontal lobe, was loud-mouthed and profane, rude and impulsive, and contemptuous of others. He no longer planned realistically for the future and was no longer motivated and industrious, as he once had been. As a result, Gage lost his job as foreman and ended up joining P. T. Barnum's circus as a sideshow exhibit at carnivals and county fairs. (Adapted from Harlow, 1848.)

Well over a century and a half has passed since the heavy metal rod tore through Phineas Gage's brain. During that time, much has been learned about the human brain—some of it puzzling and mysterious, all of it fascinating. How could Gage survive such massive damage to his brain, when a small bullet fired through a person's brain in any one of a number of different places can result in instant death? In this chapter, you'll learn how this remarkable 3-pound organ can be so tough and resilient and, at the same time, so fragile and vulnerable.

■ **neuron**
(NEW-ron) A specialized cell that conducts impulses through the nervous system and contains three major parts—a cell body, dendrites, and an axon.

■ **cell body**
The part of a neuron that contains the nucleus and carries out the metabolic functions of the neuron.

Chapter 1, the introduction to *The World of Psychology*, defined *psychology* as the scientific study of behavior and mental processes. Before you can gain an understanding and an appreciation of human behavior and mental processes, we must first explore the all-important biological connection. Every thought you think, every emotion you feel, every sensation you experience, every decision you reach, every move you make—in short, all of human behavior—is rooted in a biological event. Therefore, this chapter focuses on biology and behavior. The story begins where the action begins, in the smallest functional unit of the brain—the nerve cell, or neuron.

The Neurons and the Neurotransmitters

The Neurons

How are messages transmitted through the nervous system?

All our thoughts, feelings, and behavior can ultimately be traced to the activity of **neurons**—the specialized cells that conduct impulses through the nervous system. Neurons perform several important tasks: (1) Afferent (sensory) neurons relay messages from the sense organs and receptors—eyes, ears, nose, mouth, and skin—to the brain or spinal cord; (2) efferent (motor) neurons convey signals from the central nervous system to the glands and the muscles, enabling the body to move; and (3) interneurons, thousands of times more numerous than motor or sensory neurons, carry information between neurons in the brain and between neurons in the spinal cord.

■ **dendrites**
(DEN-drytes) In a neuron, the branchlike extensions of the cell body that receive signals from other neurons.

Anatomy of a Neuron Although no two neurons are exactly alike, nearly all are made up of three important parts: the cell body, the dendrites, and the axon. The **cell body**, or *soma*, contains the nucleus and carries out the metabolic, or life-sustaining, functions of a neuron. Branching out from the cell body are the **dendrites**, which look much like the leafless branches of a tree (*dendrite* comes from the Greek word for "tree"). The dendrites are the primary receivers of signals from other neurons, but the cell body can also receive signals directly. And dendrites do not only receive signals from other neurons and relay them to the cell body. Scientists now know that dendrites also relay messages backward—from the cell body to their own branches (a process called *back propagating*)—although this is not their primary function. These backward messages may shape the dendrites' responses to future signals they receive (Magee & Johnston, 1997; Sejnowski, 1997).

The **axon** is the slender, tail-like extension of the neuron that sprouts into many branches, each ending in a bulbous axon terminal. Signals move from the axon terminals to the dendrites or cell bodies of other neurons and to muscles, glands, and other parts of the body. In humans, some axons are short—only thousandths of an inch long. Others can be as long as a meter (39.37 inches)—long enough to reach from the brain to the tip of the spinal cord, or from the spinal cord to remote parts of the body. Figure 2.1 (on page 42) shows a neuron's structure.

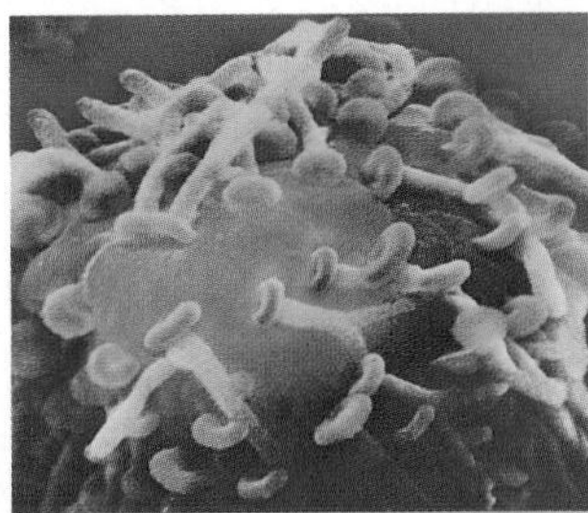

This scanning electron micrograph shows numerous axon terminals (the orange, button-shaped structures) that could synapse with the cell body of the neuron (shown in green).

Glial Cells **Glial cells** are specialized cells in the brain and spinal cord that hold the neurons together. They are smaller than neurons and make up more than one-half the volume of the human brain. Glial cells remove waste products, such as dead neurons, from the brain by engulfing and digesting them, and they handle other manufacturing, nourishing, and cleanup tasks.

The Synapse Remarkably, the billions of neurons that send and receive signals are not physically connected. The axon terminals are separated from the receiving neurons by tiny, fluid-filled gaps called *synaptic clefts*. The **synapse** is the junction where the axon terminal of a sending (presynaptic) neuron communicates with a receiving (postsynaptic) neuron across the synaptic cleft. There may be as many as 100 trillion synapses in the human nervous system (Swanson, 1995). And a single neuron may synapse with thousands of other neurons (Kelner, 1997). A technique that has recently been developed to monitor the action at the synapses may soon enable researchers to visualize the activity of all the synapses of a single neuron. If neurons aren't connected, how do they communicate with one another?

The Neural Impulse Researchers have known for some 200 years that cells in the brain, the spinal cord, and the muscles generate electrical potentials. These tiny electric charges play a part in all bodily functions. Every time you move a muscle, experience a sensation, or have a thought or a feeling, a small but measurable electrical impulse is present.

How does this biological electricity work? Even though the impulse that travels down the axon is electrical, the axon does not transmit it the way a wire conducts an electrical current. What actually changes is the **permeability** of the cell membrane (its capability of being penetrated or passed through). In other words, the membrane changes in a way that makes it easier for molecules to move through it and into the cell. This process allows ions (electrically charged atoms or molecules) to move into and out of the axon through ion channels in the membrane.

Body fluids contain ions, some with positive electrical charges and others with negative charges. Inside the axon, there are normally more negative than positive ions. When at rest (not firing), the axon membrane carries a negative electrical potential of about –70 millivolts (–70 thousandths of a volt) relative to the fluid outside the cell. This slight negative charge is referred to as the neuron's **resting potential**.

When the excitatory effects on a neuron reach a certain threshold, ion channels begin to open in the cell membrane of the axon at the point closest to the cell body, allowing positive ions to flow into the axon. This inflow of positive ions causes the membrane potential to change abruptly, to a positive value of about +50 millivolts (Pinel, 2000). This sudden reversal of the resting potential, which lasts for about 1 millisecond (1 thousandth of a second), is the **action potential**. Then, the ion channels admitting positive ions close, and other ion channels open, forcing some positive

■ **axon**
(AK-sahn) The slender, tail-like extension of the neuron that transmits signals to the dendrites or cell body of other neurons and to muscles, glands, and other parts of the body.

■ **glial cells**
(GLEE-ul) Specialized cells in the brain and spinal cord that hold neurons together, remove waste products such as dead neurons, and perform other manufacturing, nourishing, and cleanup tasks.

■ **synapse**
(SIN-aps) The junction where the axon terminal of a sending neuron communicates with a receiving neuron across the synaptic cleft.

■ **permeability**
(perm-ee-uh-BIL-uh-tee) The capability of being penetrated or passed through.

■ **resting potential**
The slight negative electrical potential of the axon membrane of a neuron at rest, about –70 millivolts.

■ **action potential**
The sudden reversal of the resting potential, which initiates the firing of a neuron.

FIGURE 2.1 The Structure of a Typical Neuron

A typical neuron has three important parts: (1) a cell body, which carries out the metabolic functions of the neuron; (2) branched fibers called dendrites, which are the primary receivers of the impulses from other neurons; and (3) a slender, tail-like extension called an axon, the transmitting end of the neuron, which sprouts into many branches, each ending in an axon terminal. The photograph shows human neurons greatly magnified.

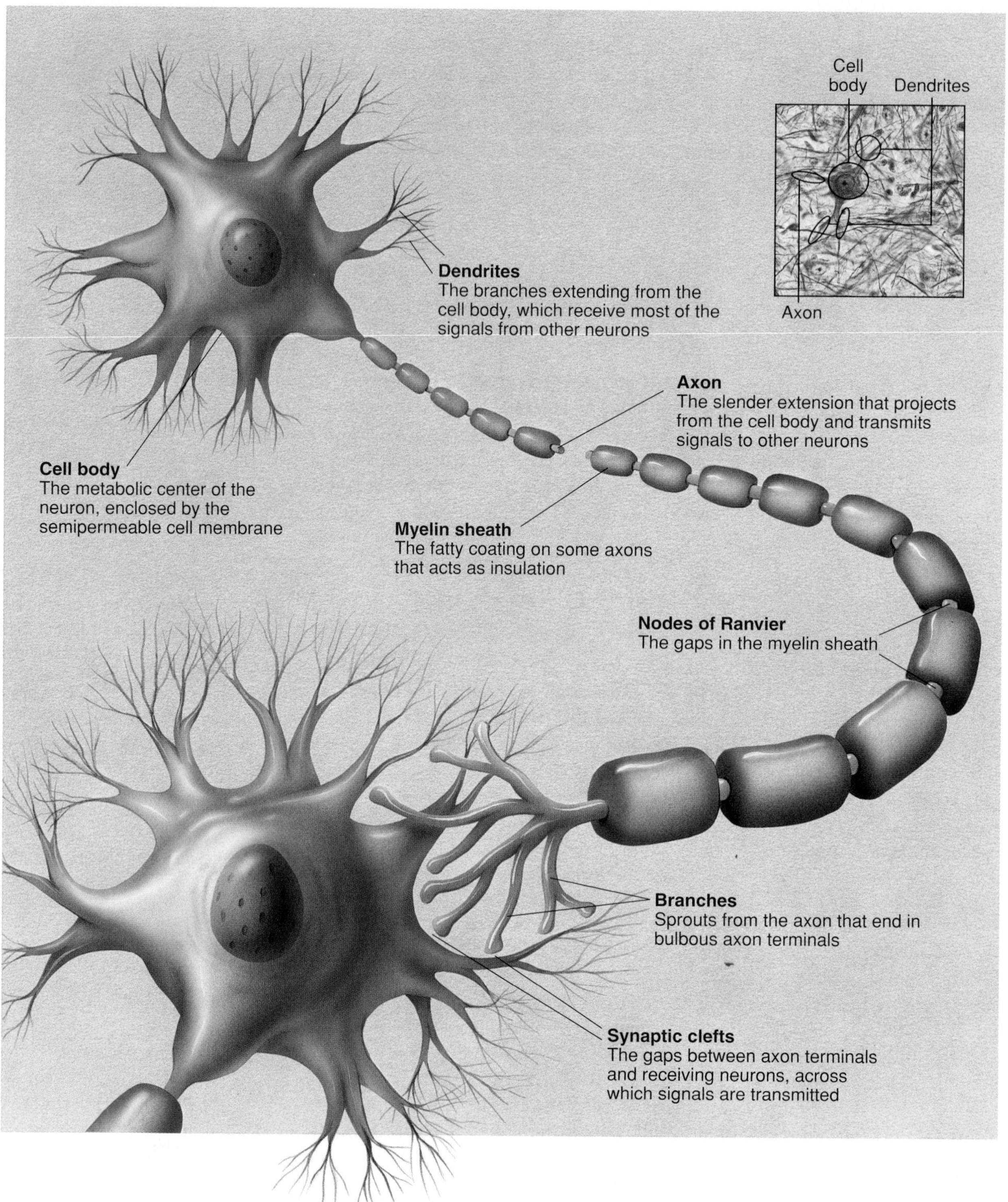
Cell body
Dendrites
Axon
Dendrites
The branches extending from the cell body, which receive most of the signals from other neurons
Axon
The slender extension that projects from the cell body and transmits signals to other neurons
Cell body
The metabolic center of the neuron, enclosed by the semipermeable cell membrane
Myelin sheath
The fatty coating on some axons that acts as insulation
Nodes of Ranvier
The gaps in the myelin sheath
Branches
Sprouts from the axon that end in bulbous axon terminals
Synaptic clefts
The gaps between axon terminals and receiving neurons, across which signals are transmitted

ions out of the axon. As a result, the original negative charge, or resting potential, is restored. The opening and closing of ion channels continues, segment by segment, down the length of the axon, causing the action potential to move along the axon (Cardoso et al., 2000). The action potential operates according to the "all or none" law—a neuron either fires completely or does not fire at all. Immediately after a neuron fires, it enters a *refractory period*, during which it cannot fire again for 1 to 2 milliseconds. But, even with these short resting periods, neurons can fire hundreds of times per second.

The Rate of Neural Firing and the Speed of the Impulse If a neuron only fires or does not fire, how can we tell the difference between a very strong and a very weak stimulus? In other words, what is the neurological distinction between feeling anxious about being disciplined by your boss for being late to work and running for your life to avoid being the victim of a criminal attacker? The answer lies in the number of neurons firing at the same time and their rate of firing. A weak stimulus may cause relatively few neurons to fire, while a strong stimulus may trigger thousands of neurons to fire at the same time. Also, a weak stimulus may be signaled by neurons firing very slowly; a stronger stimulus may incite neurons to fire hundreds of times per second.

Impulses travel at speeds from about 1 meter per second to approximately 100 meters per second (about 224 miles per hour). The most important factor in speeding the impulse on its way is the **myelin sheath**—a white, fatty coating wrapped around some axons that acts as insulation. If you look again at Figure 2.1, you will see that the coating has numerous gaps, called *nodes of Ranvier*. The electrical impulse is retriggered or regenerated at each node (or naked gap) on the axon. This regeneration makes the impulse up to 100 times faster than impulses in axons without myelin sheaths. Damage to the myelin sheath causes interruptions in the transmission of neural messages. In fact, the disease multiple sclerosis (MS) involves deterioration of the myelin sheath, resulting in loss of coordination, jerky movements, muscular weakness, and disturbances in speech.

■ **myelin sheath**
(MY-uh-lin) The white, fatty coating wrapped around some axons that acts as insulation and enables impulses to travel much faster.

■ **neurotransmitter**
(NEW-ro-TRANS-mit-er) A chemical substance that is released into the synaptic cleft from the axon terminal of a sending neuron, crosses a synapse, and binds to appropriate receptor sites on the dendrites or cell body of a receiving neuron, influencing the cell either to fire or not to fire.

■ **receptors**
Protein molecules on the surfaces of dendrites and cell bodies that have distinctive shapes and will interact only with specific neurotransmitters.

Neurotransmitters

What are neurotransmitters, and what do they contribute to nervous system functioning?

Once a neuron fires, how does it get its message across the synaptic cleft and on to another neuron? Messages are transmitted between neurons by one or more of a large group of chemical substances known as **neurotransmitters**. Where are the neurotransmitters located? Inside the axon terminal are many small, sphere-shaped containers with thin membranes called *synaptic vesicles*, which hold the neurotransmitters. (*Vesicle* comes from a Latin word meaning "little bladder.") When an action potential arrives at the axon terminal, synaptic vesicles move toward the cell membrane, fuse with it, and release their neurotransmitter molecules. This process is shown in Figure 2.2 (on page 44).

The Receptor Once released, neurotransmitters do not simply flow into the synaptic cleft and stimulate all the adjacent neurons. Each neurotransmitter has a distinctive molecular shape, as do **receptors**, which are protein molecules on the surfaces of dendrites and cell bodies. Neurotransmitters can affect only those neurons whose receptors are the right shape to receive them. In other words, each receptor is somewhat like a lock that only certain neurotransmitter keys can unlock (Cardoso et al., 2000; Restak, 1993). And as you'll learn in Chapter 4, many drugs affect the brain by mimicking the shapes of natural neurotransmitter molecules.

However, the binding of neurotransmitters with receptors is not as fixed and rigid a process as keys fitting locks or jigsaw puzzle pieces interlocking. Receptors on neurons are somewhat flexible; they can expand and contract their enclosed volumes. And

FIGURE 2.2 Synaptic Transmission

Sending neurons transmit their messages to receiving neurons by electrochemical action. When a neuron fires, the action potential arrives at the axon terminal and triggers the release of neurotransmitters from the synaptic vesicles. Neurotransmitters flow into the synaptic cleft and move toward the receiving neuron, which has numerous receptors. The receptors will bind only with neurotransmitters whose molecular shapes match their enclosed volumes. Neurotransmitters influence the receiving neuron to fire or not to fire.

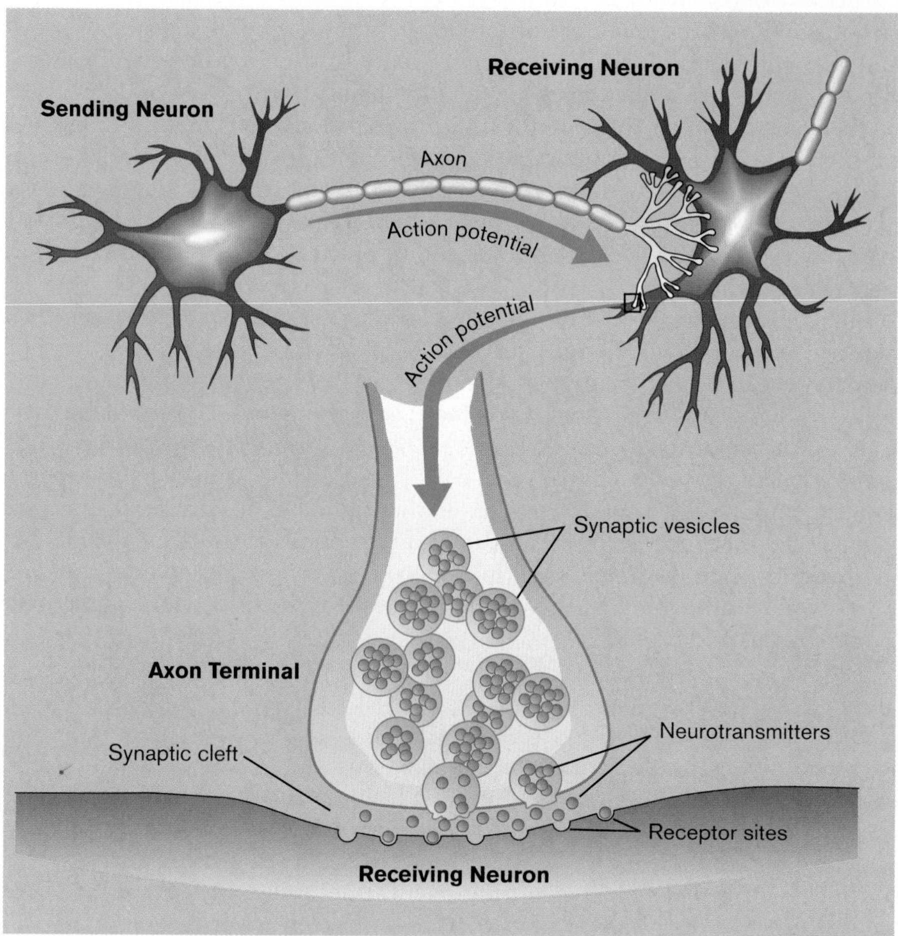

neurotransmitters of different types can have similar shapes. Thus, two different neurotransmitters may compete for the same receptor. The receptor will admit only one of the competing neurotransmitters—the one that fits it best. A receptor may receive a certain neurotransmitter sometimes, but not receive it in the presence of a better-fitting neurotransmitter whose "affinity with the receptor is even stronger. As in dating and mating, what is finally settled for is always a function of what is available" (Restak, 1993, p. 28).

An analogy may help you understand the difference between excitatory and inhibitory neurotransmitters. Why do some pots and pans have copper bottoms? You probably know that copper is a good conductor of heat, and so a copper bottom on a pan helps transmit the heat of the stove burner to the food inside the pan. An excitatory neurotransmitter is a bit like the copper bottom. It is a substance that facilitates and speeds up the transmission of neural impulses from one neuron to another. By contrast, pot handles are usually made of some kind of plastic. They prevent the heat of the pan from being transmitted to your hand because plastic is a poor conductor of heat. Inhibitory transmitters serve a similar function. They prevent or slow down the transmission of neural impulses across the synaptic cleft.

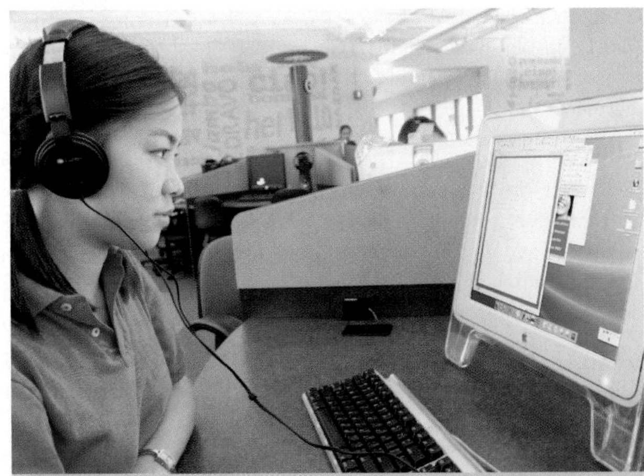
The neurotransmitter acetylcholine helps you process new information by facilitating neural transmissions involved in learning.

The Action of Neurotransmitters When neurotransmitters bind with receptors on the dendrites or cell bodies of receiving neurons, their action is either excitatory (influencing the neurons to fire) or inhibitory (influencing them not to fire). Because a single receiving neuron may synapse with thousands of other neurons at the same time, it will always be subject to both excitatory and inhibitory influences from incoming neurotransmitters. For the neuron to fire, the excitatory influences must exceed the inhibitory influences by a sufficient amount (the threshold).

You may wonder how the synaptic vesicles can continue to pour out neurotransmitters, yet have a ready supply so that the neuron can respond to continuing stimulation. First, the cell body of the neuron is always working to manufacture more of the neurotransmitter. Second, unused neurotransmitters in the synaptic cleft may be broken down into components and reclaimed by the axon terminal to be recycled and used again. Third, by an important process called **reuptake**, the neurotransmitter is taken back into the axon terminal, intact and ready for immediate use. This terminates the neurotransmitter's excitatory or inhibitory effect on the receiving neuron.

The nature of synaptic transmission—whether it is primarily chemical or electrical—was a subject of controversy during the first half of the 20th century. By the 1950s, it seemed clear that the means of communication between neurons was chemical. Yet, at some synapses, what was termed *gap junction*, or electrical transmission, occurred between the neurons. Recent research has shown that this electrical transmission may be more frequent than neuroscientists once believed (Bennett, 2000). Even though synaptic transmission of information between neurons is primarily chemical, some electrical transmission is known to occur at synapses in the retina, the olfactory bulb (sense of smell), and the cerebral cortex, which we discuss further later in this chapter.

■ **reuptake**
The process by which neurotransmitters are taken from the synaptic cleft back into the axon terminal for later use, thus terminating their excitatory or inhibitory effect on the receiving neuron.

■ **acetylcholine**
(ah-SEET-ul-KOH-leen) A neurotransmitter that plays a role in learning new information, causes the skeletal muscle fibers to contract, and keeps the heart from beating too rapidly.

The Variety of Neurotransmitters

What are the functions of some of the major neurotransmitters?

Researchers have identified 75 or more chemical substances that are manufactured in the brain, spinal cord, glands, and other parts of the body and may act as neurotransmitters (Greden, 1994).

One of the most important is **acetylcholine** (Ach). This neurotransmitter exerts excitatory effects on the skeletal muscle fibers, causing them to contract so that the body can move. But it has an inhibitory effect on the muscle fibers in the heart, which keeps the heart from beating too rapidly. Thus, when you run to make it to class on time, acetylcholine helps your leg muscles contract quickly, while, at the same time, it prevents your heart muscle from pumping so rapidly that you pass out. The differing nature of the receptors on the receiving neurons in the two kinds of muscles causes these opposite effects. Acetylcholine also plays an excitatory role in stimulating the neurons involved in learning new information. So, as you are reading this text, acetylcholine is helping you understand and store the information in your memory.

Dopamine (DA), one of four neurotransmitters called *monoamines*, produces both excitatory and inhibitory effects and is involved in several functions, including learning, attention, movement, and reinforcement. Neuroscientists have learned that many

■ **dopamine**
(DOE-pah-meen) A neurotransmitter that plays a role in learning, attention, movement, and reinforcement; neurons in the brains of those with Parkinson's disease and schizophrenia are less sensitive to its effects.

of the neurons in the brains of patients with Parkinson's disease or schizophrenia are less sensitive to the effects of dopamine than is typical in those who do not suffer from these disorders (Kurup & Kurup, 2002).

The other three monoamines also serve important functions. **Norepinephrine** (NE) has an effect on eating habits (it stimulates the intake of carbohydrates) and plays a major role in alertness and wakefulness. **Epinephrine** complements norepinephrine by affecting the metabolism of glucose and causing the nutrient energy stored in muscles to be released during strenuous exercise. **Serotonin** plays an important role in regulating mood, sleep, impulsivity, aggression, and appetite.

Two amino acids that serve as neurotransmitters are more common than any other transmitter substances in the central nervous system. **Glutamate** is the primary excitatory neurotransmitter in the brain (Riedel, 1996). It may be released by about 40% of neurons and is active in areas of the brain involved in learning, thought, and emotions (Coyle & Draper, 1996). **GABA** (short for "*g*amma-*a*mino*b*utyric *a*cid") is the main inhibitory neurotransmitter in the brain (Miles, 1999). It is thought to facilitate the control of anxiety in humans. Tranquilizers, barbiturates, and alcohol appear to have a calming and relaxing effect because they bind with and stimulate one type of GABA receptor and thus increase GABA's anxiety-controlling effect. An abnormality in the neurons that secrete GABA is believed to be one of the causes of epilepsy, a serious neurological disorder in which neural activity can become so heightened that seizures result.

More than 25 years ago, Candace Pert and her fellow researchers (1974) demonstrated that a localized region of the brain contains neurons with receptors that respond to the opiates—drugs such as opium, morphine, and heroin. Later, it was learned that the brain itself produces its own opiatelike substances, known as **endorphins**. Endorphins provide relief from pain or the stress of vigorous exercise and produce feelings of pleasure and well-being. "Runner's high" is attributed to the release of endorphins. (See Chapter 3 for more information on endorphins.)

■ **norepinephrine**
(nor-EP-ih-NEF-rin) A neurotransmitter affecting eating, alertness, and sleep.

■ **epinephrine**
(EP-ih-NEF-rin) A neurotransmitter that affects the metabolism of glucose and nutrient energy stored in muscles to be released during strenuous exercise.

■ **serotonin**
(ser-oh-TOE-nin) A neurotransmitter that plays an important role in regulating mood, sleep, impulsivity, aggression, and appetite.

■ **glutamate**
(GLOO-tah-mate) Primary excitatory neurotransmitter in the brain.

■ **GABA**
Primary inhibitory neurotransmitter in the brain.

■ **endorphins**
(en-DOR-fins) Chemicals produced naturally by the brain that reduce pain and the stress of vigorous exercise and positively affect mood.

Remember It 2.1

1. The branchlike extensions of neurons that act as the *primary* receivers of signals from other neurons are the ____________.
2. ____________ support neurons, supplying them with nutrients and carrying away their waste products.
3. The ____________ is the junction where the axon of a sending neuron communicates with a receiving neuron.
4. When a neuron fires, neurotransmitters are released from the synaptic vesicles in the ____________ into the ____________.
5. The ____________ potential is the firing of a neuron; the ____________ potential is the state in which the cell membrane is relatively impermeable.
6. Receptor sites on the receiving neuron receive only neurotransmitter molecules whose ____________ is similar to theirs.
7. The neurotransmitter called ____________ keeps the heart from beating to fast.
8. Individuals with schizophrenia may be less sensitive to the effects of ____________.
9. ____________ affects eating habits by stimulating the intake of carbohydrates.
10. ____________ are neurotansmitters that act as natural pain killers.

ANSWERS: 1. dendrites; 2. Glial cells; 3. synapse; 4. axon terminal, synaptic cleft; 5. action, resting; 6. shape; 7. acetylcholine; 8. dopamine; 9. Norepinephrine; 10. Endorphins

The Central Nervous System

Human functioning involves much more than the action of individual neurons. Collections of neurons, brain structures, and organ systems also play essential roles in the body. The nervous system is divided into two parts: (1) the **central nervous system (CNS)**, which is composed of the brain and the spinal cord, and (2) the peripheral nervous system, which connects the central nervous system to all other parts of the body (see Figure 2.3).

■ **central nervous system (CNS)** The part of the nervous system comprising the brain and the spinal cord.

The Spinal Cord

Why is an intact spinal cord important to normal functioning?

The **spinal cord** can best be thought of as an extension of the brain. A cylinder of neural tissue about the diameter of your little finger, the spinal cord reaches from the base of the brain, through the neck, and down the hollow center of the spinal column. The spinal cord is protected by bone and also by spinal fluid, which serves as a shock absorber. The spinal cord literally links the body with the brain. It transmits messages between the brain and the peripheral nervous system. Thus, sensory information can reach the brain, and messages from the brain can be sent to the muscles, the glands, and other parts of the body.

Although the spinal cord and the brain usually function together, the spinal cord can act without help from the brain to protect the body from injury. A simple withdrawal reflex triggered by a painful stimulus—touching a hot stove burner, for example—involves three types of neurons. Sensory neurons in your fingers detect the painful stimulus and relay this information to interneurons in the spinal cord. These interneurons activate motor neurons that control the muscles in your arm and cause you to jerk your hand away. All this happens within a fraction of a second, without any involvement of your brain. However, the brain quickly becomes aware and involved when the pain signal reaches it. At that point, you might plunge your hand into cold water to relieve the pain.

■ **spinal cord** An extension of the brain, from the base of the brain through the neck and spinal column, that transmits messages between the brain and the peripheral nervous system.

FIGURE 2.3 Divisions of the Human Nervous System

The human nervous system is divided into two parts: (1) the central nervous system, consisting of the brain and the spinal cord; and (2) the peripheral nervous system.

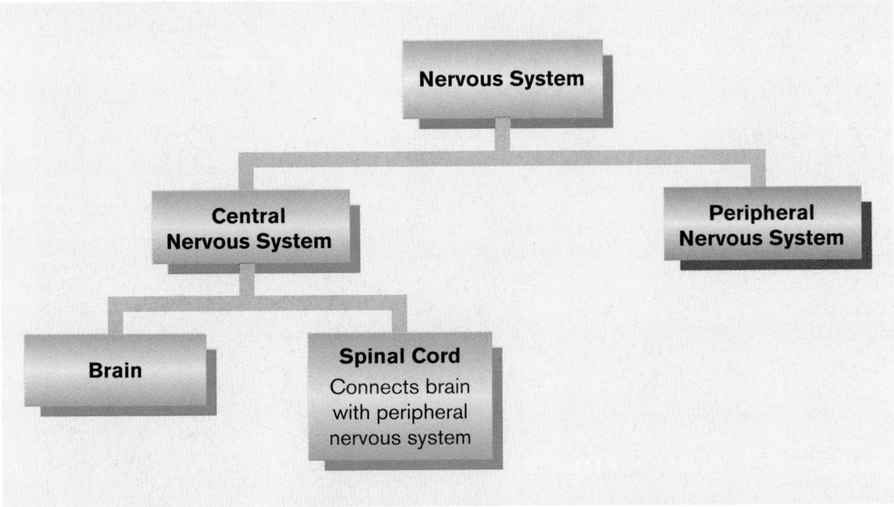

The Brainstem

What are the crucial functions handled by the brainstem?

Brain structures are often grouped into the *hindbrain*, the *midbrain*, and the *forebrain*, as shown in Figure 2.4. The part of the hindbrain known as the **brainstem** begins at the site where the spinal cord enlarges as it enters the skull. The brainstem handles functions that are so critical to physical survival that damage to it is life-threatening. The **medulla** is the part of the brainstem that controls heartbeat, breathing, blood pressure, coughing, and swallowing. Fortunately, the medulla handles these functions automatically, so you do not have to decide consciously to breathe or remember to keep your heart beating.

Extending through the central core of the brainstem into the pons is another important structure, the **reticular formation**, sometimes called the *reticular activating system* (RAS) (refer to Figure 2.4). The reticular formation plays a crucial role in arousal and attention (Kinomura et al., 1996; Steriade, 1996). Every day, our sense organs are bombarded with stimuli, but we cannot possibly pay attention to everything we see or hear. The reticular formation blocks some messages and sends others on to structures in the midbrain and forebrain for processing. For example, a driver may be listening intently to a radio program when, suddenly, a car cuts in front of him. In response, the reticular formation blocks the sensory information coming from the radio and fixes the driver's attention on the potential danger posed by the other driver's action. Once the traffic pattern returns to normal, the reticular formation allows him to attend to the radio again, while continuing to monitor the traffic situation.

The reticular formation also determines how alert we are. When it slows down, we doze off or go to sleep. But, thanks to the reticular formation, important messages

■ **brainstem**
The structure that begins at the point where the spinal cord enlarges as it enters the brain and handles functions critical to physical survival. It includes the medulla, the pons, and the reticular formation.

■ **medulla**
(muh-DUL-uh) The part of the brainstem that controls heartbeat, blood pressure, breathing, coughing, and swallowing.

■ **reticular formation**
A structure in the brainstem that plays a crucial role in arousal and attention and that screens sensory messages entering the brain.

FIGURE 2.4 Major Structures of the Human Brain

This drawing shows some of the major structures of the brain with a brief description of the function of each. The brainstem contains the medulla, the reticular formation, and the pons.

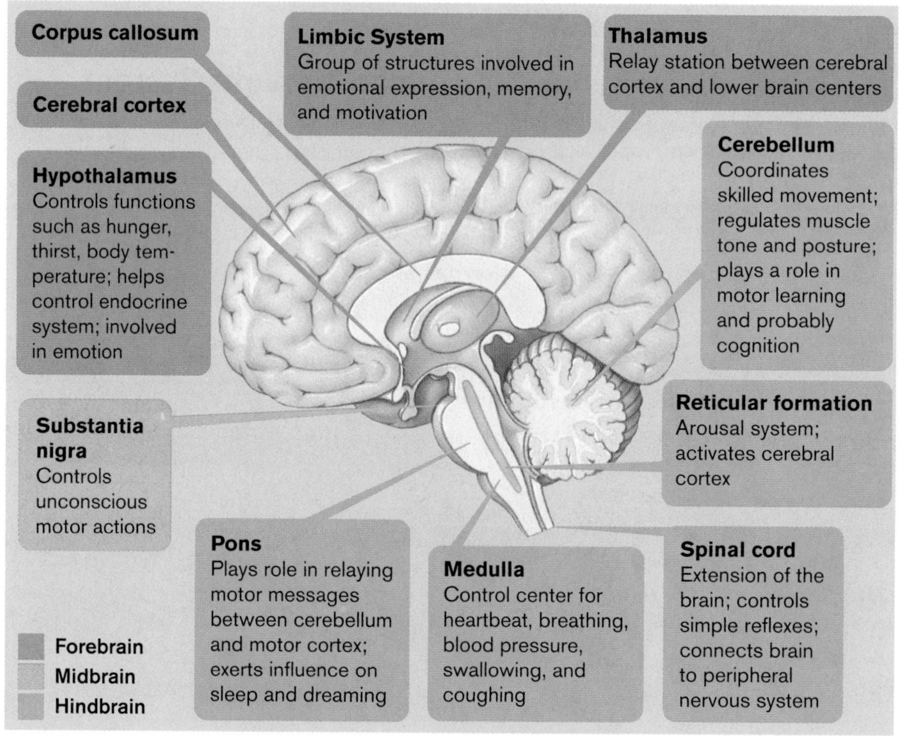
Corpus callosum
Limbic System
Group of structures involved in emotional expression, memory, and motivation
Thalamus
Relay station between cerebral cortex and lower brain centers
Cerebral cortex
Cerebellum
Coordinates skilled movement; regulates muscle tone and posture; plays a role in motor learning and probably cognition
Hypothalamus
Controls functions such as hunger, thirst, body temperature; helps control endocrine system; involved in emotion
Reticular formation
Arousal system; activates cerebral cortex
Substantia nigra
Controls unconscious motor actions
Pons
Plays role in relaying motor messages between cerebellum and motor cortex; exerts influence on sleep and dreaming
Medulla
Control center for heartbeat, breathing, blood pressure, swallowing, and coughing
Spinal cord
Extension of the brain; controls simple reflexes; connects brain to peripheral nervous system
Forebrain
Midbrain
Hindbrain

get through even when we are asleep. This is why parents may be able to sleep through a thunderstorm but will awaken to the slightest cry of their baby.

Above the medulla and at the top of the brainstem is a bridgelike structure called the *pons* that extends across the top front of the brainstem and connects to both halves of the cerebellum. The pons plays a role in body movement and even exerts an influence on sleep and dreaming.

■ **cerebellum** (sehr-uh-BELL-um) The brain structure that helps the body execute smooth, skilled movements and regulates muscle tone and posture.

The Cerebellum

What are the primary functions of the cerebellum?

The **cerebellum** makes up about 10% of the brain's volume and, with its two hemispheres, resembles the larger cerebrum that lies above it (Swanson, 1995). (Refer to Figure 2.4.) The cerebellum is critically important to the body's ability to execute smooth, skilled movements (Spencer et al., 2003). It also regulates muscle tone and posture. Furthermore, it has been found to play a role in motor learning and in retaining memories of motor activities (Lalonde & Botez, 1990). The cerebellum guides the graceful movements of the ballet dancer and the split-second timing of the skilled race car driver. But more typically, it coordinates the series of movements necessary to perform many simple activities—such as walking in a straight line or touching your finger to the tip of your nose—without conscious effort. For people who have damage to their cerebellum or who are temporarily impaired by too much alcohol, such simple acts may be difficult or impossible to perform.

Although some researchers remain skeptical, some studies suggest that the cerebellum is involved in cognitive and social functions as well as motor functions (Ellis, 2001; Fiez, 1996; Kim et al., 1994; Riva & Giorgi, 2000). The cerebellum may help to heighten our ability to focus attention on incoming sensory stimuli and to shift attention efficiently when conditions require (Allen et al., 1997). In addition, the cerebellum may increase our efficiency in acquiring sensory information and discriminating between sensory stimuli (Gao et al., 1996).

■ **substantia nigra** (sub-STAN-sha NI-gra) The structure in the midbrain that controls unconscious motor movements.

■ **thalamus** (THAL-uh-mus) The structure, located above the brainstem, that acts as a relay station for information flowing into or out of the forebrain.

The Midbrain

What important structure is located in the midbrain?

As shown in Figure 2.4, the midbrain lies between the hindbrain and forebrain. The structures of this brain region act primarily as relay stations through which the basic physiological functions of the hindbrain are linked to the cognitive functions of the forebrain. For example, when you burn your finger, the physical feeling travels through the nerves of your hand and arm, eventually reaching the spinal cord. From there, nerve impulses are sent through the midbrain to the forebrain, where they are interpreted ("I'd better drop this hot pot because it hurts a lot and may result in serious injury!").

The **substantia nigra** is located in the midbrain. This structure is comprised of darkly colored nuclei of nerve cells that control our unconscious motor actions. When you ride a bicycle or walk up stairs without giving your movements any conscious thought, the nuclei of the cells that allow you to do so are found in the substantia nigra. Recent research indicates that deficiencies in the responsiveness of these cells to various neurotransmitters may explain the inability of people with Parkinson's disease to control their physical movements (Trevitt et al., 2002).

The Thalamus and Hypothalamus

What are the functions of the thalamus and the hypothalamus?

Above the brainstem lie two extremely important structures (refer again to Figure 2.4). The **thalamus**, which has two egg-shaped parts, serves as the relay station for virtually all the information that flows into and out of the forebrain, including sensory information from all the senses except smell. (You'll learn more about the sense of smell in Chapter 3.)

■ **hypothalamus**
(HY-po-THAL-uh-mus) A small but influential brain structure that regulates hunger, thirst, sexual behavior, internal body temperature, other body functions, and a wide variety of emotional behaviors.

■ **limbic system**
A group of structures in the midbrain, including the amygdala and hippocampus, that are collectively involved in emotional expression, memory, and motivation.

■ **amygdala**
(ah-MIG-da-la) A structure in the limbic system that plays an important role in emotion, particularly in response to unpleasant or punishing stimuli.

The thalamus, or at least one small part of it, affects our ability to learn new verbal information and plays a role in the production of language (Metter, 1991). Another function of the thalamus is the regulation of sleep cycles, which is thought to be accomplished in cooperation with the pons and the reticular formation (Krosigk, 1993). The majority of people who have had acute brain injury and remain in an unresponsive "vegetative" state have suffered significant damage to the thalamus, to the neural tissue connecting it to parts of the forebrain, or to both (Adams et al., 2000).

The **hypothalamus** lies directly below the thalamus and weighs only about 2 ounces. It regulates hunger, thirst, sexual behavior, and a wide variety of emotional behaviors. The hypothalamus also regulates internal body temperature, starting the process that causes you to perspire when you are too hot and to shiver to conserve body heat when you are too cold. It also houses the biological clock—the mechanism responsible for the timing of the sleep/wakefulness cycle and the daily fluctuation in more than 100 body functions (Ginty et al., 1993). Because of the biological clock, once your body gets used to waking up at a certain time, you tend to awaken at that time every day—even if you forget to set your alarm. The physiological changes in the body that accompany strong emotion—sweaty palms, a pounding heart, a hollow feeling in the pit of your stomach—are also initiated by neurons concentrated primarily in the hypothalamus.

The Limbic System

How does the limbic system influence mental processes and behavior?

The **limbic system**, shown in Figure 2.5, is a group of structures in the midbrain, including the amygdala and the hippocampus, that are collectively involved in emotional expression, memory, and motivation. The **amygdala** plays an important role in emotion, particularly in response to unpleasant or punishing stimuli (LeDoux, 1994, 2000). Heavily involved in the learning of fear responses, the amygdala helps form vivid memories of emotional events, which enable humans and other animals to avoid dangerous situations (Cahill et al., 1995; LeDoux, 1995). The mere sight of frightened faces causes neurons in the amygdala to fire (Morris et al., 1996). Damage to the amygdala can impair a person's ability to recognize facial expressions and tones of voice that are associated with fear and anger (LeDoux, 2000; Scott et al., 1997).

FIGURE 2.5 The Principal Structures in the Limbic System

The amygdala plays an important role in emotion; the hippocampus is essential in the formation of new memories.

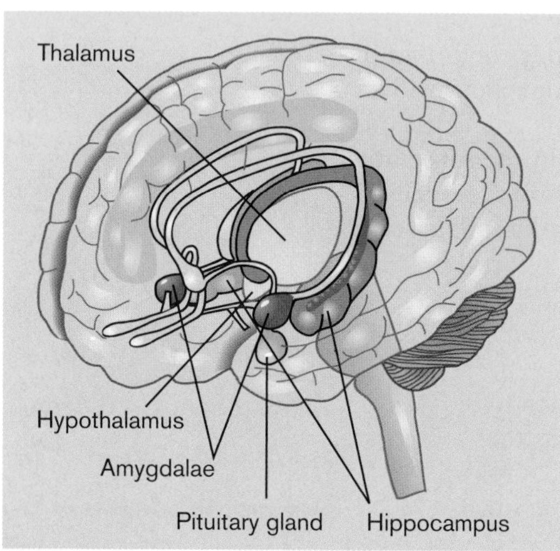

The **hippocampus** is an important brain structure of the limbic system located in the interior temporal lobes (see Figure 2.5). If your hippocampal region—the hippocampus and the underlying cortical areas—were destroyed, you would not be able to store or recall any new personal or cognitive information, such as that day's baseball score or the phone number of the person you met at dinner (Eichenbaum, 1997; Gluck & Myers, 1997; Varga-Khadem et al., 1997). Yet, memories already stored before the hippocampal region was destroyed would remain intact. However, recent research indicates the possibility of cell regeneration in the hippocampus in human adults (Robertson & Murre, 1999). You will learn more about the central role of the hippocampal region in the formation of memories in Chapter 6.

Besides its critically important role in memory, researchers have discovered that the hippocampus is an essential part of a neurological network that detects and responds to unexpected or novel stimuli (Knight, 1996). The hippocampus also plays a role in the brain's internal representation of space in the form of neural "maps" that help us learn our way about in new environments and remember where we have been (Wilson & McNaughton, 1993). An interesting study of taxi drivers in London revealed that their posterior (rear) hippocampus was significantly larger than that of participants in a control group who did not have extensive experience navigating the city's streets (Maguire et al., 2000). In fact, the more experience a taxi driver had, the larger that part of the hippocampus was. This study shows that the posterior hippocampus is important for navigational ability. More broadly, the study reveals that an important structure in the adult human brain has *plasticity*, the ability to respond to environmental demands (Maguire et al., 2000).

Autopsies performed on patients suffering from the severe memory impairment associated with Alzheimer's disease have revealed extensive damage to neurons in the hippocampus (West et al., 1994). Former President Ronald Reagan announced in 1994 that he was in the early stages of Alzheimer's disease. You will learn more about this insidious brain disease, which develops gradually, in Chapter 10.

■ **hippocampus**
(hip-po-CAM-pus) A structure in the limbic system that plays a central role in the storing of new memories, the response to new or unexpected stimuli, and navigational ability.

■ **cerebrum**
(seh-REE-brum) The largest structure of the human brain, consisting of the two cerebral hemispheres connected by the corpus callosum and covered by the cerebral cortex.

Remember It 2.2

1. The ___________ and ___________ make up the central nervous system.
2. Internal body temperature is regulated by the ___________.
3. The ___________ is associated with emotions, and the ___________ is involved in memory and learning.
4. The ___________ serves as a relay station for most sensory information.
5. The ___________ consists of the pons, medulla, and reticular formation.
6. Coordinated body movements are controlled by the ___________.

ANSWERS: 1. brain, spinal cord; 2. hypothalamus; 3. amygdala, hippocampus; 4. thalamus; 5. brainstem; 6. cerebellum

■ **cerebral hemispheres**
(seh-REE-brul) The right and left halves of the cerebrum, covered by the cerebral cortex and connected by the corpus callosum; they control movement and feeling on the opposing sides of the body.

■ **corpus callosum**
(KOR-pus kah-LO-sum) The thick band of nerve fibers that connects the two cerebral hemispheres and makes possible the transfer of information and the synchronization of activity between the hemispheres.

The Cerebrum

What functions come to mind when you think of the brain? Like most people, you probably identify this organ with logic, problem solving, language comprehension and production, and other such "higher" cognitive functions. Though other parts of the brain play important supporting roles in these functions, their primary site is the cerebrum. Indeed, the most essentially human part of our magnificent 3-pound brain is the cerebrum and its cortex.

Components of the Cerebrum

What are the components of the cerebrum?

If you could peer into your skull and look down on your brain, what you would see would resemble the inside of a huge walnut. Like a walnut, which has two matched halves connected to each other, the **cerebrum** is composed of two **cerebral hemispheres**—a left and a right hemisphere resting side by side (see Figure 2.6, on page 52). The two hemispheres are physically connected at the bottom by a thick band of nerve fibers called the **corpus callosum**. This connection makes possible the transfer of information and the coordination of activity between the hemispheres. In general, the right cerebral hemisphere controls movement and feeling on the left side of the body; the left hemisphere controls the right side of the body.

FIGURE 2.6 **Two Views of the Cerebral Hemispheres**

(a) The two hemispheres rest side by side like two matched halves, physically connected by the corpus callosum. (b) An inside view of the right hemisphere.

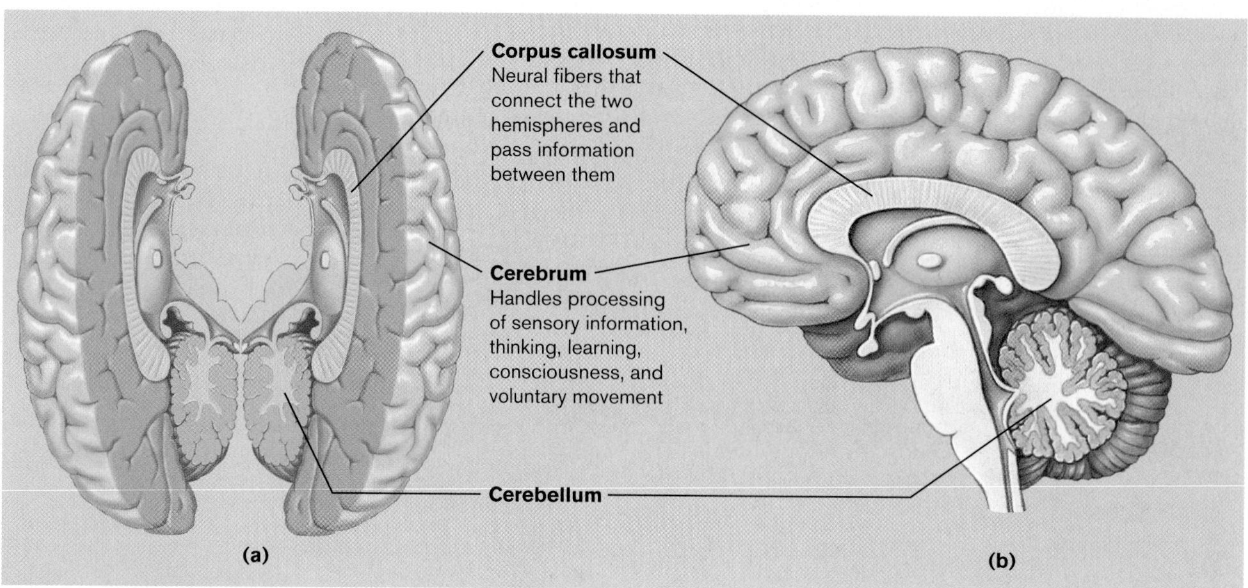

Corpus callosum
Neural fibers that connect the two hemispheres and pass information between them
Cerebrum
Handles processing of sensory information, thinking, learning, consciousness, and voluntary movement
Cerebellum
(a)
(b)

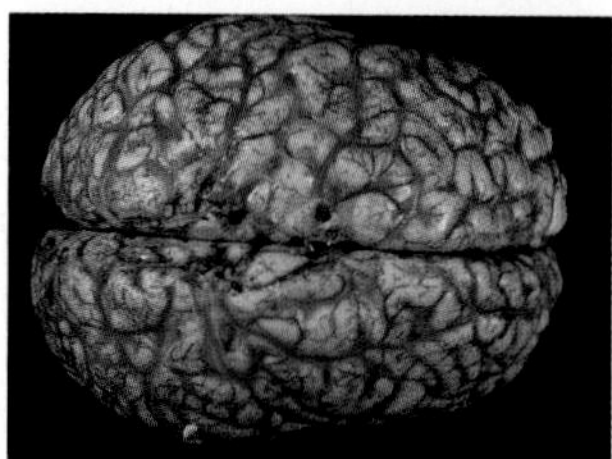
The two cerebral hemispheres show up clearly in this view looking down on an actual brain.

The cerebral hemispheres have a thin outer covering about 1/8 inch thick called the **cerebral cortex**, which is primarily responsible for the higher mental processes of language, memory, and thinking. The presence of the cell bodies of billions of neurons in the cerebral cortex gives it a grayish appearance. Thus, the cortex is often referred to as *gray matter*. Immediately beneath the cortex are the white myelinated axons (referred to as *white matter*) that connect the neurons of the cortex with those of other brain regions. Research by Andreasen and others (1993) indicated that the amount of gray matter is positively correlated with intelligence in humans.

In humans, the cerebral cortex is very large—if it were spread out flat, it would measure about 2 feet by 3 feet. Because the cortex is roughly three times the size of the cerebrum itself, it does not fit smoothly around the cerebrum. Rather, it is arranged in numerous folds or wrinkles, called *convolutions*. About two-thirds of the cortex is hidden from view in these folds. The cortex of less intelligent animals is much smaller in proportion to total brain size and, therefore, is much less convoluted. The cerebral cortex contains three types of areas: (1) sensory input areas, where vision, hearing, touch, pressure, and temperature register; (2) motor areas, which control voluntary movement; and (3) **association areas**, which house memories and are involved in thought, perception, and language. In each cerebral hemisphere, there are four lobes—the frontal lobe, the parietal lobe, the occipital lobe, and the temporal lobe (see Figure 2.7).

The Frontal Lobes

Which psychological functions are associated with the frontal lobes?

The largest of the brain's lobes, the **frontal lobes**, begin at the front of the brain and extend to the top center of the skull. They contain the motor cortex, Broca's area, and the frontal association areas.

The Motor Cortex In 1870, two physicians, Gustav Fritsch and Eduard Hitzig, used a probe to apply a weak electrical current to the cortex of a dog. (The brain itself is insensitive to pain, so probing it causes no discomfort.) When they stimulated various points on the cortex along the rear of the

FIGURE 2.7 The Cerebral Cortex of the Left Hemisphere

This illustration of the left cerebral hemisphere shows the four lobes: (1) the frontal lobe, including the motor cortex and Broca's area; (2) the parietal lobe, with the somatosensory cortex; (3) the occipital lobe, with the primary visual cortex; and (4) the temporal lobe, with the primary auditory cortex and Wernicke's area.

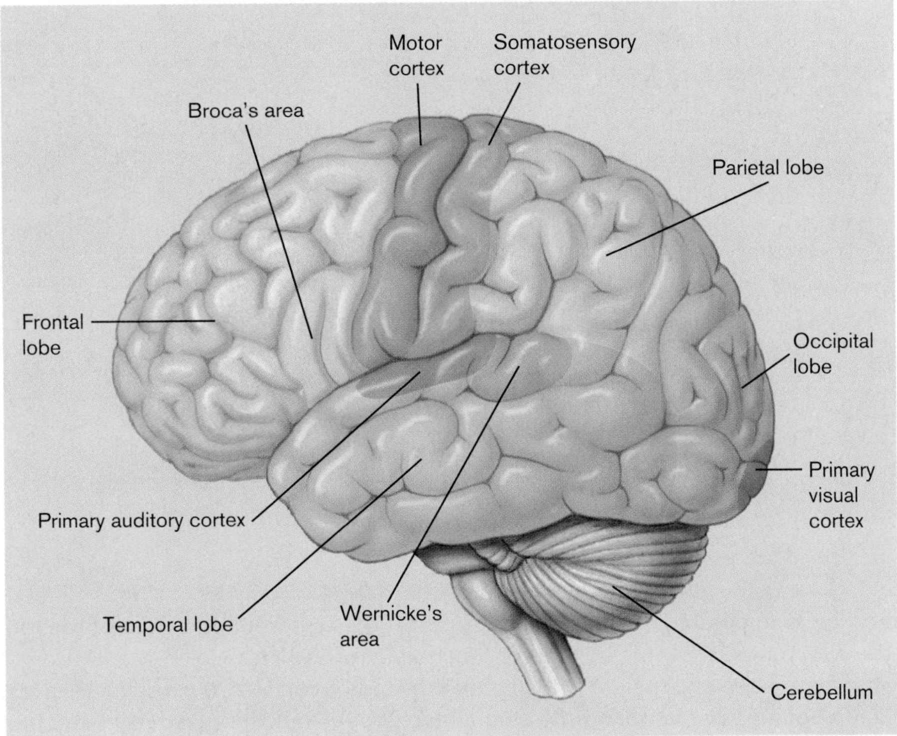

frontal lobes, specific parts of the dog's body moved. Fritsch and Hitzig had discovered the **motor cortex**—the area that controls voluntary body movement (refer to Figure 2.7). The right motor cortex controls movement on the left side of the body, and the left motor cortex controls movement on the right side of the body.

Later, in 1937, Canadian neurosurgeon Wilder Penfield applied electrical stimulation to the motor cortex of conscious human patients undergoing neurosurgery. He mapped the primary motor cortex in humans, as shown in Figure 2.8 (on page 54). Body parts are drawn in proportion to the amount of motor cortex involved in the movement of each. The parts of the body that are capable of the most finely coordinated movements, such as the fingers, lips, and tongue, have a larger share of the motor cortex. Movements in the lower parts of the body are controlled primarily by neurons at the top of the motor cortex, whereas movements in the upper body parts (face, lips, and tongue) are controlled mainly by neurons near the bottom of the motor cortex. For example, when you wiggle your right big toe, the movement is produced mainly by the firing of a cluster of brain cells at the top of the left motor cortex.

How accurately and completely does Penfield's map account for the control of body movement? Although it may be useful in a broad sense, more recent research has shown that there is not a precise one-to-one correspondence between specific points on the motor cortex and movement of particular body parts. Motor neurons that control the fingers, for example, play a role in the movement of more than a single finger. In fact, the control of movement of any single finger is handled by a network of neurons that are widely distributed over the entire hand area of the motor cortex (Sanes & Donoghue, 2000; Sanes et al., 1995; Schieber & Hibbard, 1993). Sometimes damage in the motor cortex can cause the grand mal seizures of epilepsy. On the other hand, if an

■ **cerebral cortex**
(seh-REE-brul KOR-tex) The gray, convoluted covering of the cerebral hemispheres that is responsible for the higher mental processes of language, memory, and thinking.

■ **association areas**
Areas of the cerebral cortex that house memories and are involved in thought, perception, and language.

■ **frontal lobes**
The largest of the brain's lobes, which contain the motor cortex, Broca's area, and the frontal association areas.

■ **motor cortex**
The strip of tissue at the rear of the frontal lobes that controls voluntary body movement and participates in learning and cognitive events.

FIGURE 2.8 The Motor Cortex and the Somatosensory Cortex from the Left Hemisphere

The left motor cortex controls voluntary movement on the right side of the body. The left somatosensory cortex is the site where touch, pressure, temperature, and pain sensations from the right side of the body register. The more sensitive the body parts and the more capable they are of finely coordinated movements, the greater the areas of somatosensory cortex and motor cortex dedicated to those body parts.

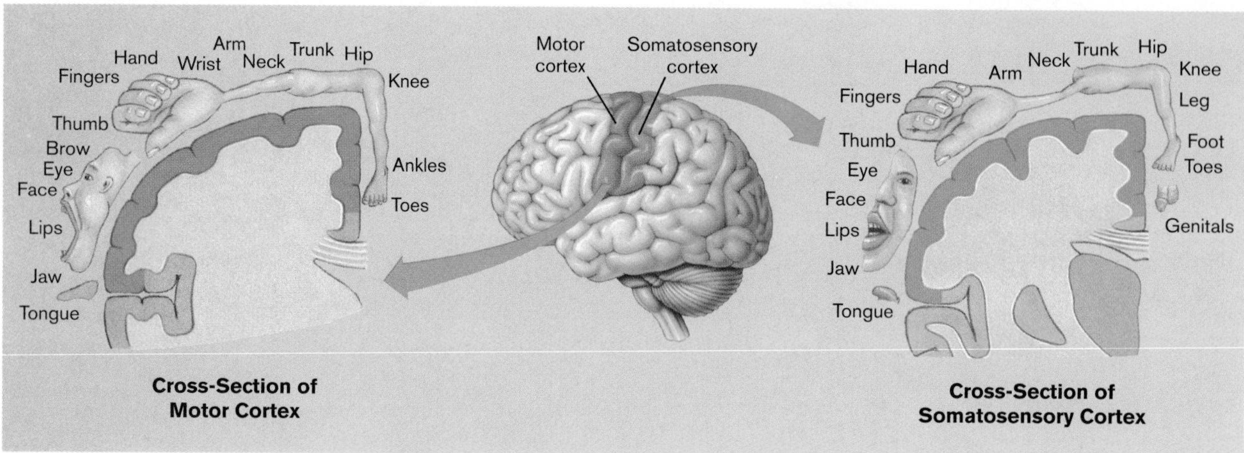

arm or leg is amputated, many of the neurons in the corresponding area of the motor cortex will eventually switch to another function (Murray, 1995).

Evidence has come to light showing that the motor cortex also participates in learning and cognitive events (Sanes & Donoghue, 2000). And the **plasticity**—the brain's capacity to adapt to changes such as brain damage—of the motor cortex is maintained throughout life. This plasticity allows synapses to strengthen and reorganize their interconnections when stimulated by experience and practice. Even mental rehearsal, or imaging, can produce changes in the motor cortex (Sanes & Donoghue, 2000), but such changes are not as powerful as those generated by real rehearsal or performance. Thus, athletes often spend time before a game visualizing their upcoming performance on the field or court—but this mental practice never replaces actual, physical practice. Moreover, the motor cortex in humans is responsive to both short-term and long-term experience (Liepert et al., 1999). Simply repeating a sequence of movements rapidly for as little as 5 to 10 minutes can alter the motor cortex (Classen et al., 1998).

plasticity The capacity of the brain to adapt to changes such as brain damage.

Broca's area (BRO-kuz) The area in the frontal lobe, usually in the left hemisphere, that controls the production of speech sounds.

Broca's aphasia (BRO-kuz uh-FAY-zyah) An impairment in the physical ability to produce speech sounds or, in extreme cases, an inability to speak at all; caused by damage to Broca's area.

aphasia (uh-FAY-zyah) A loss or impairment of the ability to use or understand language, resulting from damage to the brain.

Broca's Area In 1861, physician Paul Broca performed autopsies on two patients—one who had been totally without speech, and another who could say only four words (Jenkins et al., 1975). Broca found that both individuals had damage in the left hemisphere, slightly in front of the part of the motor cortex that controls movements of the jaw, lips, and tongue. Broca was among the first scientists to demonstrate the existence of localized functions in the cerebral cortex (Schiller, 1993). He concluded that the site of left hemisphere damage he identified through the autopsies was the part of the brain responsible for speech production, now called **Broca's area** (refer to Figure 2.7). Broca's area is involved in directing the pattern of muscle movement required to produce speech sounds.

If Broca's area is damaged as a result of head injury or stroke, **Broca's aphasia** may result. **Aphasia** is a general term for a loss or impairment of the ability to use or understand language, resulting from damage to the brain (Goodglass, 1993). Characteristically, patients with Broca's aphasia know what they want to say but can speak very little or not at all. If they are able to speak, their words are produced very slowly, with great effort, and are poorly articulated. Broca's aphasia, then, is a problem in producing language, not in understanding it (Maratsos & Matheny, 1994). Even patients who cannot speak are often able to sing songs they knew before suffering brain damage. Singing is normally controlled by the right hemisphere, and words to familiar songs are stored there (Albert & Helm-Estabrooks, 1988).

But Broca's area does more than just control the physical production of speech. A recent brain-imaging study (Embick et al., 2000) indicates that Broca's area buzzes with activity when a person makes grammatical errors, especially those involving word order. This finding confirms the existence of distinct brain structures for language knowledge and provides direct evidence of a specialization for grammar in Broca's area.

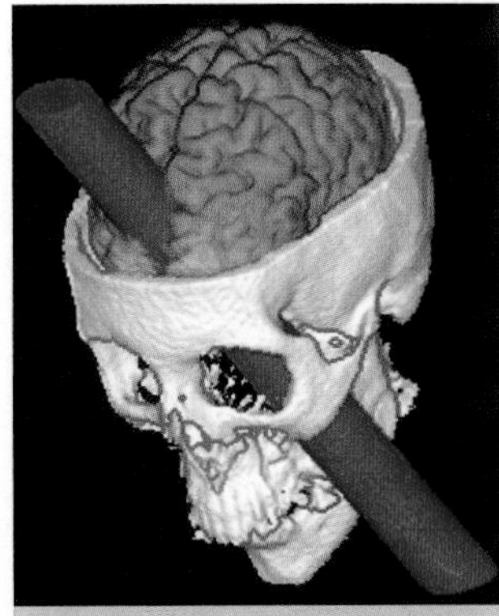

This computer-generated image shows the likely path of the bar that tore through Phineas Gage's skull.

Frontal Association Areas Much of the frontal lobes consist of association areas involved in thinking, motivation, planning for the future, impulse control, and emotional responses (Stuss et al., 1992). Damage to the frontal association areas produces deficiencies in the ability to plan and anticipate the consequences of actions. Sometimes, pronounced changes in emotional responses occur when the frontal lobes are damaged. Phineas Gage, discussed at the opening of this chapter, represents one case in which damage to the frontal lobes drastically altered impulse control and emotional responses.

The Parietal Lobes

What is the somatosensory cortex, and what does it do?

The **parietal lobes** lie directly behind the frontal lobes, in the top middle portion of the brain (refer back to Figure 2.7). The parietal lobes are involved in the reception and processing of touch stimuli. The front strip of brain tissue in the parietal lobes is the **somatosensory cortex**, the site where touch, pressure, temperature, and pain register in the cerebral cortex (Stea & Apkarian, 1992). The somatosensory cortex also makes you aware of movement in your body and the positions of your body parts at any given moment.

The two halves of the somatosensory cortex, in the left and right parietal lobes, are wired to opposite sides of the body. Also, cells at the top of the somatosensory cortex govern feeling in the lower extremities of the body. Drop a brick on your right foot, and the topmost brain cells of the left somatosensory cortex will fire and register the pain sensation. (Note: This is *not* a *Try It!*) Notice in Figure 2.8 that large somatosensory areas are connected to sensitive body parts such as the tongue, lips, face, and hand, particularly the thumb and index finger. A person with damage to the somatosensory cortex of one hemisphere loses some sensitivity to touch on the opposite side of the body. If the damage is severe enough, the person might not be able to feel the difference between sandpaper and silk, or the affected part of the body might feel numb.

Experience can affect the somatosensory cortex (Juliano, 1998). For example, compared to nonmusicians, professional musicians who play stringed instruments have a significantly larger area of the somatosensory cortex dedicated to the fingers of their left hand. And the earlier the age at which they began to play, the larger this dedicated cortical area is (Elbert et al., 1995).

Other parts of the parietal lobes are responsible for spatial orientation and sense of direction—for example, helping you to retrace your path when you take a wrong turn. The hippocampus cooperates with these parts of the parietal lobes in performing such functions, as the study of London taxi drivers discussed on page 51 indicates (Maguire et al., 2000). Other recent research reveals a gender-related difference in human navigational thinking. Female and male participants had to find their way out of a complex, three-dimensional, computer-simulated maze. Brain imaging showed that male participants relied heavily on the left hippocampus while navigating through the maze, while female participants consistently used both the right parietal cortex and the right frontal cortex (Gron et al., 2000).

■ **parietal lobes** (puh-RY-uh-tul) The lobes that contain the somatosensory cortex (where touch, pressure, temperature, and pain register) and other areas that are responsible for body awareness and spatial orientation.

■ **somatosensory cortex** (so-MAT-oh-SENS-or-ee) The strip of tissue at the front of the parietal lobes where touch, pressure, temperature, and pain register in the cerebral cortex.

■ **occipital lobes**
(ahk-SIP-uh-tul) The lobes that are involved in the reception and interpretation of visual information; they contain the primary visual cortex.

Have you ever fumbled for your keys in a coat pocket, purse, or backpack? How did you distinguish between your keys and other objects without looking? There are association areas in the parietal lobes that house memories of how objects feel against the human skin, a fact that explains why we can identify objects by touch. People with damage to these areas could hold a computer mouse, a CD, or a baseball in their hand but not be able to identify the object by touch alone.

The Occipital Lobes

Why are the occipital lobes critical to vision?

Behind the parietal lobes at the rear of the brain lie the **occipital lobes**, which are involved in the reception and interpretation of visual information (refer to Figure 2.7). At the very back of the occipital lobes is the **primary visual cortex**, the site where vision registers in the cortex.

Each eye is connected to the primary visual cortex in both the right and the left occipital lobes. Look straight ahead and draw an imaginary line down the middle of what you see. Everything to the left of the line is referred to as the left visual field and registers in the right visual cortex. Everything to the right of the line is the right visual field and registers in the left visual cortex. A person who sustains damage to one half of the primary visual cortex will still have partial vision in both eyes because each eye sends information to both the right and the left occipital lobes.

The association areas in the occipital lobes are involved in the interpretation of visual stimuli. The association areas hold memories of past visual experiences and enable us to recognize what is familiar among the things we see. That's why the face of a friend stands out in a crowd of unfamiliar people. When these areas are damaged, people can lose the ability to identify objects visually, although they will still be able to identify the same objects by touch or through some other sense.

■ **primary visual cortex**
The area at the rear of the occipital lobes where vision registers in the cerebral cortex.

■ **temporal lobes**
The lobes that are involved in the reception and interpretation of auditory information; they contain the primary auditory cortex, Wernicke's area, and the temporal association areas.

The Temporal Lobes

What are the major areas within the temporal lobes, and what are their functions?

The **temporal lobes**, located slightly above the ears, are involved in the reception and interpretation of auditory stimuli. The site in the cortex where hearing registers is known as the primary auditory cortex. The **primary auditory cortex** in each temporal lobe receives sound inputs from both ears. Injury to one of these areas results in reduced hearing in both ears, and the destruction of both areas causes total deafness.

Wernicke's Area Adjacent to the primary auditory cortex in the left temporal lobe is **Wernicke's area**, which is the language area involved in comprehending the spoken word and in formulating coherent written and spoken language (refer to Figure 2.7). In about 95% of people, Wernicke's area is in the left hemisphere. When you listen to someone speak, the sound registers first in the primary auditory cortex. The sound is then sent to Wernicke's area, where the speech sounds are unscrambled into meaningful patterns of words. The same areas that are active when you listen to someone speak are also active in deaf individuals when they watch a person using sign language (Söderfeldt et al., 1994). Wernicke's area is also involved when you select the words you want to use when speaking and writing (Nishimura et al., 1999).

Wernicke's aphasia is a type of aphasia resulting from damage to Wernicke's area. Although speech is fluent and words are clearly articulated, the actual message does not make sense to listeners (Maratsos & Matheney, 1994). The content may be vague or bizarre and may contain inappropriate words, parts of words, or a gibberish of nonexistent words. One Wernicke's patient, when asked how he was feeling, replied, "I think that there's an awful lot of mung, but I think I've a lot of net and tunged in a little wheat duhvayden" (Buckingham & Kertesz, 1974). People with Wernicke's aphasia are not aware that anything is wrong with their speech. Thus, this disorder is difficult to treat.

■ **primary auditory cortex**
The part of each temporal lobe where hearing registers in the cerebral cortex.

■ **Wernicke's area**
(VUR-nih-keys) The language area in the left temporal lobe involved in comprehending the spoken word and in formulating of coherent speech and written language.

■ **Wernicke's aphasia**
Aphasia that results from damage to Wernicke's area and in which the person's speech is fluent and clearly articulated but does not make sense to listeners.

Another kind of aphasia is *auditory aphasia*, or word deafness. It can occur if there is damage to the nerves connecting the primary auditory cortex with Wernicke's area. The person is able to hear normally but may not understand spoken language—just as when you hear a foreign language spoken and perceive the sounds but have no idea what the speaker is saying.

The Temporal Association Areas The remainder of the temporal lobes consists of the association areas that house memories and are involved in the interpretation of auditory stimuli. For example, the association area where your memories of various sounds are stored enables you to recognize the sounds of your favorite band, a computer booting up, your roommate snoring, and so on. There is also a special association area where familiar melodies are stored.

Remember It 2.3

1. The band of fibers connecting the left and right cerebral hemispheres is the ________.
2. ________ is to speech production as ________ is to speech understanding.
3. The primary auditory cortex is found in the ________ lobe, while the primary visual cortex is located in the ________ lobe.
4. A person with brain damage who has problems regulating emotion most likely has an injury to the ________ lobe.
5. The sense of touch is associated with the ________ lobe.

ANSWERS: 1. corpus callosum; 2. Broca's area, Wernicke's area; 3. temporal, occipital; 4. frontal; 5. parietal

The Cerebral Hemispheres

You've probably heard about differences between "right-brained" and "left-brained" people. For instance, "right-brained" people are sometimes described as creative, while their "left-brained" counterparts are characterized as logical. These ideas sprang from the tendency of journalists to oversimplify and misinterpret research findings (Coren, 1993). Such a notion has no scientific basis, yet it has served to heighten public interest in hemispheric specialization and neuroscience in general (Hellige, 1993). In fact, despite their specialized functions, the right and left hemispheres are always in contact, thanks to the corpus callosum (shown in Figure 2.4). But research has shown that some **lateralization** of the hemispheres exists; that is, each hemisphere is specialized to handle certain functions. Let's look at the specific functions associated with the left and right hemispheres.

■ **lateralization** The specialization of one of the cerebral hemispheres to handle a particular function.

■ **left hemisphere** The hemisphere that controls the right side of the body, coordinates complex movements, and, in most people, handles most of the language functions.

The Left Hemisphere

What are the specialized functions of the left hemisphere?

In 95% of right-handers and in about 62% of left-handers, the **left hemisphere** handles most of the language functions, including speaking, writing, reading, speech comprehension, and comprehension of the logic of written information (Hellige, 1990; Long & Baynes, 2002). But relating written information to its context involves both hemispheres. Likewise, American sign language (ASL), used by deaf persons, is processed by both hemispheres (Neville et al., 1998). The left hemisphere is also specialized for mathematical abilities, particularly calculation, and it processes information in an analytical and sequential, or step-by-step, manner (Corballis, 1989). Logic is primarily a left hemisphere activity.

The left hemisphere coordinates complex movements by directly controlling the right side of the body and by indirectly controlling the movements of the left side of the body. It accomplishes this by sending orders across the corpus callosum to the right hemisphere so that the proper movements will be coordinated and executed smoothly. (Remember that the cerebellum also plays an important role in helping coordinate complex movements.)

The Right Hemisphere

What are the specialized functions of the right hemisphere?

The **right hemisphere** is generally considered to be the hemisphere more adept at visual-spatial relations. And the auditory cortex in the right hemisphere appears to be far better able to process music than the left (Zatorre et al., 2002). When you arrange your bedroom furniture or notice that your favorite song is being played on the radio, you are relying primarily on your right hemisphere.

right hemisphere The hemisphere that controls the left side of the body and, in most people, is specialized for visual-spatial perception.

The right hemisphere also augments the left hemisphere's language-processing activities. For example, it produces the unusual verbal associations characteristic of creative thought and problem solving (Seger et al., 2000). As Van Lancker (1987) pointed out, "although the left hemisphere knows best what is being said, the right hemisphere figures out how it is meant and who is saying it" (p. 13). It is the right hemisphere that is able to understand familiar idiomatic expressions, such as "She let the cat out of the bag."

To experience an effect of the specialization of the cerebral hemispheres, try your hand at *Try It 2.1.*

Try It 2.1 A Balancing Act

Get a meter stick or yardstick. Try balancing it vertically on the end of your left index finger, as shown in the drawing. Then try balancing it on your right index finger. Most people are better with their dominant hand—the right hand for right-handers, for example. Is this true for you?

Now try this: Begin reciting the ABCs out loud as fast as you can while balancing the stick with your left hand. Do you have less trouble this time? Why should that be? The right hemisphere controls the act of balancing with the left hand. However, your left hemisphere, though poor at controlling the left hand, still tries to coordinate your balancing efforts. When you distract the left hemisphere with a steady stream of talk, the right hemisphere can orchestrate more efficient balancing with your left hand without interference.

Patients with right hemisphere damage may have difficulty understanding metaphors or orienting spatially, as in finding their way around, even in familiar surroundings. They may have attentional deficits and be unaware of objects in the left visual field, a condition called *unilateral neglect* (Deovell et al., 2000; Halligan & Marshall, 1994). Patients with this condition may eat only the food on the right side of a plate, read only the words on the right half of a page, groom only the right half of the body, or even deny that the arm on the side opposite the brain damage belongs to them (Bisiach, 1996; Chen-Sea, 2000; Posner, 1996; Tham et al., 2000). Researchers have found that a treatment combining visual training with forced movement of limbs on the neglected side helps some patients (Brunila et al., 2002).

The Right Hemisphere's Role in Emotion The right hemisphere also responds to the emotional message conveyed by another's tone of voice (LeDoux, 2000). Reading and interpreting nonverbal behavior, such as gestures and facial expressions, is another right hemisphere task (Hauser, 1993; Kucharska-Pietura & Klimkowski, 2002). For example, the subtle clues that tell us someone is lying (such as excessive blinking or lack of eye contact) are processed in the right hemisphere (Etcoff et al., 2000).

The right hemisphere is involved in the expression of emotion through tone of voice and facial expressions. The left side of the face, controlled by the right hemisphere, usually conveys stronger emotion than the right side of the face. Lawrence Miller (1988) describes the facial expressions and the voice inflection of people with right hemisphere damage as "often strangely blank—almost robotic" (p. 39).

Evidence also continues to accumulate that brain mechanisms responsible for negative emotions are located in the right hemisphere, while those responsible for positive emotions are in the left hemisphere (Hellige, 1993). Research shows that patients suffering from major depression experience decreased activity in the left prefrontal cortex, where positive emotions are produced (Drevets et al., 1997). Interestingly, too, patients with brain tumors in the right hemisphere perceive their situation more negatively than those with tumors on the left side of the brain (Salo et al., 2002). By contrast, doctors' ratings of patients' quality of life do not vary according to the hemisphere in which the tumor is located. Figure 2.9 summarizes the functions associated with the left and right hemispheres.

FIGURE 2.9 Lateralized Functions of the Brain

Assigning functions to one hemisphere or the other allows the brain to function more efficiently.

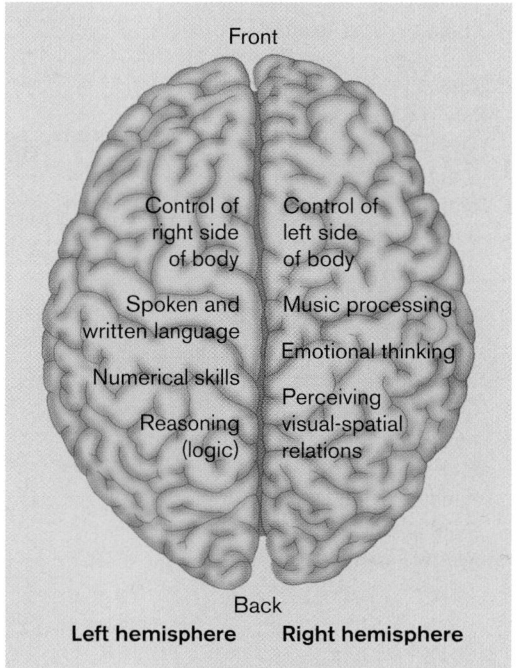

The Split Brain

What do researchers mean by the term "split brain"?

A great deal of knowledge about lateralization has been gained from studies involving individuals in whom the corpus callosum is absent or has been surgically modified. Many such individuals have had their corpus callosum severed in a drastic surgical procedure called the **split-brain operation**. Neurosurgeons Joseph Bogen and Philip Vogel (1963) found that patients with severe epilepsy, suffering frequent and uncontrollable grand mal seizures, could be helped by surgery that severed their corpus callosum, rendering communication between the two hemispheres impossible. The operation decreases the frequency of seizures in two-thirds of patients and causes minimal loss of cognitive functioning or change in personality (Washington University School of Medicine, 2003).

Research with split-brain patients by Roger Sperry (1964) and colleagues Michael Gazzaniga (1970, 1989) and Jerre Levy (1985) expanded knowledge of the unique capabilities of the individual hemispheres. Sperry (1968) found that when the brain was surgically separated, each hemisphere continued to have individual and private experiences, sensations, thoughts, and perceptions. However, most sensory experiences are shared almost simultaneously because each ear and eye has direct sensory connections to both hemispheres.

Testing the Split-Brain Patient Sperry's research, for which he won a Nobel Prize in medicine in 1981, revealed some fascinating findings. In Figure 2.10 (on page 60), a split-brain patient sits in front of a screen that separates the right and left fields of vision. If an orange is flashed to the right field of vision, it will register in the left (verbal) hemisphere. If asked what he saw, the patient will readily reply, "I saw an orange." Suppose that, instead, an apple is flashed to the left visual field and is relayed to the right (nonverbal) hemisphere. The patient will reply, "I saw nothing."

■ **split-brain operation** A surgical procedure, performed to treat severe cases of epilepsy, in which the corpus callosum is cut, separating the cerebral hemispheres.

FIGURE 2.10 Testing a Split-Brain Person

Using special equipment, researchers are able to study the independent functioning of the hemispheres in split-brain patients. In this experiment, when a visual image (an orange) is flashed on the right side of the screen, it is transmitted to the left (talking) hemisphere. When asked what he sees, the split-brain patient replies, "I see an orange." When an image (an apple) is flashed on the left side of the screen, it is transmitted only to the right (nonverbal) hemisphere. Because the split-brain patient's left (language) hemisphere did not receive the image, he replies, "I see nothing." But he can pick out the apple by touch if he uses his left hand, proving that the right hemisphere "saw" the apple. *Source*: Based on Gazzaniga (1983).

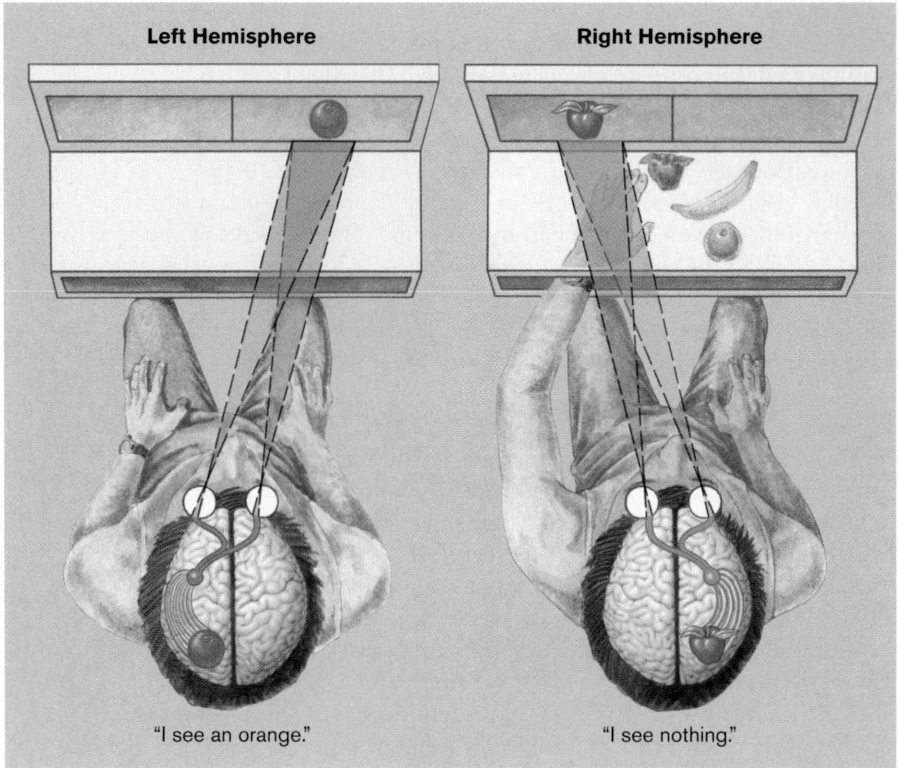

Why could the patient report that he saw the orange but not the apple? Sperry (1964, 1968) maintains that in split-brain patients, only the verbal left hemisphere can report what it sees. In these experiments, the left hemisphere does not see what is flashed to the right hemisphere, and the right hemisphere is unable to report verbally what it has viewed. But did the right hemisphere actually see the apple that was flashed in the left visual field? Yes, because with his left hand (which is controlled by the right hemisphere), the patient can pick out from behind a screen the apple or any other object shown to the right hemisphere. The right hemisphere knows and remembers what it sees just as well as the left, but unlike the left hemisphere, the right cannot name what it has seen. (In these experiments, images must be flashed for no more than 1/10 or 2/10 of a second so that the subjects do not have time to refixate their eyes and send the information to the opposite hemisphere.)

Handedness, Culture, and Genes

How are handedness and brain function related?

Since we've been discussing right and left hemispheres, you might be wondering whether right- and left-handedness have anything to do with hemispheric specialization. Investigators have identified differences in the brains of left- and right-handers that suggest that the process of hemispheric specialization and the development of handedness may be related. On average, the corpus callosum of left-handers is 11% larger and contains up to 2.5 million more nerve fibers than that of right-handers (Witelson, 1985). In general, the two sides of the brain are less specialized in left-handers (Hellige et al., 1994). There is also evidence that new learning is more easily transferred from one side of the brain to the other in left-handers (Schmidt et al., 2000).

In addition, left-handers tend to experience less language loss following an injury to either hemisphere. They are also more likely to recover, because the undamaged hemisphere can more easily take over the speech functions. On the other hand, left-handers tend to have higher rates of learning disabilities and mental disorders than right-handers, perhaps because of differences in brain organization (Grouios et al., 1999; Hernandez et al., 1997; Tanner, 1990).

It used to be believed that cultural forces were responsible for the high incidence of right-handedness. The idea was that the prevalence of right-handedness grew along with the spread of tool use among humans. There is some evidence to support this view. For instance, in cultures where there is a great deal of pressure on children to adopt a right-hand preference, there are lower proportions of left-handers than there are in societies, such as the United States, where it is widely believed that forcing children to be right-handed is detrimental to their development (Wilson, 1998). Further, the proportion of left-handers among elderly people in the United States is smaller than that for younger groups (Porac & Friesen, 2000). One possible explanation for this generational difference is that children of earlier generations who displayed a left-handed preference were more strongly pressured to switch to the right hand than were children born later. Still, right-handedness continues to predominate even in cultures that are highly tolerant of left-handedness among children. Why?

Many creative people, such as Whoopi Goldberg, are left-handed. However, language processing is lateralized to the left cerebral hemisphere in majorities of both right- and left-handed people.

Historical evidence generally supports a genetic explanation for the predominance of right-handedness among humans. Archeological studies of ancient populations show that the proportions of left- and right-handers in the human population has been about the same for several thousand years (83% right-handed, 14% left-handed, and 3% ambidexterous; Steele & Mays, 1995). And anthopological studies of ancient artwork and tools from locations all over the world have shown that right-handedness has been dominant for thousands of years (Wilson, 1998). There is even evidence that pre-human species, such as *Homo erectus*, were predominantly right-handed.

Anthropologists believe that the biologically based predominance of right-handedness explains the pervasiveness of right-left symbolism in mythology, art, and language. Cross-cultural studies show that right-handedness is typically characterized as normal, while left-handedness is associated either with evil or with exceptional abilities (Hicks & Gwynne, 1996). For example, if you examine a deck of Tarot cards, you will see that justice is right-handed, while evil is left-handed. And we are asked to raise our right hands when we take an oath of any kind. Note, however, that the positive association of left-handedness with exceptional talent seems to have some basis in fact. Left-handers are more numerous among artists, musicians, and political leaders (Wilson, 1998).

Animal studies provide further support for the genetic hypothesis. Studies indicate that right-handedness is almost as prevalent among chimpanzees as among humans (Hopkins et al., 2001). By contrast, studies involving other primate species, which are less genetically similar to humans than chimpanzees are, find a majority of individuals to be left-handed (Westergaard & Lussier, 1999).

Consistent with the genetic hypothesis, humans' handedness is evident early in life. Hepper and others (1990) found that, of the human fetuses they observed, 94.6% were sucking their right thumb and only 5.4% were sucking their left thumb. And if you carefully observe infant pointing behavior, you will see that babies almost always point with their right hand (Butterworth et al., 2002). By the age of 5, a large majority of children show a consistent preference for the right hand when manipulating objects.

Some neuroscientists believe that handedness is just one manifestation of a general "rightward bias" in the human nervous system. Even infants, for example, are more likely to attend to an object that appears in the right visual field than one that appears in the left. (Butterworth et al., 2002). And more than half of left-handers demonstrate right-side dominance with regard to motor skills that do not involve the hands, such as kicking (Bourassa et al., 1996). Moreover, only 26% of children born to two left-handed parents are left-handed themselves (McManus & Bryden, 1992). These findings suggest that a rightward bias may be a biologically based characteristic of the entire human species that has a more powerful influence on hand preference than does individual heredity.

Remember It 2.4

1. When you listen to a person talk, you most likely process her words in your ________ hemisphere.
2. You process facial expressions in your ________ hemisphere.
3. The split-brain operation is sometimes performed to cure ________.
4. Reaserch suggests that the prevalence of right-handedness among humans may be caused by an inherited ________.

ANSWERS: 1. left; 2. right; 3. epilepsy; 4. rightward bias

■ **electroencephalogram (EEG)** (ee-lek-tro-en-SEFF-uh-lo-gram) A record of brain-wave activity made by a machine called the electroencephalograph.

■ **beta wave** (BAY-tuh) The brain-wave pattern associated with mental or physical activity.

■ **alpha wave** The brain-wave pattern associated with deep relaxation.

Discovering the Brain's Mysteries

As we have seen, the first attempts to discover the mysteries of the human brain were through autopsies, such as those performed by Broca, and through clinical observations of the effects of brain injury and diseases. The next method of study was to insert electrical probes into live brains, as Fritsch and Hitzig did in 1870.

Modern researchers do not have to perform autopsies or wait for injuries to occur to learn more about the brain. Today, researchers are unlocking the mysteries of the human brain using the electroencephalograph (EEG), the microelectrode, and modern scanning techniques such as the CT scan, magnetic resonance imaging (MRI), the PET scan, functional MRI, and others (Andreasen et al., 1992).

The EEG and the Microelectrode

What does the electroencephalogram (EEG) reveal about the brain?

In 1924, Austrian psychiatrist Hans Berger invented the electroencephalograph, a machine that records the electrical activity occurring in the brain. This electrical activity, detected by electrodes placed at various points on the scalp and amplified greatly, provides the power to drive a pen across paper, producing a record of brain-wave activity called an **electroencephalogram (EEG)**. The **beta wave** is the brain-wave pattern associated with mental or physical activity. The **alpha wave** is associated with deep relaxation, and the **delta wave** with slow-wave (deep) sleep. (You will learn more about these brain-wave patterns in Chapter 4.)

A computerized EEG imaging technique shows the different levels of electrical activity occurring every millisecond on the surface of the brain (Gevins et al., 1995). It can show an epileptic seizure in progress and can be used to study neural activity in people with learning disabilities, schizophrenia, Alzheimer's disease, sleep disorders, and other neurological problems.

■ **delta wave** The brain-wave pattern associated with slow-wave (deep) sleep.

■ **microelectrode** A small wire used to monitor the electrical activity of or stimulate activity within a single neuron.

Although the EEG is able to detect electrical activity in different areas of the brain, it cannot reveal what is happening in individual neurons. However, the **microelectrode** can. A microelectrode is a wire so small that it can be inserted near or into a single neuron without damaging it. Microelectrodes can be used to monitor the electrical activity of a single neuron or to stimulate activity within it. Researchers have used microelectrodes to discover the exact functions of single cells within the primary visual cortex and the primary auditory cortex.

The CT Scan and Magnetic Resonance Imaging

How are the CT scan and MRI helpful in the study of brain structure?

Since the early 1970s, a number of techniques that provide scientists and physicians with images of the brain's structures have become available. For example, a patient undergoing a **CT scan (computerized axial tomography)** of the brain is placed inside a large, doughnut-shaped structure where an X-ray tube encircles the entire head. The tube rotates in a complete circle and shoots X-rays through the brain as it does so. A series of computerized, cross-sectional images reveal the structures within the brain as well as abnormalities and injuries, including tumors and evidence of old or more recent strokes.

Another technique, **MRI (magnetic resonance imaging)**, that became widely available in the 1980s produces clearer and more detailed images without exposing patients to potentially dangerous X-rays (Potts et al., 1993). MRI can be used to find abnormalities in the central nervous system and in other systems of the body. Although the CT scan and MRI do a remarkable job of showing what the brain looks like both inside and out, they cannot reveal what the brain is doing. But other technological marvels can.

■ CT scan (computerized axial tomography)
A brain-scanning technique that uses a rotating, computerized X-ray tube to produce cross-sectional images of the structures of the brain.

■ MRI (magnetic resonance imagery)
A diagnostic scanning technique that produces high-resolution images of the structures of the brain.

The PET Scan, fMRI, and Other Imaging Techniques

How are the PET scan and newer imaging techniques used to study the brain?

As helpful as they are, CT and MRI images show only structures. By contrast, several techniques capture images of both brain structures and their functions. The oldest of these techniques, the **PET scan (positron-emission tomography)** has been used since the mid-1970s to identify malfunctions that cause physical and psychological disorders. It has also been used to study normal brain activity. A PET scan maps the patterns of blood flow, oxygen use, and glucose consumption (glucose is the food of the brain). It can also show the action of drugs and other biochemical substances in the brain and other bodily organs (Farde, 1996).

A technique that become available in the 1990s, **functional MRI (fMRI),** has several important advantages over PET: (1) It can provide images of both brain structure and brain activity; (2) it requires no injections (of radioactive or other material); (3) it can identify locations of activity more precisely than PET can; and (4) it can detect changes that take place in less than a second, compared with about a minute for PET ("Brain Imaging," 1997).

Still other imaging devices are now available. SQUID (superconducting quantum interference device) shows brain activity by measuring the magnetic changes produced by the electric current that neurons discharge when they fire. Another imaging

■ PET scan (positron-emission tomography)
A brain-imaging technique that reveals activity in various parts of the brain, based on patterns of blood flow, oxygen use, and glucose consumption.

■ functional MRI (fMRI)
A brain-imaging technique that reveals both brain structure and brain activity more precisely and rapidly than PET.

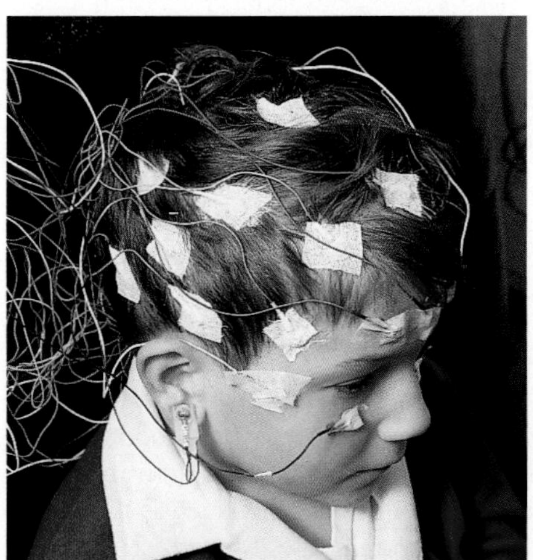

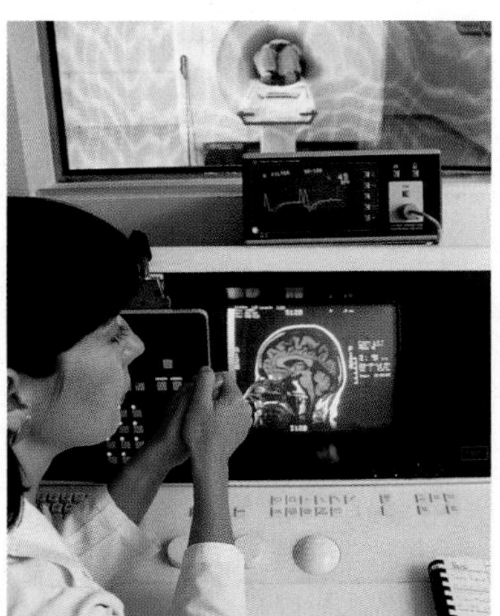

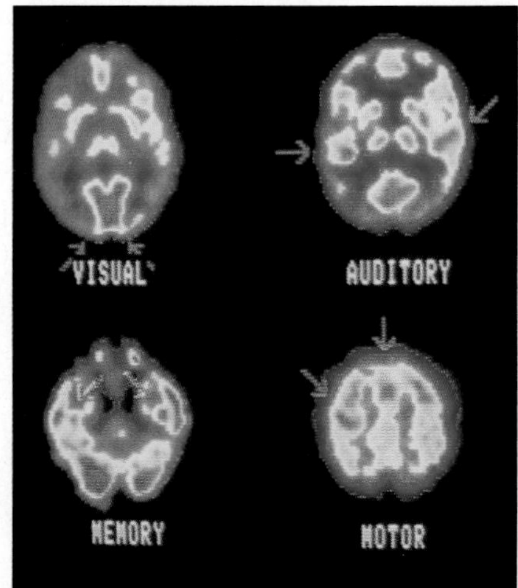

The electroencephalograph, or EEG (left), uses electrodes placed on the scalp to amplify and record electrical activity in the brain. MRI (center) is a powerful tool for revealing what the brain looks like. Unlike PET, however, it cannot show what the brain is doing. PET scans (right) show activity in specific areas of the brain.

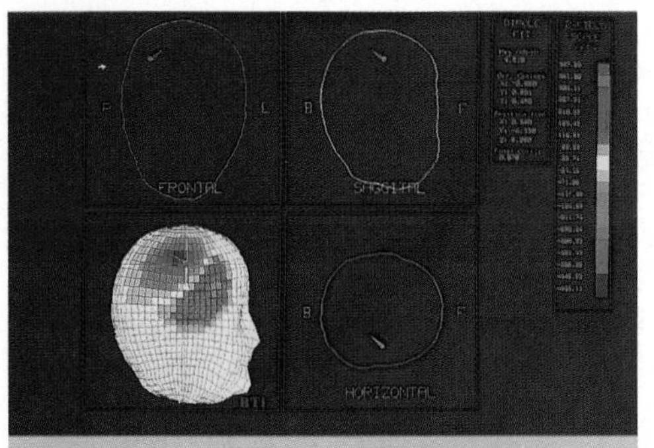

SQUID is a relatively new brain-imaging tool that measures magnetic changes in the brain.

marvel, MEG (magnetoencephalography), also measures such magnetic changes and shows neural activity within the brain as rapidly as it occurs, much faster than PET or fMRI.

Brain-imaging techniques have helped neuroscientists develop an impressive store of knowledge about normal brain functions such as memory (Zhang et al., 2003). These imaging techniques have also been used to show abnormal brain patterns peculiar to certain psychiatric disorders and to reveal where and how various drugs affect the brain (Juengling et al., 2003; Tamminga & Conley, 1997). And some neuroscientists are experimenting with combining virtual reality with fMRI to study how the brain responds to situations and environments that would be impossible to observe using conventional imaging techniques (Travis, 1996).

Remember It 2.5

1. The CT scan and MRI are used to produce images of the __________ of the brain.
2. The __________ reveals the electrical activity of the brain by producing a record of brain waves.
3. A __________ scan reveals brain activity and function, rather than the structure of the brain.
4. A newer imaging technique called __________ reveals both brain structure and brain activity.
5. Match the brain-wave pattern with the state associated with it.

____ (1) slow-wave (deep) sleep	a. beta wave
____ (2) deep relaxation	b. delta wave
____ (3) physical or mental activity	c. alpha wave

ANSWERS: 1. structures; 2. electroencephalograph; 3. PET scan; 4. fMRI; 5. (1) b, (2) c, (3) a

The Brain across the Lifespan

The principles of neurological functioning you've learned about—how action potentials occur and so on—work pretty much the same no matter what an individual's age. Still, there are some important age-related variations in brain structure and function that may contribute to psychological and behavioral age differences. You'll read about these variations in greater detail in Chapters 9 and 10; now let's discuss a few general principles of neurological development.

The Ever-Changing Brain

In what ways does the brain change across the lifespan?

Do you consider your brain to be fully matured? When do you think the brain reaches full maturity? The answer to this question might surprise you. In fact, the brain grows in spurts from conception until well into adulthood (Fischer & Rose, 1994). In childhood and adolescence, many of these spurts are correlated with major advances in physical and intellectual skills, such as the acquisition of fluency in language that happens around age 4 for most children. Each growth spurt also seems to involve a different brain area. For example, the spurt that begins around age 17 and continues into the early 20s mainly affects the frontal lobes, where, you'll recall, the abilities to plan and to control one's emotions are located. Differences between teens and adults in these abilities may be due to this growth spurt. Changes in brain function are influenced by several development processes.

Synaptogenesis Synapses develop as a result of the growth of both dendrites and axons. This process, known as *synaptogenesis*, occurs in spurts throughout the lifespan. Each spurt is followed by a period of **pruning**, the process through which the developing brain eliminates unnecessary or redundant synapses. The activity of neurotransmitters within the synapses also varies with age. For example, acetylcholine is less plentiful in the brains of children than in teens and adults. This difference may help explain age differences in memory and other functions influenced by this excitatory neurotransmitter.

There are many differences between the brains of children and adults, which may help explain why children process information less efficiently than adults do.

Myelination The process of *myelination*, or the development of myelin sheaths around axons, begins prior to birth but continues well into adulthood. For example, the brain's association areas are not fully myelinated until age 12 or so (Tanner, 1990). And the reticular formation, which, as you'll recall, regulates attention, isn't fully myelinated until the mid-20s (Spreen et al., 1995). Thus, differences in myelination may account for differences between children and adults in processing speed, memory, and other functions.

Hemispheric Specialization Some degree of hemispheric specialization is present very early in life. Language processing, for example, occurs primarily in the left hemisphere of the fetal and infant brain just as it does in the adult brain (Chilosi et al., 2001; de Lacoste et al., 1991). Other functions, such as spatial perception, aren't lateralized until age 8 or so. Consequently, children younger than 8 exhibit much poorer spatial skills than do those who are older (Roberts & Bell, 2000). For instance, children younger than 8 have difficulty using maps and distinguishing between statements such as *It's on your left* and *It's on my left*.

Plasticity As you learned earlier, the ability of the brain to reorganize, to reshape itself in response to input from both internal (within the brain) and external (environmental) sources (Clifford, 2000), and to compensate for damage is termed *plasticity*. Plasticity is greatest in young children within whom the hemispheres are not yet completely lateralized. In one case study, researchers found that a prenatal hemorrhage that prevented the development of the left side of the cerebellum in one child was evidenced only by a slight tremor at age 3 (Mancini et al., 2001). As you might suspect, an adult who lost the left side of his or her cerebellum would probably experience much more functional impairment.

However, it is probably also true that the brain retains some degree of plasticity throughout life. For example, researchers have found that the correction of hearing defects in late-middle-aged adults results in changes in all the areas of the brain that are involved in sound perception (Giraud et al., 2001). Moreover, the brains of these individuals appear to develop responses to sounds in areas in which the brains of people with normal hearing do not.

■ **pruning**
The process through which the developing brain eliminates unnecessary or redundant synapses.

Aging and Other Influences on the Brain

How do aging, learning, and stroke-related damage affect the brain?

Does the brain ever stop changing? No, the brain both gains and loses synapses throughout life. At some point in adulthood, however, losses begin to exceed gains (Huttenlocher, 1994). Brain weight begins to decline around age 30. And one brain-imaging study showed that gray matter, but not white matter, is lost with normal aging in both hemispheres of the cerebellum (Sullivan et al., 2000). Age-related deficits due to the loss of gray matter are common. For example, elderly people tend to experience problems with balance, they become less steady on their feet, and their gait is affected. However, as is true in childhood, intellectual and motor skill training can positively influence the brains of older adults.

stroke
The most common cause of damage to adult brains, arising when blockage of an artery cuts off the blood supply to a particular area of the brain or when a blood vessel bursts.

In fact, at every age, the brain is influenced by experience as well as by the presumably genetically programmed maturational process. For example, animal research suggests that stimulation of the brain during childhood spurts in synaptogenesis may be important to intellectual development (e.g., Escorihuela et al., 1994). Exposure to patterned auditory stimuli, such as those characteristic of human language, may be particularly important to the development of the primary auditory cortex in young children (Chang & Merzenich, 2003). And older adults who are better educated and more intellectually active show less atrophy of the cerebral cortex than do their peers who lack these advantages (Coffey et al., 1999).

As illustrated by Phineas Gage's story, brain damage can lead to significant changes in brain function. But injuries such as the one Gage suffered aren't the most common source of damage. In the United States, strokes are the most common cause of damage to the adult brain and the third most common cause of death. A **stroke** occurs when a blood clot or plug of fat blocks an artery and cuts off the blood supply to a particular area of the brain or when a blood vessel bursts, often as a result of high blood pressure. High doses of stimulants such as amphetamines and cocaine also increase the risk of stroke.

Stroke patients, many of whom are older adults, may be left with impaired intellect, loss of coordination or sensation, and/or paralysis. A high percentage of stroke survivors suffer from depression (Angeleri et al., 1997), and about 25% have aphasia. But patients who receive TPA (a blood clot-dissolving drug used successfully in treating heart attacks) within 3 hours of the onset of a stroke are 30% more likely to have minimal or no disability (Gorman, 1996; National Institute of Neurological Disorders, 1995).

Furthermore, physical therapy can help stroke patients of all ages recover at least partial motor functions, providing yet another example of the brain's plasticity. Indeed, though it was long believed that, once damaged, neurons in the brain were incapable of regeneration, research has shown that this may not be true. Researchers working with monkeys at Princeton Unversity have produced the first solid evidence that new neurons are generated in the lining of the ventricles deep in the center of the adult brain and then migrate to the cerebral cortex (Gould et al., 1999). Thus, the brain should be thought of as dynamic, or constantly changing, throughout the human lifespan.

Remember It 2.6

1. The brain grows in __________.
2. The fetal brain appears to be lateralized for __________.
3. __________ is a gradual process during which connections between neurons develop.
4. __________ is the most common cause of injury to the adult brain.
5. The ability of the brain to adapt and change is known as __________.

ANSWERS: 1. spurts; 2. language function; 3. Synaptogenesis; 4. Stroke; 5. plasticity

The Peripheral Nervous System

What is the difference between the sympathetic and parasympathetic nervous systems?

What makes your heart pound and palms sweat when you watch a scary movie? Such reactions result from the actions of the peripheral nervous system. The **peripheral nervous system (PNS)** is made up of all the nerves that connect the central nervous system to the rest of the body. It has two subdivisions: the somatic nervous system and the autonomic nervous system. Figure 2.11 shows the subdivisions within the peripheral nervous system.

The *somatic nervous system* consists of (1) all the sensory nerves, which transmit information from the sense receptors—eyes, ears, nose, tongue, and

FIGURE 2.11 The Human Nervous System

The nervous system is divided into two parts: the central nervous system and the peripheral nervous system. The diagram shows the relationships among the parts of the nervous system and provides a brief description of the functions of those parts.

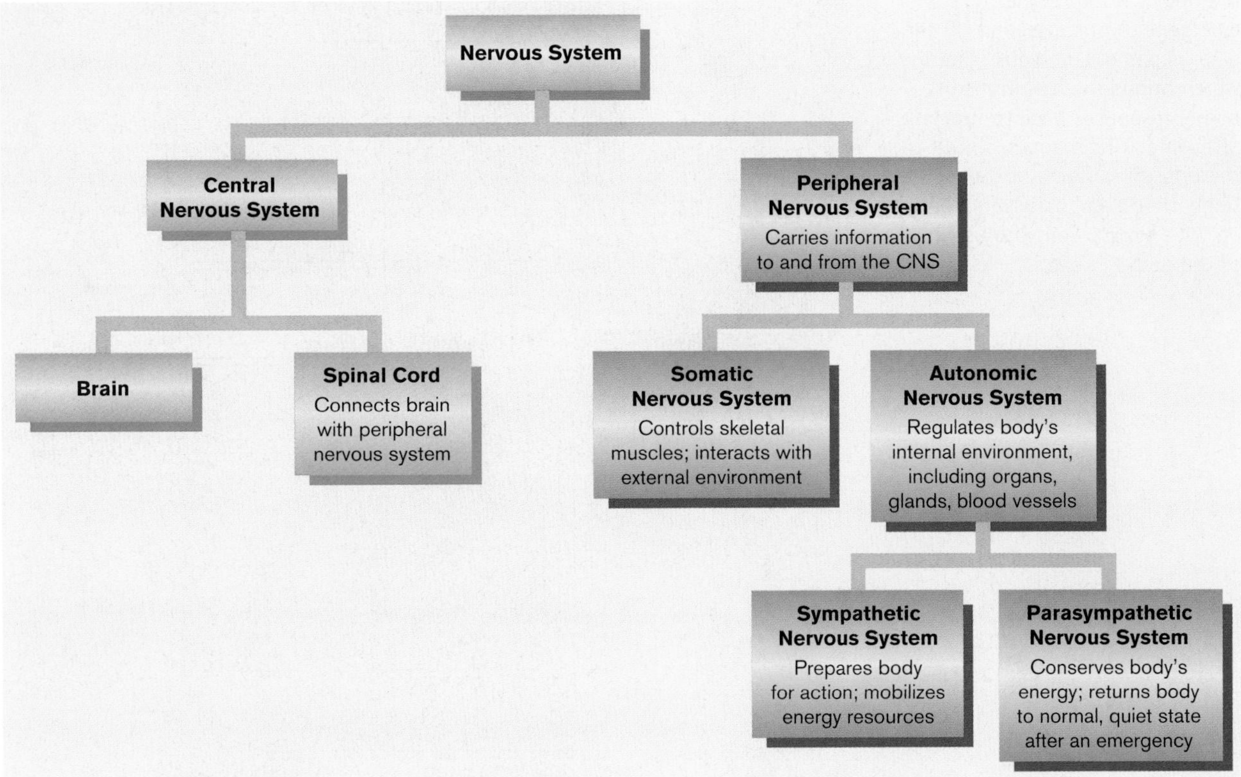

skin—to the central nervous system, and (2) all the motor nerves, which relay messages from the central nervous system to all the skeletal muscles of the body. In short, the nerves of the somatic nervous system make it possible for you to sense your environment and to move, and they are primarily under conscious control.

The *autonomic nervous system* operates without any conscious control or awareness on your part. It transmits messages between the central nervous system and the glands, the cardiac (heart) muscle, and the smooth muscles (such as those in the large arteries and the gastrointestinal system), which are not normally under voluntary control. This system is further divided into two parts—the sympathetic and the parasympathetic nervous systems.

Any time you are under stress or faced with an emergency, the **sympathetic nervous system** automatically mobilizes the body's resources, preparing you for action. This physiological arousal produced by the sympathetic nervous system was named the *fight-or-flight response* by Walter Cannon (1929, 1935). If an ominous-looking stranger started following you down a dark, deserted street, your sympathetic nervous system would automatically go to work. Your heart would begin to pound, your pulse rate would increase rapidly, your breathing would quicken, and your digestive system would nearly shut down. The blood flow to your skeletal muscles would be enhanced, and all of your bodily resources would be made ready to handle the emergency.

Once the emergency is over, the **parasympathetic nervous system** brings these heightened bodily functions back to normal. As a result of its action, your heart stops pounding and slows to normal, your pulse rate and breathing slow down, and your digestive system resumes its normal functioning. As shown in Figure 2.12 (on page 68), the sympathetic and parasympathetic branches act as opposing but complementary forces in the autonomic nervous system. Their balanced functioning is essential for health and survival.

■ **peripheral nervous system (PNS)**
(peh-RIF-er-ul) The nerves connecting the central nervous system to the rest of the body.

■ **sympathetic nervous system**
The division of the autonomic nervous system that mobilizes the body's resources during stress and emergencies, preparing the body for action.

■ **parasympathetic nervous system**
The division of the autonomic nervous system that brings the heightened bodily responses back to normal following an emergency.

FIGURE 2.12 The Autonomic Nervous System

The autonomic nervous system consists of (1) the sympathetic nervous system, which mobilizes the body's resources during emergencies or stress, and (2) the parasympathetic nervous system, which brings the heightened bodily responses back to normal afterward. This diagram shows the opposite effects of the sympathetic and parasympathetic nervous systems on various parts of the body.

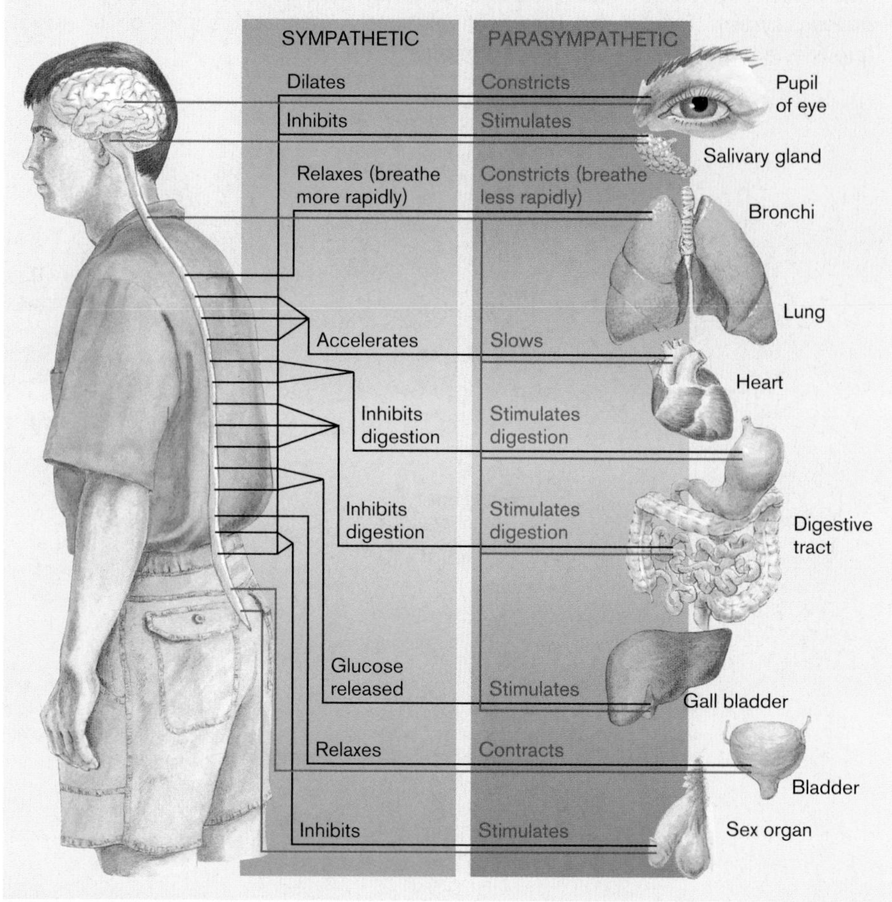

Remember It 2.7

1. The ____________ nervous system connects the brain and spinal cord to the rest of the body.
2. The ____________ nervous system mobilizes the body's resources during times of stress.
3. The ____________ nervous system restores the body's functions to normal once a crisis has passed.

ANSWERS: 1. peripheral; 2. sympathetic; 3. parasympathetic

The Endocrine System

What functions are associated with the various glands of the endocrine system?

Most people think of the reproductive system when they hear the word *hormones*. Or they may associate hormones with particular physical changes, such of those of puberty, pregnancy, or menopause. However, these substances regulate many other physical and psychological functions. And their influence reaches far beyond the reproductive system.

The **endocrine system** is a series of ductless glands, located in various parts of the body, that manufacture and secrete the chemical substances

FIGURE 2.13 The Endocrine System

The endocrine system is a series of glands that manufacture and secrete hormones. The hormones travel through the circulatory system and have important effects on many bodily functions.

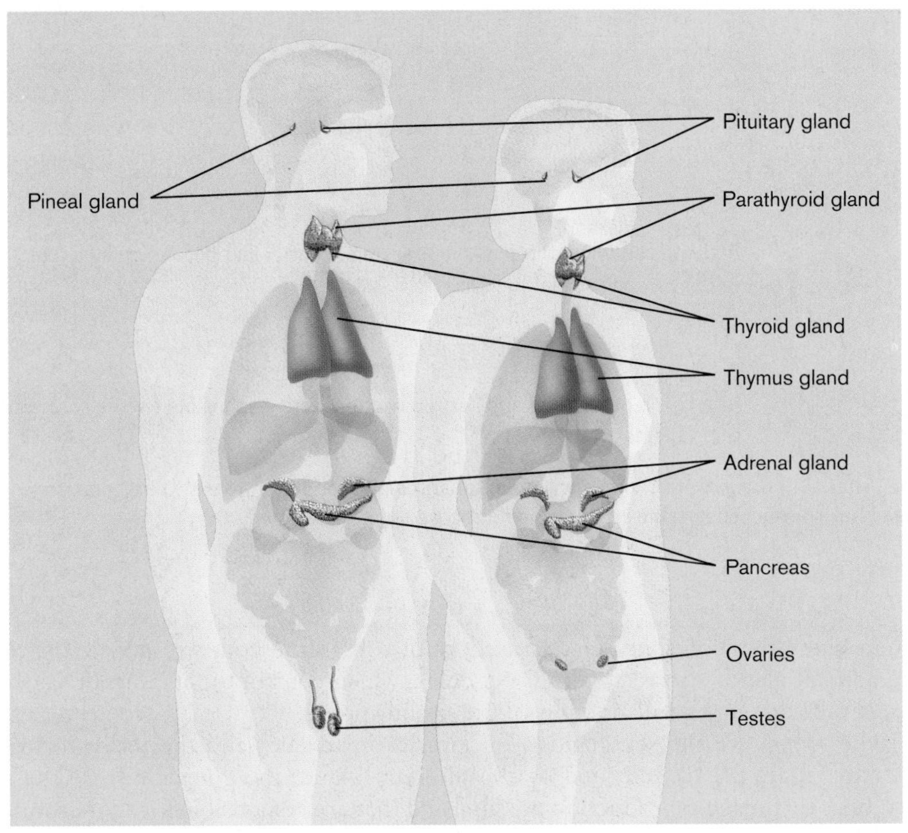

known as **hormones**, which are manufactured and released in one part of the body but have an effect on other parts of the body. Hormones are released into the bloodstream and travel throughout the circulatory system, but each hormone performs its assigned job only when it connects with the body cells that have receptors for it. Some of the same chemical substances that are neurotransmitters act as hormones as well—norepinephrine and vasopressin, to name two. Figure 2.13 shows the glands in the endocrine system and their locations in the body.

The **pituitary gland** rests in the brain just below the hypothalamus and is controlled by it (see Figure 2.13). The pituitary is considered to be the "master gland" of the body because it releases the hormones that activate, or turn on, the other glands in the endocrine system—a big job for a tiny structure about the size of a pea. The pituitary also produces the hormone that is responsible for body growth (Howard et al., 1996). Too little of this powerful substance will make a person a dwarf; too much will produce a giant.

The *thyroid gland* rests in the front, lower part of the neck just below the voice box (larynx). The thyroid produces the important hormone thyroxine, which regulates the rate at which food is metabolized, or transformed into energy. The *pancreas* regulates the body's blood sugar levels by releasing the hormones insulin and glucagon into the bloodstream. In people with diabetes, too little insulin is produced. Without insulin to break down the sugars in food, blood-sugar levels can get dangerously high.

The two **adrenal glands**, which rest just above the kidneys (as shown in Figure 2.13), produce epinephrine and norepinephrine. By activating the sympathetic nervous

■ **endocrine system** (EN-duh-krin) A system of ductless glands in various parts of the body that manufacture hormones and secrete them into the bloodstream, thus affecting cells in other parts of the body.

■ **hormone** A chemical substance that is manufactured and released in one part of the body and affects other parts of the body.

■ **pituitary gland** The endocrine gland located in the brain that releases hormones that activate other endocrine glands as well as growth hormone; often called the "master gland."

■ **adrenal glands** (ah-DREE-nal) A pair of endocrine glands that release hormones that prepare the body for emergencies and stressful situations and also release corticoids and small amounts of the sex hormones.

REVIEW *and* REFLECT 2.1

Glands, Hormones, and Their Functions

GLAND(S)	HORMONE(S)	FUNCTION
Pituitary	Growth hormone; many others	Controls growth rate; activates other endocrine glands
Thyroid	Thyroxine	Regulates metabolism
Pancreas	Insulin Glucagon	Regulates blood sugar
Adrenals	Epinephrine Norepinephrine Coticoids Sex hormones	Activate the sympathetic nervous system; control salt balance; play a role in puberty and sexual function
Gonads	Sex hormones	Regulate reproduction and sexual functions; are responsible for the secondary sex characteristics

Want to be sure you've fully absorbed the material in this chapter? Visit **www.ablongman.com/wood5e** for access to free practice tests, flashcards, interactive activities, and links developed specifically to help you succeed in psychology.

system, these two hormones play an important role in the body's response to stress. The adrenal glands also release the corticoids, which control the important salt balance in the body, and small amounts of the sex hormones.

The *gonads* are the sex glands—the ovaries in females and the testes in males (refer to Figure 2.13). Activated by the pituitary gland, the gonads release the sex hormones that make reproduction possible and that are responsible for the secondary sex characteristics—pubic and underarm hair in both sexes, breasts in females, and facial hair and a deepened voice in males. Androgens, the male sex hormones, influence sexual motivation. Estrogen and progesterone, the female sex hormones, help regulate the menstrual cycle. Although both males and females have androgens and estrogens, males have considerably more androgens, and females have considerably more estrogens. (The sex hormones and their effects are discussed in more detail in Chapter 12.)

Review and Reflect 2.1 summarizes the hormones you have just read about.

Remember It 2.8

1. The endocrine glands secrete ________ directly into the ________.
2. The ________ gland acts as a "master gland" that activates the others.
3. Blood sugar levels are regulated by the ________ through the release of ________ and ________.
4. Sex hormones are produced by both the ________ and the ________.
5. The ________ is the gland responsible for maintaining balanced metabolism.

ANSWERS: 1. hormones, bloodstream; 2. pituitary; 3. pancreas, insulin, glucagon; 4. gonads, adrenals; 5. thyroid

Genes and Behavioral Genetics

You may have heard of the Human Genome Project, a 13-year enterprise spearheaded by the U.S. Department of Energy and devoted to mapping the entire human genetic code. Remarkably, in April 2003, only 50 years after scientists James Watson and Francis Crick discovered the structure of DNA (of which genes consist), the international team of scientists involved in the project announced that they had achieved their goal (U.S. Department of Energy, 2003). The map of the human genetic code has made it possible to find specific links between genes and diseases, psychological traits, and other variables of interest to psychologists. For example, psychologists have known for a long time that heredity contributes to mental illnesses such as schizophrenia. Now, the human genome map will make it possible to determine exactly which genes on which chromosomes control this disease. Such knowledge may open new avenues to treatment (Plomin et al., 2003).

Of course, you received your own genetic code from your parents. But just how do the chemical messages that make up your genes affect your body and your behavior?

The Mechanisms of Heredity

What patterns of inheritance are evident in the transmission of genetic traits?

Genes are segments of DNA located on rod-shaped structures called **chromosomes**. The nuclei of normal body cells, with two exceptions, have 23 pairs of chromosomes (46 in all). The two exceptions are the sperm and egg cells, each of which has 23 single chromosomes. At conception, the sperm adds its 23 chromosomes to the 23 of the egg. From this union, a single cell called a *zygote* is formed; it has the full complement of 46 chromosomes (23 pairs), which contain about 30,000 genes (Baltimore, 2000). These genes carry all the genetic information needed to make a human being. The Human Genome Project is aimed at identifying the functions of all the genes and their locations on the chromosomes.

Twenty-two of the 23 pairs of chromosomes are matching pairs, called *autosomes*, and each member of these pairs carries genes for particular physical and mental traits. The chromosomes in 23rd pair are called *sex chromosomes* because they carry the genes that determine a person's sex. The sex chromosomes of females consist of two X chromosomes (XX); males have an X chromosome and a Y chromosome (XY). The egg cell always contains an X chromosome. Half of a man's sperm cells carry an X chromosome, and half carry a Y. Thus, the sex of an individual depends on which type of chromosome is carried by the sperm that fertilizes the egg. A single gene found only on the Y chromosome causes a fetus to become a male. This gene, which has been labeled *Sry*, orchestrates the development of the male sex organs (Capel, 2000).

Many traits are influenced by complementary gene pairs, one from the sperm and the other from the egg. In most cases, these gene pairs follow a set of inheritance rules known as the **dominant-recessive pattern**. The gene for curly hair, for example, is dominant over the gene for straight hair. Thus, a person having one gene for curly hair and one for straight hair will have curly hair, and people with straight hair have two recessive genes. A person who carries two copies of the same gene, whether both dominant or both recessive, is known as *homozygous*, while one who has two different genes is called *heterozygous*. Figure 2.14 (on page 72) shows two of the possible hair types of offspring of a parent who has curly hair but is heterozygous for this trait and a parent who has straight hair. What are the others?

Several neurological and psychological disorders are associated with dominant or recessive genes. For example, *Huntington's chorea*, a degenerative disease of the nervous system is transmitted by a dominant gene, and some kinds of schizophrenia are linked to recessive genes. However, most of the traits of interest to psychologists follow more complex inheritance patterns.

■ **genes**
The segments of DNA that are located on the chromosomes and are the basic units for the transmission of all hereditary traits.

■ **chromosomes**
Rod-shaped structures in the nuclei of body cells, which contain all the genes and carry all the genetic information necessary to make a human being.

■ **dominant-recessive pattern**
A set of inheritance rules in which the presence of a single dominant gene causes a trait to be expressed but two genes must be present for the expression of a recessive trait.

FIGURE 2.14 Dominant-Recessive Inheritance

Two examples of how the recessive gene for straight hair passes from parents to children.

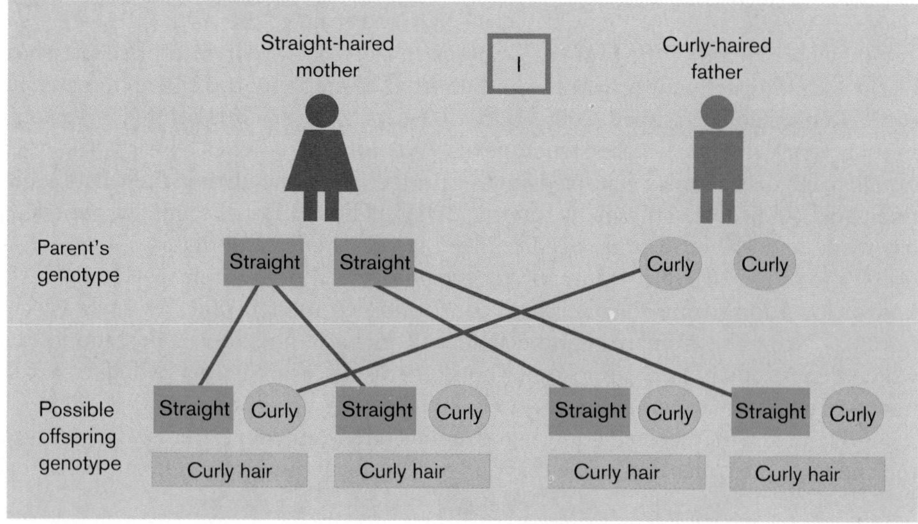

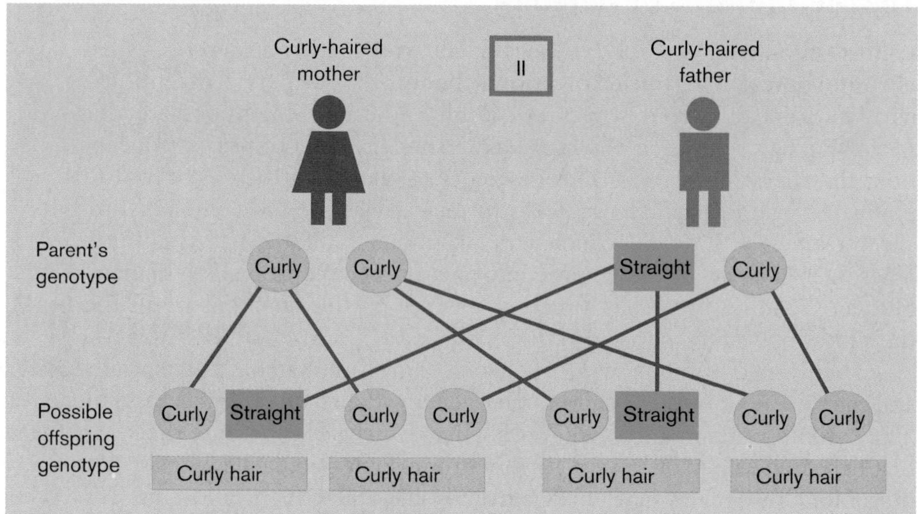

In *polygenic inheritance*, many genes influence a particular characteristic. For example, skin color is determined by several genes. When one parent has dark skin and the other is fair-skinned, the child will have skin that is somewhere between the two. Many polygenic characteristics are subject to **multifactorial inheritance**; that is, they are influenced by both genes and environmental factors. For instance, a man's genes may allow him to reach a height of 6 feet, but if he suffers from malnutrition while still growing, his height may not reach its genetic potential. As you'll learn in later chapters, both intelligence (Chapter 8) and personality (Chapter 14) are believed to be polygenic and multifactorial in nature. In addition, many neurological disorders, including Alzheimer's disease, are multifactorial (Bird, 2001).

Sex-linked inheritance involves the genes on the X and Y chromosomes. In females, the two X chromosomes function pretty much like the autosomes: If one carries a harmful gene, the other usually has a gene that offsets its effects. In males, however, if the single X chromosome carries a harmful gene, there is no offsetting gene on the Y chromosome because it is very small and carries only the genes needed to create the male body type. Consequently, disorders caused by genes on the X chromosome occur far more often in males than in females. For example, one fairly common sex-linked disorder you will read about in Chapter 3 is *red-green color blindness*. About 5% of men have the disorder, but less than 1% of women suffer from it (Neitz et al., 1996).

■ **multifactorial inheritance**
A pattern of inheritance in which a trait is influenced by both genes and environmental factors.

Apply It

Why Consider Genetic Counseling?

Do you have relatives who suffer from genetic disorders? Surveys suggest that most relatives of individuals who suffer from such disorders or who have diseases, such as breast cancer, that may have a genetic basis are eager to know their own personal risk (Kinney et al., 2001). If you consult a genetic counselor, he or she will carry out a case study involving a detailed family history as well as genetic tests. The purpose of the study will be to estimate your risk of suffering from the same disorders and diseases as your relatives. The counselor will also estimate the likelihood that you will pass genetic defects on to your children.

The goal of genetic counseling is to help people make informed decisions about their own lives and those of their children. This goal is important because most people, especially those whose relatives have genetic disorders, greatly overestimate their own chances of having a genetic defect (Quaid et al., 2001). Generally, genetic counseling leads to more realistic perceptions and feelings of relief (Tercyak et al., 2001). Moreover, parents of children who suffer from genetic diseases report that they feel less guilt about transmitting the disease to their children after receiving genetic counseling (Collins et al., 2001).

However, genetic counseling also has a downside. Once an individual's disease risk is known, especially for life-threatening illnesses such as breast cancer, it may be difficult for him or her to get health insurance (Geer et al., 2001). Although there is no evidence that insurance companies deny coverage based on the results of genetic testing, 28 states have enacted laws to prevent them from doing so in the future (Steinberg, 2000). Geneticists and genetic counselors believe that such legislation is needed because genetic testing is rapidly making prediction of future illness more accurate. Moreover, a growing number of people are seeking such testing. Experts point out that results form genetic testing do not differ much from the information on the family history that health insurers already use to accept or reject applicants (Steinberg, 2000). Thus, without legal protection in place, genetic testing could become a routine part of the application approval process for health insurance.

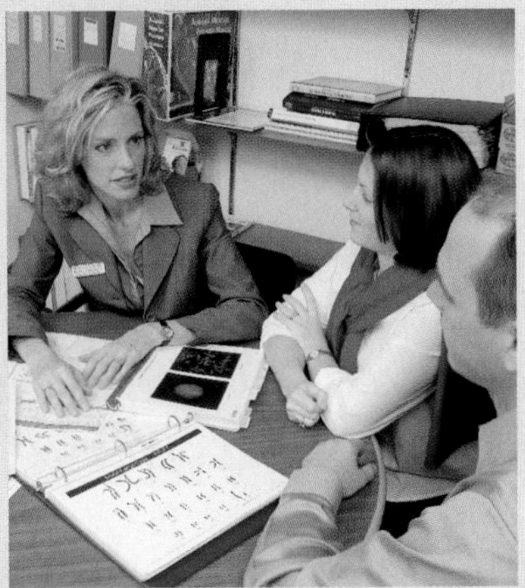

Another problem with genetic counseling is that many recipients report feeling overwhelmed by the amount of information provided by counselors and the sometimes difficult task of understanding the complex probability statements that often result from the case studies (Collins et al., 2001). Still, most people who seek genetic counseling say that, on balance, they are better off knowing the facts about potential genetic risks for themselves and their children (Collins et al., 2001).

About 1 in every 1,500 males and 1 in every 2,500 females have a far more serious sex-linked disorder called *fragile-X syndrome*, which can cause mental retardation (Adesman, 1996).

Behavioral Genetics

What kinds of studies are done by behavioral geneticists?

Behavioral genetics is a field of research that investigates the relative effects of heredity and environment—nature and nurture—on behavior (Plomin et al., 1997). In twin studies, behavioral geneticists study identical twins (monozygotic twins) and fraternal twins (dizygotic twins) to determine how much they resemble each other on a variety of characteristics. Identical twins have exactly the same genes because a single sperm of the father fertilizes a single egg of the mother, forming a cell that then splits and forms two human beings—"carbon copies." In the case of fraternal twins, two separate sperm cells fertilize two separate eggs that happen to be released at the same time during ovulation. Fraternal twins are no more alike genetically than any two siblings born to the same parents.

■ **behavioral genetics** A field of research that uses twin studies and adoption studies to investigate the relative effects of heredity and environment on behavior.

Twins who are raised together, whether identical or fraternal, have similar environments. If identical twins raised together are found to be more alike on a certain trait than fraternal twins raised together, then that trait is assumed to be more influenced by heredity. But if the identical and fraternal twin pairs do not differ on the trait, then that trait is assumed to be influenced more by environment.

In adoption studies, behavioral geneticists study children adopted shortly after birth. Researchers compare the children's abilities and personality traits to those of their adoptive parents and those of their biological parents. This strategy allows researchers to disentangle the effects of heredity and environment (Plomin et al., 1988). As you will learn in later chapters, behavioral geneticists have found that genes clearly contribute to individual differences in both intelligence (Chapter 8) and personality (Chapter 14). However, their research has also demonstrated that environmental factors, such as poverty and culture, influence these characteristics as well.

Because heredity and environment work together to influence so many of the variables of interest to psychologists, you'll be reading a great deal more in later chapters about the debate concerning their relative influence.

Remember It 2.9

1. The X and Y chromosomes are known as the ____________ chromosomes.
2. A ____________ gene will not be expressed if the individual carries only one copy of it.
3. Characteristics that are affected by both genes and environment are said to be ____________ .
4. ____________ is the field of research that investigates the relative effects of heredity and environment on behavior.
5. ____________ twins develop from a single fertilized egg.
6. Researchers use ____________ and ____________ studies to disentangle the effects of heredity and environment.

ANSWERS: 1. sex; 2. recessive; 3. multifactorial; 4. Behavioral genetics; 5. Identical; 6. twin, adoption

Summary *and* Review

The Neurons and Neurotransmitters p. 40

How are messages transmitted through the nervous system? p. 40

The action potential, the primary means by which the brain and body communicate with one another via the nervous system, is the sudden reversal (from a negative to a positive value) of the resting potential on the cell membrane of a neuron; this reversal initiates the firing of a neuron. A strong stimulus will cause many more neurons to fire and to fire much more rapidly than a weak stimulus will.

What are neurotransmitters, and what do they contribute to nervous system functioning? p. 43

Neurotransmitters are chemicals released into the synaptic cleft from the axon terminal of the sending neuron. They cross the synaptic cleft and bind to receptors on the receiving neuron, influencing the cell to fire or not to fire. Neurotransmitters thus transmit messages between neurons.

What are the functions of some of the major neurotransmitters? p. 45

Some of the major neurotransmitters are acetylcholine, dopamine, norepinephrine, epinephrine, serotonin, glutamate, GABA, and endorphins. Acetylcholine (Ach) affects muscle fibers and is involved in learning. Dopamine affects learning, attention, movement, and reinforcement. Norepinephrine and epinephrine help regulate eating and energy release. Serotonin and GABA are inhibitory neurotransmitters that help us sleep, while glutamate, an excitatory neurotransmitter, helps us stay awake. Endorphins are natural pain-killers.

The Central Nervous System p. 47

Why is an intact spinal cord important to normal functioning? p. 47

The spinal cord is an extension of the brain, connecting it to the peripheral nervous system. The spinal cord must be intact so that sensory information can reach the brain and messages from the brain can reach muscles, glands, and other parts of the body.

What are the crucial functions handled by the brainstem? p. 48

The brainstem contains both the medulla, which controls heartbeat, breathing, blood pressure, coughing, and swallowing, and the reticular formation, which plays a crucial role in arousal and attention.

What are the primary functions of the cerebellum? p. 49

The cerebellum allows the body to execute smooth, skilled movements and regulates muscle tone and posture.

What important structure is located in the midbrain? p. 49

The substantia nigra, located in the midbrain, controls unconscious motor actions, such as riding a bicycle. Damage to this structure is believed to be one cause of Parkinson's disease.

What are the functions of the thalamus and the hypothalamus? p. 49

The thalamus acts as a relay station for virtually all the information flowing into and out of the forebrain. The hypothalamus regulates hunger, thirst, sexual behavior, internal body temperature, and a wide variety of emotional behaviors.

How does the limbic system influence mental processes and behavior? p. 50

The limbic system is a group of structures in the brain, including the amygdala and the hippocampus, that are collectively involved in emotional expression, memory, and motivation.

The Cerebrum p. 51

What are the components of the cerebrum? p. 51

The cerebral hemispheres are the two halves of the cerebrum, connected by the corpus callosum and covered by the cerebral cortex, which is primarily responsible for higher mental processes such as language, memory, and thinking.

Which psychological functions are associated with the frontal lobes? p. 52

The frontal lobes contain (1) the motor cortex, which controls voluntary motor activity; (2) Broca's area, which functions in speech production; and (3) the frontal association areas, which are involved in thinking, motivation, planning for the future, impulse control, and emotional responses.

What is the somatosensory cortex, and what does it do? p. 55

The somatosensory cortex is the front portion of the parietal lobes. It is the site where touch, pressure, temperature, and pain register in the cerebral cortex.

Why are the occipital lobes critical to vision? p. 56

The occipital lobes are involved in the reception and interpretation of visual information. They contain the primary visual cortex, where vision registers in the cerebral cortex.

What are the major areas within the temporal lobes, and what are their functions? p. 56

The temporal lobes contain (1) the primary auditory cortex, where hearing registers in the cortex; (2) Wernicke's area, which is involved in comprehending the spoken word and in formulating coherent speech and written language; and (3) the temporal association areas, where memories are stored and auditory stimuli are interpreted.

The Cerebral Hemispheres p. 57

What are the specialized functions of the left hemisphere? p. 57

The left hemisphere controls the right side of the body, coordinates complex movements, and handles most of the language functions, including speaking, writing, reading, and understanding the written and the spoken word.

What are the specialized functions of the right hemisphere? p. 58

The right hemisphere controls the left side of the body. It is specialized for visual-spatial perception, the interpretation of nonverbal behavior, and the recognition and expression of emotion.

What do researchers mean by the term "split brain"? p. 59

In the split-brain operation, a surgeon cuts the corpus callosum, preventing the transfer of information between the two cerebral hemispheres. Because the two halves of the brain perceive the world differently, research on split-brain patients has extended scientific knowledge of the unique capabilities of the individual hemispheres.

How are handedness and brain function related? p. 60

On average, the corpus callosum of left-handers is larger and contains more nerve fibers than that of right-handers. In left-handers, the two sides of the brain are less specialized and new learning is more easily transferred. Learning disabilities and mental disorders are more common among left-handed individuals, perhaps because of differences in brain organization.

Discovering the Brain's Mysteries p. 62

What does the electroencephalogram (EEG) reveal about the brain? p. 62

The electroencephalogram (EEG) is a record of brain-wave activity. It can reveal an epileptic seizure and can show patterns of neural activity associated with learning disabilities, schizophrenia, Alzheimer's disease, sleep disorders, and other problems.

How are the CT scan and MRI helpful in the study of brain structure? p. 62

Both the CT scan and MRI provide detailed images of brain structures. Functional MRI (fMRI) can also provide information about brain function.

How are the PET scan and newer imaging techniques used to study the brain? p. 63

The PET scan reveals patterns of blood flow, oxygen use, and glucose metabolism in the brain. It can also show the action of drugs in the brain and other organs. PET scan studies show that different brain areas are used to perform different tasks. Two more recently developed technologies, SQUID and MEG, measure magnetic changes to reveal neural activity within the brain as it occurs.

The Brain across the Lifespan p. 64

In what ways does the brain change across the lifespan? p. 64

The brain grows in spurts, each of which is followed by a period of pruning of unnecessary synapses. The activity of transmitters within the synapses also varies with age. Few neurons are myelinated at birth, but the process of myelination continues into the adult years. Language appears to be lateralized very early in life, but other functions, such as spatial perception, aren't fully lateralized until age 8 or so.

How do aging, learning, and stroke-related damage affect the brain? p. 65

Aging eventually leads to a reduction in the number of synapses. Animal studies suggest that both maturation and aging processes, as well as learning, affect brain development. Older adults who have more education and engage in more intellectual activity show less atrophy of the cerebral cortex. Stroke is the most common cause of damage to the adult brain and can lead to impairments in both intellectual and motor functioning.

The Peripheral Nervous System p. 66

What is the difference between the sympathetic and parasympathetic nervous systems? p. 66

The peripheral nervous system, which connects the central nervous system to the rest of the body, has two subdivisions: (1) the somatic nervous system, which consists of all the nerves that make it possible for the body to sense and to move; and (2) the autonomic nervous system. The autonomic nervous system has two parts: (1) the sympathetic nervous system, which mobilizes the body's resources during emergencies or during stress; and (2) the parasympathetic nervous system, which brings the heightened bodily responses back to normal after an emergency.

The Endocrine System p. 68

What functions are associated with the various glands of the endocrine system? p. 68

The pituitary gland releases hormones that control other glands in the endocrine system and also releases a growth hormone. The thyroid gland produces thyroxine, which regulates metabolism. The pancreas produces insulin and glucagon and regulates blood sugar levels. The adrenal glands release epinephrine and norepinephrine, which prepare the body for emergencies and stressful situations; these glands also release corticoids and small amounts of the sex hormones. The gonads are the sex glands, which produce the sex hormones and make reproduction possible.

Genes and Behavioral Genetics p. 71

What patterns of inheritance are evident in the transmission of genetic traits? p. 71

Some genetic traits follow the dominant-recessive pattern, while others are polygenic and multifactorial. Both intelligence and personality are thought to be polygenic and multifactorial. Thus, they are influenced by many genes as well as factors in the environment.

What kinds of studies are done by behavioral geneticists? p. 73

Behavioral genetics is the study of the relative effects of heredity and environment on behavior. Researchers in this field use twin studies, which involve comparisons of identical and fraternal twins, and adoption studies, or studies of children adopted shortly after birth and their adoptive and biological parents. Such studies suggest that both intelligence and personality are influenced by heredity as well as by the environment.

Key Terms

acetylcholine, p. 45
action potential, p. 41
adrenal glands, p. 69
alpha wave, p. 62
amygdala, p. 50
aphasia, p. 54
association areas, p. 52
axon, p. 41
behavioral genetics, p. 73
beta wave, p. 62
brainstem, p. 48
Broca's aphasia, p. 54
Broca's area, p. 54
cell body, p. 40
central nervous system (CNS), p. 47
cerebellum, p. 49
cerebral cortex, p. 52
cerebral hemispheres, p. 51
cerebrum, p. 51
chromosomes, p. 71
corpus callosum, p. 51
CT scan (computerized axial tomography), p. 62
delta wave, p. 62
dendrites, p. 40
dominant-recessive pattern, p. 71
dopamine, p. 45
electroencephalogram (EEG), p. 62
endocrine system, p. 68
endorphins, p. 46
epinephrine, p. 46
functional MRI (fMRI), p. 63
frontal lobes, p. 52
GABA, p. 46
genes, p. 71
glial cells, p. 41
glutamate, p. 46
hippocampus, p. 50
hormone, p. 69
hypothalamus, p. 50
lateralization, p. 57
left hemisphere, p. 57
limbic system, p. 50
MRI (magnetic resonance imagery), p. 63
medulla, p. 48
microelectrode, p. 62
motor cortex, p. 53
multifactorial inheritance, p. 72
myelin sheath, p. 43
neuron, p. 40
neurotransmitter, p. 43
norepinephrine, p. 46
occipital lobes, p. 56
parasympathetic nervous system, p. 67
parietal lobes, p. 55
peripheral nervous system (PNS), p. 66
permeability, p. 41
PET scan (positron-emission tomography), p. 63
pituitary gland, p. 69
plasticity, p. 54
primary auditory cortex, p. 56
primary visual cortex, p. 56
pruning, p. 65
receptors, p. 43
resting potential, p. 41
reticular formation, p. 48
reuptake, p. 45
right hemisphere, p. 58
serotonin, p. 46
somatosensory cortex, p. 55
spinal cord, p. 47
split-brain operation, p. 59
stroke, p. 66
substantia nigra, p. 49
sympathetic nervous system, p. 67
synapse, p. 41
temporal lobes, p. 56
thalamus, p. 49
Wernicke's aphasia, p. 56
Wernicke's area, p. 56

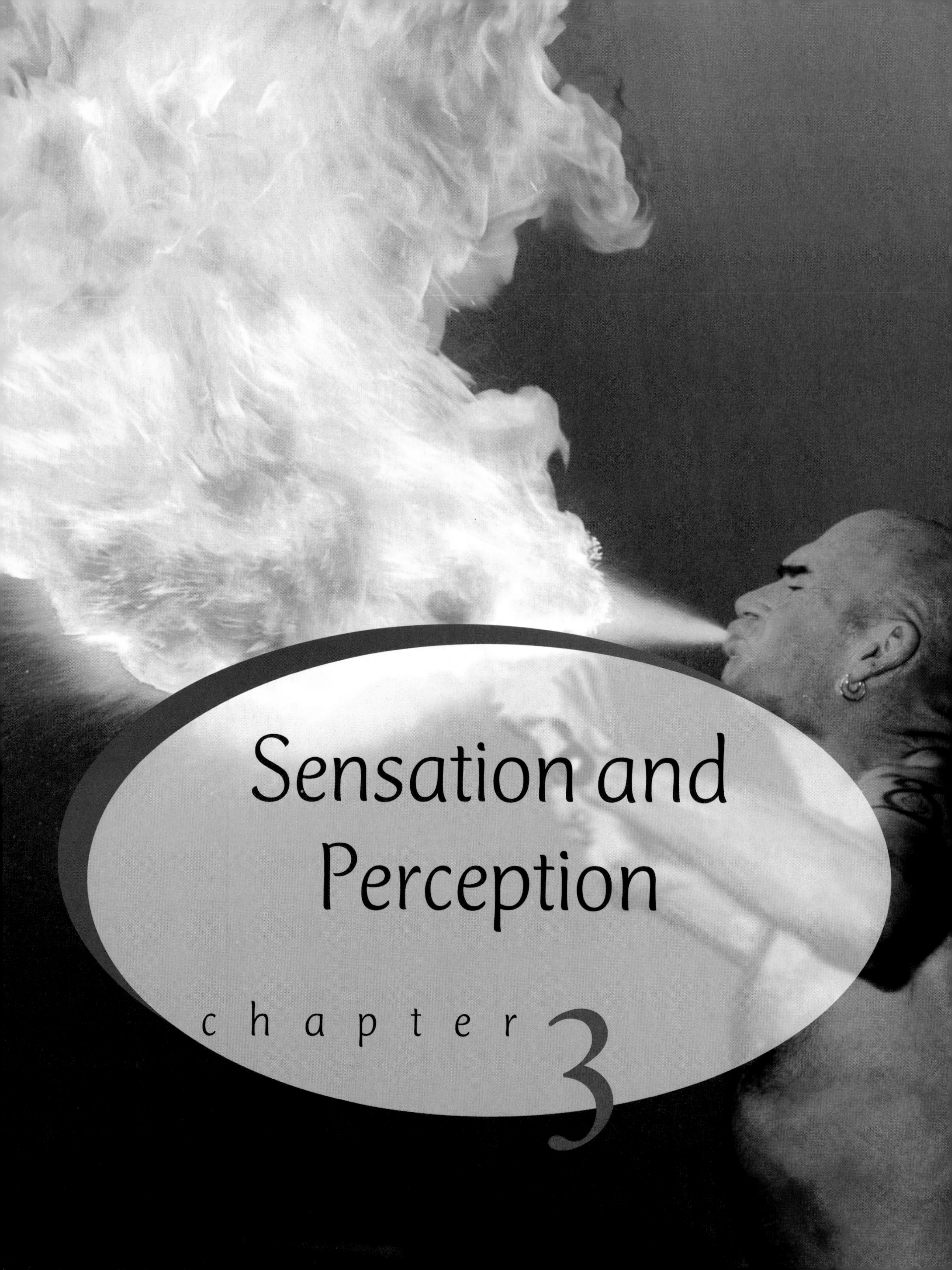

Sensation and Perception

chapter 3

The Process of Sensation

- *What is the difference between the absolute threshold and the difference threshold?*
- *How does transduction enable the brain to receive sensory information?*

Vision

- *How does each part of the eye function in vision?*
- *What path does visual information take from the retina to the primary visual cortex?*
- *How do we detect the difference between one color and another?*
- *What two major theories attempt to explain color vision?*
- *Do individuals with color blindness see the world in black and white?*

Hearing

- *What determines the pitch and loudness of a sound, and how is each quality measured?*
- *How do the outer ear, middle ear, and inner ear function in hearing?*
- *What two major theories attempt to explain hearing?*
- *What are some of the major causes of hearing loss?*

Smell and Taste

- *What path does a smell message take from the nose to the brain?*
- *What are the primary taste sensations, and how are they detected?*

The Skin Senses

- *How does the skin provide sensory information?*
- *What is the function of pain, and how is pain influenced by psychological factors, culture, and endorphins?*

The Spatial Orientation Senses

- *What kinds of information do the kinesthetic and vestibular senses provide?*

Perception

- *What are the principles that govern perceptual organization?*
- *What are some of the binocular and monocular depth cues?*
- *How does the brain perceive real and apparent motion?*
- *What are three types of puzzling perceptions?*

Influences on Perception

- *How does prior knowledge influence perception?*
- *What is inattentional blindness?*
- *Do we perceive physical objects and social stimuli in the same way?*

How much do you think you could accomplish in life if you could neither see nor hear?

You might surprise yourself. When Helen (1880–1968) was only 9 months old, a serious illness left her totally blind and deaf. Her world was limited to only three sensory avenues—taste, smell, and touch. Her overwhelming reality was permanent darkness and silence. Only the most primitive, rudimentary communication with her parents was possible (she spit out food she disliked). In fact, her ability to give and receive information was far less effective than that of most household pets. As she grew from infancy into early childhood, Helen's frustration gave way to explosive tantrums. She became a rebellious, unruly "wild child." The Keller family needed a miracle!

Finally, when Helen was 6 years old, her father learned that the Perkins Institution had achieved success in teaching the physically handicapped. So, he and the family took Helen to Boston. There, they met a talented young teacher, Anne Sullivan, who agreed to tutor Helen. Anne Sullivan used a manual alphabet to slowly spell out in the palm of Helen's hand the names of objects with her finger. In this way, she taught Helen that everything has a name—a fundamental requirement for communication.

Progress was slow at first, but one day, as Anne poured water over Helen's hand, she spelled out *w-a-t-e-r* in her other hand. The look of surprise and delight on Helen's face told Anne Sullivan that at last she had gotten through. Helen quickly learned to use her finger to write the names for virtually everything and everyone around—Mama, Papa, Anne, and, of course, Helen. The miracle had arrived.

But Helen didn't stop there. She learned to read and write Braille. Helen also learned how to understand much of what others were saying by using her thumb to sense the vibrations coming from a speaker's vocal cords and her forefinger to interpret lip movements. With her other three fingers, she could "see" facial expressions and could recognize and identify anyone she knew by the feel of their face. Helen even learned to speak quite well, a remarkable achievement for one who had never been able to hear. At 20, Helen enrolled in Radcliffe College and graduated with honors, thanks to the daily help of her tutor and companion, Anne Sullivan.

■ sensation
The process through which the senses pick up visual, auditory, and other sensory stimuli and transmit them to the brain.

■ perception
The process by which sensory information is actively organized and interpreted by the brain.

As the story of Helen Keller illustrates, sensation and perception are intimately related in everyday experience, but they are not the same. **Sensation** is the process through which the senses pick up visual, auditory, and other sensory stimuli and transmit them to the brain. **Perception** is the process by which sensory information is actively organized and interpreted by the brain. Sensation furnishes the raw material of sensory experience, while perception provides the finished product. Young Helen could sense Anne Sullivan's fingers tracing letters in her hand, but she could not perceive their symbolic character until her breakthough experience with the water.

In this chapter, we will explore the world of sensation. First, we'll consider the two dominant senses: vision and hearing. Then, we'll turn our attention to the other senses: smell, taste, touch, pain, and balance. You will learn how the senses detect sensory information and how this sensory information is actively organized and interpreted by the brain.

The Process of Sensation

Our senses serve as ports of entry for all information about our world. Yet it is amazing how little of the sensory world humans actually do sense, compared to animals. Some animals have a superior sense of hearing (bats and dolphins), others have extremely sharp vision (hawks), and still others have an amazingly keen sense of smell (bloodhounds). Nevertheless, humans have remarkable sensory and perceptual abilities.

The Absolute and Difference Thresholds

What is the difference between the absolute threshold and the difference threshold?

What is the softest sound you can hear, the dimmest light you can see, the most diluted substance you can taste? Researchers in sensory psychology have performed many experiments over the years to answer these questions. Their research has established measures for the senses known as absolute thresholds. Just as the threshold of a doorway is the dividing point between being outside a room and inside, the **absolute threshold** of a sense marks the difference between not being able to perceive a stimulus and being just barely able to perceive it. Psychologists have arbitrarily defined this absolute threshold as the minimum amount of sensory stimulation that can be detected 50% of the time. The absolute thresholds for vision, hearing, taste, smell, and touch are illustrated in Figure 3.1.

If you are listening to music, the very fact that you can hear it means that the absolute threshold has been crossed. But how much must the volume be turned up or down for you to notice a difference? Or, if you are carrying some bags of groceries, how much weight must be added or taken away for you to be able to sense that your load is heavier or lighter? The **difference threshold** is a measure of the smallest increase or decrease in a physical stimulus that is required to produce the **just noticeable difference (JND)**. The JND is the smallest change in sensation that a person is able to detect 50% of the time. If you were holding a 5-pound weight and 1 pound were added, you could easily notice the difference. But if you were holding 100 pounds and 1 additional pound were added, you could not sense the difference. Why not?

More than 150 years ago, researcher Ernst Weber (1795–1878) observed that the JND for all the senses depends on a proportion or percentage of change in a stimulus rather than on a fixed amount of change. This observation became known as **Weber's law**. A weight you are holding must increase or decrease by 1/50, or 2%, for you to notice the difference; in contrast, if you were listening to music, you would notice a difference if a tone became slightly higher or lower in pitch by about only 0.33%. According to Weber's law, the greater the original stimulus, the more it must be increased or decreased for the difference to be noticeable.

As you might suspect, the difference threshold is not the same for all the senses. A very large (1/5, or 20%) difference is necessary for some changes in taste to be detected. Moreover, Weber's law best applies to people with average sensitivities and to sensory

■ **absolute threshold**
The minimum amount of sensory stimulation that can be detected 50% of the time.

■ **difference threshold**
A measure of the smallest increase or decrease in a physical stimulus that is required to produce a difference in sensation that is noticeable 50% of the time.

■ **just noticeable difference (JND)**
The smallest change in sensation that a person is able to detect 50% of the time.

■ **Weber's law**
The law stating that the just noticeable difference (JND) for all the senses depends on a proportion or percentage of change in a stimulus rather than on a fixed amount of change.

FIGURE 3.1 Absolute Thresholds

Absolute thresholds have been established for humans for vision, hearing, taste, smell, and touch.

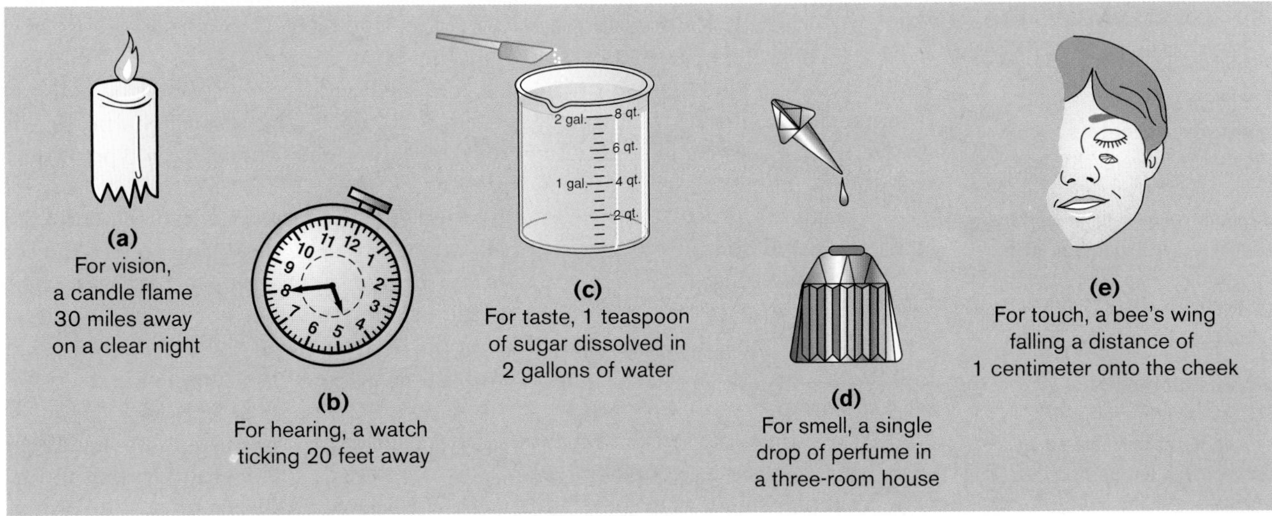

(a)
For vision, a candle flame 30 miles away on a clear night
(b)
For hearing, a watch ticking 20 feet away
2 gal.
8 qt.
6 qt.
1 gal.
4 qt.
2 qt.
(c)
For taste, 1 teaspoon of sugar dissolved in 2 gallons of water
(d)
For smell, a single drop of perfume in a three-room house
(e)
For touch, a bee's wing falling a distance of 1 centimeter onto the cheek

What is the dimmest light this lifeguard could perceive in the darkness? Researchers in sensory psychology have performed many experiments over the years to answer such questions. Their research has established measures known as absolute thresholds. Just as the threshold of a doorway is the dividing point between being outside a room and being inside it, the absolute threshold of a sense marks the difference between not being able to perceive a stimulus and being just barely able to perceive it.

stimuli that are neither very strong (loud thunder) nor very weak (a faint whisper). For instance, expert wine tasters would know if a particular vintage was a little too sweet, even if its sweetness varied by only a fraction of the 20% necessary for changes in taste. Furthermore, people who have lost one sensory ability often gain greater sensitivity in others. For example, one study found that children with early-onset blindness were more capable of correctly labeling 25 common odors than were sighted children, while another found that congenitally deaf students possessed motion-perception abilities superior to those of hearing students (Bavelier et al., 2000; Rosenbluth et al., 2000).

Transduction and Adaptation

How does transduction enable the brain to receive sensory information?

Would you be surprised to learn that our eyes do not actually see and that our ears do not hear? The sense organs provide only the beginning of sensation, which must be completed by the brain. As you learned in Chapter 2, specific clusters of neurons in specialized parts of the brain must be stimulated for us to see, hear, taste, and so on. Yet the brain itself cannot respond directly to light, sound waves, odors, and tastes. How, then, does it get the message? The answer is through the sensory receptors.

The body's sense organs are equipped with highly specialized cells called **sensory receptors**, which detect and respond to one type of sensory stimuli—light, sound waves, odors, and so on. As Figure 3.2 shows, the form of each type of sensory receptor is unique.

■ sensory receptors
Highly specialized cells in the sense organs that detect and respond to one type of sensory stimuli—light, sound, or odor, for example—and transduce (convert) the stimuli into neural impulses.

■ transduction
The process through which sensory receptors convert the sensory stimulation into neural impulses.

Through a process known as **transduction**, the sensory receptors convert the sensory stimulation into neural impulses, the electrochemical language of the brain. The neural impulses are then transmitted to precise locations in the brain, such as the primary visual cortex for vision or the primary auditory cortex for hearing. We experience a sensation only when the appropriate part of the brain is stimulated. The sense receptors provide the essential link between the physical sensory world and the brain.

After a time, the sensory receptors grow accustomed to constant, unchanging levels of stimuli—sights, sounds, or smells—so we notice them less and less, or not at all. For example, smokers become accustomed to the smell of cigarette smoke in their

FIGURE 3.2 Sensory Receptors

Each type of sensory receptor has a unique form.

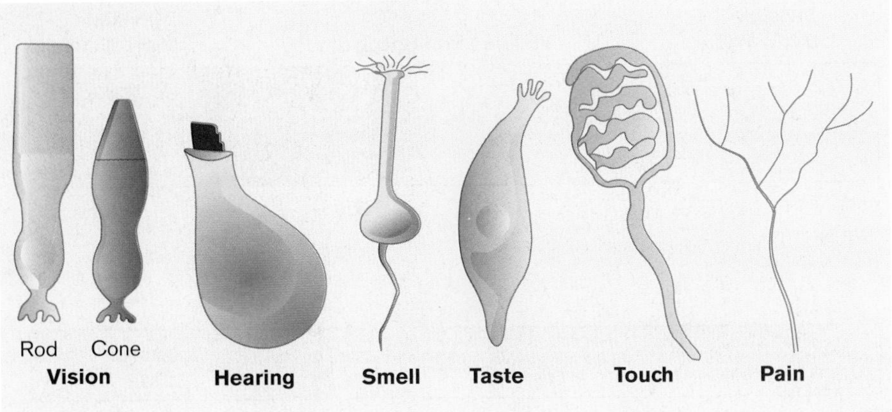

homes and on their clothing. This process is known as **sensory adaptation**. Even though it reduces our sensory awareness, sensory adaptation enables us to shift our attention to what is most important at any given moment. However, sensory adaptation is not likely to occur in the presence of a very strong stimulus, such as the smell of ammonia, an ear-splitting sound, or the taste of rancid food.

■ **sensory adaptation** The process in which sensory receptors grow accustomed to constant, unchanging levels of stimuli over time.

Remember It 3.1

1. The process through which the senses detect visual, auditory, and other sensory stimuli and transmit them to the brain is called __________ .
2. The point at which you can barely sense a stimulus 50% of the time is called the __________ threshold.
3. __________ transmit sensory information from the sense organs to the brain.
4. The process by which a sensory stimulus is converted into a neural impulse is called __________ .
5. Each day, when Jessica goes to work at a coffee house, she smells the strong odor of fresh-brewed coffee. After she is there for a few minutes, she is no longer aware of the smell. The phenomenon known as __________ accounts for Jessica's experience.

ANSWERS: 1. sensation; 2. absolute; 3. Sensory receptors; 4. transduction; 5. sensory adaptation

Vision

Which of your senses do you regard as the most valuable? If you're like most people, you value vision more than any other sensory experience. So perhaps it is not surprising that vision is the most studied of all the senses. One thing vision researchers have known for a long time is that there is a great deal more information in the sensory environment than our eyes can take in. Our eyes can respond only to visible light waves, which form a small subgroup of *electromagnetic waves*, a band called the **visible spectrum** (see Figure 3.3, on page 84). The shortest light waves we can see appear violet, while the longest visible waves appear red. But sight is much more than just response to light.

■ **visible spectrum** The narrow band of electromagnetic waves that are visible to the human eye.

FIGURE 3.3 The Electromagnetic Spectrum

Human eyes can perceive only a very thin band of electromagnetic waves, known as the visible spectrum.

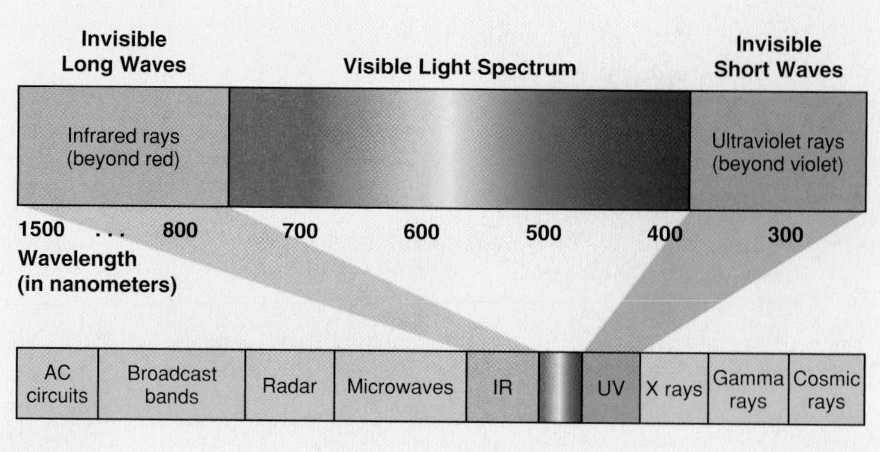

How does each part of the eye function in vision?

■ **cornea**
(KOR-nee-uh) The tough, transparent, protective layer that covers the front of the eye and bends light rays inward through the pupil.

The Eye

The globe-shaped human eyeball, shown in Figure 3.4, measures about 1 inch in diameter. It is truly one of the marvels of nature.

The Cornea, Iris, and Pupil Bulging from the eye's surface is the **cornea**—the tough, transparent, protective layer covering the front of the eye. The cornea performs the first step in vision by bending the light rays inward. It directs the light rays through the *pupil*, the small, dark opening in the center of the *iris*, or colored part of the eye. The iris dilates and contracts the pupil to regulate the amount of light entering the eye.

Suspended just behind the iris and the pupil, the **lens** is composed of many thin layers and looks like a transparent disc. The lens performs the task of focusing on viewed objects. It flattens as it focuses on objects at a distance and becomes

FIGURE 3.4 The Major Parts of the Human Eye

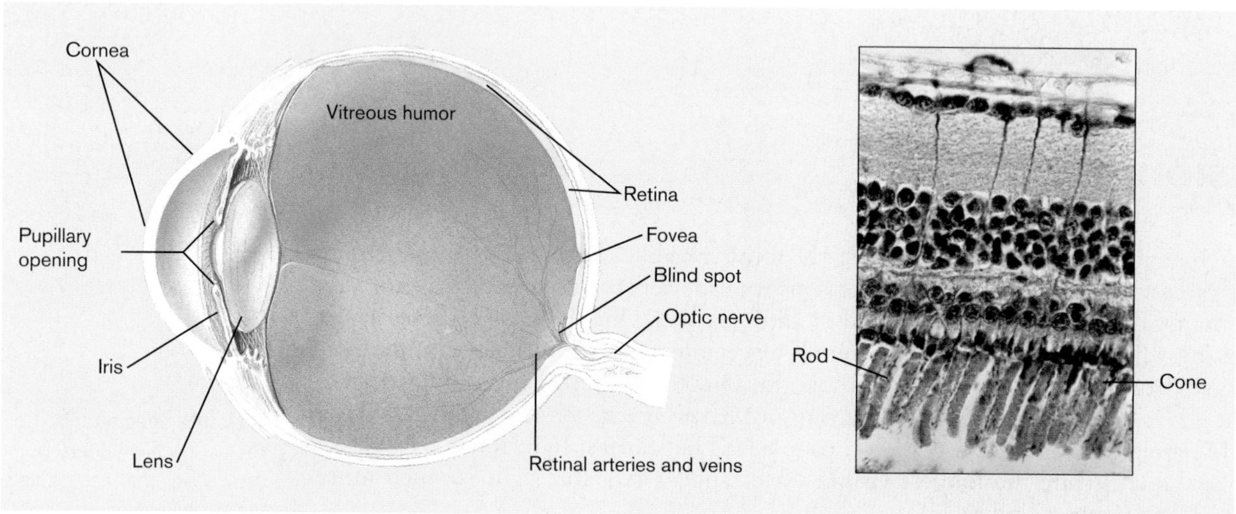

more spherical, bulging in the center, as it focuses on close objects. This flattening and bulging action of the lens is known as **accommodation**. With age, the lens loses the ability to change its shape to accommodate for near vision, a condition called *presbyopia* ("old eyes"). This is why many people over age 40 must hold a book or newspaper at arm's length or use reading glasses to magnify the print.

lens
The transparent disc-shaped structure behind the iris and the pupil that changes shape as it focuses on objects at varying distances.

accommodation
The flattening and bulging action of the lens as it focuses images of objects on the retina.

From Lens to Retina The lens focuses the incoming image onto the **retina**—a layer of tissue about the size of a small postage stamp and as thin as onion skin, located on the inner surface of the eyeball and containing the sensory receptors for vision. The image that is projected onto the retina is upside down and reversed left to right, as illustrated in Figure 3.5.

In some people, the distance through the eyeball (from the lens to the retina) is either too short or too long for proper focusing. Nearsightedness (*myopia*) occurs when the lens focuses images of distant objects in front of, rather than on, the retina. A person with this condition will be able to see near objects clearly, but distant images will be blurred. Farsightedness (*hyperopia*) occurs when the lens focuses images of close objects behind, rather than on, the retina. The individual is able to see far objects clearly, but close objects are blurred. Both conditions are correctable with eyeglasses or contact lenses or by surgical procedures.

retina
The layer of tissue that is located on the inner surface of the eyeball and contains the sensory receptors for vision.

rods
The light-sensitive receptor cells in the retina that look like slender cylinders and allow the eye to respond to as few as five photons of light.

cones
The light-sensitive receptor cells in the retina that enable humans to see color and fine detail in adequate light but do not function in very dim light.

The Rods and Cones At the back of the retina is a layer of light-sensitive receptor cells—the **rods** and the **cones**. Named for their shapes, the rods look like slender cylinders, and the cones appear shorter and more rounded. There are about 120 million rods and 6 million cones in each retina. The cones are the receptor cells that enable us to see color and fine detail in adequate light, but they do not function in very

FIGURE 3.5 From Retinal Image to Meaningful Information

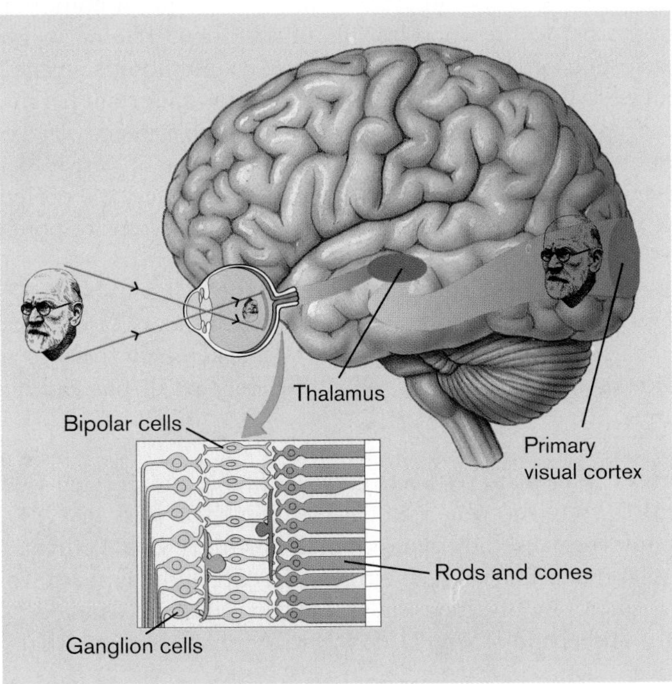

Because of the way the lens alters light rays in order to produce a clear image, images are upside down on the retina. The brain's visual processing system takes the upside-down retinal image and flips it so it is properly orientated.

dim light. By contrast, the rods in the human eye are extremely sensitive, allowing the eye to respond to as few as five photons of light (Hecht et al., 1942).

A substance called *rhodopsin* present in the rods enables us to adapt to variations in light. Rhodopsin has two components: *opsin* and *retinal* (a chemical similar to Vitamin A). In bright light, opsin and retinal break apart, as the process of *light adaptation* takes place. During *dark adaptation*, opsin and retinal bond to one another, reforming rhodopsin. So, as you've no doubt experienced, when you move from bright light to total darkness, as when you enter a darkened movie theater, you are momentarily blind until the opsin and retinal recombine. Similarly, when you leave the theater again, you become temporarily blind until the two substances break apart once again.

At the center of the retina is the **fovea**, a small area about the size of the period at the end of this sentence. When you look directly at an object, the image of the object is focused on the center of your fovea. The fovea contains no rods but has about 30,000 cones tightly packed together, providing the clearest and sharpest area of vision in the whole retina. The cones are most densely packed at the center of the fovea; their density decreases sharply just a few degrees beyond the fovea's center and then levels off more gradually to the periphery of the retina.

What path does visual information take from the retina to the primary visual cortex?

Vision and the Brain

As you can see in Figure 3.5, the brain is responsible for converting the upside-down retinal images into meaningful visual information. But the first stages of neural processing actually take place in the retina itself.

From the Retina to the Brain The rods and cones transduce, or change, light waves into neural impulses that are fed to the bipolar cells, which, in turn, pass the impulses along to the ganglion cells. The approximately 1 million axonlike extensions of the ganglion cells are bundled together in a pencil-sized cable that extends through the wall of the retina, leaving the eye and leading to the brain. There are no rods or cones where the cable runs through the retinal wall, and so this point is a **blind spot** in each eye.

Beyond the retinal wall of each eye, the cable becomes the **optic nerve** (refer to Figure 3.4). The two optic nerves come together at the *optic chiasm*, a point where some of their nerve fibers cross to the opposite side of the brain. The nerve fibers from the right half of each retina go to the right hemisphere, and those from the left half of each retina go to the left hemisphere. This crossing over is important because it allows visual information from a single eye to be represented in the primary visual cortex of both hemispheres of the brain. Moreover, it plays an important part in depth perception. But if one eye is covered and deprived of vision during a critical period of visual development early in life, the visual cortex almost completely stops responding to signals sent by that eye (Fagiolini & Hensch, 2000).

From the optic chiasm, the optic nerve fibers extend to the thalamus, where they form synapses with neurons that transmit the impulses to the primary visual cortex. Approximately one-fourth of the primary visual cortex is dedicated exclusively to analyzing input from the fovea, which, as you'll recall, is a very small but extremely important part of the retina.

The Primary Visual Cortex Thanks to researchers David Hubel and Torsten Wiesel (1959, 1979; Hubel, 1963, 1995), who won a Nobel Prize for their work in 1981, we know a great deal about how specialized the neurons of the **primary visual cortex** are. (Recall from Chapter 2 that the primary visual cortex is the part of the brain in which visual information is processed.) By inserting tiny microelectrodes into single cells in the visual cortexes of cats, Hubel and Wiesel (1959) were able to determine what was

■ **fovea**
(FO-vee-uh) A small area at the center of the retina that provides the clearest and sharpest vision because it has the largest concentration of cones.

■ **blind spot**
The point in each retina where there are no rods or cones because the cable of ganglion cells is extending through the retinal wall.

■ **optic nerve**
The nerve that carries visual information from each retina to both sides of the brain.

■ **primary visual cortex**
The part of the brain in which visual information is processed.

REVIEW *and* REFLECT 3.1

Major Structures of the Visual System

STRUCTURE	FUNCTION
Cornea	Translucent covering on the front of the eyeball that bends light rays entering the eye inward through the pupil
Iris	Colored part of the eye that adjusts to maintain a constant amount of light entering the eye through the pupil
Pupil	Opening in the center of the iris through which light rays enter the eye
Lens	Transparent disk-shaped structure behind the pupil that adjusts its shape to allow focusing on objects at varying distances
Retina	Layer of tissue on the inner surface of the eye that contains sensory receptors for vision
Rods	Specialized receptor cells in the retina that are sensitive to light changes
Cones	Specialized receptor cells in the retina that enable humans to see fine detail and color in adequate light
Fovea	Small area at the center of the retina, packed with cones, on which objects viewed directly are clearly and sharply focused
Optic nerve	Nerve that carries visual information from the retina to the brain
Blind spot	Area in each eye where the optic nerve joins the retinal wall and no vision is possible

Want to be sure you've fully absorbed the material in this chapter? Visit **www.ablongman.com/wood5e** for access to free practice tests, flashcards, interactive activities, and links developed specifically to help you succeed in psychology.

happening in individual cells when the cats were exposed to different kinds of visual stimuli. They discovered that each neuron responded only to specific patterns. Some neurons responded only to lines and angles, while others fired only when the cat saw a vertical or horizontal line. Still others were responsive to nothing but right angles or lines of specific lengths. Neurons of this type are known as **feature detectors**, and they are already coded at birth to make their unique responses. Yet we see whole images, not collections of isolated features, because visual perceptions are complete only when the primary visual cortex transmits the millions of pieces of visual information it receives to other areas in the brain, where they are combined and assembled into whole visual images (Perry & Zeki, 2000).

■ **feature detectors** Neurons in the brain that respond only to specific visual patterns (for example, to lines or angles).

The major structures of the visual system are summarized in *Review and Reflect 3.1.*

Color Vision

How do we detect the difference between one color and another?

Why does the skin of an apple appear to be red, while its flesh is perceived as an off-white color? Remember, what we actually see is reflected light. Some light waves striking an object are absorbed by it; others are reflected from it. So, why does an apple's skin look red? If you hold a red apple in bright light, light waves of all the different wavelengths strike the apple, but more of the longer red wavelengths of light are reflected from the apple's skin. The shorter wavelengths are absorbed, so you see only the reflected red. Bite into the apple, and it looks off-white. Why? You see the near-white color because, rather than being absorbed, almost all of the wavelengths of the visible spectrum are reflected from the inside part of the apple. The presence of all visible wavelengths gives the sensation

hue
The dimension of light that refers to the specific color perceived.

saturation
The purity of a color, or the degree to which the light waves producing it are of the same wavelength.

of a near-white color. If an object does indeed reflect 100% of visible wavelengths, it appears to be pure white.

Our everyday visual experience goes far beyond the colors in the rainbow. We can detect thousands of subtle color shadings. What produces these fine color distinctions? Researchers have identified three dimensions of light that combine to provide the rich world of color we experience: (1) The chief dimension is **hue,** which refers to the specific color perceived—red, blue, or yellow, for example. (2) **Saturation** refers to the purity of a color; a color becomes less saturated, or less pure, as other wavelengths of light are mixed with it. (3) **Brightness** refers to the intensity of the light energy that is perceived as a color.

Theories of Color Vision

What two major theories attempt to explain color vision?

Scientists know that the cones are responsible for color vision, but exactly how do they work to produce color sensations? Two major theories have been offered to explain color vision, and both were formulated before the development of laboratory technology capable of testing them. The **trichromatic theory**, first proposed by Thomas Young in 1802, was modified by Hermann von Helmholtz about 50 years later. This theory states that there are three kinds of cones in the retina and that each kind makes a maximal chemical response to one of three colors—blue, green, or red. Research conducted in the 1950s and the 1960s by Nobel Prize winner George Wald (1964; Wald et al., 1954) supports the trichromatic theory. Wald discovered that even though all cones have basically the same structure, the retina does indeed contain three kinds of cones. Subsequent research demonstrated that each kind of cone is particularly sensitive to one of three colors—red, green, or blue (Roorda & Williams, 1999).

brightness
The intensity of the light energy that is perceived as a color.

trichomatic theory
The theory of color vision suggesting that there are three types of cones in the retina that make a maximal chemical response to one of three colors—red, green, or blue.

opponent-process theory
The theory of color vision suggesting that three kinds of cells respond by increasing or decreasing their rate of firing when different colors are present.

afterimage
A visual sensation that remains after a stimulus is withdrawn.

color blindness
The inability to distinguish certain colors from one another.

The other major attempt to explain color vision is the **opponent-process theory**, which was first proposed by physiologist Ewald Hering in 1878 and revised in 1957 by researchers Leon Hurvich and Dorthea Jamison. According to the opponent-process theory, three kinds of cells respond by increasing or decreasing their rate of firing when different colors are present. The red/green cells increase their firing rate when red is present and decrease it when green is present. The yellow/blue cells have an increased response to yellow and a decreased response to blue. A third kind of cells increase their response rate for white light and decrease it in the absence of light.

If you look long enough at one color in the opponent-process pair and then look at a white surface, your brain will give you the sensation of the opposite color—a negative **afterimage**, a visual sensation that remains after the stimulus is withdrawn. After you have stared at one color in an opponent-process pair (red/green, yellow/blue, white/black), the cell responding to that color tires and the opponent cell begins to fire, producing the afterimage. Demonstrate this for yourself in *Try It 3.1*.

But which theory of color vision is correct? It turns out that each theory explains a different phase of color processing. It is now generally accepted that the cones perform color processing in a way that is best explained by the trichromatic theory. The cones pass on information about wavelengths of light to the ganglion cells, the site of opponent processes. And color perception appears to involve more than just these two phases. Researchers think that color processing starts at the level of the retina, continues through the bipolar and ganglion cells, and is completed in the color detectors in the visual cortex (Masland, 1996; Sokolov, 2000).

Color Blindness

Do individuals with color blindness see the world in black and white?

You may have wondered what it means if someone is "color blind." Does that person see the world in black and white? No—the term **color blindness** refers to an inability to distinguish certain colors from one

Try It 3.1 A Negative Afterimage

Stare at the dot in the green, black, and yellow flag for approximately 1 minute. Then shift your gaze to the dot in the blank rectangle. You will see the American flag in its true colors—red, white, and blue, which are the opponent-process opposites of green, black, and yellow.

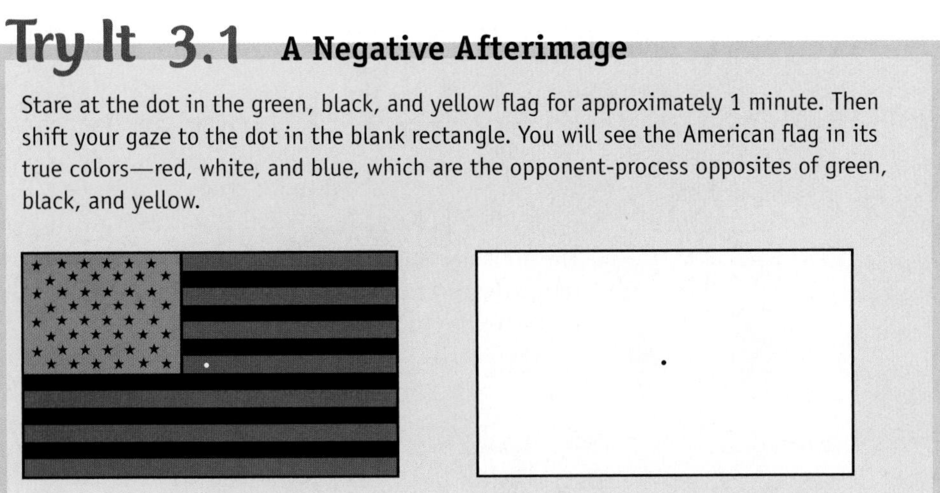

another. About 7% of males experience some kind of difficulty in distinguishing colors, most commonly red from green (Montgomery, 2003). By contrast, fewer than 1% of females suffer from color blindness. (Recall from Chapter 2 that this sex difference is explained by the fact that genes for color vision are carried on the X chromosome.)

Research has shown that color blindness can have degrees; it isn't simply a matter of either-you-have-it-or-you-don't. And why are some of us better able to make fine distinctions between colors, as we must do when sorting black and navy blue socks, for instance? These differences appear to be related to the number of color vision genes individuals have. Researchers have found that, in people with normal color vision, the X chromosome may contain as few as two or as many as nine genes for color perception (Neitz & Neitz, 1995). Those who have more of such genes appear to be better able to make very fine distinctions between colors.

On the left a hot air balloon is shown as it would appear to a person with normal color vision; on the right is the same balloon as it would appear to a person with red-green color blindness.

Remember It 3.2

1. Match each part of the eye with its description:

   ____ (1) the colored part of the eye
   ____ (2) the opening in the iris that dilates and constricts
   ____ (3) the transparent covering of the iris
   ____ (4) the transparent structure that focuses an inverted image on the retina
   ____ (5) the thin, light-sensitive membrane at the back of the eye on which the lens focuses an inverted image

   a. retina
   b. cornea
   c. pupil
   d. iris
   e. lens

2. The ____________ in the retina enable you to see in dim light.
3. The ____________ in the retina enable you to see color and detail.
4. The optic nerve carries neural impulses from the retina to the ____________, from which the impluses are passed on to the ____________.

ANSWERS: 1. (1) d, (2) c, (3) b, (4) e, (5) a; 2. rods; 3. cones; 4. thalamus, primary visual cortex

Hearing

Years ago, the frightening science fiction movie *Alien* was advertised this way: "In space, no one can hear you scream!" Although the movie was fiction, the statement is true. Light can travel through the vast nothingness of space, a vacuum, but sound cannot. In this section, you will learn why.

Sound

What determines the pitch and loudness of a sound, and how is each quality measured?

Sound requires a medium, such as air, water, or a solid object, through which to move. This fact was first demonstrated by Robert Boyle in 1660 when he suspended a ringing pocket watch by a thread inside a specially designed jar. When Boyle pumped all the air out of the jar, he could no longer hear the watch ring. But when he pumped the air back into the jar, he could again hear the watch ringing.

Frequency is determined by the number of cycles completed by a sound wave in one second. The unit used to measure a wave's frequency, or cycles per second, is known as the hertz (Hz). The *pitch*—how high or low the sound is—is chiefly determined by frequency—the higher the frequency (the more cycles per second), the higher the sound. The human ear can hear sound frequencies from low bass tones of around 20 Hz up to high-pitched sounds of about 20,000 Hz. The lowest tone on a piano sounds at a frequency of about 28 Hz, and the highest tone at about 4,214 Hz. Many mammals, such as dogs, cats, bats, and rats, can hear tones much higher in frequency than 20,000 Hz. Amazingly, dolphins can respond to frequencies up to 100,000 Hz.

The loudness of a sound is determined by a measure called **amplitude**. The force or pressure with which air molecules move chiefly determines loudness, which is measured using a unit called the *bel*, named for Alexander Graham Bell. Because the bel is a rather large unit, sound levels are expressed in tenths of a bel, or **decibels (dB)**. The threshold of human hearing is set at 0 dB, which does not mean the absence of sound but rather the softest sound that can be heard in a very quiet setting. Each

■ **frequency**
The number of cycles completed by a sound wave in one second, determining the pitch of the sound; measured in the unit called the hertz.

■ **amplitude**
The measure of the loudness of a sound; expressed in the unit called the decibel.

■ **decibel (dB)**
(DES-ih-bel) A unit of measurement for the loudness of sounds.

FIGURE 3.6 Decibel Levels of Various Sounds

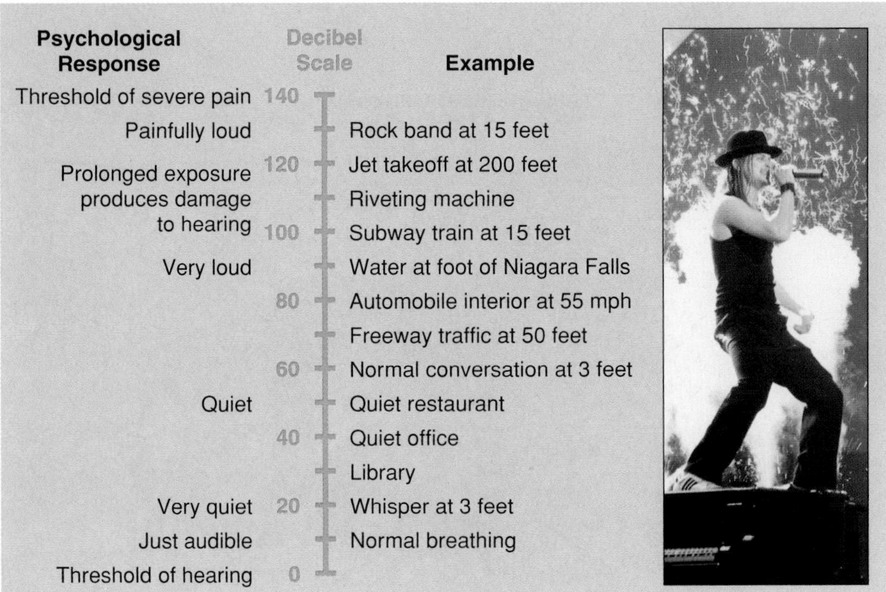

The loudness of a sound (its amplitude) is measured in decibels. Each increase of 10 decibels makes a sound 10 times louder. A normal conversation at 3 feet measures about 60 decibels, which is 10,000 times louder than a soft whisper of 20 decibels. Any exposure to sounds of 130 decibels or higher puts a person at immediate risk for hearing damage.

increase of 10 decibels makes a sound 10 times louder. Figure 3.6 shows comparative decibel levels for a variety of sounds.

Another characteristic of sound is **timbre**, the distinctive quality of a sound that distinguishes it from other sounds of the same pitch and loudness. Have you ever thought about why a given musical note sounds different when played on a piano, a guitar, and a violin, even though all three instruments use vibrating strings to produce sounds? The characteristics of the strings, the technique used to initiate the vibrations, and the way the body of the instrument amplifies the vibrations work together to produce a unique "voice," or timbre, for each instrument. Human voices vary in timbre as well, providing us with a way of recognizing individuals when we can't see their faces. Timbres vary from one instrument to another, and from one voice to another, because most sounds consist of several different frequencies rather than a single pitch. The range of those frequencies gives each musical instrument, and each human voice, its unique sound.

■ **timbre**
(TAM-burr) The distinctive quality of a sound that distinguishes it from other sounds of the same pitch and loudness.

■ **audition**
The sensation and process of hearing.

■ **outer ear**
The visible part of the ear, consisting of the pinna and the auditory canal.

The Ear

How do the outer ear, middle ear, and inner ear function in hearing?

Would you still be able to hear if you lost your ears? In fact, the part of the human body called the ear plays only a minor role in **audition**, which is the sensation and process of hearing. So, even if the visible part of your ears were cut off, your hearing would suffer very little. Let's see how each part of the ear contributes to the ability to hear.

The oddly shaped, curved flap of cartilage and skin called the *pinna* is the visible part of the **outer ear** (see Figure 3.7, on page 92). Inside the ear, the *auditory canal* is about 1 inch long, and its entrance is lined with hairs. At the end of the auditory canal is the *eardrum* (or *tympanic membrane*), a thin, flexible membrane about ⅓ inch in diameter. The eardrum moves in response to the sound waves that travel through the auditory canal and strike it.

The **middle ear** is no larger than an aspirin tablet. Inside its chamber are the *ossicles*, the three smallest bones in the human body. Named for their shapes, the ossicles—the hammer, the anvil, and the stirrup—are connected in that order, linking the eardrum

■ **middle ear**
The portion of the ear containing the ossicles, which connect the eardrum to the oval window and amplify sound waves.

FIGURE 3.7 The Anatomy of the Human Ear

Sound waves pass through the auditory canal to the eardrum, causing it to vibrate and set in motion the ossicles in the middle ear. When the stirrup pushes against the oval window, it sets up vibrations in the inner ear. This moves the fluid in the cochlea back and forth and sets in motion the hair cells, causing a message to be sent to the brain via the auditory nerve.

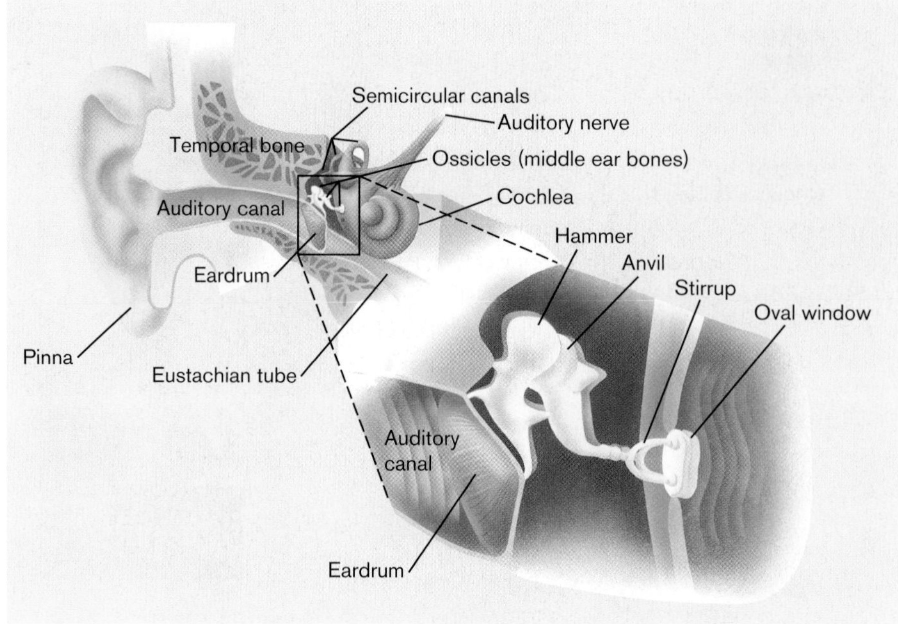

inner ear
The innermost portion of the ear, containing the cochlea, the vestibular sacs, and the semicircular canals.

cochlea
(KOK-lee-uh) The fluid-filled, snail-shaped, bony chamber in the inner ear that contains the basilar membrane and its hair cells (the sound receptors).

hair cells
Sensory receptors for hearing that are attached to the basilar membrane in the cochlea.

to the oval window (see Figure 3.7). The ossicles amplify sound waves some 22 times (Békésy, 1957). The **inner ear** begins at the inner side of the oval window, at the **cochlea**—a fluid-filled, snail-shaped, bony chamber. When the stirrup pushes against the oval window, it sets up vibrations that move the fluid in the cochlea back and forth in waves. Inside the cochlea, attached to its thin basilar membrane are about 15,000 sensory receptors called **hair cells**, each with a bundle of tiny hairs protruding from it. The tiny hair bundles are pushed and pulled by the motion of the fluid inside the cochlea. If the tip of a hair bundle is moved only as much as the width of an atom, an electrical impulse is generated, which is transmitted to the brain by way of the auditory nerve.

The ear isn't the only physical structure that contributes to hearing. We can hear some sounds through *bone conduction*, the vibrations of the bones in the face and skull. When you click your teeth or eat crunchy food, you hear these sounds mainly through bone conduction. And, if you have heard a recording of your voice, you may have thought it sounded odd. This is because recordings do not reproduce the sounds you hear through bone conduction when you speak, so you are hearing your voice as it sounds to others.

Having two ears, one on each side of the head, enables you to determine the direction from which sounds are coming (Konishi, 1993). Unless a sound is directly above, below, in front of, or behind you, it reaches one ear very shortly before it reaches the other (Spitzer & Semple, 1991). The brain detects differences as small as 0.0001 second and interprets them, revealing the direction of the sound (Rosenzweig, 1961). The source of a sound may also be determined by the difference in the intensity of the sound reaching each ear, as well as the position of the head when the sound is detected (Kopinska & Harris, 2003; Middlebrooks & Green, 1991).

What two major theories attempt to explain hearing?

Theories of Hearing

How do the parts of the ear work together to produce auditory sensations? Scientists have proposed two theories to explain hearing.

In the 1860s, Hermann von Helmholtz helped develop **place theory**. This theory of hearing holds that each individual pitch a person hears is determined by the particular spot or place along the basilar membrane that vibrates the most. Observing the living basilar membrane, researchers verified that different locations do indeed vibrate in response to differently pitched sounds (Ruggero, 1992). Even so, place theory seems to apply only to frequencies above 150 Hz.

Another attempt to explain hearing is **frequency theory**. According to this theory, the hair cells vibrate the same number of times per second as the sounds that reach them. Thus, a tone of 500 Hz would stimulate the hair cells to vibrate 500 times per second. However, frequency theory cannot account for frequencies higher than 1,000 Hz because individual neurons linked to the hair cells cannot fire more than about 1,000 times per second. So, even if a receptor vibrated as rapidly as the sound wave associated with a higher tone, the information necessary to perceive the pitch wouldn't be faithfully transmitted to the brain. Consequently, frequency theory seems to be a good explanation of how we hear low-frequency tones (below 500 Hz), but place theory better describes the way in which tones with frequencies above 1,000 Hz are heard (Matlin & Foley, 1997). Both frequency and location are involved when we hear sounds whose frequencies are between 500 and 1,000 Hz.

■ **place theory**
The theory of hearing that holds that each individual pitch a person hears is determined by the particular location along the basilar membrane of the cochlea that vibrates the most.

■ **frequency theory**
The theory of hearing that holds that hair cell receptors vibrate the same number of times per second as the sounds that reach them.

Hearing Loss

What are some of the major causes of hearing loss?

Did you know that every individual has a fairly high risk of suffering from some kind of hearing loss? About 1 infant in every 1,000 in the United States is born with a moderate to severe hearing loss, usually due to circumstances of birth (especially prematurity or lack of oxygen during birth) or to genetic defects (CDC, 2003). Many other children suffer from milder hearing losses, many of which occur after birth as a result of disease or exposure to excessive noise. And hearing loss affects many older Americans as well. In fact, hearing loss affects normal communication in 10% of people 65 or older who have a prior history of normal hearing (Willems, 2000). There are several different kinds of hearing loss, many of which are treatable or entirely preventable.

Conductive hearing loss, or *conduction deafness*, is usually caused by disease or injury to the eardrum or to the bones of the middle ear, preventing sound waves from being conducted to the cochlea. Almost all conductive hearing loss can be repaired medically or surgically. And, in rare cases, a person can be fitted with a hearing aid that bypasses the middle ear, using bone conduction to send sound vibrations to the cochlea.

Most adults with hearing loss suffer from *sensorineural hearing loss*, which involves damage to either the cochlea or the auditory nerve. Large numbers of the cochlea's delicate hair cells, which transduce sound waves into neural impulses, may be damaged or destroyed. If the damage is not too severe, a conventional hearing aid may reduce the effects of this type of hearing loss (Bramblett, 1997). And cochlear implants may help restore hearing in many cases of sensorineural hearing loss, even when the individual is totally deaf. But hearing aids and implants are useless if the damage is to the auditory nerve, which connects the cochlea to the brain; in such cases, the hearing loss is usually total.

About 75% of the cases of hearing loss in older adults appear to be caused by lifelong exposure to excessive noise rather than by aging (Kalb, 1997). Cross-cultural research supports the view that noise is a factor in age-related hearing loss. Older persons in one culture, the Mabaan tribe in the Sudan in Africa, don't appear to suffer much hearing loss as they age. In fact, when hearing tests were conducted on Mabaan tribe members, some of the 80-year-olds could hear as well as 20-year-olds from industrialized countries. The Mabaan pride themselves on their sensitive hearing, and an important tribal custom is never raising one's voice. Even tribal festivals and celebrations are quiet affairs, featuring dancing and soft singing accompanied by stringed instruments rather than drums (Bennett, 1990).

Members of some Sudanese tribes play stringed instruments rather quietly during celebrations. Perhaps because they are not exposed to much noise, these people generally have very sharp hearing.

Remember It 3.3

1. The pitch of a sound is chiefly determined by __________.
2. Loudness is chiefly determined by __________.
3. Decibels are units used to measure __________.
4. Match the part of the ear with the structures it contains.
   ____ (1) ossicles a. outer ear
   ____ (2) pinna, auditory canal b. middle ear
   ____ (3) cochlea, hair cells c. inner ear
5. The sensory receptors for hearing are found in the __________.
6. Two major theories that explain hearing are __________ theory and __________ theory.

ANSWERS: 1. frequency; 2. amplitude; 3. loudness; 4. (1) b, (2) a, (3) c; 5. cochlea; 6. frequency, place

Smell and Taste

Clearly, our sensory experiences would be extremely limited without vision and hearing, but what about the chemical senses—smell and taste?

Smell

If you suddenly lost your sense of smell, you might think, "This isn't so bad. I can't smell flowers or food, but, on the other hand, I no longer have to endure the foul odors of life." But your *olfactory system*—the technical name for the organs and brain structures involved in the sense of smell—aids your survival. You smell smoke and can escape before the flames of a fire envelop you. Your nose broadcasts an odor alarm to the brain when certain poisonous gases or noxious fumes are present. Smell, aided by taste, provides your line of defense against putting spoiled food or drink into your body. And, believe it or not, every single individual gives off a unique scent, which is genetically determined (Axel, 1995).

What path does a smell message take from the nose to the brain?

The Mechanics of Smell Did you know that the human olfactory system is capable of sensing and distinguishing 10,000 different odors? **Olfaction**, the sense of smell, is a chemical sense. You cannot smell a substance unless some of its molecules vaporize—pass from a solid or liquid into a gaseous state. Heat speeds up the vaporization of molecules, which is why food that is cooking has a stronger and more distinct odor than uncooked food. When odor molecules vaporize, they become airborne and make their way up each nostril to the **olfactory epithelium**. The olfactory epithelium consists of two 1-square-inch patches of tissue, one at the top of each nasal cavity; together these patches contain about 10 million olfactory neurons, which are the receptor cells for smell. Each of these neurons contains only one of the 1,000 different types of odor receptors (Bargmann, 1996). Because humans are able to detect some 10,000 odors, each of the 1,000 types of odor receptors must be able to respond to more than one kind of odor molecule. Moreover, some odor molecules trigger more than one type of odor receptor (Axel, 1995). The intensity of a smell stimulus—how strong or weak it is—is apparently determined by the number of olfactory neurons firing at the same time (Freeman, 1991). Figure 3.8 shows a diagram of the human olfactory system.

■ **olfaction**
(ol-FAK-shun) The sense of smell.

■ **olfactory epithelium**
Two 1-square-inch patches of tissue, one at the top of each nasal cavity, which together contain about 10 million olfactory neurons, the receptors for smell.

FIGURE 3.8 The Olfactory System

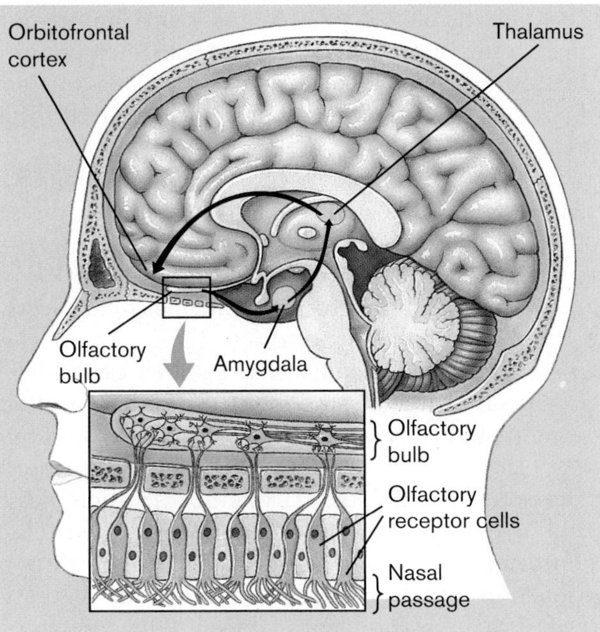

Odor molecules travel up the nostrils to the olfactory epithelium, which contains the receptor cells for smell. Olfactory receptors are special neurons whose axons form the olfactory nerve. The olfactory nerve relays smell messages to the olfactory bulbs, which pass them on to the thalamus, the orbitofrontal cortex, and other parts of the brain.

Have you ever wondered why dogs have a keener sense of smell than humans? Not only do many dogs have a long snout, but, in some breeds, the olfactory epithelium can be as large as the area of a handkerchief and can contain up to 20 times as many olfactory neurons as in humans (Engen, 1982). It is well known that dogs use scent to recognize not only other members of their species, but also the humans they live with. And humans have this ability, too. The mothers of newborns can recognize their own babies by smell within hours after birth. But can humans recognize the scents of other species—their own pets, for example? Yes, to a remarkable degree. When presented with blankets permeated with the scents of dogs, some 89% of the dog owners easily identified their own dog by smell (Wells & Hepper, 2000).

Olfactory neurons are different from all other sensory receptors: They both come into direct contact with sensory stimuli and reach directly into the brain. These neurons have a short lifespan; after functioning for only about 60 days, they die and are replaced by new cells (Buck, 1996).

The axons of the olfactory neurons relay a smell message directly to the **olfactory bulbs**—two brain structures the size of matchsticks that rest above the nasal cavities (refer to Figure 3.8). From the olfactory bulbs, the message is relayed to the thalamus and the orbitofrontal cortex, which distinguish the odor and relay that information to other parts of the brain.

The process of sensing odors is the same in every individual, but there are large differences in sensitivity to smells. For example, perfumers and whiskey blenders can distinguish subtle variations in odors that are indistinguishable to the average person. Young people are more sensitive to odors than older people, and nonsmokers are more sensitive than smokers (Matlin & Foley, 1997).

Smell and Memory Has a particular smell ever triggered a memory for you? In his novel *Remembrance of Things Past*, the French novelist Marcel Proust told the story of a character who claimed to have accessed all of his childhood memories by simply smelling a "petite Madeline" (a small cake or cookie) dipped in a cup of tea. But is there any evidence to support this idea? Indeed, brain-imaging studies of human

■ **olfactory bulbs**
Two matchstick-sized structures above the nasal cavities, where smell sensations first register in the brain.

pheromones
Chemicals excreted by humans and other animals that can have a powerful effect on the behavior of other members of the same species.

olfactory functioning have established key connections among smell, emotion, and memory (Pause & Krauel, 2000; Zald & Pardo, 2000). The association of memories with odors is thought to occur because the olfactory system first sends information to the limbic system, an area in the brain that plays an important role in emotions and memories (Horwitz, 1997). Interestingly, the brain's encoding system for smell-related memories appears to bypass the hippocampus, a structure involved in most other kinds of memories (Kaut et al., 2003).

So, you might be thinking, would my memory for psychology information be better if I splashed on a distinctive cologne while studying and then applied the same scent to my body just prior to taking an exam? Maybe, but you should be aware that the ability to associate odors with memories appears to peak between 6 and 10 years of age (Chu and Downes, 2000). Therefore, using scents as memory-enhancers, as Proust's character did, may work best for childhood memories.

Another piece of the odor-memory puzzle comes from research examining the sense of smell in Alzheimer's patients. Researchers have found that measures of olfactory function in the elderly strongly predict the onset of age-related memory problems (Royall et al., 2002; Swan & Carmelli, 2002). Those who show the greatest loss of olfaction are more likely to develop dementia. Recall from the discussion of correlation in Chapter 1 that it would be erroneous to conclude that a deficient sense of smell *causes* dementia or that improving older adults' sense of smell, or somehow preventing loss of olfactory function, will protect them against dementia. At the very least, however, these studies suggest that measurement of olfactory function in older adults may be a useful way of identifying those who are at greater risk for developing dementia, prior to their having exhibited any symptoms.

Pheromones Many animals excrete chemicals called **pheromones**, which can have a powerful effect on the behavior of other members of the same species. For example, the "queen" of an ant colony emits an odor that identifies her as such to all subordinate colony members (Vander Meer & Alonso, 2002). Animals also use pheromones to mark off territories and to signal sexual receptivity. A female mouse in heat will find the pheromone secreted from a gland on the penis of a male mouse irresistible; the same pheromone will enrage another male mouse. Higher mammals, such as monkeys, also make use of pheromones in their sexual behavior. In salamanders, pheromones emitted by predators serve as cues for the adoption of antipredator behaviors such as hiding (Sullivan et al., 2002).

Humans produce and respond to pheromones as well. When people are exposed to the hormone *androsterone*, which acts as a pheromone, physiological functions such as heart rate are affected and mood states change (DeBortoli et al., 2001). Another interesting area of pheromone research involves *menstrual synchrony*, the tendency of the menstrual cycles of women who live together to synchronize over time. In one study of women living in college dormitories, researchers found that 38% of roommate pairs developed synchronous cycles after 3 months of living together (Morofushi et al., 2000). Roommates who were synchronized showed greater olfactory sensitivity to androsterone than those who were not synchronized.

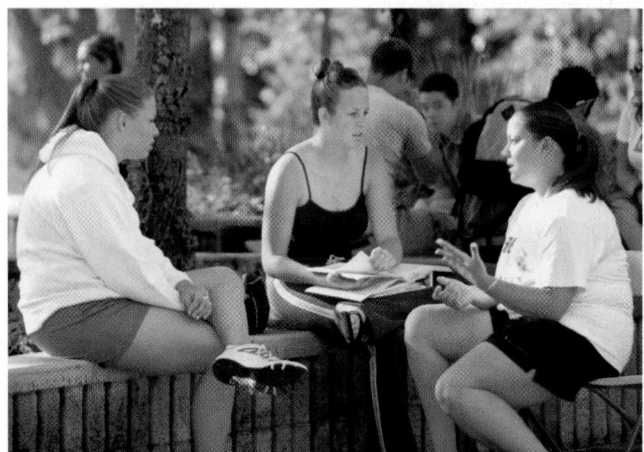

Individual differences in sensitivity to pheromones contribute to variations in menstrual synchrony among women who live in college dormitories.

Studies conducted by Viennese researcher Karl Grammar (cited in Holden, 1996) suggest that humans, although not consciously aware of it, respond to pheromones when it comes to mating. In his research, Grammar analyzed the saliva of 66 young men who had used an inhalant to sniff copulines—pheromones found in female vaginal secretions. The secretions were obtained during three different times in the menstrual cycle, but those taken at ovulation were the only ones to cause a rise in testosterone levels in the men's saliva. The men apparently recognized, though not consciously, which of the women were most likely to be fertile.

Taste

What are the primary taste sensations, and how are they detected?

Do you think you would enjoy life without the tastes of fresh-baked bread, crispy fried chicken, or luscious chocolate ice cream? Of course, even without a sense of taste, you would still feel the texture and temperature of foods you put in the mouth. And you might be surprised to learn that much of the pleasure you attribute to the sense of taste actually arises from smells, which are due to odor molecules forced up the nasal cavity by the action of the tongue, cheeks, and throat when you chew and swallow. So, without a sense of taste, your sense of smell would provide you with some taste sensations. Still, life without the ability to fully experience the tastes of the foods we love would, no doubt, be less enjoyable.

The Five Basic Tastes Psychology textbooks have long maintained that **gustation**, the sense of taste, produces four distinct kinds of taste sensations: sweet, sour, salty, and bitter. This is true. But recent research suggests that there is a fifth taste sensation in humans (Herness, 2000). This fifth taste sensation, called *umami*, is triggered by the substance glutamate, which, in the form of monosodium glutamate (MSG), is widely used as a flavoring in Asian foods (Matsunami et al., 2000). Many protein-rich foods, such as meat, milk, aged cheese, and seafood, also contain glutamate.

All five taste sensations can be detected on all locations of the tongue. Indeed, even a person with no tongue could still taste to some extent, thanks to the taste receptors found in the palate, in the mucus lining of the cheeks and lips, and in parts of the throat, including the tonsils. When tastes are mixed, the specialized receptors for each type of flavor are activated and send separate messages to the brain (Frank et al., 2003). In other words, your brain perceives the two distinctive flavors present in sweet and sour sauce quite separately. This analytical quality of the sense of taste prevents your being fooled into eating spoiled or poisoned food when the characteristic taste of either is combined with some kind of pleasant flavor.

The Taste Receptors If you look at your tongue in a mirror, you will see many small bumps called *papillae*. There are four different types of papillae, and three of them have **taste buds** along their sides (see Figure 3.9, on page 98). Each taste bud is composed of 60 to 100 receptor cells. But the lifespan of the taste receptors is very short—only about 10 days—and they are continually being replaced.

Taste Sensitivities Research indicates that humans can be divided into three groups based on taste sensitivity for certain sweet and bitter substances: nontasters, medium tasters, and supertasters (Yackinous & Guinard, 2002). Nontasters are unable to taste certain sweet and bitter compounds, but they do taste most other substances, although with less sensitivity. Supertasters taste these sweet and bitter compounds with far stronger intensity than other people. Researchers are currently investigating links between taste sensitivity, eating behaviors, and health status variables, such as obesity. For example, supertasters who are particularly sensitive to the chemical that gives fruits and vegetables a bitter taste eat less salad than medium tasters and nontasters (Yackinous & Guinard, 2002). Still, supertasters appear no more likely to be overweight than medium tasters or nontasters. In fact, among individuals who report that they never deliberately restrict their diets to try to lose weight, supertasters of the bitter chemical have less body fat than medium tasters or nontasters (Tepper & Ullrich, 2002). So, researchers know that taste sensitivity is linked to food preferences, but not how these preferences may be connected to nutritional status.

■ **gustation**
The sense of taste.

■ **taste buds**
Structures in many of the tongue's papillae that are composed of 60 to 100 receptor cells for taste.

FIGURE 3.9 **The Tongue's Papillae and Taste Buds**

(a) A photomicrograph of the surface of the tongue shows several papillae. (b) This vertical cross-section through a papillae reveals the location of the taste buds and taste receptors.

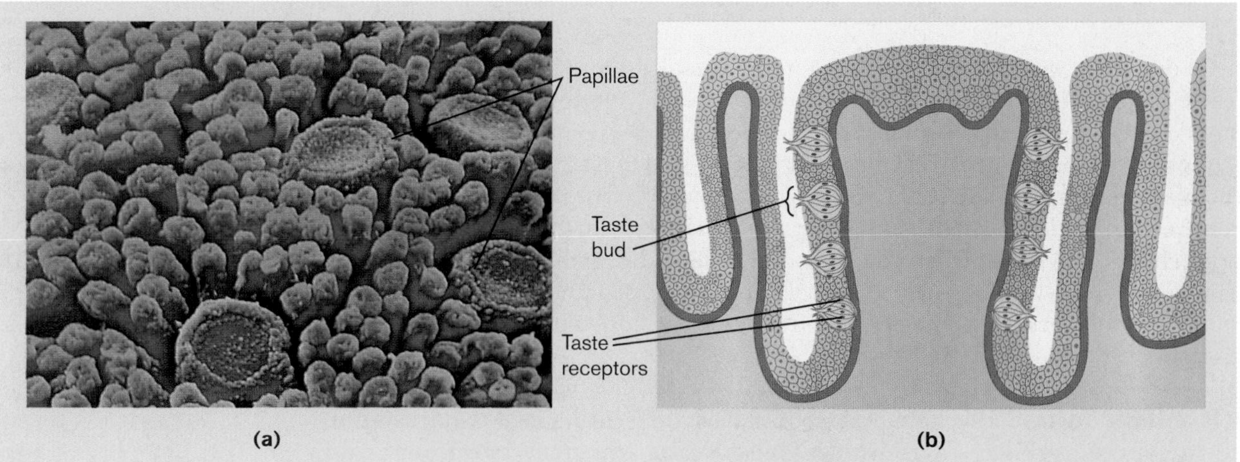

Remember It 3.4

1. The technical name for the process or sensation of smell is ________.
2. The olfactory, or smell, receptors are located in the ________.
3. The primary taste sensations are ________, ________, ________, ________, and ________.
4. Much of the pleasure we attribute to the sense of taste actually arises from ________.
5. Each ________ contains from 60 to 100 receptor cells for taste.
6. ________ taste certain sweet and bitter compounds with far stronger intensity than most people.

ANSWERS: 1. olfaction; 2. olfactory epithelium; 3. sweet, salty, sour, bitter, and umami (for glutamate); 4. smell; 5. taste bud; 6. Supertasters

The Skin Senses

How important is the sense of touch? Classic research in the mid-1980s demonstrated that premature infants who were massaged for 15 minutes three times a day gained weight 47% faster than other premature infants who received only regular intensive care treatment (Field et al., 1986). The massaged infants were more responsive and were able to leave the hospital about 6 days earlier on average than those who were not massaged. Thus, the sense of touch is not only one of the more pleasant aspects of life, but it is also critical to our survival. And it may be just as important to adult as to infant survival. For instance, you may feel a poisonous spider crawling up your arm and flick it away before it can inflict a deadly bite. The other skin sense—pain—is also vital because it serves as an early warning system for many potentially deadly conditions, as you'll learn in this section.

■ tactile
Pertaining to the sense of touch.

Touch

How does the skin provide sensory information?

Your natural clothing, the skin, is the largest organ of your body. It performs many important biological functions, while also providing much of what is known as sensual pleasure. **Tactile** information is conveyed to the brain when an object touches and depresses the skin, stimulating one or more of the several distinct types of receptors found in the nerve endings. These sensitive nerve endings in the skin send the touch message through nerve connections to the spinal cord. The message travels up the spinal cord and through the brainstem and the midbrain, finally reaching the somatosensory cortex, as shown in Figure 3.10. (Recall from Chapter 2 that the somatosensory cortex is the strip of tissue at the front of the parietal lobes where touch, pressure, temperature, and pain register.) Once the somatosensory cortex has been activated, you become aware of where and how hard you have been touched. In the 1890s, one of the most prominent researchers of the tactile sense, Max von Frey, discovered the *two-point threshold*—the measure of how far apart two points must be before they are felt as two separate touches.

If you could examine the skin from the outermost to the deepest layer, you would find a variety of nerve endings that differ markedly in appearance. Most or all of these nerve endings appear to respond in some degree to all different types of tactile stimulation. The more densely packed with these sensory receptors a part of the body's surface is, the more sensitive it is to tactile stimulation.

Pain

What is the function of pain, and how is pain influenced by psychological factors, culture, and endorphins?

Although the tactile sense delivers a great deal of pleasure, it brings us pain as well. Pain motivates us to tend to injuries, to restrict activity, and to seek medical help. Pain also teaches us to avoid pain-producing circumstances in the future. Chronic pain—pain that persists for 3 months or more—continues long after it serves any useful function and is itself a serious medical problem for some 34 million Americans (Brownlee & Schrof, 1997). The three major types of chronic pain are low-back pain, headache, and arthritis pain. For its victims, chronic pain is like a fire alarm that no one can turn off.

Scientists are not certain how pain works, but one major theory that attempts to answer this question is the *gate-control theory* of Ronald Melzack and Patrick Wall (1965, 1983). These researchers contend that there is an area in the spinal cord that

FIGURE 3.10 The Sense of Touch and the Brain

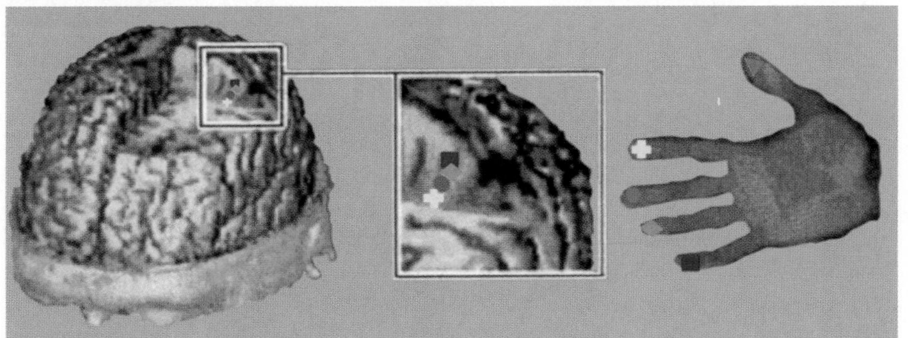

The color coding in this combined MRI/MEG image shows that the thumb and fingers of the right hand are connected in maplike fashion with areas of the left somatosensory cortex.
Source: From Rodolfo Llinás, © NAS.

can act like a "gate" and either block pain messages or transmit them to the brain. Only so many messages can go through the gate at any one time. You feel pain when pain messages carried by small, slow-conducting nerve fibers reach the gate and cause it to open. Large, fast-conducting nerve fibers carry other sensory messages from the body, and these can effectively tie up traffic at the gate so that it will close and keep many of the pain messages from getting through. What is the first thing you do when you stub your toe or pound your finger with a hammer? If you rub or apply gentle pressure to the injury, you are stimulating the large, fast-conducting nerve fibers, which get their message to the spinal gate first and block some of the pain messages from the slower nerve fibers. Applying ice, heat, or electrical stimulation to the painful area also stimulates the large nerve fibers and closes the spinal gate.

The gate-control theory also accounts for the fact that psychological factors, both cognitive and emotional, can influence the perception of pain. Melzack and Wall (1965, 1983) contend that messages from the brain to the spinal cord can inhibit the transmission of pain messages at the spinal gate and thereby affect the perception of pain. This explains why some people can undergo surgery under hypnosis and feel little or no pain. It also explains why soldiers injured in battle or athletes injured during games can be so distracted that they do not experience pain until some time after the injury.

Psychological and Cultural Influences on the Experience of Pain Chronic pain rates vary across cultures, as you can see in Figure 3.11 Why? Researchers don't have a definitive answer. However, they do know that the experience of pain has a physical and an emotional component, both of which vary from person to person. Pain experts distinguish between pain and suffering—suffering being the affective, or emotional, response to pain. Sullivan and others (1995) found that people suffered most from pain when they harbored negative thoughts about it, feared its potential threat to their well-being, and expressed feelings of helplessness. So, cross-cultural variations in chronic pain may be linked to differences in people's emotional states.

Culture also influences the way pain is experienced and expressed. The most often cited work on pain and culture is that of Zborowski (1952), who compared the responses to pain of Italian, Jewish, Irish, and native-born Anglo-Saxon patients in a large hospital in New York. Among the four groups, Jewish and Italian patients responded more emotionally and showed heightened expressions of pain.

FIGURE 3.11 Cross-Cultural Variations in the Prevalence of Chronic Pain

The prevalence of chronic pain varies widely across cultures.

Sources: Brownlee & Schrof (1997); Catala et al. (2002); Moulin et al. (2002); Ng et al. (2002); Smith et al. (2001).

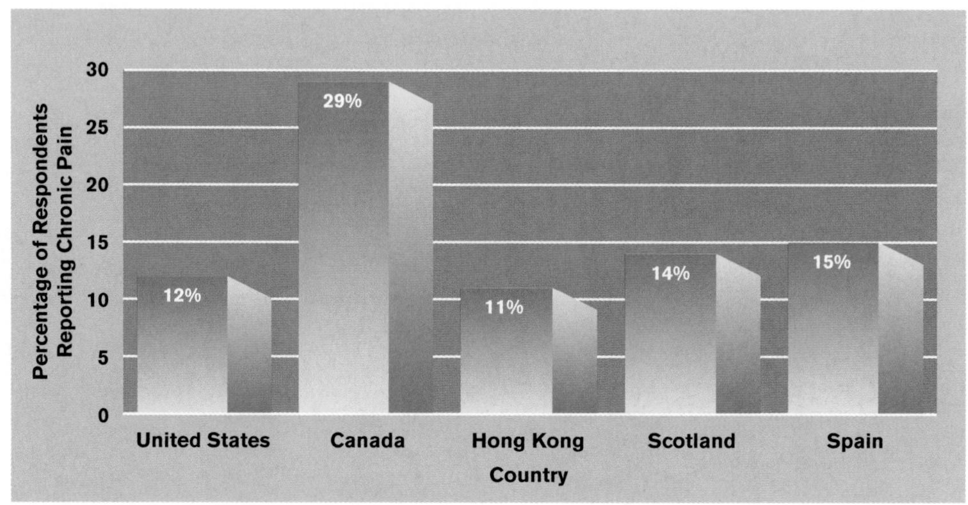

Culture even influences the experience and expression of pain during childbirth. The Chinese value silence, and Chinese women enduring the pain of childbirth typically do not engage in loud and highly emotional responses for fear they will dishonor themselves and their families (Weber, 1996). In stark contrast are some Pakistani women who believe that the greater their suffering and the louder their response to the pain, the more caring their husbands will be during the following weeks (Ahmad, 1994).

■ **endorphins**
(en-DOR-fins) The body's own natural painkillers, which block pain and produce a feeling of well-being.

Endorphins Americans spend more money trying to get rid of pain than for any other medical purpose. Over $40 billion is spent each year in the United States on treatments for chronic pain, ranging from over-the-counter medications to surgery and psychotherapy (Brownlee & Schrof, 1997). The body produces its own natural painkillers, the **endorphins**, which block pain and produce a feeling of well-being. Endorphins are released when you are injured, when you experience stress or extreme pain, and when you laugh, cry, or exercise.

Some people release endorphins even when they only *think* they are receiving pain medication but are being given, instead, a placebo in the form of a sugar pill or an injection of saline solution. Asthma, high blood pressure, and even heart disease can respond to placebo "treatment" (Brown, 1998). Why? Apparently, when patients believe that they have received a drug for pain, that belief stimulates the release of their own natural pain relievers, the endorphins.

Remember It 3.5

1. The largest organ in the body is the ________.
2. The part of the brain that is responsible for interpreting tactical information is the ________.
3. ________ in the skin respond to all kinds of tactile stimuli.
4. ________ are the body's own natural painkillers.

ANSWERS: 1. skin; 2. somatosensory cortex; 3. Nerve endings; 4. Endorphins

The Spatial Orientation Senses

What kinds of information do the kinesthetic and vestibular senses provide?

The senses you've learned about so far provide you with valuable information about your environment. But what if you could see, hear, smell, taste, and sense touch perfectly well, but your ability to orient yourself in space was disrupted? For instance, what if you couldn't sense how high to raise a hammer in order to hit a nail? You might hit yourself in the head with the hammer. How would you keep from falling if you couldn't sense whether you were standing up straight or leaning to one side? You would be forever bumping into walls as you rounded corners. Fortunately, the kinesthetic and vestibular senses keep you apprised of exactly where all parts of your body are and how the location of your body is related to your physical environment.

The **kinesthetic sense** provides information about (1) the position of body parts in relation to each other and (2) the movement of the entire body or its parts. This information is detected by receptors in the joints, ligaments, and muscles. The other senses, especially vision, provide additional information about body position and movement, but the kinesthetic sense works well on its own. Thanks to the kinesthetic

■ **kinesthetic sense**
The sense providing information about the position of body parts in relation to each other and the movement of the entire body or its parts.

FIGURE 3.12 Sensing Balance and Movement

You sense the rotation of your head in any direction because the movement sends fluid coursing through the tubelike semicircular canals in the inner ear. The moving fluid bends the hair cell receptors, which, in turn, send neural impulses to the brain.

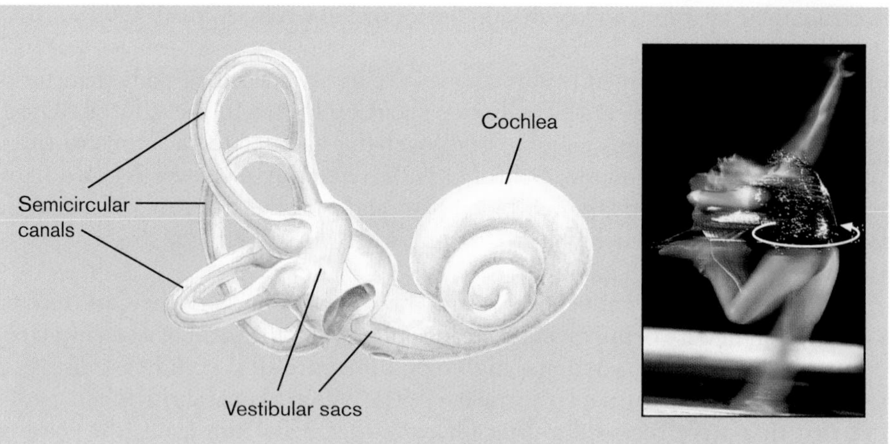

sense, we are able to perform smooth and skilled body movements without visual feedback or a studied, conscious effort. (But why do we perceive ourselves as stationary in a moving car? More on this later in the chapter.)

The **vestibular sense** detects movement and provides information about the body's orientation in space. The vestibular sense organs are located in the semicircular canals and the *vestibular sacs* in the inner ear. The **semicircular canals** sense the rotation of your head, such as when you are turning your head from side to side or when you are spinning around (see Figure 3.12). Because the canals are filled with fluid, rotating movements of the head in any direction send the fluid coursing through the tubelike semicircular canals. In the canals, the moving fluid bends the hair cells, which act as receptors and send neural impulses to the brain. Because there are three canals, each positioned on a different plane, rotation in a given direction will cause the hair cells in one canal to bend more than the hair cells in the other canals.

■ vestibular sense (ves-TIB-yu-ler) The sense that detects movement and provides information about the body's orientation in space.

■ semicircular canals Three fluid-filled tubular canals in the inner ear that sense the rotation of the head.

The semicircular canals and the vestibular sacs signal only changes in motion or orientation. If you were blindfolded and had no visual or other external cues, you would not be able to sense motion once your speed reached a constant rate. For example, in an airplane, you would feel the takeoff and the landing, as well as any sudden changes in speed. But once the plane leveled off and maintained a fairly constant cruising speed, your vestibular organs would not signal the brain that you are moving, even if you were traveling at a rate of hundreds of miles per hour.

Remember It 3.6

1. The ___________ sense provides information about the position of body parts in relation to each other.
2. The ___________ sense provides information about the body's orientation in space.
3. Vestibular sense organs are located in the ___________ and the ___________ in the inner ear.
4. Kinesthetic sense receptors are located in the ___________, ___________, and ___________.

ANSWERS: 1. kinesthetic; 2. vestibular; 3. semicircular canals, vestibular sacs; 4. joints, ligaments, muscles

Perception

Earlier in the chapter, you learned why an apple appears to be red. But why do we think of an apple as having a somewhat spherical shape, like that of a ball? And how do we tell the difference between a picture of an apple and the real thing—that is, the difference between two-dimensional and three-dimensional objects? Recall that *perception* is the process by which sensory information is actively organized and interpreted by the brain. Sensations are the raw materials of human experiences; perceptions are the finished products.

Principles of Perceptual Organization

What are the principles that govern perceptual organization?

Are our perceptions random and haphazard in nature, or do our brains provide us with rules for interpreting sensory experiences? Researchers addressing this question have found a few principles that appear to govern perceptions in all human beings.

Gestalt Principles of Perceptual Organization The Gestalt psychologists maintained that people cannot understand the perceptual world by breaking down experiences into tiny parts and analyzing them separately. When sensory elements are brought together, something new is formed. That is, the whole is more than just the sum of its parts. The German word **Gestalt** has no exact English equivalent, but it roughly refers to the whole form, pattern, or configuration that a person perceives. The Gestalt psychologists claimed that sensory experience is organized according to certain basic principles of perceptual organization:

- *Figure-ground*. As we view the world, some object (the figure) often seems to stand out from the background (the ground) (see Figure 3.13).
- *Similarity*. Objects that have similar characteristics are perceived as a unit. In Figure 3.14(a) (on page 104), dots of a similar color are perceived as belonging together to form horizontal rows on the left and vertical columns on the right.
- *Proximity*. Objects that are close together in space or time are usually perceived as belonging together. Because of their spacing, the lines in Figure 3.14(b) are perceived as four pairs of lines rather than as eight separate lines.
- *Continuity*. We tend to perceive figures or objects as belonging together if they appear to form a continuous pattern, as in Figure 3.14(c).
- *Closure*. We perceive figures with gaps in them to be complete. Even though parts of the figure in Figure 3.14(d) are missing, we use closure and perceive it as a triangle.

Gestalt (geh-SHTALT) A German word that roughly refers to the whole form, pattern, or configuration that a person perceives.

Perceptual Constancy When you say good-bye to friends and watch them walk away, the image they cast on your retina grows smaller and smaller until they finally

FIGURE 3.13 Reversing Figure and Ground

In this illustration, you can see a white vase as a figure against a black background, or two black faces in profile on a white background. Exactly the same visual stimulus produces two opposite figure-ground perceptions.

FIGURE 3.14 Gestalt Principles of Grouping

Gestalt psychologists proposed several principles of perceptual grouping, including similarity, proximity, continuity, and closure.

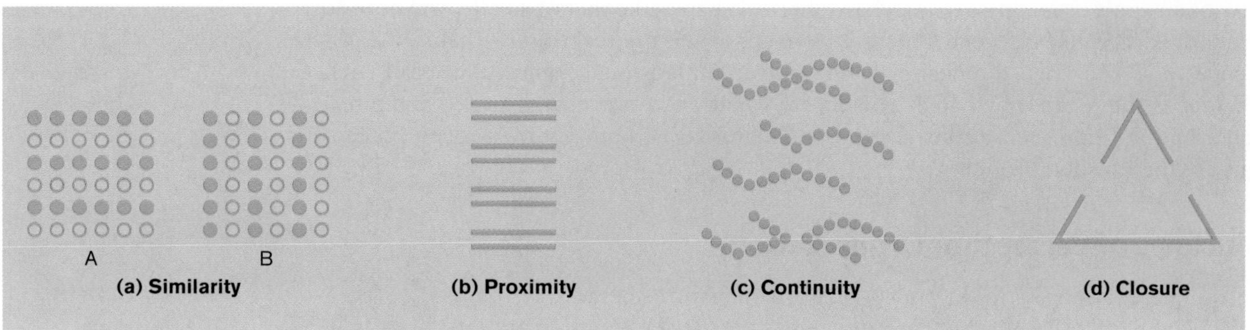

perceptual constancy The phenomenon that allows us to perceive objects as maintaining stable properties, such as size, shape, and brightness, despite differences in distance, viewing angle, and lighting.

disappear in the distance. So how does your brain know that they are still the same size? Scientists call this phenomenon **perceptual constancy**. Thanks to perceptual constancy, when you watch someone walk away, the information that the retina sends to the brain (the sensation that that person is shrinking in size) does not fool the perceptual system. As objects or people move farther away, you continue to perceive them as being about the same size. This perceptual phenomenon is known as *size constancy*. You do not make a literal interpretation about the size of an object from its retinal image—the image of the object projected onto the retina. If you did, you would believe that objects become larger as they approach and smaller as they move away.

The shape or image of an object projected onto the retina changes according to the angle from which it is viewed. But your perceptual ability includes *shape constancy*—the tendency to perceive objects as having a stable or unchanging shape, regardless of changes in the retinal image resulting from differences in viewing angle. In other words, you perceive a door as rectangular and a plate as round from whatever angle you view them (see Figure 3.15).

We normally see objects as maintaining a constant level of brightness, regardless of differences in lighting conditions—a perceptual phenomenon known as *brightness constancy*. Nearly all objects reflect some part of the light that falls on them, and white objects reflect more light than black objects. However, a black asphalt driveway at noon in bright sunlight actually reflects more light than a white shirt does indoors at night in dim lighting. Nevertheless, the driveway still looks black, and the shirt still looks white. Why? We learn to infer the brightness of objects by comparing it with the brightness of all other objects viewed at the same time.

Depth Perception

What are some of the binocular and monocular depth cues?

Depth perception is the ability to perceive the visual world in three dimensions and to judge distances accurately. We judge how far away objects and other people are. We climb and descend stairs without stumbling and perform numerous other actions requiring depth perception. Depth perception is three-dimensional. Yet each eye is able to provide only a two-dimensional view. The images cast on the retina do not contain depth; they are flat, just like a photograph. How, then, do we perceive depth so vividly?

Binocular Depth Cues Some cues to depth perception depend on both eyes working together. These are called **binocular depth cues,** and they include convergence and binocular disparity. *Convergence* occurs when the eyes turn inward to

FIGURE 3.15 Shape Constancy

The door projects very different images on the retina when viewed from different angles. But because of shape constancy, you continue to perceive the door as rectangular.

focus on nearby objects—the closer the object, the greater the convergence. Hold the tip of your finger about 12 inches in front of your nose, and focus on it. Now, slowly begin moving your finger toward your nose. Your eyes will turn inward so much that they virtually cross when the tip of your finger meets the tip of your nose. Many psychologists believe that the tension of the eye muscles as they converge conveys to the brain information that serves as a cue for depth perception. Fortunately, the eyes are just far enough apart, about 2½ inches or so, to give each eye a slightly different view of the objects being focused on and, consequently, a slightly different retinal image. The difference between the two retinal images, known as *binocular disparity* (or *retinal disparity*), provides an important cue for depth perception (see Figure 3.16, on page 106). The farther away from the eyes (up to 20 feet or so) the objects being looked at, the less is the disparity, or difference, between the two retinal images. The brain integrates the two slightly different retinal images and creates the perception of three dimensions.

Monocular Depth Cues Close one eye, and you will see that you can still perceive depth. The visual depth cues perceived with one eye alone are called **monocular depth cues**. The following is a description of seven monocular depth cues, many of which have been used by artists in Western cultures to give the illusion of depth to their paintings.

- *Interposition*. When one object partly blocks your view of another, you perceive the partially blocked object as being farther away.
- *Linear perspective*. Parallel lines that are known to be the same distance apart appear to grow closer together, or converge, as they recede into the distance.
- *Relative size*. Larger objects are perceived as being closer to the viewer, and smaller objects as being farther away.

■ **depth perception**
The ability to perceive the visual world in three dimensions and to judge distances accurately.

■ **binocular depth cues**
Depth cues that depend on both eyes working together.

■ **monocular depth cues**
(mah-NOK-yu-ler) Depth cues that can be perceived by one eye alone.

FIGURE 3.16 Retinal Disparity and Viewing a Stereogram

Retinal disparity enables most of us to perceive 3-D images in stereograms. Place this picture against the tip of your nose and then very, very slowly move the book straight back from your face. Look at the image without blinking. A 3-D picture of soccer players and their fans will suddenly appear.

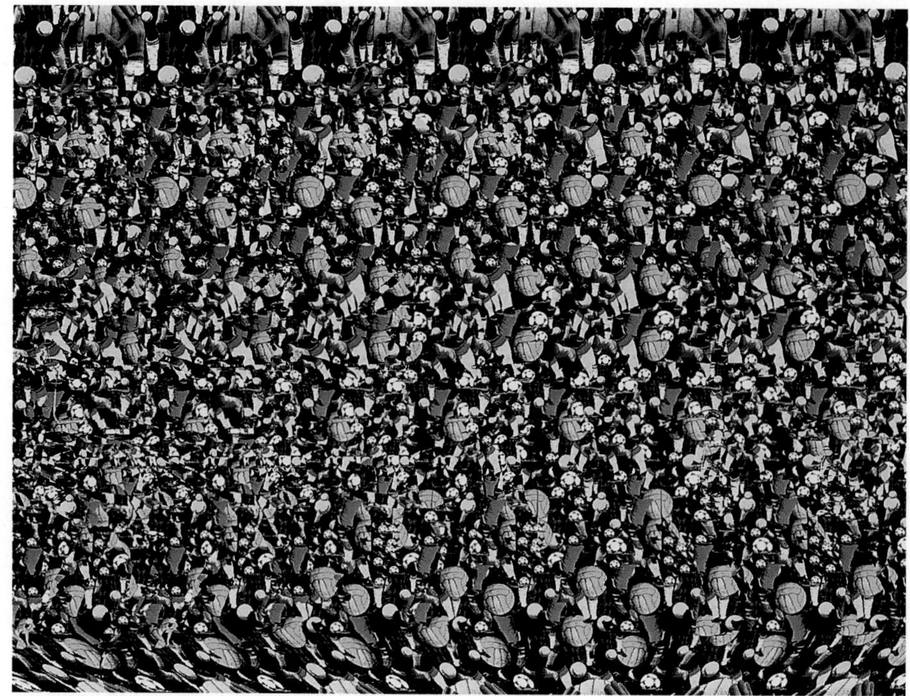

- *Texture gradient.* Objects close to you appear to have sharply defined features, and similar objects that are farther away appear progressively less well-defined or fuzzier in texture.
- *Atmospheric perspective* (sometimes called *aerial perspective*). Objects in the distance have a bluish tint and appear more blurred than objects close at hand.
- *Shadow or shading.* When light falls on objects, they cast shadows, which add to the perception of depth.
- *Motion parallax.* When you ride in a moving vehicle and look out the side window, the objects you see outside appear to be moving in the opposite direction and at different speeds; those closest to you appear to be moving faster than those in the distance. Objects very far away, such as the moon and the sun, appear to move in the same direction as the viewer.

Photos illustrating each of these cues are shown in Figure 3.17.

Perception of Motion

How does the brain perceive real and apparent motion?

Imagine you're sitting in a bus looking through the window at another bus parked parallel to the one in which you are sitting. Suddenly, you sense your bus moving; then, you realize that it is not your bus that moved but the one next to it. In other words, your ability to perceive the motion of objects has been fooled in some way. This example illustrates the complexity of motion perception, a process that is primarily visual, but that also involves auditory and kinesthetic cues. False motion perceptions are so common that psychologists have conducted a great deal of research to find out how the brain perceives real and apparent motion. These researchers use the term **real motion** to refer to perceptions of motion tied to movements of real objects through space. In contrast, the term **apparent motion** signifies perceptions of motion that seem to be psychologically constructed in response to various kinds of stimuli.

real motion Perceptions of motion tied to movements of real objects through space.

FIGURE 3.17 **Monocular Depth Cues**

Interposition
When one object partially blocks your view of another, you perceive the partially blocked object as being farther away.

Linear Perspective
Parallel lines are the same distance apart but appear to grow closer together, or converge, as they recede into the distance.

Relative Size
Larger objects are perceived as being closer to the viewer, and smaller objects as being farther away.

Texture Gradient
Objects close to you appear to have sharply defined features, and similar objects farther away appear progressively less well defined, or fuzzier in texture.

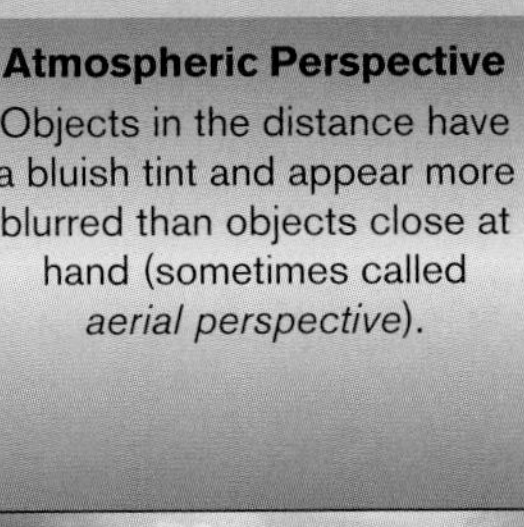

Atmospheric Perspective
Objects in the distance have a bluish tint and appear more blurred than objects close at hand (sometimes called *aerial perspective*).

Shadow or Shading
When light falls on objects, they cast shadows, which add to the perception of depth.

Motion Parallax
When you ride in a moving train and look out the window, the objects you see outside appear to be moving in the opposite direction and at different speeds; those closest to you appear to be moving faster than those in the distance.

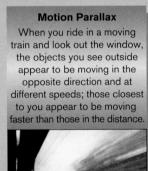

Real Motion When objects move in the field of vision, they project images that move across the retina. As you might expect, research indicates that motion detection is due to brain mechanisms linked to the retina, the edges of which appear to be especially sensitive to motion, just as the fovea is specialized for detail and color (Bach & Hoffman, 2000). However, if you walk across a room with your eyes fixed on an object—your sofa, for example—the object will move across your retina. So, movement of an image across the retina isn't sufficient for motion detection. Your own kinesthetic sense contributes to judgments of motion. Generally, you know whether you're moving or not. But have you ever watched a train go by while sitting still? It's not unusual to have the feeling that your head is moving as you watch the railroad cars whiz by. So, your kinesthetic sense is also linked to your perceptions of movement outside your own body. Brain-imaging studies show that such stimuli activate the vestibular cortex, just as real body movements do (Nishiike et al., 2001).

One of the most important contributors to our understanding of motion perception is psychologist James Gibson. Gibson points out that our perceptions of motion

■ **apparent motion**
Perceptions of motion that seem to be psychologically constructed in response to various kinds of stimuli.

■ phi phenomenon
Apparent motion that occurs when several stationary lights in a dark room are flashed on and off in sequence, causing the perception that a single light is moving from one spot to the next.

■ autokinetic illusion
Apparent motion caused by the movement of the eyes rather than the movement of the objects being viewed.

appear to be based on fundamental, but frequently changing, assumptions about stability (Gibson, 1994). Our brains seem to search for some stimulus in the environment to serve as the assumed reference point for stability. Once the stable reference point is chosen, all objects that move relative to that reference point are judged to be in motion. For example, in the bus situation, your brain assumes that the other bus is stable, and when the motion sensors linked to your retina detect movement, it concludes that your bus is moving. In the train situation, your brain assumes that the train is stable, and so your head must be moving. And when you're driving a car, you sense the car to be in motion relative to the outside environment. But your brain uses the inside of the car as the stable point of reference for your own movements. Only your movements in relation to the seat, steering wheel, and so on are sensed as motion by your brain.

Apparent Motion In one type of apparent motion study, several stationary lights in a dark room are flashed on and off in sequence, causing participants to perceive a single light is moving from one spot to the next. This type of apparent motion, called the **phi phenomenon**, was first discussed by Max Wertheimer (1912), one of the founders of Gestalt psychology. How many neon signs have you seen that caused you to perceive motion? The neon lights don't move; they simply flash on and off in a particular sequence. When you watch a motion picture, you are also perceiving this kind of apparent motion, often called *stroboscopic motion*.

The fact that the eyes are never really completely still also contributes to perceptions of apparent motion. For instance, if you stare at a single unmoving light in a dark room for a few seconds, the light will appear to begin moving, a phenomenon called the **autokinetic illusion**. However, if you look away from the light and then return to watching it, it will again appear to be stable. (Could this phenomenon account for some sightings of "unidentified flying objects"?) Two lights placed close to one another will appear to move together, as if they are linked by an invisible string. What is really happening is that your eyes, not the lights, are moving. Because of the darkness of the room, the brain has no stable visual reference point to use in deciding whether the lights are actually moving or not (Gibson, 1994). But when the room is lit up, the brain immediately "fixes" the error because it has a stable visible background for the lights.

Puzzling Perceptions

What are three types of puzzling perceptions?

Not only can we perceive motion that doesn't exist, we can also perceive objects that aren't present in a stimulus and misinterpret those that are.

Ambiguous and Impossible Figures When you are faced for the first time with an *ambiguous figure*, you have no experience to call on. Your perceptual system is puzzled and tries resolve the uncertainty by seeing the ambiguous figure first one way and then another, but not both ways at once. You never get a lasting impression of ambiguous figures because they seem to jump back and forth beyond your control. In some ambiguous figures, two different objects or figures are seen alternately. The best known of these, "Old Woman/Young Woman," by E. G. Boring, is shown in Figure 3.18(a). If you direct your gaze to the left of the drawing, you are likely to see an attractive young woman, her face turned away. But the young woman disappears when you suddenly perceive the image of the old woman. Such examples of object ambiguity offer striking evidence that perceptions are more than the mere sum of sensory parts. It is hard to believe that the same drawing (the same sum of sensory parts) can convey such dramatically different perceptions.

At first glance, many impossible figures do not seem particularly unusual—at least not until you examine them more closely. Would you invest your money in a company that manufactured the three-pronged device shown in Figure 3.18(b)? Such an object

FIGURE 3.18 **Some Puzzling Perceptions**

(a) Do you see an old woman or a young woman? (b) Why couldn't you build a replica of this three-pronged device? (c) Which horizontal line appears to be longer? (d) Which bar, A or B, is longer?
Source: "Old Woman/Young Woman" by E. G. Boring.

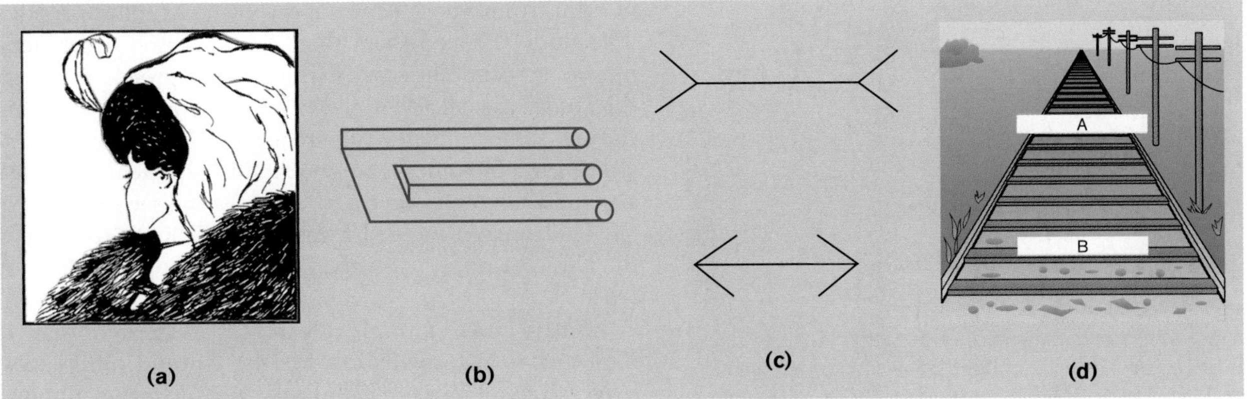

could not be made as pictured because the middle prong appears to be in two different places at the same time. However, this type of impossible figure is more likely to confuse people from Western cultures. Classic research in the 1970s showed that people in some African cultures do not represent three-dimensional visual space in their art, and they do not perceive depth in drawings that contain pictorial depth cues. These people see no ambiguity in drawings similar to the three-pronged trident, and they can draw the figure accurately from memory much more easily than people from Western cultures can (Bloomer, 1976).

Illusions An **illusion** is a false perception or a misperception of an actual stimulus in the environment. We can misperceive size, shape, or the relationship of one element to another. We need not pay to see illusions performed by magicians. Illusions occur naturally, and we see them all the time. An oar in the water appears to be bent where it meets the water. The moon looks much larger at the horizon than it does overhead. Why? One explanation of the *moon illusion* involves relative size. This idea suggests that the moon looks very large on the horizon because it is viewed in comparison to trees, buildings, and other objects. When viewed overhead, the moon cannot be directly compared with other objects, and it appears smaller.

In Figure 3.18(c), the two lines are the same length, but the diagonals extending outward from both ends of the upper line make it look longer than the lower line, which has diagonals pointing inward, a phenomenon known as the *Müller-Lyer illusion*. The *Ponzo illusion* also plays an interesting trick on our estimation of size. Look at Figure 3.18(d) Contrary to your perceptions, bars A and B are the same length. Again, perceptions of size and distance, which we trust and which are normally accurate in informing us about the real world, can be wrong. If you saw two obstructions like the ones in the illusion on real railroad tracks, the one that looks larger would indeed be larger. So the Ponzo illusion is not a natural illusion but a contrived one. In fact, all these illusions are really misapplications of principles that nearly always work properly in normal everyday experience.

Cultural Differences in the Perception of Visual Illusions Because responses to a number of illusions are universal, many psychologists believe they are inborn. However, British psychologist R. L. Gregory believed that susceptibility to the Müller-Lyer and other such illusions is not innate. Rather, the culture in which people live is

■ **illusion**
A false perception or a misperception of an actual stimulus in the environment.

Some visual illusions seem to be culture-dependent. For example, Zulus and people from other cultures in which the houses lack straight sides and corners do not perceive the Müller-Lyer illusion.

responsible to some extent for the illusions they perceive. To test whether susceptibility to the Müller-Lyer and similar illusions is due to experience, Segall and others (1966) tested 1,848 adults and children from 15 different cultures in Africa, the Philippines, and the United States. Included were a group of Zulus from South Africa and a group of Illinois residents. The study revealed that "there were marked differences in illusion susceptibility across the cultural groups included in this study" (Segall, 1994, p. 137). People from all the cultures showed some tendency to perceive the Müller-Lyer illusion, indicating a biological component, but experience was clearly a factor. Zulus, who have round houses and see few corners of any kind, are not fooled by this illusion. Illinois residents saw the illusion readily, while the Zulu tribespeople tended not to see it.

Early cross-cultural researchers suggested that race might offer an explanation for the cultural differences in perceptions of illusions (Pollack, 1970). But an important study by Stewart (1973) in response to these claims provided evidence that it is fundamentally culture, not race, that drives perceptions of illusions. When two groups of schoolchildren from Illinois (60 African Americans and 60 Whites) were shown the Müller-Lyer and other illusions, no significant differences were found in susceptibility to the illusions. And in Zambia, researchers tested five different groups of Black African schoolchildren using the same illusions. Children's tendency to see the illusions had nothing to do with race but was strongly influenced by culture. Those children who lived in areas where buildings had angles, edges, corners, and doors were likely to be fooled by the illusions; those who lived in remote villages with primarily round houses were not.

In another classic cross-cultural study of illusions, Pedersen and Wheeler (1983) studied perceptions of the Müller-Lyer illusion among two groups of Navajos. The group who lived in rectangular houses and had experienced corners, angles, and edges tended to see the illusion. The members of the other group, like the Zulus, tended not to see it because their cultural experience consisted of round houses.

Remember It 3.7

1. Retinal disparity and convergence are two ____________ depth cues.
2. Match each example with the appropriate monocular depth cue.
   - ____ (1) one building partly blocking your view of another
   - ____ (2) railroad tracks converging in the distance
   - ____ (3) closer objects appearing to move faster than objects farther away
   - ____ (4) small objects appearing to be farther away

   a. motion parallax
   b. linear perspective
   c. interposition
   d. relative size
3. The apparent motion produced by several lights flashing off and on in sequence is known as the ____________.
4. The apparent motion produced by movements of the eyes is known as the ____________.
5. A(n) ____________ is a misinterpretation of a real stimulus.
6. Responses to many illusions are ____________, but perceptions of others are influenced by ____________.

ANSWERS: 1. binocular; 2. (1) c , (2) b, (3) a, (4) d; 3. phi phenomenon; 4. autokinetic illusion; 5. illusion; 6. universal, culture

Influences on Perception

How we perceive sensory information is often determined by factors—such as the Gestalt principle of perceptual organization—that vary little from individual to individual. But individual differences can influence perceptions as well. Consequently, many sensory experiences are interpreted differently by different people.

Prior Knowledge

How does prior knowledge influence perception?

The knowledge we possess about a given sensory stimulus influences how we perceive it. Prior knowledge sometimes enhances perception, but it can lead to errors as well.

Bottom-Up and Top-Down Processing Suppose you were presented with the coded message XBDID FXI XIL. How would you go about deciphering the words? You might conclude that each word uses X to represent a letter, so X must stand for one of the more common letters in English, such as R. You might then insert R in the position of X to see if you could come up with something that makes sense. Such a strategy would involve **bottom-up processing**. This approach begins with the individual components of a stimulus that are detected by the sensory receptors. The information is then transmitted to areas in the brain where it is combined and assembled into patterns. The brain then uses prior knowledge to make inferences about these patterns. For instance, what is the next number in the sequence 2, 7, 12, 17? Your brain infers the pattern $y = x + 5$ (where x is the number that immediately precedes y) from the sequence and proposes that the next number is 22.

What if you noticed that the second and third words in XBDID FXI XIL have two letters in common and are both three letters long and then compared them to real three-letter words in English that share two letters? Or what if you compared the code words to common three-word statements in English, substituting various words until the correct letter sequences and repetitions were found? In either of these approaches, you would be using **top-down processing**. In top-down processing, previous experience and conceptual knowledge are applied in order to recognize the nature of a "whole" and then logically deduce the individual components of that whole.

Of course, we use both bottom-up and top-down processing to form perceptions. And either approach, or a combination of the two, eventually leads to the conclusion that the words in the coded message are ROSES ARE RED.

Perceptual Set If you ordered raspberry sherbet and it was colored green, would it still taste like raspberry, or might it taste more like lime? Would you eagerly bite into a hamburger patty to which someone had added green food coloring, or would you be a bit more cautious? The **perceptual set**—what we expect to perceive—determines, to a large extent, what we actually see, hear, feel, taste, and smell. Such expectations are, of course, based on prior knowledge (that lime sherbert is usually green and green meat is usually spoiled). Such expectations do seem to influence perception. So, green raspberry sherbert might, indeed, taste a bit like lime, and a green hamburger might smell and taste spoiled.

In a classic study of perceptual set, psychologist David Rosenhan (1973) and some of his colleagues were admitted as patients to various mental hospitals with "diagnoses" of schizophrenia. Once admitted, they acted normal in every way. The purpose? They wondered how long it would take the doctors and the hospital staff to realize that they were not mentally ill. But the doctors and the staff members saw what they expected to see and not what actually occurred. They perceived everything the pseudo-patients said and did, such as note taking, to be symptoms of their illness. But the real patients were not fooled; they were the first to realize that the psychologists were not really mentally ill.

■ bottom-up processing
Information processing in which individual components of a stimulus are combined in the brain and prior knowledge is used to make inferences about these patterns.

■ top-down processing
Information processing in which previous experience and conceptual knowledge are applied in order to recognize the nature of a "whole" and then logically deduce the individual components of that whole.

■ perceptual set
An expectation of what will be perceived, which can affect what actually is perceived.

Attention

What is inattentional blindness?

"That car came out of nowhere!" is a thought most of us have had after a car crash or a narrow escape. What we experienced was probably a phenomenon researchers call **inattentional blindness** (Mack & Rock, 1998; Most et al., 2001). When our visual field contains many moving objects, as in city traffic, it's quite difficult to keep track of everything at once. Consequently, we shift our focus from one object to another and, in the process, fail to notice changed positions of objects to which we are not directly paying attention (Woodman & Luck, 2003). Remember, the edges of the retina are especially sensitive to motion, so we *sense* these changes. The failure is one of perception, not sensation. Such findings have important implications for tasks that require humans to monitor constantly changing objects. For example, pilots have to simultaneously keep track of dozens of instrument read-outs and objects (such as other aircraft, birds, and mountaintops) that share the skies with the planes they fly. Consequently, designers create airplane instrument panels that help minimize the effects of inattentional blindness on pilots' in-flight decision making (Carpenter, 2001).

In many studies examining inattentional blindness, experimenters present participants with a scene and ask them to attend to a particular element in it. For example, one researcher, Daniel Simons, and colleagues (e.g. Simons & Chabris, 1999) showed participants a videotape of a basketball game in which one team wore white uniforms and the other wore black. Participants were instructed to count how many times the ball was passed from one player to another, either on the white or on the black team. Under such conditions, about a third of participants typically failed to later recall the appearance on the screen of even extremely incongruent stimuli (for example, a woman carrying an open umbrella, a man dressed in a gorilla costume). The inattentional blindness happens even when the incongruous stimulus is present on the screen for a long period of time.

■ **inattentional blindness** The phenomenon in which we shift our focus from one object to another and, in the process, fail to notice changes in objects to which we are not directly paying attention.

Dividing concentration between two different sources of sensory information also leads to attentional failures. For example, do you think you are just as good a driver when you are talking on a cell phone as when you are not? Research by David Strayer and his colleagues (2003) showed that drivers (using a simulator, not actually driving a car) often failed to perceive vehicles braking directly in front of them while they were engaged in hands-free cell phone conversations. Moreover, participants engaged in cell-phone conversations were less able than control participants to recognize other

When you look at this photograph, you can easily notice the gorilla-costumed figure. However, this photo is actually a frame from a video used in Simons's inattentional blindness studies. Participants are shown the video after being told to keep track of how many times the basketball is passed from one person to another. Under these conditions, participants typically fail to notice when the gorilla-costumed figure enters the scene. You can view clips from Simons's videos at http://viscog.beckman.uiuc.edu/grafs/demos/15.shtml.

visual stimuli, such as billboards, that were present during driving simulations. Consequently, experts believe that it's best to pull off the road when you talk on a cell phone. And many communities are banning cell phone use by drivers.

Social Perception

Do we perceive physical objects and social stimuli in the same way?

Finally, do the rules of perceptual processing you've learned so far apply to social stimuli as well as physical objects? The traditional view holds that perceptual processes in the brain are organized according to the kind of process—vision, hearing, smell, taste, touch, or kinesthetic sense—needed to perceive a particular stimulus. Thus, looking at a face or a cat should elicit the same kind of response from the brain because both are visual stimuli. It is true that visual perception occurs primarily in the same parts of the brain, no matter what you are looking at. But brain-imaging studies show that patterns of neural activation within those areas vary according to the types of objects being viewed. For example, there is one pattern for faces and another for cats (Haxby et al., 2001).

Perception of human faces appears to be particularly complex and distinctive from perceptions of other kinds of visual stimuli. Researcher James Haxby and his colleagues suggest that there is a "core system" of face perception that uses the universal features of the human face (eyes, nose, and mouth) to make judgments about people's identities (Haxby et al., 2002). We move beyond the core system when we engage in verbal and nonverbal communication with others and, in so doing, activate a larger neural network. Other researchers have found equally distinctive neural systems for processing images of human body parts (Downing et al., 2001).

The way we combine information from two sensory modalities—a process known as *cross-modal perception*—also differs for nonsocial and social stimuli. For example, how would your brain respond to the sight of an approaching train paired with the sound of a departing train? Research indicates that, when judging motion based on conflicting visual and auditory cues, we tend to rely on the auditory input (Meyer & Wuerger, 2001). So, your brain would decide that the train was moving away rather than approaching.

In the case of social perception, the opposite is true. Facial expressions, the visual cues for emotional perceptions, often take priority over the auditory cues associated with a person's speech intonation and volume, as well as the actual words spoken. Thus, a person who exhibits an angry face but speaks in a happy voice will typically be judged to be angry rather than happy (Vroomen et al., 2001). Perhaps this is why one old song suggests that we "put on a happy face."

Remember It 3.8

1. When you approach a problem by using prior knowledge to analyze its components, you are using __________ processing.
2. When you approach a problem by using prior knowledge to make assumptions about the nature of the solution, you are using __________ processing.
3. __________ refers to what people expect to perceive.
4. When individuals focus on one of several moving objects in their visual field, they often exhibit __________.
5. When visual and auditory information are in conflict, individuals tend to rely on __________ sensations when processing social information.

ANSWERS: 1. bottom-up; 2. top-down; 3. Perceptual set; 4. inattentional blindness; 5. visual

Apply It

Noise and Hearing Loss

As you learned in this chapter, noise is probably the most common cause of hearing loss. But how does noise damage hearing? In one kind of damage, an explosion, gun blast, or other extremely loud noise bursts the eardrum or fractures or dislocates the tiny ossicles in the middle ear. Often these kinds of injuries can be repaired surgically, but noise injuries to the inner ear cannot.

How much noise does it take to damage hearing? In the United States, the Occupational Health and Safety Administration requires employers to provide workers with ear protection in work environments where sound levels regularly exceed 90 decibels (Noise Pollution Council, 2003). However, many experts believe that this standard is not restrictive enough to protect workers' hearing. Indeed, according to the Environmental Protection Agency, just 3 minutes of exposure to sounds above 100 decibels can cause permanent hearing loss (Noise Pollution Council, 2003). Moreover, there are many sources of excessive noise outside the workplace.

Noisy Toys

Experts warn that children who play with toy weapons may be at risk for temporary or permanent hearing loss. In an eye-opening classic study, researchers Axelsson and Jerson (1985) tested seven squeaking toys that, at a distance of 10 centimeters, emitted sound levels loud enough to put toddlers at risk for hearing loss at only 2 minutes of daily exposure. And these researchers' tests of various toy weapons found that all exceeded the 130-decibel peak level that is considered the upper limit for exposure

to brief explosive sounds if hearing loss is to be avoided.

Fireworks

Firecrackers and other popular fireworks items pose a significant hearing hazard if they explode close enough to the ear. In one study, a number of firecrackers were tested at 3 meters, and sound levels were found to range from 130 decibels to a highly dangerous 190 decibels (Gupta & Vishwakarma, 1989).

Amplified Music

Individuals who routinely crank up the volume on their CD players to full blast expose themselves to potentially damaging sounds every day, often with little or no awareness of the threat posed to hearing. And the decibel levels common at rock concerts can damage hearing very rapidly. For example, rock musician Kathy Peck lost 40% of her hearing in a single evening after her band opened a stadium concert. Moreover, in 1986, the rock group The Who entered the *Guiness Book of World Records* as the loudest rock band on record, blasting out deafening sound intensities that measured 120 decibels at a distance of 164 feet from the speakers. Unless their ears were protected, audience members within that 164-foot radius probably suffered some irreversible hearing loss. And the band members? Pete Townsend of The Who has severely damaged hearing and, in addition, is plagued by *tinnitus,* an annoying condition that causes him to experience continuous ringing in the ears.

Power Tools

Many types of power tools emit sufficient noise to damage hearing. Experts claim that exposure to a lawn mower, for example (a noise level of about 90 decibels), for more than 8 hours in a 24-hour period can damage hearing. For every increase of 5 decibels, maximum exposure time to the tool should be cut in half: 4 hours for 95 decibels, 2 hours for 100 decibels, and 1 hour for 105 decibels.

Protect Yourself from Hearing Loss

What you can do to protect yourself from the effects of noise?

- If you must be exposed to loud noise, use earplugs (not the kind used for swimming) or earmuffs to reduce noise, or put your fingers in your ears. Leave the scene as soon as possible.
- If you must engage in an extremely noisy activity, such as cutting wood with a chain saw, limit periods of exposure so that stunned hair cells can recover.
- Keep the volume down on your portable radio or CD player. If the volume control is numbered 1 to 10, a volume above 4 probably exceeds the federal standards for noise. If you have ringing or a tickling sensation in your ears after you remove your headset, or if sounds seem muffled, you could have sustained some hearing loss.

Summary *and* Review

The Process of Sensation p. 80

What is the difference between the absolute threshold and the difference threshold? p. 81

The absolute threshold is the minimum amount of sensory stimulation that can be detected 50% of the time. The difference threshold is a measure of the smallest increase or decrease in a physical stimulus that can be detected 50% of the time.

How does transduction enable the brain to receive sensory information? p. 82

For each of the senses, the body has sensory receptors that detect and respond to sensory stimuli. Through the process of transduction, the receptors change the sensory stimuli into neural impulses, which are then transmitted to precise locations in the brain.

Vision p. 83

How does each part of the eye function in vision? p. 84

The cornea bends light rays inward through the pupil—the small, dark opening in the eye. The iris dilates and contracts the pupil to regulate the amount of light entering the eye. The lens changes its shape as it focuses images of objects at varying distances on the retina, a thin layer of tissue that contains the sensory receptors for vision. The cones detect color and fine detail; they function best in adequate light. The rods are extremely sensitive and enable vision in dim light.

What path does visual information take from the retina to the primary visual cortex? p. 86

The rods and the cones transduce light waves into neural impulses that pass from the bipolar cells to the ganglion cells, whose axons form the optic nerve beyond the retinal wall of each eye. At the optic chiasm, the two optic nerves come together, and some of the nerve fibers from each eye cross to the opposite side of the brain. They synapse with neurons in the thalamus, which transmit the neural impulses to the primary visual cortex.

How do we detect the difference between one color and another? p. 87

The perception of color results from the reflection of particular wavelengths of the visual spectrum from the surfaces of objects. For example, an object that appears to be red reflects light of longer wavelengths than one that appears to be blue.

What two major theories attempt to explain color vision? p. 88

Two major theories that attempt to explain color vision are the trichromatic theory and the opponent-process theory.

Do individuals with color blindness see the world in black and white? p. 88

No, color blindness is the inability to distinguish certain colors from one another, rather than the total absence of color vision.

Hearing p. 90

What determines the pitch and loudness of a sound, and how is each quality measured? p. 90

The pitch of a sound is determined by the frequency of the sound waves, which is measured in hertz. The loudness of a sound is determined largely by the amplitude of the sound waves, which is measured in decibels.

How do the outer ear, middle ear, and inner ear function in hearing? p. 91

Sound waves enter the pinna, the visible part of the outer ear, and travel to the end of the auditory canal, causing the eardrum to vibrate. This sets in motion the ossicles in the middle ear, which amplify the sound waves. The vibration of the oval window causes activity in the inner ear, setting in motion the fluid in the cochlea. The moving fluid pushes and pulls the hair cells attached to the thin basilar membrane, which transduce the vibrations into neural impulses. The auditory nerve then carries the neural impulses to the brain.

What two major theories attempt to explain hearing? p. 92

Two major theories that attempt to explain hearing are place theory and frequency theory.

What are some of the major causes of hearing loss? p. 93

Some causes of hearing loss are excessive noise, disease, circumstances of birth, genetic defects, injury, and aging.

Smell and Taste p. 94

What path does a smell message take from the nose to the brain? p. 94

The act of smelling begins when odor molecules reach the smell receptors in the olfactory epithelium, at the top of the nasal cavity. The axons of these receptors relay the smell message to the olfactory bulbs. From there, the smell message travels to the thalamus and the orbitofrontal cortex, which distinguish the odor and relay that information to other parts of the brain.

What are the primary taste sensations, and how are they detected? p. 97

The primary taste sensations are sweet, salty, sour, and bitter, along with a newly discovered one for glutamate, called umami. The receptor cells for taste are found in the taste buds on the tongue and in other parts of the mouth and throat.

The Skin Senses p. 98

How does the skin provide sensory information? p. 99

Sensitive nerve endings in the skin convey tactile information to the brain when an object touches and depresses the skin. The neural impulses for touch sensations ultimately register in the brain's somatosensory cortex.

What is the function of pain, and how is pain influenced by psychological factors, culture, and endorphins? p. 99

Pain can be a valuable warning and a protective mechanism, motivating people to tend to an injury, to restrict activity, and to seek medical help. Negative thinking can influence the perception of pain. Some cultures encourage individuals to suppress (or exaggerate) emotional reactions to pain. Endorphins are natural painkillers produced by the body, which block pain and produce a feeling of well-being.

The Spatial Orientation Senses p. 101

What kinds of information do the kinesthetic and vestibular senses provide? p. 101

The kinesthetic sense provides information about the position of body parts in relation to one another and movement of the entire body or its parts. This information is detected by sensory receptors in the joints, ligaments, and muscles. The vestibular sense detects movement and provides information about the body's orientation in space. Sensory receptors in the semicircular canals and the vestibular sacs sense changes in motion and the orientation of the head.

Perception p. 103

What are the principles that govern perceptual organization? p. 103

The Gestalt principles of perceptual organization include figure-ground, similarity, proximity, continuity, and closure. Perceptual constancy is the tendency to perceive objects as maintaining the same size, shape, and brightness, despite changes in lighting conditions or changes in the retinal image that result when an object is viewed from different angles and distances.

What are some of the binocular and monocular depth cues? p. 104

The binocular depth cues include convergence and binocular disparity, which depend on both eyes working together for depth perception. The monocular depth cues, those that can be perceived by one eye, include interposition, linear perspective, relative size, texture gradient, atmospheric perspective, shadow or shading, and motion parallax.

How does the brain perceive real and apparent motion? *p. 106*

The brain perceives real motion by comparing the movement of images across the retina to information derived from the spatial orientation senses. Apparent motion is the result of a psychological response to specific kinds of stimuli, such as flashing lights. The brain may also mistakenly perceive eye movement as object movement.

What are three types of puzzling perceptions? *p. 108*

Three types of puzzling perceptions are ambiguous figures, impossible figures, and illusions.

Influences on Perception p. 111

How does prior knowledge influence perception? *p. 111*

Individuals use bottom-up and top-down processing to apply their prior knowledge to perceptual problems. Expectations based on prior knowledge may predispose people to perceive sensations in a particular way.

What is inattentional blindness? *p. 112*

Inattentional blindness occurs when we shift our focus from one object to another and, in the process, fail to notice changes in objects to which we are not directly paying attention.

Do we perceive physical objects and social stimuli in the same way? *p. 113*

Research suggests that the neural systems and rules for processing information about social stimuli are distinct from those for physical objects.

Key Terms

absolute threshold, p. 81
accommodation, p. 85
afterimage, p. 88
amplitude, p. 90
apparent motion, p. 106
audition, p. 91
autokinetic illusion, p. 108
binocular depth cues, p. 104
blind spot, p. 86
bottom-up processing, p. 111
brightness, p. 88
cochlea, p. 92
color blindness, p. 88
cones, p. 85
cornea, p. 84
decibel (dB), p. 90
depth perception, p. 104
difference threshold, p. 81
endorphins, p. 101
feature detectors, p. 87
fovea, p. 86
frequency, p. 90
frequency theory, p. 93
Gestalt, p. 103
gustation, p. 97
hair cells, p. 92
hue, p. 88
illusion, p. 109
inattentional blindness, p. 112
inner ear, p. 92
just noticeable difference (JND), p. 81
kinesthetic sense, p. 101
lens, p. 84
middle ear, p. 91
monocular depth cues, p. 105
olfaction, p. 94
olfactory bulbs, p. 95
olfactory epithelium, p. 94
opponent-process theory, p. 88
optic nerve, p. 86
outer ear, p. 91
perception, p. 80
perceptual constancy, p. 104
perceptual set, p. 111
pheromones, p. 96
phi phenomenon, p. 108
place theory, p. 92
primary visual cortex, p. 86
real motion, p. 106
retina, p. 85
rods, p. 85
saturation, p. 88
semicircular canals, p. 102
sensation, p. 80
sensory adaptation, p. 83
sensory receptors, p. 82
tactile, p. 99
taste buds, p. 97
timbre, p. 91
top-down processing, p. 111
transduction, p. 82
trichromatic theory, p. 88
vestibular sense, p. 102
visible spectrum, p. 83
Weber's law, p. 81

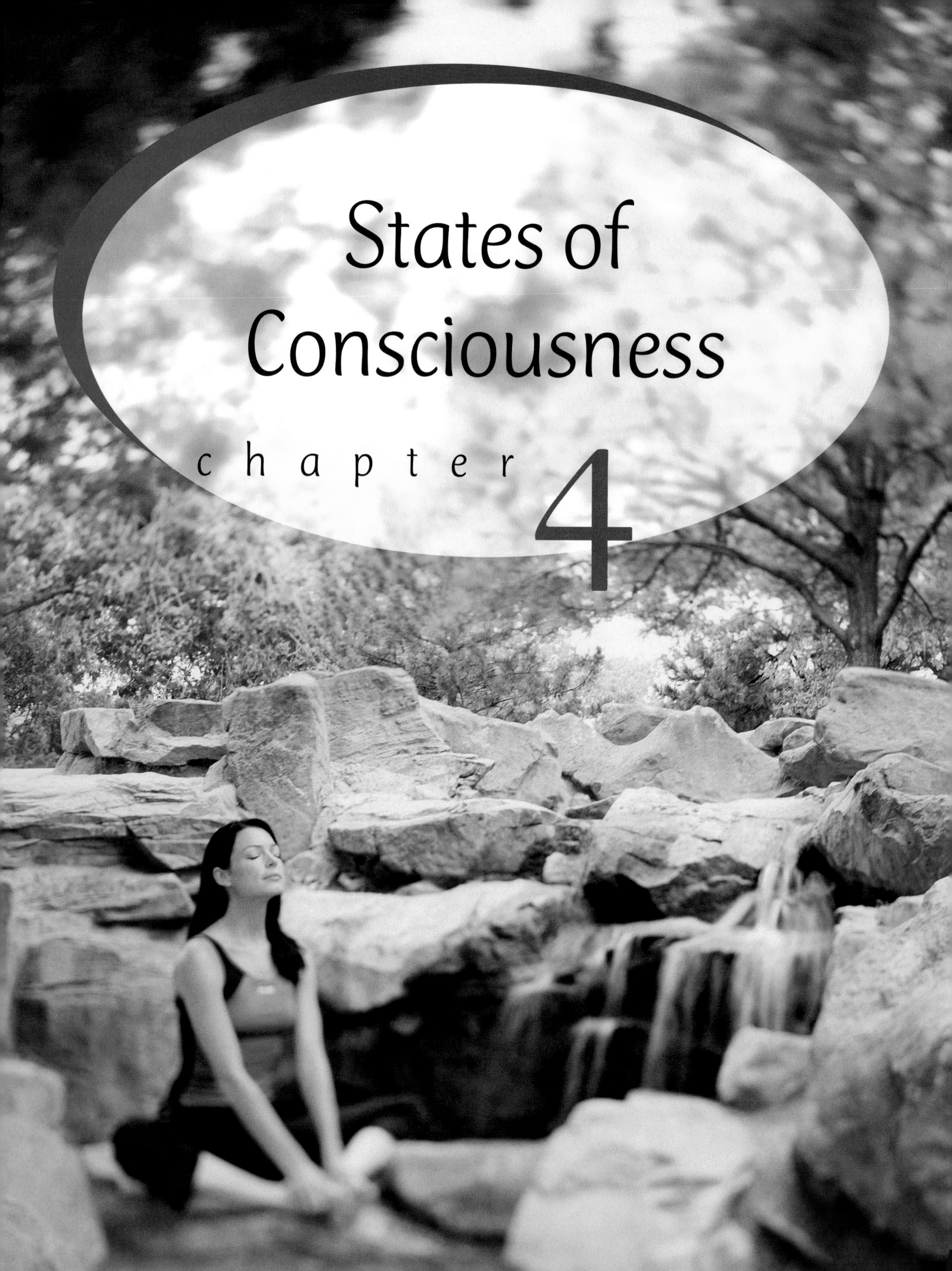

States of Consciousness

chapter 4

Explaining Consciousness

- *How have psychologists' views about consciousness changed since the early days of psychology?*

Circadian Rhythms

- *Which physiological and psychological functions are influenced by circadian rhythms?*
- *How do biological and environmental variables influence circadian rhythms?*
- *How can travelers combat the effects of jet lag?*
- *In what ways does the disruption of circadian rhythms affect shift workers?*
- *How can research linking circadian rhythms and neurological disorders be put to practical use?*

Sleep

- *How do NREM and REM sleep differ?*
- *What is the progression of NREM stages and REM sleep in a typical night of sleep?*
- *How do age and individual differences influence people's sleep patterns?*
- *What is the difference between the restorative and circadian theories of sleep?*
- *How does sleep deprivation affect behavior and neurological functioning?*
- *What have researchers learned about dreams, their content, their biological basis, and their controllability?*
- *How do the views of contemporary psychologists concerning the nature of dreams differ from those of Freud?*
- *What are the various disorders that can trouble sleepers?*

Meditation and Hypnosis

- *What are the benefits of meditation?*
- *What are the effects of hypnosis, and how do theorists explain them?*
- *What is the connection between altered states of consciousness and culture?*

Psychoactive Drugs

- *How do drugs affect the brain's neurotransmitter system?*
- *What are some risk and protective factors for substance abuse?*
- *What is the difference between physical and psychological drug dependence?*
- *What are the effects of stimulants, depressants, and hallucinogens on behavior?*
- *What are the pros and cons of using herbal remedies?*

Could a hypnotist "program" a morally upright person to become a cold-blooded killer?

Benjamin Franklin was a prominent figure in early American history, a scientist, author, and publisher. But did you know that he participated in the first scientific study of a technique for influencing consciousness called *hypnosis*? Franklin, who was the U.S. ambassador to France at the time of the study (in the early 1780s), chaired a committee of eminent scientists commissioned by the French government to assess the validity of the claims of a hypnotist named Anton Mesmer. Mesmer is generally credited with discovering the techniques for inducing hypnosis (or "mesmerism," as it was called then) that are still in use today. The findings of the Franklin Commission, published in 1784, suggested that hypnotism was a real phenomenon but that it was not capable of curing serious physical ailments, as Mesmer had often claimed (Franklin et al., 1784/2002). Other scientific examinations of too-fantastic-to-be-true claims about the power of hypnosis have yielded similar results, yet people continue to be fascinated with this phenomenon.

The frequency with which hypnotism appears as a theme in popular fiction bears witness to this fascination. One of the most powerful works of hypnosis-based fiction is the 1959 novel *The Manchurian Candidate,* written by Richard Condon. In this Cold War–era thriller, hypnosis is used to program the main character, Korean War soldier Raymond Shaw, to assassinate American political figures in response to a series of verbal and visual cues. Moreover, Shaw's fellow soldiers are programmed to say, in robot-like fashion, "Raymond Shaw is the kindest, bravest, warmest, most wonderful human being I've ever met in my life," whenever they are asked about him. The plot centers around the breakdown of the hypnosis-induced programming in one of the soldiers and his efforts to prevent Shaw from assassinating the President of the United States.

Stories like *The Manchurian Candidate* are interesting because most of us are intrigued by the idea that hypnosis can be used to make one individual's behavior conform to the will of another. But what do scientists say? Could there ever be a real-life Raymond Shaw? This and many other questions about consciousness will be answered in this chapter. But before we look more closely at altered states of consciousness, such as hypnosis, let's first consider exactly what consciousness is.

What Is Consciousness?

How have psychologists' views about consciousness changed since the early days of psychology?

What if, in the course of a middle-of-the-night phone call, your mother told you that your grandmother had had a stroke and had been in a coma for a short while, but then had regained consciousness? You would most likely understand your mother to mean that your grandmother was in a state of unawareness of her own and others' activities but then returned to a state of awareness, or wakefulness. One way of understanding the meaning of consciousness is to think of it in contrast to its opposite, unconsciousness. But, is that all there is to consciousness—simply being awake? What about when you arrive home from shopping but have no recollection of the drive from the mall to your home. Certainly, you were awake, so the reason you don't remember is *not* that you were unconscious. Thus, **consciousness** is defined as everything of which we are aware at any given time—our thoughts, feelings, sensations, and perceptions of the external environment.

The early psychologists held widely varying views of the nature of consciousness. William James likened consciousness to a flowing stream (the stream of consciousness) that sometimes is influenced by the will and sometimes is not. Sigmund Freud emphasized the notion that unconscious wishes, thoughts, and feelings are hidden from consciousness because they evoke too much anxiety. In contrast to both James and Freud, behaviorist John Watson urged psychologists to abandon the study of consciousness, claiming that it could not be studied scientifically. Because of the strong influence of behaviorism, especially in the United States, psychologists did not study consciousness for several decades (Nelson, 1996).

■ **consciousness**
Everything of which we are aware at any given time—our thoughts, feelings, sensations, and external environment.

In recent decades, though, psychological researchers have returned to the study of consciousness, in examining physiological rhythms, sleep, and **altered states of consciousness** (changes in awareness produced by sleep, meditation, hypnosis, and drugs). Modern brain-imagining techniques have allowed psychologists to accumulate a large body of evidence leading to a better understanding of the neurological basis of consciousness. Consequently, today's psychologists think about consciousness largely in neurobiological terms. In other words, psychologists tend to equate the subjective experience of consciousness with objective observations of what's actually happening in the brain during states such as sleep and hypnosis (Parvizi & Damasio, 2001).

■ **altered state of consciousness** Changes in awareness produced by sleep, meditation, hypnosis, and drugs.

Remember It 4.1

1. A synonym for consciousness is ___________.
2. Because of the influence of ___________, psychologists avoided the study of consciousness for several decades.
3. Today's psychologists focus on the ___________ aspects of consciousness.
4. Changes in awareness associated with sleep, meditation, hypnosis, and drugs are called ___________.

ANSWERS: 1. awareness; 2. behaviorism; 3. neurobiological; 4. altered states of consciousness

Circadian Rhythms

Do you notice changes in the way you feel throughout the day—fluctuations in your energy level, moods, or efficiency? Over 100 bodily functions and behaviors follow **circadian rhythms**—that is, they fluctuate regularly from a high to a low point over a 24-hour period (Dement, 1974).

The Influence of Circadian Rhythms

Which physiological and psychological functions are influenced by circadian rhythms?

Circadian rhythms play a critical role in the timing of life-sustaining processes in virtually all organisms, from humans and other vertebrates to plants, and even single-cell life forms (Kay, 1997). Physiological functions such as blood pressure, heart rate, appetite, secretion of hormones and digestive enzymes, sensory acuity, elimination, and even the body's response to medication all follow circadian rhythms (Hrushesky, 1994; Morofushi et al., 2001). Many psychological functions—including learning efficiency, the ability to perform a wide range of tasks, and even moods—ebb and flow according to these daily rhythms (Boivin et al., 1997; Johnson et al., 1992; Manly et al., 2002). Indeed, the circadian timing system is involved in the 24-hour variation of virtually every physiological and psychological variable researchers have studied (Kunz & Herrmann, 2000).

Two circadian rhythms of particular importance are the sleep/wakefulness cycle and the daily fluctuation in body temperature. Normal human body temperature ranges from a low of about 97–97.5°F between 3:00 and 4:00 a.m. to a high of about 98.6°F between 6:00 and 8:00 p.m. People sleep best when their body temperature is at its lowest, and they are most alert when their body temperature is at its daily high point. Alertness also follows a circadian rhythm, one that is quite separate from the sleep/wakefulness cycle (Monk, 1989). For most people, alertness decreases between 2:00 and 5:00 p.m. and between 2:00 and 7:00 a.m. (Webb, 1995).

■ **circadian rhythm** (sur-KAY-dee-un) Within each 24-hour period, the regular fluctuation from high to low points of certain bodily functions and behaviors.

The Suprachiasmatic Nucleus

How do biological and environmental variables influence circadian rhythms?

In their studies of circadian rhythms in mammals, researchers have found that the biological clock is the **suprachiasmatic nucleus (SCN),** located in the brain's hypothalamus (Ginty et al., 1993; Ralph, 1989; Ruby et al., 2002). The SCN, a pair of tiny brain structures, each about the size of a pinhead, controls the timing of circadian rhythms (Moore-Ede, 1993).

But the ebb and flow of circadian rhythms is not strictly biological. Environmental cues also play a part. The most significant environmental cue is bright light, particularly sunlight. Specialized cells (photoreceptors) in the retina at the back of each eye respond to the amount of light reaching the eye and relay this information via the optic nerve to the SCN. The SCN acts on this information by signaling the pineal gland, located in the center of the brain. In response, the pineal gland secretes the hormone *melatonin* from dusk to shortly before dawn but does not secrete it during daylight. Melatonin induces sleep, perhaps through its ability to lower the activity of neurons in the SCN (Barinaga, 1997).

■ suprachiasmatic nucleus (SCN) A pair of tiny structures in the brain's hypothalamus that control the timing of circadian rhythms; the biological clock.

Other types of cells may also respond to daily light-dark cycles. Researchers studying vertebrates less complex than humans have found that exposing some of the animals' bodily organs to light sets the "circadian clock" and maintains circadian rhythms. Even certain single cells from these vertebrates, when placed in cultures in the laboratory, respond directly to light-dark cycles (Abe et al., 2002; Whitmore et al., 2000).

So, circadian rhythms are clearly vital, and you may be wondering what happens when they are disrupted.

Jet Lag

How can travelers combat the effects of jet lag?

Suppose you fly from Chicago to London, and the plane lands at 12:00 a.m. Chicago time, about the time you usually go to sleep. At the same time that it is midnight in Chicago, it is 6:00 a.m. in London, almost time to get up. The clocks, the sun, and everything else in London tell you it is early morning, but you still feel like it is midnight. You are experiencing jet lag.

Jet lag is associated with a number of problems—mental illness, for example. Travelers whose psychiatric disorders are in remission are at risk of suffering relapses when they cross several time zones (Katz et al., 2002; Oyewumi, 1998). Also, chronic jet lag, such as that experienced by many airline pilots and flight attendants, produces memory deficits that may be permanent (Cho, 2001; Cho et al., 2000). You might think that airline employees who regularly fly across time zones would adjust to their schedules. However, research indicates that experienced airline workers are just as likely to suffer from jet lag as passengers on their first intercontinental flight (Criglington, 1998).

Research indicates that frequent flyers, such as these airline employees, are just as likely to suffer from jet lag when crossing several time zones as travelers who are on their first intercontinental journey.

Fortunately, supplemental melatonin has been shown to be an effective treatment for relapses of psychiatric disorders induced by jet lag (Katz et al., 1999; Katz et al., 2001). Melatonin has also been found to be helpful for alleviating jet lag in some long-distance travelers. For others, exposure to bright sunlight during the early morning hours and avoidance of bright lights during the evening may be more effective than melatonin for restoring circadian rhythms (Edwards et al., 2000; Zisapel, 2001).

Shift Work

In what ways does the disruption of circadian rhythms affect shift workers?

What about the circadian rhythms of shift workers, people who work during the night and sleep all day? On average, shift workers get 2 to 4 hours less sleep than do nonshift workers of the same age (Campbell, 1995). Moreover, alertness and performance deteriorate if people work during **subjective night,** when their biological clock is telling them to go to sleep (Åkerstedt, 1990; Folkard, 1990). During subjective night, energy and efficiency are at their lowest points, reaction time is slowest, productivity is diminished, and industrial accidents are significantly higher. For example, in one study, more than 17% of a group of commercial long-haul truck drivers admitted to having experienced "near misses" while dozing off behind the wheel (Häkkänen & Summala, 1999). Even the slight circadian disruption due to the 1-hour sleep loss when people put their clocks forward in spring for daylight saving time is associated with an increase in traffic accidents and a short-term but significant 6.5% increase in accidental deaths (Coren, 1996a, 1996b).

When people must work at night, the normal daily rhythms of many of their bodily functions are disrupted. These disruptions in circadian rhythms can cause a variety of physical and psychological problems. Shift workers have more gastrointestinal and cardiovascular problems, use more prescription drugs, experience higher levels of personal and family stress and more mood problems, and have higher divorce rates (Campbell, 1995; Garbarino et al., 2002; Moore-Ede, 1993).

Some shift workers even have to adjust to shifts that change regularly. What can be done to make such shift rotation less disruptive? Moving work schedules forward from days to evenings to nights makes adjustment easier because people find it easier to go to bed later and wake up later than the reverse. And rotating shifts every three weeks instead of every week lessens the effect on sleep even more (Pilcher et al., 2000). Some researchers have even suggested scheduling brief nap periods during shifts to help sleepy workers adjust to rotating shifts (Goh et al., 2000). Others are investigating the use of a new wakefulness drug called *modafinil* that helps people remain alert without the side effects of stimulants such as caffeine (Wesensten et al., 2002)

■ **subjective night**
The time during a 24-hour period when the biological clock is telling a person to go to sleep.

Interestingly, shift workers who temporarily reside at their workplaces, such as offshore oil rigs, appear to adjust more easily to the demands of night work than do those who live at home (Parkes, 2002). Researchers attribute this finding to, among other factors, reduced social demands. Essentially, shift workers in such settings are expected only to work. By contrast, shift workers who live at home experience more stress because they must function in a social world that revolves around their families' daytime schedules. For example, at the time when shift workers with children are arriving home and needing to sleep, the children are just getting up and are probably eager to spend time with them. So, helping shift workers' families understand the need for adjustments in the social environment may also help reduce the workers' stress.

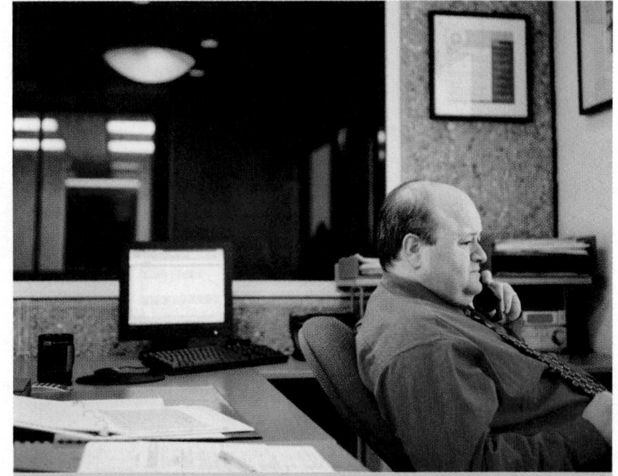

People who work at night experience disruptions in their circadian rhythms that can cause physical and psychological problems.

Light exposure is another important factor affecting adjustment to shift work. In simulated night-shift schedules, exposure to appropriately timed bright light or even light of medium intensity has been found to reset young adults' biological clocks and improve their performance (Campbell & Murphy, 1998; Martin & Eastman, 1998). Some researchers have used a device called a "light mask" to reset shift workers' biological clocks. This mask allows researchers to control the amount of light to which the closed eyelids of research participants are exposed. The findings of light mask studies suggest that exposing participants to bright light during the last 4 hours of sleep is an effective treatment for the kinds of sleep-phase delays experienced by shift workers (Cole et al., 2002). Thus, this device may become important in the treatment of sleep disorders associated with shift work.

Circadian Timing and Neurological Disorders

How can research linking circadian rhythms and neurological disorders be put to practical use?

Given the neurological basis of circadian rhythms, do you think there might be any link between these rhythms and brain injuries, neurological diseases, or psychiatric disorders? Consider the case of V.D., a 54-year-old man who sustained a head injury after falling off a scaffold (Florida Institute for Neurologic Rehabilitation, Inc., 2002). One of the many trauma-related symptoms V.D. has is difficulty in both falling asleep and waking up. Such problems are common in head-injury patients (Thaxton & Myers, 2002), perhaps because such injuries, as well as a number of neurological diseases and psychiatric disorders, are associated with disturbances in circadian functioning (Kashihara et al., 1999; Kirveskari et al. 2001; Kropyvnytskyy et al., 2001). Consequently, like many shift workers, many head-injury patients suffer from disturbed sleep-wakefulness cycles. Experts suggest that these sleep-wakefulness problems are a major source of stress for patients and should be treated with the same methods used to reset the circadian clocks of shift workers.

Research examining the link between circadian rhythms and neurological disorders may lead to new ways of diagnosing Alzheimer's disease. Abnormal circadian rhythms are common in Alzheimer's patients (Harper et al., 2001; Volicer et al., 2001). But individuals with non-Alzheimer's types of dementia do not exhibit circadian disturbances. Thus, researchers believe that tracking patients' daily variations in body temperature and other circadian variables (e.g., heart rate) may provide a fairly simple way of distinguishing those with Alzheimer's from those with other types of dementia (Cromie, 2001). The distinction is an important one because different kinds of dementia respond to different kinds of treatment. And one study of autopsies performed on individuals suspected of having Alzheimer's disease found that almost a third did not have the disease, suggesting that current methods of diagnosis are inadequate (Cromie, 2001).

Understanding disturbances in circadian timing may also be important in helping caregivers manage Alzheimer's patients. One consequence of the atypical circadian rhythms exhibited by Alzheimer's sufferers is a phenomenon called *sundowning*, a tendency to exhibit more symptoms of the disease in the afternoon and nighttime hours (Volicer et al., 2001). Caring for an Alzheimer's patient who exhibits sundowning causes many caregivers to develop their own sleep disturbances. Thus, researchers hope to learn how to modify these patterns for the benefit of both Alzheimer's patients and their caregivers.

Remember It 4.2

1. The two circadian rhythms of particular importance are the sleep/wakefulness cycle and the daily fluctuation in ________.
2. People sleep best when their body temperature is at its ________ point in the 24-hour cycle.
3. The structure that serves as the body's biological clock is the ________.
4. Exposure to ________ helps many travelers overcome the effects of jet lag.
5. Alertness and performance deteriorate when people work during ________.
6. ________ is a hormone that is believed to regulate the biological clock.

ANSWERS 1. body temperature; 2. lowest; 3. suprachiasmatic nucleus (SCN); 4. bright light; 5. subjective night; 6. Melatonin

Sleep

As noted earlier, the sleep/wakefulness cycle is a circadian rhythm. But what actually happens during our periods of sleep? Before the 1950s, there was little understanding of what goes on during the state of consciousness known as sleep. Then, in the 1950s, several universities set up sleep laboratories where people's brain waves, eye movements, chin-muscle tension, heart rate, and respiration rate were monitored through a night of sleep. From analyses of sleep recordings, known as *polysomnograms*, researchers discovered the characteristics of two major types of sleep.

■ **NREM sleep**
Non–rapid eye movement sleep, which consists of four sleep stages and is characterized by slow, regular respiration and heart rate, little body movement, an absence of rapid eye movements, and blood pressure and brain activity that are at their 24-hour low points.

NREM and REM Sleep

The two major types of sleep are NREM (non–rapid eye movement) sleep and REM (rapid eye movement) sleep.

How do NREM and REM sleep differ?

NREM Sleep **NREM** (pronounced "NON-rem") **sleep** is sleep in which there are no rapid eye movements. Heart rate and respiration are slow and regular, there is little body movement, and blood pressure and brain activity are at their lowest points of the 24-hour period. There are four stages of NREM sleep—Stages 1, 2, 3, and 4—with Stage 1 being the lightest sleep and Stage 4 being the deepest. Sleepers pass gradually rather than abruptly from one stage to the next. Each stage can be identified by its brain-wave pattern, as shown in Figure 4.1. Growth hormone is secreted primarily in Stage 3 and Stage 4 sleep (Gronfier et al., 1996; Van Cauter, 2000); this timing is significant because older people get little of this slow-wave sleep and thus may be deficient in this important hormone.

REM Sleep Most of us envision sleep as a time of deep relaxation and calm. But **REM sleep,** sometimes called "active sleep," is anything but calm, and it constitutes 20–25% of a normal night's sleep in adults. During the REM state, there is intense brain activity. In fact, within 1 to 2 minutes after REM sleep begins, brain metabolism increases, and brain temperature rises rapidly (Krueger & Takahashi, 1997). Epinephrine is released

■ **REM sleep**
A type of sleep characterized by rapid eye movements, paralysis of large muscles, fast and irregular heart and respiration rates, increased brain-wave activity, and vivid dreams.

FIGURE 4.1 **Brain-Wave Patterns Associated with Different Stages of Sleep**

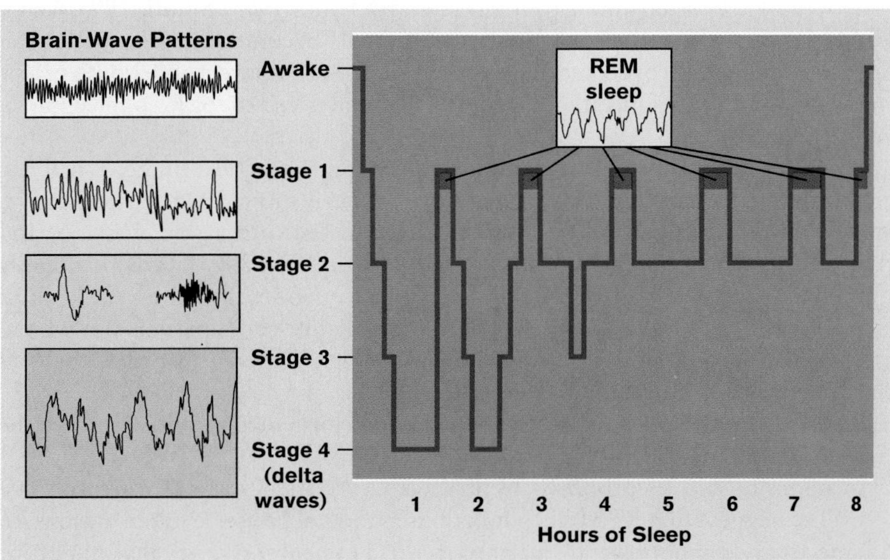

By monitoring brain-wave activity on an EEG throughout a night's sleep, researchers have identified the brain-wave patterns associated with different stages of sleep. As sleepers progress through the four NREM stages, the brain-wave pattern changes from faster, smaller waves in Stages 1 and 2 to the slower, larger delta waves in Stages 3 and 4.

into the system, causing blood pressure to rise and heart rate and respiration to become faster and less regular. Ulcer patients may secrete 3 to 20 times as much stomach acid as during the day and may awaken with stomach pains (Webb, 1975). In contrast to this storm of internal activity, there is an external calm during REM sleep. The large muscles of the body—arms, legs, trunk—become paralyzed (Chase & Morales, 1990). Some researchers suggest that this paralysis prevents people from acting out their dreams. But there is a rare condition known as *REM sleep behavior disorder*, in which individuals are not paralyzed during REM sleep. Consequently, they may become violent, causing injury to themselves and their bed partners and damage to their homes (Broughton & Shimizu, 1995; Moldofsky et al., 1995).

Observe a sleeper during the REM state, and you will see her or his eyes darting around under the eyelids. Eugene Azerinsky first discovered these bursts of rapid eye movements in 1952, and William Dement and Nathaniel Kleitman (1957) made the connection between rapid eye movements and dreaming. It is during REM sleep that the most vivid dreams occur. When awakened from REM sleep, 80% of people report that they had been dreaming (Carskadon & Dement, 1989). And, if you awaken during REM sleep and remain awake for several minutes, you may not go back into REM sleep for at least 30 minutes. This is why most people have had the disappointing experience of waking in the middle of a wonderful dream and trying to get back to sleep quickly and into the dream again, but failing to do so.

Nocturnal Erection Almost from birth, regardless of the content of their dreams, males have a full or partial erection during REM sleep, and females experience vaginal swelling and lubrication. Because sleepers are more likely to awaken naturally at the end of a period of REM sleep than during NREM sleep, men usually wake up with an erection (Campbell, 1985). In males suffering from impotence, the presence of an erection during REM sleep, even occasionally, indicates that the impotence is psychological; the consistent absence of an erection indicates that the impotence is likely to be physiological in origin.

The Function of REM Sleep You may have already found out through personal experience that studying all night before a big exam can cause you to yawn frequently and nod off when you take the actual test. But did you know that you can also short-circuit the learning process by engaging in this popular, though ineffective, method of exam preparation? Researchers say that REM sleep aids in information processing, helping people sift through daily experiences in order to organize and store in memory information that is relevant to them. Animal studies provide strong evidence for a relationship between REM sleep and learning (Hennevin et al., 1995; Smith, 1995; Winson, 1990). However, research also suggests that animals become tolerant of REM sleep deprivation after 4 days or so and return to pre-deprivation levels of learning performance (Kennedy, 2002). Thus, the final verdict on the necessity of REM sleep for efficient learning has yet to be reached.

In humans, researchers have found that sleep may be critical to the consolidation of memories after learning. Several experiments have shown that participants' performance on previously acquired motor and verbal tasks improves after a period of normal sleep (Fenn et al., 2003; Nader, 2003; Walker et al., 2003). Other studies have suggested that the brain carries out the important function of memory consolidation during REM sleep. Karni and others (1994) found that research participants who were learning a new perceptual skill showed an improvement in performance, with no additional practice, 8 to 10 hours later if they had a normal night's sleep or if the researchers disturbed only their NREM sleep. Performance did not improve, however, in those who were deprived of REM sleep.

An opposite view is proposed by Francis Crick and Graeme Mitchison (1983, 1995). They suggest that REM sleep functions as mental housecleaning, erasing trivial and unnecessary memories and clearing overloaded neural circuits that might interfere with memory and rational thinking. In other words, they say, people dream in order to forget.

There is no doubt that REM sleep serves an important function, even if psychologists do not know precisely what that function is. The fact that newborns show such a high percentage of REM sleep has led to the conclusion that this type of sleep is necessary for maturation of the brain during infancy (Marks et al., 1995). Furthermore, when people are deprived of REM sleep as a result of general sleep loss or illness, they will make up for the deprivation by getting an increased amount of REM sleep afterward, a phenomenon called **REM rebound.** Because the intensity of REM sleep is increased during a REM rebound, nightmares often occur. Alcohol, amphetamines, cocaine, and LSD suppress REM sleep, and withdrawal from these drugs results in a REM rebound (Porte & Hobson, 1996).

■ **REM rebound**
The increased amount of REM sleep that occurs after REM deprivation; often associated with unpleasant dreams or nightmares.

■ **sleep cycle**
A period of sleep lasting about 90 minutes and including one or more stages of NREM sleep, followed by REM sleep.

Sleep Cycles

What is the progression of NREM stages and REM sleep in a typical night of sleep?

You may be surprised to learn that sleep follows a fairly predictable pattern each night. We all sleep in cycles. During each **sleep cycle,** which lasts about 90 minutes, a person has one or more stages of NREM sleep, followed by a period of REM sleep. Let's look closely at a typical night of sleep for a young adult.

The first sleep cycle begins with a few minutes in Stage 1 sleep, sometimes called "light sleep." Stage 1 is actually a transition stage between waking and sleeping. Then sleepers descend into Stage 2 sleep, in which they are somewhat more deeply asleep and harder to awaken. (About 50% of a total night's sleep is spent in Stage 2 sleep.) As sleep gradually becomes deeper, brain activity slows, and more **delta waves** (slow waves) appear in the electroencephalogram (EEG). When the EEG registers 20% delta waves, sleepers enter Stage 3 sleep, the beginning of **slow-wave sleep** (or deep sleep). Delta waves continue to increase, and when they reach more than 50%, people enter **Stage 4 sleep**—the deepest sleep, from which they are hardest to awaken (Carskadon & Rechtschaffen, 1989; Cooper, 1994). Perhaps you have taken an afternoon nap and woke up confused, not knowing whether it was morning or night, a weekday or a weekend. If so, you probably awakened during Stage 4 sleep.

In Stage 4 sleep, delta waves may reach nearly 100% on the EEG, but after about 40 minutes in this stage, brain activity increases and the delta waves begin to disappear. Sleepers ascend back through Stage 3 and Stage 2 sleep, then enter their first REM period, which lasts 10 or 15 minutes. At the end of this REM period, the first sleep cycle is complete, and the second sleep cycle begins. Unless people awaken after the first sleep cycle, they go directly from REM into Stage 2 sleep. They then follow the same progression as in the first sleep cycle, through Stages 3 and 4 and back again into REM sleep.

After the first two sleep cycles of about 90 minutes each (3 hours total), the sleep pattern changes, and sleepers usually get no more Stage 4 sleep. From this point on, during each 90-minute sleep cycle, people alternate mainly between Stage 2 and REM sleep for the remainder of the night. With each sleep cycle, the REM period (and therefore dreaming time) get progressively longer. The last REM period of the night may last 30 to 40 minutes. Most people have about five sleep cycles (7 to 8 hours) and average 1 to 2 hours of slow-wave sleep and 1 to 2 hours of REM sleep. Figure 4.1 shows the progression through NREM and REM sleep during a typical night.

■ **delta wave**
The slowest brain-wave pattern; associated with Stage 3 and Stage 4 NREM sleep.

■ **slow-wave sleep**
Deep sleep; associated with Stage 3 and Stage 4 sleep.

■ **Stage 4 sleep**
The deepest stage of NREM sleep, characterized by an EEG pattern of more than 50% delta waves.

Variations in Sleep

How do age and individual differences influence people's sleep patterns?

Have you ever compared notes with a friend about how much sleep it takes to make you feel alert and rested the next day? If so, you have probably noticed that the amount of sleep people get varies a lot from one person to another. But how much sleep do we need? Many of us have heard that 8 hours of sleep are required for optimal health. Research suggests that this is not true. In a longitudinal study begun in 1982, more than a million Americans were asked about their sleep habits. Twenty years later, people who reported sleeping 6 or fewer hours per night, along with those who slept more than 8, showed somewhat higher death rates than adults who slept about 7 hours each night (Kripke et al., 2002).

Do such findings mean that we should all strive to sleep exactly 7 hours each night? Not at all, because these findings are correlational. We cannot infer from them that differences in amount of sleep cause differences in death rates. People who have diseases that result in early death may sleep less because of their symptoms or because of anxiety about their health status. Moreover, such studies deal with averages. There is considerable individual variation in the amount of sleep people need, and, for each individual, a certain amount of sleep may be sufficient at one point in life but insufficient at another. A few major factors influence how much sleep we need.

Sleep Changes over the Life Span Which age group sleeps the greatest number of hours per day? Most people think it's teenagers. But it is actually infants and young children who have the longest sleep time and the highest percentages of REM and slow-wave sleep. However, infants and children also have more erratic sleep patterns than individuals in other age groups. By contrast, children from age 6 to puberty are the most consistent sleepers and wakers. They fall asleep easily, sleep soundly for 8 to 9 hours at night, and feel awake and alert during the day. Moreover, they tend to fall asleep and wake up at about the same time every day. Contrary to popular belief, teenagers average just 7.2 hours of sleep a night (Carskadon et al., 1997).

As people age, the quality and quantity of sleep usually decrease (Reyner & Horne, 1995). In one large study of 9,000 participants aged 65 and over, only 12% reported no sleep problems (Foley et al., 1995). Older adults have more difficulty falling asleep than younger people do and typically sleep more lightly. Moreover, they spend more time in bed but less time asleep, averaging about 6 hours of sleep a night (Prinz et al., 1990). However, while slow-wave sleep decreases substantially from age 30 to age 50 (Mourtazaev et al., 1995; Van Cauter, 2000), the percentage of REM sleep stays about the same (Moran & Stoudemire, 1992).

Larks and Owls Are you a lark or an owl? Larks (early risers) awaken early every morning and leap out of bed with enthusiasm, eager to start the day. Owls (night people) fumble for the alarm clock and push a snooze button to get a few more precious minutes of sleep. Larks find it hard to keep from yawning after 10:00 p.m. and have an overwhelming urge to get to bed. But this is precisely the time when the owls come to life.

As you might suspect, differences between larks and owls are due to variations in circadian rhythms. About 25% of people are larks, people whose body temperature rises rapidly after they awaken and stays high until about 7:30 p.m. Larks turn in early and have the fewest sleep problems. Then there are the 25% of people who are owls and the 50% who are somewhere in between. The body temperature of an owl gradually rises throughout the day, peaking in the afternoon and not dropping until later in the evening.

How much sleep does the average person need? The need for sleep varies across individuals, but this person is obviously not getting enough!

Guthrie and others (1995) compared the performance of several hundred college students who had been classified as either larks or owls. They found that the larks made better grades in early morning classes, while the owls made higher grades in classes they took later in the day. One of the genes that run the biological clock is responsible, in part, for the differences between larks and owls (Katzenberg et al., 1998). To find out which you are, complete *Try It 4.1*.

What accounts for such differences? Genetics appears to play a part. Identical twins, for example, have

Try It 4.1 Lark or Owl?

Answer the following questions and score each choice as 1 point, 3 points, or 5 points, as indicated in parentheses.

1. On days when I can get up when I choose, I am usually up:
   ____ Before 7 a.m. (1)
   ____ Between 7 and 9 a.m. (3)
   ____ After 9 a.m. (5)
2. For me, getting out of bed on school or work days is:
   ____ Fairly easy (1)
   ____ Sometimes difficult (3)
   ____ Very difficult (5)
3. When I get up in the morning, I usually feel:
   ____ Alert/fresh (1)
   ____ It varies (3)
   ____ Sleepy/tired (5)
4. If I could go to bed whenever I chose, it would probably be:
   ____ By 10:30 p.m. (1)
   ____ Between 10:30 p.m. and midnight (3)
   ____ After midnight (5)
5. About an hour or two before going to bed on school days, I usually feel:
   ____ Very tired/sleepy (1)
   ____ Moderately tired (3)
   ____ Not very tired (5)

Add all your points together: ______________

Total score

5–10 Chirp! You are a lark. Be sure to take some photos of those beautiful sunrises for the rest of us—just don't wake us up to see them.

11–19 Ahh, mediocrity. You are neither a lark nor an owl, but don't worry . . . 50% of the population is right there with you.

20–25 Congratulations—you and your fellow owls keep the late-night talk shows on the air.

strikingly similar sleep patterns, while those of fraternal twins tend to differ (Webb & Campbell, 1983). Researchers have even bred laboratory animals to be short or long sleepers. Still, there is no doubt that, whatever our preferred sleep pattern, we don't perform as well when we are deprived of sleep. Clearly, then, sleep serves an important psychological and physiological function.

Explaining the Function of Sleep

What is the difference between the restorative and circadian theories of sleep?

Are you one of those people who regards sleep as a waste of time—especially when you have a term paper due the next day? (Of course, you wouldn't be facing a sleepless night if you hadn't procrastinated about the paper in the first place!) In fact, consistent sleep habits are probably important to getting good grades. Why?

Two complementary theories have been advanced to explain why we need to sleep. Taken together, they provide us with a useful explanation. One, the **restorative theory of sleep**, holds that being awake produces wear and tear on the body and the brain, while sleep serves the function of restoring body and mind (Gökcebay et al., 1994). There is now convincing evidence for this theory: The functions of sleep do include the restoration of energy and the consolidation of memory (Kunz & Herrmann, 2000). The second explanation, the **circadian theory of sleep,** sometimes called the *evolutionary theory*, is based on the premise that sleep evolved to keep humans out of harm's way during the dark of night, possibly from becoming prey for some nocturnal predator.

Alexander Borbely (1984; Borbely et al., 1989) explains how a synthesis of the circadian and restorative theories can be used to explain the function of sleep. That people feel sleepy at certain times of day is consistent with the circadian theory. And that sleepiness increases the longer a person is awake is consistent with the restorative theory. In

■ **restorative theory of sleep** The theory that the function of sleep is to restore body and mind.

■ **circadian theory of sleep** The theory that sleep evolved to keep humans out of harm's way during the night; also known as the evolutionary theory.

other words, the urge to sleep is partly a function of how long a person has been awake and partly a function of the time of day (Webb, 1995).

Sleep Deprivation

How does sleep deprivation affect behavior and neurological functioning?

What is the longest you have ever stayed awake—about 48 hours? According to the *Guinness Book of World Records*, Robert McDonald stayed awake 453 hours and 40 minutes (almost 19 days) in a 1986 rocking-chair marathon. Unlike McDonald, most people have missed no more than a few consecutive nights of sleep, perhaps studying for final exams. If you have ever missed two or three nights of sleep, you may remember having had difficulty concentrating, lapses in attention, and general irritability. Research indicates that even the rather small amount of sleep deprivation associated with delaying your bedtime on weekends leads to decreases in cognitive performance and increases in negative mood on Monday morning (Yang & Spielman, 2001). Thus, the familiar phenomenon of the "Monday morning blues" may be the result of staying up late on Friday and Saturday nights.

After 60 hours without sleep, cognitive performance declines substantially. Some people deprived of this much sleep even have minor hallucinations. Most people who try to stay awake for long periods of time will experience **microsleeps,** 2- to 3-second lapses from wakefulness into sleep. You may have experienced a microsleep if you have ever caught yourself nodding off for a few seconds in class or on a long automobile trip. Note that if you do become sleepy while driving, you should not rely on a blast of cold air or higher volume on your radio to keep you awake for more than about 30 minutes (Reyner & Horne, 1998).

A meta-analysis using data from more than 1,900 subjects indicated that sleep deprivation seriously impairs human functioning (Pilcher & Huffcutt, 1996). It negatively impacts mood, alertness, and performance and reduces the body's ability to warm itself, even at relatively comfortable temperatures (Bonnet & Arand, 1995; Landis et al., 1998). And partial sleep loss, even for one night, can significantly reduce the effectiveness of the human immune system. After one full night of sleep, however, the immune function appears to return to normal (Irwin et al., 1994).

Sleep Deprivation and the Brain How does a lack of sleep affect the brain? Researchers have known for some time that sleep deprivation impairs a variety of cognitive functions, such as the retrieval of recently learned information from memory, in both children and adults (Harrison & Horne, 2000; Raz et al., 2001; Sadeh et al., 2003). But the specific brain areas that are most (and least) active when sleep-deprived and non–sleep-deprived individuals perform cognitive tasks remained unidentified until recently.

Drummond and others (2000) used brain-imaging techniques to map the patterns of brain activity during a verbal learning task in two groups of participants: those in an experimental group who were deprived of sleep for about 35 hours, and those in a control group who slept normally. In the control group, the prefrontal cortex was highly active, as were the temporal lobes. As expected, on average, these rested participants scored significantly higher on the learning task than did their sleep-deprived counterparts. Surprisingly, however, areas of the prefrontal cortex were even more active in the sleep-deprived participants than in those who slept normally. Moreover, the temporal lobes that were so active in the rested group were almost totally inactive in the sleep-deprived group. The parietal lobes of the latter group became highly active, however, as if to compensate for their sleep-deprived condition. And, the more active the parietal lobes, the higher a sleep-deprived participant scored on the learning task.

This study, the first to use brain-imaging techniques to examine the effects of sleep deprivation on verbal learning, indicates that the cognitive functions used in such learning are significantly impaired by sleep deprivation. It also shows that there are

■ microsleep
A brief lapse (2 to 3 seconds long) from wakefulness into sleep, usually occurring when a person has been sleep-deprived.

compensatory mechanisms in the parietal lobes that can reduce this impairment to some degree (Drummond et al., 2000).

Dreams

What have researchers learned about dreams, their content, their biological basis, and their controllability?

What does a young woman mean when she says, "I met the guy of my dreams last night?" Or how about a telemarketer who promises you a "dream vacation" in exchange for listening to a sales pitch? Most of the time, we think of dreaming as a pleasant, imaginative experience. But when a fellow student exclaims, "That exam was a nightmare!" he or she means, of course, that the exam was somewhat less than pleasant, like a frightening dream. Good or bad, just exactly what is a dream?

The vivid dreams people remember and talk about are usually **REM dreams,** the type that occur almost continuously during each REM period. But people also have **NREM dreams,** which occur during NREM sleep, although these are typically less frequent and less memorable than REM dreams (Foulkes, 1996). REM dreams have a storylike or dreamlike quality and are more visual, vivid, and emotional than NREM dreams (Hobson, 1989). Blind people who lose their sight before age 5 usually do not have visual dreams, although they do have vivid dreams involving the other senses.

The Content of Dreams What do people dream about? Griffith and others (1958) asked 250 college students about the themes of their dreams. The most common themes, reported by 70% or more of the sample, were falling, being attacked or chased, trying repeatedly to do something, and studying. How many of these have you dreamed about?

Because dreams are notoriously hard to remember, the features that stand out tend to be those that are bizarre or emotional. Indeed, individuals who suffer from delusional disorders, such as schizophrenia, report more bizarre dreams than do individuals without such disorders (Watson, 2001). But researchers don't know whether the dreams of people with these mental illnesses really are more bizarre or if their disorders cause them to focus more on the dreams' bizarre qualities.

REM Sleep, Dreaming, and the Brain Brain-imaging studies suggest that the general perception that events in REM dreams are stranger and more emotion-provoking than waking experiences is probably true. The areas of the brain responsible for emotions, as well as the primary visual cortex, are active during REM dreams (Braun et al., 1998). By contrast, the prefrontal cortex, the more rational part of the brain, is suppressed during REM sleep, suggesting that the bizarre events that happen in REM dreams result from the inability of the brain to structure perceptions logically during that type of sleep. Areas associated with memory are also suppressed during REM sleep, which may explain why REM dreams are difficult to remember.

Furthermore, different neurotransmitters are dominant in the cortex during wakefulness and during REM sleep (Gottesmann, 2000). When we are awake, powerful inhibiting influences exert control over the functioning of the cortex, keeping us anchored to reality, less subject to impulsive thoughts and acts, and more or less "sane." These inhibiting influences are maintained principally by cortical neurons that are responding to serotonin and norepinephrine. These neurotransmitters are far less plentiful during REM dreaming, when a higher level of dopamine causes other cortical neurons to show intense activity. This uninhibited, dopamine-stimulated activity of the dreaming brain has been likened to a psychotic mental state (Gottesmann, 2000).

Some researchers have questioned an assumption held by many sleep experts that dreaming is simply the brain's effort to make sense of the random firing of neurons that occurs during REM sleep. There is mounting evidence, says British researcher Mark Solms (2000), that dreaming and REM sleep, while normally occurring together,

■ **REM dream**
A type of dream occurring almost continuously during each REM period and having a storylike quality; typically more vivid, visual, and emotional than NREM dreams.

■ **NREM dream**
A type of dream occurring during NREM sleep that is typically less frequent and memorable than REM dreams are.

lucid dream
A dream that an individual is aware of dreaming and whose content the individual is often able to influence while the dream is in progress.

manifest content
Freud's term for the content of a dream as recalled by the dreamer.

latent content
Freud's term for the underlying meaning of a dream.

activation-synthesis hypothesis of dreaming
The hypothesis that dreams are the brain's attempt to make sense of the random firing of brain cells during REM sleep.

are not one and the same. The REM state is controlled by neural mechanisms in the brainstem, while areas in the forebrain provide the neural pathway for the complex and often vivid mental experiences we call dreams. In fact, vivid REM dreams are associated with distributions of activity in the forebrain that are very similar to those exhibited by individuals with delusional disorders while they are awake (Schwartz & Maquet, 2002). These findings suggest the network of neurons associated with dreaming can be activated whether an individual is asleep or not.

Lucid Dreaming Have you ever been troubled by a frightening, recurring dream? People who have such dreams seem to experience a greater number of minor physical complaints, greater stress, and more anxiety and depression than other people do (Brown & Donderi, 1986). Is there anything that can be done to stop recurring dreams? Although most adults do not believe that the content of dreams can be controlled (Woolley & Boerger, 2002), some people have been taught to deliberately control dream content in order to stop unwanted, recurrent dreams. In **lucid dreams,** people attempt to exert control over a dream while it is in progress. Research suggests that individuals who are good at controlling their thoughts when awake are also successful at lucid dreaming (Blagrove & Hartnell, 2000). Lucid dreaming has even been advocated as an intervention for depression, although its effects appear to be inconsistent among depressed individuals (Newell & Cartwright, 2000), perhaps because the ability to control thoughts is impaired in many of these people. *Try It 4.2* introduces you to a technique for lucid dreaming.

Try It 4.2 Lucid Dreaming

Next time you wake up during a dream, try the following steps to see if you can engage in lucid dreaming.

1. Relax.
2. Close your eyes and focus on an imaginary spot in your field of vision.
3. Focus on your intention to have a lucid dream.
4. Tell yourself that you're going to dream about whatever you want.
5. Imagine yourself in a dream of the type you want to have.
6. Repeat the steps until you fall asleep.

How do the views of contemporary psychologists concerning the nature of dreams differ from those of Freud?

Interpreting Dreams

You may have wondered whether dreams, especially those that frighten us or that recur, have hidden meanings. Sigmund Freud believed that dreams function to satisfy unconscious sexual and aggressive desires. Because such wishes are unacceptable to the dreamer, they have to be disguised and therefore appear in dreams in symbolic forms. Freud (1900/1953a) claimed that objects like sticks, umbrellas, tree trunks, and guns symbolize the male sex organ; objects such as chests, cupboards, and boxes represent the female sex organ. Freud differentiated between the **manifest content** of a dream—the content of the dream as recalled by the dreamer—and the **latent content**—or the underlying meaning of the dream—which he considered more significant.

In recent years, there has been a major shift away from the Freudian interpretation of dreams. Now there is a greater focus on the manifest content—the actual dream itself—which is seen as an expression of a broad range of the dreamer's concerns rather than as an expression of sexual impulses (Webb, 1975). And, from an evolutionary viewpoint, dreams are viewed as a mechanism for simulating threatening and dangerous events so that the dreamer can "rehearse" and thus enhance her or his chances for survival (Revensuo, 2000).

Well-known sleep researcher J. Allan Hobson (1988) rejects the notion that nature would equip humans with the capability of having dreams that would require a specialist to interpret. Hobson and McCarley (1977) advanced the **activation-synthesis hypothesis of dreaming.** This hypothesis suggests that dreams are simply the brain's attempt to make sense of the random firing of brain cells during REM sleep. Just as people try to make sense of input from the environment during their waking hours, they try to find meaning in the conglomeration of sensations and memories that are generated internally by this random firing of brain cells. Hobson (1989) believes that dreams also have psychological significance, because the meaning a person imposes on the random mental activity reflects that person's experiences, remote memories, associations, drives, and fears. (As noted earlier, some researchers have questioned Hobson's position.)

If you dream you are trapped in a virtual reality matrix, does your dream mean that you have problems in your relationship with your parents, or perhaps an unconscious fear of video games? Freud might think so, but it's more likely that your dream resembles a movie you saw recently.

Sleep Disorders

What are the various disorders that can trouble sleepers?

So far, our discussion has centered on a typical night for a typical sleeper. But what about the significant number of people who report sleep problems (Rosekind, 1992)?

Parasomnias Do you walk or talk in your sleep? Or have you ever had a relative or roommate who did so? Psychologists use the term *parasomnia* to refer to such behaviors. **Parasomnias** are sleep disturbances in which behaviors and physiological states that normally occur only in the waking state take place during sleep (Schenck & Mahowald, 2000). For example, sleepwalking **(somnambulism)** occurs during a partial arousal from Stage 4 sleep in which the sleeper does not come to full consciousness. Sleepwalkers may get up and roam through the house, or simply stand for a short time and then go back to bed. Occasionally, they get dressed, eat a snack, or go to the bathroom. Some sleepwalkers have even been known to drive during an episode (Schenck & Mahowald, 1995). Typically, though, there is no memory of the episode the following day (Moldofsky et al., 1995).

Sleep terrors also happen during partial arousal from Stage 4 sleep. Sleep terrors usually begin with a piercing scream. The sleeper springs up in a state of panic—eyes open, perspiring, breathing rapidly, with the heart pounding at two or more times the normal rate (Karacan, 1988). Episodes usually last from 5 to 15 minutes, and then the person falls back to sleep. Up to 5% of children have sleep terrors (Keefauver & Guilleminault, 1994), but only about 1% of adults experience them (Partinen, 1994). Parents should not be unduly alarmed by sleep terrors in young children, but episodes that continue through adolescence into adulthood are more serious (Horne, 1992). Sleep terrors in adults often indicate extreme anxiety or other psychological problems.

Unlike sleep terrors, **nightmares** are very frightening dreams that occur during REM sleep and are likely to be remembered in vivid detail. The most common themes are falling and being chased, threatened, or attacked. Nightmares can be a reaction to traumatic life experiences, and they are more frequent at times of high fevers, anxiety, and emotional upheaval. REM rebound during drug withdrawal or following long periods without sleep can also produce nightmares. While sleep terrors occur early in

■ **parasomnias**
Sleep disturbances in which behaviors and physiological states that normally take place only in the waking state occur while a person is sleeping.

■ **somnambulism**
Sleepwalking; a parasomnia that occurs during partial arousal from Stage 4 sleep.

■ **sleep terrors**
A sleep disturbance that occurs during partial arousal from Stage 4 sleep, in which the sleeper springs up in a state of panic.

■ **nightmares**
Frightening dreams that occur during REM sleep and are likely to be remembered in vivid detail.

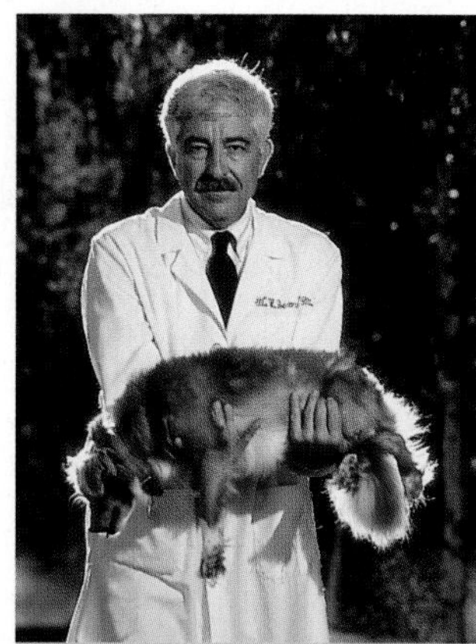

Sleep researcher William Dement holds a dog that is experiencing a narcoleptic sleep attack. Much has been learned about narcolepsy through research with dogs.

the night during Stage 4 sleep, anxiety nightmares occur toward morning, when the REM periods are longest. Frequent nightmares may be associated with psychological maladjustment (Berquier & Aston, 1992).

Sleeptalking **(somniloquy)** can occur during any sleep stage and is more frequent in children than in adults. There is no evidence at all that sleeptalking is related to a physical or psychological disturbance—not even to a guilty conscience. Sleeptalkers rarely reply to questions, and they usually mumble words or phrases that make no sense to the listener.

Major Sleep Disorders Some sleep disorders can be so debilitating that they affect a person's entire life. For instance, **narcolepsy** is an incurable sleep disorder characterized by excessive daytime sleepiness and uncontrollable attacks of REM sleep, usually lasting 10 to 20 minutes (American Psychiatric Association, 1994). People with narcolepsy, who number from 250,000 to 350,000 in the United States alone, tend to be involved in accidents virtually everywhere—while driving, at work, and at home (Broughton & Broughton, 1994). Narcolepsy is caused by an abnormality in the part of the brain that regulates sleep, and it appears to have a strong genetic component (Billiard et al., 1994; Partinen et al., 1994). Some dogs are subject to narcolepsy, and much has been learned about the genetics of this disorder from research on canine subjects (Lamberg, 1996). Although there is no cure for narcolepsy, stimulant medications improve daytime alertness in most patients (Guilleminault, 1993; Mitler et al., 1994). Experts also recommend scheduled naps to relieve sleepiness (Garma & Marchand, 1994).

Over 1 million Americans—mostly obese men—suffer from another sleep disorder, **sleep apnea**. Sleep apnea consists of periods during sleep when breathing stops, and the individual must awaken briefly in order to breathe (White, 1989). The major symptoms of sleep apnea are excessive daytime sleepiness and extremely loud snoring, often accompanied by snorts, gasps, and choking noises. A person with sleep apnea will drop off to sleep, stop breathing altogether, and then awaken struggling for breath. After gasping several breaths in a semi-awakened state, the person falls back to sleep and stops breathing again. People with severe sleep apnea may partially awaken as many as 800 times a night to gasp for air. Alcohol and sedatives aggravate the condition (Langevin et al., 1992).

Severe sleep apnea can lead to chronic high blood pressure, heart problems, and even death (Lavie et al., 1995). Neuroscientists have also found that sleep apnea may cause mild brain damage (Macey et al., 2002). Physicians sometimes treat sleep apnea by surgically modifying the upper airway (Sher et al., 1996). When the surgery is effective, sleep apnea sufferers not only sleep better, they also exhibit higher levels of performance on tests of verbal learning and memory (Dahloef et al., 2002). These findings suggest that the interrupted sleep experienced by individuals with this disorder affects cognitive as well as physiological functioning.

Approximately one-third of adults in the United States suffer from **insomnia**, a sleep disorder characterized by difficulty falling or staying asleep, by waking too early, or by sleep that is light, restless, or of poor quality. Any of these symptoms can lead to distress and impairment in daytime functioning (Costa E Silva et al., 1996; Roth, 1996b; Sateia et al., 2000). Transient (temporary) insomnia, lasting 3 weeks or less, can result from jet lag, emotional highs (as when preparing for an upcoming wedding) or lows (losing a loved one or a job), or a brief illness or injury that interferes with sleep (Reite et al., 1995). Much more serious is chronic insomnia, which lasts for months or even years and plagues about 10% of the adult population (Roth, 1996b). The percentages are even higher for women, the elderly, and people suffering from psychiatric and medical disorders (Costa E Silva et al., 1996). Chronic insomnia may begin as a reaction to a psychological or medical problem but persist long after the problem is resolved. Individuals with chronic insomnia experience "higher psychological distress [and] greater impairments of daytime functioning, are involved in more fatigue-related accidents, take more sick leave, and utilize health care resources more often than good sleepers" (Morin & Wooten, 1996, p. 522).

■ **somniloquy**
Sleeptalking; a parasomnia that can occur during any sleep stage.

■ **narcolepsy**
An incurable sleep disorder characterized by excessive daytime sleepiness and uncontrollable attacks of REM sleep.

■ **sleep apnea**
A sleep disorder characterized by periods during sleep when breathing stops and the individual must awaken briefly in order to breathe.

■ **insomnia**
A sleep disorder characterized by difficulty falling or staying asleep, by waking too early, or by sleep that is light, restless, or of poor quality.

Remember It 4.3

1. In __________ sleep, heart rate and respiration are slow and regular.
2. There is intense brain activity and large muscle paralysis during __________ sleep.
3. Match each NREM sleep stage with its characteristics.
   ____ (1) Transition between waking and sleeping
   ____ (2) The deepest sleep occurs
   ____ (3) The beginning of slow-wave sleep
   ____ (4) About 50% of each night's sleep

   a. Stage 1
   b. Stage 2
   c. Stage 3
   d. Stage 4
4. __________ and __________ have the highest percentages of REM and slow-wave sleep of any age group.
5. The two main theories that attempt to explain the function of sleep are the __________ and the __________ theories.
6. The least memorable dreams occur during __________ sleep.
7. The __________ hypothesis suggests that dreams are the brain's attempt to make sense of the random firing of brain cells during REM sleep.
8. Match each sleep problem with its description or associated symptom.
   ____ (1) Uncontrollable sleep attacks during the day
   ____ (2) Very frightening REM dream
   ____ (3) Cessation of breathing during sleep
   ____ (4) Difficulty falling or staying asleep

   a. Narcolepsy
   b. Sleep apnea
   c. Insomnia
   d. Nightmare

ANSWERS: 1. NREM; 2. REM; 3. (1) a, (2) d, (3) c, (4) b; 4. Infants, young children; 5. restorative, circadian (evolutionary); 6. NREM; 7. activation-synthesis; 8. (1) a, (2) d, (3) b, (4) c

Meditation and Hypnosis

We all have to sleep. Even if you fight it, your body will eventually force you to sleep. But there are other forms of altered consciousness that we may experience only if we choose to do so. Meditation and hypnosis are two of these.

Meditation

What are the benefits of meditation?

Do you know that a mental and physical relaxation technique can actually induce an altered state of consciousness? **Meditation** (the concentrative form) is a group of techniques that involve focusing attention on an object, a word, one's breathing, or one's body movements in order to block out all distractions, to enhance well-being, and to achieve an altered state of consciousness. Some forms of concentrative meditation, such as yoga, Zen, and transcendental meditation (TM), have their roots in Eastern religions and are practiced by followers of those religions to attain a higher spiritual state. In the United States, these approaches are often used to increase relaxation, reduce arousal, or expand consciousness. Brain-imaging studies support the conclusion that meditation, in addition to being relaxing, induces an altered state of consciousness (Newberg et al., 2001).

■ meditation (concentrative) A group of techniques that involve focusing attention on an object, a word, one's breathing, or one's body movements in order to block out all distractions, to enhance well-being, and to achieve an altered state of consciousness.

In practicing yoga, a meditator typically assumes a cross-legged position (known as the lotus) and gazes at a visual stimulus—a mandala (a symbolic circular pattern) or an object such as a vase or a flower. During Zen meditation, the individual counts breaths or concentrates on the breathing process. In transcendental meditation, the meditator uses a mantra, a secret word assigned by a teacher. The meditator sits quietly with closed eyes and silently repeats the mantra over and over during meditation. With all three approaches, the meditator's goal is to block out unwanted thoughts and facilitate the meditative state.

Is a special mantra really necessary for effective meditation? Studies demonstrating that prayer induces psychological and physiological states very much like those associated with meditation suggest that this is not the case (Bernardi et al., 2001). Indeed, in 1975, psychologist Herbert Benson claimed that the beneficial effects of meditation can be achieved through simple relaxation techniques. Since that time, many individuals have found Benson's approach to be effective. Here are the steps he proposed:

Step 1. Find a quiet place and sit in a comfortable position.
Step 2. Close your eyes.
Step 3. Relax all your muscles deeply. Begin with your feet and move slowly upward, relaxing the muscles in your legs, buttocks, abdomen, chest, shoulders, neck, and, finally, your face. Allow your whole body to remain in this deeply relaxed state.
Step 4. Now, concentrate on your breathing, and breathe in and out through your nose. Each time you breathe out, silently say the word *one* to yourself. If a distracting thought comes to mind, just ignore it.
Step 5. Repeat this process for 20 minutes. (You can open your eyes to look at your watch periodically but don't use an alarm.) When you are finished, remain seated for a few minutes—first with your eyes closed, then with them open.
Step 6. Practice this exercise one or two times each day, but not within 2 hours of your last meal. Digestion interferes with the relaxation response.

Meditation has benefits beyond relaxation and stress relief. Researchers have found that regular meditation helps individuals, even those who are severely depressed, learn to control their emotions (Segal et al., 2001). Such findings have implications for professionals whose clients are interested in alternative approaches to mental health care. They are also helpful to mental health professionals who practice in non-Western societies where meditation is highly valued, such as India (Clay, 2002). Studies demonstrating the mental health benefits of meditation provide justification for its inclusion in culturally sensitive therapy (see Chapter 16).

But what about physical health? Meditation may be helpful here as well. It appears that meditation may lower blood pressure, cholesterol levels, and other measures of cardiovascular health (Seeman et al., 2003). Thus, researchers think that meditation may be an important component of a comprehensive approach to preventing and treating cardiovascular disease (Fields et al., 2002). Keep in mind, though, that meditation isn't a "quick fix" for either mental or physical health problems. Deriving benefits from meditation requires self-discipline and commitment (Murray, 2002). First, you have to practice your meditation technique until you become proficient. Then, meditation must become part of your daily routine.

Hypnosis

What are the effects of hypnosis, and how do theorists explain them?

The chapter opening mentioned people's longstanding fascination with hypnosis. Now, let's consider the scientific basis of this phenomenon. **Hypnosis** may be formally defined as a procedure through which one person, the hypnotist, uses the power of suggestion to induce changes in thoughts, feelings, sensations, perceptions, or behavior in another person, the subject. Under hypnosis, people suspend their usual rational and logical ways of thinking and perceiving and allow themselves to experience distortions in perceptions, memories, and thinking. They may experience positive hallucinations, in which they see, hear, touch, smell, or taste things that are not present in the environment. Or they may have negative hallucinations, in which they fail to perceive things that are actually present.

About 80–95% of people are hypnotizable to some degree, but only 5% can reach the deepest levels of the hypnotic state (Nash & Baker, 1984). The ability to become completely absorbed in imaginative activities is characteristic of highly hypnotizable people (Nadon et al., 1991). Silva and Kirsch (1992) found that individuals' fantasy-proneness and their expectation of responding to hypnotic suggestions are predictors of their hypnotizability.

hypnosis
A procedure through which one person, the hypnotist, uses the power of suggestion to induce changes in thoughts, feelings, sensations, perceptions, or behavior in another person, the subject.

Myths about Hypnosis There are many misconceptions about hypnosis, some of which probably stem from its long association with stage entertainers. Have you ever believed one of these myths?

- *Hypnotized people are under the complete control of the hypnotist and will violate their moral values if told to do so.* Hypnosis is not something that is done to people. Subjects retain the ability to refuse to comply with the hypnotist's suggestions, and they will not do anything that is contrary to their true moral beliefs.
- *People can demonstrate superhuman strength and perform amazing feats under hypnosis.* Subjects are not stronger or more powerful under hypnosis (Druckman & Bjork, 1994).
- *Memory is more accurate under hypnosis.* Although it is true that hypnotized subjects supply more information and are more confident of their recollections, the information is often inaccurate (Dywan & Bowers, 1983; Kihlstrom & Barnhardt, 1993; Nogrady et al., 1985; Weekes et al., 1992). And in the process of trying to help people recall certain events, hypnotists may instead create in them false memories, or *pseudomemories* (Lynn & Nash, 1994; Yapko, 1994).
- *People under hypnosis will reveal embarrassing secrets.* Hypnosis is not like a truth serum. Subjects can keep secrets or lie under hypnosis.
- *People under hypnosis can relive an event that occurred when they were children and can function mentally as if they were that age.* Careful reviews of studies on hypnotic age regression have found no evidence to support this claim. "Although hypnotically regressed subjects may undergo dramatic changes in demeanor and subjective experience, their performance is not accurately childlike" (Nash, 1987, p. 50).

Medical Uses of Hypnosis Hypnosis has come a long way from the days when it was used mainly by entertainers. It is now recognized as a viable technique to be used in medicine, dentistry, and psychotherapy (Lynn et al., 2000). Hypnosis is accepted by the American Medical Association, the American Psychological Association, and the American Psychiatric Association. Hypnosis has been particularly helpful in the control of pain (Hilgard, 1975; Kihlstrom, 1985; Montgomery et al., 2000). Experimental studies have shown that patients who are hypnotized and exposed to suggestions designed to induce relaxation prior to surgery experience less postsurgery pain than do non-hypnotized patients (Montgomery et al., 2002).

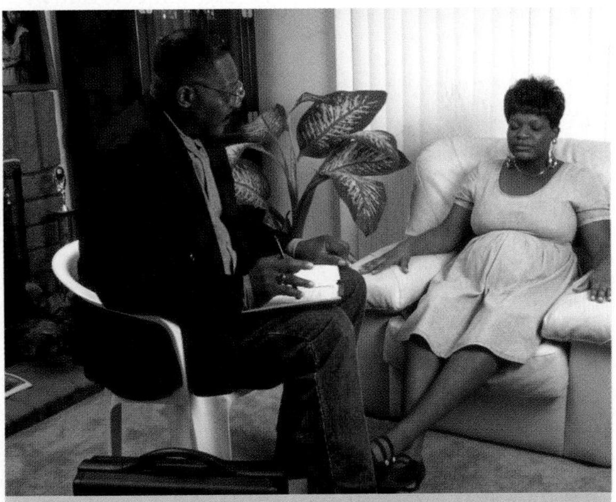
A hypnotized person is in a state of heightened suggestibility. This hypnotherapist may therefore be able to help the woman control chronic or post-surgery pain.

Hypnosis has also been used successfully to treat a wide range of disorders, including high blood pressure, bleeding, psoriasis, severe morning sickness, and the side effects of chemotherapy. Other problems that have responded well to hypnosis are asthma, severe insomnia, some phobias (Orne, 1983), dissociative identity disorder (Kluft, 1992),

■ sociocognitive theory of hypnosis
A theory suggesting that the behavior of a hypnotized person is a function of that person's expectations about how subjects behave under hypnosis.

■ neodissociation theory of hypnosis
A theory proposing that hypnosis induces a split, or dissociation, between two aspects of the control of consciousness: the planning function and the monitoring function.

■ theory of dissociated control
The theory that hypnosis is an authentic altered state of consciousness in which the control the executive function exerts over other subsystems of consciousness is weakened.

and posttraumatic stress disorder (Cardena, 2000). Furthermore, there are studies suggesting that hypnosis can be useful in treating warts (Ewin, 1992), pain due to severe burns (Patterson & Ptacek, 1997), repetitive nightmares (Kingsbury, 1993), and sexual dysfunctions such as inhibited sexual desire and impotence (Crasilneck, 1992; Hammond, 1992). Suppose you are overweight, or you smoke or drink heavily. Could a visit to a hypnotist rid you of overeating or other bad habits? Probably not. Hypnosis has been only moderately effective in weight control and virtually useless in overcoming drug and alcohol abuse or nicotine addiction (Abbot et al., 2000; Green & Lynn, 2000; Orne, 1983).

For the most hypnotizable people, hypnosis can be used instead of a general anesthetic in surgery. In one remarkable case, a young Canadian dentist had gall bladder surgery, using only hypnosis. From the time of the first incision until the operation was over, the patient maintained a steady pulse rate and blood pressure. Unbelievably, he claimed that he felt nothing that could be described as pain, only a tugging sensation (Callahan, 1997). Did this patient have the world's greatest hypnotist? No, most experts in hypnosis believe that "hypnotic responsiveness depends more on the efforts and abilities of the person hypnotized than on the skill of the hypnotist" (Kirsch & Lynn, 1995, p. 846).

Theories of Hypnosis According to the **sociocognitive theory of hypnosis**, the behavior of a hypnotized person is a function of that person's expectations about how subjects behave under hypnosis. People are motivated to be good subjects, to follow the suggestions of the hypnotist, and to fulfill the social role of the hypnotized person as they perceive it (Spanos, 1986, 1991, 1994). Does this mean that hypnotized people are merely acting or faking it? No, "most hypnotized persons are neither faking nor merely complying with suggestions" (Kirsch & Lynn, 1995, p. 847). In fact, using the single most effective and reliable indicator of deception in the laboratory—skin conductance, which indicates emotional response by measuring perspiration—Kinnunen and others (1994) found that 89% of supposedly hypnotized people had been truly hypnotized.

Ernest Hilgard (1986, 1992) has proposed a theory to explain why hypnotized individuals can accomplish very difficult acts, even undergoing surgery without anesthesia. According to his **neodissociation theory of hypnosis**, hypnosis induces a split, or dissociation, between two aspects of the control of consciousness: the planning function and the monitoring function. During hypnosis, it is the planning function that carries out the suggestions of the hypnotist and remains a part of the subject's conscious awareness. The monitoring function monitors or observes everything that happens to the subject, but without his or her conscious awareness. Hilgard called the monitoring function, when separated from conscious awareness, "the hidden observer."

The ritualized spinning dance of the whirling dervishes produces an altered state of consciousness that is recognized as part of their religious practice.

Bowers and his colleagues (Bowers, 1992; Woody & Bowers, 1994) have proposed a view of hypnosis as an authentic altered state of consciousness. Their **theory of dissociated control** maintains that hypnosis does not induce a splitting of different aspects of consciousness, as Hilgard's model suggests. Rather, they believe that hypnosis weakens the control of the executive function over other parts (subsystems) of consciousness, allowing the hypnotist's suggestions to contact and influence those subsystems directly. Bowers further believes that the hypnotized person's responses are automatic and involuntary, like reflexes, and not controlled by normal cognitive functions (Kirsch & Lynn, 1995). And, indeed, some research supports this viewpoint (Bowers & Woody, 1996; Hargadon et al., 1995).

Although the majority of hypnosis researchers seem to support the sociocognitive theory, most clinicians, and some influential researchers in the field, apparently believe that hypnosis is a unique altered state of consciousness (Kirsch & Lynn, 1995; Nash, 1991; Woody & Bowers, 1994). Kihlstrom (1986) has suggested that a more complete picture of hypnosis could emerge from some combination of the sociocognitive and neodissociation theories. But even though researchers still have theoretical differences, hypnosis is being increasingly used in clinical practice and in selected areas of medicine and dentistry.

Culture and Altered States of Consciousness

What is the connection between altered states of consciousness and culture?

In every culture around the world, and throughout recorded history, human beings have found ways to induce altered states of consciousness. Some means of inducing altered states that are used in other cultures may seem strange and exotic to most Westerners. Entering ritual trances and experiencing spirit possession are seen in many cultures in religious rites and tribal ceremonies. Typically, people induce ritual trance by flooding the senses with repetitive chanting, clapping, or singing; by whirling in circles until they achieve a dizzying speed; or by burning strong, pungent incense.

The fact that so many different means of altering consciousness are practiced by members of so many cultures around the world has led some experts to wonder whether "there may be a universal human need to produce and maintain varieties of conscious experiences" (Ward, 1994, p. 60). This may be why some people use drugs to deliberately induce altered states of consciousness.

Remember It 4.4

1. According to Herbert Benson, the beneficial effects of meditation can be achieved with simple __________.
2. Researchers have found that meditation may be useful in the prevention and treatment of __________.
3. About __________ of people can attain a deep state of hypnosis.
4. Information recalled while under hypnosis is often __________.
5. The three main theories proposed to explain hypnosis are the __________, __________, and __________.

ANSWERS: 1. relaxation techniques; 2. cardiovascular disease; 3. 5%; 4. inaccurate; 5. sociocognitive theory, neodissociation theory, theory of dissociated control

Psychoactive Drugs

The last time you took a pain reliever or an antibiotic, you probably didn't think of yourself as engaging in a mind-altering experience. However, all chemical substances, even the aspirin you take for a headache and the penicillin your doctor prescribes to cure an ear or sinus infection, affect the brain because they alter the functioning of neurotransmitters (Munzar et al., 2002). As you can probably guess, most such substances have no noticeable effect on your state of consciousness. Some drugs, however, have especially powerful effects on the brain and induce dramatically altered states of consciousness.

A **psychoactive drug** is any substance that alters mood, perception, or thought. When psychoactive drugs, such as antidepressants, are approved for medical use, they are called *controlled substances*. The term *illicit* denotes psychoactive drugs that are illegal. Many *over-the-counter drugs*, such as antihistamines and decongestants, as well as many herbal preparations, are psychoactive. And, certain foods, such as chocolate, may also

■ **psychoactive drug** Any substance that alters mood, perception, or thought; called a controlled substance if approved for medical use.

alter our moods (Dallard et al., 2001). Note to restaurant servers: Giving customers a piece of chocolate along with their checks increases tips (Strohmetz et al., 2002).

How Drugs Affect the Brain

How do drugs affect the brain's neurotransmitter system?

Did you know that all kinds of physical pleasure have the same neurological basis? Whether derived from sex, a psychoactive chemical, or any other source, a subjective sense of physical pleasure is brought about by an increase in the availability of the neurotransmitter dopamine in a part of the brain's limbic system known as the *nucleus accumbens* (Gerrits et al., 2002; Robinson et al., 2001). Thus, it isn't surprising that researchers have found that a surge of dopamine is involved in the rewarding and motivational effects produced by most psychoactive drugs (Carlson, 1998), including marijuana, heroin (Tanda et al., 1997), and nicotine (Pich et al., 1997; Pontieri et al., 1996). Why, then, does the altered state associated with alcohol feel different from that associated with nicotine or marijuana? Because the effect drugs have on the dopamine system is just the beginning of a cascade of effects that involve the brain's entire neurotransmitter system. Each drug influences the whole system differently and is associated with a distinctive altered state of consciousness. Consider a few examples of how different drugs act on neurotransmitters and the associated beneficial effects:

- Opiates such as morphine and heroin mimic the effects of the brain's own endorphins, chemicals that have pain-relieving properties and produce a feeling of well-being. For this reason, opiates are useful in pain management.
- Depressants such as alcohol, barbiturates, and benzodiazepines (Valium and Librium, for example) act on GABA receptors to produce a calming, sedating effect (Harris et al., 1992). Thus, depressants can play a role in reducing a patient's nervousness prior to undergoing a medical procedure.
- Stimulants such as amphetamines and cocaine mimic the effects of epinephrine, the neurotransmitter that triggers the sympathetic nervous system. The effects of the sympathetic nervous system include suppressed hunger and digestion; this is why "diet pills" typically contain some kind of stimulant, such as caffeine.

However, as we all know, drugs don't always have solely beneficial effects. Why? Because too much of a good thing, or the wrong combination of good things, can lead to disaster. For example, opiates, when taken regularly, will eventually completely suppress the production of endorphins. As a result, natural pain management systems break down, and the brain becomes dependent on the presence of opiates to function normally. Similarly, if ingestion of too much alcohol, or of a combination of alcohol and other depressants, floods the brain with GABA, consciousness will be lost and death may follow. And excessive amounts of a stimulant can send heart rates and blood pressure levels zooming; death can even result from the ingestion of a single, large dose.

Reasons for Substance Abuse

What are some risk and protective factors for substance abuse?

What motivates people to abuse psychoactive drugs when the possible side effects can be so devastating? One possibility is that many people are unaware of just how harmful these drugs can be (Johnston et al., 1997). Or drug abusers may believe that they aren't ingesting enough of a particular drug to cause permanent harm to their bodies. Other, possibly more important, factors may also underlie substance abuse.

Neurobiological Factors The pleasant physiological state produced by stimulation of the nucleus accumbens is one reason for substance abuse. But pleasure seeking alone doesn't fully explain drug abuse. Brain-imaging studies have also shown that the irrationality caused by drugs' effects on brain structures other than the nucleus accumbens is also a contributing factor (Porrino & Lyons, 2000; Volkow & Fowler, 2000). It is now known that the irrational behavior of substance abuse is associated with changes in the orbitofrontal cortex and other brain structures to which it is connected. Impaired decision making, irresistible craving for the abused substance, and the willingness to do anything to get it are all sustained, in part, by this drug-disabled brain area (London et al., 2000).

Where is the orbitofrontal cortex? Point your index finger between your eyes where your nose meets your skull. You are pointing directly toward your orbitofrontal cortex, which lies at the very front of the cortex at its lowermost point, just behind the eye sockets. This brain structure is anatomically connected to the association areas for all five of your senses, to structures in the limbic system (such as the amygdala, which has so much to do with emotions), and to other regions in the frontal cortex that handle decision making (Bechara et al., 2000). Thus, the orbitofrontal cortex is intimately involved in everything you see, hear, touch, taste, and smell, in the emotions you feel, and even in the decisions you make. Now, imagine what happens when this brain area is abnormally activated by illicit drugs. It is no wonder that addictive behavior is so irrational.

Researchers Norma Volkow and others (1999) were the first to pinpoint the part of the orbitofrontal cortex associated with the craving for cocaine in addicts. The right side of this brain area (but not the left) produced this craving in the addicts when it was activated. Interestingly, this same area was found to be abnormal in people diagnosed with obsessive-compulsive disorder (Volkow & Fowler, 2000).

Heredity Individual differences in the way people respond physiologically to drugs also contribute to substance abuse. For example, some people feel intoxicated after drinking very small amounts of alcohol, while others require a much larger "dose." People who have to drink more to experience intoxication are more likely to become alcoholics, and genetic researchers are currently searching for the gene or genes that contribute to low response to alcohol (Schuckit et al., 2001).

Moreover, the genetic underpinnings of alcoholism and other addictions appear to involve physiological differences beyond those associated with drug responses. Neuroscientist Henri Begleiter and his colleagues have accumulated a large body of evidence suggesting that the brains of alcoholics respond differently to visual and auditory stimuli than do those of nonalcoholics (Hada et al., 2000; Prabhu et al., 2001). Further, many relatives of alcoholics, even children and adults who have never consumed any alcohol in their lives, display the same types of response patterns (Hada et al., 2001; Zhang et al., 2001). And relatives of alcoholics who display these patterns are more likely to become alcoholics themselves or to suffer from other types of addictions (Anokhin et al., 2000; Bierut et al., 1998). Begleiter has suggested that the kinds of brain-imaging techniques he uses in his research may someday be used to determine which relatives of alcoholics are genetically predisposed to addiction and which are not (Porjesz et al., 1998).

Psychological and Social Factors Psychological factors also strongly influence a person's response to a drug. Impulsivity, for instance, is associated with both experimentation with drugs and addiction (Simons & Carey, 2002). And stress-related variables, both early in life and in adulthood, are reliable predictors of substance abuse (Gordon, 2002; Sussman & Dent, 2000). For example, recent research indicates that family violence strongly predicts drug use (Easton et al., 2000). One study found that females are much more likely than males to use drugs to cope with family dysfunction and the symptoms that arise from internalizing various forms of abuse (Dakof, 2000).

The earlier adolescents start using drugs (most start with alcohol and nicotine), the more likely they are to progress to more serious drugs and full-blown addiction (Kandel & Davies, 1996; Zinkernagel et al., 2001). As you can see in Figure 4.2 (on page 142), the proportion of teens who have tried illegal drugs is lower than it was

FIGURE 4.2 Results of a Survey of 8th, 10th, and 12th Graders about Their Use of Any Illicit Drug during the Previous 12 Months

The graph shows the percentage of high school seniors for 1976 through 2000 and the percentages of 8th and 10th graders for 1991 through 2000 who reported using any illicit (illegal) drug during the previous 12 months. After declining steeply from 1982 to 1992, the use of illicit drugs began to increase dramatically in 1992 and continued to climb until 1997. Then, drug use decreased slightly in 1997 and 1998 but began to creep upward again in 1999.

Source: Data from Johnston et al. (2001).

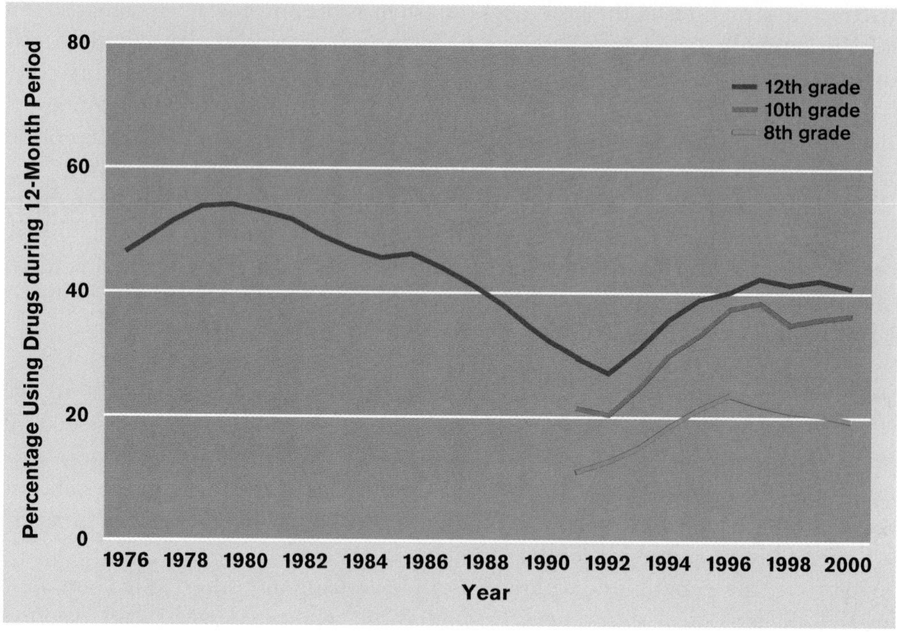

25 years ago (Johnston et al., 2001). Still, most experts regard current levels of adolescent drug use to be unacceptable.

Adolescents who use drugs seek out peers who also use and, in turn, are influenced by those peers (Curran et al., 1997). In a 16-year longitudinal study that followed 552 7th, 8th, and 9th graders into adulthood, Newcomb (1997) found that drug use and abuse in adolescents was associated with a number of problem behaviors, including "cigarette use, alcohol abuse, . . . precocious sexual involvement, academic problems, frequency of various sexual activities, deviant attitudes, and delinquent behavior" (p. 65). Substance abuse among adolescents is also related to the propensity to take risks, and a significant percentage of risk-taking drug users (15%) reported suffering injuries while engaging in substance use (Spirito et al., 2000).

Protective Factors Several protective factors tend to lower the risk of drug use by young people. These include parental support, behavioral coping skills, academic and social competence (Newcomb, 1997; Wills & Cleary, 1996; Wills et al., 1996), and traditional religious beliefs (Kendler et al., 1997). Cultural variables contribute to protection from drug abuse as well. In one study of more than 400 California teens, researchers found that adolescents of Chinese and Asian/Pacific Island backgrounds were far more likely to abstain from alcohol than peers in other groups (Faryna & Morales, 2000). (See Figure 4.3.) Remarkably, 9% of European American and 12% of Latin American youths reported using alcohol every day. Researchers attribute these

FIGURE 4.3 Alcohol Use among Adolescents of Diverse Ethnicities

In this study involving more than 400 California high school students, researchers found that those with Chinese and Asian/Pacific Island backgrounds were less likely to use alcohol than were their peers from other ethnic groups. The researchers suggested that differences in cultural values and family structure help to account for these differences. Chinese American and Asian American/Pacific Islander teens were more likely to come from homes in which both parents were present. Further, European American, Latin American, and African American teens spent more time with peers than with their families, but the reverse was true for the Chinese American and Asian American/Pacific Islander high school students.

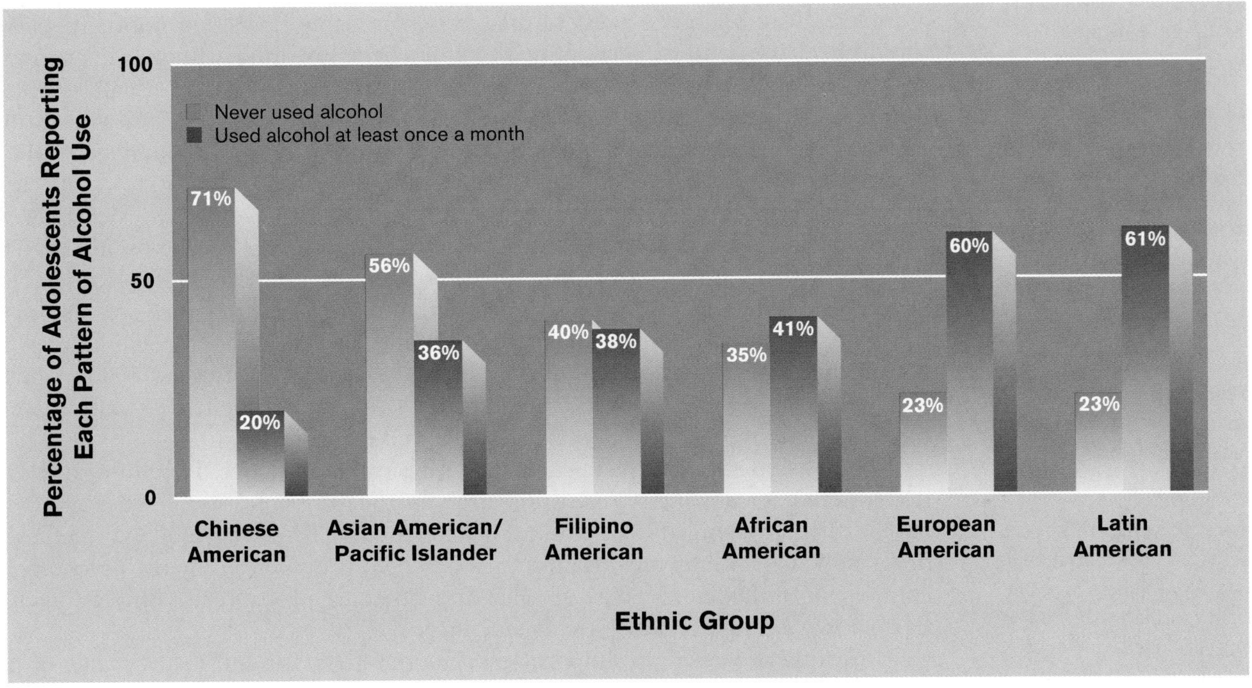

differences to healthy social influences, such as an environment that promotes abstinence and a greater likelihood of having an intact family among Americans of Chinese and Asian/Pacific Island backgrounds. Also, young Asian Americans spend more time with their families and less time with friends and other peers, thus minimizing potentially bad influences and peer group pressures (Au & Donaldson, 2000).

Drug Addiction

What is the difference between physical and psychological drug dependence?

The trip from first use to abuse of a drug may be long or very short. *Substance abuse* may be defined as continuing drug use that interferes with a person's major life roles at home, in school, at work, or elsewhere and contributes to legal difficulties or any psychological problems (American Psychiatric Association, 1994). Four factors influence the addictive potential of a drug: (1) how fast the effects of the drug are felt, (2) how pleasurable the drug's effects are in producing euphoria or in extinguishing pain, (3) how long the pleasurable effects last, and (4) how much discomfort is experienced when the drug is discontinued (Medzerian, 1991). The pleasurable effects of the most addictive drugs are felt almost immediately, and they are short-lived. For example, the intense, pleasurable effects of crack cocaine are felt in 7 seconds and last only about 5 minutes. The addictive potential of an addictive

■ physical drug dependence
A compulsive pattern of drug use in which the user develops a drug tolerance coupled with unpleasant withdrawal symptoms when the drug use is discontinued.

■ drug tolerance
A condition in which the user becomes progressively less affected by the drug and must take larger and larger doses to maintain the same effect or high.

■ withdrawal symptoms
The physical and psychological symptoms (usually the exact opposite of the effects produced by the drug) that occur when a regularly used drug is discontinued and that terminate when the drug is taken again.

■ psychological drug dependence
A craving or irresistible urge for a drug's pleasurable effects.

■ stimulants
A category of drugs that speed up activity in the central nervous system, suppress appetite, and can cause a person to feel more awake, alert, and energetic; also called "uppers."

drug is higher if it is injected rather than taken orally, and slightly higher still if it is smoked rather than injected.

Some drugs create a physical or chemical dependence; others create a psychological dependence. **Physical drug dependence** comes about as a result of the body's natural ability to protect itself against harmful substances by developing a **drug tolerance**. This means that the user becomes progressively less affected by the drug and must take larger and larger doses to get the same effect or high (Ramsay & Woods, 1997). Tolerance occurs because the brain adapts to the presence of the drug by responding less intensely to it. In addition, the liver produces more enzymes to break down the drug. The various bodily processes adjust in order to continue to function with the drug in the system.

Once drug tolerance is established, a person cannot function normally without the drug. If the drug is taken away, the user begins to suffer withdrawal symptoms. The **withdrawal symptoms**, both physical and psychological, are usually the exact opposite of the effects produced by the drug. For example, withdrawal from stimulants leaves a person exhausted and depressed; withdrawal from tranquilizers leaves a person nervous and agitated. Since taking the drug is the only way to escape these unpleasant symptoms, withdrawal can lead to relapse into addiction. Moreover, the lasting behavioral and cognitive effects of abused substances on the brain also often interfere with attempts to stop using the substances. Among other effects, researchers have learned that addiction is associated with attention and memory deficits, loss of the ability to accurately sense the passage of time, and decreased capacity to plan and control behavior (Bates et al., 2002; Buhusi & Meck, 2002; Lyvers, 2000). Abusers need all of these skills to overcome addiction and rebuild their lives, but regaining them once drug abuse has stopped takes time and determination.

There is more to drug addiction than physical dependence. **Psychological drug dependence** is a craving or irresistible urge for the drug's pleasurable effects, and it is more difficult to combat than physical dependence (O'Brien, 1996). Continued use of drugs to which an individual is physically addicted is influenced by the psychological component of the habit. There are also drugs that are probably not physically addictive but may create psychological dependence.

Learning processes are important in the development and maintenance of psychological dependence. For example, because of classical conditioning, drug-taking cues—the people, places, and things associated with using—can produce a strong craving for the abused substance (Hillebrand, 2000). In fact, some researchers have found that people addicted to opiates selectively pay attention to drug-related cues, ignoring virtually all non-drug cues any time the drug cues are present (Lubman et al., 2000). However, "selective attention" probably isn't the most descriptive term for what is happening in a drug addict's brain. PET scans of cocaine addicts' brains indicate that such cues arouse a cue-specific neural network, which may explain why it is difficult for addicts to divert their attention from them (Bonson et al., 2002). Further, research with animals indicates that drug-related cues elicit the same responses in the brain as the drugs themselves (Kiyatkin & Wise, 2002). These findings underscore the necessity of changes in addicts' physical and social environment in the treatment of both physical and psychological drug dependence.

The Behavioral Effects of Psychoactive Drugs

What are the effects of stimulants, depressants, and hallucinogens on behavior?

Have you ever advised a friend to "switch to decaf"? This advice comes from a bit of drug knowledge we all share: Caffeine can make us jumpy. But what are the specific behavioral effects associated with other kinds of drugs? Let's begin with a look at the stimulants, the group to which caffeine belongs.

Stimulants **Stimulants**, often called "uppers," speed up activity in the central nervous system, suppress appetite, and can make a person feel more awake, alert, and energetic. Stimulants increase pulse rate, blood pressure, and respiration rate, and they reduce cerebral blood flow (Mathew & Wilson, 1991). In higher doses, stimulants make people feel nervous, jittery, and restless, and they can cause shaking or trembling and interfere with sleep.

Caffeine Coffee, tea, cola drinks, chocolate, and more than 100 prescription and over-the-counter drugs contain caffeine. Caffeine makes people more mentally alert and can help them stay awake (Wesensten et al., 2002). When moderate to heavy caffeine users abstain, they suffer withdrawal symptoms such as nervousness, instability, headaches, drowsiness, and decreased alertness. Using EEGs and sonograms, researchers looked at the effects of caffeine withdrawal symptoms on the brain and were able to correlate the symptoms with significant increases in blood pressure and in the velocity of blood flow in all four of the cerebral arteries. The EEGs also showed an increase in slower brain waves, which correlates with decreased alertness and drowsiness (Jones et al., 2000).

Nicotine Like caffeine, nicotine increases alertness, but few people who have tried to quit smoking doubt its addictive power. (The many serious health problems associated with smoking are discussed in Chapter 13.) Many treatment methods advertised as being helpful to smokers trying to quit appear to have limited value. For example, Green and Lynn (2000) reviewed the results of 59 studies of hypnosis and smoking and concluded that hypnosis cannot be considered effective in helping smokers break the habit. However, experiments have shown that over-the-counter nicotine patches help about 1 in 5 smokers quit and enable many others to cut down on the number of cigarettes they smoke (Jolicoeur et al., 2003).

Amphetamines Amphetamines increase arousal, relieve fatigue, improve alertness, suppress the appetite, and give a rush of energy. Animal research suggests that amphetamines stimulate the release of dopamine in the frontal cortex as well as in the nucleus accumbens, which may account for some of their desirable cognitive effects such as increases in attention span and concentration (Frantz et al., 2002). In high doses (100 milligrams or more), however, amphetamines can cause confused and disorganized behavior, extreme fear and suspiciousness, delusions and hallucinations, aggressiveness and antisocial behavior, even manic behavior and paranoia. The powerful amphetamine methamphetamine (known as "crank" or "speed") comes in a smokable form ("ice"), which is highly addictive and can be fatal.

Withdrawal from amphetamines leaves a person physically exhausted; he or she will sleep for 10 to 15 hours or more, only to awaken in a stupor, extremely depressed and intensely hungry. Stimulants constrict the tiny capillaries and the small arteries. Over time, high doses can stop blood flow, causing hemorrhaging and leaving parts of the brain deprived of oxygen. In fact, victims of fatal overdoses of stimulants usually have multiple hemorrhages in the brain.

Amphetamines affect the parts of the brain that control attention and concentration, as well as the nucleus accumbens. This helps explain why these stimulants are useful in the treatment of attention problems in schoolchildren.

Cocaine Cocaine, a stimulant derived from coca leaves, can be sniffed as a white powder, injected intravenously, or smoked in the form of crack. The effects of snorting cocaine are felt within 2 to 3 minutes, and the high lasts 30 to 45 minutes. The euphoria from cocaine is followed by an equally intense crash, marked by depression, anxiety, agitation, and a powerful craving for more of the drug.

Cocaine stimulates the reward, or "pleasure," pathways in the brain, which use the neurotransmitter dopamine (Landry, 1997). With continued use, these reward systems fail to function normally, and the user becomes incapable of feeling any pleasure except from the drug. The main withdrawal symptoms are psychological—the inability to feel pleasure and the craving for more cocaine.

Cocaine constricts the blood vessels, raises blood pressure, speeds up the heart, quickens respiration, and can even cause epileptic seizures in people who have no history of epilepsy (Pascual-Leone et al., 1990). Over time, or even quickly in high doses, cocaine can cause heart palpitations, an irregular heartbeat, and heart attacks, and high doses can cause strokes in healthy young individuals. Chronic cocaine use can also result in holes in the nasal septum (the ridge of cartilage running down the middle of the nose) and in the palate (the roof of the mouth) (Armstrong & Shikani, 1996; Sastry et al., 1997).

Animals become addicted more readily to cocaine than to any other drug, and those who are addicted to multiple substances prefer cocaine when offered a choice of drugs (Manzardo, et al., 2002). Given unlimited access to cocaine, animals will lose interest in everything else, including food, water, and sex, and will rapidly and continually self-administer cocaine. They tend to die within 14 days, usually from cardiopulmonary collapse (Gawin, 1991). Cocaine-addicted monkeys will press a lever as many as 12,800 times to get one cocaine injection (Yanagita, 1973).

Crack, or "rock," the most dangerous form of cocaine, can produce a powerful dependency in several weeks. Users who begin with cocaine in powder form are likely to progress to crack, while users who start on crack are more likely to continue using it exclusively. When both powder and crack are used interchangeably, a mutual reinforcement seems to occur, and the user develops a dependence on both forms of cocaine (Shaw et al., 1999).

Depressants Another class of drugs, the **depressants** (sometimes called "downers"), decrease activity in the central nervous system, slow down bodily functions, and reduce sensitivity to outside stimulation. Within this category are the sedative-hypnotics (alcohol, barbiturates, and minor tranquilizers) and the narcotics (opiates). When different depressants are taken together, their sedative effects are additive and, thus, potentially dangerous.

depressants
A category of drugs that decrease activity in the central nervous system, slow down bodily functions, and reduce sensitivity to outside stimulation; also called "downers."

Alcohol The more alcohol a person consumes, the more the central nervous system is depressed. As drinking increases, the symptoms of drunkenness mount—slurred speech, poor coordination, staggering. Men tend to become more aggressive (Pihl et al., 1997) and more sexually aroused (Roehrich & Kinder, 1991) but less able to perform sexually (Crowe & George, 1989). (We will discuss the health consequences of alcohol abuse in detail in Chapter 13.) Alcohol also decreases the ability to form new memories (Kirchner & Sayette, 2003). That's why an episode of heavy drinking is often followed by a "morning after," during which the drinker is unable to remember the events that occurred while he or she was under the influence of alcohol. Interestingly, though, alcohol placebos have similar effects on memory function, so a drinker's expectations contribute to alcohol's effects to some extent (Assefi & Garry, 2003).

Some people feel intoxicated after drinking very small amounts of alcohol, while others require a much larger "dose." People who have to drink more to experience intoxication are more likely to become alcoholics.

Barbiturates Barbiturates depress the central nervous system, and, depending on the dose, a barbiturate can act as a sedative or a sleeping pill. People who abuse barbiturates become drowsy and confused, their thinking and judgment suffer, and their coordination and reflexes are affected (Henningfield & Ator, 1986). Barbiturates can kill if taken in overdose, and a lethal dose can be as little as only three times the prescribed dose. Alcohol and barbiturates, when taken together, are a potentially fatal combination.

Minor tranquilizers The popular minor tranquilizers, the *benzodiazepines*, came on the scene in the early 1960s and are sold under the brand names Valium, Librium, Dalmane, and, more recently, Xanax (also used as an antidepressant). About 90 million prescriptions for minor tranquilizers are filled each year. Benzodiazepines are prescribed for several medical and psychological disorders. Abuse of these drugs is associated with both temporary and permanent impairment of memory and other cognitive functions (Paraherakis et al., 2001). (A more detailed discussion of tranquilizers can be found in Chapter 16.)

Narcotics **Narcotics** are derived from the opium poppy and produce both pain-relieving and calming effects. Opium affects mainly the brain, but it also paralyzes the intestinal muscles, which is why it is used medically to treat diarrhea. If you have ever taken paregoric, you have had a tincture (extract) of opium. Because opium suppresses the cough center, it is used in some cough medicines. Morphine and codeine, natural constituents of opium, may be found in some drugs prescribed for pain relief. Such drugs, including Oxycontin and Vicodin, are addictive and are sold illegally to millions of people in the United States every year (Drug Enforcement Administration, 2003).

A highly addictive narcotic derived from morphine is heroin. Heroin addicts describe a sudden "rush" of euphoria, followed by drowsiness, inactivity, and impaired concentration. Withdrawal symptoms begin about 6 to 24 hours after use, and the addict becomes physically sick. Nausea, diarrhea, depression, stomach cramps, insomnia, and pain grow worse and worse until they become intolerable—unless the person gets another "fix."

Hallucinogens

The **hallucinogens**, or *psychedelics*, are drugs that can alter and distort perceptions of time and space, alter mood, and produce feelings of unreality. As the name implies, hallucinogens also cause hallucinations, sensations that have no basis in external reality (Andreasen & Black, 1991; Miller & Gold, 1994). Hallucinogens have been used in religious rituals and ceremonies and recreationally in diverse cultures since ancient times (Millman & Beeder, 1994). Rather than producing a relatively predictable effect like most other drugs, hallucinogens usually magnify the mood of the user at the time the drug is taken. And, contrary to the belief of some, hallucinogens hamper rather than enhance creative thinking (Bourassa & Vaugeois, 2001).

Marijuana *THC* (tetrahydrocannabinol), the ingredient in marijuana that produces the high, remains in the body "for days or even weeks" (Julien, 1995). Marijuana impairs attention and coordination and slows reaction time, and these effects make operating complex machinery such as an automobile dangerous, even after the feeling of intoxication has passed. Marijuana can interfere with concentration, logical thinking, and the ability to form new memories. It can produce fragmentation in thought and confusion in remembering recent occurrences (Herkenham, 1992). A 17-year longitudinal study of Costa Rican men supports the claim that long-term use of marijuana has a negative impact on short-term memory and the ability to focus sustained attention (Fletcher et al., 1996). Many of the receptors for THC are in the hippocampus, which explains why the drug affects memory (Matsuda et al., 1990).

Chronic use of marijuana has been associated with loss of motivation, general apathy, and decline in school performance, referred to as *amotivational syndrome* (Andreasen & Black, 1991). Studies comparing marijuana users who began before age 17 with those who started later show that early marijuana use is associated with a somewhat smaller brain volume and a lower percentage of the all-important gray matter in the brain's cortex. Marijuana users who started younger were also shorter and weighed less than users who started when older (Wilson et al., 2000). Further, marijuana smoke contains many of the same carcinogenic chemicals as cigarette smoke.

However, an advisory panel of the National Institute on Drug Abuse, after reviewing the scientific evidence, concluded that marijuana shows promise as a treatment for

■ **narcotics**
A class of depressant drugs derived from the opium poppy that produce both pain-relieving and calming effects.

■ **hallucinogens**
(hal-LU-sin-o-jenz) A category of drugs that can alter and distort perceptions of time and space, alter mood, produce feelings of unreality, and cause hallucinations; also called *psychedelics*.

Rave dances continue to be popular among North American and European teens. When attending raves, many teens use designer drugs such as Ecstasy because they believe these drugs will increase the pleasure they derive from these events.

certain medical conditions. It has been found effective for treating the eye disease glaucoma, for controlling nausea and vomiting in cancer patients receiving chemotherapy, and for improving appetite and curtailing weight loss in some AIDS patients (Fackelmann, 1997). But there is a continuing controversy over whether marijuana should be legalized for medical purposes.

LSD (lysergic acid diethylamide) LSD is lysergic acid diethylamide, sometimes referred to simply as "acid." The average LSD "trip" lasts for 10 to 12 hours and usually produces extreme perceptual and emotional changes, including visual hallucinations and feelings of panic (Miller & Gold, 1994). On occasion, bad LSD trips have ended tragically in accidents, death, or suicide. Former LSD users sometimes experience *flashbacks*, brief recurrences of previous trips that occur suddenly and without warning. Some develop a syndrome called *hallucinogen persisting perception disorder (HPPD)*, in which the visual cortex becomes highly stimulated whenever the individuals shut their eyes, causing them to experience chronic visual hallucinations whenever they try to sleep (Abraham & Duffy, 2001).

Designer drugs Designer drugs are so called because they are specially formulated to mimic the pleasurable effects of other drugs without, supposedly, their negative side effects. STP (for Serenity, Tranquility, and Peace) and Ecstasy are two common designer drugs. All designer drugs are derived from amphetamines but have hallucinogenic as well as stimulant effects. One reason for their popularity is that most are metabolized by the body differently than are the drugs they imitate (Drug Free Workplace, 2002). As a result, conventional drug tests do not detect the presence of designer drugs in an individual's system. As drug testing has become more common prior to employment and on a random basis in workplaces and some schools, designer drugs have become more popular.

As you have probably heard, Ecstasy, or MDMA (methylene-dioxy-methamphetamine), is a popular drug of abuse with teenagers, especially at "raves" (Schwartz & Miller, 1997). Long popular in Britain, these dances gained quite a following among American adolescents and young adults in the 1990s, and their popularity continues to grow in the 21st century. Typically, rave dances are held in large facilities, where as many as 2,000 partygoers, tightly packed together, dance all night to heavily mixed, electronically generated music accompanied by stunning laser light shows. This may sound like fun, but officials at the National Institute on Drug Abuse and others have become alarmed, not because of the dancing, but because MDMA has become so closely identified with raves that it is virtually synonymous with them. Indeed, the largest ongoing study of teenagers and drug use, the "Monitoring the Future Survey," conducted at the University of Michigan, revealed the alarming news that MDMA use nearly doubled among American teenagers in only 3 years, between 1998 and 2001. (Johnston et al., 2002).

Users of MDMA describe a wonderfully pleasant state of consciousness, in which even the most backward, bashful, self-conscious people shed their inhibitions (U.S. Department of Health and Human Services, 2001). Pretenses melt away, and the users become "emotionally synthesized" with other ravers and with the music and the lighting effects. Users feel that the drug allows them to be who they "really are." They report an immediate and deep acceptance and understanding of others; interpersonal barriers disappear, along with emotional and sexual inhibitions. It is said that the frequent, spontaneous outbursts of mass hugging and kissing make MDMA users feel that they are accepted, even loved. But there is a price to be paid for entering this "joyous" state.

MDMA is known to impair a variety of cognitive functions, including memory, sustained attention, analytical thinking, and self-control (National Institute on Drug

Abuse, 2001). More specifically, the drug is believed to have devastating effects on the critically important neurotransmitter serotonin, by depleting the brain's serotonin receptors. Serotonin, as you learned in Chapter 2, influences cognitive performance (including memory), as well as moods, sleep cycles, and the ability to control impulses (Reneman et al., 2000; Volkow & Fowler, 2000). Overdoses of MDMA can be fatal (Drug Enforcement Administration, 2003).

Review and Reflect 4.1 provides a summary of the effects and withdrawal symptoms of the major psychoactive drugs.

REVIEW *and* REFLECT 4.1

The Effects and Withdrawal Symptoms of Some Psychoactive Drugs

PSYCHOACTIVE DRUG	EFFECTS	WITHDRAWAL SYMPTOMS
Stimulants		
Caffeine	Produces wakefulness and alertness; increases metabolism but slows reaction time	Headache, depression, fatigue
Nicotine (tobacco)	Effects range from alertness to calmness; lowers appetite for carbohydrates; increases pulse rate and other metabolic processes	Irritability, anxiety, restlessness, increased appetite
Amphetamines	Increase metabolism and alertness; elevate mood, cause wakefulness, suppress appetite	Fatigue, increased appetite, depression, long periods of sleep, irritability, anxiety
Cocaine	Brings on euphoric mood, energy boost, feeling of excitement; suppresses appetite	Depression, fatigue, increased appetite, long periods of sleep, irritability
Depressants		
Alcohol	First few drinks stimulate and enliven while lowering anxiety and inhibitions; higher doses have a sedative effect, slowing reaction time, impairing motor control and perceptual ability	Tremors, nausea, sweating, depression, weakness, irritability, and in some cases hallucinations
Barbiturates	Promote sleep, have calming and sedative effect, decrease muscular tension, impair coordination and reflexes	Sleeplessness, anxiety; sudden withdrawal can cause seizures, cardiovascular collapse, and death
Tranquilizers (e.g., Valium, Xanax)	Lower anxiety, have calming and sedative effect, decrease muscular tension	Restlessness, anxiety, irritability, muscle tension, difficulty sleeping
Narcotics	Relieve pain; produce paralysis of intestines	Nausea, diarrhea, cramps, insomnia
Hallucinogens		
Marijuana	Generally produces euphoria, relaxation; affects ability to store new memories	Anxiety, difficulty sleeping, decreased appetite, hyperactivity
LSD	Produces excited exhilaration, hallucinations, experiences perceived as insightful and profound	
MDMA (Ecstasy)	Typically produces euphoria and feelings of understanding others and accepting them; lowers inhibitions; often causes overheating, dehydration, nausea; can cause jaw clenching, eye twitching, and dizziness	Depression, fatigue, and in some cases a "crash," during which the person may be sad, scared, or annoyed

Want to be sure you've fully absorbed the material in this chapter? Visit **www.ablongman.com/wood5e** for access to free practice tests, flashcards, interactive activities, and links developed specifically to help you succeed in psychology.

Apply It

Should You Kick Your Caffeine Habit?

The most popular caffeine-containing beverage in the United States is coffee. Americans drink more than half a billion cups of coffee daily, with most coffee drinkers consuming at least two cups. In addition to appreciating coffee's flavor and aroma, coffee drinkers say that it makes them feel more energetic and alert. The caffeine in coffee improves muscular coordination, thus facilitating work activities such as typing, and it may improve memory and reasoning. For people with tight airways, it opens breathing passages. It is also a mild diuretic. Caffeine, in short, is a natural stimulant. And other foods and beverages—chocolate, tea, and cola, for example—contain caffeine. Thus, even if you aren't a coffee drinker, you probably consume more caffeine than you realize.

Does Caffeine Cause Health Problems?

During the past two decades, extensive research has been conducted on possible links between caffeine use and health problems. The results have been mixed: For every study that implicates caffeine as a possible health risk, another finds no connection. For example, coffee consumption had been linked to increased risk of coronary artery disease and heart attack, but a 1996 study found that when researchers adjusted for cigarette smoking among coffee drinkers, the link disappeared (Mayo Clinic, 1997).

This is not to say that caffeine is entirely harmless. Even a couple of cups of coffee can make you nervous, anxious, and irritable. It can produce heartburn and irritate existing ulcers, and it causes bladder irritation in some people. It can also cause a temporary rise in blood pressure.

Who Is Most Likely to Be Affected by Caffeine?

Any health problems related to caffeine consumption are usually found only in people who drink large quantities of coffee—eight or more cups a day (Mayo Clinic, 1997). Thus, the effects of caffeine on an individual depend on the amount consumed, the frequency of consumption, the individual's metabolism, and the individual's sensitivity to caffeine.

Is Caffeine Addictive?

Some people say that they are "addicted" to coffee because they feel unable to start the day without it. What they really mean is that they depend on caffeine's stimulant effects to get them going. It has been suggested that dependence on caffeine is similar to dependence on alcohol or tobacco. The major evidence for this is that halting caffeine consumption abruptly can cause withdrawal symptoms such as headaches, fatigue, and depression. It is also true that regular consumption leads to a tolerance for many of the effects of caffeine. However, caffeine consumption patterns differ from those associated with serious drug dependence: Caffeine use does not result in a craving for ever-higher doses, and it is not very difficult to stop consuming it. And most consumers of caffeine do not exhibit the compulsive behavior characteristic of those dependent on illicit drugs. According to the World Health Organization, "There is no evidence whatsoever that caffeine use has even remotely comparable physical and social consequences [compared to those] associated with serious drugs of abuse" (quoted in IFIC, 1998).

Should You Try to Kick Your Caffeine Habit?

If you are particularly sensitive to caffeine or have been consuming it in large quantities, you may be experiencing side effects such as excessive nervousness—"coffee nerves"—and insomnia. If so, you may wish to cut back on or eliminate caffeine. This does not mean that you have to suffer withdrawal symptoms. Experts agree that these can be avoided by tapering off your consumption gradually—the slower the tapering, the easier the withdrawal. While you're cutting back, decaffeinated coffee, tea, and soft drinks can provide the flavor you're used to without the stimulant effects. Finally, if you're not trying to eliminate caffeine altogether, consider avoiding it for 3 days every 2 or 3 weeks to give your body a rest from the continual stimulation.

What are the pros and cons of using herbal remedies?

Herbal Remedies and Supplements

Have you ever heard a radio or television commercial touting a "natural" remedy that works just as well as some prescription drug? Such advertisements are becoming more frequent because public interest in alternative approaches to health care has grown tremendously in the past few years. One survey of college students found that about half used herbal supplements

(Newberry, et al., 2001). The use of herbs as medicines is an ancient practice that is still very common in some cultures.

Herbal supplements are growing in popularity. However, the effectiveness of most of them has not been tested scientifically.

Many herbs have the same kinds of effects on the brain as drugs do. However, the kinds of placebo-controlled studies that are common in pharmacological research are still rare in research on herbal treatments. In the few studies that have been done, researchers have found that many herbal preparations do live up to their claims. Both kava and valerian can make you feel calmer and help you sleep (Mischoulon, 2002; Wheatley, 2001). Kava, in particular, may someday play an important role in the treatment of serious anxiety disorders (Watkins et al., 2001), just as St. John's wort may be used to treat depression (Rivas-Vasquez, 2001). Other herbs appear to be effective in treating attention deficit disorder (Lyon et al., 2001) and in relieving symptoms of premenstrual syndrome and menopause (Chavez & Spitzher, 2002).

Many people think that something called "natural" must be safe. But research has yet to establish effective and safe dosages for herbal treatments. The dosage issue is an important one because excessive consumption of herbal supplements has been linked to allergic reactions, heightened risk for sunburn, asthma, liver failure, hypertension, mania, depression, and potentially dangerous interactions with prescription medications (Escher et al., 2001; Halemaskel et al., 2001; Pyevich & Bogenschutz, 2001; Rivas-Vasquez, 2001). Moreover, people who use herbal therapies to treat illnesses may delay seeking necessary medical care (Brienza et al., 2002).

Clearly, many of us find herbal preparations to be helpful. However, we need to keep in mind that their ability to affect both mind and body shouldn't be underestimated just because they seem more "natural" than manufactured drugs.

Remember It 4.5

1. All addictive drugs increase the effect of the neurotransmitter __________ in the __________.

2. The irrationality associated with substance abuse is probably caused by the effects of drugs on the __________.

3. Physical dependence on a drug begins with the development of ________, followed by __________ whenever the drug is discontinued.

4. Classify each drug by matching it with the appropriate category.

____ (1) marijuana		a. depressant
____ (2) caffeine		b. stimulant
____ (3) Ecstasy		c. narcotic
____ (4) STP		d. hallucinogen
____ (5) heroin		e. designer drug
____ (6) LSD		
____ (7) amphetamine		
____ (8) cocaine		
____ (9) nicotine		
____ (10) alcohol		

ANSWERS: 1. dopamine, nucleus accumbens; 2. orbitofrontal cortex; 3. drug tolerance, withdrawal symptoms; 4. (1) d, (2) b, (3) e, (4) e, (5) a, (6) d, (7) b, (8) b, (9) b, (10) a

Summary *and* Review

What Is Consciousness? p. 120

How have psychologists' views about consciousness changed since the early days of psychology? p. 120

Early psychologists saw consciousness, or awareness, as psychological in nature. Freud distinguished between conscious and unconscious experience. James emphasized the continuous flow of thought and feeling in consciousness. The rise of behaviorism, which claimed that consciousness could not be studied scientifically, led to a loss of interest in the phenomenon for several decades among psychologists in the United States. Today's psychologists use brain-imaging techniques to identify patterns of brain activity associated with different states of consciousness. Thus, they view consciousness as a neurobiological phenomenon, rather than an exclusively psychological one.

Circadian Rhythms p. 121

Which physiological and psychological functions are influenced by circadian rhythms? p. 121

Circadian rhythms regulate all vital life functions (e.g., heart rate, blood pressure), as well as learning efficiency and moods. These rhythms also affect sleep patterns and alertness.

How do biological and environmental variables influence circadian rhythms? p. 122

The suprachiasmatic nucleus (SCN) is the body's biological clock, which regulates circadian rhythms and signals the pineal gland to secrete or suppress secretion of melatonin, a hormone that acts to induce sleep. The amount of melatonin released by the pineal gland depends on the amount of light perceived by specialized photoreceptor cells on the retina. Environmental cues, especially bright light, also influence circadian rhythms.

How can travelers combat the effects of jet lag? p. 122

Supplemental melatonin has been found to be helpful in alleviating jet lag. Exposure to bright sunlight during the early morning hours and avoidance of bright lights during the evening may also restore circadian rhythms in jet lag sufferers.

In what ways does the disruption of circadian rhythms affect shift workers? p. 123

People working night shifts and especially rotating shifts experience a disruption in their circadian rhythms that can cause sleep difficulties as well as lowered alertness, efficiency, productivity, and safety during subjective night.

How can research linking circadian rhythms and neurological disorders be put to practical use? p. 124

Finding ways to restore circadian timing may improve quality of life for those who suffer from various neurological disorders. Alzheimer's patients show distinctive circadian rhythms, and restoring them to normal circadian functioning may help both the patients and their caregivers.

Sleep p. 125

How do NREM and REM sleep differ? p. 125

During NREM sleep, heart rate and respiration are slow and regular, and blood pressure and brain activity are at a 24-hour low point; there is little body movement and no rapid eye movements. During REM sleep, the large muscles of the body are paralyzed, respiration and heart rate are fast and irregular, brain activity increases, and rapid eye movements and vivid dreams occur. Many psychologists believe that important neurological tasks, such as the consolidation of new learning, take place during REM sleep.

What is the progression of NREM stages and REM sleep in a typical night of sleep? p. 127

During a typical night of sleep, a person goes through about five sleep cycles, each lasting about 90 minutes. The first sleep cycle contains Stages 1, 2, 3, and 4 of NREM sleep as well as a period of REM sleep; the second contains Stages 2, 3, and 4 of NREM sleep and a period of REM sleep. In the remaining sleep cycles, the sleeper alternates mainly between Stage 2 and REM sleep, with each sleep cycle having progressively longer periods of REM.

How do age and individual differences influence people's sleep patterns? *p. 127*

Infants and young children have the longest sleep time and largest percentages of REM and slow-wave sleep. Children from age 6 to puberty sleep best. The elderly typically have shorter total sleep time, more awakenings, and substantially less slow-wave sleep. Larks wake up early and are alert in the morning and maintain their alertness throughout the day; owls do not reach their peak of alertness until the afternoon or early evening. Such differences may be partly due to genetics.

What is the difference between the restorative and circadian theories of sleep? *p. 129*

The restorative theory of sleep claims that being awake causes stress on the body and the brain; repairs are made during sleep. The circadian (evolutionary) theory maintains that circadian rhythms, which evolved to protect humans from predators during the night, dictate periods of sleep and alertness.

How does sleep deprivation affect behavior and neurological functioning? *p. 130*

Sleep deprivation can lead to lapses in concentration and emotional irritability. It impacts performance and alertness and reduces the body's ability to warm itself. It can also reduce the effectiveness of the human immune system. Microsleeps are common among the sleep-deprived. Research examining the effects of sleep deprivation on verbal learning have shown that sleep deprivation may lead to suppression of neurological activity in the temporal lobes. However, the brain attempts to compensate by increasing activity in the prefrontal cortex and the parietal lobes.

What have researchers learned about dreams, their content, their biological basis, and their controllability? *p. 131*

REM dreams have a storylike or dreamlike quality and are more visual, vivid, and emotional than NREM dreams. Common dream themes include falling or being attacked or chased. Dreams tend to be less emotional and bizarre than people remember them. During REM dreams, areas of the brain responsible for emotions and the primary visual cortex are active, but the neurotransmitters serotonin and norepinephrine are less plentiful. Lucid dreaming is a set of techniques that enable dreamers to exert cognitive control over the content of their dreams.

How do the views of contemporary psychologists concerning the nature of dreams differ from those of Freud? *p. 132*

Freud believed that dreams carry hidden meanings and function to satisfy unconscious sexual and aggressive desires. He claimed that the manifest content of dreams differs from their latent content. Today, some psychologists support the activation-synthesis hypothesis, which claims that dreams are the brain's attempt to make sense of the random firing of brain cells during REM sleep.

What are the various disorders that can trouble sleepers? *p. 133*

Parasomnias such as somnambulism and sleep terrors occur during a partial arousal from Stage 4 sleep, and the person does not come to full consciousness. In a sleep terror, the sleeper awakens in a panicked state with a racing heart. Episodes last 5 to 15 minutes, and then the person falls back to sleep. Nightmares are frightening dreams that occur during REM sleep and are usually remembered in vivid detail. Somniloquy can occur during any sleep stage and is more common in children than adults. The symptoms of narcolepsy include excessive daytime sleepiness and sudden attacks of REM sleep. Sleep apnea is a serious sleep disorder in which a sleeper's breathing stops and the person must awaken briefly to breathe. Its major symptoms are excessive daytime sleepiness and extremely loud snoring. Insomnia is a sleep disorder characterized by difficulty falling or staying asleep, by waking too early, or by sleep that is light, restless, or of poor quality.

Meditation and Hypnosis p. 135

What are the benefits of meditation? *p. 135*

Meditation is used to promote relaxation, reduce arousal, or expand consciousness. It may also help prevent and treat cardiovascular disease.

What are the effects of hypnosis, and how do theorists explain them? *p. 136*

Hypnosis is a procedure through which a hypnotist uses the power of suggestion to induce changes in the thoughts, feelings, sensations, perceptions, or behavior of a subject. It has been used most successfully for the control of pain. The three main theories proposed to explain hypnosis are the sociocognitive theory, the neodissociation theory, and the theory of dissociated control. In sociocognitive theory, hypnosis is believed to be the result of the hypnotized person's expectations about how a person is supposed to behave under hypnosis. In neodissociation theory, the hypnotized person experiences a split between the planning and the monitoring functions of the mind. According to the theory of dissociated control, hypnosis weakens the executive function over subsystems of consciousness, allowing the hypnotizer to gain influence over those subsystems.

What is the connection between altered states of consciousness and culture? p. 139

Practices in many cultures allow individuals to deliberately induce altered states, often as part of tribal ceremonies or religious rituals. For instance, whirling dances and repetitive chanting are capable of producing such states.

Psychoactive Drugs p. 139

How do drugs affect the brain's neurotransmitter system? p. 140

All chemical substances alter neurotransmitter function. Psychoactive drugs increase the availability of dopamine in the nucleus accumbens. Beyond that, each drug has a unique influence on a specific neurotransmitter or group of neurotransmitters. Consequently, each psychoactive drug is associated with a distinctive altered state of consciousness.

What are some risk and protective factors for substance abuse? p. 140

Risk factors for substance abuse include craving for the drug, genetics, impulsivity, association with drug-using peers, family violence, and sexual abuse. Age is a risk factor: The younger a teen is when he or she first uses drugs, the more likely he or she is to abuse them. Protective factors include parental support, behavioral coping skills, academic and social competence, and traditional religious beliefs. Cultural background may also have a protective effect.

What is the difference between physical and psychological drug dependence? p. 143

With physical drug dependence, the user develops a drug tolerance, and so larger and larger doses of the drug are needed to get the same effect or high. Withdrawal symptoms appear when the drug is discontinued and disappear when the drug is taken again. Psychological drug dependence involves an intense craving for the drug's pleasurable effects.

What are the effects of stimulants, depressants, and hallucinogens on behavior? p. 144

Stimulants (amphetamines, cocaine, caffeine, and nicotine) speed up activity in the central nervous system, suppress appetite, and make a person feel more awake, alert, and energetic. Depressants decrease activity in the central nervous system, slow down bodily functions, and reduce sensitivity to outside stimulation. Depressants include sedative-hypnotics (alcohol, barbiturates, and minor tranquilizers) and narcotics (opiates such as opium, codeine, morphine, and heroin), which have both pain-relieving and calming effects. Hallucinogens—including marijuana, LSD, and MDMA—can alter and distort perception's of time and space, alter mood, produce feelings of unreality, and cause hallucinations.

What are the pros and cons of using herbal remedies? p. 150

Many herbs affect the brain in much the same way as drugs do. Some herbs have been shown to help in the treatment of anxiety, insomnia, depression, attention deficit disorder, premenstrual syndrome, and menopause symptoms. However, effective dosage guidelines have yet to be established, and excessive consumption of herbal supplements can have very serious effects on health.

Key Terms

activation-synthesis hypothesis of dreaming, p. 133
altered state of consciousness, p. 121
circadian rhythm, p. 121
circadian theory of sleep, p. 129
consciousness, p. 120
delta wave, p. 127
depressants, p. 146
drug tolerance, p. 144
hallucinogens, p. 147
hypnosis, p. 136
insomnia, p. 134
latent content, p. 132
lucid dream, p. 132
manifest content, p. 132
meditation (concentrative), p. 135
microsleep, p. 130
narcolepsy, p. 134
narcotics, p. 147
neodissociation theory of hypnosis, p. 138
nightmares, p. 133
NREM dream, p. 131
NREM sleep, p. 125
parasomnias, p. 133
physical drug dependence, p. 144
psychoactive drug, p. 139
psychological drug dependence, p. 144
REM dream, p. 131
REM rebound, p. 127
REM sleep, p. 125
restorative theory of sleep, p. 129
sleep apnea, p. 134
sleep cycle, p. 127
sleep terrors, p. 133
slow-wave sleep, p. 127
sociocognitive theory of hypnosis, p. 138
somnambulism, p. 133
somniloquy, p. 134
Stage 4 sleep, p. 127
stimulants, p. 144
subjective night, p. 123
suprachiasmatic nucleus (SCN), p. 122
theory of dissociated control, p. 138
withdrawal symptoms, p. 144

Learning

chapter 5

Classical Conditioning: The Original View

- *What kind of learning did Pavlov discover?*
- *How is classical conditioning accomplished?*
- *What kinds of changes in stimuli and learning conditions lead to changes in conditioned responses?*
- *How did Watson demonstrate that fear could be classically conditioned?*

Classical Conditioning: The Contemporary View

- *According to Rescorla, what is the critical element in classical conditioning?*
- *What did Garcia and Koelling discover about classical conditioning?*
- *What types of everyday responses can be subject to classical conditioning?*
- *Why doesn't classical conditioning occur every time unconditioned and conditioned stimuli occur together?*

Operant Conditioning

- *What did Thorndike conclude about learning by watching cats try to escape from his puzzle box?*
- *What was Skinner's major contribution to psychology?*
- *What is the process by which responses are acquired through operant conditioning?*
- *What is the goal of both positive reinforcement and negative reinforcement, and how is that goal accomplished with each?*
- *What are the four types of schedules of reinforcement, and which type is most effective?*
- *Why don't consequences always cause changes in behavior?*
- *How does punishment differ from negative reinforcement?*
- *When is avoidance learning desirable, and when is it maladaptive?*
- *What are some applications of operant conditioning?*

Cognitive Learning

- *What is insight, and how does it affect learning?*
- *What did Tolman discover about the necessity of reinforcement?*
- *How do we learn by observing others?*

How do you suppose animal trainers get their "students" to perform unnatural behaviors such as riding a bicycle or jumping through a hoop?

Training a dolphin to leap high in the air might seem to be fairly simple. After all, wild dolphins jump out of the water at times. Of course, they jump when they feel like it, not when another being signals them to do it. To perform the leaping trick, and to learn to do it at the right time, a dolphin has to acquire several skills.

The process begins with relationship building; the dolphin learns to associate the trainer with things it enjoys, such as food, stroking, and fetching games. These interactions also help the trainer to learn each individual dolphin's personality characteristics: Some enjoy being touched more than playing, some prefer to play "fetch" rather than get stroked, and so on. The pleasant stimuli associated with the trainers serve as potential rewards for desirable behavior.

Once the dolphin is responsive to some kind of reward, a long pole with a float on the end is used to teach it to follow directions. Trainers touch the dolphin with the float and then reward it. Next, the float is placed a few feet from the dolphin. When it swims over and touches the float, a reward is administered. The float is moved farther and farther away from the dolphin until the dolphin has been led to the particular location in the tank where the trainer wants it to begin performing the trick.

The pole-and-float device is then used to teach the dolphin to jump. Remember, it has been rewarded for touching the float. To get the dolphin to jump, the trainer raises the float above the water level. The dolphin jumps up to touch the float and receives its reward. The float is raised a little higher each time, until the animal must jump completely out of the water to receive the reward. The process continues until the dolphin has learned to jump to the desired height.

Suppressing unwanted behaviors is also part of the training process. But the training program cannot include any unpleasant consequences (e.g., beating, electric shocks) because such techniques are regarded as unethical and are forbidden by law in many places. So, to get dolphins to suppress unwanted behaviors, trainers remain completely motionless and silent whenever undesired behaviors occur. This helps the dolphins learn that rewards will be available only after desired behaviors have been performed. The final step in the training process is to teach the dolphin to respond to a unique signal that tells it when to perform the trick. Again, trainers use rewards to teach the dolphin to associate a specific hand gesture or verbal command with the desired behavior.

This process might seem to be very time-consuming, but there is one important shortcut in training dolphins: observational learning. Trainers have found that it is much easier to teach an untrained dolphin to perform desired behaviors when a more experienced dolphin participates in the training. In fact, park-bred babies are usually allowed to accompany their mothers during shows so that they learn all of the show behaviors through observation. Some aspects of training must still be accomplished individually, but, like humans, dolphins appear to have a very great capacity for learning complex behaviors by observing others of their species.

The principles of animal training are the same, whether the "students" are marine mammals or dogs.

Dolphin training takes advantage of all the principles of learning covered in this chapter. Psychologists define **learning** as a relatively permanent change in behavior, knowledge, capability, or attitude that is acquired through experience and cannot be attributed to illness, injury, or maturation. Several parts of this definition warrant further explanation. First, defining learning as a "relatively permanent change" excludes temporary changes that could result from illness, fatigue, or fluctuations in mood. Second, limiting learning to changes that are "acquired through experience" excludes some readily observable changes in behavior that occur as a result of brain injuries or certain diseases. Also, certain observable changes that occur as individuals grow and mature have nothing to do with learning. For example, technically speaking, infants do not *learn* to crawl or walk. Basic motor skills and the maturational plan that governs their development are a part of the genetically programmed behavioral repertoire of every species. The first kind of learning we'll consider is classical conditioning.

Classical Conditioning: The Original View

Why do images of Adolf Hitler, the mere mention of the IRS, and the sight of an American flag waving in a gentle breeze evoke strong emotional responses? Each stirs up our emotions because it carries certain associations: Hitler with evil, the IRS with paying taxes, and the American flag with national pride. How do such associations occur? **Classical conditioning** is a type of learning through which an organism learns to associate one stimulus with another. A **stimulus** (the plural is *stimuli*) is any event or object in the environment to which an organism responds. People's lives are profoundly influenced by the associations learned through classical conditioning, which is sometimes referred to as *respondent conditioning*, or *Pavlovian conditioning*.

Pavlov and Classical Conditioning

What kind of learning did Pavlov discover?

Ivan Pavlov (1849–1936) organized and directed research in physiology at the Institute of Experimental Medicine in St. Petersburg, Russia, from 1891 until his death 45 years later. There, he conducted his classic experiments on the physiology of digestion, which won him a Nobel Prize in 1904—the first time a Russian received this honor.

Pavlov's contribution to psychology came about quite by accident. To conduct his study of the salivary response in dogs, Pavlov made a small incision in the side of each dog's mouth. Then he attached a tube so that the flow of saliva could be diverted from inside the animal's mouth, through the tube, and into a container, where the saliva was collected and measured. Pavlov's purpose was to collect the saliva that the dogs would secrete naturally in response to food placed inside the mouth. But he noticed that, in many cases, the dogs would begin to salivate even before the food was presented. Pavlov observed drops of saliva collecting in the containers when the dogs heard the footsteps of the laboratory assistants coming to feed them. He observed saliva collecting when the dogs heard their food dishes rattling, saw the attendant who fed them, or spotted their food. How could an involuntary response such as salivation come to be associated with the sights and sounds involved in feeding? Pavlov spent the rest of his life studying this question. The type of learning he studied is known today as classical conditioning.

Just how meticulous a researcher Pavlov was is reflected in this description of the laboratory he planned and built in St. Petersburg more than a century ago:

> The windows were covered with extra thick sheets of glass; each room had double steel doors which sealed hermetically when closed; and the steel girders which supported the floors were embedded in sand. A deep moat filled with straw encircled the building. Thus,

■ **learning**
A relatively permanent change in behavior, knowledge, capability, or attitude that is acquired through experience and cannot be attributed to illness, injury, or maturation.

■ **classical conditioning**
A type of learning through which an organism learns to associate one stimulus with another.

■ **stimulus**
(STIM-yu-lus) Any event or object in the environment to which an organism responds; plural is *stimuli*.

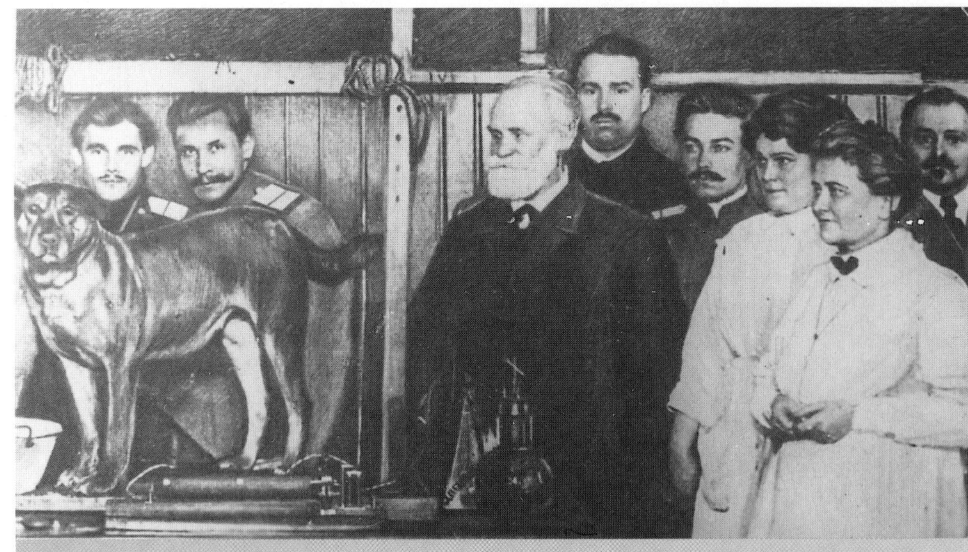
Ivan Pavlov (1849–1936) earned fame by studying the conditioned reflex in dogs.

vibration, noise, temperature extremes, odors, even drafts were eliminated. Nothing could influence the animals except the conditioning stimuli to which they were exposed. (Schultz, 1975, pp. 187–188)

■ reflex
An involuntary response to a particular stimulus, such as the eyeblink response to a puff of air or salivation when food is placed in the mouth.

The dogs were isolated inside soundproof cubicles and placed in harnesses to restrain their movements. From an adjoining cubicle, an experimenter observed the dogs through a one-way mirror. Food and other stimuli were presented, and the flow of saliva measured by remote control (see Figure 5.1). What did Pavlov and his colleagues learn?

The Process of Classical Conditioning

How is classical conditioning accomplished?

The Reflex A **reflex** is an involuntary response to a particular stimulus. Two examples are salivation in response to food placed in the mouth and the eyeblink response to a puff of air (Green & Woodruff-Pak, 2000). There are two kinds of reflexes: conditioned and unconditioned. Think of the term *conditioned* as meaning "learned" and the term *unconditioned* as meaning "unlearned." Salivation in response to food is an unconditioned reflex because it is an inborn, automatic, unlearned response to a particular stimulus.

When Pavlov observed that his dogs would salivate at the sight of food or the sound of rattling dishes, he realized that this salivation reflex was the result of learning. He called these learned involuntary responses **conditioned reflexes**.

■ conditioned reflex
A learned involuntary response.

■ unconditioned response (UR)
A response that is elicited by an unconditioned stimulus without prior learning.

■ unconditioned stimulus (US)
A stimulus that elicits a specific unconditioned response without prior learning.

The Conditioned and Unconditioned Stimulus and Response Pavlov (1927/1960) used tones, bells, buzzers, lights, geometric shapes, electric shocks, and metronomes in his conditioning experiments. In a typical experiment, food powder was placed in the dog's mouth, causing salivation. Because dogs do not need to be conditioned to salivate to food, salivation to food is an unlearned response, or **unconditioned response (UR).** Any stimulus, such as food, that without prior learning will automatically elicit, or bring forth, an unconditioned response is called an **unconditioned stimulus (US).**

Following is a list of some common unconditioned reflexes, showing their two components: the unconditioned stimulus and the unconditioned response.

FIGURE 5.1 The Experimental Apparatus Used in Pavlov's Classical Conditioning Studies

In Pavlov's classical conditioning studies, the dog was restrained in a harness in the cubicle and isolated from all distractions. An experimenter observed the dog through a one-way mirror and, by remote control, presented the dog with food and other conditioning stimuli. A tube carried the saliva from the dog's mouth to a container where it was measured.

UNCONDITIONED REFLEXES

Unconditioned Stimulus (US)	*Unconditioned Response (UR)*
food	salivation
loud noise	startle response
light in eye	contraction of pupil
puff of air in eye	eyeblink response

Pavlov demonstrated that dogs could be conditioned to salivate to a variety of stimuli never before associated with food, as shown in Figure 5.2 (on page 162). During the conditioning process, the researcher would present a neutral stimulus such as a musical tone shortly before placing food powder in the dog's mouth. The food powder would cause the dog to salivate. Pavlov found that after the tone and the food were paired many times, usually 20 or more, the tone alone would elicit salivation (Pavlov, 1927/1960, p. 385). Pavlov called the tone the learned stimulus, or **conditioned stimulus (CS)**, and salivation to the tone the learned response, or **conditioned response (CR)**.

■ conditioned stimulus (CS) A neutral stimulus that, after repeated pairing with an unconditioned stimulus, becomes associated with it and elicits a conditioned response.

■ conditioned response (CR) The learned response that comes to be elicited by a conditioned stimulus as a result of its repeated pairing with an unconditioned stimulus.

Higher-Order Conditioning Think about what happens when you have to have some kind of blood test. Typically, you sit in a chair next to a table on which are arranged materials such as needles, syringes, and such. Next, some kind of constricting device is tied around your arm, and the nurse or technician pats on the surface of your skin until a vein becomes visible. Each step in the sequence tells you that the unavoidable "stick" of the needle and the pain, which is largely the result of reflexive muscle tension, is coming. The stick itself is the unconditioned stimulus, to which you reflexively respond. But all the steps that precede it are conditioned stimuli that cause you to anticipate the pain of the stick itself. And with each successive step, a conditioned response occurs, as your muscles respond to your anxiety by contracting a bit

FIGURE 5.2 Classically Conditioning a Salivation Response

A neutral stimulus (a tone) elicits no salivation until it is repeatedly paired with the unconditioned stimulus (food). After many pairings, the neutral stimulus (now called the conditioned stimulus) alone produces salivation. Classical conditioning has occurred.

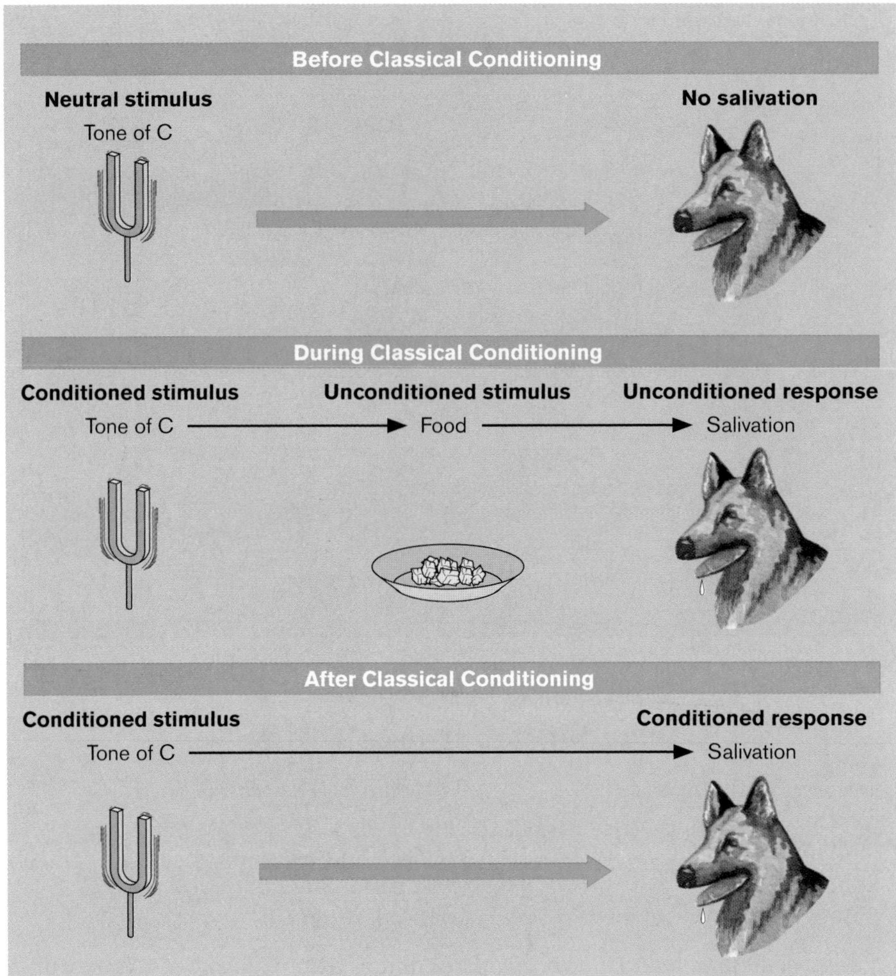

■ **higher-order conditioning** Conditioning that occurs when conditioned stimuli are linked together to form a series of signals.

■ **extinction** In classical conditioning, the weakening and eventual disappearance of the conditioned response as a result of repeated presentation of the conditioned stimulus without the unconditioned stimulus.

■ **spontaneous recovery** The reappearance of an extinguished response (in a weaker form) when an organism is exposed to the original conditioned stimulus following a rest period.

more in anticipation of the stick. When conditioned stimuli are linked together to form a series of signals, a process called **higher-order conditioning** occurs.

Changing Conditioned Responses

What kinds of changes in stimuli and learning conditions lead to changes in conditioned responses?

After conditioning an animal to salivate to a tone, what would happen if you continued to sound the tone but no longer paired it with food? Pavlov found that without the food, salivation to the tone became weaker and weaker and then finally disappeared altogether—a process known as **extinction.** After the response had been extinguished, Pavlov allowed the dog to rest for 20 minutes and then brought it back to the laboratory. He found that the dog would again salivate to the tone. Pavlov called this recurrence **spontaneous recovery.** But the spontaneously recovered response was weaker and shorter in duration than the original conditioned response. Figure 5.3 shows the processes of extinction and spontaneous recovery.

FIGURE 5.3 Extinction of a Classically Conditioned Response

When a classically conditioned stimulus (a tone) was presented in a series of trials without the unconditioned stimulus (food), Pavlov's dogs salivated less and less until there was virtually no salivation. But after a 20-minute rest, one sound of the tone caused the conditioned response to reappear in a weakened form (producing only a small amount of salivation), a phenomenon Pavlov called *spontaneous recovery*.

Source: Data from Pavlov (1927/1960), p. 58.

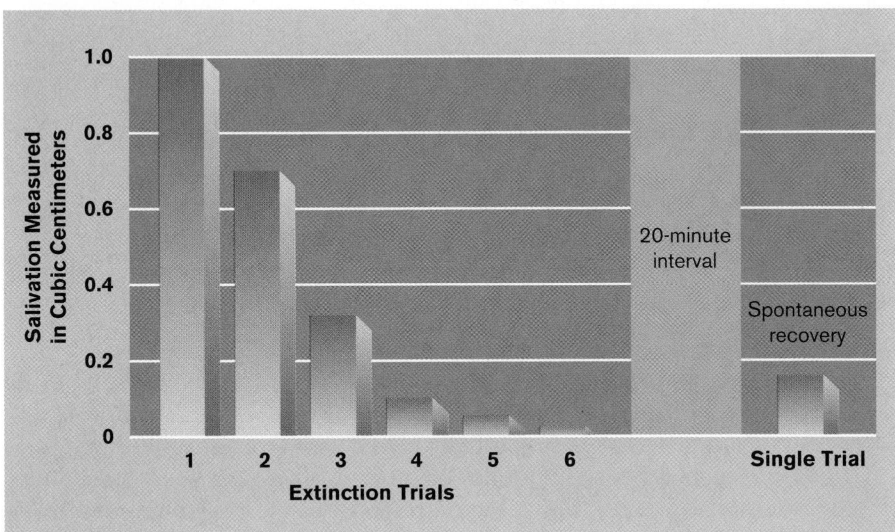

Smell and taste are closely associated because the smell of a particular food is a signal for its taste and the physical sensations associated with eating it. Consequently, a food's odor is a conditioned stimulus that elicits the same emotional and even physiological responses as the food itself. In fact, seeing a photo of someone smelling a particularly pungent food may also act as a conditioned stimulus. When you look at this photo, can you imagine how the peach smells? When you imagine the smell, do you recall the food's taste and texture? Are you starting to get hungry?

Some research indicates that extinction is context-specific (Bouton, 1993; Bouton & Ricker, 1994). When a conditioned response is extinguished in one setting, it can still be elicited in other settings where extinction training has not occurred. Pavlov did not discover this because his experiments were always conducted in the same setting.

Assume that you have conditioned a dog to salivate when it hears the tone middle C played on the piano. Would it also salivate if you played B or D? Pavlov found that a tone similar to the original conditioned stimulus would produce the conditioned response (salivation), a phenomenon called **generalization.** But the salivation decreased the farther the tone was from the original conditioned stimulus, until the tone became so different that the dog would not salivate at all.

Pavlov was able to demonstrate generalization using other senses, such as touch. He attached a small vibrator to a dog's thigh and conditioned the dog to salivate when the thigh was stimulated. Once generalization was established, salivation also occurred when other parts of the dog's body were stimulated. But the farther away the point of stimulation was from the thigh, the weaker the salivation response became (see Figure 5.4, on page 164).

It is easy to see the value of generalization in daily life. For instance, if you enjoyed being in school as a child, you probably feel more positively about your college experiences than your classmates who enjoyed school less. Because of generalization, we do not need to learn a conditioned response to every stimulus that may differ only slightly from an original one. Rather, we learn to approach or avoid a range of stimuli similar to the one that produced the original conditioned response.

Let's return to the example of a dog being conditioned to a musical tone to trace the process of **discrimination,** the learned ability to distinguish between similar stimuli so that the conditioned response occurs only to the original conditioned stimuli but not to similar stimuli.

■ **generalization**
In classical conditioning, the tendency to make a conditioned response to a stimulus that is similar to the original conditioned stimulus.

■ **discrimination**
The learned ability to distinguish between similar stimuli so that the conditioned response occurs only to the original conditioned stimulus but not to similar stimuli.

FIGURE 5.4 Generalization of a Conditioned Response

Pavlov attached small vibrators to different parts of a dog's body. After conditioning salivation to stimulation of the dog's thigh, he stimulated other parts of the dog's body. Due to generalization, the salivation also occurred when other body parts were stimulated. But the farther away from the thigh the stimulus was applied, the weaker the salivation response.

Source: From Pavlov (1927/1960).

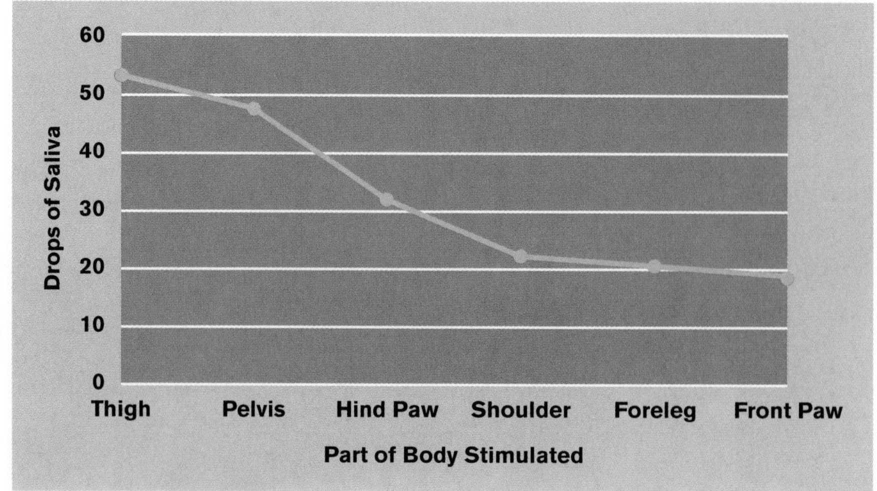

Step 1. The dog is conditioned to salivate in response to the tone C.

Step 2. Generalization occurs, and the dog salivates to a range of musical tones above and below C. The dog salivates less and less as the tone moves away from C.

Step 3. The original tone C is repeatedly paired with food. Neighboring tones are also sounded, but they are not followed by food. The dog is being conditioned to discriminate. Gradually, the salivation response to the neighboring tones (A, B, D, and E) is extinguished, while salivation to the original tone C is strengthened.

Like generalization, discrimination has survival value. Discriminating between the odors of fresh and spoiled milk will spare you an upset stomach. Discriminating between a rattlesnake and a garter snake could save your life.

John Watson and Emotional Conditioning

How did Watson demonstrate that fear could be classically conditioned?

In 1919, John Watson (1878–1958) and his assistant, Rosalie Rayner, conducted a now-famous study to prove that fear could be classically conditioned. The subject of the study, known as Little Albert, was a healthy and emotionally stable 11-month-old infant. When tested, he showed no fear except of the loud noise Watson made by striking a hammer against a steel bar near his head.

In the laboratory, Rayner presented Little Albert with a white rat. As Albert reached for the rat, Watson struck the steel bar with a hammer just behind Albert's head. This procedure was repeated, and Albert "jumped violently, fell forward and began to whimper" (Watson & Rayner, 1920, p. 4). A week later, Watson continued the experiment, pairing the rat with the loud noise five more times. Then, at the sight of the white rat alone, Albert began to cry.

When Albert returned to the laboratory 5 days later, the fear had generalized to a rabbit and, somewhat less, to a dog, a seal coat, Watson's hair, and a Santa Claus mask (see Figure 5.5). After 30 days, Albert made his final visit to the laboratory. His fears were still evident, although they were somewhat less intense. Watson concluded that conditioned fears "persist and modify personality throughout life" (Watson & Rayner, 1920, p. 12).

Although Watson had formulated techniques for removing conditioned fears, Albert moved out of the city before they could be tried on him. Since Watson apparently knew that Albert would be moving away before these fear-removal techniques could be applied, he clearly showed a disregard for the child's welfare. The American Psychological Association now has strict ethical standards for the use of human and animal participants in research experiments and would not sanction an experiment such as Watson's.

FIGURE 5.5 The Conditioned Fear Response

Little Albert's fear of a white rat was a conditioned response that was generalized to other stimuli, including a rabbit and, to a lesser extent, a Santa Claus mask.

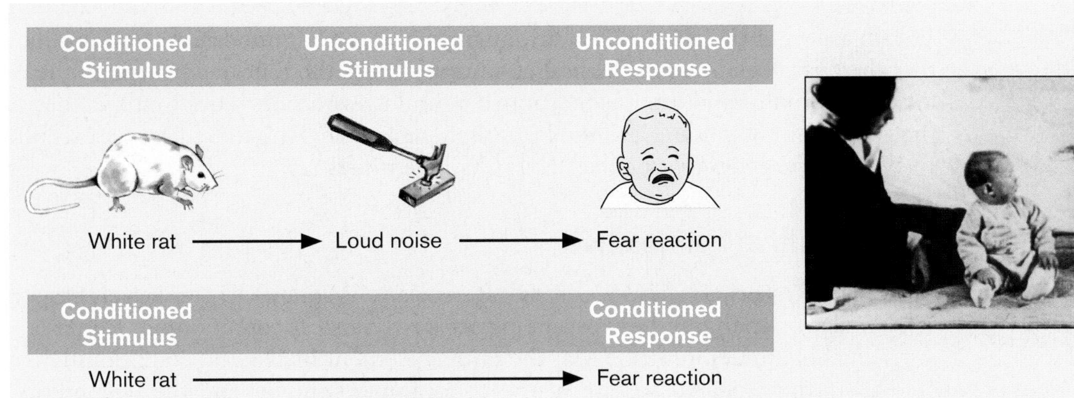

Some of Watson's ideas for removing fears laid the groundwork for certain behavior therapies used today. Three years after his experiment with Little Albert, Watson and a colleague, Mary Cover Jones (1924), found 3-year-old Peter, who, like Albert, was afraid of white rats. He was also afraid of rabbits, a fur coat, feathers, cotton, and a fur rug. Peter's fear of the rabbit was his strongest fear, and this became the target of Watson's fear-removal techniques. Peter was brought into the laboratory, seated in a high chair, and given candy to eat. A white rabbit in a wire cage was brought into the room but kept far enough away from Peter that it would not upset him. Over the course of 38 therapy sessions, the rabbit was brought closer and closer to Peter, who continued to enjoy his candy. Occasionally, some of Peter's friends were brought in to play with the rabbit at a safe distance from Peter so that he could see firsthand that the rabbit did no harm. Toward the end of Peter's therapy, the rabbit was taken out of the cage and eventually put in Peter's lap. By the final session, Peter had grown fond of the rabbit. What is more, he had lost all fear of the fur coat, cotton, and feathers, and he could tolerate the white rats and the fur rug.

So far, we have considered classical conditioning primarily in relation to Pavlov's dogs and Watson's human subjects. How is classical conditioning viewed today?

Remember It 5.1

1. Classical conditioning was discovered by ___________.
2. A dog's salivation in response to a musical tone is a(n) ___________ response.
3. The weakening of a conditioned response that occurs when a conditioned stimulus is presented without the unconditioned stimulus is called ___________.
4. Five-year-old Mia was bitten by her grandmother's labrador retriever. She won't go near that dog but seems to have no fear of other dogs, even other labradors. Her behavior is best explained by the principle of ___________.
5. For ___________ conditioning to occur, conditioned stimuli are linked together to form a series of signals.
6. In Watson's experiment with Little Albert, the white rat was the ___________ stimulus, and Albert's crying when the hammer struck the steel bar was the ___________ response.
7. Albert's fear of the white rat transferred to a rabbit, a dog, a fur coat, and a mask, in a learning process known as ___________.

ANSWERS: 1. Pavlov; 2. conditioned; 3. extinction; 4. discrimination; 5. higher-order; 6. conditioned, unconditioned; 7. generalization

Classical Conditioning: The Contemporary View

Which aspect of the classical conditioning process is most important? Pavlov believed that the critical element in classical conditioning was the repeated pairing of the conditioned stimulus and the unconditioned stimulus, with only a brief interval between the two. Beginning in the late 1960s, though, researchers began to discover exceptions to some of the general principles Pavlov had identified.

The Cognitive Perspective

According to Rescorla, what is the critical element in classical conditioning?

Robert Rescorla (1967, 1968, 1988; Rescorla & Wagner, 1972) is largely responsible for changing how psychologists view classical conditioning. Rescorla was able to demonstrate that the critical element in classical conditioning is not the repeated pairing of the conditioned stimulus and the unconditioned stimulus. Rather, the important factor is whether the conditioned stimulus provides information that enables the organism to reliably *predict* the occurrence of the unconditioned stimulus. How was Rescorla able to prove that prediction is the critical element?

Using rats as his subjects, Rescorla used a tone as the conditioned stimulus and a shock as the unconditioned stimulus. For one group of rats, the tone and shock were paired 20 times—the shock always occurred during the tone. The other group of rats also received a shock 20 times while the tone was sounding, but this group also received 20 shocks that were not paired with the tone. If the only critical element in classical conditioning were the number of pairings of the conditioned stimulus and the unconditioned stimulus, both groups of rats should have developed a conditioned fear response to the tone, because both groups experienced exactly the same number of pairings of tone and shock. But this was not the case. Only the first group, for which the tone was a reliable predictor of the shock, developed the conditioned fear response to the tone. The second group showed little evidence of conditioning, because the shock was just as likely to occur without the tone as with it. In other words, for this group, the tone provided no additional information about the shock.

But what about Pavlov's belief that almost any neutral stimulus could serve as a conditioned stimulus? Later research revealed that organisms' biological predispositions can limit the associations they can form through classical conditioning.

Biological Predispositions

What did Garcia and Koelling discover about classical conditioning?

Remember that Watson conditioned Little Albert to fear the white rat by pairing the presence of the rat with the loud noise of a hammer striking against a steel bar. Do you think Watson could just as easily have conditioned a fear response to a flower or a piece of ribbon? Probably not. Research has shown that humans are more easily conditioned to fear stimuli, such as snakes, that can have very real negative effects on their well-being (Ohman & Mineka, 2003). Moreover, fear of snakes and other potentially threatening animals is just as common in apes and monkeys as in humans, suggesting a biological predisposition to develop these fearful responses.

According to Martin Seligman (1972), most common fears "are related to the survival of the human species through the long course of evolution" (p. 455). Seligman (1970) has suggested that humans and other animals are prepared to associate only certain stimuli with particular consequences. One example of this preparedness is the tendency to develop **taste aversions**—the intense dislike and/or avoidance of particular foods that have been associated with nausea or discomfort.

Chemotherapy treatments can result in a conditioned taste aversion, but providing patients with a "scapegoat" target for the taste aversion can help them maintain a proper diet.

Experiencing nausea and vomiting after eating a certain food is often enough to condition a long-lasting taste aversion. Taste aversions can be classically conditioned when the delay between the conditioned stimulus (food or drink) and the unconditioned stimulus (nausea) is as long as 12 hours. Researchers believe that many taste aversions begin when children are between 2 and 3 years old, so adults may not remember how their particular aversions originated (Rozin & Zellner, 1985).

In a classic study on taste aversion, Garcia and Koelling (1966) exposed rats to a three-way conditioned stimulus: a bright light, a clicking noise, and flavored water. For one group of rats, the unconditioned stimulus was being exposed to either X-rays or lithium chloride, either of which produces nausea and vomiting several hours after exposure; for the other group, the unconditioned stimulus was an electric shock to the feet. The rats that were made ill associated the flavored water with the nausea and avoided it at all times, but they would still drink unflavored water when the bright light and the clicking sound were present. The rats receiving the electric shock continued to prefer the flavored water over unflavored water, but they would not drink at all in the presence of the bright light or the clicking sound. The rats in one group associated nausea only with the flavored water; those in the other group associated electric shock only with the light and the sound.

Garcia and Koelling's research established two exceptions to traditional ideas of classical conditioning. First, the finding that rats formed an association between nausea and flavored water ingested several hours earlier contradicted the principle that the conditioned stimulus must be presented shortly before the unconditioned stimulus. Second, the finding that rats associated electric shock only with noise and light and nausea only with flavored water revealed that animals are apparently biologically predisposed to make certain associations and that associations cannot be readily conditioned between just any two stimuli.

Other research on conditioned taste aversions has led to the solution of such practical problems as controlling predators and helping cancer patients. Gustavson and others (1974) used taste aversion conditioning to stop wild coyotes from attacking lambs in the western United States. They set out lamb flesh laced with lithium chloride, a poison that made the coyotes extremely ill but was not fatal. The plan was so successful that after one or two experiences, the coyotes would get sick even at the sight of a lamb.

Knowledge about conditioned taste aversion is useful in solving other problems as well. Bernstein and others (1982; Bernstein, 1985) devised a technique to help cancer patients avoid developing aversions to desirable foods. A group of cancer patients were given a novel-tasting, maple-flavored ice cream before chemotherapy. The nausea caused by the treatment resulted in a taste aversion to the ice cream. The researchers found that when an unusual or unfamiliar food becomes the "scapegoat," or target for a taste aversion, other foods in the patient's diet may be protected, and the patient will continue to eat them regularly. So, cancer patients should refrain from eating preferred or nutritious foods prior to chemotherapy. Instead, they should be given an unusual-tasting food shortly before treatment. As a result, they are less likely to develop aversions to foods they normally eat and, in turn, are more likely to maintain their body weight during treatment.

■ **taste aversion**
The intense dislike and/or avoidance of a particular food that has been associated with nausea or discomfort.

Classical Conditioning in Everyday Life

What types of everyday responses can be subject to classical conditioning?

Do certain songs have special meaning because they remind you of a current or past love? Do you find the scent of a particular perfume or after-shave pleasant or unpleasant because it reminds you of a certain person? Many of our emotional responses, whether positive or negative, result from classical conditioning. Clearly, classical conditioning is an important, even essential, component of the array of learning capacities characteristic of humans. Indeed, recent research suggests that the inability to acquire classically conditioned responses may be the first sign of Alzheimer's disease, a sign that appears prior to any memory loss (Woodruff-Pak, 2001).

You may have a fear or phobia that was learned through classical conditioning. For example, many people who have had painful dental work develop a dental phobia. Not only do they come to fear the dentist's drill, but they develop anxiety in response to a wide range of stimuli associated with it—the dental chair, the waiting room, even the building where the dentist's office is located. In the conditioning of fear, a conditioned stimulus (CS), such as a tone, is paired with an aversive stimulus (US), such as a foot shock, in a new or unfamiliar environment (context). After just one pairing, an animal exhibits a long-lasting fear of the CS and of the context.

Through classical conditioning, environmental cues associated with drug use can become conditioned stimuli and later produce the conditioned responses of drug craving (Field & Duka, 2002; London et al., 2000). The conditioned stimuli associated with drugs become powerful, often irresistible forces that lead individuals to seek out and use those substances (Porrino & Lyons, 2000). Consequently, drug counselors strongly urge recovering addicts to avoid any cues (people, places, and things) associated with their past drug use. Relapse is far more common in those who do not avoid such associated environmental cues.

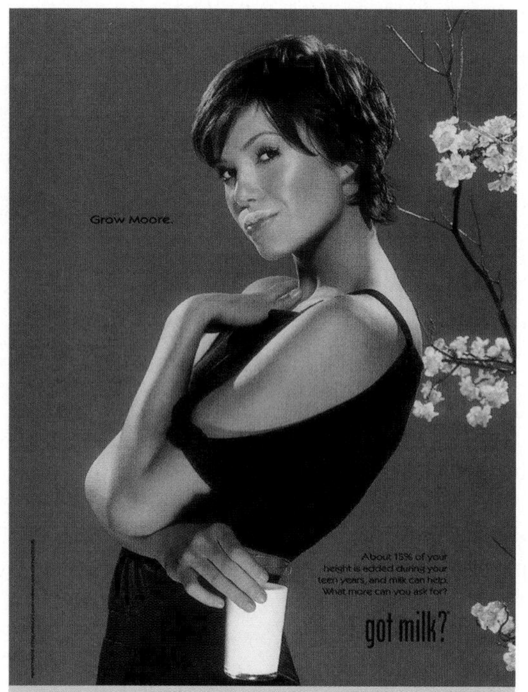

Classical conditioning has proved to be a highly effective tool for advertisers. Here, a neutral product (milk) is paired with an image of an attractive celebrity.

Advertisers seek to classically condition consumers when they show products being used by great-looking models or celebrities or in situations where people are enjoying themselves. Advertisers reason that if the "neutral" product is associated with people, objects, or situations consumers particularly like, in time the product will elicit a similarly positive response. Pavlov found that presenting the tone just before the food was the most efficient way to condition salivation in dogs. Television advertisements, too, are most effective when the products are presented before the beautiful people or situations are shown (van den Hout & Merckelbach, 1991).

Research indicates that even the immune system is subject to classical conditioning (Ader, 1985; Ader & Cohen, 1982, 1993; Exton et al., 2000). In the mid-1970s, Robert Ader was conducting an experiment with rats, conditioning them to avoid saccharin-sweetened water. Immediately after drinking the sweet water (which rats consider a treat), the rats were injected with a tasteless drug (cyclophosphamide) that causes severe nausea. The conditioning worked, and from that time on, the rats would not drink the sweet water, with or without the drug. Attempting to reverse the conditioned response, Ader force-fed the sweet water to the rats for many days; later, unexpectedly, many of them died. Ader was puzzled, because the sweet water was in no way lethal. When he checked further into the properties of the tasteless drug, he learned that it suppresses the immune system. A few doses of an immune-suppressing drug paired with sweetened water had produced a conditioned response. As a result, the sweet water alone continued to suppress the immune system, causing the rats to die.

Ader and Cohen (1982) successfully repeated the experiment, with strict controls to rule out other explanations. The fact that a neutral stimulus such as sweetened water can produce effects similar to those of an immune-suppressing drug shows how powerful classical conditioning can be.

Bovbjerg and others (1990) found that in some cancer patients undergoing chemotherapy, environmental cues in the treatment setting (context) eventually came to elicit nausea and immune suppression. These were the same conditioned responses that the treatment alone had caused earlier. Other researchers showed that classical conditioning could be used to suppress the immune system in order to prolong the survival of mice heart tissue transplants (Grochowicz et al., 1991). And not only can classically conditioned stimuli suppress the immune system, they can also be used to boost it (Exton et al., 2000; Markovic et al., 1993).

Neurological Basis of Classical Conditioning An intact amygdala is required for the conditioning of fear in both humans and animals, and context fear conditioning also depends on the hippocampus (Anagnostaras et al., 2000; Cheng et al., 2003). Research clearly indicates that the cerebellum is the essential brain structure for motor (movement) conditioning and also the storage site for the memory traces formed during such conditioning (Steinmetz, 2000; Thompson et al., 2000).

Factors Influencing Classical Conditioning

Why doesn't classical conditioning result every time unconditioned and conditioned stimuli occur together?

In summary, four major factors facilitate the acquisition of a classically conditioned response:

1. *How reliably the conditioned stimulus predicts the unconditioned stimulus.* Rescorla (1967, 1988) has shown that classical conditioning does not occur automatically just because a neutral stimulus is repeatedly paired with an unconditioned stimulus. The neutral stimulus must also reliably predict the occurrence of the unconditioned stimulus. A tone that is always followed by food will elicit more salivation than one that is followed by food only some of the time.
2. *The number of pairings of the conditioned stimulus and the unconditioned stimulus.* In general, the greater the number of pairings, the stronger the conditioned response. But one pairing is all that is needed to classically condition a taste aversion or a strong emotional response to cues associated with some traumatic event, such as an earthquake or rape.
3. *The intensity of the unconditioned stimulus.* If a conditioned stimulus is paired with a very strong unconditioned stimulus, the conditioned response will be stronger and will be acquired more rapidly than if the conditioned stimulus were paired with a weaker unconditioned stimulus (Gormezano, 1984). For example, striking the steel bar with the hammer produced stronger and faster conditioning in Little Albert than if Watson had merely clapped his hands behind Albert's head.
4. *The temporal relationship between the conditioned stimulus and the unconditioned stimulus.* Conditioning takes place fastest if the conditioned stimulus occurs shortly before the unconditioned stimulus. It takes place more slowly or not at all when the two stimuli occur at the same time. Conditioning rarely takes place when the conditioned stimulus follows the unconditioned stimulus (Gallistel & Gibbon, 2000; Spetch et al., 1981; Spooner & Kellogg, 1947). The ideal time between presentation of conditioned and unconditioned stimuli is about ½ second, but this varies according to the type of response being conditioned and the nature and intensity of the conditioned stimulus and the unconditioned stimulus (see Wasserman & Miller, 1997).

Remember It 5.2

1. According to Rescorla, the most critical element in classical conditioning is ________ .
2. Garcia and Koelling's research suggests that classical conditioning is influenced by ________ .
3. Conditioning of a ________ contradicts the general principle of classical conditioning that the unconditioned stimulus should occur immediately after the conditioned stimulus and the two should be paired repeatedly.
4. In everyday life, ________ and ________ are often acquired through classical conditioning.
5. Classical conditioning can suppress or boost the ________ .

ANSWERS: 1. prediction; 2. biological predispositions; 3. taste aversion; 4. fears, phobias; 5. immune system

Operant Conditioning

■ **trial-and-error learning** Learning that occurs when a response is associated with a successful solution to a problem after a number of unsuccessful responses.

Understanding the principles of classical conditioning can provide a great deal of insight into human behavior. But is there more to human learning than simply responding reflexively to stimuli? Think about a ringing telephone, for example. Do you respond to this stimulus because it has been paired with a natural stimulus of some kind or because of a consequence you anticipate when you hear it? The work of two psychologists, Edward L. Thorndike and B. F. Skinner, helps answer this question.

Thorndike and the Law of Effect

What did Thorndike conclude about learning by watching cats try to escape from his puzzle box?

Have you ever watched a dog learn how to turn over a trash can, or a cat learn how to open a door? If so, you probably observed the animal fail several times before finding just the right physical technique for accomplishing the goal. According to American psychologist Edward Thorndike (1874–1949), **trial-and-error learning** is the basis of most behavioral changes. Based on his observations of animal behavior, Thorndike formulated several laws of learning, the most important being the law of effect (Thorndike, 1911/1970). The **law of effect** states that the consequence, or effect, of a response will determine whether the tendency to respond in the same way in the future will be strengthened or weakened. Responses closely followed by satisfying consequences are more likely to be repeated. Thorndike (1898) insisted that it was "unnecessary to invoke reasoning" to explain how the learning took place.

In Thorndike's best-known experiments, a hungry cat was placed in a wooden box with slats, which was called a *puzzle box*. The box was designed so that the animal had to manipulate a simple mechanism—pressing a pedal or pulling down a loop—to escape and claim a food reward that lay just outside the box. The cat would first try to squeeze through the slats; when these attempts failed, it would scratch, bite, and claw the inside of the box. In time, the cat would accidentally trip the mechanism, which would open the door. Each time, after winning freedom and claiming the food reward, the cat was returned to the box. After many trials, the cat learned to open the door almost immediately after being placed in the box.

■ **law of effect** One of Thorndike's laws of learning, which states that the consequence, or effect, of a response will determine whether the tendency to respond in the same way in the future will be strengthened or weakened.

Thorndike's law of effect was the conceptual starting point for B. F. Skinner's work in operant conditioning.

B. F. Skinner: A Pioneer in Operant Conditioning

What was Skinner's major contribution to psychology?

Most people in the United States know something about B. F. Skinner because his ideas about learning have strongly influenced American education, parenting practices, and approaches to business management. As a boy growing up in Susquehanna, Pennsylvania, Burrhus Frederic Skinner (1904–1990) became fascinated at an early age by the complex tricks he saw trained pigeons perform at country fairs. He was also interested in constructing mechanical devices and in collecting an assortment of animals, which he kept as pets. These interests were destined to play a major role in his later scientific achievements (Bjork, 1993).

After a failed attempt at becoming a writer following his graduation from college, Skinner began reading the books of Pavlov and Watson. He became so intrigued that he entered graduate school at Harvard and completed his Ph.D. in psychology in 1931. Like Watson before him, Skinner believed that the causes of behavior are in the environment and are not rooted in inner mental events such as thoughts, feelings, or perceptions. Instead, Skinner claimed that these inner mental events are themselves behaviors and, like any other behaviors, are shaped and determined by environmental forces.

Skinner conducted much of his research in operant conditioning at the University of Minnesota in the 1930s and wrote *The Behavior of Organisms* (1938), now a classic. Gaining more attention was his first novel, *Walden Two* (1948b), set in a fictional utopian community where reinforcement principles are used to produce happy, productive, and cooperative citizens. In 1948, Skinner returned to Harvard and continued his research and writing. There, he wrote *Science and Human Behavior* (1953), which provides a description of the process of operant conditioning.

In a later and highly controversial book, *Beyond Freedom and Dignity* (1971), Skinner was critical of society's preoccupation with the notion of freedom. He maintained that free will is a myth and that a person's behavior is always shaped and controlled by others—parents, teachers, peers, advertising, television. He argued that rather than leaving the control of human behavior to chance, societies should systematically shape the behavior of their members for the larger good.

Although Skinner's social theories generated controversy, little controversy exists about the significance of his research in operant conditioning.

■ operant conditioning
A type of learning in which the consequences of behavior are manipulated in order to increase or decrease the frequency of an existing response or to shape an entirely new response.

■ reinforcer
Anything that follows a response and strengthens it or increases the probability that it will occur.

The Process of Operant Conditioning

What is the process by which responses are acquired through operant conditioning?

Most of us know that we learn from consequences, but what is the actual process involved in such learning? In **operant conditioning,** the consequences of behavior are manipulated in order to increase or decrease the frequency of an existing response or to shape an entirely new response. Behavior that is reinforced—that is, followed by rewarding consequences—tends to be repeated. A **reinforcer** is anything that strengthens or increases the probability of the response it follows.

Operant conditioning permits the learning of a broad range of new responses. For example, humans can learn to modify their brain-wave patterns through operant conditioning if they are given immediate positive reinforcement for the brain-wave changes that show the desired direction. Such operantly conditioned changes can result in better performance on motor tasks and faster responses on a variety of cognitive tasks (Pulvermüller et al., 2000).

Shaping Behavior In the description of dolphin training at the beginning of the chapter, you learned that the tricks are learned in small steps rather than all at once, an operant conditioning technique called **shaping.** B. F. Skinner demonstrated that shaping is particularly effective in conditioning complex behaviors. With shaping, rather than waiting for the desired response to occur and then reinforcing it, a researcher (or parent or animal trainer) reinforces any movement in

■ shaping
An operant conditioning technique that consists of gradually molding a desired behavior (response) by reinforcing any movement in the direction of the desired response, thereby gradually guiding the responses toward the ultimate goal.

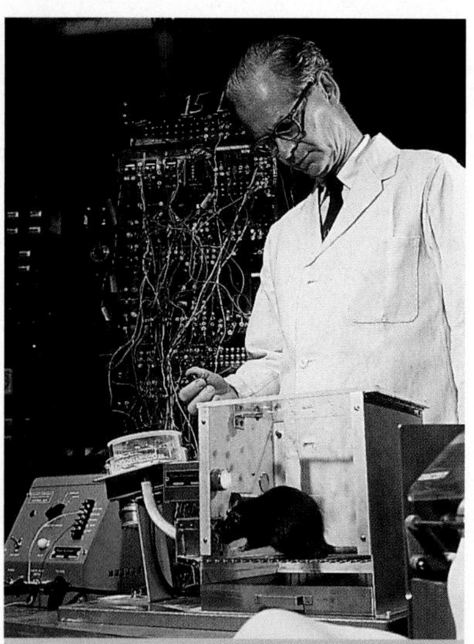

B. F. Skinner shapes a rat's bar-pressing behavior in a Skinner box.

the direction of the desired response, thereby gradually guiding the responses toward the ultimate goal.

Skinner designed a soundproof apparatus, commonly called a **Skinner box,** with which he conducted his experiments in operant conditioning. One type of box is equipped with a lever, or bar, that a rat presses to gain a reward of food pellets or water from a dispenser. A record of the animal's bar pressing is registered on a device called a *cumulative recorder*, also invented by Skinner. Through the use of shaping, a rat in a Skinner box is conditioned to press a bar for rewards. It may be rewarded first for simply turning toward the bar. The next reward comes only when the rat moves closer to the bar. Each step closer to the bar is rewarded. Next, the rat must touch the bar to receive a reward; finally, it is rewarded only when it presses the bar.

Shaping—rewarding **successive approximations** of the desired response—has been used effectively to condition complex behaviors in people as well as other animals. Parents may use shaping to help their children develop good table manners, praising them each time they show an improvement. Teachers often use shaping with disruptive children, reinforcing them at first for very short periods of good behavior and then gradually expecting them to work productively for longer and longer periods. Through shaping, circus animals have learned to perform a wide range of amazing feats, and pigeons have learned to bowl and play Ping-Pong.

Of course, the motive of the shaper is very different from that of the person or animal whose behavior is being shaped. The shaper seeks to change another's behavior by controlling its consequences. The motive of the person or animal whose behavior is being shaped is to gain rewards or avoid unwanted consequences.

Superstitious Behavior Why do athletes develop habits such as wearing their "lucky socks" whenever they play? Sometimes a reward follows a behavior, but the two are not related. Superstitious behavior occurs if an individual falsely believes that a connection exists between an act and its consequences. A gambler in Las Vegas blows on the dice just before he rolls them and wins $1,000. On the next roll, he follows the same ritual and wins again. Although a rewarding event follows the ritual of blowing on the dice, the gambler should not assume a connection between the two.

Superstitious behavior is not confined to humans. Skinner (1948a) developed superstitious behavior in pigeons by giving food rewards every 15 seconds regardless of the pigeons' behavior. Whatever response the pigeons happened to be making was reinforced, and before long, each pigeon developed its own ritual, such as turning counterclockwise in the cage several times or making pendulum movements with its head.

Extinction What happens when reinforcement is no longer available? In operant conditioning, **extinction** occurs when reinforcers are withheld. A rat in a Skinner box will eventually stop pressing a bar when it is no longer rewarded with food pellets.

In humans and other animals, the withholding of reinforcement can lead to frustration or even rage. Consider a child having a temper tantrum. If whining and loud demands do not bring the reinforcer, the child may progress to kicking and screaming. If a vending machine takes your coins but fails to deliver candy or soda, you might shake the machine or even kick it before giving up. When we don't get something we expect, it makes us angry.

The process of *spontaneous recovery*, which we discussed in relation to classical conditioning, also occurs in operant conditioning. A rat whose bar pressing has been extinguished may again press the bar a few times when it is returned to the Skinner box after a period of rest.

Generalization and Discrimination Skinner conducted many of his experiments with pigeons placed in a specially designed Skinner box. The box contained small illu-

■ **Skinner box**
A soundproof chamber with a device for delivering food to an animal subject; used in operant conditioning experiments.

■ **successive approximations**
A series of gradual steps, each of which is more similar to the final desired response.

■ **extinction**
In operant conditioning, the weakening and eventual disappearance of the conditioned response as a result of the withholding of reinforcement.

minated disks that the pigeons could peck to receive bits of grain from a food tray. Skinner found that **generalization** occurs in operant conditioning, just as in classical conditioning. A pigeon reinforced for pecking at a yellow disk is likely to peck at another disk similar in color. The less similar a disk is to the original color, the lower the rate of pecking will be.

Discrimination in operant conditioning involves learning to distinguish between a stimulus that has been reinforced and other stimuli that may be very similar. Discrimination develops when the response to the original stimulus is reinforced but responses to similar stimuli are not reinforced. For example, to encourage discrimination, a researcher would reinforce the pigeon for pecking at the yellow disk but not for pecking at the orange or red disk. Pigeons have even been conditioned to discriminate between a cubist-style Picasso painting and a Monet with 90% accuracy. However, they weren't able to tell a Renoir from a Cezanne ("Psychologists' pigeons . . . ," 1995).

Certain cues come to be associated with reinforcement or punishment. For example, children are more likely to ask their parents for a treat when the parents are smiling than when they are frowning. A stimulus that signals whether a certain response or behavior is likely to be rewarded, ignored, or punished is called a **discriminative stimulus.** If a pigeon's peck at a lighted disk results in a reward but a peck at an unlighted disk does not, the pigeon will soon be pecking exclusively at the lighted disk. The presence or absence of the discriminative stimulus—in this case, the lighted disk—will control whether the pecking takes place.

Why do children sometimes misbehave with a grandparent but not with a parent, or make one teacher's life miserable yet be model students for another? The children may have learned that in the presence of some people (the discriminative stimuli), their misbehavior will almost certainly lead to punishment, but in the presence of certain other people, it may even be rewarded.

■ **generalization**
In operant conditioning, the tendency to make the learned response to a stimulus similar to that for which the response was originally reinforced.

■ **discriminative stimulus**
A stimulus that signals whether a certain response or behavior is likely to be rewarded, ignored, or punished.

■ **reinforcement**
Any event that follows a response and strengthens or increases the probability that the response will be repeated.

Reinforcement

What is the goal of both positive reinforcement and negative reinforcement, and how is that goal accomplished with each?

Positive and Negative Reinforcement How did you learn the correct sequence of behaviors involved in using an ATM machine? Simple—a single mistake in the sequence will prevent you from getting your money, so you learn to do it correctly. What about paying bills on time? Doesn't prompt payment allow you to avoid those steep late-payment penalties? In each case, your behavior is reinforced, but in a different way.

Reinforcement is a key concept in operant conditioning and may be defined as any event that follows a response and strengthens or increases the probability of the response being repeated. There are two types of reinforcement, positive and negative. **Positive reinforcement,** which is roughly the same thing as a reward, refers to any pleasant or desirable consequence that follows a response and increases the probability that the response will be repeated. The money you get when you use the correct ATM procedure is a positive reinforcer.

Just as people engage in behaviors to get positive reinforcers, they also engage in behaviors to avoid or escape aversive, or unpleasant, conditions, such as late-payment penalties. With **negative reinforcement,** a person's or animal's behavior is reinforced by the termination or avoidance of an unpleasant condition. If you find that a response successfully ends an aversive condition, you are likely to repeat it. You will turn on the air conditioner to avoid the heat and will get out of bed to turn off a faucet and end the annoying "drip, drip, drip." Heroin addicts will do almost anything to obtain heroin to terminate their painful withdrawal symptoms. In these instances, negative reinforcement involves putting an end to the heat, the dripping faucet, and the withdrawal symptoms.

Primary and Secondary Reinforcers Are all reinforcers created equal? Not necessarily. A **primary reinforcer** is one that fulfills a basic physical need for survival and does not depend on learning. Food, water, sleep, and termination of pain are examples of primary reinforcers. And sex is a powerful reinforcer that fulfills a basic physical

■ **positive reinforcement**
Any pleasant or desirable consequence that follows a response and increases the probability that the response will be repeated.

■ **negative reinforcement**
The termination of an unpleasant condition after a response, which increases the probability that the response will be repeated.

■ **primary reinforcer**
A reinforcer that fulfills a basic physical need for survival and does not depend on learning.

need for survival of the species. Fortunately, learning does not depend solely on primary reinforcers. If that were the case, people would need to be hungry, thirsty, or sex starved before they would respond at all. Much observed human behavior occurs in response to secondary reinforcers. A **secondary reinforcer** is acquired or learned through association with other reinforcers. Some secondary reinforcers (money, for example) can be exchanged at a later time for other reinforcers. Praise, good grades, awards, applause, attention, and signals of approval, such as a smile or a kind word, are all examples of secondary reinforcers.

secondary reinforcer
A reinforcer that is acquired or learned through association with other reinforcers.

Schedules of Reinforcement

What are the four types of schedules of reinforcement, and which type is most effective?

Think about the difference between an ATM machine and a slot machine. Under the right conditions, you can get money from either of them. But the ATM machine gives you a reinforcer every time you use the right procedure, while the slot machine does so only intermittently. How is your behavior affected in each case?

Initially, Skinner conditioned rats by reinforcing each bar-pressing response with a food pellet. Reinforcing every correct response, known as **continuous reinforcement,** is the kind of reinforcement provided by an ATM machine, and it is the most effective way to condition a new response. However, after a response has been conditioned, partial or intermittent reinforcement is often more effective in maintaining or increasing the rate of response. How many people punch buttons on ATM machines just for fun? And how long will you keep on trying to get money from an ATM machine that hasn't responded to a couple of attempts in which you know you did everything right? Yet people will spend hours playing slot machines without being rewarded. **Partial reinforcement** (the slot machine type) is operating when some but not all responses are reinforced. In real life, reinforcement is almost never continuous; partial reinforcement is the rule.

continuous reinforcement
Reinforcement that is administered after every desired or correct response; the most effective method of conditioning a new response.

partial reinforcement
A pattern of reinforcement in which some but not all correct responses are reinforced.

Partial reinforcement may be administered according to any of several types of **schedules of reinforcement.** Different schedules produce distinct rates and patterns of responses, as well as varying degrees of resistance to extinction when reinforcement is discontinued. The effects of reinforcement schedules can vary somewhat with humans, depending on any instructions given to participants that could change their expectations (Lattal & Neef, 1996).

The two basic types of schedules are ratio and interval schedules. Ratio schedules require that a certain number of responses be made before one of the responses is reinforced. With interval schedules, a given amount of time must pass before a reinforcer is administered. These types of schedules are further subdivided into fixed and variable categories. (See Figure 5.6.)

For many students, studying with classmates reduces the nervousness they feel about an upcoming exam. They respond to their test anxiety by joining a study group and studying more. Discussing the exam with other students helps alleviate the anxiety, as well. Thus, for these students, test anxiety is an important source of negative reinforcement.

The Fixed-Ratio Schedule On a **fixed-ratio schedule,** a reinforcer is given after a fixed number of correct, nonreinforced responses. If the fixed ratio is set at 30 responses (FR-30), a reinforcer is given after 30 correct responses. When wages are paid to factory workers according to the number of units produced and to migrant farm workers for each bushel of fruit they pick, those payments are following a fixed-ratio schedule.

The fixed-ratio schedule is a very effective way to maintain a high response rate, because the number of reinforcers received depends directly on the response

FIGURE 5.6 Four Types of Reinforcement Schedules

Skinner's research revealed distinctive response patterns for four partial reinforcement schedules (the reinforcers are indicated by the diagonal marks). The ratio schedules, based on the number of responses, yielded a higher response rate than the interval schedules, which are based on the amount of time elapsed between reinforcers.

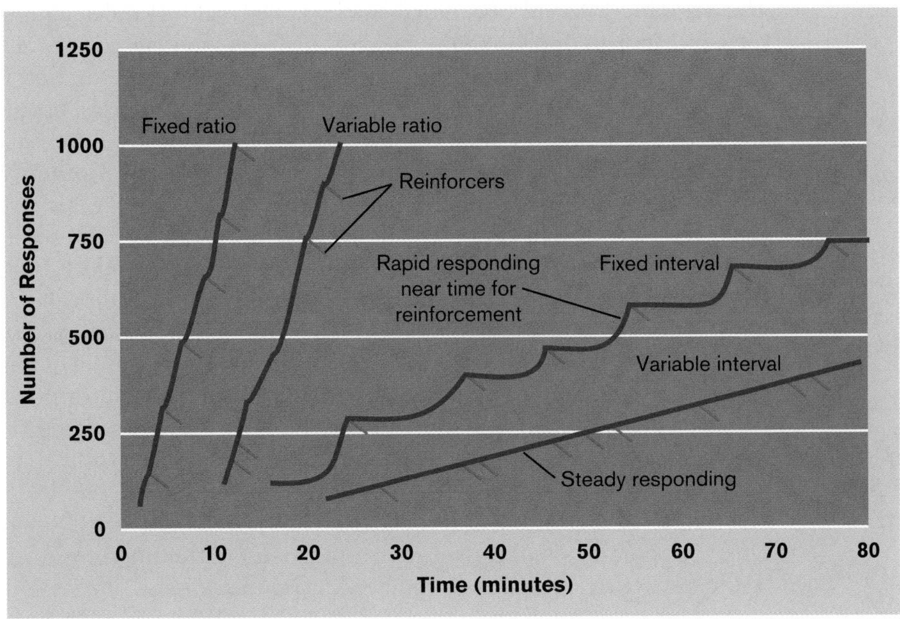

rate. The faster people or animals respond, the more reinforcers they earn and the sooner they earn them. When large ratios are used, people and animals tend to pause after each reinforcement but then return to the high rate of responding.

The Variable-Ratio Schedule The pauses after reinforcement that occur with a high fixed-ratio schedule normally do not occur with a variable-ratio schedule. On a **variable-ratio schedule,** a reinforcer is given after a varying number of nonreinforced responses, based on an average ratio. With a variable ratio of 30 responses (VR-30), people might be reinforced one time after 10 responses, another after 50, another after 30 responses, and so on. It would not be possible to predict exactly which responses will be reinforced, but reinforcement would occur 1 in 30 times, on average.

Variable-ratio schedules result in higher, more stable rates of responding than do fixed-ratio schedules. Skinner (1953) reported that, on this type of schedule, "a pigeon may respond as rapidly as five times per second and maintain this rate for many hours" (p. 104). The best example of the power of the variable-ratio schedule is found in the gambling casino. Slot machines, roulette wheels, and most other games of chance pay on this type of schedule. In general, the variable-ratio schedule produces the highest response rate and the most resistance to extinction.

The Fixed-Interval Schedule On a **fixed-interval schedule,** a specific period of time must pass before a response is reinforced. For example, on a 60-second fixed-interval schedule (FI-60), a reinforcer is given for the first correct response that occurs 60 seconds after the last reinforced response. People who are on salary, rather than paid an hourly rate, are reinforced on the fixed-interval schedule.

■ **schedule of reinforcement**
A systematic process for administering partial reinforcement that produces a distinct rate and pattern of responses and degree of resistance to extinction.

■ **fixed-ratio schedule**
A schedule in which a reinforcer is given after a fixed number of correct, nonreinforced responses.

■ **variable-ratio schedule**
A schedule in which a reinforcer is given after a varying number of nonreinforced responses, based on an average ratio.

■ **fixed-interval schedule**
A schedule in which a reinforcer is given following the first correct response after a specific period of time has elapsed.

Two examples of variable-ratio schedules of reinforcement: Gamblers can't predict when the payoff (reinforcement) will come, so they are highly motivated to keep playing. Likewise, many computer users find themselves in the predicament of knowing they should stop playing solitaire and get to work, but they just can't seem to tear themselves away from the game. Why? The power of variable-ratio reinforcement motivates them to stick with the game until the next win, and the next, and the next. . . .

Unlike ratio schedules, reinforcement on interval schedules does not depend on the number of responses made, only on the one correct response made after the time interval has passed. Characteristic of the fixed-interval schedule is a pause or a sharp decline in responding immediately after each reinforcement and a rapid acceleration in responding just before the next reinforcer is due.

The Variable-Interval Schedule Variable-interval schedules eliminate the pause after reinforcement typical of the fixed-interval schedule. On a **variable-interval schedule,** a reinforcer is given after the first correct response following a varying time of nonreinforced responses, based on an average time. Rather than being given every 60 seconds, for example, a reinforcer might be given after a 30-second interval, with others following after 90-, 45-, and 75-second intervals. But the average time elapsing between reinforcers would be 60 seconds (VI-60). This schedule maintains remarkably stable and uniform rates of responding, but the response rate is typically lower than that for ratio schedules, because reinforcement is not tied directly to the number of responses made. Random drug testing in the workplace is an excellent example of application of the variable-interval schedule that appears to be quite effective.

Review and Reflect 5.1 summarizes the characteristics of the four schedules of reinforcement.

The Effect of Continuous and Partial Reinforcement on Extinction One way to understand extinction in operant conditioning is to consider how consistently a response is followed by reinforcement. On a continuous schedule, a reinforcer is expected without fail after each correct response. When a reinforcer is withheld, it is noticed immediately. But on a partial-reinforcement schedule, a reinforcer is not expected after every response. Thus, no immediate difference is apparent between the partial-reinforcement schedule and the onset of extinction.

When you put money in a vending machine and pull the lever but no candy or soda appears, you know immediately that something is wrong with the machine. But if you were playing a broken slot machine, you could have many nonreinforced responses before you would suspect the machine of malfunctioning.

Partial reinforcement results in greater resistance to extinction than does continuous reinforcement (Lerman et al., 1996). This result is known as the **partial-reinforcement effect.** There is an inverse relationship between the percentage of responses that have been reinforced and resistance to extinction. That is, the lower the percentage of responses that are reinforced, the longer extinction will take when reinforcement is withheld. The strongest resistance to extinction ever observed occurred in one experiment in which pigeons were conditioned to peck at a disk. Holland and Skinner (1961) report that "after the response had been maintained on a fixed ratio of 900 and reinforcement was then discontinued, the pigeon emitted 73,000 responses during the first 4½ hours of extinction" (p. 124).

Parents often wonder why their children continue to whine in order to get what they want, even though the parents usually do not give in to the whining. Unwittingly, parents are reinforcing whining on a variable-ratio schedule, which results in the most persistent behavior. This is why experts always caution parents to be consistent. If parents never reward whining, the behavior will stop; if they give in occasionally, it will persist and be extremely hard to extinguish.

Reward seeking is indeed a powerful motivating force for both humans and animals. There is little doubt that rewards are among the most important of the influences that shape behavior (Elliott et al., 2000). However, the results of more than 100 studies suggest that the overuse of tangible rewards may have certain long-term nega-

■ **variable-interval schedule**
A schedule in which a reinforcer is given after the first correct response that follows a varying time of nonreinforcement, based on an average time.

■ **partial-reinforcement effect**
The greater resistance to extinction that occurs when a portion, rather than all, of the correct responses are reinforced.

REVIEW *and* REFLECT 5.1

Reinforcement Schedules Compared

SCHEDULE OF REINFORCEMENT	RESPONSE RATE	PATTERN OF RESPONSES	RESISTANCE TO EXTINCTION
Fixed-ratio schedule	Very high	Steady response with low ratio. Brief pause after each reinforcement with very high ratio.	The higher the ratio, the more resistance to extinction.
Variable-ratio schedule	Highest response rate	Constant response pattern, no pauses.	Most resistance to extinction.
Fixed-interval schedule	Lowest response rate	Long pause after reinforcement, followed by gradual acceleration.	The longer the interval, the more resistance to extinction.
Variable-interval schedule	Moderate	Stable, uniform response.	More resistance to extinction than fixed-interval schedule with same average interval.

Want to be sure you've fully absorbed the material in this chapter? Visit **www.ablongman.com/wood5e** for access to free practice tests, flashcards, interactive activities, and links developed specifically to help you succeed in psychology.

tive effects, such as undermining people's intrinsic motivation to regulate their own behavior (Deci et al., 1999).

Factors Influencing Operant Conditioning

Why don't consequences always cause changes in behavior?

What factors, other than reinforcement schedules, influence learning from consequences? We have seen that the schedule of reinforcement influences both response rate and resistance to extinction. Three other factors affect response rate, resistance to extinction, and how quickly a response is acquired:

1. *The magnitude of reinforcement.* In general, as the magnitude of reinforcement increases, acquisition of a response is faster, the rate of responding is higher, and resistance to extinction is greater (Clayton, 1964). For example, in studies examining the influence of cash incentives on drug addicts' ability to abstain from taking the drug, researchers have found that the greater the amount of the incentive, the more likely the addicts are to abstain over extended periods of time (Dallery et al., 2001; Katz et al., 2002).
2. *The immediacy of reinforcement.* In general, responses are conditioned more effectively when reinforcement is immediate. As a rule, the longer the delay before reinforcement, the more slowly a response is acquired (Church, 1989; Mazur, 1993). (See Figure 5.7, on page 178.) In animals, little learning occurs when there is any delay at all in reinforcement, because even a short delay obscures the relationship between the behavior and the reinforcer. In humans, a reinforcer sometime in the future is usually no match for immediate reinforcement in controlling behavior. Overweight people have difficulty changing their eating habits partly because of the long delay between their behavior change and the rewarding consequences of weight loss.
3. *The level of motivation of the learner.* If you are highly motivated to learn to play tennis, you will practice more and learn faster than if you have no interest in the game. Skinner (1953) found that when food is the reinforcer, a hungry animal

FIGURE 5.7 **The Effect of a Delay in Reinforcement on the Conditioning of a Response**

In general, responses are conditioned more effectively when reinforcement is immediate. The longer the delay in reinforcement, the lower the probability that a response will be acquired.

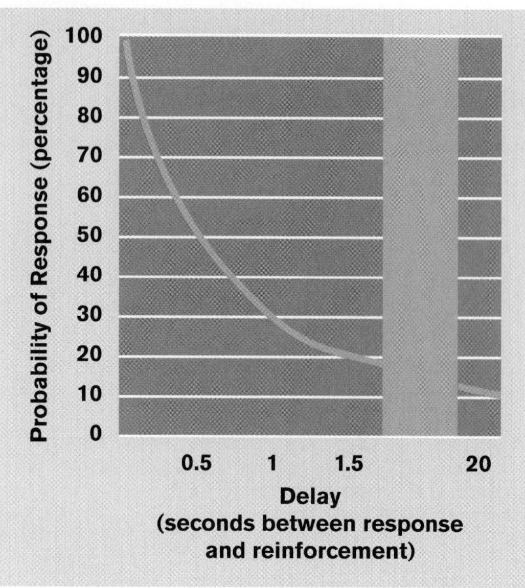

will learn faster than a full animal. To maximize motivation, he used rats that had been deprived of food for 24 hours and pigeons that were maintained at 75–80% of their normal body weight.

Comparing Classical and Operant Conditioning Are you having difficulty distinguishing between classical and operant conditioning? In fact, the processes of generalization, discrimination, extinction, and spontaneous recovery occur in both classical and operant conditioning. And both types of conditioning depend on associative learning. However, in classical conditioning, an association is formed between two stimuli—for example, a tone and food, a white rat and a loud noise, a product and a celebrity. In operant conditioning, the association is established between a response and its consequences—for example, bar pressing and food, studying hard and a high test grade. Furthermore, in classical conditioning, the focus is on what precedes the response. Pavlov focused on what led up to the salivation in his dogs, not on what happened after they salivated. In operant conditioning, the focus is on what follows the response. If a rat's bar pressing or your studying is followed by a reinforcer, that response is more likely to occur in the future. Generally, too, in classical conditioning, the subject is passive and responds to the environment rather than acting on it. In operant conditioning, the subject is active and operates on the environment. Children do something to get their parents' attention or their praise.

Punishment

How does punishment differ from negative reinforcement?

You may be wondering about one of the most common types of consequences, punishment. **Punishment** is the opposite of reinforcement. Punishment usually lowers the probability of a response by following it with an aversive or unpleasant consequence. However, punishment can be accomplished by either adding an unpleasant stimulus or removing a pleasant stimulus. The added unpleasant stimulus might take the form of criticism, a scolding, a disapproving look, a fine, or a prison sentence. The removal of a pleasant stimulus might consist of withholding affection and attention, suspending a driver's license, or taking away a privilege such as watching television.

It is common to confuse punishment and negative reinforcement because both involve an unpleasant condition, but there is a big difference between the two. With punishment, an unpleasant condition may be added, but with negative reinforcement, an unpleasant condition is terminated or avoided. Moreover, the two have opposite effects: Unlike punishment, negative reinforcement increases the probability of a desired response by removing an unpleasant stimulus when the correct response is made. "Grounding" can be used as either punishment or negative reinforcement. If a teenager fails to clean her room after many requests to do so, her parents could ground her for the weekend—a punishment. An alternative approach would be to tell her she is grounded until the room is clean—negative reinforcement. Which approach is more likely to be effective?

■ **punishment**
The removal of a pleasant stimulus or the application of an unpleasant stimulus, thereby lowering the probability of a response.

The Disadvantages of Punishment Thus, if punishment can suppress behavior, why do so many people oppose its use? A number of potential problems are associated with the use of punishment:

1. According to Skinner, punishment does not extinguish an undesirable behavior; rather, it suppresses that behavior when the punishing agent is present. But the behavior is apt to continue when the threat of punishment is removed and in settings where punishment is unlikely. If punishment (imprisonment, fines, and so on) reliably extinguished unlawful behavior, there would be fewer repeat offenders in the criminal justice system.
2. Punishment indicates that a behavior is unacceptable but does not help people develop more appropriate behaviors. If punishment is used, it should be administered in conjunction with reinforcement or rewards for appropriate behavior.
3. The person who is severely punished often becomes fearful and feels angry and hostile toward the punisher. These reactions may be accompanied by a desire to retaliate or to avoid or escape from the punisher and the punishing situation. Many runaway teenagers leave home to escape physical abuse. Punishment that involves a loss of privileges is more effective than physical punishment and engenders less fear and hostility (Walters & Grusec, 1977).
4. Punishment frequently leads to aggression. Those who administer physical punishment may become models of aggressive behavior, by demonstrating aggression as a way of solving problems and discharging anger. Children of abusive, punishing parents are at greater risk than other children of becoming aggressive and abusive themselves (Widom, 1989).

If punishment can cause these problems, what can be done to discourage undesirable behavior?

Alternatives to Punishment Are there other ways to suppress behavior? Many psychologists believe that removing the rewarding consequences of undesirable behavior is the best way to extinguish a problem behavior. According to this view, parents should extinguish a child's temper tantrums not by punishment but by never giving in to the child's demands during a tantrum. A parent might best extinguish problem behavior that is performed merely to get attention by ignoring it and giving attention to more appropriate behavior. Sometimes, simply explaining why a certain behavior is not appropriate is all that is required to extinguish the behavior.

Using positive reinforcement such as praise will make good behavior more rewarding for children. This approach brings with it the attention that children want and need—attention that often comes only when they misbehave.

It is probably unrealistic to believe that punishment will ever become unnecessary. If a young child runs into the street, puts a finger near an electrical outlet, or reaches for a hot pan on the stove, a swift punishment may save the child from a potentially disastrous situation.

Making Punishment More Effective When punishment is necessary (e.g., to stop destructive behavior), how can we be sure that it will be effective? Research has revealed several factors that influence the effectiveness of punishment: its timing, its intensity, and the consistency of its application (Parke, 1977).

1. Punishment is most effective when it is applied during the misbehavior or as soon afterward as possible. Interrupting the problem behavior is most effective because doing so abruptly halts its rewarding aspects. The longer the delay between the response and the punishment, the less effective the punishment is in suppressing the response (Camp et al., 1967). When there is a delay, most animals do not make the connection between the misbehavior and the punishment. For example, anyone who has tried to housebreak a puppy knows that it is necessary to catch the animal in the act of soiling the carpet for the punishment to be effective. With humans, however, if the punishment must be delayed, the punisher should remind the perpetrator of the incident and explain why the behavior was inappropriate.
2. Ideally, punishment should be of the minimum severity necessary to suppress the problem behavior. Animal studies reveal that the more intense the punishment,

Culture shapes ideas about punishment. Because ideas about what is and is not humane punishment have changed in Western society, public humiliation is no longer considered to be an appropriate punishment, regardless of its potential for reducing crime.

the greater the suppression of the undesirable behavior (Church, 1963). But the intensity of the punishment should match the seriousness of the misdeed. Unnecessarily severe punishment is likely to produce the negative side effects mentioned earlier. The purpose of punishment is not to vent anger but, rather, to modify behavior. Punishment meted out in anger is likely to be more intense than necessary to bring about the desired result. Yet, if the punishment is too mild, it will have no effect. Similarly, gradually increasing the intensity of the punishment is not effective because the perpetrator will gradually adapt, and the unwanted behavior will persist (Azrin & Holz, 1966). At a minimum, if a behavior is to be suppressed, the punishment must be more punishing than the misbehavior is rewarding. In human terms, a $200 ticket is more likely to suppress the urge to speed than a $2 ticket.

3. To be effective, punishment must be applied consistently. A parent cannot ignore misbehavior one day and punish the same act the next. And both parents should react to the same misbehavior in the same way. An undesired response will be suppressed more effectively when the probability of punishment is high. Would you be tempted to speed if you saw a police car in your rear-view mirror?

Culture and Punishment Do you think stoning is an appropriate punishment for adultery? Probably not, unless you come from a culture in which such punishments are acceptable. Punishment is used in every culture to control and suppress people's behavior. It is administered when important values, rules, regulations, and laws are violated. But not all cultures share the same values or have the same laws regulating behavior. U.S. citizens traveling in other countries need to be aware of how different cultures view and administer punishment. For example, selling drugs is a serious crime just about everywhere. In the United States, it carries mandatory prison time; in some other countries, it is a death penalty offense.

Can you imagine being beaten with a cane as a legal punishment for vandalism? A widely publicized 1994 incident involving a young man named Michael Fay continues to serve as one of the best real-life examples of the sharp differences in concepts of crime and punishment between the United States and Singapore. Fay, an 18-year-old American living in Singapore, was arrested and charged with 53 counts of vandalism, including the spray painting of dozens of cars. He was fined approximately $2,000, sentenced to 4 months in jail, and received four lashes with a rattan cane, an agonizingly painful experience. In justifying their system of punishment, the officials in Singapore were quick to point out that their city, about the same size as Los Angeles, is virtually crime-free. Among Americans, sentiment about the caning was mixed. Some, including Fay's parents, viewed it as barbarous and cruel. But many Americans (51% in a CNN poll) expressed the view that caning might be an effective punishment under certain circumstances. What do you think?

When is avoidance learning desirable, and when is it maladaptive?

Escape and Avoidance Learning

Remember the earlier example about paying bills on time to avoid late fees? Learning to perform a behavior because it prevents or terminates an aversive event is called *escape learning*, and it reflects the power of negative reinforcement. Running away from a punishing situation and taking aspirin to relieve a pounding headache are examples of escape behavior. In these situations, the aversive event has begun, and an attempt is being made to escape it.

Avoidance learning, in contrast, depends on two types of conditioning. Through classical conditioning, an event or condition comes to signal an aversive state. Drinking and driving may be associated with automobile accidents and death. Because of such associations, people may engage in behaviors to avoid the anticipated aversive consequences. Making it a practice to avoid riding in a car with a driver who has been drinking is sensible avoidance behavior.

Much avoidance learning is maladaptive, however, and occurs in response to phobias. Students who have had a bad experience speaking in front of a class may begin to fear any situation that involves speaking before a group. Such students may avoid taking courses that require class presentations or taking leadership roles that necessitate public speaking. Avoiding such situations prevents them from suffering the perceived dreaded consequences. But the avoidance behavior is negatively reinforced and thus strengthened through operant conditioning. Maladaptive avoidance behaviors are very difficult to extinguish, because people never give themselves a chance to learn that the dreaded consequences probably will not occur, or that they are greatly exaggerated.

There is an important exception to the ability of humans and other animals to learn to escape and avoid aversive situations: **Learned helplessness** is a passive resignation to aversive conditions, learned by repeated exposure to aversive events that are inescapable or unavoidable. The initial experiment on learned helplessness was conducted by Overmeier and Seligman (1967). Dogs in the experimental group were strapped into harnesses from which they could not escape and were exposed to electric shocks. Later, these same dogs were placed in a box with two compartments separated by a low barrier. The dogs then experienced a series of trials in which a warning signal was followed by an electric shock administered through the box's floor. However, the floor was electrified only on one side, and the dogs could have escaped the electric shocks simply by jumping the barrier. Surprisingly, the dogs did not do so. Dogs in the control group had not previously experienced the inescapable shock and behaved in an entirely different manner and quickly learned to jump the barrier when the warning signal sounded and thus escaped the shock. Seligman (1975) later reasoned that humans who have suffered painful experiences they could neither avoid nor escape may also experience learned helplessness. Then, they may simply give up and react to disappointment in life by becoming inactive, withdrawn, and depressed (Seligman, 1991).

■ **avoidance learning**
Learning to avoid events or conditions associated with aversive consequences or phobias.

■ **learned helplessness**
A passive resignation to aversive conditions that is learned through repeated exposure to inescapable or unavoidable aversive events.

Applications of Operant Conditioning

You have probably realized that operant conditioning is an important learning process that we experience almost every day. Operant conditioning can also be used intentionally by one person to change another person's or an animal's behavior.

What are some applications of operant conditioning?

Shaping the Behavior of Animals The principles of operant conditioning are used effectively to train animals not only to perform entertaining tricks but also to help physically challenged people lead more independent lives. Dogs and monkeys have been trained to help people who are paralyzed or confined to wheelchairs, and for years, seeing-eye dogs have been trained to assist the blind.

Through the use of shaping, animals at zoos, circuses, and marine parks have been conditioned to perform a wide range of amazing feats. After conditioning thousands of animals from over 38 different species to perform numerous feats for advertising and entertainment purposes, Breland and Breland (1961) concluded that biological predispositions in various species can affect how easily responses can be learned. When an animal's instinctual behavior runs counter to the behavior being conditioned, the animal will eventually resume its instinctual behavior, a phenomenon known as *instinctual drift.* For example, picking up coins and depositing them in a bank is a task that runs counter to the natural tendencies of raccoons and pigs. In time, a raccoon will hold the coins and rub them together instead of dropping them in the bank, and the pigs will drop them on the ground and push them with their snouts.

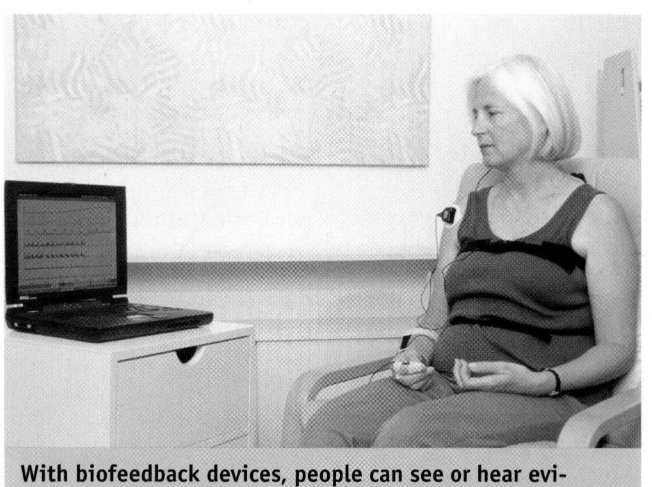

With biofeedback devices, people can see or hear evidence of internal physiological states and learn how to control them through various mental strategies.

Biofeedback Training your dog to roll over is one thing, but can you train yourself to control your body's responses to stress? For years, scientists believed that internal responses such as heart rate, brain-wave patterns, and blood flow were not subject to operant conditioning. It is now known that when people are given very precise feedback about these internal processes, they can learn, with practice, to exercise control over them. **Biofeedback** is a way of getting information about internal biological states. Biofeedback devices have sensors that monitor slight changes in these internal responses and then amplify and convert them into visual or auditory signals. Thus, people can see or hear evidence of internal physiological processes, and by trying out various strategies (thoughts, feelings, or images), they can learn which ones routinely increase, decrease, or maintain a particular level of activity.

Biofeedback has been used to regulate heart rate and to control migraine and tension headaches, gastrointestinal disorders, asthma, anxiety tension states, epilepsy, sexual dysfunctions, and neuromuscular disorders such as cerebral palsy, spinal cord injuries, and stroke (Kalish, 1981; L. Miller, 1989; N. E. Miller, 1985).

Behavior Modification Can operant conditioning help you get better grades? Perhaps, if you apply its principles to your study behavior. **Behavior modification** is a method of changing behavior through a systematic program based on the learning principles of classical conditioning, operant conditioning, or observational learning (which we will discuss soon). The majority of behavior modification programs use the principles of operant conditioning. *Try It 5.1* challenges you to come up with your own behavior modification plan.

Many institutions, such as schools, mental hospitals, homes for youthful offenders, and prisons, have used behavior modification programs with varying degrees of success. Such institutions are well suited for the use of these programs because they provide a restricted environment where the consequences of behavior can be more strictly controlled. Some prisons and mental hospitals use a **token economy**—a program that motivates socially desirable behavior by reinforcing it with tokens. The tokens (poker chips or coupons) may later be exchanged for desired items like candy or cigarettes and privileges such as weekend passes, free time, or participation in desired activities. People in the program know in advance exactly what behaviors will be reinforced and how they will be reinforced. Token economies have been used effectively in mental hospitals to encourage patients to attend to grooming, to interact with other patients, and to carry out housekeeping tasks (Ayllon & Azrin, 1965, 1968). Although the positive behaviors generally stop when the tokens are discontinued, this does not mean that the programs are not worthwhile. After all, most people who are employed would probably quit their jobs if they were no longer paid.

Many classroom teachers and parents use *time out*—a behavior modification technique in which a child who is misbehaving is removed for a short time from sources of positive reinforcement. (Remember, according to operant conditioning, a behavior that is no longer reinforced will extinguish.)

■ **biofeedback**
The use of sensitive equipment to give people precise feedback about internal physiological processes so that they can learn, with practice, to exercise control over them.

■ **behavior modification**
A method of changing behavior through a systematic program based on the learning principles of classical conditioning, operant conditioning, or observational learning.

■ **token economy**
A program that motivates socially desirable behavior by reinforcing it with tokens that can be exchanged for desired items or privileges.

Try It 5.1 Using Behavior Modification

Use conditioning to modify your own behavior.

1. *Identify the target behavior.* It must be both observable and measurable. You might choose, for example, to increase the amount of time you spend studying.
2. *Gather and record baseline data.* Keep a daily record of how much time you spend on the target behavior for about a week. Also note where the behavior takes place and what cues (or temptations) in the environment precede any slacking off from the target behavior.
3. *Plan your behavior modification program.* Formulate a plan and set goals to either decrease or increase the target behavior.
4. *Choose your reinforcers.* Any activity you enjoy more can be used to reinforce any activity you enjoy less. For example, you could reward yourself with a movie after a specified period of studying.
5. *Set the reinforcement conditions and begin recording and reinforcing your progress.* Be careful not to set your reinforcement goals so high that it becomes nearly impossible to earn a reward. Keep in mind Skinner's concept of shaping through rewarding small steps toward the desired outcome. Be perfectly honest with yourself and claim a reward only when you meet the goals. Chart your progress as you work toward gaining more control over the target behavior.

Behavior modification is also used successfully in business and industry to increase profits and to modify employee behavior related to health, safety, and job performance. In order to keep their premiums low, some companies give annual rebates to employees who do not use up the deductibles in their health insurance plan. To reduce costs associated with automobile accidents and auto theft, insurance companies offer incentives in the form of reduced premiums for installing airbags and burglar alarm systems. To encourage employees to take company-approved college courses, some companies offer tuition reimbursement to employees who complete such courses with acceptable grades. Many companies promote sales by giving salespeople bonuses, trips, and other prizes for increasing sales. One of the most successful applications of behavior modification has been in the treatment of psychological problems ranging from phobias to addictive behaviors. In this context, behavior modification is called behavior therapy (discussed in Chapter 16).

Remember It 5.3

1. The process of reinforcing successive approximations of a behavior is known as ________.
2. When reinforcers are withheld, ________ of a response occurs.
3. Taking aspirin to relieve a headache is an example of ________ reinforcement; studying to get a good grade on a test is an example of ________ reinforcement.
4. Glen and Megan are hired to rake leaves. Glen is paid $1 for each bag of leaves he rakes; Megan is paid $4 per hour. Glen is paid according to a ________ schedule; Megan is paid according to a ________ schedule.
5. Negative reinforcement ________ behavior, while punishment ________ behavior.
6. Victims of spousal abuse who have repeatedly failed to escape or avoid the abuse may eventually passively resign themselves to it, a condition known as ________.
7. The use of sensitive electronic equipment to monitor physiological processes in order to bring them under conscious control is called ________.
8. Applying learning principles to eliminate undesirable behavior and/or encourage desirable behavior is called ________.

ANSWERS: 1. shaping; 2. extinction; 3. negative, positive; 4. fixed-ratio; fixed-interval; 5. strengthens, suppresses; 6. learned helplessness; 7. biofeedback; 8. behavior modification

Cognitive Learning

By now, you are probably convinced of the effectiveness of both classical and operant conditioning. But can either type of conditioning explain how you learned a complex mental function like reading? Behaviorists such as Skinner and Watson believed that any kind of learning could be explained without reference to internal mental processes. Today, however, a growing number of psychologists stress the role of mental processes. They choose to broaden the study of learning to include such **cognitive processes** as thinking, knowing, problem solving, remembering, and forming mental representations. According to cognitive theorists, understanding these processes is critically important to a more complete, more comprehensive view of learning. We will consider the work of three important researchers in the field of cognitive learning: Wolfgang Köhler, Edward Tolman, and Albert Bandura.

Learning by Insight

What is insight, and how does it affect learning?

Have you ever been worried about a problem, only to have a crystal clear solution suddenly pop into your mind? If so, you experienced an important kind of cognitive learning first described by Wolfgang Köhler (1887–1967). In his book *The Mentality of Apes* (1925), Köhler described experiments he conducted on chimpanzees confined in caged areas. In one experiment, Köhler hung a bunch of bananas inside the caged area but overhead, out of reach of the chimps; boxes and sticks were left around the cage. Köhler observed the chimps' unsuccessful attempts to reach the bananas by jumping up or swinging sticks at them. Eventually, the chimps solved the problem by piling the boxes on top of one another and climbing on the boxes until they could reach the bananas.

Köhler observed that the chimps sometimes appeared to give up in their attempts to get the bananas. However, after an interval, they returned with the solution to the problem, as if it had come to them in a flash of **insight.** They seemed to have suddenly realized the relationship between the sticks or boxes and the bananas. Köhler insisted that insight, rather than trial-and-error learning, accounted for the chimps' successes, because they could easily repeat the solution and transfer this learning to similar problems. In human terms, a solution gained through insight is more easily learned, less likely to be forgotten, and more readily transferred to new problems than a solution learned through rote memorization (Rock & Palmer, 1990).

■ **cognitive processes**
(COG-nuh-tiv) Mental processes such as thinking, knowing, problem solving, remembering, and forming mental representations.

■ **insight**
The sudden realization of the relationship between elements in a problem situation, which makes the solution apparent.

Latent Learning and Cognitive Maps

What did Tolman discover about the necessity of reinforcement?

Like Köhler, Edward Tolman (1886–1959) held views that differed from the prevailing ideas on learning. First, Tolman (1932) believed that learning could take place without reinforcement. Second, he differentiated between learning and performance. He maintained that **latent learning** could occur; that is, learning could occur without apparent reinforcement and not be demonstrated until the organism was motivated to do so. A classic experimental study by Tolman and Honzik (1930) supports this position.

Three groups of rats were placed in a maze daily for 17 days. The first group always received a food reward at the end of the maze. The second group never received a reward, and the third group did not receive a food reward until the 11th day. The first group showed a steady improvement in performance over the 17-day period. The second group showed slight, gradual improvement. The third group, after being rewarded on the 11th day, showed a marked improvement the next day and, from then on, outperformed the rats that had been rewarded daily (see Figure 5.8). The rapid improvement of the third group indicated to Tolman that latent learning had

■ **latent learning**
Learning that occurs without apparent reinforcement and is not demonstrated until the organism is motivated to do so.

FIGURE 5.8 **Latent Learning**

Rats in Group 1 were rewarded every day for running the maze correctly, while rats in Group 2 were never rewarded. Group 3 rats were rewarded only on the 11th day and thereafter outperformed the rats in Group 1. The rats had "learned" the maze but were not motivated to perform until rewarded, demonstrating that latent learning had occurred.
Source: From Tolman & Honzik (1930).

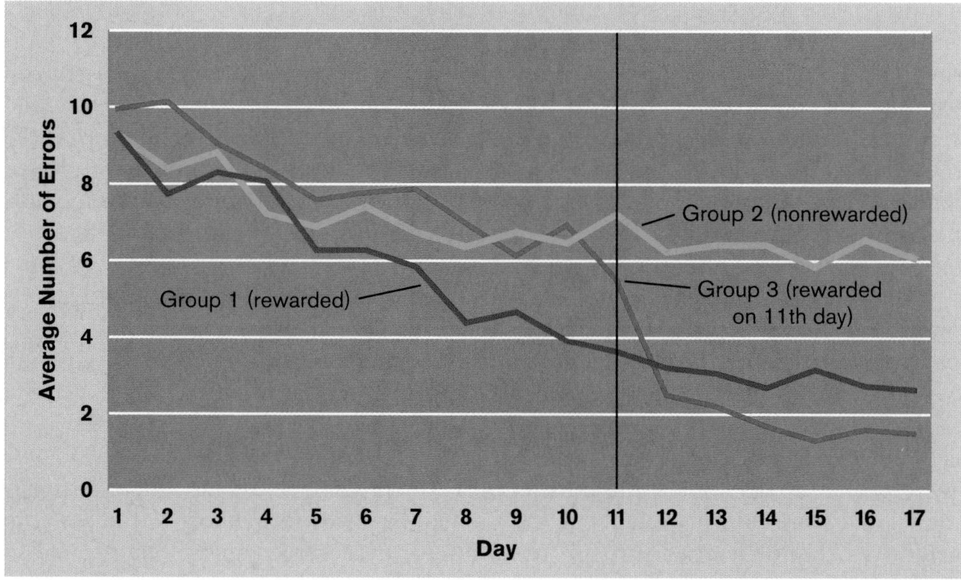

occurred—that the rats had actually learned the maze during the first 11 days but were not motivated to display this learning until they were rewarded for it.

Skinner was still in graduate school in 1930, when Tolman provided this exception to a basic principle of operant conditioning—that reinforcement is required for learning new behavior. The rats in the learning group did learn something before reinforcement and without exhibiting any evidence of learning by overt, observable behavior. But what did they learn? Tolman concluded that the rats had learned to form a **cognitive map,** a mental representation or picture, of the maze but had not demonstrated their learning until they were reinforced. In later studies, Tolman showed how rats quickly learn to rearrange their established cognitive maps and readily find their way through increasingly complex mazes.

The very notion of explaining the rats' behavior with the concept of cognitive maps is counter to Skinner's most deeply held belief—that mental processes do not explain the causes of behavior. But the concepts of cognitive maps and latent learning have a far more important place in psychology today than was true in Tolman's lifetime. They provide a cognitive perspective on operant conditioning.

■ **cognitive map**
A mental representation of a spatial arrangement such as a maze.

■ **observational learning**
Learning by observing the behavior of others and the consequences of that behavior; learning by imitation.

■ **modeling**
Another name for observational learning.

Observational Learning

How do we learn by observing others?

Have you ever wondered why you slow down when you see another driver getting a speeding ticket? In all likelihood, no one has ever reinforced you for slowing down under these conditions, so why do you do it? Psychologist Albert Bandura (1986) contends that many behaviors or responses are acquired through observational learning, or as he calls it, *social-cognitive learning.* **Observational learning,** sometimes called **modeling,** results when people observe the behavior of others and note the consequences of that behavior. Thus, you slow down when you see another driver getting a ticket because you assume their consequence will also be your consequence. The same process is involved when we see another person get a free soft drink by hitting the side of a vending machine. We assume that if we hit the machine, we will also get a free drink.

A person who demonstrates a behavior or whose behavior is imitated is called a **model.** Parents, movie stars, and sports personalities are often powerful models for children. The effectiveness of a model is related to his or her status, competence, and power. Other important factors are the age, sex, attractiveness, and ethnicity of the model. Whether learned behavior is actually performed depends largely on whether the observed models are rewarded or punished for their behavior and whether the observer expects to be rewarded for the behavior (Bandura, 1969, 1977a). Recent research has also shown that observational learning is improved when several sessions of observation (watching the behavior) precede attempts to perform the behavior and are then repeated in the early stages of practicing it (Weeks & Anderson, 2000).

But repetition alone isn't enough to cause an observer to learn from a model: An observer must be physically and cognitively capable of performing the behavior in order to learn it. In other words, no matter how much time you devote to watching Serena Williams play tennis or Tiger Woods play golf, you won't be able to acquire skills like theirs unless you possess physical talents that are equal to theirs. Likewise, it is doubtful that a kindergartener will learn geometry from watching her high-school-aged brother do his homework. Furthermore, the observer must pay attention to the model and store information about the model's behavior in memory. Ultimately, to exhibit a behavior learned through observation, the observer must be motivated to perform the behavior on her or his own.

A model does not have to be a person. For example, when you buy a piece of furniture labeled "assembly required," it usually comes with diagrams and instructions showing how to put it together. Typically, the instructions break down the large task of assembling the piece into a series of smaller steps. Similarly, Chapter 1 opens with an explanation of the SQ3R method that provides step-by-step instructions on how to incorporate the features of this textbook, such as the questions in the chapter outlines, into an organized study method. These instructions serve as a model, or plan, for you to follow in studying each chapter. As is true of learning from human models, you must believe that imitating this kind of verbal model will be beneficial to you. Moreover, you must remember the steps and be capable of applying them as you read each chapter. You will be more likely to keep using the SQ3R method if your experiences motivate you to do so. That is, once you use the model and find that it helps you learn the information in a chapter, you will be more likely to use it for another chapter.

One way people learn from observation is to acquire new responses, a kind of learning called the **modeling effect.** Do you remember learning how to do math problems in school? Most likely, when your teachers introduced a new kind of problems, they demonstrated how to solve them on a chalkboard or overhead projector. Your task was then to follow their procedures, step by step, until you were able to work the new problems independently. For you and your classmates, solving each new kind of problem was a new behavior acquired from a model.

Another kind of observational learning is particularly common in unusual situations. Picture yourself as a guest at an elaborate state dinner at the White House. Your table setting has more pieces of silverware than you have ever seen before. Which fork should be used for what? How should you proceed? You might decide to take your cue from the First Lady. In this case, you wouldn't be learning an entirely new behavior. Instead, you would be using a model to learn how to modify a known behavior (how to use a fork) to fit the needs of a unfamiliar situation. This kind of observational learning is known as the **elicitation effect.**

■ **model**
The individual who demonstrates a behavior or whose behavior is imitated.

■ **modeling effect**
Learning a new behavior from a model through the acquisition of new responses.

■ **elicitation effect**
Exhibiting a behavior similar to that shown by a model in an unfamiliar situation.

REVIEW *and* REFLECT 5.2

Cognitive Learning

TYPE OF LEARNING	MAJOR CONTRIBUTORS	CLASSIC RESEARCH
Insight Sudden realization of how to solve a problem	Wolfgang Köhler	Observations of chimpanzees' attempts to retrieve bananas suspended from the tops of their cages
Latent learning Learning that is hidden until it is reinforced	Edward Tolman	Comparisons of rats that were rewarded for learning to run a maze with others that were allowed to explore it freely
Observational learning Learning from watching others	Albert Bandura	Comparisons of children who observed an adult model behaving aggressively with those who did not observe such an aggressive model

Want to be sure you've fully absorbed the material in this chapter? Visit **www.ablongman.com/wood5e** for access to free practice tests, flashcards, interactive activities, and links developed specifically to help you succeed in psychology.

Sometimes, models influence us to exhibit behaviors that we have previously learned to suppress, a process called the **disinhibitory effect.** For example, we have all learned not to belch in public. However, if we are in a social setting in which others are belching and no one is discouraging them from doing so, we are likely to follow suit. And adolescents may lose whatever resistance they have to drinking, drug use, or sexual activity by seeing or hearing about peers or characters in movies or television shows engaging in these behaviors without experiencing any adverse consequences.

However, we may also suppress a behavior upon observing a model receive punishment for exhibiting it (the **inhibitory effect**). This is the kind of observational learning we are displaying when we slow down upon seeing another driver receiving a ticket. When schoolchildren see a classmate punished for talking out, the experience has a tendency to suppress that behavior in all of them. Thus, a person does not have to experience the unfortunate consequences of dangerous or socially unacceptable behaviors in order to avoid them.

Fears, too, can be acquired through observational learning. Gerull and Rapee (2002) found that toddlers whose mothers expressed fear at the sight of rubber snakes and spiders displayed significantly higher levels of fear of these objects when tested later than did control group children whose mothers did not express such fears. Conversely, children who see "a parent or peer behaving nonfearfully in a potentially fear-producing situation may be 'immunized'" to feeling fear when confronting a similar frightening situation at a later time (Basic Behavioral Science Task Force, 1996, p. 139).

Review and Reflect 5.2 compares the three types of cognitive learning we've discussed.

Learning from Television and Other Media Close your eyes and picture a local TV news program. Is the anchor in your imaginary newscast a White or minority person? Research demonstrating the influence of models on behavior has raised concerns about what viewers, particularly children, learn from television. Racial stereotypes, for instance, are common in television programs. Moreover, minorities are shown in high-status roles far less often than Whites. Figure 5.9 (on page 188), for example, shows the percentages of various ethnic groups who serve as anchors for local news programs. Thus, many psychologists believe that television watching can lead to the development and maintenance of racial stereotypes.

■ **disinhibitory effect** Displaying a previously suppressed behavior because a model does so without receiving punishment.

■ **inhibitory effect** Suppressing a behavior because a model is punished for displaying the behavior.

FIGURE 5.9 Ethnicities of Local Television News Anchors

A survey of 818 television stations across the United States revealed that the vast majority of local television news anchors are White. Some psychologists believe that the lack of sufficient representation of minorities in such high-status roles may lead viewers to develop or maintain racial stereotypes.
Source: Papper & Gerhard (2002).

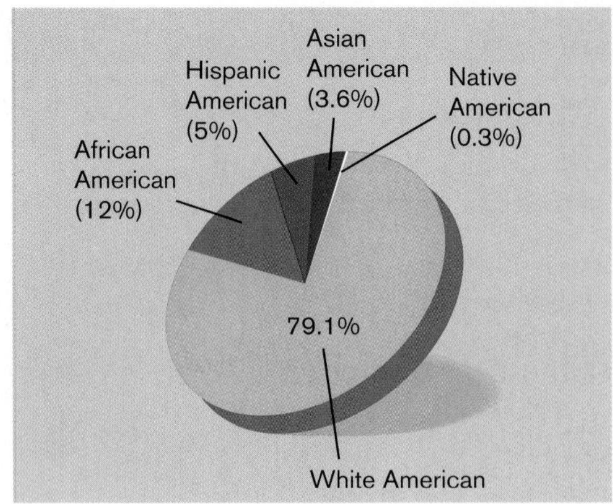

Albert Bandura suspected that aggression and violence on television programs, including cartoons, tend to increase aggressive behavior in children. His pioneering work has greatly influenced current thinking on these issues. In several classic experiments, Bandura demonstrated how children are influenced by exposure to aggressive models. One study involved three groups of preschoolers. Children in one group individually observed an adult model punching, kicking, and hitting a 5-foot, inflated plastic "Bobo Doll" with a mallet, while uttering aggressive phrases (Bandura et al., 1961, p. 576). Children in the second group observed a nonaggressive model who ignored the Bobo Doll and sat quietly assembling Tinker Toys. The children in the control group were placed in the same setting with no adult present. Later, each child was observed through a one-way mirror. Those children exposed to the aggressive model imitated much of the aggression and also engaged in significantly more nonimitative aggression than did children in either of the other groups. The group that observed the nonaggressive model showed less aggressive behavior than the control group.

A further study compared the degree of aggression in children following exposure to (1) an aggressive model in a live situation, (2) a filmed version of the same situation, or (3) a film depicting an aggressive cartoon character using the same aggressive behaviors in a fantasylike setting (Bandura et al., 1963). A control group was not exposed to any of the three situations of aggression. The groups exposed to aggressive models used significantly more aggression than the control group. The researchers concluded that "of the three experimental conditions, exposure to humans on film portraying aggression was the most influential in eliciting and shaping aggressive behavior" (p. 7).

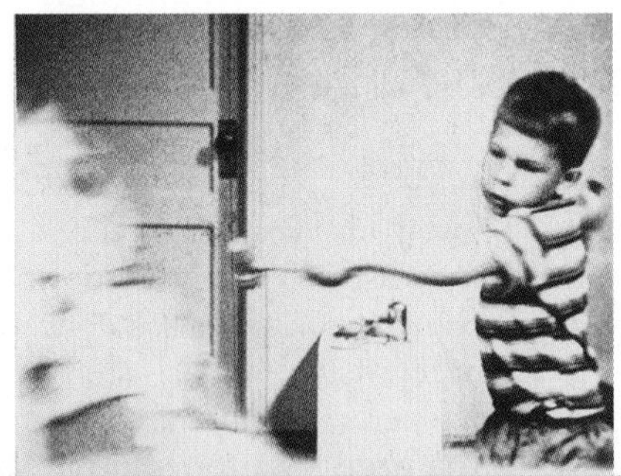

In Bandura's observational learning research, children learned to copy aggression by observing adult models act aggressively toward a Bobo doll.

Portrayals on television showing violence as an acceptable way to solve problems tend to encourage aggressive behavior in children.

Bandura's research sparked interest in studying the effects of violence and aggression portrayed in other entertainment media. For example, researchers have also shown in a variety of ways—including carefully controlled laboratory experiments with children, adolescents, and young adults—that violent video games increase aggressive behavior (Anderson & Bushman, 2001). Moreover, the effects of media violence are evident whether the violence is presented in music, music videos, or advertising or on the Internet (Villani, 2001). Such research has spawned a confusing array of rating systems that parents may refer to when choosing media for their children. However, researchers have found that labeling media as "violent" may enhance children's desire to experience it, especially in boys over the age of 11 years (Bushman & Cantor, 2003).

But, you might argue, if televised violence is followed by appropriate consequences, such as an arrest, it may actually teach children not to engage in aggression. However, experimental research has demonstrated that children do not process information about consequences in the same ways as adults do (Krcmar & Cooke, 2001). Observing consequences for aggressive acts does seem to help preschoolers learn that violence is morally unacceptable. By contrast, school-aged children appear to judge the rightness or wrongness of an act of violence on the basis of provocation; that is, they believe that violence demonstrated in the context of retaliation is morally acceptable even if it is punished by an authority figure.

Remarkably, too, recently published longitudinal evidence shows that the effects of childhood exposure to violence persist well into the adult years. Psychologist L. Rowell Huesman and his colleagues (2003) found that individuals who had watched the greatest number of violent television programs in childhood were the most likely to have engaged in actual acts of violence as young adults. This study was the first to show that observations of media violence during childhood are linked to real acts of violence in adulthood.

But just as children imitate the aggressive behavior they observe on television, they also imitate the prosocial, or helping, behavior they see there. Programs like *Mister Rogers' Neighborhood* and *Sesame Street* have been found to have a positive influence on children. And, hopefully, the findings of Huesman and his colleagues also apply to the positive effects of television.

Many avenues of learning are available to humans and other animals. Luckily, people's capacity to learn seems practically unlimited. Certainly, advances in civilization could not have been achieved without the ability to learn.

Remember It 5.4

1. The sudden realization of the relationship between the elements in a problem situation that results in the solution to the problem is called ____________.
2. Learning not demonstrated until the organism is motivated to perform the behavior is called ____________ learning.
3. Grant has been afraid of mice for as long as he can remember, and his mother has the same paralyzing fear. Grant most likely acquired his fear through ____________ learning.
4. Match each psychologist with the subject(s) of his research.

____ (1) Edward Tolman	a. observational learning
____ (2) Albert Bandura	b. cognitive maps
____ (3) Wolfgang Köhler	c. learning by insight
	d. latent learning

ANSWERS: 1. insight; 2. latent; 3. observational; 4. (1) b, d, (2) a, (3) c

Apply It

How to Win the Battle against Procrastination

Have you often thought that you could get better grades if only you had more time? Do you often find yourself studying for an exam or completing a term paper at the last minute? If so, it makes sense for you to learn how to overcome the greatest time waster of all—procrastination. Research indicates that academic procrastination arises partly out of a lack of confidence in one's ability meet expectations (Wolters, 2003). But anyone can overcome procrastination, and gain self-confidence in the process, by using behavior modification techniques. Systematically apply the following suggestions to keep procrastination from interfering with your studying:

- *Identify the environmental cues that habitually interfere with your studying.* Television, computer or video games, and even food can be powerful distractors that consume hours of valuable study time. However, these distractors can be useful positive reinforcers to enjoy *after* you've finished studying.
- *Schedule your study time and reinforce yourself for adhering to your schedule.* Once you've scheduled it, be just as faithful to your schedule as you would be to a work schedule set by an employer. And be sure to schedule something you enjoy to immediately follow the study time.
- *Get started.* The most difficult part is getting started. Give yourself an extra reward for starting on time and, perhaps, a penalty for starting late.
- *Use visualization.* Much procrastination results from the failure to consider its negative consequences. Visualizing the consequences of not studying, such as trying to get through an exam you haven't adequately prepared for, can be an effective tool for combating procrastination.
- *Beware of jumping to another task when you reach a difficult part of an assignment.* This procrastination tactic gives you the feeling that you are busy and accomplishing something, but it is, nevertheless, an avoidance mechanism.
- *Beware of preparation overkill.* Procrastinators may actually spend hours preparing for a task rather than working on the task itself. For example, they may gather enough library materials to write a book rather than a five-page term paper. This enables them to postpone writing the paper.
- *Keep a record of the reasons you give yourself for postponing studying or completing important assignments.* If a favorite rationalization is "I'll wait until I'm in the mood to do this," count the number of times in a week you are seized with the desire to study. The mood to study typically arrives after you begin, not before.

Don't procrastinate! Begin now! Apply the steps outlined here to gain more control over your behavior and win the battle against procrastination.

Summary and Review

Classical Conditioning: The Original View p. 159

What kind of learning did Pavlov discover? p. 159

Pavlov's study of a conditioned reflex in dogs led him to discover a model of learning called classical conditioning.

How is classical conditioning accomplished? p. 160

In classical conditioning, a neutral stimulus (a tone in Pavlov's experiments) is presented shortly before an unconditioned stimulus (food in Pavlov's experiments), which naturally elicits, or brings forth, an unconditioned response (salivation for Pavlov's dogs). After repeated pairings, the conditioned stimulus alone (the tone) comes to elicit the conditioned response.

What kinds of changes in stimuli and learning conditions lead to changes in conditioned responses? p. 162

If the conditioned stimulus (tone) is presented repeatedly without the unconditioned stimulus (food), the conditioned response (salivation) becomes progressively weaker and eventually disappears, a process called extinction. Generalization occurs when an organism makes a conditioned response to a stimulus that is similar to the original conditioned stimulus. Discrimination is the ability to distinguish between similar stimuli, allowing the organism to make the conditioned response only to the original conditioned stimulus.

How did Watson demonstrate that fear could be classically conditioned? p. 164

Watson showed that fear could be classically conditioned by presenting a white rat to Little Albert along with a loud, frightening noise, thereby conditioning the child to fear the white rat. He also used the principles of classical conditioning to remove the fears of a boy named Peter.

Classical Conditioning: The Contemporary View p. 166

According to Rescorla, what is the critical element in classical conditioning? p. 166

Rescorla found that the critical element in classical conditioning is whether the conditioned stimulus provides information that enables the organism to reliably predict the occurrence of the unconditioned stimulus.

What did Garcia and Koelling discover about classical conditioning? p. 166

Garcia and Koelling conducted a study in which rats formed an association between nausea and flavored water ingested several hours earlier. This represented an exception to the principle that the conditioned stimulus must be presented shortly before the unconditioned stimulus. The finding that rats associated electric shock only with noise and light and nausea only with flavored water proved that animals are biologically predisposed to make certain associations and that associations cannot be readily conditioned between any two stimuli.

What types of everyday responses can be subject to classical conditioning? p. 168

Types of responses acquired through classical conditioning include positive and negative emotional responses (including likes, dislikes, fears, and phobias), responses to environmental cues associated with drug use, and conditioned immune system responses.

Why doesn't classical conditioning result every time unconditioned and conditioned stimuli occur together? p. 169

Whenever unconditioned and conditioned stimuli occur close together in time, four factors determine whether classical conditioning results: (1) how reliably the conditioned stimulus predicts the unconditioned stimulus, (2) the number of pairings of the conditioned stimulus and unconditioned stimulus, (3) the intensity of the unconditioned stimulus, and (4) the temporal relationship between the conditioned stimulus and the unconditioned stimulus (the conditioned stimulus must occur first).

Operant Conditioning p. 170

What did Thorndike conclude about learning by watching cats try to escape from his puzzle box? p. 170

Thorndike concluded that most learning occurs through trial and error. He claimed that the consequences of a response determine whether the tendency to respond in the same way in the future will be strengthened or weakened (the law of effect).

What was Skinner's major contribution to psychology? p. 171

Skinner's major contribution to psychology was his extensive and significant research on operant conditioning.

What is the process by which responses are acquired through operant conditioning? p. 171

Operant conditioning is a method for manipulating the consequences of behavior in order to shape a new response or to increase or decrease the frequency of an existing response. In shaping, a researcher selectively reinforces small steps toward the desired response until that response is achieved. Extinction occurs when reinforcement is withheld.

What is the goal of both positive reinforcement and negative reinforcement, and how is that goal accomplished with each? p. 173

Both positive reinforcement and negative reinforcement are used to strengthen or increase the probability of a response. With positive reinforcement, the desired response is followed by a reward; with negative reinforcement, it is followed by the termination of an aversive stimulus.

What are the four types of schedules of reinforcement, and which type is most effective? p. 174

The four types of schedules of reinforcement are the fixed-ratio, variable-ratio, fixed-interval, and variable-interval schedules. The variable-ratio schedule provides the highest response rate and the most resistance to extinction. The partial-reinforcement effect is the greater resistance to extinction that occurs when responses are maintained under partial reinforcement, rather than under continuous reinforcement.

Why don't consequences always cause changes in behavior? p. 177

In operant conditioning, response rate, resistance to extinction, and how quickly a response is acquired are influenced by the magnitude of reinforcement, the immediacy of reinforcement, and the motivation level of the learner. If the incentive is minimal, the reinforcement delayed, or the learner minimally motivated, consequences will not necessarily cause behavior changes.

How does punishment differ from negative reinforcement? p. 178

Punishment is used to decrease the frequency of a response; thus, an unpleasant stimulus may be added. Negative reinforcement is used to increase the frequency of a response, and so an unpleasant stimulus is terminated or avoided. Punishment generally suppresses rather than extinguishes behavior; it does not help people develop more appropriate behaviors. And it can cause fear, anger, hostility, and aggression in the punished person. Punishment is most effective when it is given immediately after undesirable behavior, when it is consistently applied, and when it is just intense enough to suppress the behavior.

When is avoidance learning desirable, and when is it maladaptive? p. 180

Avoidance learning involves acquisition of behaviors that remove aversive stimuli. Avoidance learning is desirable when it leads to an beneficial response, such as running away from a potentially deadly snake or buckling a seat belt to stop the annoying sound of a buzzer. It is maladaptive when it occurs in response to fear. For example, fear of speaking to a group may lead you to skip class on the day your oral report is scheduled.

What are some applications of operant conditioning? p. 181

Applications of operant conditioning include training animals to provide entertainment or to help physically challenged people, using biofeedback to gain control over internal physiological processes, and using behavior modification techniques to eliminate undesirable behavior and/or encourage desirable behavior in individuals or groups.

Cognitive Learning p. 184

What is insight, and how does it affect learning? p. 184

Insight is the sudden realization of the relationship of the elements in a problem situation that makes the solution apparent; this solution is easily learned and transferred to new problems.

What did Tolman discover about the necessity of reinforcement? p. 184

Tolman demonstrated that rats could learn to run to the end of a maze just as quickly when allowed to explore it freely as when they were reinforced with food for getting to the end. His hypothesis was that the rats formed a cognitive map of the maze. He also maintained that latent learning occurs without apparent reinforcement, but it is not demonstrated in the organism's performance until the organism is motivated to do so.

How do we learn by observing others? p. 185

Learning by observing the behavior of others (called models) and the consequences of that behavior is known as observational learning. We learn from models when we assume that the consequences they experience will happen to us if we perform their behaviors. Research has demonstrated that children can acquire aggressive behavior from watching televised acts of aggression. However, they can also learn prosocial behavior from television.

Key Terms

Memory

chapter 6

Remembering

- *What are the characteristics of each component of memory in the Atkinson-Shiffrin model?*
- *How does the levels-of-processing model differ from that proposed by Atkinson and Shiffrin?*
- *What are the three methods used by psychologists to measure memory?*

The Nature of Remembering

- *What is meant by the statement "Memory is reconstructive in nature"?*
- *What conditions reduce the reliability of eyewitness testimony?*
- *What is the controversy regarding the therapy used to recover repressed memories of childhood sexual abuse?*
- *What does research evidence say about flashbulb and photographic memories?*
- *How does culture influence memory?*

Factors Influencing Retrieval

- *What happens when information must be recalled in a particular order?*
- *How does environmental context affect memory?*
- *How do emotions and altered states of consciousness affect memory?*

Biology and Memory

- *What roles do the hippocampus and the hippocampal region play in memory?*
- *Why is long-term potentiation important?*
- *How do memories of threatening situations that elicit the "fight or flight response" compare with ordinary memories?*

Forgetting

- *What did Ebbinghaus discover about forgetting?*
- *What causes forgetting?*

Improving Memory

- *How can organization, overlearning, spaced practice, and recitation improve memory?*

How accurate is your memory?

Suppose you are a woman who was attacked by a knife-wielding rapist—would you remember his face? You might be surprised at just how faulty our memories can be, as the case of rape victim Jennifer Thompson illustrates. While being brutally raped, Thompson steeled herself to study the rapist—his facial features, scars, tattoos, voice, and mannerisms—vowing to herself that she would remember the man well enough to send him to prison.

Hours after her ordeal, Thompson viewed police photos of potential suspects, searching for those of her rapist, his pencil-thin moustache, eyebrows, nose, and other features. She then selected a composite photo that looked like the rapist. A week later, she viewed six suspects holding cards numbered 1 to 6. Thompson looked at suspect number 5 and announced with total confidence, "That's the man who raped me."

The man was Ronald Cotton, who had already served a year and a half in prison for attempted sexual assault. In court, Thompson was unshakably confident, sure that this man had raped her. Cotton was nervous and frightened. His alibis didn't check out, and a piece missing from one of his shoes resembled a piece found at the crime scene. But it was the confident, unwavering testimony of the only eyewitness, Jennifer Thompson, that sealed his fate. The jury found him guilty and sentenced him to life in prison, just as she had hoped.

"God knows I'm innocent," said Cotton, and he vowed to prove it somehow. Remarkably, after Cotton had been in prison for more than a year, a new inmate, Bobby Poole, who had been convicted of a series of brutal rapes, joined him at his work assignment in the kitchen. When Cotton told Poole that he had been convicted of raping Jennifer Thompson, Poole laughed and bragged that Cotton was doing some of his time.

Finally, after Cotton had served 11 years, law professor Richard Rosen heard his story and agreed to help him. Rosen knew that DNA tests could be performed that were far more sophisticated than those that had been available 11 years earlier. It was Cotton's DNA samples that cleared him of the crime. Bobby Poole's DNA samples, however, proved that he had raped Jennifer Thompson.

A nightmare now plagued Thompson: She had sent an innocent man to prison. But she met with Ronald Cotton and, in tears, expressed her sorrow for his ordeal. Cotton responded softly, "I'm not mad at you. I just want you to have a good life." Thompson tearfully thanked him for his forgiveness.

Ronald Cotton is now married with a beautiful daughter, Raven. With Jennifer Thompson's help, he got a six-figure settlement from the state government. (Adapted from O'Neil, 2000.)

Does this case reflect rare and unusual aspects of human memory, or are such memory errors common? This and many other questions you may have about memory will be answered in this chapter.

Remembering

encoding
The process of transforming information into a form that can be stored in memory.

What enables us to remember something? Psychologists think of memory as involving three processes: encoding, storage, and retrieval. The first process, **encoding**, is the transformation of information into a form that can be stored in memory. For example, if you witness a car crash, you might try to form a mental picture of it to

FIGURE 6.1 The Processes Required for Remembering

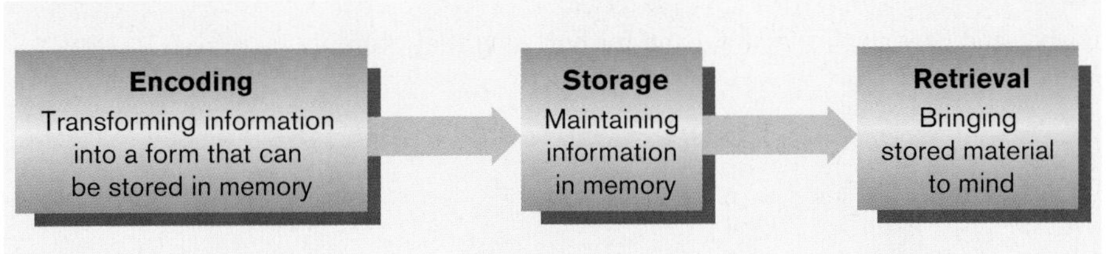

The act of remembering requires successful completion of all three of these processes: encoding, storage, and retrieval.

enable yourself to remember it. The second memory process, **storage**, involves keeping or maintaining information in memory. For encoded information to be stored, some physiological change must take place in the brain—a process called **consolidation**. The final process, **retrieval**, occurs when information stored in memory is brought to mind. To remember something, you must perform all three processes—encode the information, store it, and then retrieve it. A memory lapse can result from the failure of any one of the three (see Figure 6.1).

■ **storage**
The process of keeping or maintaining information in memory.

■ **consolidation**
A physiological change in the brain that allows encoded information to be stored in memory.

■ **retrieval**
The process of bringing to mind information that has been stored in memory.

The Atkinson-Shiffrin Model

What are the characteristics of each component of memory in the Atkinson-Shiffrin model?

How are memories stored? Most current efforts to understand human memory are conducted within a framework known as the *information-processing approach* (Klatzky, 1984). This approach makes use of modern computer science and related fields to provide models that help psychologists understand the processes involved in memory (Kon & Plaskota, 2000).

According to one widely accepted information-processing memory model, the *Atkinson-Shiffrin model*, there are three different, interacting memory systems: sensory memory, short-term memory, and long-term memory (Atkinson & Shiffrin, 1968; Broadbent, 1958). We will examine each of these three memory systems, which are shown in Figure 6.2.

Sensory Memory Imagine yourself driving down a city street. How many separate pieces of information are you sensing? You are probably seeing, hearing, feeling, and smelling millions of tiny bits of information every minute. But how many of them do you remember? Very few, most likely. That's because, although virtually everything we see, hear, or otherwise sense is held in **sensory memory**, each piece of information is stored only for the briefest period of time. As shown in Figure 6.3 (on page 198), sensory memory normally holds visual images for a fraction of a second and sounds for

■ **sensory memory**
The memory system that holds information from the senses for a period of time ranging from only a fraction of a second to about 2 seconds.

FIGURE 6.2 The Three Memory Systems

According to the Atkinson-Shiffrin model, there are three separate memory systems: sensory memory, short-term memory, and long-term memory.

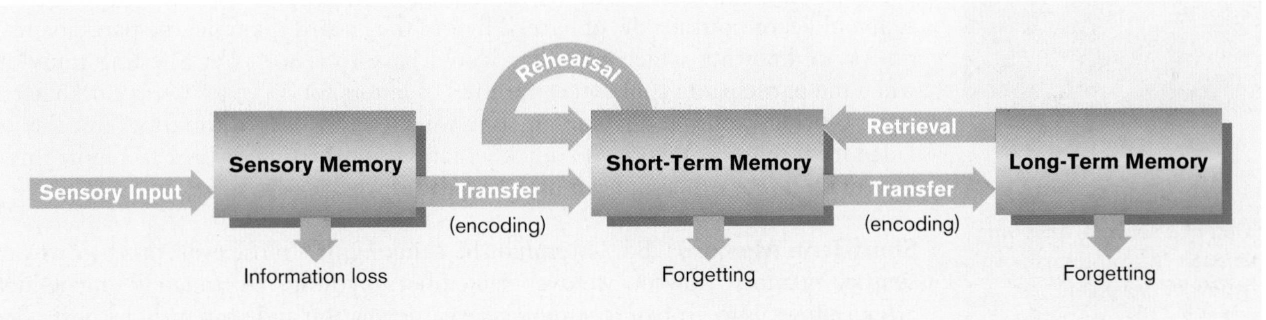

FIGURE 6.3 Characteristics of and Processes Involved in the Three Memory Systems

The three memory systems differ in what and how much they hold and for how long they store it.
Source: Peterson & Peterson (1959).

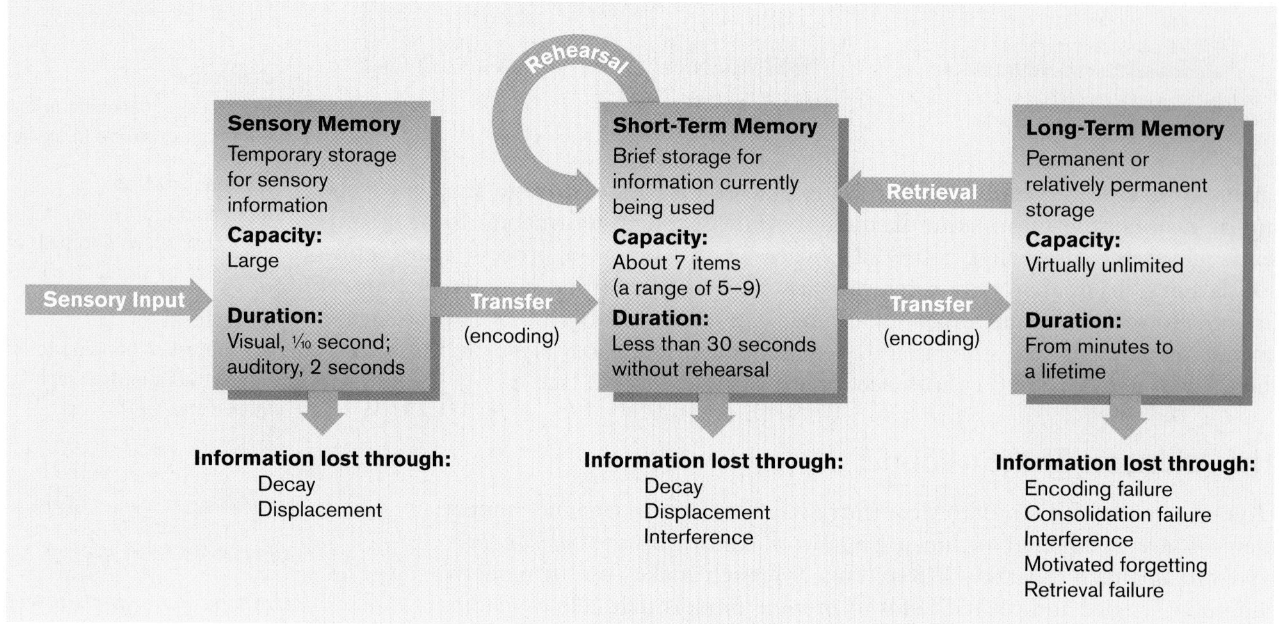

about 2 seconds (Crowder, 1992; Klatzky, 1980). Visual sensory memory lasts just long enough to keep whatever you are viewing from disappearing when you blink your eyes. You experience auditory sensory memory when the last few words someone has spoken seem to echo briefly in your head. So, sensory memory functions a bit like a strainer; that is, most of what flows into it immediately flows out again.

Exactly how long does visual sensory memory last? Glance at the three rows of letters shown below for a fraction of a second, and then close your eyes. How many of the letters can you recall?

X B D F
M P Z G
L C N H

Most people can correctly recall only four or five of the letters when they are briefly presented. Does this indicate that visual sensory memory can hold only four or five letters at a time? To find out, researcher George Sperling (1960) briefly flashed 12 letters, as shown above, to participants. Immediately upon turning off the display, he sounded a high, medium, or low tone that signaled the participants to report only the top, middle, or bottom row of letters. Before they heard the tone, the participants had no way of knowing which row they would have to report. Yet Sperling found that, when the participants could view the rows of letters for $^{15}/_{1000}$ to $^{1}/_{2}$ second, they could report correctly all the items in any one row nearly 100% of the time. But the items faded from sensory memory so quickly that during the time it took to report three or four of them, the other eight or nine had already disappeared.

Sensory memory holds a visual image, such as a lightning bolt, for a fraction of a second—just long enough for you to perceive a flow of movement.

Short-Term Memory So, you might be thinking, if almost everything flows out of sensory memory, how do we ever remember anything? Fortunately, our ability to attend allows us to grab onto some sensory information and send it to the next stage of processing, **short-term memory (STM)**. Whatever you are thinking about right now is in your STM (see Figure 6.3). Unlike sensory memory, which holds virtually the exact sensory stimulus, short-term memory usually codes information according to sound. For example, the letter *T* is coded as the sound "tee," not as the shape T.

Short-term memory has a very limited capacity—about seven (plus or minus two) different items or bits of information at one time. This is just enough for phone numbers and ordinary zip codes. (Nine-digit zip codes strain the capacity of most people's STM.) When short-term memory is filled to capacity, displacement can occur. In **displacement**, each new, incoming item pushes out an existing item, which is then forgotten. Think of what happens when the top of your desk gets too crowded. Things start to "disappear" under other things; some items even fall off the desk. So, you can remember that short-term memory is the limited component of the memory system by associating it with the top of your desk: The desk is limited in size, causing you to lose things when it gets crowded, and the same is true of short-term memory.

One way to overcome the limitation of seven or so bits of information is to use a strategy that George A. Miller (1956), a pioneer in memory research, calls **chunking**—organizing or grouping separate bits of information into larger units, or chunks. A *chunk* is an easily identifiable unit such as a syllable, a word, an acronym, or a number (Cowan, 1988). For example, nine digits, such as 5 2 9 7 3 1 3 2 5, can be divided into three more easily memorized chunks, 529 73 1325. (Notice that this is the form of social security numbers in the United States.)

Anytime you chunk information on the basis of knowledge stored in long-term memory, that is, by associating it with some kind of meaning, you increase the effective capacity of short-term memory (Lustig & Hasher, 2002). And when you increase the effective capacity of short-term memory, you are more likely to transfer information to long-term memory. (*Hint:* The headings and subheadings, Remember It questions, and margin questions in this textbook help you sort information into manageable chunks. You will remember more of a chapter if you use them as organizers for your notes and as cues to recall information when you are reviewing for an exam.)

The duration of short-term memory Items in short-term memory are lost in less than 30 seconds unless you repeat them over and over to yourself. This process is known as **rehearsal**. But rehearsal is easily disrupted. It is so fragile, in fact, that an interruption can cause information to be lost in just a few seconds. Distractions that are stressful are especially likely to disrupt short-term memory. And a threat to survival certainly does, as researchers showed when they pumped the odor of a feared predator, a fox, into a laboratory where rats were performing a task requiring short-term memory—the rats' performance plummeted (Morrison et al., 2002; Morrow et al., 2000).

How long does short-term memory last if rehearsal is prevented? In a series of early studies, participants were briefly shown three consonants (such as H, G, and L) and then asked to count backward by threes from a given number (738, 735, 732, and so on) (Peterson & Peterson, 1959). After intervals lasting from 3 to 18 seconds, participants were instructed to stop counting backward and recall the three letters. Following a delay of 9 seconds, the participants could recall an average of only one of the three letters. After 18 seconds, there was practically no recall whatsoever. An 18-second distraction had completely erased the three letters from short-term memory.

Short-term memory as working memory Allan Baddeley (1990, 1992, 1995) has suggested that "working memory" is a more fitting term than short-term memory. This memory system is where you work on information to understand it, remember it, or use it to solve a problem or to communicate with someone. Research shows that the prefrontal cortex is the brain area primarily responsible for working memory (Courtney et al., 1997; Rao et al., 1997).

So, just what kind of "work" goes on in working memory? One of the most important working memory processes is the application of *memory strategies*, such as

■ **short-term memory (STM)**
The memory system that codes information according to sound and holds about seven (from five to nine) items for less than 30 seconds without rehearsal; also called working memory.

■ **displacement**
The event that occurs when short-term memory is filled to capacity and each new, incoming item pushes out an existing item, which is then forgotten.

■ **chunking**
A memory strategy that involves grouping or organizing bits of information into larger units, which are easier to remember.

■ **rehearsal**
The act of purposely repeating information to maintain it in short-term memory.

■ elaborative rehearsal
A memory strategy that involves relating new information to something that is already known.

■ long-term memory (LTM)
The memory system with a virtually unlimited capacity that contains vast stores of a person's permanent or relatively permanent memories.

■ declarative memory
The subsystem within long-term memory that stores facts, information, and personal life events that can be brought to mind verbally or in the form of images and then declared or stated; also called explicit memory.

■ episodic memory
(ep-ih-SOD-ik) The type of declarative memory that records events as they have been subjectively experienced.

■ semantic memory
The type of declarative memory that stores general knowledge, or objective facts and information.

Declarative memories involve facts, information, and personal life events, such as a trip to a foreign country. Nondeclarative memory encompasses motor skills, such as the expert swing of professional golfer Tiger Woods. Once learned, such movements can be carried out with little or no conscious effort.

chunking. Using a memory strategy involves manipulating information in ways that make it easier to remember. We use some memory strategies almost automatically, but others require more effort. For example, sometimes we repeat information over and over again until we can recall it easily. (Remember learning those multiplication tables in elementary school?) This strategy, sometimes called *rote rehearsal*, may work well for remembering telephone numbers, license plate numbers, and even the multiplication tables, especially when combined with chunking. However, it isn't the best way to remember more complex information, such as the kind you find in a textbook. For this kind of information, the best memory is probably **elaborative rehearsal**, which involves relating new information to something you already know.

How does elaborative rehearsal work? Here is an example. Suppose you are taking a French class and have to learn the word *éscaliers*, which is equivalent to *stairs* in English. You might remember the meaning of *éscaliers* by associating it with the English word *escalator*.

Long-Term Memory What happens next? If information is processed effectively in short-term memory, it makes its way to long-term memory. **Long-term memory (LTM)** is a person's vast storehouse of permanent or relatively permanent memories (refer to Figure 6.3). There are no known limits to the storage capacity of this memory system, and long-term memories can last for years, some of them for a lifetime. Information in long-term memory is usually stored in semantic form, although visual images, sounds, and odors can be stored there, as well.

Some experts believe that there are two main subsystems within long-term memory. The first, **declarative memory** (also called *explicit memory*) stores facts, information, and personal life events that can be brought to mind verbally or in the form of images and then declared or stated. It holds information that we intentionally and consciously recollect. There are two types of declarative memory: episodic memory and semantic memory.

Episodic memory is the type of declarative memory that records events as they have been subjectively experienced (Wheeler et al., 1997). It is somewhat like a mental diary, a record of the episodes of your life—the people you have known, the places you have seen, and the personal experiences you have had. According to Canadian psychologist Endel Tulving (1989), "episodic memory enables people to travel back in time, as it were, into their personal past, and to become consciously aware of having witnessed or participated in events and happenings at earlier times" (p. 362). Using episodic memory, a person might make this statement: "I remember being in Florida on my vacation last spring, lying on the sand, soaking up some rays, and listening to the sound of the waves rushing to the shore."

Semantic memory, the other type of declarative memory, is memory for general knowledge, or objective facts and information. In other words, semantic memory is a mental dictionary or encyclopedia of items like these:

Dictionary is spelled d-i-c-t-i-o-n-a-r-y.

10 times 10 equals 100.

The three memory systems are sensory, short-term, and long-term.

Brain-imaging studies show that the left hemisphere shows more activity than the right when a person is accessing semantic memory (Koivisto & Revensuo, 2000). Does this imply that the two types of declarative memory work independently? Could major damage be done to semantic memory without affecting episodic memory? Not according to Tulving (1995), who hypothesizes that episodic memory is dependent on the functioning of semantic memory; see Figure 6.4(a). However, researchers have recently demonstrated that some people who have suffered selective damage to their long-term semantic memory can still learn and remember using episodic memory (Graham et al., 2000). Patients with "semantic dementia" perform poorly on semantic tasks, such as picture naming, giving examples of general categories (e.g., household

FIGURE 6.4 Two Models of the Relationship of Episodic and Semantic Memory

(a) Tulving's (1995) model shows the dependence of episodic memory on semantic memory.
(b) The model of Graham and others (2000) shows the reliance of episodic memory on perceptual input and semantic memory.

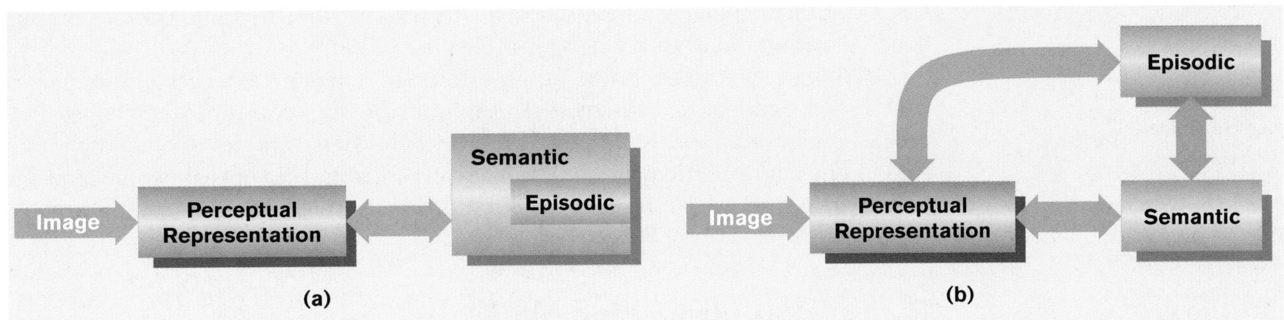

items), and sorting words or pictures into specified categories (e.g., living versus nonliving things). Yet their episodic memory is mainly unaffected (Hodges et al., 1995; Snowden et al., 1996). Figure 6.4(b) shows that although episodic and semantic memory are connected, episodic memory can store perceptual information without direct aid from or dependence on semantic memory (Graham et al., 2000).

Nondeclarative memory (also called *implicit memory*) is the subsystem within long-term memory that stores motor skills, habits, and simple classically conditioned responses (Squire et al., 1993). Motor skills are acquired through repetitive practice and include such things as eating with a fork, riding a bicycle, or driving a car. Although acquired slowly, once learned, these skills become habit, are quite reliable, and can be carried out with little or no conscious effort. For example, you probably use the keyboard on a computer without consciously being able to name the keys in each row from left to right. Figure 6.5 shows the two subsystems of long-term memory.

■ **nondeclarative memory** The subsystem within long-term memory that stores motor skills, habits, and simple classically conditioned responses; also called implicit memory.

FIGURE 6.5 Subsystems of Long-Term Memory

Declarative memory can be divided into two subsystems: episodic memory, which stores memories of personally experienced events, and semantic memory, which stores facts and information. Nondeclarative memory consists of motor skills acquired through repetitive practice, habits, and simple classically conditioned responses.

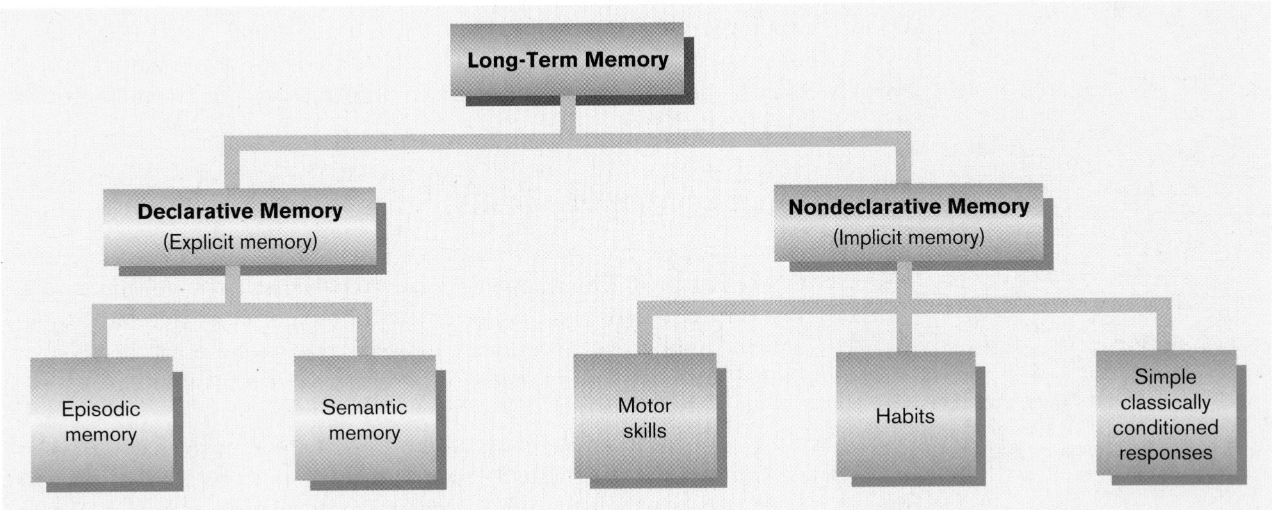

■ priming
The phenomenon by which an earlier encounter with a stimulus (such as a word or a picture) increases the speed or accuracy of naming that stimulus or a related stimulus at a later time.

Associated with nondeclarative, or implicit, memory is a phenomenon known as **priming**, by which an earlier encounter with a stimulus (such as a word or a picture) increases the speed or accuracy of naming that stimulus or a related stimulus at a later time. Such improvement occurs without the person's conscious awareness of having previously seen or heard the stimulus. For example, a researcher might flash the word *elephant* on a computer screen so briefly that it is not consciously perceived by a viewer. But if asked later to name as many animals as come to mind, the viewer is quite likely to include "elephant" on the list (Challis, 1996).

Priming can influence not only performance, but preferences and behavior as well. Individuals exposed briefly (even subliminally) to pictures of abstract art showed greater preferences for that type of art than did others who did not see the pictures. And in one study, participants subliminally exposed to faces of real people later interacted with those people more than did individuals not exposed to the photos (Basic Behavioral Science Task Force, 1996).

The Levels-of-Processing Model

How does the levels-of-processing model differ from that proposed by Atkinson and Shiffrin?

Not all psychologists support the notion of three memory systems. Craik and Lockhart (1972) proposed instead a **levels-of-processing model**. They suggested that whether people remember something for a few seconds or a lifetime depends on how deeply they process the information. With the shallowest levels of processing, a person is merely aware of incoming sensory information. Deeper processing takes place only when the person does more with the new information, such as forming relationships, making associations, attaching meaning to a sensory impression, or engaging in active elaboration on new material. However, the deeper levels of processing that establish a memory also require background knowledge, so that lasting connections can be formed between the person's existing store of knowledge and the new information (Willoughby et al., 2000).

■ levels-of-processing model
A model of memory that holds that retention depends on how deeply information is processed.

Craik and Tulving (1975) tested the levels-of-processing model. They had participants answer "yes" or "no" to questions asked about words just before the words were flashed to them for 1/5 of a second. The participants had to process the words in three ways: (1) visually (is the word in capital letters?); (2) acoustically (does the word rhyme with another particular word?); and (3) semantically (does the word make sense when used in a particular sentence?). Thus, this test required shallow processing for the first question, deeper processing for the second question, and still deeper processing for the third question. Later retention tests showed that the deeper the level of processing, the higher the accuracy of memory. But this conclusion is equally valid for the three-system model. Some brain-imaging studies with fMRI revealed that semantic (deeper) encoding causes greater activity in the left prefrontal cortex (Gabrieli et al., 1996). Other studies of how brain activity is related to depth of (semantic) processing reveal two kinds of memory-related activity: information search and information retrieval (Rugg et al., 2000).

Three Kinds of Memory Tasks

What are the three methods used by psychologists to measure memory?

How many times have you recognized someone without being able to recall his or her name? This happens to everyone because recognition is an easier memory task than recall. A great deal of memory research has focused on understanding the differences between the two. Researchers have also studied another kind of memory task known as relearning.

Recall Do you do well on essay tests? Most students prefer other kinds of exams, because essay tests usually require test takers to recall a lot of information. In **recall,** a person must produce required information simply by searching memory. Trying to remember someone's name, the items on a shopping list, or the words of a speech or a poem is a recall task. Which of the following test questions do you think is more difficult?

> What are the three basic memory processes?
>
> Which of the following is *not* one of the three basic memory processes?
>
> a. encoding   b. storage   c. retrieval   d. relearning

Most people think the second question is easier because it requires only recognition, whereas the first involves recall.

A recall task may be made a little easier if cues are provided to jog memory. A **retrieval cue** is any stimulus or bit of information that aids in retrieving a particular memory. Such a cue might consist of providing the first letters of the required words for fill-in-the-blank questions:

> The three processes involved in memory are e____________, s____________, and r____________.

Are you better at remembering faces than names? Have you ever wondered why? It's because the task involves recognition rather than recall. You must recall the name but merely recognize the face.

Sometimes *serial recall* is required; that is, information must be recalled in a specific order. This is the way you learned your ABCs, memorized poems, and learned any sequences that had to be carried out in a certain order. Serial recall is often easier than *free recall*, or remembering items in any order. In serial recall, each letter, word, or task may serve as a cue for the one that follows. Indeed, research suggests that, in recall tasks, order associations are more resistant to distractions than meaningful associations are (Howard, 2002).

You may fail to recall information in a memory task even if you are given many retrieval cues, but this does not necessarily mean that the information is not in long-term memory. You might be able to remember it if a recognition task is used.

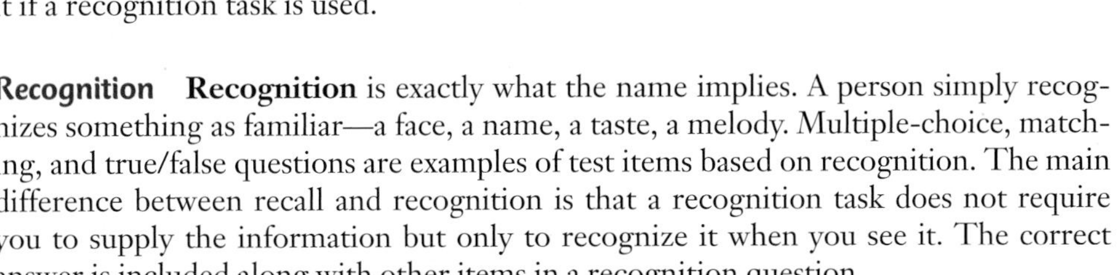

Recognition **Recognition** is exactly what the name implies. A person simply recognizes something as familiar—a face, a name, a taste, a melody. Multiple-choice, matching, and true/false questions are examples of test items based on recognition. The main difference between recall and recognition is that a recognition task does not require you to supply the information but only to recognize it when you see it. The correct answer is included along with other items in a recognition question.

Recent brain-imaging studies have discovered that the hippocampus plays an extensive role in memory tasks involving recognition and that the degree of hippocampal activity varies depending on the exact nature of the task. When the task is recognizing famous faces, widespread brain activity takes place in both hemispheres, involving the prefrontal and temporal lobes and including the hippocampus and the surrounding hippocampal region. Less widespread brain activity is observed during the recognition of recently encoded faces or the encoding of faces seen for the first time (Henson et al., 2002). Studies with monkeys whose brain damage is limited to the hippocampal region show conclusively that this region is absolutely essential for normal recognition tasks (Teng et al., 2000; Zola et al., 2000).

Relearning There is another, more sensitive way to measure memory. With the **relearning method**, retention is expressed as the percentage of time saved when material is relearned relative to the time required to learn the material originally. Suppose it took you 40 minutes to memorize a list of words, and 1 month later you were tested on those words, using recall or recognition. If you could not recall or recognize a single word, would this mean that you had absolutely no memory of anything on the list? Or could it mean that the recall and recognition tasks were not sensitive enough

■ **recall**
A memory task in which a person must produce required information by searching memory.

■ **retrieval cue**
Any stimulus or bit of information that aids in retrieving particular information from long-term memory.

■ **recognition**
A memory task in which a person must simply identify material as familiar or as having been encountered before.

■ **relearning method**
A measure of memory in which retention is expressed as the percentage of time saved when material is relearned compared with the time required to learn the material originally.

savings score
The percentage of time saved when relearning material compared with the amount of time required for the original learning.

to measure what little information you may have stored? How could a researcher measure such a remnant of former learning? Using the relearning method, a researcher could time how long it would take you to relearn the list of words. If it took 20 minutes to relearn the list, this would represent a 50% savings over the original learning time of 40 minutes. The percentage of time saved—the **savings score**—reflects how much material remains in long-term memory.

College students demonstrate the relearning method each semester when they study for comprehensive final exams. Relearning material for a final exam takes less time than it took to learn the material originally.

Remember It 6.1

1. Transforming information into a form that can be stored in memory is the process of __________; bringing to mind the material that has been stored is the process of __________.
2. Match each memory system with the best description of its capacity and the duration of time it holds information.
   ____ (1) sensory memory
   ____ (2) short-term memory
   ____ (3) long-term memory
   a. virtually unlimited capacity; long duration
   b. large capacity; short duration
   c. very limited capacity; short duration
3. __________ memory does not require consciousness.
4. Match each task with the corresponding method of measuring memory:
   ____ (1) identifying a suspect in a lineup
   ____ (2) answering a fill-in-the-blank question on a test
   ____ (3) having to study less for a comprehensive final exam than for all of the previous exams put together
   ____ (4) answering a matching or multiple-choice question on a test
   ____ (5) reciting one's lines in a play
   a. recognition
   b. relearning
   c. recall

ANSWERS: 1. encoding, retrieval; 2. (1) b, (2) c, (3) a; 3. Nondeclarative; 4. (1) a, (2) c, (3) b, (4) a, (5) c

The Nature of Remembering

Do you agree with Wilder Penfield (1969), a Canadian neurosurgeon, who claimed that experiences leave a "permanent imprint on the brain . . . as though a tape recorder had been receiving it all" (p. 165)? Penfield (1975) performed over 1,100 operations on patients with epilepsy. He found that when parts of the temporal lobes were stimulated with an electrical probe, 3.5% of patients reported flashback experiences, as though they were actually reliving parts of their past. After reviewing Penfield's findings, other researchers offered different explanations for his patients' responses. Neisser (1967) suggested that the experiences patients reported were "comparable to the content of dreams," rather than the recall of actual experiences (p. 169). Does human memory really function like a tape or video recorder? Probably not.

What is meant by the statement "Memory is reconstructive in nature"?

Memory as a Reconstruction

Other than Penfield's work, there is no research to suggest that memory works like a video recorder, capturing every part of an experience exactly as it happens. Normally, what a person recalls is not an exact replication of an event, according to Elizabeth Loftus, a leading memory researcher. Rather a memory is a **reconstruction**—an account pieced together from a few highlights, using information that may or may not be accurate (Loftus & Loftus, 1980). Put another way, "memory is not so much like reading a book as it is like writing one from fragmentary notes" (Kihlstrom, 1995, p. 341). Ample evidence indicates that memory is quite often inaccurate. "Critical details of an experience can be forgotten or become distorted, their source and order may be misremembered, and under certain circumstances completely new details may be incorporated into a memory" (Conway et al., 1996, p. 69). Recall is, even for people with the most accurate memories, partly truth and partly fiction. This was the finding of another pioneer in memory research, Englishman Sir Frederick Bartlett.

The Work of Frederick Bartlett Sir Frederick Bartlett (1886–1969) studied memory by giving participants stories to read and drawings to study; then, after varying time intervals, he had them reproduce the original material. Accurate reports were rare. The participants seemed to reconstruct the material they had learned, rather than actually remember it. They recreated the stories, making them shorter and more consistent with their own individual viewpoints. They adapted puzzling features of the stories to fit their own expectations and often changed details, substituting more familiar objects or events. Errors in memory increased with time, and Bartlett's participants were not aware that they had partly remembered and partly invented. Ironically, the parts his participants had created were often the parts they most adamantly claimed to have remembered (Bartlett, 1932).

Bartlett concluded that people systematically distort the facts and the circumstances of experiences. Information already stored in long-term memory exerts a strong influence on how people remember new information and experiences. As Bartlett (1932) put it, "the past is being continually remade, reconstructed in the interest of the present" (p. 309).

■ reconstruction
An account of an event that has been pieced together from a few highlights, using information that may or may not be accurate.

■ schemas
The integrated frameworks of knowledge and assumptions a person has about people, objects, and events, which affect how the person encodes and recalls information.

Schemas and Memory Bartlett suggested that his participants' inaccuracies in memory reflected their **schemas**—the integrated frameworks of knowledge and assumptions they had about people, objects, and events. Schemas aid in processing large amounts of material, because they provide frameworks into which people can incorporate new information and experience. Schemas also provide association cues that can help in retrieval.

Once formed, schemas influence what we notice and how we encode and recall information. When we encounter new information or have a new experience related to an existing schema, we try to make it fit or be consistent with that schema. To accomplish this, we may have to distort some aspects of the information and ignore or forget other aspects. Some of the distorting and ignoring occurs as the material is being encoded; more can occur when we try to remember or reconstruct the original experience.

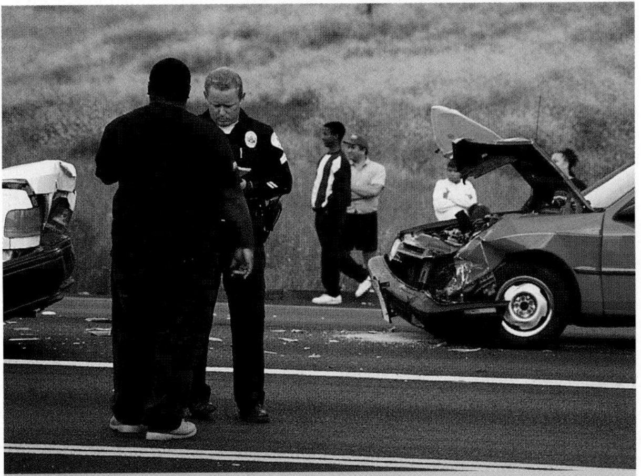

When people recall an event, such as a car accident, they are actually reconstructing it from memory by piecing together bits of information that may or may not be totally accurate.

Distortion in Memory When people reconstruct memories, they do not purposely try to distort the actual experience—unless, of course, they are lying. But people tend to omit some details that actually occurred and to supply other details from their own imaginations. *Distortion* occurs when people alter the memory of an event or an experience in order to fit their beliefs, expectations, logic, or prejudices. The tendency toward systematic distortion of actual events has been proven many times. *Try It 6.1* (on page 206) demonstrates distortion in memory.

Try It 6.1 Creating a False Memory

Read this list of words aloud at a rate of about one word per second. Then close your book, and write down all the words you can remember.

bed	awake	dream	snooze	nap	snore
rest	tired	wake	doze	yawn	slumber

Now check your list. Did you "remember" the word *sleep*? Many people do, even though it is not one of the words on the list (Deese, 1959).

The *Try It* shows that we are very likely to alter or distort what we see or hear to make it fit with what we believe to be true. All the words on the list are related to sleep, so it seems logical that *sleep* should be one of the words. In experiments using word lists similar to the one in the *Try It*, between 40% and 55% of the participants "remembered" a key related word that was not on the list (Roediger & McDermott, 1995). If you added the word *sleep* when doing the *Try It*, you created a false memory, which probably seemed as real to you as a true memory (Dodson et al., 2000).

The tendency to distort makes the world more understandable and enables people to organize their experiences into their existing systems of beliefs and expectations. But this tendency often causes gross inaccuracies in what people remember. And they usually distort memories of their own lives in a positive direction. Bahrick and others (1996) found that 89% of college students accurately remembered the A's they earned in high school, but only 29% accurately recalled the D's. The most dramatic examples of systematic distortion often occur in eyewitness testimony.

Eyewitness Testimony

What conditions reduce the reliability of eyewitness testimony?

Recall from this chapter's opening story that Ronald Cotton was a victim of faulty eyewitness identification. Is his case an isolated incident? Unfortunately not. According to Elizabeth Loftus (1993a), a staggering number of wrongful convictions in the United States each year are based on eyewitness testimony. According to Huff (1995), the number is probably at least 10,000. Yet it was not until October 1999 that the U.S. Department of Justice prepared the first national guidelines for the collection of eyewitness evidence (Wells et al., 2000).

Studies on the accuracy of human memory suggest that eyewitness testimony is highly subject to error, and that it should always be viewed with caution (Loftus, 1979). Nevertheless, it does play a vital role in the U.S. justice system. According to Loftus (1984), "We can't afford to exclude it legally or ignore it as jurors. Sometimes, as in cases of rape, it is the only evidence available, and it is often correct" (p. 24).

Fortunately, eyewitness mistakes can be minimized. Eyewitnesses to crimes typically identify suspects from a lineup. If shown photographs of a suspect before viewing the lineup, eyewitnesses may mistakenly identify that suspect in the lineup because the person looks familiar. Research suggests that it is better to have an eyewitness first describe the perpetrator and then search for photos matching that description than to have the eyewitness start by looking through photos and making judgments as to their similarity to the perpetrator (Pryke et al., 2000).

The composition of the lineup is also important. Other subjects in a lineup must resemble the suspect in age, body build, and certainly race. Even then, if the lineup does not contain the guilty party, eyewitnesses may identify the person who most closely resembles the perpetrator (Gonzalez et al., 1993). Eyewitnesses are less likely to make errors if a sequential lineup is used—that is, if the members of the lineup are viewed one after the other, rather than simultaneously (Loftus, 1993a). Some police officers and researchers prefer a "showup," in which the witness sees only one suspect at a time and indicates whether or not that person is the perpetrator. There are fewer misidentifications with a showup, but also more failures to make a positive identification (Wells, 1993).

The composition of this police lineup is consistent with research findings that suggest that all individuals in a lineup should be similar to the suspect with respect to age, race, body build, and other physical characteristics.

Eyewitnesses are more likely to identify the wrong person if the person's race is different from their own. According to Egeth (1993), misidentifications are approximately 15% higher in cross-race than in same-race identifications. Misidentification is also somewhat more likely to occur when a weapon is used in a crime. The witnesses may pay more attention to the weapon than to the physical characteristics of the criminal (Steblay, 1992).

Even the questioning of witnesses after a crime can influence what they later remember. Because leading questions can substantially change a witness's memory of an event, it is critical that the interviewers ask neutral questions (Leichtman & Ceci, 1995). Misleading information supplied after the event can result in erroneous recollections of the actual event, a phenomenon known as the *misinformation effect* (Kroll et al., 1988; Loftus & Hoffman, 1989). Loftus (1997) and her students have conducted "more than 20 experiments involving over 20,000 participants that document how exposure to misinformation induces memory distortion" (p. 71). Furthermore, after eyewitnesses have repeatedly recalled information, whether it is accurate or inaccurate, they become even more confident when they testify in court because the information is so easily retrieved (Shaw, 1996).

Witnessing a crime is highly stressful. How does stress affect eyewitness accuracy? Research suggests that eyewitnesses do tend to remember the central, critical details of the event, even though their arousal is high, but the memory of less important details suffers (Burke et al., 1992; Christianson, 1992).

Furthermore, as was demonstrated by Jennifer Thompson in this chapter's opening story, the confidence eyewitnesses have in their testimony is not necessarily an indication of its accuracy (Loftus, 1993a; Sporer et al., 1995). In fact, eyewitnesses who perceive themselves to be more objective have more confidence in their testimony, regardless of its accuracy, and are more likely to include incorrect information in their verbal descriptions (Geiselman et al., 2000). When witnesses make incorrect identifications with great certainty, they can be highly persuasive to judges and jurors alike. "A false eyewitness identification can create a real-life nightmare for the identified person, friends, and family members. . . . False identifications also mean that the actual culprit remains at large—a double injustice" (Wells, 1993, p. 568).

Recovering Repressed Memories

What is the controversy regarding the therapy used to recover repressed memories of childhood sexual abuse?

Do you believe that unconscious memories of childhood abuse can lead to serious psychological disorders? Perhaps because of the frequency of such cases in fictional literature, on television, and in movies, many people in the United States apparently do believe that so-called repressed memories can cause problems in adulthood (Stafford & Lynn, 2002). Such beliefs have also been fostered by self-help books such as *The Courage to Heal*, published in 1988, by Ellen Bass and Laura Davis. This best-selling book became the "bible" for sex abuse victims and the leading "textbook" for some therapists who specialized in treating them. Bass and Davis not only sought to help survivors who remember having suffered sexual abuse, but also reached out to other people who had no memory of any sexual abuse and tried to help them determine whether they might have been abused. They suggested that "if you are unable to remember any specific instances . . . but still have a feeling that something abusive happened to you, it probably did" (p. 21). They offered a definite conclusion: "If you think you were abused and your life shows the symptoms, then you were" (p. 22). And they freed potential victims of sexual abuse from the responsibility of establishing any proof: "You are not responsible for proving that you were abused" (p. 37).

However, many psychologists are skeptical about such "recovered" memories, claiming that they are actually false memories created by the suggestions of therapists. Critics "argue that repression of truly traumatic memories is rare" (Bowers & Farvolden, 1996, p. 355). Moreover, they maintain that "when it comes to a serious trauma, intrusive thoughts and memories of it are the most characteristic reaction" (p. 359). Repressed-memory therapists believe, however, that healing hinges on their patients' being able to recover their repressed memories.

Critics further charge that recovered memories of sexual abuse are suspect because of the techniques therapists usually use to uncover them—namely, hypnosis and guided imagery. As you have learned (in Chapter 4), hypnosis does not improve the accuracy of memory, only the confidence that what one remembers is accurate. And a therapist using guided imagery might tell a patient something similar to what Wendy Maltz (1991) advocates in her book:

> Spend time imagining that you were sexually abused, without worrying about accuracy, proving anything, or having your ideas make sense. . . . Ask yourself . . . these questions: What time of day is it? Where are you? Indoors or outdoors? What kind of things are happening? (p. 50)

Can merely imagining experiences in this way lead people to believe that those experiences had actually happened to them? Yes, according to some studies. Many research participants who are instructed to imagine that a fictitious event happened do, in fact, develop a false memory of that imagined event (Hyman et al., 1995; Hyman & Pentland, 1996; Loftus & Pickrell, 1995; Mazzoni & Memon, 2003; Worthen & Wood, 2001).

False childhood memories can also be experimentally induced. Garry and Loftus (1994) were able to implant a false memory of being lost in a shopping mall at 5 years of age in 25% of participants aged 18 to 53, after verification of the fictitious experience by a relative. Repeated exposure to suggestions of false memories can create those memories (Zaragoza & Mitchell, 1996). Further, researchers have found that adults who claim to have recovered memories of childhood abuse or of abduction by extraterrestrials are more vulnerable to experimentally induced false memories than are adults who do not report such recovered memories (McNally, 2003). So, individual differences in suggestibility may play a role in the recovery of memories.

Critics are especially skeptical of recovered memories of events that occurred in the first few years of life; in part because the hippocampus, vital in the formation of episodic memories, is not fully developed then. And neither are the areas of the cortex where memories are stored (Squire et al., 1993). Furthermore, young children, who are still limited in language ability, do not store semantic memories in categories that are accessible to them later in life. The relative inability of older children and adults to recall events from the first few years of life is referred to as **infantile amnesia**.

In light of these developmental limitations, is it possible that some individuals cannot recall incidents of childhood sexual abuse? Widom and Morris (1997) found that 64% of a group of women who had been sexually abused as children reported no memory of the abuse in a 2-hour interview 20 years later. Following up on women who had documented histories of sexual victimization, Williams (1994) found that 38% of them did not report remembering the sexual abuse some 17 years later. Memories of abuse were better when the victimization took place between the ages of 7 and 17 than when it occurred in the first 6 years of life. Keep in mind, however, that it is

■ **infantile amnesia**
The relative inability of older children and adults to recall events from the first few years of life.

possible that some of these women may have remembered the abuse but, for whatever reason, chose not to admit it.

The American Psychological Association (1994), the American Psychiatric Association (1993), and the American Medical Association (1994) have issued status reports on memories of childhood abuse. The position of all three groups is that current evidence supports both the possibility that repressed memories exist and the likehood that false memories can be constructed in response to suggestions of abuse. This position suggests that recovered memories of abuse should be verified independently before they are accepted as facts. Taking such a position is critically important. As you saw in *Try It 6.1*, false memories are easily formed. And, once formed, they are often relied on with great confidence (Dodson et al., 2000; Henkel et al., 2000).

■ flashbulb memory
An extremely vivid memory of the conditions surrounding one's first hearing the news of a surprising, shocking, or highly emotional event.

■ eidetic imagery
(eye-DET-ik) The ability to retain the image of a visual stimulus for several minutes after it has been removed from view and to use this retained image to answer questions about the visual stimulus.

Unusual Memory Phenomena

What does research evidence say about flashbulb and photographic memories?

Flashbulb Memories: Extremely Vivid Memories Do you remember where you were and what you were doing when you heard about the tragic events of September 11, 2001? Most people do. Likewise, most people over age 50 claim to have vivid memories of exactly when and where they received the news of the assassination of President John F. Kennedy. And many of their parents have very clear memories of learning about the attack on Pearl Harbor on December 7, 1941, which marked the entry of the United States into World War II. This type of extremely vivid memory is called a **flashbulb memory** (Bohannon, 1988). Brown and Kulik (1977) suggest that a flashbulb memory is formed when a person learns of an event that is very surprising, shocking, or highly emotional. You might have a flashbulb memory of when you received the news of the death or the serious injury of a close family member or a friend.

Pillemer (1990) argues that flashbulb memories do not constitute a completely different type of memory. Rather, he suggests, all memories can vary on the dimensions of emotion, consequentiality (the importance of the consequences of the event), and rehearsal (how often people think or talk about the event afterwards). Flashbulb memories rank high in all three dimensions and thus are extremely memorable.

However, several studies suggest that flashbulb memories are not as accurate as people believe them to be. Neisser and Harsch (1992) questioned university freshmen about the televised explosion of the space shuttle *Challenger* the following morning. When the same students were questioned again 3 years later, one-third gave accounts that differed markedly from those given initially, but these individuals were extremely confident about their recollections. Further, flashbulb memories appear to be forgotten at about the same rate and in the same ways as other kinds of memories (Curci et al., 2001).

Eyewitnesses to the aftermath of the terrorist attacks on the World Trade Center almost certainly formed flashbulb memories of the horrific events they witnessed. Do you remember where you were and what you were doing when you heard the news on September 11, 2001?

Eidetic Imagery Have you ever wished you had a photographic memory? Psychologists doubt that there are more than a few rare cases of a truly photographic memory, one that captures all the details of an experience and retains them perfectly. But some studies do show that about 5% of children have something like a photographic memory, an ability psychologists call **eidetic imagery** (Haber, 1980). These children can retain the image of a visual stimulus, such as a picture, for several minutes after it has been removed from view and use this retained image to answer questions about the visual stimulus (see Figure 6.6, on page 210).

Children with eidetic imagery generally have no better long-term memory than others their age. And virtually all children with eidetic imagery lose it before adulthood. One exceptional case, however, is Elizabeth, a teacher and a skilled artist. She can create on canvas an exact duplicate of a remembered scene in all its rich detail. Just as remarkable is her ability to retain visual

FIGURE 6.6 Test for Eidetic Imagery

Researchers test children for eidetic imagery by having them stare for 30 seconds at a picture like the one in (a). A few minutes later, the drawing in (b) is shown to the children, who are asked to report what they see. Those with eidetic imagery usually claim that they see a face and describe the composite sketch in (c). The face can be perceived only if the child retains the image of the first picture and fuses it with the middle drawing.

Source: Haber (1980).

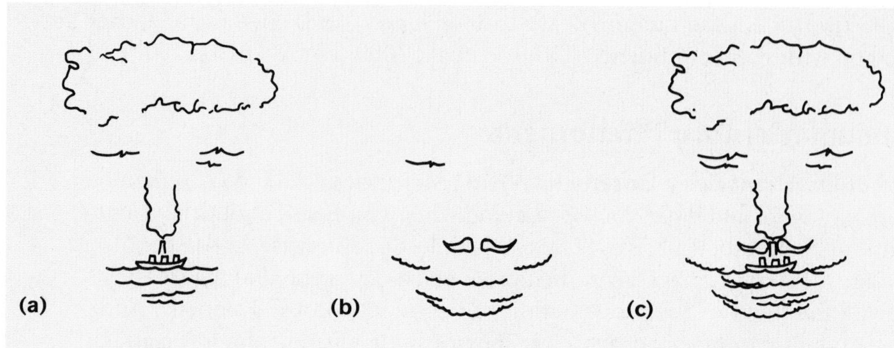

images of words. "Years after having read a poem in a foreign language, she can fetch back an image of the printed page and copy the poem from the bottom line to the top line as fast as she can write" (Stromeyer, 1970, p. 77).

Memory and Culture

How does culture influence memory?

Sir Frederick Bartlett (1932) believed that some impressive memory abilities operate within a social or cultural context and cannot be completely understood as a process. He stated that "both the manner and matter of recall are often predominantly determined by social influences" (p. 244). Studying memory in a cultural context, Bartlett (1932) described the amazing ability of the Swazi people of Africa to remember the slight differences in individual characteristics of their cows. One Swazi herdsman, Bartlett claimed, could remember details of every cow he had tended the year before. Such a feat is less surprising when you consider that the key component of traditional Swazi culture is the herds of cattle the people tend and depend on for their living. Do the Swazi people have super memory powers? Bartlett asked young Swazi men and young European men to recall a message consisting of 25 words. In this case, the Swazi had no better recall ability than the Europeans.

In many traditional cultures, elders are oral historians, remembering and passing on the details of tribal traditions and myths as well as genealogical data.

Among many tribal peoples in Africa, the history of the tribe is preserved orally by specialists, who must be able to encode, store, and retrieve huge volumes of historical data (D'Azevedo, 1982). Elders of the Iatmul people of New Guinea are also said to have committed to memory the lines of descent for the various clans of their people, stretching back for many generations (Bateson, 1982). The unerring memory of the elders for the kinship patterns of their people are used to resolve disputed property claims (Mistry & Rogoff, 1994).

Barbara Rogoff, an expert in cultural psychology, maintains that such phenomenal, prodigious memory feats are best explained and understood in their cultural context (Rogoff & Mistry, 1985). The tribal elders perform their impressive memory feats because it is an integral and critically important part of the culture in which they live. Most likely, their ability to remember nonmeaningful information would be no better than your own.

A study examining memory for location among a tribal group in India, the Asur, who do not use artificial lighting of any kind, provides further information about the influence of culture on memory (Mishra & Singh, 1992). Researchers hypothesized that members of this group would perform better on tests of memory for locations than on memory tests involving word pairs, because, without artificial light, they have to remember where things are in order to be able to move around in the dark without bumping into things. When the tribe members were tested, the results supported this hypothesis: They remembered locations better than word pairs.

In classic research, cognitive psychologists have also found that people more easily remember stories set in their own cultures than those set in others. In one of the first of these studies, researchers told women in the United States and Aboriginal women in Australia a story about a sick child (Steffensen & Calker, 1982). Participants were randomly assigned to groups for whom story outcomes were varied. In one version, the girl got well after being treated by a physician. In the other, a traditional native healer was called in to help the girl. Aboriginal participants better recalled the story with the native healer, while the American women were more accurate in their recall of the story in which a physician treated the girl.

Remember It 6.2

1. __________ found that, rather than accurately recalling information detail by detail, people often reconstruct and systematically distort facts to make them more consistent with past experiences.
2. When a person uses __________ to process information, both encoding and retrieval can be affected.
3. __________ memories are vivid memories of where and when an individual learned of a particularly dramatic event.
4. __________ is the ability to retain the image of a visual stimulus for several minutes after it has been removed from view.

ANSWERS: 1. Bartlett; 2. schemas; 3. Flashbulb; 4. Eidetic imagery

Factors Influencing Retrieval

Why are some kinds of information easier to pull up out of memory than others? Researchers in psychology have identified several factors that influence memory. A person can control some of these factors, but not all of them.

serial position effect The finding that, for information learned in a sequence, recall is better for the beginning and ending items than for the middle items in the sequence.

What happens when information must be recalled in a particular order?

The Serial Position Effect

What would happen if you were introduced to a dozen people at a party? You would most likely recall the names of the first few people you met and the last one or two, but forget many of the names in the middle. The reason is the **serial position effect**—the finding that, for information learned in a sequence, recall is better for items at the beginning and the end than for items in the middle of the sequence.

■ **primacy effect**
The tendency to recall the first items in a sequence more readily than the middle items.

■ **recency effect**
The tendency to recall the last items in a sequence more readily than those in the middle.

Information at the beginning of a sequence is subject to the **primacy effect**—the tendency to recall the first items in a sequence more readily than the middle items. Such information is likely to be recalled because it already has been placed in long-term memory. Information at the end of a sequence is subject to the **recency effect**—the tendency to recall the last items in a sequence more readily than those in the middle. This information has an even higher probability of being recalled because it is still in short-term memory. The poorer recall of information in the middle of a sequence occurs because that information is no longer in short-term memory and has not yet been placed in long-term memory. The serial position effect lends strong support to the notion of separate systems for short-term and long-term memory (Postman & Phillips, 1965).

Environmental Context and Memory

How does environmental context affect memory?

Have you ever stood in your living room and thought of something you needed from your bedroom, only to forget what it was when you got there? Did the item come to mind again when you returned to the living room? Tulving and Thompson (1973) suggest that many elements of the physical setting in which a person learns information are encoded along with the information and become part of the memory. If part or all of the original context is reinstated, it may serve as a retrieval cue. That is why returning to the living room elicits the memory of the object you intended to get from the bedroom. In fact, just visualizing yourself in the living room might do the trick (Smith et al., 1978). (*Hint:* Next time you're taking a test and having difficulty recalling something, try visualizing yourself in the room where you studied.)

Godden and Baddeley (1975) conducted one of the early studies of context and memory with members of a university diving club. Participants memorized a list of words when they were either 10 feet underwater or on land. They were later tested for recall of the words in the same environment or in a different environment. Words learned underwater were best recalled underwater, and words learned on land were best recalled on land. In fact, when the divers learned and recalled the words in the same context, their scores were 47% higher than when the two contexts were different (see Figure 6.7).

In a more recent study of context-dependent memory, participants viewed videotapes and then were tested on their memory of the videos in two separate interviews conducted 2 days apart. The memory context was the same for all the participants, with one exception. Half the participants were questioned by different interviewers, whereas the

FIGURE 6.7 Context-Dependent Memory

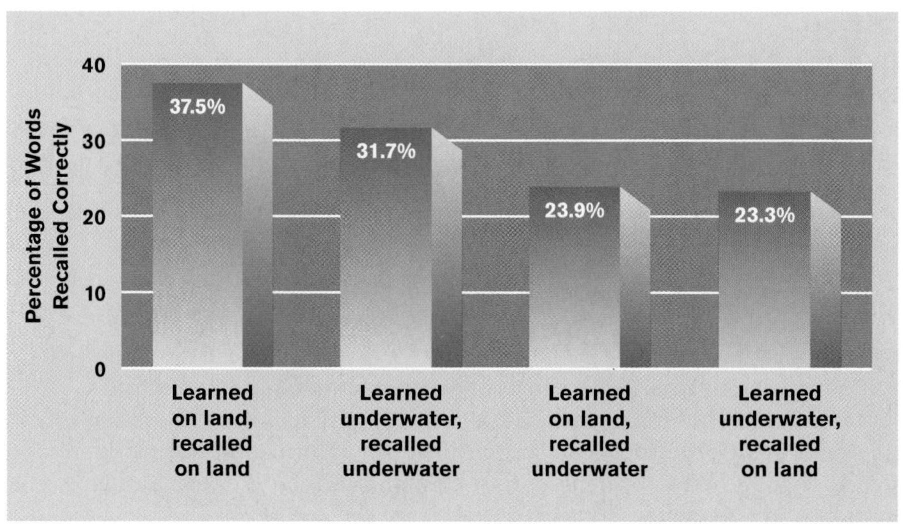

Godden and Baddeley showed the strong influence of environmental context on recall. Divers who memorized a list of words, either on land or underwater, had significantly better recall in the same physical context in which the learning had taken place.
Source: Data from Godden & Baddeley (1975).

other half were questioned by the same interviewer in both sessions. As you might expect, participants who were questioned twice by the same interviewer (same context) performed better than the other participants on the memory task (Bjorklund et al., 2000).

Odors can also supply powerful and enduring retrieval cues for memory. In a study by Morgan (1996), participants were placed in isolated cubicles and exposed to a list of 40 words. They were instructed to perform a cognitive task using the words but were not asked to remember them. Then, back in the cubicle 5 days later, participants were unexpectedly tested for recall of the 40 words. Experimental participants who experienced a pleasant odor during learning and again when tested 5 days later had significantly higher recall than did control participants who did not experience the odor during both learning and recall.

The State-Dependent Memory Effect

How do emotions and altered states of consciousness affect memory?

As we have seen, the external environment can influence performance on memory tasks, but might a person's internal state (happy or sad, intoxicated or sober) also do so? The answer is yes. People tend to recall information better if they are in the same internal state (psychological or pharmacological) as when the information was encoded. Psychologists call this the **state-dependent memory effect**.

Some studies have shown a state-dependent memory effect for alcohol and drugs such as marijuana, amphetamines, and barbiturates (Eich, 1980). Participants learned (encoded) material while sober or intoxicated and were later tested in either the sober or the intoxicated state. Recall was found to be best when the participants were in the same state for both learning and testing (Weingartner et al., 1976). As in other studies, the state-dependent memory effect was evident for recall but not for recognition.

Researchers have not been able to show conclusively that recall is best if participants are in the same happy or sad mood when they encode or learn material as when they try to recall it. However, evidence does suggest that anxiety and fear influence memory. For example, people going through significant life stress—death of a loved one, loss of a job, divorce—do more poorly on tests of recent memories. Further, when researchers exposed college students to spiders and/or snakes while they were learning lists of words, the students recalled more words when the creatures were also present during tests of recall (Lang et al., 2001).

Adults who are clinically depressed tend to recall more negative life experiences (Clark & Teasdale, 1982) and are likely to recall their parents as unloving and rejecting (Lewinsohn & Rosenbaum, 1987). Moreover, a meta-analysis of 48 studies revealed a significant relationship between depression and memory impairment. And recognition and recall were more impaired in younger depressed patients than in older ones (Burt et al., 1995). But, as depression lifts, the tendency toward negative recall and associated memory impairments reverses itself.

■ **state-dependent memory effect**
The tendency to recall information better if one is in the same pharmacological or psychological state as when the information was encoded.

Remember It 6.3

1. When children learn the alphabet, they often can recite "A, B, C, D, ..." and "..., W, X, Y, Z" before they can recite the letters in between. This is because of the ____________.
2. Both ____________ and ____________ can provide retrieval cues for memories.
3. The ____________ happens when individuals acquire information while in a pharmacologically altered state of consciousness or when experiencing a particular emotion.

ANSWERS: 1. serial position effect; 2. context, odors; 3. state-dependent memory effect

Biology and Memory

Obviously, a person's vast store of memories must exist physically somewhere in the brain. But where?

The Hippocampus and Hippocampal Region

What roles do the hippocampus and the hippocampal region play in memory?

Researchers continue to identify specific locations in the brain that house and mediate functions and processes in memory. One important source of information comes from people who have suffered memory loss resulting from damage to specific brain areas. One especially significant case is that of H.M., a man who suffered from such severe epilepsy that, out of desperation, he agreed to a radical surgical procedure. The surgeon removed the part of the brain believed to be causing H.M.'s seizures—the medial portions of both temporal lobes, containing the amygdala and the **hippocampal region**, which includes the hippocampus itself and the underlying cortical areas. It was 1953, and H.M. was 27 years old.

After his surgery, H.M. remained intelligent and psychologically stable, and his seizures were drastically reduced. But unfortunately, the tissue cut from H.M.'s brain housed more than the site of his seizures. It also contained his ability to use working memory to store new information in long-term memory. Though the capacity of his short-term memory remains the same, and he remembers life events that were stored before the operation, H.M. suffers from **anterograde amnesia**. He has not been able to remember a single event that has occurred since the surgery. And though H.M. is in his late 70s, as far as his conscious long-term memory is concerned, it is still 1953 and he is still 27 years old.

Surgery affected only H.M.'s declarative, long-term memory—his ability to store facts, personal experiences, names, faces, telephone numbers, and the like. But researchers were surprised to discover that he could still form nondeclarative memories; that is, he could still acquire skills through repetitive practice, although he could not remember having done so. For example, since the surgery, H.M. has learned to play tennis and improve his game, but he has no memory of ever having played (Milner, 1966, 1970; Milner et al., 1968).

Animal studies support the conclusion that the parts of H.M.'s brain that were removed are critical to working memory function (Ragozzino et al., 2002). Moreover, other patients who have suffered similar brain damage show the same types of memory loss (Squire, 1992).

Most recent research supports the hypothesis that the hippocampus is especially important in forming episodic memories (Eichenbaum, 1997; Eichenbaum & Fortin, 2003; Gluck & Myers, 1997; Spiers et al., 2001). Semantic memory, however, depends not only on the hippocampus, but also on the other parts of the hippocampal region (Vargha-Khadem et al., 1997). Once stored, memories can be retrieved without the involvement of the hippocampus (Gluck & Myers, 1997; McClelland et al., 1995). Consequently, many researchers argue that neurological underpinnings of episodic and semantic memories are entirely separate (e.g., Tulving, 2002). But the degree to which the brain processes associated with episodic and semantic memories can be clearly distinguished is being questioned by some neuroscientists. Research involving older adults who suffer from semantic dementia due to frontal lobe damage shows that many of them suffer from deficiencies in episodic memory (Nestor et al., 2002). Moreover, other studies show that damage to the temporal and occipital lobes can also affect episodic memory (Wheeler & McMillan, 2001).

An interesting recent study (Maguire et al., 2000), which was described briefly in Chapter 2, suggests that the hippocampus may serve special functions in addition to those already known. A part of the hippocampus evidently specializes in navigational

■ **hippocampal region**
A part of the limbic system, which includes the hippocampus itself and the underlying cortical areas, involved in the formation of semantic memories.

■ **anterograde amnesia**
The inability to form long-term memories of events occurring after a brain injury or brain surgery, although memories formed before the trauma are usually intact and short-term memory is unaffected.

FIGURE 6.8 **MRI Scans Showing the Larger Size of the Posterior Hippocampus in the Brain of an Experienced Taxi Driver**

The posterior (rear) hippocampus of an experienced London taxi driver, shown in red in MRI scan (a), is significantly larger than the posterior hippocampus of a research participant who was not a taxi driver, shown in red in scan (b).

Source: Adapted from Maguire et al. (2000).

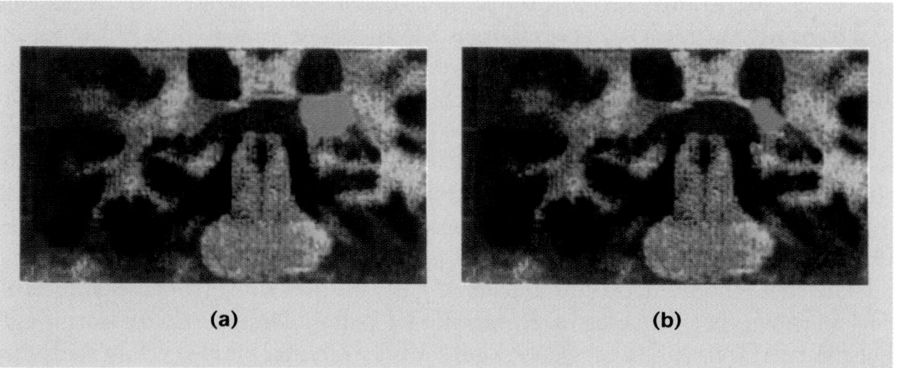

skills by helping to create intricate neural spatial maps. Using magnetic resonance imaging (MRI) scans, researchers found that the rear (posterior) region of the hippocampus of London taxi drivers was significantly larger than that of participants in a matched control group whose living did not depend on navigational skills (see Figure 6.8). In addition, the more time spent as a taxi driver, the greater the size of this part of the hippocampus. Further, in many small mammals and birds, the size of the hippocampus increases seasonally, as navigational skills and spatial maps showing where food is hidden become critical for survival (Clayton, 1998; Colombo & Broadbent, 2000). Moreover, recent animal studies show that the hippocampus also plays an important role in the reorganization of previously learned spatial information (Lee & Kesner, 2002).

Thus, research has established that the hippocampus is critically important for storing and using mental maps to navigate in the environment. And the observed size increase in the hippocampus of the more experienced London taxi drivers confirms that brain plasticity in response to environmental demands can continue into adulthood. These findings also raise the possibility of *neurogenesis* (the growth of new neurons) in the adult hippocampus.

We have considered how researchers have identified and located some of the brain structures that play a role in memory. But what happens within these brain structures as they change, reshape, and rearrange to make new memories?

Neuronal Changes and Memory

Why is long-term potentiation important?

Some researchers are exploring memory at deeper levels than the structures of the brain. Some look at the actions of single neurons; others study collections of neurons and their synapses and the neurotransmitters whose chemical action begins the process of recording and storing a memory. The first close look at how memory works in single neurons was provided by Eric Kandel and his colleagues, who traced the effects of learning and memory in the sea snail *Aplysia* (Dale & Kandel, 1990). Using tiny electrodes implanted in several single neurons in this snail, the researchers mapped the neural circuits that are formed and maintained as the animal learns and remembers. They also discovered the different types of protein synthesis that facilitate short-term and long-term memory (Sweatt & Kandel, 1989). Kandel won a Nobel Prize in 2000 for his work.

■ **long-term potentiation (LTP)**
An increase in the efficiency of neural transmission at the synapses that lasts for hours or longer.

But the studies of learning and memory in *Aplysia* reflect only simple classical conditioning, which is a type of nondeclarative memory. Other researchers studying mammals report that physical changes occur in the neurons and synapses in brain regions involved in declarative memory (Lee & Kesner, 2002).

As far back as the 1940s, Canadian psychologist Donald O. Hebb (1949) argued that learning and memory must involve the enhancement of transmission at the synapses between neurons. The most widely studied model for learning and memory at the level of the neurons meets the requirements of the mechanism Hebb described (Fischbach, 1992). **Long-term potentiation (LTP)** is an increase in the efficiency of neural transmission at the synapses that lasts for hours or longer (Bliss & Lomo, 2000; Martinez & Derrick, 1996; Nguyen et al., 1994). (*To potentiate* means "to make potent, or to strengthen.") Long-term potentiation does not take place unless both the sending and the receiving neurons are activated at the same time by intense stimulation. Also, the receiving neuron must be depolarized (ready to fire) when the stimulation occurs, or LTP will not happen. LTP is common in the hippocampal region, which, as you have learned, is essential in the formation of declarative memories (Eichenbaum & Otto, 1993).

If the changes in synapses produced by LTP are the same changes that take place during learning, then blocking or preventing LTP should interfere with learning. And it does. When Davis and others (1992) gave rats a drug that blocks certain receptors in doses large enough to interfere with a maze-running task, they discovered that LTP in the rats' hippocampi was also disrupted. In contrast, Riedel (1996) found that LTP was enhanced and the rats' memory improved when a drug that excites those same receptors was administered shortly after maze training.

Researchers now believe that LTP has the required characteristics to be a process involved in consolidating new memories (Cotman & Lynch, 1989). However, controversy continues as to whether the relatively long-lasting increase in synaptic efficiency that constitutes LTP is the result of an increase in the amount of neurotransmitter released, an increase in the number of receptors at the synapses, or both (Bennett, 2000).

Hormones and Memory

How do memories of threatening situations that elicit the "fight or flight response" compare with ordinary memories?

The strongest and most lasting memories are usually those fueled by emotion. Research by Cahill and McGaugh (1995) suggests that there may be two pathways for forming memories—one for ordinary information and another for memories that are fired by emotion. When a person is emotionally aroused, the adrenal glands release the hormones epinephrine (adrenalin) and norepinephrine (noradrenaline) into the bloodstream. Long known to be involved in the "fight or flight response," these hormones enable humans to survive, and they also imprint powerful and enduring memories of the circumstances surrounding threatening situations. Such emotionally laden memories activate the amygdala (known to play a central role in emotion) and other parts of the memory system. This widespread activation in the brain may be the most important factor in explaining the intensity and durability of flashbulb memories.

Other hormones may have important effects on memory. Excessive levels of the stress hormone *cortisol*, for example, have been shown to interfere with memory in patients who suffer from diseases of the adrenal glands, the site of cortisol production (Jelicic & Bonke, 2001). Furthermore, people whose bodies react to experimenter-induced stressors, such as forced public speaking, by releasing higher than average levels of cortisol perform less well on memory tests than those whose bodies release lower than average levels in the same situations (Al'absi et al., 2002).

Estrogen, the female sex hormone, appears to improve working memory efficiency (Dohanich, 2003). This hormone, along with others produced by the ovaries, also plays some role in the development and maintenance of synapses in areas of the brain known to be associated with memory (e.g, the hippocampus). This finding caused researchers to hypothesize that hormone replacement therapy might prevent or reverse the effects of Alzheimer's disease (Dohanich, 2003). However, recent research shows that postmenopausal women who take a combination of synthetic estrogen and progesterone, the two hormones that regulate the menstrual cycle, may actually increase their risk of developing dementia (Rapp et al., 2003; Shumaker et al., 2003).

The strongest and most lasting memories are usually fueled by emotion. That's why most people have vivid memories of the events and circumstances that surround the experience of falling in love.

Remember It 6.4

1. The hippocampus is involved primarily in the formation of __________ memories; the rest of the hippocampal region is involved primarily in the formation of __________ memories.
2. H.M. retained his ability to add to his __________ memory.
3. __________ is the long-lasting increase in the efficiency of neural transmission at the synapses; it may be the basis for learning and memory at the level of the neurons.
4. Memories of circumstances surrounding threatening situations that elicit the "fight or flight response" activate the __________.

ANSWERS: 1. episodic, semantic; 2. nondeclarative; 3. Long-term potentiation; 4. amygdala

Forgetting

Wouldn't it be depressing if you remembered in exact detail every bad thing that ever happened to you? Most people think of forgetting as a problem to be overcome, but it's actually not always unwelcome. Still, when you need to remember particular information to answer an exam question, forgetting can be very frustrating.

Ebbinghaus and the First Experimental Studies on Forgetting

What did Ebbinghaus discover about forgetting?

Hermann Ebbinghaus (1850–1909) conducted the first experimental studies on learning and memory. Realizing that some materials are easier than others to understand and remember, Ebbinghaus faced the task of finding items that would all be equally difficult to memorize. So he invented the **nonsense syllable**, a consonant-vowel-consonant combination that is not an actual word. Examples are LEJ, XIZ, LUK, and ZOH. Using nonsense syllables in his research largely accomplished Ebbinghaus's goal. But did you notice that some of the syllables sound more like actual words than others and would, therefore, be easier to remember?

Ebbinghaus (1885/1964) conducted his studies on memory using 2,300 nonsense syllables as his material and himself as the only participant. He carried out all his experiments at about the same time of day in the same surroundings, eliminating all possible distractions. Ebbinghaus memorized lists of nonsense syllables by repeating them over and over at a constant rate of 2.5 syllables per second, marking time with a

nonsense syllable
A consonant-vowel-consonant combination that does not spell a word and is used in memory research.

FIGURE 6.9 Ebbinghaus's Curve of Forgetting

After memorizing lists of nonsense syllables similar to those at left, Ebbinghaus measured his retention after varying intervals of time using the relearning method. Forgetting was most rapid at first, as shown by his retention of only 58% after 20 minutes and 44% after 1 hour. Then, the rate of forgetting tapered off, with a retention of 34% after 1 day, 25% after 6 days, and 21% after 31 days.
Source: Data from Ebbinghaus (1885/1913).

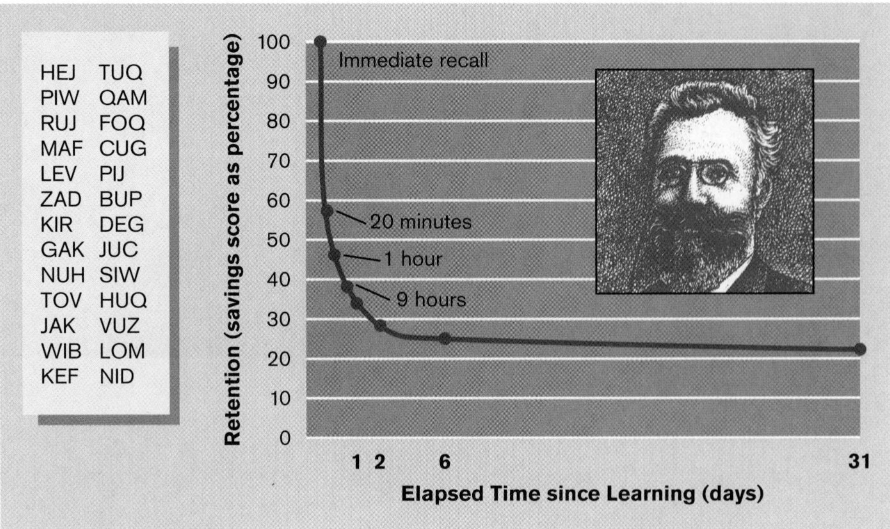

metronome or a ticking watch. He repeated a list until he could recall it twice without error, a measure he called *mastery*.

Ebbinghaus recorded the amount of time or the number of trials it took to memorize his lists to mastery. Then, after different periods of time had passed and forgetting had occurred, he recorded the amount of time or number of trials needed to relearn the same list to mastery. Ebbinghaus compared the time or number of trials required for relearning with that for original learning and then computed the percentage of time saved. This savings score represented the percentage of the original learning that remained in memory.

Ebbinghaus learned and relearned more than 1,200 lists of nonsense syllables to discover how rapidly forgetting occurs. Figure 6.9 shows his famous curve of forgetting, which consists of savings scores at various time intervals after the original learning. The curve of forgetting shows that the largest amount of forgetting occurs very quickly, after which forgetting tapers off. Of the information Ebbinghaus retained after a day or two, very little more would be forgotten even a month later. But, remember, this curve of forgetting applies to nonsense syllables. Meaningful material is usually forgotten more slowly, as is material that has been carefully encoded, deeply processed, and frequently rehearsed.

What Ebbinghaus learned about the rate of forgetting is relevant for everyone. Do you, like most students, cram before a big exam? If so, don't assume that everything you memorize on Monday can be held intact until Tuesday. So much forgetting occurs within the first 24 hours that it is wise to spend at least some time reviewing the material on the day of the test. The less meaningful the material is to you, the more you will forget and the more necessary a review is. Recall from Chapter 4 that the quantity and quality of sleep you get between studying and taking the test also influences how much you will remember.

When researchers measured psychology students' retention of names and concepts, they found that the pattern of forgetting was similar to Ebbinghaus's curve. Forgetting of names and concepts was rapid over the first several months, leveled off in approximately 36 months, and remained about the same for the next 7 years (Conway et al., 1991).

What causes forgetting?

The Causes of Forgetting

Why do we fail to remember, even when we put forth a lot of effort aimed at remembering? There are many reasons.

Encoding Failure When you can't remember something, could it be because the item was never stored in memory to begin with? Of course, there is a distinction between forgetting and not being able to remember. *Forgetting* is the inability to recall something that you could recall previously. But often when people say they cannot remember, they have not actually forgotten. The inability to remember is sometimes a result of **encoding failure**—the information was never put into long-term memory in the first place.

Of the many things we encounter every day, it is surprising how little we actually encode. Can you recall accurately, or even recognize, something you have seen thousands of times before? Read *Try It 6.2* to find out.

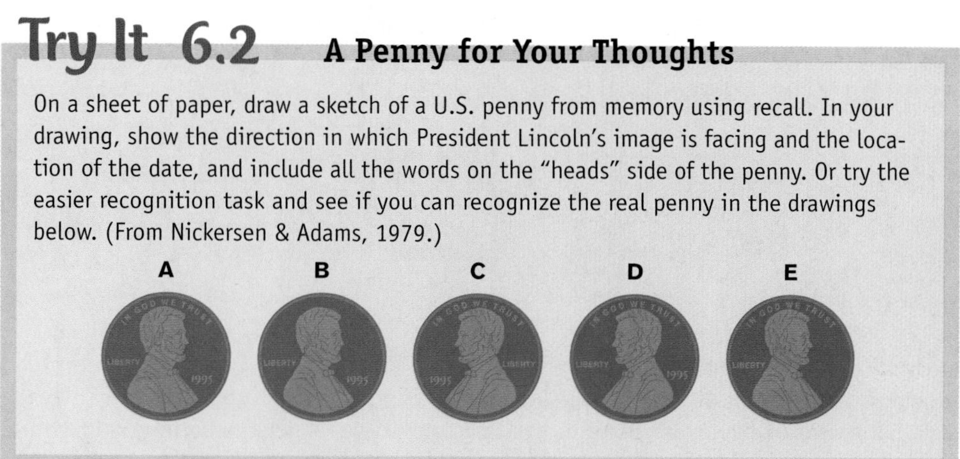

Try It 6.2 A Penny for Your Thoughts

On a sheet of paper, draw a sketch of a U.S. penny from memory using recall. In your drawing, show the direction in which President Lincoln's image is facing and the location of the date, and include all the words on the "heads" side of the penny. Or try the easier recognition task and see if you can recognize the real penny in the drawings below. (From Nickersen & Adams, 1979.)

In your lifetime, you have seen thousands of pennies, but unless you are a coin collector, you probably have not encoded the details of a penny's appearance. If you did poorly on the *Try It*, you have plenty of company. After studying a large group of participants, Nickerson and Adams (1979) reported that few people could reproduce a penny from recall. In fact, only a handful of participants could even recognize an accurate drawing of a penny when it was presented along with incorrect drawings. (The correct penny is the one labeled A in the *Try It*.)

When preparing for tests, do you usually take on a passive role? Do you merely read and reread your textbook and your notes and assume that this process will eventually result in learning? If you don't test yourself by reciting the material, you may find that you have been the unwilling victim of encoding failure. Textbook features such as margin questions and end-of-section reviews can help you by providing structure for rehearsing information to ensure that is encoded.

Decay **Decay theory**, probably the oldest theory of forgetting, assumes that memories, if not used, fade with time and ultimately disappear entirely. The word *decay* implies a physiological change in the neurons that recorded the experience. According to this theory, the neuronal record may decay or fade within seconds, days, or even much longer periods of time.

Most psychologists now accept that decay, or the fading of memories, is a cause of forgetting in sensory and short-term memory but not in long-term memory. There does not appear to be a gradual, inevitable decay of long-term memories. In one study, Harry Bahrick and others (1975) found that after 35 years, participants could recognize 90% of their high school classmates' names and photographs, the same percentage as for recent graduates.

Interference A major cause of forgetting that affects people every day is **interference**. Whenever you try to recall any given memory, two types of interference can hinder the

■ **encoding failure**
A cause of forgetting that occurs when information was never put into long-term memory.

■ **decay theory**
The oldest theory of forgetting, which holds that memories, if not used, fade with time and ultimately disappear altogether.

■ **interference**
A cause of forgetting that occurs because information or associations stored either before or after a given memory hinder the ability to remember it.

FIGURE 6.10 Retroactive and Proactive Interference

As shown in Example 1, retroactive interference occurs when new learning hinders the ability to recall information learned previously. As shown in Example 2, proactive interference occurs when prior learning hinders new learning.

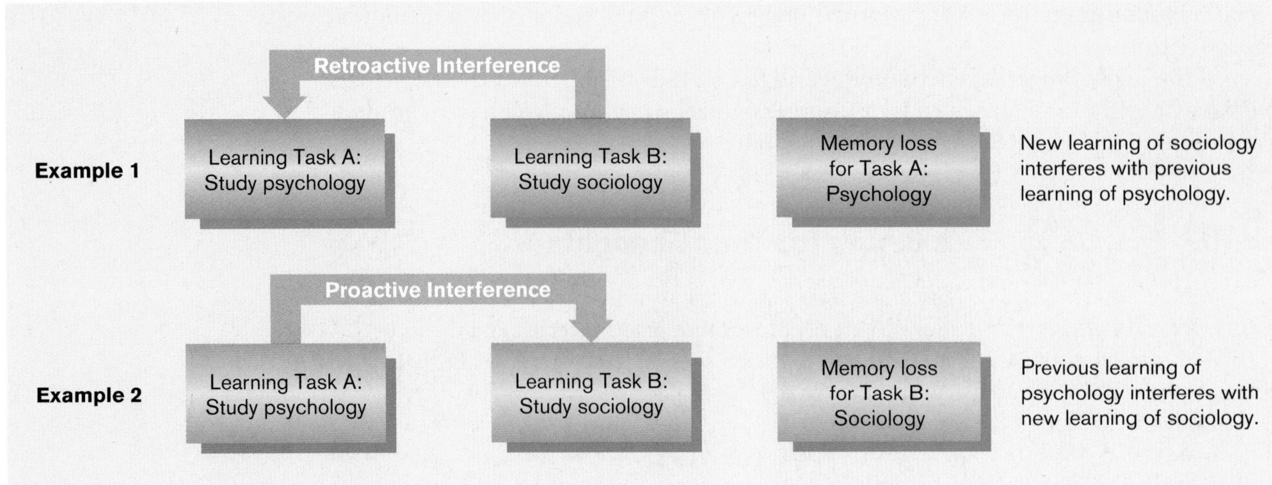

effort. Information or associations stored either *before* or *after* a given memory can interfere with the ability to remember it (see Figure 6.10). Interference can reach either forward or backward in time to affect memory—it gets us coming and going. Also, the more similar the interfering associations are to the information a person is trying to recall, the more difficult it is to recall the information (Underwood, 1964).

Proactive interference occurs when information or experiences already stored in long-term memory hinder the ability to remember newer information (Underwood, 1957). For example, Laura's romance with her new boyfriend, Todd, got off to a bad start when she accidentally called him "Dave," her former boyfriend's name. One explanation for proactive interference is the competition between old and new responses (Bower et al., 1994).

Retroactive interference happens when new learning interferes with the ability to remember previously learned information. The more similar the new material is to that learned earlier, the more interference there is. For example, when you take a psychology class, it may interfere with your ability to remember what you learned in your sociology class, especially with regard to theories (e.g., psychoanalysis) that are shared by the two disciplines but applied and interpreted differently.

Consolidation Failure *Consolidation* is the process by which encoded information is stored in memory. When a disruption in this process occurs, a long-term memory usually does not form. **Consolidation failure** can result from anything that causes a person to lose consciousness—a car accident, a blow to the head, a grand mal epileptic seizure, or an electroconvulsive shock treatment given for severe depression. Memory loss of the experiences that occurred shortly before the loss of consciousness is called **retrograde amnesia**.

Researchers Nader and others (2000) demonstrated that conditioned fears in rats can be erased by infusing into the rats' brains a drug that prevents protein synthesis (such synthesis is necessary for memory consolidation). Rats experienced a single pairing of a tone (the conditioned stimulus, CS) and a foot shock (the unconditioned stimulus, US). Later, the rats were exposed to the sound of the tone alone (CS) and showed a fear response, "freezing" (becoming totally immobile as if frozen with fright). Clearly, the rats remembered the feared stimulus. Twenty-four hours later, the rats were again exposed to the tone alone, and it elicited fear, causing them to freeze.

■ **consolidation failure** Any disruption in the consolidation process that prevents a long-term memory from forming.

■ **retrograde amnesia** (RET-ro-grade) A loss of memory for experiences that occurred shortly before a loss of consciousness.

Immediately, the drug anisomycin, which prevents protein synthesis in the brain, was infused into the rats' amygdalae (the part of the brain that processes fear stimuli). After the drug was infused, the rats were shocked again, but they showed no fear response (freezing). The rats in the study had already consolidated the memory of the fear, but it was completely wiped out after the drug prevented protein synthesis from occurring. This means that fear memories, once activated, must be "reconsolidated," or they may disappear.

This finding has positive implications. If fear memories can be activated and then wiped out with drugs that prevent protein synthesis, a new therapy may be on the horizon for people who suffer from debilitating fears (Nader et al., 2000).

We have discussed ways to avoid forgetting, but there are occasions when people may want to avoid remembering—times when they want to forget.

Motivated Forgetting Victims of rape or physical abuse, war veterans, and survivors of airplane crashes or earthquakes all have had terrifying experiences that may haunt them for years. These victims are certainly motivated to forget their traumatic experiences, but even people who have not suffered any trauma use **motivated forgetting** to protect themselves from experiences that are painful, frightening, or otherwise unpleasant.

With one form of motivated forgetting, *suppression*, a person makes a conscious, active attempt to put a painful, disturbing, anxiety- or guilt-provoking memory out of mind, but the person is still aware that the painful event occurred. With another type of motivated forgetting, **repression**, unpleasant memories are literally removed from consciousness, and the person is no longer aware that the unpleasant event ever occurred (Freud, 1922). People who have **amnesia** (partial or complete memory loss) that is not due to loss of consciousness or brain damage have repressed the events they no longer remember. Motivated forgetting is probably used by more people than any other method to deal with unpleasant memories. It seems to be a natural human tendency to forget the unpleasant circumstances of life and to remember the pleasant ones (Linton, 1979; Meltzer, 1930).

Prospective forgetting—not remembering to carry out some intended action (e.g., forgetting to go to your dentist appointment)—is another type of motivated forgetting. People are most likely to forget to do the things they view as unimportant, unpleasant, or burdensome. They are less likely to forget things that are pleasurable or important to them (Winograd, 1988).

However, as you probably know, prospective forgetting isn't always motivated by a desire to avoid something. Have you ever arrived home and suddenly remembered that you had intended to go to the bank to deposit your paycheck? Or you may have seen a review of a concert in the newspaper and suddenly remembered that you had intended to buy a ticket for it. In such cases, prospective forgetting is more likely to be the result of interference or consolidation failure.

Retrieval Failure How many times have these experiences happened to you? You are with a friend when you meet an acquaintance, but you can't introduce the two because you cannot recall the name of the acquaintance. Or, while taking a test, you can't remember the answer to a question that you are sure you know. Often, people are certain they know something, but are not able to retrieve the information when they need it. This type of forgetting is called *retrieval failure*.

Endel Tulving (1974) claims that much of what people call forgetting is really an inability to locate the needed information. The information is in long-term memory, but the person cannot retrieve it. In his experiments, Tulving found that participants could recall a large number of items they seemed to have forgotten if he provided retrieval cues to jog their memory. For example, odors often provide potent reminders of experiences from the past, and certain odors can serve as retrieval cues for information that was learned when those odors were present (Schab, 1990).

■ **motivated forgetting**
Forgetting through suppression or repression in order to protect oneself from material that is painful, frightening, or otherwise unpleasant.

■ **repression**
Completely removing unpleasant memories from one's consciousness, so that one is no longer aware that a painful event occurred.

■ **amnesia**
A partial or complete loss of memory due to loss of consciousness, brain damage, or some psychological cause.

■ **prospective forgetting**
Not remembering to carry out some intended action.

A common experience with retrieval failure is known as the *tip-of-the-tongue (TOT) phenomenon* (Brown & McNeil, 1966). You have surely experienced trying to recall a name, a word, or some other bit of information, knowing that you knew it but not able to come up with it. You were on the verge of recalling the word or name, perhaps aware of the number of syllables and the beginning or ending letter. It was on the tip of your tongue, but it just wouldn't quite come out.

Remember It 6.5

1. __________ invented the nonsense syllable, conceived the relearning method for retention, and plotted the curve of forgetting.
2. Match each cause of forgetting with the appropriate example.

____ (1) encoding failure	a. failing to remember the answer on a test until after you turn the test in
____ (2) consolidation failure	b. forgetting a humiliating childhood experience
____ (3) retrieval failure	c. not being able to describe the back of a dollar bill
____ (4) repression	d. calling a friend by someone else's name
____ (5) interference	e. waking up in the hospital and not remembering you had an automobile accident

3. To minimize interference, it is best to follow learning with __________.
4. According to the text, the major cause of forgetting is __________.

ANSWERS: 1. Ebbinghaus; 2. (1) c, (2) e, (3) a, (4) b, (5) d; 3. sleep; 4. interference

Improving Memory

How can organization, overlearning, spaced practice, and recitation improve memory?

Have you ever wished there was a magic pill you could take before studying for an exam, one that would make you remember everything in your textbook and lecture notes? Sorry, but there are no magic formulas for improving your memory. Remembering is a skill that, like any other, requires knowledge and practice. In this section, we consider several study habits and techniques that can improve your memory.

Are you the kind of person who has a place for everything in your home or office, or do you simply toss things anywhere and everywhere? If you're the everything-in-its-place type, you probably have an easier time finding things than do people who are the "wherever" type. Memory works the same way. How information is organized strongly influences your ability to remember it. For example, almost anyone can name the months of the year in about 10 seconds, but how long would it take to recall them in alphabetical order? These 12 well-known items are much harder to retrieve in alphabetical order, because they are not organized that way in memory. Similarly, you are giving your memory an extremely difficult task if you try to remember large amounts of information in a haphazard fashion. Try to organize items you want to remember in alphabetical order, or according to categories, historical sequence, size, or shape, or in any other way that will make retrieval easier for you.

FIGURE 6.11 Overlearning

When a person learns material only to the point of one correct repetition, forgetting is very rapid. Just 22% is retained after 1 day, 3% after 4 days, and 2% after 14 days. When participants spend 50% more time going over the material, the retention increases to 36% after 1 day, 30% after 4 days, and 21% after 14 days.

Source: Data from Krueger (1929).

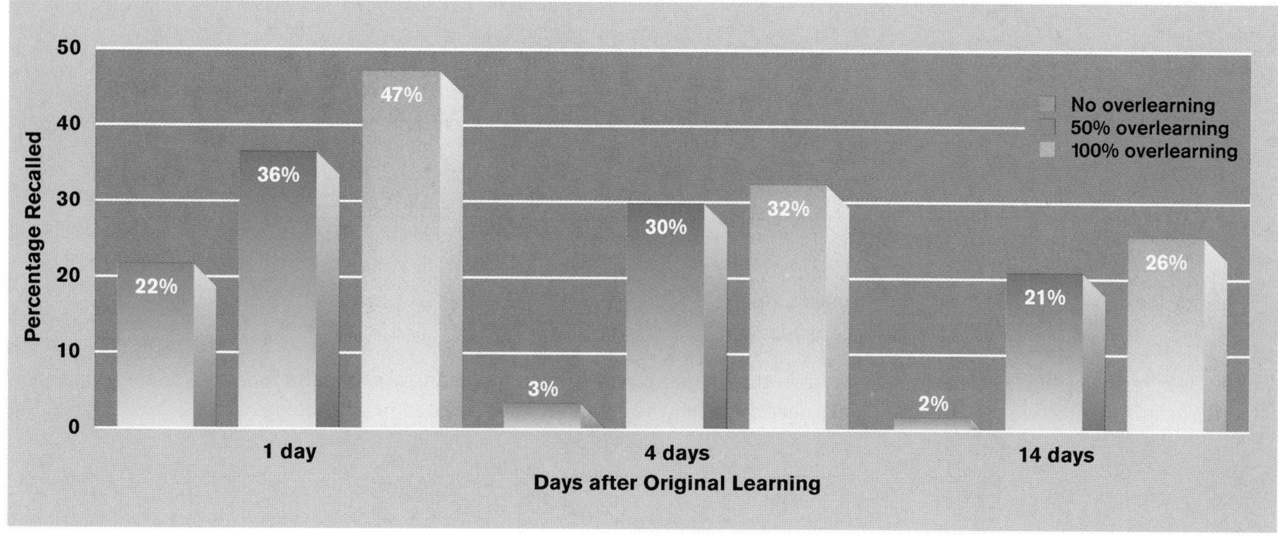

Do you still remember the words to songs that were popular when you were in high school? Can you recite many of the nursery rhymes you learned as a child even though you haven't heard them in years? You probably can because of **overlearning,** practicing or studying material beyond the point where it can be repeated once without error. Suppose you wanted to memorize a list of words, and you studied until you could recite them once without error. Would this amount of study or practice be sufficient? Research suggests that people remember material better and longer if they overlearn it (Ebbinghaus, 1885/1964). A pioneering study in overlearning by Krueger (1929) showed very substantial long-term gains for participants who engaged in 50% and 100% overlearning (see Figure 6.11). Furthermore, overlearning makes material more resistant to interference and is perhaps the best insurance against stress-related forgetting. So, the next time you study for a test, don't stop studying as soon as you think you know the material. Spend another hour or so going over it, using features of your textbook such as margin questions and end-of-section review questions; you will be surprised at how much more you will remember.

Most students have tried cramming for examinations, but spacing study over several sessions is generally more effective than **massed practice**, learning in one long practice session without rest periods (Glover & Corkill, 1987). You will remember more with less total study time if you space your study over a number of sessions. Long periods of memorizing make material particularly subject to interference and often result in fatigue and lowered concentration. Also, when you space your practice, you probably create new memories that may be stored in different places, thus increasing your chances for recall. The spacing effect applies to learning motor skills as well as to learning facts and information. Music students can tell you that it is better to practice for half an hour each day, every day, than to practice many hours in a row once a week.

Furthermore, recent research suggests that significant improvement in learning results when spaced study sessions are accompanied by short, frequent tests of the material being studied (Cull, 2000). Thus, you should be doing well in this course if you are answering the questions in the *Remember It* boxes at the ends of sections in this textbook.

■ **overlearning**
Practicing or studying material beyond the point where it can be repeated once without error.

■ **massed practice**
Learning in one long practice session without rest periods.

REVIEW and REFLECT 6.1

Examples of Strategies for Improving Memory

STRATEGY	EXAMPLE
Organization	Write each heading and subheading of a textbook chapter on an index card; take notes on each section and subsection on the cards; keep them in order by chapter and use them to review for exams.
Overlearning	Memorize information that is easily organized into a list (e.g., the functions associated with the left and right cerebral hemispheres) until you can recall each item on the list automatically without error.
Spaced practice	When you have an hour to study, break it up into three 15-minute study periods with 5-minute breaks between them.
Recitation	After you finish studying this *Review and Reflect* table, close your eyes and see how much of the information you can repeat aloud.

Want to be sure you've fully absorbed the material in this chapter? Visit **www.ablongman.com/wood5e** for access to free practice tests, flashcards, interactive activities, and links developed specifically to help you succeed in psychology.

Do you ever reread a chapter just before a test? Research over many years shows that you will recall more if you increase the amount of recitation in your study. For example, it is better to read a page or a few paragraphs and then recite or practice recalling what you have just read. Then, continue reading, stop and practice reciting again, and so on. When you study for a psychology test and review the assigned chapter, try to answer each of the questions in the *Summary and Review* section at the end of the chapter. Then, read the material that follows each question and check to see if you answered the question correctly. This will be your safeguard against encoding failure. Don't simply read each section and assume that you can answer the question. Test yourself before your professor does.

A. I. Gates (1917) tested groups of students who spent the same amount of time in study, but who spent different percentages of that time in recitation and rereading. Participants recalled two to three times more if they increased their recitation time up to 80% and spent only 20% of their study time rereading.

Review and Reflect 6.1 provides examples for each of the memory improvement techniques discussed in this section.

Remember It 6.6

1. When studying for an exam, it is best to spend:
   a. more time reciting than rereading.
   b. more time rereading than reciting.
   c. equal time rereading and reciting.
   d. all of the time reciting rather than rereading.

2. The ability to recite a number of nursery rhymes from childhood is probably due mainly to __________.

ANSWERS: 1. a; 2. overlearning

Apply It

Improving Memory with Mnemonic Devices

Writing notes, making lists, writing on a calendar, or keeping an appointment book is often more reliable and accurate than trusting to memory (Intons-Peterson & Fournier, 1986). But what if you need information at some unpredictable time, when you do not have external aids handy? Several *mnemonics*, or memory devices, have been developed over the years to aid memory (Bower, 1973; Higbee, 1977; Roediger, 1980).

Rhyme

Rhymes are a common aid to remembering material that otherwise might be difficult to recall. Perhaps as a child you learned to recite "*i* before *e* except after *c*" when you were trying to spell a word containing that vowel combination.

The Method of Loci

The *method of loci* is a mnemonic device that can be used when you want to remember a list of items such as a grocery list, or when you give a speech or a class report and need to make your points in order without using notes. The word *loci* (pronounced "LOH-sye") is the plural form of *locus*, which means "location" or "place."

Figure 6.12 shows how to use the method of loci. Select any familiar place—your home, for example—and simply associate the items to be remembered with locations there. Progress in an orderly fashion: For example, visualize the first item or idea you want to remember in its place on the driveway, the second in the garage, the third at the front door, and so on, until you have associated each item you want to remember with a specific location. You may find it helpful to conjure up oversized images of the items that you place at each location. When you want to recall the items, take an imaginary walk starting at the first place—the first item will pop into your mind. When you think of the second place, the second item will come to mind, and so on.

(continued on page 226)

FIGURE 6.12 The Method of Loci

Begin by thinking of locations, perhaps in your home, that are in a sequence. Then, visualize one of the items to be remembered in each location.

Apply It

(continued)

The First-letter Technique

Another useful technique is to take the first letter of each item to be remembered and form a word, a phrase, or a sentence with those letters (Matlin, 1989). For example, suppose you had to memorize the seven colors of the visible spectrum in their proper order:

Red
Orange
Yellow
Green
Blue
Indigo
Violet

You could make your task easier by using the first letter of each color to form the name Roy G. Biv. Three chunks are easier to remember than seven different items.

The Pegword System

Another mnemonic that has been proven effective is the *pegword system* (Harris & Blaiser, 1997). Developed in England around 1879, it uses rhyming words: *one = bun; two = shoe; three = tree; four = door; five = hive; six = sticks; seven = heaven; eight = gate; nine = wine; ten = hen*. The rhyming words are memorized in sequence and then linked through vivid associations with any items you wish to remember in order, as shown in Figure 6.13.

For example, suppose you want to remember to buy five items at the store: milk, bread, grapefruit, laundry detergent, and eggs. Begin by associating the milk with a bun (your first pegword) by picturing milk being poured over a bun. Next, picture a shoe, the second pegword, kicking a loaf of bread. Then, continue by associating each item on your list with a pegword. To recall the items, simply go through your list of pegwords, and the associated word will immediately come to mind.

FIGURE 6.13 The Pegword System

Each item to be recalled is associated with a pegword using a mental image. *Source:* Adapted from Bower (1973).

Item Number	Pegword	Peg Image	Item to Be Recalled	Connecting Image	
1	bun	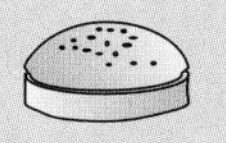	milk		 *Milk* pouring onto a soggy hamburger *bun*
2	shoe		bread		 A *shoe* kicking and breaking a brittle loaf of French *bread*

Summary *and* Review

Remembering p. 196

What are the characteristics of each component of memory in the Atkinson-Shiffrin model? p. 197

Sensory memory holds information coming in through the senses for up to 2 seconds. This is just long enough for the nervous system to begin to process the information and send some of it on to short-term memory. Short-term (working) memory holds about seven (plus or minus two) unrelated items of information for less than 30 seconds without rehearsal. Short-term memory also acts as a mental workspace for carrying out any mental activity. Long-term memory is the permanent or relatively permanent memory system with virtually unlimited capacity. Its subsystems are (1) declarative memory, which holds facts and information (semantic memory) along with personal life experiences (episodic memory); and (2) nondeclarative memory, which consists of motor skills acquired through repetitive practice, habits, and simple classically conditioned responses.

How does the levels-of-processing model differ from that proposed by Atkinson and Shiffrin? p. 202

The levels-of-processing model, proposed by Craik and Lockhart, is based on deep and shallow processing of information rather than separate memory stores. With deep processing, a person associates the incoming information with some form of meaning; with shallow processing, a person is merely aware of the incoming sensory information.

What are the three methods used by psychologists to measure memory? p. 202

Three methods of measuring retention of information in memory are (1) recall, where information must be supplied with few or no retrieval cues; (2) recognition, where information must simply be recognized as having been encountered before; and (3) the relearning method, which measures retention in terms of time saved when relearning material compared with the time required to learn it originally.

The Nature of Remembering p. 204

What is meant by the statement "Memory is reconstructive in nature"? p. 204

Memory does not work like a video recorder. People reconstruct memories, piecing them together from a few highlights and using information that may or may not be accurate. Sir Frederick Bartlett found that people systematically reconstruct and distort memories to fit information already stored in memory. Bartlett suggested that reconstructive memory involves the application of schemas, or integrated frameworks of prior knowledge and assumptions, during the encoding and retrieval phases of remembering.

What conditions reduce the reliability of eyewitness testimony? p. 206

The reliability of eyewitness testimony is reduced when witnesses view a photograph of the suspect before viewing the lineup, when members of a lineup don't sufficiently resemble each other; when members of a lineup are viewed at the same time rather than one by one, when the perpetrator's race is different from that of the eyewitness, when a weapon has been used in the crime, and when leading questions are asked to elicit information from the witness.

What is the controversy regarding the therapy used to recover repressed memories of childhood sexual abuse? p. 207

Critics argue that therapists using hypnosis and guided imagery to help their patients recover repressed memories of childhood sexual abuse are actually implanting false memories in those patients. Therapists who use these techniques believe that a number of psychological problems can be treated successfully by helping patients recover repressed memories of sexual abuse.

What does research evidence say about flashbulb and photographic memories? p. 209

Flashbulb memories, which are formed when a person learns of events that are surprising, shocking, or highly emotional, may not be as accurate as people believe they are. Researchers have also found that some of the details in flashbulb memories change over time. Something similar to photographic memory, called eidetic imagery, appears to exist in about 5% of children.

How does culture influence memory? p. 210

The existence of oral historians in some cultures suggests that the ability to remember certain kinds of material may be influenced by culture. The status of the role and the importance of the particular information to members of the culture motivate individuals to store and retrieve large amounts of such information. Their memory for other kinds of information, however, is no better than that of others. In addition, we more easily remember stories set in our own culture.

Factors Influencing Retrieval p. 211

What happens when information must be recalled in a particular order? p. 211

The serial position effect is the tendency, when recalling a list of items, to remember the items at the beginning of the list (primacy effect) and the items at the end of the list (recency effect) better than items in the middle.

How does environmental context affect memory? p. 212

People tend to recall material more easily if they are in the same physical location during recall as during the original learning.

How do emotions and altered states of consciousness affect memory? p. 213

The state-dependent memory effect is the tendency to recall information better if one is in the same pharmacological or psychological state as when the information was learned.

Biology and Memory p. 214

What roles do the hippocampus and the hippocampal region play in memory? p. 214

The hippocampus itself is involved primarily in the formation of episodic memories; the rest of the hippocampal region is involved in forming semantic memories.

Why is long-term potentiation important? p. 215

Long-term potentiation (LTP) is a long-lasting increase in the efficiency of neural transmission at the synapses. LTP is important because it may be the basis for learning and memory at the level of the neurons.

How do memories of threatening situations that elicit the "fight or flight response" compare with ordinary memories? p. 216

Memories of threatening situations tend to be more powerful and enduring than ordinary memories, perhaps because of the strong emotions aroused in such situations.

Forgetting p. 217

What did Ebbinghaus discover about forgetting? p. 217

In conducting the first experimental studies of learning and memory, Ebbinghaus invented the nonsense syllable, used the relearning method as a test of memory, and plotted the curve of forgetting. He discovered that the largest amount of forgetting occurs very quickly, then it tapers off.

What causes forgetting? p. 218

Encoding failure happens when an item is perceived as having been forgotten but, in fact, was never stored in memory. Information that has not been retrieved from memory for a long time may fade and ultimately disappear entirely (decay theory). Consolidation failure results from a loss of consciousness as new memories are being encoded. Interference occurs when information or associations stored either before or after a given memory hinder the ability to remember it. Sometimes, we forget because we don't want to remember something, a process called motivated forgetting. Other times, an item is stored in memory, but we are unable to retrieve it (retrieval failure).

Improving Memory p. 222

How can organization, overlearning, spaced practice, and recitation improve memory? p. 222

Organization, as in using outlines based on chapter headings, provides retrieval cues for information. Overlearning means practicing or studying material beyond the point where it can be repeated once without error. You remember overlearned material better and longer, and it is more resistant to interference and stress-related forgetting. Short study session at different times (spaced practice) allow time for consolidation of new information. Recitation of newly learned material is more effective than simply rereading it.

Key Terms

amnesia, p. 221
anterograde amnesia, p. 214
chunking, p. 199
consolidation, p. 197
consolidation failure, p. 220
decay theory, p. 219
declarative memory, p. 200
displacement, p. 199
eidetic imagery, p. 209
elaborative rehearsal, p. 200
encoding, p. 196
encoding failure, p. 219
episodic memory, p. 200
flashbulb memory, p. 209
hippocampal region, p. 214
infantile amnesia, p. 208
interference, p. 219
levels-of-processing model, p. 202
long-term memory (LTM), p. 200
long-term potentiation (LTP), p. 216
massed practice, p. 223
motivated forgetting, p. 221
nondeclarative memory, p. 201
nonsense syllable, p. 217
overlearning, p. 223
primacy effect, p. 212
priming, p. 202
prospective forgetting, p. 221
recall, p. 202
recency effect, p. 212
recognition, p. 203
reconstruction, p. 205
rehearsal, p. 199
relearning method, p. 203
repression, p. 221
retrieval, p. 197
retrieval cue, p. 203
retrograde amnesia, p. 220
savings score, p. 204
schemas, p. 205
semantic memory, p. 200
sensory memory, p. 197
serial position effect, p. 212
short-term memory (STM), p. 199
state-dependent memory effect, p. 213
storage, p. 197

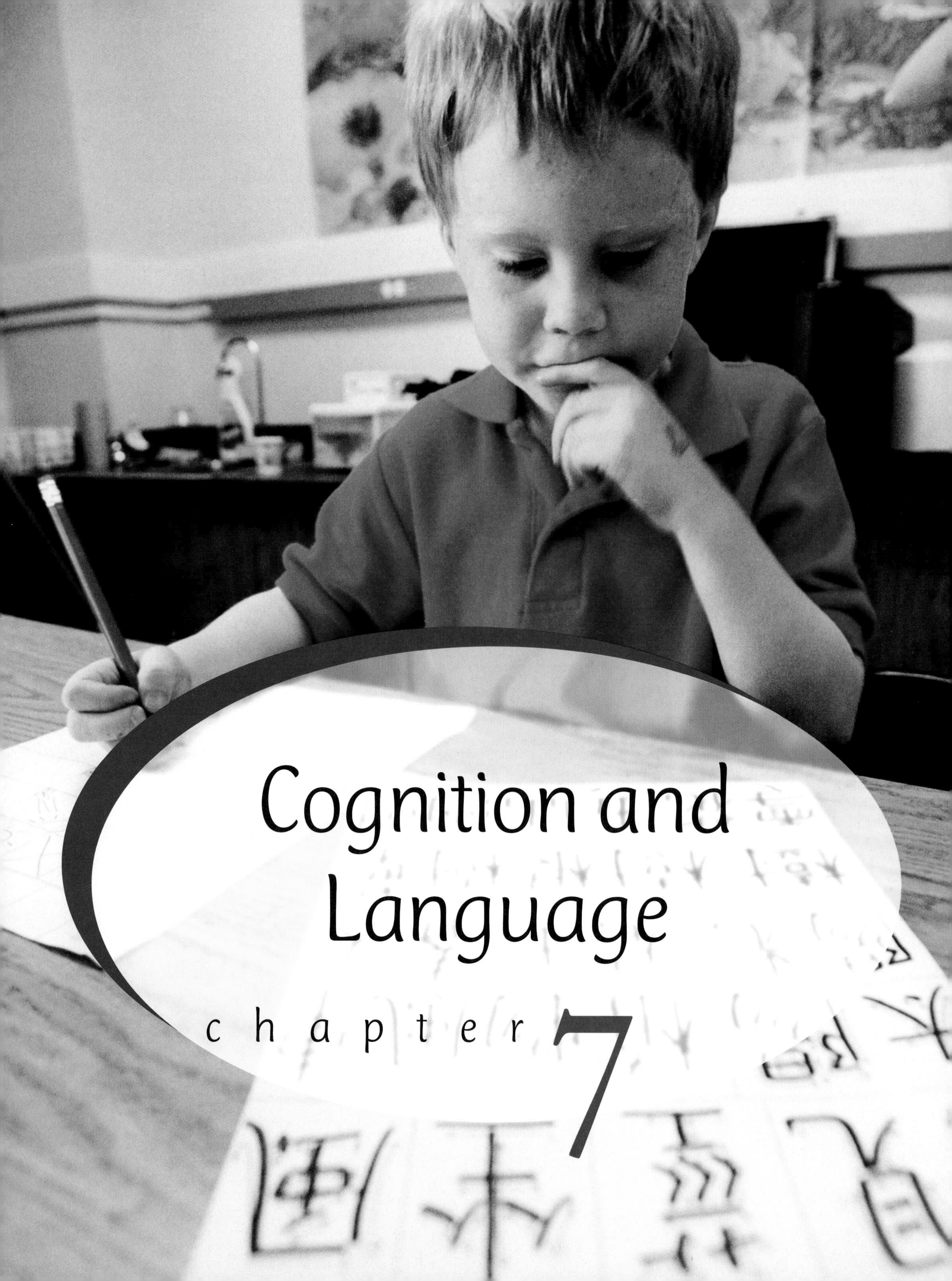

Cognition and Language

chapter 7

Imagery, Concepts, and Reasoning

- *How do we form images, and how does imagery help us think?*
- *How do formal and natural concepts differ?*
- *What is the difference between deductive and inductive reasoning?*

Decision Making

- *How are the additive strategy and elimination by aspects used in decision making?*
- *What are the strengths and weaknesses of the availability and representativeness heuristics?*
- *How does framing help with decision making?*

Problem Solving

- *What are three basic approaches to problem solving, and how do they differ?*
- *How do functional fixedness and mental set impede problem solving?*

High-Tech Applications of Cognition

- *In what ways does artificial intelligence resemble human cognition?*
- *How do scientists use artificial neural networks?*
- *What are some practical applications of robotics?*

Language

- *What are the necessary components of any language?*
- *What areas of the brain are involved in producing and comprehending language?*
- *How does animal communication differ from that of humans?*
- *In what ways does thinking influence language?*
- *What is the best time in life to learn a second language, and why?*

Can technology produce an artificial limb that a person can control as precisely as a real limb by using brain power alone?

Researcher John Chapin and colleagues demonstrated that brain cell activity (thinking) alone can cause robotic arms to move just like normal limbs (Whitehouse, 2000). Rats were trained to obtain water from a robotic arm by pushing a small lever. Electrodes were implanted in the motor cortex of each rat's brain to record the electrical activity of the brain cells used to press the lever. Researchers identified the specific brain cells that drove the movement of the rat's paws and linked these cells to a lever-pressing mechanism. The rats soon learned that they could obtain water by merely "thinking about" pushing the lever.

In subsequent studies with humans, researchers demonstrated that brain activity alone could control the movements of artificial limbs with virtually the same accuracy and speed as normal arm movements (Taylor et al., 2002). Surprisingly, only a small group of neurons in the brain's motor cortex appear to be required. Moreover, practice (thinking) improves the accuracy of the movements even more (König & Verschure, 2002).

The implications of this kind of research for the physically handicapped are astounding. For example, paralyzed patients could be fitted with artificial limbs that can be controlled at will, simply by thought, just as normal limbs are controlled (Whitehouse, 2000).

Until modern times, could anyone have envisioned the development of technology capable of using the power of thinking alone to move objects in such a precise and predictable fashion? Surprisingly, the ancient Greek thinker Aristotle (382–322 B.C.), who furthered the study of human cognition by inventing laws for reasoning and who stressed the importance of mental imagery, foresaw something similar: "If every instrument could accomplish its own work, obeying or anticipating the will of others. . . . If the shuttle could weave, and the pick touch the lyre, without a hand to guide them, chief workmen would not need servants, nor masters slaves." What Aristotle envisioned when he wrote these words over 2,300 years ago were machines much like the modern robots that guide manufacturing processes and the computerized sound systems that assist rock bands. What Aristotle foresaw now exists. But even Aristotle would be amazed by artificial vision for the blind and other modern achievements in artificial intelligence and robotics.

■ **cognition**
The mental processes that are involved in acquiring, storing, retrieving, and using information and that include sensation, perception, memory, imagery, concept formation, reasoning, decision making, problem solving, and language.

Accomplishments such as those just described rely on research that helps psychologists understand human cognition. The findings of cognition studies, in turn, enable programmers to figure out how to "teach" computers to perform tasks similar to those carried out by the human brain. But just what is cognition? **Cognition** refers collectively to the mental processes involved in acquiring, storing, retrieving, and using information (Matlin, 1989).

In earlier chapters, we discussed the cognitive processes of sensation, perception, and memory. In this chapter, we first consider several other cognitive processes: imagery, concept formation, reasoning, decision making, and problem solving. Then, we will explore recent developments in artificial intelligence and robotics—two high-tech applications of cognition. Finally, we will look at language, which plays a vital role in both cognition and communication.

Imagery, Concepts, and Reasoning

Have you ever heard the famous quote attributed to the great French philosopher René Descartes (1596–1650), "I think, therefore I am"? Unfortunately, Descartes did not describe the act of thinking itself. All of us have an intuitive notion of what thinking is. We say, "I think it's going to rain" (a prediction); "I think this is the right answer" (a choice); "I think I will resign" (a decision). But our everyday use of the word *think* does not suggest the processes we use to perform the act itself. Sometimes, thinking is free-flowing rather than goal-oriented. At other times, it is directed and aimed at a goal such as solving a problem or making a decision. Just how is the act of thinking accomplished? There is general agreement that it makes use of at least two tools: images and concepts.

Imagery

How do we form images, and how does imagery help us think?

Can you imagine hearing a recording of your favorite song or someone calling your name? Can you picture yourself jogging, walking, or kissing someone you love? In your imagination, can you smell ammonia or taste your favorite ice cream? In doing these things, you take advantage of your ability to use **imagery**—that is, to represent or picture a sensory experience mentally. Albert Einstein is said to have done much of his thinking in images.

How We Form Images An analog camera captures a complete image on film, while a digital camera builds a picture by assembling digitally encoded bits and pieces of it. Which process is more like the way our brains form images? According to psychologist Stephen Kosslyn (1988), we mentally construct the objects we image, one part at a time, somewhat like the digital camera. Studies suggest that two types of processes are used in the formation of visual images. First, stored memories of how parts of an object look are retrieved, and then mental processes are used to arrange or assemble those parts into the proper whole. Both the left and the right hemispheres participate in the processes of forming visual images. Kosslyn (1975) also discovered that the processes of imaging objects and perceiving their counterparts in the real world are strongly related. For example, it takes people longer to form large mental images than to conjure up small ones, just as it takes longer to visually scan an elephant than an ant.

■ **imagery**
The representation in the mind of a sensory experience—visual, auditory, gustatory, motor, olfactory, or tactile.

This similarity between imagery and reality is not limited to visual imaging. You can form a realistic image of an action involving motion and tactile sensations, such as carrying a heavy load or a light load. Think of yourself as carrying a bowling ball across your living room. Next, think of walking the same distance holding a balloon. Did you imagine yourself walking faster when holding the balloon? This was the experience of participants in a similar imaging experiment (Intons-Peterson & Roskos-Ewoldsen, 1989). Why should this be true? This study suggests that imaging involves more than simply calling up visual images; it also involves knowing how different objects behave under different circumstances in the real world. If you had not factored in the realization that you tend to walk faster when holding light objects than when lugging heavy objects, your imaginary walk across the room would have been equally fast with either the balloon or the bowling ball.

Not only can we form a mental image of an object, but we can manipulate and move it around mentally, much as we would if we were actually holding and looking at the object (Cooper & Shepard, 1984; Farah, 1995; Kosslyn & Sussman, 1995). In an early study, Shepard & Metzler (1971) asked eight research participants to judge some 1,600 pairs of drawings like the ones in Figure 7.1. Participants had to rotate the objects mentally to see if they matched. Try doing this before reading further. As you may have discovered, the objects in parts (a) and (b) of Figure 7.1 match; those in part (c) do not. The more the objects had to be rotated mentally, the longer it took participants to decide whether they matched. This is precisely what would happen if the participants had rotated real objects—the more the objects needed to be rotated, the longer it would take to make the decision. And, as happens with actual physical performance, younger adults can carry out mental rotation tasks more rapidly than those who are elderly (Band & Kok, 2000).

FIGURE 7.1 Samples of Geometric Patterns in Shepard and Metzler's Mental Rotation Study

Mentally rotate one of the patterns in each pair—(a), (b), and (c)—and decide whether the two patterns match. Do you find that the more you have to rotate the objects mentally, the longer it takes to decide if they match?

Source: Shepard & Metzler, (1971).

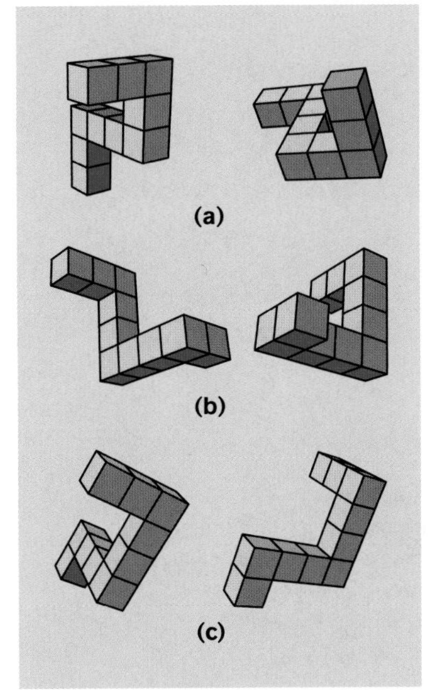

How We Use Imagery Studies examining our ability to hold both mental images and images of real objects in working memory at the same time also suggest that similar mental processes are involved in both. In an early study, Segal and Fusella (1970) asked student participants to form either a visual image of a tree or an auditory image of the sound of a typewriter.

Many professional athletes use visualization to improve performance.

The researchers then made a faint sound on a harmonica or flashed a small, dimly lighted blue arrow, or did nothing at all. Participants who were holding the visual image of a tree were more likely to miss seeing the blue arrow but more likely to hear the harmonica. But participants imaging the sound of a typewriter had the opposite experience. Presumably, interference occurs when the brain is trying to use the same processes simultaneously on two different tasks.

Professionals in many fields—mathematicians, scientists, writers, artists, and musicians—use imaging effectively. A professional pianist, Liu Chi Kung, was imprisoned for 7 years during China's cultural revolution. Soon after being released, he was back on the tour circuit playing better than ever, according to critics who judged his performances. How did he do it without practicing for 7 long years? Using mental imagery, he rehearsed every day, playing every piece he knew in his imagination (Garfield, 1986). And sports psychologists have found that athletes skilled in visualization can actually improve their performance by practicing mentally (Schwartz, 2000; Ungerleider, 1992). The link between visualization and performance is assumed to be based on the close correspondence between brain activation during imagery and that which occurs when an individual actually engages in the imagined task.

Imagery and the Brain What happens in the brain when we use imagery? PET scans reveal that the mental operations performed are similar whether a person is constructing a visual image or perceiving a stimulus that is physically present (Kosslyn et al., 1993; Posner & Raichle, 1995). Another study, which measured participants' regional cerebral blood flow (rCBF), revealed that engaging in imaging based on verbal descriptions alone activated regions of the brain known to be involved in higher-level visual processing (Mellet et al., 2000). And research examining the brain's responses to stimuli indicate that the same areas are activated when we hear a sound as when we imagine hearing a sound (Yoo & Lee, 2002).

With regard to imaging of physical activities such as rotating an object, playing an instrument, or performing such actions as hitting a baseball, brain-imaging studies show that, in general, the same brain areas are activated whether a person is performing a given task or mentally rehearsing the task using imagery (Stephan et al., 1995). Brain-imaging studies indicate that the same regions in the motor cortex and related areas that are involved in the physical movements required for rotation of objects are also very active during mental imaging, although the cerebellum is more active during actual performance than during visualization (Lotze et al., 1999; Richter et al., 2000).

Concepts

How do formal and natural concepts differ?

Suppose your professor tells you that an upcoming exam will be "conceptual" in nature. What do you think she means? You would probably conclude that she wants you to grasp the big ideas in the material and to link relevant details to them. Psychologists use the word **concept** to refer to a mental category that represents a class or group of objects, people, organizations, events, situations, or relations that share common characteristics or attributes. *Furniture*, *tree*, *student*, *college*, and *wedding* are all examples of concepts. As fundamental units of thought, concepts are useful tools that help us to order our world and to think and communicate with speed and efficiency.

concept
A mental category used to represent a class or group of objects, people, organizations, events, situations, or relations that share common characteristics or attributes.

How do we learn concepts? Some concepts are learned in an orderly, systematic way. For example, elementary school students learn that, by definition, a triangle has three sides. In Chapter 6, you learned that working memory has limited capacity. Such concepts are **formal concepts**; they are clearly defined by a set of rules, a formal definition, or a classification system. Formal concepts are common in the sciences and other academic disciplines.

But what about concepts that are a bit more "fuzzy"? Most of the concepts we form and use are **natural concepts**, acquired not from definitions but through everyday perceptions and experiences. We acquire many natural concepts through experiences with *examples*, or positive instances of the concept. When children are young, parents may point out examples of a car—the family car, the neighbor's car, cars on the street, and pictures of cars in books. But if a child points to some other type of moving vehicle and says "car," the parent will say, "No, that is a truck," or "This is a bus." Truck and bus are negative instances, or *nonexamples*, of the concept of car. After experience with positive and negative instances of the concept, a child begins to grasp some of the properties of a car that distinguish it from other wheeled vehicles.

How do our minds use natural concepts as thinking tools? In using natural concepts, we are likely to picture a **prototype** of the concept—an example that embodies its most common and typical features. What is your prototype for the concept of bird? Chances are it is not a penguin, an ostrich, or a kiwi. All three are birds that cannot fly. A more likely bird prototype is a robin or perhaps a sparrow. Most birds can fly, but not all; most mammals cannot fly, but bats are mammals, have wings, and can fly. So not all examples of a natural concept fit it equally well. This is why natural concepts often seem less clear-cut than formal ones. Nevertheless, a prototype most closely fits a given natural concept, and other examples of the concept most often share more attributes with that prototype than with the prototype of any other concept.

A different view of concept formation suggests that concepts are represented by their **exemplars**—individual instances, or examples, of a concept that are stored in memory from personal experience (Estes, 1994). To decide whether an unfamiliar item belongs to a concept, we compare it with exemplars (other examples) of that concept.

Do you think that people who know a great deal about a particular topic think about its concepts differently from those who know little about it? Researchers Lynch and others (2000) asked participants who were experts on trees and those who were knew little about trees to rate 48 trees according to how well the trees represented the concept of tree. For the novices, familiarity determined the ratings of trees as good examples of the concept. A person who lived in an area where pine trees are abundant would offer the pine tree as an good exemplar, while another who was more familiar with oaks would propose that an oak tree is the best example of the concept. The tree experts, in contrast, often selected the "ideal" tree, the best of the best, as the most representative example; for instance, experts selected trees that were extremely tall, not those of average height. Therefore, goodness-of-example ratings depend more on the knowledge and experience of the rater than on the attributes or qualities of the selections being rated (Lynch et al., 2000).

Like expert knowledge, language appears to be important to conceptual thinking, especially in young children. In one clever study, researcher Linda Smith (2003) provided children with replicas of everyday objects along with three-dimensional representations of those objects that were made up entirely of geometric shapes, as shown in Figure 7.2 (on page 236). Smith wanted to know whether the children would play with the geometric shapes in the same way as they would with the replicas. In other words, would children be just as likely to pretend to eat a geometric pizza shape as a pizza replica? Smith assumed that, when children pretended to eat both, they recognized

■ **formal concept**
A concept that is clearly defined by a set of rules, a formal definition, or a classification system.

■ **natural concept**
A concept acquired not from a definition but through everyday perceptions and experiences.

■ **prototype**
An example that embodies the most common and typical features of a concept.

■ **exemplars**
The individual instances, or examples, of a concept that are stored in memory from personal experience.

A prototype is an example that embodies the most typical features of a concept. Which of the animals shown here best fits your prototype for the concept of bird?

FIGURE 7.2 **Replica and Geometric Representation of An Everyday Object**

Researcher Linda Smith tested toddlers to see whether they responded to different representations of everyday objects in the same way. Those with the greatest knowledge of object names were most likely to regard replicas and geometric representations of objects as exemplars of the same category.

Source: Smith (2003).

each as an exemplar of the concept of pizza. She also tested the young participants to find out how many of 200 everyday objects each could identify by name. Smith found that children who knew the most object names were the most likely to play with replicas and geometric representations in the same way.

You might be wondering how the vast number of concepts stored in our long-term memories are related to one another. The concepts we form do not exist in isolation, but rather in hierarchies, or nested categories. For example, the canary and the cardinal are subsets of the concept of bird; at a higher level, birds form a subset of the concept of animal; and at a still higher level, animals are a subset of the concept of living things. Thus, concept formation has a certain logic to it, as does the type of logical thinking called *reasoning*, which we consider next.

Reasoning

What is the difference between deductive and inductive reasoning?

What comes to mind when you think of "reasoning" is probably a deliberate, analytical thought process. That's a fairly good definition for everyday use. Psychologists formally define **reasoning** as a form of thinking in which conclusions are drawn from a set of facts. The two basic forms of reasoning are deductive reasoning and inductive reasoning. In Aristotle's time, the use of formal logic was considered to be the surest path to sound conclusions, and deductive reasoning was considered to be the foundation of logic (Haberlandt, 1997).

Reasoning by Deduction **Deductive reasoning** is reasoning from the general to the specific, or drawing particular conclusions from general principles. Aristotle introduced a formal method for deductive reasoning—the syllogism. A **syllogism** is a scheme for logical reasoning in which two statements known as *premises* (the major premise and the minor premise) are followed by a valid conclusion. The power of the syllogism is not in its content but in its form. It is organized in such a way that the conclusion must be true if both premises are true and if the premises follow the rules of formal logic.

Consider this syllogism:

Major premise: All standard cars have four wheels.
Minor premise: Maria's vehicle is a standard car.
Conclusion: Therefore, Maria's vehicle has four wheels.

Clearly, the conclusion is valid because the entire class of standard cars fits within the larger class of four-wheeled vehicles. Maria's vehicle is within "standard cars" and thus also within the larger class, "four-wheeled vehicles."

Now consider this syllogism, which does not adhere to the rules of formal logic:

Major premise: All standard cars have four wheels.
Minor premise: Maria's vehicle has four wheels.
Conclusion: Therefore, Maria's vehicle is a standard car.

The conclusion is invalid. Even though the major and minor premises are both true, a valid conclusion does not follow from them. The minor premise is too general to be used deductively: Some trucks and other vehicles, such as tractors, also have four wheels. Therefore, we cannot logically conclude that Maria's vehicle is a standard car.

Reasoning by Induction **Inductive reasoning** is a form of reasoning in which general conclusions are drawn from particular facts or individual cases. This kind of reasoning results in conclusions that *might* be true. Therefore, premises can be judged to be false on the basis of conclusions, but they cannot be judged to be true. Thus, inductive reasoning stands in sharp contrast to deductive reasoning, in which true premises always yield true conclusions.

For example, given the number series 737373737, what would you predict the next number to be? A reasonable conclusion would be that the next number will be 3. The premise of this conclusion is a general rule derived from the series: 7 is always followed by 3. If the next number is 5, you know the premise is false. However, if the next number is 3, you still don't know whether the premise is true because its predictions may not hold up in the future. You only know that it was supported in this particular instance.

Individual Differences in Reasoning Ability How good do you think your formal reasoning abilities are? Many people, especially those who don't listen carefully to instructions or follow them well, have difficulty with formal reasoning problems. In one study, researchers presented a set of several premises to participants, told them that only one premise of the set was true, and asked them to select that premise. After the participants had selected the premise they believed to be true, they were not convinced that all the others were false. Even when researchers used only two premises and stated that one of them was true and one was false, some of the participants were still not totally convinced that one of the premises had to be false. Only when the researchers told the participants to check their conclusions again, remembering that only one premise was true, were the participants totally convinced none of the others could be true (Goldvarg & Johnson-Laird, 2000).

Don't despair if you think you don't reason well. There is hope! Research suggests that people can improve their reasoning skills when exposed to step-by-step instruction and practice in formal reasoning (Leshowitz et al., 2002). Moreover, laboratory experiments may underestimate people's ability to reason because we tend to reason more effectively on problems drawn from domains in which we have a great deal of knowledge (Johnson-Laird, 2001). Consequently, a baseball fan can reason more logically when thinking about the probabilities of a given team's winning a league championship than when considering problems about which he or she has little relevant knowledge.

■ **reasoning**
A form of thinking in which conclusions are drawn from a set of facts.

■ **deductive reasoning**
Reasoning from the general to the specific, or drawing particular conclusions from general principles.

■ **syllogism**
A scheme for logical reasoning in which two statements known as premises are followed by a valid conclusion.

■ **inductive reasoning**
Reasoning in which general conclusions are drawn from particular facts or individual cases.

Deduction, Induction, and the Scientific Method Do the descriptions of deductive and inductive reasoning remind you of the scientific method you learned about in Chapter 1? Both inductive and deductive reasoning are used in the scientific method. First, scientists observe. Next, they use inductive reasoning to formulate a hypothesis, or tentative explanation, based on their observations. The next step is to design a study to test the hypothesis. The design of a study is deductive in nature. Once formulated, the hypothesis becomes a major premise, and the method used to test it, a minor premise. The outcome of the study is the conclusion. Because the major premise is arrived at through inductive reasoning, the logic of scientific research is often referred to as *hypothetico-deductive* rather than truly deductive. This term implies that the conclusion is based on a premise hypothesized to be true, rather than one that is known to be true.

An example will help to clarify: Given that everyday observations of human memory indicate that we are better able to remember a short list of items than a long list, a psychologist hypothesizes that the number of items humans can memorize at one time is limited. She decides to test the hypothesis by asking participants to memorize lists of 5 words and lists of 10 words. She finds that the participants are able to recall, on average, 100% of the 5-word lists and 70% of the 10-word lists. The experiment can be formally stated as follows.

Major premise (hypothesis): The number of items humans can memorize at one time is limited.

Minor premise (method): If the major premise is true, then memory performance will differ when participants are compared on 5- and 10-word lists.

Conclusion (results): Participants remembered a higher percentage of words on the 5-word lists than on the 10-word lists.

Note that the researcher knows that she compared memory performance on lists of different lengths and what the results of the experiment were, so there is no doubt that the minor premise and conclusion are true. It is the major premise (or hypothesis) that remains in doubt. If the participants had performed equally well on 5- and 10-word lists, then the major premise could be judged to be false, since only a single erroneous prediction causes it to be false. However, participants may have performed better on 5-word than 10-word lists for some reason other than that stated in the major premise. Therefore, the psychologist can only conclude that the results support the major premise, but do not rule out the possibility of another outcome in the future that would falsify that hypothesis. For this reason, scientific studies, no matter which science is involved or how convincing the results may seem to be, must always be repeated. Scientists are obligated to continue searching for the one experimental outcome that will falsify the hypothesis.

Remember It 7.1

1. The two most common forms of imagery are ________ and ________.
2. A mental category that represents a class or group of items that share common characteristics or attributes is called a(n) ________.
3. Concepts learned in school are likely to be ________ concepts, while those acquired through everyday experience are likely to be ________ concepts.
4. A(n) ________ is the most typical example of a concept.
5. A person uses ________ reasoning to draw general conclusions from particular facts or individual cases.
6. Syllogisms involve ________ reasoning.

ANSWERS: 1. visual, auditory; 2. concept; 3. formal, natural; 4. prototype; 5. inductive; 6. deductive

Decision Making

When was the last time, in everyday life, that you engaged in formal reasoning? It may have been in connection with an important decision you had to make. Reasoning, both deductive and inductive, is a vital component of decision making. And the quality of our lives is strongly influenced by the decisions we make. **Decision making** is the process of considering alternatives and choosing among them. Psychologists have identified various approaches to decision making. Let's examine some of these approaches.

■ **decision making**
The process of considering alternatives and choosing among them.

■ **additive strategy**
A decision-making approach in which each alternative is rated on each important factor affecting the decision, and the alternative rated highest overall is chosen.

The Additive and Elimination by Aspects Strategies

How are the additive strategy and elimination by aspects used in decision making?

Suppose you wanted to rent an apartment starting next semester. How would you go about deciding among different apartments? You could use the **additive strategy**—a decision-making approach in which each alternative is rated on each of the important factors affecting the decision and the alternative with the highest overall rating is chosen. Two important factors in choosing where to live are location and price. So, your goal would be to find an apartment that is in a safe location near your workplace or school and is within your price range.

A variation on the additive strategy is **elimination by aspects** (Tversky, 1972). With this approach, the factors on which the alternatives are to be evaluated are ordered from most important to least important. Any alternative that does not satisfy the most important factor is automatically eliminated. The process of elimination continues as each factor is considered in order. The alternative that survives is the one chosen. For example, if the most important factor for your apartment search was that the maximum rent you could afford was $800 per month, then you would automatically eliminate all the apartments that rented for more than that. Then, if the second most important factor was availability of parking, you would take the lists of apartments that cost $800 or less per month and weed out those without appropriate parking. You would then continue with your third most important factor, and so on, until you had whittled the list down to a single alternative.

■ **elimination by aspects**
A decision-making approach in which alternatives are eliminated if they do not satisfy a set of factors that have been ordered from most to least important.

■ **heuristic**
(yur-RIS-tik) A rule of thumb that is derived from experience and used in decision making and problem solving, although there is no guarantee of its accuracy or usefulness.

Heuristics

What are the strengths and weaknesses of the availability and representativeness heuristics?

Have you ever made a decision based on the belief that an event or a set of circumstances carried a certain probability? For example, have you ever left your home a bit earlier than necessary in order to allow time for a possible traffic jam, overcrowded subway, or missed bus? Such probability assumptions are often based on **heuristics**—rules of thumb that are derived from experience and used in decision making and problem solving, although there is no guarantee of their accuracy or usefulness.

The Availability Heuristic Decision making is quite likely to be influenced by how quickly and easily information bearing on the decision comes to mind—that is, how readily available that information is in memory. The cognitive rule of thumb that the probability of an event or the importance assigned to it is based on its availability in memory is known as the **availability heuristic**. This is why ads that use humor, emotional appeals, or even sexual innuendos are more memorable than others. When you think about buying a new car, for example, the type of car you associate with a memorable TV commercial or magazine ad is likely to come to mind more rapidly than others.

Any information affecting a decision, whether it is accurate or not, is more likely to be considered if it is readily available. Are travelers more likely to die in a plane or

■ **availability heuristic**
A cognitive rule of thumb that bases the probability of an event or the importance assigned to it on its availability in memory.

How do you decide which fast-food restaurant to patronize when you want a quick bite to eat? Chances are you use a representativeness heuristic, a prototype that guides your expectations about how long it will take to get your food and what it will taste like. Fast-food chains use the same ingredients and food preparation methods at every location in order to maintain patrons' representativeness heuristics as guides for their future fast-food buying decisions.

an automobile accident? Although it is common knowledge that many more deaths result from automobile accidents, some people have an inordinate fear of flying. This arises because every fatal plane crash is publicized—some, like the intentional plane crashes of September 11, 2001, dramatically and persistently. Thus, images of plane crashes are typically more readily available in memory.

The Representativeness Heuristic Another common heuristic used in decision making, in judging people, or in predicting the probability of certain events is the representativeness heuristic. The **representativeness heuristic** is a thinking strategy based on how closely a new object or situation is judged to resemble or match an existing prototype of that object or situation (Pitz & Sachs, 1984). The representativeness heuristic can lead to good decisions if the new object or situation truly matches the appropriate prototype.

■ representativeness heuristic
A thinking strategy based on how closely a new object or situation is judged to resemble or match an existing prototype of that object or situation.

Suppose you were playing a coin-tossing game in which you had to predict whether the outcome of each toss would be heads or tails. Let's say the first five coin tosses came up heads. What would you predict the next toss to be? Many people would predict tails to be more likely on the next toss, because a sample of coin tosses should be approximately 50% heads. Thus, a tail is long overdue, they reason. Nevertheless, the next toss is just as likely to be a head as a tail. After 100 coin tosses, the proportions of heads and tails should be about equal, but for each individual coin toss, the probability still remains 50–50. This example illustrates how people tend to base their estimate of the probability of something turning out a certain way not on the actual likelihood of it being that way, but rather on their own mental representation of the likelihood.

Another example of the use of the representativeness heuristic occurs when people judge others based on stereotypes. A person may expect someone from California to be either a surfer or an actor because that fits the person's mental representation of a Californian. In reality, however, most Californians are neither surfers nor actors; only a small fraction fit these stereotypes.

Framing

How does framing help with decision making?

Let's consider another strategy that is widely used for decision making. Suppose you have an important decision to make—should you go to a movie or study for your psychology exam? You might think of the decision in terms of the gains—enjoying the movie or getting a high score on the exam. Alternatively, you might think of it in terms of losses—missing the movie or failing the exam. Either way, you would be engaging in a decision-making process psychologists call *framing*. **Framing** refers to the way information is presented so as to emphasize either a potential gain or a potential loss as the outcome of a decision based on that information. To study the effects of framing on decision making, Kahneman and Tversky (1984) presented the following options to a group of participants.

■ framing
The way information is presented so as to emphasize either a potential gain or a potential loss as the outcome of a decision based on that information.

> The United States is preparing for the outbreak of a dangerous disease, which is expected to kill 600 people. There have been designed two alternative programs to combat the disease. If program A is adopted, 200 people will be saved. If program B is adopted, there is a one-third probability that all 600 will be saved and a two-thirds probability that no people will be saved.

REVIEW *and* REFLECT 7.1

Approaches to Decision Making

APPROACH	DESCRIPTION
Additive strategy	Each alternative is rated on each important factor; the option with the highest total rating is chosen.
Elimination by aspects	Factors on which alternatives are to be evaluated are ordered from most to least important; any alternatives that do not satisfy the most important factor are eliminated; elimination of alternatives then continues factor by factor until one choice remains.
Availability heuristic	Information that comes easily to mind determines the decision that is made.
Representativeness heuristic	The decision is based on how closely an object or situation resembles or matches an existing prototype.
Framing	Potential gains and losses associated with alternatives are emphasized and influence the decision.

Want to be sure you've fully absorbed the material in this chapter? Visit **www.ablongman.com/wood5e** for access to free practice tests, flashcards, interactive activities, and links developed specifically to help you succeed in psychology.

The researchers found that 72% of the participants selected the "sure thing" of program A over the "risky gamble" of program B. Now, consider the options as they were reframed:

> If program C is adopted, 400 people will die. If program D is adopted, there is a one-third probability that nobody will die and a two-thirds probability that all 600 people will die.

The first version of the problem was framed to focus attention on the number of lives that could be saved. And when people are primarily motivated to achieve gains (save lives), they are more likely to choose a safe option (program A). However, 78% of research participants given the second version chose program D, even though program D has the same consequences as program B in the earlier version. Whereas the first version emphasized gains, the second version was framed in terms of losses, so people were more willing to choose the "risky" option.

There are numerous practical applications of framing to decision making. Customers are more readily motivated to buy products if they are on sale than if they are simply priced lower than similar products to begin with. As a result, customers focus on what they save—a gain—rather than on what they spend—a loss. People seem more willing to purchase an $18,000 car and receive a $1,000 rebate (a gain) than to simply pay $17,000 for the same car.

Review and Reflect 7.1 summarizes the approaches to decision making you have learned about.

Remember It 7.2

1. The __________ strategy allows the more desirable aspects of a situation to compensate for other less desirable aspects.
2. The approach called __________ eliminates options that do not meet the decision maker's most important goals.
3. When sales of flood insurance rise dramatically after major flooding, purchasers' decisions to buy it have most likely been influenced by the __________ heuristic.
4. __________ refers to the way information is presented so as to focus on a potential gain or loss.

ANSWERS: 1. additive; 2. elimination by aspects; 3. availability; 4. Framing

Problem Solving

When you think about "problem solving" you might have visions of struggling with a mathematical equation. But we all face problems that must be solved in everyday life—problems both great and small. For instance, how can you make your paycheck last longer? Or how can you equitably divide housekeeping chores with a roommate? **Problem solving** refers to using the thoughts and actions required to achieve a desired goal that is not readily attainable.

What are three basic approaches to problem solving, and how do they differ?

Approaches to Problem Solving

As you may have observed, individuals appear to differ widely in terms of how they go about solving problems. Careful examination of these apparent differences, though, would probably uncover some common underlying patterns. In fact, we commonly use three basic approaches to solving problems: trial and error, algorithms, and heuristics.

Trial and Error Perhaps you have solved a problem by **trial and error,** an approach in which one solution after another is tried in no particular order until a solution is found. This approach can often lead to a solution. Moreover, it may be the most appropriate strategy when you have little or no knowledge relevant to the problem. For example, suppose that every time it rains, a small amount of water collects on the sill of one of the windows in your home. If you know nothing about construction but don't want to spend hundreds of dollars hiring a contractor, you might try caulking around the window panes to stop the leak. If the leakage continues, you might caulk around the wood that frames the window on the outside of the building. Eventually, you would arrive at a solution, or else determine that the problem is beyond your ability to solve.

When you possess relevant background knowledge, using that knowledge to find a solution to a problem is more efficient than using trial and error. For example, suppose your car had a mechanical problem. How efficient would it be to replace one part after another until you hit on the right one? However, if you have a great deal of mechanical know-how, you can reflect on the problem and come up with a reasonable hypothesis about what's wrong. And if you don't have such knowledge, you are better off consulting someone who does—a professional mechanic—instead of replacing parts randomly until you happen to fix the problem.

Algorithms Another major problem-solving method is the algorithm (Newell & Simon, 1972). An **algorithm** is a systematic, step-by-step procedure that guarantees a solution to a problem of a certain type if the algorithm is executed properly. For example, if you follow the correct procedure for solving algebraic equations, you will always get a value of 2 for x in the equation $4x + 9 = 17$. Scientific and mathematical formulas, such as Einstein's famous $E = mc^2$, are algorithms. Another type of algorithm is a systematic strategy for exploring every possible solution to a problem until the correct one is reached. In some cases, millions or billions or even more possibilities may have to be considered before the solution is found. Often, computers are programmed to solve problems using such algorithms, because with a computer an accurate solution is guaranteed and millions of possible solutions can be tried in a few seconds.

Heuristics Heuristics are used in problem solving in much the same way as in decision making. One heuristic that is effective for solving some problems is **working backwards**, sometimes called the *backward search*. This approach starts with the solution, a known condition, and works back through the problem. Once the backward search has revealed the steps to be taken and their order, the problem can be solved. Try working backwards to solve the water lily problem in *Try It 7.1*.

problem solving
Using thoughts and actions to achieve a desired goal that is not readily attainable.

trial and error
An approach to problem solving in which one solution after another is tried in no particular order until an answer is found.

algorithm
A systematic, step-by-step procedure that guarantees a solution to a problem of a certain type if the algorithm is executed properly.

working backwards
A heuristic strategy in which a person discovers the steps needed to solve a problem by starting with the solution and working back through the problem.

Try It 7.1 Water Lily Problem

Water lilies double the area they cover every 24 hours. At the beginning of the summer there is one water lily on a pond. It takes 60 days for the pond to become covered with water lilies. On what day is the pond half covered? (From Fixx, 1978.)

Answer: The most important fact is that the lilies double in number every 24 hours. If the pond is to be completely covered on the 60th day, it has to be half covered on the 59th day.

If your professor assigns a term paper, you do not simply sit down and write it. Instead, you probably use a popular heuristic known as **means-end analysis**. In means-end analysis, the current position is compared with a desired goal, and a series of steps is formulated and then taken to close the gap between the two (Sweller & Levine, 1982). Many problems are large and complex and must be broken down into smaller steps or subproblems before a solution can be reached. For example, in writing a term paper, you must determine how you will deal with your topic, research the topic, make an outline, and then write the sections over a period of time. After this is done, you are ready to assemble the complete term paper, write several drafts, and put the finished product in final form before handing it in.

Another problem-solving strategy is the **analogy heuristic**—applying a solution used for a past problem to a current problem that shares many similar features. Situations with many features in common are said to be analogous. When faced with a new problem to solve, you can look for commonalities between the new problem and other problems you have solved before, and then you can apply a strategy similar to one that has worked in the past. For example, if your car is making strange sounds and you take it to an auto mechanic, the mechanic may be able to diagnose the problem by analogy—the sounds your car is making are comparable to sounds she has heard before and can associate with a particular problem.

■ **means-end analysis**
A heuristic strategy in which the current position is compared with a desired goal, and a series of steps is formulated and then taken to close the gap between the two.

■ **analogy heuristic**
A heuristic strategy that applies a solution used for a past problem to a current problem that shares many similar features.

■ **functional fixedness**
The failure to use familiar objects in novel ways to solve problems because of a tendency to view objects only in terms of their customary functions.

Impediments to Problem Solving

How do functional fixedness and mental set impede problem solving?

Have you ever faced a problem that seemed to defy solution despite your best efforts to solve it? You may have lacked the relevant knowledge or experience to solve it, or you may not have had sufficient material resources. Do you have any problems that could be solved if money were no object? There are other impediments to problem solving that serve as stumbling blocks for many. Two of these are functional fixedness and mental set.

Functional Fixedness Do you think of a butter knife as nothing more than an object used to butter bread—or might it also serve as a screwdriver? Many of us are hampered in our efforts to solve problems in daily life because of **functional fixedness**—

Many of us are hampered in our efforts to solve problems in daily life because of functional fixedness, the failure to use familiar objects in novel ways to solve problems.

the failure to use familiar objects in novel ways to solve problems because of a tendency to think only of their customary functions. Just think of all the items you use daily—tools, utensils, and other equipment—that help you perform certain functions. Often, the traditional functions of objects become so fixed in your thinking that you do not consider using them in new and creative ways.

Suppose you injured your leg and knew that you should apply ice to prevent swelling, but you had no ice cubes or ice bag in your refrigerator. Or what if you wanted a cup of coffee, but the decanter for your coffeemaker was broken? If you suffered from functional fixedness, you might come to the conclusion that there was nothing you could do to solve your problem at that moment. But, rather than thinking about the object or utensil that you don't have, think about the function that will solve your problem. In the first instance, what you need is something very cold, not necessarily an ice bag or ice cubes per se; a cold can of soda or a bag of frozen peas might be a solution. In the second case, what you need is something to catch the coffee, maybe a bowl or a coffee mug.

Mental Set Perhaps you found a way to solve a problem once in the past and continue to use the same technique in similar situations, even though it is not highly effective or efficient. If so, you are exhibiting another impediment to problem solving—mental set. **Mental set** is the tendency to apply a familiar strategy to solve a problem even though another approach might be better. For instance, what do you do when you face the problem of needing to study for a test? Do you, like many students, habitually procrastinate until the last minute and then spend hours cramming the day before the test? If so, your study habits are being influenced by mental set. And if you find that this strategy allows you to achieve passing grades, the positive reinforcement you receive may make you continue to rely on this approach. However, you could probably dramatically improve your test grades by breaking this mental set and adopting more effective study strategies.

■ **mental set**
The tendency to apply a familiar strategy to solve a problem even though another approach might be better.

Humans are not unique as problem solvers. Many animals can also solve problems. And what about machines?

Remember It 7.3

1. A(n) __________ is a problem-solving strategy that guarantees a correct answer.
2. Working backwards and means-end analysis are examples of __________ .
3. The __________ heuristic involves applying a solution that worked for a past problem to a problem that shares many similar features.
4. Rich uses a wastebasket to keep a door from closing. In solving his problem, he was not hindered by __________ .

ANSWERS: 1. algorithm; 2. heuristics; 3. analogy; 4. functional fixedness

High-Tech Applications of Cognition

Artificial Intelligence

In what ways does artificial intelligence resemble human cognition?

Can a computer really think like a human being? Yes and no, as you'll see. Although there are important differences between the ways computers and human brains process information, amazing progress has been made in the field of artificial intelligence since the term was first used by researcher John McCarthy in 1956. **Artificial intelligence (AI)** refers to the programming of computer systems to simulate human thinking in solving problems and in making judgments and decisions. The first successful effort to program computers to mimic human thinking was made by Allen Newell and Herbert A. Simon in 1972. They developed programs that could play chess as well as a human expert could, although not as well as master players. Eventually, AI experts at IBM created a computer called Deep Blue, which defeated long-time world chess champion Garry Kasparov in 1997. (In 2003, a match between Kasparov and a smaller, slower version of Deep Blue known as Deep Junior ended in a draw.)

Some experts have stated that chess-playing computers such as Deep Blue could not really think on their own. These experts insist that even the most sophisticated "thinking" of computers is not really analogous to human cognition, because, unlike humans, these machines are merely following a set of rules, no matter how complex those rules may be. Stunned by his defeat, Kasparov disagreed with Deep Blue's critics. As the match proceeded, he felt that the computer was showing signs of humanlike cognitive ability in the form of strategic understanding. Somewhere along the way, the tactics (specific rules for playing chess) that had been programmed into Deep Blue had apparently been transformed into strategy—the formulation of an overall game plan.

Decades before Deep Blue's stunning defeat of the reigning world chess champion, Newell and Simon had opened the door for computer systems able to do far more than play chess like an expert. Today's expert systems "perform a substantial number of human tasks at a professional level" (Simon, 1995, p. 507). **Expert systems** are computer programs designed to carry out highly specific functions within a limited domain. One of the first medical expert systems was MYCIN, a computerized diagnostician in the area of blood diseases and meningitis. Other expert systems perform a range of functions in medicine, space technology, military defense, weather prediction, and a variety of other fields.

Expert systems operate in well-defined domains; that is, such a system's knowledge base, or store of information, is not inordinately large and is limited to a specific area of expertise (Hendler, 1994). Outside its area of expertise, an expert system cannot function. Expert systems, then, are useful only as assistants to humans; they cannot stand alone. For example, expert systems can be used by physicians to confirm

■ **artificial intelligence (AI)** Programming of computer systems to simulate human thinking in solving problems and in making judgments and decisions.

■ **expert systems** Computer programs designed to carry out highly specific functions within a limited domain.

World champion Garry Kasparov contemplates a move against Deep Blue, an IBM computer that exhibited artificial intelligence in the area of top-level chess play.

diagnoses or to suggest diagnoses doctors haven't thought of (Brunetti et al., 2002). Yet, these systems far surpass the human brain in their ability to retrieve massive amounts of stored data and to use that data to make decisions based on specific facts and rules that have been preprogrammed into their software. In addition, because they run on computers, expert systems are vastly superior to humans in carrying out complex mathematical operations at lightning speed.

Moreover, the idea that expert systems can't stand alone is being challenged. For example, some studies show that psychotherapy clients can be helped just as effectively by interacting with expert systems as in face-to-face sessions with a human therapist (Taylor & Luce, 2003). Remember, though, that any expert system relies on the accumulated knowledge of human experts. Thus, it is impossible for computers to totally replace human professionals.

Artificial Neural Networks

How do scientists use artificial neural networks?

Scientists are devising ever more sophisticated computer systems, based on their understanding of how neurons in certain parts of the brain are connected and how those connections develop (Buonomano & Merzenich, 1995; Hinton et al., 1995). Computer systems that are intended to mimic the human brain are called **artificial neural networks (ANNs)**. Like synaptic connections in the brain, the connections in an ANN can be strengthened or weakened as a result of experience. Many of the newer expert systems utilize ANNs, making them not only able to process information like human experts but also to learn from experience just as those experts do (Brunetti et al., 2002). However, even some of the simplest cognitive tasks that people accomplish without conscious effort can be very difficult to program into a computer system. For example, ANNs that can learn how to distinguish between moving beings, such as humans, horses, cows, and so on, have only recently been developed (Tabb et al., 2002).

Understanding what people say to us seems to be a fairly simple task, one that we take for granted. However, comprehension of natural human language is by far the biggest challenge for ANN designers. In one of the pioneering studies in this field, computer scientist Alex Waibel and colleagues developed a system "programmed to modify itself according to whatever signals come into the system . . . the speech recognizer actually learns how to identify sounds and words" (Peterson, 1993, p. 254). Voice recognition systems are already used by banks and credit card companies and in other commercial settings. But, unlike humans, such computer systems cannot understand the subtleties of language—tone of voice, accompanying nonverbal behavior, or even level of politeness (Peterson, 1993).

Many other aspects of language processing also are extremely difficult for computers to manage. For example, what kind of scene comes to mind when you hear the word *majestic*? Perhaps you see a range of snow-capped mountains. At present, computer scientists are working to develop programs that can enable computers to retrieve images on the basis of such vague, abstract cues (Kuroda, 2002).

It's important to note here that a simple if-then program would allow a computer to call up an image of a mountain range when the word *majestic* was keyed in. So, the point of research with ANNs is not just to use a computer to bring about a particular result, but to be able to program the computer to produce the result in the same way that the human mind does. Perhaps you visualize mountains when you hear the word *majestic* because this word is linked to height as a scene feature. The concept of height is, in turn, associated with mountains. However, skyscrapers are tall as well, so why don't you see them in your mind's eye when you hear *majestic*? Perhaps some people do. If so, why does one person see skyscrapers while another sees mountains? Is there a particular experience or piece of knowledge that leads to this difference? These are the kinds of cognitive pathways that network designers attempt to identify in human

■ **artificial neural networks (ANNs)** Computer systems that are intended to mimic the human brain.

thinking and duplicate in computer programs. In so doing, these scientists not only program computers to accomplish tasks that seemed nearly impossible just a few short decades ago but, at the same time, gain insight into human cognition.

robotics The science of automating human and animal functions.

Robotics

What are some practical applications of robotics?

Do you recall the discussion about artificial limbs at the beginning of this chapter? One area in which human cognition has been applied to develop technological marvels is **robotics**—the science of automating human and animal functions. In some cases, robotics has made it possible to manipulate variables in experiments that previously could only be investigated in correlational studies. Scientists studying the mating behavior of bowerbirds, for example, observed the females of the species repeatedly crouching during the attraction phase of mating (Patricelli et al., 2002). To examine the crouching variable in an experiment, they built a robotic version of a female bowerbird whose crouching actions could be remotely controlled. By systematically exposing male bowerbirds to crouching and noncrouching behavior, and by varying the amount and frequency of crouching, they were able to learn that males use females' crouching behavior as cues to initiate displays of their colorful plumage.

Experiments involving robotic birds may seem very far removed from any kind of practical application. However, projects such as this one help scientists and engineers learn more about how to build and program robots to behave like their living counterparts. And the resulting technology has tremendous potential for a wide variety of applications. Some impressive achievements in robotics include the following:

- Robots help stroke patients toward recovery by assisting them in exercise movement.
- Robotic surgical assistants help surgeons make remarkable gains in precision for some difficult surgeries.
- Robotic filling stations will keep satellites aloft.
- Miniature robots will assist tomorrow's soldiers.
- Robots can perform many duties too dangerous for humans (cleaning up toxic spills, finding and destroying land mines, cleaning up nuclear waste sites, etc.).

Some of the applications of robotics and artificial intelligence are so remarkable that it is easy to lose sight of how they came to be. Keep in mind that the real power lies not in the machines, but in their creator—human cognition.

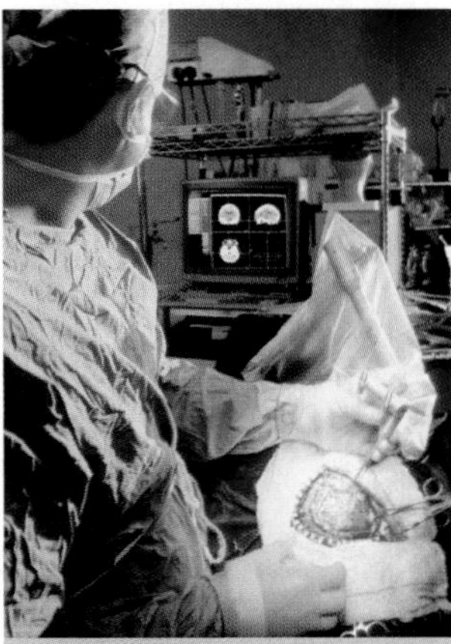

High-tech robotics has enhanced many human skills, including those involved in brain surgery. Here, the exact position of a tumor is located and displayed to a surgeon on a monitor; the surgeon guides the computer-controlled robotic arm, called a "magic wand," to remove the tumor with pinpoint accuracy.

Remember It 7.4

1. Programming computers to simulate human cognition is called ________.
2. ________ are primarily used to assist human experts.
3. Computer systems intended to mimic the functioning of the human brain are called ________.
4. One of the most difficult aspects of human cognition for computers to master is the processing of natural ________.
5. The science of ________ involves developing machines that can carry out motor functions very much like those of humans and animals.

ANSWERS: 1. artificial intelligence; 2. Expert systems; 3. artificial neural networks; 4. language; 5. robotics

Language

Can we think without using language? Research on imagery indicates that we can. But, without language, each of us would live in a largely solitary and isolated world, unable to communicate or receive much information. Scientists define **language** as a means of communicating thoughts and feelings, using a system of socially shared but arbitrary symbols (sounds, signs, or written symbols) arranged according to rules of grammar.

Think for a minute about how amazing language really is. It allows us to form and comprehend a virtually infinite number of meaningful sentences. If this were not the case, we would be limited to merely repeating statements we had heard or read. Moreover, language is not bound by space or time. Language enables us to communicate about things that are abstract or concrete, present or not present, and about what has been, is now, or conceivably might be. Thanks to language, we can profit from the experience, the knowledge, and the wisdom of others, and we can benefit others with our own. Language makes available the wisdom of the ages from every corner of the world. In Chapter 10, we will discuss how language is acquired by infants. Here, we explore the structure and the components of this amazing form of human communication.

The Structure of Language

What are the necessary components of any language?

Psycholinguistics is the study of how language is acquired, produced, and used and how the sounds and symbols of language are translated into meaning. Psycholinguists devote much effort to the study of the structure of language and the rules governing its use. These vital components of language are phonemes, morphemes, syntax, semantics, and pragmatics.

Phonemes The smallest units of sound in a spoken language are known as **phonemes**. Phonemes form the basic building blocks of a spoken language. Three phonemes together form the sound of the word *cat*—the *c* (which sounds like *k*), *a*, and *t*. Phonemes do not sound like the single letters of the alphabet as you recite them, *a-b-c-d-e-f-g*, but like the sounds of the letters as they are used in words, like the *b* in *boy*, the *p* in *pan*, and so on. The sound of the phoneme *c* in the word *cat* is different from the sound of the phoneme *c* in the word *city*.

Letters combined to form sounds, such as *th* in *the* and *ch* in *child*, are also phonemes. The same sound (phoneme) may be represented by different letters in different words, as the *a* in *stay* and the *ei* in *sleigh*. And, as you saw with *c*, the same letter can serve as different phonemes. The letter *a*, for example, is sounded as four different phonemes in *day*, *cap*, *watch*, and *law*.

How many phonemes are there? About 100 or so different sounds could serve as phonemes, but most languages have far fewer. English uses about 45 phonemes, while some languages may have as few as 15 and others as many as 85 (Solso, 1991). However, phonemes do not provide meaning. Meaning is conveyed by the next component of a language, the morphemes.

Morphemes **Morphemes** are the smallest units of meaning in a language. In almost all cases in the English language, a morpheme is made of two or more phonemes. But a few phonemes also serve as morphemes, such as the article *a* and the personal pronoun *I*. Many words in English are single morphemes—*book*, *word*, *learn*, *reason*, and so on. In addition to root words, morphemes may also be prefixes (such as *re-* in *relearn*) or suffixes (such as *-ed* to show past tense, as in *learned*). The word *reasonable* consists of two morphemes: *reason* and *able*. The addition of the prefix *un-* (another morpheme) forms *unreasonable*, reversing the meaning. The letter *s* gives a plural meaning to a word and is thus a morpheme. The morpheme *book* (singular) becomes two morphemes, *books* (plural).

language
A means of communicating thoughts and feelings, using a system of socially shared but arbitrary symbols (sounds, signs, or written symbols) arranged according to rules of grammar.

psycholinguistics
The study of how language is acquired, produced, and used, and how the sounds and symbols of language are translated into meaning.

phonemes
The smallest units of sound in a spoken language.

morphemes
The smallest units of meaning in a language.

So, morphemes, singly and in combination, form the words in a language and provide meaning. But single words alone do not constitute a language. A language also requires rules for structuring, or putting together, words in orderly and meaningful fashion. This is where syntax enters the picture.

Syntax **Syntax** is the aspect of grammar that specifies the rules for arranging and combining words to form phrases and sentences. For example, an important rule of syntax in English is that adjectives usually come before nouns. English speakers refer to the residence of the U.S. President as the White House. But in Spanish, the noun usually comes before the adjective, and Spanish speakers would say, "la Casa Blanca" (the House White). In English, we ask, "Do you speak German?" But speakers of German would ask, "Sprechen sie Deutsch?" (Speak you German?). So, the rules of word order, or syntax, differ from one language to another.

Semantics **Semantics** refers to the meaning derived from morphemes, words, and sentences. The same word can have different meanings, depending on how it is used in sentences: "I don't mind." "You mind your manners." "He has lost his mind."

The noted linguist and creative theorist Noam Chomsky (1986, 1990) maintained that the ability to glean a meaningful message from a sentence is stored in a different area of the brain than are the words used to compose the sentence. Moreover, he distinguished between the surface structure and the deep structure of a sentence. The **surface structure** of a sentence refers to the literal words that are spoken or written (or signed). The **deep structure** is the underlying meaning of the sentence.

In some sentences, the surface structure and the deep structure are the same. This is true of the sentence "Lauren read the book." But if this sentence is rewritten in the passive voice—"The book was read by Lauren"—the surface structure changes, yet the deep structure remains the same. Alternatively, a single sentence may have one or more different deep structures. For example, in the sentence "John enjoys charming people," two competing deep structures produce ambiguity. Does John enjoy people who are charming, or does he enjoy exercising his charm on other people?

Pragmatics How do you know whether a person is making a statement or asking a question? The pragmatic characteristics of a language help you tell the difference. **Pragmatics** is defined as the characteristics of spoken language that help you decipher the social meaning of utterances. For example, one aspect of pragmatics is *prosody*, or intonation. Every language has prosodic rules that are followed when producing statements or questions. In English, statements fall in intonation at the end, while questions rise. So, if someone sitting near you in an airport says to you, "newspaper," with rising intonation at the end of the word, you know that she is saying "Would you like this newspaper?" Other nonverbal cues may accompany the question. She may be holding a newspaper out to you or motioning to a newspaper lying on a table. Such gestures represent another aspect of pragmatics.

■ syntax
The aspect of grammar that specifies the rules for arranging and combining words to form phrases and sentences.

■ semantics
The meaning derived from morphemes, words, and sentences.

■ surface structure
The literal words of a sentence that are spoken or written (or signed).

■ deep structure
The underlying meaning of a sentence.

■ pragmatics
The characteristics of spoken language, such as intonation and gestures, that indicate the social meaning of utterances.

Language and the Brain

What areas of the brain are involved in producing and comprehending language?

How would you pronounce the nonword *zat*? Most English speakers would probably pronounce it to rhyme with *bat*. But other nonwords are not as easy to pronounce. For instance, how should *mough* be pronounced? Should it rhyme with *rough*, *bough*, *dough*, or *cough*? This is just one example of the many confusing inconsistencies in the way English words are spelled and pronounced. However, some languages, such as Italian, have very few inconsistencies in the way words are spelled and pronounced. Thus, speakers of Italian should be able to pronounce written words more easily and more quickly than those who speak English—and they do, according to research by Paulesu and others (2000).

Paulesu and his colleagues (2000) conducted brain-imaging studies comparing English and Italian speakers. These researchers chose these two languages because English spelling and pronunciation are inconsistent, while Italian spelling and pronunciation are highly consistent. The experiments suggest that speakers of these two languages process written words and nonwords in different regions in their brains.

These researchers used PET (positron emission tomography) scans to view activity in areas of the brains of Italian and English speakers while these participants read aloud a list of words and nonwords. The English speakers took longer than the Italian speakers to begin reading the words and even longer to begin reading the nonwords. As a control measure to find out if the English speakers were just slower than the Italians, both groups were compared on another test, in which they had to produce the words for pictured objects. In this test, no difference in performance time was found between Italian and English participants, most likely because naming pictured objects does not require a translation from spelling to pronunciation.

The PET scans of all participants in this study revealed heightened activity in a widespread area of the brain known to be associated with reading, as was expected. But the new information that Paulesu and colleagues (2000) uncovered is that the brain activity in specific regions varied according to the speaker's native language. Compared with the English speakers, the Italian speakers showed greater brain activity in an upper area of the left temporal lobe when reading both words and nonwords. English speakers showed increased brain activity in the left frontal lobe and in an upper region of the left temporal lobe when reading only nonwords. This study assumed that the more proficient and the more expert a person is at a given task, the greater the neural activity in the brain structure that handles that task. Research provides some support for this assumption. For example, compared with nonmusicians, piano players show greater activity in the motor-related regions of the brain while performing a finger-moving task (Hund-Georgiadis & von Cramon, 1999).

What parts of the brain are key in processing syntactical and semantic aspects of language? Two brain areas that are important for processing language are Broca's area and Wernicke's area (as you learned in Chapter 2). The role of Broca's area was long believed to be largely restricted to the physical production of speech. But a recent brain-imaging study (Ni et al., 2000) revealed that Broca's area was highly activated when participants were processing errors in syntax, as in the sentence "Trees can grew." Other research has confirmed the role of Broca's area in syntactical processing (Dogil et al., 2002). Further, both Wernicke's area and part of the cerebellum are activated when we make judgments about the grammatical characteristics of language.

Animal Language

How does animal communication differ from that of humans?

What capability most reliably sets humans apart from all other species? Most people think it's language, and for good reason. As far as scientists know, humans are the only species to have developed this rich, varied, and complex system of communication. But even though they have never developed their own language, could our nearest cousins, the chimpanzees, learn to master our language if we taught them? The earliest attempts to answer this question date back 70 years, to the early 1930s, and they met with little success.

Chimpanzee Communication You may have heard or read about chimpanzees who can communicate using sign language. One of the most famous was Washoe. Psychologists Allen and Beatrix Gardner (1969) taught this chimp sign language beginning when she was 1 year old. Washoe learned signs for objects and for certain concepts and commands such as "flower," "more", "give me," "come," and "open." By the end of her 5th year, she had mastered about 160 signs (Fleming, 1974).

Psychologist David Premack taught another chimp, Sarah, to use an artificial language he had developed. Its symbols consisted of magnetized chips of various shapes,

FIGURE 7.3 Sarah's Symbols

A chimpanzee named Sarah learned to communicate using plastic chips of various shapes, sizes, and colors to represent words in an artificial language developed by her trainer, David Premack.

Source: Premack (1971).

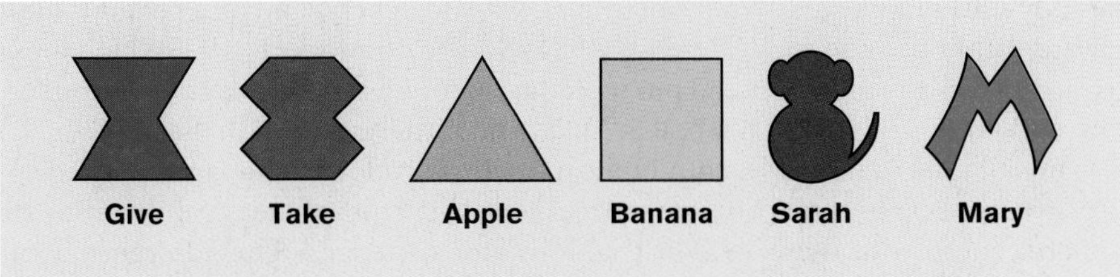

sizes, and colors, as shown in Figure 7.3. Premack used operant conditioning techniques to teach Sarah to select the chip representing a fruit and place it on a magnetic language board. The trainer would then reward Sarah with the fruit she had requested. Sarah mastered the notions of similarities and differences, and eventually she could signal whether two objects were the same or different with nearly perfect accuracy (Premack & Premack, 1983). She even performed well on part-whole relationships and could match such things as half an apple and a glass half filled with water. Despite Sarah's accomplishments, Premack firmly maintained that it is unlikely that animals are capable of language (Premack & Premack, 1983).

At the Yerkes Primate Research Center at Emory University, a chimp named Lana participated in a computer-controlled language-training program. She learned to press keys imprinted with geometric symbols that represented words in an artificial language called Yerkish. One day, her trainer, Tim, had an orange that she wanted. Lana had available symbols for many fruits, but none for an orange. Yet, there was a colored symbol for the color orange. So, Lana improvised and signaled, "Tim give apple which is orange" (Savage-Rumbaugh, 1986).

Was human-like language being displayed in these studies with primates? Not according to Herbert Terrace (1981), who examined the research of others and conducted his own. Terrace and his coworkers taught sign language to a chimp they called Nim Chimpsky (after the famed linguist Noam Chomsky) and reported Nim's progress from the age of 2 weeks to 4 years. Nim learned 125 symbols, which is respectable, but does not amount to language. Rather, chimps like Nim simply imitate their trainers and make responses to get reinforcers, according to the principles of operant conditioning, not the rules of language (Terrace, 1985, 1986).

The most impressive performance to date is that of a pygmy chimpanzee, Kanzi, who developed an amazing ability to communicate with his trainers. Kanzi eventually demonstrated an advanced understanding (for chimps) of spoken English and could respond correctly even to new commands, such as "Go to the refrigerator and get out a tomato" (Savage-Rumbaugh, 1990; Savage-Rumbaugh et al., 1992). By the time Kanzi was 6 years old, the team of researchers who worked with him had recorded more than 13,000 "utterances" and reported that the chimp could communicate using some 200 different geometric symbols (Gibbons, 1991). Reportedly, Kanzi could respond just as well when requests were made over earphones so that no one else in the room could signal to him purposely or inadvertently.

Communication in Other Animals Most animal species studied by language researchers are limited to motor responses, such as using signs, gestures, or magnetic symbols or pressing keys on symbol boards. But these limitations do not extend to some bird species, such as parrots, which are capable of making human-like speech sounds. One remarkable case is Alex, an African grey parrot who not only mimics human speech, but seems to do so intelligently. Able to recognize and name various colors, objects, and shapes, Alex answers questions about them in English (Pepperberg, 1991, 1994b). And he can count as well. When asked such questions as "How many red blocks?" Alex answers correctly about 80% of the time (Pepperberg, 1994a).

Research with sea mammals such as whales and dolphins has established that they apparently use complicated systems of grunts, whistles, clicks, and other sounds to communicate within their species (Herman, 1981; Savage-Rumbaugh, 1993). Dolphins can also learn to pick out an object and put it on the right or left of a basket, for example, and follow such commands as "in the basket" and "under the basket" (Chollar, 1989).

Many of the remarkable communication feats reported for animal species are impressive, especially those of chimpanzees. Clearly, chimpanzees can learn to string together requests. But these are constructions, not sentences. The difference between a construction—such as Lana's "Tim give apple which is orange"—and a sentence (a fundamental element of human language) was captured by the philosopher Bertrand Russell. Someone once asked Russell if apes might ever learn to speak. He is said to have answered that he would be persuaded of an ape's grasp of language if the animal could demonstrate understanding of a sentence such as "My father was poor but honest" (quoted in Restak, 1988, p. 202).

Language and Thinking

In what ways does language influence thinking?

If language is unique to humans, then does language drive human thinking? Does the fact that you speak English mean that you reason, think, and perceive your world differently than does someone who speaks Spanish, or Chinese, or Swahili? According to one hypothesis presented more than 45 years ago, it does.

Benjamin Whorf (1956) put forth his **linguistic relativity hypothesis,** which suggests that the language a person speaks largely determines the nature of that person's thoughts. According to this hypothesis, a person's worldview is constructed primarily using the words available in his or her language. As proof, Whorf offered his classic example: The languages used by the Eskimo people have a number of different words for snow, including "*apikak*, first snow falling; *aniv*, snow spread out; *pukak*, snow for drinking water," while the English-speaking world has but one word, *snow* (Restak, 1988, p. 222). Whorf claimed that such a rich and varied selection of words to represent snow enables Eskimos to think differently about it than do people whose languages lack specific words for various snow conditions. No matter what language you speak, however, you can perceive and think about snow according to whether it is falling or on the ground, powdery or slushy, fluffy or packed, without having specific words for snow in those conditions.

Eleanor Rosch (1973) tested whether people whose language contains many names for colors are better at discriminating among colors than people whose language has only a few color names. Her subjects were English-speaking Americans and members of the Dani, a remote tribe in New Guinea, whose language has only two names for colors—*mili* for dark, cool colors, and *mola* for bright, warm colors. Rosch showed members of both groups single-color chips of 11 colors—black, white, red, yellow, green, blue, brown, purple, pink, orange, and gray—for 5 seconds each. Then, after 30 seconds, she had the participants select the 11 colors they had viewed from an assortment of 40 color chips. Rosch found no significant differences between the Dani and the Americans in discriminating or remembering the 11 colors.

■ linguistic relativity hypothesis
The notion proposed by Whorf that the language a person speaks largely determines the nature of that person's thoughts.

Rosch's study did not support the linguistic relativity hypothesis. And neither did an earlier and larger study of 98 different languages by Berlin and Kay (1969). These researchers found a consistent pattern in establishing names for colors in all the cultures they studied. They concluded that people in cultures throughout the world think about colors in much the same way, regardless of the language they speak. Thought both influences and is influenced by language, and language appears to reflect cultural differences more than it determines them (Pinker, 1994; Rosch, 1987).

Consider the vast number of words that have been added to the English language within the last few decades—*CD, fax, e-mail, Internet,* and a host of others from the fields of medicine, science, engineering, and so on. New ideas preceded the introduction of these and other words. But once new words appear, they are used in thinking of other ideas. Although we think both with and without language (as in imagery), a large and rich vocabulary is one of our most important tools for thinking. And there is a strong, consistent correlation between one's vocabulary and one's performance on most of the widely accepted tests for measuring intelligence.

Along the border between the United States and Mexico, Spanish-English bilingualism is common. Businesses and government agencies must be prepared to communicate with clients in both languages.

Sexism in Language Does it really matter whether we use "he" or "she" to refer to an unspecified person who represents a particular profession? Consider the generic use of the pronoun *he* to refer to any member of a group of people. If your professor says, "I expect each student in this class to do the best he can," does this announcement mean the same to males and females? Studies confirm that the generic use of *he, him,* and *his* is interpreted heavily in favor of males (Gastil, 1990; Hamilton, 1988; Henley, 1989; Ng, 1990). If this were not the case, the following sentence would not seem unusual at all: "Like other mammals, man bears his offspring live."

Bilingualism

What is the best time in life to learn a second language, and why?

Do you speak more than one language? Most native-born Americans speak only English. But in many other countries around the world, the majority of citizens speak two or even more languages (Snow, 1993). In European countries, most students learn English in addition to the languages of the countries bordering their own. Dutch is the native language of the Netherlands, but all Dutch schoolchildren learn German, French, and English. College-bound German students also typically study three languages (Haag & Stern, 2003). English instruction begins for most Germans in elementary school. During the intermediate years, German children study either Latin or French. Then, in high school, most study Spanish. By contrast, children in the United States who study any language other than English typically study only one.

However, given the changing demographics of the United States population, many Americans are finding it necessary to learn at least a few words in languages other than English in order to be able to communicate in their everyday lives (see Figure 7.4, on page 254). In some cities in the United States, more than 100 languages are spoken. And, according to the U.S. Census Bureau (2001), about one-third of schoolchildren in the United States speak a language other than English at home. Many of these children learn English at school, or from their playmates, while also learning the language of their parents. But what about the effect of learning two languages on the process of language development itself? (You'll learn more about this process in Chapter 9.)

Research suggests that there are both advantages and disadvantages to learning two languages early in life. One of the pluses is that, among preschool and school-age children, bilingualism is associated with better *metalinguistic skills,* the capacity to think about language (Bialystok et al., 2000; Mohanty & Perregaux, 1997). On the downside, even in adulthood, bilingualism is sometimes associated with decreased efficiency in memory tasks involving words (Gollan & Silverberg, 2001; McElree et al., 2000). However, bilinguals appear to develop compensatory strategies that allow

FIGURE 7.4 Numbers of Individuals over 5 Years Old in the United States Whose First Language Is Other Than English

The number of Spanish speakers in the United States far exceeds that of any other language group.

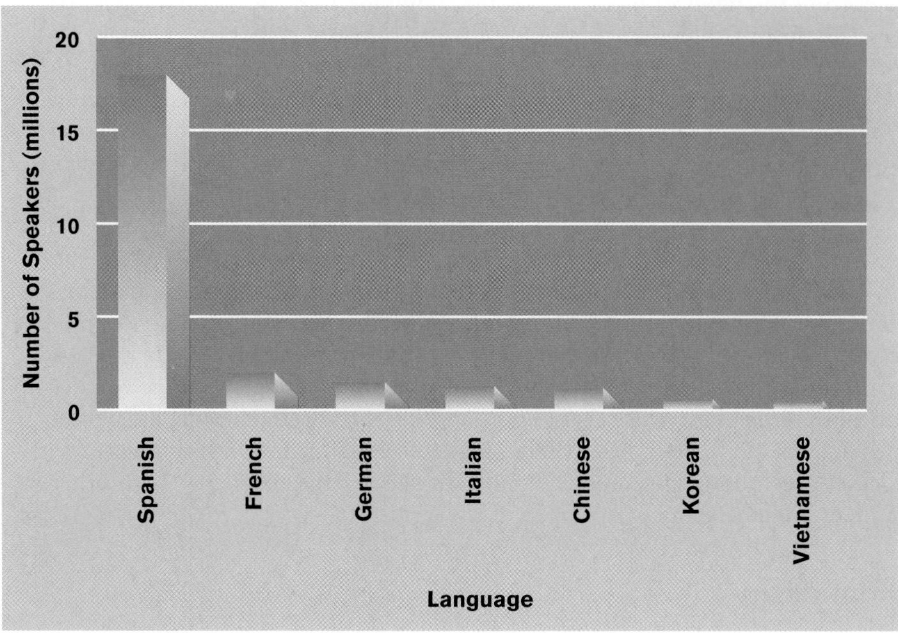

them to make up for these inefficiencies. Consequently, they often perform such tasks as accurately as monolinguals, though they may respond more slowly. Many people would argue, however, that the advantages associated with fluency in two languages are worth giving up a bit of cognitive efficiency.

So, you may ask, what about people who did not have the good fortune to grow up bilingual? Is it still possible to become fluent in a second language after reaching adulthood? Researchers have found that there is no age at which it is impossible to acquire a new language. While it is true that those who begin earlier reach higher levels of proficiency, age is not the only determining factor. Kenji Hakuta and his colleagues (2003) used census data to examine relationships among English proficiency, age at entry into the United States, and educational attainment for Chinese- and Spanish-speaking immigrants. The results of their study are shown in Figure 7.5. As you can see, even when immigrants entered the United States in middle and late adulthood, their ability to learn English was predicted by their educational backgrounds. And other studies have shown that the more you know about your first language—its spelling rules, grammatical structure, and vocabulary—the easier it will be for you to learn another language (Meschyan & Hernandez, 2002).

There is one clear advantage to learning two languages earlier in life, however. People who are younger when they learn a new language are far more likely to be able to speak it with an appropriate accent (McDonald, 1997). One reason for this difference between early and late language learners may have to do with slight variations in neural processing in Broca's area, the area of the brain that controls speech production. Research by Kim and others (1997) suggests that bilinguals who learned a second

FIGURE 7.5 English Proficiency in Chinese- and Spanish-Speaking Immigrants to the United States

These research results, based on census data involving more than 2 million individuals, suggest that it is never too late to learn a second language.
Source: Hakuta et al. (2003).

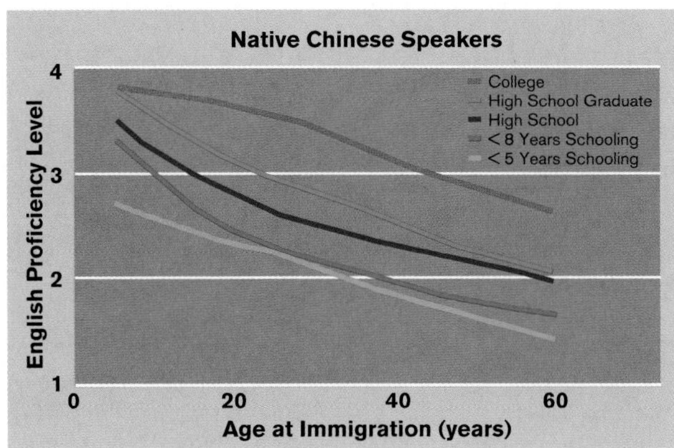

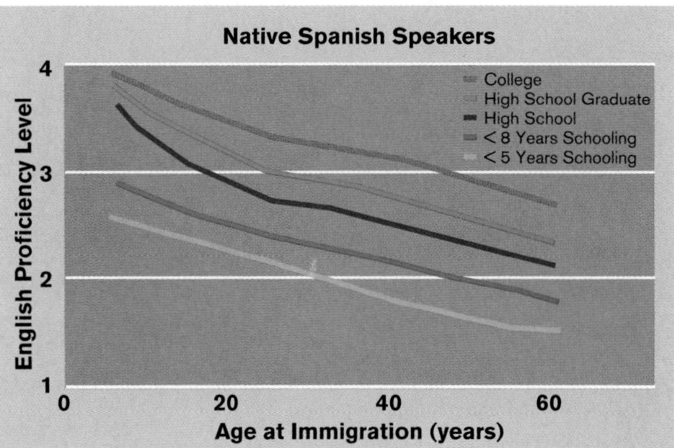

language early (younger than age 10 or 11) rely on the same patch of tissue in Broca's area for both of the languages they speak. But in those who learned a second language at an older age, two different sections of Broca's area are active while they are performing language tasks—one section for the first language and another for the second language. Yet, the two sections are very close, only 1/3 inch apart.

As noted earlier, Americans in general lag far behind citizens of most other technologically advanced nations in their knowledge of languages other than their native tongue and have much catching up to do. The ability to communicate in more than one language will surely become increasingly important as we move further into the 21st century.

Remember It 7.5

1. Match each description with the correct component of language.
   - (1) ___ the smallest units of meaning
   - (2) ___ the meaning of utterances
   - (3) ___ grammatical rules
   - (4) ___ the social aspects of language
   - (5) ___ the smallest units of sound

   a. pragmatics
   b. syntax
   c. morphemes
   d. semantics
   e. phonemes

2. Sentences are more likely to be ambiguous if they have two or more ___________ structures.
3. Chimpanzees can communicate with humans using symbols or ___________.
4. According to the ___________, thinking can be limited by language.
5. The ability to reach high levels of proficiency when learning a second language ___________ as people get older.

ANSWERS: 1. (1) c, (2) d, (3) b, (4) a, (5) e; 2. deep; 3. sign language; 4. linguistic relativity hypothesis; 5. declines

Apply It

How to Build a Powerful Vocabulary

Of all the cognitive skills humans possess, none is more important for clarity of thinking and academic success than vocabulary. How, then, can you build a more powerful vocabulary? The best way is to realize that almost all words belong to larger networks of meaning, and to understand that your mind is already geared toward organizing information in terms of meaning. Thus, with a little effort, you can greatly increase your vocabulary by supporting the kind of learning your brain is already trying to do. Here are a few techniques you can apply.

- *Learn to think analytically about words you already know and relate new words to them.* What do the words *antiseptic* and *septic tank* have in common? You use an *antiseptic* to prevent bacterial infection of a wound; a *septic tank* is used for removing harmful bacteria from water containing human waste. A logical conclusion would be that *septic* has something to do with bacteria. Knowing this, what do you think a doctor means when she says that a patient is suffering from *sepsis*? By linking *sepsis* to *septic tank* and *antiseptic,* you can guess that she is referring to some kind of bacterial infection.
- *Be aware of word connections that may be hidden by spelling differences.* You may know that both *Caesar* and *Czar* refer to some kind of ruler or leader. But you may not know that they are exactly the same word, spoken and spelled somewhat differently in Ancient Rome (*Caesar*) and in Russia (*Czar*). Now, if you're taking a history class in which you learn about *Kaiser* Wilhelm, who led Germany during World War I, thinking analytically about his title may help you realize that it is exactly the same word as *Caesar* and *Czar,* with a German spelling. Here's another example: Can you guess something about the location and climate of the nation of Ecuador by relating its name to a word that differs from it only slightly in spelling?
- *Use your knowledge of word parts to actively seek out new words.* Don't learn new words one at a time. Instead, be on the lookout for "word families"—root words and prefixes and suffixes. Here is one important root word: *spect,* which means "look," "look at," "watch," and "see." And *spect* appears in dozens of different words, such as *inspect.* What do you do when you *inspect* something? You look closely at it. Equipped with this knowledge, other *spect* words may start to come to mind, along with an entirely new way of thinking about their meanings: *spectacular, spectator, spectacle, spectacles, perspective, prospect, respect, disrespect, retrospect, suspect,* and so on. The word *circumspect* may be new to you. Look it up in a dictionary, and think about how the literal meaning of the word ("look around") relates to the way this word is frequently used. And, when you read Chapter 1, do you think it would have been easier to understand and remember the meaning of Wundt's research method, *introspection,* if you had thought about the *spect* part of the word? Probably so.

A strong vocabulary based on root words and prefixes and suffixes will yield the word power that will "literally" profit you in many ways. If you put this Apply It into practice, you will be able to build a powerful vocabulary.

Summary *and* Review

Imagery, Concepts, and Reasoning p. 232

How do we form images, and how does imagery help us think? p. 233

Imagery is the mental representation of sensory experiences—visual, auditory, gustatory, motor, olfactory, or tactile. The mental images are constructed one part at a time. Imagery is helpful for learning new skills and for practicing those we already know.

How do formal and natural concepts differ? p. 234

A concept is a mental category that represents a class or group of objects, people, organizations, events, situations, or relations that share common characteristics or attributes. A formal concept is one that is clearly defined by a set of rules, a formal definition, or a classification system. A natural concept is formed on the basis of everyday perceptions and experiences and can be somewhat "fuzzy."

What is the difference between deductive and inductive reasoning? p. 236

Deductive reasoning involves reasoning from the general to the specific, or drawing particular conclusions from general principles. In inductive reasoning, general conclusions are drawn from particular facts or individual cases.

Decision Making p. 239

How are the additive strategy and elimination by aspects used in decision making? p. 239

In the additive strategy for decision making, each alternative is rated on each important factor affecting the decision and the alternative with the highest overall rating is chosen. Elimination by aspects is most useful when a decision involves many alternatives and multiple factors. With this approach, the multiple factors are ordered according to their importance, and alternatives that do not satisfy the ordered factors are eliminated until one alternative remains.

What are the strengths and weaknesses of the availability and representativeness heuristics? p. 239

The availability heuristic is a rule of thumb that says that the probability of an event or the importance assigned to it is based on its availability in memory, that is, the ease with which the information comes to mind. The representativeness heuristic is a thinking strategy that assesses how closely a new object or situation matches an existing prototype of that object or situation. Both of these strategies help us quickly make probability assumptions. However, errors in judgment can cause either strategy to result in an inappropriate decision.

How does framing help with decision making? p. 240

Framing is the way information is presented so as to emphasize either a potential gain or a potential loss as the outcome of a decision based on that information.

Problem Solving p. 242

What are three basic approaches to problem solving, and how do they differ? p. 242

Three basic approaches to problem solving are trial and error, algorithms, and heuristics. Trial and error can be time-consuming, but may be the most appropriate strategy when you have little or no knowledge relevant to the problem. Algorithms are systematic, step-by-step procedures that always lead to correct answers, but there are many problems for which there is no algorithm. Applying heuristic strategies to problems can lead to speedy solutions. However, we may not always choose the most appropriate heuristic.

How do functional fixedness and mental set impede problem solving? p. 243

Functional fixedness, or the tendency to view objects only in terms of their customary functions, results in a failure to use the objects in novel ways to solve problems. Mental set is the tendency to apply a familiar strategy that was successful in the past to solve new problems, even though it may not be appropriate for their special requirements.

High-Tech Applications of Cognition p. 245

In what ways does artificial intelligence resemble human cognition? p. 245

Artificial intelligence refers to the programming of computer systems to simulate human thinking in solving problems and in making judgments and decisions. With such programming, computers can efficiently apply expert knowledge to problems. Moreover, computers can access data more rapidly and comprehensively than many human experts.

How do scientists use artificial neural networks? p. 246

Artificial neural networks (ANNs) are used to simulate human thinking. These networks can effectively process information like human experts and learn from experience. One ANN has helped scientists learn more about speech recognition.

What are some practical applications of robotics? p. 246

Robotics have been used to perform tasks too dangerous for humans, to assist in difficult surgeries, to help stroke patients exercise, and to improve prostheses for individuals who have lost a limb.

Language p. 248

What are the necessary components of any language? p. 248

The components of any language are (1) phonemes, the smallest units of sound in a spoken language; (2) morphemes, the smallest units of meaning; (3) syntax, the aspect of grammar that specifies the rules for arranging and combining words to form phrases and sentences; (4) semantics, the meaning derived from phonemes, morphemes, and sentences; and (5) pragmatics, which includes characteristics such as intonation and gestures that indicate the social meaning of utterances.

What areas of the brain are involved in producing and comprehending language? p. 249

The tasks of reading aloud words and nonwords have been found to elicit different patterns of activity in the left frontal and temporal lobes of English and Italian speakers. Broca's area is important in the processing of grammatical errors as well as in speech production. Wernicke's area and some parts of the cerebellum appear to be involved in other grammar processing.

How does animal communication differ from that of humans? p. 250

Chimpanzees' communication with humans uses sign language or symbols and consists of constructions strung together rather than actual sentences.

In what ways does thinking influence language? p. 252

In general, thinking has a greater influence on language than vice versa. Whorf's linguistic relativity hypothesis has not been supported by research. However, words referring to gender (e.g., *policeman*) do cause hearers and readers to infer that the individual to whom the term refers is male. Thus, language does sometimes influence thinking.

What is the best time in life to learn a second language, and why? p. 253

The best time to learn a second language is childhood. Those who learn a second language when they are younger than 10 or 11 usually speak it without an accent and reach a higher level of proficiency than do those who are older when they learn another language.

Key Terms

additive strategy, p. 239
algorithm, p. 242
analogy heuristic, p. 243
artificial intelligence (AI), p. 245
artificial neural networks (ANNs), p. 246
availability heuristic, p. 239
cognition, p. 232
concept, p. 234
decision making, p. 239
deductive reasoning, p. 236
deep structure, p. 249
elimination by aspects, p. 239
exemplars, p. 235
expert systems, p. 245
formal concept, p. 234
framing, p. 240
functional fixedness, p. 243
heuristic, p. 239
imagery, p. 233
inductive reasoning, p. 237
language, p. 248
linguistic relativity hypothesis, p. 252
means-end analysis, p. 243
mental set, p. 244
morphemes, p. 248
natural concept, p. 234
phonemes, p. 248
pragmatics, p. 249
problem solving, p. 242
prototype, p. 235
psycholinguistics, p. 248
reasoning, p. 236
representativeness heuristic, p. 240
robotics, p. 246
semantics, p. 249
surface structure, p. 249
syllogism, p. 236
syntax, p. 249
trial and error, p. 242
working backwards, p. 242

chapter 8

Intelligence and Creativity

The Nature of Intelligence

- *What factors underlie intelligence, according to Spearman and Thurstone?*
- *What types of intelligence did Gardner and Sternberg identify?*

Measuring Intelligence

- *What is Binet's major contribution to intelligence testing?*
- *How did the work of Terman and Wechsler influence intelligence testing in the United States?*
- *Why are reliability, validity, and standardization important in intelligence testing?*

The Range of Intelligence

- *What does the term "bell curve" mean when applied to IQ test scores?*
- *According to the Terman study, how do the gifted differ from the general population?*
- *What two criteria must a person meet to be classified as mentally retarded?*
- *What is the relationship between intelligence and the efficiency and speed of neural processing?*

The IQ Controversy

- *Of what are intelligence tests good predictors?*
- *What are some abuses of intelligence tests?*
- *What is the nature–nurture controversy regarding intelligence, and how do twin studies support the view that intelligence is inherited?*
- *What are Jensen's and Herrnstein and Murray's controversial views on race and IQ?*
- *What kinds of evidence suggest that IQ is changeable rather than fixed?*
- *How might parental expectations and teaching methods influence scores on standardized tests?*

Emotional Intelligence

- *What are the personal components of emotional intelligence?*
- *What are the interpersonal components of emotional intelligence?*

Creativity

- *What are the four stages in the creative problem-solving process?*
- *How does creative thinking differ from other forms of cognition?*
- *What are some tests that have been used to measure creativity?*
- *What are some characteristics of creative people?*
- *How do savants differ from other people?*

Who has the highest IQ score ever recorded on an intelligence test?

The name of Albert Einstein may quickly come to mind and perhaps a host of other great thinkers of the past—perhaps mostly men. However, the person with the highest IQ score ever recorded happens to be a woman.

Marilyn Mach, born in St. Louis, Missouri, in 1946, scored an amazing 230 on the Stanford-Binet IQ test when she was a 10-year-old elementary school student. How high is a 230 IQ? The average Stanford-Binet IQ score is set at 100, and a score of 116—only about half as high as Mach's lofty score—places a person in the top 16% of the population. Not only does Mach have no peer when it comes to measured intelligence, she doesn't even have a competitor. Her score is nearly 30 points higher than that of her nearest rival.

Descended from the Austrian philosopher and physicist Ernst Mach, who did pioneering work in the physics of sound (Mach 1, Mach 2), Marilyn Mach added her mother's birth name as an adult and became known as Marilyn Mach vos Savant. She completed about 2 years of college courses but has no college degree. Her primary intellectual interest is creative writing, and she has written 12 books and 3 plays. Her first published work was the *Omni IQ Quiz Contest*. Mach lives with her husband in New York, where she writes the "Ask Marilyn" column for *Parade* magazine, lectures on intelligence, and pursues various other interests.

Now consider Dr. Robert Jarvik, the world-famous inventor of the Jarvik artificial heart. Dr. Jarvik combined his medical knowledge and his mechanical genius to produce the world's first functioning artificial heart. But his path wasn't easy. Unlike Marilyn Mach vos Savant, Jarvik was a poor test taker. In fact, he scored too low on intelligence and admissions tests to be admitted to any medical school in the United States. Eventually, despite his low test scores, he was accepted by a medical school in Italy, where he completed his studies and received his M.D. degree. Then, he returned to practice in the United States and made his contribution to medical science—one that kept alive many gravely ill heart patients until a suitable heart transplant could be performed.

How difficult do you think it would be for Dr. Jarvik to improve his IQ test score? Well, he might ask his wife, Marilyn Mach vos Savant-Jarvik, for some help with that.

Like Dr. Jarvik, many highly creative individuals have tested poorly in school. Some of the most prominent are the famous American inventor Thomas A. Edison; Winston Churchill, whose teachers thought he was mentally limited; and even the great Albert Einstein, who was labeled a dunce in math.

In this chapter, we explore cognitive and emotional intelligence and creativity. You will learn about the nature of intelligence and how it is measured. Where does human intelligence come from—genes, experiences provided by the environment, or both? We will look at the extremes in intelligence—the mentally gifted and the mentally retarded. We will also consider how creative people think.

■ **intelligence**
An individual's ability to understand complex ideas, to adapt effectively to the environment, to learn from experience, to engage in various forms of reasoning, and to overcome obstacles through mental effort.

First, let's ask the most obvious question: What is intelligence? A task force of experts from the American Psychological Association (APA) defined **intelligence** as possessing several basic facets: an individual's "ability to understand complex ideas, … to adapt effectively to the environment, … to learn from experience, to engage in various forms of reasoning, and to overcome obstacles by taking thought" (Neisser et al., 1996, p. 77). As you'll learn in this chapter, though, there's more to intelligence than any simple definition can encompass.

The Nature of Intelligence

The Search for Factors Underlying Intelligence

Is intelligence a single trait or capability, or is it many capabilities unrelated to each other? Stop and think about how you would respond to this question before reading about the diverse answers psychologists have proposed over the past century or so.

What factors underlie intelligence, according to Spearman and Thurstone?

Spearman and General Intelligence Traditionally, intelligence has been considered as more or less a single entity. This notion was first suggested by English psychologist Charles Spearman (1863–1945), who observed that people who are good at one type of thinking or cognition tend to do well at other types as well. In other words, they tend to be generally intelligent. Spearman (1927) came to believe that intelligence is composed of a general ability, or ***g* factor**, which underlies all intellectual functions.

Spearman arrived at his *g* factor theory when he found positive relationships among scores on the subtests of intelligence tests. He theorized that this positive relationship meant that the tests were measuring something in common—that general ability was being assessed to some degree in all of them. This, said Spearman, was evidence of general intelligence, the *g* factor.

But some of the correlations between subtests were much higher than others. Therefore, some other abilities in addition to the *g* factor must be being assessed by some subtests. Spearman named these other abilities *s factors*, for specific abilities. Spearman concluded that intelligence tests measure a person's *g* factor, or general intelligence, and a number of *s* factors, or specific intellectual abilities. Spearman's influence can be seen in those intelligence tests, such as the Stanford-Binet, that yield one IQ score to indicate the level of general intelligence.

Spearman's theory continues to be influential, according to some leading researchers in the field of intelligence. For example, Robert Plomin (1999) asserts that the *g* factor is among the most valid and reliable measures of intelligence, better than other measures in predicting success in social, educational, and occupational endeavors.

Where in the brain might processing related to high general intelligence be located? It was expected that tasks related to general intelligence would show a broad, diffuse pattern of brain function. But, instead, brain-imaging studies show that general intelligence tasks, whether they involve verbal or perceptual skills or geometry, are associated with specific areas of the frontal cortex in one or both hemispheres (Duncan et al., 2000).

■ ***g* factor**
Spearman's term for a general ability that underlies all intellectual functions.

■ **primary mental abilities**
According to Thurstone, seven relatively distinct abilities that, singly or in combination, are involved in all intellectual activities.

Thurstone's Primary Mental Abilities Another early researcher, Louis L. Thurstone (1938), rejected Spearman's notion of a general intellectual ability, or *g* factor. After analyzing the scores of many research participants on 56 separate tests, Thurstone identified seven **primary mental abilities**: verbal comprehension, numerical ability, spatial relations, perceptual speed, word fluency, memory, and reasoning. He maintained that all intellectual activities involve one or more of these primary mental abilities. Thurstone believed that a single IQ score obscures more than it reveals and suggested that a profile showing relative strengths and weaknesses on the seven primary abilities would provide a more accurate picture of a person's mental ability. With his wife, Thelma G. Thurstone, he developed the Primary Mental Abilities Tests to measure these seven abilities.

Intelligence: More Than One Type?

What types of intelligence did Gardner and Sternberg identify?

Some theorists, instead of searching for the factors that underlie intelligence, propose that different types of intelligence exist. Two such modern theorists are Howard Gardner and Robert Sternberg.

These soccer players would probably get high scores on a measure of the ability Gardner calls *bodily-kinesthetic intelligence.*

Gardner's Theory of Multiple Intelligences Harvard psychologist Howard Gardner (1983; Gardner & Hatch, 1989) also denies the existence of a *g* factor. Instead, he proposes eight independent forms of intelligence, or *frames of mind*, as illustrated in Figure 8.1. The eight frames of mind are linguistic, logical-mathematical, spatial, bodily-kinesthetic, musical, interpersonal, intrapersonal, and naturalistic.

Gardner (1983) first developed his theory by studying patients with different types of brain damage that affect some forms of intelligence but leave others intact. He also studied reports of people with *savant syndrome*, who show a combination of mental retardation and unusual talent or ability. (You'll read more about this phenomenon later in this chapter.) Finally, Gardner considered how various abilities and skills have been valued differently in other cultures and periods of history.

Perhaps the most controversial aspect of Gardner's theory is his view that all forms of intelligence are of equal importance. In fact, different cultures assign varying degrees of importance to the types of intelligence. For example, linguistic and logical-mathematical intelligences are valued most in the United States and other Western cultures; bodily-kinesthetic intelligence is more highly prized in cultures that depend on hunting for survival.

Gardner's theory "has enjoyed wide popularity, especially among educators, but [his] ideas are based more on reasoning and intuition than on the results of empirical research studies" (Aiken, 1997, p. 196). Gardner's critics doubt that all

FIGURE 8.1 Gardner's Eight Frames of Mind

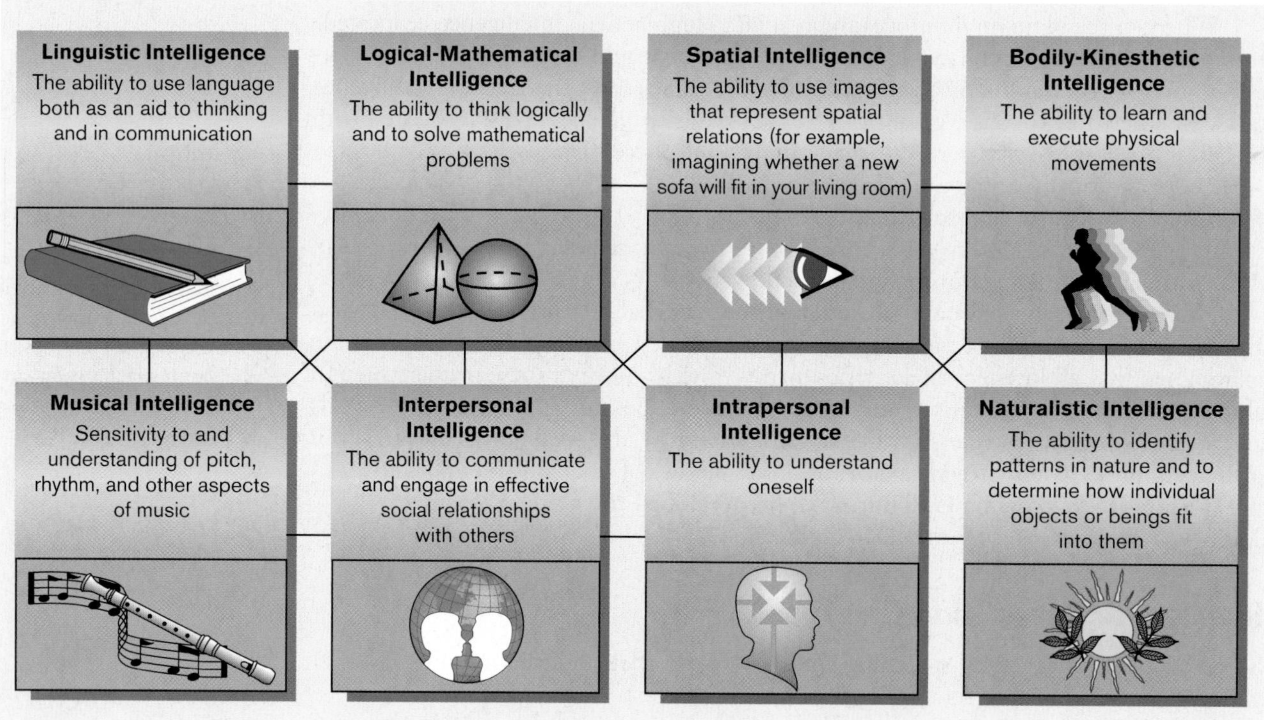
Linguistic Intelligence
The ability to use language both as an aid to thinking and in communication
Logical-Mathematical Intelligence
The ability to think logically and to solve mathematical problems
Spatial Intelligence
The ability to use images that represent spatial relations (for example, imagining whether a new sofa will fit in your living room)
Bodily-Kinesthetic Intelligence
The ability to learn and execute physical movements
Musical Intelligence
Sensitivity to and understanding of pitch, rhythm, and other aspects of music
Interpersonal Intelligence
The ability to communicate and engage in effective social relationships with others
Intrapersonal Intelligence
The ability to understand oneself
Naturalistic Intelligence
The ability to identify patterns in nature and to determine how individual objects or beings fit into them

the forms of intelligence he proposes are of equal value in education and in life. Robert Sternberg (1985b) claims that "the multiple intelligences might better be referred to as multiple talents" (p. 1114). He asks whether an adult who is tone-deaf and has no sense of rhythm can be considered mentally limited in the same way as one who has never developed any verbal skills. In addition to differing with Gardner, Sternberg (2000) is also critical of heavy reliance on Spearman's *g* factor for measuring intelligence. But Sternberg is not merely a critic; he has developed his own theory of intelligence.

triarchic theory of intelligence Sternberg's theory that there are three types of intelligence—componential (analytical), experiential (creative), and contextual (practical).

Sternberg's Triarchic Theory of Intelligence Robert Sternberg (1985a; 1986a) has formulated a **triarchic theory of intelligence**, which proposes that there are three types of intelligence (see Figure 8.2). The first type, *componential intelligence*, refers to the mental abilities most closely related to success on conventional IQ and achievement tests. Sternberg claims that traditional IQ tests measure only componential, or analytical, intelligence.

The second type, *experiential intelligence*, is reflected in creative thinking and problem solving. People with high experiential intelligence are able to solve novel problems and deal with unusual and unexpected challenges. Another aspect of experiential intelligence is finding creative ways to perform common daily tasks more efficiently and effectively.

The third type, *contextual intelligence*, or practical intelligence, might be equated with common sense or "street smarts." People with high contextual intelligence are survivors, who capitalize on their strengths and compensate for their weaknesses. They either adapt well to their environment, change the environment so that they can succeed, or, if necessary, find a new environment.

Sternberg and others (1995, 2000) argue that IQ-test performance and real-world success are based on two different types of knowledge: *formal academic knowledge*, or the knowledge we acquire in school, and *tacit knowledge*. Unlike formal academic

FIGURE 8.2 Sternberg's Triarchic Theory of Intelligence

According to Sternberg, there are three types of intelligence: componential, experiential, and contextual.

Componential Intelligence
Mental abilities most closely related to success on traditional IQ and achievement tests

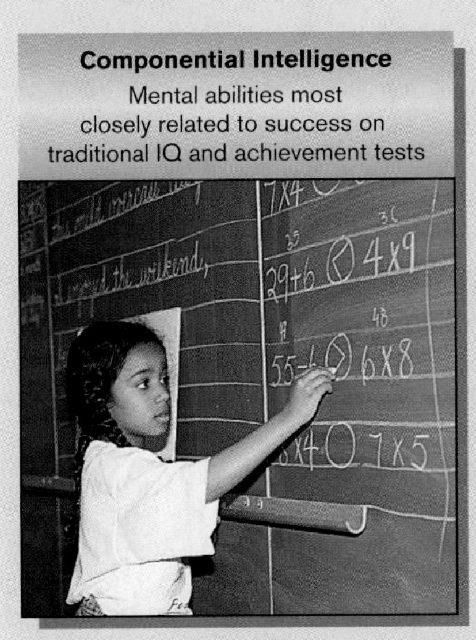

Experiential Intelligence
Creative thinking and problem solving

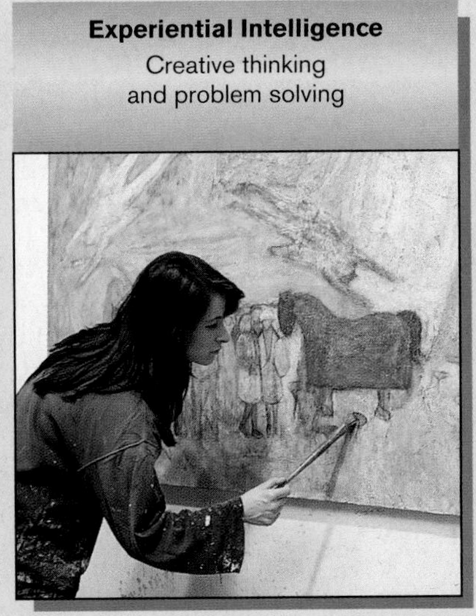

Contextual Intelligence
Practical intelligence or "street smarts"

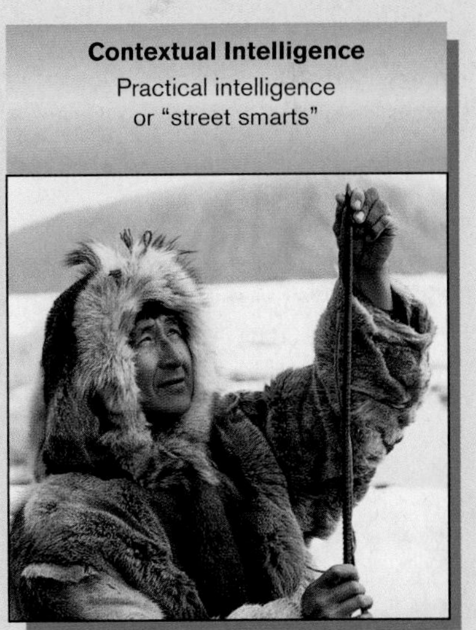

REVIEW and REFLECT 8.1

Theories of Intelligence

THEORY	DESCRIPTION
Spearman's *g* factor	Intelligence consists of a single factor known as *g*, which represents a general intellectual ability.
Thurstone's primary mental abilities	Intelligence has seven separate components: verbal comprehension, numerical ability, spatial relations, perceptual speed, word fluency, memory, and reasoning.
Gardner's frames of mind	There are eight independent forms of intelligence: linguistic, logical-mathematical, spatial, bodily-kinesthetic, musical, interpersonal, intrapersonal, and naturalistic.
Sternberg's triarchic theory	There are three types of intelligence: componential, experiential, and contextual.

Want to be sure you've fully absorbed the material in this chapter? Visit **www.ablongman.com/wood5e** for access to free practice tests, flashcards, interactive activities, and links developed specifically to help you succeed in psychology.

knowledge, tacit knowledge is action-oriented and is acquired without direct help from others. According to Sternberg, tacit knowledge is more important to successful real-world performance. Research supports Sternberg's contention that the two forms of knowledge are different (Taub et al., 2001). However, investigators have found that measures of formal academic knowledge, such as traditional IQ tests, better predict real-world success than do Sternberg's tests of practical intelligence. Sternberg and those who agree with him contend that imperfections in the tests themselves are responsible for such results. Thus, in recent years, Sternberg and his colleagues have focused on developing a reliable and valid intelligence test that measures each of the three hypothesized types of intelligence (Sternberg et al., 2001).

Sternberg's ideas have become popular among educators. Several studies have shown that teaching methods designed to tap into all three types of intelligence can be effective with students who are low achievers (Grigorenko et al., 2002). In such instruction, teachers emphasize the practical relevance of formal academic knowledge and help students apply it to real-world problems.

Review and Reflect 8.1 summarizes the various theories of intelligence.

Remember It 8.1

1. According to Spearman, different kinds of cognitive tasks may appear to use different abilities, but they are all tied to a single type of intelligence called the ____________ .
2. Thurstone proposed seven different kinds of intelligence he called ____________ .
3. The theory proposing eight distinct types of intellectual abilities was developed by ____________ .
4. Match each of Sternberg's three types of intelligence with its definition:

___ (1) experiential intelligence	a. practical intelligence, or "street smarts"
___ (2) componential intelligence	b. creative thinking and problem solving
___ (3) contextual intelligence	c. success on IQ and achievement tests

ANSWERS: 1. *g* factor; 2. primary mental abilities; 3. Gardner; 4. (1) b, (2) c, (3) a

Measuring Intelligence

Binet and the First Successful Intelligence Test

What is Binet's major contribution to intelligence testing?

Have you ever seen films depicting early attempts to construct a flying machine? Looking back, you might wonder why anyone ever believed some of those designs would work. Some of the early intelligence tests might appear to be just as far-fetched. For instance, one early researcher, Franz Gall (1758–1828), proposed that measurements of the size and shape of an individual's skull could be used to estimate intelligence. As you might expect, Gall's attempt to correlate the physical characteristics of people's skulls with their intellectual functioning failed miserably.

Like airplanes, today's intelligence tests have grown from humble, often stumbling, beginnings to become a prominent feature of modern life. In fact, many people regard intelligence testing as the most useful contribution of psychological science to society (Benson, 2003). Even those who would argue that intelligence tests do not deserve such high praise would grant that they are one of psychology's greatest success stories.

Most of the early intelligence tests, like Gall's skull measurements, were developed to test the hypothesis that intelligence is a physiologically based genetic trait. Interestingly, though, the first successful effort to measure intelligence resulted not from a theoretical approach, but as a practical means of solving a problem in the schools of France. At the very beginning of the 20th century, the Ministry of Public Instruction in Paris was struggling with the problem of trying to find some objective means of sorting out children whose intelligence was too low for them to profit from regular classroom instruction. The ministry wanted to ensure that average or brighter children would not be wrongly assigned to special classes and that children of limited ability would not be subjected to the regular program of instruction. In 1903, a commission was formed to study the problem, and one of its members was French psychologist Alfred Binet (1857–1911).

With the help of his colleague, psychiatrist Theodore Simon, Binet began testing the schoolchildren of Paris in 1904. The two men used a wide variety of tests, and they kept only those items on which the performance of older and younger children clearly differed. Binet and Simon published their intelligence scale in 1905 and revised it in 1908 and again in 1911. The Binet-Simon Intelligence Scale was an immediate success.

Test items on the scale were ordered according to difficulty, with the easiest item first and each succeeding item becoming more difficult (see Table 8.1, on page 268). Children went as far as they could, and then their progress was compared with that of other children of the same age. A child with the mental ability of a normal 5-year-old could be said to have a mental age of 5. Binet established the concept that mental retardation and mental superiority are a function of the difference between chronological age (actual age in years) and mental age. An 8-year-old with a mental age of 8 is normal or average. An 8-year-old with a mental age of 5 is mentally deficient; an 8-year-old with a mental age of 11 is mentally superior.

Binet believed that children whose mental age was 2 years below their chronological age were retarded and should be placed in special education classes. But there was a flaw in his thinking. A 4-year-old with a mental age of 2 is far more retarded than a 12-year-old with a mental age of 10. How could a similar degree of retardation be expressed for individuals of different ages? German psychologist William Stern (1914) provided an answer. In 1912, he devised a simple formula for calculating an index of intelligence—the *intelligence quotient*. He divided a child's mental age by his or her chronological age to obtain this index.

TABLE 8.1 Subtests of the Binet-Simon Intelligence Scale

SUBTEST	EXAMINEE MUST . . .
1. Visual fixation	Visually track the movement of a flame (lighted match).
2. Tactile grasp	Grasp an object that touches the hand.
3. Visual grasp	Grasp an object within the visual field.
4. Food recognition	Make distinctions between food and nonfood objects.
5. Search for food	Uncover or unwrap a food item.
6. Response to instructions	Follow simple instructions and imitate simple gestures.
7. Body part names	Point to body parts when named.
8. Picture names	Point to pictures of objects (e.g., a broom) when named.
9. Object naming	Produce names of pictured objects (e.g., dog).
10. Length comparison	Identify which of two lines is longer.
11. Number repetition	Repeat a series of random numbers.
12. Weight comparison	Identify which of two objects is heavier.
13. Suggestibility	Resist suggestions to name nonpresent objects (e.g., the examiner asks, "Which of these objects is a button?" when no button is present).
14. Verbal definitions	State definitions for objects such as houses and eating utensils.
15. Sentence repetition	Repeat 15-word sentences.
16. Object comparisons	Explain how similar objects (e.g., paper and cardboard) differ.
17. Picture memory	Recall the names of 13 pictured items viewed for 30 seconds each.
18. Design memory	Draw a design from memory after viewing it for 10 seconds.
19. Number repetition	Repeat another series of random numbers.
20. Object comparisons	Explain how objects are similar (e.g., stop sign and blood are the same color).
21. Length comparison	Identify which of two lines is longer (differs from subtest 10 in that the lines are much closer in length).
22. Weight ordering	Order five objects from heaviest to least heavy.
23. Gap in weights	Identify which of the ordered weights from subtest 22 has been removed.
24. Rhyme exercise	Supply rhymes for words.
25. Verbal gaps	Fill in the blanks in sentences (e.g., "The crow _____ his feathers with his beak").
26. Sentence synthesis	Combine three words supplied by the examiner to form a sentence.
27. Abstract question	Answer a question such as "When you need advice, what should you do?"
28. Clock hands reversal	State the time resulting from a reversal of the short and long hands of a clock (e.g., if the long and short hands currently indicate 2:45, the time would be 9:10 if they were reversed).
29. Paper cutting	Correctly name a figure resulting from a cutout in a folded piece of paper (e.g., if a piece of paper is folded in half and a triangle is cut out with the fold as one side of the triangle, what figure will appear when the paper is unfolded?).
30. Abstract definitions	Explain the difference between concepts such as esteem and affection.

Source: Binet (1905).

Intelligence Testing in the United States

As we have seen, intelligence testing began in Europe. However, two American psychologists, Lewis Terman and David Wechsler, are credited with developing the two best-known measures of intelligence.

How did the work of Terman and Wechsler influence intelligence testing in the United States?

The Stanford-Binet Intelligence Scale Lewis M. Terman, a psychology professor at Stanford University, published a thorough revision of the Binet-Simon scale in 1916. Terman revised and adapted the items for American children, added new items, and established new **norms**—standards based on the test scores of a large number of individuals and used as bases for comparison. Within 2½ years, 4 million children had taken Terman's revision, known as the **Stanford-Binet Intelligence Scale**. It was the first test to make use of Stern's formula for the intelligence quotient, which Terman improved by multiplying the result by 100 to eliminate the decimal. He also introduced the abbreviation IQ. Here is Terman's formula for the **intelligence quotient (IQ),** along with a few examples:

$$(\text{Mental Age} \div \text{Chronological Age}) \times 100 = \text{IQ}$$

A 10-year-old with a mental age of 12: $(12 \div 10) \times 100 = 120$

A 6-year-old with a mental age of 3: $(3 \div 6) \times 100 = 50$

A 12-year-old with a mental age of 12: $(12 \div 12) \times 100 = 100$

The highly regarded Stanford-Binet Intelligence Scale is an individually administered IQ test for those aged 2 to 23. It contains four subscales: verbal reasoning, quantitative reasoning, abstract visual reasoning, and short-term memory. An overall IQ score is derived from scores on the four subscales, and the test scores correlate well with achievement test scores (Laurent et al., 1992).

The Wechsler Intelligence Tests Intelligence testing became increasingly popular in the United States in the 1920s and 1930s, but it quickly became obvious that the Stanford-Binet Intelligence Scale was not useful for testing adults. The original IQ formula could not be applied to adults, because at a certain age people achieve maturity in intelligence. According to the original IQ formula, a 40-year-old with the same IQ test score as the average 20-year-old would be considered mentally retarded, with an IQ of only 50. Obviously, something was wrong with the formula when applied to populations of all ages.

Today, psychologists still use IQ scores for adults, but now such a score is a **deviation score,** derived by comparing an individual's score with the scores of others of the same age on whom the intelligence test was normed. The deviation score is a contribution of David Wechsler, another pioneer in mental testing. In 1939, Wechsler developed the first successful individual intelligence test for adults, designed for those age 16 and older. His original test has been revised, restandardized, and renamed the **Wechsler Adult Intelligence Scale (WAIS-III),** and it is one of the most widely used psychological tests. The test contains both verbal and performance (nonverbal) subtests, which yield separate verbal and performance IQ scores as well as an overall IQ score. This represents a departure from the Stanford-Binet scale, which yields a single IQ score.

Wechsler also published the Wechsler Intelligence Scale for Children (WISC-III) and the Wechsler Preschool and Primary Scale of Intelligence (WPPSI), which is normed for children aged 4 to 6½. Table 8.2 (on page 270) describes the types of tasks found on the Wechsler Intelligence Scale for Children.

One advantage of the Wechsler scales is their ability to identify intellectual strengths in nonverbal as well as verbal areas. Wechsler also believed that differences in a person's scores on the various verbal and performance subtests could be used for diagnostic purposes. In fact, the Wechsler Memory Scale (WMS-R) is frequently used to assess memory function in adults and to evaluate patients with epilepsy (Cañizares et al., 2000).

■ **norms**
Standards based on the test scores of a large number of individuals and used as bases of comparison for other test takers.

■ **Stanford-Binet Intelligence Scale**
An individually administered IQ test for those aged 2 to 23; Terman's revision of the Binet-Simon scale.

■ **intelligence quotient (IQ)**
An index of intelligence originally derived by dividing mental age by chronological age and then multiplying by 100; now derived by comparing an individual's score with the scores of others of the same age.

■ **deviation score**
An IQ test score calculated by comparing an individual's score with the scores of others of the same age.

■ **Wechsler Adult Intelligence Scale (WAIS-III)**
An individual intelligence test for adults that yields separate verbal and performance (nonverbal) IQ scores as well as an overall IQ score.

TABLE 8.2 Typical Subtests on the Wechsler Intelligence Scale for Children (WISC-III)

VERBAL SUBTEST	SAMPLE ITEM	PERFORMANCE SUBTEST	SAMPLE ITEM
Information	How many wings does a bird have?	Picture arrangement	Arrange a series of cartoon panels to make a meaningful story.
Digit span	Repeat from memory a series of digits, such as 3 1 0 6 7 4 2 5, after hearing it once.	Picture completion	What is missing from these pictures?
General comprehension	What is the advantage of keeping money in a bank?	Block design	Copy designs using blocks
Arithmetic	If 2 apples cost 15¢, what will be the cost of a dozen apples?		
Similarities	In what way are a lion and a tiger alike?		
Vocabulary	This test consists simply of asking, "What is a ________?" or "What does ________ mean?" The words cover a wide range of difficulty or familiarity.	Object assembly	Put together a jigsaw puzzle.
		Digit symbol	Fill in the missing symbols:

1	2	3	4
X	III	I	O

3	4	1	3	4	2	1	2

Group Intelligence Tests Administering individual intelligence tests such as the Stanford-Binet and Wechsler scales is expensive and time-consuming. The tests must be given to one person at a time by a qualified professional. For testing large numbers of people in a short period of time on a limited budget, group intelligence tests are the answer. Group intelligence tests—such as the California Test of Mental Maturity, the Cognitive Abilities Test, and the Otis-Lennon Mental Ability Test—are widely used.

Why are reliability, validity, and standardization important in intelligence testing?

Reliability, Validity, and Standardization

If your watch gains 5 or 6 minutes one day and loses 3 or 4 minutes the next day, would you rely on it to get you to class on time? Like a watch, an intelligence test must have **reliability**; that is, the test must consistently yield nearly the same score when the same people are tested and then retested with it or an alternative form of it. The higher the correlation between the test and retest scores, the more reliable the test. A correlation coefficient of 1.0 would indicate perfect reliability. Most widely used tests, such as the Stanford-Binet and Wechsler scales and the Scholastic Assessment Test (SAT), boast high reliabilities, with correlations of about .90. Some researchers, however, have stated that the index scores for WISC-III should be interpreted cautiously: When used with children who are not members of the mainstream cultural group on which the tests were normed, the scores have poor reliability (Caruso & Cliff, 2000).

Tests can be highly reliable but worthless if they are not valid. **Validity** is the ability of a test to measure what it is intended to measure. For example, a thermometer is a valid instrument for measuring temperature; a bathroom scale is valid for measuring weight. But no matter how reliable your bathroom scale is, it will not take your temperature—it is valid only for weighing. The validity of some of the WISC-III subtests as social intelligence measures has been questioned. Some researchers have claimed that the picture arrangement subtest is unrelated to social functioning and that the general comprehension subtest has limited clinical significance when used with children who have attention-deficit/hyperactivity disorder (ADHD) (Beebe et al., 2000).

Aptitude tests are designed to predict a person's achievement or performance at some future time. Selecting students for admission to college or graduate schools is based partly on the predictive validity of aptitude tests such as the Scholastic Assessment Test (SAT), the American College Testing Program (ACT), and the Graduate Record Examination (GRE). How well do SAT scores predict success in college? Moderately, at best. The correlation between SAT scores and the grades of college freshmen is about .40 (Linn, 1982).

Once a test is shown to have reliability and validity, the next requirement is **standardization**. There must be standard procedures for administering and scoring the test. Exactly the same directions must be given, whether written or oral, and the same amount of time must be allowed for every test taker. Even more important, standardization means establishing norms by which all scores are interpreted. A test is standardized by administering it to a large sample of individuals representative of those who will be taking the test in the future. The group's scores are analyzed, and then the average score, standard deviation, percentile rankings, and other measures are computed. These comparative scores become the norms used as the standard against which all other scores on that test are interpreted.

After studying the performance of Black and White South African children on WISC-R (the predecessor of WISC-III), researchers claimed that the validity of such traditional tests is questionable for cultural groups other than those on which the tests were normed (Skuy et al., 2000). Test items that are valid in one cultural context may lose their validity in a different context (Knowles & Condon, 2000). Moreover, intelligence tests must undergo continuous revision to maintain their validity. The wording of test items is critical, especially since some items may be as old or older than the grandparents of today's young test takers (Strauss et al., 2000). Also, the nature of the U.S. population is changing rapidly. Thus, when new tests are normed and standardized or when existing tests are renormed, the increasing diversity of the test takers must be considered. Researchers Okazaki and Sue (2000) point out that Asian Americans, in particular, have been severely underrepresented in the validation studies of the Wechsler scales.

■ reliability
The ability of a test to yield nearly the same score when the same people are tested and then retested on the same test or an alternative form of the test.

■ validity
The ability of a test to measure what it is intended to measure.

■ aptitude test
A test designed to predict a person's achievement or performance at some future time.

■ standardization
The process of establishing both norms for interpreting scores on a test and standard procedures for administering the test.

Remember It 8.2

1. The first successful attempt to measure intelligence was made by ________ .
2. According to Stern's formula, as revised by Terman, the IQ of a child with a mental age of 12 and a chronological age of 8 is ________ .
3. The ________ and ________ intelligence tests must be administered individually to test takers.
4. The first intelligence test for adults was developed by ________ .
5. A test that measures what it claims to measure has ________ .
6. A test that gives consistent results shows ________ .

ANSWERS: 1. Binet; 2. 150; 3. Stanford-Binet, Wechsler; 4. Wechsler; 5. validity; 6. reliability

The Range of Intelligence

When we refer to a person as "smart," what we usually mean is that she is smart*er* than most people. In other words, we have the idea that "smartness," or intelligence, varies in quantity from one person to another. What can IQ test scores reveal about how much variation there is in intelligence? And is there a physiological basis for such variations?

The Bell Curve

What does the term "bell curve" mean when applied to IQ test scores?

You may have heard of a bell curve and wondered just exactly what it is. When large populations are measured on intelligence or on physical characteristics, such as height or blood pressure, a graph of the frequencies of all the test scores or results usually conforms to a bell-shaped distribution known as the *normal curve*, or sometimes as the *bell curve*. The majority of the scores cluster around the mean (average). The more the scores deviate, or the farther away they are, from the mean—either above or below—the fewer there are. And the curve is perfectly symmetrical, that is, there are just as many scores above as below the mean.

The average IQ test score for all people in the same age group is arbitrarily assigned an IQ score of 100. On the Wechsler intelligence tests, approximately 50% of the scores are in the average range, between 90 and 110. About 68% of the scores fall between 85 and 115, and about 95% fall between 70 and 130. About 2% of the scores are above 130, which is considered superior, and about 2% fall below 70, in the range of mental retardation (see Figure 8.3).

FIGURE 8.3 The Normal Curve

When a large number of IQ test scores are compiled and graphed, they are typically distributed in a normal (bell-shaped) curve. On the Wechsler scales, the average or mean IQ score is set at 100. About 68% of the scores fall between 15 IQ points (1 standard deviation) above and below 100 (from 85 to 115), and about 95.5% of the scores fall between 30 points (2 standard deviations) above and below 100 (from 70 to 130).

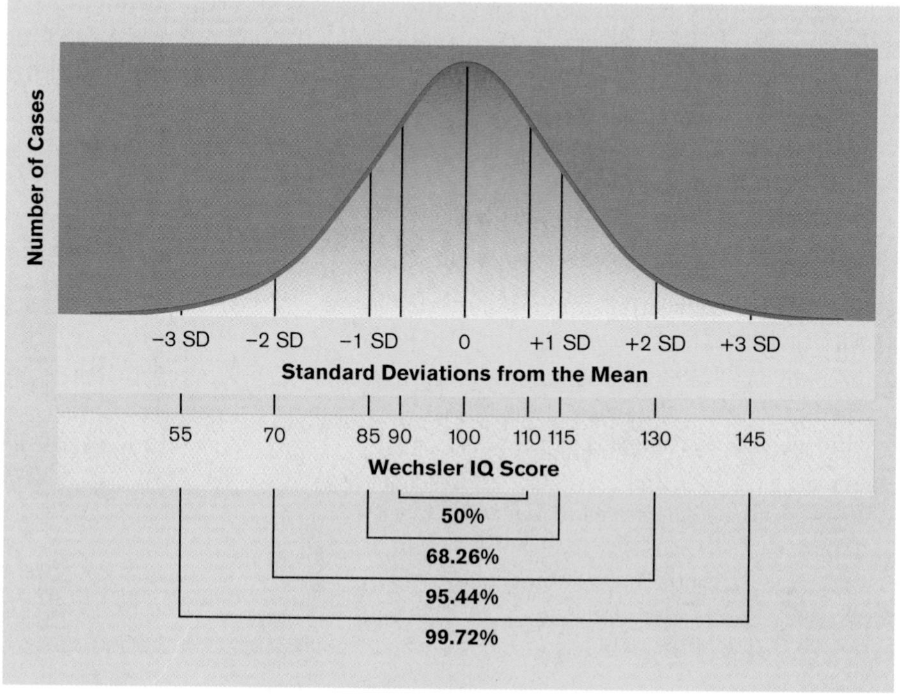

Giftedness

According to the Terman study, how do the gifted differ from the general population?

What is the meaning of variations in IQ scores? One way of examining this question is to study individuals whose scores lie at one extreme or the other of the bell curve.

Terman's Study of "Genius" In 1921, Lewis Terman (1925) launched a longitudinal study, now a classic, in which 1,528 students with "genius" IQs were measured at different ages throughout their lives. The participants, 857 males and 671 females, had an average IQ of 151, with Stanford-Binet scores ranging from 135 to 200. Terman assumed that the Stanford-Binet measured innate intelligence and that IQ was fixed at birth (Cravens, 1992).

Terman's early findings put an end to the myth that mentally superior people are more likely to be physically inferior. In fact, Terman's gifted participants excelled in almost all of the abilities he studied—intellectual, physical, emotional, moral, and social. Terman also exploded many other myths about the mentally gifted (Terman & Oden, 1947). For example, you may have heard the saying that there is a thin line between genius and madness. Actually, Terman's gifted group enjoyed better mental health than the general population. Also, you may have heard that mentally gifted people are long on "book sense" but short on "common sense." In reality, Terman's participants earned more academic degrees, achieved higher occupational status and higher salaries, were better adjusted both personally and socially, and were healthier than their less mentally gifted peers. However, most women at that time did not pursue careers outside of the home, so the findings related to occupational success applied primarily to the men. Terman (1925) concluded that "there is no law of compensation whereby the intellectual superiority of the gifted is offset by inferiorities along nonintellectual lines" (p. 16).

The Terman study continues today, with the surviving participants in their 80s or 90s. In a report on Terman's study, Shneidman (1989) states its basic findings—that "an unusual mind, a vigorous body, and a relatively well-adjusted personality are not at all incompatible" (p. 687).

Who Are the Gifted? Beginning in the early 1920s, the term *gifted* was used to describe the intellectually superior, those with IQs in the upper 2–3% of the U.S. population. Today, the term also includes both the exceptionally creative and those who excel in the visual or performing arts.

Traditionally, special programs for the gifted have involved either acceleration or enrichment. *Acceleration* enables students to progress at a rate that is consistent with their ability. Students may skip a grade, progress through subject matter at a faster rate, be granted advanced placement in college courses, or enter college early. *Enrichment* aims to broaden students' knowledge by giving them special courses in foreign language, music appreciation, and the like or by providing special experiences designed to foster advanced thinking skills.

mental retardation Subnormal intelligence reflected by an IQ below 70 and by adaptive functioning that is severely deficient for one's age.

Mental Retardation

What two criteria must a person meet to be classified as mentally retarded?

At the opposite end of the bell curve from the intellectually gifted are the 2% of the U.S. population whose IQ scores place them in the range of **mental retardation**. Individuals are not classified as mentally retarded unless (1) their IQ score is below 70 and (2) they have a severe deficiency in everyday adaptive functioning—the ability to care for themselves and relate to others (Grossman, 1983). Degrees of retardation range from mild to profound. Individuals with IQs ranging from 55 to 70 are considered mildly retarded; from 40 to 55, moderately retarded; from 25 to 40, severely retarded; and below 25, profoundly retarded. Table 8.3 (on page 274) shows the level of functioning expected for various categories of mental retardation.

TABLE 8.3 Mental Retardation as Measured on the Wechsler Scales

CLASSIFICATION	IQ RANGE	PERCENTAGE OF THE MENTALLY RETARDED	CHARACTERISTICS OF RETARDED PERSONS AT EACH LEVEL
Mild	55–70	90%	Are able to grasp learning skills up to 6th-grade level. May become self-supporting and can be profitably employed in various vocational occupations.
Moderate	40–55	6%	Probably are not able to grasp more than 2nd-grade academic skills but can learn self-help skills and some social and academic skills. May work in sheltered workshops.
Severe	25–40	3%	Can be trained in basic health habits; can learn to communicate verbally. Learn through repetitive habit training.
Profound	Below 25	1%	Have rudimentary motor development. May learn very limited self-help skills.

Among the many causes of mental retardation are brain injuries, chromosomal abnormalities such as Down syndrome, chemical deficiencies, and hazards present during fetal development. And studies continue to document the enduring mental deficits produced by early exposure to lead (Garavan et al., 2000; Morgan et al., 2000).

Before the late 1960s, mentally retarded children in the United States were educated almost exclusively in special schools. Since then, there has been a movement toward **inclusion**—educating mentally retarded students in regular schools. Inclusion, or *mainstreaming*, may involve placing these students in classes with nonretarded students for part of the day or in special classrooms in regular schools.

■ **inclusion**
Educating mentally retarded students in regular schools by placing them in classes with nonhandicapped students for part of the day or in special classrooms in regular schools; also known as *mainstreaming*.

Resources spent on training programs for the mentally retarded are proving to be sound investments. Such programs, which rely heavily on behavior modification techniques, are making it possible for some retarded citizens to become employed workers who earn the minimum wage or better. Everyone benefits—the individual, the family, the community, and society as a whole.

Intelligence and Neural Processing

What is the relationship between intelligence and the efficiency and speed of neural processing?

What causes intelligence to vary so widely from one person to another? One clue to the cause of variations in intelligence is the fact that there are many genetic and chromosomal defects that cause mental retardation. One such condition is *Down syndrome*, in which a person has an extra chromosome in the 21st pair. These defects cause biochemical errors that are assumed to be the causal factors underlying the effects on intelligence. Consequently, some scientists believe that biochemical differences may explain variations in normal intelligence as well.

One possibility is that biochemical differences lead to variations in neural processing speed, a variable that has been shown to be strongly influenced by genes (Luciano et al., 2001, 2003). Presumably, according to this hypothesis, higher IQ test scores are associated with faster processing. To test the hypothesis, researchers are using PET scans to compare the efficiency and speed of neural processing in people with a range of intelligence levels. (A PET scan, as you will recall from Chapter 2, reveals the location and amount of brain activity by measuring how much glucose and oxygen are used during the performance of various mental tasks.) Researchers have reported that the speed at which certain simple mental tasks are performed is related to intelligence test scores (Neisser et al., 1996). Many people perform less well on intelligence tests than they otherwise could because they are inefficient in terms of processing speed, sometimes called *inspection time.* Spending too much time puzzling over a single question robs many test takers of time they could be using on other questions that they might be able to answer correctly much more quickly.

Individuals with mental retardation can learn to do many kinds of jobs that are both beneficial to society and personally rewarding to themselves.

Some researchers have found that processing speed is related to intelligence and accelerates as children get older (Fry & Hale, 1996). But studies of processing speed have a methodological problem. It is hard to separate neural processing time from physical reaction time (Brody, 1992). For example, suppose a participant must decide whether two objects flashed on a screen are the same or different and then respond physically by pushing one of two buttons, labeled "S" and "D." The time taken for the mental task (processing speed) may be affected by the time needed for the physical task (reaction time), and that physical factor may have nothing to do with intelligence. A research technique that measures inspection time is a better way to gauge processing speed (Deary & Stough, 1996; Scheuffgen et al., 2000).

A typical inspection-time task is shown in Figure 8.4. In this very simple experiment, an image of the incomplete stimulus, part (a), is flashed to the participant very briefly and then immediately masked by a stimulus that covers it, part (b). The participant is then asked whether the long side of the original stimulus appeared on the left or the right. The relevant factor is how much inspection time (from a few hundred milliseconds to 10 milliseconds or less) is needed for a participant to consistently achieve a given level of accuracy, say 75% or 85%. The shorter the inspection time, the more rapidly information must be processed (Deary & Stough, 1996).

Is inspection time (processing speed) related to intelligence? Apparently so. Deary and Stough claim that "inspection time is, to date, the only single information-processing index that accounts for approximately 20% of intelligence-test variance" (p. 599). Even so, experts in intelligence still lack sufficient understanding of the relationship between inspection time and intelligence (Brody, 1992).

FIGURE 8.4 A Typical Inspection-Time Task

Participants view (a) briefly; after which (b) is superimposed over (a), masking it. The researcher then asks whether the long arm of (a) was on the right or left. The variable measured is how much time the participant must view (a) before she or he is able to respond correctly.
Source: Deary & Stough (1996).

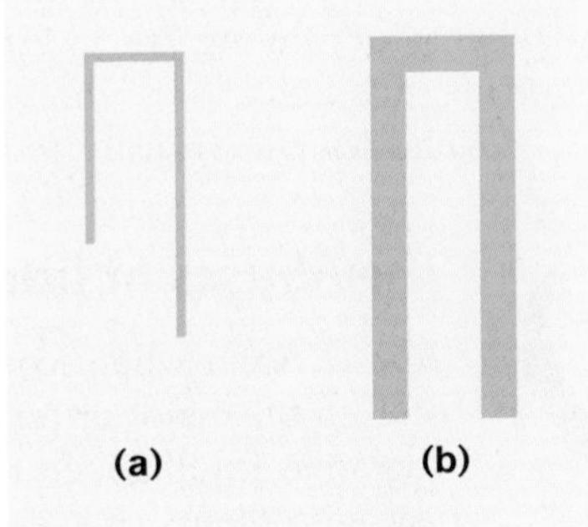

Remember It 8.3

1. The ___________ is the shape of the frequency distribution of variables such as height and intelligence.
2. Fifty percent of individuals score between ___________ and ___________ on standardized IQ tests.
3. The research of ___________ with intellectually gifted children ended the myth that individuals who are cognitively superior to others are physically inferior to them.
4. People are considered mentally retarded if they are clearly deficient in adaptive functioning and their IQ is below ___________ .

ANSWERS: 1. bell curve; 2. 90, 110; 3. Terman; 4. 70

The IQ Controversy

How important is an individual's IQ? Many Americans have come to believe that a "magical" number—an IQ score, a percentile rank, or some other derived score—unfalteringly portrays a person's intellectual capacity, ability, or potential. It's true that IQ tests are reliable and do predict some important things about a person, but they have limitations as well.

Of what are intelligence tests good predictors?

The Uses of Intelligence Tests

What do IQ tests actually predict? IQ scores are fairly good predictors of academic performance. The correlation between school grades and IQ scores is about .50, which means that about 25% of the variance in school grades can be accounted for by IQ score. Consequently, the remaining 75% must be explained by factors other than IQ alone. According to Neisser and others (1996), "successful school learning depends on many personal characteristics other than intelligence, such as persistence, interest in school, and willingness to study" (p. 81).

Is there a high correlation between IQ and success in life? Although the average IQ score of people in the professions (doctors, dentists, lawyers) tends to be higher than that of people in lower-status occupations, the exact relationship between IQ score and occupational status is not clearly understood. Nevertheless, studies indicate that intelligence test scores are related to a wide range of social outcomes, including job performance, income, social status, and years of education completed (Neisser et al., 1996).

Teenagers who score higher on intelligence tests are significantly less likely than their lower-scoring peers to engage in early sexual activity (Halpern et al., 2000). In fact, a higher IQ score appears to be a protective factor against a wide spectrum of risky sexual behaviors among 7th to 12th graders, while a lower score represents a risk factor for such behaviors, whose consequences can include unwanted pregnancies and sexually transmitted diseases.

What are some abuses of intelligence tests?

The Abuses of Intelligence Tests

Abuses occur when scores on intelligence or aptitude tests are the only or even the major criterion for admitting people to various educational programs. Intelligence tests do not measure attitude and motivation, critical ingredients of success. Many people are admitted to educational programs who probably should not be, while others who could profit from the experience and possibly make significant contributions to society are denied admission. (Think of Dr. Robert Jarvik, described at the beginning of this chapter.)

Early categorization based solely on IQ scores can doom children to slow-track educational programs that are not appropriate for them. Many poor and minority children (particularly those for whom English is a second language) and visually or hearing-impaired children have been erroneously placed in special education programs. IQ tests predicted that they were not mentally able to profit from regular classroom instruction. There would be no problem if IQ test results were unfailingly accurate, but, in fact, they are not. Indeed, since the early 1970s, federal law in the United States has prohibited schools from classifying children as mentally retarded on the basis of IQ scores alone. As you'll learn later in this chapter, the law requires that a variety of assessment techniques be used to diagnose mental retardation.

Another problem with intelligence tests is that they are sometimes designed in such a way that their results reflect cultural bias. However, several attempts have been made to develop **culture-fair intelligence tests**. In general, the questions on such tests do not penalize individuals whose cultural background and/or language differs from that of the White middle and upper classes. Here is an example of a test question that might be culturally unfair:

> Choose the best answer to complete the analogy below.
>
> Caesar is to salad as ______________ is to brandy.
>
> a. Churchill   b. Napoleon   c. Hitler   d. Lincoln

If the test takers' cultures did not expose them to Caesar salad and Napoleon brandy, this question could prove more difficult than intended. See Figure 8.5 for an example of the type of test items found on culture-fair intelligence tests.

A comparative study using a culture-fair nonverbal ability test, the Naglieri Nonverbal Ability Test, with 7,890 participants, revealed only small differences between matched samples of White Americans (2,306) and African Americans (2,306). Minimal differences were also found between Whites (1,176) and Hispanics (1,176) and between Whites (466) and Asians (466). Scores on the test correlated moderately well with achievement. Results of the study suggest that this nonverbal ability test provides a means of fair assessment for both White and minority children (Naglieri & Ronning, 2000).

■ **culture-fair intelligence test**
An intelligence test that uses questions that will not penalize those whose cultural background and/or language differs from that of the White middle and upper classes.

FIGURE 8.5 **An Example of an Item on a Culture-Fair Test**

This culture-fair test item does not penalize test takers whose language or cultural experiences differ from those of the White middle and upper classes. Subjects are to select, from the six samples on the right, the patch that would complete the pattern. Patch number 3 is the correct answer.

Source: Adapted from the Raven Standard Progressive Matrices Test.

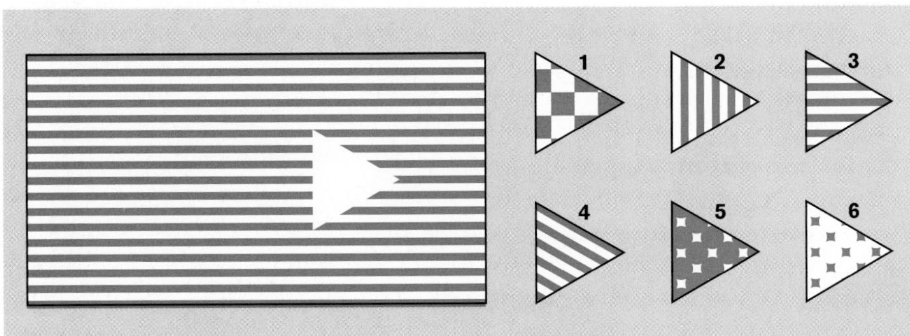

The Heritability of Intelligence

What is the nature-nurture controversy regarding intelligence, and how do twin studies support the view that intelligence is inherited?

Do you think of intelligence as an inherited or a learned characteristic? Even though it has been debated for about 130 years, the **nature-nurture controversy** is still very much alive. British researcher Sir Francis Galton (1822–1911) coined this term when he initiated the debate over whether intelligence is predominantly the result of heredity (nature) or the environment (nurture) (Galton, 1874). After studying many prominent English families, Galton concluded that intelligence is inherited—that nature, not nurture, is responsible for intelligence. Environmentalists disputed Galton's claim and just as strongly insisted that intelligence is the product of one's environment—the result of nurture. Today, most psychologists agree that both nature and nurture contribute to intelligence, but they continue to debate the relative contributions of these two factors (Petrill, 2003).

■ nature-nurture controversy The debate over whether intelligence (or another trait) is primarily the result of heredity (nature) or the environment (nurture).

■ heritability A measure of the degree to which a characteristic is estimated to be influenced by heredity.

You should remember from Chapter 2 that behavioral genetics is the field of study in which scientists attempt to determine the relative contributions of nature and nurture to variables such as intelligence. Many of the most important studies in the field involve twins. Twins, whether identical or fraternal, who are raised together have similar environments. If identical twins raised together are found to be more alike on a certain trait than are fraternal twins raised together, then that trait is assumed to be more influenced by heredity. But if identical and fraternal twins from similar environments do not differ on a trait, then that trait is assumed to be influenced more by environment. The **heritability** of a trait is a measure of the degree to which a characteristic is estimated to be influenced by heredity. Figure 8.6 shows the strong contribution that genetic factors make to intelligence.

FIGURE 8.6 Correlations between the IQ Scores of Persons with Various Relationships

The more closely related two individuals are, the more similar their IQ scores tend to be. Thus, there is a strong genetic contribution to intelligence.

Source: Based on data from Bouchard & McGue (1981); Erlenmeyer-Kimling & Jarvik (1963).

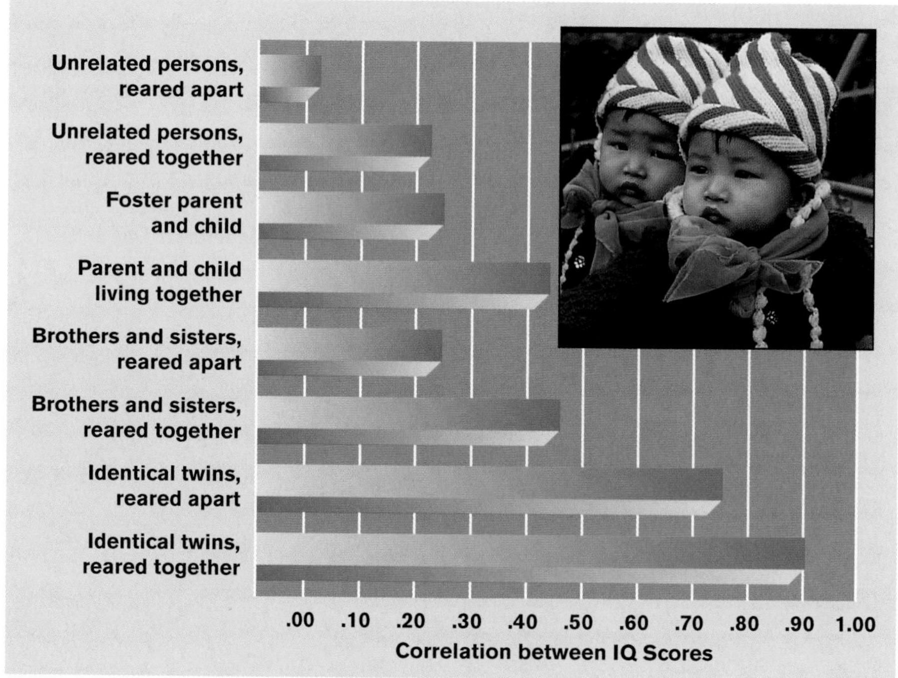

Minnesota—home of the twin cities and the Minnesota Twins—is also, fittingly, the site of the most extensive U.S. study of identical and fraternal twins. The Minnesota Center for Twin and Adoption Research has assembled the Minnesota Twin Registry, which in 1998 included more than 10,000 twin pairs (Bouchard, 1998). Since 1979, Minnesota researchers, headed by Thomas Bouchard, have studied about 60 pairs of fraternal twins and 80 pairs of identical twins who were reared apart. Of all the traits Bouchard and his colleagues studied, the most heritable trait turned out to be intelligence. Bouchard (1997) reported that various types of twin studies have consistently yielded heritabilities of .60 to .70 for intelligence. (A heritability of 1.00 would mean that all of the variation in intelligence is due to genes.)

The IQ scores of adopted children have been found to correlate more strongly with those of their biological than with those of their adoptive parents. However, the correlation is far from perfect, leaving ample opportunity for adoptive parents to influence the cognitive functioning of their children.

Not all researchers agree with Bouchard's estimate of the heritability of intelligence. Combining data from a number of twin studies, Plomin and others (1994) found the heritability estimate for general intelligence to be .52. Similar findings emerged from meta-analyses using dozens of adoption studies and twin studies involving more than 10,000 pairs of twins. These analyses concluded that the heritability of general cognitive ability was about .50 (McClearn et al., 1997). Psychologists who consider environmental factors as the chief contributors to differences in intelligence also take issue with Bouchard's findings. They claim that most separated identical twins are raised by adoptive parents who have been matched as closely as possible to the biological parents. This fact, the critics say, could account for the similarity in the identical twins' IQ scores. In response to his critics, Bouchard (1997) points out that children who are not related biologically but are raised in the same home are no more similar in intelligence once they reach adulthood than are complete strangers.

Researchers also use the **adoption study method**, an approach that involves studying children who were adopted very early in life. Adoption studies reveal that children adopted shortly after birth have IQs more closely resembling those of their biological parents than those of their adoptive parents. The family environment has an influence on IQ early in life, but that influence seems to diminish with age. Twin and adoption studies indicate that, as people reach adulthood, genetic factors are most closely correlated with IQ (Loehlin et al., 1988, 1989; McCartney et al., 1990; Plomin & Rende, 1991). In fact, the influence of genes seems to increase predictably as people age, with a heritability of .30 in infancy, .40 in childhood, .50 in adolescence, and about .60 in adulthood (McGue et al., 1993). A large study in Sweden of pairs of identical twins and same-sex fraternal twins who had been reared together and had reached the age of 80 or more revealed a heritability estimate of .62 for general cognitive ability (McClearn et al., 1997).

Bouchard and others (1990) claim that "although parents may be able to affect their children's rate of cognitive skill acquisition, they may have relatively little influence on the ultimate level attained" (p. 225). A great deal of convincing research does argue for the importance of genes in determining intelligence, including language skills (Plomin & Dale, 2000). But a great deal of room is still left for environmental forces to have a significant influence. Thus, the nature-nurture controversy remains unresolved.

■ **adoption study method** A method researchers use to assess the relative effects of heredity and environment by studying children who were adopted very early in life.

Race and IQ

What are Jensen's and Herrnstein and Murray's controversial views on race and IQ?

Historically, most studies have shown that Blacks score, on average, about 15 points lower than Whites on standardized IQ tests in the United States (e.g., Loehlin et al., 1975). Other studies have shown similar differences for Blacks and Whites in other nations (e.g., Rushton & Jensen, 2003). But why? Two publications addressing this question stimulated heated debate about the link between race and intelligence in the scientific community and the general public.

In 1969, psychologist Arthur Jensen published an article in which he attributed the IQ gap to genetic differences between the races. Further, he claimed that the genetic influence on intelligence is so strong that the environment cannot make a significant difference. Jensen even went so far as to claim that Blacks and Whites possess qualitatively different kinds of intelligence.

The late psychologist Richard Herrnstein (1930–1994) and political scientist Charles Murray added fresh fuel to the controversy during the mid-1990s with their book *The Bell Curve* (Herrnstein & Murray, 1994). They argued that IQ differences among individuals and between groups explain how those at the top of the ladder in U.S. society got there and why those on the lower rungs remain there. Herrnstein and Murray largely attributed the social ills of modern society—including poverty, welfare dependency, crime, and illegitimacy—to low IQ, which they implied is primarily genetic and largely immune to change by environmental intervention. Yet, their own estimate was that 60% of IQ is genetically inherited, "which, by extension, means that IQ is about 40% a matter of environment" (p. 105). That 40% would seem to leave a lot of room for improvement.

The Bell Curve offered correlational data to show a relationship between IQ and many other variables—poverty, for example. Critics of *The Bell Curve* were quick to point out that correlational data cannot be used to conclude that low IQ causes poverty or, for that matter, that poverty causes low IQ (Kamin, 1995). Herrnstein and Murray's most ominous conclusion rests heavily on the notion that IQ is destiny, and their book warns of castelike divisions in modern society based on IQ. Those in the highest 5–10% of the intelligence distribution will be even more firmly entrenched at the top of society, they write. And those with low IQs will remain a permanent underclass. But the frightening outcomes envisioned by Herrnstein and Murray are inescapable only to the degree that IQ is not affected by environmental factors.

Jensen's and Herrnstein and Murray's views run counter to the belief that an enriched, stimulating environment can overcome the deficits of poverty and cultural disadvantage and thus reduce any negative effects these have on IQ. The studies you'll read about in the next section suggest that changes in environment can increase IQ scores. Moreover, a new testing technique called *dynamic assessment* also supports this idea. In dynamic assessment, examinees are taught the goal and format of each IQ subtest before actually being tested. The rationale behind the technique is the assumption that children from middle-class backgrounds have more experience with testing procedures and better understand that the goal of testing is to demonstrate competency. Studies of dynamic assessment show that it significantly increases the number of minority children who achieve above-average IQ scores (Lidz & Macrine, 2001).

Indeed, if average IQ differences were genetically determined by race, then the mean IQ scores of mixed-race individuals should fall somewhere between the mean scores for African Americans and Whites. But studies over the decades have not found such a relationship between IQ and mixed ancestry (Loehlin et al., 1973; Scarr et al., 1977). At the end of World War II, American soldiers stationed in Germany, both Black and White, fathered thousands of children with German women. Fifteen years later, Eyeferth (1961) randomly selected samples of these children. The mean IQs of the two groups were virtually identical. Having a White father conferred no measurable IQ advantage at all.

Intelligence: Fixed or Changeable?

What kinds of evidence suggest that IQ is changeable rather than fixed?

Clearly, the high degree of similarity in the intelligence scores of identical twins who have been reared apart makes a strong case for the powerful influence of genetics. But it's important to keep in mind that none of us inherits a specific IQ score. Instead, our genes probably set the boundaries of a fairly wide range of possible performance levels, called the *reaction range*. Our environments determine where we end up within that range.

Adoption Studies In general, the IQ scores of adopted children tend to resemble those of their biological parents more than those of their adopted parents. However, almost three decades ago, Sandra Scarr and Richard Weinberg (1976) found a different pattern among adopted children whose biological and adoptive parents differed both in race and in socioeconomic status. Their study involved 130 Black and interracial children who had been adopted by highly educated, upper-middle-class White families; 99 of the children had been adopted in the first year of life. The adoptees were fully exposed to middle-class cultural experiences and vocabulary, the "culture of the tests and the school" (p. 737).

How did the children perform on IQ and achievement tests? The average IQ score of the 130 adoptees was 106.3. And their achievement test scores were slightly above the national average, not below. On average, the earlier the children were adopted, the higher their IQs. The mean IQ score of the 99 early adoptees was 110.4, about 10 IQ points above the average for Whites. Studies in France have also shown that IQ scores and achievement are substantially higher when children from lower-class environments are adopted by middle-class and upper-middle-class families (Duyme, 1988; Schiff and Lewontin, 1986).

Early Childhood Interventions In addition to these adoption studies, research examining the effects of preschool programs involving infants and young children from poor families clearly indicates that early educational experiences can affect intellectual functioning (Brooks-Gunn, 2003). Some of the best known of these interventions have been carried out by developmental psychologist Craig Ramey (Burchinal et al., 1997; Campbell & Ramey, 1994; Ramey, 1993; Ramey & Campbell, 1987). And unlike many studies of early interventions, Ramey's research focuses on true experiments—so we know that the outcomes are caused by the interventions.

In one of Ramey's programs, 6- to 12-month-old infants of low-IQ, low-income mothers were randomly assigned either to an intensive, 40-hour-per-week day-care program that continued throughout the preschool years or to a control group that received only medical care and nutritional supplements. When the children reached school age, half in each group (again based on random assignment) were enrolled in a special after-school program that helped their families learn how to support school learning with educational activities at home. Ramey followed the progress of children in all four groups through age 12, giving them IQ tests at various ages.

Figure 8.7 (on page 282) shows that children who participated in Ramey's infant and preschool program scored higher on IQ tests than their peers who received either no intervention or only the school-age intervention. Perhaps more important, during the elementary school years, about 40% of the control group participants had IQ scores classified as borderline or retarded (scores below 85), compared to only 12.8% of those who were in the infant program. Further, recent research shows that the cognitive advantage enjoyed by the infant intervention group has persisted into adulthood (Campbell et al., 2001, 2002). Clearly, Ramey's work shows that the environment has great potential to influence IQ scores.

Changes in Standard of Living The IQ scores of Americans and of citizens of other developed nations have gained about 3 points per decade since 1940, a finding most often attributed to widespread changes in the standard of living. James Flynn (1987, 1999; Dickens & Flynn, 2001) analyzed 73 studies involving some 7,500 participants ranging in age from 12 to 48 and found that "every Binet and Wechsler sample from 1932 to 1978 has performed better than its predecessor" (p. 225). Studies in developing countries, such as Kenya, have shown that IQ gains can happen over much shorter periods of time when the standard of living improves drastically (Daley et al., 2003). The consistent improvement in IQ scores over time that accompanies an increase in the standard of living is known as the *Flynn effect*.

Some researchers suggest that the Flynn effect is caused by those parts of IQ tests that measure learning rather than the *g* factor (Flynn, 2003; Kane & Oakland, 2000).

FIGURE 8.7 **Ramey's Infant Intervention Program**

The positive effects of Ramey's intervention program for young children were still evident when participants reached age 12.

Source: Campbell, F., & Ramey, C. (1994). Effects of achievement: A follow-up study of children from low-income families, Fig. 1, p. 690, *Child Development, 65,* 684–698. By permission of the Society for Research in Child Development.

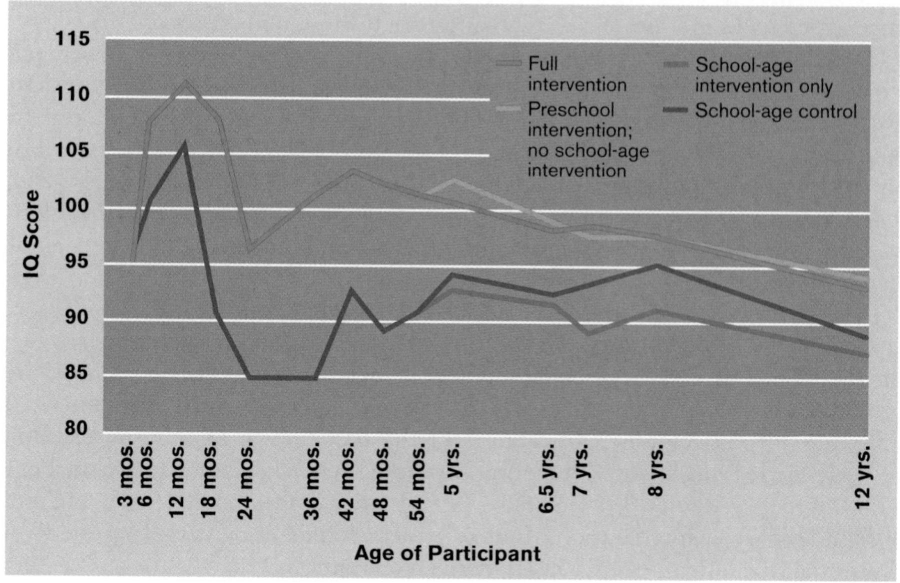

In other words, from their perspective, people today possess more knowledge but do not necessarily possess a greater quantity of intelligence, as Spearman defined it. In support of their view, these psychologists point out that average scores on the Wechsler subtests of arithmetic, vocabulary, and general information have not changed over time. These subtests, they argue, are more strongly correlated with *g* than are the subtests that show changes in average scores. In response, Flynn claims that the similarities subtest, the one on which scores have changed the most, reflects the kind of thinking and problem solving needed in modern society. Therefore, he claims, the gains are still real and socially significant, whether they represent gains in *g* or not (Flynn, 2003).

Some observers suggest that physiological variables underlie the association between improved standards of living and IQ score gains. They claim that improved nutrition and prenatal care are responsible for gains in neurological functioning that have resulted in increased IQ scores (Flynn, 2003). However, Flynn argues that such changes should affect those at the bottom of the IQ scale more than those at the top. He points out that there has been just as much change among high scorers as among those whose scores are below average. Consequently, Flynn argues that more general cultural changes, such as the increased popularity of cognitively demanding leisure activities, have produced these gains.

Another general cultural change, noted by Zajonc and Mullally (1997), is decreased family size. According to their research, first- and second-born children tend to do better on intelligence and achievement tests than do children born later in larger families. The decrease in average family size has increased the proportions of first-borns and second-borns in the population as a whole.

Like Flynn, some psychologists believe that changes in standards of living may also be narrowing the Black-White IQ gap. Researcher Ken Vincent (1991) presents data suggesting that the gap is smaller (about 7 or 8 IQ points) among younger children than among older children and adults. Vincent (1993) attributes the rapid mean gains by African American children to environmental changes in economic and educational opportunity. These conclusions are supported by studies in which low-income families are given vouchers to pay for housing in more affluent neighborhoods (Leventhal & Brooks-Gunn, 2003). Although these studies do not deal directly with IQ, they have demonstrated that children whose families move from low- to moderate-income neighborhoods demonstrate significant gains in academic functioning within a very short period of time.

Expectations, Effort, and Standardized Test Scores

How might parental expectations and teaching methods influence scores on standardized tests?

How do you think the standardized test scores of American students compare to those of their peers in other countries? In one classic study of cross-national differences in achievement test scores, Harold Stevenson and others (1986) compared the math scores of randomly selected elementary schoolchildren from three comparable cities: Taipei in Taiwan, Sendai in Japan, and Minneapolis in the United States. Though all groups were fairly equal at the beginning of school, by the 5th grade, the Asian students were outscoring the Americans by about 15 points. And the Asian superiority held firmly from the highest to the lowest achievement levels. The Japanese children scored the highest of the three groups in 5th grade, and even the lowest-scoring Japanese classes did better than the top-scoring classes in the United States. How can such differences in achievement in children from different cultures be explained?

Cultural Beliefs Many studies have shown that Western and Asian cultures foster different beliefs about the nature of learning and achievement (Li, 2003). Moreover, these beliefs influence child-rearing practices. For instance, Stevenson and his colleagues (1990) interviewed the parents of their study participants. The Chinese and Japanese mothers considered academic achievement to be the most important pursuit of their children, whereas American parents did not value it as a central concern. The Asian, but not the American, families structured their home activities to promote academic achievement as soon as their first child started elementary school.

Significantly, too, the Asian parents downplayed the importance of innate ability but emphasized the value of hard work and persistence (Stevenson, 1992). American parents, in contrast, believed more firmly in genetic limitations on ability and achievement. More recent research indicates that, as preschoolers, children in the United States display beliefs about the effort-achievement connection that are similar to those of Asian children (Heyman et al., 2003). However, apparently as a result of both adult and peer influence, by the time they reach the age of 11 years, American children have acquired the belief that achievement results more from ability than effort (Altermatt & Pomerantz, 2003; Heyman et al., 2003). As Stevenson states, "when [adults] believe success in school depends for the most part on ability rather than effort, they are less likely to foster [children's] participation in activities related to academic achievement" (1992, p. 73). As a result, the ability-achievement belief affects the amount of academic effort put forth by the children and becomes a self-fulfilling prophecy.

In follow-up studies, Stevenson and others (1993) found that the achievement gap between Asian and American students persisted over a 10-year period. Some critics of Stevenson's work have argued that cross-national differences in high school achievement are explained in part by the fact that the American students spend more time working at part-time jobs and socializing than their Asian counterparts do (Fuligni & Stevenson, 1995; Larson & Verma, 1999). However, a comparison of German and Japanese students found that German teens, like their American agemates, are less likely to attribute academic success to effort (Randel et al., 2000). Moreover, German students' achievement test scores were found to be lower than those of Japanese teens. These findings support the contention that Western beliefs about ability and learning contribute to cross-national differences in achievement.

But do Asian students pay a psychological price for their strong academic achievement? Are they more likely than students in the United States to be stressed and heavily burdened by pressures to maintain academic excellence? A large cross-cultural study comparing 11th-grade students from Japan, Taiwan, and the United States did find a correlation between achievement in mathematics and psychological distress—but, surprisingly, for the American students, not the Asian students (Crystal et al., 1994). And the study of German teens cited earlier produced similar findings: German adolescents are more likely than their Japanese peers to have emotional difficulties (Randel et al., 2000).

How can such findings be explained? The researchers suggest that Asian teenagers typically enjoy support and encouragement for their academic achievement from family and peers alike (Crystal et al., 1994). In contrast, high-achieving teenagers in the United States are often torn between studying harder to excel academically and pursuing nonacademic social interests. Such interests may be strongly encouraged by their peers and often by parents who want their children to be "well-rounded." Moreover, many colleges consider extracurricular activities in deciding which applicants to admit.

Another possible explanation is that Western teens may experience a greater discrepancy between expectations and outcomes in mathematics achievement than do their peers in Asian countries. For instance, German teens express greater confidence in their abilities than Japanese teens do (Randel et al., 2000). Other studies have shown that adolescents in most Asian countries express a general lack of confidence in their mathematics abilities, despite their high levels of achievement (Leung, 2002). For this reason, some psychologists believe that Western teens experience more disappointment than Asian adolescents when they compare their achievement expectations to their actual performance. As a result, they experience more achievement-related anxiety and depression.

Formal Education More comprehensive studies than those of Stevenson and his colleagues suggest that attribution of cross-national differences in math scores exclusively to differences in cultural values is overly simplistic. For many years, the National Center for Educational Statistics (NCES), a branch of the U.S. Department of Education, has tracked the math and science achievement test scores of thousands of children all over the world in a study called *Trends in International Mathematics and Science Study (TIMSS)*. As Table 8.4 shows, in many European countries and Canada, societies with cultural values quite similar to those of the United States, scores are comparable to those in Asian nations (NCES, 2000).

Asian students consistently score higher on math achievement tests than do their American counterparts. Cultural beliefs and parental expectations explain some of this difference, but variations in teaching methods across the two cultures are contributing factors.

Because of the data from TIMSS and other studies like it, researchers, including Stevenson, have looked at other kinds of environmental factors besides differences in cultural values. For example, in Singapore, the nation ranked first in mathematics in the TIMSS data, parents begin teaching their children about numbers and the relationships among numbers long before the children enter school (Sharpe, 2002). Moreover, Singaporean parents specifically tailor this home teaching, and their selection of formal preschool experiences, to the mathematics curricula of the early grades in public schools. Consequently, by the tender age of 5 or 6, Singaporean youngsters are already ahead of their peers in other nations.

Teaching methods, too, can vary widely from one country to another. In one frequently cited study, Stigler and Stevenson (1991) observed math teachers in Japan, Taiwan, and the United States. They found that the Asian teachers spent more time on each kind of problem and did not move on to another until they were certain that students understood the first. By contrast, the American teachers introduced many kinds of problems within a

TABLE 8.4 **Selected Math and Science Achievement Rankings Based on Data from *Trends in International Mathematics and Science Study (TIMSS)***

Out of 38 countries that participated in TIMSS, the United States ranked 19th in math achievement and 18th in science achievement. Hungary was the only non-Asian country to rank among the top 5 in either math or science.

COUNTRY	MATH RANKING	SCIENCE RANKING
Singapore	1	2
South Korea	2	5
Chinese Taipei	3	1
Hong Kong SAR	4	15
Japan	5	4
Belgium	6	12
Netherlands	7	6
Slovak Republic	8	11
Hungary	9	3
Canada	10	14
Russia	12	16
Australia	13	7
Finland	14	10
United States	19	18
England	20	9
New Zealand	21	19
Italy	23	21
Thailand	27	24
Israel	28	26
Turkey	31	33
Iran	33	31
Chile	35	35
South Africa	38	38

single class period and did not allow time for students to master any of them. More recent studies have produced similar findings (NCES, 2003).

Another important aspect of math teaching, emphasis on computational fluency, has been found to contribute to math achievement differences both across cultures and across classrooms within the United States (Geary et al., 1999; Kail & Hall, 1999). *Computational fluency* is the ability to produce answers to simple calculations automatically. Many critics of teaching practices in the United States claim that math curricula in American elementary schools seldom include criteria that encourage students to develop computational fluency (Murray, 1998). As a result, these critics say, elementary school students in the United States are not adequately prepared to tackle the more advanced mathematical concepts of algebra, geometry, and calculus.

This conclusion may be correct, as evidenced by comparisons of calculator use and other aspects of instruction in secondary school math classes. Data collected as part of the TIMSS study in recent years show that Japanese 8th graders rarely use calculators in their algebra classes, while their counterparts in the United States use them almost every day (NCES, 2003). Moreover, Japanese 8th graders can handle more complex problems—ones involving four or more steps—than American students can. Another important finding is that the Japanese students are able to infer connections between different kinds of algebra problems. By contrast, teachers in American 8th-grade algebra classes must devote more time than Japanese teachers to explicit explanations of the links between different kinds of problems and to reviews of information students are supposed to have learned in earlier grades.

Remember It 8.4

1. IQ tests are good predictors of __________ success.
2. Twin studies suggest that variation in IQ scores is strongly influenced by __________ .
3. The studies of Weinberg and Scarr suggest that IQ is __________ .
4. The finding that early childhood intervention programs can improve IQ scores is associated with the research of __________ .
5. The __________ refers to the historical change in average IQ scores that has accompanied improved standards of living.
6. The work of Stevenson and his colleagues suggests that Western cultures associate intellectual achievement with __________ , while Asian cultures attribute academic success to __________ .

ANSWERS: 1. academic; 2. heredity; 3. changeable; 4. Ramey; 5. Flynn effect; 6. ability, effort

Emotional Intelligence

You probably see how the kinds of intellectual abilities described so far have important consequences for everyday living. But you might also believe that other abilities are equally important. For example, can you imagine anyone being successful without the ability to manage his or her feelings? **Emotional intelligence** is the ability to apply knowledge about emotions to everyday life (Salovey & Pizarro, 2003). And emotional management is just one aspect of emotional intelligence. Two leading researchers in the field, Peter Salovey and David Pizarro (2003), propose that emotional intelligence also includes the ability to perceive emotions, the capacity to use emotions to aid cognitive processes, and a comprehension of emotions. These abilities are separate from IQ, they argue, but are equally necessary for success in the workplace, in intimate personal relations, and in social interactions. Research supports this view, showing that emotional intelligence is unrelated to IQ scores (Lam & Kirby, 2002; van der Zee et al., 2002). Moreover, scores on tests of emotional intelligence predict both academic and social success (Rozell et al., 2002).

■ emotional intelligence The ability to apply knowledge about emotions to everyday life; this type of intelligence involves an awareness of and an ability to manage one's own emotions, self-motivation, empathy, and the ability to handle relationships.

Those who are high in emotional intelligence often emerge as leaders. Successful leaders can empathize with their followers, understanding their needs and wants. If you want to be an influential leader, a top salesperson, a therapist, or a marriage counselor, or if you want to have fulfilling intimate relationships, learn to understand and manage your own emotions and to respond appropriately to the emotions of others. To find out what your Emotional Quotient (EQ) is, complete *Try It 8.1*.

Try It 8.1 Find Your EQ

Emotional intelligence may be just as important to success in your chosen career as your actual job skills. Take this short test to assess your EQ by checking one response for each item.

1. I'm always aware of even subtle feelings as I have them.

   ___ Always ___ Usually ___ Sometimes ___ Rarely ___ Never

2. I can delay gratification in pursuit of my goals instead of getting carried away by impulse.

   ___ Always ___ Usually ___ Sometimes ___ Rarely ___ Never

3. Instead of giving up in the face of setbacks or disappointments, I stay hopeful and optimistic.

   ___ Always ___ Usually ___ Sometimes ___ Rarely ___ Never

4. My keen sense of others' feelings makes me compassionate about their plight.

   ___ Always ___ Usually ___ Sometimes ___ Rarely ___ Never

5. I can sense the pulse of a group or relationship and state unspoken feelings.

   ___ Always ___ Usually ___ Sometimes ___ Rarely ___ Never

6. I can soothe or contain distressing feelings, so that they don't keep me from doing things I need to do.

   ___ Always ___ Usually ___ Sometimes ___ Rarely ___ Never

Score your responses as follows: Always = 4 points, Usually = 3 points, Sometimes = 2 points, Rarely = 1 point, Never = 0 points. The closer your total number of points is to 24, the higher your EQ probably is.

Personal Components of Emotional Intelligence

What are the personal components of emotional intelligence?

The foundation of emotional intelligence is said to be self-knowledge, which involves an awareness of emotions, an ability to manage those emotions, and self-motivation.

Awareness and Management of One's Emotions Being aware of one's own emotions—recognizing and acknowledging feelings as they happen—is at the very heart of emotional intelligence. And this awareness encompasses not only moods, but also thoughts about those moods. People who are able to monitor their feelings as they arise are less likely to be ruled by them and are thus better able to manage their emotions.

Managing emotions does not mean suppressing them; nor does it mean giving free rein to every feeling. Daniel Goleman (1995), one of several authors who have popularized the notion of emotional intelligence, insists that the goal is balance and that every feeling has value and significance. As Goleman says, "A life without passion would be a dull wasteland of neutrality, cut off and isolated from the richness of life itself" (p. 56). Thus, we manage our emotions by expressing them in an appropriate manner. Emotions can also be managed by engaging in activities that cheer us up, soothe our hurts, or reassure us when we feel anxious.

Clearly, awareness and management of emotions are not independent. For instance, you might think that individuals who seem to experience their feelings more intensely than others would be less able to manage them. However, a critical component of awareness of emotions is the ability to assign meaning to them—to know why we are experiencing a particular feeling or mood. Psychologists have found that, among individuals who experience intense emotions, individual differences in the ability to assign meaning to those feelings predict differences in the ability to manage them (Gohm, 2003). In other words, if two individuals are intensely angry, the one who is better able to understand why he or she is angry will also be better able to manage the anger.

Self-Motivation Self-motivation refers to strong emotional self-control, which enables a person to get moving and pursue worthy goals, persist at tasks even when frustrated, and resist the temptation to act on impulse. Resisting impulsive behavior is, according to Goleman (1995), "the root of all emotional self-control" (p. 81).

Of all the attributes of emotional intelligence, the ability to postpone immediate gratification and to persist in working toward some greater future gain is most closely related to success—whether one is trying to build a business, get a college degree, or even stay on a diet. One researcher has found that 4-year-old children who have mastered the art of delaying instant gratification in order to advance toward some future goal will be "far superior as students" when they graduate from high school than will 4-year-olds who are not able to resist the impulse to satisfy their immediate wishes (Shoda et al., 1990).

Interpersonal Components of Emotional Intelligence

What are the interpersonal components of emotional intelligence?

The interpersonal components of emotional intelligence are empathy and the ability to handle relationships.

Empathy Empathy, a sensitivity to the needs and feelings of others, appears to be a quality that reflects a high level of emotional development and springs from self-awareness. If we have no insight into our own emotions, it is unlikely that we will develop a sensitivity to and understanding of those of others.

One key indicator, or hallmark, of empathy as a component of emotional intelligence is the ability to read and interpret nonverbal behavior—the gestures, vocal inflections, tones of voice, and facial expressions of others. Nonverbal behavior is, in a sense, the language of the emotions, because our feelings are most genuinely expressed this way. People may fail to communicate their feelings verbally or even lie about them, but their nonverbal behavior will most often reveal their true feelings.

A person with high emotional intelligence shows empathy, recognizing nonverbal signals from others and making appropriate responses.

Handling Relationships For most people, hardly anything in life is more important than their relationships—an intimate love relationship, relationships with family and friends, and professional or work relationships. Without rewarding relationships, life would be lonely indeed. And emotional intelligence has a great deal to do with forming and maintaining successful relationships.

Two components of emotional intelligence that are necessary for success in handling relationships are (1) the ability to manage one's own emotions and (2) empathy. These two components combine to produce the ability to respond appropriately to emotions in others.

Remember It 8.5

1. Identify the category in which each component of emotional intelligence belongs.

___ (1) empathy — a. personal
___ (2) awareness of one's own emotions — b. interpersonal
___ (3) self-motivation
___ (4) ability to handle relationships

ANSWERS: (1) b, (2) a, (3) a, (4) b

Creativity

Have you ever known a person who was intellectually bright, but lacked creativity? **Creativity** can be thought of as the ability to produce original, appropriate, and valuable ideas and/or solutions to problems. And research indicates that there is only a weak to moderate correlation between creativity and IQ (Lubart, 2003). Remember the mentally gifted individuals studied by Lewis Terman? Not one of them has produced a highly creative work (Terman & Oden, 1959). No Nobel laureates, no Pulitzer prizes. Geniuses, yes; creative geniuses, no. Thus, high intelligence does not necessarily mean high creativity.

creativity
The ability to produce original, appropriate, and valuable ideas and/or solutions to problems.

The Creative Process

What are the four stages in the creative problem-solving process?

Cartoonists often illustrate creative thinking as a flash of insight, a lightbulb that suddenly turns on in the mind. But research studies indicate that useful and genuine creativity rarely appears in the form of sudden flashes (Haberlandt, 1997). For the most part, creative ideas that come to conscious awareness have been incubating for some time. And most experts agree that genuine creativity "is an accomplishment born of intensive study, long reflection, persistence and interest" (Snow, 1993, p. 1033).

There are basically four stages in the creative problem-solving process (Goleman et al., 1992):

1. *Preparation*—searching for information that may help solve the problem
2. *Incubation*—letting the problem "sit" while the relevant information is digested
3. *Illumination*—being suddenly struck by the right solution
4. *Translation*—transforming the insight into useful action

The incubation stage, perhaps the most important part of the process, takes place below the level of awareness.

divergent thinking
The ability to produce multiple ideas, answers, or solutions to a problem for which there is no agreed-on solution.

The Nature of Creative Thinking

How does creative thinking differ from other forms of cognition?

What is unique about creative thought? According to psychologist J. P. Guilford (1967), who studied creativity for several decades, creative thinkers are highly proficient at divergent thinking. **Divergent thinking** is the ability to produce multiple ideas, answers, or solutions to a problem for which there is no agreed-on solution (Guilford, 1967). More broadly, divergent thinking is novel, or original, and involves the synthesis of an unusual association of ideas; it is flexible, switching quickly and smoothly from one stream of thought or set of ideas to another; and it requires fluency, or the ability to formulate an abundance of ideas (Csikszentmihalyi, 1996). In contrast to divergent thinking, Guilford defined *convergent thinking* as the type of mental activity measured by IQ and achievement tests; it consists of solving precisely defined, logical problems for which there is a known correct answer.

However, divergent and convergent thinking are not always separate phenomena. Both are required for most cognitive tasks. For example, in order to be creative, a person must develop divergent thinking, but convergent thinking is required to discriminate between good and bad ideas (Csikszentmihalyi, 1996). Similarly, solving precisely defined problems can involve divergent thinking, as one tries to think of possible solutions.

Researchers are identifying the different brain areas involved in convergent and divergent thinking. In general, convergent thinking is characterized by greater activity in the left frontal cortex, while divergent thinking is marked by higher levels of activity in the right frontal cortex (Razoumnikova, 2000). Other studies show that processes involved in convergent thinking, such as searching for patterns in events, are carried out in the left hemisphere (Wolford et al., 2000). And studies by Carlsson and others (2000) that measured regional cerebral blood flow (rCBF) revealed striking differences in frontal lobe activity between participants who were engaged in highly creative thinking and those who were not. Figure 8.8(a) shows the frontal lobe activity during highly creative thinking. There is activity in both hemispheres but a significantly greater amount in the right frontal cortex. In contrast, Figure 8.8(b) shows that during periods when no creative thinking is occurring, the left frontal lobe is highly active, and there is very little activity in the right hemisphere.

Some psychologists have criticized what might be called the *trait approach* to the study of creativity—the notion that creativity is a unique type of thought characteristic of certain people. For example, cognitive psychologist John Baer argues that creativity is a domain-specific set of cognitive skills. In other words, people develop or learn it in connection with particular tasks (Baer, 1998). To support his view, he cites research showing that people can be trained to engage in divergent thinking in response to a specific task such as poetry writing. But when researchers then test these

FIGURE 8.8 Maps of Regional Cerebral Blood Flow (rCBF)

(a) Highly creative thinking is associated with activity in both hemispheres, but with significantly higher levels in the right hemisphere (red indicates activity). (b) During thinking that is not creative, activity is largely restricted to the left hemisphere.

Source: Adapted from Carlsson et al. (2000).

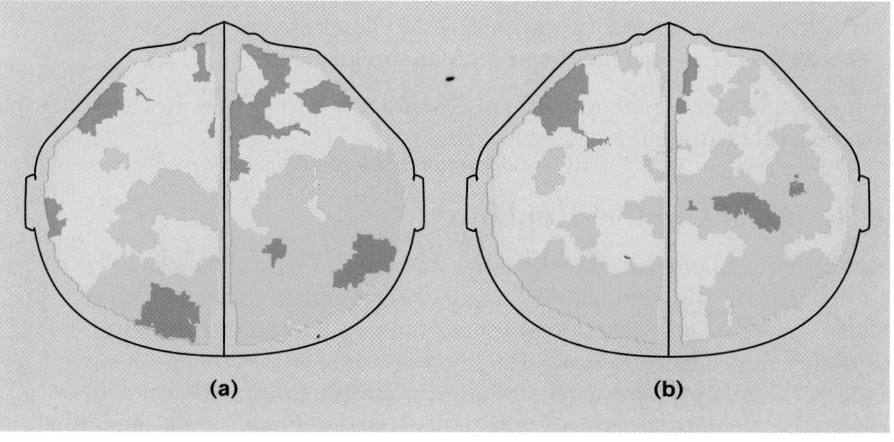

participants' capacity for divergent thinking with other tasks, they demonstrate no more divergent thinking than do participants who have received no training (Baer, 1996). Thus, according to Baer and those who agree with him, divergent thinking is like any other form of thought and should be studied within the information-processing framework rather than as a special trait or ability possessed by few people.

Measuring Creativity

What are some tests that have been used to measure creativity?

How might individual differences in creativity be measured? Tests designed to measure creativity emphasize original approaches to arriving at solutions for open-ended problems or to producing artistic works (Gregory, 1996). One creativity test, the Unusual Uses Test, asks respondents to name as many uses as possible for an ordinary object (such as a brick). Another measure of creativity is the Consequences Test, which asks test takers to list as many consequences as they can that would be likely to follow some basic change in the world (such as the force of gravity being reduced by 50%). And researchers Mednick and Mednick (1967), who reasoned that the essence of creativity consists of the creative thinker's ability to fit together ideas that to the noncreative thinker might appear remote or unrelated, created the Remote Associates Test (RAT).

However, tests of creativity are, at best, mediocre predictors of real-life creative achievements (Hocevar & Bachelor, 1989). The main weakness of such tests is that they measure creativity in the abstract. They treat creativity as a general trait, as though the same set of abilities could explain the creative accomplishments of inventors, composers, artists, and architects (Amabile, 1983, 1990). It is rare indeed for one individual to excel in more than one creative domain.

Characteristics of Creative People

What are some characteristics of creative people?

Creative people share a number of characteristics that distinguish them from less creative individuals. Among the most important of these traits are expertise, openness to experience, independence of mind, intrinsic motivation, and perseverance.

Expertise Expertise in a specific area of endeavor is built up over years of disciplined practice. Although expertise alone does not produce creativity, genuine creative accomplishments are rooted in this quality (Ericsson & Charness, 1994). Benjamin Bloom (1985) and his associates studied 120 case histories of people who had made notable creative contributions in six different fields. Every one of these individuals had unquestioned expertise, based on high-quality training, as well as unyielding determination.

Openness to Experience Creative individuals are open to experience and will entertain, at least initially, even seemingly irrational thoughts that uncreative people might dismiss. Creative people are typically less close-minded and less inhibited than others in their feelings and fantasies (Lack, et al., 2003; McCrae, 1987). Moreover, they seem to be inherently curious and inquisitive (Sternberg, 1985a). They are comfortable with ambiguity and apparently don't need immediate resolution of conflicting and contradictory ideas. During the early stages of creative work, these individuals are not on a quest for certainty, but rather a journey of discovery. And, along the way, they are not bothered by loose or dead ends. Rather, they work their way through failures and out of blind alleys, persisting until they succeed.

Independence of Mind Creative people tend to be independent thinkers. They cherish this independence and, especially in their area of creative expertise, prefer to go their own way. They can easily spend long periods alone and are not influenced by

One characteristic of creative people is intrinsic motivation. They enjoy the process of creation for its own sake—the end result may be a whimsical toy rather than a practical tool.

the opinions of others as much as their less creative counterparts are. They will take unpopular stands if they must and are often seen as nonconformists. But, then, by its very nature, creativity is unconventional and uncommon. Such unconventionality is, however, typically confined to the work of creative people. Otherwise, they do not appear to be especially eccentric or out-of-the-ordinary.

Intrinsic Motivation Unlike people who are readily influenced by the opinions of others and motivated by extrinsic (external) rewards, creative individuals are more likely to be intrinsically (internally) motivated. Creative people are moved by—and sometimes carried away by—the anticipation, excitement, and enjoyment associated with their work, whether it is inventing, producing works of art, or advancing scientific knowledge. For these people, the sheer joy of creative activity itself carries its own reward. In short, they "enjoy the process of creation for its own sake" (Csikszentmihalyi, 1996, p. 40).

Perseverance Creative endeavor requires intelligence and hard work. Creativity is not poured from empty vessels or fashioned by idle hands. Thomas A. Edison, who held 1,093 patents, claimed that his magnificently creative contributions were accomplished through 2% inspiration and 98% perspiration. Albert Einstein published 248 papers and persevered (perspired) for 10 years on his theory of relativity before it was finished. And Mozart, when he died at age 35, had created 609 musical compositions (Haberlandt, 1997).

Savant Syndrome

How do savants differ from other people?

Perhaps you have seen the movie *Rain Man,* in which Dustin Hoffman plays an autistic man whose ability to keep track of cards that have been played enables his brother, played by Tom Cruise, to win a great deal of money at blackjack. Raymond, Hoffman's character, was a *savant.*

Savant syndrome, an unusual combination of mental retardation and genius, is a condition that allows an individual whose level of general intelligence is very low to perform certain highly creative or difficult mental feats. The term is derived from the French term for such a person: *idiot savant* (*idiot* means "poorly informed or untutored" and *savant* means "wise one"). Savants demonstrate high levels of performance in a variety of domains. Some are exceptionally gifted in musical performance. Others can identify the day of the week corresponding to any specific date in the past or in the future. Still others can carry out complex calculations in their heads. Arthur is such a person.

■ savant syndrome
A condition that allows an individual whose level of general intelligence is very low to perform highly creative or difficult mental feats.

> "Arthur, how much is 6,427 times 4,234?" Arthur turned his head in my direction and said slowly but without hesitation, "27 million, 211 thousand, 918." His voice was stilted but

> precise. His eyes never lost their blank stare, and now he returned to gazing into space, without seeing anything, a handsome, impassive 8-year-old. (Rimland, 1978, p. 69)

Arthur can multiply multidigit numbers in his head faster than you could do it on a calculator, and he never makes a mistake. Yet, his measured IQ is extremely low.

Alonzo Clemons is not able to speak in complete sentences, cannot read or count, and, at almost 50 years of age, has the mental ability of an average 6-year-old child. He lives in a facility for the mentally retarded near Denver, Colorado. But Alonzo, the retarded genius, is making a name for himself in the art world, creating bronze sculptures, which collectors are eagerly buying for hundreds of dollars each, or more for special pieces. In only 4 months after his first show, Alonzo, the sculptor, sold $30,000 worth of his work through a Denver art gallery.

Another rare combination of genius and low IQ is Arnold, who is identified as an autistic savant. Although his IQ of 80 is low, it is too high to allow him to be considered retarded. Arnold is employed at a Goodwill store, doing assembly work. But his mother describes him this way:

> He reads and understands books on electronics and uses the theories to build devices. He recently put together a tape recorder, a fluorescent light, and a small transistor radio with some other components, so that music from the tape was changed to light energy in the light and then back to music in the radio. By passing his hand between the recorder and the light, he could stop the music. He understands the concepts of electronics, astronomy, music, navigation and mechanics. He knows an astonishing amount about how things work and is familiar with technical terms. (Rimland, 1978, p. 70)

The puzzle of savant syndrome is slowly being unraveled by scientists. For instance, psychologists have known for a long time that the prevalence of *absolute pitch*, the ability to identify musical tones merely by hearing them, is greater among individuals with autism than in the general population. Recently, though, researchers have found that people with autism are more sensitive than other people to sounds, and to changes in pitch, in general (Bonnel et al., 2003). Moreover, savants who can rapidly determine day-date associations in the past and future, known as *calendrical savants*, appear to have enhanced abilities to calculate and to associate all kinds of verbal and numerical stimuli (Cowan et al., 2003; Pring & Hermelin, 2002). Many researchers hope that further investigation of the puzzling aspects of savant syndrome will lead to a clearer understanding of intelligence and creativity.

Remember It 8.6

1. Creativity and IQ scores are __________ related.
2. Match each stage of the creative process with its associated activity.
   - ___ (1) preparation
   - ___ (2) incubation
   - ___ (3) illumination
   - ___ (4) translation

   a. letting the problem "sit" while digesting information
   b. transforming the new insight into useful action
   c. searching for relevant information
   d. being suddenly struck by the right solution
3. Divergent thinking is associated with activity in the __________ of the brain.
4. Fred is autistic but can play any piece of music he hears on the piano immediately after listening to it. Fred exhibits __________.

ANSWERS: 1. weakly; 2. (1) c, (2) a, (3) d, (4) b; 3. right frontal cortex; 4. savant syndrome

Apply It

Boosting Your Standardized Test Scores

As you probably know, standardized testing doesn't end when you graduate from high school. Many states require college students to pass standardized tests before qualifying for graduation. Moreover, graduates entering fields such as nursing and teaching have to take exams for state certification or licensure. And a sizeable proportion of college graduates take an entrance exam, such as the Graduate Record Exam (GRE), the Law School Aptitude Test (LSAT), the Graduate Management Admission Test (GMAT), or the Medical College Aptitude Test (MCAT), for admission to graduate or professional school.

When your future depends on a test result, you want to do your best. Knowing this, test preparation services, along with the publishers of test preparation books and software, often promise potential buyers a substantial increase in their chances of obtaining the desired score. Research supports the notion that special preparation activities can improve scores, but the degree of improvement is seldom as great as advocates of these programs and materials suggest (Powers & Rock, 1999). And self-study with free materials provided by a test publisher can be just as effective as expensive courses and books (Koenig & Leger, 1997).

Of course, it's important to realize that standardized exams used to establish qualifications for professional licensure or to help graduate and professional schools make admission decisions are designed to test examinees on knowledge and skills that are assumed to have been accumulated over a period of many years. For this reason, you are not likely to improve your scores on such exams with last-minute cramming. But focused preparation spread over a period of weeks or months can make a difference. Here are a few general guidelines you can follow the next time you have to take a standardized test:

- *Become familiar with the test format.* Before you take the test, you should know what kinds of skills it measures (e.g., vocabulary, reading comprehension, problem solving) and the types of items (e.g., multiple choice) it includes. You can probably learn enough about the test from the publisher's free materials, but you may want to invest in a preparation book or a commercial review course.
- *Take practice tests under simulated test conditions.* Most standardized tests are timed, and many publishers provide practice tests. Some even sell actual exams that have been used in the past. When you take practice tests, impose the same time limitations on yourself as will be in effect when you take the real exam. If you can't finish within the allotted time, keep practicing until you can.
- *Review skills you haven't used for a while.* Many graduate and professional school entrance exams cover subject matter you may not have studied for several years. If you plan to take the GRE, for instance, and you haven't taken a math course for several years, a review will probably help. Moreover, calculator speed is correlated with math performance on such tests (Scheuneman et al., 2002), so practice your calculator skills! Similarly, the MCAT tests your basic knowledge of sciences such as biology and chemistry, so you may want to brush up a bit in these areas.
- *Know how the test is scored.* Some standardized tests deduct more points for missed items than for those that are left blank. Obviously, it helps to know this when you're taking the test. In addition, many tests require examinees to write essays. It's critical that you know how an essay will be assessed. You should also know the rules regarding repetition of a test. Most tests can be repeated a limited number of times, and some professional school entrance exam scores are reported as an average of all the scores an examinee has received.
- *Relax.* The greatest benefit of preparation may be to increase your confidence allowing you to relax and decreasing your test anxiety.

Summary and Review

The Nature of Intelligence p. 263

What factors underlie intelligence, according to Spearman and Thurstone? p. 263

Spearman believed that intelligence is composed of a general ability (*g* factor), which underlies all intellectual functions, and a number of specific abilities (*s* factors). Thurstone identified seven primary mental abilities, which, singly or in combination, are involved in all intellectual activities.

What types of intelligence did Gardner and Sternberg identify? p. 263

Gardner claims that there are eight independent types of intelligence: linguistic, logical-mathematical, musical, spatial, bodily-kinesthetic, interpersonal, intrapersonal, and naturalistic. Sternberg's triarchic theory of intelligence identifies three types: componential (conventional intelligence), experiential (creative intelligence), and contextual (practical intelligence).

Measuring Intelligence p. 267

What is Binet's major contribution to intelligence testing? p. 267

Binet worked with Simon in Paris in the early 20th century to develop the Binet-Simon Intelligence Scale, the first standardized, age-normed test of intelligence. A child's score on the test was expressed as a mental age.

How did the work of Terman and Wechsler influence intelligence testing in the United States? p. 269

Terman revised the Binet-Simon scale and established norms for his version of the test—the Stanford-Binet Intelligence Scale. Terman also introduced the abbreviation IQ for the intelligence quotient, a score derived by dividing a person's mental age by his or her chronological age and then multiplying by 100. Wechsler developed the first individual intelligence test for adults, the Wechsler Adult Intelligence Scale (WAIS-III). He was also the first to calculate the IQ score as a deviation score so that it could be applied to populations of all ages.

Why are reliability, validity, and standardization important in intelligence testing? p. 270

To be useful, an intelligence test must be reliable and valid and must be standardized. Reliability is the ability of a test to yield nearly the same score each time a person takes the test or an alternative form of the test. Validity is the ability of a test to measure what it is intended to measure. Standardization involves following prescribed procedures for administering a test as well as establishing norms for the test by using a representative sample of the population to whom the test will be given.

The Range of Intelligence p. 272

What does the term "bell curve" mean when applied to IQ test scores? p. 272

Graphing the frequencies of a large number of IQ scores produces a symmetrical curve (the normal curve) shaped like a bell. Exactly 50% of IQ scores fall above and below the average score of 100 on this curve.

According to the Terman study, how do the gifted differ from the general population? p. 273

Terman's longitudinal study revealed that, in general, gifted individuals enjoy better physical and mental health and are more successful than members of the general population.

What two criteria must a person meet to be classified as mentally retarded? p. 273

To be classified as mentally retarded, an individual must have an IQ score below 70 and show a severe deficiency in everyday adaptive functioning.

What is the relationship between intelligence and the efficiency and speed of neural processing? p. 274

People who are more intelligent generally use less mental energy and have a faster neural processing speed than less intelligent people.

The IQ Controversy p. 276

Of what are intelligence tests good predictors? p. 276

IQ scores are fairly good predictors of academic performance.

What are some abuses of intelligence tests? p. 276

Abuses occur when IQ tests are the only or the major criterion for admitting people to educational programs or for placing children in special educational programs. Many people claim that IQ tests are culturally biased in favor of the White middle and upper classes.

What is the nature-nurture controversy regarding intelligence, and how do twin studies support the view that intelligence is inherited? p. 278

The nature-nurture controversy is the debate over whether intelligence is primarily determined by heredity or by the environment. Twin studies provide evidence that intelligence is primarily inherited because identical twins are more alike in intelligence than are fraternal twins, even if they have been reared apart.

What are Jensen's and Herrnstein and Murray's controversial views on race and IQ? p. 279

These researchers claimed that the difference in average IQ scores between Blacks and Whites is due to genetic differences between the races that cannot be changed significantly through environmental intervention.

What kinds of evidence suggest that IQ is changeable rather than fixed? p. 280

Several adoption studies have revealed that when infants from disadvantaged environments are adopted by middle- or upper-middle-class parents, their IQ scores are higher on average than would otherwise be expected. Research involving infants and young children from poor families has demonstrated that early educational experiences can affect intellectual functioning. Also, IQ scores have been rising steadily over the past 60 years in many developed and developing nations, presumably because of changes in the standard of living.

How might parental expectations and teaching methods influence scores on standardized tests? p. 283

Some studies show that Asian parents have higher expectations for their children's academic performance, which may help explain why Asian students score higher, on average, on math achievement tests than American children do. But teaching methods may also play a role. Asian teachers allow students to master each kind of problem before moving on to a new one. Moreover, teachers in Asian schools emphasize computational fluency to a greater degree than do teachers in the United States.

Emotional Intelligence p. 286

What are the personal components of emotional intelligence? p. 287

The personal components of emotional intelligence are an awareness of one's emotions, an ability to manage those emotions, and self-motivation.

What are the interpersonal components of emotional intelligence? p. 288

The interpersonal components of emotional intelligence are empathy and the ability to handle relationships.

Creativity p. 289

What are the four stages in the creative problem-solving process? p. 289

The four stages in the creative problem-solving process are preparation, incubation, illumination, and translation.

How does creative thinking differ from other forms of cognition? p. 289

Guilford suggests that creativity involves divergent thinking, which is more flexible and fluent than convergent thinking. Baer argues that creativity flows naturally from accumulated knowledge in an area of expertise.

What are some tests that have been used to measure creativity? p. 291

Some tests used to measure creativity are the Unusual Uses Test, the Consequences Test, and the Remote Associates Test (RAT). But these tests are only mediocre predictors of real-life creative achievement.

What are some characteristics of creative people? *p. 291*

Creative people share some distinguishing characteristics: expertise, openness to experience, independence of mind, intrinsic motivation, and perseverance.

How do savants differ from other people? *p. 292*

Savants are individuals whose level of general intelligence is very low but who can perform certain highly creative or difficult mental feats. For example, they may be able to do complex calculations very rapidly in their heads.

Key Terms

adoption study method, p. 279
aptitude test, p. 271
creativity, p. 289
culture-fair intelligence test, p. 277
deviation score, p. 269
divergent thinking, p. 289
emotional intelligence, p. 286
g factor, p. 263
heritability, p. 278
inclusion, p. 274
intelligence, p. 262
intelligence quotient (IQ), p. 269
mental retardation, p. 273
nature-nurture controversy, p. 278
norms, p. 269
primary mental abilities, p. 263
reliability, p. 270
savant syndrome, p. 292
standardization, p. 271
Stanford-Binet Intelligence Scale, p. 269
triarchic theory of intelligence, p. 265
validity, p. 270
Wechsler Adult Intelligence Scale (WAIS-III), p. 269

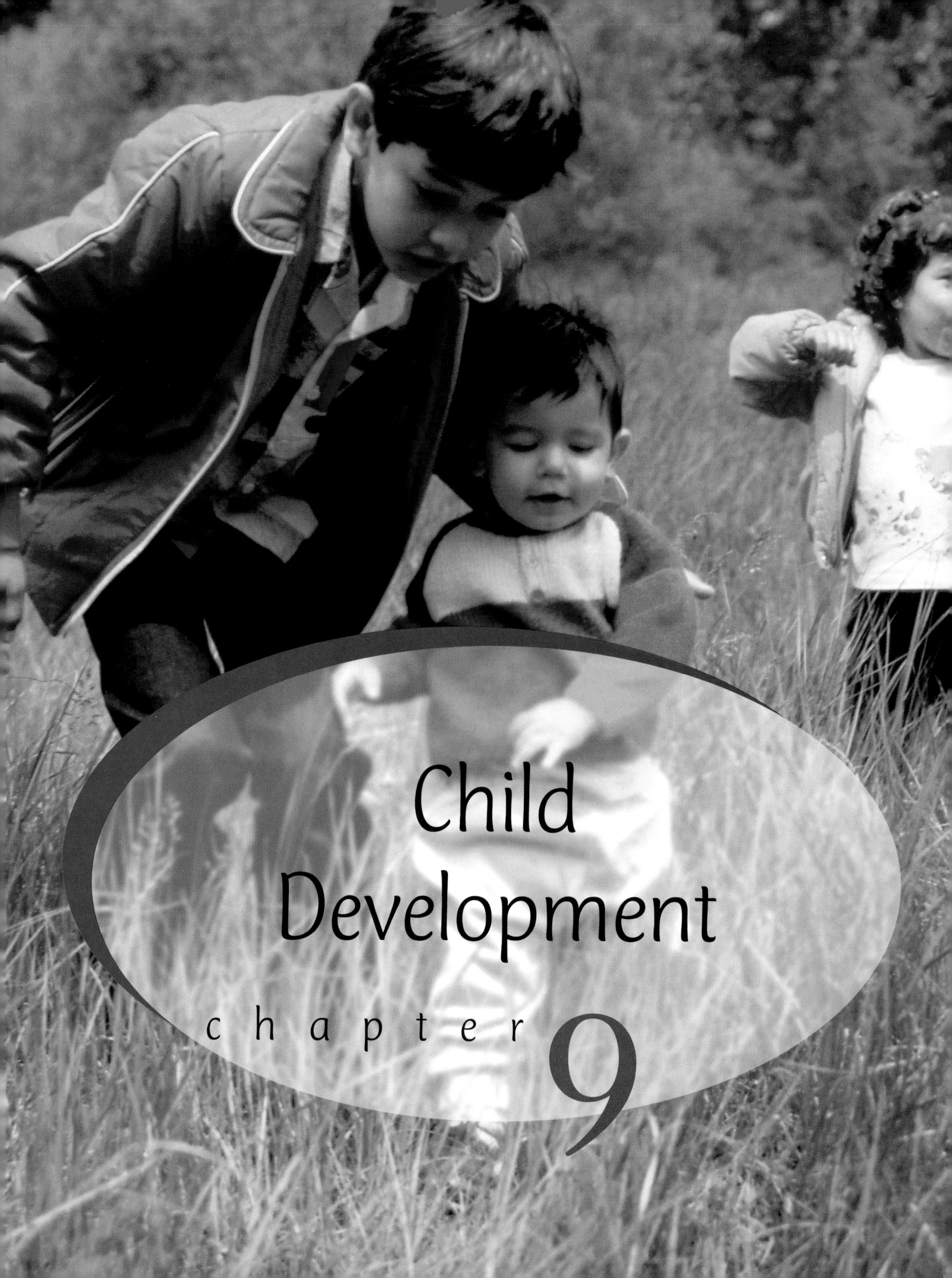

Child Development

chapter 9

Developmental Psychology: Basic Issues and Methodology

- *What three issues are frequently debated among developmental psychologists?*
- *What methods do developmental psychologists use to investigate age-related changes?*

Prenatal Development

- *What happens in each of the three stages of prenatal development?*
- *What have scientists learned about fetal behavior in recent years?*
- *What are some negative influences on prenatal development, and when is their impact greatest?*

Infancy

- *How do the motor behaviors of a newborn compare to those of an older infant?*
- *What are the sensory and perceptual abilities of a newborn?*
- *What types of learning occur in infancy?*
- *What is temperament, and what are the three temperament types identified by Thomas, Chess, and Birch?*
- *What did the research of Harlow, Bowlby, and Ainsworth reveal about the process of infant-caregiver attachment?*
- *How do fathers affect children's development?*

Piaget's Theory of Cognitive Development

- *How did Piaget use the concepts of scheme, assimilation, and accommodation to explain cognitive development?*
- *What occurs during each of Piaget's stages of cognitive development?*
- *What are some important criticisms of Piaget's work?*

Other Approaches to Cognitive Development

- *In Vygotsky's view, how do private speech and scaffolding contribute to cognitive development?*
- *What three cognitive abilities have information-processing researchers studied extensively?*

Language Development

- *What is the sequence of language development from babbling through the acquisition of grammatical rules?*
- *How do learning theory and the nativist position explain the acquisition of language?*
- *What is phonological awareness, and why is it important?*

Socialization of the Child

- *What are the three parenting styles identified by Baumrind, and which does she find most effective?*
- *How do peers contribute to the socialization process?*
- *What are some of the positive and negative effects of television?*
- *How does Bronfenbrenner explain the influence of culture on children's development?*

What was your worst childhood experience, and how did you overcome it?

During the early 1990s in the Sudan, children, some as young as 4 years of age, were caught in the middle of a bloody civil war, in which Christians and animists, adults and children both, were ruthlessly slaughtered by the Sudanese government. Literally running for their lives, groups of boys, who became known as the "Lost Boys of the Sudan," crossed hundreds of miles of hostile East African desert, a deadly hot and dry land more than twice the size of

Texas. Many starved to death or died from disease, bad water, or tainted or poisonous food. Often, at night, a howling pack of hyenas would stalk a group of boys. On some occasions, as many as five boys in a group would be lost to these predators. The terrified survivors could do nothing but climb a tree and watch until the hyenas had finished turning their human prey into small piles of cleaned bones.

In a testimony to human resilience, thousands of the Lost Boys made their way to refugee camps in Kenya, where relief agencies helped them emigrate to European and North American nations. Some were adopted into families; others lived in group homes. Most adapted well to their new homes. Today, the Lost Boys are young adults who are going to college, starting careers, establishing families of their own, and doing all the other things that young adults in their adopted societies do.

How do you think you would have fared if your early life had included something like the experiences of the Lost Boys? Child development is often seen as a fragile process in which potentially damaging influences can easily push an individual toward a poor outcome. Although it's preferable to have positive experiences in one's early years, early negative influences often seem to be compensated for in some way. The Lost Boys, for example, developed intense emotional bonds with one another and continue to maintain those bonds as young adults, many years after their traumatic experiences. Is it possible that these bonds protected them to some degree from the potentially damaging effects of their experiences? Psychologists study such questions in their research on human development, as you will learn in this chapter.

Developmental Psychology: Basic Issues and Methodology

Developmental psychology is the study of how humans grow, develop, and change throughout the life span. Some developmental psychologists specialize in the study of a particular age group on the continuum from infancy, childhood, and adolescence, through early, middle, and late adulthood, to the end of the life span. Others concentrate on a specific area of interest, such as physical, cognitive, or language development or emotional or moral development.

What three issues are frequently debated among developmental psychologists?

Controversial Issues in Developmental Psychology

In turning to the study of development, we encounter an age-old question: Which is more important, heredity or environment? Chapter 8 discussed the nature-nurture controversy regarding differences in intelligence. Among developmental psychologists, interest in these two sets of factors extends far beyond the domain of intelligence. Obviously, heredity imposes some limits on what a person can become. The best possible home environment, education, and nutrition are not enough to produce an Albert Einstein or a Marilyn Mach vos Savant (whose 230 IQ is the highest ever recorded). But parental neglect, poor nutrition, ill health, abuse, and lack of education can prevent even the brightest child from becoming the best his or her genes would allow. Still, many individuals have achieved normal or exceptional lives despite childhood deprivation.

Some developmental psychologists have argued that the best way to resolve the nature-nurture debate—and to explain why some children exhibit *resilience* (the capacity to bounce back) in response to unsupportive or harmful environments—is to think of each child as being born with certain *vulnerabilities*, such as a difficult temperament or a genetic disorder (Masten, 2001; Masten et al., 1999). Each child is also born with some *protective factors*, such as high intelligence, good coordination, or an easy-going personality, that tend to increase resilience. Through childhood and adolescence, vulnerabilities and protective factors interact with variables in the environment so that the same environment can have different effects, depending on the characteristics of each child. For example, a shy child who has few friends might be damaged more by parental emotional abuse than one who is more outgoing and has a greater number of relationships outside the family.

We often say that a child who is acting out in some way is going through a "phase" or a "stage." But are there really phases or stages in development that differ qualitatively? This is one of the most important questions in developmental psychology. To understand how developmentalists think about this question, consider what happens as children become taller. Children change *quantitatively* as they grow taller. In other words, the characteristic of height is the same at all ages. Older children simply have more of it than those who are younger. However, changes in other developmental variables—logical thinking, for example—occur in stages. Such changes are *qualitative* in nature. In other words, the logic of a 10-year-old is completely different from that of a 3-year-old. The older child doesn't just have more logic; he thinks in an entirely different way. In this chapter, we will explore one of the most important stage theories in developmental psychology: Piaget's theory of cognitive development. In Chapter 10, you will read about Erikson's psychosocial stages and Kohlberg's stages of moral reasoning.

Developmentalists also attempt to answer questions about the extent to which personal traits, such as intelligence and personality, are stable over time. How do developmental psychologists study changes over the lifespan?

■ **developmental psychology**
The study of how humans grow, develop, and change throughout the life span.

■ **longitudinal study**
A type of developmental study in which the same group of participants is followed and measured at different ages.

■ **cross-sectional study**
A type of developmental study in which researchers compare groups of participants of different ages on various characteristics to determine age-related differences.

Approaches to Studying Developmental Change

What methods do developmental psychologists use to investigate age-related changes?

How would you go about finding out how individuals change with age? You could follow a group of people as they get older, or you could compare individuals of different ages. Developmental psychologists use both approaches in their research.

A **longitudinal study** is one in which the same group of participants is followed and measured at different ages, over a period of years. Such studies allow researchers to observe age-related changes in individuals. There are some drawbacks to a longitudinal study, however. It is time-consuming and expensive, and participants may drop out of the study or die, possibly leaving the researcher with a biased sample.

A **cross-sectional study** is a less expensive and less time-consuming method in which researchers compare groups of participants of different ages to determine age-related differences in some characteristics. But, in a cross-sectional study, differences

To find out about developmental changes, is it better to compare older and younger people, like those in this photo, or to begin studying individuals when they are young and follow them as they age? Developmental psychologists use both approaches, and each has advantages and disadvantages.

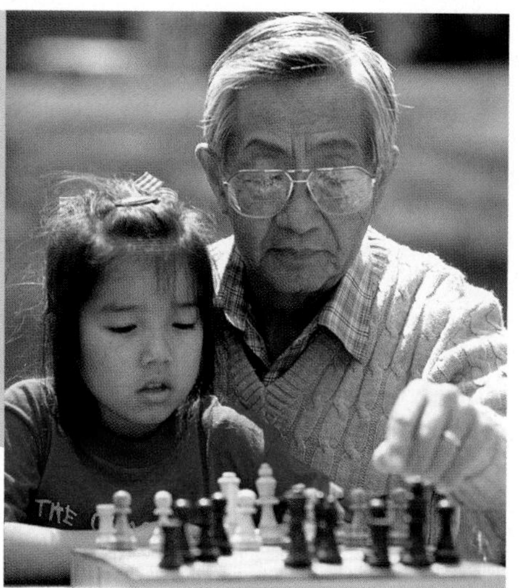

across age groups are based on group averages, so this approach cannot be used to answer certain questions. For example, it could not be used to determine if individual temperament is stable over time. Moreover, certain relevant differences in groups of participants may have less to do with the participants' ages than with the eras in which they grew up, a problem known as the *cohort effect*. Figure 9.1 compares longitudinal and cross-sectional studies.

Development is a fascinating and remarkable process that begins even before birth, and we will trace its course from the very beginning.

FIGURE 9.1 A Comparison of Longitudinal and Cross-Sectional Studies

To study age-related changes using a longitudinal study, researchers examine the same group of participants at several times over an extended period. When using a cross-sectional study, researchers examine and compare groups of different ages at one point in time.

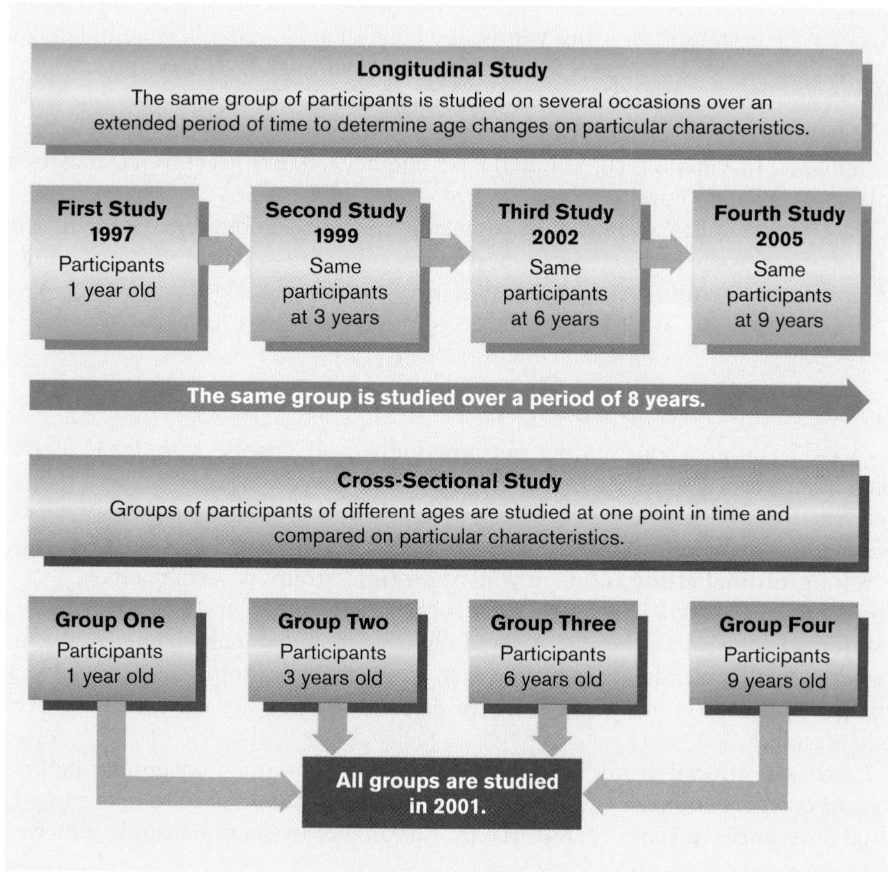

Remember It 9.1

1. Developmental psychologists study changes that happen during
   a. childhood.
   b. adulthood.
   c. old age.
   d. the entire lifespan.
2. One of the controversies in developmental psychology is whether development occurs in ________.
3. The finding that older children think more logically than younger children is an example of a(n) ________ change.
4. Identify the characteristics of cross-sectional studies with the letter *c* and the characteristics of longitudinal studies with the letter *l*.
   ___ (1) Groups of different ages are tested at the same time.
   ___ (2) A single group is studied at different times.
   ___ (3) The less expensive of the two research methods.
   ___ (4) The method that can reveal individual change over time.
   ___ (5) Participants may drop out or die.
   ___ (6) Differences may be due to factors other than development, such as the era in which participants grew up.

ANSWERS: (1) d; 2. stages; 3. qualitative; 4. (1) c, (2) l, (3) c, (4) l, (5) l, (6) c

Prenatal Development

Stages of Prenatal Development

Many people divide the 9 months of pregnancy into *trimesters*, three periods of 3 months' duration: The first begins at conception and ends at 3 months, the second spans the period from 3 to 6 months, and the third extends from 6 to 9 months. However, the division of pregnancy into trimesters is arbitrary and has no significance with regard to prenatal development. In fact, each of the three stages of **prenatal development,** or development from conception to birth, is marked by a specific event at its beginning and another at its end. Moreover, you may be surprised to learn, by the time the first trimester of pregnancy is over, the third stage of prenatal development has already begun.

Conception Conception occurs the moment a sperm cell fertilizes the ovum (egg cell), forming a single-celled **zygote.** You should remember from Chapter 2 that the zygote carries the full complement of 46 chromosomes (23 from the father's sperm and 23 from the mother's ovum) that are necessary for the development of a human being. These chromosomes carry genes, the biochemical instructions that determine many of the new individual's characteristics, such as eye color and genetic disorders. Other genetic instructions, in combination with environmental influences, will shape the individual's development throughout the lifespan. These include genes that influence intelligence, personality, and the development of chronic health conditions such as diabetes and heart disease.

Sometimes, for an unknown reason, the zygote divides into two cells, resulting in identical, or *monozygotic*, twins. There are even cases of identical triplets, quadruplets, and quintuplets. In fact, the famous Dionne quintuplets, born in Canada in the 1930s, were identical. There are also times when two (or more) eggs unite with two (or more) sperm, resulting in fraternal, or *dizygotic*, twins.

■ prenatal development Development that occurs between conception and birth and consists of three stages (germinal, embryonic, and fetal).

■ zygote The single cell that forms when a sperm and egg unite.

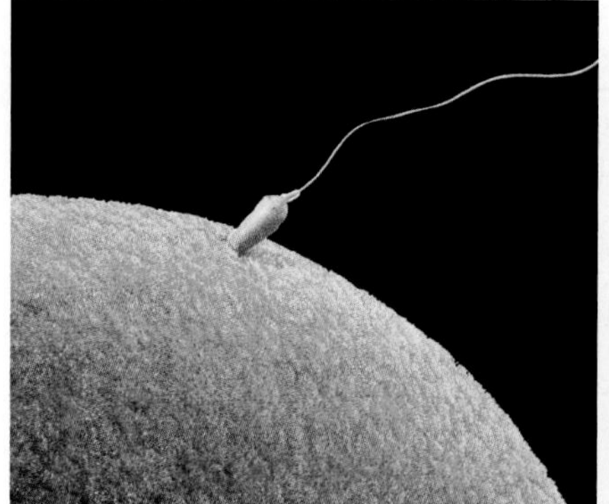
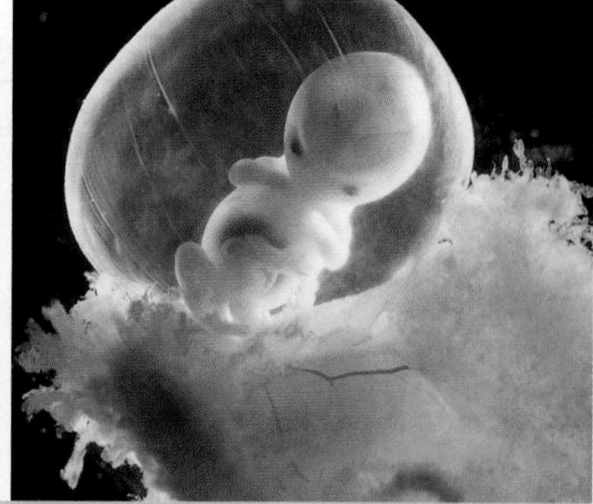
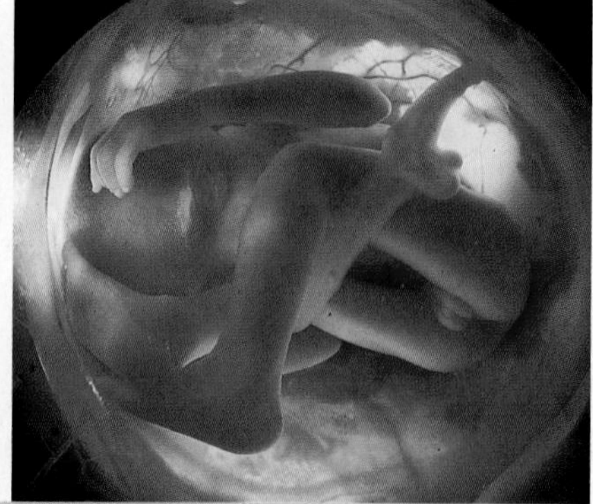

This sequence of photos shows the fertilization of an egg by a sperm (left), an embryo at 7 weeks (center), and a fetus at 22 weeks (right).

What happens in each of the three stages of prenatal development?

embryo
The developing human organism during the period from week 3 through week 8, when the major systems, organs, and structures of the body develop.

fetus
The developing human organism during the period from week 9 until birth, when rapid growth and further development of the structures, organs, and systems of the body occur.

The Germinal, Embryonic, and Fetal Stages Conception usually takes place in one of the fallopian tubes, and within the next 2 weeks, the zygote travels to the uterus and attaches itself to the uterine wall. During this 2-week period, called the germinal stage, rapid cell division occurs. Once the zygote is successfully attached, the germinal stage is over. At the end of this stage, the zygote is only the size of the period at the end of this sentence.

The second stage is the *embryonic stage*, during which the developing human organism, now called an **embryo,** forms all of the major body systems, organs, and structures. Lasting from the beginning of week 3 through week 8, this period begins when the zygote attaches itself to the uterine wall and ends when the first bone cells form. Only 1 inch long and weighing 1/7 of an ounce, the embryo already resembles a human being, with limbs, fingers, toes, and many internal organs that have begun to function.

The final stage of prenatal development, the *fetal stage*, lasts from the beginning of week 9, when bone cells begin to form, until birth. The developing human organism is now called a **fetus,** and it experiences rapid growth and further development of body structures, organs, and systems. Table 9.1 summarizes the stages of prenatal development.

TABLE 9.1 **Stages of Prenatal Development**

STAGE	TIME AFTER CONCEPTION	MAJOR ACTIVITIES OF THE STAGE
Germinal	1 to 2 weeks	Zygote attaches to the uterine lining. At 2 weeks, zygote is the size of the period at the end of this sentence.
Embryonic	3 to 8 weeks	Major systems, organs, and structures of the body develop. Stage ends when first bone cells appear. At 8 weeks, embryo is about 1 inch long and weighs 1/7 of an ounce.
Fetal	9 weeks to birth (38 weeks)	Rapid growth and further development of the body structures, organs, and systems.

Fetal Behavior

What have scientists learned about fetal behavior in recent years?

Would you be surprised to learn that a human fetus is very responsive to sounds as early as the 25th week of gestation (Joseph, 2000)? Over the past few decades, scientists have learned a great deal about the behavior of fetuses because of the availability of such technologies as ultrasonagraphy, which allow them to observe fetal behavior directly. Thus, we know that fetal responses to sound are both physical, such as turning the head toward a sound, and neurological (Moore et al., 2001).

Several studies of newborns have shown that they remember sounds to which they were exposed as fetuses. In one frequently cited study, researchers DeCasper and Spence (1986) had 16 pregnant women read *The Cat in the Hat* to their developing fetuses twice a day during the final 6 weeks of pregnancy. A few days after birth, the infants could adjust their sucking on specially designed, pressure-sensitive nipples to hear their mother reading either *The Cat in the Hat* or *The King, the Mice, and the Cheese*, a story they had never heard before. By their sucking behavior, the infants showed a clear preference for the familiar sound of *The Cat in the Hat*. Other research has demonstrated that newborns remember such prenatal stimuli as their mother's heartbeats, the odor of the amniotic fluid, and music they heard in the womb (Righetti, 1996; Schaal et al., 1998).

Does prenatal learning contribute to intellectual development in infancy or even later in childhood? Researchers don't yet know the answer to this question. However, experiments are currently underway in which the cognitive development of children who were systematically exposed to prenatal stimuli is being compared to that of children not so exposed. In one of these studies, pregnant women strapped small speakers to their abdomens during the later weeks of pregnancy in order to expose their babies to many hours of classical music (Lafuente et al., 1997). Babies who were exposed to the music prior to birth were found to be more advanced in cognitive development at 6 months of age than infants in the control group, who were not exposed to the music (Lafuente et al., 1997). Of course, the long-term significance of such findings is unknown.

Stable individual differences are also evident during prenatal development. For instance, fetuses exhibit a wide range of differences in activity level. Longitudinal research has demonstrated that highly active fetuses grow into young children who are very active (DiPietro et al., 2002). Moreover, in the elementary school years, parents and teachers are more likely to label such children "hyperactive." By contrast, low levels of fetal activity are associated with mental retardation (Accardo, et al., 1997).

Some sex differences appear early in prenatal development as well. One such difference is the frequent finding that male fetuses, on average, are more physically active than females (DePietro et al., 1996a, 1996b). Another difference is that female fetuses appear to be more responsive than male fetuses to sounds and other external stimuli (Groome et al., 1999).

Negative Influences on Prenatal Development

What are some negative influences on prenatal development, and when is their impact greatest?

Most of the time, prenatal development progresses smoothly and ends in the birth of a normal, healthy infant. However, there are a few factors that increase the risks of various kinds of problems. Maternal illness, for one, can interfere with the process. A chronic condition such as diabetes, for example, can cause problems that may include retardation or acceleration of fetal growth (Levy-Shiff et al., 2002).

When the mother suffers from a viral disease such as rubella, chicken pox, or HIV, she may deliver an infant with physical and behavioral abnormalities (Amato, 1998; Kliegman, 1998). Some of these effects, such as the heart problems that are associated with rubella, can be lifelong. In addition, these viral diseases can be passed

Drinking alcohol during pregnancy can result in the birth of an infant with fetal alcohol syndrome, a permanent condition that involves mental retardation and physical and behavioral abnormalities.

from mother to child. In the case of HIV, prenatal transmission of the virus is likely to lead to the development of full-blown AIDS in the child after birth. Viruses and other harmful agents, including drugs, X-rays, and environmental toxins, that can have a negative impact on prenatal development are called **teratogens**.

A teratogen's impact depends on both its intensity and the time during prenatal development when it is present. Drugs, environmental hazards such as X-rays and toxic waste, and diseases such as rubella generally have their most devastating consequences during the embryonic stage. During this time, there are **critical periods** when certain body structures develop. If drugs or infections interfere with development during a critical period, a particular body structure will not form properly, nor will it develop later (Kopp & Kaler, 1989). For example, maternal alcohol intake early in prenatal development can lead to facial deformities as well as mental retardation and behavior problems, a condition known as **fetal alcohol syndrome**. Exposure to teratogens during the fetal stage is more likely to result in various types of intellectual and social impairments than to cause physical abnormalities. Table 9.2 lists a number of teratogens and other factors that may negatively affect prenatal development.

One of the most serious effects of teratogens is that they increase the risks of **low birth weight**, a birth weight less than 5.5 pounds. There are two types of low-birth-weight infants: preterm and small-for-date. *Preterm infants* are those who are born early, specifically, before 38 weeks of gestation. *Small-for-date infants* are those who have birth weights lower than expected for their gestational age. Of the two types, small-for-date infants are more likely to die or have permanent disabilities because their size is the result of some prenatal factor, such as maternal malnutrition, that caused them to grow too slowly. By contrast, preterm infants have experienced appropriate growth rates but may have organs, especially the lungs, that are not yet ready to function independently.

Finally, things sometimes go wrong during the birth process. When infants are exposed to life-threatening complications during birth, such as collapse of the umbilical cord, they are at increased risk of experiencing many negative developmental outcomes. For example, lack of sufficient oxygen can damage the brain. Moreover, birth complications are related to behavior problems, such as excessive aggressiveness, later in childhood and adolescence (Arseneault et al., 2002).

■ **teratogens**
Viruses and other harmful agents that can have a negative impact on prenatal development.

■ **critical period**
A period during the embryonic stage when certain body structures are developing and can be harmed by negative influences in the prenatal environment.

■ **fetal alcohol syndrome**
A condition that is caused by maternal alcohol intake early in prenatal development and that leads to facial deformities as well as mental retardation.

■ **low birth weight**
A weight at birth of less than 5.5 pounds.

Remember It 9.2

1. Match each stage of prenatal development with its description.

___ (1) germinal
___ (2) embryonic
___ (3) fetal

a. first 2 weeks of life
b. rapid growth and further development of body structures and systems
c. development of major systems, organs, and structures of the body

2. Fetal variations in ___________ are related to the diagnosis of hyperactivity during childhood.

3. Because many body structures are at critical periods of development during this time, a teratogen is most likely to cause defects during the ___________ stage.

ANSWERS: 1. (1) a, (2) c, (3) b; 2. activity level; 3. embryonic

TABLE 9.2 **Negative Influences on Prenatal Development**

TERATOGENS	POSSIBLE EFFECTS ON FETUS
Maternal Diseases/ Conditions	
Malnutrition	Poor growth, mental retardation
Diabetes	Growth abnormalities
Rubella	Heart defects, blindness, deafness
Cytomegalovirus	Mental retardation, deafness; disease can be transmitted to fetus
Herpes	Nerve damage; disease can be transmitted to fetus
HIV	Disease can be transmitted to fetus
Cancer	Fetal or placental tumor
Toxoplasmosis	Brain swelling, spinal abnormalities
Chicken pox	Scars, eye damage
Parvovirus	Anemia
Hepatitis B	Hepatitis
Chlamydia	Conjunctivitis, pneumonia
Syphillis	Blindness, deafness, mental retardation
Gonorrhea	Blindness
Tuberculosis	Pneumonia or tuberculosis
Drugs	
Alcohol	Fetal alcohol syndrome (FAS; facial deformities, mental retardation, behavior problems)
Heroin	Addiction, tremors, erratic sleep patterns, vomiting, prematurity
Cocaine	Prematurity, physical defects, sleep difficulties, tremors
Marijuana	Tremors, sleep difficulties
Tobacco	Low birth weight, sudden infant death syndrome
Caffeine	Consumption of more than 300 mg/day (about 3 cups of brewed coffee) linked to low birth weight
Inhalants	FAS-like syndrome, prematurity
Accutane/Vitamin A	Facial, ear, heart deformities
Streptomycin	Deafness
Penicillin	Skin disorders
Tetracycline	Tooth deformities
Diet pills	Low birth weight

Source: Amato (1998); Kliegman (1998).

Infancy

Reflexes and Motor Development

How do the motor behaviors of a newborn compare to those of an older infant?

If you have observed the behavior of a newborn baby, you probably noticed that his or her movements seem fairly erratic when compared to those of an older infant. During the first few days after birth, the movements of **neonates** (newborn babies up to 1 month old) are dominated by **reflexes**, which are inborn, unlearned, automatic responses to certain stimuli. These behaviors are needed to ensure survival in their new world. Sucking, swallowing, coughing, and blinking are some important behaviors that newborns can perform right away. Newborns will move an arm, a leg, or other body part away from a painful stimulus and will try to remove a blanket or cloth placed over the face. Stroke a baby on the cheek, and you will trigger the *rooting reflex*—the baby opens its mouth and actively searches for a nipple.

Neonates also have some reflexes that serve no apparent function and are believed to be remnants of humans' evolutionary past. As the brain develops, some behaviors that were initially reflexive (controlled by structures in the hindbrain) gradually come under the voluntary control of parts of the forebrain. The presence of these reflexes at birth and their disappearance between the 2nd and 4th months of age provide researchers with a means of assessing development of the nervous system.

In time, most reflexes give way to more deliberate, coordinated motor behavior. Most motor milestones (shown in Figure 9.2) result from **maturation**, each infant's own genetically determined, biological pattern of development. Although infants follow their own individual timetables, the basic motor skills usually appear in a particular sequence. Physical and motor development proceeds from the head downward to the trunk and legs. So, babies lift their heads before they sit, and they sit before they walk. Development also proceeds from the center of the body outward—trunk to shoulders to arms to fingers. Thus, control of the arms develops before control of the fingers.

But what about experience? What influence does it exert on motor development? The rate at which the motor milestones are achieved is delayed when an infant is subjected to extremely unfavorable environmental conditions, such as severe malnutrition or illness. And experiences that restrict infants' freedom of movement, including cultural practices such as strapping babies to "papoose" boards, also delay motor development. However, once babies are free to move about, they quickly acquire the same level of motor skill development as others their age who have not been restricted.

Experience may also accelerate motor development. In some African cultures, mothers use special motor training techniques that enable their infants to attain some of the major motor milestones earlier than most infants in the United States (Kilbride & Kilbride, 1975; Super, 1981). But maturation limits the effects of experience. No amount of training will cause a one-month-old infant to walk; when the baby is near the typical age for walking, special exercises may facilitate acquisition of the skill. Moreover, speeding up infant motor development has no effect on a child's future physical abilities.

neonate
A newborn infant up to 1 month old.

reflexes
Inborn, unlearned, automatic responses (such as blinking, sucking, and grasping) to certain environmental stimuli.

maturation
Each infant's own genetically determined, biological pattern of development.

Sensory and Perceptual Development

What are the sensory and perceptual abilities of a newborn?

Did you know that the five senses, although not fully developed, are functional at birth? Moreover, a newborn already has preferences for certain types of stimuli.

Vision At birth, an infant's vision is about 20/600, and it doesn't approach the 20/20 level until the child is about 2 years old (Courage & Adams, 1990; Held, 1993). Newborns focus best on objects about 9 inches

FIGURE 9.2 The Progression of Motor Development

Most infants develop motor skills in the sequence shown. The ages indicated are only averages, so normal, healthy infants may develop any of these milestones a few months earlier or several months later than the average.

Source: Frankenburg et al. (1992).

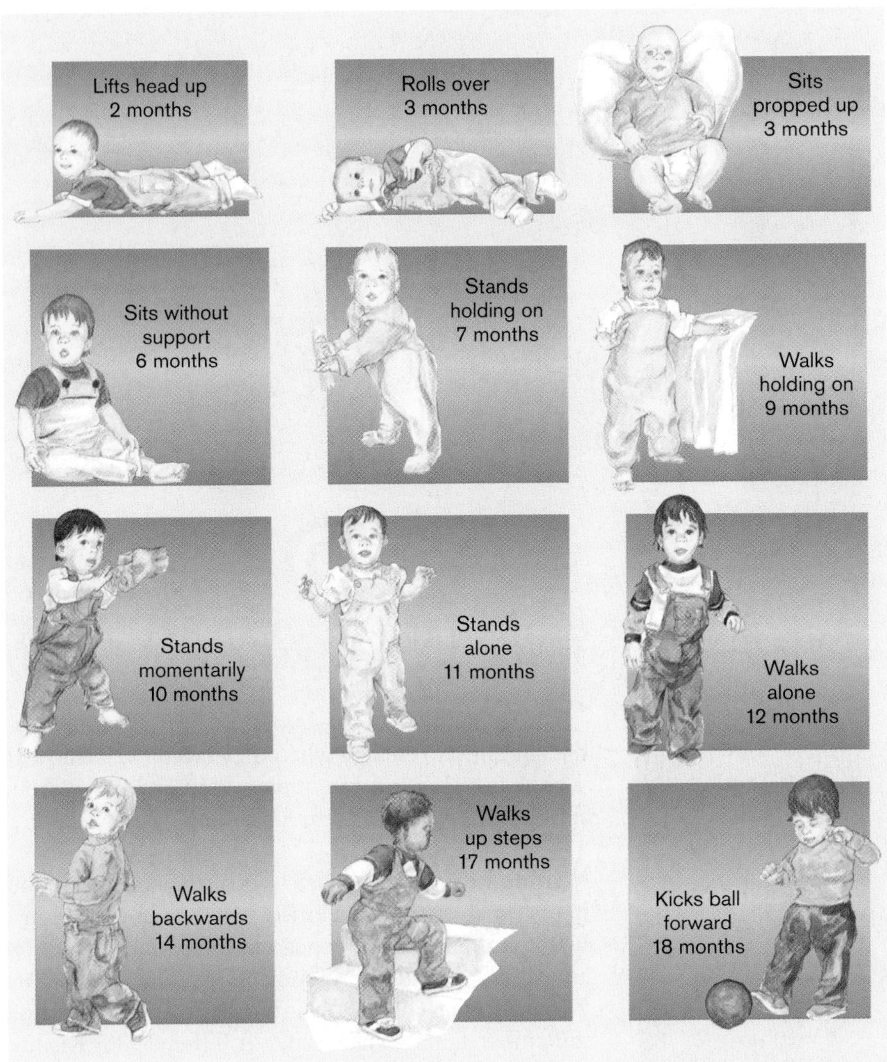

away, and they can follow a slowly moving object. By 2 to 3 months of age, most infants prefer human faces to other visual images (Fantz, 1961; see Figure 9.3, on page 310). Although newborns prefer colored stimuli to gray ones, they can't distinguish all of the colors adults normally can until they are about 2 months old (Brown, 1990). Then, they prefer red, blue, green, and yellow (Bornstein & Marks, 1982).

Depth Perception Gibson and Walk (1960) designed an apparatus called the **visual cliff** (shown in the photograph on page 310) to measure infants' ability to perceive depth. When 36 babies, aged 6 to 14 months, were placed on the center board, most could be coaxed by their mothers to crawl to the shallow side, but only three would crawl onto the deep side. Gibson and Walk concluded that most babies "can discriminate depth as soon as they can crawl" (p. 64). Campos and others (1970) also found that 6-week-old infants had distinct changes in heart rate when they faced the deep side of

■ **visual cliff**
An apparatus used to measure infants' ability to perceive depth.

FIGURE 9.3 Results of Fantz's Study

Using a device called a *viewing box* to observe and record infants' eye movements, Fantz (1961) found that they preferred faces to black-and-white abstract patterns.

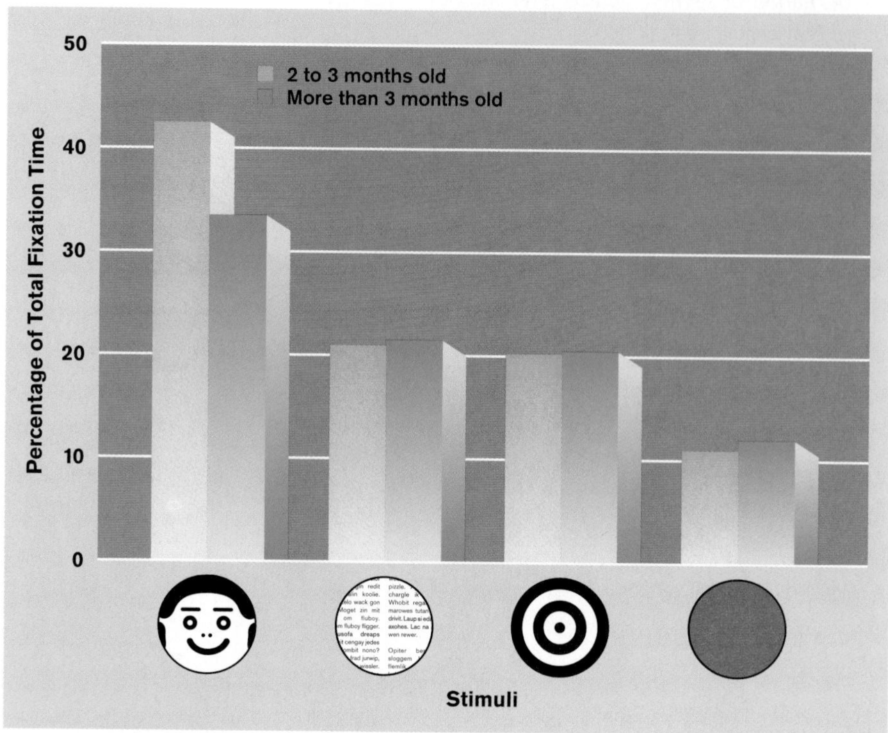

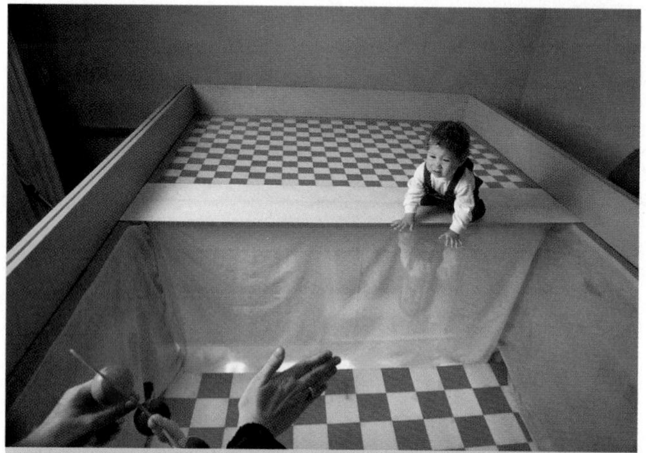

When placed on the visual cliff, most infants older than 6 months will not crawl out over the deep side, indicating that they can perceive depth.

the cliff, but no change when they faced the shallow side. The change in heart rate indicated interest or apprehension and showed that the infants could perceive depth.

Hearing and Other Senses At birth, a newborn's hearing is much better developed than her or his vision. An infant is able to turn the head in the direction of a sound and shows a general preference for female voices. Newborns also prefer their own mother's voice to that of an unfamiliar female (DeCasper & Fifer, 1980; Kisilevsky et al., 2003), but a preference for the father's voice over a strange male voice does not develop until later.

Neonates are able to discriminate among and show preferences for certain odors and tastes (Bartoshuk & Beauchamp, 1994; Leon, 1992). They show a favorable response to sweet tastes and are able to differentiate between salty, bitter, and sour solutions. Newborns are also sensitive to pain (Porter et al., 1988) and are particularly responsive to touch, reacting positively to stroking and fondling.

What types of learning occur in infancy?

Learning

Earlier in the chapter, you read that learning takes place even in the womb, so you won't be surprised to hear that several types of learning are evident in newborns. The simplest evidence of learning in infants is the phenomenon of **habituation**. When presented with a new stimulus, infants respond with a general quieting, their heart rate slows, and they fixate on the stimulus. But when they become accustomed to the stimulus, they stop responding—that is, they habituate to it. Later, if the familiar stimulus is presented along with a new stimulus, the infants will usually pay more attention to the new stimulus, indicating that they remember the original stimulus but prefer the new one.

■ **habituation**
A decrease in response or attention to a stimulus as an infant becomes accustomed to it.

Using habituation, Swain and others (1993) demonstrated that 3-day-old newborns could retain in memory for 24 hours a speech sound that had been presented repeatedly to them the day before. When the same sound was repeated the following day, the babies quickly showed habituation by turning their head away from the familiar sound and toward a novel sound. And infants 2 to 3 months old can form memories of their past experiences that last for days, and even longer as they get older (Rovee-Collier, 1990).

Other researchers have demonstrated both classical conditioning and operant conditioning in newborns (Lipsitt, 1990). And a study by Meltzoff (1988a) demonstrated observational learning in 14-month-olds. After watching an adult on television playing with a toy in an unusual way, the babies were able to imitate the behavior when presented with the same toy 24 hours later.

Temperament

What is temperament, and what are the three temperament types identified by Thomas, Chess, and Birch?

Have you ever heard the parent of a newborn describe him or her as "shy" or "outgoing" and thought they were reading more into their infant's behaviors than was warranted? You might have been wrong, because research shows that such differences among infants can be identified even in the earliest days of life. In fact, current thinking and research in developmental psychology suggest that each baby is born with an individual behavioral style or characteristic way of responding to the environment—a particular **temperament**.

Differences in Temperament One of the most important studies of temperament began in 1956. Alexander T. Thomas, Stella C. Chess, and Herbert B. Birch (1970) studied a group of 2- to 3-month-old infants and followed them into adolescence and adulthood. They found that "children do show distinct individuality in temperament in the first weeks of life independently of their parents' handling or personality style" (p. 104). Three general types of temperament emerged from the study: easy, difficult, and slow-to-warm-up.

"Easy" children—40% of the group—had generally pleasant moods, were adaptable, approached new situations and people positively, and established regular sleeping, eating, and elimination patterns. "Difficult" children—10% of the group—had generally unpleasant moods, reacted negatively to new situations and people, were intense in their emotional reactions, and showed irregularity of bodily functions. "Slow-to-warm-up" children—15% of the group—tended to withdraw, were slow to adapt, and were prone to negative emotional states. The remaining 35% of the children studied were too inconsistent to categorize.

Researchers now view infants as possessing different degrees of several dimensions of temperament. An individual baby might be higher than average in all of them, or high in some and low in others, or below average for all of the dimensions. While there is still debate over the definitions of these proposed dimensions of temperament, a few of them that are accepted by almost all developmental psychologists are listed in Table 9.3 (on page 312).

■ **temperament**
A person's behavioral style or characteristic way of responding to the environment.

Origins and Significance of Temperamental Differences Research indicates that temperament is strongly influenced by heredity (e.g., Caspi, 2000; Plomin, 2001). However, environmental factors, such as parents' child-rearing style, also affect tem-

TABLE 9.3 Dimensions of Temperament	
Activity level	Quantity and quality of physical movement; how often and how strongly a baby moves
Sociability *or* Approach	A tendency to move toward rather than away from new people and things; often accompanied by positive emotion
Inhibition *or* Shyness	A tendency to respond with fear or withdrawal to new people or situations or to situations in which there is too much stimulation (e.g., a children's birthday party)
Negative emotionality	A tendency to respond with anger, fussing, loudness, or irritability
Effortful control	The ability to stay focused and manage attention and effort; to persist until a task is complete

perament (Richter et al., 2000). For example, mothers' responses to toddlers can serve to either increase or decrease shyness (Rubin et al., 2002). When mothers criticize toddlers' shy behavior, it increases; by contrast, toddlers of mothers who are more tolerant of their children's shyness become more outgoing as they get older.

Studies suggest that the various dimensions of temperament can predict behavioral problems that may appear later in childhood or in adolescence (Pierrehumbert et al., 2000). Children who are impulsive at a young age tend to become aggressive, danger-seeking, impulsive adolescents (Hart et al., 1997), with strong negative emotions (Caspi & Silva, 1995). On the other hand, overcontrolled children have been found to be "more prone to social withdrawal" (Hart et al., 1997) and lacking in social potency as adolescents; that is, "they were submissive, not fond of leadership roles, and had little desire to influence others" (Caspi & Silva, 1995, p. 495).

Attachment

What did the research of Harlow, Bowlby, and Ainsworth reveal about the process of infant-caregiver attachment?

You may have noticed that, once they reach a certain age, most babies cry or protest when separated from their parents. The cultural emphasis on individualism and independence may lead some adults in the United States and other Western nations to see such behavior as a sign that an infant is developing an undesirable trait. But this view is wrong. One of the most important concepts in developmental psychology is **attachment**, the early, close relationship formed between infant and caregiver (Thompson, 2000). In fact, failure to develop an attachment relationship in infancy can seriously compromise later development.

Attachment in Infant Monkeys For many years, it was believed that the main ingredient in infant-caregiver attachment was the fact that the caregiver provides the infant with the nourishment that sustains life. However, a series of classic studies conducted by psychologist Harry Harlow on attachment in rhesus monkeys suggests that physical nourishment alone is not enough to bind infants to their primary caregivers. To systematically investigate the nature of attachment and the effects of maternal deprivation on infant monkeys, Harlow constructed two surrogate (artificial) monkey "mothers." One was a plain wire-mesh cylinder with a wooden head; the other was a wire-mesh cylinder that was padded, covered with soft terrycloth, and fitted with a somewhat more monkey-like head. A baby bottle could be attached to either surrogate mother for feeding.

attachment
The early, close relationship formed between infant and caregiver.

Newborn monkeys were placed in individual cages where they had equal access to a cloth surrogate and a wire surrogate. The source of their nourishment (cloth or wire surrogate) was unimportant. "The infants developed a strong attachment to the cloth mothers and little or none to the wire mothers" (Harlow & Harlow, 1962, p. 141). Harlow found that it was contact comfort—the comfort supplied by bodily contact—rather than nourishment that formed the basis of the infant monkey's attachment to its mother.

If infant monkeys were placed with the cloth mother for the first 5½ months of life, their attachment was so strong that it persisted even after an 18-month separation. Their attachment to the cloth mother was almost identical to the attachment normal monkeys have to their real mothers. However, unlike real mothers, the cloth mothers were unresponsive, so the emotional development of monkeys attached to cloth mothers was quite different from that of their peers who had access to real mothers. Monkeys with cloth mothers would not interact with other monkeys, and they showed inappropriate aggression. Their sexual behavior was grossly abnormal, and they would not mate. If impregnated artificially, they became terrible mothers, whose behavior ranged from ignoring their babies to violently abusing them (Harlow et al., 1971). The only aspect of development not affected was learning ability. Thus, Harlow concluded that contact comfort might be sufficient for attachment, but something more was required for normal emotional development: active affection and responsiveness.

Harlow found that infant monkeys developed a strong attachment to a cloth-covered surrogate mother and little or no attachment to a wire surrogate mother—even when the wire mother provided nourishment.

The Development of Attachment in Humans Numerous studies have supported Harlow's conclusion that parental affection and responsiveness are necessary for the development of attachment in human infants (e.g., Posada et al., 2002). The primary caregiver holds, strokes, and talks to the baby and responds to the baby's needs. In turn, the baby gazes at, listens to, and moves in synchrony with the caregiver's voice. Even crying can promote attachment: The caregiver is motivated to relieve the baby's distress and feels rewarded when the crying stops. Like Harlow's monkeys, babies cling to their mothers and, when old enough to crawl, will move to stay near them.

The infant's attachment to the mother develops over time and is usually quite strong by age 6 to 8 months (Bowlby, 1969). According to developmentalist John Bowlby, attachment behavior serves the evolutionary function of protecting the infant from danger (Bretherton, 1992). Once the attachment has formed, infants begin to show **separation anxiety**—fear and distress when the parent leaves them. Occurring from about 8 to 24 months of age, separation anxiety peaks between 12 and 18 months of age (Fox & Bell, 1990). Infants who previously voiced no distress when left with a babysitter may now scream when their parents leave.

At about 6 or 7 months of age, infants develop a fear of strangers called **stranger anxiety**, which increases in intensity until about 12½ months and then declines in the second year (Marks, 1987). Stranger anxiety is greater in an unfamiliar setting, when the parent is not close at hand, and when a stranger abruptly approaches or touches the child. Interestingly, stranger anxiety is not directed at unfamiliar children until age 19 to 30 months (P. K. Smith, 1979).

Ainsworth's Attachment Categories Practically all infants reared in a family develop an attachment to a familiar caregiver by the age of 2 years. But there are vast differences in the quality of attachment. In a classic study of mother-child attachment, Mary Ainsworth (1973, 1979) observed mother-child interactions in the home during the infants' first year and then again at age 12 months in a laboratory, using a procedure called the "strange situation." Based on infants' reactions to their mothers after brief periods of separation, Ainsworth and others (1978; Main & Solomon, 1990) identified four patterns of attachment: *secure*, *avoidant*, *resistant*, and *disorganized/disoriented*. Table 9.4 (on page 314) describes these attachment patterns.

■ **separation anxiety**
The fear and distress shown by infants and toddlers when the parent leaves, occurring from 8 to 24 months and reaching a peak between 12 and 18 months.

■ **stranger anxiety**
A fear of strangers common in infants at about 6 or 7 months of age, which increases in intensity until about 12½ months and then declines.

TABLE 9.4 Attachment Patterns

PATTERN	PREVALENCE	DESCRIPTION
Secure	About 65% of infants	Infants show distress on separation from mother and happiness when mother returns; use mother as safe base for exploration.
Avoidant	About 20% of infants	Infants do not show distress when mother leaves and are indifferent when mother returns.
Resistant	Approximately 10% of infants	Infants may cling to mother before she leaves and show anger when mother returns; may push mother away; do not explore environment when mother is present; difficult to comfort when upset.
Disorganized/ Disoriented	About 5% of infants	Infants may show distress when mother leaves and alternate between happiness, indifference, and anger when mother returns; often look away from mother or look at her with expressionless face.

Secure attachment is the most common pattern across cultures. However, cross-cultural research revealed a higher incidence of insecure attachment in Israel, Japan, and West Germany than in the United States (Collins & Gunnar, 1990). Thus, Ainsworth's procedure may not be valid for all cultures.

Origins and Significance of Attachment Differences Some studies show that depression in the mother is related to insecure attachment (Hipwell et al., 2000). Infant temperament is associated with attachment quality as well (Bee & Boyd, 2003). Easy infants are more likely to be securely attached than are difficult or slow-to-warm-up babies.

Other researchers have studied infant-caregiver attachment in foster families. In these settings, the primary factor affecting attachment seems to be the age of the infant at the time of placement in a foster home. Children who were less than 1 year old at the time of placement tended to develop secure attachments, while those who were older than 1 year at placement were more likely to develop insecure attachments (Stovall and Dozier, 2000).

Variations in the quality of infant attachment persist into adulthood and predict behavior (Tideman et al., 2002). In childhood and adolescence, securely attached infants are likely to be more socially competent than less securely attached infants (Weinfield et al., 1997). Their interactions with friends tend to be more harmonious and less controlling (Park & Waters, 1989). Attachment style also seems to have an impact on the quality of adult love relationships (Collins, 1996). In addition, secure attachment seems to protect infants from the potentially adverse effects of risk factors such as poverty (Belsky & Fearon, 2002). And parents who were securely attached infants are more responsive to their own babies (van IJzendoorn, 1995).

The Father-Child Relationship

How do fathers affect children's development?

Father-child interactions have enduring influences on children. On the negative side, children whose fathers exhibit antisocial behavior, such as deceitfulness and aggression, are more likely to demonstrate such behavior themselves (Jaffee et al., 2003). More often, though, fathers exert a positive influence on their children's development. For instance, children who experience regular interaction with their fathers tend to have higher IQs and to do better in social situations and at coping with frustration than children lacking such interaction. They also persist longer in solving problems and are less impulsive and less likely to become violent (Adler, 1997; Bishop & Lane, 2000; Roberts & Moseley, 1996). Positive father-son relationships are also associated with parenting behavior by sons when they have children of their own (Shears et al., 2002). In other words, research supports the commonsense notion that fathers serve as important role models for the fathering skills that will be exhibited by their sons later in life.

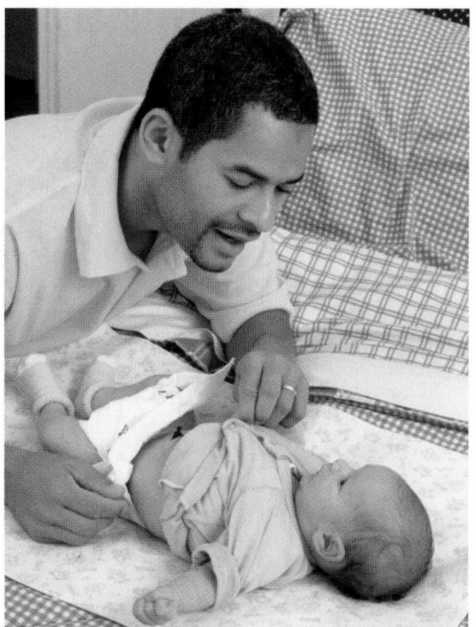

Fathers tend to engage in more physical play with their children than mothers. However, many fathers today share basic child-care responsibilities, such as feeding and diaper changing, with mothers.

Because the effects of fathers on children's development are generally positive, father absence is associated with many undesirable developmental outcomes. For example, children in homes without fathers experience poorer school performance, lower grade point average, lower school attendance, and higher dropout rate. Father absence is also related to children's reduced self-confidence in problem solving, low self-esteem, depression, suicidal thoughts, and behavioral problems such as aggression and delinquency (Bishop & Lane, 2000). And, for girls, father absence predicts early sexual behavior and teenage pregnancy (Ellis et al., 2003).

The presence or absence of the father may affect development because mothers and fathers interact differently with infants and children. In general, fathers do not appear to be as affectionate as mothers (Berndt et al., 1993; Hoosain & Roopnarine, 1994). However, fathers engage in more exciting and arousing physical play with children (McCormick & Kennedy, 2000). Mothers are more likely to cushion their children against overstimulation, while fathers tend to pour it on, producing a wider range of arousal. Fathers tend "to get children worked up, negatively or positively, with fear as well as delight, forcing them to learn to regulate their feelings" (Lamb, quoted in Roberts & Moseley, 1996, p. 53).

Some developmentalists believe that fathers are more supportive than mothers of children's confidence and identity development (Moradi, cited in Adler, 1997). A mother may instill a sense of caution in a child, but a father may encourage the child (especially if male) to be more daring. For example, fathers allow infants to crawl farther away, up to twice as far as mothers usually do. And fathers remain farther away as the infant explores novel stimuli and situations. Mothers tend to move in closer when the child confronts the unknown.

Ideally, children need both sets of influences. Moreover, when the mother and the father have a good relationship, fathers tend to spend more time with and interact more with their children (Willoughby & Glidden, 1995). However, about 38% of American children live apart from their biological fathers today—more than twice the percentage (17.5%) who did in 1960. And more than half of American children will not have a father present for at least part of their childhood (Shapiro & Schrof, 1995).

Remember It 9.3

1. __________ is the main factor in motor development.
2. __________ is better developed at birth than vision.
3. Two-month-old Carter was entranced by the multicolored ball in his crib for a couple of days, but then seemed to lose interest. This phenomenon is called __________.
4. Children who have pleasant moods and positive attitudes toward new situations and people have __________ temperaments.
5. Ainsworth found that most infants showed __________ attachment.
6. Fathers help children develop a sense of __________.

ANSWERS: 1. Maturation; 2. Hearing; 3. habituation; 4. easy; 5. secure; 6. individual identity

Piaget's Theory of Cognitive Development

Can you determine what is happening in this scenario? A parent gives his 3-year-old a cookie. When the child bites into the cookie, it breaks into several pieces. The child begins to cry and complains that his cookie is now "ruined" and demands a new one. The parent responds that the cookie is still the same whether broken or not, but the child is inconsolable until the parent provides him with an intact cookie. Why was the parent unable to convince the 3-year-old that a broken cookie is just as good as an unbroken one? Thanks to the work of Swiss psychologist Jean Piaget (pronounced "PEE-ah-ZHAY"), psychologists have gained insights about how children think and solve problems. After reading this section, see if you can understand why the parent's logic had little effect on the 3-year-old.

Schemes: The Foundation of Cognitive Development

How did Piaget use the concepts of scheme, assimilation, and accommodation to explain cognitive development?

The primary way in which human knowledge develops, according to Piaget, is through the application of a mental process called **organization**. Through organization, we use specific experiences to make inferences that can be generalized to new experiences. These inferences result in the construction of **schemes**—plans of action to be used in similar circumstances. For instance, once you've experienced the series of actions involved in using a fast-food restaurant's drive-through service, you can construct a drive-through scheme and apply it to any such restaurant. Each time you use this scheme at a different restaurant, there will be a few differences from your experience at other places, but the basic plan of action you follow will be the same. The point is that you don't have to start from scratch every time you go to a new fast-food restaurant; the mental process of organization has provided you with a general plan of action—a scheme—to follow.

The essence of cognitive development, for Piaget, is the refinement of schemes. For example, an infant who has had experience playing with rubber balls has constructed a scheme that she uses whenever she encounters a ball-like object. The scheme leads her to expect that anything resembling a ball will bounce. Consequently, when she is presented with an orange, her ball scheme (her mental plan of action to be applied to ball-like objects) leads her to throw the orange to the floor, expecting it to bounce. Piaget used the term **assimilation** to refer to the mental process by which new objects, events, experiences, and information are incorporated into existing schemes.

Of course, oranges don't bounce, so what happens to the ball scheme? According to Piaget, a mental process called **equilibration** is at work when the results of our actions conflict with our expectations. Equilibration is a characteristic of human intelligence that motivates us to keep our schemes in balance with the realities of the environment. So, when the infant sees that the orange doesn't bounce, her ball scheme changes (although she may try bouncing oranges a few more times just to be sure!). This change of scheme will result in a better intellectual adaptation to the real world (a better *equilibrium*, to use Piaget's term), because the revised scheme includes the knowledge that some ball-like objects bounce but others do not. Piaget used the term **accommodation** for the mental process of modifying existing schemes and creating new ones to incorporate new objects, events, experiences, and information.

Accommodation, however, is not the end of the process. As a result of her discovery that oranges don't bounce, the infant will be motivated to experiment on every ball-like object she sees (back to assimilation again) so that she can learn to discriminate between those that bounce and those that don't. The goal of her actions is to add to the scheme a set of rules that can be used to tell the difference between bouncing and nonbouncing balls (accommodation). One such rule might be "if you can eat it, it doesn't bounce." Once a workable set of rules is constructed, her ball scheme will be

■ **organization**
Piaget's term for a mental process that uses specific experiences to make inferences that can be generalized to new experiences.

■ **scheme**
A plan of action, based on previous experiences, to be used in similar circumstances.

■ **assimilation**
The mental process by which new objects, events, experiences, and information are incorporated into existing schemes.

■ **equilibration**
The mental process that motivates humans to keep schemes in balance with the real environment.

■ **accommodation**
The mental process of modifying existing schemes and creating new ones in order to incorporate new objects, events, experiences, and information.

finished (or *equilibrated*, in Piaget's terms), and she will stop trying to bounce every round object that comes her way. Children develop cognitively through this back-and-forth process of using schemes to act on the world (assimilation), changing them when things don't go as expected (accommodation), and acting on the world with the new schemes until they fit reality (equilibration).

Piaget's Stages of Cognitive Development

What occurs during each of Piaget's stages of cognitive development?

Piaget's primary research method was to observe children in natural settings, formulate hypotheses about their behavior, and devise problems that would allow him to test his hypotheses. He and his research assistants presented these problems to children individually, posing questions to gain insight into how each child thought about a problem and to determine whether he or she could give the right answer. Piaget's problems have been used by thousands of developmental psychologists, working in many different cultures. The result of all this research is the discovery that logical thinking in human beings develops in a universal sequence.

Piaget thought of this sequence as a series of universal *stages*, each of which represents a better set of schemes (Piaget, 1963, 1964; Piaget & Inhelder, 1969). In recent years, Piaget's notion of stages, and their relationship to children's ages, has been challenged by other developmentalists. However, the sequence of development for cognitive skills that he first discovered remains one of the most enduring sets of findings in all of psychology. So, before we explore the debate about stages and ages, we will discuss that sequence using Piaget's terminology.

The Sensorimotor Stage (Ages Birth to 2 Years) In the **sensorimotor stage**, infants gain an understanding of the world through their senses and their motor activities (actions or body movements). The child learns to respond to and manipulate objects and to use them in goal-directed activity. These manipulations are physical at first but become transformed into "mental action" and representational thought in the second half of the stage (Beilin & Fireman, 1999).

The major achievement of the sensorimotor stage is the development of **object permanence**, which is the realization that objects (including people) continue to exist even when they are out of sight. The concept of object permanence develops gradually and is complete when the child is able to represent objects mentally in their absence. The attainment of this ability marks the end of the sensorimotor period.

■ **sensorimotor stage**
Piaget's first stage of cognitive development (ages birth to 2 years), in which infants gain an understanding of their world through their senses and their motor activities; culminates with the development of object permanence and the beginning of representational thought.

■ **object permanence**
The realization that objects continue to exist even when they are out of sight.

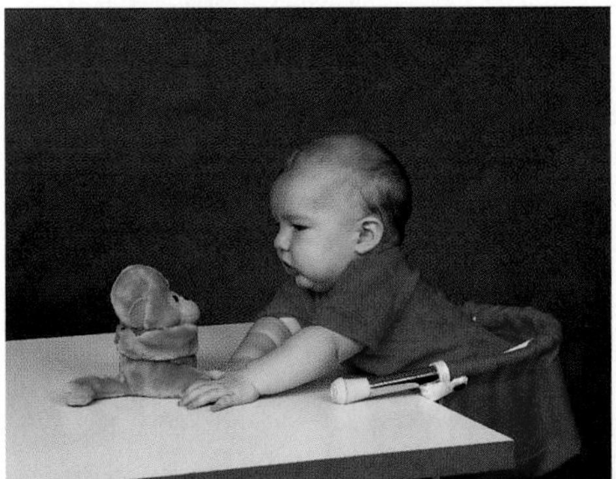

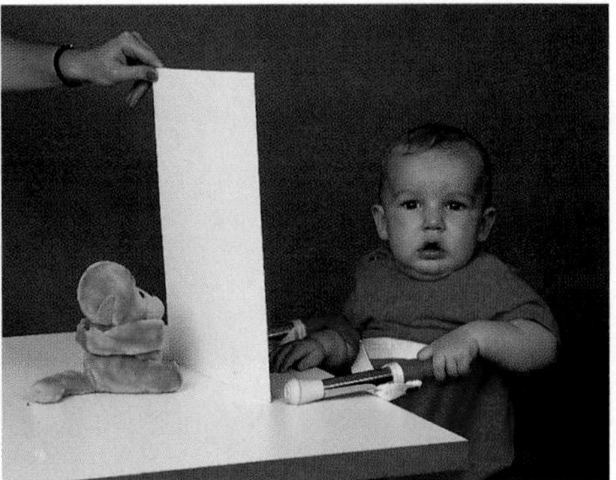

According to Piaget, this infant has not yet developed object permanence—the understanding that objects continue to exist even when they are out of sight. He makes no attempt to look for the toy after the screen is placed in front of it.

The Preoperational Stage (Ages 2 to 6 Years) The ability to mentally represent objects at the end of the sensorimotor stage makes it possible for the infant to construct a scheme for symbolic representation—that is, the idea that one thing can stand for another. For example, the word *ball* can stand for all round objects; a half-eaten piece of toast can stand for a car when the infant pushes it around and makes a motor sound; a doll can represent an imaginary baby that may be rocked and fed. The development and refinement of schemes for symbolic representation is the theme of the **preoperational stage.**

The ability to use symbols greatly advances the child's ability to think beyond what was possible in the sensorimotor stage. However, the child's ability to use logic is still quite restricted. Thinking is dominated by perception, and children at this stage exhibit *egocentrism* in thought. They believe that everyone sees what they see, thinks as they think, and feels as they feel. And they may display *animistic thinking*, the belief that inanimate objects are alive (e.g., "Why is the moon following me?").

■ **preoperational stage**
Piaget's second stage of cognitive development (ages 2 to 6 years), which is characterized by the development and refinement of schemes for symbolic representation.

■ **centration**
A preoperational child's tendency to focus on only one dimension of a stimulus.

The preoperational stage is so named because children are not yet able to perform mental operations (manipulations) that follow logical rules. If you know a child of preschool age and have the parents' permission, try the experiment illustrated in *Try It 9.1.*

Piaget proposed that young children have difficulty with logic because of a flaw in their thinking that he called **centration**, the tendency to focus on only one dimension of a stimulus. For example, in the *Try It*, the child focuses on the tallness of the glass and fails to notice that it is also narrower. And the child with the broken cookie, discussed earlier, can only think of the cookie in its present state, not the fact that it still has the same mass and makeup as before it broke.

Try It 9.1 Conservation of Volume

Show a preschooler two glasses of the same size and then fill them with the same amount of juice. After the child agrees they are the same, pour the juice from one glass into a taller, narrower glass and place that glass beside the other original one. Now ask the child if the two glasses have the same amount of juice, or if one glass has more than the other. Children at this stage will insist that the taller, narrower glass has more juice, although they will quickly agree that you neither added juice nor took any away.

Now, repeat the procedure with a school-aged child. The older child will be able to explain that even though there appears to be more liquid in the taller glass, pouring liquid into a different container doesn't change its quantity.

Because of egocentrism and centration, children in the preoperational stage have problems understanding any activity that is governed by rules. Two young children playing a board game may move their pieces around randomly on the board and have little or no sense of what it means to win. The end of the stage is marked by a shift in play preferences that may first be seen in shared pretending. A group of children playing "house" may make up rules such as "the smallest one has to be the baby."

Another piece of evidence that a child is leaving this stage is his realization that costumes and masks don't change his identity. A 3-year-old may be frightened by seeing himself in a mirror wearing a Halloween mask. He may be unsure as to whether the mask causes him to temporarily become the character it represents. By contrast, most 5-year-olds think masks are fun because they know that changing their outward appearance doesn't change who they are on the inside. Piaget would say that they are beginning to make the transition to a more mature form of thought.

The Concrete Operations Stage (Ages 6 to 11 or 12 Years) In the third stage, the **concrete operations stage**, children gradually construct schemes that allow them to *decenter* their thinking—that is, to attend to two or more dimensions of a stimulus at the same time. These schemes also allow them to understand **reversibility**, the fact that when only the appearance of a substance has been changed, it can be returned to its original state. So, the child in this stage who works on the problem in *Try It 9.1* can think about both the height and the width of the liquid in the two containers and can mentally return the poured juice to the original glass. As a result, the child realizes that the two glasses of juice are equal, a concept Piaget called **conservation**—the understanding that a given quantity of matter (a given number, mass, area, weight, or volume of matter) remains the same if it is rearranged or changed in its appearance, as long as nothing is added or taken away. Children's ability to apply concrete operational schemes to different kinds of quantities develops gradually (see Figure 9.4, on page 320).

Children at this stage, however, are able to apply logical operations only to problems that can be tested in the real world. For example, consider this deductive reasoning problem: If John has three apples, and Lucy has two, how many do they have together? A child can verify a proposed solution of "five" by taking three objects, combining them with two others, and counting the total. Now, consider a deductive problem that cannot be tested in the real world: If Farmer Brown has three green sheep, and one of them is named Suzie, what color is Suzie? Given this problem, a child in Piaget's concrete operations stage is likely to say that Suzie is white or gray or that he or she doesn't know the answer. The child may also propose a concrete explanation for the color of the sheep: "Suzie is green because she's been rolling around in the grass" (Rosser, 1994). The child's confusion results from the fact that there are no green sheep in the real world. Thus, even though children in this stage are quite good at applying logical schemes to problems with real-world referents, they can't yet think logically about hypothetical or abstract problems. In fact, according to Piaget, when children can respond correctly to problems with unreal elements like green sheep, they have equilibrated the concrete operations stage and are moving on to the next one.

The Formal Operations Stage (Ages 11 or 12 Years and Beyond) To get beyond the concrete operations stage, children must construct a scheme that allows them to coordinate present reality with other possible realities. Let's say, for example, that Joe is a 16-year-old who doesn't have a car but who imagines himself buying one. Of course, when he was younger, he could imagine owning a car. However, he couldn't construct a mental bridge between the reality of not having a car and the imagined goal of getting one that would actually result in his owning a car. The schemes of Piaget's fourth and final stage, the **formal operations stage**, allow him to do so. Joe can use these schemes to apply logical thinking to a series of hypothetical propositions

■ **concrete operations stage**
Piaget's third stage of cognitive development (ages 6 to 11 or 12 years), during which a child acquires the concepts of reversibility and conservation and is able to attend to two or more dimensions of a stimulus at the same time.

■ **reversibility**
The fact that when only the appearance of a substance has been changed, it can be returned to its original state.

■ **conservation**
The understanding that a given quantity of matter remains the same if it is rearranged or changed in its appearance, as long as nothing is added or taken away.

■ **formal operations stage**
Piaget's fourth and final stage of cognitive development (ages 11 or 12 years and beyond), which is characterized by the ability to apply logical thinking to abstract problems and hypothetical situations.

FIGURE 9.4 Piaget's Conservation Tasks

Pictured here are several of Piaget's conservation tasks. The ability to answer correctly develops over time, at approximately the ages indicated for each task.
Source: Berk (1994a).

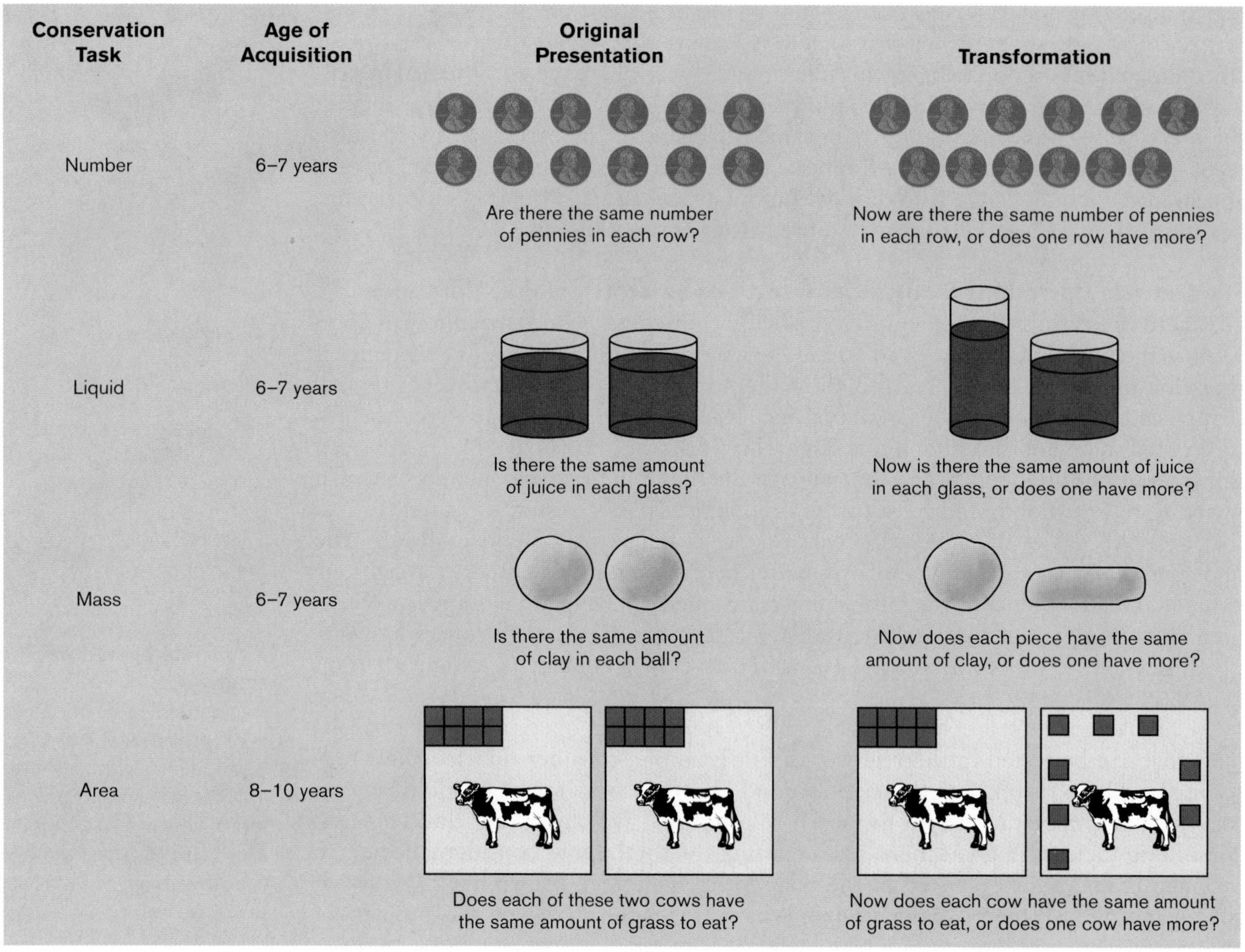

Conservation Task	Age of Acquisition	Original Presentation	Transformation
Number	6–7 years	Are there the same number of pennies in each row?	Now are there the same number of pennies in each row, or does one row have more?
Liquid	6–7 years	Is there the same amount of juice in each glass?	Now is there the same amount of juice in each glass, or does one have more?
Mass	6–7 years	Is there the same amount of clay in each ball?	Now does each piece have the same amount of clay, or does one have more?
Area	8–10 years	Does each of these two cows have the same amount of grass to eat?	Now does each cow have the same amount of grass to eat, or does one cow have more?

that will result in a plan for buying a car: "If I get a job that pays *X*...; if I save all my money for *X* months...; if I can find a car for *X* amount of money...," and so on. Joe's plan may be flawed because of his lack of financial experience, but it will be a plan that is far superior, in a logical sense, to any he might have constructed a few years earlier.

Because of their ability to construct an imaginary reality that is linked to present reality, adolescents exhibit types of thinking that are virtually nonexistent in younger children. One is the kind of thinking required for scientific experimentation. Adolescents can formulate a hypothesis and devise a way of testing it: "I think Jennifer likes me. I'll say 'hi' to her at lunch today, and, if she smiles at me, I'll know she likes me."

Even though formal operational schemes represent a huge leap in cognitive development, they still must be put to work in the real world (just like the infant's ball scheme) in order to become equilibrated. Teenagers' attempts to do this have varying results. Teens display a type of thinking Piaget called *naive idealism* (Piaget & Inhelder, 1969) when they come up with elaborate plans to end world hunger or to achieve total disarmament. Naive idealism may also be evident in their personal plans, as when two

17-year-olds plan to marry immediately after high school graduation and use their earnings from their minimum wage jobs both to live on and to attend college. Adults have a hard time convincing adolescents that they are wrong because the plans are so perfectly worked out in the adolescents' own minds. Did you construct any seemingly perfect plan in your teen years that didn't go quite as you thought it would when you tried to put it into action?

Another manifestation of teenagers' newly constructed formal operational schemes is *adolescent egocentrism* (Elkind, 1967, 1974). Do you remember, as a teenager, picturing how your friends would react to the way you looked when you made your grand entrance at a big party? At this stage of life, it never occurs to teens that most of the people at the party are preoccupied not with others, but with the way they themselves look and the impression they are making. This *imaginary audience* of admirers (or critics) that adolescents conjure up exists only in their imagination, "but in the young person's mind, he/she is always on stage" (Buis & Thompson, 1989, p. 774).

Teenagers also have an exaggerated sense of their own uniqueness, known as the *personal fable*. They cannot fathom that anyone has ever felt as deeply as they feel or has ever loved as they love. Some psychologists claim that this compelling sense of personal uniqueness may cause adolescents to believe that they are somehow indestructible and protected from the misfortunes that befall others, such as unwanted pregnancies, auto accidents, or drug overdoses. However, research suggests that the personal fable may also lead to exaggerated estimates of risk (Quadrel et al., 1993). For the formal operational teenager, hypothesized reality, whether good or bad, is the basis for many behavioral choices.

Piaget's stages of cognitive development are summarized in *Review and Reflect 9.1* (on page 322).

An Evaluation of Piaget's Contribution

What are some important criticisms of Piaget's work?

Although Piaget's genius and his monumental contribution to scientists' knowledge of mental development are rarely disputed, some of his findings and conclusions have been criticized (Halford, 1989). Today's developmental psychologists point out that Piaget relied on observation and on the interview technique, which depends on verbal responses. Newer techniques requiring nonverbal responses—sucking, looking, heart-rate changes, reaching, and head turning—have shown that infants and young children are more competent than Piaget proposed (Flavell, 1992; Johnson, 2000). For example, recent research indicates that an infant's knowledge of hidden objects may be more advanced than Piaget originally believed (Johnson et al., 2003; Mareschal, 2000). And there is some evidence that awareness of object permanence may begin as early as 3½ months (Baillargeon & DeVos, 1991).

Few developmental psychologists believe that cognitive development takes place in the general stagelike fashion proposed by Piaget. If it did, children's cognitive functioning would be similar across all cognitive tasks and content areas (Flavell, 1992). *Neo-Piagetians* believe that there are important general patterns in cognitive development, but there is also more variability in how children perform on certain tasks than Piaget described (Case, 1992). This variability results from expertise children acquire in different content areas through extensive practice and experience (Flavell, 1992). Even adults who use formal operational reasoning fall back on concrete operational thinking when they approach a task outside their areas of expertise.

Cross-cultural studies have verified the sequence of cognitive development, but they have also revealed differences in the rate of such development. Whereas the children in Piaget's research began to acquire the concept of conservation between ages 5 and 7, Australian Aboriginal children show this change between the ages of 10 and 13 (Dasen, 1994). Yet the Aboriginal children function at the concrete operations stage

REVIEW and REFLECT 9.1

Piaget's Stages of Cognitive Development

STAGE		DESCRIPTION
Sensorimotor (0 to 2 years)		Infants experience the world through their senses, actions, and body movements. At the end of this stage, toddlers develop the concept of object permanence and can mentally represent objects in their absence.
Preoperational (2 to 6 years)		Children are able to represent objects and events mentally with words and images. They can engage in imaginary play (pretend), using one object to represent another. Their thinking is dominated by their perceptions, and they are unable to consider more than one dimension of an object at the same time (centration). Their thinking is egocentric; that is, they fail to consider the perspective of others.
Concrete operations (6 to 11 or 12 years)		Children at this stage become able to think logically in concrete situations. They acquire the concepts of conservation and reversibility, can order objects in a series, and can classify them according to multiple dimensions.
Formal operations (11 or 12 years and beyond)		At this stage, adolescents learn to think logically in abstract situations, learn to test hypotheses systematically, and become interested in the world of ideas. Not all people attain full formal operational thinking.

Want to be sure you've fully absorbed the material in this chapter? Visit **www.ablongman.com/wood5e** for access to free practice tests, flashcards, interactive activities, and links developed specifically to help you succeed in psychology.

earlier on spatial tasks than on quantification (counting) tasks, and the reverse is true for Western children.

Another criticism comes from research showing that formal operational thought is not universal. Not only do many people fail to show formal operational thinking, but those who do attain it usually apply it only in those areas in which they are most proficient (Ault, 1983; Martorano, 1977). And in non-Western cultures, some studies of adults have found no evidence of formal operational thinking. Consequently, some psychologists have suggested that formal operational thought may be more a product of formal education and specific learning experiences than of a universal developmental process, as Piaget hypothesized.

According to Flavell (1996), "Piaget's greatest contribution was to found the field of cognitive development as we currently know it" (p. 200). And Piaget's theories remain works in progress because of their continuing impact on psychology and education (Beilin & Fireman, 1999).

Remember It 9.4

1. Which statement reflects Piaget's thinking about the stages of cognitive development?
   a. All people pass through the same stages but not necessarily in the same order.
   b. All people progress through the stages in the same order but not at the same rate.
   c. All people progress through the stages in the same order and at the same rate.
   d. Very bright children sometimes skip stages.
2. Eight-month-old Amala spots a dead bug on the living room floor, picks it up, and puts it in her mouth. She is using the mental process Piaget called __________ .
3. Four-year-old Madeleine rolls a ball of clay into a sausage shape to "make more" clay. Her actions demonstrate that she has not acquired the concept of __________ .
4. Not all individuals reach Piaget's __________ stage.
5. Match the stage with the relevant concept.

___ (1) abstract thought	a. sensorimotor stage
___ (2) conservation, reversibility	b. preoperational stage
___ (3) object permanence	c. concrete operations stage
___ (4) egocentrism, centration	d. formal operations stage

ANSWERS: 1. c; 2. assimilation; 3. conservation; 4. formal operations; 5. (1) d, (2) c, (3) a, (4) b

Other Approaches to Cognitive Development

As you might imagine, developmental psychologists have proposed other ways of looking at cognitive development that differ somewhat from Piaget's approach. Two important frameworks are Vygotsky's sociocultural theory and the information-processing approach.

Vygotsky's Sociocultural View

In Vygotsky's view, how do private speech and scaffolding contribute to cognitive development?

Have you ever noticed children talking to themselves as they assemble a puzzle or paint a picture? Russian psychologist Lev Vygotsky (1896–1934) believed that this and other spontaneous language behaviors exhibited by children are important to the process of cognitive development. Vygotsky maintained that human infants come equipped with basic skills such as perception, the ability to pay attention, and certain capacities of memory not unlike those of many other animal species (Vygotsky 1934/1986). During the first 2 years of life, these skills grow and develop naturally through direct experiences and interactions with the child's sociocultural world. In due course, children develop the mental ability to represent objects, activities, ideas, people, and relationships in a variety of ways, but primarily through language (speech). With their new ability to represent ideas, activities, and so on through speech, children are often observed "talking to themselves." Vygotsky believed that talking to oneself—*private speech*—is a key component in cognitive development. Through private speech, children can specify the components of a problem and verbalize steps in a process to help them work through a puzzling activity or situation. As young children develop greater competence, private speech fades into barely audible mumbling and muttering, and finally becomes simply thinking.

Vygotsky saw a strong connection among social experience, speech, and cognitive development. He also maintained that a child's readiness to learn resides within a *zone of proximal development* (*proximal* means "potential"). This zone, according to Vygotsky, is a range of cognitive tasks that the child cannot yet perform alone but can learn to perform with the instruction and guidance of a parent, teacher, or more advanced peer. This kind of help, in which a teacher or parent adjusts the quality and degree of instruction and guidance to fit the child's present level of ability or performance, is often referred to as *scaffolding*. In scaffolding, direct instruction is given, at first, for unfamiliar tasks (Maccoby, 1992). But as the child shows increasing competence, the teacher or parent gradually withdraws from direct and active teaching, and the child may continue toward independent mastery of the task.

The Information-Processing Approach

What three cognitive abilities have information-processing researchers studied extensively?

The information-processing approach sees the human mind as a system that functions like a computer (see Chapters 1 and 6). Psychologists who use this approach view cognitive development as a gradual process through which specific information-processing skills are acquired, rather than a series of cognitive "leaps," as Piaget's stage theory suggests (Klahr, 1992; Kuhn, 1992). Researchers using the information-processing approach have done extensive work on age-related changes in three cognitive abilities: processing speed, memory, and metacognition.

Processing Speed Developmental psychologist Robert Kail (2000) has found that processing speed increases dramatically as children move from infancy through childhood. This increase in speed is evident in a number of tasks, including perceptual-motor tasks such as responding quickly to a stimulus (e.g., pushing a button when a tone is heard) and cognitive tasks such as mental arithmetic. Increased processing speed is also associated with improved memory. Thus, age differences in this variable may explain why younger children are less efficient learners than those who are older.

Memory Short-term memory develops dramatically during an infant's first year. Babies under 8 months of age who watch an object being hidden have trouble remembering its location if they are distracted for a short time and are not allowed to reach for the object immediately—out of sight, out of short-term memory. At 15 months, though, children's short-term memory has developed to the point that they can remember where an object is hidden even when they are not allowed to reach for it until 10 seconds have passed (Bell & Fox, 1992).

This father teaching his daughter to ride a bike is using Vygotsky's technique called *scaffolding*. A parent or teacher provides direct and continuous instruction at the beginning of the learning process and then gradually withdraws from active teaching as the child becomes more proficient at the new task or skill.

Children increasingly use strategies for improving memory as they mature cognitively. One universal strategy for holding information in short-term memory is *rehearsal*, or mentally repeating information over and over. You use rehearsal when you silently repeat a new phone number long enough to dial it. Although certain aspects of rehearsal may be observed in preschoolers, in general, they have not learned how to use this strategy effectively to help them retain information (Bjorklund & Coyle, 1995). Rehearsal becomes a more valuable strategy for storing information by the time children reach age 6, and the majority of children use rehearsal routinely by age 8 (Lovett & Flavell, 1990).

Organization is a very practical strategy for storing information in such a way that it can be retrieved without difficulty. By about age 9, children tend to use organization to help them remember. *Elaboration*, another useful strategy, is not widely used until age 11 or older (Schneider & Pressley, 1989). Elaboration requires creating relationships or connections between items that are to be remembered but have no inherent connection.

Metacognition A fundamental developmental task for children is coming to understand that people differ greatly in what they know and believe (Miller, 2000). Reaching a level of cognitive maturity in which an individual is aware of his or her own thoughts and has an understanding about how thinking operates involves acquiring what is referred to as a *theory of mind*. More broadly, the process of thinking about how you or others think is known as *metacognition*. We use metacognition when we see ourselves and others as having various mental states such as beliefs, perceptions, and desires (Johnson, 2000). Children learn very young (at about 3 years of age) that people, including themselves, have different mental states during thinking, remembering, forgetting, pretending, wishing, imagining, guessing, and daydreaming. In short, they can distinguish between thinking and other mental states.

Some research suggests that children as young as 18 months of age are aware when adults are imitating their behavior, gestures, or words and have been observed purposely testing the adults to see if the "imitation" will continue (Aspendorf et al., 1996). Children older than 2½ years know the difference between reality and pretending. And 3-year-olds typically know that thinking is an activity that occurs inside one's head and that they can think about something without seeing, hearing, or touching it (Flavell et al., 1995).

Development of theory of mind and metacognition is related to children's language skills: The more advanced they are in language, the greater their ability to think about their own and others' thoughts (Astington & Jenkins, 1999; Deak et al., 2003). In addition, theory of mind seems to grow when children engage in shared pretending with others their age (Tan-Niam et al., 1998). The importance of social interactions to metacognition is also illustrated by research showing that children with disorders that interfere with social interactions—such as deafness, autism, and schizophrenia—lag far behind others their age in the development of theory of mind (Jarrold et al., 2000; Lundy, 2002; Pilowsky et al., 2000; Sarfati, 2000).

Remember It 9.5

1. Vygotsky believed that children's __________ aids their cognitive development.
2. __________ is a way of helping children accomplish tasks they aren't quite ready to do on their own.
3. A child who understands how thinking operates has acquired a __________.
4. Researchers who focus on how processing speed, memory, and metacognition develop and change with age are using the __________ approach.

ANSWERS: 1. private speech 2. Scaffolding 3. theory of mind; 4. information-processing

Language Development

Think about how remarkable it is that, at birth, an infant's only means of communication is crying, but at age 17, an average high school graduate has a vocabulary of 80,000 words (Miller & Gildea, 1987). From age 18 months to 5 years, a child acquires about 14,000 words, an amazing average of 9 new words per day (Rice, 1989). But children do much more than simply add new words to their vocabulary. In the first 5 years of life, they also acquire an understanding of the way words are put together to form sentences (syntax) and the way language is used in social situations.

What is the sequence of language development from babbling through the acquisition of grammatical rules?

The Sequence of Language Development

Have you ever tried to learn another language? It's difficult, isn't it? Yet children acquire most of their language without any formal teaching and discover the rules of language on their own. They do so during the first 3 years of life, in a sequence shown in Table 9.5 (on page 326). The process begins in the early weeks of life with *cooing*, the familiar "ooh" and "aah" sounds uttered by all babies. At about 6 months, cooing

TABLE 9.5 **Language Development during the First 3 Years of Life**

AGE	LANGUAGE ACTIVITY
2–3 months	Makes cooing sounds when alone; responds with smiles and cooing when talked to.
20 weeks	Mixes various vowel and consonant sounds with cooing.
6 months	Babbles; utters phonemes of all languages.
8 months	Focuses on the phonemes, rhythm, and intonation of native tongue.
12 months	Says single words; mimics sounds; understands some words.
18–20 months	Uses two-word sentences; has vocabulary of about 50 words; overextension common.
24 months	Has vocabulary of about 270 words; acquires suffixes and function words in a fixed sequence.
30 months	Uses telegraphic speech.
36 months	Begins acquisition of grammar rules; overregularization common.

begins to evolve into **babbling**. Babbling is the vocalization of **phonemes**, the basic units of sound in any language. By about 1 year of age, babies have restricted the sounds they utter to those that fit the language they are learning. So a 1-year-old French baby's babbling sounds different from that of a 1-year-old Chinese baby. In fact, babies of this age can no longer hear subtle distinctions between sounds that differentiate the accents of one language from that of another (Werker & Desjardins, 1995). This is why Japanese speakers may have difficulty distinguishing between the [l] and [r] sounds in English.

Sometime during the second year, infants begin to use words to communicate. Single words may function as whole sentences, called *holophrases* by linguists. Depending on the context, an infant who says "cookie" might mean "I want a cookie" or "This is a cookie" or "Where is the cookie?"

Once children know about 50 words, they stop using holophrases and start combining words into two-word sentences. As is true for holophrases, the meanings of these two-word sentences have to be determined using the child's tone of voice, intonation, and the context in which they are spoken as clues. The utterance "eat cookie" may mean many different things.

By the end of the second year, most children use nearly 300 words (Brown, 1973). However, they don't always use them correctly. Sometimes, as when a child uses "doggie" to refer to all four-legged animals, they exhibit **overextension**. They may also display **underextension**, or the failure to apply a word to other members of the class to which it applies. For example, the family beagle is a "doggie," but the German shepherd next door is not.

Children's language advances considerably between 2 and 3 years of age as they begin to use sentences of three words, which linguists call **telegraphic speech** (Brown, 1973). These short sentences follow a rigid word order and contain only essential content words, leaving out plurals, possessives, conjunctions, articles, and prepositions. Telegraphic speech reflects the child's understanding of *syntax*—the rules governing how words are ordered in a sentence. When a third word is added to a sentence, it is usually the word missing from the two-word sentence (for example, "Mama eat cookie").

■ **babbling**
Vocalization of the basic units of sound (phonemes).

■ **phonemes**
The basic units of sound in any language.

■ **overextension**
The application of a word, on the basis of some shared feature, to a broader range of objects than is appropriate.

■ **underextension**
The restriction of a word to only a few, rather than to all, members of a class of objects.

■ **telegraphic speech**
Short sentences that follow a rigid word order and contain only three or so essential content words.

After age 3, children experience a phase linguists refer to as the *grammar explosion*, meaning that they acquire the grammatical rules of language very rapidly. Most become fluent speakers by about age 5. But they still make errors. One kind of error is **overregularization,** which happens when children inappropriately apply grammatical rules for forming plurals and past tenses to irregular nouns and verbs. For example, a 3-year-old might say "I breaked my cookie," to which the parent replies "You mean you broke your cookie." In response, the child overcorrects and says "I broked it" or even "I brokeded it." Sometimes, parents and teachers worry about overregularization errors, but they actually represent an advance in language development since they indicate that a child has acquired some grammatical rules. Through observation and practice, the child will learn which words do not follow the rules.

■ overregularization
The act of inappropriately applying the grammatical rules for forming plurals and past tenses to irregular nouns and verbs.

Theories of Language Development

How do learning theory and the nativist position explain the acquisition of language?

Exactly how does language development happen? The same sequence of language development can be found in every culture in the world, but there has been considerable debate about how best to explain it.

Learning Theory Learning theorists have long maintained that language is acquired in the same way as other behaviors are acquired—as a result of learning through reinforcement and imitation. B. F. Skinner (1957) asserted that language is shaped through reinforcement. He claimed that parents selectively criticize incorrect speech and reinforce correct speech through praise, approval, and attention. Thus, the child's utterances are progressively shaped in the direction of grammatically correct speech. Others believe that children acquire vocabulary and sentence construction mainly through imitation (Bandura, 1977a).

Problems arise, however, when learning theory is considered the sole explanation for language acquisition. Imitation cannot account for patterns of speech such as telegraphic speech or for systematic errors such as overregularization. Children do not hear telegraphic speech in everyday life, and "I comed" and "he goed" are not forms commonly used by parents. There are also problems with reinforcement as the major cause of language acquisition. Parents seem to reward children more for the content of the utterance than for the correctness of the grammar (Brown et al., 1968). And parents are much more likely to correct them for saying something untrue than for making a grammatical error.

The Nativist Position The nativist view asserts that the language learning process is an inborn characteristic of all members of the human species, quite similar to the developmental sequence of motor milestones you read about earlier in this chapter (Lenneberg, 1967). For the nativists, the only environmental factor required for language development is the presence of language. Neither instruction nor reinforcement is necessary.

Nativist and linguist Noam Chomsky (1968) maintains that the brain contains a *language acquisition device (LAD)*, which enables children to sort the stream of speech they hear around them in ways that allow them to discover grammar rules. So, a child listening to English quickly figures out that adjectives (such as *big*) usually precede the nouns they describe (such as *house*). By contrast, a child learning Spanish infers the opposite, the noun *casa* comes before the adjective *grande*.

Chomsky also suggests that the LAD determines the sequence of language development—babbling at about 6 months, the one-word stage at about 1 year, and the two-word stage at 18 to 20 months. In fact, although English- and Spanish-speaking children learn different rules for adjective-noun order, they apply those rules to their own speech at the same point in their development. Thus, the universality of the sequence of language development supports the nativist view. Morever, research demonstrating that deaf children exposed to sign language from birth proceed along the same schedule also supports this view (Meier, 1991; Petitto & Marentette, 1991).

Deaf mothers use sign language to communicate with their young children, but they do so in *motherese,* signing slowly and with frequent repetitions.

Nature and Nurture: An Interactionist Perspective The interactionist perspective acknowledges the importance of both learning and an inborn capacity for acquiring language (Chapman, 2000). One's first language, after all, is acquired in a social setting, where the experiences one has must have some influence on language development. And, of course, heredity plays a role in every human capability.

Recent research reveals that language learning proceeds in a piecewise fashion, which calls into question the assumptions of Chomsky's nativist approach (Tomasello, 2000). Children learn the concrete language expressions they hear around them, and then they imitate and build on those. One way parents support the language-learning process is by adjusting their speech to their infant's level of development. Parents often use *motherese*—highly simplified speech with shorter phrases and sentences and simpler vocabulary, which is uttered slowly, at a high pitch, and with exaggerated intonation and much repetition (Fernald, 1993). Deaf mothers communicate with their infants in a similar way, signing more slowly and with exaggerated hand and arm movements and frequent repetition (Masataka, 1996).

Reading to children and with them also supports language development. Parents should comment and expand on what a child says and encourage the child to say more by asking questions. According to Rice (1989), "Most children do not need to be taught language, but they do need opportunities to develop language" (p. 155).

Learning to Read

What is phonological awareness, and why is it important?

Learning spoken language seems to be largely a natural process, but what about learning to understand written language? As you might expect, many aspects of the development of spoken language are critical to the process of learning to read. **Phonological awareness**, or sensitivity to the sound patterns of a language and how they are represented as letters, is particularly important. Children who can answer questions such as "What would *bat* be if you took away the [b]?" by the age of 4 or so learn to read more rapidly than peers who cannot (de Jong & van der Leij, 2002). Moreover, children who have good phonological awareness skills in their first language learn to read more easily even if reading instruction takes place in an entirely new language (McBride-Chang & Treiman, 2003; Mumtaz & Humphreys, 2002; Quiroga et al., 2002). And blind children who have poor phonological awareness skills are slower at learning to read Braille than are their peers with better skills (Gillon & Young, 2002).

phonological awareness Sensitivity to the sound patterns of a language and how they are represented as letters.

Children seem to learn phonological awareness skills through word play. Among English-speaking children, learning nursery rhymes facilitates the development of these skills (Layton et al., 1996). Japanese parents foster phonological awareness in their children by playing a game called *shiritori*, in which one person says a word and another must supply a word that begins with its ending sound (Serpell & Hatano, 1997). Activities in which parents and children work together to read or write a story also foster the development of phonological awareness (Aram & Levitt, 2002).

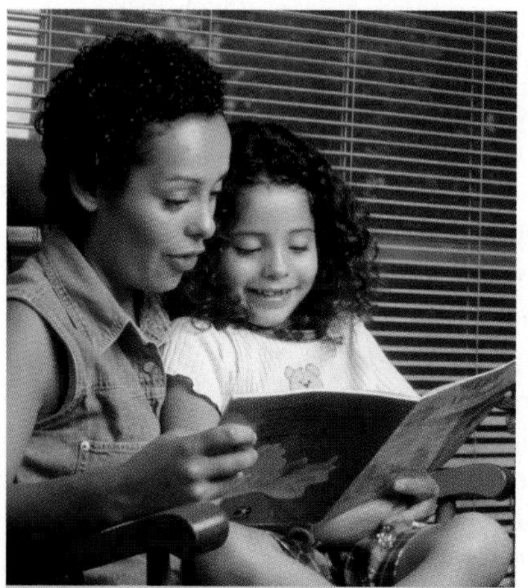

Reading to children and engaging them in word play helps them acquire phonological awareness.

The formal reading instruction that children receive when they start school helps them improve their phonological awareness skills (Shu et al., 2000). Once children have mastered the basic symbol-sound decoding process, they become better readers by learning about root words, suffixes, and prefixes (Adams & Henry, 1997). Teachers also facilitate the development of reading comprehension by helping children learn skills such as identifying the main idea of a passage or story (Pressley & Wharton-McDonald, 1997). Moreover, at every stage in the process, children benefit from exposure to good stories, both those they read on their own and those that are read to them by parents and teachers.

Remember It 9.6

1. Match each utterance with the linguistic term that describes it.

___ (1) "ba-ba-ba"	a. telegraphic speech
___ (2) "He eated the cookies."	b. holophrase
___ (3) "Mama see ball."	c. overregularization
___ (4) "oo," "ah"	d. babbling
___ (5) "kitty," meaning a lion	e. overextension
___ (6) "ball," meaning "look at the ball"	f. cooing

2. The nativist position suggests that language ability is largely ________.

3. When asked to supply a word that rhymes with *cat*, 3-year-old Jenny says "hat." Jenny's response indicates that she has developed ________.

ANSWERS: 1. (1) d, (2) c, (3) a, (4) f, (5) e, (6) b; 2. innate; 3. phonological awareness

Socialization of the Child

To function effectively and comfortably in society, children must acquire the patterns of behavior considered to be desirable and appropriate. The process of learning socially acceptable behaviors, attitudes, and values is called **socialization**. Although parents play the major role in socialization, peers, school, the media, and religion are also important influences.

The Parents' Role in the Socialization Process

What are the three parenting styles identified by Baumrind, and which does she find most effective?

Have you ever read William Golding's novel *Lord of the Flies*? The story implies that, without adult influence, children will grow up to be ignorant of important facts about the natural and social world, subject to superstitious beliefs, cruel to one another, and highly aggressive. Do you agree with this view?

Most people, whether laypersons or psychologists, believe that parents' role in the socialization process is to set examples, to teach, and to provide discipline. Research supports this view and has demonstrated that parents are usually most effective when they are loving, warm, nurturing, and supportive (Maccoby & Martin, 1983). In fact, a longitudinal study that followed individuals from age 5 to age 41 revealed that "children of warm, affectionate parents were more likely to be socially accomplished adults who, at age 41, were mentally healthy, coping adequately, and psychosocially mature in work, relationships, and generativity" (Franz et al., 1991, p. 593). Families are dysfunctional when the roles are reversed, and the children nurture and control their parents (Maccoby, 1992).

To be effective, socialization must ultimately result in children having the ability to regulate their own behavior. The attainment of this goal is undermined when parents control their children's behavior by asserting power over them (Maccoby, 1992). Diane Baumrind (1971, 1980, 1991) studied the continuum of parental control and identified three parenting styles: authoritarian, authoritative, and permissive. She related these styles to different patterns of behavior in predominantly White, middle-class children.

■ **socialization**
The process of learning socially acceptable behaviors, attitudes, and values.

■ **authoritarian parents**
Parents who make arbitrary rules, expect unquestioned obedience from their children, punish misbehavior, and value obedience to authority.

Authoritarian Parents **Authoritarian parents** make arbitrary rules, expect unquestioned obedience from their children, punish misbehavior (often physically), and value obedience to authority. Rather than giving a rationale for a rule, authoritarian parents

■ **authoritative parents** Parents who set high but realistic and reasonable standards, enforce limits, and encourage open communication and independence.

■ **permissive parents** Parents who make few rules or demands and usually do not enforce those that are made; they allow children to make their own decisions and control their own behavior.

■ **neglecting parents** Parents who are permissive and are not involved in their children's lives.

consider "because I said so" a sufficient reason for obedience. Parents using this style tend to be uncommunicative, unresponsive, and somewhat distant. Baumrind (1967) found preschool children disciplined in this manner to be withdrawn, anxious, and unhappy.

Parents' failure to provide a rationale for rules makes it hard for children to see any reason for following them. Saying "Do it because I said so" or "Do it, or you'll be punished" may succeed in making the child do what is expected when the parent is present, but it is ineffective when the parent is not around. The authoritarian style has been associated with low intellectual performance and lack of social skills, especially in boys (Maccoby & Martin, 1983). Also, if not blindly obeyed, extremely authoritarian parents tend to respond with anger, which has potentially negative long-term consequences. In fact, anger is precisely the wrong emotion to direct at children if they are to thrive, to achieve, to be well adjusted and happy, and to become effective parents themselves someday (Denham et al., 2000).

Authoritative Parents **Authoritative parents** set high but realistic and reasonable standards, enforce limits, and, at the same time, encourage open communication and independence. They are willing to discuss rules and supply rationales for them. Knowing why the rules are necessary makes it easier for children to internalize them and to follow them, whether their parents are present or not. Authoritative parents are generally warm, nurturing, supportive, and responsive, and they show respect for their children and their opinions. Their children are usually mature, happy, self-reliant, self-controlled, assertive, socially competent, and responsible. The authoritative parenting style is associated with higher academic performance, independence, higher self-esteem, and internalized moral standards in middle childhood and adolescence (Aunola et al., 2000; Lamborn et al., 1991; Steinberg et al., 1989).

The positive effects of authoritative parenting have been found across all ethnic groups in the United States (Querido et al., 2002; Steinberg & Dornbusch, 1991). The one exception is that the authoritarian style is more strongly associated with academic achievement among first-generation Asian immigrants (Chao, 2001). Developmental psychologist Ruth Chao suggests that this finding may be explained by the traditional idea in Asian culture that making a child obey is an act of affection. Moreover, strict parenting tends to be tempered by emotional warmth in Asian families, so the children probably get the idea that their parents expect unquestioning obedience because they love them (Chao, 2001).

Permissive Parents Although they are rather warm and supportive, **permissive parents** make few rules or demands and usually do not enforce those that are made. They allow children to make their own decisions and control their own behavior. Children raised in this manner are often immature, impulsive, and dependent, and they seem to have less self-control and be less self-reliant.

Neglecting Parents Based on their own research, developmental psychologists Eleanor Maccoby and John Martin (1983) identified a fourth parenting style, in addition to the three proposed by Baumrind. **Neglecting parents** are permissive and are not involved in their children's lives. Infants of neglecting parents are more likely than others to be insecurely attached and to continue to experience difficulties in social relationships throughout childhood and into their adult years. Lack of parental monitoring during adolescence places children of neglecting parents at increased risk of becoming delinquent, of using drugs or alcohol, or of engaging in sexual activity in the early teen years (Maccoby & Martin, 1983; Patterson et al., 1992; Pittman & Chase-Lansdale, 2001).

How do peers contribute to the socialization process?

Peer Relationships

The stereotypical view of peer influence is that it is negative. But is this belief justified? Probably not. For one thing, interest in peers seems to be an innate response. Infants begin to show an interest in each other at a very young age. At only 6 months of age, they already demonstrate an interest in other infants by looking, reaching, touching, smiling, and vocalizing (Vandell & Mueller, 1980). Friendships begin to develop by 3 or 4 years of age, and relationships with peers become increasingly important. These early relationships are usually based on shared activities; two children think of themselves as friends while they are playing together. By middle childhood, friendships tend to be based on mutual trust (Dunn et al., 2002), and membership in a peer group is usually seen as central to a child's happiness. Peer groups are usually composed of children of the same race, sex, and social class (Schofield & Francis, 1982). Moreover, during the school years, peer groups tend to be homogeneous with regard to academic achievement (Chen et al., 2003).

The peer group serves a socializing function by providing models of behavior, dress, and language. It is a continuing source of both reinforcement for appropriate behavior and punishment for deviant behavior. The peer group also provides an objective measure against which children can evaluate their own traits and abilities—how smart or how good at sports they are, for example. In their peer groups, children learn how to get along with age-mates—how to share and cooperate, develop social skills, and regulate aggression.

Physical attractiveness is a major factor in peer acceptance even in children as young as 3 to 5, although it seems to be more important for girls than for boys (Krantz, 1987; Langlois, 1985). Negative traits are often inappropriately attributed to unattractive children. Athletic ability and academic success in school are also valued by the peer group. The more popular children are usually energetic, happy, cooperative, sensitive, and thoughtful. Popular children have social skills that lead to positive social outcomes and facilitate the goals of their peers. But they are also able to be assertive and aggressive when the situation calls for it (Newcomb et al., 1993). Popular children tend to have parents who use an authoritative parenting style (Dekovic & Janssens, 1992).

Low acceptance by peers can be an important predictor of later mental health problems (Kupersmidt et al., 1990). Most often excluded from the peer group are neglected children, who are shy and withdrawn, and rejected children, who typically exhibit aggressive and inappropriate behavior and who are likely to start fights (Dodge, Cole, et al., 1990). Children abused at home tend to be unpopular with their classmates, who typically view them as aggressive and uncooperative (Salzinger et al., 1993). Rejection by peers is linked to feelings of loneliness, unhappiness, alienation, and poor achievement; in middle childhood, it is linked with delinquency and dropping out of school (Asher & Paquette, 2003; Gazelle & Ladd, 2003; Kupersmidt & Coie, 1990; Parker & Asher, 1987).

Television as a Socializing Agent

What are some of the positive and negative effects of television?

How important was television to you when you were growing up? For most children in the industrialized world, television is a powerful influence. Indeed, many parents and others continue to have concerns about how repeated viewing of the horrific events of September 11, 2001 will affect children. Because those events were so bizarre and shocking, developmental psychologists have little research on which to base predictions about their long-term effects (Atwood & Donnelly, 2002). However, there is a great deal of evidence about how the more typical stimuli provided by television influence children.

Surveys indicate that most parents are keenly aware of the potentially damaging effects of television, especially violent programs, on their children's development (Bushman & Cantor, 2003). Their concerns are well founded because, in the United States, children spend more time watching television than peforming any other activity except sleeping (Tuncer & Yalcin, 2000). By the time the average American child is 2 years old, he or she watches about 27 hours of television per week (Cooke, 1992). And, on average, American children have viewed more than 100,000 violent acts on

Television's strong influence on most children begins before they go to school. Programs such as *Mr. Rogers' Neighborhood* help teach children positive social values and behaviors.

television by the time they finish elementary school (Gerbner & Signorielli, 1990). Even the youngest children prefer to watch cartoons that are violent in nature. Literally thousands of studies suggest that TV violence leads to aggressive behavior in children and teenagers (Slaby et al., 1995). Other studies show that excessive TV viewing is linked to childhood obesity (Tuncer & Yalcin, 2000). Still other research has reported a relationship between too much TV watching and sleep disturbances (Owens et al., 2000).

Television can also shape the child's view of the world, and heavy viewers perceive the world as a "mean and scary place" (Donnerstein et al., 1994). Children's preferences and beliefs are easily manipulated by TV programming, and television socializes children to become active consumers. Moreover, the socializing effect of television begins before that of schools, religious institutions, and peers. In fact, researchers have found that the attitudes of children as young as 12 months towards specific objects, such as products featured in commercials, can be influenced by the facial expressions of people on television (Mumme & Fernald, 2003).

Much of children's commercial programming is marked by rapid activity and change and an "intense auditory and visual barrage" (Wright & Huston, 1983, p. 837). Singer and Singer (1979) suggest that such programming can lead to a shortened attention span. Others contend that television "promotes passive rather than active learning, induces low-level cognitive processing, and takes away time and energy from more creative or intellectually stimulating activities" (Wright and Huston, 1983, p. 835).

Despite its potential for negatively influencing development, television can be an effective educational medium. *Mister Rogers' Neighborhood* was found to increase prosocial behavior, imaginative play, and task persistency in preschoolers (Stein & Friedrich, 1975). Children viewing *Sesame Street* at ages 3 and 4 had larger vocabularies and better prereading skills at age 5 (Rice et al., 1990). Jerome and Judith Singer (cited in Leland, 1997) found that *Barney* encouraged creative play among 2- to 3-year-olds, but *Power Rangers* led to fighting.

Clearly, many factors contribute to child development. For all of life, from conception onward, it is the interplay of nature and nurture that drives and shapes us. In Chapter 10, we will continue to explore human development, moving from adolescence through old age.

Culture and Child Development

How does Bronfenbrenner explain the influence of culture on children's development?

You learned earlier that first-generation Asian immigrants tend to display an authoritarian parenting style because of beliefs rooted in the traditional Asian cultures from which they emigrated. This is one example of the influence of culture on children's development. But just how do such variables as cultural beliefs influence individual children?

Developmental psychologist Urie Bronfenbrenner (1979, 1989, 1993) proposes that the environment in which a child grows up is a system of interactive, layered **contexts of development** (see Figure 9.5). At the core of the system are what he calls *microsystems*, which include settings in which the child has personal experience (e.g., the family). The next layer, known as *exosystems*, includes contexts that the child does not experience directly but that affect the child because of their influence on microsystems (e.g., parents' jobs). Finally, the *macrosystem* includes all aspects of the larger culture.

■ contexts of development Bronfenbrenner's term for the interrelated and layered settings (family, neighborhood, culture, etc.) in which a child grows up.

The ideas and institutions of the macrosystem filter down to the child through the exosystems and microsystems. Bronfenbrenner's explanation of the process can be best understood by using this question as an example: Why do some cultures provide public schools for all children and require them to attend while other cultures do not, and how does this cultural difference affect individual children? One reason for cross-cultural variations in schooling might be that, at the level of the macrosystem, societies with public schools believe strongly in the value of education for all people. At

FIGURE 9.5 Bronfenbrenner's Contexts of Development

Bronfenbrenner's theory proposes that children grow up in an environment of interconnected and layered contexts that have significant effects on their development.

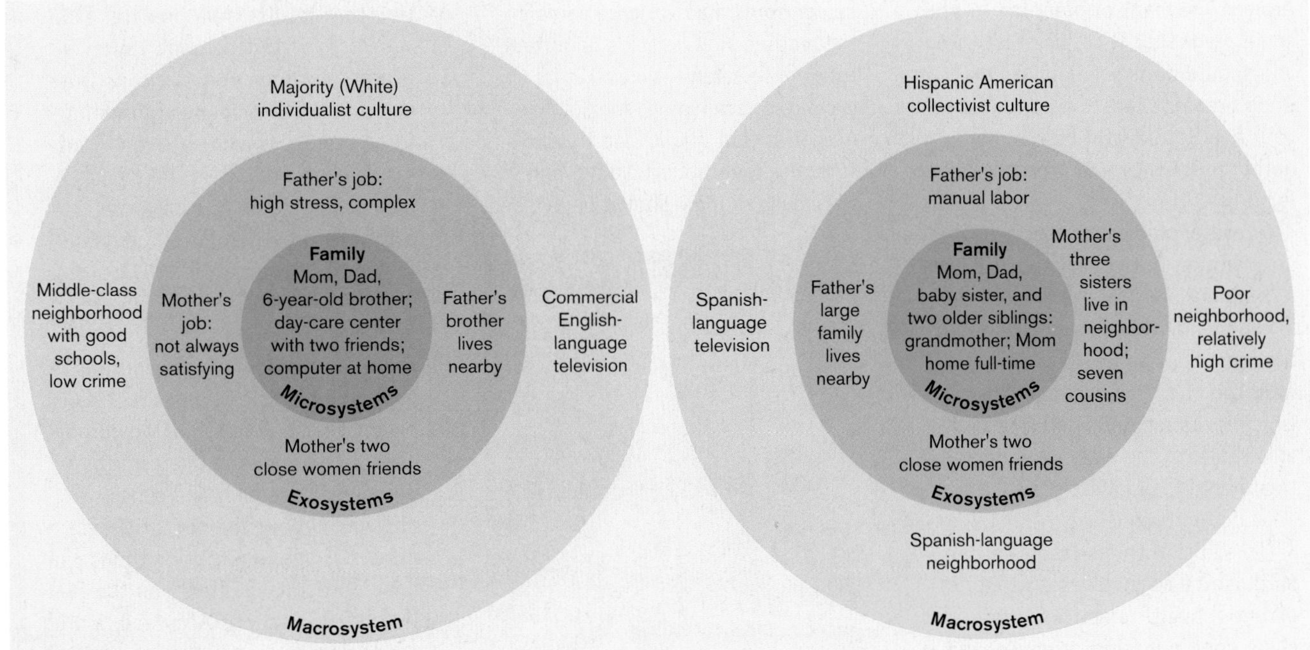

the exosystem level, this belief is put into practice when governmental authorities allocate funds for schools and make laws requiring parents to enroll their children. In a culture where there is no such belief, or where the belief is present but there are no funds to pay for public education, there will be no schools.

Even so, the microsystem may ultimately determine whether a culture's beliefs and practices regarding education will reach the individual child. In countries without public schools, wealthy parents may send their children to private schools, middle-class parents may pinch pennies to do likewise, and poor parents may do their best to teach their children at home. In countries with a public school system—some parents may choose not to enroll their children, even at the risk of facing legal sanctions. They might do so because they need the children to stay home to care for younger siblings or to do agricultural work. Or they may have ideological reasons for keeping their children at home. A child's own abilities, attitudes, and behaviors may also determine the individual effects of the macrosystem and exosystem. A child who has a learning disability will respond to school differently than a child who doesn't have learning problems. A child's like or dislike of the school environment and her or his ability to behave appropriately in the classroom will also contribute to the impact of schooling on that child's individual development. Conversely, in a culture without public schools, a child who is very curious and determined may find ways to educate herself or himself. Thus, every level of the system is involved in determining whether and how cultural variables affect individual children.

Clearly, the values and decisions associated with each level of Bronfenbrenner's system have a strong and lasting impact on children's development. With regard to schooling, developmental psychologists know that formal education is strongly associated with progression through Piaget's stages of cognitive development as well as with the acquisition of information-processing skills (Mishra, 1997). Children who attend school advance more rapidly through the concrete operations stage and have more memory strategies than do their peers who do not go to school. And, as teens and adults, those with formal education are more likely to develop formal operational thinking. Obviously, children benefit most when all contexts of development work together toward the same goals for them.

Apply It

The Importance of Prenatal Care

Are you pregnant or planning to become pregnant? If so, the first thing you should do is see your doctor. Good prenatal care is essential to your health and your baby's, both during pregnancy and after the baby is born.

Prenatal medical care usually begins with an initial visit that includes a complete physical examination, followed by monthly checkups early in the pregnancy and weekly ones toward the end. These regular exams, which include blood and urine tests, are critical to the early detection and treatment of complications that may arise during pregnancy.

In addition to medical care, prenatal care also involves a variety of maternal health practices. These include good nutrition, exercise, and avoidance of cigarettes, alcohol, and any drugs that might harm the fetus. It is also important to reduce stress during pregnancy.

Nutrition

Although it is commonplace to say that a pregnant woman is "eating for two," a woman's nutritional needs actually increase by only 300 calories a day during pregnancy. Those extra calories should come from the major food groups and be supplemented with an extra serving of milk or other dairy product (to provide calcium for bone formation) and about 10 more grams of protein (for cell formation). Fats should not be increased beyond the recommended 30% or less of total calories.

Exercise

Pregnancy is a normal condition, not an illness, and there is no reason for pregnant women to stop exercising. Moderate aerobic exercise increases the flow of oxygen and nutrients to the fetus and reduces fluid retention, hemorrhoids, and varicose veins in the mother. However, it's important to exercise safely—by walking, cycling, or swimming, for example. Activities that might lead to falls—such as skiing, rollerblading, and horseback riding—should be avoided.

Smoking

If you are a smoker and planning to become a mother, there couldn't be a better time to stop. Smoking has a variety of effects on the reproductive system, including lowering a woman's ability to conceive and making a man's sperm less viable. It is also hazardous to the health of the fetus. A woman who smokes is almost twice as likely as one who doesn't to have a low-birth-weight baby. Smoking can also cause a miscarriage, stillbirth, or premature birth. Children born to mothers who smoke tend to have respiratory problems such as chronic coughing and are twice as likely to develop asthma. They may also be retarded in their physical and intellectual development. In short, the evidence is overwhelming: A pregnant woman should not smoke or be exposed to secondhand smoke.

Alcohol

In this chapter, you read about fetal alcohol syndrome, a serious condition that results from prenatal exposure to excessive alcohol. However, experts disagree on what constitutes an "excessive" amount of drinking for pregnant women. The American Academy of Pediatrics therefore recommends that women avoid alcohol altogether during pregnancy (McAnulty & Burnette, 2001).

Drugs

Every drug a woman takes during pregnancy reaches the fetus. This means that before taking any drug, even a common one like aspirin, a pregnant woman should consult a physician about the potential side effects. Some prescription drugs can have devastating effects on the fetus. One example is Accutane, a drug used to treat acne, which has been found to cause birth defects in many cases. Also harmful to the fetus are illegal drugs such as cocaine and heroin. Use of these drugs can lead to several dangerous conditions, including premature birth, cerebral hemorrhage, and sudden infant death syndrome.

Stress

Stressors in a pregnant woman's life—relationship problems, job difficulties, financial woes—can also affect prenatal development. Such sources of maternal stress are linked to high blood pressure in the woman and to premature birth and low birth weight in the newborn. Consequently, physicians suggest that pregnant women find effective ways to relax.

In sum, having regular medical checkups, watching your diet, exercising, avoiding harmful substances, and finding time to relax will put you on track for a normal pregnancy, a trouble-free delivery, and a healthy baby.

Remember It 9.7

1. Match each approach to discipline with the related parenting style.

   ___ (1) expecting unquestioned obedience
   ___ (2) setting high standards, giving rationale for rules
   ___ (3) setting few rules or limits
   ___ (4) lack of involvement in children's lives

   a. permissive
   b. authoritative
   c. authoritarian
   d. neglecting

2. The __________ can have either a negative or a positive effect on development.

3. Which is not an effect of television on children?
   a. reducing racial and sexual stereotypes
   b. shortening attention span
   c. contributing to childhood obesity
   d. increasing aggressive behavior through exposure to televised violence

4. Identify each of the following as belonging to one of Bronfenbrenner's contexts of development.

   ___ (1) a child's parents
   ___ (2) cultural beliefs about punishment
   ___ (3) public funding for day care centers
   ___ (4) the social status of a family's neighborhood
   ___ (5) a racial group's sense of ethnic identity

   a. macrosystem
   b. exosystem
   c. microsystem

ANSWERS: 1. (1) c, (2) b, (3) a, (4) d; 2. peer group; 3. a; 4. (1) c, (2) a, (3) b, (4) b, (5) a

Summary *and* Review

Developmental Psychology: Basic Issues and Methodology p. 300

What three issues are frequently debated among developmental psychologists? p. 300
Many questions in developmental psychology are rooted in the nature-nurture controversy. Others stem from the assertion that development occurs in stages. Another point of debate is whether certain characteristics, such as personality traits, remain stable across the entire lifespan.

What methods do developmental psychologists use to investigate age-related changes? p. 301
To investigate age-related changes, developmental psychologists use the longitudinal study and the cross-sectional study. In longitudinal research, a single group of individuals is studied at different ages. Cross-sectional research compares groups of participants of different ages at the same time.

Prenatal Development p. 303

What happens in each of the three stages of prenatal development? p. 304
In the germinal stage, from conception to 2 weeks, the egg is fertilized, and the zygote attaches itself to the uterine wall. During the embryonic stage, from week 3 to week 8, all of the major systems, organs, and structures form. In the fetal stage, from week 9 until birth, the fetus experiences rapid growth and body systems, structures, and organs continue their development.

What have scientists learned about fetal behavior in recent years? p. 305
Fetuses can hear and remember sounds that they hear repeatedly. Some individual and sex differences in behavior are evident during prenatal development.

What are some negative influences on prenatal development, and when is their impact greatest? p. 305
Some common negative influences on prenatal development include certain prescription and nonprescription drugs, psychoactive drugs, environmental hazards, poor maternal nutrition, and maternal illness. Their impact depends on their timing during pregnancy. Exposure is most harmful when it occurs during critical periods of development for the various body structures.

Infancy p. 308

How do the motor behaviors of a newborn compare to those of an older infant? p. 308

The motor behavior of newborns is dominated by reflexes. As maturation proceeds, controlled motor skills, such as grasping and walking, develop. Experience can retard or accelerate motor development, but the sequence of motor milestones is universal.

What are the sensory and perceptual abilities of a newborn? p. 308

All of a newborn's senses are functional at birth, and the infant already shows preferences for certain odors, tastes, sounds, and visual patterns.

What types of learning occur in infancy? p. 310

Newborns are capable of habituation, and they can acquire new responses through classical and operant conditioning and observational learning.

What is temperament, and what are the three temperament types identified by Thomas, Chess, and Birch? p. 311

Temperament refers to an individual's behavioral style or characteristic way of responding to the environment. The three temperament types identified by Thomas, Chess, and Birch are easy, difficult, and slow-to-warm-up. Current research indicates that dimensions of temperament include activity level, sociability inhibition, negative emotionality, and effortful control.

What did the research of Harlow, Bowlby, and Ainsworth reveal about the process of infant–caregiver attachment? p. 312

Harlow found that the basis of attachment in infant monkeys is contact comfort, and that monkeys raised with surrogate mothers show normal learning ability but abnormal social, sexual, and emotional behavior. According to Bowlby, the infant has usually developed a strong attachment to the mother at age 6 to 8 months. Ainsworth identified four attachment patterns in infants: secure, avoidant, resistant, and disorganized/disoriented.

How do fathers affect children's development? p. 314

Fathers' patterns of interaction with children differ from those of mothers. Thus, mothers and fathers exert unique influences on children's development, and, ideally, children need both influences. Children who interact regularly with their fathers tend to have higher IQs, do better in social situations, and manage frustration better than children lacking such interaction. Father absence is associated with low self-esteem, depression, suicidal thoughts, behavioral problems, and teen pregnancy.

Piaget's Theory of Cognitive Development p. 316

How did Piaget use the concepts of scheme, assimilation, and accommodation to explain cognitive development? p. 316

Piaget proposed that humans construct schemes, or general action plans, on the basis of experiences. Schemes change through assimilation and accommodation until they work effectively in the real world.

What occurs during each of Piaget's stages of cognitive development? p. 317

During the sensorimotor stage (ages birth to 2 years), infants understand their world through their senses and motor activities and develop object permanence. Children at the preoperational stage (ages 2 to 6 years) are increasingly able to represent objects and events mentally, but they exhibit egocentrism and centration. When working real-world problems, children at the concrete operations stage (ages 6 to 11 or 12 years) are able to apply logical operations only to problems that can be tested in the real world. At the formal operations stage (ages 11 or 12 years and beyond), adolescents are able to apply logical thinking to abstract problems and hypothetical situations.

What are some important criticisms of Piaget's work? p. 321

Piaget may have underestimated the cognitive skills of infants and young children. Formal operations does not appear in all individuals or in all cultures.

Other Approaches to Cognitive Development p. 323

In Vygotsky's view, how do private speech and scaffolding contribute to cognitive development? p. 323

Private speech, or self-guided talk, helps children to specify the components of a problem and verbalize the steps in a process to help them solve it. Scaffolding is a process in which a teacher or parent adjusts the quality and degree of instruction or guidance to fit the child's present level of ability. It allows a child to gradually perform a task independently.

What three cognitive abilities have information-processing researchers studied extensively? p. 324

The three cognitive abilities studied extensively by information-processing researchers are processing speed, memory, and metacognition.

Language Development p. 325

What is the sequence of language development from babbling through the acquisition of grammatical rules? **p. 325**

Babbling begins at age 6 months, followed by single words or holophrases sometime during the second year, two-word sentences at ages 18 to 20 months, and telegraphic speech between 2 and 3 years of age, and then the acquisition of grammatical rules.

How do learning theory and the nativist position explain the acquisition of language? **p. 327**

Learning theory suggests that language is acquired through imitation and reinforcement. The nativist position is that language ability is largely innate, because it is acquired in stages that occur in a fixed order at the same ages in most children throughout the world.

What is phonological awareness, and why is it important? **p. 328**

Phonological awareness is sensitivity to the sound patterns of a language and how those patterns are represented as letters. Children who acquire good phonological awareness skills before going to school have an easier time learning to read than do peers with lower skill levels.

Socialization of the Child p. 329

What are the three parenting styles identified by Baumrind, and which does she find most effective? **p. 329**

The three parenting styles identified by Baumrind are authoritarian, authoritative, and permissive. She claims the authoritative style is the most effective.

How do peers contribute to the socialization process? **p. 330**

The peer group serves a socializing function by modeling and reinforcing behaviors it considers appropriate, by punishing inappropriate behaviors, and by providing an objective measure against which children can evaluate their own traits and abilities.

What are some of the positive and negative effects of television? **p. 331**

Television can increase prosocial behavior, imaginative play, and vocabulary and improve prereading and number skills. But it can also lead to aggressive behavior, obesity, racial and sexual stereotyping, and a shortened attention span.

How does Bronfenbrenner explain the influence of culture on children's development? **p. 332**

Bronfenbrenner thinks of the environment in which a child grows up as a system of interactive, layered contexts of development. Cultural influences, found at the macrosystem level, filter down to the individual child through the exosystems and microsystems in which the child lives. A child's own characteristics are also part of the microsystem and contribute to how much or how little of the cultural effects actually influence her or his development.

Key Terms

accommodation, p. 316
assimilation, p. 316
attachment, p. 312
authoritarian parents, p. 329
authoritative parents, p. 330
babbling, p. 326
centration, p. 318
concrete operations stage, p. 319
conservation, p. 319
contexts of development, p. 332
critical period, p. 306
cross-sectional study, p. 301
developmental psychology, p. 300
embryo, p. 304
equilibration, p. 316
fetal alcohol syndrome, p. 306
fetus, p. 304
formal operations stage, p. 319
habituation, p. 311
longitudinal study, p. 301
low birth weight, p. 306
maturation, p. 308
neglecting parents, p. 330
neonate, p. 308
object permanence, p. 317
organization, p. 316
overextension, p. 326
overregularization, p. 327
permissive parents, p. 330
phonemes, p. 326
phonological awareness, p. 328
prenatal development, p. 303
preoperational stage, p. 318
reflexes, p. 308
reversibility, p. 319
scheme, p. 316
sensorimotor stage, p. 317
separation anxiety, p. 313
socialization, p. 329
stranger anxiety, p. 313
telegraphic speech, p. 326
temperament, p. 311
teratogens, p. 306
underextension, p. 326
visual cliff, p. 309
zygote, p. 303

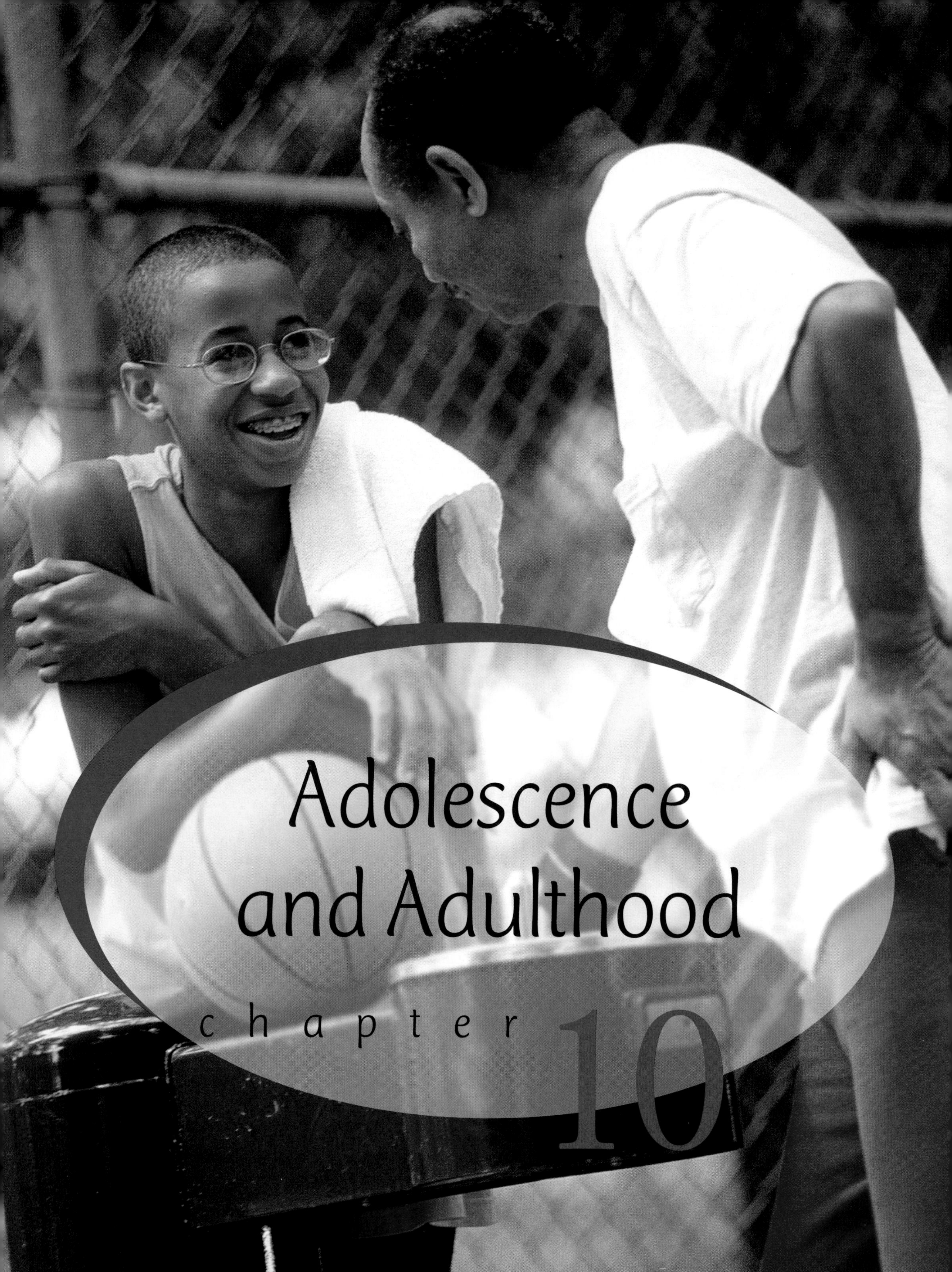

Adolescence and Adulthood

chapter 10

The Lifespan Perspective

- *How does Erikson's theory of psychosocial development differ from other developmental theories?*
- *What does research suggest about the accuracy of Erikson's theory?*

Adolescence

- *What physical and psychological changes occur as a result of puberty?*
- *What cognitive abilities develop during adolescence?*
- *What are the differences among Kohlberg's three levels of moral reasoning?*
- *What outcomes are often associated with the authoritative, authoritarian, and permissive parenting styles?*
- *What are some of the beneficial functions of the adolescent peer group?*
- *What are some of the consequences of teenage pregnancy?*

Early and Middle Adulthood

- *What is the difference between primary and secondary aging?*
- *In what ways do cognitive functions change between the ages of 20 and 60?*
- *How does attending college affect adult development?*
- *What are some current trends in lifestyle patterns among young adults?*

Later Adulthood

- *What are some physical changes associated with later adulthood?*
- *What happens to mental ability in later adulthood?*
- *How does Alzheimer's disease affect the brain?*
- *What does research indicate about older adults' life satisfaction?*
- *In what ways do the experiences of older adults differ across cultures?*
- *According to Kübler-Ross, what stages do terminally ill patients experience as they come to terms with death?*

What do you picture yourself doing in your later years?

Do you see yourself lying on a sun-drenched beach in some exotic locale, enjoying your retirement benefits, with all the cares and worries of your career behind you? Or do you see yourself confined to a nursing home because of a debilitating chronic condition? When views of older adulthood are negative, they often reflect the influence of *ageism*, the tendency to associate old age with inactivity and/or incompetence. But researchers are publishing studies almost every day showing that such stereotypes have little or no basis in fact (Dittmann, 2003). Indeed, some people seem to be just entering the "prime" of their lives in their late 50s and early 60s and are neither eager for retirement nor on the brink of physical incapacitation. Consider, for instance, Dr. Ruth Simmons, president of Brown University.

On July 3, 1945, Ruth Simmons entered the world as the 12th child in an East Texas family headed by a sharecropper and his wife, who did housework for White families in their small town. Growing up in those rigidly segregated times, Simmons was often called hateful and demeaning names. But in spite of the obstacles she faced, she persevered, impressing her parents and teachers with her academic prowess. When Simmons won a scholarship to Dillard University, her high school teachers took up a collection to buy her some clothes and a coat to take with her. Once in college, she excelled in her studies, majoring in French. Simmons went on to graduate school at Harvard University, earning a Ph.D. in romance languages.

After graduate school, Simmons embarked on an academic career. She became a professor and later the president of prestigious Smith College. But the crowning success of her career came in 2001, when she became president of Brown University, the first African American ever to become head of an Ivy League college or university. Still, Simmons remains humble and credits her mother's commitment to hard work, civility, kindness, and "always doing one's best, no matter what the circumstances or conditions of life" as her principle source of inspiration. Although Simmons is approaching what many people think of as "retirement" age, she continues to be a dynamic leader who appears to be just now entering the peak years of her career. So, don't be surprised if you hear even more about her accomplishments in the future.

The lifespan perspective is the view that changes across all developmental domains—physical, cognitive, and social—occur throughout the entire human lifespan, from conception to death.

Of course, middle and late adulthood aren't the only periods of life associated with stereotypes. As you'll see, many commonly held beliefs about adolescence simply aren't true. In this chapter, we examine some of these beliefs as we trace physical, cognitive, social, and personality development from adolescence to the end of life.

The Lifespan Perspective

How do you view the years from adolescence to old age? Historically, both psychologists and laypersons have considered adolescence to be a period of great change, adulthood a time of stability, and old age a period of decline. But today, developmental psychologists' approach to all these periods is strongly influenced by the **lifespan perspective,** the view that developmental changes happen throughout the entire human lifespan, literally from "womb to tomb" (Baltes et al., 1980). Thus, understanding change in adulthood is just as important as understanding change in childhood and adolescence. Moreover, research based in many disciplines—anthropology, sociology, economics, political science, and biology, as well as psychology—is required to fully comprehend human development. One of the most important theoretical influences for the lifespan perspective has been Erikson's theory of psychosocial development.

■ lifespan perspective The view that developmental changes happen throughout the human lifespan and that interdisciplinary research is required to fully understand human development.

Erikson's Psychosocial Theory

How does Erikson's theory of psychosocial development differ from other developmental theories?

Erik Erikson (1902–1994) proposed the only major theory of development to include the entire lifespan. According to Erikson, individuals progress through eight **psychosocial stages** during the lifespan. As Table 10.1 (on page 342) shows, each stage is defined by a conflict that arises from the individual's relationship with the social environment and that must be resolved satisfactorily in order for healthy development to occur. The stages are named for the contrasting attitudes that result, depending on how the conflict is resolved (Erikson, 1980). Although failure to resolve a particular conflict impedes later development, the resolution may occur at a later stage and reverse any damage done previously.

Erikson believed that a healthy adult personality depends on acquiring the appropriate basic attitudes in the proper sequence during childhood and adolescence. Moreover, he suggested that the themes of each of his adult stages shape the ways in which adults of various ages approach major life events. The loss of a spouse, for example, has different meanings for and effects on young, middle-aged, and elderly adults.

Research Support for Erikson's Theory

What does research suggest about the accuracy of Erikson's theory?

How accurately do Erikson's stages apply to your own experiences to this point in your life? Most people find Erikson's general notions about the major themes of development during certain age periods to be helpful in organizing and analyzing their experiences. However, research examining Erikson's stages has focused primarily on the conflicts facing infants (trust vs. mistrust), adolescents (identity vs. role confusion), and middle-aged adults (generativity vs. stagnation), and results have been mixed.

Infants' Trust In Chapter 9, you learned about Harlow's research demonstrating that a strong emotional bond between infant and caregiver, in which the infant is certain of the caregiver's availability as a source of comfort, is vital to the child's future social and personality development. Such findings support Erikson's idea that the development of trust in infancy is essential to later development.

Moreover, research examining the effects of nonparental care provides additional support for Erikson's theory. Infants who are placed in poor-quality settings, such as in child care centers with too few workers to adequately care for the number of infants present, are more likely to develop insecure attachments to their parents (NICHD, 1997). As a result, they are at greater risk for the negative outcomes associated with insecure attachment, which, as you learned in Chapter 9, can persist into adulthood. By contrast, children placed in high-quality child care settings show either no differences from home-reared peers or higher levels of social competence.

■ psychosocial stages Erikson's eight developmental stages through which individuals progress during their lifespan; each stage is defined by a conflict involving the individual's relationship with the social environment, which must be resolved satisfactorily in order for healthy development to occur.

The Identity Crisis Erikson coined the term **identity crisis,** by which he meant the emotional turmoil a teenager experiences when trying to answer the question "Who am I?" Psychologist James Marcia (1980) expanded on Erikson's concept of an identity crisis in his proposal that adolescent identity development involves alternating between several different statuses of crisis and commitment. A mature sense of personal identity isn't attained until the teenager reaches *identity achievement*, a firm commitment to self-chosen occupational and personal goals.

■ identity crisis The emotional turmoil a teenager experiences when trying to establish a sense of personal identity.

TABLE 10.1 Erikson's Psychosocial Stages of Development

STAGE	AGES	DESCRIPTION
Trust vs. mistrust	Birth to 1 year	Infants learn to trust or mistrust depending on the degree and regularity of care, love, and affection provided by parents or caregivers.
Autonomy vs. shame and doubt	1 to 3 years	Children learn to express their will and independence, to exercise some control, and to make choices. If not, they experience shame and doubt.
Initiative vs. guilt	3 to 6 years	Children begin to initiate activities, to plan and undertake tasks, and to enjoy developing motor and other abilities. If not allowed to initiate or if made to feel stupid and considered a nuisance, they may develop a sense of guilt.
Industry vs. inferiority	6 years to puberty	Children develop industriousness and feel pride in accomplishing tasks, making things, and doing things. If not encouraged or if rebuffed by parents and teachers, they may develop a sense of inferiority.
Identity vs. role confusion	Adolescence	Adolescents must make the transition from childhood to adulthood, establish an identity, develop a sense of self, and consider a future occupational identity. Otherwise, role confusion can result.
Intimacy vs. isolation	Young adulthood	Young adults must develop intimacy—the ability to share with, care for, and commit themselves to another person. Avoiding intimacy brings a sense of isolation and loneliness.
Generativity vs. stagnation	Middle adulthood	Middle-aged people must find some way of contributing to the development of the next generation. Failing this, they may become self-absorbed and emotionally impoverished and reach a point of stagnation.
Ego integrity vs. despair	Late adulthood	Individuals review their lives, and if they are satisfied and feel a sense of accomplishment, they will experience ego integrity. If dissatisfied, they may sink into despair.

Again, as with Erikson's theory, many people have found Marcia's ideas about identity to be useful. However, both he and Erikson may have been wrong about the timing of the identity crisis. Research has shown that identity development may begin in adolescence, but it is not complete until early adulthood (Waterman, 1985). Many college students, for example, are in *moratorium*, the type of crisis in which options are explored. Most haven't settled on a major or a future career, and they use their classroom experiences to make these important decisions. Some are in *foreclosure;* that is, they are pursuing the academic goals that others have chosen for them. For instance, a student may be majoring in biology because her parents expect her to become a physician. Another student may have chosen to major in business because his employer provides tuition reimbursements for such classes. Other students may be in *identity diffusion*, just "hanging out," not taking their classes seriously or thinking about job opportunities but rather waiting for something to come along that will push them in one direction or another.

One reason for the delay before identity achievement is attained may be that advances in logical reasoning, such as those associated with Piaget's formal operations stage, are strongly related to identity development (Klaczynski et al., 1998). As you learned in Chapter 9, formal operational thinking evolves slowly during the adolescent years. Consequently, people may not be able to engage in the kind of thinking necessary for identity achievement until their early adult years.

Generativity A number of studies have examined Erikson's concept of *generativity*, an interest in contributing to the development of the next generation. In one cross-sectional study of young, midlife, and older women, researchers found that generativity did increase in middle adulthood (Zucker et al., 2002). However, it did not decline in late adulthood. The oldest group of study participants, with an average age of 66, cited generativity concerns as being important to them just as frequently as the middle-aged group did. Thus, generativity may be more characteristic of middle than of early adulthood, as Erikson suggested, but it appears to continue to be important in late adulthood.

According to Erikson, in middle adulthood, people develop generativity—an interest in guiding the next generation.

Differences in generativity, as Erikson predicted, are related to variations in behavior. For example, a study involving parents of adolescents found that those with the most acute sense of generativity were more likely than those with lower levels of generativity to display an authoritative parenting style. However, the relationship between generativity and authoritative parenting was much stronger for mothers than for fathers (Pratt et al., 2001). Thus, Erikson's conflict for middle age may be more applicable to women than to men.

There is also some research support for Erikson's claim that generativity is related to mental health in middle age. In a study of midlife adults, generativity was positively related to satisfaction in life and work, and it was a strong predictor of emotional well-being (Ackerman et al., 2000). In another study, which measured middle-aged women's sense of being burdened by caring for elderly parents, those who exhibited the highest levels of generativity felt the least burdened (Peterson, 2002).

Erikson's lifespan perspective was a key factor that influenced 20th-century developmentalists to look more closely at the transition from childhood to adulthood commonly known as *adolescence*.

Remember It 10.1

1. According to Erikson, the poor resolution of conflicts in early stages affects an individual's ability to ___________.

2. Match each description of child behavior with the appropriate psychosocial stage.

   ___ (1) needs consistent attention to physical, social, and emotional needs

   ___ (2) initiates play and motor activities, asks questions

   ___ (3) strives for sense of independence

   ___ (4) undertakes projects, makes things

   a. trust vs. mistrust
   b. autonomy vs. shame and doubt
   c. initiative vs. guilt
   d. industry vs. inferiority

3. Match each description of adolescent or adult behavior with the appropriate psychosocial stage.

   ___ (1) searches for a life partner

   ___ (2) seeks to answer the question "Who am I?"

   ___ (3) concerned with influencing future generations

   ___ (4) reflects on life's accomplishments to achieve a sense of satisfaction

   a. identity vs. role confusion
   b. intimacy vs. isolation
   c. generativity vs. stagnation
   d. ego integrity vs. despair

4. Most research on Erikson's theory has focused on his three stages of ___________, ___________, and ___________.

ANSWERS: 1. resolve conflicts in later stages; 2. (1) a, (2) c, (3) b, (4) d; 3. (1) b, (2) a, (3) c, (4) d; 4. trust vs. mistrust, identity vs. role confusion, generativity vs. stagnation

Adolescence

What personal associations do you have with the beginning of adolescence? You might remember your first day of secondary school, or the realization that the clothing and shoes sold in children's stores no longer fit you, or perhaps your first serious "crush." In some cultures, young teens participate in formal ceremonies known as *rites of passage*, which publicly mark the passage from childhood to adulthood. In the Western industrialized world, however, there is a long transitional period between childhood and adulthood, which is marked by many less formal experiences, such as a first job, that help young people acquire the skills necessary to live independently. The term **adolescence** refers to this developmental stage that begins at puberty.

The concept of adolescence did not exist until 1904, when psychologist G. Stanley Hall first wrote about it in his book by that name. He portrayed adolescence as characterized by "storm and stress," resulting from the biological changes that occur during the period. Anna Freud (1958), daughter of Sigmund Freud, even considered a stormy adolescence a necessary part of normal development. And though it does appear to be true that turbulent, unsettled periods occur more often in adolescence than in any other period of human development, Hall and Freud overstated the case (Arnett, 1999).

■ **adolescence**
The developmental stage that begins at puberty and encompasses the period from the end of childhood to the beginning of adulthood.

The somewhat exaggerated claims of Hall and Freud about the emotional upheavals of adolescence have probably contributed to a number of negative stereotypes. Many see adolescence as a period of emotional instability, punctuated by inevitable associations with socially deviant peers and experimentation with risky behaviors, such as alcohol abuse and unprotected sexual intercourse. However, the truth is that most teens are psychologically healthy and have primarily positive developmental experiences (Takanishi, 1993). Most enjoy good relationships with their families and friends, and researchers say that the majority of them are happy and self-confident (Diener & Diener, 1996).

Contrary to popular belief, adolescence is not stormy and stressful for most teenagers.

Perhaps few teens have the experiences stereotypically associated with adolescence because most are too busy doing exactly what they should be doing during these years: learning the skills they will need for adulthood. But if adolescence is defined as the period of life when people acquire the skills needed for independent living, exactly when does it end? The answer to this question depends on how long a transition is required by the particular culture in which a young person is growing up. In fact, in societies such as the United States, the college years may be thought of as an extended adolescence because college students are still engaged in learning skills they will need to function independently from their parents. Consequently, adolescence can vary in length from person to person.

Puberty

What physical and psychological changes occur as a result of puberty?

Finding the dividing line between adolescence and adulthood is far more difficult than determining when adolescence begins. A dramatic series of physiological changes clearly mark, at least in a physical sense, the transition from childhood to adolescence. **Puberty** is a collective term that includes all of these changes. Thus, puberty is not a single event. Rather, it is a period of several years' duration that is marked by rapid physical growth and physiological changes and that culminates in sexual maturity. Although the average onset of puberty is at age 10 for girls and age 12 for boys, the normal range extends from 7 to 14 for girls and from 9 to 16 for boys (Chumlea, 1982). Every person's individual timetable for puberty is influenced primarily by heredity, although environmental factors, such as diet and exercise, also exert some influence.

puberty
A period of several years in which rapid physical growth and physiological changes occur, culminating in sexual maturity.

secondary sex characteristics
Those physical characteristics that are not directly involved in reproduction but distinguish the mature male from the mature female.

The Physical Changes of Puberty Puberty begins with a surge in hormone production, which, in turn, causes a number of physical changes. For instance, do you remember outgrowing a new pair of shoes in just a few days or weeks during your early teen years? Such experiences are common because the most startling change during puberty is the marked acceleration in growth known as the *adolescent growth spurt*. On the average, the growth spurt occurs from age 10 to 13 in girls and about 2 years later in boys, from age 12 to 15 (Tanner, 1990). Because various parts of the body grow at different rates, the adolescent often has a lanky, awkward appearance. Girls attain their full height between ages 16 and 17, and boys, between ages 18 and 20.

During puberty, the reproductive organs in both sexes mature, and **secondary sex characteristics** appear—those physical characteristics that are not directly involved in reproduction but distinguish the mature male from the mature female. In girls, the breasts develop and the hips round; in boys, the voice deepens, and facial and chest hair appears; and in both sexes, pubic and underarm (axillary) hair grows.

The major landmark of puberty for males is the first ejaculation, which occurs, on average, at age 13 (Jorgensen & Keiding, 1991). For females, it is *menarche*, the onset of menstruation, which occurs, on average, between ages 12 and 13, although the normal range is considered to extend from 10 to 16 (Tanner, 1990). The age of menarche is influenced by heredity, but a girl's diet and lifestyle contribute as well. Regardless of genes, a girl must have a certain proportion of body fat to attain menarche. Consequently, girls who eat high-fat diets and who are not physically active begin menstruating earlier than girls whose diets contain less fat and whose activities involve fat-reducing exercise (e.g., ballet, gymnastics). And girls living in poor countries where they experience malnutrition or in societies in which children are expected to perform physical labor also begin menstruating at later ages.

The Timing of Puberty The timing of puberty can have important psychological and social consequences. Early-maturing boys, taller and stronger than their classmates, have an advantage in sports and in capturing attention from girls. They are likely to have a positive body image, to feel confident, secure, independent, and happy, and to be successful academically as well (Alsaker, 1995; Blyth et al., 1981; Peterson, 1987). Late-maturing boys often show the opposite effects: poor body image, less confidence, and so on.

However, early puberty isn't always positive for boys. Sometimes, it interacts with other factors to produce more negative developmental outcomes. For example, among African American boys who live in poor neighborhoods, early puberty is associated with higher levels of aggressive behavior (Ge et al., 2002).

For girls, early maturation brings increased self-consciousness and, often, dissatisfaction with their developing bodies (Ohring et al., 2002). Consequently, early-maturing girls are more likely than their peers to develop bulimia and other eating disorders (Kaltiala-Heino et al., 2001). In addition, they may have to deal with the sexual advances of older boys before they are emotionally or psychologically mature (Peterson, 1987). In addition to having earlier sexual experiences and more unwanted pregnancies than late-maturing girls, early-maturing girls are more likely to be exposed to alcohol and drug use (Caspi et al., 1993; Lanza & Collins, 2002). And those who have had such experiences tend to perform less well academically than their agemates (Stattin & Magnusson, 1990).

Sexuality Puberty, of course, brings with it the capacity for sexual intercourse. Before the 1960s, the surging sex drive of adolescents was held in check primarily by societal influences. Parents, religious leaders, the schools, and the media were united

FIGURE 10.1 Sexual Activity among High School Students in the United States

This graph is based on surveys of more than 15,000 high school students conducted in 1999.

Source: CDC (2000).

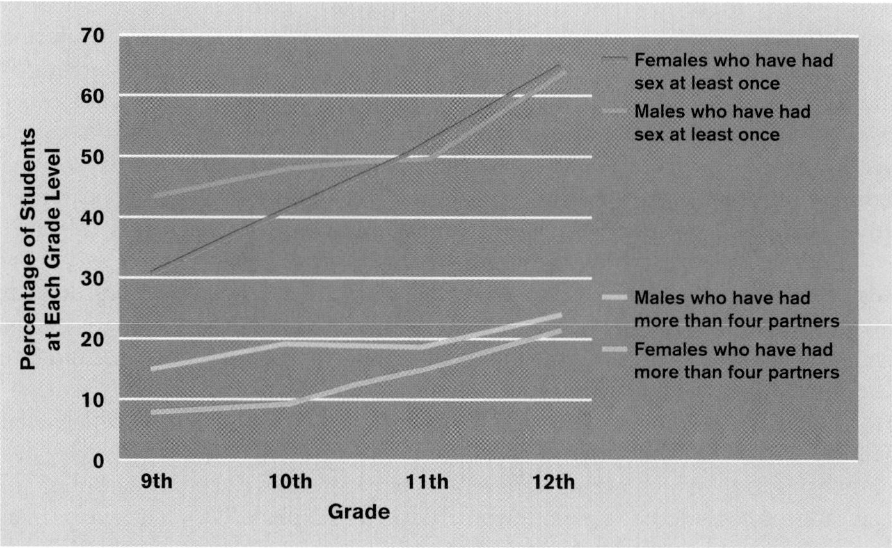

in delivering the same message: Premarital sex is wrong. Then, sexual attitudes began to change. Today, as Figure 10.1 shows, high school students in the United States are very sexually active, with about 25% of them having had four or more sex partners by the time they are seniors (CDC, 2000). Still, research has demonstrated that sex education that includes the message that postponing sex until adulthood is a good decision can reduce teen pregnancy rates (Doniger et al., 2001).

Early intercourse is associated with an increased risk of pregnancy (Morgan et al., 1995) and sexually transmitted diseases. The less sexually experienced teens typically attend religious services frequently and live with both biological parents, who are neither too permissive nor too strict in their discipline and rules (White & DeBlassie, 1992). The presence of a girl's father in her home appears to be particularly important in predicting early sexual behavior among teenage girls; girls in father-absent homes are more likely to become sexually active in their early teens (Ellis et al., 2003). Moreover, early intercourse is less prevalent among adolescents whose academic achievement is above average and whose parents have a harmonious relationship (Brooks-Gunn & Furstenberg, 1989).

Cognitive Development

What cognitive abilities develop during adolescence?

In Chapter 9, you read about Piaget's formal operations stage, in which teenagers acquire the capacity to think hypothetically. Many other improvements in cognitive abilities also occur during these years.

A classic study of the processing of expository text (the type of text you are reading right now), conducted by psychologists Ann Brown and Jeanne Day (1983), illustrates these changes quite well. Experimenters asked 10-, 13-, 15-, and 18-year-olds to read and summarize a 500-word passage (about the same as a page in a typical college textbook). The researchers predicted that participants would use four rules in writing summaries: (1) Delete trivial information; (2) use categories to organize information (e.g., use terms such as *animals* rather than specific names of animals); (3) incorporate topic sentences from the text's paragraphs; and (4) invent topic sentences for paragraphs that lacked them. All participants, regardless of age, included more general information than details in their summaries, suggesting that they had all used the first rule. However, there was far less evidence suggestive of the remaining three rules in the summaries of the 10- and 13-year-olds than in those written by the 15- and 18-year-olds. In addition, only the 18-year-olds used topic sentences consistently.

metamemory
The ability to think about and control one's own memory processes.

Other research has shown that metamemory skills also improve dramatically during adolescence (Winsler & Naglieri, 2003). **Metamemory** is the ability to think about and control one's own memory processes. In one frequently cited early study, researchers instructed 10- and 14-year-olds to engage in an activity for precisely 30 minutes and provided them with a clock to keep track of time (Ceci & Bronfenbrenner, 1985). A much greater proportion of the 14-year-olds than the 10-year-olds periodically checked the clock to determine how many minutes had elapsed since they had begun the activity. As you might expect, fewer than half of the 10-year-olds succeeded in stopping on time, compared to more than 75% of the 14-year-olds. The difference between the two groups was most likely due to the more efficient working memories of the teenagers. In other words, the 14-year-olds were able to keep both the time limit and the activity in mind at the same time. By contrast, the 10-year-olds' working memories were less able to manage the dual demands of keeping up with elapsed time while also engaging in an activity.

These results, along with many other similar ones, indicate that teenagers are much more able than children to organize information efficiently. As a result, adolescents are more effective learners than children are. Moreover, information-processing skills continue to improve well into late adolescence and early adulthood. So, you are far better equipped to handle the intellectual demands of college than you would have been just a few years ago. And it isn't just because you have more knowledge. You manage the knowledge you have, as well as new information you encounter, in an entirely different way.

Moral Development

What are the differences among Kohlberg's three levels of moral reasoning?

Does the clear cognitive advantage of adolescents over children also extend to other domains such as moral reasoning? What about teenagers' capacity to think about moral issues? Lawrence Kohlberg (1981, 1984, 1985) believed, as did Piaget before him, that moral reasoning is closely related to cognitive development and that it, too, evolves in stages. Kohlberg (1969) studied moral development by presenting a series of moral dilemmas to male participants from the United States and other countries. Here is one of his best-known dilemmas:

> In Europe a woman was near death from a special kind of cancer. There was one drug the doctors thought might save her. It was a form of radium that a druggist in the same town had recently discovered. The drug was expensive to make, and the druggist was charging ten times what it cost him. He paid $200 for the radium and charged $2,000 for a small dose of the drug. The sick woman's husband, Heinz, went to everyone he knew to borrow the money, but he could only get together $1,000, which was half of what the drug cost. He told the druggist that his wife was dying and asked him to sell it cheaper or let him pay later. But the druggist said, "No, I discovered the drug, and I am going to make money from it." So Heinz got desperate and broke into the man's store to steal the drug for his wife (Colby et al., 1983, p. 77).

What moral judgment would you make about this dilemma? Should Heinz have stolen the drug? Why or why not? Kohlberg was less interested in whether the participants judged Heinz's behavior right or wrong than in the reasons for their responses. He found that moral reasoning could be classified into three levels, with each level having two stages.

preconventional level Kohlberg's first level of moral reasoning, in which moral reasoning is governed by the standards of others rather than the person's own internalized standards of right and wrong; acts are judged as good or bad based on their physical consequences.

conventional level Kohlberg's second level of moral reasoning, in which the individual has internalized the standards of others and judges right and wrong in terms of those standards.

postconventional level Kohlberg's highest level of moral reasoning, in which moral reasoning involves weighing moral alternatives and realizing that laws may conflict with basic human rights.

The Levels of Moral Reasoning Kohlberg's first level of moral reasoning is the **preconventional level**, where moral reasoning is governed by the standards of others rather than the individual's own internalized standards of right and wrong. An act is judged good or bad based on its physical consequences. In Stage 1, "right" is whatever avoids punishment. In Stage 2, "right" is whatever is rewarded, benefits the individual, or results in a favor being returned. "You scratch my back, and I'll scratch yours" is the type of thinking common at this stage.

At Kohlberg's second level of moral reasoning, the **conventional level**, the individual has internalized the standards of others and judges right and wrong in terms of those standards. In Stage 3, sometimes called the *good boy–nice girl orientation*, "good behavior is that which pleases or helps others and is approved by them" (Kohlberg, 1968, p. 26). In Stage 4, the orientation is toward "authority, fixed rules, and the maintenance of the social order. Right behavior consists of doing one's duty, showing respect for authority, and maintaining the given social order for its own sake" (p. 26).

Kohlberg believed that a person must function at Piaget's concrete operations stage to reason morally at the conventional level. Thus, theoretically at least, conventional moral reasoning should appear some time between the ages of 6 and 12. However, Kohlberg's research and that of others demonstrated that moral reasoning lags behind cognitive development. Consequently, most school-age children, though proficient at concrete operational thinking, do not yet reason about moral dilemmas at the conventional level, as shown in Figure 10.2.

Kohlberg's highest level of moral reasoning is the **postconventional level.** At this level, people weigh moral alternatives, realizing that at times laws may conflict with basic human rights. In Stage 5, the person believes that laws are formulated to protect both society and the individual and should be changed if they fail to do so. In Stage 6, ethical

FIGURE 10.2 Changes in Moral Reasoning from Childhood to Early Adulthood

Researchers Ann Colby and Lawrence Kohlberg studied changes in participants' responses to the Heinz dilemma and similar moral problems over more than 20 years. As you can see, preconventional reasoning predominated until participants were approaching adolescence.

Source: Colby et al. (1983), Figure 1, p. 46. Copyright: The Society for Research in Child Development.

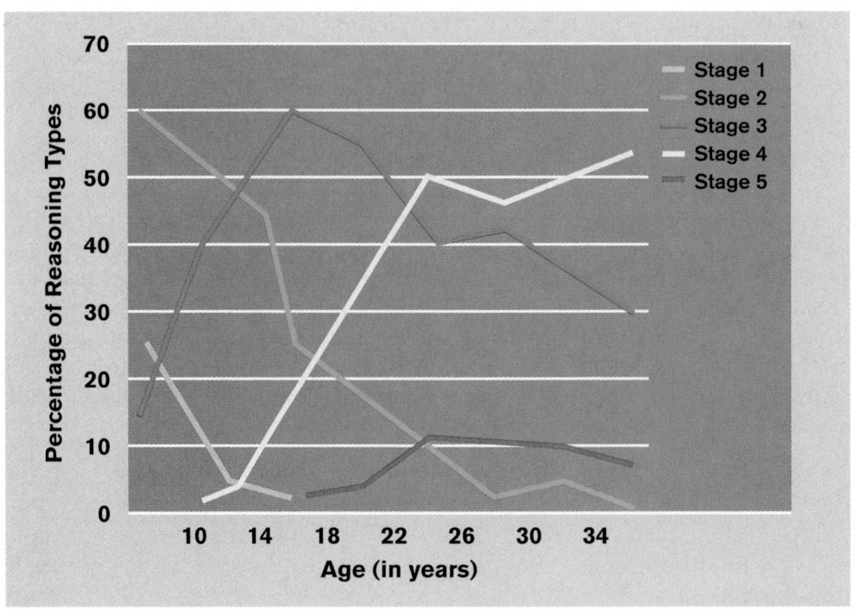

decisions are based on universal ethical principles, which emphasize respect for human life, justice, equality, and dignity for all people. People who reason morally at Stage 6 believe that they must follow their conscience, even if it results in a violation of the law.

According to Kohlberg, postconventional moral reasoning requires the ability to think at Piaget's stage of formal operations. However, attainment of formal operational thought does not guarantee that an individual will reach Kohlberg's postconventional level. Postconventional reasoning is strongly related to education and is most often found among middle-class, college-educated adults.

Review and Reflect 10.1 summarizes Kohlberg's six stages of moral reasoning.

The Development of Moral Reasoning Kohlberg claimed that people progress through his stages of moral reasoning one stage at a time, in a fixed order. As you learned earlier, moral and cognitive development are correlated, but attaining a high level of cognitive development does not guarantee advanced moral reasoning. And, as Kohlberg came to realize, discussion of moral dilemmas does not reliably improve moral behavior. He eventually agreed that direct teaching of moral and ethical values is necessary and compatible with his theory (Higgins, 1995; Power et al., 1989).

Research on Kohlberg's Theory In a review of 45 studies of Kohlberg's theory conducted in 27 countries, Snarey (1985) found support for the universality of Stages 1 through 4 and for the invariant sequence of these stages in all groups studied.

REVIEW *and* REFLECT 10.1

Kohlberg's Stages of Moral Reasoning

LEVEL	STAGE
Level I: Preconventional level Moral reasoning is governed by the standards of others; an act is good or bad depending on its physical consequences—whether it is punished or rewarded.	**Stage 1** The stage in which behavior that avoids punishment is right. Children obey out of fear of punishment. **Stage 2** The stage of self-interest. What is right is what benefits the individual or gains a favor in return. "You scratch my back, and I'll scratch yours."
Level II: Conventional level The child internalizes the standards of others and judges right and wrong according to those standards.	**Stage 3** The morality of mutual relationships. The "good boy–nice girl orientation." Child acts to please and help others. **Stage 4** The morality of the social system and conscience. Orientation toward authority. "Right" is doing one's duty, respecting authority, and maintaining the social order.
Level III: Postconventional level Moral conduct is under internal control; this is the highest level and the mark of true morality.	**Stage 5** The morality of contract; respect for individual rights and laws that are democratically agreed on. Rational valuing of the wishes of the majority and the general welfare. Belief that society is best served if citizens obey the law. **Stage 6** The morality of universal ethical principles. The person acts according to internal standards, independent of legal restrictions or opinions of others. The highest stage of the highest level of moral reasoning.

Want to be sure you've fully absorbed the material in this chapter? Visit **www.ablongman.com/wood5e** for access to free practice tests, flashcards, interactive activities, and links developed specifically to help you succeed in psychology.

Although extremely rare, Stage 5 was found in almost all samples from urban or middle-class populations and was absent in all of the tribal or village folk societies studied. More recent research conducted by Snarey (1995) supports the conclusions reached a decade earlier.

In a cross-cultural study of the moral reasoning of adults and children from India and the United States, Miller and Bersoff (1992) found great differences between the two cultures. The postconventional moral reasoning common in India stresses interpersonal responsibilities over obligations to further justice. In contrast, Americans emphasize individual rights over responsibilities to others. Such findings, along with Snarey's observations about Stage 5 reasoning, suggest that Kohlberg's postconventional level of moral reasoning may be more strongly associated with culture than are his lower levels.

Gilligan's Alternative Approach Kohlberg indicated that the majority of women remain at Stage 3, while most men attain Stage 4. Do men typically attain a higher level of moral reasoning than women? Carol Gilligan (1982) asserts that Kohlberg's theory is gender-biased. Not only did Kohlberg fail to include females in his original research, Gilligan points out, but he limits morality to abstract reasoning about moral dilemmas. Moreover, Kohlberg's highest level, Stage 6, emphasizes justice and equality but not mercy, compassion, love, or concern for others. Gilligan suggests that females, more than males, tend to view moral behavior in terms of compassion, caring, and concern for others. More recent evidence suggests that females do tend to emphasize care and compassion in resolving moral dilemmas, while males tend to stress justice or at least to give it equal standing with caring (Garmon et al., 1996; Wark & Krebs, 1996). And researchers other than Kohlberg have found that females score as high as males in moral reasoning (Walker, 1989).

What outcomes are often associated with the authoritative, authoritarian, and permissive parenting styles?

Parental Relationships

You may recall from Chapter 9 that many teens use their newfound cognitive abilities to devise idealistic plans, which give rise to many parent-teen conflicts. For instance, a 14-year-old might protest against doing algebra homework because he envisions himself becoming a professional athlete, who would, of course, have no need for algebra. Parents counter that, athlete or not, algebra is required for high school graduation and the homework, therefore, must be done. You probably had some arguments with your parents during your high school years, but research does not support the view that adolescents' relationships with their parents are dominated by conflicts. In fact, secure attachments to parents, along with effective parenting practices, are just as critical to a teen's development as they are to that of an infant or child (Allen et al., 2003; Cassidy et al., 2003; Galambos et al., 2003).

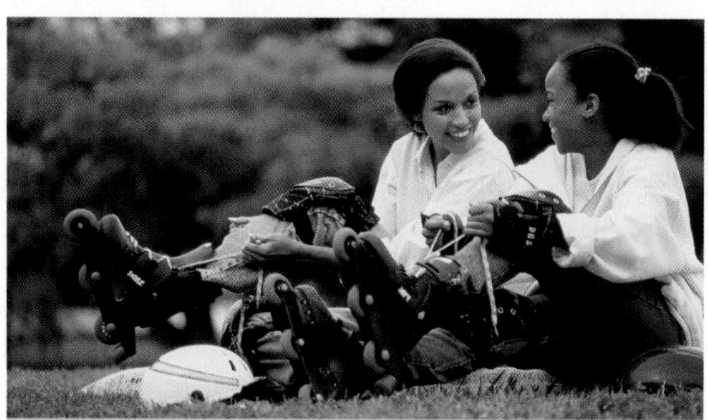

Most adolescents and their parents have good relationships and enjoy doing things together.

Of the three parenting styles discussed in Chapter 9 (authoritative, authoritarian, and permissive), the authoritative style is most effective and the permissive least effective for adolescents (Baumrind, 1991; Steinberg et al., 1994). In a study of about 2,300 adolescents, those with permissive parents were more likely to use alcohol and drugs and to have conduct problems and less likely to be engaged in school than were those with authoritative or authoritarian parents (Lamborn et al., 1991). The authoritarian style was related to more psychological distress and less self-reliance and self-confidence in adolescents. The authoritative parenting style was associated with psychosocial competence for adolescents of all racial and ethnic groups and with academic success for those who are White and middle-class (Aunola et al., 2000; Steinberg et al., 1994). But the authoritarian rather than the authoritative style has been found to be associated with high academic achievement by Asian American and African American adolescents (Steinberg, 1992). Why? With regard to Asian American teens, Steinberg (1992) suggests that authoritarian parenting is tied to parents' strong belief that a child's accomplishments are attributable to both the child's own efforts and those of his family. In the case of African American adolescents, though, authoritarian parenting may help overcome potentially negative peer influences. According to Steinberg (1992), "African American students are more likely than others to be caught in a bind between performing well in school and being popular among their peers" (p. 728). Thus, when peer values and norms do not support academic pursuits, African American parents may adopt an authoritarian approach because they believe it will best serve their child's long-term interests.

Other research suggests that the relationship between parenting style and developmental outcomes is more complex than researchers once believed. For instance, when parents become increasingly authoritarian in response to their teenage children's deviant behavior, researchers have found that the deviant behavior decreases (Galambos et al., 2003). Also, firm parental control over teenagers' behavior helps to counteract the adverse effects of peers who engage in deviant behavior. Further, parents who monitor the activities and relationships of teenagers who have a history of delinquency increase those teens' chances of getting their lives on a more positive developmental track (Laird et al., 2003). So, good parenting for teens may not necessarily mean adoption of any single style. Instead, it may be more important for parents to be flexible and to exhibit the style of parenting that is most appropriate for their own teenager.

The Peer Group

What are some of the beneficial functions of the adolescent peer group?

Clearly, parents are important to adolescent development, but friends can also be a vital source of emotional support and approval. Indeed, interactions with peers may be critical while young people are fashioning their identities. Adolescents can try out different roles and observe the reactions of their friends to their behavior and their appearance. The peer group provides teenagers with a standard of comparison for evaluating their own attributes as well as a vehicle for developing social skills (Berndt, 1992).

A controversial book, *The Nurture Assumption*, by Judith Harris (1998), suggests that peers have more influence on young people than parents do. But such a claim implies that the environmental influence of peers is strong enough to override both parents' genetic contribution (nature) and their environmental influence (nurture). In fact, peer and parental influences are not necessarily opposing forces. Often, parents know and like the friends of their teenage children. Moreover, adolescents are not assigned to peer groups at random; they usually choose to associate with those similar to themselves (Duck, 1983; Epstein, 1983; Hamm, 2000). For example, an academically inclined teen is likely to gravitate to a peer group with academic interests (Altermatt & Pomerantz, 2003). Associating with academically successful peers will reinforce this teenager's achievement. In such cases, then, peer influence complements parental influence.

However, peer influences can be negative as well. For instance, aggressive teens tend to associate with peers who are equally aggressive (Espelage et al., 2003). And, like the peers of academically inclined teens, the friends of teens who are aggressive reinforce their behavior. Moreover, associating with peers who use tobacco, alcohol, or other substances increases the odds that a teenager will adopt these practices (Cleveland & Wiebe, 2003). In these cases, peer influence and parental influence are in opposition. Still, as noted earlier, when parents adapt their approaches to parenting to a teenager's behavior and his or her peer associations, their influence can counteract the negative effects of deviant peers (Laird et al., 2003). Thus, peer influences can render parenting more complex when children reach their teen years, but peer influence does not generally outweigh the effects of good parenting.

Teen Pregnancy

What are some of the consequences of teenage pregnancy?

Why do 5–10% of adolescent girls in the United States become pregnant each year (Federal Interagency Forum on Child and Family Statistics, 2000)? Although teen pregnancy rates are lower in other countries, research indicates that similar risk factors underlie this phenomenon, no matter where it occurs.

Risk Factors for Teen Parenthood Many of the same factors predispose both girls and boys to becoming teenage parents: poverty, poor school performance, drug use, early dating, early sexual activity, multiple sex partners, peer rejection, aggressive behavior, and delinquency (Guagliardo et al., 1999; Xie et al., 2001). Family variables also contribute. Boys who grow up without a father in the home are more likely to impregnate a girl (Furstenberg & Weiss, 2000). Further, both boys and girls whose parents are addicted to alcohol or drugs are at greater risk of adolescent parenthood than peers whose parents don't have such problems (Goodyear et al., 2002).

Fulfillment of idealized gender roles may also be a factor in teen parenthood. This appears to be particularly true for boys who regard impregnating a girl, or several girls, as a sign of masculinity (Goodyear et al., 2000). Likewise, many teenage girls are eager to take on the mother role and appear to be quite committed to being good parents (Dallas et al., 2000; Davies et al., 2001). What are the developmental consequences for teenage parents, their children, and their families?

The Consequences for Mother and Child Because pregnant teens are more likely than older pregnant women to come from poor backgrounds, they are less likely to receive early prenatal medical care and adequate nutrition. As a result, pregnant teenagers are at higher risk for miscarriage, stillbirth, and complications during delivery. They are also more likely to deliver premature or low-birth-weight babies, who have a higher infant mortality rate (Fraser et al., 1995; Goldenberg & Klerman, 1995; Scholl et al., 1996).

Among young women who give birth before age 18 and choose to keep their babies, half never complete high school. Because many teenage mothers are single parents living in poverty, researchers typically find that their children display poor developmental outcomes more frequently than those of older mothers (Turley, 2003). For instance, in school, these children typically score lower on intelligence tests and are more likely to exhibit disruptive behavior (Berk, 1997).

Nevertheless, teen pregnancy does not inevitably lead to poor outcomes for mother and child. Programs to help teen mothers stay in school and to learn how to take care of their babies do make a difference. In addition, when the parents of adolescent mothers help them with finances, child care, and educational decisions, these girls are more likely to remain in school (Birch, 1998). Finishing school, in turn, has benefits for both the mother and the baby. For instance, those who graduate from high school are less likely than their peers who drop out to require long-term public assistance, such as food stamps and welfare payments (Morris et al., 2003).

The Consequences for Teen Fathers Historically, research on the causes and consequences of adolescent parenthood has focused on mothers and babies (Levandowski, 2001). This is because the mothers typically have custody of the babies; in one study involving 144 custodial teenage parents, only 2 were fathers (Greenberg, 2001). Thus, it has often been assumed that the mother is the one who bears most, if not all, of the consequences of teen parenthood. However, in the past decade, developmentalists have begun to question this assumption.

One important longitudinal study of teen fatherhood is the Pittsburgh Youth Study, funded by the U.S. Department of Justice (Thornberry et al., 2000). Researchers have followed several hundred inner-city, mostly minority, male teenagers, beginning in 7th grade. By age 20, about 12% of participants had became fathers, some as early as age 14. Many of these young men had more than one child. The 62 fathers in the study had a total of 82 children while still in their teens. One surprising finding was that becoming a father while a teenager was associated with a large increase in delinquent behavior in the year following the baby's birth. Consequently, the teen fathers were more likely than their peers who did not have children to be incarcerated. Researchers have not yet been able to explain this increase in delinquency. However, the school drop-out rate was also dramatically higher for the teen fathers: about 60% of them left school, compared to just over 20% of the nonfathers. The unstructured time available to drop-outs, who probably have difficulty finding employment, may be a contributing factor to the increase in delinquency. The teens who became fathers were also more likely to use alcohol and drugs.

While there are many support programs for teen mothers, there are very few for teen fathers. Thus, developmentalists don't know whether such programs might help reduce the negative impact of early parenthood for boys, just as they do for girls. Moreover, pregnancy prevention programs focus heavily on the consequences of pregnancy for girls. Findings such as those of the Pittsburgh study suggest that adding components designed to address risk factors and consequences for boys may make these prevention programs more effective.

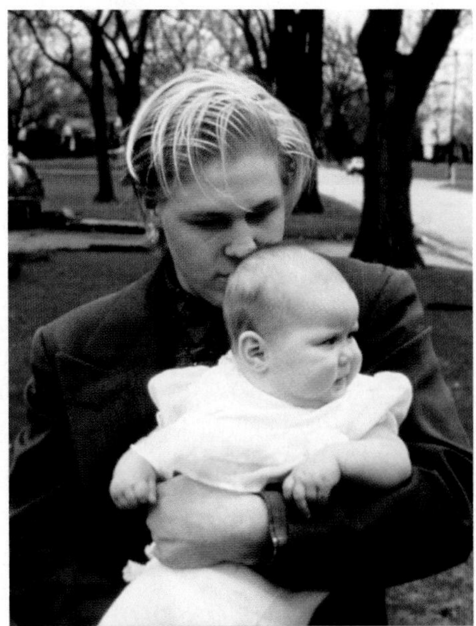

Like teen motherhood, adolescent fatherhood is associated with a number of risk factors and negative consequences. However, interventions for teen fathers may be helpful in increasing their involvement with children and decreasing negative outcomes, such as dropping out of school.

Remember It 10.2

1. According to __________ and __________, adolescence is a period of storm and stress.
2. __________ sex characteristics are physical characteristics that are not directly involved in reproduction.
3. The ability to consciously monitor memory function, known as __________, dramatically improves during adolescence.
4. Match each rationale for engaging in a behavior with one of Kohlberg's levels of moral reasoning.

   ___ (1) to avoid punishment or gain a reward
   ___ (2) to ensure that human rights are protected
   ___ (3) to gain approval or follow the law

   a. conventional level
   b. preconventional level
   c. postconventional level
5. For adolescents, the most effective parenting style is the __________ style; the least effective is the __________ style.
6. Peers can be an important source of __________ for teens.

ANSWERS: 1. G. Stanley Hall, Anna Freud; 2. Secondary; 3. metamemory; 4. (1) b, (2) c, (3) a; 5. authoritative, permissive; 6. emotional support

Early and Middle Adulthood

When do you think a person attains adulthood? An 18-year-old is physically and legally an adult. However, a full-fledged adult—in the social sense of the term—is an individual who is living independently from his or her parents. But, as noted earlier, considerable change can occur in the adult years. Clearly, a 25-year-old differs from a 45-year-old in important ways. To help in studying developmental differences among adults, psychologists divide adulthood into early, middle, and late periods. We consider the early and middle periods in this section and the late period in the next section. Generally, developmentalists regard the years from ages 20 to 40 as *early adulthood* and those from ages 40 to 65 as *middle adulthood*. Several physical, cognitive, and social changes occur across these years.

What is the difference between primary and secondary aging?

Physical Changes

You probably won't be surprised to learn that adults in their 20s are in their top physical condition. It is in this decade that physical strength, reaction time, reproductive capacity, and manual dexterity all peak. During the 30s, there is a slight decline in these physical capacities, which is barely perceptible to most people other than professional athletes. People in their 40s and 50s often complain about a loss of physical vigor and endurance.

Researchers divide the events associated with aging into two categories: *primary aging* and *secondary aging*. Primary aging is biological and generally unavoidable. For example, one unavoidable change in the mid- to late 40s is the development of **presbyopia**, a condition in which the lenses of the eyes no longer accommodate adequately for near vision, and reading glasses or bifocals are often required for reading. Secondary aging is the result of poor health-related habits and lifestyle choices. For instance, the loss of strength many adults experience as they get older is more likely to be due to lack of exercise than to biological aging processes. Thus, declines associated with advancing age are attributable to the combination of primary and secondary aging. Moreover, changing controllable factors, such as diet and exercise, may slow down these declines. (You'll read more about this intriguing idea in Chapter 13.)

One important milestone of primary aging for women during middle age is **menopause**, the cessation of menstruation, which usually occurs between ages 45 and 55 and marks the end of reproductive capacity. Although life expectancy for females in developed countries increased by 30 years during the 20th century, the span of their fertile years, during which conception is possible, has not increased. The duration of women's reproductive capability is apparently unaffected by the factors that control longevity (Brody et al., 2000).

presbyopia
(prez-bee-O-pee-uh) A condition, developing in the mid- to late 40s, in which the lenses of the eyes no longer accommodate adequately for near vision, and reading glasses or bifocals are required for reading.

menopause
The cessation of menstruation, which usually occurs between ages 45 and 55 and marks the end of reproductive capacity.

The most common symptom associated with menopause and the accompanying sharp decrease in the level of estrogen is hot flashes, sudden feelings of being uncomfortably hot. Some women also experience symptoms such as anxiety, irritability, and/or mood swings, and about 10% become depressed. However, most women do not experience psychological problems in connection with menopause (Busch et al., 1994; Matthews, 1992).

Although men do not have a physical event equivalent to menopause, they do experience a gradual decline in testosterone from age 20 until about age 60. During late middle age, many men also experience a reduction in semen production and in the sex drive. However, though women are not able to conceive after menopause, many men can and do father children during late adulthood.

In what ways do cognitive functions change between the ages of 20 and 60?

Intellectual Abilities

Are there any middle-aged adults in your psychology class? If so, do you think they will perform as well as younger students? The answer might depend on the kind of learning required. Younger adults outperform older adults on tests requiring speed or rote memory. On tests measuring general information, vocabulary, reasoning ability, and social judgment, however, older participants usually do better than younger ones because of their greater experience and education (Horn, 1982). Adults actually continue to gain knowledge and skills over the years, particularly when they lead intellectually challenging lives. Thus, it isn't surprising that most middle-aged college students are academically successful.

Intellectual gains across early and middle adulthood have been documented in longitudinal studies. For example, psychologist Walter Schaie (1994, 1995) analyzed data from the Seattle Longitudinal Study, which assessed the intellectual abilities of some 5,000 participants. Many of the participants were tested six times over the course of 35 years. Schaie found that in five areas—verbal meaning, spatial orientation, inductive reasoning, numerical reasoning, and word fluency—participants showed modest gains from young adulthood to their mid-40s (see Figure 10.3). Decline did not occur, on average, until after age 60, and even then the decline was modest until participants were in their 80s. Even at age 81, half of the participants showed no decline over the previous 7 years. The study also revealed several gender differences: Females performed better on tests of verbal meaning and inductive reasoning, while males tended to do better on tests of numerical reasoning and spatial orientation.

Further, in a classic study of intellectual productivity, Dennis (1968) looked at the productivity of 738 persons who had lived at least 79 years and had attained eminence as scholars, scientists, or artists. For almost every one of these individuals, the decade of the 40s was most productive. Historians, philosophers, and literary scholars enjoyed high productivity from their 40s all the way through their 70s. Scientists were highly productive from their 40s through their 60s, but showed a significant decline in productivity in their 70s. Those in the arts peaked earliest and showed a dramatic decline in their 70s. Of course, the researchers did not interview Michelangelo, Pablo Picasso, Georgia O'Keeffe, Duke Ellington, Irving Berlin, or any of the many other individuals who have been artistically potent and vital into their 80s and 90s.

FIGURE 10.3 Age Differences in Performance on Tests of Five Mental Abilities

This graph shows the average scores of participants in the Seattle Longitudinal Study on tests of five mental abilities. Participants were tested six times over a period of 35 years and showed gains from young adulthood until their mid-40s. Very little decline occurred until after age 60.

Source: Based on Schaie (1994).

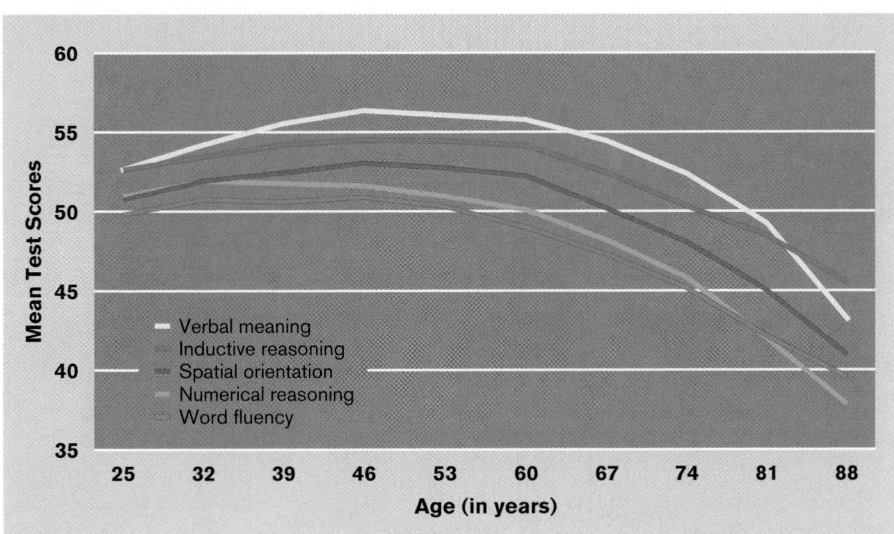

How does attending college affect adult development?

The Impact of College Attendance

Have you ever wondered whether college is really worth the trouble? The answer is yes, if the measure of worth is income. As you can see in Figure 10.4, some college is better than none, but there is a clear income advantage for degree-holders. These income differences exist because, compared to nongraduates, college graduates get more promotions, are less likely to experience long periods of unemployment, are less likely to be discriminated against on the basis of race or gender, and are regarded more favorably by potential employers (Pascarella & Terenzi, 1991). But college attendance has benefits beyond increased income.

College Attendance and Development The longer individuals attend college, even if they don't graduate, the more likely they are to be capable of formal operational thinking and other forms of abstract logical thought (Lehman & Nisbett, 1990; Pascarella, 1999). Years of attendance is also correlated with how efficiently people manage problems in their everyday lives, such as balancing family and work schedules. Longitudinal

FIGURE 10.4 Level of Education and Income

These statistics make it clear that, the longer you stay in school, the more money you are likely to earn. However, note that, even with equal education, men's earnings greatly exceed women's. Reasons for the differences include (1) women are more likely to be working part-time; (2) traditionally female professions (e.g., teaching) do not pay as well as traditionally male occupations (e.g., engineering), even when educational requirements are the same; and (3) most women have spent fewer years in the workforce than have their male counterparts.
Source: U.S. Census Bureau (1998).

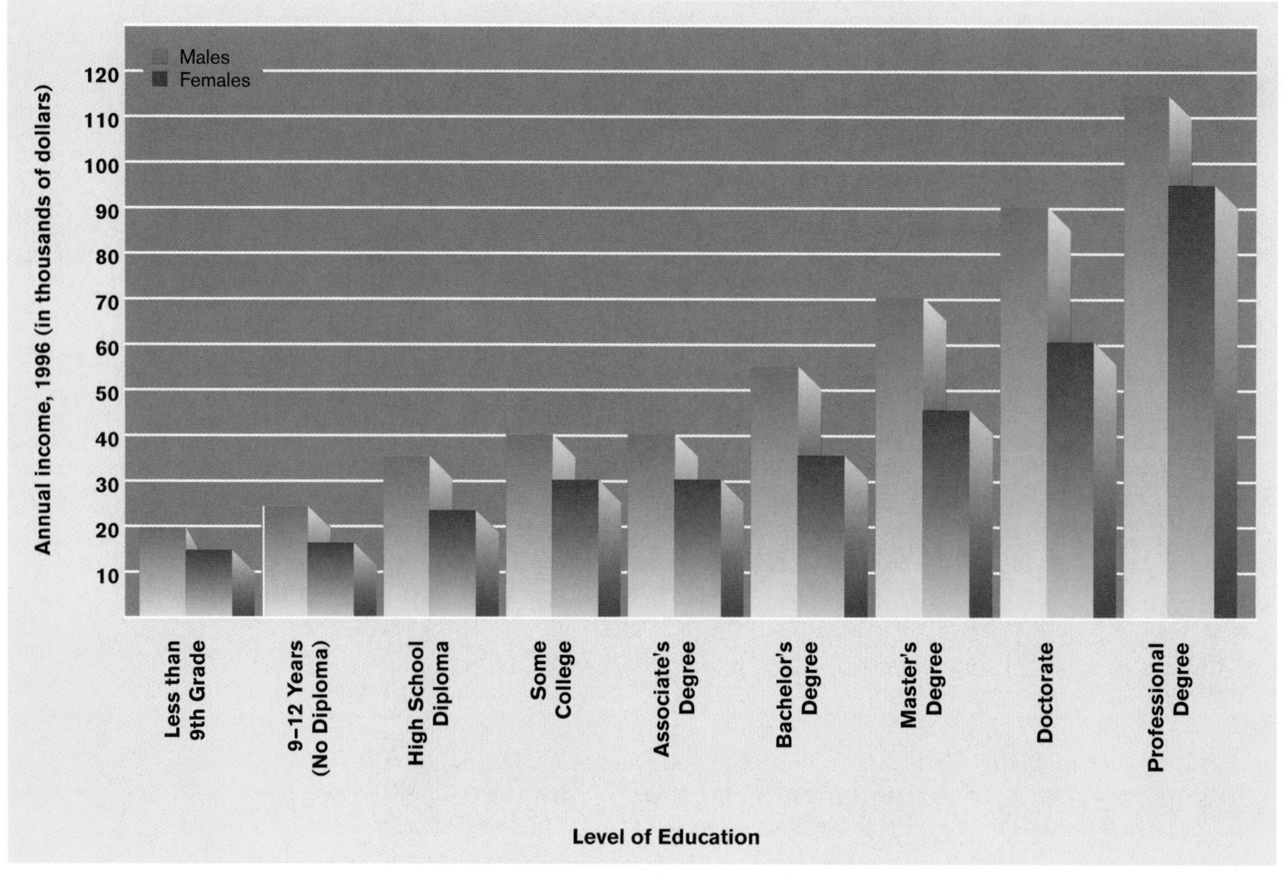

studies show that these cognitive gains happen between the first and later years of college. Such findings mean that two individuals who are of equal intellectual ability, as measured by acceptance by a college or university, are likely to diverge from one another in cognitive skills if one leaves school while the other persists.

College also offers adults the opportunity to sharpen their self-perceptions (Pascarella & Terenzi, 1991). For example, researchers have found that many biology majors enter college with the goal of becoming physicians (Pearsall et al., 1997). Their experiences in biology classes modify these goals. Some realize that becoming a science teacher is a more realistic goal. For others, the goal of a career in medicine is reinforced when they discover that they are more competent in science than they believed prior to taking college-level biology classes. Integrating goals with actual academic experiences helps college graduates achieve a better understanding of where they can best fit into the workforce.

College attendance influences social development as well. For many students, college is their first opportunity to meet people of ethnicities and nationalities that are different from theirs. And students, particularly those who live on campus, learn to establish social networks that eventually replace parents as their primary source of emotional support. The extensive opportunities for social interaction may explain associations that researchers (Chickering & Reisser, 1993; Pascarella & Terenzi, 1991) have found among college attendance, capacity for empathy, and moral reasoning.

Traditional and Nontraditional Students What are the factors other than intellectual ability that predict success in college? You may be surprised to learn that one such factor is authoritative parenting (Wintre & Yaffe, 2000). As is true for elementary and secondary school students, college students whose parents display the authoritative style are more academically successful than peers who parents exhibit other styles. More important than parenting style, though, is a group of factors that researchers use to classify students as *traditional* or *nontraditional*. These factors are given in *Try It 10.1* (on page 358). What type of student are you?

Traditional students make up roughly one-third of the college population in the United States. The remaining two-thirds are distributed across the three nontraditional categories explained in the *Try It*. Most students who enroll in college full-time directly after high school do so because they have financial support from parents, have received scholarships, or qualify for substantial financial aid awards. But the desire to please parents is also a major reason (*Chronicle of Higher Education*, 1997). This may be one area of life in which doing something to please one's parents pays off: About two-thirds of traditional students obtain a degree within 5 years, a much higher graduation rate than that for any of the nontraditional categories. The more nontraditional students are, the less likely they are to graduate (NCES, 1997). Among minimally nontraditional students, just over half get degrees within 5 years of first enrolling; moderately nontraditional students have about a 40% graduation rate; and fewer than 30% of highly nontraditional students graduate.

One reason for the lower graduation rates of nontraditional students may be that they, in contrast to traditional students, are concentrated in 2-year colleges (NCES, 1997). These institutions are less likely to have counseling centers and other support services that help students with academic and personal problems. Two-year schools also offer fewer opportunities for social interaction, so students don't develop the kinds of social support networks that are common among students at 4-year colleges. Thus, a major goal of most community and junior colleges in recent years has been finding ways to better support students in order to decrease drop-out rates.

Gender, Race, and College Completion Gender is also related to college completion. At all degree levels, women are more likely than men to graduate (NCES, 1997). Why? One reason is that female students use more effective study strategies than their male counterparts do (Braten & Olaussen, 1998; Pearsall et al., 1997). In addition,

Try It 10.1 Are You Traditional?

Researchers use seven factors to classify students as *traditional* (no factors present), *minimally nontraditional* (one to two factors present), *moderately nontraditional* (three to four factors present), or *highly nontraditional* (five or more factors present). The factors are (1) delaying college entry more than a year after graduating from high school, (2) living independently from parents, (3) being employed while in school, (4) enrolling part-time rather than full-time, (5) being a parent, (6) having a GED rather than a high school diploma, and (7) being a custodial parent who is single. Using these factors, how would you classify yourself?

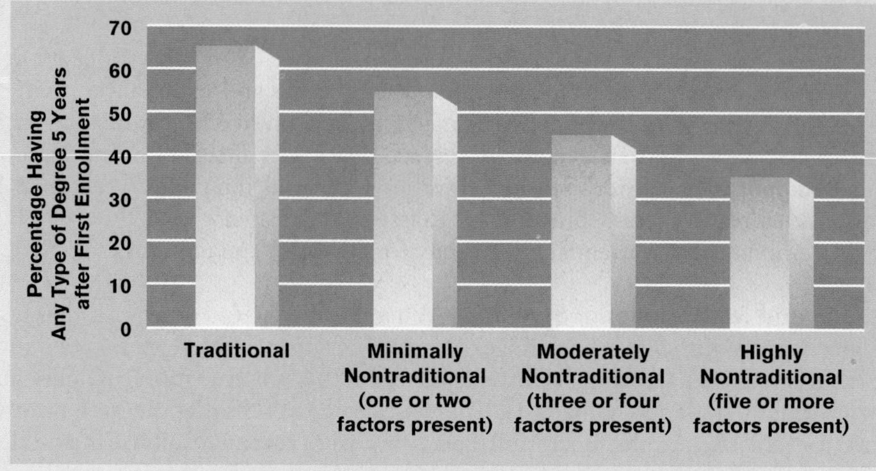

Source: NCES (1997).

male students are more likely to cheat and to be negatively influenced by peers in making decisions about behaviors such as binge drinking (Senchak et al., 1998; Thorpe et al., 1999).

Race is linked to graduation rates as well. As you can see in Figure 10.5, White American students are more likely to drop out than are Asian American, Native American, and Hispanic American students. However, African American students have the highest drop-out rate of all these groups. About 44% leave college and do not return. The reason most often cited for leaving is the perception of racial hostility in the college environment (Schwitzer et al., 1999; Zea et al., 1997). Many African American students have their first experiences with overt racism when they go to college and often feel that they are outsiders in the college community (Gossett et al., 1998).

A greater sense of belonging may explain why African American students who attend historically Black institutions show more gains in both cognitive and social competence than their peers who attend predominantly White colleges (Flowers, 2002; Flowers & Pascarella, 1999). In addition, attending historically Black colleges may help African American students achieve a stronger sense of racial identity, a factor which is correlated with persistence in college (Rowley, 2000). Thus, when these students graduate, they may be better prepared for the demands of graduate and professional programs than are peers who graduate from colleges where African Americans are in the minority. Indeed, this was the path followed by Ruth Simmons: She attended Dillard University, a historically Black college, before going on to Harvard to do graduate work.

FIGURE 10.5 **College Drop-Out Rates in the United States**

Drop-out rates vary widely across ethnic groups in the United States.
Source: NCES (1997).

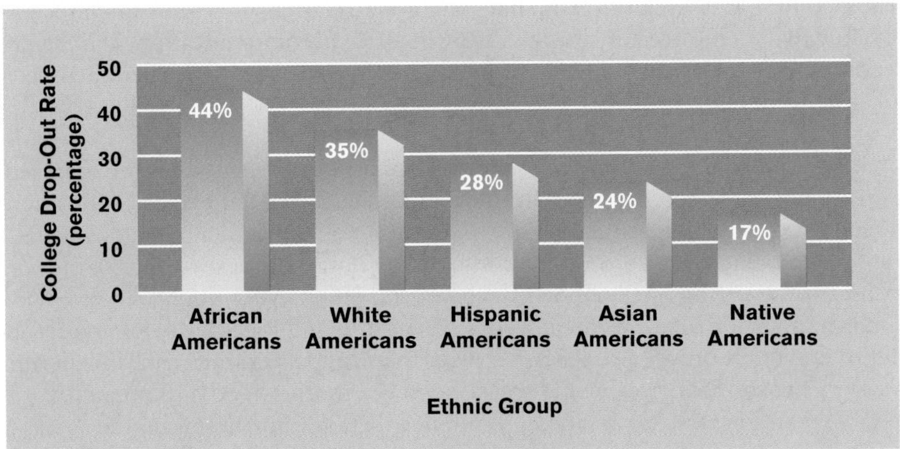

Lifestyle Patterns in Adulthood

Is the "average household" in the United States still headed by a married couple? Yes, the majority of people (53%) live in a household headed by a married couple who may or may not have children under age 18 (U.S. Census Bureau, 2001). Figure 10.6 shows the percentages of the U.S. population living in various household arrangements. Let's consider some of these lifestyle patterns.

What are some current trends in lifestyle patterns among young adults?

Singles Some people believe that if unburdened by a spouse, they will be able to pursue their careers and their interests and have a more interesting and exciting life. Yet the happiest singles seem to be those who have relationships that provide emotional support. Some single people who want a relationship choose living together rather than making the commitment of marriage. At present, in the United States,

FIGURE 10.6 **Household Composition in the United States**

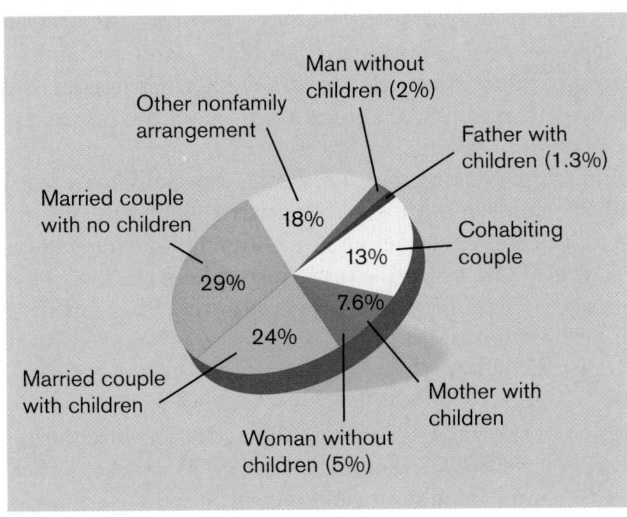

Although households headed by married couples have decreased over the last several decades, 53% of the U.S. population lives in such households. About 25% live alone or with nonfamily members.
Source: Data from U.S. Census Bureau (2001).

about 43% of women under age 40 have been in at least one cohabiting relationship, and cohabiting couples currently represent about 13% of all households (U.S. Census Bureau, 2001). Perhaps surprisingly, the divorce rate for couples who live together before marrying is higher than the divorce rate for couples who do not (Heaton, 2002). Research suggests that cohabiting relationships prior to marriage are associated with emotionally negative, unsupportive communication and behavior patterns during marriage, a factor that may help explain this higher divorce rate (Cohan & Kleinbaum, 2002).

Marriage The mating culture of today's singles is not as oriented toward marriage as it was in the past. A recent report from the National Marriage Project, sponsored by Rutgers University and entitled "The State of Our Unions, 2000," suggests that the dating scene today is one of low commitment, a culture of "sex without strings, relationships without rings" (Poponoe & Whitehead, 2000). Most young singles, 66% of the men and 58.5% of the women, were in favor of living together before marriage in order to find out more about each other prior to making a commitment. Furthermore, 54% of the women said they would consider unwed motherhood if they could not find a suitable man to marry (Poponoe & Whitehead, 2000). Furthermore, the age at first marriage keeps rising for both males and females: In 1960, the median age at first marriage was 20 for females and 23 for males; today, the median age is 25 for females and 27 for males (Poponoe & Whitehead, 2000).

Despite these changes, most people marry at least once in their lives and may be better off as a result. In a review of 93 studies, Wood and others (1989) found that married people report much higher levels of well-being than unmarried people do, and that married women report slightly higher levels than married men. Inglehart (1990) analyzed studies done in Europe and North America and reported that married couples are happier than people who are unmarried, separated, or divorced. Lesbian couples, too, report being happier than lesbian women living alone (Wayment & Peplau, 1995).

Divorce Today's divorce rate is more than twice that of 40 years ago: In 1960, there were 9 divorces per 1,000 married women age 15 or older; today, there are approximately 20 divorces per 1,000 married women age 15 or older (Poponoe & Whitehead, 2000). The marriages most likely to fail are marriages between teenagers, nonreligious marriages in which the bride was pregnant, and marriages of people whose parents had divorced (Poponoe & Whitehead, 2000). But the marriages that do survive are not necessarily happy. Many couples stay together for reasons other than love: because of religious beliefs, for the sake of the children, for financial reasons, or out of fear of facing the future alone.

Even for the "miserable marrieds," divorce does not always solve the problems. "Alcoholism, drug abuse, depression, psychosomatic problems, and accidents are more common among divorced than nondivorced adults" (Hetherington et al., 1989, pp. 307–308). Yet, most people who get divorced are not soured on the institution of marriage, because the majority of them do remarry.

Divorce often radically alters the course of an adult's life, especially for a woman. For one thing, women who have children often experience a reduced standard of living after divorce. For another, both women and men must often find new networks of friends and often new places to live. On a positive note, research shows that the new friendship networks of divorced mothers help them cope with the effects of divorce (Albeck & Kaydar, 2002). Their networks are larger than those of married women, and the relationships are emotionally closer.

Parenthood Several studies have shown that marital satisfaction declines after the birth of the first child (Belsky et al., 1989; Cowan & Cowan, 1992; Hackel & Ruble, 1992). The problem appears to center mainly on the division of work—that is, who does what. Even though men are helping with children more than in the past, child care still generally ends up being primarily the responsibility of the woman. Unless she holds very traditional views of gender roles, a woman's dissatisfaction after the birth of the first child often relates to the discrepancy between how much help with child care and housework she expected from her husband and how much help she actually receives (Hackel & Ruble, 1992). Thus, you probably won't be surprised to learn that researchers have found that equitable sharing of responsibilities results in a more satisfying marriage (Erel & Burman, 1995).

Parenthood can cause stress and conflict in a marriage, but it is also immensely satisfying for most couples.

Sharing responsibilities may be especially important when both parents work outside the home. One of the most important trends among U.S. adults in the last 30 years is the growing percentage of women with children who are employed. Currently, about 68% of women with children younger than 6 are employed; more than 80% of the mothers of school-aged children work (U.S. Census Bureau, 2001).

Reinke's Life Course for Women Some theorists believe that theory and research examining adult development have focused more on models that apply to men than on those that may better explain women's experiences. Reinke and her colleagues (1985) interviewed 124 middle-class women aged 30 to 60 to gain information about their marriages, families, employment, life satisfactions and dissatisfactions, and life changes. The researchers found major transitional periods in which participants seemed to reappraise their lives and consider changes. Some of these transitional periods were related to specific chronological ages, but the researchers believe that married women's development is best viewed in terms of six phases in the family cycle: (1) the no-children phase, (2) the starting-a-family/preschool phase, (3) the school-age phase, (4) the adolescent phase, (5) the launching phase (beginning when the first child leaves home and ending when the last child leaves), and (6) the post-parental phase.

Changes were reliably associated with each of the six family-cycle phases, regardless of whether women had experienced major transitions. Women experiencing a major transition at the starting-a-family/preschool phase were more likely to report changes in themselves, as well as marital separation or divorce. The 40% of participants who reported a transition at the launching phase became more introspective and assertive, but very few experienced the *empty nest syndrome* (feelings of emptiness and depression when children grow up and leave home). Indeed, Wink and Helson (1993) found that after children leave home, most women work at least part-time and tend to experience an increase in self-confidence and a heightened sense of competence and independence. Contrary to the popular stereotype of the empty nest syndrome, most parents seem to be happier when their children are on their own (Norris & Tindale, 1994). Thus, the empty nest syndrome is a popular stereotype of middle age that seems to have little basis in reality.

When their children leave home to go to college or get a job, most parents do not experience the sadness associated with the "empty nest syndrome" but instead are able to adjust successfully.

Remember It 10.3

1. Most people reach their physical peak while they are in their ___________.
2. From the 20s to the 40s, intellectual performance tends to ___________.
3. While attending college, young adults form ___________ that serve as the primary source of social support.
4. Higher levels of life satisfaction are reported by adults who are ___________.

ANSWERS: 1. 20s; 2. increase; 3. social networks; 4. married

Later Adulthood

Physical Changes in Later Adulthood

What are some physical changes associated with later adulthood?

Do you know which age group in the United States is increasing in size most rapidly? You have probably heard that it is the elderly. But did you know that it is the oldest group of elders, those over the age of 85, that is increasing at the most rapid rate (FIFARS, 2000)? By 2050, there will be nearly 1 million people over the age of 100 in the United States, compared to about 60,000 today (U.S. Census Bureau, 1999). This is the phenomenon to which social scientists are referring when they speak of the "graying" of society. Not only are the elderly more numerous than ever, but more of them are enjoying life in relatively good health (Morley & van den Berg, 2000). In fact, the majority of older adults are active, healthy, and self-sufficient (Schaie & Willis, 1996). Still, the effects of primary aging are far more evident in later than in middle adulthood.

Primary and Secondary Aging Effects One primary aging effect is the breakdown of the myelin sheaths of individual neurons in the brain, which causes a general slowing of behavior (Birren & Fisher, 1995; Peters et al., 1994; Wickelgren, 1996). A decrease in the rate at which the body supplies oxygen to the brain also help explain the slowing-down phenomenon (Mehagnoul-Schipper et al., 2002).

Primary aging affects sensory abilities as well. With advancing age, people typically become more farsighted and have increasingly impaired night vision (Long & Crambert, 1990). They suffer hearing loss in the higher frequencies and often have difficulty following a conversation when there is competing background noise (Slawinski et al., 1993). Their sense of smell isn't as sharp as when they were younger, and they may have trouble with balance because of a deterioration in the vestibular sense.

Secondary aging takes a toll in later adulthood as well. About 80% of Americans over age 65 have one or more chronic conditions such as arthritis, rheumatism, heart problems, or high blood pressure, many of which are caused or made worse by poor health habits. For example, a high ratio of total cholesterol to high-density lipoprotein (HDL) increases the risk of mortality from all causes (heart disease, cancer, stroke, etc.) in men aged 65 and older. But an increased level of HDL (good cholesterol) alone seems to protect against mortality from all causes in men between 65 and 74. High HDL levels are associated with a diet low in saturated fats. It's never too late to gain the benefits of improved health habits, and many elderly people learn that they can positively affect their health by making such changes (Kasch et al., 1999).

Some fortunate individuals also seem to have an intrinsic hardiness that protects them against environmental disease agents, such as viruses, and even from their own poor health behaviors. An interesting study of the "oldest old"—those over 85—

revealed that members of this group are often in better mental and physical condition than adults 20 years younger (Perls, 1995). They often remain employed and sexually active through their 90s and carry on "as if age were not an issue" (p. 70). How do they do it? They appear to have a genetic advantage that makes them particularly resistant to the diseases that kill or disable most people at younger ages.

Sex and the Senior Citizen Are you surprised to learn that people in their 90s are sexually active? Older adults are less sexually active than those who are younger, but not by much. Surveys indicate that more than 70% of adults over age 65 in the United States are still sexually active. Moreover, in a survey of adults aged 80 to 102 who were not taking medication, 70% of the men and 50% of the women admitted fantasizing about intimate sexual relations often or very often. And 63% of the men and 30% of the women were doing more than fantasizing—they were still having sex (McCarthy, 1989).

Declines in testosterone associated with aging in both men and women are partly responsible for diminished sexual activity and pleasure. However, research suggests that older adults compensate for these primary aging effects with sexual experimentation. For example, elderly women are more likely to be willing to watch sexually explicit films with their partners than are younger women (Purnine & Carey, 1998). Clearly, sexual activity remains an important component of adults' lives, no matter how old they are.

Successful Aging A recent concept in *gerontology* (the scientific study of aging) is that of successful aging. First proposed by gerontologists John Rowe and Robert Kahn (1998), the *successful aging perspective* provides researchers with a comprehensive theoretical framework from which to derive hypotheses about aging. Essentially, Rowe and Kahn maintain that successful aging is a function of an elderly individual's status and characteristics across three domains: physical health, cognitive functioning, and social engagement. Individuals are deemed as having aged successfully if they effectively integrate their levels of functioning in the three domains. In other words, if an elderly woman has a physical ailment that limits her activities, she may compensate for this limitation in the cognitive domain by reading more or listening to music.

■ **crystallized intelligence**
A type of intelligence comprising verbal ability and accumulated knowledge, which tend to increase over the lifespan.

■ **fluid intelligence**
A type of intelligence comprising abstract reasoning and mental flexibility, which peak in the early 20s and decline slowly as people age.

Cognitive Changes in Later Adulthood

What happens to mental ability in later adulthood?

Intellectual decline in later adulthood is not inevitable. Older adults who keep mentally and physically active tend to retain their mental skills. They do well on tests of vocabulary, comprehension, and general information, and their ability to solve practical problems is generally higher than that of young adults. And they are just as capable as younger adults at learning new cognitive strategies (Saczynski et al., 2002).

Researchers often distinguish between two types of intelligence (Horn, 1982): **Crystallized intelligence**—verbal ability and accumulated knowledge—tends to increase over the lifespan. **Fluid intelligence**—abstract reasoning and mental flexibility—peaks in the early 20s and declines slowly as people age. The rate at which people process information also slows gradually with age (Hertzog, 1991; Lindenberger et al., 1993; Salthouse, 1996). This explains, in part, why older adults perform more poorly on mental tasks requiring speed. When tasks do not involve speed, however, elderly adults perform just as well as those who are younger.

Older adults take more time to learn new skills, but, once learned, they apply new skills as accurately as those who are younger.

Several factors are positively correlated with good cognitive functioning in the elderly. They are education level (Anstey et al., 1993), a complex work environment, a long marriage to an intelligent spouse, and a higher income (Schaie, 1990). Gender is a factor as well: Women not only outlive men; they generally show less cognitive decline during old age. But intellectual functioning during later adulthood can be hampered by physical problems (Manton et al., 1986) or by psychological problems such as depression (Flint & Rifat, 2000). A study by Shimamura and others (1995) revealed that people who continue to lead intellectually stimulating and mentally active lives are far less likely to suffer mental decline as they age. Moreover, there is some evidence that physical exercise positively affects cognitive functioning in old age (Colcombe & Kramer, 2003).

Alzheimer's Disease—the Most Common Dementia

How does Alzheimer's disease affect the brain?

Athough most older adults are in full possession of their intellectual faculties, the rapid population growth among the elderly has brought an increase in the number of individuals who suffer from severe, age-related cognitive disabilities. As adults get older, the likelihood that they will develop one of several dementias increases. The **dementias** are a group of neurological disorders in which problems with memory and thinking affect an individual's emotional, social, and physical functioning. Some kind of dementia afflicts about 5–8% of adults over age 65, 15–20% of those over 75, and 25–50% of those over 85 (American Psychiatric Association, 1997). Dementias are caused by physical deterioration of the brain. They can result from cerebral arteriosclerosis (hardening of the arteries in the brain), chronic alcoholism, or irreversible damage by a series of small strokes. But about half of all cases of dementia result from **Alzheimer's disease**, a progressive and uncurable disorder that involves widespread degeneration and disruption of brain cells.

■ **dementias**
A group of neurological disorders in which problems with memory and thinking affect an individual's emotional, social, and physical functioning; caused by physical deterioration of the brain.

■ **Alzheimer's disease**
A progressive and incurable disorder that involves widespread degeneration and disruption of brain cells, resulting in dementia.

At first, victims of Alzheimer's disease show a gradual impairment in memory and reasoning, and in their efficiency in carrying out everyday tasks. Many have difficulty finding their way around in familiar locations. Alzheimer's patients, even in early stages, have difficulty with temporal memory (time sequences), especially when distractors are present (Putzke et al., 2000). As the disorder progresses, Alzheimer's patients become increasingly unable to care for themselves. Even motor skills, habits, and simple classically conditioned responses are eventually lost (Bäckman et al., 2000). If Alzheimer's patients live long enough, they reach a stage where they do not respond when spoken to and no longer recognize even their spouse or children.

Compared with healthy people of similar age, Alzheimer's patients in one study averaged 68% fewer neurons in parts of the hippocampus, the area of the brain important in the formation and retention of memories (West et al., 1994). Alzheimer's patients also show memory impairment beyond that involving the hippocampal region (Hamann et al., 2002; Kensinger et al., 2002). Autopsies of Alzheimer's patients reveal that the cerebral cortex as well as the hippocampus contain neurons clogged with twisted, stringy masses (called *neurofibrillary tangles*) and surrounded by dense deposits of proteins and other materials (called *plaques*) (de Leon et al., 1996; Peskind, 1996; Riley et al., 2002).

Heredity is a major factor in early-onset Alzheimer's, which accounts for about 10% of the disease's victims and develops before age 65—in some cases, as early as the 40s. Heredity is also a major factor in late-onset Alzheimer's, which generally affects people over 65 (Bergem et al., 1997). Alzheimer's has been linked to genes on 4 of the 23 human chromosomes (Selkoe, 1997).

Results from a study of older Americans from various ethnic groups who were suffering from Alzheimer's disease showed that African Americans were less debilitated by the disease than were their Asian, White, and Hispanic counterparts. Compared to the

As Alzheimer's disease worsens, those afflicted with it need constant reminders of the locations and names of common household items if they are to perform any routine tasks.

other ethnic groups, African Americans had less depression, less anxiety, and fewer sleep problems (Chen et al., 2000).

Can Alzheimer's disease be delayed? According to researchers, a high IQ coupled with lifelong intellectual activity may delay or lessen the symptoms of Alzheimer's in those who are at risk for the disease (Alexander et al., 1997; Wilson & Bennett, 2003). Interestingly, certain anti-inflammatory drugs (such as ibuprofen) and the antioxidant Vitamin E may also provide a measure of protection (Nash, 1997; Sano et al., 1997). Clinical trials with an anti-inflammatory drug called indomethacin have shown promising results (Hull et al., 1999). Other substances and drugs currently being studied for use in the prevention of Alzheimer's include folic acid (Reynolds, 2002), Vitamin C (Brown et al., 2002), and nicotine (Murray & Abeles, 2002).

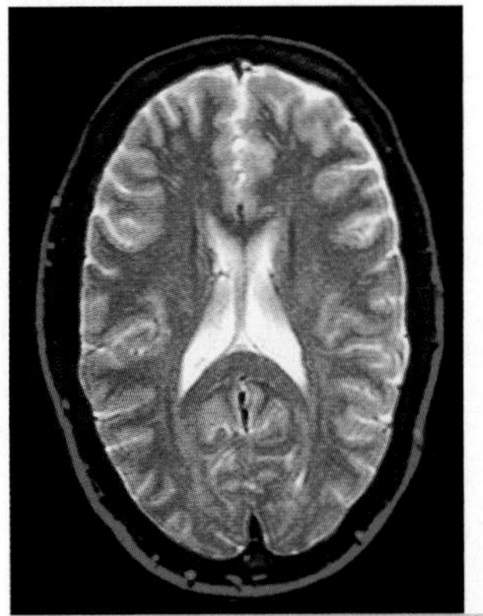
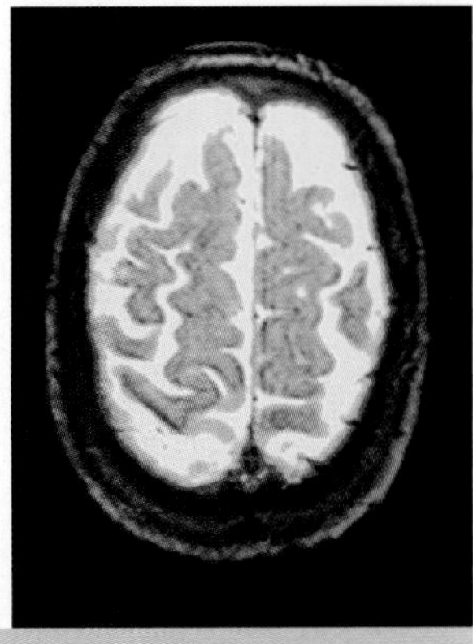

Compared with a normal adult brain (left), the brain of an Alzheimer's patient (right) has a smaller volume and many twisted, stringy masses called *neurofibrillary tangles.*

Social Development and Adjustment in Later Adulthood

What does research indicate about older adults' life satisfaction?

In several major national surveys, life satisfaction and feelings of well-being were about as high in older adults as in younger ones (Inglehart, 1990) (see Figure 10.7). Life satisfaction appears to be most strongly related to good health, as well as to a feeling of control over one's life (Schulz & Heckhausen, 1996). Elders who tend to have an optimistic outlook on life also report higher levels of satisfaction (Hagberg et al., 2002). Further, the incidence of optimism itself increases as adults age, perhaps due to the tendency to recall fewer negative experiences (Charles et al., 2003). Adequate income, participation in religious and social activities, and a satisfactory marital relationship are also associated with high levels of life satisfaction in later adulthood (Harlow & Cantor, 1996; Levenson et al., 1993; Pinquart & Sörensen, 2000).

Contrary to some stereotypes, older adults vary widely in economic status. About 10.5% of Americans over age 65 live below the poverty line, and among them are disproportionately high numbers of African Americans (25.4%) and Hispanic Americans (23.5%) (U.S. Census Bureau, 2001). Moreover, elderly persons, especially those with cognitive or physical impairments who are struggling to live on small incomes, are especially vulnerable to financial exploitation (Tueth, 2000). But many adults in the 65-plus group live comfortably. With homes that are paid for and no children to support, people over 65 tend to view their financial situation more positively than do younger adults.

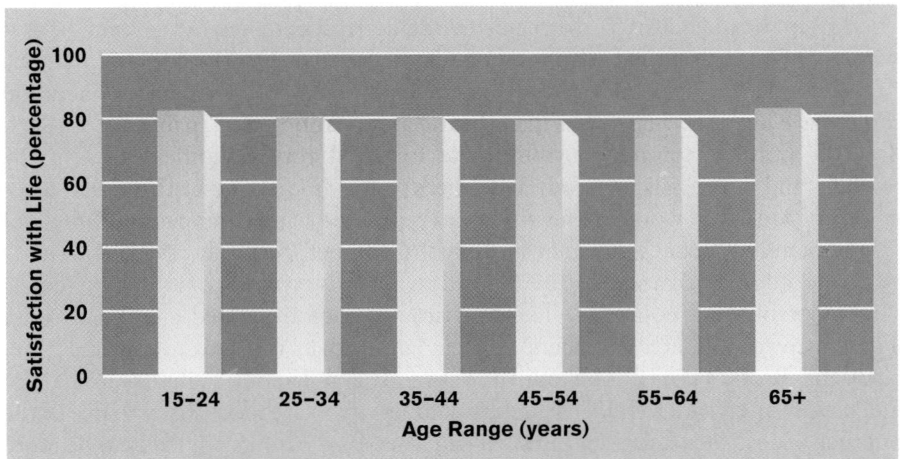

FIGURE 10.7

Age and Life Satisfaction

Surveys including participants from many nationalities reveal that levels of life satisfaction and happiness remain much the same and relatively high (about 80%) throughout the lifespan.
Source: Data from Inglehart (1990).

Yet old age undoubtedly involves many losses. Health declines, friends die, and some older adults who do not wish to retire must do so because of company policies or for health reasons. When life becomes more burdensome than enjoyable, an older person can fall victim to depression, a serious problem that affects about 15% of the elderly and can even be deadly. White males over age 75 have the highest suicide rate of any age group in the United States (U.S. Census Bureau, 1997). But the rate of major depression seems to be lower among the elderly than among younger persons (Benazzi, 2000).

Another factor affecting life satisfaction involves older adults' career-related decisions. Most older adults in the United States (about 88%) are retired (U.S. Census Bureau, 2001). Despite stereotypes, most of them are happy to leave work and do not experience a great deal of stress in adjusting to retirement. Generally, the people most reluctant to retire are those who are better educated, hold high-status jobs with a good income, and find fulfillment in their work. Bosse and others (1991) found that only 30% of retirees reported finding retirement stressful, and most of those were likely to be in poor health and to have financial problems.

Another common event that may affect life satisfaction for older adults is the loss of a spouse. For most people, losing a spouse is the most stressful event in a lifetime. Disruption of sleep patterns is among the many physical effects associated with this loss (Steeves, 2002). These physical effects take their toll on the bereaved elderly and lead to tiredness and anxiety. In addition, both widows and widowers are at a greater risk for health problems due to suppressed immune function and have a higher mortality rate, particularly within the first 6 months, than their age-mates who are not bereaved (Martikainen & Valkonen, 1996).

Cultural Differences in Care for the Elderly

In what ways do the experiences of older adults differ across cultures?

As you have learned, the United States, along with some other industrialized countries, will soon have a great many more elderly people to care for and not enough young people to serve as their caretakers. How will these changes affect Americans in different ethnic groups? Can we learn some lessons about elder care from other cultures?

Older African Americans as well as older Asian and Hispanic Americans are more likely to live with and be cared for by their adult children than are other elderly Americans. African Americans are more likely than White Americans to regard elderly persons with respect and to feel that children should help their older parents (Mui, 1992). Still, multigenerational households are by no means commonplace in the United States, regardless of ethnicity. For the most part, older Americans have a strong preference for maintaining their independence and living in their own homes, although they and their adult children express a desire to live near each other (Bengtson et al., 1990).

Such separate living arrangements are not typical of other countries around the world, where economic necessity and social norms often dictate living arrangements. In many Latin American countries, the majority of elderly people live in the same household with younger generations in an extended family setting (De Vos, 1990). In Korea, 80% of the elderly are cared for by family members (Sung, 1992). And three-generation households have been the rule rather than the exception among the Japanese.

How do attitudes toward providing care for aged relatives differ between the United States and Japan? Elaine Brody and others (1984) studied these attitudes in three generations of American women. Her study was replicated with a comparable sample of three generations of Japanese women in Tokyo (Campbell & Brody, 1985). Women's attitudes were studied because the care of aged relatives is typically provided by female family members in both countries. The American women expressed a stronger sense of obligation toward elderly members of their family than the Japanese women did. Campbell and Brody (1985) point out, however, that in Japan daughters-in-law, not daughters, most often care for elderly family members, who are more likely to live in the home of their oldest son. Relations between daughters and parents are likely to be more positive than relations between daughters-in-law and parents-in-law.

Older African Americans and older members of other minority groups are more likely than older White Americans to live with relatives. However, among all ethnic groups in the United States, aging adults prefer to maintain their independence by living alone. This pattern of living arrangements contrasts sharply with that in many other cultures around the world.

Brody and others (1992) found that married daughters who are providing parent care experience less strain and less depression than caregiving daughters who are single, divorced, or widowed. Also, African Americans caring for elderly relatives suffering from Alzheimer's disease report less stress and depression than do their White American counterparts (Hayley et al., 1996).

Death and Dying

Death, of course, can come at any age. Still, for most people, one of the developmental tasks of old age is to accept the inevitability of death and to prepare for it. Research suggests that impending death may lead to certain psychological responses that are common to dying individuals of all ages.

According to Kübler-Ross, what stages do terminally ill patients experience as they come to terms with death?

Kübler-Ross on Death and Dying Elisabeth Kübler-Ross (1969) interviewed about 200 terminally ill people and found that they shared common reactions to their impending death. In her book *On Death and Dying*, she identifies five stages people go through in coming to terms with death.

In the first stage, *denial*, most patients react to the diagnosis of their terminal illness with shock and disbelief. (Surely, the doctors must be wrong.) The second stage, *anger*, is marked by feelings of resentment toward and envy of those who are young and healthy. In the third stage, *bargaining*, the person attempts to postpone death in return for a promise of "good behavior." An individual may offer God some special service or a promise to live a certain kind of life in exchange for an opportunity to attend a child's wedding or a grandchild's graduation. The fourth stage, *depression*, brings a great sense of loss and may take two forms: depression over past losses and depression over impending losses. Given enough time, patients may reach the final stage, *acceptance*, in which they stop struggling against death and contemplate its coming without fear or despair. Kübler-Ross claims that immediate family members also go through stages similar to those experienced by the patient.

Critics deny the universality of Kübler-Ross's proposed stages and their invariant sequence (Butler & Lewis, 1982; Kastenbaum, 1992). Each person is unique. The reactions of all terminally ill people cannot be expected to conform to some rigid sequence of stages.

Decisions about Death Death comes too soon for most people, but not soon enough for others. Some who are terminally ill and subject to intractable pain may welcome an end to their suffering. Should dying patients be left with no choice but to suffer to the end? In answer to this highly controversial question, Dr. Jack Kevorkian has said "No!" and has defied both laws and criticism to help many terminally ill patients end their lives. Although Dr. Kevorkian was convicted and jailed for his work, he brought to the nation's attention the plight of many hopelessly, terminally ill individuals who wish to end their lives. Today, physician-assisted suicide ("requested death") has become the focus of a social movement (McInerney, 2000). The state of Oregon legalized physician-assisted suicide in 1997. Most patients who "request" death cite as their reasons loss of control of bodily functions, loss of autonomy, and inability to take part in activities that make life enjoyable (Sullivan, Hedberg, et al., 2000).

To avoid leaving surviving family members with staggering medical bills, many people write living wills. Under the terms of a typical living will, hospitals and medical professionals are not to use heroic measures or life-support systems to delay the death of a patient who cannot possibly recover, but may linger indefinitely in a comatose state.

A rapidly growing alternative to hospitals and nursing homes is hospice care. *Hospices* are agencies that care for the needs of the dying in ways that differ from traditional hospital care. A hospice follows a set of guidelines attuned to patients' personal needs and preferences. These guidelines include the following:

- The patient and his or her family will control decisions about the patient's care.
- The patient's pain will be managed so that the patient's remaining time is more livable.
- Professional personnel will be available as needed, at any time of the day or night.
- Facilities will be less clinical and more homelike than typical hospital environments are.
- Family members may work with the hospice team as caregivers.
- Family members may receive counseling before and after the patient dies and be helped through the grieving process.

Bereavement Many of us have experienced the grieving process—the period of bereavement that follows the death of a loved one and sometimes lingers long after the person has gone. Contrary to what many believe, bereaved individuals who suffer the most intense grief initially, who weep inconsolably and feel the deepest pain, do not get through their bereavement more quickly than others (Bonanno et al., 1995). According to one proposed model for how married people cope with bereavement, the grieving spouse at times actively confronts and at other times avoids giving full vent to grief. This dual-process coping, with periods of grieving and periods of relief, seems effective in dealing with the stress of losing a spouse (Stroebe & Schut, 1999).

Researchers have also studied bereavement in those who care for loved ones dying of AIDS. Folkman and her colleagues (1996) interviewed male partners who were caregivers for AIDS patients. From several interviews conducted both before and after the patient's death, they concluded that the gay partners experienced basically the same grieving process as married heterosexuals in similar circumstances did.

Death and dying are not easy subjects to discuss, but doing so helps us remember that each day alive should be treasured like a precious gift.

Remember It 10.4

1. Which of the following statements is true of older adults as compared to younger adults?

   a. They are less satisfied with life.

   b. They are less likely to be poor.

2. Alzheimer's disease is associated with neurons clogged with ___________ and surrounded by ___________.

3. Younger adults outperform older adults on cognitive tasks requiring ___________.

4. According to Kübler-Ross, the first stage experienced by terminally ill patients in coming to terms with death is ___________; the last stage is ___________.

5. An agency that is an alternative to a hospital or nursing home as a provider of care for the dying is a ___________.

ANSWERS: 1. b; 2. neurofibrillary tangles, plaques; 3. speed; 4. denial, acceptance; 5. hospice

Apply It

Building a Good Relationship

Decide whether each of the following statements about intimate relationships is true or false:

- The best relationships are free from conflict.
- Voicing complaints to one's partner undermines happiness in the relationship.
- Anger in all its forms is a negative emotion that is destructive in a relationship.
- The best way to maintain a relationship is to have a realistic view of one's partner.

All of these statements are true, right? Wrong. Every one of them is false. In studies of couples married 20 years or more, John Gottman (1994) and his colleagues gained some interesting insights on how different aspects of conflict affect relationship quality.

Complaints

A complaint is limited to a specific situation and states how you feel: "I am upset because you didn't take out the garbage tonight." Complaints may actually make a relationship stronger. In fact, Gottman believes that complaining "is one of the healthiest activities that can occur in a marriage" (1994, p. 73). Why? Because it is better to express your feelings through complaints than to let them seethe until they crystallize into deep-seated resentment.

This is not to say that all complaining is useful. Cross-complaining, in which you counter your partner's complaint with one of your own and ignore what your partner has said, obviously serves no useful purpose. And spouting off a long list of complaints all at once—what Gottman calls "kitchen-sinking"—is not productive either.

Criticism

A complaint is likely to begin with "I," but criticisms typically begin with "you": "You never remember to take out the trash. You promised you would do it, and you broke your promise again." Criticisms also tend to be global, often including the word *always* or *never:* "You never take me anywhere"; "You're always finding fault with me." Criticizing thus goes beyond merely stating a feeling; a criticism is an accusation, sometimes even a personal attack. Frequent criticism can destroy a relationship.

Contempt

Even more damaging than criticism is contempt. As Gottman points out, "what separates contempt from criticism is the intention to insult and psychologically abuse your partner" (1994, p. 79). Contempt basically adds insult to criticism. The insult can take a variety of forms, including name calling, hostile humor, mockery, and body language such as sneering and rolling the eyes. According to Gottman, words such as *jerk, fat,* and *stupid* "are such dangerous assault weapons that they ought to be outlawed" (1994, p. 80).

Anger

While criticism and contempt definitely have negative effects on relationships, anger does not. Anger has negative effects on a relationship only if it is expressed along with criticism or contempt. In fact, according to Gottman, "expressing anger and disagreement—airing a complaint—though rarely pleasant, makes the [relationship] stronger in the long run than suppressing the complaint" (1994, p. 73).

Hints for Resolving Conflicts

Learning to manage conflicts is essential to good relationships (Fincham, 2003). But how can you solve a conflict without resorting to complaining, criticism, contempt, and anger? Try applying these guidelines for resolving conflicts:

- *Be gentle with complaints.* Kindness works wonders when stating a complaint. And remember to avoid criticism.
- *Don't get defensive when your partner makes requests.* Remain positive, and comply willingly and as quickly as possible.
- *Stop conflicts before they get out of hand.* Don't let negative thoughts about your partner grow into criticism or contempt. Do whatever it takes to put the brakes on negativity. Relive in your memory the happiest moments you and your partner have spent together.

Finally, it helps to have a positive, even idealistic, perception of one's partner. Research by Sandra Murray and her colleagues (1996a, 1996b) has shown that in the best relationships partners overlook each other's faults and embellish each other's virtues. A full and accurate assessment of one's partner's imperfections leads to dissatisfaction.

Summary and Review

The Lifespan Perspective p. 340

How does Erikson's theory of psychosocial development differ from other developmental theories? p. 341

Most developmental theories focus on childhood. By contrast, Erikson believed that individuals progress through eight psychosocial stages that span the entire period from birth to death. Each stage is defined by a conflict involving the individual's relationship with the social environment. A positive resolution of each conflict makes it more likely that an individual will be successful in later stages.

What does research suggest about the accuracy of Erikson's theory? p. 341

The periods of life most studied using Erikson's stages have been infancy, adolescence, and middle adulthood. Research supports many of Erikson's general ideas, including the idea that development of trust in infancy is essential to later development. However, studies suggest that the adolescent identity crisis occurs later than he claimed. In addition, those in late adulthood value generativity as much as middle-aged adults do, and Erikson's ideas about middle adulthood may be more applicable to women than to men.

Adolescence p. 344

What physical and psychological changes occur as a result of puberty? p. 344

Puberty is characterized by the adolescent growth spurt, further development of the reproductive organs, and the appearance of the secondary sex characteristics. Early maturation provides enhanced status for boys, because of their physical advantage in sports and greater attractiveness to girls. Late maturation puts boys at a disadvantage in these areas, resulting in a lack of confidence that can persist into adulthood. Early-maturing girls are often self-conscoius and dissatisfied with their bodies. They are also more likely to be exposed prematurely to alcohol and drug use and to have early sexual experiences and unwanted pregnancies.

What cognitive abilities develop during adolescence? p. 346

Teenagers acquire hypothetical thinking in Piaget's formal operations stage. Their advanced information-processing skills, compared to those of preadolescents, allow them to better organize text and to keep track of their own memory processes.

What are the differences among Kohlberg's three levels of moral reasoning? p. 347

At the preconventional level, moral reasoning is governed by the standards of others, and the physical consequences of an act determine whether it is judged as good or bad. At the conventional level of moral reasoning, judgments of right and wrong are based on the internalized standards of others. Postconventional moral reasoning involves weighing moral alternatives and realizing that laws may conflict with basic human rights.

What outcomes are often associated with the authoritative, authoritarian, and permissive parenting styles? p. 350

Authoritative parenting is most effective and is associated with psychosocial competence in all groups and with academic success in White middle-class teens. Adolescents with authoritarian parents are typically the most psychologically distressed and the least self-reliant and self-confident. Permissive parenting is least effective and is often associated with adolescent drug use and behavior problems.

What are some of the beneficial functions of the adolescent peer group? p. 351

The adolescent peer group (usually composed of teens with similar interests) provides a vehicle for developing social skills and a standard of comparison against which teens' attributes can be evaluated.

What are some of the consequences of teenage pregnancy? p. 352

Teens are at higher risk for delivering premature or low-birth-weight babies. Half of teenage mothers never finish high school, and many eventually depend on welfare. Their children are more likely to receive inadequate parenting, nutrition, and health care and to have behavior and academic problems in school. Some research indicates that teen fathers exhibit higher levels of delinquency after the birth. There is less support for teen fathers than for teen mothers.

Early and Middle Adulthood p. 354

What is the difference between primary and secondary aging? p. 354

Primary aging is caused by biological processes and is unavoidable; secondary aging results from poor health-related behaviors and lifestyle choices. Physical changes associated with middle age are a loss of physical vigor and endurance, a need for reading glasses, and the end of reproductive capacity (menopause) in women and a decline in testosterone levels in men.

In what ways do cognitive functions change between the ages of 20 and 60? p. 354

Although younger people tend to do better on mental tasks requiring speed or rote memory, the intellectual performance of adults shows modest gains until the mid-40s. A modest decline occurs from the 60s to the 80s.

How does attending college affect adult development? p. 356

Adults who attend college earn more money and possess better cognitive skills than those who do not. They also exhibit higher levels of moral reasoning and empathy. College helps some adults sharpen their self-perceptions, and it influences social development as well.

What are some current trends in lifestyle patterns among young adults? p. 359

About 53% of the U.S. population live in households headed by a married couple with or without children under 18. Couples are waiting longer to get married and to have children. Marital satisfaction often declines after the birth of the first child, and 68% of married women with children under age 6 hold full-time or part-time jobs outside the home. Research indicates that most middle-aged adults are happy, rather than distressed, when their children leave home.

Later Adulthood p. 362

What are some physical changes associated with later adulthood? p. 362

Physical changes associated with later adulthood include a general slowing of behavior, a decline in sensory capacity and in heart, lung, kidney, and muscle function, and an increase in chronic conditions such as arthritis, heart problems, and high blood pressure.

What happens to mental ability in later adulthood? p. 363

Crystallized intelligence tends to increase over the lifespan; fluid intelligence peaks in the early 20s and declines slowly as people age. Although older adults perform cognitive tasks more slowly, if they keep mentally and physically active, they can usually maintain their mental skills as long as their health holds out.

How does Alzheimer's disease affect the brain? p. 364

Alzheimer's disease is an incurable form of dementia characterized by a progressive deterioration of intellect and personality, resulting from widespread degeneration of brain cells.

What does research indicate about older adults' life satisfaction? p. 365

Surveys indicate that life satisfaction is about as high in older adults as in those who are younger. Life satisfaction in old age is related to good health, a sense of control over one's life, optimism, adequate income, social and religious involvement, and marital satisfaction.

In what ways do the experiences of older adults differ across cultures? p. 366

In the United States, older adults are more likely to live with family members if they are Hispanic, Asian, or African American. However, older Americans of all ethnic groups are more likely to live alone than are their peers in other countries around the world.

According to Kübler-Ross, what stages do terminally ill patients experience as they come to terms with death? p. 367

Kübler-Ross maintains that terminally ill patients go through five stages in coming to terms with death: denial, anger, bargaining, depression, and acceptance.

Key Terms

adolescence, p. 344
Alzheimer's disease, p. 364
conventional level, p. 348
crystallized intelligence, p. 363
dementias, p. 364
fluid intelligence, p. 363
identity crisis, p. 341
lifespan perspective, p. 340
menopause, p. 354
metamemory, p. 347
postconventional level, p. 348
preconventional level, p. 348
presbyopia, p. 354
psychosocial stages, p. 341
puberty, p. 344
secondary sex characteristics, p. 345

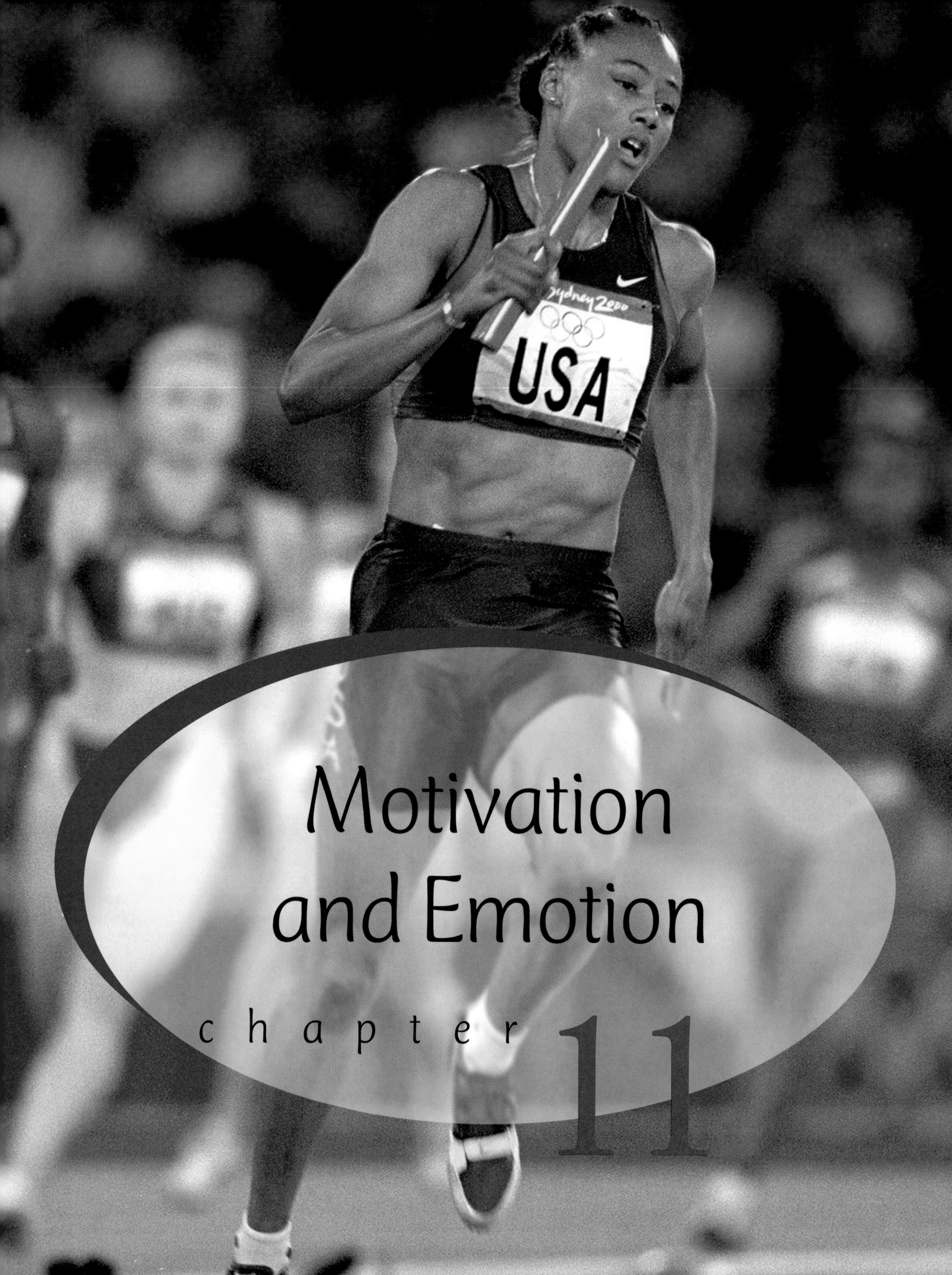

chapter 11
Motivation and Emotion

What Is Motivation?

- *What is the difference between intrinsic and extrinsic motivation?*
- *How do instinct theories explain motivation?*
- *How does drive-reduction theory explain motivation?*
- *How does arousal theory explain motivation?*
- *What is Maslow's hierarchy of needs?*

The Primary Drives

- *Under what conditions do the two types of thirst occur?*
- *How do internal and external hunger cues influence eating behavior?*
- *What are some factors that account for variations in body weight?*
- *Why is it almost impossible to maintain weight loss by cutting calories alone?*
- *What are the symptoms of anorexia nervosa and bulimia nervosa?*

Social Motives

- *What is Murray's contribution to the study of motivation?*
- *What is work motivation, and how can it be increased?*

The What and Why of Emotions

- *What are the three components of emotions?*
- *According to the various theories of emotion, what sequence of events occurs when an individual experiences an emotion?*
- *What brain structure processes the emotion of fear?*
- *What does a polygraph measure?*

The Expression of Emotion

- *What are basic emotions?*
- *How does the development of facial expressions in infants suggest a biological basis for emotional expression?*
- *What evidence is there to suggest that facial expressions have the same meanings all over the world?*
- *How do display rules for emotions differ across cultures?*
- *Why is emotion considered a form of communication?*

Experiencing Emotion

- *How do facial expressions influence internal emotional states?*
- *In what ways do males and females differ with regard to emotions?*
- *How does emotion influence thought?*
- *How does Sternberg's triangular theory of love account for the different kinds of love?*

Why do people behave in the ways they do?

This question assumes that there is a cause for every behavior and that causes can be identified. Moreover, it implies that behavior results from a rational process. For instance, why are you reading this book? You probably have a rational goal, such as wanting to succeed in your psychology course. But motivation isn't always so easily explained. Indeed, many questions about human motivation have proven extremely difficult to answer. For example, philosophers and psychologists have long grappled with the question of why people put their lives at risk to help others. To do so, individuals must put aside what must be the strongest motive of all: the will to survive. Moreover, in most cases, they have no rational expectation of a reward. So, why do they do it? Let's consider an example.

On the morning of September 11, 2001, Orio Palmer, a 20-year veteran of the Fire Department of New York (FDNY) and chief of Manhattan's Ladder 12 Engine 3 Battalion 7, went to work, just as he had hundreds of times before. Taped to his refrigerator was the motto "Live while you're alive." And on September 11, 2001, living, for Chief Palmer, meant responding to the call that took him and the rest of his battalion to the smoldering World Trade Center.

Recordings of walkie-talkie communications reveal that Palmer was the first firefighter to reach the 78th floor of the south tower, the lowest of the building's seven floors directly hit by the plane. When he arrived, he reported that there were numerous people on the floor who had survived the plane's impact, but who were too badly injured to descend on their own. He devised an evacuation plan for them and radioed emergency medical personnel, describing the various injuries so that survivors could be transported to the most appropriate treatment facilities. Palmer also quickly put together a plan for extinguishing several fires that he was able to see from his vantage point in the floor's express elevator lobby. People who have heard the tapes say that there was no panic or fear in his voice, just focused determination, geared toward getting the survivors out of the building as quickly as possible and putting out the fires. Sadly, only a few of the injured on the 78th floor, those who were able to walk on their own, got out of the building. Chief Palmer lost his life in the building's collapse, along with 15 other firefighters from Battalion 7. He left a wife and three children. In September 2002, a street in the Bronx, where he grew up, was named after him.

Why did Chief Palmer and the other FDNY firefighters place their own lives at peril? The stock answer we most often hear about such heroics is that emergency personnel are trained to respond in just this way. But what does this statement really mean? Does it mean that human beings must have special training before they can be motivated to put their own interests aside for the sake of others? If so, then what about the countless ordinary citizens who risked their own safety to bravely assist people who needed help to get out of the smoking Pentagon and crumbling World Trade Center, or those who gave their lives trying to prevent Flight 93 from reaching its hijackers' intended target? And how do we explain the motivations of those whose suicide mission initiated the infamous events of September 11, 2001?

You may remember from Chapter 1 that, to be useful, a psychological theory has to account for most, or preferably all, of the relevant data. Thus, a full explanation of human motivation must cover the motives that drove both the heroes and the villains of September 11. So far, psychologists haven't come up with a single, comprehensive theory that can explain the entire range of human motivation. Consequently, researchers who study motivation assume that a variety of factors—biological, cognitive, emotional, behavioral, social, and cultural—in various combinations influence the motivation underlying any given behavior. Researchers today are thus more likely to study particular kinds of motivated behavior than to look for a general theory that explains all such behavior (Petri, 1996).

What Is Motivation?

What is the difference between intrinsic and extrinsic motivation?

Have you ever been in a situation in which you needed to do something, but you just weren't motivated to do it? We often talk about "being motivated," but have you ever thought about exactly what that means? For psychologists, **motivation** is a very broad term that encompasses all the processes that initiate, direct, and sustain behavior. Generally, psychologists consider motivation to have three components: activation, persistence, and intensity. *Activation* is the initiation of motivated behavior; it involves taking the first steps required to achieve a goal or complete a project. So, when you say you're not motivated to study for an exam, you're most likely talking about the activation component of motivation. *Persistence* is the faithful and continued effort put forth in order to achieve a goal or finish a project. Once you take that first step of opening your text or notebook, do you stick with it, or are you easily distracted? In other words, the persistence component includes whatever pushes you to keep moving toward your goal or in the opposite direction. *Intensity* refers to the focused energy and attention applied in order to achieve a goal or complete a project. If you persist in studying, do you get caught up in the subject matter, or is the possibility of getting a good grade so enticing that it keeps you going? In either case, it's the intensity component of motivation that's at work.

At any given time, your behavior might be explained by one or a combination of **motives**—needs or desires that energize and direct behavior toward a goal. Motives can arise from an internal source, such as when you keep studying because you find the subject matter interesting. When activities are pursued as ends in themselves, simply because they are enjoyable or satisfying, not because any external reward is attached, the type of motivation we experience is known as **intrinsic motivation**. Other motives originate from outside sources, as when some external stimulus, or **incentive**, pulls or entices you to act. When the desire to get a good grade, or to avoid a bad grade, causes you to study, the grade is serving as an incentive. When we act in order to gain some external reward or to avoid some undesirable consequence, we are pulled by **extrinsic motivation**.

Intrinsic and extrinsic motivation have different effects on behavior. Generally, activities that are intrinsically motivating are more likely to become a permanent part of our behavioral repertoire than those to which incentives are applied or for which we receive extrinsic rewards. For instance, in one study, researchers examined differences in physical education teachers' messages about the potential intrinsic rewards of exercise. They found that students whose teachers helped them identify the intrinsically rewarding aspects of exercise were more likely to engage in voluntary physical activities outside of class than were their peers whose teachers provided little information about intrinsic motivation (Standage et al., 2003). In actuality, though, the motives for many activities are both intrinsic and extrinsic. You may love your job, but would you continue going to work if your salary, an important extrinsic motivator, were taken away?

Another way of classifying motives has to do with whether they are learned or unlearned. *Biological motives* are programmed into our nature; they are unlearned. For instance, no one had to teach you how to be sexually attracted to another person. By contrast, *social motives* are learned as a result of living in human society. From your social environment, you have acquired ideas about the importance of physical attractiveness. Attraction itself is biological, but discriminating between two potential partners on the basis of their physical attractiveness involves a social motive, or one that has been learned. What do researchers say about the sources of these different types of motives? Let's consider some theories of motivation.

■ **motivation**
All the processes that initiate, direct, and sustain behavior.

■ **motives**
Needs or desires that energize and direct behavior toward a goal.

■ **intrinsic motivation**
The desire to behave in a certain way because it is enjoyable or satisfying in and of itself.

■ **incentive**
An external stimulus that motivates behavior (for example, money or fame).

■ **extrinsic motivation**
The desire to behave in a certain way in order to gain some external reward or to avoid some undesirable consequence.

How do instinct theories explain motivation?

Instinct Theories

Perhaps you have seen a flock of birds migrating south for the winter. No doubt, you have heard that such behavior results from *instincts*—inborn, unlearned, fixed patterns of behavior characteristic of an entire species. Indeed, scientists have learned much about instincts by observing animal behavior. An instinct does not improve with practice, and an animal will behave in the same instinctual way even if it has never seen another member of its species.

But can human motivation be explained by **instinct theory**—the notion that human behavior is motivated by certain inborn, unlearned tendencies, or instincts, that are shared by all individuals? Instinct theory was widely accepted by many early psychologists, and thousands of instincts (e.g., the maternal instinct) were proposed to explain human behavior. However, most psychologists today reject instinct theory, as observation alone suggests that human behavior is too richly diverse, and often too unpredictable, to be considered fixed and invariant across the entire species.

■ **instinct theory**
A theory of motivation suggesting that human behavior is motivated by certain inborn, unlearned tendencies, or instincts, that are shared by all individuals.

How does drive-reduction theory explain motivation?

Drive-Reduction Theory

Another major attempt to explain motivation is **drive-reduction theory**, which was popularized by Clark Hull (1943). According to Hull, all living organisms have certain biological needs that must be met if they are to survive. A need gives rise to an internal state of tension or arousal called a **drive**, which the organism is motivated to reduce. For example, when you are deprived of food or go too long without water, your biological need causes a state of tension—in this case, the hunger or thirst drive. You become motivated to seek food or water to reduce the drive and satisfy your biological need.

Drive-reduction theory is derived largely from the biological concept of **homeostasis**—the natural tendency of the body to maintain a balanced internal state in order to ensure physical survival. Body temperature, blood sugar, water, oxygen—in short, everything required for physical existence—must be maintained in a state of equilibrium, or balance. When this state is disturbed, a drive is created to restore the balance, as shown in Figure 11.1.

However, drive-reduction theory only accounts for a part of the broad range of human motivation. It is true that people are sometimes motivated to reduce tension, but often they are just as motivated to increase it. Many people seek out activities, such as hang gliding, bungee jumping, and viewing horror movies, that actually create a state of tension. Why do animals and humans alike engage in exploratory behavior when it does not serve to reduce any primary drive?

■ **drive-reduction theory**
A theory of motivation suggesting that biological needs create internal states of tension or arousal called drives, which organisms are motivated to reduce.

■ **drive**
An internal state of tension or arousal that is brought about by an underlying need and that an organism is motivated to reduce.

How does arousal theory explain motivation?

Arousal Theory

Arousal theory states that people are motivated to maintain an optimal level of **arousal,** which is a state of alertness and mental and physical activation. Arousal levels can range from no arousal (when a person is comatose), to moderate arousal (when pursuing normal day-to-day activities), to high arousal (when excited and highly stimulated). Unlike drive-reduction theory, arousal theory does not suggest that people are always motivated to reduce arousal. If the level of arousal is less than optimal, we do something to stimulate it; if arousal exceeds the optimal level, we seek to reduce the stimulation.

Biological needs, such as the need for food and water, increase arousal. However, people also become aroused when they encounter new stimuli or when the intensity of stimuli is increased, as with loud noises, bright lights, or foul odors. And, of course,

■ **homeostasis**
The natural tendency of the body to maintain a balanced internal state in order to ensure physical survival.

FIGURE 11.1 Drive-Reduction Theory

Drive-reduction theory is based on the biological concept of homeostasis—the natural tendency of a living organism to maintain a state of internal balance, or equilibrium. When the equilibrium becomes disturbed (by a biological need such as thirst), a drive (an internal state of arousal or tension) emerges. Then, the organism is motivated to take action to satisfy the need, thus reducing the drive and restoring equilibrium.

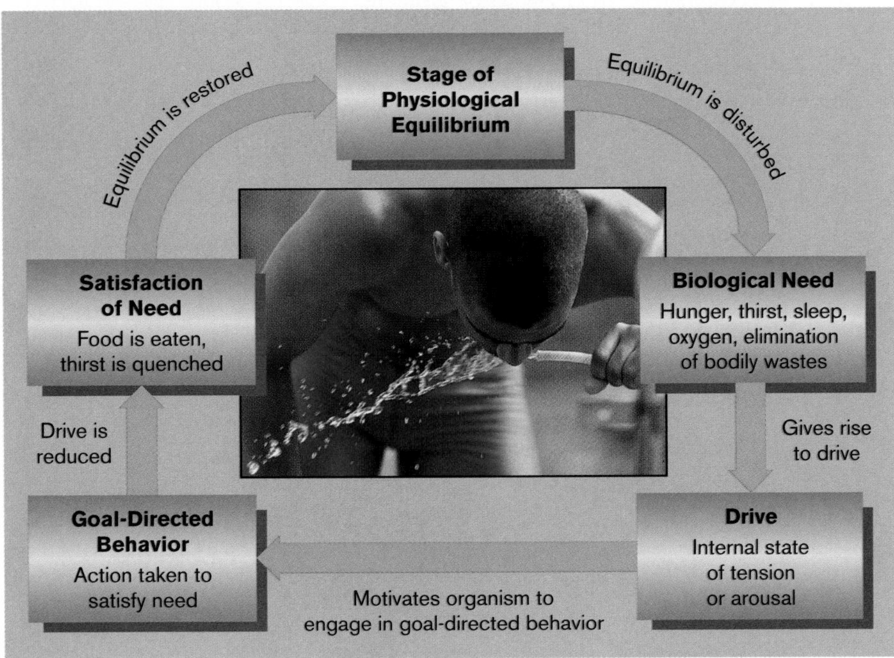

certain kinds of drugs—stimulants such as caffeine, nicotine, amphetamines, and cocaine—increase arousal.

When the level of arousal is too low, **stimulus motives**, such as curiosity and the motives to explore, to manipulate objects, and to play—cause humans and other animals to increase stimulation. Young monkeys will play with mechanical puzzles for long periods just for the stimulation (Harlow, 1950). A very early study found that rats will explore intricate mazes when they are neither thirsty nor hungry and when no reinforcement is provided (Dashiell, 1925). According to Berlyne (1960), rats will spend more time exploring novel objects than familiar objects. So will humans.

There is often a close link between arousal and performance. According to the **Yerkes-Dodson law**, performance on tasks is best when the arousal level is appropriate for the difficulty of the task. Performance on simple tasks is better when arousal is relatively high. Tasks of moderate difficulty are best accomplished when arousal is moderate; complex or difficult tasks, when arousal is lower (see Figure 11.2, on page 378). But performance suffers when the arousal level is either too high or too low for the task. You may have experienced too much or too little arousal when taking an exam. Perhaps your arousal level was so low that your mind was sluggish, and you didn't finish the test; or you might have been so keyed up that you couldn't remember much of what you had studied.

People differ in the level of arousal they normally prefer. Some people are sensation seekers, who love the thrill of new experiences and adventure. Sensation seekers are willing, even eager, to take risks. They are easily bored and experience little fear or uncertainty (McCourt et al., 1993). Other people are the opposite: They enjoy the routine

arousal theory
A theory of motivation suggesting that people are motivated to maintain an optimal level of alertness and physical and mental activation.

arousal
A state of alertness and mental and physical activation.

stimulus motives
Motives that cause humans and other animals to increase stimulation when the level of arousal is too low (examples are curiosity and the motive to explore).

Yerkes-Dodson law
The principle that performance on tasks is best when the arousal level is appropriate to the difficulty of the task: higher arousal for simple tasks, moderate arousal for tasks of moderate difficulty, and lower arousal for complex tasks.

FIGURE 11.2 The Yerkes-Dodson Law

The optimal level of arousal varies according to the difficulty of the task. Arousal levels should be relatively high for simple tasks, moderate for moderately difficult tasks, and lower for difficult tasks.

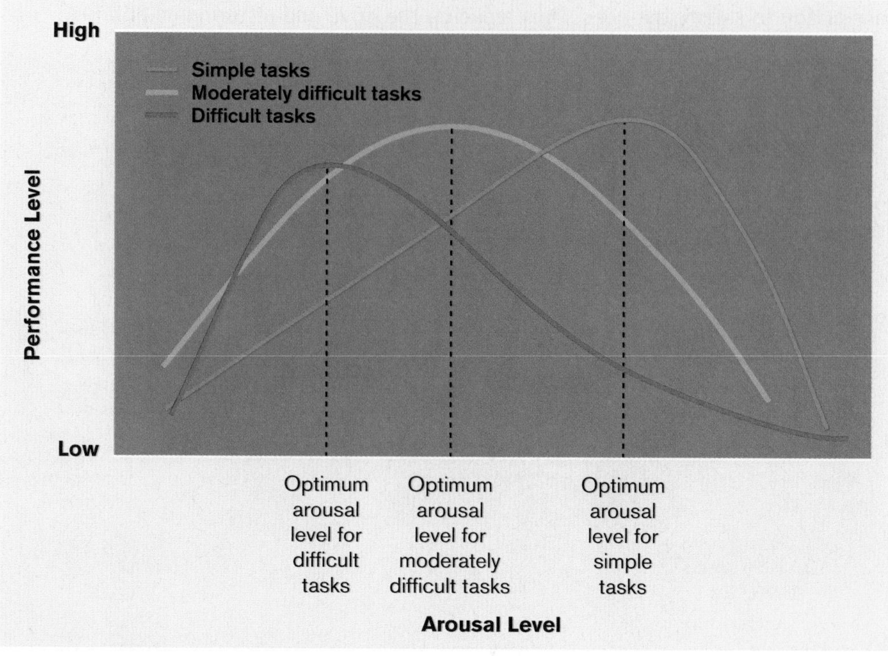

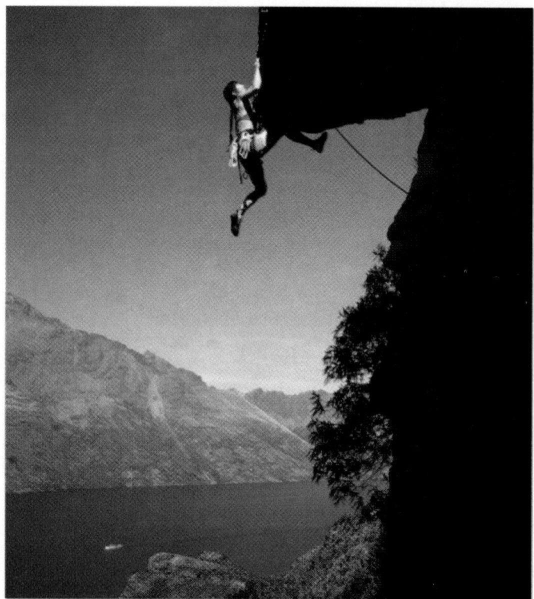

People vary greatly in the amount of arousal they can tolerate. For some people, the heightened level of arousal they experience when hanging from the surface of a sheer cliff like this one is enjoyable. Others prefer less arousing activities.

and the predictable, avoid risk, and fare best when arousal is relatively low. There may be gender and cultural differences in sensation-seeking tendencies. Researchers have found that males tend to score higher than females on this characteristic, and White Americans tend to score higher than African Americans (Zuckerman, 1979).

How do you suppose it would feel to have no stimulation at all? In an early experiment, Bexton and others (1954) at McGill University gave student volunteers the opportunity to find out when they studied the effects of **sensory deprivation**—a condition in which sensory stimulation is reduced to a minimum or eliminated. Students had to lie motionless in a specially designed sensory deprivation chamber in which stimulation was severely restricted. They wore translucent goggles that reduced visual input to a diffused light. Their hands were placed in cotton gloves, and cardboard cuffs were placed over their lower arms, preventing the sensation of touch. The only sound they heard was the hum of an air conditioner through a foam-rubber headpiece. The participants could eat, drink, and go to the bathroom when they wanted to. Occasionally, they would take tests of motor and mental function. Otherwise, they were confined to their sensationless prison.

Did they enjoy the experience? Hardly! Half the participants quit the experiment after the first 2 days. Eventually, the remaining participants became irritable, confused, and unable to concentrate. They began to have visual hallucinations. Some began to hear imaginary voices and music and felt as if they were receiving electric shocks or being hit by pellets. Their performance on motor and cognitive tasks deteriorated, and none of the participants said they enjoyed the experience.

sensory deprivation A condition in which sensory stimulation is reduced to a minimum or eliminated.

Maslow's Hierarchy of Needs

What is Maslow's hierarchy of needs?

The motivational theories you've learned about so far emphasize physiological processes such as homeostasis and arousal. But what about more complex needs, such as the desire for friendship or the quest for success in a career? Another view of motivation, which is associated with the humanistic personality theory of Abraham Maslow, suggests that physiological motivations are the foundation for so-called higher-level motives. As shown in Figure 11.3, Maslow proposed that our need for *self-actualization* depends on how well our needs for physical well-being, safety, belonging, and esteem have been met. His theory claims that we are motivated by the lowest unmet need. Thus, we don't worry about safety when we are in need of food. Similarly, love and esteem are of little concern when we are in danger. Maslow believed that these motivational processes are central to the human personality, so you'll be reading more about his theory in Chapter 14.

Review and Reflect 11.1 (on page 380) summarizes the theoretical approaches to motivation we have discussed in this section.

FIGURE 11.3 Maslow's Hierarchy of Needs

According to humanistic psychologist Abraham Maslow, "higher" motives, such as the need for esteem, go unheeded when "lower" motives, such as the need for safety, have not been met.

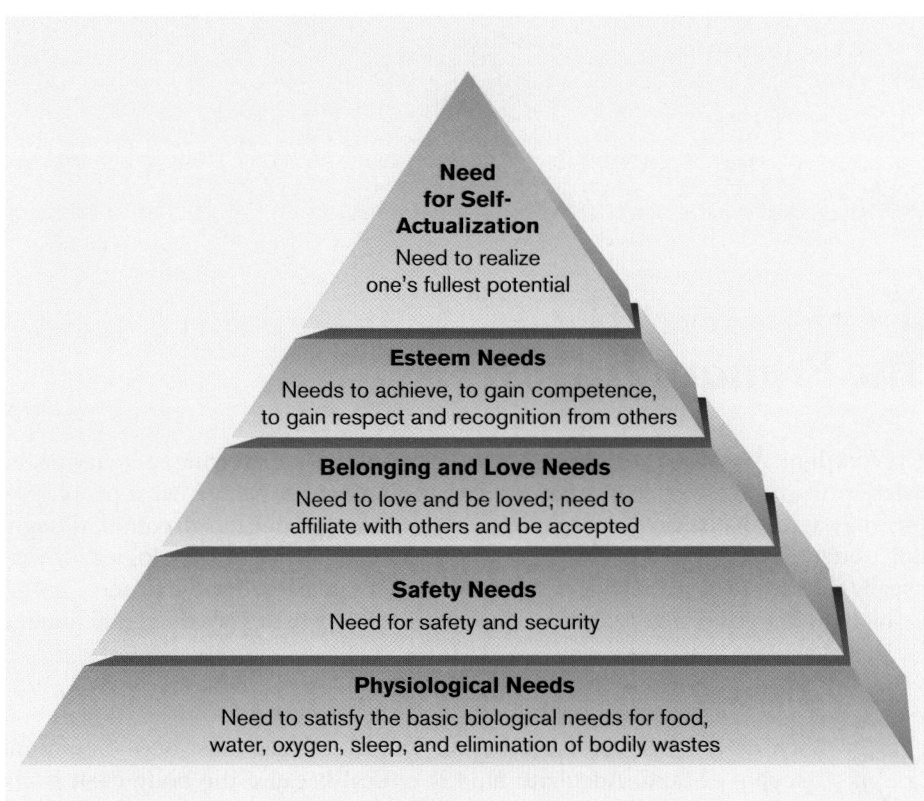

REVIEW and REFLECT 11.1

Theories of Motivation

THEORY	VIEW	EXAMPLE
Instinct theory	Behavior is the result of innate, unlearned tendencies. (This view has been rejected by most modern psychologists.)	Two people fighting because of their aggressive instinct
Drive-reduction theory	Behavior results from the need to reduce an internal state of tension or arousal.	Eating to reduce hunger
Arousal theory	Behavior results from the need to maintain an optimal level of arousal.	Climbing a mountain for excitement; listening to classical music for relaxation
Maslow's hierarchy of needs	Lower needs must be met before higher needs will motivate behavior.	Schoolchildren unable to focus on achievement because they are hungry or don't feel safe

Want to be sure you've fully absorbed the material in this chapter? Visit **www.ablongman.com/wood5e** for access to free practice tests, flashcards, interactive activities, and links developed specifically to help you succeed in psychology.

Remember It 11.1

1. When you engage in an activity in order to gain a reward or to avoid an unpleasant consequence, your motivation is __________.
2. Drive-reduction theory focuses primarily on __________ needs and the drives they produce.
3. __________ theory suggests that human behavior is motivated by innate, unlearned tendencies shared by all individuals.
4. According to arousal theory, people seek __________ levels of arousal.
5. In Maslow's view, __________ and __________ needs must be met before a person can be motivated by needs for social belonging, esteem, and self-actualization.

ANSWERS: 1. extrinsic; 2. biological; 3. Instinct; 4. optimal; 5. physiological, safety

The Primary Drives

■ **primary drive**
A state of tension or arousal that arises from a biological need and is unlearned.

Do you think Maslow was right? Can you concentrate on studying, a behavior motivated by the need for esteem, when you are feeling hunger pangs? Most people would probably agree that at times, physiological drives demand our full attention, though we don't often think of them as being psychologically important. Physiological drives are usually referred to as **primary drives**, those that are unlearned and that serve to satisfy biological needs. Two of the most important primary drives are thirst and hunger.

Under what conditions do the two types of thirst occur?

Thirst

Thirst is a basic biological drive, for all animals must have a continuous supply of fluid. Adequate fluid is critical because the body itself is about 75% water. Without any intake of fluids, a person can survive only about 4 or 5 days.

There are two types of thirst. *Extracellular thirst* occurs when fluid is lost from the body tissues. If you are exercising heavily or doing almost anything in hot weather, you will perspire and lose bodily fluid. Bleeding, vomiting, and diarrhea also rob your body of fluid. In addition, alcohol increases extracellular fluid loss. This is why people awaken with a powerful thirst after drinking heavily the night before.

Intracellular thirst involves the loss of water from inside the body cells. When you eat a lot of salty food, the water-sodium balance in the blood and in the tissues outside the cells is disturbed, so the cells release some of their own water into surrounding tissues to restore the balance. As the body cells become dehydrated, thirst is stimulated and you drink to increase their water volume (Robertson, 1983). This explains why so many bars offer customers free salted nuts, chips, or pretzels—to stimulate their thirst for more drinks.

Internal and External Hunger Cues

How do internal and external hunger cues influence eating behavior?

You probably won't be surprised to learn that hunger, the other major primary drive, is a bit more complex than thirst. We'll look at hunger and eating from a biological perspective, before turning to its psychological and social aspects. What happens in the body to make you feel hungry, and what causes *satiety*—the feeling of being full or satisfied?

The Hypothalamus Researchers have found two areas of the hypothalamus that are of central importance in regulating eating behavior and thus affect the hunger drive (Steffens et al., 1988). As researchers discovered long ago, the **lateral hypothalamus (LH)** acts as a feeding center to incite eating. Stimulating the feeding center causes animals to eat even when they are full (Delgado & Anand, 1953). And when the feeding center is destroyed, animals initially refuse to eat (Anand & Brobeck, 1951).

The **ventromedial hypothalamus (VMH)** apparently acts as a satiety (fullness) center that inhibits eating (Hernandez & Hoebel, 1989). If the satiety center is electrically stimulated, animals stop eating (Duggan & Booth, 1986). If the VMH is surgically removed, animals soon eat their way to gross obesity (Hetherington & Ranson, 1940; Parkinson & Weingarten, 1990). Gorging to obesity occurs immediately after the destruction of a rat's VMH; refusing to eat at all is the consequence of destruction of the LH. Some time after the surgery, the rat begins to establish more normal eating patterns. But the obese rats continue to maintain above-average body weight, and the noneating rats eventually establish a below-average body weight (Hoebel & Teitelbaum, 1966).

■ **lateral hypothalamus (LH)** The part of the hypothalamus that acts as a feeding center to incite eating.

■ **ventromedial hypothalamus (VMH)** The part of the hypothalamus that acts as a satiety (fullness) center to inhibit eating.

A rat whose satiety center has been destroyed can weigh up to six times as much as a normal rat—in this case, 1080 grams, enough to exceed the capacity of the scale.

Other Internal Hunger and Satiety Signals Other body structures and processes contribute to feelings of hunger and satiety. For example, the fuller the stomach, even when the substance with which it is filled is a non-nourishing one such as water, the less hunger we feel. (Remember this the next time you are trying to curb your appetite.) Moreover, some of the substances secreted by the gastrointestinal tract during digestion, such as the hormone cholecystokinin (CCK), act as satiety signals (Bray, 1991; Flood et al., 1990; Woods & Gibbs, 1989).

Changes in blood sugar level and the hormones that regulate it also contribute to sensations of hunger. Blood levels of glucose are monitored by nutrient detectors in the liver that send this information to the brain (Friedman et al., 1986). Hunger is stimulated when the brain receives the message that blood levels of glucose are low. Similarly, insulin, a hormone produced by the pancreas, chemically converts glucose into energy that is usable by the cells. Elevations in insulin cause an increase in hunger, in food intake, and in a desire for

Just the sight of mouth-watering foods can make us want to eat, even when we aren't actually hungry.

sweets (Rodin et al., 1985). In fact, chronic oversecretion of insulin stimulates hunger and often leads to obesity.

External Signals Sensory cues such as the taste, smell, and appearance of food stimulate the appetite. For many, the hands of a clock alone, signaling mealtime, are enough to prompt a quest for food. Even eating with others tends to stimulate people to eat more than they would if they were eating alone (de Castro & de Castro, 1989). For some individuals, simply seeing or thinking about food can cause an elevated level of insulin, and such people have a greater tendency to gain weight (Rodin, 1985).

Table 11.1 summarizes the factors that stimulate and inhibit eating.

Variations in Body Weight

What are some factors that account for variations in body weight?

Obviously, body weight can vary tremendously from one individual to another, even when two people are the same size in other dimensions, such as height and shoe size. Extremes in either fatness or thinness can pose health risks, as you'll learn in Chapter 13. In some cases, these extremes result from variations in the hunger-satiety system itself rather than simply from differences in eating and exercise patterns.

Heredity Across all weight classes, from very thin to very obese, children adopted from birth tend to resemble their biological parents more than their adoptive parents in body size. In adoptees, thinness seems to be even more influenced by genes than obesity is (Costanzo & Schiffman, 1989). A review of studies encompassing more than 100,000 participants found that 74% of identical twin pairs had similar body weights. Only 32% of fraternal twins, however, had comparable body weights. The researchers reported an estimated heritability for body weight of between .50 and .90 (Barsh et al., 2000).

TABLE 11.1 Biological and Environmental Factors That Inhibit and Stimulate Eating

	BIOLOGICAL	ENVIRONMENTAL
Factors that inhibit eating	Activity in ventromedial hypothalamus	Unappetizing smell, taste, or appearance of food
	Raised blood glucose levels	Acquired taste aversions
	Distended (full) stomach	Learned eating habits
	CCK (hormone that acts as satiety signal)	Desire to be thin
	Sensory-specific satiety	Reaction to stress or unpleasant emotional state
Factors that stimulate eating	Activity in lateral hypothalamus	Appetizing smell, taste, or appearance of food
	Low blood levels of glucose	Acquired food preferences
	Increase in insulin	Being around others who are eating
	Stomach contractions	Foods high in fat and sugar
	Empty stomach	Learned eating habits
		Reaction to boredom, stress, or unpleasant emotional state

A gene map for human obesity has been constructed; it contains information about 15 different chromosome regions (Perusse et al., 1999). More than 40 genes appear to be related to obesity and the regulation of body weight (Barsh et al., 2000). Moreover, these genes interact in complex ways (Grigorenko, 2003), and so genetically based obesity isn't simply a matter of inheriting a gene or two from one's parents. At present, scientists don't know why one person who has a particular obesity-related genetic profile is obese, while another is not. Once the functioning of such genes is clearly understood, perhaps new weight-loss drugs or even high-tech treatments such as gene therapy can be developed to fight obesity more effectively than currently available methods.

Because of the health risks associated with obesity, some people, such as *Today* personality Al Roker, resort to a surgical solution. Gastric bypass surgery reduced the capacity of Roker's stomach, thereby limiting the amount of food he can consume at any one time. As a result, Roker's weight has decreased dramatically.

Hormones But what exactly do people inherit that affects body weight? Researchers Friedman and others identified the hormone *leptin*, which directly affects the feeding and satiety centers in the brain's hypothalamus and is known to be a key element in the regulation of body weight (Friedman, 1997, 2000; Kochavi et al., 2001). Leptin is produced by the body's fat tissues, and the amount produced is a direct measure of body fat: The more leptin produced, the higher the level of body fat. Decreases in body fat cause lower levels of leptin in the body, and lower levels of leptin stimulate food intake. When leptin levels increase sufficiently, energy expenditure exceeds food intake, and people lose weight. Obese mice injected with leptin lost 30% of their body weight within 2 weeks (Halaas et al., 1995). In humans, a mutation of the leptin receptor gene can cause obesity as well as pituitary abnormalities (Clément et al., 1998). Changes in the body's leptin levels can affect the immune and reproductive systems, as well as the processes involved in bone formation. Thus, leptin plays a key role in linking nutrition to overall human physiology (Friedman, 2000).

Metabolic Rate The rate at which the body burns calories to produce energy is called the **metabolic rate**, and it may also be subject to genetic influences. Physical activity uses up only about one-third of your energy intake; the other two-thirds is consumed by the maintenance processes that keep you alive. When there is an imbalance between energy intake (how much you eat) and output (how much energy you use), your weight changes. Generally, if your caloric intake exceeds your daily energy requirement, you gain weight. If your daily energy requirement exceeds your caloric intake, you lose weight.

Researchers studying human metabolism from the perspective of thermodynamics have learned that obesity can result when energy intake (eating) exceeds energy expenditure (body heat and exercise) by only a small amount over an extended time period (Lowell & Spiegelman, 2000). There are, however, significant individual differences in the efficiency with which energy is burned. Even if two people are the same age and weight and have the same build and level of activity, one may be able to consume more calories each day without gaining weight.

Fat-Cell Theory Fat-cell theory proposes that obesity is related to the number of **fat cells** (adipose cells) in the body. It is estimated that people of normal weight have between 25 and 35 billion fat cells, while those whose weight is twice normal may have between 100 and 125 billion fat cells (Brownell & Wadden, 1992). The number of fat cells is determined by both genes and eating habits (Grinker, 1982). These cells serve as storehouses for liquefied fat. When a person loses weight, he or she does not lose fat cells themselves, but rather the fat that is stored in them; the cells simply shrink (Dietz, 1989).

Researchers once believed that all the fat cells a person would ever have were formed early in life. This is no longer the accepted view. Researchers now believe that when people overeat beyond their fat cells' capacity, the number of fat cells continues to increase (Rodin & Wing, 1988).

■ **metabolic rate**
(meh-tuh-BALL-ik) The rate at which the body burns calories to produce energy.

■ **fat cells**
Cells (also called *adipose cells*) that serve as storehouses for liquefied fat in the body; their number is determined by both genes and eating habits, and they decrease in size but not in number with weight loss.

set point
The weight the body normally maintains when one is trying neither to gain nor to lose weight.

Set-Point Theory Set-point theory suggests that humans are genetically programmed to carry a certain amount of body weight (Keesey, 1988). **Set point**—the weight the body normally maintains when one is trying neither to gain nor to lose weight—is affected by the number of fat cells in the body and by metabolic rate, both of which are influenced by the genes (Gurin, 1989). Yet, people with a genetic propensity to be thin can become overweight if they overeat steadily for long periods, because they will gradually develop more and more fat cells.

According to set-point theory, an internal homeostatic system functions to maintain set-point weight, much as a thermostat works to keep temperature near the point at which it is set. When body weight falls below set point, appetite increases, whether an individual is lean, overweight, or average. When weight climbs above set point, appetite decreases so as to restore the original weight. The rate of energy expenditure is also adjusted to maintain the body's set-point weight (Keesey & Powley, 1986). When people gain weight, metabolic rate increases (Dietz, 1989). But when they restrict calories to lose weight, the metabolic rate lowers, causing the body to burn fewer calories and thus making further weight loss more difficult. Increasing the amount of physical activity—exercising during and after weight loss—is the best way to lower the set point so that the body will store less fat (Forey et al., 1996).

Dieting

Why is it almost impossible to maintain weight loss by cutting calories alone?

Are you currently on some kind of weight-loss diet? If so, you have a lot of company. National surveys show that nearly 60% of Americans are actively attempting to lose weight (Sutherland, 2002). All types of weight-reduction diets—no matter what approach they use—result in some weight loss in most people who try them (French et al., 1999; Serdula et al., 1993; Wadden, 1993). However, the weight loss is often temporary. Why?

The complexities of the processes involved in appetite regulation and energy metabolism explain why diets often do not work (Campbell & Dhand, 2000). To be effective, any weight-loss program must help people decrease energy intake (eat less), increase energy expenditure (exercise more), or both (Bray & Tartaglia, 2000). Unfortunately, most people who are trying to lose weight focus only on cutting calories. At first, when overweight people begin to diet and cut their calories, they do lose weight. But after a few pounds are shed initially, the dieter's metabolic rate slows down as if to conserve the remaining fat store because fewer calories are being consumed (Hirsch, 1997). Morever, when a person restricts calories too severely, even exercise cannot reverse the body's drastic lowering of metabolism and its natural tendency to conserve remaining fat (Ballor et al., 1990).

Understanding the complexities of the hunger regulation system can help an overweight person realize that successful weight loss involves more than simply counting calories. For instance, calories eaten in the form of fat are more likely to be stored as body fat than are calories eaten as carbohydrates. Miller and others (1990) found that even when obese and thin people have the same caloric intake, thin people derive about 29% of their calories from fats, while obese people average 35% from fat. So, the composition of the diet may have as much to do with weight gain as the amount of food eaten and the lack of exercise. Counting and limiting the grams of fat or more effectively balancing proteins and carbohydrates may be more beneficial than counting calories in helping a person achieve and maintain a desirable body weight.

What are the symptoms of anorexia nervosa and bulimia nervosa?

Eating Disorders

Eating disorders constitute a category of mental disorder in which eating and dieting behaviors go far beyond the common, everyday experiences of overeating and dieting. Sadly, there has been an increase in the incidence of these disorders in recent years (Halmi, 1996).

Anorexia Nervosa **Anorexia nervosa** is characterized by an overwhelming, irrational fear of gaining weight or becoming fat, compulsive dieting to the point of self-starvation, and excessive weight loss. Some anorexics lose as much as 20–25% of their original body weight.

Anorexia typically begins in adolescence, and most of those afflicted are females. About 1% of females between ages 12 and 40 suffer from this disorder (Johnson et al., 1996). The greater prevalence of eating disorders among females appears to be a general phenomenon, rather than a culturally specific one. In a large sample of Norwegian adults, for example, women were twice as likely as men to have an eating disorder (Augestad, 2000). Although it has been established that females are significantly more at risk for eating disorders than males are, a study of the relationship of eating problems to self-concept and other emotional/behavioral measures found that 20% of the females and, surprisingly, 10% of the males in a sample of 471 college students had symptoms of anorexia. This study, although small, suggests that eating disorders may be more prevalent among males than has been thought (Nelson et al., 1999).

Jamie-Lynn Sigler, famous for her role as Meadow on the hit series *The Sopranos,* is one of many young women who have struggled with anorexia. Some psychologists believe that women who suffer from eating disorders have developed distorted ideas about an "ideal" body type, based on media images of very thin women.

There are important differences between dieting, or even obsessive dieting, and anorexia nervosa. For one, anorexics' perception of their body size is grossly distorted. No matter how emaciated they become, they continue to perceive themselves as fat. Researchers have learned that anorexics' unrealistic perceptions of their own bodies may result from a general tendency toward distorted thinking (Tchanturia et al., 2001). Moreover, an unusually high rate of *obsessive-compulsive disorder*—a psychological disorder characterized by an obsessive need for control—has been found among anorexics (Milos et al., 2002). These findings suggest that, for some sufferers, anorexia may be only one component of a larger set of problems.

Frequently, anorexics not only starve themselves but also exercise relentlessly in an effort to accelerate the weight loss. Further, anorexics don't necessarily avoid food or the ritual of eating. Indeed, most anorexics are fascinated with food and the process of preparing it (Faunce, 2002). Many become skilled in giving the appearance of eating while not actually swallowing food. To accomplish this, some anorexics habitually chew and spit out their food, often with such dexterity that others with whom they eat don't notice (Kovacs et al., 2002).

Among young female anorexics, progressive and significant weight loss eventually results in amenorrhea (cessation of menstruation). Anorexics may also develop low blood pressure, impaired heart function, dehydration, electrolyte disturbances, and sterility (American Psychiatric Association, 1993a), as well as decreases in the gray matter volume in the brain, which are thought to be irreversible (Lambe et al., 1997). Unfortunately, up to 20% of those suffering from anorexia nervosa eventually die of starvation or complications from organ damage (Brotman, 1994).

It is difficult to pinpoint the cause of this disorder. Most anorexic individuals are well-behaved and academically successful (Vitousek & Manke, 1994). Psychological risk factors for eating disorders include being overly concerned about physical appearance, worrying about perceived attractiveness, and feeling social pressure in favor of thinness (Whisenhunt et al., 2000). Some investigators believe that young women who refuse to eat are attempting to control a portion of their lives, which they may feel unable to control in other respects.

Anorexia is very difficult to treat. Most anorexics are steadfast in their refusal to eat, while insisting that nothing is wrong with them. The main thrust of treatment, therefore, is to get the anorexic individual to gain weight. The patient may be admitted to a hospital, fed a controlled diet, and given rewards for small weight gains and increases in food intake. The treatment usually includes some type of psychotherapy and/or a self-help group.

■ **anorexia nervosa**
An eating disorder characterized by an overwhelming, irrational fear of gaining weight or becoming fat, compulsive dieting to the point of self-starvation, and excessive weight loss.

Bulimia Nervosa Up to 50% of anorexics also develop **bulimia nervosa**, a chronic disorder characterized by repeated and uncontrolled (and often secretive) episodes of binge eating (American Psychiatric Association, 1993a). Individuals who are not anorexic may also develop bulimia. Many bulimics come from families in which family

■ **bulimia nervosa**
An eating disorder characterized by repeated and uncontrolled (and often secretive) episodes of binge eating.

members make frequent negative comments about others' physical appearances (Crowther et al., 2002).

An episode of binge eating has two main features: (1) the consumption of much larger amounts of food than most people would eat during the same period of time, and (2) a feeling that one cannot stop eating or control the amount eaten. Binges—which generally involve foods that are rich in carbohydrates, such as cookies, cake, and candy—are frequently followed by purging. Purging consists of self-induced vomiting and/or the use of large quantities of laxatives and diuretics. Bulimics may also engage in excessive dieting and exercise. Athletes are especially susceptible to this disorder. But many bulimics are of average size and purge after an eating binge simply to maintain their weight.

Bulimia nervosa can cause a number of physical problems. The stomach acid in vomit eats away at the teeth and may cause them to rot, and the delicate balance of body chemistry is destroyed by excessive use of laxatives and diuretics. The bulimic may have a chronic sore throat as well as a variety of other symptoms, including dehydration, swelling of the salivary glands, kidney damage, and hair loss. The disorder also has a strong emotional component: The bulimic person is aware that the eating pattern is abnormal and feels unable to control it. Depression, guilt, and shame accompany both binging and purging.

Bulimia nervosa tends to appear in the late teens and affects about 1 in 25 women (Kendler et al., 1991). Like anorexics, bulimics have high rates of obsessive-compulsive disorder (Milos et al., 2002). Further, perhaps as many as a third of bulimics have engaged in other kinds of self-injurious behavior, such as cutting themselves intentionally (Paul et al., 2002). Many experts agree that "bulimia nervosa is most likely to develop in dieters who are at risk of obesity and psychiatric disorder in general" (Fairburn et al., 1997). About 10–15% of all bulimics are males, and homosexuality or bisexuality seems to increase the risk for bulimia in males (Carlat et al., 1997). In addition, researchers are finding evidence of a cultural component to bulimia. Westernized attitudes in Turkey, for example, are clashing with the country's traditional values and, according to researchers, creating an increase in cases of bulimia (Elal et al., 2000). Apparently, some Turkish citizens succumb to Western media pressure to have an ultrathin body.

Bulimia, like anorexia, is difficult to treat. Sometimes treatment is complicated by the fact that a person with an eating disorder is likely to have a personality disorder as well or be too shy to interact effectively with therapists (Goodwin & Fitzgibbon, 2002; Rosenvinge et al., 2000). Some behavior modification programs have helped extinguish bulimic behavior (Traverso et al., 2000), and cognitive-behavioral therapy has been used successfully to help bulimics modify their eating habits and their abnormal attitudes about body shape and weight (Halmi, 1996; Johnson et al., 1996). Certain antidepressant drugs have been found to reduce the frequency of binge eating and purging and to result in significant attitudinal change (Agras et al., 1994; "Eating disorders," 1997).

Remember It 11.2

1. All of the following are hunger signals except
   a. activity in the lateral hypothalamus
   b. low levels of glucose in the blood
   c. the hormone CCK
   d. a high insulin level
2. Your ________ rate is responsible for how fast your body burns calories to produce energy.
3. According to ________ theory, the body works to maintain a certain weight.
4. Adopted children are more likely to be very thin if their ________ parents are very thin.
5. Effective weight loss programs must include ________ as well as reduced caloric intake.
6. Compulsive dieting to the point of self-starvation is the defining symptom of ________.

ANSWERS: 1. c; 2. metabolic; 3. set-point; 4. biological; 5. exercise; 6. anorexia nervosa

Social Motives

Now we turn from biological motives to those that are social in nature. For instance, when you feel lonely, you may call a friend or go to your favorite coffee house. The need for *affiliation*, as psychologists call it, is one kind of **social motive**. Unlike the primary drives, social motives are learned through experience and interaction with others. This group of motives includes the need for achievement and the kinds of motivations most of us experience in the workplace.

■ social motives
Motives (such as the needs for affiliation and achievement) that are acquired through experience and interaction with others.

The Need for Achievement

What is Murray's contribution to the study of motivation?

Why are some students satisfied with a C, while others must get an A at all costs? To answer this and other questions about the motivational underpinnings of academic and career achievement, psychologists have developed a number of research instruments and techniques. One of the most important was developed by Henry Murray (1938). Murray's **Thematic Apperception Test (TAT)** consists of a series of pictures of ambiguous situations. The person taking the test is asked to write a story about each picture—to describe what is going on in the picture, what the person or persons pictured are thinking about, what they may be feeling, and what is likely to be the outcome of the situation. The stories are presumed to reveal the test taker's needs and the strength of those needs.

One of the social motives identified by Murray was the **need for achievement (*n* Ach)**, or the motive "to accomplish something difficult . . . . To overcome obstacles and attain a high standard. To excel . . . . To rival and surpass others. To increase self-regard by the successful exercise of talent" (p. 164). The need for achievement, rather than being satisfied with accomplishment, seems to grow as it is fed.

Complete *Try It 11.1*, which describes a game that is said to reveal a high or low need for achievement.

■ Thematic Apperception Test (TAT)
An instrument for assessing an individual's needs and their strength; the test consists of a series of pictures of ambiguous situations, about which the test taker writes stories.

■ need for achievement (*n* Ach)
The need to accomplish something difficult and to perform at a high standard of excellence.

Characteristics of Achievers The need for achievement has been researched more vigorously than any other of Murray's needs, and researchers David McClelland and John Atkinson have conducted many of these studies (McClelland, 1958, 1961, 1985;

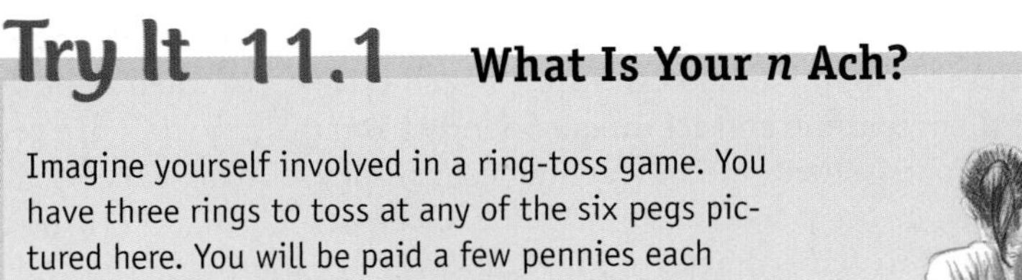

Try It 11.1 What Is Your *n* Ach?

Imagine yourself involved in a ring-toss game. You have three rings to toss at any of the six pegs pictured here. You will be paid a few pennies each time you are able to ring a peg.

Which peg would you try to ring with your three tosses—peg 1 or 2 nearest you, peg 3 or 4 at a moderate distance, or peg 5 or 6 at the far end of the row?

People with a high need for achievement relish opportunities to take on new challenges. For example, after a successful career as an actor, Arnold Schwarzenegger ran for (and won) the office of governor in the state of California.

McClelland et al., 1953). People with a high need for achievement pursue goals that are challenging, yet attainable through hard work, ability, determination, and persistence. Goals that are too easy, those anyone can reach, offer no challenge and hold no interest, because success would not be rewarding (McClelland, 1985). Impossibly high goals and high risks are also not pursued, because they offer little chance of success and are considered a waste of time. Further, goals are self-determined and linked to perceived abilities; thus, they tend to be realistic (Conroy et al., 2001). By contrast, people with a low need for achievement are not willing to take chances when it comes to testing their own skills and abilities. They are motivated more by fear of failure than by hope and expectation of success. This is why they set either ridiculously low goals, which anyone can attain, or else impossibly high goals (Geen, 1984). After all, who can fault a person for failing to reach a goal that would be impossible for almost anyone?

In view of this description, which peg in the ring-toss game in the *Try It* would people low in achievement motivation try for? If you guessed peg 1 or 2, or peg 5 or 6, you are right. People low in achievement motivation are likely to stand right over peg 1 so that they can't possibly fail. Or they may toss the rings at peg 6, hoping that they might be lucky. If they fail, no one can blame them for not attaining a nearly impossible goal. A chance to win a few cents is certainly no incentive for people with a high need for achievement, so they tend to toss their rings at peg 3 or 4, an intermediate distance that offers some challenge. Which peg did you choose?

People with a high need for achievement see their success as a result of their own talents, abilities, persistence, and hard work (Kukla, 1972). They typically do not credit luck or the influence of other people for their successes, or blame luck or others for their failures. When people with a low need for achievement fail, they usually give up quickly. They believe that luck or fate, rather than effort or ability, is responsible for accomplishment (Weiner, 1974).

In a young person, the need for achievement may be expressed as a need to excel in school. Neumann and others (1988) found that high achievement motivation is related to college students' accomplishments and grades. Those who were underachievers in high school showed less persistence later in completing college, keeping a job, and sustaining a successful marriage (McCall, 1994).

Developing Achievement Motivation Some experts believe that child-rearing practices and values in the home are important factors in developing achievement motivation (McClelland & Pilon, 1983). Parents can foster *n* Ach if they give their children responsibilities, teach them to think and act independently from the time they are very young, stress excellence, persistence, and independence, and praise them sincerely for their accomplishments (Ginsberg & Bronstein, 1993; Gottfried et al., 1994). Birth order appears to be related to achievement motivation, with first-born and only children showing higher *n* Ach than younger siblings (Falbo & Polit, 1986). Younger siblings, however, tend to be more sociable and likable than first-born or only children, and this has its rewards, too.

Work Motivation

What is work motivation, and how can it be increased?

What motivates workers to perform well, or to perform poorly, on the job? Psychologists who apply their knowledge in the workplace are known as **industrial/organizational (I/O) psychologists**. (You'll read more about their field in Chapter 18.) Although I/O psychologists are interested in many aspects of the workplace—organizational design, decision making, personnel selection, training and evaluation, work-related stress—they are vitally interested in work motivation and job performance. **Work motivation** can be thought of as "the conditions and processes that account for the arousal, direction, magnitude, and maintenance of effort in a person's job" (Katzell & Thompson, 1990, p. 144). Two of the most effective ways to increase employee motivation and improve performance are reinforcement and goal setting.

industrial/organizational (I/O) psychologists Psychologists who apply their knowledge in the workplace and are especially interested in work motivation and job performance.

work motivation The conditions and processes responsible for the arousal, direction, magnitude, and maintenance of effort of workers on the job.

To use reinforcement, I/O psychologists help design behavior modification techniques to increase performance and productivity. Reinforcers or incentives include bonuses, recognition awards, praise, time off, posting of individual performance, better offices, more impressive titles, and/or promotions. Companies may discourage ineffective behaviors through such measures as docking the pay of employees who miss work.

Using goal setting to increase performance involves establishing specific, difficult goals, which leads to higher levels of performance than simply telling people to do their best in the absence of assigned goals (Locke & Latham, 1990). An organization can enhance employees' commitment to goals by (1) having them participate in the goal setting, (2) making goals specific, attractive, difficult, and attainable, (3) providing feedback on performance, and (4) rewarding the employees for attaining the goals (Katzell & Thompson, 1990).

Several theories have been applied to research on work motivation. According to one of these—*expectancy theory*—motivation to engage in a given activity is determined by (1) *expectancy,* a person's belief that more effort will result in improved performance; (2) *instrumentality,* the person's belief that doing a job well will be noticed and rewarded; and (3) *valence,* the degree to which a person values the rewards that are offered. Several studies have supported expectancy theory by showing that employees work harder when they believe that more effort will improve their performance, when they think that a good performance will be acknowledged and rewarded, and when they value the rewards that are offered (Tubbs et al., 1993; van Eerde & Thierry, 1996).

The aspects of a job workers consider most rewarding are interesting work, good pay, sufficient resources and authority, and friendly and cooperative co-workers. Conversely, some factors undermine job satisfaction. For one, workers become dissatisfied when their workload is increased beyond their perceived capacity to perform (Yousef, 2002). For another, job satisfaction declines when workers believe that there is no fair, systematic process for resolving grievances (Kickul et al., 2002).

Supervisors' beliefs can affect job satisfaction. In one study, supervisors led to believe that certain employees were intrinsically motivated gave those employees more autonomy and were more supportive of them (Pelletier & Vallerand, 1996). Other studies have shown that the impact of stress on the job, which affects job satisfaction and performance, is buffered by social support. Workers who have social support still experience stress, but without the significant increases in heart rate or blood pressure seen in workers who lack such support (Steptoe, 2000).

I/O psychologists redesign jobs to make them more interesting, satisfying, and attractive—an approach called *job enrichment.* For example, assembly-line workers might become involved in the production of a whole item instead of repeating the same single task day after day. Workers might also be given a greater voice in how their work will be accomplished. On-the-job productivity tends to be higher when workers are given incentives, when they think their work is important, and when the effort level required is challenging but not excessive (Shepperd, 1993).

Remember It 11.3

1. Social motives are acquired through ________.
2. Individuals who have a high need for achievement set goals that are of ________ difficulty.
3. Industrial/organizational psychologists use reinforcement and goal setting to increase ________.

ANSWERS: 1. learning; 2. moderate; 3. employee motivation

The What and Why of Emotions

What do you do when you feel angry? For most people, anger leads to some kind of action directed toward the source of the anger. So, an important component of motivation is emotion—and not just anger. Think about the kinds of actions that result from feelings of disgust or sadness or fear. In fact, the root of the word *emotion* means "to move," indicating the close relationship between emotion and motivation. But what, precisely, are emotions?

Explaining the Components of Emotions

What are the three components of emotions?

An **emotion** is an identifiable feeling state, something we all recognize when we feel it. But how can subjective feelings be studied? Typically, psychologists have studied emotions in terms of three components: the physical, the cognitive, and the behavioral (Wilken et al., 2000). The physical component is the physiological arousal (the internal body state) that accompanies the emotion. The cognitive component, the way we perceive or interpret a stimulus or situation, determines the specific emotion we feel. The behavioral component of emotions is their outward expression.

■ emotion
An identifiable feeling state involving physiological arousal, a cognitive appraisal of the situation or stimulus causing that internal body state, and an outward behavior expressing the state.

The three components appear to be interdependent. For instance, in one study, participants who were better at detecting changes in heart rate (the physical component) rated their subjective experiences of emotion (the cognitive component) as being more intense than did participants who were less able to detect such physical changes (Wilken et al., 2000). Thus, any satisfactory explanation of emotion must consider these interdependencies.

Theories of Emotion

According to the various theories of emotion, what sequence of events occurs when an individual experiences an emotion?

The idea that an emotion has components seems to make sense, but in exactly what sequence do we experience the physical, cognitive, and behavioral components? As you might suspect, there is a long-standing debate among psychologists about which component comes first in the overall experience of emotion.

The James-Lange Theory American psychologist William James (1884) argued that the sequence of events in an emotional experience is exactly the reverse of what subjective experience tells us. James claimed that only after an event causes physiological arousal and a physical response does the individual perceive or interpret the physical response as an emotion. In other words, saying something stupid causes you to blush, and you interpret your physical response, blushing, as an emotion, embarrassment. James (1890) went on to suggest that "we feel sorry because we cry, angry because we strike, afraid because we tremble" (p. 1066).

At about the same time that James proposed his theory, a Danish physiologist and psychologist, Carl Lange, independently formulated a very similar theory. The two have been combined into the **James-Lange theory of emotion** (Lange & James, 1922), which suggests that different patterns of arousal in the autonomic nervous system produce the different emotions people feel, and that the physiological arousal appears before the emotion is perceived (see Figure 11.4.)

■ James-Lange theory of emotion
The theory that emotional feelings result when an individual becomes aware of a physiological response to an emotion-provoking stimulus (for example, feeling fear because of trembling).

But if physical arousal causes what we know as emotion, there would have to be distinctly different bodily changes associated with each emotion. Otherwise, you wouldn't know whether you were sad, embarrassed, frightened, or happy.

The Cannon-Bard Theory Another early theory of emotion that challenged the James-Lange theory was proposed by Walter Cannon (1927), who did pioneering

FIGURE 11.4 The James-Lange Theory of Emotion

The James-Lange theory of emotion is the exact opposite of what subjective experience tells us. If a dog growls at you, the James-Lange interpretation is that the dog growls, your heart begins to pound, and only after perceiving that your heart is pounding do you conclude that you must be afraid.

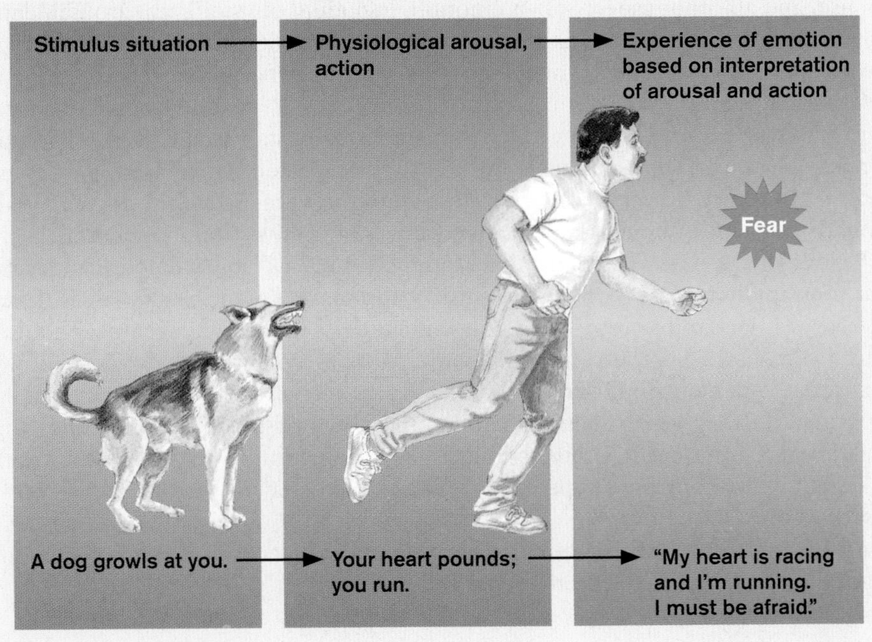

Stimulus situation
Physiological arousal, action
Experience of emotion based on interpretation of arousal and action
Fear
A dog growls at you.
Your heart pounds; you run.
"My heart is racing and I'm running. I must be afraid."

work on the fight-or-flight response and the concept of homeostasis. Cannon claimed that the bodily changes caused by the various emotions are not sufficiently distinct to allow people to distinguish one emotion from another.

Cannon's original theory was later expanded by physiologist Philip Bard (1934). The result, the **Cannon-Bard theory of emotion,** suggests that the following chain of events occurs when we feel an emotion: Emotion-provoking stimuli are received by the senses and then relayed simultaneously to the cerebral cortex, which provides the conscious mental experience of the emotion, and to the sympathetic nervous system, which produces the physiological state of arousal. In other words, your feeling of emotion (fear, for example) occurs at about the same time that you experience physiological arousal (a pounding heart). One does not cause the other.

■ Cannon-Bard theory of emotion
The theory that an emotion-provoking stimulus is transmitted simultaneously to the cerebral cortex, providing the conscious mental experience of the emotion, and to the sympathetic nervous system, causing the physiological arousal.

The Schachter-Singer Theory Stanley Schachter believed that the early theories of emotion left out a critical component—the subjective cognitive interpretation of why a state of arousal has occurred. Schachter and his colleague, Jerome Singer, proposed a two-factor theory (Schachter & Singer, 1962). According to the **Schachter-Singer theory of emotion,** two things must happen in order for a person to feel an emotion: (1) The person must first experience physiological arousal; (2) there must then be a cognitive interpretation or explanation of the physiological arousal so that the person can label it as a specific emotion. Thus, Schachter concluded, a true emotion can occur only if a person is physically aroused and can find some reason for it. When people are in a state of physiological arousal but do not know why they are aroused, they tend to label the state as an emotion that is appropriate to their situation at the time.

■ Schachter-Singer theory of emotion
A two-factor theory stating that for an emotion to occur, there must be (1) physiological arousal and (2) a cognitive interpretation or explanation of the arousal, allowing it to be labeled as a specific emotion.

Some attempts to replicate the findings of Schachter and Singer have been unsuccessful (Marshall & Zimbardo, 1979). Also, the notion that arousal is general rather than specific has been questioned by later researchers who have identified some distinctive

Lazarus theory of emotion
The theory that a cognitive appraisal is the first step in an emotional response and all other aspects of an emotion, including physiological arousal, depend on it.

patterns of arousal for some of the basic emotions (Ekman et al., 1983; Levenson, 1992; Scherer & Wallbott, 1994).

The Lazarus Theory The theory of emotion that most heavily emphasizes the cognitive aspect has been proposed by Richard Lazarus (1991a, 1991b, 1995). According to the **Lazarus theory of emotion**, a cognitive appraisal is the first step in an emotional response, and all other aspects of an emotion, including physiological arousal, depend on that cognitive appraisal. This theory is most compatible with the subjective experience of an emotion's sequence of events—the sequence that James reversed long ago. Faced with a stimulus, an event, a person first appraises it. This cognitive appraisal determines whether the person will have an emotional response and, if so, what type of response. The physiological arousal and all other aspects of the emotion flow from the appraisal. In short, Lazarus contends that emotions are provoked when cognitive appraisals of events or circumstances are positive or negative—but not neutral.

Critics of the Lazarus theory have pointed out that some emotional reactions occur too rapidly to pass through a cognitive appraisal (Zajonc, 1980, 1984). Lazarus (1984, 1991a, 1991b) has responded that some mental processing occurs without conscious awareness. And there must be some form of cognitive realization, however brief, or else a person would not know what he or she is responding to or what emotion to feel. Further, researchers have found that reappraisal, or changing one's thinking about an emotional stimulus, is related to a reduction in physiological response (Gross, 2002). By contrast, suppression of emotional behavior without cognitive reappraisal is not.

Review and Reflect 11.2 summarizes the four major theories of emotion: James-Lange, Cannon-Bard, Schachter-Singer, and Lazarus.

REVIEW *and* REFLECT 11.2

Theories of Emotion

THEORY	VIEW	EXAMPLE
James-Lange theory	An event causes physiological arousal. You experience an emotion only *after* you interpret the physical response.	You are walking home late at night and hear footsteps behind you. Your heart pounds and you begin to tremble. You interpret these physical responses as *fear*.
Cannon-Bard theory	An event causes a physiological *and* an emotional response simultaneously. One does not cause the other.	You are walking home late at night and hear footsteps behind you. Your heart pounds, you begin to tremble, *and* you feel afraid.
Schachter-Singer theory	An event causes physiological arousal. You must then be able to identify a reason for the arousal in order to label the emotion.	You are walking home late at night and hear footsteps behind you. Your heart pounds and you begin to tremble. You know that walking alone at night can be dangerous, and so you feel afraid.
Lazarus theory	An event occurs, a cognitive appraisal is made, and then the emotion and physiological arousal follow.	You are walking home late at night and hear footsteps behind you. You think it could be a mugger. So you feel afraid, and your heart starts to pound and you begin to tremble.

Want to be sure you've fully absorbed the material in this chapter? Visit **www.ablongman.com/wood5e** for access to free practice tests, flashcards, interactive activities, and links developed specifically to help you succeed in psychology.

Emotion and the Brain

What brain structure processes the emotion of fear?

What happens in the brain when we experience an emotion? More than any other emotion, fear has stimulated research by neuroscientists (LeDoux, 1996, 2000). And the brain structure most closely associated with fear is the amygdala (see Figure 11.5). Information comes to the amygdala directly from all of the senses and is acted on there immediately, without initial involvement of the primary "thinking" area of the brain, the cortex. But, as with reflex actions, the cortex does become involved as soon as it "catches up" with the amygdala (LeDoux, 2000). Thus, an emotion can be stirred up even before the cortex knows what is going on.

When the emotion of fear first materializes, much of the brain's processing is nonconscious. We become conscious of it later, of course, but the amygdala is activated before we are aware that a threat is present (Damasio, 1994, 1999). Interestingly, the amygdala becomes more highly activated when a person looks at photos of angry or fearful-looking faces than it does when the person views photos of happy faces (LeDoux, 2000).

Emotions may also be lateralized. Sad feelings, for example, are associated with greater activity in the left cerebral hemisphere (Papousek & Schulter, 2002). Researchers using electroencephalographs to track mood changes have found that reductions in both anxiety and depression are associated with a shift in electrical activity from the left to the right side of the brain. Perception of others' emotions appears to be lateralized on the right side of the brain. This pattern of lateralization may be more pronounced in females than in males. In one study, participants listened to emotional expressions alternately with the left and right ears. (Recall that the left ear sends auditory signals to the right side of the brain, while the right ear sends them to the left side.) A left-ear advantage for accurate identification of a speaker's emotional state was evident only for women (Voyer & Rodgers, 2002). Another interesting and possibly related finding is that women who describe themselves as being high in emotional expressivity are more likely to turn the left side of their face to the camera when asked to pose for a picture than those who report less emotional sensitivity (Nicholls et al., 2002). Researchers speculate that their behavior is motivated by an unconscious sense of the left-ear advantage in emotional perception.

FIGURE 11.5 Emotion and the Amygdala

The amygdala plays an important role in emotion. It is activated by fear before any direct involvement of the cerebral cortex occurs.

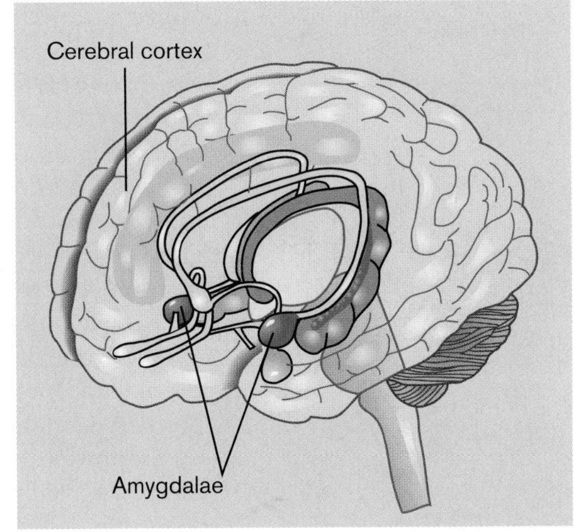

The Polygraph Test

What does a polygraph measure?

Why do you suppose that the results of "lie detector" tests, while they are extremely useful investigative tools, are not admissible as evidence in United States courtrooms? The answer to this question lies in the nature of the test. A **polygraph**, commonly called a "lie detector," is a device designed to detect changes in heart rate, blood pressure, respiration rate, and skin conductance response. The assumption behind the use of the polygraph is that lying causes changes in these physiological functions that can be accurately measured and recorded by the device (Rosenfeld, 1995). However, a polygraph is not really a lie detector; it cannot distinguish lying from fear, sexual arousal, anxiety, anger, or general emotional arousal.

■ **polygraph**
A device designed to detect the changes in heart rate, blood pressure, respiration rate, and skin conductance response that typically accompany arousal.

How accurate is the polygraph? Some experts say that the percentage of innocent people falsely accused of lying may be as high as one out of three (Kleinmuntz & Szucko, 1984), as illustrated in Figure 11.6 (on page 394) . What about guilty people? One out of four who were shown to have lied on a polygraph test were judged to be

FIGURE 11.6 **The Unreliability of Polygraph Tests**

Polygraph tests are far from infallible. In one study, one out of three innocent people were judged guilty and one out of four guilty people were judged innocent. People who can lie easily often show little physical arousal and therefore may be evaluated as telling the truth.

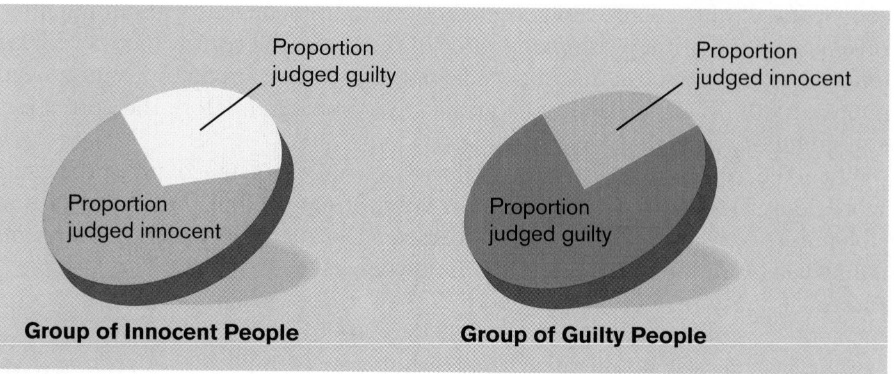

telling the truth. Does this mean it's possible to beat the lie detector? Inveterate, or habitual, liars, those who lie easily without any emotional disturbance or physiological arousal, are more likely to be evaluated as telling the truth. It has been suggested that failing to pay close attention or being distracted during questioning also lowers physiological responses.

In one classic study of polygraph accuracy, volunteer participants distracted themselves by counting backward by sevens throughout the examination, and they were able to lie without being detected more often than when they were not using such distraction (Waid et al., 1981). Lykken (1981) found that increasing arousal by tensing muscles and thinking about something exciting during neutral questions could also alter the results. Apparently, even taking tranquilizers before the test can reduce the physiological response that usually accompanies lying.

The less-than-satisfactory reliability of lie detectors has led to increasing restrictions on their use (Lykken, 1985). However, the polygraph continues to be an important research tool in the study of criminal behavior. For example, in one study, researchers used polygraph examinations to obtain estimates of the proportion of sex offenders who under-report previous charges and convictions and who over-report sexual victimization during their own childhoods (Hindman & Peters, 2001). Researchers are studying other ways to gauge physiological indicators of truth telling, including *thermal imaging*, a technique for measuring different levels of heat emanating from the face (Pavlidis et al., 2002).

Remember It 11.4

1. Emotion involves ________, ________, and ________ components.
2. The ________ theory of emotion holds that you feel a true emotion only when you become physically aroused and can identify some cause for the arousal.
3. The ________ theory suggests that you would feel fearful *because* you were trembling.
4. The ________ theory suggests that the feeling of an emotion and the physiological response to an emotional situation occur at about the same time.
5. The ________ theory suggests that the physiological arousal and the emotion flow from a cognitive appraisal of an emotion-provoking event.
6. When fear strikes, the ________ is activated before the ________.
7. A polygraph measures ________.

ANSWERS: 1. physical, cognitive, behavioral; 2. Schachter-Singer; 3. James-Lange; 4. Cannon-Bard; 5. Lazarus; 6. amygdala, cerebral cortex; 7. arousal

The Expression of Emotion

Who taught you how to smile and frown? No one did, of course. Expressing emotions comes as naturally to humans as breathing. And the facial expressions of certain basic emotions are similar in all cultures.

The Range of Emotion

What are basic emotions?

How many emotions are there? Two leading researchers on emotion, Paul Ekman (1993) and Carroll Izard (1992), insist that there are a limited number of basic emotions. **Basic emotions** are unlearned and universal; that is, they are found in all cultures, are reflected in the same facial expressions, and emerge in children according to their biological timetable of development. Fear, anger, disgust, surprise, happiness or joy, and sadness or distress are usually considered basic emotions. Izard (1992, 1993) suggests that there are distinct neural circuits that underlie each of the basic emotions, and Levenson and others (1990) point to specific autonomic nervous system activity associated with the basic emotions.

■ basic emotions
Emotions that are unlearned and universal, that are reflected in the same facial expressions across cultures, and that emerge in children according to their biological timetable of development; fear, anger, disgust, surprise, happiness, and sadness are usually considered basic emotions.

In studying the range of emotion, Ekman (1993) has suggested that emotions should be considered as families. The anger family might range from annoyed to irritated, angry, livid, and, finally, enraged. Furthermore, if perceived as a family, anger should also include various forms of its expression, according to Ekman (1993). Resentment, for example, is a form of anger "in which there is a sense of grievance" (p. 386). Other forms are indignation and outrage, which seem to be justifiable anger focused on a wrongful or unjust action against self or others. Vengefulness is anger that retaliates, or gets revenge for an injustice or misdeed by another. In its most intense form, anger may be expressed as blind rage, in which a person loses control and may commit brutal atrocities against the target of the rage. Just as there are many words in the English language to describe the variations in the range of any emotion, there are subtle distinctions in the facial expression of a single emotion that convey its intensity (Ekman, 1993).

How does the development of facial expressions in infants suggest a biological basis for emotional expression?

The Development of Facial Expressions

Emotional expressions are natural, but what patterns are associated with their development? Newborn babies don't even smile, but 1-year-olds exhibit almost as many facial expressions as older children and adults. Like the motor skills of crawling and walking, facial expressions of emotions develop according to a biological timetable of maturation. Even newborns are capable of expressing some emotions—specifically, distress, pleasure, and interest in the environment. By 3 months of age, babies can express happiness and sadness (Lewis, 1995), and laughter appears somewhere between 3 and 4 months (Provine, 1996). Between the ages of 4 and 6 months, the emotions of anger and surprise appear, and by about 7 months, infants show fear. The self-conscious emotions do not emerge until later. Between 18 months and 3 years, children begin to show first empathy, envy, and embarrassment, followed by shame, guilt, and pride (Lewis, 1995).

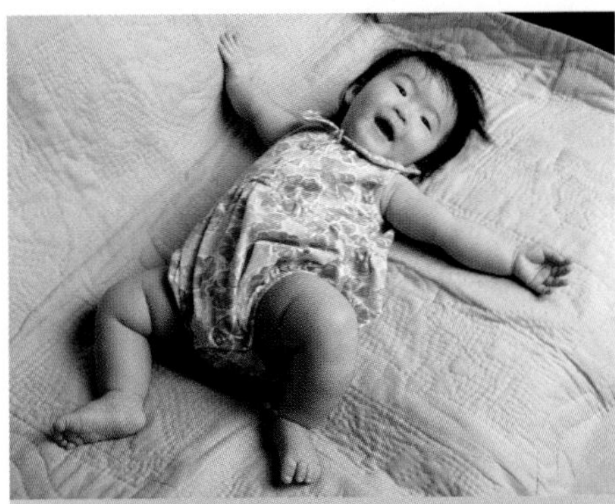

Even infants who are blind or deaf smile and frown, suggesting that facial expressions are biologically programmed, universal expressions of emotion.

The consistency of emotional development across individual infants and across cultures supports the idea that emotional expression is inborn. Another strong indication that the facial expressions of emotion are biologically determined comes from research on children who have been blind and deaf since birth. Their smiles and frowns, laughter and crying, and facial expressions of anger, surprise, and pouting are the same as those of children who can hear and see (Eibl-Eibesfeldt, 1973).

Try It 11.2 Recognizing Basic Emotions

Look carefully at the six photographs. Which basic emotion is portrayed in each? Match the photograph with the letter of the basic emotion it conveys.

a. happiness b. sadness c. fear d. anger e. surprise f. disgust

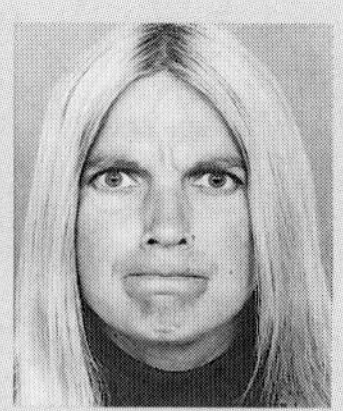

1. ________

2. ________

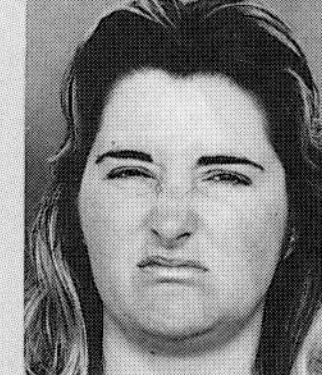

3. ________

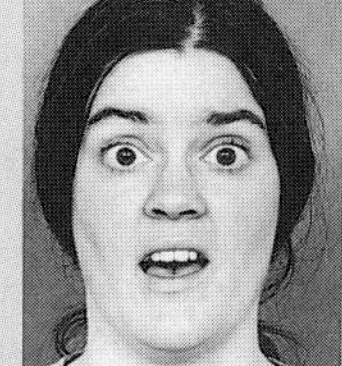

4. ________

5. ________

6. ________

ANSWERS: 1. d 2. c 3. f 4. e 5. a 6. b

What evidence is there to suggest that facial expressions have the same meanings all over the world?

The Universality of Facial Expressions

Do you think that facial expressions have the same meaning for every individual and in every culture? Use the photos in *Try It 11.2* to find out whether people you know agree about what these facial expressions mean.

The relationship between emotions and facial expressions was first studied by Charles Darwin (1872/1965). He believed that the facial expression of emotion was an aid to survival, because it enabled people to communicate their internal states and react to emergencies before they developed language. Darwin maintained that most emotions, and the facial expressions that convey them, are genetically inherited and characteristic of the entire human species. To test his belief, he asked missionaries and people of different cultures around the world to record the facial expressions that accompany the basic emotions. Based on those data, he concluded that facial expressions were similar across cultures. Modern researchers agree that Darwin was right.

Other researchers have found evidence for universality as well as for cultural variations. Scherer and Wallbott (1994) found very extensive overlap in the patterns of emotional experiences reported across cultures in 37 different countries on 5 continents. They also found important cultural differences in the ways emotions are elicited and regulated and in how they are shared socially. Recent research suggests that Asians pay more attention to indicators of emotion, such as tone of voice, than Westerners do (Ishii et al., 2003).

Moreover, each culture appears to have an "accent" for facial expressions (Marsh et al., 2003). This accent is a pattern of minute muscle movements that are used by most members of a culture when they exhibit a particular facial expression. In other words, there is a Japanese way to make a happy face, an American way to make a happy face that is somewhat different, and a German way of making a happy face that differs from both. In fact, these differences are enough to influence perceptions of emotion even when individuals come from very similar cultural backgrounds. In one classic study, researchers found that White Americans more quickly identified the facial expressions of other White Americans than did White Europeans (Izard, 1971).

How do display rules for emotions differ across cultures?

Cultural Rules for Displaying Emotion

Do you remember what you did at age 8 when you opened Aunt Sally's birthday gift and discovered it was a hideous sweater you would never wear? You probably said "yuck," or something similar. But what happened when you had a similar experience at age 18? By then, you had learned to smile and pretend you loved Aunt Sally's gift. In other words, you had learned a **display rule**—a cultural rule that dictates how an emotion should generally be expressed and when and where its expression is appropriate (Ekman, 1993; Ekman & Friesen, 1975; Scherer & Wallbott, 1994).

There are many situations in which people must disguise their emotions to comply with the display rules of their culture, which dictate when and how feelings should be expressed. For example, these Buckingham palace guards are expected to remain expressionless, even if it means hiding their true feelings.

Often, a society's display rules require people to give evidence of certain emotions that they may not actually feel or to disguise their true feelings. For example, we are expected to look sad at funerals, to hide disappointment when we lose at games, and to refrain from making facial expressions of disgust if the food we are served tastes bad. In one study, Cole (1986) found that 3-year-old girls, when given an unattractive gift, smiled nevertheless. They had already learned a display rule and signaled an emotion they very likely did not feel. Davis (1995) found that among 1st, 2nd, and 3rd graders, girls were better able to hide disappointment than boys were.

Different cultures, neighborhoods, and even families may have very different display rules. Display rules in Japanese culture dictate that negative emotions must be disguised when other people are present (Ekman, 1972; Triandis, 1994). In many societies in the West, women are expected to smile often, whether they feel happy or not. And in East Africa, young males from traditional Masai society are expected to appear stern and stony-faced and to "produce long, unbroken stares" (Keating, 1994). Thus, the emotions people show are sometimes not truly felt, but merely reflect compliance with display rules.

Not only can emotions be displayed and not felt, they can also be felt and not displayed (Russell, 1995). Consider Olympic medalists waiting to receive their gold, silver, or bronze medals. Though brimming with happiness, the athletes display few smiles until their medals have been presented and they are interacting with the authorities and responding to the crowd (Fernández-Dols & Ruiz-Belda, 1995). Further, researchers have learned that, in the United States, teens conform to unspoken display rules acquired from peers that discourage public displays of emotion. The resulting subdued emotional expressions can cause them to appear aloof, uncaring, and even rude to parents and other adults (Salisch, 2001). Psychologists speculate that conformity to these peer-based display rules may be the basis of much miscommunication between teens and their parents and teachers.

Most of us learn display rules very early and abide by them most of the time. Yet you may not be fully aware that the rules you have learned dictate where, when, how, and even how long certain emotions should be expressed. You will learn more about reading emotions and detecting the probable motives of others when we explore nonverbal behavior—the language of facial expressions, gestures, and body positions—in Chapter 17.

■ **display rules**
Cultural rules that dictate how emotions should generally be expressed and when and where their expression is appropriate.

Emotion as a Form of Communication

Why is emotion considered a form of communication?

Often, we communicate emotions in order to motivate others to action. If you communicate sadness or distress, then people close to you are likely to be sympathetic and try to help. Emotional expressions allow infants to communicate their feelings and needs before they are able to speak.

In an early study, Katherine Bridges (1932) observed emotional expression in Canadian infants over a period of months. She reported that the first emotional expression to appear is that of distress. In survival terms, the expression of distress enables helpless newborns to get the attention of their caretakers so that their needs can be met. More recent research indicates that adults are quite adept at interpreting infants' nonverbal emotional signals; they can even correctly determine whether a baby is looking at a new or familiar object by simply observing the change in the baby's facial expression and body language (Camras et al., 2002).

Do you feel happier when you are around others who are happy? You may already know that emotions are contagious. Mothers seem to know this intuitively when they display happy expressions in an effort to improve their babies' moods (Keating, 1994). Researchers have found that mothers in many cultures—Trobriand Island, Yanomamo, Greek, German, Japanese, and American—attempt to regulate the moods of their babies through facial communication of emotions (Kanaya et al., 1989; Keller et al., 1988; Termine & Izard, 1988).

From an evolutionary perspective, there is survival value in the ability to interpret various states instantly and reliably and then emulate them. In many species, if a single member of the group or herd senses a predator and communicates the emotion of fear, the other members also become afraid, which prepares them to flee for their lives. For humans, too, quick and accurate recognition of facial expressions that communicate anger or a threat clearly has adaptive value. And research indicates that such recognition is indeed fast and efficient (Fox et al., 2000b; Horstmann, 2003).

Humans begin to perceive the emotions of others early in the first year of life and use this information to guide behavior. Infants pay close attention to the facial expressions of others, especially their mothers. And when they are confronted with an ambiguous situation, they use the mother's emotion as a guide to whether they should approach or avoid the situation. This phenomenon is known as *social referencing* (Klinnert et al., 1983).

But what happens when false and thus deceptive emotions are being conveyed? Evolutionary psychologists, who study how humans adapt their behavior for the purpose of passing on their genes (as noted in Chapter 1), have presented evidence indicating that both males and females use emotional deception in the context of mating behavior. In a study involving some 200 male and female university students, women admitted that they had flirted with, smiled at, and played up to men, leading them on when they had no romantic interest in the men or any intention of having sex with them. Men admitted intentionally deceiving women about the depth of their emotional commitment. Asked whether they had ever exaggerated the depth of their feelings for a partner in order to get sex, more than 70% of the male students said yes, compared with 39% of the female students. When asked whether they thought that a man had ever exaggerated his feelings to get sex, a staggering 97% of the female students said yes (Buss, 1994, 1999).

Evolutionary psychologists would say that this study shows how males have adapted their behavior so that they can mate with as many females as possible and pass on their genes to the offspring. Females, on the other hand, seek to gain emotional commitment from males before procreation, so that the resulting children will be provided for. Devastating negative emotions can result if a woman consents to having sex with a man and later learns that he was lying about his emotional commitment. False emotions are almost always detected, so emotional honesty is the best policy in any relationship.

Remember It 11.5

1. The basic emotions emerge in children as a result of their ______ of development.
2. Each culture appears to have its own pattern of minute ______ that are used to exhibit a particular facial expression.
3. Because of cultural ______, people sometimes express emotions they do not really feel.
4. According to evolutionary pychologists, both men and women use ______ in their mating behaviors.

ANSWERS: 1. biological timetable; 2. muscle movements; 3. display rules; 4. emotional deception

Experiencing Emotion

How is the expression of emotion related to the experience of emotion? Some researchers go so far as to suggest that the facial expression alone can actually produce the feeling.

The Facial-Feedback Hypothesis

How do facial expressions influence internal emotional states?

Do you think that making particular facial expressions can affect your emotions? Nearly 125 years ago, Darwin wrote, "Even the simulation of an emotion tends to arouse it in our minds" (1872/1965, p. 365). Researcher Sylvan Tomkins (1962, 1963) went a step further. He claimed that the facial expression itself—that is, the movement of the facial muscles producing the expression—triggers both the physiological arousal and the conscious feeling associated with the emotion. The notion that the muscular movements involved in certain facial expressions produce the corresponding emotions is called the **facial-feedback hypothesis** (Izard, 1971, 1977, 1990; Strack et al., 1988).

In classic research using 16 participants (12 professional actors and 4 scientists), Ekman and colleagues (1983) documented the effects of facial expressions on physiological indicators of emotion. The participants were guided to contract specific muscles in the face so that they could assume the facial expressions of six basic emotions—surprise, disgust, sadness, anger, fear, and happiness. They were never actually told to smile, frown, or put on an angry face, however. The participants were monitored by electronic instruments, which recorded physiological changes in heart rate, galvanic skin response (to measure perspiring), muscle tension, and hand temperature. Measurements were taken as the participants made each facial expression. The participants were also asked to imagine or relive an experience in which they had felt each of the six emotions.

Ekman reported that a distinctive physiological response pattern emerged for each of the emotions of fear, sadness, anger, and disgust, whether the participants relived one of their emotional experiences or simply made the corresponding facial expression. In fact, in some cases the physiological measures of emotion were greater when the actors and scientists made the facial expression than when they imagined an emotional experience (Ekman et al., 1983). The researchers found that both anger and fear accelerate heart rate, but fear produces colder fingers than does anger.

If facial expressions can activate emotions, is it possible that intensifying or weakening a facial expression might intensify or weaken the corresponding feeling state? Izard (1990) believes that learning to self-regulate emotional expression can help in controlling emotions. You might learn to change the intensity of an emotion by inhibiting, weakening, or amplifying its expression. Or you might change the emotion itself by simulating the expression of another emotion. Izard proposes that this approach to the regulation of emotion might be a useful adjunct to psychotherapy. Regulating or modifying an emotion by simulating an expression of its opposite may be effective if the emotion is not unusually intense.

Does it really matter whether we control our emotions? You may have heard that "venting" emotions, a process known as *catharsis*, is good for mental health. In reality, the opposite is true. Venting anger makes a person angrier and may even make him or her more likely to express the anger aggressively (Bushman, 2002). Better control of emotions is associated with a lower incidence of drug problems (Simons & Carey, 2002). Presumably, the better we are at controlling our own emotions, the less likely we are to resort to chemical means of regulating them.

■ **facial-feedback hypothesis**
The idea that the muscular movements involved in certain facial expressions produce the corresponding emotions (for example, smiling makes one feel happy).

Gender Differences in Experiencing Emotion

In what ways do males and females differ with regard to emotions?

Do females and males differ significantly in the way they experience their emotions? Do women tend to be more intensely emotional than men? According to evolutionary psychologists, the answer to both questions is yes. Intense emotions are frequently experienced in the context of sexual behavior, and evolutionary psychologist David Buss (1999, 2000b) has reported that women are far more likely than men to feel anger when their partner is sexually aggressive. Men, on the other hand, experience greater anger than women do when their partner withholds sex.

There are other gender differences with respect to the emotion of anger. According to the evolutionary perspective, your answer to the following question is likely to be gender-specific: What emotion would you feel first if you were betrayed or harshly criticized by another person? When asked to respond to this question, male research participants in a classic study were more likely to report that they would feel angry; female participants were more likely to say that they would feel hurt, sad, or disappointed (Brody, 1985). Of course, both males and females express anger, but typically not in the same ways. Women are just as likely as men to express anger in private (at home) but much less likely than men to express it publicly (Cupach & Canary, 1995).

Research by evolutionary psychologists also suggests clear and consistent differences between the sexes concerning feelings of jealousy. Men, more than women, experience jealousy over evidence or suspicions of sexual infidelity. A woman, however, is more likely than a man to be jealous of her partner's emotional attachment and commitment to another and of attention, time, and resources diverted from the relationship (Buss, 1999, 2000a; Pietrzak et al., 2002; White & Mullen, 1989).

Within married couples, women appear to be more attuned to the relationship's overall emotional climate and are more likely to be its "emotional manager" (Gottman, 1994). The most puzzling gender difference in emotional experience is the following: In surveys of happiness, women report greater happiness and life satisfaction than men do (Wood et al., 1989). Paradoxically, women also report more sadness than men, are twice as likely to report being depressed, and admit to greater fear than men do (Scherer et al., 1986).

How can women be both happier and sadder than men? Perhaps this is why men often complain that they don't understand women. However, understanding another gender difference may help. Researchers have found sex differences in the intensity of emotional response. Grossman and Wood (1993) tested male and female participants for the intensity of emotional responses on five basic emotions—joy, love, fear, sadness, and anger. They found that "women reported more intense and more frequent emotions than men did, with the exception of anger" (p. 1013). More joy, more sadness, more fear, more love! But these were self-reports. How did Grossman and Wood know that the female participants actually felt four of the five emotions more intensely than the males? The researchers also measured physiological arousal. The participants viewed slides depicting the various emotions while they were hooked up to an electromyograph, which measured tension in the facial muscles. The researchers found that "women not only reported more intense emotional experience than men, but they also generated more extreme physiological reactions" (p. 1020). Other researchers agree that, in general, women respond with greater emotional intensity than men and thus can experience both greater joy and greater sorrow (Fujita et al., 1991).

In a recent study, men were found to process emotions, especially positive ones, predominantly in the left hemisphere of the brain, while women were found to use both cerebral hemispheres more equally for processing emotions (Coney & Fitzgerald, 2000). This finding could account for some of the emotional difference between the genders.

Emotion and Cognition

How does emotion affect thought? Is it possible to think logically without so much as a hint of emotion, as Mr. Spock does in *Star Trek*? You learned in Chapter 6 that an individual's emotional state can affect the way the person remembers a particular event. For example, when people feel sad, they recall more negative events than when they are happy. Thus, emotion is clearly an integral part of human thought processes. So, what happens when, instead of trying to recall the past, we think about the future while in one emotional state or another?

How does emotion influence thought?

There is a good deal of evidence suggesting that emotions help us formulate risk assessments and develop appropriate behavioral responses (Schupp et al., 2003). In fact, emotion allows us to detect risk more quickly than we could using rational thought alone (Dijksterhuis & Aarts, 2003). Suppose you get on a bus late one night and see a passenger methodically sharpening a knife. Will you engage in a cool-headed logical analysis of the likelihood that he will use his knife to attack you? Probably not. Chances are, your emotions will steer you toward the more efficient course of staying clear of the threatening passenger or getting off the bus as soon as you can.

The connection between emotion and risk assessment was demonstrated particularly well in a series of studies conducted by psychologist Jennifer Lerner and several colleagues. They examined how people's emotional responses to the terrorist attacks of September 11, 2001, influenced their ability to assess the risk of future events of the same kind (Lerner et al., 2003). First, Lerner and her associates examined whether naturally occurring individual differences in emotional responses to the attacks were related to differences in risk perception. Their first surveys were carried out within 9 to 23 days of the attacks. They found that people who responded with anger, as measured on a "desire for vengeance" scale, were less likely to believe that another major attack would occur within a year than were those who responded with fear. And they found that the initial emotional reactions continued to predict differences in risk assessment 6 to 10 weeks later.

Next, this group of researchers asked whether experimentally induced emotions would color risk perceptions in the same way. To examine this question, the researchers randomly assigned participants to conditions in which they were exposed to stimuli designed to elicit specific emotions. For instance, in the anger condition, the participants were first asked to explain what about the attacks made them most angry; these participants then watched a video portraying celebrations of the attacks in Middle Eastern countries. In the fear condition, participants were first asked what about the attacks made them most afraid; next, they were shown a video depicting postal workers taking measures to protect themselves from anthrax exposure. After the questions and videos, participants in both groups were asked to predict the probability that at some time within the next 12 months, they personally would be victimized by terrorism and that there would be attacks on other Americans. Lerner and her colleagues (2003) found that the the probability estimates, both personal and general, given by participants in the fear group were higher than those given by participants in the anger group.

What would cause an angry person to be more optimistic than a fearful person? One clue may lie in the participants' views of possible policy responses to terrorist attacks. Anger, both naturally occurring and experimentally induced, was associated with endorsement of specific actions against potential perpetrators of terrorism, such as strict policies requiring immediate deportation of individuals who enter the United States illegally. By contrast, fear, again both natural and experimentally induced, was associated with precautionary approaches such as universal vaccinations against possible biological weapons. Thus, it is possible that the anger-optimism link arises from confidence, whether justified or not, in concrete measures directed toward people who are perceived as potentially threatening.

Love

How does Sternberg's triangular theory of love account for the different kinds of love?

What emotion do you think has the most positive influence on our experiences? Most people would say that love is the most life-enhancing of all emotions. Although people often use the term rather loosely or casually ("I *love* ice cream," "I *love* to dance"), love is usually experienced as a deep and abiding affection for parents, children, and, ideally, friends, neighbors, and other fellow humans. There is also love of country and love of learning. But what about romantic love? Is it different from other forms of this emotion?

Robert Sternberg (1986b, 1987), whose triarchic theory of intelligence was discussed in Chapter 8, has also proposed a **triangular theory of love**. Its three components are intimacy, passion, and commitment. Sternberg explains intimacy as "those feelings in a relationship that promote closeness, bondedness, and connectedness" (1987, p. 339). Passion refers to those drives in a loving relationship "that lead to romance, physical attraction, [and] sexual consummation" (1986b, p. 119). The commitment component consists of (1) a short-term aspect, the decision that one loves another person, and (2) a long-term aspect, a commitment to maintaining that love over time.

Sternberg proposes that these three components, singly and in various combinations, produce seven different kinds of love (see Figure 11.7):

triangular theory of love Sternberg's theory that three components—intimacy, passion, and commitment—singly and in various combinations, produce seven different kinds of love.

consummate love According to Sternberg's theory, the most complete form of love, consisting of all three components—intimacy, passion, and commitment.

1. *Liking* includes only one of the love components—intimacy. In this case, liking is not used in a trivial sense. Sternberg says that this intimate liking characterizes true friendships, in which a person feels a bondedness, a warmth, and a closeness with another but not intense passion or long-term commitment.
2. *Infatuated love* consists solely of passion and is often what is felt as "love at first sight." But without the intimacy and the commitment components of love, infatuated love may disappear suddenly.
3. *Empty love* consists of the commitment component without intimacy or passion. Sometimes, a stronger love deteriorates into empty love, in which the commitment remains, but the intimacy and passion have died. In cultures in which arranged marriages are common, relationships often begin as empty love.

FIGURE 11.7 Sternberg's Triangular Theory of Love

Sternberg identifies three components of love—passion, intimacy, and commitment—and shows how the three, singly and in various combinations, produce seven different kinds of love. Consummate love, the most complete form of love, has all three components.
Source: Sternberg (1986b).

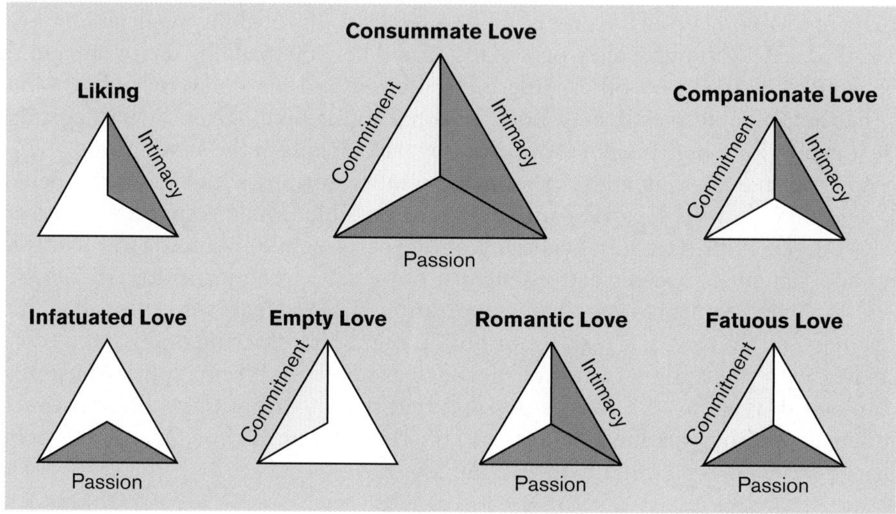

4. *Romantic love* is a combination of intimacy and passion. Romantic lovers are bonded emotionally (as in liking) and physically through passionate arousal.
5. *Fatuous love* has the passion and the commitment components but not the intimacy component. This type of love can be exemplified by a whirlwind courtship and marriage in which a commitment is motivated largely by passion, without the stabilizing influence of intimacy.
6. *Companionate love* consists of intimacy and commitment. This type of love is often found in marriages in which the passion has gone out of the relationship, but a deep affection and commitment remain.
7. *Consummate love* is the only type of love that includes all three components—intimacy, passion and commitment. **Consummate love** is the most complete form of love, and it represents the ideal love relationship for which many people strive but which apparently few achieve. Sternberg cautions that maintaining a consummate love may be even harder than achieving it. He stresses the importance of translating the components of love into action. "Without expression," he warns, "even the greatest of loves can die" (1987, p. 341).

According to Sternberg, romantic love has both emotional and physical components.

Apply It

The Quest for Happiness

"Life, Liberty and the pursuit of Happiness"—these ringing words from the Declaration of Independence are familiar to most of us, and most of us would agree that happiness is a desirable goal. But what exactly is happiness, and how can one attain it? These questions are not as easily answered as you might expect.

Psychologists usually equate happiness with the feeling of well-being, the pervasive sense that life is good. As David G. Myers, a leader in the field of happiness research, puts it, well-being "is an ongoing perception that this time of one's life, or even life as a whole, is fulfilling, meaningful, and pleasant" (1992, p. 23). Happiness is closely related to life satisfaction—people who feel happy also tend to believe that their lives are satisfying. Of course, there are factors in everyone's life that can't be changed, and some of them can result in unhappiness. However, people can use certain strategies to exercise greater control over the way they respond emotionally to their life situations.

- *Count your blessings.* One important factor affecting happiness is the tendency to compare one's situation with that of other people. If you feel that you are struggling to make ends meet while everyone around you appears to be living in comfort and security, you will feel less joy and more stress. Indeed, surveys have shown that perceived wealth matters more than absolute wealth. So, you should try to appreciate what you have rather than focusing on what you lack.
- *Smile.* Smiling really does induce feelings of happiness. Smile at other people—even people you don't like a lot. As the song goes, "Put on a happy face." Don't worry if it feels like pretending; after a while, it will come naturally.
- *Stay connected to people.* Another way to make your life happier is to make the most of social occasions—phone calls, visits, meals with friends. Such occasions often require you to behave as if you were happy, which can actually serve to free you from unhappiness.
- *Keep busy.* You will also feel happier if you get so caught up in an activity that you become oblivious to your surroundings. Psychologists refer to this state as *flow*. To be in flow is to be unselfconsciously absorbed (Csikszentmihalyi, 1990). People who are engaged in some activity that engages their skills—whether it is work, play, or simply driving a car—report more positive feelings.

You may not be able to control every aspect of your life situation, but you do have some control over how you respond to it.

Remember It 11.6

1. The idea that making a happy, sad, or angry face can actually trigger the physiological response and the feeling associated with the emotion is called the __________.
2. Women are more likely than men to experience jealousy in response to a partner's __________ infidelity.
3. Sternberg's theory claims that the three components of romantic love are __________, __________, and __________.
4. According to Sternberg, the most complete form of love is __________ love.

ANSWERS: 1. facial-feedback hypothesis; 2 emotional; 3. intimacy, passion, commitment; 4. consummate

Summary *and* Review

What Is Motivation? p. 375

What is the difference between intrinsic and extrinsic motivation? p. 375

With intrinsic motivation, an act is performed because it is satisfying or pleasurable in and of itself; with extrinsic motivation, an act is performed in order to gain a reward or to avert an undesirable consequence.

How do instinct theories explain motivation? p. 376

Instinct theories suggest that human behavior is motivated by certain inborn, unlearned tendencies, or instincts, that are shared by all people.

How does drive-reduction theory explain motivation? p. 376

Drive-reduction theory suggests that a biological need creates an internal state of arousal or tension called a drive, which the organism is motivated to reduce.

How does arousal theory explain motivation? p. 376

Arousal theory suggests that the aim of motivation is to maintain an optimal level of arousal. If arousal is less than optimal, a person engages in activities that stimulate arousal; if arousal exceeds the optimal level, the person seeks to reduce stimulation.

What is Maslow's hierarchy of needs? p. 379

According to Maslow, higher needs cannot be addressed until lower needs are met. Lower needs include both physical needs (e.g., for food) and the need for safety. Once these are satisfied, behavior can be motivated by higher needs, such as the needs for belonging, esteem, and self-actualization.

The Primary Drives p. 380

Under what conditions do the two types of thirst occur? p. 380

Extracellular thirst results from a loss of fluid from the body tissues. This can be caused by perspiring, vomiting, bleeding, diarrhea, or excessive intake of alcohol. Intracellular thirst results from loss of water inside the body cells. This can be caused by excessive intake of salt, which disturbs the water-sodium balance in the blood and tissues.

How do internal and external hunger cues influence eating behavior? p. 381

The lateral hypothalamus (LH) signals us to eat when we are hungry, and the ventromedial hypothalamus (VMH) motivates us to stop eating when we are full. Other internal hunger signals are low blood glucose levels and high insulin levels. Some satiety signals are high blood glucose levels and the presence in the blood of other satiety substances (such as CCK) that are secreted by the gastrointestinal tract during digestion. External hunger cues, such as the taste, smell, and appearance of food, eating with other people, and the time of day, can cause people to eat more food than they actually need.

What are some factors that account for variations in body weight? p. 382

Variations in body weight are influenced by genes, hormones, metabolic rate, activity level, number of fat cells, and eating habits. Fat-cell theory claims that individuals who are overweight have more fat cells in their bodies. Set-point theory suggests that an internal homeostatic system functions to maintain body weight by adjusting appetite and metabolic rate.

Why is it almost impossible to maintain weight loss by cutting calories alone? p. 384

It is almost impossible to maintain weight loss by cutting calories alone because a dieter's metabolic rate slows down to compensate for the lower intake of calories. Exercise both prevents the lowering of metabolic rate and burns up additional calories.

What are the symptoms of anorexia nervosa and bulimia nervosa? p. 384

The symptoms of anorexia nervosa are an overwhelming, irrational fear of being fat, compulsive dieting to the point of self-starvation, and excessive weight loss. The symptoms of bulimia nervosa are repeated and uncontrolled episodes of binge eating, usually followed by purging.

Social Motives p. 387

What is Murray's contribution to the study of motivation? p. 387

Murray developed the Thematic Apperception Test (TAT) to assess a person's needs and the strength of those needs. He described a motive called the need for achievement (*n* Ach), which is the need to accomplish something difficult and to perform at a high standard of excellence. People high in the need for achievement enjoy challenges and like to compete. They tend to set goals of moderate difficulty, are more motivated by hope of success than fear of failure, and attribute their success to their ability and hard work.

What is work motivation, and how can it be increased? p. 388

Work motivation can be thought of as the conditions and processes responsible for the arousal, direction, magnitude, and maintenance of effort on the job. Two effective techniques for increasing work motivation are reinforcement and goal setting.

The What and Why of Emotions p. 390

What are the three components of emotions? p. 390

The three components of emotions are the physiological arousal that accompanies the emotion, the cognitive appraisal of the stimulus or situation, and the outward behavioral expression of the emotion.

According to the various theories of emotion, what sequence of events occurs when an individual experiences an emotion? p. 390

According to the James-Lange theory of emotion, environmental stimuli produce a physiological response, and then awareness of this response causes the emotion to be experienced. The Cannon-Bard theory suggests that emotion-provoking stimuli received by the senses are relayed simultaneously to the cortex, providing the mental experience of the emotion, and to the sympathetic nervous system, producing physiological arousal. The Schachter-Singer theory states that for an emotion to occur, (1) there must be physiological arousal, and (2) the person must perceive some reason for the arousal in order to label the emotion. According to the Lazarus theory, an emotion-provoking stimulus triggers a cognitive appraisal, which is followed by the emotion and the physiological arousal.

What brain structure processes the emotion of fear? p. 393

The emotion of fear is processed by the amygdala, without initial involvement of the brain's cortex.

What does a polygraph measure? p. 393

A polygraph monitors changes in heart rate, blood pressure, respiration rate, and skin conductance response, which typically accompany emotional arousal.

The Expression of Emotion p. 395

What are basic emotions? p. 395

The basic emotions (happiness, sadness, disgust, and so on) are those that are unlearned and universal and that emerge in children according to their biological timetable of development.

How does the development of facial expressions in infants suggest a biological basis for emotional expression? p. 395

The facial expressions of different emotions develop in a particular sequence in infants and seem to be the result of maturation rather than learning. The same sequence occurs even in children who have been blind and deaf since birth.

What evidence is there to suggest that facial expressions have the same meanings all over the world? p. 396

Charles Darwin first studied the universality of facial expressions because he believed that the ability to read others' emotions was an aid to survival. His research demonstrated that facial expressions are similar across cultures. Later studies confirmed Darwin's findings but also indicated that there is variation across cultures in the ways emotions are elicited and regulated and how they are shared socially.

How do display rules for emotions differ across cultures? p. 396

The customs of an individual's culture determine when, where, and under what circumstances various emotions are exhibited. Children learn these rules as they mature so that, as adults, they will be able to suppress and exhibit emotions in accordance with the rules of their cultures. Violating a culture's display rules can cause a person's behavior to be interpreted as rude or offensive.

Why is emotion considered a form of communication? p. 397

Emotions enable people to communicate desires, intentions, and needs more effectively than just words alone and thus make it more likely that others will respond.

Experiencing Emotion p. 399

How do facial expressions influence internal emotional states? p. 399

The facial-feedback hypothesis suggests that the muscular movements involved in certain facial expressions trigger corresponding emotions (for example, smiling triggers happiness).

In what ways do males and females differ with regard to emotions? p. 400

When exposed to similar stimuli, men and women respond with different emotions. Moreover, emotions such as anger and jealousy are linked to different experiences in males and females. Women may be better than men at interpreting emotions and often serve as the "emotional managers" in relationships. Men process emotion predominately in the left hemisphere of the brain, while women use both cerebral hemispheres.

How does emotion influence thought? p. 401

Emotional states affect memory. Emotions also influence attention and allow us to make rapid assessments of threatening conditions. Fear increases our perceptions of risk, while anger reduces them.

How does Sternberg's triangular theory of love account for the different kinds of love? p. 402

In his triangular theory of love, Sternberg proposes that, singly and in various combinations, three components—intimacy, passion, and commitment—produce seven different kinds of love: liking, infatuated, empty, romantic, fatuous, companionate, and consummate love.

Key Terms

anorexia nervosa, p. 385
arousal theory, p. 376
arousal, p. 376
basic emotions, p. 395
bulimia nervosa, p. 385
Cannon-Bard theory of emotion, p. 391
consummate love, p. 403
display rules, p. 397
drive, p. 376
drive-reduction theory, p. 376
emotion, p. 390
extrinsic motivation, p. 375
facial-feedback hypothesis, p. 399
fat cells, p. 383
homeostasis, p. 376
incentive, p. 375
industrial/organizational (I/O) psychologists, p. 388
instinct theory, p. 376
intrinsic motivation, p. 375
James-Lange theory of emotion, p. 390
lateral hypothalamus (LH), p. 381
Lazarus theory of emotion, p. 392
metabolic rate, p. 383
motivation, p. 375
motives, p. 375
need for achievement (*n* Ach), p. 387
polygraph, p. 393
primary drive, p. 380
Schachter-Singer theory of emotion, p. 391
sensory deprivation, p. 378
set point, p. 384
social motives, p. 387
stimulus motives, p. 377
Thematic Apperception Test (TAT), p. 387
triangular theory of love, p. 402
ventromedial hypothalamus (VMH), p. 381
work motivation, p. 388
Yerkes-Dodson law, p. 377

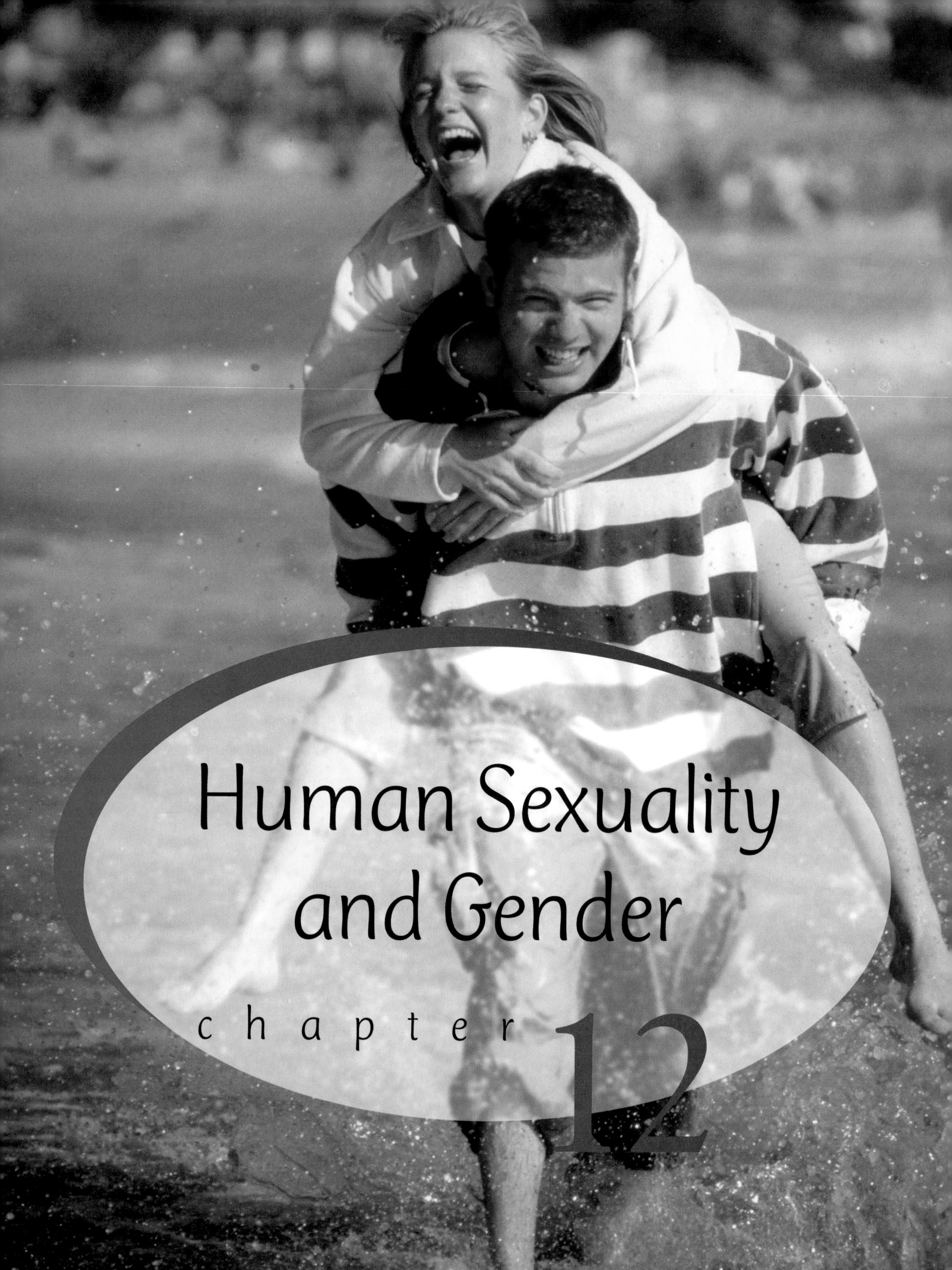

Human Sexuality and Gender

chapter 12

Sex, Gender, and Gender Roles

- *What is the difference between sex and gender?*
- *How do the various theoretical perspectives explain gender role development?*

Gender Differences

- *According to evolutionary psychologists, how do the relative parental investments of men and women shape mating behavior?*
- *For what cognitive abilities have gender differences been proven?*
- *What gender differences are found in social behavior and personality?*
- *Do good adjustment and high self-esteem seem to be related to masculine, feminine, or androgynous traits?*

Sexual Attitudes and Behavior

- *How do sexual attitudes and behaviors vary across cultures, ethnic groups, and genders?*
- *According to Masters and Johnson, what are the phases of the human sexual response cycle?*
- *What are some of the factors that contribute to sexual violence?*

Sexual Orientation

- *What are the various factors that have been suggested as possible determinants of a gay or lesbian sexual orientation?*
- *How have attitudes toward homosexuality changed in recent decades?*

Sexual Dysfunctions

- *What are the defining features of two sexual desire disorders?*
- *What are the defining features of the sexual arousal disorders?*
- *How do orgasmic and sexual pain disorders affect men's and women's sexual experiences?*

Sexually Transmitted Diseases

- *What are the major bacterial sexually transmitted diseases, and how are they treated?*
- *What viral diseases are transmitted through sexual contact?*
- *In what ways can HIV/AIDS affect an individual's physical and psychological health?*
- *What are the most effective methods of protection against sexually transmitted diseases?*

How did you find out about sex?

Alfred Kinsey and his associates did research in the 1940s that brought the subject of sex out into the open in the United States. They interviewed thousands of men and women about their sexual behaviors and attitudes, publishing the results in a two-volume report—*Sexual Behavior in the Human Male* (1948) and *Sexual Behavior in the Human Female* (1953)—which shocked the public. More than half a century later, Kinsey's work continues to be controversial.

When first published, Kinsey's report shattered common ideas about sexuality. For instance, despite the fact that sex outside marriage was widely condemned in those days, Kinsey found that 50% of the females and nearly 90% of the males reported having sexual intercourse before marriage. He also reported that about a quarter of the married women and half of the married men admitted to having had extramarital affairs. Advocates of psychological and cultural approaches to sexuality, such as anthropologist Margaret Mead, criticized Kinsey for taking a strictly biological approach to the subject. Many laypersons were surprised to learn that women and men were equally capable of sexual arousal and orgasm. Although some people attacked Kinsey's work on moral and theoretical grounds, many others—especially women—found it to be enlightening and empowering.

Another important criticism focused on Kinsey's methods. The survey participants were volunteers, mostly college-educated, and from middle-class backgrounds. Kinsey reported no information on African Americans or other minorities. Moreover, most of those who answered the 300 to 500 survey questions were under age 35. Another limitation was that Kinsey's surveys were just that—surveys. Thus, his findings depended largely on the truthfulness of participants.

Despite the limitations of his methods, Alfred Kinsey is credited with having introduced the scientific method into the study of sexuality. Indeed, the publication of his findings served as a catalyst for the thousands of studies of human sexuality that have been done since his name became a household word in the late 1940s. Moreover, the topic of sexuality is discussed more openly now than was true before Kinsey's landmark research findings became known. As these were his primary goals, it is fair to say that he accomplished exactly what he set out to do.

Of course, sex represents only one arena of experience in which gender is relevant. Everyday observations of men and women—and of boys and girls—suggest that the two genders dress differently, are attracted to different leisure and occupational activities, experience emotions differently, and, perhaps, think differently. But are these observations really accurate? Are males and females really as different as we often judge them to be? If so, are these differences "natural," or do they arise from social experiences? As you'll learn in this chapter, psychologists are interested in finding out the relevance and significance of "maleness" and "femaleness" in every area of life.

■ sex chromosomes
The pair of chromosomes that determines the biological sex of a person (XX in females and XY in males).

■ biological sex
Physiological status as male or female.

■ gonads
The sex glands; the ovaries in females and the testes in males.

■ androgens
Male sex hormones.

Sex, Gender, and Gender Roles

Do you use the words *sex* and *gender* interchangeably? Most people do, but the words have different meanings. Generally speaking, *sex* is a biological term, while *gender* is more commonly used to refer to the psychological and social variables associated with one's sex. As you might imagine, there is considerable debate about how the two are related.

Sex and Gender

What is the difference between gender and sex?

As you learned in Chapter 2, the **sex chromosomes**, XX in females and XY in males, determine one's **biological sex**. In the early weeks of prenatal development, the **gonads**, or sex glands, of the male and female fetus are identical. During the 7th week of prenatal development, a single gene found only on the Y chromosome (Capel, 2000) and known as *Sry*, sets in motion the forces that lead to the development of testes in male fetuses (Hanley et al., 2000). If the Sry gene is absent or not functioning, ovaries will develop about 12 weeks after conception (Wertz & Herrmann, 2000). But the story does not end here.

The presence or absence of **androgens,** or male sex hormones, determines whether an embryo develops male or female **genitals,** also called the **primary sex characteristics.** In the male embryo, androgens produced and secreted by the primitive testes cause the male genitals—the penis, testes, and scrotum—to develop. If androgens are not present, female genitals—the ovaries, uterus, and vagina—develop (Breedlove, 1994). A genetic male (XY) can develop female genitals if androgens are absent, and a genetic female (XX) can develop male genitals if an abnormally high level of androgens is present. But androgens affect more than the physical development of the genitals. These hormones also have a tremendous influence on the brain during fetal development, causing the brains of males and females to begin to develop in somewhat different ways (S. Kelly et al., 2000; Lazar, 2000), and they may even affect the immune system (Martin, 2000).

At puberty, the hypothalamus sends a signal to the pituitary gland, which in turn sets in motion the maturing of the genitals and the appearance of the **secondary sex characteristics**. These are the physical characteristics that are associated with sexual maturity but not directly involved in reproduction: pubic and underarm hair in both sexes, breasts in females, and facial and chest hair and a deepened voice in males.

Besides the strictly physiological determinants of sex, each individual has characteristics associated with his or her **gender**—the psychological and sociocultural definition of masculinity or femininity based on the expected behaviors for males and females. Cultures define **gender roles** for the two sexes. For instance, in most cultures, males are expected to be strong, dominant, independent, competitive, assertive, logical, decisive, confident, and unemotional; females are expected to be warm, nurturing, caring, sensitive, supportive, emotional, passive, submissive, and dependent. Children display behavior consistent with their culture's gender roles in their play fairly early in life, by age 2 or so. The process by which individuals acquire the traits, behaviors, attitudes, preferences, and interests that the culture considers appropriate for their biological sex is known as **gender typing.**

■ **genitals**
(JEN-uh-tulz) The internal and external reproductive organs of males or females.

■ **primary sex characteristics**
The internal and external reproductive organs; the genitals.

■ **secondary sex characteristics**
The physical characteristics that appear at puberty and are associated with sexual maturity but not directly involved in reproduction.

■ **gender**
(JEN-der) The psychological and sociocultural definition of masculinity or femininity, based on the expected behaviors for males and females.

■ **gender roles**
Cultural expectations about the behaviors appropriate to each gender.

■ **gender typing**
The process by which individuals acquire the traits, behaviors, attitudes, preferences, and interests that the culture considers appropriate for their biological sex.

Theories of Gender Role Development

How do the various theoretical perspectives explain gender role development?

Psychologists offer a number of explanations for gender role development and gender typing. According to the biological view, the genes and the influence of prenatal sex hormones are important to gender role development, but most developmentalists agree that both biological and environmental factors contribute to the process.

Psychoanalytic theory proposes that gender role development is a largely unconscious process governed by the child's emotions. According to Freud, children's ideas about gender arise out of a conflict concerning their feelings toward their parents. They want to bond to the opposite-sex parent, but fear the jealous reaction of the same-sex parent. To resolve the conflict, they connect to the same-sex parent, adopting his or her gender-related ideas and behavior. At the same time, they defer their love for the opposite-sex parent in the hope that someday they will be able to achieve a sexual relationship with a partner who is similar to him or her. The idea is that the better job they do of becoming like the same-sex parent, the

Gender typing begins early in life, when girls and boys learn to engage in activities that are considered typically female or male.

more likely it is that they will be able to attract a partner who is like the opposite-sex parent (a popular song in the early 20th century was even titled "I Want a Girl Just Like the Girl Who Married Dear Old Dad").

For social learning theorists, environmental influences—parental modeling, stereotypes in the media, and so forth—are more important than biological forces and emotional factors in explaining gender role development (Mischel, 1966). These theorists point out that children are usually reinforced for imitating behaviors considered appropriate for their gender. When behaviors are not appropriate (a boy puts on lipstick, or a girl pretends to shave her face), children are quickly informed, often in a tone of reprimand, that boys or girls do not do that. However, there is little evidence that parents reinforce behavior that is gender-role appropriate often enough to account for the early age at which children begin to exhibit gender typing (Fagot, 1995). Developmental psychologists have found that boys in father-absent homes exhibit the same levels of gender-typed behavior as boys in father-present homes do (Stevens et al., 2002). Thus, imitation and reinforcement probably play some part in gender role development, but they do not provide a full explanation of this phenomenon.

Cognitive developmental theory, proposed by Lawrence Kohlberg (1966; Kohlberg & Ullian, 1974), suggests that an understanding of gender is a prerequisite to gender role development. According to Kohlberg, children go through a series of stages in acquiring the concept of gender. Between ages 2 and 3, children acquire **gender identity,** the sense of being a male or a female. Between ages 4 and 5, children grasp the concept of **gender stability**, awareness that boys are boys and girls are girls for a lifetime. Finally, between ages 6 and 8, children acquire **gender constancy**, the understanding that gender does not change, regardless of the activities people engage in or the clothes they wear. Moreover, according to Kohlberg, when children realize that their gender is permanent, they are motivated to seek out same-sex models and learn to act in ways considered appropriate for that gender.

■ **gender identity**
The sense of being male or female; acquired between ages 2 and 3.

■ **gender stability**
The awareness that gender is a permanent characteristic; acquired between ages 4 and 5.

■ **gender constancy**
The understanding that activities and clothes do not affect gender stability; acquired between ages 6 and 8.

Cross-cultural studies reveal that Kohlberg's stages of gender identity, gender stability, and gender constancy occur in the same order in cultures as different as those in Samoa, Kenya, Nepal, and Belize (Munroe et al., 1984). Moreover, progression through the stages is correlated with other advances in cognitive development (Trautner et al., 2003). However, Kolberg's theory fails to explain why many gender-role appropriate behaviors and preferences are observed in children as young as age 2 or 3, long before gender constancy is acquired (Bussey & Bandura, 1999; Jacklin, 1989; Martin & Little, 1990).

Children are often reinforced for imitating the gender-typed behaviors of adults.

Gender schema theory, proposed by Sandra Bem (1981) provides a more complete explanation of gender-role development. Like social learning theory, gender schema theory suggests that young children are motivated to pay attention to and behave in ways consistent with the gender-based standards and stereotypes of their culture. Like cognitive developmental theory, gender schema theory stresses that children begin to use gender as a way to organize and process information (Bussey & Bandura, 1999). But gender schema theory holds that this process occurs earlier, with the acquisi-

REVIEW and REFLECT 12.1

Theories of Gender Role Development

THEORY	FACTORS PROPOSED TO EXPLAIN GENDER ROLE DEVELOPMENT
Biological approach	Genes, hormones, and other physiological factors
Psychoanalytic theory	Emotional conflicts brought about by attempts to bond with opposite-sex parent
Social learning theory	Role models, imitation, and reinforcement
Cognitive developmental theory	Series of stages necessary to develop concept of gender
Gender schema theory	Acquisition of stereotypes associated with gender labels

Want to be sure you've fully absorbed the material in this chapter? Visit **www.ablongman.com/wood5e** for access to free practice tests, flashcards, interactive activities, and links developed specifically to help you succeed in psychology.

tion of gender identity rather than gender constancy (Bem, 1985). Once gender identity is established, children develop strong preferences for sex-appropriate toys and clothing, and they favor same-sex friends over those of the other sex (Powlishta, 1995). To a large extent, children's self-concept and self-esteem depend on the match between their abilities and behaviors and the cultural definition of what is desirable for their gender. Consequently, the desire to maintain self-esteem, according to gender schema theory, motivates children to align their behavior with culturally defined gender roles.

gender schema theory A theory suggesting that young children are motivated to attend to and behave in ways consistent with gender-based standards and stereotypes of their culture.

The various theoretical explanations of gender role development are summarized in *Review and Reflect 12.1*.

Remember It 12.1

1. The sex chromosomes in a male are __________; while the sex chromosomes in a female are __________.

2. If __________ are not present, female genitals will develop, regardless of whether the sex chromosomes are those of a male or a female.

3. __________ is the process by which individuals acquire the traits, behaviors, attitudes, preferences, and interests that the culture considers gender appropriate.

4. For social learning theorists, __________ influences take precedence over biological and emotional factors in explanations of gender role development.

5. Match each theoretical perspective with its explanation of gender role development.

___ (1) gender schema theory	a. role models and reinforcement
___ (2) biological approaches	b. stages in understanding of gender concepts
___ (3) social learning theory	c. hormones
___ (4) psychoanalytic theory	d. unconscious emotional conflicts
___ (5) cognitive developmental theory	e. gender stereotypes

ANSWERS: 1. XY, XX; 2. androgens; 3. Gender typing; 4. environmental; 5. (1) e, (2) c, (3) a, (4) d, (5) b

Gender Differences

In the discussion of income and education in Chapter 10 (see especially Figure 10.4), you saw that, at every level of education, women's average pay is less than that of men. One reason for the difference is that women are more likely to pursue careers in lower-paying fields, such as nursing and teaching, while men are more frequently found in higher-paying jobs, such as accounting and engineering (Hattiangadi & Habib, 2000). So, even if a man and a woman possess the same educational credentials—a bachelor's degree, for instance—his degree is more likely to qualify him for a high-paying job. (You'll read more about job-related gender issues, including gender discrimination and sexual harassment, in Chapter 18.)

Why do men and women display these different patterns? It has sometimes been argued that women choose professions such as nursing and teaching because of their "natural" ability to nurture others. By contrast, men's attraction to fields involving mathematics and science has been viewed as representing their superior reasoning abilities. But are these stereotypes justified? And if so, what causes these differences?

The Evolutionary and Sociocultural Perspectives on Gender Differences

According to evolutionary psychologists, how do the relative parental investments of men and women shape mating behavior?

Before examining the data on gender differences, let's look at two very different ways of explaining them. Evolutionary psychologists often explain these differences as resulting from the influence of evolution on men's and women's mating behaviors. According to this perspective, a male can maximize the number of copies of his genes by sowing his seed as "wildly" as he can, having sex with as many different women as possible, as often as possible. But a female, as a result of nature's constraints, has a limited number of eggs carrying her genes and a limited window of opportunity during which she can conceive. Further biological restrictions dictate that she spend nearly a year bringing a single pregnancy to term. A male can sire hundreds of offspring during that time.

Evolutionary psychologists use the term **parental investment** to denote the amount of time and effort men or women must devote to parenthood. According to parental investment theory, women and men have adopted mating strategies that correspond to their respective investments in parenting (Buss, 1999, 2000b). Men are assumed to be interested in making only a short-term biological investment in parenting, and so they typically seek women who are young, healthy (physical attractiveness is taken as a sign of good health), and well suited for child bearing. Because parenting requires a greater investment from women (9 months of pregnancy and a long period of dependency), they tend to prefer men who are somewhat older, more stable and with sufficient resources, generous, emotionally attached, and strong enough to provide protection for the family (Buss, 1999). These and related gender differences are apparently not culture-specific, since they have been found in 37 different countries (Buss, 1994).

That is, over time, men and women have developed traits that maximize their chances of attracting a desirable mate. Thus, if evolutionary psychologists are right, men are motivated to enter higher-paying fields because their earning power will help them attract a youthful, fertile female. Women are less concerned than men about the financial rewards associated with a career because earning power is not one of the characteristics men look for in a mate. Women also look for careers that allow them time for child rearing.

■ parental investment
A term used by evolutionary psychologists to denote the amount of time and effort men or women must devote to parenthood.

Other researchers question whether women's reported mate preferences are thoroughly biological in nature. Researchers Eagly and Wood (1999) cite research demonstrating that gender differences in mate preferences are significantly smaller when economic and social conditions for males and females are more equal, as they are becoming in developed countries in the 21st century. In other words, when women are economically dependent on men, the mating "rules" described by evolutionary psychologists may apply; however, gender differences in mate preferences decline as women gain independence. Under conditions of equality, physical attractiveness in a mate would be likely to be just as important to women as to men. And a woman's earning capacity might be more highly valued by men.

Eagly and Wood may be right. Recent research indicates that, in societies with egalitarian attitudes about gender roles, marital status and income are correlated. Longitudinal, prospective research has shown that the higher a woman's economic status, the more likely she is to get married (Ono, 2003). So, today's men may be looking for more in their mates than good looks and child-bearing potential.

Gender Differences in Cognitive Abilities

For what cognitive abilities have gender differences been proven?

There is some evidence that men and women have different intellectual strengths. For example, Figure 12.1 (on page 416) shows some types of problems on which each gender tends to excel. But you need to keep two important points in mind: First, in general, the differences within each gender are greater than the differences between the genders. Second, even though gender differences in cognitive abilities have been generally small on average, there tends to be more variation in such abilities among males than among females (that is, the range of test scores is typically greater for males).

Gender Differences in Verbal Ability Girls as young as 18 months of age have been found to have, on average, larger vocabularies than boys of the same age, a difference that persists throughout childhood (Lutchmaya et al., 2002). In one frequently cited large-scale study, Hedges and Nowell (1995) analyzed the results of the National Assessment of Educational Progress (NAEP), which has tested a nationally representative sample of 70,000 to 100,000 9-, 13-, and 17-year-olds annually in reading comprehension, writing, math, and science. The researchers compared the achievements of the 17-year-olds from 1971 through 1992 and reported that females outperformed males in reading and writing, while males did better in science and math. Although average gender differences were small, there was one prominent exception: "Females performed substantially better than males in writing every year" (p. 44). Furthermore, Hedges and Nowell reported that more males than females were near the bottom of the distribution, not only in writing, but also in reading comprehension.

Gender Differences in Math Achievement As noted above, analyses of NAEP data show that boys display higher levels of achievement in mathematics than girls. Some data indicate that hormonal differences between males and females contribute to the math achievement gender gap (Josephs et al., 2003). However, most researchers agree that social influences are probably more important.

One possible social factor influencing the difference in math achievement is that parents often expect boys to do better than girls in math (Tiedemann, 2000). Could parental expectations become a self-fulfilling prophecy, leading girls to lack confidence in their math ability and to decide not to pursue advanced math courses? Yes, says sex difference researcher Jacqueline Eccles. Eccles's longitudinal research has shown that parents' beliefs about their children's talents at age 6 predict those children's beliefs about their own abilities at age 17 (Fredricks & Eccles, 2002). However, Eccles's research has also revealed that the gender gap in beliefs about math ability is

FIGURE 12.1 Problem-Solving Tasks Favoring Women and Men

(a) A series of problem-solving tasks on which women generally do better than men.
(b) Problem-solving tasks on which men do better.
Source: Kimura (1992).

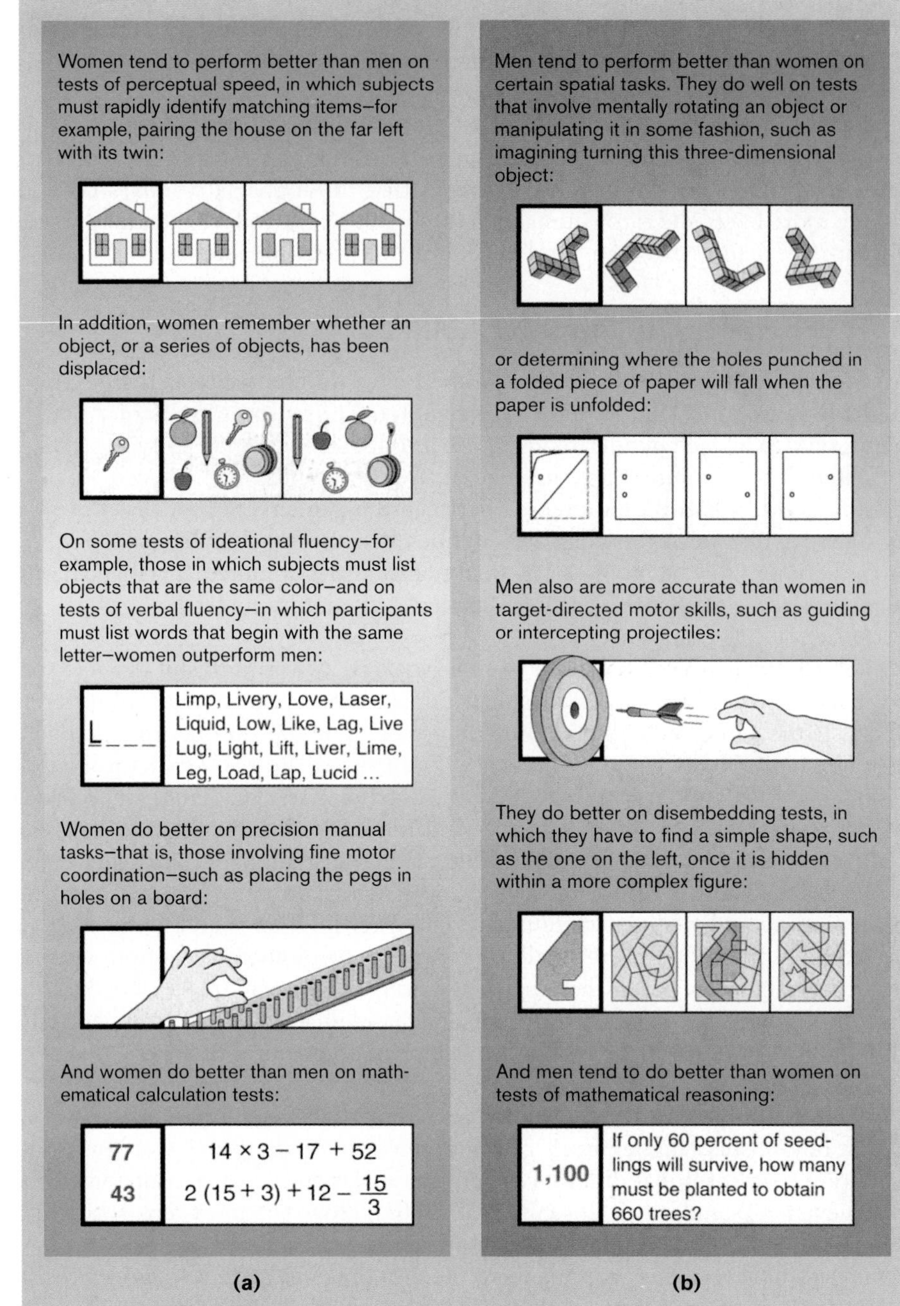

somewhat smaller among today's high school students than it was in the past, suggesting that educators' efforts to increase girls' interest and success in mathematics have been effective.

Women tend to perform better than men on tests of perceptual speed, in which subjects must rapidly identify matching items–for example, pairing the house on the far left with its twin:
In addition, women remember whether an object, or a series of objects, has been displaced:
On some tests of ideational fluency–for example, those in which subjects must list objects that are the same color–and on tests of verbal fluency–in which participants must list words that begin with the same letter–women outperform men:
L - - -
Limp, Livery, Love, Laser, Liquid, Low, Like, Lag, Live Lug, Light, Lift, Liver, Lime, Leg, Load, Lap, Lucid ...
Women do better on precision manual tasks–that is, those involving fine motor coordination–such as placing the pegs in holes on a board:
And women do better than men on mathematical calculation tests:
77
43
14 × 3 − 17 + 52
2 (15 + 3) + 12 − 15/3
(a)
Men tend to perform better than women on certain spatial tasks. They do well on tests that involve mentally rotating an object or manipulating it in some fashion, such as imagining turning this three-dimensional object:
or determining where the holes punched in a folded piece of paper will fall when the paper is unfolded:
Men also are more accurate than women in target-directed motor skills, such as guiding or intercepting projectiles:
They do better on disembedding tests, in which they have to find a simple shape, such as the one on the left, once it is hidden within a more complex figure:
And men tend to do better than women on tests of mathematical reasoning:
1,100
If only 60 percent of seedlings will survive, how many must be planted to obtain 660 trees?
(b)

Another way in which parents influence boys' and girls' ideas about math competence is their tendency to see academically successful girls as "hard workers" and academically successful boys as "talented" (Ratty et al., 2002). Thus, parents' beliefs may help explain why teenage girls who obtain top scores on standardized mathematics tests typically explain their scores as resulting from effort, while their male peers believe that their scores are due to superior natural mathematical talent (Rebs & Park, 2001). Thus, even girls with extraordinary levels of mathematical achievement may see themselves as lacking in ability. Perhaps it isn't surprising that mathematically gifted girls are far less likely than similarly gifted boys to choose math-oriented careers (Webb et al., 2002).

Gender Differences in Spatial Ability Researchers have found that, in general, males tend to perform somewhat better than females on some, but not all, spatial tasks (Geary, 1996; Kimura, 1992, 2000). Some research has shown that spatial abilities appear to be enhanced by prenatal exposure to high levels of androgens (Berenbaum et al., 1995). Further, high blood levels of testosterone in men are associated with good performance on spatial tasks such as route learning (Choi & Silverman, 2002). However, these findings do not minimize the role of social experiences and expectations in shaping children's abilities and interests. Further, women outperform men on some kinds of spatial tasks.

Gender Differences in Social Behavior and Personality

What gender differences are found in social behavior and personality?

You may already be familiar with one important gender difference in social behavior: Most researchers agree that greater physical aggression in males is one of the most consistent and significant gender differences. However, females are aggressive, just in a different way: Girls and women are more likely than their male peers to use indirect forms of aggression, such as gossip, spreading rumors, and rejecting, ignoring, or avoiding the target of aggression (Björkqvist et al., 1992). Thus, it isn't true to say that males are aggressive, and females aren't.

Females appear to have strengths in the area of communication. Researchers have consistently found that, compared to men, women appear to be more attuned to others'

Boys show higher levels of physical aggression, but girls tend to use indirect forms of aggression, such as gossiping about and rejecting others.

verbal and nonverbal expressions of feelings and less reluctant to discuss their personal experiences and reveal their own feelings (Dindia & Allen, 1992). Some evidence suggests that females tend to be relatively more people-oriented, while males are relatively more object-oriented. And this gender difference appears to hold across the lifespan (McGuinness, 1993). As this hypothesis would predict, women consistently outperform men on tasks involving facial recognition (Lewin & Herlitz, 2002).

As children, from the time they enter school, males are more likely to dominate classroom discussions (Sadker & Sadker, 1994). Boys also tend to favor competitive activities and situations, while girls are more likely to prefer cooperative ones (Geary, 1996). Males are more apt to thrive and females to suffer when exposed to highly competitive school or work environments (Hoyenga & Hoyenga, 1993).

Adjustment and Gender Typing

Do good adjustment and high self-esteem seem to be related to masculine, feminine, or androgynous traits?

Traditionally, masculinity and femininity have been considered to represent opposite ends of a continuum. But are masculine traits and feminine traits mutually exclusive? Must an individual be either independent, competent, and assertive or nurturing, sensitive, and warm? Sandra Bem (1974, 1977, 1985) proposed that "masculine" and "feminine" characteristics are separate and independent dimensions of personality rather than being at opposite ends of a continuum. A person can be high or low on one or both dimensions. People who are low on both masculine and feminine characteristics are labeled *undifferentiated*. **Androgyny** is a combination of desirable masculine and feminine characteristics in one person, who is said to be *androgynous*.

Some researchers claim that androgynous individuals are better equipped to meet the challenges of the work world and to succeed in personal relationships (Bem, 1975). But research suggests that for both males and females, masculine traits are most strongly associated with self-esteem, adjustment, creativity, and mental health (Aubé & Koestner, 1992; Hittner & Daniels, 2002; Moeller-Leimkuehler et al., 2002). To the extent that androgynous people possess the desired masculine traits, they are likely to be better adjusted and have higher self-esteem than people who are feminine or undifferentiated. Moreover, androgynous men are more likely to help their female partners with domestic tasks such as housework and child care (Gana et al., 2001).

■ **androgyny** (an-DROJ-uh-nee) A combination of desirable masculine and feminine characteristics in one person.

Remember It 12.2

1. According to evolutionary psychologists, men and women employ different mating strategies because they differ in __________.
2. For each cognitive ability, indicate whether males or females, in general, tend to score higher on tests of that ability.
   ___ (1) writing a. males
   ___ (2) science b. females
   ___ (3) spatial ability
   ___ (4) reading comprehension
   ___ (5) mathematics
3. Physical aggression is more common among __________.

ANSWERS: 1. parental investment; 2. (1) b, (2) a, (3) a, (4) b, (5) a; 3. males

Sexual Attitudes and Behavior

You learned at the start of this chapter that Alfred Kinsey's research opened the door to the scientific study of sexuality. Since his work was published, research examining this important part of life has proliferated. As a result, we know far more about sexual attitudes and behavior today than in the past.

Gender and Cultural Differences

How do sexual attitudes and behaviors vary across cultures, ethnic groups, and genders?

Do you think men and women have different ideas about sex? You may be interested to learn about classic research examining the "closing time effect" (Pennebaker et al., 1979). In studies involving bar patrons, researchers found that both men's and women's judgments of the attractiveness and desirability of opposite-sex patrons increased as closing time approached. However, men's ratings rose more than those of women. Interestingly, later studies demonstrated no relationship between the consumption of alcohol and the closing time effect (e.g., Gladue & Delaney, 1990). Subsequent research also suggested that judgments of the attractiveness of female patrons do not change as closing time approaches among men who are already in a relationship (Madey et al., 1996). These findings provide support for the hypothesis that availability of a sexual partner can drive attractiveness judgments. Evolutionary psychologists say that men focus on availability because, as noted earlier, they are primarily interested in maximizing reproductive opportunities in the short term (Buss, 1999). Women, by contrast, are interested in establishing long-term relationships that are in their, and their children's, best interests (Buss, 1999).

Of course, many men are interested in a long-term relationship, and many women are looking only for casual sex. However, research does show that, on average, men are more interested in sex and think about it more often than women do (Peplau, 2003). And they are more likely than women to be interested in purely physical sex and to have more permissive attitudes toward sex (Baldwin & Baldwin, 1997; Dantzker & Eisenman, 2003). A study of first-year college students illustrates this difference quite well (Cohen & Shotland, 1996). These researchers found that the male students expected sexual intercourse to become part of a dating relationship far sooner than the female students did. Nearly all of the men in the study expressed a willingness to have sex on a basis of physical attraction only, with no emotional involvement; fewer than two-thirds of the women were willing to do so. Approximately 30% of the men but only 5% of the women admitted to having had sex with someone they were neither attracted to nor emotionally involved with.

Sexual attitudes and behaviors differ across cultural groups as well as across gender. As you can see in Figure 12.2 (on page 420), surveys reveal that rates of sexual activity vary widely around the world (Durex Global Sex Survey, 2002). Ethnic groups in the United States also show varying rates of sexual activity. According to Sprecher and Hatfield (1996), African American college students tend to have more permissive premarital sexual standards than White American college students do, while their Mexican American peers have more conservative attitudes than either of these groups.

■ **coitus**
(KOY-tus) Penile-vaginal intercourse.

Sexual Desire and Arousal

According to Masters and Johnson, what are the phases of the human sexual response cycle?

Although, for most people, intimate relationships are not restricted to the physical realm, the physiological aspects of sex are critical to its enjoyment. In 1954, Dr. William Masters and Dr. Virginia Johnson conducted the first laboratory investigations of the human sexual response and its culmination in **coitus** (penile-vaginal intercourse). They monitored volunteer participants, who engaged in sex while connected

FIGURE 12.2 Frequency of Sexual Intercourse around the World

Results of an international survey conducted by the Durex Corporation, a manufacturer of condoms, shows that the frequency of intercourse varies from country to country. *Source:* Durex Global Sex Survey (2002).

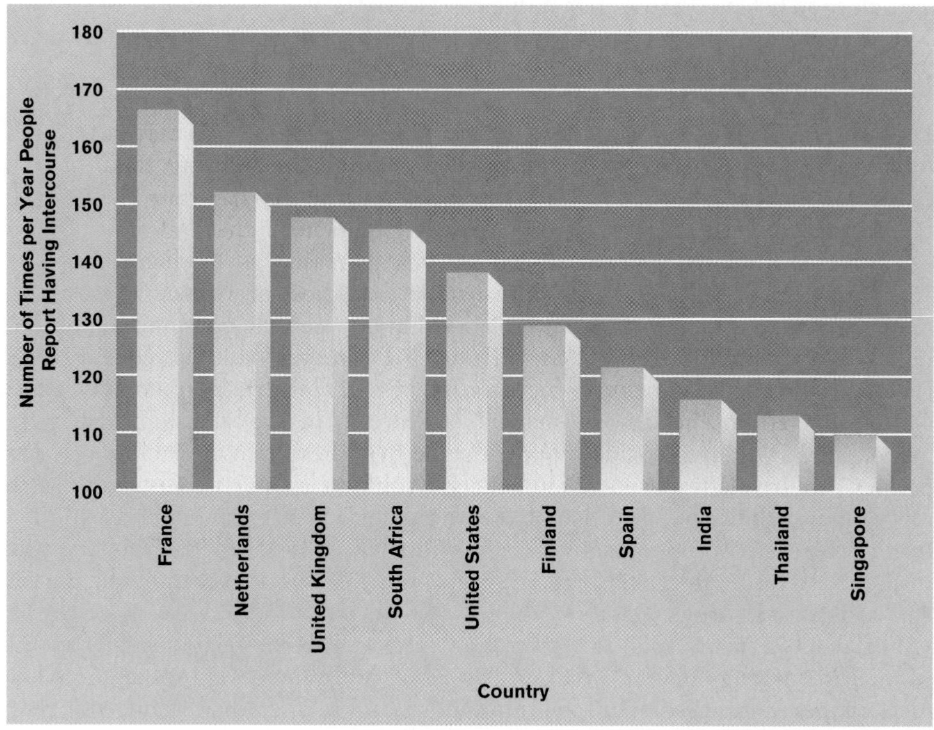

■ **sexual response cycle**
According to Masters and Johnson, the typical pattern of the human sexual response in both males and females, consisting of four phases: excitement, plateau, orgasm, and resolution.

■ **excitement phase**
The first stage of the sexual response cycle, characterized by an erection in males and a swelling of the clitoris and vaginal lubrication in females.

■ **plateau phase**
The second stage of the sexual response cycle, during which muscle tension and blood flow to the genitals increase in preparation for orgasm.

■ **orgasm**
The third stage of the sexual response cycle, marked by a sudden discharge of accumulated sexual tension and involuntary muscle contractions.

to electronic sensing devices. Masters and Johnson (1966) concluded that both males and females experience a **sexual response cycle** with four phases (see Figure 12.3).

The **excitement phase** is the beginning of the sexual response cycle. Visual cues like watching a partner undress are more likely to initiate the excitement phase in men than in women. Tender, loving touches coupled with verbal expressions of love arouse women more readily than visual stimulation. And men can become aroused almost instantly, while arousal for women may be a more gradual, building process. For both partners, muscular tension increases, heart rate quickens, and blood pressure rises. As additional blood is pumped into the genitals, the male's penis becomes erect, and the female feels a swelling of the clitoris. Vaginal lubrication occurs as the inner two-thirds of the vagina expands and its inner lips enlarge. In women, especially, the nipples harden and stand erect.

After the excitement phase, the individual enters the **plateau phase**, when excitement builds steadily. Blood pressure and muscle tension increase still more, and breathing becomes heavy and more rapid. The man's testes swell, and drops of liquid, which could contain live sperm cells, may drip from the penis. The outer part of the woman's vagina swells as the increased blood further engorges the area in preparation for orgasm. The clitoris withdraws under the clitoral hood, its skin covering, and the breasts become engorged with blood.

The **orgasm**, the shortest of the phases, is the highest point of sexual pleasure, marked by a sudden discharge of accumulated sexual tension. Involuntary muscle contractions may seize the entire body during orgasm, and the genitals contract rhythmically. Orgasm is a two-stage experience for the male. In the first stage, he is aware that

FIGURE 12.3 **The Sexual Response Cycle**

Masters and Johnson found that the components of sexual response occur in a predictable sequence in both males and females.

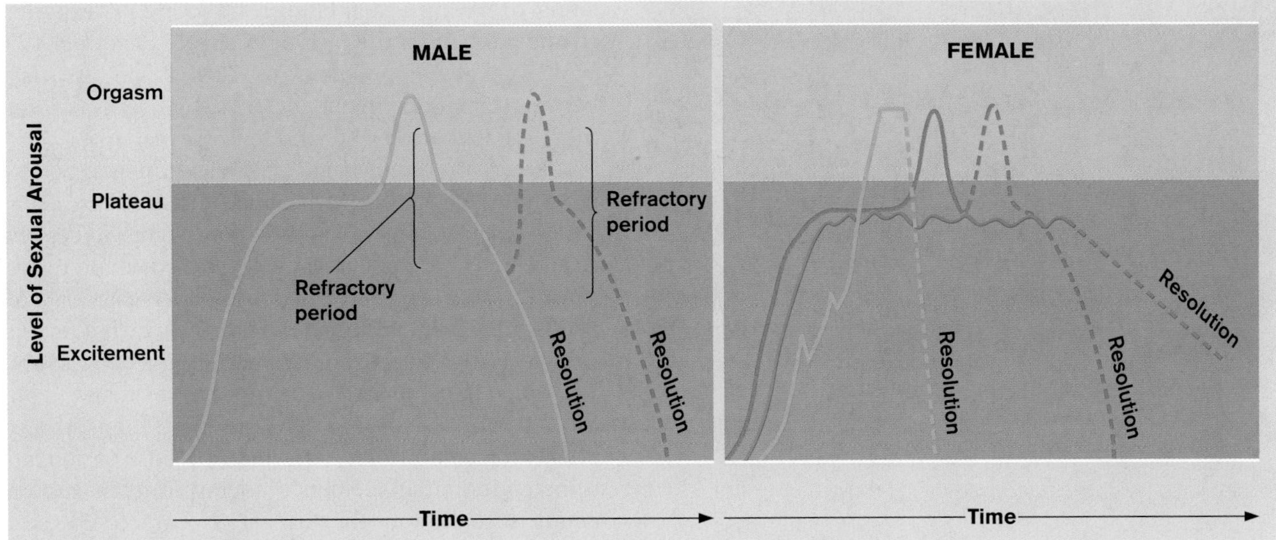

ejaculation is near and that he can do nothing to stop it; the second stage consists of the ejaculation itself, when semen is released from the penis in forceful spurts. The experience of orgasm in women builds in much the same way as for men. Marked by powerful, rhythmic contractions, the female's orgasm usually lasts longer than that of the male.

The orgasm gives way to the **resolution phase**, a tapering-off period, when the body returns to its unaroused state. Men experience a refractory period in the resolution phase, during which they cannot have another orgasm. The refractory period may last from only a few minutes for some men to as much as several hours for others. Women do not have a refractory period and may, if restimulated, experience another orgasm right away.

The sexual response cycle is strongly influenced by hormones. The sex glands manufacture hormones—estrogen and progesterone in the ovaries, and androgens in the testes. The adrenal glands in both sexes also produce small amounts of these hormones. **Estrogen** promotes the secondary sex characteristics in females and controls the menstrual cycle; **progesterone** aids in the regulation of the menstrual cycle and prepares the lining of the uterus for pregnancy. Females have considerably more estrogen and progesterone than males do, so these are known as the female sex hormones. Males have considerably more androgens, the male sex hormones.

Testosterone, the most important androgen, influences the development and maintenance of male sex characteristics as well as sexual motivation. Males must have a sufficient level of testosterone in order to maintain sexual interest and have an erection. Females, too, need small amounts of testosterone in the bloodstream to maintain sexual interest and responsiveness (Anderson & Cyranowski, 1995). Deficiencies in sexual interest and activity can sometimes be reversed in men or women with the use of testosterone patches or ointments (Meyer, 1997).

Psychological factors play a large role in sexual arousal. Part of the psychological nature of sexual behavior stems from the preferences and practices people learn from their culture. And cultural norms for sexual behavior vary widely, covering everything from the age at which initiation of sexual behavior is proper to the partners, conditions, settings, positions, and specific sexual acts that are considered acceptable. Moreover, what is perceived as sexually attractive in males and females may differ dramatically from culture to culture.

resolution phase
The final stage of the sexual response cycle, during which the body returns to an unaroused state.

estrogen
(ES-truh-jen) A female sex hormone that promotes the secondary sex characteristics in females and controls the menstrual cycle.

progesterone
(pro-JES-tah-rone) A female sex hormone that plays a role in the regulation of the menstrual cycle and prepares the lining of the uterus for pregnancy.

testosterone
(tes-TOS-tah-rone) The most important androgen, which influences the development and maintenance of male sex characteristics and sexual motivation and, in small amounts, maintains sexual interest and responsiveness in females.

Psychological factors play an important role in sexual attraction and arousal. Such factors involve preferences and attitudes we learn from our culture.

Sexual fantasies also influence sexual arousal. Men's fantasies generally involve more specific visual imagery, while women's fantasies have more emotional and romantic content. Although 95% of males and females admit to having sexual fantasies, about 25% experience strong guilt about them (Leitenberg & Henning, 1995). However, research seems to suggest an association between a higher incidence of sexual fantasies and a more satisfactory sex life and fewer sexual problems.

External stimuli, such as images in magazines or movies, can also influence arousal. Men are more likely to seek out such sources of stimulation. Some studies reveal that people may come to value their partner and relationship less after exposure to erotic sexual material. Also, people may feel disappointed with their own sexual performance after comparing it to performances by actors.

Of course, there is much more to sex than the physical response. According to Masters and Johnson, a couple's "total commitment, in which all sense of obligation is linked to mutual feelings of loving concern, sustains a couple sexually over the years" (1975, p. 268). Research supports this assertion: Both men and women experience greater sexual satisfaction in relationships that are emotionally satisfying and supportive (Greeff & Malherbe, 2001; Waite & Joyner, 2001).

What are some of the factors that contribute to sexual violence?

Sexual Violence

Unfortunately, not all sex occurs within the context of a loving relationship. **Sexual violence** is any kind of sexual contact in which one or more participants are either unable to give consent or are forced into participation (National Center for Injury Prevention and Control [NCIPC], 2002). Clearly, this definition is very broad and includes a number of different kinds of sexual contact, including the following:

- *Sexual assault*—forcing or coercing another person into engaging in any kind of sexual activity
- *Rape*—sexual assault that includes penetration
- *Date/acquaintance rape*—rape that occurs in the context of a social relationship
- *Sexual abuse*—sexual assault directed toward a vulnerable individual (e.g., a child or elderly person)

Sexual Violence against Women Women are far more likely than men to be victimized by sexual violence (Murphy, 2003). In the United States, about 28% of women, compared to 8% of men, have experienced some type of sexual violence by the time they reach college age (NCIPC, 2000). Surveys of older women show that about 40% have been victims of sexual violence. In most cases, the perpetrator is a current or former intimate partner. In the United States, rates of sexual violence involving an intimate partner are among the highest in the world, as you can see in Figure 12.4.

When statistical analyses are narrowed to include only rape, hospital emergency room records and police reports show an annual prevalence rate for rape in the United States of about 70 rapes per 100,000 women (NCIPC, 2000). However, national surveys indicate that more than 80% of rapes are never reported to the police. Thus, the true prevalence of rape is difficult to determine. In more than 90% of reported rapes, the perpetrator is a friend, acquaintance, or intimate partner of the victim (NCIPC, 2000).

■ **sexual violence**
Any kind of sexual contact in which one or more participants are either unable to give consent or are forced into participation.

FIGURE 12.4 Percentages of Women Who Have Been Sexually Victimized by an Intimate Partner

A fairly large percentage of women all over the world have experienced sexual violence within an intimate relationship. But percentages are much higher in some countries than in others, presumably because of differences in cultural factors, such as the economic status of women.

Sources: Basile (2002); WHO (2002).

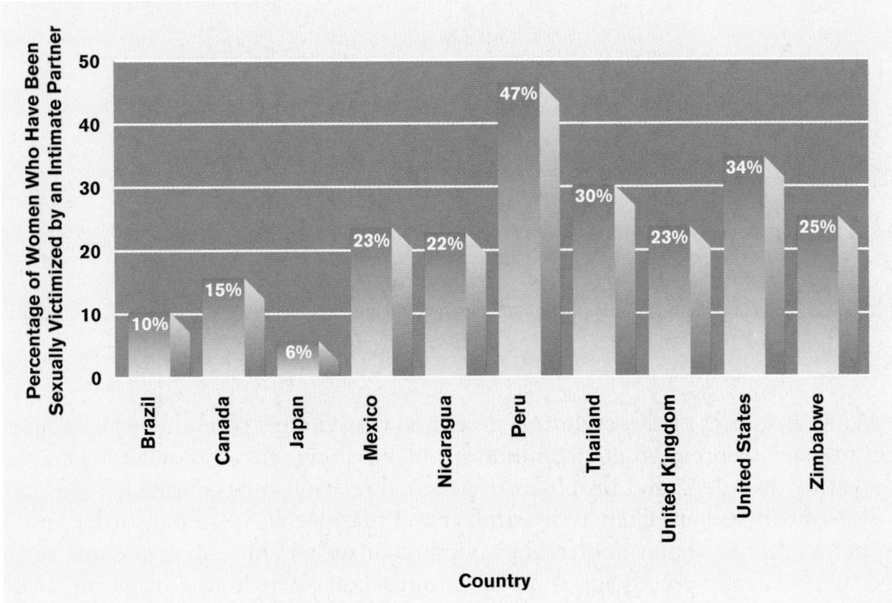

Interestingly, the World Health Organization reports that the factors contributing to sexual violence against women are similar throughout the world (WHO, 2002a). In addition to these factors, shown in Table 12.1 (on page 424), some other individual characteristics are associated with sexual violence. For example, rapists are less able to empathize with their victims than are perpetrators of other kinds of crimes, a deficit that may arise from their own sexual victimization experiences in childhood (Fernandez & Marshall, 2003; Simons et al., 2002). Moreover, sex offenders are more likely than other criminal offenders to believe that men should be dominant over women (Murnen et al., 2002).

The consequences of rape can include pregnancy (4% of victims), sexually transmitted disease (3.5% of victims), and physical injury (3% of victims). Moreover, rape victims, as well as victims of other kinds of sexual violence, often experience long-term emotional problems, including depression and posttraumatic stress disorder (NCIPC, 2000). Victims of all types of sexual violence are more likely than nonvictimized peers to tell researchers that they do not enjoy sex (Maitra & Schensul, 2002).

Sexual Abuse of Children To many people, sexual abuse of children is the worst type of sexual violence. Unfortunately, it is all too common. In the United States, more than 100,000 cases of child sexual abuse are reported to authorities each year (NCIPC, 2002). Experts estimate that about 17% of women and 8% of men were sexually abused as children (Putnam, 2003). According to the World Health Organization, girls under the age of 15 are sexually assaulted more often than adult women in most countries (WHO, 2002b). In the United States, about 60% of sexual assault victims are females under age 15, and 29% are under age 10.

TABLE 12.1 Factors Contributing to Sexual Violence against Women

AMONG PERPETRATORS	AMONG VICTIMS
History of early sexual contact or victimization	Reluctance to report sexual violence to authorities
Extreme views about sex-role stereotypes	Nonforceful verbal resistance of unwanted advances
Hostility toward women	Extreme views about sex-role stereotypes
Fantasies about sexual violence	Acceptance of rape myths
Involvement with pornography	Poverty
Association with sexually aggressive peers	Alcohol and/or drug use
Acceptance of rape myths (e.g., women enjoy being raped)	
Poverty	
Alcohol and/or drug use	

Sources: NCIPC (2000); WHO (2002b).

What are some of the enduring problems that victims of child sexual abuse are likely to face? Depression is a common problem, along with low self-esteem, anger, guilt, eating disorders, and problems in personal relationships (Putnam, 2003). Sexually abused children are likely to live in fear and to experience sleep disorders and loss of appetite. As they enter adolescence, victims of sexual abuse may become sexually active at a relatively young age and even promiscuous, may abuse drugs and alcohol, and may have suicidal thoughts and tendencies. Some become delinquent or run away to escape their abusive environment (Kendall-Tackett et al., 1993).

Some researchers have suggested that a tendency toward *pedophilia* (a preference for children as sexual partners) may be the result of hypersexuality due to a brain disorder, especially in the front part of the right frontal or temporal lobe (Burns & Swerdlow, 2003); Mendez et al., 2000). Therapies to treat those who sexually abuse children are likely to focus on deviant sexual fantasies, which are believed to serve as "triggers," pushing the abuser to act (Swaffer et al., 2000).

Remember It 12.3

1. __________ tend to have more permissive attitudes toward premarital sex than __________ do.
2. The human sexual response cycle consists of __________ phases.
3. With regard to the sexual response cycle, the most important sex hormone in both men and women is __________.
4. Match each type of sexual violence with its definitions.

   ___ (1) sexual assault
   ___ (2) rape
   ___ (3) sexual abuse
   ___ (4) date/acquaintance rape

   a. sexual assault with penetration
   b. any type of forced or coerced sexual contact
   c. forced or coerced sexual contact within the context of a social relationship
   d. sexual contact with a vulnerable person who is unable to give consent

ANSWERS: 1. Men, women; 2. four; 3. testosterone; 4. (1) b, (2) a, (3) d, (4) c

Sexual Orientation

So far, we have discussed many aspects of human sexual response and sexual arousal, but we have not considered **sexual orientation**—the direction of an individual's sexual preference, erotic feelings, and sexual activity. In heterosexuals, the human sexual response is oriented toward members of the opposite sex; in homosexuals, toward those of the same sex; and in bisexuals, toward members of both sexes.

Homosexuality has been reported in all societies throughout recorded history (Carrier, 1980; Ford & Beach, 1951). Kinsey and his associates (1948, 1953) estimated that 4% of their male respondents had had exclusively homosexual relations throughout life, and about 2–3% of their female participants had been in mostly or exclusively lesbian relationships. In what is said to be the most definitive and reliable sex survey to date, Laumann and others (1994) reported that the percentages of people who identified themselves as homosexual or bisexual were 2.8% of men and 1.4% of women. But 5.3% of men and 3.5% of women said that they had had a sexual experience with a person of the same sex at least once since puberty. And even larger percentages of those surveyed—10% of males and 9% of females—said that they had felt some same-sex desires.

In 1988, actor Ian McKellen ("Gandalf" in the *Lord of the Rings* films) became one of the first well-known British actors to reveal his homosexual orientation. Despite warnings that the revelation would ruin his career, McKellen has received numerous honors and awards since then—including being knighted by Queen Elizabeth II in 1991.

However, other surveys suggest that a completely accurate measure of the prevalence of homosexuality may still be lacking. For one thing, a truly exclusive homosexual orientation appears to be rare. For example, Sell and his colleagues (1995) reanalyzed the results of an 1988 Harris Poll to include both homosexual attraction and behavior. They found that 6% of the male and 3–4% of the female respondents identified themselves as predominantly homosexual in both attraction and behavior. However, only 1% of these poll respondents claimed to have had no sexual contact whatever with members of the opposite sex in the previous 5 years.

Moreover, demographic studies indicate that homosexuality is not equally prevalent in all ethnic groups or in all locales. College-educated White American men who live in large cities are more likely to identify themselves as homosexual than are men in other groups. Some studies suggest that the prevalence of homosexuality among such men may be as high as 14% (Binson et al., 1995). Notably, though, almost all prevalence studies suggest that homosexuality is twice as common in males as in females.

Determinants of Sexual Orientation

What are the various factors that have been suggested as possible determinants of a gay or lesbian sexual orientation?

Psychologists continue to debate whether sexual orientation is biologically fixed or acquired through learning and experience. Although Freud argued that homosexuality results from early childhood experiences (Mitchell, 2002), many psychologists believe that biological factors largely determine sexual orientation (Bailey & Pillard, 1994; Isay, 1989; LeVay, 1993). Still others lean toward an interaction theory, which holds that both nature and nurture play a part (Breedlove, 1994; Byne, 1994; Patterson, 1995). Could hormones play a role?

Some have suggested that abnormal levels of androgens during prenatal development, or at any other time in development, might influence sexual orientation (Collaer & Hines, 1995; McFadden, 2002). Too high or too low a level of androgens at critical periods of brain development might masculinize or feminize the brain of the developing fetus, making a homosexual orientation more likely (Berenbaum & Snyder, 1995). A few studies have revealed an increase in the incidence of lesbianism among females who had been exposed prenatally to synthetic estrogen (Meyer-Bahlburg et al., 1995) or to an excess of androgens (Ehrhardt et al., 1968; Money & Schwartz, 1977).

■ **sexual orientation**
The direction of one's sexual preference, erotic feelings, and sexual activity—toward members of the opposite sex (heterosexuality), toward one's own sex (homosexuality), or toward both sexes (bisexuality).

Sexual Orientation and the Brain Neuroscientist Simon LeVay (1991) reported that an area in the hypothalamus governing sexual behavior is about twice as large in heterosexual men as in homosexual men. This part of the hypothalamus, no larger than a grain of sand, is about the same size in heterosexual females as in homosexual males. LeVay admits that his research offers no direct evidence that the brain differences he found cause homosexuality (LeVay & Hamer, 1994), and critics were quick to point out that all of the gay men included in his research sample died of AIDS. It is known that AIDS is associated with abnormalities in certain brain areas. Therefore, some researchers questioned whether the brain differences LeVay observed might have resulted from AIDS, rather than being associated with sexual orientation (Byne, 1993b). Others have suggested that the brain differences could be the cause or the consequence of variables as yet unidentified that may interact with the brain in determining sexual orientation.

Swaab and Hofman (1995) contend that structural differences in the hypothalamus might be related to sexual orientation and that sexual differentiation of the hypothalamus takes place between about 4 years of age and puberty. However, the researchers caution that these observations await further confirmation and that their exact functional implications are not yet understood. Bailey and Zucker (1995) maintain that empirical evidence supports the notion that "childhood sex-typed behavior and sexual orientation are subject to similar hormonal influences (whether or not they are affected by the same brain structures)" (p. 50).

Researchers looking for a genetic contribution to sexual orientation suggest that a number of "feminizing" genes work together to shift male brain development in the female direction (Miller, 2000). If only a few of these feminizing genes are active, males who inherit them tend to be more gentle and sensitive. But if many such genes are active during development, their effect probably contributes to homosexuality. Moreover, a similar effect may occur with other genes, resulting in lesbianism in females (Miller, 2000). In earlier research on the influence of heredity on sexual orientation, Bailey and Pillard (1991) studied gay males who had twin brothers. They found that 52% of the gay identical twins and 22% of the gay fraternal twins had a gay twin brother. Among adoptive brothers of the gay twins, however, only 11% shared a homosexual orientation. In a similar study, Whitam and others (1993) found that 66% of the identical twins and 30% of the fraternal twins of gay males studied were also gay. Such studies indicate a substantial genetic influence on sexual orientation, but suggest that nongenetic influences are at work as well.

According to Bailey and Benishay (1993), "female homosexuality appears to run in families" (p. 277). They found that 12.1% of their lesbian participants had a sister who was also lesbian, compared with 2.3% of heterosexual female participants. Bailey and others (1993) report that in a study of lesbians, 48% of their identical twins, 16% of their fraternal twins, 14% of their nontwin biological sisters, and 6% of their adopted sisters were also lesbian. Bailey and Pillard (1994) claim that, according to their statistical analysis, the heritability of sexual orientation is about 50%.

Hamer and others (1993) found that brothers of gay participants had a 13.5% chance of also being gay. Furthermore, male relatives on the mother's side of the family, but not on the father's side, had a significantly higher rate of homosexuality. This led the researchers to suspect that a gene influencing sexual orientation might be located on the X chromosome, the sex chromosome contributed by the mother. After studying the DNA on the X chromosomes of 40 pairs of gay brothers, the researchers found that 33 of the pairs carried matching genetic information on the end tip of the X chromosome. However, no particular gene has been singled out among the several hundred genes carried on that end tip. And precisely how the gene might influence sexual orientation is not known (LeVay & Hamer, 1994; Rahman & Wilson, 2003). Some researchers have questioned the validity of Hamer's findings, and a colleague has charged that Hamer excluded from the study some pairs of brothers whose sexual orientations contradicted his findings (Horgan, 1995).

Do the findings of LeVay, Bailey and Pillard, and Hamer and others provide convincing evidence that sexual orientation is biologically determined? Some researchers (Byne, 1993a; Byne & Parsons, 1993, 1994) maintain that, in the absence of studies of identical twins reared apart, the influence of environment cannot be ruled out as the cause of a higher incidence of homosexuality in certain families. Furthermore, they suggest that if one or more genes are involved, they may not be genes directly influencing sexual orientation. Rather, they could be genes affecting personality or temperament, which could influence how people react to environmental stimuli (Byne, 1994). Let's explore early environmental influences.

Childhood Experiences of Gay Men and Lesbians What evidence is there that homosexuality is linked to some kind of formative experience in childhood? In classic research examining this question, Alan P. Bell, Martin Weinberg, and Sue Kiefer Hammersmith (1981) conducted extensive face-to-face interviews with 979 homosexual participants (293 women, 686 men) and 477 heterosexual controls. The researchers found no single condition of family life or childhood experience that in and of itself appeared to be a factor in either homosexual or heterosexual development. But, as children, the homosexuals they interviewed did not feel that they were like others of their sex.

Using meta-analysis, Bailey and Zucker (1995) found that cross-gender behavior exhibited in early childhood could be a predictor of homosexuality for both females and males. In one study, Bailey and others (1995) found a strong association between sexual orientation and sex-typed behavior in childhood, as recalled by both gay men and their mothers. However, some gay men exhibited masculine sex-typed behavior, and some heterosexual men were "feminine" boys. In another study, Phillips and Over (1995) found that lesbian women were more likely to recall imagining themselves as males, preferring boy's games and being called "tomboys." Yet, some heterosexual women recalled childhood experiences similar to those of the majority of lesbians, and some lesbians recalled experiences more like those of the majority of heterosexual women.

■ **homophobia**
An intense, irrational hostility toward or fear of homosexuals.

Clearly, there are no certain predictors of homosexuality. And so, researchers continue to disagree on the genesis of sexual orientation. Psychologist Charlotte Patterson (1995) suggests that the relationship between sexual orientation and human development can be studied more profitably as a complex interaction of nature and nurture.

How have attitudes toward homosexuality changed in recent decades?

Social Attitudes toward Gays and Lesbians

The American Psychiatric Association considered homosexuality a disorder until 1973, but now views it as such only if the individual considers it a problem. Thanks to such changes, more gay men and lesbians are "coming out," preferring to acknowledge and express their sexual orientation. Such individuals appear to be as healthy psychologically as heterosexuals (Strickland, 1995).

Homophobia is an intense, irrational hostility toward or fear of homosexuals that can lead to discrimination against gays and lesbians, or even motivate acts of violence against them. Fortunately, most people's views of homosexuality stop short of full-blown homophobia, although negative attitudes toward homosexuality are still common in U.S. society (Herek, 2002). Generally, men are more likely to express such views. For instance, in one survey, 45% of male respondents believed gays should "stay in the closet"; only 30% of female respondents expressed such a belief (Moore, 1993). Thirty-four percent of males, compared with 42% of females, considered homosexuality an acceptable lifestyle (Hugick, 1992). Most adults hold more negative attitudes about gay males than about lesbians (Herek, 2002; Louderback & Whitley, 1997).

Social attitudes toward homosexuality appear to be moving slowly toward acceptance. One indication is the popularity of the TV sitcom *Will & Grace,* with its gay lead characters Will Truman and Jack McFarland.

Importantly, though, most people are opposed to discrimination based on sexual orientation. (Moreover, such discrimination is illegal.) Surveys show that more than three-quarters of Americans believe that homosexuality should not be a factor in hiring public school teachers (Herek, 2002). Similarly, an overwhelming majority of Americans, including those who are strongly opposed to homosexual behavior, adamantly support the rights of homosexuals to speak out and to try to influence public policy. Thus, objections to homosexuality appear to be focused on the behavior itself and not on those who exhibit it.

Remember It 12.4

1. Sexual __________ is the direction of a person's sexual preference.
2. Statistics suggest that homosexuality is twice as common in __________ as in __________.
3. Indicate whether or not each of the statements about the origins of homosexuality is supported by research.

 ___ (1) Homosexual and heterosexual adults have different levels of sex hormones.

 ___ (2) Homosexual men and women are more likely than heterosexuals to recall cross-gender childhood experiences.

 ___ (3) Genetics may play a role in sexual orientation.

 ___ (4) Differences between homosexual and heterosexual individuals are not evident before puberty.

 ___ (5) Exposure to androgens during prenatal development may influence an individual's sexual orientation.

 a. supported by research

 b. not supported by research

ANSWERS: 1. orientation; 2. males, females; 3. (1) b, (2) a, (3) a, (4) b, (5) a

Sexual Dysfunctions

■ **sexual dysfunction**
A persistent or recurrent problem that causes marked distress and interpersonal difficulty and that may involve some combination of the following: sexual desire, sexual arousal or the pleasure associated with sex, or orgasm.

Have you seen advertisements for drugs or herbal preparations that enhance sexual performance? The prevalence of such ads should tell you that the desire to improve the quality of one's sexual experiences is common. Further, a sizable number of women and men are plagued by serious sexual dysfunctions, which eliminate or at least decrease the pleasures of sex. A **sexual dysfunction** is a persistent or recurrent problem that causes marked distress and interpersonal difficulty and may involve any or a combination of the following: sexual desire, sexual arousal or the pleasure associated with sex, or orgasm.

Sexual Desire Disorders

What are the defining features of two sexual desire disorders?

Disorders of sexual desire involve a lack of sexual desire and/or an aversion to genital sexual contact. One of the most common complaints of people who see sex therapists is low or nonexistent sexual desire or interest in sexual activity. This condition is known as **hypoactive sexual desire disorder** (Beck, 1995). Such people may be unreceptive to the sexual advances of their partners, or they may participate despite their lack of desire. Loss of desire or lack of interest can stem from depression, emotional stress, marital dissatisfaction, or repeated unsuccessful attempts at intercourse. In men who are middle-aged and older, a decline in sexual interest may be related to a decline in testosterone levels that occurs with aging (Brody, 1995).

■ **hypoactive sexual desire disorder**
A sexual dysfunction marked by low or nonexistent sexual desire or interest in sexual activity.

A more severe problem is **sexual aversion disorder**, an "aversion to and active avoidance of genital contact with a sexual partner" (American Psychiatric Association, 1994, p. 499). People with this condition experience emotions ranging from anxiety or fear to disgust when confronted with a sexual situation. In some cases, a sexual aversion stems from a sexual trauma such as rape or incest.

■ sexual aversion disorder
A sexual dysfunction characterized by an aversion to and active avoidance of genital contact with a sexual partner.

Sexual Arousal Disorders

Some individuals have a normal interest in sex but are unable to become aroused. A woman with **female sexual arousal disorder** may not feel sexually aroused in response to sexual stimulation, or she may be unable to achieve or sustain "an adequate lubrication-swelling response to sexual excitement" (American Psychiatric Association, 1994, p. 500). The problem may stem from the trauma of rape or childhood sexual abuse, from resentment toward one's partner, or from vaginal dryness due to reduced estrogen production.

What are the defining features of the sexual arousal disorders?

A common sexual dysfunction reported in men is **male erectile disorder**, the repeated inability to have or sustain an erection firm enough for coitus. This disorder (more widely known as *impotence* or *erectile dysfunction*) can take different forms: the inability to have an erection at all, having one but losing it, or having a partial erection that is not adequate for intercourse. Some men have firm erections under some conditions but not under others (with one sexual partner but not with another, or during masturbation but not during intercourse). The term *erectile disorder* does not apply to the failures all males have on occasion as a result of fear, anxiety, physical fatigue, illness, or drinking too much alcohol.

In a study of 1,290 men aged 40 to 70, 52% were found to have some degree of erectile disorder, with the likelihood increasing with age. The prevalence of complete erectile disorder ranged from 5% in men aged 40 to 15% in men aged 70 (Feldman et al., 1994). Male erectile disorder may be physical or psychological in origin, but most cases involve some combination of the two (Ackerman & Carey, 1995; Rosen, 1996). Physical causes may include diabetes, alcoholism, and drugs such as cocaine, amphetamines, barbiturates, tranquilizers, and blood pressure medication. When the cause is physical, the problem usually develops gradually over a period of months or years, and the man always has difficulty achieving an erection, in all circumstances (Lizza & Cricco-Lizza, 1990). But if a man awakens to find himself with an erection, even occasionally, he can usually rule out a physical cause.

The most common cause of male erectile disorder is performance anxiety. When a man fails repeatedly to achieve an erection, his worst psychological enemy is the fear that he will not be able to have an erection when he most wants one. A number of medical treatments, particularly the drug sildenafil (Viagra), have been found to be effective in treating this problem (Rosen, 1996). Moreover, research has shown that a combination of pycogenol (an antioxidant derived from tree bark) with L-arginine (an amino acid) may be helpful, though its effects may not be evident until several weeks after treatment has begun (Stanislavov & Nikolova, 2003). Sufferers from erectile disorder would do well to be wary of the claims associated with many "natural" treatments, because most of them are not based on controlled studies (Rowland & Tai, 2003). Moreover, self-treatment with supplements and herbal remedies may cause a serious underlying medical condition to go undiagnosed and, as a result, untreated.

■ female sexual arousal disorder
A sexual dysfunction in which a woman may not feel sexually aroused in response to sexual stimulation or may be unable to achieve or sustain an adequate lubrication-swelling response to sexual excitement.

■ male erectile disorder
A sexual dysfunction in which a man experiences the repeated inability to have or sustain an erection firm enough for coitus; also known as erectile dysfunction or impotence.

■ female orgasmic disorder
A sexual dysfunction in which a woman is persistently unable to reach orgasm or delays in reaching orgasm, despite adequate sexual stimulation.

Orgasmic and Sexual Pain Disorders

The most common sexual dysfunction in women is **female orgasmic disorder,** a persistent inability to reach orgasm or a delay in reaching orgasm despite adequate sexual stimulation. Some women with this disorder have never been able to reach orgasm; others who were formerly orgasmic no longer can achieve orgasm. Some women are able to have orgasms only under certain circumstances or during certain types of sexual activity, while others have orgasms only from time to time. Women with this disorder may be uninterested in sex, or they may still find it exciting, satisfying, and enjoyable, despite the lack of orgasms.

How do orgasmic and sexual pain disorders affect men's and women's sexual experiences?

male orgasmic disorder A sexual dysfunction in which a man experiences the absence of ejaculation, or ejaculation occurs only after strenuous effort over a prolonged period.

premature ejaculation A chronic or recurring orgasmic disorder in which orgasm and ejaculation occur with little stimulation, before, during, or shortly after penetration and before the man wishes; the most common sexual dysfunction in males.

dyspareunia (dis-PAH-roo-nee-yah) A sexual pain disorder marked by genital pain associated with sexual intercourse; more common in females than in males.

vaginismus (VAJ-ah-NIZ-mus) A sexual pain disorder in which involuntary muscle contractions tighten and even close the vagina, making intercourse painful or impossible.

In **male orgasmic disorder,** there is an absence of ejaculation, or ejaculation occurs only after strenuous effort over an extremely prolonged period. Sometimes, both partners may nearly collapse from exhaustion before the male finally reaches orgasm or gives up. The delay in or absence of ejaculation usually occurs during intercourse, rather than during manual or oral stimulation or during masturbation. Suspected causes include alcoholism or use of drugs (illicit or prescription), stressful or traumatic life situations, and fear of impregnating one's partner (Kaplan, 1974).

The most common sexual dysfunction in males is **premature ejaculation**, a chronic or recurring orgasm disorder in which orgasm and ejaculation occur with little stimulation, before, during, or shortly after penetration and before the man wishes (American Psychiatric Association, 1994). This condition may have its origins in early sexual experiences that called for quick ejaculation, such as hurried masturbation. However, biological factors may be more important. Some research suggests that SSRI antidepressants (those that increase the action of the neurotransmitter serotonin) are effective in helping some men with this problem (Balon, 1996; Rowland et al., 2003).

Sexual pain disorders are common in women but infrequent in men (Rosen & Leiblum, 1995). **Dyspareunia**, genital pain associated with sexual intercourse, is much more common in women. Inadequate lubrication is the major cause, although vaginal infections, sexually transmitted diseases, and various psychological factors may also be involved.

Vaginismus is a sexual pain disorder in which involuntary muscle contractions tighten and even close the vagina, making intercourse painful or impossible. The problem may stem from a rigid religious upbringing in which sex was looked on as sinful and dirty. It may also stem from past experiences of extremely painful intercourse or from a fear of men, rape, or other traumatic experiences associated with intercourse (Kaplan, 1974).

Remember It 12.5

Match each sexual disorder with the appropriate description.

___ (1) male erectile disorder	a. inability to reach orgasm
___ (2) vaginismus	b. inability to control ejaculation
___ (3) premature ejaculation	c. lack of sexual interest
___ (4) female orgasmic disorder	d. inability to have or maintain an erection
___ (5) female sexual arousal disorder	e. an involuntary closing of the vagina
___ (6) hypoactive sexual desire disorder	f. inability to feel sexually excited and to lubricate sufficiently

ANSWERS: (1) d, (2) e, (3) b, (4) a, (5) f, (6) c

Sexually Transmitted Diseases

sexually transmitted diseases (STDs) Infections that are spread primarily through intimate sexual contact.

What is the most common infectious disease in the United States? You might be surprised to learn that it isn't the common cold or the flu. It's a sexually transmitted disease called *chlamydia* (St. Louis County Department of Health, 2003).

Sexually transmitted diseases (STDs) are infections spread primarily through intimate sexual contact. Each year, about 15 million Americans contract a sexually transmitted disease, and a total of 65 million Americans have been infected with an incurable STD-causing virus other than HIV (CDC, 2000). Minority populations in U.S. inner cities are experiencing an epidemic in STDs, as are people in developing countries (CDC, 2000). Worldwide, more than 30 million people contract curable STDs each year (WHO, 1996). Millions more are diagnosed each year with incurable STDs—including about 5 million cases of HIV/AIDS (NIH, 2003).

The incidence of many sexually transmitted diseases has increased dramatically since the early 1970s. This can be explained in part by more permissive attitudes toward sex and an increase in sexual activity among young people, some of whom have had sexual contact with multiple partners (Turner et al., 1995). Another factor is the greater use of nonbarrier methods of contraception such as the pill. Barrier methods, such as condoms and vaginal spermicide, provide some protection against STDs. Some of the more serious sexually transmitted diseases are bacterial infections such as chlamydia, gonorrhea, and syphilis, which are curable, and viral infections such as genital warts, genital herpes, and AIDS, which are not curable.

How much do you already know about the major sexually transmitted diseases? To find out, complete *Try It 12.1*.

■ **chlamydia**
(klah-MIH-dee-uh) A highly infectious bacterial STD that is found in both sexes and can cause infertility in females.

■ **pelvic inflammatory disease (PID)**
An infection in the female pelvic organs, which can result from untreated chlamydia or gonorrhea and can cause pain, scarring of tissue, and even infertility or an ectopic pregnancy.

Try It 12.1 Knowledge about STDs

Choose the correct answer to each item.

1. 45 million Americans currently have ______________.
   a. HIV/AIDS   b. genital herpes   c. chlamydia
2. Which of the following bacterial STDs is common among teenaged and young adult women?
   a. scabies   b. chlamydia   c. trichomoniasis
3. Which of the following STDs can be cured?
   a. genital herpes   b. gonorrhea   c. genital warts
4. For women, the most common symptom of chlamydia or gonorrhea infection is ______________.
   a. vaginal discharge   b. genital sores/blisters   c. a lack of symptoms

ANSWERS: 1. b 2. b 3. b 4. c

Bacterial STDs

What are the major bacterial sexually transmitted diseases, and how are they treated?

There are many types of bacteria that cause sexually transmitted diseases. Fortunately, in most cases, bacterial STDs, including chlamydia, gonorrhea, and syphilis, can be cured with antibiotics.

Chlamydia is a highly infectious disease. Rates of infection among young people are especially high. For example, studies involving teenagers confined to juvenile detention center have found that as many as 15% of them test positive for chlamydia (CDC, 2001a). And in 1999, about 5% of men inducted into the United States Army were found to have the disease.

Men with chlamydia are likely to have symptoms that alert them to the need for treatment, but they suffer no adverse reproductive consequences from the infection. Women, on the other hand, typically have only mild symptoms or no symptoms at all when chlamydia begins in the lower reproductive tract. Therefore, the infection often goes untreated and spreads to the upper reproductive tract, where it can cause **pelvic inflammatory disease (PID)**. PID often produces scarring of tissue in the fallopian

■ gonorrhea (gahn-ah-REE-ah) A bacterial STD that, in males, causes a puslike discharge from the penis and painful urination; if untreated, females can develop pelvic inflammatory disease and possibly infertility.

■ syphilis A bacterial STD that progresses through three predictable stages; if untreated, it can eventually be fatal.

■ genital warts Growths on the genitals that are caused by the human papillomavirus (HPV).

■ human papillomavirus (HPV) A virus that causes genital warts; also believed to contribute to cervical cancer.

■ genital herpes An STD that is caused by the herpes simplex virus and results in painful blisters on the genitals; presently incurable, the infection usually recurs and is highly contagious during outbreaks.

tubes, which can result in infertility or an *ectopic pregnancy*—in which the fertilized ovum is implanted outside of the uterus (Temmerman, 1994; Weström, 1994).

In 2000, in the United States, 358,995 cases of **gonorrhea** were reported to the Centers for Disease Control; this number represented nearly 133 cases for every 100,000 people in the U.S. population. The rate rose from 122 cases per 100,000 people in 1997 (CDC, 2001a). Within the first 2 weeks after contracting gonorrhea, 95% of men develop a puslike discharge from the penis and experience painful urination (Schwebke, 1991a). Most seek treatment and are cured. If there are no symptoms present or if the individual does not seek treatment within 2 to 3 weeks, the infection may spread to the internal reproductive organs and eventually cause sterility. The bad news for women is that 50–80% of women who contract gonorrhea do not have early symptoms. The infection spreads from the cervix through the other internal reproductive organs, causing inflammation and scarring. About 20% of women with untreated gonorrhea develop PID (Schwebke, 1991a). Gonorrhea can be cured with antibiotics (Levine et al., 1994).

About 31,575 cases of **syphilis** were reported in the United States in 2000 (CDC, 2001a). The rate is particularly high "among inner city ethnic groups of low socioeconomic status" (Schwebke, 1991b, p. 44). Syphilis has been linked to the use of illicit drugs, particularly crack, because addicts often exchange sex for drugs (Gunn et al., 1995).

Left untreated, syphilis progresses in predictable stages. In the primary stage, a painless sore, or chancre (pronounced "SHANK-er"), appears where the spirochete ("SPY-ro-keet"), the microorganism that causes syphilis, entered the body. This sore may go unnoticed, but even without treatment, it will heal. In the second stage of syphilis, a painless rash appears on the body, usually accompanied by a fever, sore throat, loss of appetite, fatigue, and headache. Again, without treatment, these symptoms eventually disappear. Then, the spirochetes enter the various tissues and organs of the body, where they may be inactive for anywhere from several years to a lifetime. About 30–50% of people with untreated syphilis enter the final and terrible third stage, in which blindness, paralysis, heart failure, mental illness, and death result.

A pregnant woman in any stage of syphilis will infect the fetus. But syphilis can be stopped at any point in its development, except in the third stage, with strong doses of penicillin (Levine et al., 1994).

What viral diseases are transmitted through sexual contact?

Viral STDs

Unlike the bacterial infections, the viral infections—genital warts, genital herpes, and AIDS—are incurable. Moreover, they can lead to more serious diseases, including cancer. For example, **genital warts** are caused by the **human papillomavirus (HPV)**. Even after the warts are removed or disappear spontaneously, the virus remains latent in the body for years and may eventually cause genital cancer, particularly cervical cancer (Koutsky et al., 1992; Tinkle, 1990). In fact, HPVs may be linked to 85% or more of the cervical cancer cases in the United States (Ochs, 1994). Prevalence studies in the United States show that 25% of women between 20 and 29 years of age, and 10% of women 30 and over, are infected with HPV (Stone et al., 2002).

According to the Centers for Disease Control and Prevention (CDC, 2001b), 20% of adults in the United States, or about 45 million people, are infected with the virus that causes most cases of **genital herpes** (CDC, 2001b). The type 2 virus—herpes simplex—produces 80–90% of the cases of genital herpes and is transmitted through direct contact with infected genitals. However, the type 1 virus—the herpes virus more commonly associated with cold sores and fever blisters in the mouth—can also cause genital herpes and can be transmitted via oral or genital sex.

In genital herpes, painful blisters form on the genitals (or around the anus in homosexual men), fill with pus, and then burst, leaving open sores. It is at this point that a person is most contagious. After the blisters heal, the virus travels up nerve fibers to an area around the base of the spinal cord, where it remains in a dormant state but can flare up anew at any time. The first herpes episode is usually the most severe (Apuzzio, 1990); recurring attacks are typically milder and briefer. Although genital herpes is most contagious during an outbreak, it can be transmitted even when an infected person has no symptoms (Dawkins, 1990).

Acquired Immune Deficiency Syndrome (AIDS)

In what ways can HIV/AIDS affect an individual's physical and psychological health?

No sexually transmitted disease has more devastating consequences than **acquired immune deficiency syndrome (AIDS)**. By the end of 2002, about 900,000 cases of AIDS and 501,669 deaths from AIDS had been reported to the Centers for Disease Control (NIH, 2003). Worldwide, 3.1 million people died from AIDS and 42 million people are infected with HIV (NIH, 2003). Although the first case was diagnosed in this country in 1981, there is still no cure for AIDS, but progress is being made in the development of a vaccine to protect against it (National Institutes of Health, 2002). How much do you know about AIDS? Test your knowledge by completing *Try It 12.2.*

AIDS is caused by the **human immunodeficiency virus (HIV)**, often referred to as the *AIDS virus*. When a person is first infected, HIV enters the bloodstream. This initial infection usually causes no symptoms, and the immune system begins to produce HIV antibodies. It is these antibodies that are detected in a blood test for AIDS. Individuals then progress to the asymptomatic carrier state, in which they experience no symptoms whatsoever and thus can unknowingly infect others.

HIV attacks the immune system until it becomes essentially nonfunctional. The diagnosis of AIDS is made when the immune system is so damaged that victims develop rare forms of cancer or pneumonia or other opportunistic infections. Such infections are not usually serious in people with normal immune responses, but in those with a very impaired immune system, they can be very serious and even life-threatening. At this point, patients typically experience progressive weight loss, weakness, fever, swollen lymph nodes, and diarrhea; 25% develop a rare cancer that

■ **acquired immune deficiency syndrome (AIDS)** A devastating and incurable illness that is caused by HIV and progressively weakens the body's immune system, leaving the person vulnerable to opportunistic infections that usually cause death.

■ **human immunodeficiency virus (HIV)** The virus that causes AIDS.

Try It 12.2 Knowledge about AIDS

1. AIDS is a single disease. (true/false)
2. AIDS symptoms vary widely from country to country, and even from risk group to risk group. (true/false)
3. Those at greatest risk for getting AIDS are people who have sex without using condoms, drug users who share needles, and infants born to AIDS-infected mothers. (true/false)
4. AIDS is one of the most highly contagious diseases. (true/false)
5. One way to avoid contracting AIDS is to use an oil-based lubricant with a condom. (true/false)

ANSWERS:
1. False: AIDS is not a single disease. Rather, a severely impaired immune system leaves a person with AIDS highly susceptible to a whole host of infections and diseases.
2. True: In the United States and Europe, AIDS sufferers may develop Kaposi's sarcoma (a rare form of skin cancer), pneumonia, and tuberculosis. In Africa, people with AIDS usually waste away with fever, diarrhea, and symptoms caused by tuberculosis.
3. True: Those groups are at greatest risk. Screening of blood donors and testing of donated blood have greatly reduced the risk of contracting AIDS through blood transfusions. Today, women make up the fastest-growing group of infected people worldwide, as AIDS spreads among heterosexuals, especially in Africa.
4. False: AIDS is not among the most highly infectious diseases. You cannot get AIDS from kissing, shaking hands, or using objects handled by people who have AIDS.
5. False: *Do not* use oil-based lubricants, which can eat through condoms. Latex condoms with an effective spermicide are safer. Learn the sexual history of any potential partner, including HIV test results. Don't have sex with prostitutes.

In 2002, writers and producers of the PBS television show *Sesame Street* introduced an HIV-positive Muppet character to help educate children about HIV and AIDS.

produces reddish-purple spots on the skin. Other infections develop as the immune system weakens further.

Before developing a full-blown case of AIDS, some people develop less severe symptoms related to immune system dysfunction, such as unexplained fevers, chronic diarrhea, and weight loss. The average time from infection with HIV to advanced AIDS is about 10 years, but the time may range from 2 years to as long as 15 years or more (Nowak & McMichael, 1995). The disease progresses faster in smokers, in the very young, in people over 50, and, apparently, in women. AIDS also progresses faster in those who are repeatedly exposed to the virus and in those who were infected by someone in an advanced stage of the disease.

Currently, researchers are testing many drugs on people infected with HIV, and early detection of HIV infection can lead to life-prolonging medical intervention. Researchers have discovered that drugs known as *protease inhibitors*, in combination with drugs such as AZT, can cause significant reductions in blood levels of HIV (Collier et al., 1996).

The Transmission of AIDS Researchers believe that HIV is transmitted primarily through the exchange of blood, semen, or vaginal secretions during sexual contact or when IV (intravenous) drug users share contaminated needles or syringes. In the United States, about 25% of those with AIDS are IV drug users, but homosexual men represent the largest number of HIV carriers and AIDS cases (CDC, 2001c). Infection rates among gay men are high because many gay men have multiple sex partners and are likely to have anal intercourse. Anal intercourse is more dangerous than coitus, because rectal tissue often tears during penetration, allowing HIV ready entry into the bloodstream. However, it is a mistake to view AIDS as a disease confined to gay men; about 30% of AIDS suffers are women. Figure 12.5 illustrates the rates of HIV infection among three risk groups in the United States: homosexual men, intravenous drug users, and the sexual partners of homosexual men and IV drug users.

The Psychological Impact of HIV Infection and AIDS What are the psychological effects on people who struggle to cope with this fearsome disease? The reaction to the news that one is HIV-positive is frequently shock, bewilderment, confusion, or disbelief. Stress reactions to the news are typically so common and so acute that experts strongly recommend pretest counseling so that those who do test positive may know in advance what to expect (Maj, 1990). Another common reaction is anger—at past or present sexual partners, family members, health care professionals, or society in general. Often, a person's response includes guilt, a sense that one is being punished for homosexuality or drug abuse. Other people exhibit denial, ignoring medical advice

FIGURE 12.5 How HIV Was Transmitted in AIDS Cases in the United States

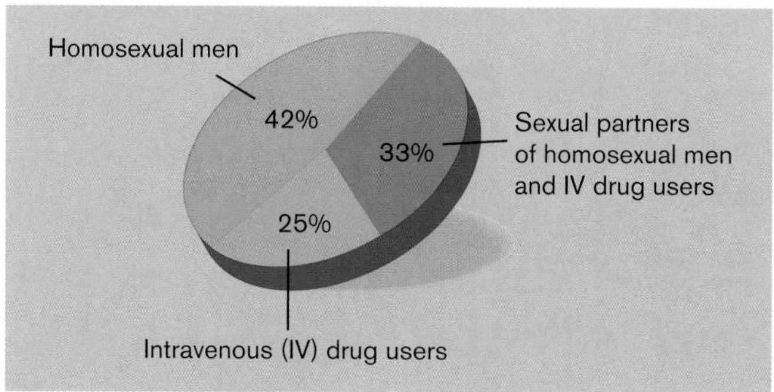

Source: CDC (2001c).

and continuing to act as if nothing has changed in their lives. Then, of course, there is fear—of death, of mental and physical deterioration, of rejection by friends, family, and co-workers, of sexual rejection, of abandonment. Experiencing emotional swings ranging from shock to anger to guilt to fear can lead to serious clinical depression and apathy (Tate et al., 2003). Once apathy sets in, HIV patients may become less likely to comply with treatment (Dorz et al., 2003).

To cope psychologically, AIDS patients and those infected with HIV, and their loved ones, need education and information about the disease. They can be helped by psychotherapy, self-help groups, and medications such as antidepressants and anti-anxiety drugs. Self-help groups and group therapy may serve as an extended family for some patients. A concern voiced by most patients in psychotherapy is whether to tell others, and if so, what to tell them and how. Patients may feel a compelling need to confide in others and, at the same time, to conceal their condition.

Protection against Sexually Transmitted Diseases

What are the most effective methods of protection against sexually transmitted diseases?

There are only two foolproof ways to protect oneself from becoming infected with a sexually transmitted disease through intimate sexual contact. The first is obvious: Abstain from sexual contact. The second is to have a mutually faithful (monogamous) relationship with a partner who is free of infection. Any other course of action will place a person at risk.

Discharges, blisters, sores, rashes, warts, odors, or any other unusual symptoms are warning signs of sexually transmitted diseases. Yet, many people who have no visible symptoms carry STDs. What you don't know can hurt you. People who choose to practice risky sex cannot be safe but can reduce the risks by using a latex condom along with a spermicide such as an intravaginal contraceptive foam, jelly, or cream.

The potential for risky sexual behavior is increased when people are under the influence of alcohol and other drugs (Leigh & Stall, 1993). People put themselves at risk for AIDS when they have multiple sex partners or have sex with prostitutes, IV drug users, or anyone carrying HIV (Bellis et al., 2002). Anyone who fears that he or she might have been exposed to an STD should go to a doctor or clinic to be tested. Many STDs are easily treated, and serious complications can be avoided if the treatment is prompt. Obviously, anyone who has an STD should tell his or her partner so that the partner can be checked and treated.

STDs were curable until genital warts, herpes, and AIDS came on the scene. But, today, engaging in sexual intimacy with multiple partners or casual acquaintances is indeed a dangerous way to satisfy the sex drive. Much has been written in recent decades about the joy of sex. It is true that the pleasures sex brings to life are many, but fear of STDs may interfere with those pleasures. Thus, safe sex practices are essential—not only for health, but also for the enjoyment of sex.

Remember It 12.6

1. If left untreated, __________, a bacterial STD, can be fatal.
2. Genital __________ causes painful blisters on the genitals and is usually recurring, highly contagious during outbreaks, and incurable.
3. The two STDs most likely to cause infertility in women are __________ and __________.
4. HIV eventually causes a breakdown of the __________ system.
5. The group in the United States at highest risk of being infected with HIV is __________.

ANSWERS: 1. syphilis; 2. herpes; 3. chlamydia, gonorrhea; 4. immune; 5. homosexual men

Apply It

How to Get a Date

You think you have met Mr. or Ms. Right. So, what do you do? How do you go about making a date? Psychologists have learned that we can enhance our social skills, including our date-seeking skills, through the technique of *successive approximations.* That means that we can practice a series of tasks that are graded in difficulty, honing our social skills and gaining self-confidence at each step. We can try out some of our skills on friends, who can role-play the prospective date and give honest feedback about our behavior.

Here is a series of graduated (step-by-step) tasks that may help you sharpen your own date-seeking skills.

Easy Practice Level

- Select a person with whom you are friendly, but whom you have no desire to date. Practice making small talk about the weather, new films, TV shows, concerts, museum shows, political events, and personal hobbies.
- Select a person you might have some interest in dating. Smile when you pass this person at work, school, or elsewhere, and say, "Hi." Engage in this activity with other people of both genders to increase your skills at greeting others.

Medium Practice Level

- Sit down next to the person you want to date, and engage in small talk. If you are in a classroom, talk about a homework assignment, the seating arrangement, or the instructor (be kind). If you are at work, talk about the building or some recent interesting event in the neighborhood. Ask your intended date how he or she feels about the situation.
- Engage in small talk about the weather and local events. Channel the conversation into an exchange of personal information. Give your "name, rank, and serial number"—who you are, your major field or your occupation, where you're from, and why or how you came to the school or company. The other person is likely to reciprocate and provide equivalent information.
- Rehearse asking the person out before your mirror, a family member, or a confidant. You may wish to suggest a cup of coffee or a film. It is somewhat less threatening to ask someone out to a gathering at which "some of us will be getting together." Or you may rehearse asking the person to accompany you to a cultural event, such as an exhibition at a museum or a concert—it's sort of a date, but less anxiety-inducing.

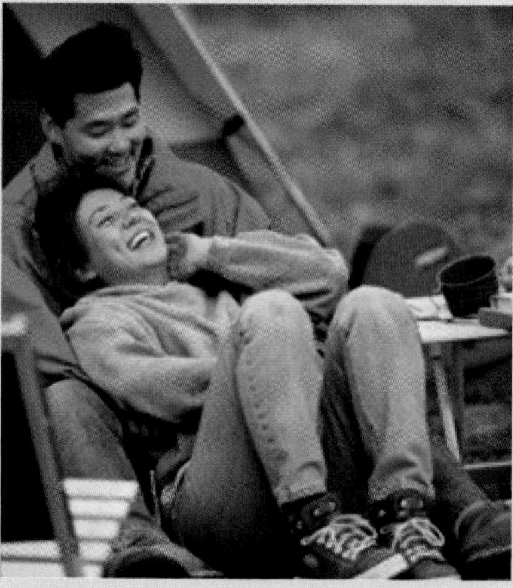

Target Behavior Level

- Ask the person out on a date in a manner that is consistent with your behavior rehearsal. If the person says he or she has a previous engagement or can't make it, you might wish to say something like "That's too bad" or "I'm sorry you can't make it" and add something like "Perhaps another time." You should be able to get a feeling for whether the person you asked out was just seeking an excuse or has a genuine interest in you and could not, in fact, accept the specific invitation.
- Before asking the person out again, pay attention to his or her apparent comfort level when you return to small talk on a couple of occasions. If there is still a chance, the other person should smile and return your eye contact; he or she might also offer you an invitation. In any event, if you are turned down twice, do not ask a third time. And don't make a catastrophe out of the refusal. Look up. Note that the roof hasn't fallen in. The birds are still chirping in the trees. You are still paying taxes. Then give someone else a chance to appreciate your fine qualities.

Source: Rathus et al. (2000).

Summary *and* Review

Sex, Gender, and Gender Roles p. 410

What is the difference between sex and gender? p. 411

Generally, sex is a biological term, while gender refers to the psychological and social variables associated with sex. At conception, the sex chromosomes are set—XY in males and XX in females. Gender typing is the process by which people acquire psychological gender.

How do the various theoretical perspectives explain gender role development? p. 411

The biological perspective emphasizes the influence of genes and hormones on gender role behavior. Psychoanalytic theory focuses more on same-sex parent bonding, based on unconscious emotional conflicts. According to social learning theory, models and rewards shape gender-related behavior. Kohlberg's cognitive developmental theory claims that gender concepts develop in stages of gender identity, gender stability, and gender constancy. Gender schema theory holds that once gender identity is attained, children develop strong preferences for sex-appropriate items.

Gender Differences p. 414

According to evolutionary psychologists, how do the relative parental investments of men and women shape mating behavior? p. 414

Evolutionary psychologists claim that men look for mates who are available and appear healthy, and women seek partners who can provide support and stability. The proposed explanation for this difference is that men's investment in parenting is restricted to the provision of sperm, while women's investment in nurturing children to adulthood is much greater. Thus, men focus on the physical attributes of potential mates, and women are more concerned with long-term support.

For what cognitive abilities have gender differences been proven? p. 415

Females outperform males in reading and writing. Males seem to do better in science, math, and some spatial tasks.

What gender differences are found in social behavior and personality? p. 417

The most consistent and significant gender difference in behavior is that males tend to be more physically aggressive than females. Females are more likely to use indirect aggression, to be more attuned to the feelings of others, and to be more people-oriented. Males tend to be more dominant, more object-oriented, and more competitive.

Do good adjustment and high self-esteem seem to be related to masculine, feminine, or androgynous traits? p. 418

Masculine traits appear to be most strongly related to good adjustment and high self-esteem.

Sexual Attitudes and Behavior p. 419

How do sexual attitudes and behaviors vary across cultures, ethnic groups, and genders? p. 419

The frequency of sexual activity varies across cultures. Among Americans, African American college students have more permissive premarital sexual standards than do White college students, while Mexican American students have more conservative sexual standards. Men are more likely than women to think of sex in purely physical terms and to have more permissive attitudes toward sex.

According to Masters and Johnson, what are the phases of the human sexual response cycle? p. 419

The sexual response cycle consists of four phases: the excitement phase, the plateau phase, orgasm, and the resolution phase. Hormones influence the cycle in both men and women.

What are some of the factors that contribute to sexual violence? p. 422

Sexual violence includes sexual assault, rape, date/acquaintance rape, and sexual abuse. Factors that contribute to sexual violence include abuse of alcohol and other substances, poverty, acceptance of rape myths, and a history of early sexual contact or victimization.

Sexual Orientation p. 425

What are the various factors that have been suggested as possible determinants of a gay or lesbian sexual orientation? p. 425

The biological factors suggested as possible causes of a gay or lesbian sexual orientation are (1) abnormal levels of androgens during prenatal development, which could masculinize or feminize the brain of the developing fetus; (2) structural differences in an area of the hypothalamus of gay men; and (3) genetic factors. Bell, Weinberg, and Hammersmith were unable to trace differences between gay men and lesbians and heterosexuals to conditions of family life or childhood experiences. The only commonality was that as children, gays did not feel that they were like others of their sex.

How have attitudes toward homosexuality changed in recent decades? p. 427

Prior to 1973, homosexuality was considered to be a disorder by mental health professionals. Today, most people are opposed to discrimination based on homosexuality.

Sexual Dysfunctions p. 428

What are the defining features of two sexual desire disorders? p. 428

Hypoactive sexual desire disorder is characterized by little or no sexual desire or interest in sexual activity. Sexual aversion disorder is defined by an aversion to genital contact with a sexual partner.

What are the defining features of the sexual arousal disorders? p. 429

A woman with female sexual arousal disorder may not feel sexually aroused or become sufficiently lubricated in response to sexual stimulation. Male erectile disorder, or impotence, involves the repeated inability to have or sustain an erection firm enough for coitus.

How do orgasmic and sexual pain disorders affect men's and women's sexual experiences? p. 429

Female orgasmic disorder is the persistent inability of a woman to reach orgasm or a delay in reaching orgasm despite adequate sexual stimulation. In male orgasmic disorder, there is an absence of ejaculation, or it occurs only after strenuous effort over an extremely prolonged period. In premature ejaculation, the male ejaculates with little stimulation, before he desires it. Women are more likely than men to suffer from sexual pain disorders.

Sexually Transmitted Diseases p. 430

What are the major bacterial sexually transmitted diseases, and how are they treated? p. 431

The major sexually transmitted diseases caused by bacteria are chlamydia, gonorrhea, and syphilis. All can be cured with antibiotics. However, chlamydia and gonorrhea pose a particular threat to women because, unlike men, women with these infections typically have no symptoms or very mild symptoms, making prompt diagnosis and treatment less likely. If the infection spreads, it may result in infertility or an ectopic pregnancy.

What viral diseases are transmitted through sexual contact? p. 432

Viral STDs include genital warts, genital herpes, and AIDS. Viral infections presently are not curable. Genital herpes causes painful blisters on the genitals, is usually recurring, and is highly contagious during outbreaks.

In what ways can HIV/AIDS affect an individual's physical and psychological health? p. 433

HIV gradually renders the immune system nonfunctional. The diagnosis of AIDS is made when the person succumbs to various opportunistic infections. Persons with HIV must take precautions against transmitting the infection to others. Sufferers may react to the diagnosis with shock, denial, and/or anger and then experience emotional mood swings that can lead to serious clinical depression and apathy. Psychotherapy, self-help groups, and antidepressant medication can be helpful to those coping with HIV.

What are the most effective methods of protection against sexually transmitted diseases? *p. 435*

Abstinence or a monogamous relationship with a partner who is free of infection is the only foolproof way to protect yourself from acquiring an STD through intimate sexual contact. The risk of infection can be reduced by avoiding sex with multiple or anonymous partners, being on the lookout for symptoms of these diseases in a potential partner, and using a latex condom with a spermicide.

Key Terms

acquired immune deficiency syndrome (AIDS), p. 433
androgens, p. 411
androgyny, p. 418
biological sex, p. 411
chlamydia, p. 431
coitus, p. 419
dyspareunia, p. 430
estrogen, p. 421
excitement phase, p. 420
female orgasmic disorder, p. 429
female sexual arousal disorder, p. 429
gender, p. 411
gender constancy, p. 412
gender identity, p. 412
gender roles, p. 411
gender schema theory, p. 412
gender stability, p. 412
gender typing, p. 411
genital herpes, p. 432
genital warts, p. 432
genitals, p. 411
gonads, p. 411
gonorrhea, p. 432
homophobia, p. 427
human immunodeficiency virus (HIV), p. 433
human papillomavirus (HPV), p. 432
hypoactive sexual desire disorder, p. 428
male erectile disorder, p. 429
male orgasmic disorder, p. 430
orgasm, p. 420
parental investment, p. 414
pelvic inflammatory disease (PID), p. 431
plateau phase, p. 420
premature ejaculation, p. 430
primary sex characteristics, p. 411
progesterone, p. 421
resolution phase, p. 421
secondary sex characteristics, p. 411
sex chromosomes, p. 411
sexual aversion disorder, p. 428
sexual dysfunction, p. 428
sexual orientation, p. 425
sexual response cycle, p. 420
sexual violence, p. 422
sexually transmitted diseases (STDs), p. 430
syphilis, p. 432
testosterone, p. 421
vaginismus, p. 430

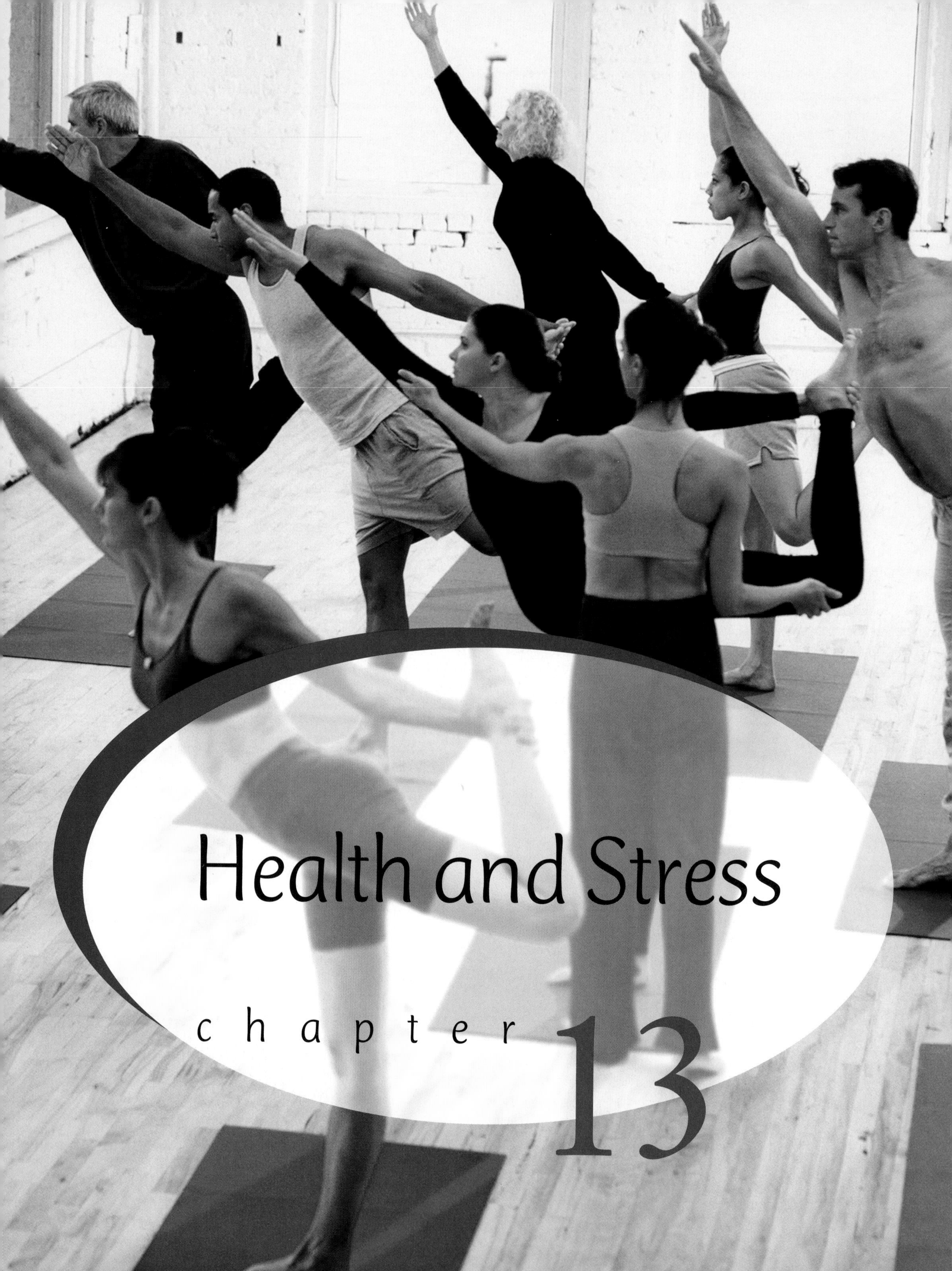

Health and Stress

chapter 13

Sources of Stress

- *What was the Social Readjustment Rating Scale designed to reveal?*
- *What roles do hassles and uplifts play in the stress of life, according to Lazarus?*
- *How do approach-approach, avoidance-avoidance, and approach-avoidance conflicts differ?*
- *How do the unpredictability and lack of control over a stressor affect its impact?*
- *For people to function effectively and find satisfaction on the job, what nine variables should fall within their comfort zone?*
- *How do people typically react to catastrophic events?*
- *How might historical racism affect the health of African Americans?*

Responding to Stress

- *What is the general adaptation syndrome?*
- *What are the roles of primary and secondary appraisals when a person is confronted with a potentially stressful event?*
- *What is the difference between problem-focused and emotion-focused coping?*

Health and Illness

- *How do the biomedical and biopsychosocial models differ in their approaches to health and illness?*
- *What are the Type A and Type B behavior patterns?*
- *How do psychological factors influence cancer patients' quality of life?*
- *What are the effects of stress on the immune system?*
- *What four personal factors are associated with health and resistance to stress?*
- *What are the relationships among gender, ethnicity, and health?*

Lifestyle and Health

- *What is the most dangerous health-threatening behavior?*
- *What are some health risks of alcohol abuse?*
- *What are some benefits of regular aerobic exercise?*
- *What are the benefits and risks associated with alternative medicine?*

How would you react to the news that you had a life-threatening disease?

Perhaps you remember Michael J. Fox as Alex P. Keaton, an endearing teenager on the hit 1980s TV series *Family Ties*. Or you may have seen him first as Marty McFly, who raced back and forth in time in the *Back to the Future* trilogy. Or you might have come to know him when he returned to prime-time television, portraying Michael Flaherty, New York's deputy mayor on ABC's *Spin City*.

In 1998, many were stunned when this popular star announced that he was a victim of Parkinson's disease, which he had been battling in secret for 7 years. Parkinson's is a debilitating degenerative disease that strikes the neural circuits and the inner workings of neurons in the brain that control movement. Symptoms include slow or jerky movements, tremors that range from mild to uncontrollable shaking, and garbled speech. Clearly, this is a particularly devastating disease for an actor. Can you imagine the stress Fox had to endure in keeping his illness a secret? Concerns about someone finding out or about how long he could physically and emotionally continue as an actor must have weighed heavily on him. Acting was his living, the way he supported his family.

Fox was deeply stressed, but not devastated. In fact, he didn't even slow down. He even wrote a book about his life titled *Lucky Man: A Memoir* (Fox, 2002). How could a person struggling with an ever-worsening, debilitating terminal disease consider himself lucky? Fox knows that his joys far outweigh his troubles. Not only has he had a very successful career in a highly competitive field, but more importantly, he has the love and support of his wife, actress Tracy Pollen, and their children.

Michael J. Fox is more than a successful actor who has been stricken with a terrible disease. He has turned tragedy into triumph and now spends his time, his financial resources, and his talents trying to help others. He chairs the Michael J. Fox Foundation for Parkinson's Disease Research to raise awareness of the disease and secure funds to help find a cure. And he knows, firsthand, that one's health is far more important than fame and fortune.

In this chapter, we explore many aspects of health and stress. We begin our exploration by looking at stress, which is necessary for survival, but which, if chronic and excessive, can become disabling or even deadly.

■ stress
The physiological and psychological response to a condition that threatens or challenges a person and requires some form of adaptation or adjustment.

■ fight-or-flight response
A response to stress in which the parasympathetic nervous system triggers the release of hormones that prepare the body to fight or flee.

■ stressor
Any stimulus or event capable of producing physical or emotional stress.

Sources of Stress

What do you mean when you say you are "stressed out"? Most psychologists define **stress** as the physiological and psychological response to a condition that threatens or challenges an individual and requires some form of adaptation or adjustment. Stress is associated with the **fight-or-flight response,** in which the body's parasympathetic nervous system triggers the release of hormones that prepare the body to fight or escape from a threat (see Chapter 2). Most of us frequently experience other kinds of **stressors,** stimuli or events that are capable of producing physical or emotional stress.

Holmes and Rahe's Social Readjustment Rating Scale

What was the Social Readjustment Rating Scale designed to reveal?

Researchers Holmes and Rahe (1967) developed the **Social Readjustment Rating Scale (SRRS)** to measure stress by ranking different life events from most to least stressful and assigning a point value to each event. Life events that produce the greatest life changes and require the greatest adaptation are considered the most stressful, regardless of whether the events are positive or negative. The 43 life events on the scale range from death of a spouse (assigned 100 stress points) to minor law violations such as getting a traffic ticket (11 points). Find your life stress score by completing *Try It 13.1* (on page 444).

Holmes and Rahe claim that there is a connection between the degree of life stress and major health problems. People who score 300 or more on the SRRS, the researchers say, run about an 80% risk of suffering a major health problem within the next 2 years. Those who score between 150 and 300 have a 50% chance of becoming ill within a 2-year period (Rahe et al., 1964). More recent research has shown that the weights given to life events by Holmes and Rahe continue to be appropriate for adults in North America and that SRRS scores are correlated with a variety of health indicators (Hobson & Delunas, 2001; Scully et al., 2000).

Even positive life events, such as getting married, can cause stress.

Some researchers have questioned whether a high score on the SRRS is a reliable predictor of future health problems (Krantz et al., 1985; McCrae, 1984). One of the main shortcomings of the SRRS is that it assigns a point value to each life change without taking into account how an individual copes with that stressor. One study found that SRRS scores did reliably predict disease progression in multiple sclerosis patients (Mohr et al., 2002). But the patients who used more effective coping strategies displayed less disease progression than did those who experienced similar stressors but coped poorly with them.

■ **Social Readjustment Rating Scale (SRRS)** Holmes and Rahe's measure of stress, which ranks 43 life events from most to least stressful and assigns a point value to each.

Daily Hassles and Uplifts

What roles do hassles and uplifts play in the stress of life, according to Lazarus?

Which is more stressful—major life events or those little problems and frustrations that seem to crop up every day? Richard Lazarus believes that the little stressors, which he calls **hassles,** cause more stress than major life events do. Daily hassles are the "irritating, frustrating, distressing demands and troubled relationships that plague us day in and day out" (Lazarus & DeLongis, 1983, p. 247). Kanner and others (1981) developed the Hassles Scale to assess various categories of hassles. Unlike the Holmes and Rahe scale, the Hassles Scale takes into account the facts that items may or may not represent stressors to individuals and that the amount of stress produced by an item varies from person to person. People completing the scale indicate the items that have been a hassle for them and rate those items for severity on a 3-point scale. Table 13.1 shows the ten hassles most frequently reported by college students.

■ **hassles** Little stressors, including the irritating demands that can occur daily, that may cause more stress than major life changes do.

■ **uplifts** The positive experiences in life, which may neutralize the effects of many hassles.

■ **approach-approach conflict** A conflict arising from having to choose between equally desirable alternatives.

DeLongis and others (1988) studied 75 American couples over a 6-month period and found that daily stress (as measured on the Hassles Scale) related significantly to present and future "health problems such as flu, sore throat, headaches, and backaches" (p. 486). Research also indicates that minor hassles that accompany stressful major life events, such as those measured by the SRRS, are better predictors of a person's level of psychological distress than the major events themselves (Pillow et al., 1996).

According to Lazarus, **uplifts,** or positive experiences in life, may neutralize the effects of many hassles. Lazarus and his colleagues also constructed an Uplifts Scale. As with the Hassles Scale, people completing this scale make a cognitive appraisal of what they consider to be an uplift. Items viewed as uplifts by some people may actually be stressors for others. For middle-aged people, uplifts are often health- or family-related, whereas for college students uplifts often take the form of having a good time (Kanner et al., 1981).

Making Choices

How do approach-approach, avoidance-avoidance, and approach-avoidance conflicts differ?

What happens when you have to decide which movie to see or which new restaurant to try? Simply making a choice, even among equally desirable alternatives (an **approach-approach conflict**), can be stressful. Some approach-approach

Try It 13.1 Finding a Life Stress Score

To assess your level of life changes, check all of the events that have happened to you in the past year. Add up the points to derive your life stress score. (Based on Holmes & Masuda, 1974.)

Rank	Life Event	Life Change Unit Value	Your Points
1	Death of spouse	100	____
2	Divorce	73	____
3	Marital separation	65	____
4	Jail term	63	____
5	Death of close family member	63	____
6	Personal injury or illness	53	____
7	Marriage	50	____
8	Getting fired at work	47	____
9	Marital reconciliation	45	____
10	Retirement	45	____
11	Change in health of family member	44	____
12	Pregnancy	40	____
13	Sex difficulties	39	____
14	Gain of new family member	39	____
15	Business readjustment	39	____
16	Change in financial state	38	____
17	Death of close friend	37	____
18	Change to different line of work	36	____
19	Change in number of arguments with spouse	35	____
20	Taking out loan for major purchase (e.g., home)	31	____
21	Foreclosure of mortgage or loan	30	____
22	Change in responsibilities at work	29	____
23	Son or daughter leaving home	29	____
24	Trouble with in-laws	29	____
25	Outstanding personal achievement	28	____
26	Spouse beginning or stopping work	26	____
27	Beginning or ending school	26	____
28	Change in living conditions	25	____
29	Revision of personal habits	24	____
30	Trouble with boss	23	____
31	Change in work hours or conditions	20	____
32	Change in residence	20	____
33	Change in schools	20	____
34	Change in recreation	19	____
35	Change in church activities	19	____
36	Change in social activities	18	____
37	Taking out loan for lesser purchase (e.g., car or TV)	17	____
38	Change in sleeping habits	16	____
39	Change in number of family get-togethers	15	____
40	Change in eating habits	15	____
41	Vacation	13	____
42	Christmas	12	____
43	Minor violation of the law	11	____
		Life stress score:	____

TABLE 13.1 The Ten Most Common Hassles for College Students

HASSLE	PERCENTAGE OF TIMES CHECKED
1. Troubling thoughts about future	76.6
2. Not getting enough sleep	72.5
3. Wasting time	71.1
4. Inconsiderate smokers	70.7
5. Physical appearance	69.9
6. Too many things to do	69.2
7. Misplacing or losing things	67.0
8. Not enough time to do the things you need to do	66.3
9. Concerns about meeting high standards	64.0
10. Being lonely	60.8

Source: Kanner et al. (1981).

conflicts are minor, such as deciding which movie to see. Others can have major consequences, such as the conflict between building a promising career or interrupting that career to raise a child. In an **avoidance-avoidance conflict,** a person must choose between two undesirable alternatives. For example, you may want to avoid studying for an exam, but at the same time you want to avoid failing the test. An **approach-avoidance conflict** involves a single choice that has both desirable and undesirable features. The person facing this type of conflict is simultaneously drawn to and repelled by a choice—for example, wanting to take a wonderful vacation but having to empty a savings account to do so.

■ **avoidance-avoidance conflict**
A conflict arising from having to choose between undesirable alternatives.

■ **approach-avoidance conflict**
A conflict arising when the same choice has both desirable and undesirable features.

Unpredictability and Lack of Control

How do the unpredictability and lack of control over a stressor affect its impact?

"Good morning, class. Today, we are going to have a pop quiz," your professor says. Do these words cause a fight-or-flight response in your body? Such reactions are common, because unpredictable stressors are more difficult to cope with than predictable stressors. Laboratory tests have shown that rats receiving electric shocks without warning develop more ulcers than rats given shocks just as often but only after receiving a warning (Weiss, 1972). Likewise, humans who are warned of a stressor before it occurs and have a chance to prepare themselves for it experience less stress than those who must cope with an unexpected stressor.

Our physical and psychological well-being is profoundly influenced by the degree to which we feel a sense of control over our lives (Rodin & Salovey, 1989). Langer and Rodin (1976) studied the effects of control on nursing-home residents. Residents in one group were given some measure of control over their lives, such as choices in arranging their rooms and in the times they could see movies. They showed improved health and well-being and had a lower death rate than another group who were not given such control. Within 18 months, 30% of the residents given no choices had died, compared with only 15% of those who had been given some control over their lives. Control is important for cancer patients, too. Some researchers suggest that a sense of control over their daily physical symptoms and emotional reactions may be even more important for cancer patients than control over the course of the disease itself (Thompson et al., 1993).

Several studies suggest that we are less subject to stress when we have the power to do something about it, whether we exercise that power or not. Glass and Singer (1972) subjected two groups of participants to the same loud noise. Participants in one group were told that they could, if necessary, terminate the noise by pressing a switch. These participants suffered less stress, even though they never did exercise the control they were given. Friedland and others (1992) suggest that when people experience a loss of control because of a stressor, they are motivated to try to reestablish control in the stressful situation. Failing this, they often attempt to increase their sense of control in other areas of their lives.

For people to function effectively and find satisfaction on the job, what nine variables should fall within their comfort zone?

Stress in the Workplace

Perhaps there is no more troublesome source of stress than the workplace. Everyone who works is subject to some job-related stress, but the amount and sources of the stress differ, depending on the type of job and the kind of organization. Albrecht (1979) suggests that if people are to function effectively and find satisfaction on the job, the following nine variables must fall within their comfort zone (see also Figure 13.1):

- *Workload.* Too much or too little to do can cause people to feel anxious, frustrated, and unrewarded.
- *Clarity of job description and evaluation criteria.* Anxiety arises from confusion about job responsibilities and performance criteria or from a job description that is too rigidly defined to leave room for individual initiative.
- *Physical variables.* Temperature, noise, humidity, pollution, amount of workspace, and the physical positions (standing or sitting) required to carry out job duties should fall within a person's comfort zone.
- *Job status.* People with very low-paying, low-status jobs may feel psychological discomfort; those with celebrity status often cannot handle the stress that fame brings.

FIGURE 13.1 Variables in Work Stress

For a person to function effectively and find satisfaction on the job, these nine variables should fall within the person's comfort zone.
Source: Albrecht (1979).

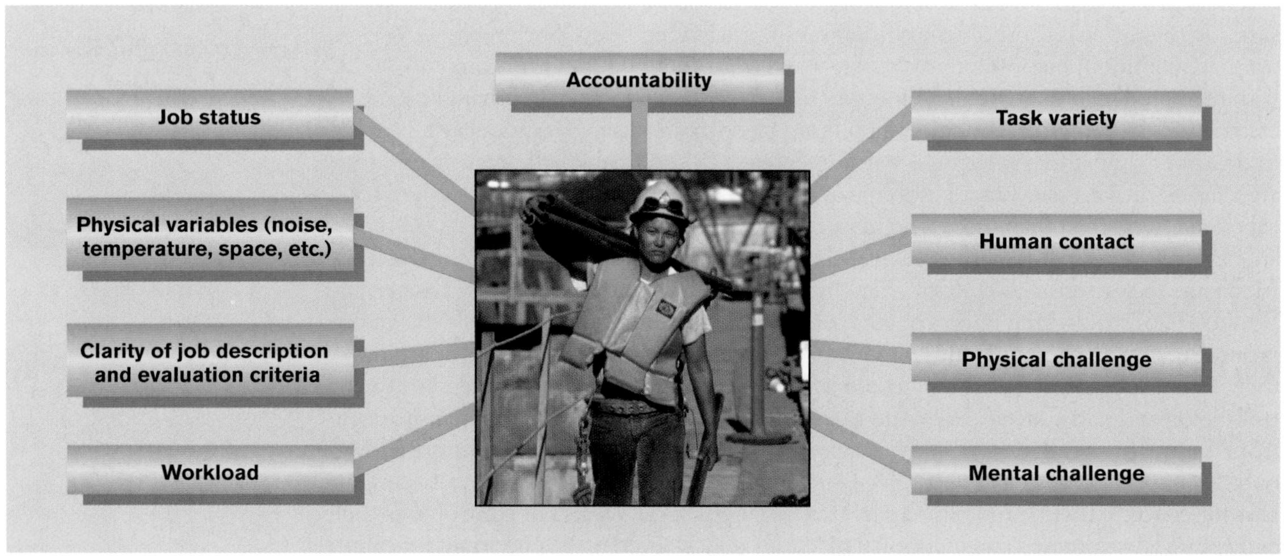

- *Accountability*. Accountability overload occurs when people have responsibility for the physical or psychological well-being of others but only a limited degree of control (air-traffic controllers, emergency room nurses and doctors); accountability underload occurs when workers perceive their jobs as meaningless.
- *Task variety*. To function well, people need a comfortable amount of variety and stimulation.
- *Human contact*. Some workers have virtually no human contact on the job (forest-fire lookouts); others have almost continuous contact with others (welfare and employment office workers). People vary greatly in how much interaction they enjoy or even tolerate.
- *Physical challenge*. Jobs range from being physically demanding (construction work, professional sports) to requiring little to no physical activity. Some jobs (firefighting, police work) involve physical risk.
- *Mental challenge*. Jobs that tax people beyond their mental capability, as well as those that require too little mental challenge, can be frustrating.

Air-traffic controllers have an extremely high-stress job. The on-the-job stress they experience increases the risk of coronary disease and stroke.

Workplace stress can be especially problematic for women because of sex-specific stressors, including sex discrimination and sexual harassment in the workplace and difficulties in combining work and family roles. These added stressors have been shown to increase the negative effects of occupational stress on the health and well-being of working women (Swanson, 2000).

Job stress can have a variety of consequences. Perhaps the most frequently cited is reduced effectiveness on the job. But job stress can also lead to absenteeism, tardiness, accidents, substance abuse, and lower morale. However, as you might predict, unemployment is far more stressful for most people than any of the variables associated with on-the-job stress (Price et al., 2002). Given a choice between a high-stress job and no job at all, most of us would choose the former.

Catastrophic Events

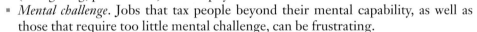

How do people typically react to catastrophic events?

Catastrophic events such as the terrorist attacks of September 11, 2001, and the crash of the space shuttle Columbia in early 2003 are stressful both for those who experience them directly and for people who learn of them via news media. Most people are able to manage the stress associated with such catastrophes. However, for some, these events lead to **posttraumatic stress disorder (PTSD)**, a prolonged and severe stress reaction to a catastrophic event (such as a plane crash or an earthquake) or to severe, chronic stress (such as that experienced by soldiers engaged in combat or residents of neighborhoods in which violent crime is a daily occurrence) (Kilpatrick et al., 2003).

The potential impact of catastrophic events on the incidence of PTSD is illustrated by surveys conducted before and after September 11, 2001. Prior to the terrorist attacks, most surveys found that between 1% and 2% of Americans met the diagnostic criteria for PTSD (Foa & Meadows, 1997). Two months after the attacks, about 17% of Americans surveyed by researchers at the University of California–Irvine reported symptoms of PTSD. When the researchers conducted follow-up interviews with survey participants 6 months after the attacks, 6% of them were still experiencing distress. Other researchers have found additional lingering effects associated with September 11 (see Figure 13.2, on page 448).

People with posttraumatic stress disorder often have flashbacks, nightmares, or intrusive memories that make them feel as though they are actually re-experiencing

■ **posttraumatic stress disorder (PTSD)**
A prolonged and severe stress reaction to a catastrophic event or to severe, chronic stress.

FIGURE 13.2 **Americans' Stress Levels after September 11, 2001**

Researchers have found that Americans continued to experience increased levels of stress and anxiety several months after the terrorist attacks of September 11, 2001.

Sources: Clay (2002), Clay et al. (2002), Schlenger et al. (2002), Silver et al. (2002).

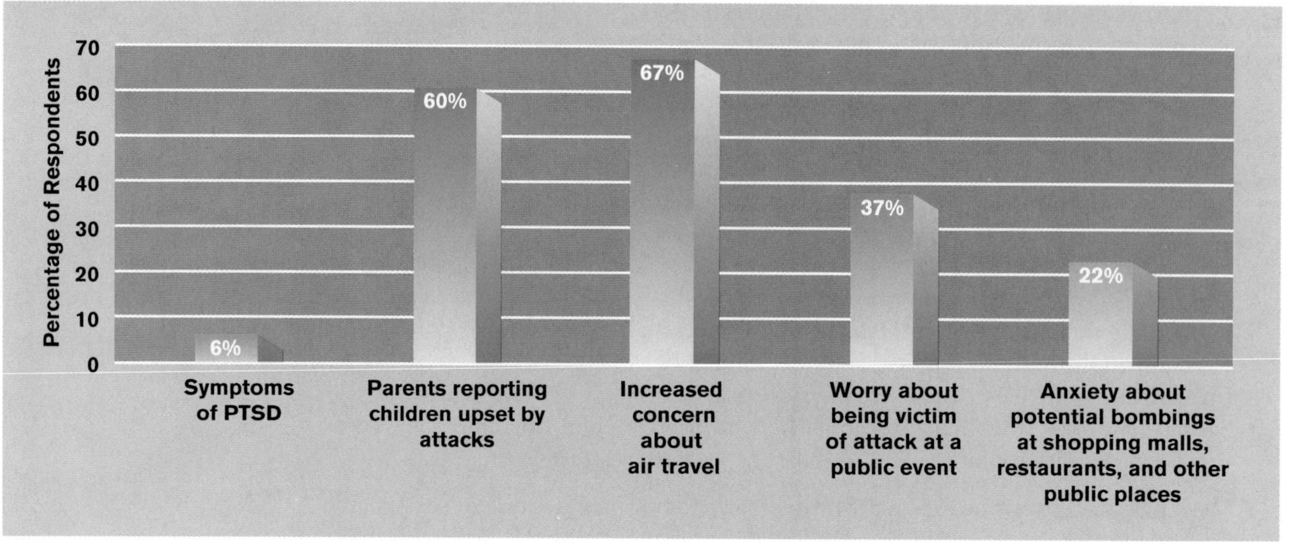

the traumatic event. They suffer increased anxiety and startle easily, particularly in response to anything that reminds them of the trauma (Green et al., 1985). Many survivors of war or catastrophic events experience *survivor guilt* because they lived while others died; some feel that perhaps they could have done more to save others. Extreme combat-related guilt in Vietnam veterans is a risk factor for suicide or preoccupation with suicide (Hendin & Haas, 1991). One study of women with PTSD revealed that they were twice as likely as women without PTSD to experience first-onset depression and three times as likely to develop alcohol problems (Breslau et al., 1997). PTSD sufferers also experience cognitive difficulties, such as poor concentration (Vasterling et al., 2002).

Racism and Stress

How might historical racism affect the health of African Americans?

A significant source of chronic stress is being a member of a minority group in a majority culture. A study of White and African American participants' responses to a questionnaire about ways of managing stress revealed that a person may experience racial stress from simply being one of the few or only members of a particular race in any of a variety of settings, such as a classroom, the workplace, or a social situation (Plummer & Slane, 1996). The feelings of stress experienced in such situations can be intense, even in the absence of racist attitudes, discrimination, or any other overt evidence of racism.

Some theorists have proposed that a phenomenon called *historical racism*—experienced by members of groups that have a history of repression—can also be a source of stress (Troxel et al., 2003). Researchers interested in the effects of historical racism have focused primarily on African Americans. Many of these researchers claim that the higher incidence of high blood pressure among African Americans is attributable to stress associated with historical racism. Surveys have shown that African Americans experience more race-related stress than members of other minority groups do (Utsey et al., 2002). Those African Americans who express the highest levels of concern about racism display higher levels of cardiovascular reactivity to experimentally induced stressors, such as sudden loud noises, than do peers who express less concern (Bowen-Reid & Harrell, 2002). Thus, there may indeed be a link between perceptions of historical racism and high blood pressure.

However, African Americans are also more likely than members of other minority groups to have a strong sense of ethnic identity, a factor that helps moderate the effects of racial stress (Utsey et al., 2002). But some studies show that personal characteristics, such as hostility, may increase the effects of racial stress (Fang & Myers, 2001; Raeikkoenen et al., 2003). So, the relationship between historical racism and cardiovascular health is probably fairly complex and varies considerably across individuals. Moreover, some researchers believe that the association must be studied more thoroughly in other historically repressed groups, such as Native Americans, before firm conclusions can be drawn (Belcourt-Dittloff & Stewart, 2000).

A strong sense of ethnic identity helps African Americans cope with the stress that may arise from living with racism.

Remember It 13.1

1. According to Holmes and Rahe, health may be adversely affected if a person experiences many stressful __________ in a short period of time.
2. According to Lazarus, __________ typically cause more stress than major life events do.
3. Rich cannot decide whether to go out with friends or stay home and study for tomorrow's test. This is an example of an __________ conflict.
4. The belief that one has __________ over a situation can moderate the effects of stress.
5. The nine variables proposed by Albrecht to account for most job-related stress are __________, __________, __________, __________, __________, __________, __________, __________, and __________.
6. __________ is a prolonged and severe stress reaction that can result from experiencing a catastrophic event.
7. Some researchers have found links between __________ and high-blood pressure in African Americans.

ANSWERS: 1. life events; 2. hassles; 3. approach-avoidance; 4. control; 5. workload, job status, physical variables, clarity of job description, accountability, task variety, human contact, physical challenge, mental challenge; 6. Posttraumatic stress disorder; 7. historical racism

Responding to Stress

How do you respond to stress? Psychologists have different views of the ways in which people respond to stressful experiences. Each approach can help us gain insight into our own experiences and, perhaps, deal more effectively with stress.

general adaptation syndrome (GAS) The predictable sequence of reactions (alarm, resistance, and exhaustion stages) that organisms show in response to stressors.

Selye and the General Adaptation Syndrome

What is the general adaptation syndrome?

Hans Selye (1907–1982), the researcher most prominently associated with the effects of stress on health, established the field of stress research. At the heart of Selye's concept of stress is the **general adaptation syndrome (GAS),** the predictable sequence of reactions that organisms show in response to stressors. It consists of three stages: the alarm stage, the resistance stage, and the exhaustion stage (Selye, 1956). (See Figure 13.3, on page 450.)

FIGURE 13.3 The General Adaptation Syndrome

The three stages in Selye's general adaptation syndrome are (1) the alarm stage, during which there is emotional arousal and the defensive forces of the body are mobilized for fight or flight; (2) the resistance stage, in which intense physiological efforts are exerted to resist or adapt to the stressor; and (3) the exhaustion stage, when the organism fails in its efforts to resist the stressor.
Source: Selye (1956).

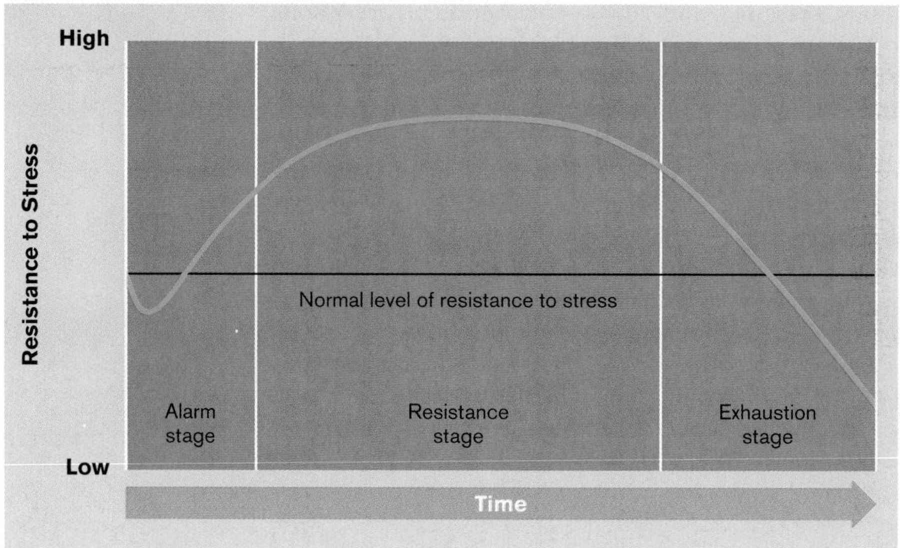

■ alarm stage
The first stage of the general adaptation syndrome, in which the person experiences a burst of energy that aids in dealing with the stressful situation.

■ resistance stage
The second stage of the general adaptation syndrome, when there are intense physiological efforts to either resist or adapt to the stressor.

■ exhaustion stage
The third stage of the general adaptation syndrome, which occurs if the organism fails in its efforts to resist the stressor.

The first stage of the body's response to a stressor is the **alarm stage,** in which the adrenal cortex releases hormones called *glucocorticoids* that increase heart rate, blood pressure, and blood-sugar levels, supplying a burst of energy that helps the person deal with the stressful situation (Pennisi, 1997). Next, the organism enters the **resistance stage**, during which the adrenal cortex continues to release glucocorticoids to help the body resist stressors. The length of the resistance stage depends both on the intensity of the stressor and on the body's power to adapt. If the organism finally fails in its efforts to resist, it reaches the **exhaustion stage,** at which point all the stores of deep energy are depleted, and disintegration and death follow.

Selye found that the most harmful effects of stress are due to the prolonged secretion of glucocorticoids, which can lead to permanent increases in blood pressure, suppression of the immune system, weakening of muscles, and even damage to the hippocampus (Stein-Behrens et al., 1994). Thanks to Selye, the connection between extreme, prolonged stress and certain diseases is now widely accepted by medical experts.

Lazarus's Cognitive Theory of Stress

What are the roles of primary and secondary appraisals when a person is confronted with a potentially stressful event?

Is it the stressor itself that upsets us, or the way we think about it? Richard Lazarus (1966; Lazarus & Folkman, 1984) contends that it is not the stressor that causes stress, but a person's perception of it. According to Lazarus, when people are confronted with a potentially stressful event, they engage in a cognitive process that involves a primary and a secondary appraisal. A **primary appraisal** is an evaluation of the meaning and significance of the situation—whether its effect on one's well-being is positive, irrelevant, or negative. An event appraised as stressful could involve (1) harm or loss, that is, damage that has already occurred; (2) threat, or the potential for harm or loss; or (3) challenge, that is, the opportunity to grow or to gain. An appraisal of threat, harm, or loss can occur in relation to anything important to you—a friendship, a part of your body, your property, your finances, your self-esteem. When people appraise a situation as involving threat, harm, or loss, they experience negative emotions such as anxiety, fear, anger, and resentment (Folkman, 1984). An appraisal that sees a challenge, on the other hand, is usually accompanied by positive emotions such as excitement, hopefulness, and eagerness.

■ primary appraisal
A cognitive evaluation of a potentially stressful event to determine whether its effect is positive, irrelevant, or negative.

During **secondary appraisal**, if people judge the situation to be within their control, they make an evaluation of available resources—physical (health, energy, stamina), social (support network), psychological (skills, morale, self-esteem), material (money, tools, equipment), and time. Then, they consider the options and decide how to deal with the stressor. The level of stress they feel is largely a function of whether their resources are adequate to cope with the threat, and how severely those resources will be taxed in the process. Figure 13.4 summarizes the Lazarus and Folkman psychological model of stress. Research supports their claim that the physiological, emotional, and behavioral reactions to stressors depend partly on whether the stressors are appraised as challenging or threatening.

secondary appraisal A cognitive evaluation of available resources and options prior to deciding how to deal with a stressor.

coping Efforts through action and thought to deal with demands that are perceived as taxing or overwhelming.

Coping Strategies

What is the difference between problem-focused and emotion-focused coping?

If you're like most people, the stresses you have experienced have helped you develop some coping stratgies. **Coping** refers to a person's efforts through action and thought to deal with demands perceived as taxing or overwhelming. **Problem-focused coping** is direct; it consists of reducing, modifying, or eliminating the source of stress itself. If you are getting a poor grade in history and appraise this as a threat, you may study harder, talk over your problem with your professor, form a study group with other class members, get a tutor, or drop the course.

problem-focused coping A direct response aimed at reducing, modifying, or eliminating a source of stress.

FIGURE 13.4 Lazarus and Folkman's Psychological Model of Stress

Potentially Stressful Event

↓

Primary Appraisal
Person evaluates event as positive, neutral, or negative.
Negative appraisal can involve:
- **Harm or loss** (damage has already occurred)
- **Threat** (the potential for harm or loss)
- **Challenge** (the opportunity to grow or gain)

↓

Secondary Appraisal
If the situation is judged to be within the person's control:
1. Person evaluates coping resources (physical, social, psychological, material) to determine if they are adequate to deal with stressor.
2. Person considers options in dealing with stressor.

↓

Stress Response
- **Physiological:** Autonomic arousal, fluctuations in hormones
- **Emotional:** Anxiety, fear, grief, resentment, excitement
- **Behavioral:** Coping behaviors (including problem-focused and emotion-focused coping strategies)

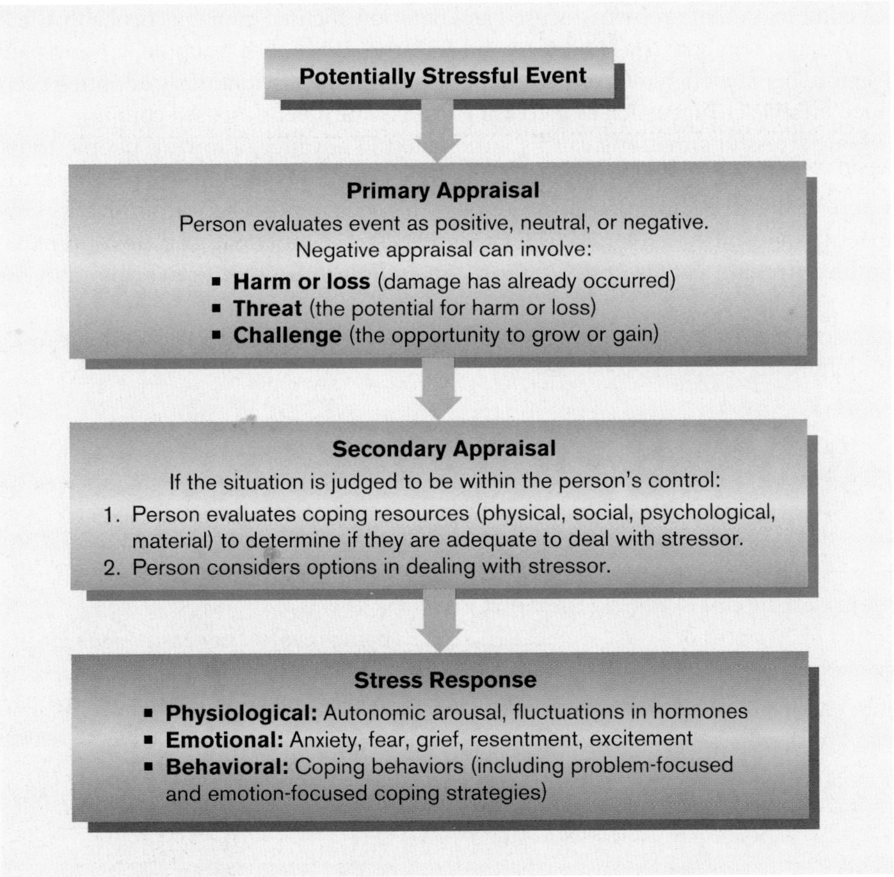

Lazarus and Folkman emphasize the importance of a person's perceptions and appraisal of stressors. The stress response depends on the outcome of the primary and secondary appraisals, whether the person's coping resources are adequate to cope with the threat, and how severely the resources are taxed in the process.
Source: Folkman (1984).

REVIEW *and* REFLECT 13.1

Theories of Stress Responses

THEORY	DESCRIPTION
Selye's general adaptation syndrome (GAS)	Three stages: alarm, resistance, and exhaustion
Lazarus's cognitive theory	Primary appraisal (evaluation of stressor), followed by secondary appraisal (evaluation of resources and options)
Coping strategies	Problem-focused coping, directed toward stressor; emotion-focused coping, directed toward the emotional response to the stressor

Want to be sure you've fully absorbed the material in this chapter? Visit **www.ablongman.com/wood5e** for access to free practice tests, flashcards, interactive activities, and links developed specifically to help you succeed in psychology.

Emotion-focused coping involves reappraising a stressor in order to reduce its emotional impact. If you lose your job, you may decide that it isn't a major tragedy and instead view it as a challenge, an opportunity to find a better job with a higher salary. Despite what you may have heard, ignoring a stressor—one form of emotion-focused coping—can be an effective way of managing stress. Researchers studied 116 people who had experienced heart attacks (Ginzburg et al., 2002). All of the participants reported being worried about suffering another attack. However, those who tried to ignore their worries were less likely to exhibit anxiety-related symptoms such as nightmares and flashbacks. Other emotion-focused strategies, though, such as keeping a journal in which you write about your worries and track how they change over time, may be even more effective (Pennebaker & Seagal, 1999; Solano et al., 2003).

A combination of problem-focused and emotion-focused coping is probably the best stress-management strategy (Folkman and Lazarus, 1980). For example, a heart patient may ignore her anxiety (emotion-focused coping) while conscientiously adopting recommended lifestyle changes such as increasing exercise (problem-focused coping).

Some stressful situations can be anticipated in advance, allowing people to use a strategy called **proactive coping,** which consists of efforts or actions taken in advance of a potentially stressful situation to prevent its occurrence or to minimize its consequences (Aspinwall & Taylor, 1997). Proactive copers anticipate and then prepare for upcoming stressful events and situations, including those that are certain and those that are only likely.

Review and Reflect 13.1 summarizes the key aspects of the various theories concerning humans' response to stress.

■ **emotion-focused coping** A response involving reappraisal of a stressor to reduce its emotional impact.

■ **proactive coping** Active measures taken in advance of a potentially stressful situation in order to prevent its occurrence or to minimize its consequences.

Remember It 13.2

1. Selye focused on the __________ aspects of stress, but Lazarus focused on its __________ aspects.
2. Match each stage of the GAS with its description.
   ____ (1) alarm stage
   ____ (2) resistance stage
   ____ (3) exhaustion stage
   a. depletion of all stores of deep energy
   b. intense physiological efforts to adapt to the stressor
   c. emotional arousal and preparation for fight or flight
3. During __________ appraisal, a person evaluates his or her coping resources and considers options for dealing with a stressor.
4. __________ coping involves adjusting one's emotions to deal with a stressor, while __________ coping involves modifying or eliminating a particular stressor.

ANSWERS: 1. physiological, psychological; 2. (1) c, (2) b, (3) a; 3. secondary; 4. Emotion-focused, problem-focused

Health and Illness

Have you heard the term *wellness* and wondered exactly what was meant by it? This word is associated with a new approach to thinking about health, used by both professionals and laypersons. This approach encompasses a growing emphasis on lifestyle, preventive care, and the need to maintain wellness rather than thinking of health matters only when the body is sick. Health psychologists are discovering how stress, through its influence on the immune system, may affect people's health. They are also examining how personal and demographic factors are related to both illness and wellness.

■ **biomedical model** A perspective that explains illness solely in terms of biological factors.

■ **biopsychosocial model** A perspective that focuses on health as well as illness and holds that both are determined by a combination of biological, psychological, and social factors.

Two Approaches to Health and Illness

For many decades, the predominant view in medicine was the **biomedical model**, which explains illness in terms of biological factors. Today, physicians and psychologists alike recognize that the **biopsychosocial model** provides a fuller explanation of both health and illness (see Figure 13.5) (Engel, 1977, 1980; Schwartz, 1982). This model considers health and illness to be determined by a combination of biological, psychological, and social factors.

How do the biomedical and biopsychosocial models differ in their approaches to health and illness?

FIGURE 13.5 The Biopsychosocial Model of Health and Illness

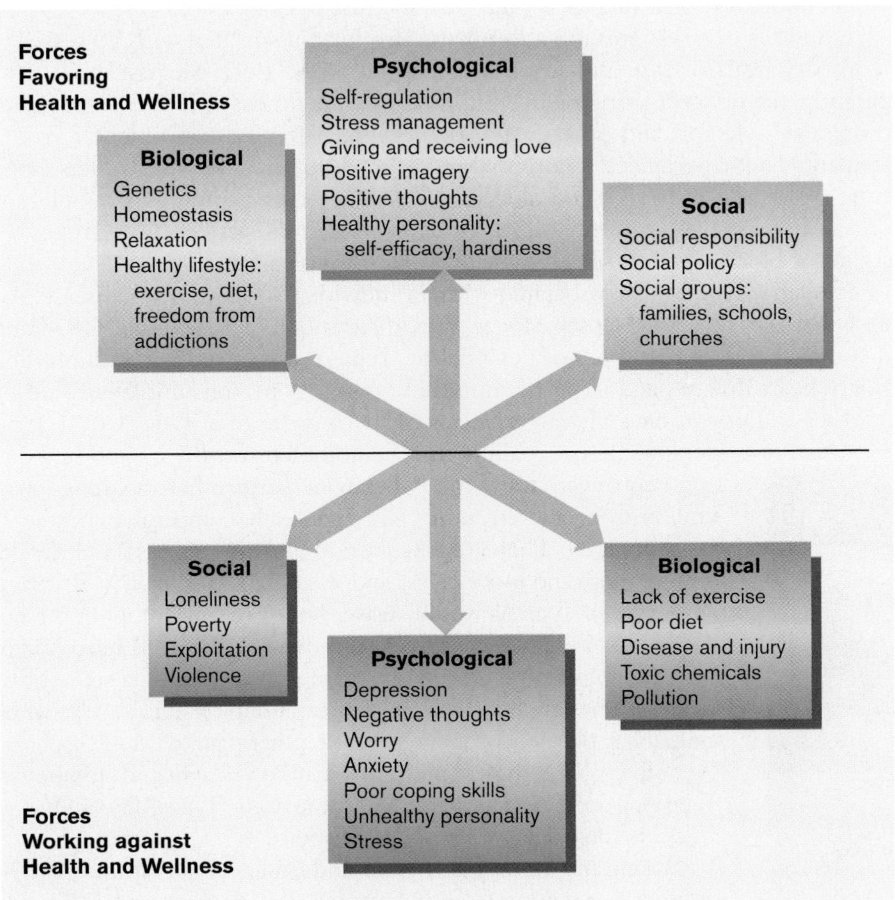

The biopsychosocial model focuses on health as well as on illness and holds that both are determined by a combination of biological, psychological, and social factors. Most health psychologists endorse the biopsychosocial model.
Source: Green & Shellenberger (1990).

health psychology The subfield within psychology that is concerned with the psychological factors that contribute to health, illness, and recovery.

Growing acceptance of the biopsychosocial approach has given rise to a new subfield, **health psychology**, which is "the field within psychology devoted to understanding psychological influences on how people stay healthy, why they become ill, and how they respond when they do get ill" (Taylor, 1991, p. 6). Health psychology is particularly important today because several prevalent diseases, including heart disease and cancer, are related to unhealthy lifestyles and stress (Taylor & Repetti, 1997).

Coronary Heart Disease

What are the Type A and Type B behavior patterns?

In order to survive, the heart muscle requires a steady, sufficient supply of oxygen and nutrients carried by the blood. Coronary heart disease is caused by the narrowing or the blockage of the coronary arteries, the arteries that supply blood to the heart muscle. Although coronary heart disease remains the leading cause of death in the United States, responsible for 31% of all deaths, deaths due to this cause have declined 50% during the past 30 years (National Center for Health Statistics, 2000).

A health problem of modern times, coronary heart disease is largely attributable to lifestyle and is therefore an important field of study for health psychologists. A *sedentary lifestyle*—one that includes a job at which one spends most of the time sitting and less than 20 minutes of exercise three times per week—is the primary modifiable risk factor contributing to death from coronary heart disease (Gallo et al., 2003). Other modifiable risk factors are high serum cholesterol level, cigarette smoking, and obesity.

Though not modifiable, another important risk factor is family history. The association between family history and coronary heart disease is both genetic and behavioral. For instance, individuals whose parents have high blood pressure, but who have not yet developed the disorder themselves, exhibit the same kinds of emotional reactivity and poor coping strategies as their parents (Frazer et al., 2002).

Type A behavior pattern A behavior pattern marked by a sense of time urgency, impatience, excessive competitiveness, hostility, and anger; considered a risk factor in coronary heart disease.

Type B behavior pattern A behavior pattern marked by a relaxed, easygoing approach to life, without the time urgency, impatience, and hostility of the Type A pattern.

High levels of stress and job strain have also been associated with increased risk for coronary heart disease and stroke (Rosengren et al., 1991; Siegrist et al., 1990). Apparently, the effects of stress enter the bloodstream almost as if they were injected intravenously. Malkoff and others (1993) report that after an experimental group of participants had experienced laboratory-induced stress, their blood platelets (special clotting cells) released large amounts of a substance that promotes the buildup of plaque in blood vessels and may lead to heart attack and stroke. No changes were found in the blood platelets of unstressed control-group participants.

Personality type is also associated with an individual's risk of heart disease. After extensive research, cardiologists Meyer Friedman and Ray Rosenman (1974) concluded that there are two types of personality: Type A, associated with a high rate of coronary heart disease, and Type B, commonly found in persons unlikely to develop heart disease. Do you have characteristics similar to those of a Type A or a Type B person? Before reading further, complete *Try It 13.2* and find out.

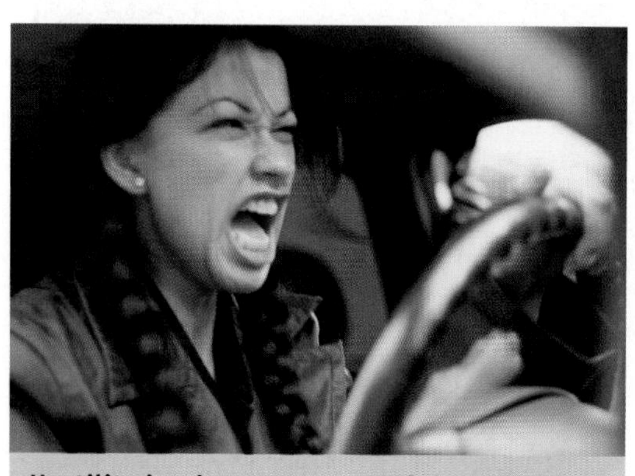

Hostility is a key component of the Type A behavior pattern.

People with the **Type A behavior pattern** have a strong sense of time urgency and are impatient, excessively competitive, hostile, and easily angered. They are "involved in a chronic, incessant struggle to achieve more and more in less and less time" (Friedman & Rosenman, 1974, p. 84). Type A's would answer "true" to most or all of the questions in the *Try It*. In contrast, people with the **Type B behavior pattern** are relaxed and easygoing and are not driven by a sense of time urgency. They are not impatient or hostile and are able to relax without guilt. They play for fun and relaxation rather than to exhibit superiority over others. Yet, a Type B individual may be as bright and ambitious as a Type A person, and more successful as well. Type B's would answer "false" to most or all of the *Try It* questions.

Using meta-analysis, Miller and others (1991) found that 70% of middle-aged men with coronary heart disease exhibited the

Try It 13.2 Type A or Type B?

Answer true (T) or false (F) for each of the statements below. (Adapted from Friedman & Rosenman, 1974.)

____ 1. I forcefully emphasize key words in my everyday speech.

____ 2. I usually walk and eat quickly.

____ 3. I get irritated and restless around slow workers.

____ 4. When talking to others, I get impatient and try to hurry them along.

____ 5. I get very irritated, even hostile, when the car in front of me drives too slowly.

____ 6. When others are talking, I often think about my own concerns.

____ 7. I usually think of or do at least two things at the same time.

____ 8. I get very impatient when I have to wait.

____ 9. I usually take command and move the conversation to topics that interest me.

____ 10. I usually feel guilty when I relax and do nothing.

____ 11. I am usually too absorbed in my work to notice my surroundings.

____ 12. I keep trying to do more and more in less time.

____ 13. I sometimes punctuate my conversation with forceful gestures such as clenching my fists or pounding the table.

____ 14. My accomplishments are due largely to my ability to work faster than others.

____ 15. I don't play games just for fun. I play to win.

____ 16. I am more concerned with acquiring things than with becoming a better person.

____ 17. I usually use numbers to evaluate my own activities and the activities of others.

Type A behavior pattern, compared to 46% of healthy middle-aged men. Research indicates that the lethal core of the Type A personality is not time urgency but anger and hostility, which fuel an aggressive, reactive temperament (Miller et al., 1996; Smith & Ruiz, 2002; Williams, 1993). Hostility is not only highly predictive of coronary heart disease but also associated with ill health in general (Miller et al., 1996).

How do psychological factors influence cancer patients' quality of life?

Cancer

Cancer is the second leading cause of death in the United States, accounting for 23% of all deaths (National Center for Health Statistics, 2000). Cancer strikes frequently in the adult population, and about 30% of Americans—over 75 million people—will develop cancer at some time in their lives. The young are not spared the scourge of cancer, for it takes the lives of more children aged 3 to 14 than any other disease.

Cancer, a collection of diseases rather than a single illness, can invade cells in any part of a living organism—humans, other animals, and even plants. Normal cells in all parts of the body divide, but fortunately they have built-in instructions about when to stop dividing. Unlike normal cells, cancer cells do not stop dividing. And, unless caught in time and destroyed, they continue to grow and spread, eventually killing the organism. Health psychologists point out that an unhealthy diet, smoking, excessive alcohol consumption, promiscuous sexual behavior, or becoming sexually active in the early teens (especially for females) are all behaviors that increase the risk of cancer.

This group of cancer patients is involved in art therapy, which is believed to lower the stress level associated with having a serious illness.

The more than 1 million people in the United States who are diagnosed with cancer each year have the difficult task of adjusting to a potentially life-threatening disease and the chronic stressors associated with it. Thus, researchers claim that cancer patients need more than medical treatment. Their therapy should include help with psychological and behavioral factors that can influence their quality of life. Carver and others (1993) found that 3 months and 6 months after surgery, breast cancer patients who maintained an optimistic outlook, accepted the reality of their situation, and maintained a sense of humor experienced less distress. Patients who engaged in denial—refusal to accept the reality of their situation—and had thoughts of giving up experienced much higher levels of distress. Dunkel-Schetter and others (1992) found that the most effective elements of a strategy for coping with cancer were social support (such as through self-help groups), a focus on the positive, and distraction. Avoidant coping strategies such as fantasizing, denial, and social withdrawal were associated with more emotional distress.

The Immune System and Stress

What are the effects of stress on the immune system?

Composed of an army of highly specialized cells and organs, the immune system works to identify and search out and destroy bacteria, viruses, fungi, parasites, and any other foreign matter that may enter the body. The key components of the immune system are white blood cells known as **lymphocytes**, which include B cells and T cells. *B cells* are so named because they are produced in the bone marrow. *T cells* derive their name from the thymus gland where they are produced. All cells foreign to the body, such as bacteria, viruses, and so on, are known as *antigens*. B cells produce proteins called *antibodies*, which are highly effective in destroying antigens that live in the bloodstream and in the fluid surrounding body tissues (Paul, 1993). For defeating harmful foreign invaders that have taken up residence inside the body's cells, however, T cells are critically important.

The immune system may turn on healthy cells or specific organs and attack them, as happens in autoimmune diseases such as juvenile diabetes, multiple sclerosis, rheumatoid arthritis, and lupus. Moreover, the system itself may be the target of a disease-causing organism. In Chapter 12, you learned about *acquired immune deficiency syndrome (AIDS)*, which is caused by the *human immunodeficiency virus (HIV)*. The virus attacks the T cells, gradually but relentlessly weakening the immune system until it is essentially nonfunctional.

Psychoneuroimmunology is a field of study in which psychologists, biologists, and medical researchers combine their expertise to learn the effects of psychological factors—emotions, thinking, and behavior—on the immune system (Cohen, 1996). Researchers now know that the immune system is not just a means for fighting off foreign invaders. Rather, it is an incredibly complex, interconnected defense system working with the brain to keep the body healthy (Ader, 2000).

Psychological factors, emotions, and stress are all related to immune system functioning (Kiecolt-Glaser et al., 2002). The immune system exchanges information with the brain, and what goes on in the brain can apparently enhance or suppress the immune system. In one study, researchers gave volunteers nasal drops containing a cold virus. Within the next few days, symptoms of the viral infection rose sharply in some of the 151 women and 125 men who participated in the study, but less so or not at all in others. Participants with a rich social life in the form of frequent interactions with others—spouses, children, parents, co-workers, friends, and volunteer and religious groups—seemed to enjoy a powerful shield of protection against the virus infection. This pattern of protection held across age and racial groups, for both sexes, at all educational levels, and at every season of the year (Ader, 2000; Cohen et al., 1997).

Close social ties—to family, friends, and others—apparently have good effects on the immune system. Ill effects often come from stress. Periods of high stress are correlated with increased symptoms of many infectious diseases, including oral and genital

■ **lymphocytes**
The white blood cells—including B cells and T cells—that are the key components of the immune system.

■ **psychoneuroimmunology**
(sye-ko-NEW-ro-IM-you-NOLL-oh-gee) A field in which psychologists, biologists, and medical researchers combine their expertise to study the effects of psychological factors on the immune system.

herpes, mononucleosis, colds, and flu. Stress can cause decreased levels of the immune system's B and T cells. Kiecolt-Glaser and others (1996) found that elderly men and women experiencing chronic stress as a result of years of caring for a spouse with Alzheimer's disease showed an impaired immune response to flu shots. Physicians have long observed that stress and anxiety can worsen autoimmune diseases. And "if fear can produce relapses [in autoimmune diseases], then even the fear of a relapse may become a self-fulfilling prophecy" (Steinman, 1993, p. 112). Stress is also associated with an increase in illness behaviors—reporting physical symptoms and seeking medical care (Cohen & Herbert, 1996; Cohen & Williamson, 1991).

Stress has the power to suppress the immune system long after the stressful experience is over. An experimental group of medical students who were enduring the stress of major exams was compared with a control group of medical students who were on vacation from classes and exams. When tested for the presence of disease-fighting antibodies, participants in the exam group, but not those in the control group, had a significant reduction in their antibody count because of the stress. The lowered antibody count was still present 14 days after the exams were over. At that point, the students were not even aware that they were still stressed and reported feeling no stress (Deinzer et al., 2000).

In addition to academic pressures, poor marital relationships and sleep deprivation have been linked to lowered immune response (Kiecolt-Glaser et al., 1987; Maier & Laudenslager, 1985). Several researchers have reported that severe, incapacitating depression is also related to lowered immune system activity (Herbert & Cohen, 1993). For several months after the death of a spouse, the widow or widower suffers weakened immune system function and is at a higher risk of mortality. Severe bereavement weakens the immune system, increasing a person's chance of suffering from a long list of physical and mental ailments for up to 2 years following a partner's death (Prigerson et al., 1997).

Personal Factors Reducing the Impact of Stress and Illness

What four personal factors are associated with health and resistance to stress?

There are several personal factors that seem to offer protection against the effects of stress and illness.

Optimism People who are generally optimistic tend to cope more effectively with stress, and this, in turn, may reduce their risk of illness (Seligman, 1990). An important characteristic optimists share is that they generally expect good outcomes. Such positive expectations help make them more stress-resistant than pessimists, who tend to expect bad outcomes. An especially lethal form of pessimism is hopelessness. A longitudinal study of a large number of Finnish men revealed that participants who reported feeling moderate to high hopelessness died from all causes at two to three times the rates of those reporting low or no hopelessness (Everson et al., 1996).

Hardiness Studying male executives with high levels of stress, psychologist Suzanne Kobasa (1979; Kobasa et al., 1982) found three psychological characteristics that distinguished those who remained healthy from those who had a high incidence of illness. The three qualities, which she referred to collectively as **hardiness**, are *commitment*, *control*, and *challenge*. Hardy individuals feel a strong sense of commitment to both their work and their personal life. They see themselves not as victims of whatever life brings, but as people who have control over consequences and outcomes. They act to solve their own problems, and they welcome challenges in life, viewing them not as threats but as opportunities for growth and improvement.

Florian and others (1995) found that commitment and control alone are apparently sufficient to produce hardiness. In stressful situations, commitment and control are compatible, complementary attributes. Commitment ensures a continuing involvement in the situation and provides the staying power to see it through. A

■ hardiness
A combination of three psychological qualities—commitment, control, and challenge—shared by people who can handle high levels of stress and remain healthy.

person who is committed does not give up. Control provides confidence that the person is in charge of the situation and is capable of finding the right solution to solve the problems at hand.

Religious Involvement Another personal factor that contributes to resistance to stress and illness is religious faith (Miller & Thoresen, 2003). One longitudinal study (conducted over a period of 28 years) revealed that frequent attendance at religious services is correlated with better health habits (Strawbridge et al., 1997). A meta-analysis of 42 separate studies combined data on some 126,000 individuals and revealed that religious involvement is positively associated with measures of physical health and lower rates of cancer, heart disease, and stroke (McCullough et al., 2000). Also, measures of religious involvement were reliable predictors of greater longevity when all causes of mortality were considered. The specific measures of religious involvement most closely related to a lower mortality rate were regular attendance at worship services, religious orthodoxy, and a personal sense of comfort and strength from one's religion (McCullough et al., 2000). This study and others have found the association between religious involvement and lower mortality to be stronger for women than for men (Hummer et al., 1999; Strawbridge et al., 1997).

Why is religious involvement linked to health? Researchers are currently examining a number of hypotheses (Powell et al., 2003). One proposal is that individuals who frequent religious services experience proportionately more positive emotions than those who do not attend. Another is that religious involvement provides people with a stronger form of social support than is available to those who are not religious. Essentially, this hypothesis claims that social support may be more meaningful, and more effective, when it comes from others who share your world view. Researchers have also proposed that religious practices, specifically meditation and prayer, may have positive effects on health-related physiological variables such as blood pressure (Seeman et al., 2003).

■ **social support**
Tangible and/or emotional support provided in time of need by family members, friends, and others; the feeling of being loved, valued, and cared for by those toward whom we feel a similar obligation.

Social Support Another factor contributing to better health is **social support** (Cohen, 1988; Kaplan et al., 1994). Social support is support provided, usually in time of need, by a spouse, other family members, friends, neighbors, colleagues, support groups, or others. It can involve tangible aid, information, and advice, as well as emotional support. It can also be viewed as the feeling of being loved, valued, and cared for by those toward whom we feel a similar obligation.

Social support appears to have positive effects on the body's immune system as well as on the cardiovascular and endocrine systems (Holt-Lunstad et al., 2003; Miller et al., 2002; Uchino et al., 1996). Social support may help encourage health-promoting behaviors and reduce the impact of stress so that people are less likely to resort to unhealthy methods of coping, such as smoking or drinking. Further, social support has been shown to reduce depression and enhance self-esteem in individuals who suffer from chronic illnesses such as kidney disease (Symister & Friend, 2003). And a large study of soldiers who had enlisted in the U.S. Army showed that a high level of social support from peers was an essential ingredient in reducing stress (Bliese & Castro, 2000). People with social support recover more quickly from illnesses and lower their risk of death from specific diseases. Social support may even increase the probability of surviving a heart attack because it buffers the impact of stress on cardiovascular function (Steptoe, 2000). A longitudinal study of 4,775 people over a 9-year period found that those low in

A strong social support network can help a person recover faster from an illness.

social support died at twice the rate of those high in social support (Berkman & Syme, 1979).

In recent years, social support researchers have begun to distinguish between *perceived support*, the degree to which a person believes help is available when needed, and *received support*, the actual help a person receives from others. Interestingly, many have found that perceived support is more important than received support (Norris & Kaniasty, 1996). Other research has shown that high levels of perceived social support are associated with lower levels of depression and even with recovery from depression (Lara et al., 1997). Such perceived support may be more a function of individual personality than of the actual availability of family and friends who can offer help. One longitudinal study found that college-aged participants who had sociable, outgoing personalities were more likely to report having high levels of perceived social support later in adulthood (Von Dras & Siegler, 1997). These results underscore the importance of psychological variables in health.

Gender, Ethnicity, and Health

What are the relationships among gender, ethnicity, and health?

The degree of wellness and the leading health risk factors are not the same for all Americans (CDC, 2003), but rather differ across gender and among various cultural and ethnic groups. The good news is that efforts to erase the gender and race disparities in medical research and treatment are underway.

The Gender Gap Researchers have found that women are more likely than men to seek medical care (Addis & Mahalik, 2003). Nevertheless, most medical research in the past, much of it funded by the U.S. government, rejected women as participants in favor of men (Matthews et al., 1997). One area where the failure to study women's health care needs has been particularly evident is in research examining mortality risk following open-heart surgery. Women are more likely to die after such surgery than are men. To date, studies have shown that the gender gap in surgical survival narrows with age, but researchers are still investigating why women's postsurgical mortality rate is higher than men's (Vaccarino et al., 2002).

Women are also slighted in general health care and treatment (Rodin & Ickovics, 1990). Physicians are more likely to see women's health complaints as "emotional" in nature rather than due to physical causes (Council on Ethical and Judicial Affairs, American Medical Association [AMA], 1991). The AMA released a major report in 1991 revealing that of men and women who received an abnormal reading on a heart scan, 40% of the men but only 4% of the women were referred for further testing and possible bypass surgery. Women are less likely than men to receive kidney dialysis or a kidney transplant (Council on Ethical and Judicial Affairs, AMA, 1991).

African Americans African Americans make up 12% of the U.S. population (U.S. Census Bureau, 2001). They are represented in every socioeconomic group from the poorest to the richest, but their overall poverty rate is about three times higher than that of White Americans. As a result, many African Americans are at higher risk for disease and death and are more likely to suffer from inadequate health care. Their life expectancy trailed behind that of the total U.S. population throughout the 20th century. African American infants are at twice the risk of death within their first year of life as White American infants.

Compared to White Americans, African Americans have higher rates of diabetes, arthritis, and, as you learned earlier in this chapter, high blood pressure (Kington & Smith, 1997). African Americans are 40% more likely than White Americans to die of heart disease and 30% more likely to die of cancer. Even when African and White Americans of the same age suffer from similar illnesses, the mortality rate of African Americans is higher (CDC, 2003). And the rate of AIDS is more than three times higher among African Americans than among White Americans.

Hispanic Americans By the end of the 20th century, Hispanic Americans, the fastest-growing U.S. minority group, represented about 13% of the total population (U.S. Census Bureau, 2001). However, Hispanic Americans account for more than 20% of new tuberculosis cases in the United States (CDC, 2003). Hypertension and diabetes are also more prevalent among Hispanic Americans than among non-Hispanic White Americans, but heart problems are less prevalent (Kington & Smith, 1997). Cigarette smoking and alcohol abuse are more common among Hispanic American teenagers than among teenagers in other U.S. ethnic groups. Further, Hispanic Americans are at high risk of death from accidental injuries (automobile accidents and other causes), homicide, cirrhosis and other chronic liver diseases, and AIDS (Public Health Service, 1991).

Native Americans Native Americans, the smallest of all minority groups in the United States, number about 2 million. The fact that a large proportion of Native Americans die before the age of 45 partly accounts for their statistically low rates of heart disease and cancer, which are more common among older people. Alcohol represents another serious risk factor for Native Americans and plays a leading role in their high homicide and suicide rates. Native Americans under age 35 are at least 10 times more likely than other Americans to die from diseases directly related to alcoholism (Sandfur et al., 1996). Rates of diabetes are also dramatically higher among Native Americans than for other groups (CDC, 2003).

Asian Americans Asian Americans, who make up 3.6% of the U.S. population, are comparatively very healthy. The overall age-adjusted death rate for Asian American males is 40% lower than that for White American males, but their death rate from stroke is 8% higher. Of all U.S. ethnic groups, infant mortality is lowest for Chinese Americans, at 3 deaths per 1,000 births, compared with 7 per 1,000 for the overall population (National Center for Health Statistics, 2000).

Remember It 13.3

1. The biomedical model focuses on __________; the biopsychosocial model also emphasizes __________.
2. Research suggests that the most harmful component of the Type A behavior pattern is __________.
3. Quality of life is associated with __________ among cancer patients.
4. HIV attacks the __________ cells of the immune system.
5. Lowered immune response has been associated with __________.
6. Hardiness includes __________, __________, and __________.

ANSWERS: 1. illness, health; 2. hostility; 3. optimism; 4. T; 5. stress; 6. commitment, control, challenge

Lifestyle and Health

Think about your own health for a moment. What do you think is the greatest threat to your personal well-being and longevity? For most Americans, health enemy number one is their own habits—lack of exercise, too little sleep, alcohol or drug abuse, an unhealthy diet, and overeating. What can make someone change an unhealthy lifestyle? Perhaps vanity is the key. Researchers have found that people are more likely to adopt healthy behaviors if they believe behavioral change will make them look better or appear more youthful than if they simply receive information about the health benefits of the suggested change (Mahler et al., 2003). Still, there are some health-threatening behaviors that carry such grave risks that everyone ought to take them seriously. The most dangerous unhealthy behavior of all is smoking.

Smoking and Health

What is the most dangerous health-threatening behavior?

Smoking remains the foremost cause of preventable diseases and deaths in the United States (U.S. Department of Health and Human Services, 2000). That message appears to be taking root because the prevalence of smoking among American adults has been decreasing and is currently under 25% (National Center for Health Statistics, 2000). Moreover, smoking is more likely to be viewed as a socially unacceptable behavior now than in the past (Chassin et al., 2003). But there are wide variations in smoking habits according to gender and ethnic group. The highest rates of smoking are found among Native American men (41%) and women (29%), while the lowest rates are reported for Asian American men (18%) and women (11%) (U.S. Department of Health and Human Services, 2000).

Even though the prevalence of smoking is decreasing, every year more than 1 million young Americans become regular smokers, and more than 400,000 American adults die from diseases related to tobacco use (U.S. Department of Health and Human Services, 2000). Smoking increases the risk for heart disease, lung cancer, other cancers that are smoking-related, and emphysema. It is now known that smoking suppresses the action of T cells in the lungs, increasing susceptibility to respiratory tract infections and tumors (McCue et al., 2000).

Other negative consequences from smoking include the widespread incidence of chronic bronchitis and other respiratory problems; the deaths and injuries from fires caused by smoking; and the low birthweight and retarded fetal development in babies born to smoking mothers. Furthermore, mothers who smoke during pregnancy tend to have babies who are at greater risk for anxiety and depression and are five times more likely to become smokers themselves (Cornelius et al., 2000). And millions of nonsmokers engage in *passive smoking* by breathing smoke-filled air—with proven ill effects. Research indicates that nonsmokers who are regularly exposed to *second-hand smoke* have twice the risk of heart attack of those who are not exposed (Kawachi et al., 1997)

Because smoking is so addictive, smokers have great difficulty breaking the habit. Even so, 90% of ex-smokers quit smoking on their own (Novello, 1990). The average smoker makes five or six attempts to quit before finally succeeding (Sherman, 1994). Some aids, such as nicotine gum and the nicotine patch, help many people kick the habit. A meta-analysis involving 17 studies and over 5,000 participants revealed that 22% of people who used the nicotine patch stopped smoking compared with only 9% of those who received a placebo. And 27% of those receiving the nicotine patch plus antismoking counseling or support remained smoke-free (Fiore, cited in Sherman, 1994). But even with the patch, quitting is difficult, because the patch only lessens withdrawal symptoms, which typically last 2 to 4 weeks (Hughes, 1992). Half of all relapses occur within the first 2 weeks after people quit, and relapses are most likely when people are experiencing stressful negative emotions or are using alcohol. It takes just one cigarette, sometimes only one puff, to cause a relapse.

Researchers have found smoking rates to be high in people suffering from drug and alcohol abuse and schizophrenia. Furthermore, a link has been found between smoking and major depression, both of which are thought to be influenced by genetic factors (Breslau et al., 1993; Kendler, Neale, MacLean, et al., 1993). Some smokers who try to quit are at higher risk for major depression. Withdrawal brings on depression in more than 85% of those with a history of depression compared with only 20% of those with no such history (Glassman, 1993). Consequently, depressed smokers are much less likely to succeed at quitting (Borrelli et al., 1996; Stage et al., 1996).

What are some health risks of alcohol abuse?

Alcohol Abuse

Do you use alcohol regularly? Many Americans do. Recall from Chapter 4 that *substance abuse* is defined as continued use of a substance that interferes with a person's major life roles at home, in school, at work, or elsewhere and contributes to legal difficulties or any psychological problems (American Psychiatric Association, 1994). Alcohol is perhaps the most frequently abused substance of all, and the health costs of alcohol abuse are staggering—in fatalities, medical bills, lost work, and family problems.

Approximately 10 million Americans are alcoholics (Neimark et al., 1994). Alcohol abuse is three times more prevalent in males than in females (Grant et al., 1991). And people who begin drinking before age 15 are four times more likely than those who begin later to become alcoholics (Grant & Dawson, 1998). For many, alcohol provides a method of coping with life stresses they feel otherwise powerless to control (Seeman & Seeman, 1992). As many as 80% of men and women who are alcoholics complain of episodes of depression. A large study of almost 3,000 alcoholics concluded that some depressive episodes are independent of alcohol, whereas others are substance-induced (Schuckit et al., 1997).

Alcohol can damage virtually every organ in the body, but it is especially harmful to the liver and is the major cause of cirrhosis, which kills 26,000 people each year (Neimark et al., 1994). Other causes of death are more common in alcoholics than in nonalcoholics as well. One Norwegian longitudinal study involving more than 40,000 male participants found that the rate of death prior to age 60 was significantly higher among alcoholics than nonalcoholics (Rossow & Amundsen, 1997). Alcoholics are about three times as likely to die in automobile accidents or of heart disease as nonalcoholics, and they have twice the rate of deaths from cancer.

Shrinkage in the cerebral cortex of alcoholics has been found by researchers using MRI scans (Jernigan et al., 1991). CT scans also show brain shrinkage in a high percentage of alcoholics, even in those who are young and in those who show normal cognitive functioning (Lishman, 1990). Moreover, heavy drinking can cause cognitive impairment that continues for several months after the drinking stops (Sullivan et al., 2002). The only good news in recent studies is that some of the effects of alcohol on the brain seem to be partially reversible with prolonged abstinence.

Alcoholism's toll goes beyond the physical damage to the alcoholic. In 1995, alcohol was involved in 41% of the traffic fatalities in the United States, which numbered almost 17,300 (National Safety Council, 1997). Alcohol has been implicated in 20–36% of suicides, 53% of falls, and 48% of burns (U.S. House, Committee on Energy and Commerce, 1991).

Since the late 1950s, the American Medical Association has maintained that alcoholism is a disease, and once an alcoholic, always an alcoholic. According to this view, even a small amount of alcohol can cause an irresistible craving for more, leading alcoholics to lose control of their drinking (Jellinek, 1960). Thus, total abstinence is seen as the only acceptable and effective method of treatment. Alcoholics Anonymous (AA) also endorses both the disease concept and the total abstinence approach to treatment. And there is a drug that may make abstinence somewhat easier. German researchers report that the drug acamprosate helps prevent relapse in recovering alcoholics (Sass et al., 1996).

Some studies suggest a genetic influence on alcoholism and lend support to the disease model. For example, neuroscientist Henri Begleiter and his colleagues have accumulated a large body of evidence suggesting that the brains of alcoholics respond differently to visual and auditory stimuli than those of nonalcoholics (Hada et al., 2000, 2001; Prabhu et al., 2001). Further, many relatives of alcoholics, even children and adults who have never consumed any alcohol in their lives, display the same types of response patterns (Zhang et al., 2001). The relatives of alcoholics who do display these patterns are more likely to become alcoholics themselves or to suffer from other types of addictions (Anokhin et al., 2000; Bierut et al., 1998). Consequently, Begleiter has suggested that the brain-imaging techniques he uses in his research may someday be used to determine which relatives of alcoholics are genetically predisposed to addiction (Porjesz et al., 1998).

Exercise

What are some benefits of regular aerobic exercise?

How much exercise do you get? Many studies show that regular exercise pays rich dividends in the form of physical and mental fitness. However, many people still express reluctance to exercise. Some simply prefer not to be physically active; others blame such factors as the cost of joining a health club or even the unpredictability of the weather for their lack of physical activity (Salmon et al., 2003). Such individuals are missing out on one of the simplest and most effective ways of enhancing one's health.

Aerobic exercise (such as running, swimming, brisk walking, bicycling, rowing, and jumping rope) is exercise that uses the large muscle groups in continuous, repetitive action and increases oxygen intake and breathing and heart rates. To improve cardiovascular fitness and endurance and to lessen the risk of heart attack, an individual should perform aerobic exercise regularly—three or four times a week for 20–30 minutes, with additional 5–10-minute warm-up and cool-down periods (Alpert et al., 1990; Shepard, 1986). Less than 20 minutes of aerobic exercise three times a week has "no measurable effect on the heart," and more than 3 hours per week "is not known to reduce cardiovascular risk any further" (Simon, 1988, p. 3). However, individuals who engage in more than 3 hours of aerobic activity each week are more successful at losing excess weight and keeping it off than are those who exercise less (Votruba et al., 2000).

aerobic exercise (ah-RO-bik) Exercise that uses the large muscle groups in continuous, repetitive action and increases oxygen intake and breathing and heart rates.

In case you are not yet convinced, consider the following benefits of exercise (Fiatarone et al., 1988):

- Increases the efficiency of the heart, enabling it to pump more blood with each beat, and reduces the resting pulse rate and improves circulation
- Raises levels of HDL (the good blood cholesterol), which (1) helps rid the body of LDL (the bad blood cholesterol) and (2) removes plaque buildup on artery walls
- Burns up extra calories, enabling you to lose weight or maintain your weight
- Makes bones denser and stronger, helping to prevent osteoporosis in women
- Moderates the effects of stress
- Gives you more energy and increases your resistance to fatigue
- Benefits the immune system by increasing natural killer cell activity

Regular aerobic exercise improves cardiovascular fitness in people of all ages.

Alternative Medicine

What are the benefits and risks associated with alternative medicine?

Do you take vitamins or herbal supplements in hopes of positively influencing your health? According to surveys, Americans spend billions of dollars each year on unconventional treatments—herbs, massage, self-help groups, megavitamins, folk remedies, and homeopathy—for a variety of illnesses and conditions. In one such survey, the National Science Foundation (NSF, 2002) found that 88% of Americans believe that there are valid ways of preventing and curing illnesses that are not recognized by the medical professional. And college-educated Americans are more likely to use unconventional treatments than those who have less education.

The National Science Foundation (2002) defines **alternative medicine** as any treatment or therapy that has not been scientifically demonstrated to be effective. Even a simple practice such as taking vitamins sometimes falls into this category. For instance, *scurvy* (a condition whose symptoms include bleeding gums and easy bruising) has been scientifically determined to be caused by Vitamin C deficiency. So, taking Vitamin C to prevent or cure scurvy is not considered an alternative therapy. However, if you take Vitamin C to

alternative medicine Any treatment or therapy that has not been scientifically demonstrated to be effective.

protect yourself against the common cold, you are using alternative medicine because Vitamin C has not been scientifically proven to prevent colds.

If alternative treatments lack scientific support, why do so many people believe in them? One possibility is that it is easier to take a vitamin than to make a lifestyle change. But it is also true that people who do their own research about alternative therapies may happen upon effective treatments of which their physicians are unaware. However, most patients who use alternative treatments do not inform their physicians about them. Health professionals cite this tendency toward secrecy as a major risk factor in the use of alternative medicine (Yale-New Haven Hospital, 2003). They point out that many therapies, especially those that involve food supplements, have pharmacological effects that can interfere with treatments prescribed by physicians. Consequently, individuals who use alternative treatments should tell their physicians about them. While doctors may be skeptical about the utility of the alternative treatments, they need to have this information about their patients in order to practice conventional medicine effectively. Moreover, faith in an alternative treatment may cause an individual to delay seeking necessary conventional medical treatment.

Although it is true that some alternative therapies may be helpful in both preventing and treating illness, most health professionals agree that lifestyle changes bring greater health benefits than do any methods of alternative medicine. Unfortunately, many people resist making lifestyle changes because they see them as taking too long to be effective or being too difficult to carry out. A smoker may think, "I've been smoking so long, quitting now won't make a difference." An obese person may be so overwhelmed by the amount of weight loss necessary to attain an ideal weight that she or he gives up. However, Table 13.2 shows that the benefits of various lifestyle changes, some of which are fairly easy to achieve, can be well worth the effort. And remember, to be healthier, you don't have to make *all* of the changes. You might consider starting with just one. Even if you never make another change, you are likely to live longer and be healthier than you would have otherwise.

TABLE 13.2 Benefits of Lifestyle Changes

LIFESTYLE CHANGE	BENEFITS
If overweight, lose just 10 pounds.	34% reduction in triglyceride levels; 16% decrease in total cholesterol; 18% increase in HDL ("good" cholesterol); significant reduction in blood pressure; decreased risk of diabetes, sleep apnea, and osteoarthritis (Still, 2001).
Add 20 to 30 grams of fiber to your diet each day.	Improved bowel function; reduced risk of colon cancer and other digestive system diseases; decrease in total cholesterol; reduced blood pressure; improved insulin function in both diabetics and nondiabetics (HCF, 2003).
Engage in moderate physical activity every day (e.g., walk up and down stairs for 15 minutes; spend 30 minutes washing a car).	Reduced feelings of anxiety and sadness; increased bone density; reduced risk of diabetes, heart disease, high blood pressure, and many other life-shortening diseases (CDC, 1999).
Stop smoking at any age, after any number of years of smoking.	*Immediate:* improved circulation; reduced blood level of carbon monoxide; stabilization of pulse rate and blood pressure; improved sense of smell and taste; improved lung function and endurance; reduced risk of lung infections such as pneumonia and bronchitis. *Long-term:* reduced risk of lung cancer (declines substantially with each year of abstinence); decreased risk of other smoking-related illnesses such as emphysema and heart disease; decreased risk of cancer recurrence in those who have been treated for some form of cancer (National Cancer Institute, 2000).

Remember It 13.4

1. The greatest threat to Americans' health and longevity is a(n) __________.
2. __________ is the leading preventable cause of disease and death.
3. Excessive intake of __________ can damage virtually every organ in the body.
4. Cardiovascular fitness and endurance can be improved through __________.

ANSWERS: 1. unhealthy lifestyle; 2. Smoking; 3. alcohol; 4. aerobic exercise

Apply It

Interpreting Health Information on the Internet

An increasing number of people are turning to the Internet for information about their health. One study of 188 women with breast cancer found that about half of them used the Internet to find out more about the disease (Fogel et al., 2002). Surveys of older adults and HIV-positive individuals have shown that using the Internet helps them gain a sense of control over their health care decisions (Kalichman et al., 2003; McMellon & Schiffman, 2002). Chat rooms devoted to specific diseases may represent an important source of social support for patients, especially those suffering from rare disorders (Kummervold et al., 2002). And using email to coach and encourage patients in the management of chronic diseases such as diabetes has proven to be effective both for patients' health and for health care professionals' time management (McKay et al., 2002).

But how reliable is the information available on the Internet? In a large-scale study of health-related Web sites sponsored by the American Medical Association, researchers found that the quality of information varied widely from one site to another (Eysenbach et al., 2002). A study of Internet-based advice for managing children's fever sponsored by the British Medical Association found that most Web sites contained erroneous information. Moreover, in a follow-up study 4 years later, the researchers found that about half the sites were no longer available; those that remained showed little improvement in the quality of information.

Despite these difficulties, physicians' organizations acknowledge the potential value of the Internet in helping patients learn about and manage their own health. And because so many older adults are using the Internet to learn about health issues, the American Association of Retired Persons (2002) has published a list of points to keep in mind when surfing the Web for health information and advice:

- *Remember that there are no rules governing what is published on the Internet.* Unlike scientific journal articles, which are usually written and reviewed by experts in the field, Internet articles can be posted by anyone, without review of any kind. Without expert knowledge, it is extremely difficult to tell whether the information and advice these articles contain are valid.
- *Consider the source.* Generally, Web sites sponsored by medical schools, government agencies, and public health organizations are reliable. Others, especially those promoting a health-related product, should be considered suspect.
- *Get a second opinion.* Ask your health care provider about Internet-based information, or read what's available from several different sources on the topic.
- *Examine references.* Sites that refer to credible sources (e.g., books, other Web sites) that you can find on the Internet or in a library or bookstore are probably more reliable than sites that offer no references to support their advice.
- *How current is the information?* Health-related information changes frequently. Be certain that you are reading the most current findings and recommendations.
- *Is it too good to be true?* As in all areas of life, if something sounds too good to be true (e.g., a vitamin that cures cancer), it probably is. Try to find experimental, placebo-controlled studies that support any claims.

Using these guidelines, you can become a better consumer of Internet-based health information.

Summary and Review

Sources of Stress p. 442

What was the Social Readjustment Rating Scale designed to reveal? p. 442

The SRRS assesses stress in terms of life events, positive or negative, that necessitate change and adaptation. Holmes and Rahe found a relationship between degree of life stress (as measured on the scale) and major health problems.

What roles do hassles and uplifts play in the stress of life, according to Lazarus? p. 443

According to Lazarus, daily hassles typically cause more stress than major life changes. Positive experiences in life—or uplifts—can neutralize the effects of many of the hassles, however.

How do approach-approach, avoidance-avoidance, and approach-avoidance conflicts differ? p. 443

In an approach-approach conflict, a person must decide between equally desirable alternatives. In an avoidance-avoidance conflict, the choice is between two undesirable alternatives. In an approach-avoidance conflict, a person is both drawn to and repelled by a single choice.

How do the unpredictability and lack of control over a stressor affect its impact? p. 445

Stressors that are unpredictable and uncontrollable have greater impact than those that are predictable and controllable.

For people to function effectively and find satisfaction on the job, what nine variables should fall within their comfort zone? p. 446

The nine variables that should fall within a worker's comfort zone are workload, clarity of job description and evaluation criteria, physical variables, job status, accountability, task variety, human contact, physical challenge, and mental challenge.

How do people typically react to catastrophic events? p. 447

Most people cope quite well with catastrophic events. However, some people develop posttraumatic stress disorder (PTSD), a prolonged, severe stress reaction, often characterized by flashbacks, nightmares, or intrusive memories of the traumatic event.

How might historical racism affect the health of African Americans? p. 448

Some researchers believe that African Americans have higher levels of high blood pressure than members of other groups because of stress due to historical racism. African Americans who express high levels of concern about racism display larger cardiovascular responses to experimentally induced stressors than do their peers who express lower levels of concern.

Responding to Stress p. 449

What is the general adaptation syndrome? p. 449

The general adaptation syndrome (GAS) proposed by Selye is the predictable sequence of reactions that organisms show in response to stressors. It consists of the alarm stage, the resistance stage, and the exhaustion stage.

What are the roles of primary and secondary appraisals when a person is confronted with a potentially stressful event? p. 450

Lazarus maintains that, when confronted with a potentially stressful event, a person engages in a cognitive appraisal process consisting of (1) a primary appraisal, to evaluate the relevance of the situation to one's well-being (whether it will be positive, irrelevant, or negative), and (2) a secondary appraisal, to evaluate one's resources and determine how to cope with the stressor.

What is the difference between problem-focused and emotion-focused coping? p. 451

Problem-focused coping is a direct response, aimed at reducing, modifying, or eliminating the source of stress; emotion-focused coping involves reappraising a stressor in order to reduce its emotional impact.

Health and Illness p. 453

How do the biomedical and biopsychosocial models differ in their approaches to health and illness? p. 453

The biomedical model focuses on illness rather than on health and explains illness in terms of biological factors. The biopsychosocial model focuses on health as well as on illness and holds that both are determined by a combination of biological, psychological, and social factors.

What are the Type A and Type B behavior patterns? p. 454

The Type A behavior pattern, often cited as a risk factor for coronary heart disease, is characterized by a sense of time urgency, impatience, excessive competitive drive, hostility, and easily aroused anger. The Type B behavior pattern is characterized by a relaxed, easygoing approach to life, without the time urgency, impatience, and hostility of the Type A pattern.

How do psychological factors influence cancer patients' quality of life? p. 455

Cancer patients can improve their quality of life by maintaining an optimistic outlook, accepting the reality of their situation, and maintaining a sense of humor. Social support and psychotherapy can help them do so.

What are the effects of stress on the immune system? p. 456

Stress has been associated with lowered immune response and with increased symptoms of many infectious diseases.

What four personal factors are associated with health and resistance to stress? p. 457

Personal factors related to health and resistance to stress are optimism, hardiness, religious involvement, and social support.

What are the relationships among gender, ethnicity, and health? p. 459

Women are more likely than men to seek medical care, but women's needs have often been ignored by medical researchers and health care providers. African Americans, Hispanic Americans, and Native Americans have higher rates of many diseases than do White Americans. Asian Americans are comparatively very healthy.

Lifestyle and Health p. 460

What is the most dangerous health-threatening behavior? p. 461

Smoking is considered the most dangerous health-related behavior because it is directly related to over 400,000 deaths each year, including deaths from heart disease, lung cancer, respiratory diseases, and stroke.

What are some health risks of alcohol abuse? p. 462

Alcohol abuse damages virtually every organ in the body, including the liver, stomach, skeletal muscles, heart, and brain. Alcoholics are three times as likely to die in motor vehicle accidents as nonalcoholics.

What are some benefits of regular aerobic exercise? p. 463

Regular aerobic exercise reduces the risk of cardiovascular disease, increases muscular strength, moderates the effects of stress, makes bones denser and stronger, and helps one maintain a desirable weight.

What are the benefits and risks associated with alternative medicine? p. 463

Alternative medicine, or the use of any treatment that has not been proven scientifically to be effective, can benefit individuals who find alternative treatments that are effective. However, many patients increase their risk of poor outcomes by not telling their physicians about their use of alternative treatments. And some people delay seeking necessary conventional medical treatment because they believe that alternative approaches will work.

Key Terms

aerobic exercise, p. 463
alarm stage, p. 450
alternative medicine, p. 463
approach-approach conflict, p. 443
approach-avoidance conflict, p. 445
avoidance-avoidance conflict, p. 445
biomedical model, p. 453
biopsychosocial model, p. 453
coping, p. 451
emotion-focused coping, p. 452
exhaustion stage, p. 450
fight-or-flight response, p. 442
general adaptation syndrome (GAS), p. 449
hardiness, p. 457
hassles, p. 443
health psychology, p. 454
lymphocytes, p. 456
posttraumatic stress disorder (PTSD) p. 447
primary appraisal, p. 450
proactive coping, p. 452
problem-focused coping, p. 451
psychoneuroimmunology, p. 456
resistance stage, p. 450
secondary appraisal, p. 451
Social Readjustment Rating Scale (SRRS), p. 442
social support, p. 458
stress, p. 442
stressor, p. 442
Type A behavior pattern, p. 454
Type B behavior pattern, p. 454
uplifts, p. 443

Personality Theory and Assessment

chapter 14

Sigmund Freud and Psychoanalysis

- *What are the three levels of awareness in consciousness?*
- *What are the roles of the id, the ego, and the superego?*
- *What is the purpose of defense mechanisms?*
- *What are the psychosexual stages, and why did Freud consider them important in personality development?*
- *How are Freud's ideas evaluated by modern psychologists?*

The Neo-Freudians

- *How do the views of the neo-Freudians differ from those of Freud?*

Learning Theories and Personality

- *What are the components of Bandura's concept of reciprocal determinism and Rotter's locus of control?*

Humanistic Personality Theories

- *What are the contributions of humanistic theorists to the study of personality?*
- *What have psychologists learned about self-esteem?*

Trait Theories

- *What were some of the ideas proposed by early trait theorists?*
- *What do factor theorists consider to be the most important dimensions of personality?*
- *What is the situation-trait debate about?*

Nature, Nurture, and Personality

- *What have twin and adoption studies revealed about the influence of genes on personality?*
- *How are neurotransmitters and personality traits linked?*
- *Why do personality researchers distinguish between shared and nonshared environments?*
- *How does personality differ across cultures?*

Personality Assessment

- *How do psychologists use observations, interviews, and rating scales?*
- *What is an inventory, and what are the MMPI-2 and the CPI designed to reveal?*
- *How do projective tests provide insight into personality, and what are some of the most commonly used projective tests?*

Personality Theories: A Final Comment

How much did your parents influence your personality?

According to Sigmund Freud, the creator of psychoanalysis, parent-child relationships are central to personality development. Though he died more than six decades ago, many of Freud's ideas continue to be controversial. To understand why, let's look at the context in which many in the United States heard about Freud's theory for the first time.

In 1924, two 18-year-old Chicago men, Nathan Leopold and Richard Loeb, brutally killed a 13-year-old boy in an effort to prove their intellectual superiority. They believed that their superior cognitive abilities not only exempted them from society's rules but would enable them to avoid detection by the intellectually inferior authorities. However, the police were able to trace a pair of glasses Leopold carelessly left at the murder scene and arrested the two a few days after the crime.

Leopold and Loeb confessed, and their wealthy families hired well-known attorney Clarence Darrow to try to save them from the death penalty. Arguing from several books and articles by Sigmund Freud, Darrow tried to convince the judge that the young men's parents were at least partially responsible for the crime because they had deprived their sons of emotional warmth in childhood (Higdon, 1975). Darrow hired psychiatric experts to testify that the two murderers were emotionally equivalent to young children and should not be put to death for their crime.

At the end of the trial, the judge sided with Darrow and sentenced the two young men to life in prison. However, he stated that his decision was not based on the life histories or psychological analysis of Leopold and Loeb but solely on their youth. Still, a new approach to criminal defense had emerged. Childhood experiences are often cited today by attorneys as mitigating circumstances that a judge or jury ought to consider before sentencing an individual convicted of a crime. Moreover, testimony by experts in psychology and psychiatry regarding the mental health of victims, witnesses, and other individuals involved in a case has become increasingly common.

Publicity surrounding the Leopold and Loeb trial was the means by which Freud's theory first became widely known among the general public in the United States (Torrey, 1992). The notion that two murderers' parents might be morally responsible for their heinous crime rendered Freud's theory repugnant to many. Of course, Freud was still living and working at the time and might have been able to moderate the effects of the bad press his theory was receiving. However, he refused to comment on the case when asked by reporters to do so.

Many concepts associated with Freud's theories are controversial. But the hypothesis that adult behavior can be influenced by early childhood emotional trauma may be Freud's most enduring contribution to the field of psychology. However, neither Freud's theory nor any other theory claims that a history of childhood trauma can be used to relieve an individual of moral responsibility for the commission of a horrendous crime. To paraphrase one of the many comments made by legal scholars of the era about the Leopold and Loeb case, society must protect itself against individuals who would violate the rights of others even if, according to expert opinion, they are emotionally immature due to childhood trauma (Olson et al., 1924). Remember, it was Leopold and Loeb's attorney, Clarence Darrow, not Freud, who turned Freud's theory into a "blame your parents" legal defense.

Even though most people agree that variations in early childhood experiences contribute to differences among adults, most also realize that many other factors must be taken into account in order to explain the full range of behaviors collectively referred to as "personality"—all the ways in which one person differs from another. **Personality** is formally defined as an individual's characteristic patterns of behaving, thinking, and feeling (Carver & Scheier, 1996). In this chapter, we explore some of the theories, including Freud's, that have been proposed to explain personality.

■ **personality**
A person's characteristic patterns of behaving, thinking, and feeling.

Sigmund Freud and Psychoanalysis

When you hear the term **psychoanalysis**, do you picture a psychiatrist treating a troubled patient on a couch? Many people do, but the term refers not only to a therapy for treating psychological disorders devised by Sigmund Freud, but also to the influential personality theory he proposed. The central idea of psychoanalytic theory is that unconscious forces shape human thought and behavior.

■ **psychoanalysis** (SY-co-ah-NAL-ih-sis) Freud's term for his theory of personality and his therapy for treating psychological disorders.

The Conscious, the Preconscious, and the Unconscious

What are the three levels of awareness in consciousness?

Freud believed that there are three levels of awareness in consciousness: the conscious, the preconscious, and the unconscious. The **conscious** consists of whatever we are aware of at any given moment—thoughts, feelings, sensations, or memories. The **preconscious** is somewhat like long-term memory: It contains all the memories, feelings, experiences, and perceptions that we are not consciously thinking about at the moment, but that may be easily brought to consciousness.

The most important of the three levels is the **unconscious**, which Freud believed to be the primary motivating force of human behavior. The unconscious holds memories that once were conscious but were so unpleasant or anxiety-provoking that they were repressed (involuntarily removed from consciousness). The unconscious also contains all of the instincts (sexual and aggressive), wishes, and desires that have never been allowed into consciousness. Freud traced the roots of psychological disorders to these impulses and repressed memories.

■ **conscious** (KON-shus) The thoughts, feelings, sensations, or memories of which a person is aware at any given moment.

The Id, the Ego, and the Superego

What are the roles of the id, the ego, and the superego?

Freud also proposed three systems of personality. Figure 14.1 shows these three systems and how they relate to his conscious, preconscious, and unconscious levels of awareness. These systems do not exist physically; they are only concepts, or ways of looking at personality.

The **id** is the only part of the personality that is present at birth. It is inherited, primitive, inaccessible, and completely unconscious. The id contains (1) the life instincts, which are the sexual instincts and the biological urges such as hunger and

FIGURE 14.1 Freud's Conception of Personality

According to Freud, personality, which may be conceptualized as a giant iceberg, is composed of three structures: the id, the ego, and the superego. The id, completely unconscious, is wholly submerged, floating beneath the surface. The ego is largely conscious and visible, but partly unconscious. The superego also operates at both the conscious and unconscious levels.

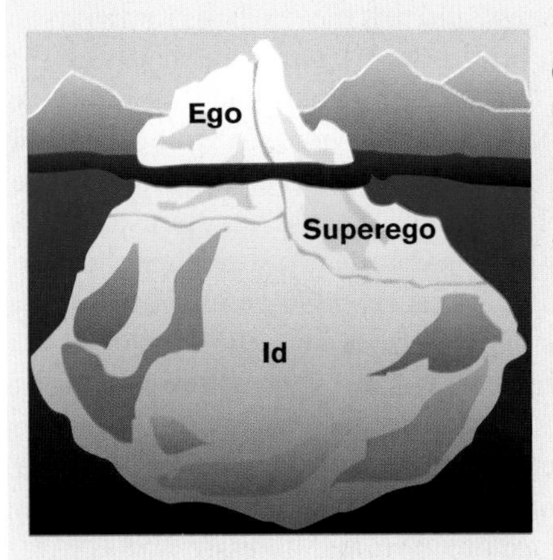

■ **preconscious** The thoughts, feelings, and memories that a person is not consciously aware of at the moment but that may be easily brought to consciousness.

■ **unconscious** (un-KON-shus) For Freud, the primary motivating force of human behavior, containing repressed memories as well as instincts, wishes, and desires that have never been conscious.

■ **id** (ID) The unconscious system of the personality, which contains the life and death instincts and operates on the pleasure principle; source of the libido.

Sigmund Freud (1856–1939), with his daughter Anna.

thirst, and (2) the death instinct, which accounts for aggressive and destructive impulses (Freud, 1933/1965). Operating according to the *pleasure principle*, the id tries to seek pleasure, avoid pain, and gain immediate gratification of its wishes. The id is the source of the *libido*, the psychic energy that fuels the entire personality; yet, the id can only wish, image, fantasize and demand.

The **ego** is the logical, rational, realistic part of the personality. The ego evolves from the id and draws its energy from the id. One of the ego's functions is to satisfy the id's urges. But the ego, which is mostly conscious, acts according to the *reality principle*. It considers the constraints of the real world in determining appropriate times, places, and objects for gratification of the id's wishes. The art of the possible is its guide, and sometimes compromises must be made—such as settling for a McDonald's hamburger instead of steak or lobster.

When a child is age 5 or 6, the **superego**, the moral component of the personality, is formed. The superego has two parts: (1) The *conscience* consists of all the behaviors for which the child has been punished and about which he or she feels guilty; (2) the *ego ideal* comprises the behaviors for which the child has been praised and rewarded and about which he or she feels pride and satisfaction. At first, the superego reflects only the parents' expectations of what is good and right, but it expands over time to incorporate teachings from the broader social world. In its quest for moral perfection, the superego sets guidelines that define and limit the ego's flexibility. A harsher judge than any external authority, including one's parents, the superego judges not only behavior, but also thoughts, feelings, and wishes.

■ **ego**
(EE-go) In Freud's theory, the logical, rational, largely conscious system of personality, which operates according to the reality principle.

Defense Mechanisms

What is the purpose of defense mechanisms?

All would be well if the id, the ego, and the superego had compatible aims. But the id's demands for pleasure are often in direct conflict with the superego's desire for moral perfection. At times the ego needs some way to defend itself against the anxiety created by the excessive demands of the id and the harsh judgments of the superego. When it cannot solve problems directly, the ego may use a **defense mechanism**, a technique used to defend against anxiety and to maintain self-esteem. All people use defense mechanisms to some degree, but research supports Freud's view that the overuse of defense mechanisms can adversely affect mental health (Watson, 2002).

According to Freud, **repression** is the most frequently used defense mechanism. It involves removing painful or threatening memories, thoughts, or perceptions from consciousness and keeping them in the unconscious. It may also prevent unconscious sexual and aggressive impulses from breaking into consciousness. Several studies have shown that people do indeed try to repress unpleasant thoughts (Koehler et al., 2002). Freud believed that repressed thoughts lurk in the unconscious and can cause psychological disorders in adults. He thought that the way to cure such disorders was to bring the repressed material back to consciousness, and this was the basis for his system of therapy—psychoanalysis.

There are several other defense mechanisms that people may use from time to time. They use **projection** when they attribute their own undesirable impulses, thoughts, personality traits, or behavior to others or when they minimize the undesirable in themselves and exaggerate it in others. For example, a sexually promiscuous husband or wife may accuse his or her spouse of being unfaithful. A dishonest businessperson may think everyone is out to cheat him or her. Projection allows people to avoid acknowledging unacceptable traits and thereby to maintain self-esteem, but it seriously distorts their perception of the external world.

Denial is a refusal to acknowledge consciously the existence of danger or a threatening condition. Many people who abuse alcohol and drugs deny that they have a problem. Yet, denial is sometimes useful as a temporary means of getting through a crisis until a more permanent adjustment can be made, as when someone initially denies the existence of a terminal illness.

■ **superego**
(sue-per-EE-go) The moral system of the personality, which consists of the conscience and the ego ideal.

■ **defense mechanism**
A means used by the ego to defend against anxiety and to maintain self-esteem.

■ **repression**
A defense mechanism in which one involuntarily removes painful or threatening memories, thoughts, or perceptions from consciousness or prevents unconscious sexual and aggressive impulses from breaking into consciousness.

■ **projection**
A defense mechanism in which one attributes one's own undesirable thoughts, impulses, personality traits, or behavior to others or minimizes the undesirable in oneself and exaggerates it in others.

Rationalization occurs when a person unconsciously supplies a logical, rational, or socially acceptable reason rather than the real reason for an action or event. Rationalization can be used to justify past, present, or future behaviors or to soften the disappointment associated with not attaining a desired goal. When people rationalize, they make excuses for, or justify, failures and mistakes. A student who did not study and then failed a test might complain, "The test was unfair."

Sometimes, when frustrated or anxious, people may use **regression** and revert to behavior that might have reduced anxiety at an earlier stage of development. A 5-year-old with a new baby sister or brother may regress by reverting to thumb sucking or dragging a baby blanket around. An adult whose new computer keeps crashing may have a temper tantrum or throw things.

Reaction formation is at work when people express exaggerated ideas and emotions that are the opposite of their disturbing, unconscious impulses and desires. In reaction formation, the conscious thought or feeling masks the unconscious one. Unconscious hatred may be expressed as love and devotion, or cruelty as kindness. Reaction formation may be occurring when a behavior is extreme, excessive, and compulsive, as when a former chain smoker becomes irate and complains loudly at the faintest whiff of cigarette smoke. Reaction formation can be viewed as a barrier that a person unconsciously erects to keep from acting on an unacceptable impulse.

Displacement occurs when a person substitutes a less threatening object or person for the original object of a sexual or aggressive impulse. If your boss makes you angry, you may take out your hostility on your boyfriend or girlfriend, or husband or wife. By contrast, with **sublimation**, people rechannel sexual or aggressive energy into pursuits or accomplishments that society considers acceptable or even praiseworthy. An aggressive person may rechannel the aggression and become a football or hockey player, a surgeon, or a butcher. Freud viewed sublimation as the only completely healthy ego defense mechanism. In fact, Freud (1930/1962) considered all advancements in civilization to be the result of sublimation.

Review and Reflect 14.1 (on page 474) lists these defense mechanisms.

■ **denial**
A defense mechanism in which one refuses to acknowledge consciously the existence of danger or a threatening condition.

■ **rationalization**
A defense mechanism in which one supplies a logical, rational, or socially acceptable reason rather than the real reason for an action or event.

■ **regression**
A defense mechanism in which one reverts to a behavior that might have reduced anxiety at an earlier stage of development.

■ **reaction formation**
A defense mechanism in which one expresses exaggerated ideas and emotions that are the opposite of one's disturbing unconscious impulses and desires.

■ **displacement**
A defense mechanism in which one substitutes a less threatening object or person for the original object of a sexual or aggressive impulse.

What are the psychosexual stages, and why did Freud consider them important in personality development?

The Psychosexual Stages of Development

The sex instinct, Freud said, is the most important factor influencing personality. It is present at birth and then develops through a series of **psychosexual stages**. Each stage centers on a particular part of the body that provides pleasurable sensations (an *erogenous zone*) and around which a conflict arises (Freud, 1905/1953b; 1920/1963b). If the conflict is not readily resolved, the child may develop a **fixation**. This means that a portion of the libido (psychic energy) remains invested at that particular stage, leaving less energy to meet the challenges of future stages. Overindulgence at any stage may leave a person psychologically unwilling to move on to the next stage, whereas too little gratification may leave the person trying to make up for unmet needs. Freud believed that certain personality characteristics develop as a result of difficulty at one or another of the stages.

Review and Reflect 14.2 (on page 475) summarizes Freud's psychosexual stages.

The Oral Stage (Birth to 1 Year) During the *oral stage*, the mouth is the primary source of an infant's sensual pleasure, which Freud (1920/1963b) considered to be an expression of infantile sexuality. The conflict at this stage centers on weaning. Too much or too little gratification may result in an oral fixation—an excessive preoccupation with oral activities such as eating, drinking, smoking, gum chewing, nail biting, and even kissing. (Freud's 20-cigars-a-day habit probably qualifies as an oral fixation, according to his theory.) Freud claimed that difficulties at the oral stage can result in certain personality traits: either excessive dependence, optimism, and gullibility (the tendency to believe anything) or extreme pessimism, sarcasm, hostility, and aggression.

■ **sublimation**
A defense mechanism in which one rechannels sexual or aggressive energy into pursuits or accomplishments that society considers acceptable or admirable.

■ **psychosexual stages**
A series of stages through which the sexual instinct develops; each stage is defined by an erogenous zone around which conflict arises.

■ **fixation**
Arrested development at a psychosexual stage occurring because of excessive gratification or frustration at that stage.

REVIEW and REFLECT 14.1

Freud's Defense Mechanisms

DEFENSE MECHANISM	DESCRIPTION	EXAMPLE
Repression	Involuntarily removing an unpleasant memory, thought, or perception from consciousness or barring disturbing sexual and aggressive impulses from consciousness	Jill forgets a traumatic incident from childhood.
Projection	Attributing one's own undesirable traits, thoughts, behavior, or impulses to another	A very lonely divorced woman accuses all men of having only one thing on their minds.
Denial	Refusing to acknowledge consciously the existence of danger or a threatening situation	Amy fails to take a tornado warning seriously and is severely injured.
Rationalization	Supplying a logical, rational, or socially acceptable reason rather than the real reason for an action or event	Fred tells his friend that he didn't get the job because he didn't have connections.
Regression	Reverting to a behavior that might have reduced anxiety at an earlier stage of development	Susan bursts into tears whenever she is criticized.
Reaction formation	Expressing exaggerated ideas and emotions that are the opposite of disturbing, unconscious impulses and desires	A former purchaser of pornography, Bob is now a tireless crusader against it.
Displacement	Substituting a less threatening object or person for the original object of a sexual or aggressive impulse	After being spanked by his father, Bill hits his baby brother.
Sublimation	Rechanneling sexual and aggressive energy into pursuits or accomplishments that society considers acceptable or even admirable	Tim goes to a gym to work out when he feels hostile and frustrated.

Want to be sure you've fully absorbed the material in this chapter? Visit **www.ablongman.com/wood5e** for access to free practice tests, flashcards, interactive activities, and links developed specifically to help you succeed in psychology.

The Anal Stage (1 to 3 Years) During the *anal stage*, children derive sensual pleasure, Freud believed, from expelling and withholding feces. But a conflict arises when toilet training begins, because this is one of parents' first attempts to have children give up or postpone gratification. When parents are harsh in their approach, children may rebel openly, defecating whenever and wherever they please. This may lead to an *anal expulsive personality*—someone who is sloppy, irresponsible, rebellious, hostile, and destructive. Other children may defy their parents and gain attention by withholding feces. They may develop an *anal retentive personality*, gaining security through what they possess and becoming stingy, stubborn, rigid, excessively neat and clean, orderly, and precise (Freud, 1933/1965). Do these patterns remind you of Monica on the TV series *Friends* or of Oscar and Felix on the old series *The Odd Couple?*

■ **Oedipus complex** (ED-uh-pus) Occurring in the phallic stage, a conflict in which the child is sexually attracted to the opposite-sex parent and feels hostility toward the same-sex parent.

The Phallic Stage (3 to 5 or 6 Years) During the *phallic stage*, children learn that they can derive pleasure from touching their genitals, and masturbation is common. They become aware of the anatomical differences in males and females. One of the most controversial features of Freud's theory is the central theme of the phallic stage, the **Oedipus complex** (named after the central character in the Greek tragedy *Oedipus Rex*, by Sophocles). Freud claimed that, during the phallic stage, "boys concentrate

REVIEW and REFLECT 14.2

Freud's Psychosexual Stages of Development

STAGE	PART OF THE BODY	CONFLICTS/EXPERIENCES	ADULT TRAITS ASSOCIATED WITH PROBLEMS AT THIS STAGE
Oral (birth to 1 year)	Mouth	Weaning Oral gratification from sucking, eating, biting	Optimism, gullibility, dependency, pessimism, passivity, hostility, sarcasm, aggression
Anal (1 to 3 years)	Anus	Toilet training Gratification from expelling and withholding feces	Excessive cleanliness, orderliness, stinginess, messiness, rebelliousness, destructiveness
Phallic (3 to 5 or 6 years)	Genitals	Oedipal conflict Sexual curiosity Masturbation	Flirtatiousness, vanity, promiscuity, pride, chastity
Latency (5 or 6 years to puberty)	None	Period of sexual calm Interest in school, hobbies, same-sex friends	
Genital (from puberty on)	Genitals	Revival of sexual interests Establishment of mature sexual relationships	

Want to be sure you've fully absorbed the material in this chapter? Visit **www.ablongman.com/wood5e** for access to free practice tests, flashcards, interactive activities, and links developed specifically to help you succeed in psychology.

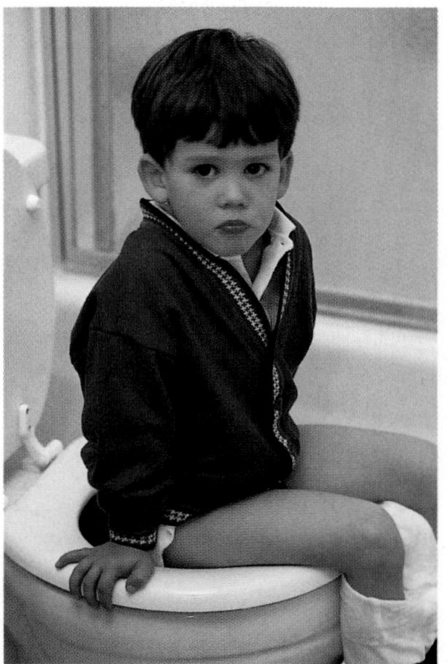

Freud believed that a fixation at the anal stage, resulting from harsh parental pressure, could lead to an anal retentive personality—characterized by excessive stubbornness, rigidity, and neatness.

their sexual wishes upon their mother and develop hostile impulses against their father as being a rival" (1925/1963a, p. 61). The boy usually resolves the Oedipus complex by identifying with his father and repressing his sexual feelings for his mother. With identification, the child takes on his father's behaviors, mannerisms, and superego standards; in this way, the superego develops (Freud, 1930/1962).

Freud proposed an equally controversial developmental process for girls in the phallic stage. When they discover they have no penis, girls in this stage develop "penis envy," and they turn to their father because he has the desired organ (Freud, 1933/1965). They feel sexual desires for him and develop jealousy and rivalry toward their mother. But eventually girls, too, experience anxiety as a result of their hostile feelings. They repress their sexual feelings toward the father and identify with the mother, leading to the formation of their superego (Freud, 1930/1962).

According to Freud, failure to resolve these conflicts can have serious consequences for both boys and girls: Tremendous guilt and anxiety may be carried over into adulthood and cause sexual problems, great difficulty relating to members of the opposite sex, or homosexuality.

The Latency Period (5 or 6 Years to Puberty) Following the stormy phallic stage, the *latency period* is one of relative calm. The sex instinct is repressed and temporarily sublimated in school and play activities, hobbies, and sports. During this period, children prefer same-sex friends and playmates.

The Genital Stage (from Puberty On) In the *genital stage*, the focus of sexual energy gradually shifts to the opposite sex for the vast majority of people, culminating in heterosexual love and the attainment of full adult sexuality. Freud believed that the few who reach the genital stage without having fixations at earlier stages can achieve the state of psychological health that he equated with the ability to love and work.

Evaluating Freud's Contribution

How are Freud's ideas evaluated by modern psychologists?

Some of Freud's ideas may seem odd or even bizarre to you, but psychology is indebted to Freud for introducing the idea that unconscious forces may motivate behavior and for emphasizing the influence of early childhood experiences on later development. Moreover, psychoanalysis is still viewed as a useful therapeutic technique (Bartlett, 2002). And Freud's concept of defense mechanisms provides a useful way of categorizing the cognitive strategies that people use to manage stress (Fauerbach et al., 2002; Tori & Bilmes, 2002). However, critics charge that much of Freud's theory defies scientific testing. Too much of the time, any act of behavior or even no act of behavior at all can be interpreted to support Freud's theory. How, for instance, can we ever test the idea that little boys are in love with their mothers and want to get rid of their fathers? How can we verify or falsify the idea that one component of personality is motivated entirely by the pursuit of pleasure? Chiefly because of the difficulty involved in finding scientific answers to such questions, there are very few strict Freudians among today's psychologists.

Remember It 14.1

1. __________ is both a theory of personality and a therapy for the treatment of psychological disorders.
2. Freud considered the __________ to be the primary motivating force of human behavior.
3. According to Freud, the part of the personality that makes you want to eat, drink, and be merry is your __________.
4. You just found a gold watch in a darkened movie theater. Your __________ would urge you to turn it in to the lost-and-found.
5. The part of the personality that Freud believed determines appropriate ways to satisfy biological urges is the __________.
6. Match each defense mechanism with the appropriate example.

   ____ (1) sublimation
   ____ (2) repression
   ____ (3) displacement
   ____ (4) rationalization

   a. forgetting a traumatic childhood experience
   b. supplying a logical reason for arriving late
   c. crafting a creative work (art, music, writing, etc.)
   d. snapping at a friend after getting a speeding ticket from a police officer

7. Match each psychosexual stage with its associated conflict or theme.

   ____ (1) oral stage
   ____ (2) anal stage
   ____ (3) phallic stage
   ____ (4) latency stage
   ____ (5) genital stage

   a. the Oedipus complex
   b. the attainment of adult sexuality
   c. weaning
   d. toilet training
   e. preference for same-sex friend and playmates

ANSWERS: 1. Psychoanalysis; 2. unconscious; 3. id; 4. superego; 5. ego; 6. (1) c, (2) a, (3) d, (4) b; 7. (1) c, (2) d, (3) a, (4) e, (5) b

The Neo-Freudians

Is it possible to construct a theory of personality that builds on the strengths of Freud's approach and avoids its weaknesses? Several personality theorists, referred to as *neo-Freudians*, have attempted to do so. Most started their careers as followers of Freud but began to disagree on certain basic principles of psychoanalytic theory.

How do the views of the neo-Freudians differ from those of Freud?

Carl Jung

One of the most important neo-Freudians, Carl Jung (1875–1961), did not consider the sexual instinct to be the main factor in personality; nor did he believe that the personality is almost completely formed in early childhood. For Jung (1933), middle age was an even more important period for personality development. Jung conceived of the personality as consisting of three parts: the ego, the personal unconscious, and the collective unconscious, as shown in Figure 14.2 (on page 478). He saw the ego as the conscious component of personality, which carries out normal daily activities. Like Freud, he believed the ego to be secondary in importance to the unconscious.

The **personal unconscious** develops as a result of one's own experience and is therefore unique to each person. It contains all the experiences, thoughts, and perceptions accessible to the conscious, as well as repressed memories, wishes, and impulses. The

personal unconscious In Jung's theory, the layer of the unconscious that contains all of the thoughts, perceptions, and experiences accessible to the conscious, as well as repressed memories, wishes, and impulses.

FIGURE 14.2 Jung's Conception of Personality

Like Freud, Jung saw three components in personality. The ego and the personal unconscious are unique to each individual. The collective unconscious accounts for the similarity of myths and beliefs in diverse cultures.

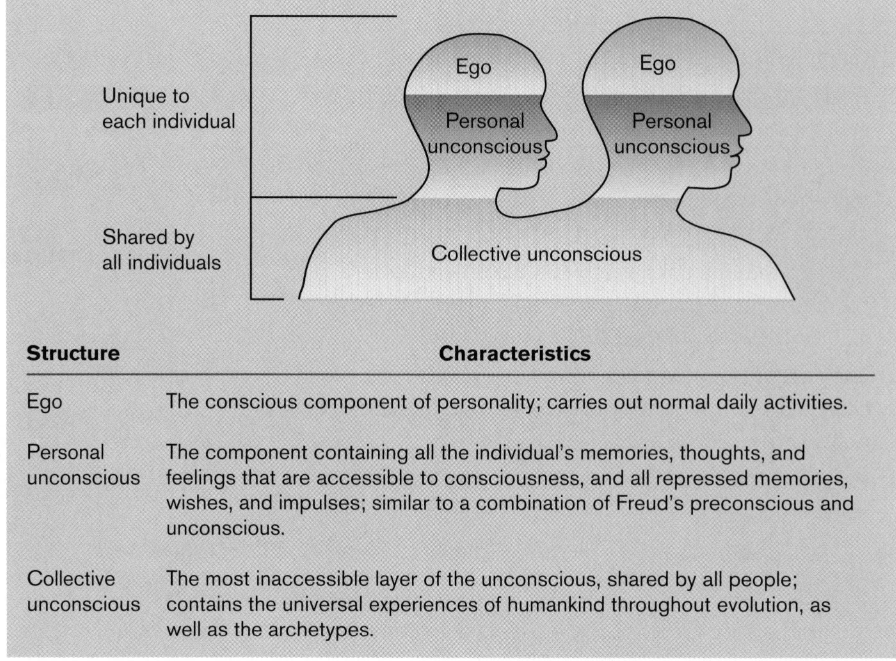

Structure	Characteristics
Ego	The conscious component of personality; carries out normal daily activities.
Personal unconscious	The component containing all the individual's memories, thoughts, and feelings that are accessible to consciousness, and all repressed memories, wishes, and impulses; similar to a combination of Freud's preconscious and unconscious.
Collective unconscious	The most inaccessible layer of the unconscious, shared by all people; contains the universal experiences of humankind throughout evolution, as well as the archetypes.

Carl Gustav Jung (1875–1961)

collective unconscious, the most inaccessible layer of the unconscious, contains the universal experiences of humankind throughout evolution. This is how Jung accounted for the similarity of certain myths, dreams, symbols, and religious beliefs in cultures widely separated by distance and time. Moreover, the collective unconscious contains what he called **archetypes**, inherited tendencies to respond to universal human situations in particular ways. Jung would say that the tendencies of people to believe in a god, a devil, evil spirits, and heroes all result from inherited archetypes that reflect the shared experience of humankind.

Jung named several archetypes that he believed exert a major influence on the personality. The *persona* is the public face one shows to the world—"a kind of mask, designed on the one hand to make a definite impression on others, and, on the other, to conceal the true nature of the individual" (Jung, 1966, p. 192). The persona is consistent with the roles an individual plays and helps him or her to function socially. But problems result if the person confuses the persona (the mask) with the real self behind it. The *shadow* represents "the 'negative side' of the personality, the sum of all those unpleasant qualities we like to hide" (Jung, 1917/1953, par. 103). To deny the shadow, or to fail to be conscious of it, gives it more power. And ironically, the qualities we condemn most in others may be lurking in our own shadow, unadmitted and unknown.

Jung also argued that each of us has qualities of the opposite sex within our unconscious, although usually in an underdeveloped state. The *anima* is Jung's term for the "inner feminine figure" within the unconscious of every man, and the *animus* is the "inner masculine figure" within the unconscious of every woman (Jung, 1961, p. 186). Both masculine and feminine qualities must be consciously acknowledged and integrated, Jung thought, for a healthy personality to develop.

The *self* represents the full development of the personality and is attained only when the opposing internal forces are integrated and balanced. The self encompasses the conscious and the unconscious, the persona, the shadow, the masculine and the feminine qualities, and the tendency toward extraversion or introversion (terms originated by Jung). *Extraversion* is the tendency to be outgoing, adaptable, and sociable; *introversion* is

collective unconscious In Jung's theory, the most inaccessible layer of the unconscious, which contains the universal experiences of humankind throughout evolution.

archetype (AR-ka-type) Existing in the collective unconscious, an inherited tendency to respond to universal human situations in particular ways.

the tendency to focus inward and to be reflective, retiring, and nonsocial. Jung claimed that the integration and balancing of opposing internal forces begin in midlife. For some, this change may be accompanied by a *midlife crisis*, which Jung himself experienced. Because he emphasized personality development in midlife, many consider Jung the conceptual founder of the psychology of adult development (Moraglia, 1994).

Alfred Adler

Another neo-Freudian, Alfred Adler (1870–1937), emphasized the unity of the personality rather than the separate warring components of id, ego, and superego. Adler (1927, 1956) also maintained that the drive to overcome feelings of inferiority acquired in childhood motivates most of our behavior. He (1956) claimed that people develop a "style of life" at an early age—a unique way in which the child and later the adult will go about the struggle to achieve superiority. Sometimes inferiority feelings are so strong that they prevent personal development, a condition Adler called the *inferiority complex* (Dreikurs, 1953). Because Adler's theory stresses the uniqueness of each individual's struggle to achieve superiority and refers to the "creative self," a conscious, self-aware component of an individual's personality, it is known as *individual psychology*.

Karen Horney

The work of neo-Freudian Karen Horney (1885–1952) centered on two main themes: the neurotic personality (Horney, 1937, 1945, 1950) and feminine psychology (Horney, 1967). Horney did not accept Freud's division of personality into id, ego, and superego, and she flatly rejected his psychosexual stages and the concepts of the Oedipus complex and penis envy. Furthermore, Horney thought Freud overemphasized the role of the sexual instinct and neglected cultural and environmental influences on personality. While she did stress the importance of early childhood experiences, Horney (1939) believed that personality could continue to develop and change throughout life.

Horney argued forcefully against Freud's notion that a woman's desire to have a child and a man is nothing more than a conversion of the unfulfilled wish for a penis. Horney (1945) believed that many of women's psychological difficulties arise from failure to live up to an idealized version of themselves. To be psychologically healthy, she claimed, women—and men, for that matter—must learn to overcome irrational beliefs about the need for perfection. Her influence may be seen in modern cognitive-behavioral therapies, which we will explore in Chapter 16.

Remember It 14.2

1. In Jung's theory, the inherited part of the personality that stores the experiences of humankind is the __________ unconscious.

2. Match each archetype with its description.

____ (1) self
____ (2) anima or animus
____ (3) shadow
____ (4) persona

a. the dark side of one's nature
b. one's public face
c. the full development of the integrated and balanced personality
d. the qualities of the opposite sex within each person's unconscious

3. __________ believed that the basic human drive is to overcome and compensate for feelings of inferiority.

4. __________ believed that Freud was wrong about the concept of penis envy.

ANSWERS: 1. collective; 2. (1) c, (2) d, (3) a, (4) b; 3. Alfred Adler; 4. Karen Horney

Learning Theories and Personality

What are the components of Bandura's concept of reciprocal determinism and Rotter's locus of control?

Do you recall the importance of reinforcement in B. F. Skinner's principles of operant conditioning? As you might expect, learning theorists view personality as just one more result of learning. Thus, according to Skinner, we consistently exhibit certain behaviors, called "personality" by most, because we have been reinforced for doing so. And, of course, behaviors and reinforcements are far more easily observed than are internal factors such as Freud's id, ego, and superego. For this reason, many psychologists regard explanations of personality that are based on learning theories as more scientific than Freud's psychoanalysis. However, learning theories are often criticized for paying too little attention to emotions and other internal processes.

Social-Cognitive Theory

reciprocal determinism Bandura's concept of a mutual influential relationship among behavior, cognitive factors, and environment.

self-efficacy The perception a person has of his or her ability to perform competently whatever is attempted.

One learning theory that does take internal factors into account is the *social-cognitive approach* of Albert Bandura (1977a, 1986). He maintains that cognitive factors (such as an individual's stage of cognitive development), individual behaviors, and the external environment are all influenced by each other (Bandura, 1989). This mutual relationship Bandura calls **reciprocal determinism** (see Figure 14.3).

One of the cognitive factors that Bandura (1997a; 1997b) considers especially important is **self-efficacy**, the perception people have of their ability to perform competently whatever they attempt. Cross-cultural researchers examining self-efficacy in 25 countries found it to be an important individual difference in all of them (Scholz et al., 2002). According to Bandura, people high in self-efficacy approach new situations confidently, set high goals, and persist in their efforts because they believe success is

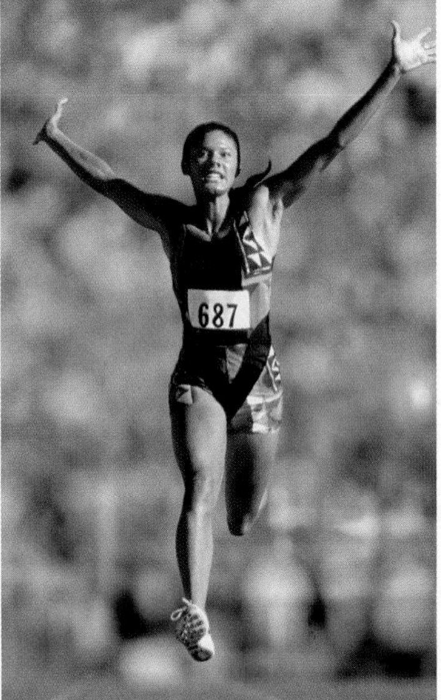

Individuals who are high in self-efficacy pursue challenging goals and persist in their efforts until they reach them.

FIGURE 14.3

Bandura's Reciprocal Determinism

Bandura takes a social-cognitive view of personality. He suggests that three components—the external environment, individual behaviors, and cognitive factors, such as beliefs, expectancies, and personal dispositions—are all influenced by each other and play reciprocal roles in determining personality.

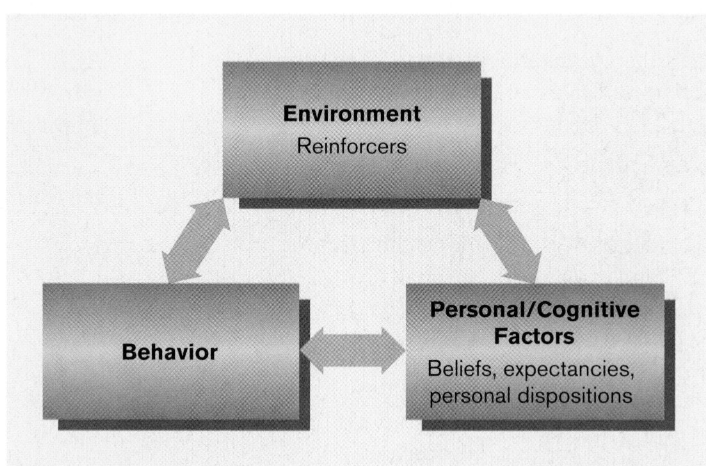

likely. People low in self-efficacy, on the other hand, expect failure; consequently, they avoid challenges and typically give up on tasks they find difficult. Bandura's research has shown that people with high self-efficacy are less likely to experience depression than those with low self-efficacy (Bandura, 1997b).

Locus of Control

Julian Rotter proposes a similar cognitive factor, **locus of control**. Some people see themselves as primarily in control of their behavior and its consequences. This perception Rotter (1966, 1971, 1990) defines as an *internal locus of control*. Other people perceive that whatever happens to them is in the hands of fate, luck, or chance. These individuals exhibit an *external locus of control* and may claim that it does not matter what they do because "whatever will be, will be." Rotter contends that people with an external locus of control are less likely to change their behavior as a result of reinforcement, because they do not see reinforcers as being tied to their own actions. Students who have an external locus of control tend to be procrastinators and, thus, are less likely to be academically successful than those with an internal locus of control (Janssen & Carton, 1999). Further, external locus of control is associated with lower levels of life satisfaction (Kirkcaldy et al., 2002). Where is your locus of control? To find out, complete *Try It 14.1*.

■ **locus of control**
Rotter's concept of a cognitive factor that explains how people account for what happens in their lives—either seeing themselves as primarily in control of their behavior and its consequences (internal locus of control) or perceiving what happens to them to be in the hands of fate, luck, or chance (external locus of control).

Try It 14.1 Where Is Your Locus of Control?

For each statement, indicate which choice best expresses your view.

1. Heredity determines most of a person's personality.
   a. strongly disagree c. neutral e. strongly agree
   b. disagree d. agree
2. Chance has a lot to do with being successful.
   a. strongly disagree c. neutral e. strongly agree
   b. disagree d. agree
3. Whatever plans you make, something will always interfere.
   a. strongly disagree c. neutral e. strongly agree
   b. disagree d. agree
4. Being at the right place at the right time is essential for getting what you want in life.
   a. almost never c. sometimes e. most of the time
   b. rarely d. quite often
5. Intelligence is a given, and it cannot be improved.
   a. strongly disagree c. neutral e. strongly agree
   b. disagree d. agree
6. If I successfully accomplish a task, it's because it was an easy one.
   a. strongly disagree c. neutral e. strongly agree
   b. disagree d. agree
7. You cannot change your destiny.
   a. strongly disagree c. neutral e. strongly agree
   b. disagree d. agree
8. School success is mostly a result of one's socioeconomic background.
   a. strongly disagree c. neutral e. strongly agree
   b. disagree d. agree
9. People are lonely because they are not given the chance to meet new people.
   a. strongly disagree c. neutral e. strongly agree
   b. disagree d. agree
10. If you set realistic goals, you can succeed at almost anything.
    a. strongly disagree c. neutral e. strongly agree
    b. disagree d. agree

Score your responses as follows: a = 10 points, b = 7.5, c = 5, d = 2.5, e = 0. A perfect score is 100 points, and the higher your total score, the more internal your locus of control is. The more internal your locus of control, the more likely you are to succeed in life!

Remember It 14.3

1. According to ____________, behavior is dependent on reinforcement rather than on internal traits.
2. Bandura's concept of ____________ refers to the mutual effects of behavior, cognitive factors, and the environment.
3. People who are high in ____________ persist in their efforts to accomplish goals.
4. ____________ proposed the concept of locus of control.

ANSWERS: 1. B. F. Skinner; 2. reciprocal determinism; 3. self-efficacy; 4. Julian Rotter

Humanistic Personality Theories

In *humanistic psychology*, people are assumed to have a natural tendency toward growth and the realization of their fullest potential. Thus, humanistic personality theories are more optimistic than Freud's psychoanalytic theory and more sensitive to emotional experiences than the learning theories. However, like Freud's theory, these perspectives are often criticized as being difficult to test scientifically.

Two Humanistic Theories

What are the contributions of humanistic theorists to the study of personality?

For humanistic psychologist Abraham Maslow (1908–1970), motivational factors are at the root of personality. You may remember from Chapter 11 that Maslow constructed a hierarchy of needs, ranging from physiological needs at the bottom upward to safety needs, belonging and love needs, esteem needs, and finally to the highest need—self-actualization (see Figure 11.3 on page 379). **Self-actualization** means developing to one's fullest potential. A healthy person is continually striving to become all that he or she can be.

In his research, Maslow found self-actualizers to be accurate in perceiving reality—able to judge honestly and to spot quickly the fake and the dishonest. Most of them believe they have a mission to accomplish or the need to devote their life to some larger good. Self-actualizers tend not to depend on external authority or other people but seem to be inner-driven, autonomous, and independent. Finally, the hallmark of self-actualizers is having frequently occurring *peak experiences*—experiences of deep meaning, insight, and harmony within themselves and with the universe. Current researchers have modified Maslow's definition of self-actualization to include effective personal relationships as well as peak experiences (Hanley & Abell, 2002).

■ **self-actualization** Developing to one's fullest potential.

■ **conditions of worth** Conditions on which the positive regard of others rests.

According to another humanistic psychologist, Carl Rogers (1902–1987), our parents set up **conditions of worth**, or conditions on which their positive regard hinges. Conditions of worth force us to live and act according to someone else's values rather than our own. In our efforts to gain positive regard, we deny our true selves by inhibiting some of our behavior, denying or distorting some of our perceptions, and closing off parts of our experience. In so doing, we experience stress and anxiety, and our whole self-structure may be threatened.

Abraham Maslow (1908–1970)

For Rogers, a major goal of psychotherapy is to enable people to open themselves up to experiences and begin to live according to their own values rather than living by the values of others in an attempt to gain positive regard. He called his therapy *person-centered therapy*, preferring not to use the term *patient* (Rogers's therapy will be discussed further in Chapter 16). Rogers believed that the therapist must give the client **unconditional positive regard**—that is, unqualified caring and nonjudgmental acceptance, no matter what the client says, does, has done, or is thinking of doing. Unconditional positive regard is designed to reduce threat, eliminate conditions of worth, and bring the person back in tune with his or her true self. If successful, the therapy helps the client become what Rogers called a *fully functioning person*, one who is functioning at an optimal level and living fully and spontaneously according to his or her own inner value system.

unconditional positive regard
Unqualified caring and nonjudgmental acceptance of another.

Self-Esteem

What have psychologists learned about self-esteem?

No doubt you have heard discussions of the importance of self-esteem to one's mental health. Though humanists have been criticized for being unscientific and for seeing, hearing, and finding no evil within the human psyche, they have inspired the study of positive personality qualities, including altruism, cooperation, love, acceptance of others, and especially self-esteem. Complete *Try It 14.2* to estimate your current level of self-esteem.

How does self-esteem develop? One source of variations in self-esteem arises from comparisons of actual to desired traits. For example, a tone-deaf person who desires to be an accomplished musician might suffer from low self-esteem. However, most of us do not form a global idea about our own self-worth on the basis of a single area of competence. Instead, we view ourselves in terms of strengths and weaknesses. When our strengths lie in areas that we value and believe to be important, we have high self-esteem. Conversely, even outstanding achievements in areas we consider to be of little value may not affect our self-esteem. So, a person who is a great plumber, but who believes that being a good plumber isn't very important, is likely to have low self-esteem. At the same time, a person who feels incompetent because he has to pay a plumber a handsome sum to fix a leaking faucet might be in awe of the plumber's skill.

Developmental psychologists have found that self-esteem is fairly stable from childhood through the late adult years (Trzesniewski et al., 2003). So, the self-worth beliefs we adopt in childhood can affect us for a lifetime. Children and adolescents form ideas about their competencies in various domains—academics, sports, fine arts—that become increasingly stable across the elementary and secondary school years (Harter, 1990). And by age 7, most children have a sense of global self-esteem as well. These judgments come from both actual experiences and information provided by others. Thus, to develop high self-esteem, children need to experience success in domains they view as important and to be encouraged to value themselves by parents, teachers, and peers.

Try It 14.2 Gauging Your Self-Esteem

For each statement below, choose the option that best reflects your feelings:

a. strongly agree b. agree c. neutral d. disagree e. strongly disagree

_____ 1. I feel confident in most social situations.

_____ 2. I believe I have something worthwhile to offer in life.

_____ 3. I feel that others respect my opinion.

_____ 4. I compare favorably with most people I know.

_____ 5. I feel that, on the whole, other people like me.

_____ 6. I deserve the love and respect of others.

Compute your score as follows: a = 4 points, b = 3, c = 2, d = 1, e = 0. A total score of 20–24 points indicates that you have excellent self-esteem; 15–19 means good, 10–14 is fair, and below 10 indicates that you could work on this quality.

Remember It 14.4

1. __________ maintained that human beings have a natural tendency toward self-actualization.
2. __________ believed that individuals require unconditional positive regard to become fully functioning persons.
3. Self-esteem results from the comparison of __________ to __________ characteristics.

ANSWERS: 1. Abraham Maslow; 2. Carl Rogers; 3. actual, desired

Trait Theories

trait
A personal quality or characteristic, which is stable across situations, that is used to describe or explain personality.

Traits are personal qualities or characteristics that make it possible for us to face a wide variety of situational demands and deal with unforeseen circumstances (De Raad & Kokkonen, 2000). *Trait theories* are attempts to explain personality and differences among people in terms of personal characteristics that are stable across situations.

What were some of the ideas proposed by early trait theorists?

Early Trait Theories

One of the early trait theorists, Gordon Allport (1897–1967), claimed that each person inherits a unique set of raw materials for given traits, which are then shaped by experiences (Allport & Odbert, 1936). A *cardinal trait* is "so pervasive and so outstanding in a life that . . . almost every act seems traceable to its influence" (Allport, 1961, p. 365). It is so strong a part of a person's personality that he or she may become identified with or known for that trait. For example, what comes to mind when you hear the name *Einstein?* Most likely, you associate this name with intellectual genius; in fact, it is sometimes used as a synonym for genius. Thus, for Albert Einstein, genius is a cardinal trait. *Central traits* are those, said Allport (1961), that we would "mention in writing a careful letter of recommendation" (p. 365).

Raymond Cattell (1950) referred to observable qualities of personality as *surface traits*. Using observations and questionnaires, Cattell studied thousands of people and found certain clusters of surface traits that appeared together time after time. He thought these were evidence of deeper, more general, underlying personality factors, which he called *source traits*. People differ in the degree to which they possess each source trait. For example, Cattell claimed that intelligence is a source trait: Everyone has it, but the amount possessed varies from person to person.

Cattell found 23 source traits in normal individuals, 16 of which he studied in great detail. Cattell's Sixteen Personality Factor Questionnaire, commonly called the *16PF*, yields a personality profile (Cattell et al., 1950, 1977). This test continues to be widely used in research (e.g., Brody et al., 2000) and for personality assessment in career counseling, schools, and employment settings. Results from the 16PF are usually plotted on a graph such as that shown in Figure 14.4.

What do factor theorists consider to be the most important dimensions of personality?

Factor Models of Personality

The early trait theories represented the beginning of a movement that continues to be important in personality research. Cattell's notion of personality factors has been especially influential. One factor model that has shaped a great deal of personality research is that of British psychologist

FIGURE 14.4 The 16PF Personality Profile

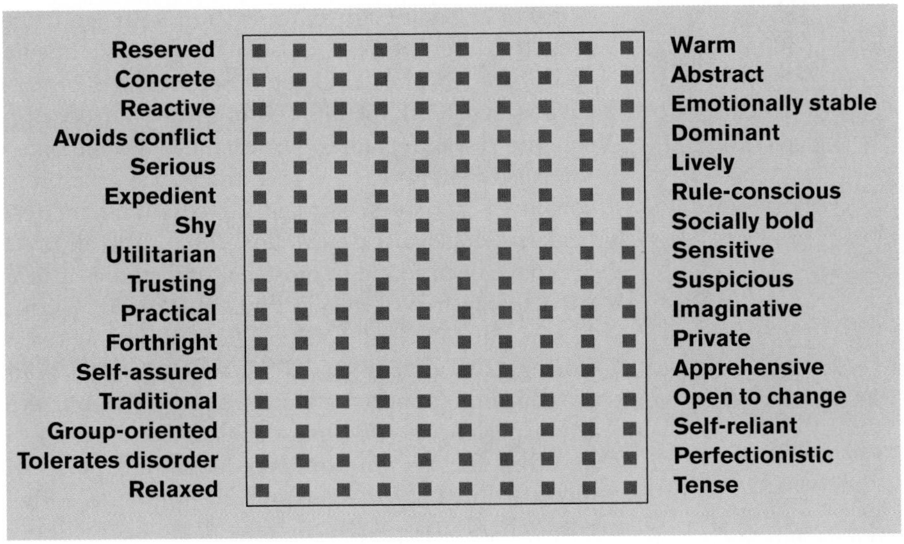

Reserved	■	■	■	■	■	■	■	■	■	■	Warm
Concrete	■	■	■	■	■	■	■	■	■	■	Abstract
Reactive	■	■	■	■	■	■	■	■	■	■	Emotionally stable
Avoids conflict	■	■	■	■	■	■	■	■	■	■	Dominant
Serious	■	■	■	■	■	■	■	■	■	■	Lively
Expedient	■	■	■	■	■	■	■	■	■	■	Rule-conscious
Shy	■	■	■	■	■	■	■	■	■	■	Socially bold
Utilitarian	■	■	■	■	■	■	■	■	■	■	Sensitive
Trusting	■	■	■	■	■	■	■	■	■	■	Suspicious
Practical	■	■	■	■	■	■	■	■	■	■	Imaginative
Forthright	■	■	■	■	■	■	■	■	■	■	Private
Self-assured	■	■	■	■	■	■	■	■	■	■	Apprehensive
Traditional	■	■	■	■	■	■	■	■	■	■	Open to change
Group-oriented	■	■	■	■	■	■	■	■	■	■	Self-reliant
Tolerates disorder	■	■	■	■	■	■	■	■	■	■	Perfectionistic
Relaxed	■	■	■	■	■	■	■	■	■	■	Tense

Results from Cattell's 16PF can be plotted on a chart like this one. The profile is represented by a line connecting an individual's score points on each dimension (e.g., reserved–warm). How would you draw your own profile? Circle the point along each of the dimensions, and connect them with a line to find out.

Hans Eysenck (1990), who places particular emphasis on two dimensions: Extroversion (extroversion versus introversion) and Neuroticism (emotional stability versus instability). Extroverts are sociable, outgoing, and active, whereas introverts are withdrawn, quiet, and introspective. Emotionally stable people are calm, even-tempered, and often easygoing, while emotionally unstable people are anxious, excitable, and easily distressed.

Extroversion and Neuroticism are also important dimensions in the most talked-about personality theory today—the **five-factor theory**, also known as the *Big Five* (Wiggins, 1996). We will consider the Big Five personality dimensions and the traits associated with them using the names assigned by Robert McCrae and Paul Costa (1987; McCrae, 1996), the most influential proponents of the five-factor theory.

1. *Extroversion.* This dimension contrasts such traits as sociable, outgoing, talkative, assertive, persuasive, decisive, and active with more introverted traits such as withdrawn, quiet, passive, retiring, and reserved.
2. *Neuroticism.* People high on Neuroticism are prone to emotional instability. They tend to experience negative emotions and to be moody, irritable, nervous, and inclined to worry. This dimension differentiates people who are anxious, excitable, and easily distressed from those who are emotionally stable and thus calm, even-tempered, easygoing, and relaxed.
3. *Conscientiousness.* This dimension differentiates individuals who are dependable, organized, reliable, responsible, thorough, hard-working, and persevering from those who are undependable, disorganized, impulsive, unreliable, irresponsible, careless, negligent, and lazy.
4. *Agreeableness.* This dimension is composed of a collection of traits that range from compassion to antagonism toward others. A person high on Agreeableness would be a pleasant person, who is good-natured, warm, sympathetic, and cooperative; one low on Agreeableness would tend to be unfriendly, unpleasant, aggressive, argumentative, cold, even hostile and vindictive.
5. *Openness to Experience.* This dimension contrasts individuals who seek out varied experiences and who are imaginative, intellectually curious, and broad-minded with those who are concrete-minded and practical and whose interests are narrow. Researchers have found that being high on Openness to Experience is a requirement for creative accomplishment (King et al., 1996).

■ **five-factor theory**
A trait theory that attempts to explain personality using five broad dimensions, each of which is composed of a constellation of personality traits.

According to the five-factor theory of personality, extroverts are sociable, outgoing, and active—both Britney Spears and Jay Leno could be considered extroverts, even though their personalities differ. How do they differ from introverts?

To measure the Big Five dimensions of personality, Costa and McCrae (1985, 1992, 1997) developed the NEO Personality Inventory (NEO-PI) and, more recently, the Revised NEO Personality Inventory (NEO-PI-R). The NEO and other measures of the Big Five are currently being used in a wide variety of personality research studies. For example, psychologists in the Australian army have used the test to measure personality differences between effective and ineffective leaders (McCormack & Mellor, 2002). And all five factors have been found in cross-cultural studies involving participants from Canada, Finland, Poland, Germany, Russia, Hong Kong, Croatia, Italy, South Korea, and Portugal (McCrae et al., 2000; Paunonen et al., 1996).

But how important are the Big Five in our everyday experiences? One line of research addressing this question focuses on connections among personality, physical health, and mental health. For instance, researchers have learned that high scores on the dimension of Neuroticism are associated with peptic ulcer disease (Goodwin & Stein, 2003). Individuals with such high scores are also more likely to suffer from attention problems (Szymura & Wodniecka, 2003). Understanding the connection between personality traits and problems such as these may help prevent these problems in the future or may help health professionals more effectively treat individuals who suffer from them.

Researchers have also found connections between the Big Five and other domains of behavior such as music preferences. For instance, the higher an individual's score on the dimension of Openness to Experience, the more likely she is to prefer classical, jazz, or rock music to country or rap (Rentfrow & Gosling, 2003). Moreover, scores on the Big Five are related to the physical characteristics of an individual's home (Gosling et al., 2002). For instance, those who score high on Extroversion are likely to arrange their living spaces in ways that are cheerful, colorful, and stylish, but a bit cluttered and unconventional. People who score high on Conscientiousness create efficient furniture arrangements and organize their possessions so that they can be easily located. Thus, it appears that the different ways in which people respond to questions on personality inventories are, indeed, meaningfully linked to everyday behavior.

The Situation versus Trait Debate

What is the situation-trait debate about?

How well do trait theories explain behavior? This question has been addressed by one of the severest critics of trait theories, Walter Mischel (1968). Mischel initiated the *situation-trait debate*, an ongoing discussion among psychologists about the relative importance of factors within the situation and factors within the person in accounting for behavior (Rowe, 1987). For instance, you probably wouldn't steal money from a store, but what if you see a stranger unknowingly drop a $5 bill? Mischel and those who agree with him say that characteristics of the two situations dictate your behavior, not a trait such as honesty. Stealing from a store might require devising and carrying out a complicated plan, and it would carry a heavy penalty if you were caught, so you opt for honesty. Picking up a $5 bill is easy and may only result in embarrassment if you get caught, so you may do it. Mischel (1973, 1977) later modified his original position and admitted that behavior is influenced by both the person and the situation. Mischel views a trait as a conditional probability that a particular action will occur in response to a particular situation (Wright & Mischel, 1987).

Advocates of the trait side of the situation-trait debate point out that support for trait theories has come from many longitudinal studies (McCrae, 2002; Pesonen et al., 2003). McCrae and Costa (1990) studied personality traits of subjects over time and found them to be stable for periods of 3 to 30 years. Typically, personality changes very little with age. As McCrae (1993) puts it, "Stable individual differences in basic dimensions are a universal feature of adult personality" (p. 577). Indeed, a large meta-analysis demonstrated that consistency of personality traits actually increases over the adult years (Roberts & DelVecchio, 2000).

Research on personality suggests that some traits, such as agreeableness, actually increase as we get older.

The weight of evidence supports the view that there are internal traits that strongly influence behavior across situations (Carson, 1989; McAdams, 1992). Still, situational variables do affect personality traits. In one study of elderly women, researchers found that life changes such as decreases in social support and increases in physical disability resulted in increases in Neuroticism (Maiden et al., 2003). Similarly, the organizational demands of adult life appear to lead to increases in Conscientiousness throughout adulthood that are most marked between the ages of 20 and 30 (Srivastava et al., 2003). (There's hope for even the most disorganized among us!) And, researchers say, the stereotype of "grumpy old men" is a myth; agreeableness actually increases as we get older (Srivastava et al., 2003). Thus, characteristic traits determine how we behave most of the time, not all of the time.

Remember It 14.5

1. According to Gordon Allport, the kind of trait that is a defining characteristic of one's personality is a ___________ trait.
2. According to ___________, the differences among people are explained by the number of source traits they possess.
3. ___________ claimed that psychologists can best understand personality by assessing people on two major dimensions—Extroversion and Neuroticism.
4. According to a growing consensus among trait theorists, there are ___________ major dimensions of personality.

ANSWERS: 1. cardinal; 2. Raymond Cattell; 3. Hans Eysenck; 4. five

Nature, Nurture, and Personality

So, you might be wondering, how do we acquire our personality traits? This question leads us back to the great debate we have encountered before—the nature-nurture controversy. Recall from Chapter 2 that *behavioral genetics* is the field of study that uses twin studies and adoption studies to investigate the relative effects of heredity and environment on behavior. Personality traits have been studied extensively by researchers in this field.

Twin and Adoption Studies

What have twin and adoption studies revealed about the influence of genes on personality?

As you learned in Chapter 8, one of the best known studies in psychology, the Minnesota twin study, revealed that the IQ scores of identical twins are strongly correlated, regardless of whether the twins are raised in the same or different environments (Bouchard, 1997). Using data from the same participants, Tellegen and others (1988) found that identical twins are also quite similar on several personality factors, again regardless of whether they are raised together or apart.

In another classic twin study, Rushton and colleagues (1986) found that nurturance, empathy, and assertiveness are substantially influenced by heredity. Even altruism and aggressiveness, traits we might expect to be strongly influenced by parental upbringing, are actually more heavily influenced by heredity. A meta-analysis by Miles and Carey (1997) revealed that the heritability of aggressiveness may be as high as .50 (or 50%). Moreover, a number of longitudinal studies indicate that heredity makes substantial contributions to individual differences in the Big Five personality dimensions, as shown in Figure 14.5 (Bouchard, 1994; Caspi, 2000; Loehlin, 1992). Thus, genetically based similarities in personality, rather than modeling, may be responsible for the ways in which our adult lives relate to those of our parents.

Other twin studies have revealed a genetic influence on social attitudes such as traditionalism, whether a person endorses traditional moral values and follows rules and authority (Finkel & McGue, 1997). The risk of divorce appears to have a heritability of .55 for women and .59 for men. This is not to say that there is a gene for

FIGURE 14.5 Estimated Influence of Heredity and Environment on the Big Five Personality Dimensions

The Minnesota study of twins reared apart yielded an average heritability estimate of .41 (41%) for the Big Five personality factors; the Loehlin twin studies, a heritability estimate of .42 (42%). Both studies found the influence of the shared environment to be only about .07 (7%). The remaining percentage represents a combination of nonshared environmental influences and measurement error.

Source: Adapted from Bouchard (1994).

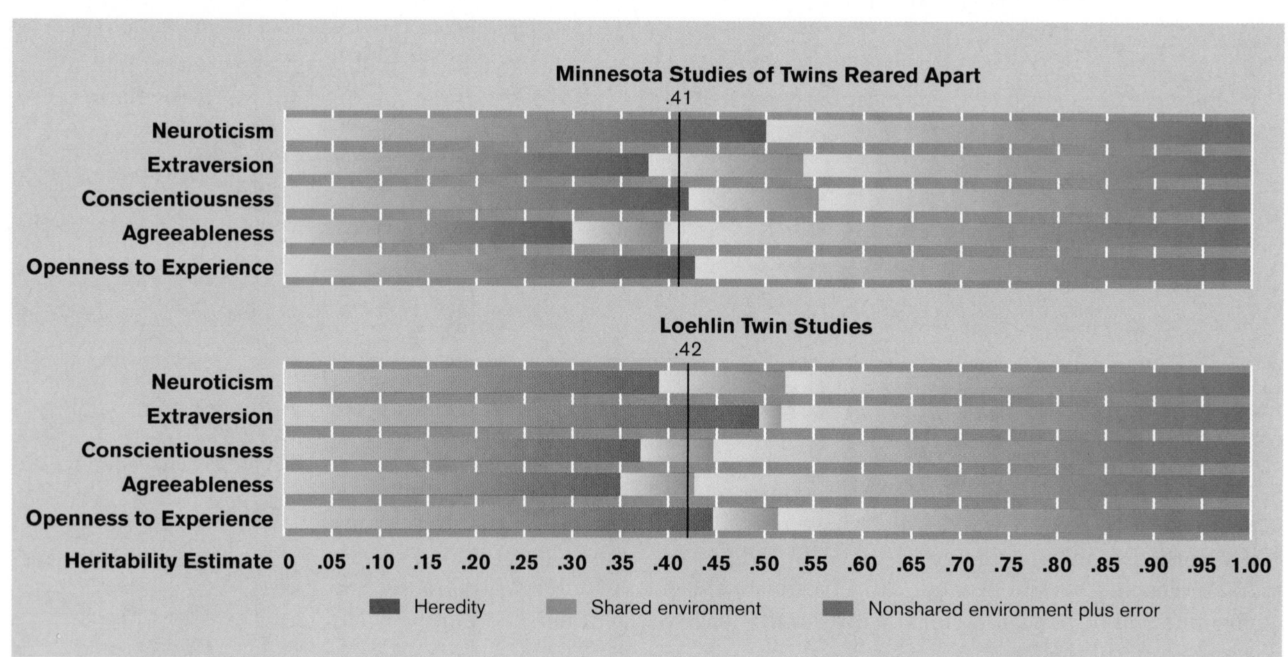

divorce; rather, the risk derives from the genetic influence on certain personality factors (Jockin et al., 1996). Genes also influence personality factors that correlate with psychological disorders, as measured by the Minnesota Multiphasic Personality Inventory (DiLalla et al., 1996). There even seems to be a genetic influence on people's sense of well-being (Lykken & Tellegen, 1996), their interests (Lykken et al., 1993), how they tend to view their environment (Chipuer et al., 1993), and how they perceive life events, particularly controllable ones (Plomin & Rende, 1991).

Adoption studies have also shown that heredity strongly influences personality. Loehlin and others (1987) assessed the personalities of 17-year-olds who had been adopted at birth. When the adopted children were compared to other children in the family, the researchers found that the shared family environment had virtually no influence on their personalities. In another study, Loehlin and colleagues (1990) measured change in personality of adoptees over a 10-year period and found that children tended "to change on the average in the direction of their genetic parents' personalities" (p. 221). The prevailing thinking among behavioral geneticists, then, is that the shared environment plays a negligible role in the formation of personality (Loehlin et al., 1988), although there has been some opposition to this view (Rose et al., 1988).

Neurotransmitters and Personality

How are neurotransmitters and personality traits linked?

Just exactly how do genes contribute to personality? Researchers have recently begun to search for answers to this question. Most hypothesize that genes contribute to personality through their influence on the brain's systems for production, transport, and reuptake of neurotransmitters (Ebstein et al., 2003). For instance, do you like to visit new restaurants and try new foods, or do you prefer to stick to the same eating-out routines and menus? Individual differences in dopamine activity may be associated with such variations in *novelty-seeking behavior*, a component of Extroversion. For some time, researchers have suspected that there is a link between dopamine-controlling genes on chromosome 11 and disorders associated with novelty seeking, such as alcoholism and attention-deficit hyperactivity disorder (Ebstein et al., 2003). However, research results are mixed: Some studies support the link (e.g., Hansenne et al., 2002); others find no evidence for it (e.g., Soyka et al., 2002).

Findings regarding a link between serotonin and Neuroticism are more consistent (Lesch, 2003). Researchers propose that people who are emotionally unstable possess a serotonin system that is unusually sensitive to dangers and threats. As a result, they may perceive threat in situations where others do not, and they may react to universally threatening circumstances with higher levels of anxiety than shown by their more emotionally stable peers. These differences, say researchers, result from variations in genes on chromosome 8 that control the serotonin system (Ebstein et al., 2003). Several DNA studies have shown direct links between the characteristics of these genes and individuals' emotional stability (Lesch, 2003). Moreover, at least one fMRI study has shown a link between these genetic differences and variations in the activity of brain areas associated with emotional responses to fear-provoking stimuli (Hariri et al., 2002).

Shared and Nonshared Environments

Why do personality researchers distinguish between shared and nonshared environments?

Clearly, heredity, perhaps through its influence on neurotransmitter activity, influences personality. However, it is equally clear that personality is not determined by genes in the same way as physical traits such as eye color and blood type are. Instead, according to many psychologists, genes *constrain* the ways in which environments affect personality traits (Kagan, 2003). For example, a child who has a genetic tendency toward shyness may be encouraged by parents to be more sociable. As a result, he will be more outgoing than he would have been without such encouragement but will still be less sociable than a child who is genetically predisposed to be extroverted.

To help explain how environmental influences contribute to personality, researchers point out that such influences arise in two ways: through the shared environment and through the nonshared environment. The *shared environment* consists of those environmental influences that tend to make family members similar. If the shared environmental influences were high, then you would expect siblings raised in the same household to be more alike than different. But the shared environmental influences on personality have a modest effect at best (Bouchard, 1994; Loehlin, 1992).

The *nonshared environment* consists of influences that operate in different ways among children in the same family (Rowe, 1994). These influences "cause family members to differ regardless of whether the locus of influence is the family (such as differential treatment by parents) or outside the family (such as different experiences at school or with peers)" (Plomin & Daniels, 1987, p. 7). Nonshared influences can occur because individual children tend to elicit different responses from their parents for a variety of reasons—their temperament, gender, or birth order, or accidents and illnesses they may have had (Plomin, 1989). Bouchard claims that twins can experience nonshared environmental influences even in the womb if the positioning of the twin embryos in the uterus leads to differences in fetal nutrition (Aldhous, 1992).

Personality and Culture

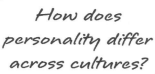

How does personality differ across cultures?

Important environmental influences on personality also arise from the diverse cultures in which humans live and work. In classic research, Hofstede (1980, 1983) analyzed questionnaire responses measuring the work-related values of more than 100,000 IBM employees in 53 countries around the world. Factor analysis revealed four separate dimensions related to culture and personality, of which one, the **individualism/collectivism dimension**, is of particular interest here. In individualist cultures, more emphasis is placed on individual achievement than on group achievement. High-achieving individuals are accorded honor and prestige in individualist cultures. People in collectivist cultures, on the other hand, tend to be more interdependent and define themselves and their personal interests in terms of their group membership. Asians, for example, have highly collectivist cultures, and collectivism is compatible with Confucianism, the predominant religion of these Eastern cultures. In fact, according to the Confucian values, the individual finds his or her identity in interrelatedness, as a part of the larger group. Moreover, this interrelatedness is an important ingredient of happiness for Asians (Kitayama & Markus, 2000).

For these native Alaskans, participating in the traditional blanket toss ceremony is one manifestation of their culture's values related to community and cooperation.

Hofstede rank-ordered the 53 countries from the IBM study on each of the four dimensions. The United States ranked as the most individualist culture in the sample, followed by Australia, Great Britain, Canada, and the Netherlands. At the other end of the continuum were the most collectivist cultures: Guatemala, Ecuador, Panama, Venezuela, and Colombia, all Latin American countries.

Although, according to Hofstede, the United States ranks first in individualism, there are many distinct minority cultural groups in the United States, which may be decidedly less individualist. Native Americans number close to 2 million, but even within this relatively small cultural group, there are over 200 different tribes, and no single language, religion, or culture (Bennett, 1994). Yet, Native Americans have many shared (collectivist) values, such as the importance of family, community, cooperation, and generosity. Native Americans value a generous nature as evidenced by gift giving and helpfulness. Such behaviors bring more honor and prestige than accumulating property and building individual wealth.

Hispanic Americans, who represent about 13% of the U.S. population (U.S. Census Bureau, 2001) also tend to be more collectivist than individualist. Despite significant cultural differences among various Hispanic American groups, there are striking similarities as well. The clearest shared cultural value is a strong identification with and attachment to the extended family. Another important value is *simpatía*, the desire for smooth and harmonious social relationships, which includes respect for the dignity of others, avoidance of confrontation, and avoidance of words or actions that might hurt another's feelings (Marín, 1994).

■ individualism/collectivism dimension
A measure of a culture's emphasis on either individual achievement or social relationships.

Although the Native American and Hispanic subcultures are more collectivist than individualist does not mean that any one member of these cultures is necessarily less individualist than any given member of the majority American culture. Moreover, many people may value both orientations—being individualist at work, for example, and collectivist in the home and community (Kagitcibasi, 1992).

It is important to note that some psychologists warn against overemphasizing cultural differences in personality. For example, Constantine Sedikides and her colleagues have argued that the goal of all individuals, regardless of cultural context, is to enhance self-esteem (Sedikides et al., 2003). That is, even in collectivist cultures, the process of conforming to one's culture is motivated by an individualistic concern, the desire for self-esteem. Consequently, at least to some degree, an individualist orientation is universal. Furthermore, while members of different cultures display varying commitments to an individualistic philosophy, autonomy—a sense of personal control over one's life—predicts well-being in all cultures (Ryan et al., 2003).

Remember It 14.6

1. Many behavioral geneticists believe that as much as __________ of personality may be inherited.
2. Research indicates that the neurotransmitter __________ is linked to the personality trait Neuroticism.
3. Behavioral geneticists have found that the __________ environment has a greater effect on personality than the __________ environment.
4. People in collectivist cultures tend to be more __________ than people in individualist cultures.

ANSWERS: 1. 50%; 2. serotonin; 3. nonshared, shared; 4. interdependent

Personality Assessment

Have you ever taken a personality test? You may have as part of a job application and screening process. Personality assessment is commonly used in business and industry to aid in hiring decisions, as you'll learn in Chapter 18. Various ways of measuring personality are used by clinical psychologists, psychiatrists, and counselors in the diagnosis of patients and in the assessment of progress in therapy.

Observation, Interviews, and Rating Scales

How do psychologists use observations, interviews, and rating scales?

Psychologists use observation in personality assessment in a variety of settings—hospitals, clinics, schools, and workplaces. Behaviorists, in particular, prefer observation to other methods of personality assessment. Using an observational technique known as *behavioral assessment*, psychologists can count and record the frequency of particular behaviors. This method is often used in behavior modification programs in settings such as psychiatric hospitals, where psychologists may chart patients' progress toward reducing aggressive acts or other undesirable or abnormal behaviors. However, behavioral assessment is time-consuming, and behavior may be misinterpreted. Probably the most serious limitation is that the very presence of the observer can alter the behavior being observed.

Clinical psychologists and psychiatrists use interviews to help in the diagnosis and treatment of patients. Counselors use interviews to screen applicants for admission to college or other special programs, and employers use them to evaluate job applicants and employees for job promotions. Interviewers consider not only a person's answers to questions but the person's tone of voice, speech, mannerisms, gestures, and general appearance as well. Interviewers often use a *structured interview*, in which the content of the questions and even the manner in which they are asked are carefully planned ahead of time. The interviewer tries not to deviate in any way from the structured format so that more reliable comparisons can be made between different subjects.

Examiners sometimes use *rating scales* to record data from interviews or observations. Such scales are useful because they provide a standardized format, including a list of traits or behaviors to evaluate. A rating scale helps to focus the rater's attention on all the relevant traits to be considered so that none is overlooked or weighed too heavily. The major limitation of these scales is that the ratings are often subjective. A related problem is the *halo effect*—the tendency of raters to be excessively influenced in their overall evaluation of a person by one or a few favorable or unfavorable traits. Often, traits or attributes that are not even on the rating scale, such as physical attractiveness or similarity to the rater, heavily influence a rater's perception of an individual. To overcome these limitations, it is often necessary to have individuals rated by more than one interviewer.

Personality Inventories

What is an inventory, and what are the MMPI-2 and the CPI designed to reveal?

As useful as observations, interviews, and rating scales are, another method of measuring personality offers greater objectivity. This method is the **inventory**, a paper-and-pencil test with questions about an individual's thoughts, feelings, and behaviors, which measures several dimensions of personality and can be scored according to a standard procedure. Psychologists favoring the trait approach prefer the inventory because it reveals where people fall on various dimensions of personality, and it yields a personality profile.

The most widely used personality inventory is the **Minnesota Multiphasic Personality Inventory (MMPI)** or its revision, the MMPI-2. The MMPI is the most heavily researched personality test for diagnosing psychiatric problems and disorders (Butcher & Rouse, 1996). There have been more than 115 recognized translations of the MMPI, and it is used in more than 65 countries (Butcher & Graham, 1989).

Developed in the late 1930s, and early 1940s by researchers J. Charnley McKinley and Starke Hathaway, the MMPI was originally intended to identify tendencies toward various types of psychiatric disorders. The researchers administered over 1,000 questions about attitudes, feelings, and specific symptoms to groups of psychiatric patients at the University of Minnesota hospital who had been clearly diagnosed with various specific disorders and to a control group of individuals who had no diagnosed disorders. They retained the 550 items that differentiated the specific groups of psychiatric patients from the group of participants considered to be normal.

Because the original MMPI had become outdated, the MMPI-2 was published in 1989 (Butcher et al., 1989). Most of the original test items were retained, but new items were added to more adequately cover areas such as alcoholism, drug abuse, suicidal tendencies, eating disorders, and the Type A behavior pattern. The MMPI had often been unreliable for African Americans, women, and adolescents (Levitt & Duckworth, 1984). Thus, new norms were established to reflect national census data and achieve a better geographical, racial, and cultural balance (Ben-Porath & Butcher, 1989).

■ **inventory**
A paper-and-pencil test with questions about a person's thoughts, feelings, and behaviors, which measures several dimensions of personality and can be scored according to a standard procedure.

■ **Minnesota Multiphasic Personality Inventory (MMPI)**
The most extensively researched and widely used personality test, which is used to screen for and diagnose psychiatric problems and disorders; revised as MMPI-2.

TABLE 14.1 The Clinical Scales of the MMPI-2

SCALE NAME	INTERPRETATION
1. Hypochondriasis (Hs)	High scorers exhibit an exaggerated concern about their physical health.
2. Depression (D)	High scorers are usually depressed, despondent, and distressed.
3. Hysteria (Hy)	High scorers complain often about physical symptoms that have no apparent organic cause.
4. Psychopathic deviate (Pd)	High scorers show a disregard for social and moral standards.
5. Masculinity/femininity (Mf)	High scorers show "traditional" masculine or feminine attitudes and values.
6. Paranoia (Pa)	High scorers demonstrate extreme suspiciousness and feelings of persecution.
7. Psychasthenia (Pt)	High scorers tend to be highly anxious, rigid, tense, and worrying.
8. Schizophrenia (Sc)	High scorers tend to be socially withdrawn and to engage in bizarre and unusual thinking.
9. Hypomania (Ma)	High scorers are usually emotional, excitable, energetic, and impulsive.
10. Social introversion (S)	High scorers tend to be modest, self-effacing, and shy.

Table 14.1 shows the 10 clinical scales of the MMPI-2. Following are examples of items on the test, which are to be answered "true," "false," or "cannot say."

I wish I were not bothered by thoughts about sex.
When I get bored, I like to stir up some excitement.
In walking I am very careful to step over sidewalk cracks.
If people had not had it in for me, I would have been much more successful.

A high score on any of the scales does not necessarily mean that a person has a problem or a psychiatric symptom. Rather, the psychologist looks at the individual's MMPI profile—the pattern of scores on all the scales—and then compares it to the profiles of normal individuals and those with various psychiatric disorders.

But what if someone lies on the test in order to appear mentally healthy? Embedded in the test to provide a check against lying are questions such as these:

Once in a while, I put off until tomorrow what I ought to do today.
I gossip a little at times.
Once in a while, I laugh at a dirty joke.

Most people would almost certainly have to answer "true" in response to such items—unless, of course, they were lying. Another scale controls for people who are faking psychiatric illness, as in the case of someone hoping to be judged not guilty of a crime by reason of insanity. Research seems to indicate that the validity scales in the MMPI-2 are effective in detecting test takers who were instructed to fake a psychological disturbance or to lie to make themselves appear more psychologically healthy (Bagby et al., 1994; Butcher et al., 1995). Even when given specific information about various psychological disorders, test takers could not produce profiles similar to those of people who actually suffered from the disorder (Wetter et al., 1993).

The MMPI-2 is reliable, easy to administer and score, and inexpensive to use. It is useful in the screening, diagnosis, and clinical description of abnormal behavior, but it does not reveal normal personality differences very well. A special form of the test, the MMPI-A, was developed for adolescents in 1992. The MMPI-A includes some items that are especially relevant to adolescents, such as those referring to eating disorders, substance abuse, and problems with school and family. The MMPI-2 has been translated for use in Belgium, Chile, China, France, Hong Kong, Israel, Korea, Italy, Japan, Norway, Russia, Spain, and Thailand (Butcher, 1992). Lucio and others (1994) administered the Mexican (Spanish) version of MMPI-2 to more than 2,100 Mexican college students. They found the profiles of these students "remarkably similar" to profiles of U.S. college students.

An important limitation of the MMPI-2, though, is that it was designed specifically to assess abnormality. By contrast, the **California Personality Inventory (CPI)** is a highly regarded personality test developed especially for normal individuals aged 13 and older. Similar to the MMPI, the CPI even has many of the same questions, but it does not include any questions designed to reveal psychiatric illness (Gough, 1987). The CPI is valuable for predicting behavior, and it has been "praised for its technical competency, careful development, cross-validation and follow-up, use of sizable samples and separate sex norms" (Domino, 1984, p. 156). The CPI was revised in 1987, to make it provide "a picture of the subject's life-style and the degree to which his or her potential is being realized" (McReynolds, 1989, p. 101). The CPI is particularly useful in predicting school achievement in high school and beyond, leadership and executive success, and the effectiveness of police, military personnel, and student teachers (Gregory, 1996).

The **Myers-Briggs Type Indicator (MBTI)** is another personality inventory that is useful for measuring normal individual differences. This test is based on Jung's personality theory. The MBTI is a forced-choice, self-report inventory that is scored on four separate bipolar dimensions:

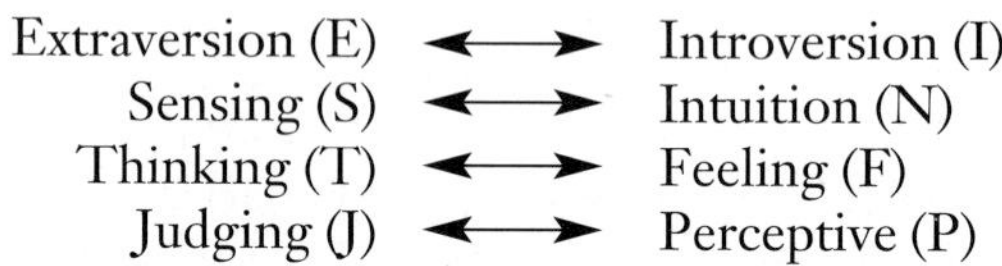

A person can score anywhere along a continuum for each of the four bipolar dimensions, and these individual scores are usually summarized according to a system of personality types. Sixteen types of personality profiles can be derived from the possible combinations of the four bipolar dimensions. For example, a person whose scores were more toward the Extraversion, Intuition, Feeling, and Perceptive ends of the four dimensions would be labeled an ENFP personality type, which is described as follows:

> Relates more readily to the outer world of people and things than to the inner world of ideas (E); prefers to search for new possibilities over working with known facts and conventional ways of doing things (N); makes decisions and solves problems on the basis of personal values and feelings rather than relying on logical thinking and analysis (F); and prefers a flexible, spontaneous life to a planned and orderly existence (P). (Gregory, 1996)

The MBTI is growing in popularity, especially in business and educational settings. Critics point to the absence of rigorous, controlled validity studies of the inventory (Pittenger, 1993). And it has also been criticized for being interpreted too often by unskilled examiners, who have been accused of making overly simplistic interpretations (Gregory, 1996). However, sufficiently sophisticated methods for interpreting the MBTI do exist, as revealed by almost 500 research studies to date (Allen, 1997). Many of these studies have shown that the MBTI personality types are associated with career choices and job satisfaction. For example, physicians who choose different specialties (e.g., pediatrics, surgery) tend to have different MBTI types (Stilwell et al., 2000). Consequently, the MBTI continues to enjoy popularity among career counselors.

■ **California Personality Inventory (CPI)**
A highly regarded personality test developed especially for normal individuals aged 13 and older.

■ **Myers-Briggs Type Indicator (MBTI)**
A personality inventory useful for measuring normal individual differences; based on Jung's theory of personality.

Projective Tests

How do projective tests provide insight into personality, and what are some of the most commonly used projective tests?

Responses on interviews and questionnaires are conscious responses and, for this reason, are less useful to therapists who wish to probe the unconscious. Such therapists may choose a completely different technique called a projective test. A **projective test** is a personality test consisting of inkblots, drawings of ambiguous human situations, or incomplete sentences for which there are no obvious correct or incorrect responses. People respond by projecting their inner thoughts, feelings, fears, or conflicts onto the test materials.

One of the oldest and most popular projective tests is the **Rorschach Inkblot Method** developed by Swiss psychiatrist Hermann Rorschach (ROR-shok) in 1921. It consists of 10 inkblots, which the test taker is asked to describe (see Figure 14.6). To develop his test, Rorschach put ink on paper and then folded the paper so that symmetrical patterns would result. Earlier, psychologists had used standardized series of inkblots to study imagination and other variables, but Rorschach was the first to use inkblots to investigate personality. He experimented with thousands of inkblots on different groups of people and found that 10 of the inkblots could be used to discriminate among different diagnostic groups, such as manic depressives, paranoid schizophrenics, and so on. These 10 inkblots—5 black and white, and 5 with color—were standardized and are still widely used.

The Rorschach can be used to describe personality, make differential diagnoses, plan and evaluate treatment, and predict behavior (Ganellen, 1996; Weiner, 1997). For the last 20 years, it has been second in popularity to the MMPI for use in research and clinical assessment (Butcher & Rouse, 1996). The test taker is shown the 10 inkblots and asked to tell everything that he or she thinks about what each inkblot looks like or resembles. The examiner writes down the test taker's responses and then goes through the cards again, asking questions to clarify what the test taker has reported. In scoring the Rorschach, the examiner considers whether the test taker has used the whole inkblot in the description or only parts of it. The test taker is asked whether the shape of the inkblot, its color, or something else prompted the response. The examiner also considers whether the test taker sees movement, human figures or parts, animal figures or parts, or other objects in the inkblots.

Until the 1990s, the main problem with the Rorschach was that the results were too dependent on the interpretation and judgment of the examiner. In response to such criticisms, Exner (1993) developed the Comprehensive System, a more reliable procedure for scoring the Rorschach. It provides some normative data so that the responses of a person taking the test can be compared to those of others with known personality characteristics. Using this system, some researchers have found high

■ **projective test**
A personality test in which people respond to inkblots, drawings of ambiguous human situations, or incomplete sentences by projecting their inner thoughts, feelings, fears, or conflicts onto the test materials.

■ **Rorschach Inkblot Method**
(ROR-shok) A projective test composed of 10 inkblots that the test taker is asked to describe; used to assess personality, make differential diagnoses, plan and evaluate treatment, and predict behavior.

FIGURE 14.6 An Inkblot Similar to One Used for the Rorschach Inkblot Method

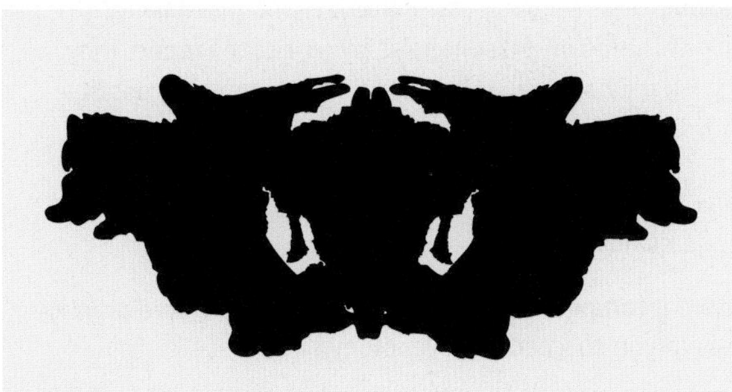

Thematic Apperception Test (TAT)
A projective test consisting of drawings of ambiguous human situations, which the test taker describes; thought to reveal inner feelings, conflicts, and motives, which are projected onto the test materials.

agreement among different raters interpreting the same responses (interrater agreement) (McDowell & Acklin, 1996). Others believe that more research is necessary before it can be concluded that the Comprehensive System yields reliable and valid results (Wood et al., 1996). However, a number of meta-analysis indicate that the Rorschach Inkblot Method has "psychometric soundness and practical utility" (Weiner, 1996).

Another projective test is the **Thematic Apperception Test (TAT)** developed by Henry Murray and his colleagues in 1935 (Morgan & Murray, 1935; Murray, 1938). You may remember from Chapter 11 that researchers have used the TAT to study the need for achievement, but it is also useful for assessing other aspects of personality. The TAT consists of 1 blank card and 19 other cards showing vague or ambiguous black-and-white drawings of human figures in various situations. If you were taking the TAT, this is what you would be told:

> This is a test of your creative imagination. I shall show you a picture, and I want you to make up a plot or story for which it might be used as an illustration. What is the relation of the individuals in the picture? What has happened to them? What are their present thoughts and feelings? What will be the outcome? (Morgan & Murray, 1962, p. 532)

REVIEW and REFLECT 14.3

Three Approaches to Personality Assessment

METHOD	EXAMPLES	DESCRIPTION
Observation and rating	Observation Interviews Rating scales	Performance (behavior) is observed in a specific situation, and personality is assessed based on the observation. In interviews, the responses to questions are taken to reveal personality characteristics. Rating scales are used to score or rate test takers on the basis of traits, behaviors, or results of interviews. Assessment is subjective, and accuracy depends largely on the ability and experience of the evaluator.
Inventories	Minnesota Multiphasic Personality Inventory-2 (MMPI-2) California Personality Inventory (CPI) Myers-Briggs Type Indicator (MBTI)	Test takers reveal their beliefs, feelings, behavior, and/or opinions on paper-and-pencil tests. Scoring procedures are standardized, and responses of test takers are compared to group norms.
Projective tests	Rorschach Inkblot Method Thematic Apperception Test (TAT) Sentence completion method	Test takers respond to ambiguous test materials and presumably reveal elements of their own personalities by what they report they see in inkblots, by themes they write about scenes showing possible conflict, or by how they complete sentences. Scoring is subjective, and accuracy depends largely on the ability and experience of the evaluator.

Want to be sure you've fully absorbed the material in this chapter? Visit **www.ablongman.com/wood5e** for access to free practice tests, flashcards, interactive activities, and links developed specifically to help you succeed in psychology.

What does the story you write have to do with your personality or your problems or motives? Murray (1965) stresses the importance of "an element or theme that recurs three or more times in the series of stories" (p. 432). For example, if a person uses many story themes about illness, sex, fear of failure, aggression, power, or interpersonal conflict, such a recurring theme is thought to reveal a problem in the person's life. Murray (1965) also claims that the strength of the TAT is "its capacity to reveal things that the patient is unwilling to tell or is unable to tell because he [or she] is unconscious of them" (p. 427).

The TAT is time-consuming and difficult to administer and score. Although it has been used extensively in research, it suffers from the same weaknesses as other projective techniques: (1) It relies heavily on the interpretation skills of the examiner, and (2) it may reflect too strongly a person's temporary motivational and emotional states and not indicate more permanent aspects of personality.

Review and Reflect 14.3 summarizes the various approaches to personality assessment.

Remember It 14.7

1. In __________, psychologists ask a standard set of questions to assess an individual's personality.
2. Match each personality test with its description.
   - ____ (1) MMPI-2
   - ____ (2) Rorschach
   - ____ (3) TAT
   - ____ (4) CPI
   - ____ (5) MBTI

   a. inventory used to diagnose psychopathology
   b. inventory used to assess normal personality
   c. projective test using inkblots
   d. projective test using drawings of ambiguous human situations
   e. inventory used to assess personality types
3. George has an unconscious resentment toward his father. Which type of personality test might best detect this?

ANSWERS: 1. structured interviews; 2. (1) a, (2) c, (3) d, (4) b, (5) a; 3. projective

Personality Theories: A Final Comment

In this chapter, we have explored the major theories of personality. You may be wondering which perspective best captures the elusive concept of personality. Some psychologists adhere strictly to a single theory and are followers of Skinner or Rogers, for example. However, it seems clear that all of the theories contribute to scientific knowledge, but that none by itself can adequately explain the whole of human personality.

Apply It

Practicing a More Positive Psychology

Why, given the same situation, do some people—typically called *optimists*—expect good things to happen, while their opposites—*pessimists*—believe that bad outcomes are more likely? According to psychologist Martin Seligman who has studied optimists and pessimists for many years, pessimists tend to believe that bad events are their own fault and are an inescapable part of their lives. Optimists, in contrast, tend to believe that a bad event is just a temporary setback, that its causes are unique, and that it is due to circumstances, bad luck, or other people. Consequently, in the face of illness, failure, or other difficulties, optimists keep trying to overcome obstacles. As a result, they feel more in control of their lives.

The ABCs of Pessimism

Seligman believes that an individual can learn to be more optimistic and thereby improve his or her general health and sense of well-being. First, though, we must learn to identify our pessimistic thoughts. Seligman (1990) has developed a method for identifying a sequence of events associated with pessimism; he calls it the *ABC method*—adversity, beliefs, and consequences. Here is how this method might work (Seligman, 1990, pp. 214–215):

- *Adversity* (anything that causes you to feel discouraged): I decided to join a gym, and when I walked into the place, I saw nothing but firm, toned bodies all around me.
- *Belief* (how you explain the adversity): What am I doing here? I look like a beached whale compared to these people! I should get out of here while I still have my dignity.
- *Consequences* (the way you feel about the adverse event): I felt totally self-conscious and ended up leaving after 15 minutes.

The method can also identify a series of thoughts that will produce optimism:

- *Adversity*: I decided to join a gym, and when I walked into the place, I saw nothing but firm, toned bodies all around me.
- *Belief*: What am I doing here? I look like a beached whale compared to these people! I can't wait until my new exercise regime gives me a body like theirs!
- *Consequences:* I felt totally self-conscious, but I focused on how my body was going to look in the future instead of how embarrassed I felt about how out-of-shape I looked in my workout clothes.

What You Can Do

If your reactions to adversity consistently follow a pessimistic pattern, you can do several specific things to change your thought patterns. Seligman (1990) has identified three useful techniques: distraction, disputation, and distancing.

- *Distraction*. Start by attempting to distract yourself—slap your hand against the wall and shout "Stop!" Then, try to think about something else.
- *Disputation*. Argue with yourself about the adverse event. Take a close look at the facts. "The most convincing way of disputing a negative belief is to show that it is factually incorrect" (Seligman, 1990, p. 221). An advantage of this technique is that it is realistic. Learned optimism is based on accuracy, not merely on making positive statements. For example, a student whose grades are somewhat below expectations might say, "I'm blowing things out of proportion. I hoped to get all As, but I got a B, a B+, and a B–. Those aren't awful grades. I may not have done the best in the class, but I didn't do the worst in the class either" (p. 219).
- *Distancing*. Still another way of dealing with pessimistic beliefs is distancing. Try to dissociate yourself from your pessimistic thoughts, at least long enough to judge their accuracy objectively. Recognize that simply believing something doesn't make it so.

Once you have challenged your pessimistic beliefs and convinced yourself that bad events are temporary and will not affect everything you do for the rest of your life, you will be able to look forward to better times in the future.

Summary *and* Review

Sigmund Freud and Psychoanalysis p. 471

What are the three levels of awareness in consciousness? p. 471

The three levels of awareness in consciousness are the conscious, the preconscious, and the unconscious. The conscious mind includes everything we are thinking about at any given moment. The preconscious includes thoughts and feelings we can easily bring to mind. The unconscious contains thoughts and feelings that are difficult to call up because they have been repressed.

What are the roles of the id, the ego, and the superego? p. 471

The id is the primitive, unconscious part of the personality, which contains the instincts and operates on the pleasure principle. The ego is the rational, largely conscious system, which operates according to the reality principle. The superego is the moral system of the personality, consisting of the conscience and the ego ideal.

What is the purpose of defense mechanisms? p. 472

A defense mechanism is a means used by the ego to defend against anxiety and to maintain self-esteem. For example, through repression, (1) painful memories, thoughts, ideas, or perceptions are involuntarily removed from consciousness, and (2) disturbing sexual or aggressive impulses are prevented from breaking into consciousness.

What are the psychosexual stages, and why did Freud consider them important in personality development? p. 473

Freud believed that the sexual instinct is present at birth and develops through a series of psychosexual stages, providing the driving force for all feelings and behaviors. The stages are the oral stage, anal stage, phallic stage (followed by the latency period), and genital stage. One of the most controversial features of Freud's stage theory is the Oedipus complex, a conflict that arises during the phallic stage, in which the child is sexually attracted to the opposite-sex parent and feels hostility toward the same-sex parent.

How are Freud's ideas evaluated by modern psychologists? p. 476

Freud is credited with calling attention to the unconscious, the importance of early childhood experiences, and the role of defense mechanisms. However, his theory is often criticized because it defies scientific testing.

The Neo-Freudians p. 477

How do the views of the neo-Freudians differ from those of Freud? p. 477

Jung conceived of the personality as having three parts: the ego, the personal unconscious, and the collective unconscious. Adler claimed that the predominant force of the personality is not sexual in nature but rather the drive to overcome and compensate for feelings of weakness and inferiority and to strive for superiority or significance. Horney took issue with Freud's sexist view of women and added the feminine dimension to the world of psychology.

Learning Theories and Personality p. 480

What are the components of Bandura's concept of reciprocal determinism and Rotter's locus of control? p. 480

The external environment, behavior, and cognitive factors are the three components of reciprocal determinism, each influencing and being influenced by the others. According to Rotter, people with an internal locus of control see themselves as primarily in control of their behavior and its consequences; those with an external locus of control believe their destiny is in the hands of fate, luck, or chance.

Humanistic Personality Theories p. 482

What are the contributions of humanistic theorists to the study of personality? p. 482

According to Maslow, the goal of personality development is to reach a level where most behavior is motivated by self-actualization, the drive to attain one's fullest potential. According to Rogers, individuals often do not become fully functioning persons because in childhood they did not receive unconditional positive regard from their parents. To gain positive regard, they had to meet their parents' conditions of worth.

What have psychologists learned about self-esteem? p. 483

The sense of self-esteem is influenced by comparisons of one's real self to one's desired self. Most people's self-esteem is based on what they perceive to be their strengths and weaknesses rather than on a single desired accomplishment or trait. By age 7, most children have a global sense of self-esteem and continue developing beliefs about their competencies in specific domains (e.g., sports) for several years.

Trait Theories p. 484

What were some of the ideas proposed by early trait theorists? p. 484

Trait theories of personality are attempts to explain personality differences in terms of people's personal characteristics. Allport defined a cardinal trait as a personal quality that pervades a person's personality to the point where he or she may become identified with that trait. A central trait is the type you might mention when writing a letter of recommendation. Cattell used the term *surface traits* to refer to observable qualities of personality. Source traits, which underlie the surface traits, are possessed in varying amounts by people.

What do factor theorists consider to be the most important dimensions of personality? p. 484

Eysenck considers the two most important dimensions of personality to be Extroversion (extroversion versus introversion) and Neuroticism (emotional stability versus instability). According to McCrae and Costa, personality is influenced by five dimensions. The Big Five are Neuroticism, Extroversion, Conscientiousness, Agreeableness, and Openness to Experience.

What is the situation-trait debate about? p. 486

The situation-trait debate mainly concerns the degree to which situations influence the manifestation of personality traits. The trait side says that behavior is strongly influenced by traits in all situations. The situation side says that situations are more strongly related to behavior. Most evidence supports the trait view, but there is also research supporting the idea that the ways in which traits and behavior are related are influenced by situations. For example, a person who demonstrates the trait of honesty most of the time might steal under certain circumstances.

Nature, Nurture, and Personality p. 487

What have twin and adoption studies revealed about the influence of genes on personality? p. 488

Both twin and adoption studies have shown that heredity strongly influences personality.

How are neurotransmitters and personality traits linked? p. 489

Some researchers believe that genes influence personality by exercising control over the amounts of various neurotransmitters in the brain. For example, serotinin has been linked to Neuroticism.

Why do personality researchers distinguish between shared and nonshared environments? p. 489

Researchers say that children raised in the same family are different in personality because most environmental influences are unique to individuals (i.e., nonshared), although perhaps dependent on genetic traits. Studies that separate shared and nonshared environmental influences help psychologists determine the separate roles of genes and environment as well as provide information about how genetic traits and environmental influences are related.

How does personality differ across cultures? *p. 490*
The cultural dimension known as individualism/collectivism is associated with personality. Individualist cultures encourage people to view themselves as separate from others and to value independence and assertiveness. Collectivist cultures emphasize social connectedness among people and encourage individuals to define themselves in terms of their social relationships.

Personality Assessment p. 491

How do psychologists use observations, interviews, and rating scales? *p. 491*
During observations, psychologists count behaviors that may be representative of an individual's personality. They use structured interviews to compare the responses of one interviewee to those of others given under similar circumstances. Rating scales are used to quantify behaviors that occur during observations or interviews.

What is an inventory, and what are the MMPI-2 and the CPI designed to reveal? *p. 492*
An inventory is a paper-and-pencil test with questions about a person's thoughts, feelings, and behaviors, which measures several dimensions of personality and can be scored according to a standard procedure. The MMPI-2 is designed to screen and diagnose psychiatric problems, and the CPI is designed to assess the normal personality.

How do projective tests provide insight into personality, and what are some of the most commonly used projective tests? *p. 495*
In a projective test, people respond to inkblots, drawings of ambiguous human situations, or incomplete sentences by projecting their inner thoughts, feelings, fears, or conflicts onto the test materials. Examples are the Rorschach Inkblot Method and the Thematic Apperception Test (TAT).

Key Terms

archetype, p. 478
California Personality Inventory (CPI), p. 494
collective unconscious, p. 478
conditions of worth, p. 482
conscious, p. 471
defense mechanism, p. 472
denial, p. 472
displacement, p. 473
ego, p. 472
five-factor theory, p. 485
fixation, p. 473
id, p. 471
individualism/collectivism dimension, p. 490
inventory, p. 492
locus of control, p. 481
Minnesota Multiphasic Personality Inventory (MMPI), p. 492
Myers-Briggs Type Indicator (MBTI), p. 494
Oedipus complex, p. 474
personal unconscious, p. 477
personality, p. 470
preconscious, p. 471
projection, p. 472
projective test, p. 495
psychoanalysis, p. 471
psychosexual stages, p. 473
rationalization, p. 473
reaction formation, p. 473
reciprocal determinism, p. 480
regression, p. 473
repression, p. 472
Rorschach Inkblot Method, p. 495
self-actualization, p. 482
self-efficacy, p. 480
sublimation, p. 473
superego, p. 472
Thematic Application Test (TAT), p. 496
trait, p. 484
unconditional positive regard, p. 483
unconscious, p. 471

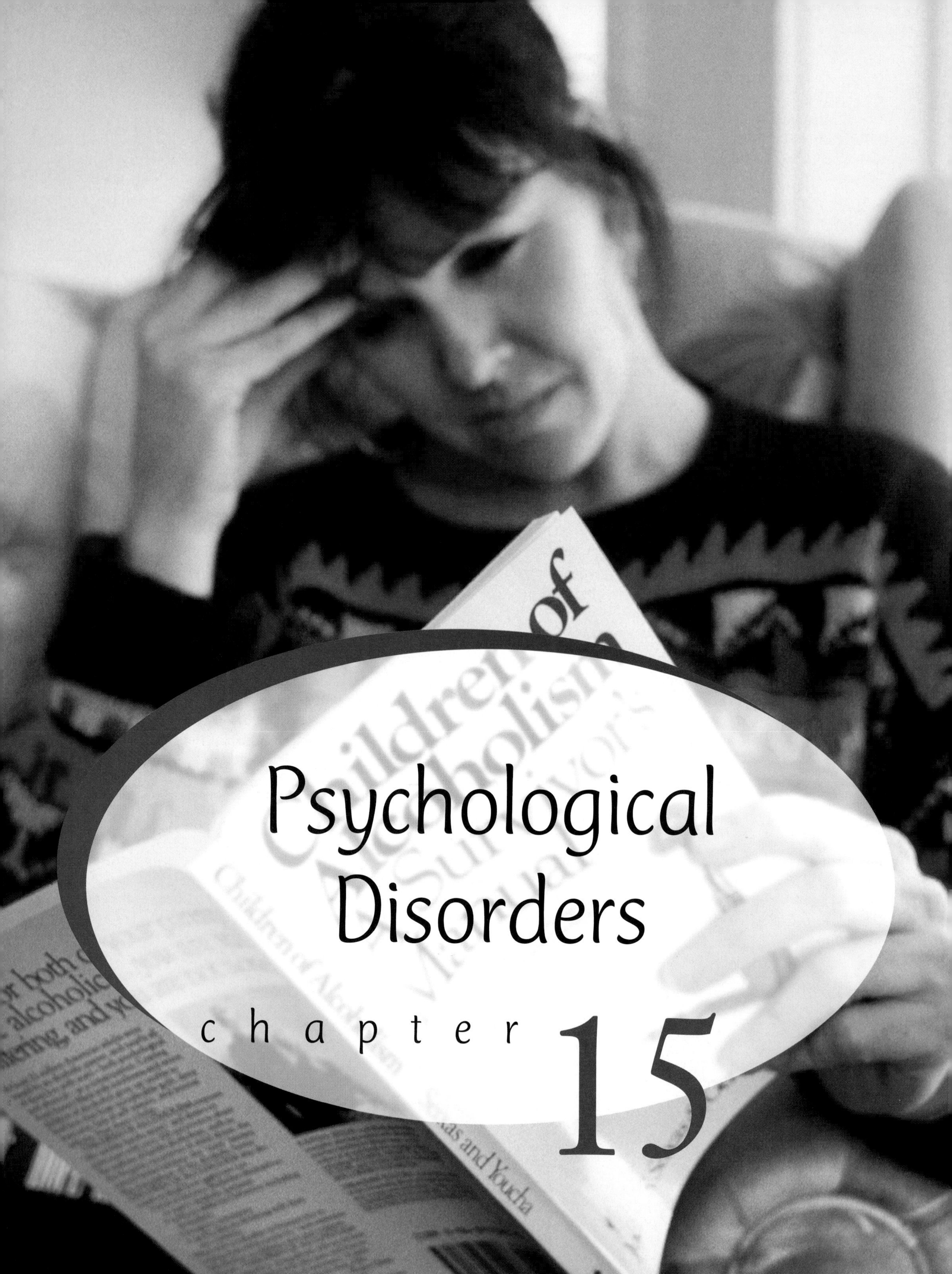

Psychological Disorders

chapter 15

What Is Abnormal?

- *What criteria can be used to determine whether behavior is abnormal?*
- *How prevalent are psychological disorders?*
- *What are the theoretical approaches that attempt to explain the causes of psychological disorders?*

Anxiety Disorders

- *How is generalized anxiety disorder manifested?*
- *How does panic disorder affect the lives of those who suffer from it?*
- *What are the characteristics of the three categories of phobias?*
- *What thought and behavior patterns are associated with obsessive-compulsive disorder?*

Mood Disorders

- *What are the symptoms of major depressive disorder?*
- *How are culture, gender, and depression related?*
- *What are the extremes of mood suffered by those with bipolar disorder?*
- *What are some suggested causes of mood disorders?*
- *What are some of the risk factors for suicide?*

Schizophrenia

- *What are the major positive symptoms of schizophrenia?*
- *What normal functions are reduced or absent in schizophrenics?*
- *What does research indicate about the neurological functioning of schizophrenics?*
- *What are the four types of schizophrenia?*
- *What factors increase the risk of developing schizophrenia?*

Somatoform and Dissociative Disorders

- *What are two somatoform disorders, and what symptoms do they share?*
- *How do the various dissociative disorders affect behavior?*

Other Psychological Disorders

- *What are the main characteristics of the various sexual disorders?*
- *What behaviors are associated with personality disorders in Clusters A, B, and C?*

When was the last time you had the "blues"?

Most of us experience feelings of sadness from time to time. Fortunately, we usually bounce back from these emotional lows fairly quickly. But for some individuals, feelings of hopelessness persist for weeks or months, sometimes with deadly consequences.

In the fall of 1985, 60-year-old William Styron had long been recognized as one of the finest writers of his time. His novels had brought him financial and critical success, and he had won many awards, including the Pulitzer Prize for his 1968 novel *The Confessions of Nat Turner.* Having received news of yet another award, this time a prestigious European prize, Styron looked forward to the October trip to Paris to accept. But as the trip approached, he began to fall into a deep, debilitating depression. He struggled with intense anxiety, had difficulty sleeping, and could not concentrate sufficiently to write. While in Paris, he suddenly realized that he had to get psychiatric help immediately or he would succumb to suicidal thoughts that were growing in frequency and intensity every day. In his memoir of the depression, *Darkness Visible: A Memoir of Madness,* Styron wrote of the afternoon he received the award: "It was past four o'clock, and my brain had begun to endure its familiar siege: panic and dislocation and a sense that my thought processes were being engulfed by a toxic and unnameable tide that obliterated any enjoyable response to the living world.... I was feeling in my mind a sensation close to, but indescribably different from, actual pain" (p. 16).

Styron returned home and entered treatment, but the relief he had hoped to get from antidepressant medications didn't come. Instead, his depression became worse. Plagued by feelings of self-hatred, he could no longer engage in normal conversation. He couldn't sleep for more than an hour or so at a time, yet he could not force himself to get out of bed. His concentration was so poor that he did not trust himself to drive a car. Finally, on a December evening in the midst of a dinner party in his home, he decided to end his life.

But in the early morning hours of the next day, he sat thinking about his wife and the home they had shared for many years. Memories of his children's early years, and even of the many pets the family had owned over the years, flooded his mind. He suddenly realized that he was not yet ready to leave his family behind. The next day, he committed himself to a mental hospital in the hope of saving his life.

William Styron was fortunate. After months of intense treatment, he recovered from his depression and continued to write. As he pointed out in *Darkness Visible,* many other artists have not been so lucky. As a group, artistic individuals appear to suffer higher rates of mental illness—especially emotional disorders like depression—than others. And the ranks of artists who have died from suicide include many well-known names: Vincent van Gogh, Ernest Hemmingway, Sylvia Plath, Marilyn Monroe, Kurt Cobaine.

psychological disorders Mental processes and/or behavior patterns that cause emotional distress and/or substantial impairment in functioning.

What causes people, even those who are enormously successful in life and appear to have so much to live for, to become so despondent that they no longer want to live? Psychologists don't yet have a definitive answer to this question, but they have learned a great deal about **psychological disorders** in recent years. This chapter explores the symptoms and possible causes of these mental processes or behavior patterns that cause emotional distress and/or substantial impairment in functioning. But first let's ask the obvious question: What is abnormal?

What Is Abnormal?

Defining Mental Disorders

What criteria can be used to determine whether behavior is abnormal?

Human behavior lies along a continuum, from well adjusted to maladaptive. But where along the continuum does behavior become abnormal? Several questions can help determine when behavior is abnormal:

- *Is the behavior considered strange within the person's own culture?* What is considered normal and abnormal in one culture is not necessarily considered so in another. In some cultures, it is normal for women to appear in public bare-breasted, but it would be abnormal for a female executive in an industrialized culture to go to work that way.
- *Does the behavior cause personal distress?* When people experience considerable emotional distress without any life experience that warrants it, they may be diagnosed as having a psychological or mental disorder. Some people may be sad and depressed, and some anxious; others may be agitated or excited, and still others frightened, or even terrified, by delusions and hallucinations.
- *Is the behavior maladaptive?* Some experts believe that the best way to differentiate between normal and abnormal behavior is to consider whether it leads to healthy or impaired functioning. Washing your hands before you eat is adaptive; washing them 100 times a day is maladaptive.
- *Is the person a danger to self or others?* Another consideration is whether people pose any danger to themselves or others. To be committed to a mental hospital, a person must be judged both mentally ill and a danger to self or others.
- *Is the person legally responsible for his or her acts?* Often, the term *insanity* is used to label those who behave abnormally, but mental health professionals do not use this term. It is a legal term used by the courts to declare people not legally responsible for their acts. Mass murderer Jeffrey Dahmer was ruled legally responsible for his acts, yet his behavior was clearly abnormal.

Abnormal behavior is defined by each culture. For example, homelessness is considered abnormal in some cultures and completely normal in others.

FIGURE 15.1 **Annual Prevalence Rates of Selected Mental Disorders among Adults in the United States**

Source: NIMH (2001).

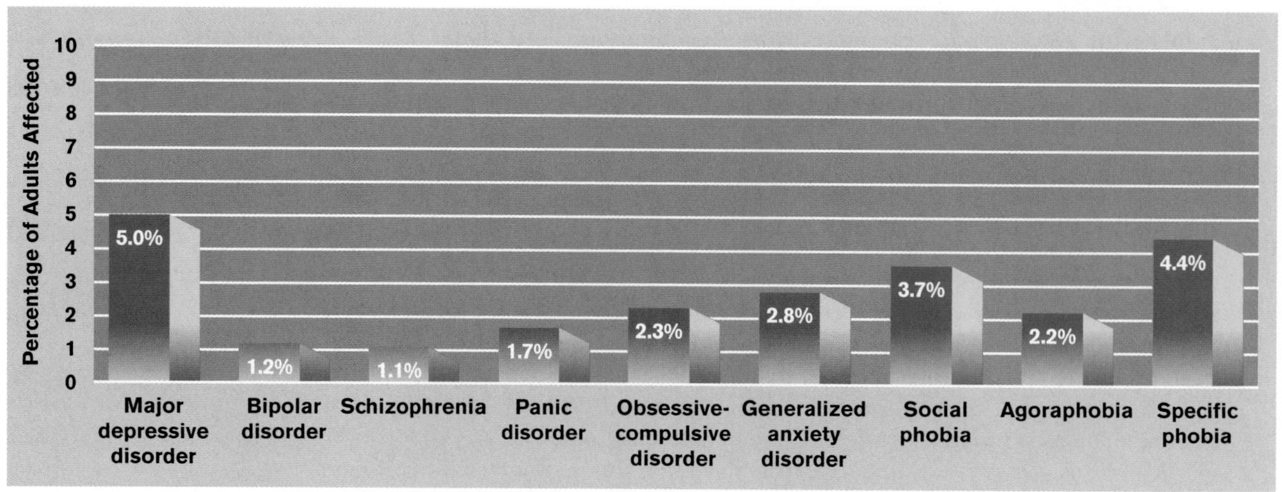

Prevalence of Psychological Disorders

How prevalent are psychological disorders?

Would you be surprised to learn that psychological disorders are more common than many physical ailments? For instance, each year in the United States, less than 1% of adults, about 1.3 million people, are diagnosed with cancer (American Cancer Society, 2002). By contrast, 22%, or more than 44 million adults, are diagnosed with a mental disorder of some kind (NIMH, 2001). Figure 15.1 shows the annual prevalence rates of a few of the more common mental disorders.

FIGURE 15.2 **Lifetime Prevalence of Psychological Disorders**

The percentages of males and females in the United States who suffer from various psychological disorders during their lifetime are based on the findings of the National Comorbidity Survey. Males and females had about the same rate for experiencing some type of disorder. Males had higher rates for substance abuse and antisocial personality disorder. Females had higher rates for anxiety disorders and mood disorders.

Source: Data from Kessler et al. (1994).

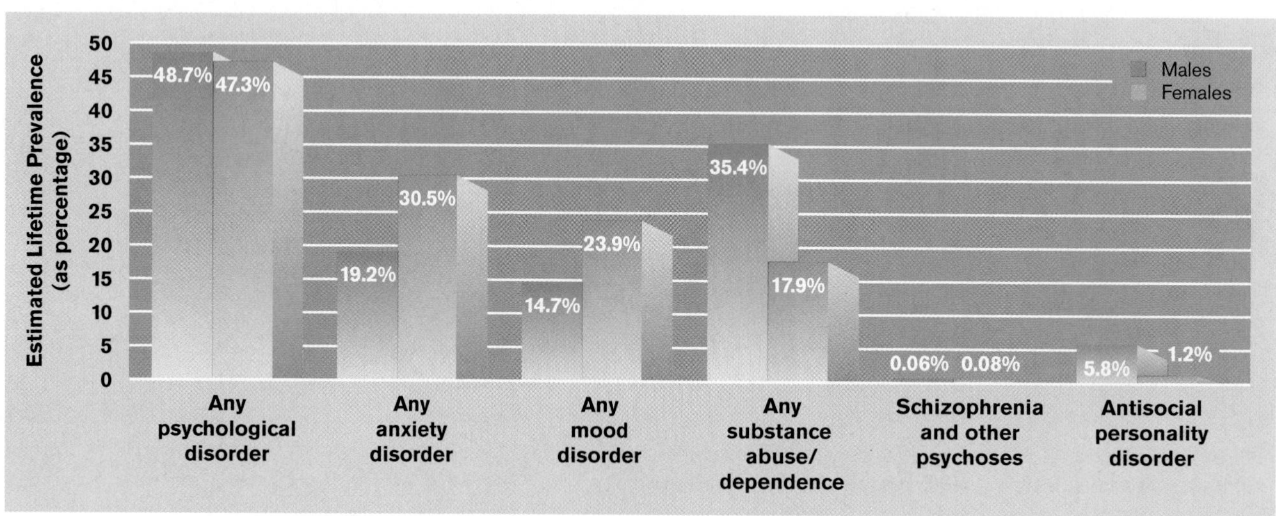

Another way of thinking about the frequency of a disorder is to examine how likely an individual is to be diagnosed with it in his or her lifetime. The lifetime prevalence rate of cancer in the United States is about 30%; in other words, about 30% of Americans will be diagnosed with cancer sometime in their lives (NCHS, 2000). Again, mental disorders are more common, with a lifetime prevalence rate of nearly 50% (Kessler et al., 1994). Lifetime rates of a few disorders are shown in Figure 15.2. Clearly, mental disorders represent a significant source of personal misery for individuals and of lost productivity for society. Thus, research aimed at identifying their causes and treatments is just as important as research examining the causes and treatments of physical diseases.

Explaining Psychological Disorders

What are the theoretical approaches that attempt to explain the causes of psychological disorders?

What causes psychological disorders, and how can they be treated? This is the question addressed by the various theoretical approaches summarized in *Review and Reflect 15.1*. Each perspective has its place in the description, analysis, and treatment of psychological disorders.

The *biological perspective* views abnormal behavior as arising from a physical cause, such as genetic inheritance, biochemical abnormalities or imbalances, structural abnormalities within the brain, and/or infection. Thus, its adherents favor biological treatments such as drug therapy.

REVIEW and REFLECT 15.1

Perspectives on Psychological Disorders

PERSPECTIVE	CAUSES OF PSYCHOLOGICAL DISORDERS	TREATMENT
Biological perspective	A psychological disorder is a symptom of an underlying physical disorder caused by a structural or biochemical abnormality in the brain, by genetic inheritance, or by infection.	Diagnose and treat like any other physical disorder Drugs, electroconvulsive therapy, or psychosurgery
Biopsychosocial perspective	Psychological disorders result from a combination of biological, psychological, and social causes.	An eclectic approach employing treatments that include both drugs and psychotherapy
Psychodynamic perspective	Psychological disorders stem from early childhood experiences and unresolved, unconscious sexual or aggressive conflicts.	Bring disturbing repressed material to consciousness and help patient work through unconscious conflicts Psychoanalysis
Learning perspective	Abnormal thoughts, feelings, and behaviors are learned and sustained like any other behaviors, or there is a failure to learn appropriate behaviors.	Use classical and operant conditioning and modeling to extinguish abnormal behavior and to increase adaptive behavior Behavior therapy Behavior modification
Cognitive perspective	Faulty thinking or distorted perceptions can cause psychological disorders.	Change faulty, irrational, and/or negative thinking Beck's cognitive therapy Rational-emotive therapy

Want to be sure you've fully absorbed the material in this chapter? Visit **www.ablongman.com/wood5e** for access to free practice tests, flashcards, interactive activities, and links developed specifically to help you succeed in psychology.

The *biopsychosocial perspective* agrees that physical (biological) causes are of central importance but also recognizes the influence of psychological and social factors in the study, identification, and treatment of psychological disorders. Consequently, biopsychosocial psychologists often advocate treatment strategies that include both drugs and psychotherapy.

Originally proposed by Freud, the *psychodynamic perspective* maintains that psychological disorders stem from early childhood experiences and unresolved, unconscious conflicts, usually of a sexual or aggressive nature. The cause assumed by the psychodynamic approach also suggests the cure—psychoanalysis, which Freud developed to uncover and resolve such unconscious conflicts.

According to the *learning perspective*, psychological disorders are thought to be learned and sustained in the same way as any other behavior. According to this view, people who exhibit abnormal behavior either are victims of faulty learning or have

TABLE 15.1 Major DSM-IV Categories of Mental Disorders

DISORDER	SYMPTOMS	EXAMPLES
Schizophrenia and other psychotic disorders	Disorders characterized by the presence of psychotic symptoms, including hallucinations, delusions, disorganized speech, bizarre behavior, and loss of contact with reality	Schizophrenia, paranoid type Schizophrenia, disorganized type Schizophrenia, catatonic type Delusional disorder, jealous type
Mood disorders	Disorders characterized by periods of extreme or prolonged depression or mania or both	Major depressive disorder Bipolar disorder
Anxiety disorders	Disorders characterized by anxiety and avoidance behavior	Panic disorder Social phobia Obsessive-compulsive disorder Posttraumatic stress disorder
Somatoform disorders	Disorders in which physical symptoms are present that are psychological in origin rather than due to a medical condition	Hypochondriasis Conversion disorder
Dissociative disorders	Disorders in which one handles stress or conflict by forgetting important personal information or one's whole identity, or by compartmentalizing the trauma or conflict into a split-off alter personality	Dissociative amnesia Dissociative fugue Dissociative identity disorder
Personality disorders	Disorders characterized by long-standing, inflexible, maladaptive patterns of behavior beginning early in life and causing personal distress or problems in social and occupational functioning	Antisocial personality disorder Histrionic personality disorder Narcissistic personality disorder Borderline personality disorder
Substance-related disorders	Disorders in which undesirable behavioral changes result from substance abuse, dependence, or intoxication	Alcohol abuse Cocaine abuse Cannabis dependence
Disorders usually first diagnosed in infancy, childhood, or adolescence	Disorders that include mental retardation, learning disorders, communication disorders, pervasive developmental disorders, attention-deficit and disruptive behavior disorders, tic disorders, and elimination disorders	Conduct disorder Autistic disorder Tourette's syndrome Stuttering
Eating disorders	Disorders characterized by severe disturbances in eating behavior	Anorexia nervosa Bulimia nervosa

Source: Based on DSM-IV (American Psychiatric Association, 1994).

failed to learn appropriate patterns of thinking and acting. Behavior therapists use the learning principles of classical and operant conditioning to eliminate distressing behavior and to establish new, more appropriate behavior in its place.

The *cognitive perspective* suggests that faulty thinking or distorted perceptions can contribute to some types of psychological disorders. Treatment based on this perspective is aimed at changing thinking, which presumably will lead to a change in behavior. Moreover, the cognitive perspective offers advice that may prevent psychological disorders. For example, one step toward healthy thinking is to recognize and avoid five cognitive traps: (1) setting unrealistic standards for yourself; (2) negative "what if" thinking (such as "What if I lose my job?"); (3) turning a single negative event, such as a poor grade, into a catastrophe ("I'll never pass this course"); (4) judging anything short of perfection to be a failure; and (5) demanding perfection in yourself and others. If your happiness depends on any of these conditions, you are setting the stage for disappointment, or even depression.

Regardless of their theoretical perspective, all clinicians and researchers use the same set of criteria to classify psychological disorders. These criteria can be found in a manual published by the American Psychiatric Association. The most recent edition, the *Diagnostic and Statistical Manual of Mental Disorders*, 4th edition, commonly known as the **DSM-IV**, appeared in 1994. An updated version, the DSM-IV-TR (Text Revision), was published in 2000. The major categories used in the DSM-IV-TR to classify psychological disorders are listed in Table 15.1.

■ **DSM-IV**
The *Diagnostic and Statistical Manual of Mental Disorders,* 4th Edition, a manual published by the American Psychiatric Association, which describes the criteria used to classify and diagnose mental disorders.

Remember It 15.1

1. To be defined as abnormal, a person's behavior must be considered strange in the __________ in which it occurs.
2. About __________ of people in the United States will suffer from a psychological disorder at some time in their lives.
3. Match the theoretical perspective with its suggested cause of abnormal behavior.

____ (1) psychodynamic perspective	a. faulty learning
____ (2) biological perspective	b. unconscious, unresolved conflicts
____ (3) learning perspective	c. genetic inheritance or biochemical or structural abnormalities in the brain
____ (4) biopsychosocial perspective	d. faulty thinking
____ (5) cognitive perspective	e. combination of biological, psychological, and social factors

ANSWERS: 1. culture; 2. 50%; 3. (1) b, (2) c, (3) a, (4) e, (5) d

Anxiety Disorders

According to chronically anxious comic strip hero Charlie Brown, the secret to life is to "replace one worry with another." Everyone worries to some degree. But, as Charlie Brown suggests, for some people, worrying is a way of life. And when vague, fearful thoughts about what might happen in the future (a state of mind referred to as *anxiety* by psychologists) become so frequent that they interfere with a person's social and occupational functioning, worrying can develop into a serious psychological disorder. In fact, **anxiety disorders** are the most common category of mental disorders and account for more than 4 million visits to doctors' offices each year in the United

■ **anxiety disorders**
Psychological disorders characterized by frequent fearful thoughts about what might happen in the future.

FIGURE 15.3 Lifetime Prevalence of Anxiety Disorders

The percentages of males and females in the United States who have suffered from various anxiety disorders during their lifetime are based on the findings of the National Comorbidity Survey.
Source: Data from Kessler et al. (1994).

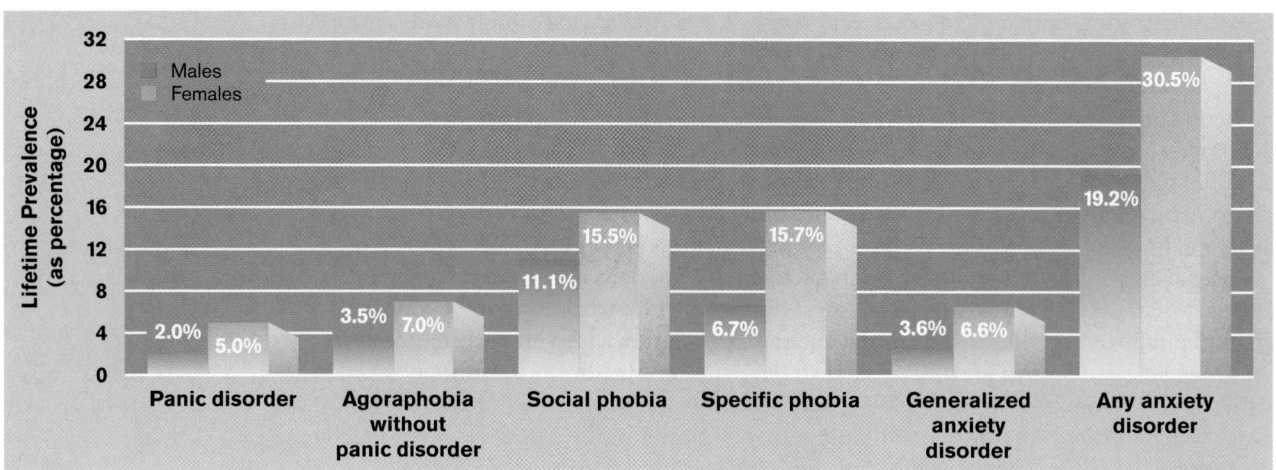

States (NCHS, 2002b). Figure 15.3 shows the percentages of males and females in the United States who have suffered from various anxiety disorders during their lifetimes. Take a minute now to complete the anxiety disorder checklist in *Try It 15.1*.

How is generalized anxiety disorder manifested?

Generalized Anxiety Disorder

Generalized anxiety disorder is the diagnosis given to people who are plagued by chronic, excessive worry for 6 months or more. These people expect the worst; their worrying is either unfounded or greatly exaggerated

Try It 15.1 Identifying Anxiety Disorders

Read each of the four descriptions below, and place a checkmark beside each description that sounds like you or someone you know.

____ 1. You are always worried about things, even when there are no signs of trouble. You have frequent aches and pains that can't be traced to physical illness or injury. You tire easily, and yet you have trouble sleeping. Your body is constantly tense.

____ 2. Out of the blue, your heart starts pounding. You feel dizzy. You can't breathe. You feel like you are about to die. You've had these symptoms over and over again.

____ 3. Every day, you fear you will do something embarrassing. You've stopped going to parties because you're afraid to meet new people. When other people look at you, you break out in a sweat and shake uncontrollably. You stay home from work because you're terrified of being called on in a staff meeting.

____ 4. You are so afraid of germs that you wash your hands repeatedly until they are raw and sore. You can't leave the house until you check the locks on every window and door over and over again. You are terrified that you will harm someone you care about. You just can't get those thoughts out of your head.

As you continue through this section of the chapter, you'll learn which anxiety disorders these symptoms represent. (From NIMH, 1999a.)

and, thus, difficult to control. They may be unduly worried about their finances, their own health or that of family members, their performance at work, or their ability to function socially. Their excessive anxiety may cause them to feel tense, tired, and irritable, and to have difficulty concentrating and sleeping. Other symptoms may include trembling, palpitations, sweating, dizziness, nausea, diarrhea, or frequent urination. This disorder affects twice as many women as men and leads to considerable distress and impairment (Brawman-Mintzer & Lydiard, 1996, 1997; Kranzler, 1996). The heritability of generalized anxiety disorder is estimated to be about 30% (Kendler et al., 1992). But, as troubling as this disorder is, it is less severe than panic disorder.

generalized anxiety disorder
An anxiety disorder in which people experience chronic, excessive worry for 6 months or more.

Panic Disorder

How does panic disorder affect the lives of those who suffer from it?

For some anxiety disorder sufferers, feelings of fear and dread happen in spurts rather than continuously. During **panic attacks**—episodes of overwhelming anxiety, fear, or terror—people commonly report a pounding heart, uncontrollable trembling or shaking, and sensations of choking or smothering. Some say they believe they are going to die or are "going crazy." Recent studies have revealed that the more catastrophic such beliefs are, the more intense the panic attack is likely to be (Hedley et al., 2000). People who suffer from recurring panic attacks may be diagnosed with **panic disorder**. Panic disorder sufferers must cope both with repeated attacks and with anxiety about the occurrence and consequences of further attacks. This anxiety can lead people to avoid situations that have been associated with previous panic attacks. About 2% of men and 5% of women in the United States suffer from panic disorder (Kessler et al., 1994).

Panic disorder can have significant social and health consequences (Sherbourne et al., 1996). Panic disorder sufferers visit doctors' offices and emergency rooms quite frequently (Katon, 1996) and are at increased risk for abuse of alcohol and other drugs (Marshall, 1997a). However, effective treatments for this disorder are available. Most individuals with panic disorder respond to a combination of medication and psychotherapy (Biondi & Picardi, 2003).

panic attack
An episode of overwhelming anxiety, fear, or terror.

panic disorder
An anxiety disorder in which a person experiences recurring, unpredictable episodes of overwhelming anxiety, fear, or terror.

Phobias

What are the characteristics of the three categories of phobias?

Is there some situation or object of which you are dreadfully afraid? Perhaps you fear snakes, insects, heights, or closed-in spaces such as elevators. Such fears are quite common. A **phobia** is a persistent, irrational fear of some specific object, situation, or activity that poses no real danger (or whose danger is blown out of proportion). Phobics realize their fears are irrational, but they nevertheless feel compelled to avoid the feared situations or objects. The phobia most likely to drive people to seek professional help is **agoraphobia**. An agoraphobic has an intense fear of being in a situation from which immediate escape is not possible or in which help would not be available if she or he should become overwhelmed by anxiety or experience a panic attack or panic-like symptoms. In some cases, a person's entire life is planned around avoiding feared situations such as busy streets, crowded stores, restaurants, and/or public transportation. An agoraphobic often will not leave home unless accompanied by a friend or family member, and, in severe cases, not even then. Women are four times more likely than men to be diagnosed with agoraphobia (Bekker, 1996).

Although agoraphobia can occur without panic attacks, it typically begins during the early adult years with repeated panic attacks (Horwath et al., 1993). The intense fear of having another attack causes the person to avoid any place or situation where previous attacks have occurred. Panic disorder with agoraphobia (PDA) is one of the most debilitating of psychological disorders, and it is more common in women than in

phobia
(FO-bee-ah) A persistent, irrational fear of some specific object, situation, or activity that poses little or no real danger.

agoraphobia
(AG-or-uh-FO-bee-ah) An intense fear of being in a situation from which escape is not possible or in which help would not be available if one experienced overwhelming anxiety or a panic attack.

men. It can affect most areas of life—physical, psychological, social, occupational, interpersonal, and economic.

People who suffer from **social phobia** are intensely afraid of any social or performance situation in which they might embarrass or humiliate themselves in front of others— by shaking, blushing, sweating, or in some other way appearing clumsy, foolish, or incompetent. Social phobia may take the specific form of *performance anxiety*. Surprisingly, many professional entertainers experience this kind of specific social phobia; Barbra Streisand's extreme performance anxiety kept her from appearing live in concert for many years. About one-third of social phobics only fear speaking in public (Kessler et al., 1998). And in a survey of 449 individuals who had not been formally diagnosed with social phobia, one-third said they would experience excessive anxiety if they had to speak in front of a large audience (Stein et al., 1996). If you are one of the millions who are afraid of public speaking, see the *Apply It* at the end of this chapter for advice on overcoming your fear.

Although less debilitating than agoraphobia, social phobia can be a disabling disorder (Stein & Kean, 2000). In its extreme form, it can seriously affect people's performance at work, preventing them from advancing in their careers or pursuing an education and severely restricting their social lives (Bruch et al., 2003; Greist, 1995; Stein & Kean, 2000). Often, those with social phobia turn to alcohol and tranquilizers to lessen their anxiety in social situations. Baseball legend Mickey Mantle, for example, used alcohol to calm himself when making public appearances (Jefferson, 1996).

A **specific phobia** is a marked fear of a specific object or situation. This general label is applied to any phobia other than agoraphobia and social phobia. Faced with the object or situation they fear, people afflicted with a specific phobia experience intense anxiety, even to the point of shaking or screaming. They will go to great lengths to avoid the feared object or situation. The categories of specific phobias, in order of frequency of occurrence, are (1) situational phobias (fear of elevators, airplanes, enclosed places, heights, tunnels, or bridges); (2) fear of the natural environment (fear of storms or water); (3) animal phobias (fear of dogs, snakes, insects, or mice); and (4) blood-injection-injury phobia (fear of seeing blood or an injury, or of receiving an injection) (Fredrikson et al., 1996). Two types of situational phobias—*claustrophobia* (fear of closed spaces) and *acrophobia* (fear of heights)—are the specific phobias treated most often by therapists.

The causes of phobias vary, depending on the type of phobia. However, heredity is an important factor in the development of phobias. A person has three times the risk of developing a phobia if a close relative suffers from one (Fyer, 1993). Heredity appears to be especially important in the development of agoraphobia.

Beyond genetics, frightening experiences appear to set the stage for the acquisition of phobias. Many specific and social phobias are acquired in childhood or adolescence through direct conditioning, modeling, or the transmission of information (Rachman, 1997). For instance, a person may be able to trace the beginning of a specific phobia to a traumatic childhood experience with the feared object or situation (Hirschfeld, 1995; Jefferson, 1996; Stemberger et al., 1995). Phobias may be acquired, as well, through observational learning. For example, children who hear their parents talk about a frightening encounter with a dog may develop a fear of dogs.

Principles of learning are often used to treat phobias. A therapist may use classical conditioning principles to teach patients to associate pleasant emotions with feared objects or situations. For example, a child who fears dogs might be given ice cream while in a room where a dog is present. Behavior modification, in which patients are reinforced for exposing themselves to fearful stimuli, may also be useful. Observation of models who do not exhibit fear in response to the object or situation of which a phobic is afraid has also been an effective treatment technique. Finally, antidepressant drugs have been shown to help agoraphobics overcome their fears (Kampman et al., 2002; Marshall, 1997c).

■ **social phobia**
An irrational fear and avoidance of any social or performance situation in which one might embarrass or humiliate oneself in front of others by appearing clumsy, foolish, or incompetent.

■ **specific phobia**
A marked fear of a specific object or situation; a general label for any phobia other than agoraphobia and social phobia.

Obsessive-Compulsive Disorder

What thought and behavior patterns are associated with obsessive-compulsive disorder?

What would your life be like if every time you left your home you were so fearful of having left your door unlocked that you had to go back and check it again and again? **Obsessive-compulsive disorder (OCD)** is an anxiety disorder in which a person suffers from recurrent obsessions or compulsions, or both. **Obsessions** are persistent, involuntary thoughts, images, or impulses that invade consciousness and cause a person great distress. People with obsessions might worry about contamination by germs or about whether they performed a certain act, such as turning off the stove or locking the door (Insel, 1990). Other types of obsessions center on aggression, religion, or sex. One minister reported obsessive thoughts of running naked down the church aisle and shouting obscenities at his congregation.

A person with a **compulsion** feels a persistent, irresistible, irrational urge to perform an act or ritual repeatedly. The individual knows such acts are senseless but cannot resist performing them without experiencing an intolerable buildup of anxiety—which can be relieved only by yielding to the compulsion. Many of us have engaged in compulsive behavior like stepping over cracks on the sidewalk, counting stairsteps, or performing little rituals from time to time. The behavior becomes a psychological problem only if the person cannot resist performing it, if it is very time-consuming, and if it interferes with the person's normal activities and relationships with others.

■ obsessive-compulsive disorder (OCD)
An anxiety disorder in which a person suffers from recurrent obsessions and/or compulsions.

■ obsession
A persistent, involuntary thought, image, or impulse that invades consciousness and causes great distress.

■ compulsion
A persistent, irresistible, and irrational urge to perform an act or ritual repeatedly.

Compulsions exhibited by people with obsessive-compulsive disorder often involve cleaning and washing behaviors, counting, checking, touching objects, hoarding, and excessive organizing. These cleaning and checking compulsions affect 75% of OCD patients receiving treatment (Ball et al., 1996). Sometimes, compulsive acts or rituals seem to reflect superstitious thinking in that they must be performed faithfully to ward off some danger. People with OCD do not enjoy the endless counting, checking, or cleaning. They realize that their behavior is not normal, but they simply cannot help themselves, as shown in the following example.

> Mike, a 32-year-old patient, performed checking rituals that were preceded by a fear of harming other people. When driving, he had to stop the car often and return to check whether he had run over people, particularly babies. Before flushing the toilet, he had to check to be sure that a live insect had not fallen into the toilet, because he did not want to be responsible for killing a living thing. At home he repeatedly checked to see that the doors, stoves, lights, and windows were shut or turned off. . . . Mike performed these and many other checking rituals for an average of 4 hours a day. (Kozak et al., 1988, p. 88)

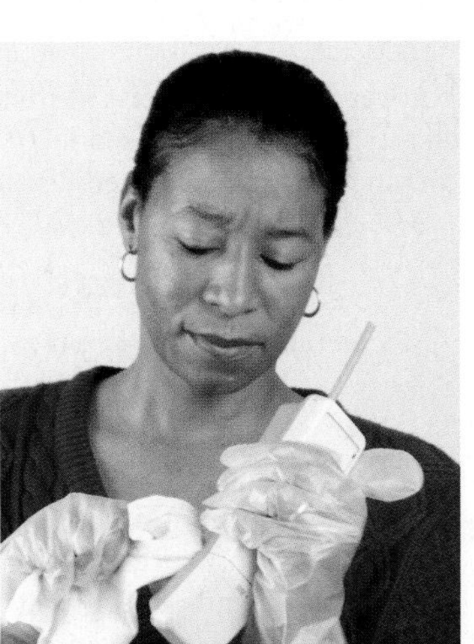
Like this woman, many people with obsessive-compulsive disorder take great pains to avoid contamination from germs and dirt.

Mike's checking compulsion is quite extreme, but it has been estimated that perhaps 2–3% of the U.S. population will suffer from OCD at some time in life. Fairly similar rates have been reported in studies in Canada, Puerto Rico, Germany, Korea, and New Zealand (Weissman et al., 1994).

Studies have shown that early autoimmune system diseases, early strep infections, and changes in the brain caused by infection may predispose a person to develop OCD (Giedd et al., 2000; Hamilton & Swedo, 2001). Several twin and family studies suggest that a genetic factor is involved in the development of OCD as well (Nestadt et al., 2000; Rasmussen & Eisen, 1990). Genes affecting serotonin functioning are suspected of causing OCD in some people, many of whom are helped by antidepressant drugs that increase serotonin levels in the brain (Pigott, 1996).

Remember It 15.2

1. Match each example of behavior with the disorder it is most likely to reflect.

   ____ (1) Reba refuses to eat in front of others for fear her hand will shake.

   ____ (2) John is excessively anxious about his health and his job, even though there is no concrete reason for him to feel this way.

   ____ (3) Tawana has been housebound for 4 years.

   ____ (4) Jackson gets hysterical when a dog approaches him.

   ____ (5) Ling has incapacitating attacks of anxiety that come on her suddenly.

   ____ (6) Max repeatedly checks his doors, windows, and appliances before he goes to bed.

   a. panic disorder
   b. agoraphobia
   c. specific phobia
   d. generalized anxiety disorder
   e. social phobia
   f. obsessive-compulsive disorder (OCD)

2. Some therapists use ____________ to help phobics learn to associate pleasant stimuli with feared objects.

3. Obsessive-compulsive disorder appears to be caused primarily by ____________ factors.

ANSWERS: 1. (1) e, (2) d, (3) b, (4) c, (5) a, (6) f; 2. classical conditioning; 3. biological

Mood Disorders

■ mood disorders
Disorders characterized by extreme and unwarranted disturbances in emotion or mood.

You read about novelist William Styron's severe depression at the beginning of this chapter. Depression is one of many **mood disorders,** which are characterized by extreme and unwarranted disturbances in emotion or mood.

Major Depressive Disorder

What are the symptoms of major depressive disorder?

Like William Styron at the depths of his illness, people with **major depressive disorder** feel an overwhelming sadness, despair, and hopelessness, and they usually lose their ability to experience pleasure. They may have changes in appetite, weight, or sleep patterns, loss of energy, and difficulty in thinking or concentrating. Key symptoms of major depressive disorder are psychomotor disturbances (Sobin & Sackeim, 1997). For example, body movements, reaction time, and speech may be so slowed that some depressed people seem to be doing everything in slow motion. Others experience the opposite extreme and are constantly moving and fidgeting, wringing their hands, and pacing. Depression can be so severe that its victims suffer from delusions or hallucinations, which are symptoms of *psychotic depression.* And the more deeply a person descends into depression over an extended period, the more she or he withdraws from social activities (Judd et al., 2000).

■ major depressive disorder
A mood disorder marked by feelings of great sadness, despair, and hopelessness as well as the loss of the ability to experience pleasure.

According to the American Psychiatric Association (1994), 1 year after their initial diagnosis of major depressive disorder, 40% of patients are without symptoms;

40% are still suffering from the disorder; and 20% are depressed, but not enough to warrant a diagnosis of major depression. Slightly less than one-half of those hospitalized for major depressive disorder are fully recovered after 1 year (Keitner et al., 1992). For many, recovery is aided by antidepressant drugs. However, some studies show that psychotherapy can be just as effective (Hollon et al., 2002). Some people suffer only one major depressive episode, but 50–60% of patients will have a recurrence. Risk of recurrence is greatest for females (Winokur et al., 1993) and for individuals with an onset of depression before age 15 (Brown, 1996). Recurrences may be frequent or infrequent, and for 20–35% of patients, the episodes are chronic, lasting 2 years or longer.

Culture, Gender, and Depression

How are culture, gender, and depression related?

How is it possible to study depression, or any mental disorder for that matter, across cultures, since cultural context must be taken into consideration when defining abnormality? Indeed, it is extremely difficult to construct surveys or other instruments for measuring mental disorders that are valid in a variety of cultures (Girolamo & Bassi, 2003). Nevertheless, a few researchers have managed to produce a limited, but informative, body of data about cross-cultural differences in depression (Girolamo & Bassi, 2003). One large study involving participants from 10 countries revealed that the lifetime risk for developing depression varied greatly around the world (see Figure 15.4), with Asian countries (Taiwan and Korea) having significantly lower rates of the disorder (Weissman et al., 1996). Despite these variations, major depressive disorder is the number one cause of disability throughout the world (NIMH, 1999c), especially in women.

In most countries, the rate of depression for females is about twice that of males (Culbertson, 1997). Before boys reach puberty, they are more likely than girls to be depressed, but a dramatic reversal of the gender-related depression rates takes place in adolescence (Cyranowski et al., 2000). Not only are women more likely than men to suffer from depression, they are also more likely to be affected by negative consequences as a result. Early-onset major depressive disorder adversely affects the educational attainment

FIGURE 15.4 Lifetime Risk for Developing Depression in 10 Countries

The lifetime prevalence of depression for 38,000 men and women in 10 different countries reveals that women are more susceptible to depression worldwide.
Source: Data from Weissman et al. (1996).

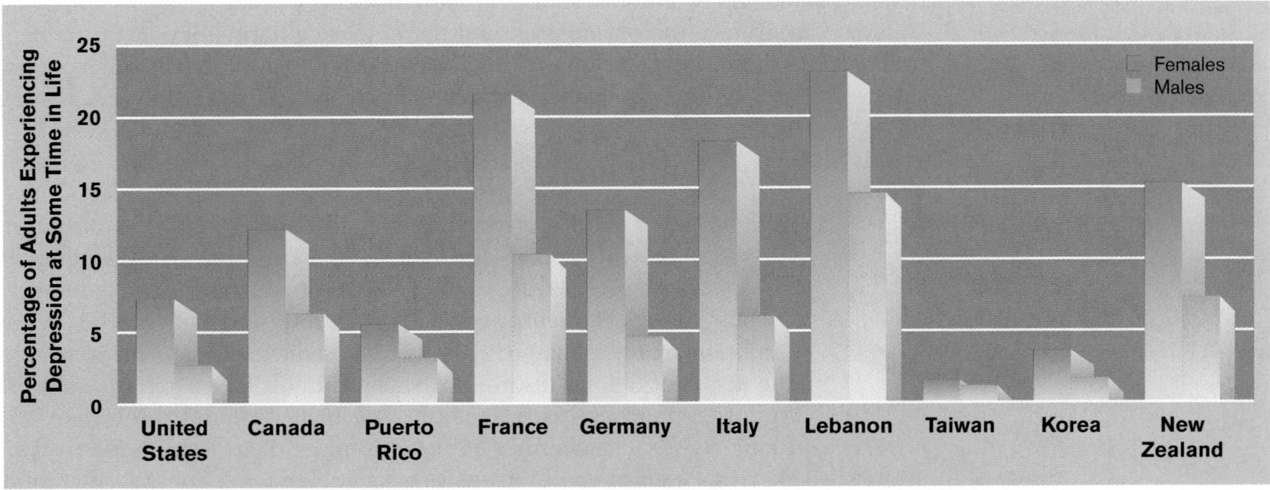

and earning power of women, but not men (Berndt et al., 2000). The National Task Force on Women and Depression suggests that the higher rate of depression in women is largely due to social and cultural factors. In fulfilling her many roles—mother, wife, lover, friend, daughter, neighbor—a woman is likely to put the needs of others ahead of her own.

Bipolar Disorder

What are the extremes of mood suffered by those with bipolar disorder?

Have you ever heard about the bizarre episode in which painter Vincent van Gogh cut off his own ear? Based on analyses of his artistic productivity and personal writings, mental health professionals believe that van Gogh suffered from **bipolar disorder** (Blumer, 2002). Individuals with bipolar disorder exhibit two radically different moods—the extreme highs of manic episodes (or *mania*) and the extreme lows of major depression—usually with relatively normal periods in between.

Van Gogh's ear-cutting episode occurred in the aftermath of a violent argument with another artist, Paul Gauguin, most likely in the context of a **manic episode.** Such episodes are marked by excessive euphoria, inflated self-esteem, wild optimism, and hyperactivity. People in a manic state have temporarily lost touch with reality and frequently have delusions of grandeur along with their euphoric highs. They may waste large sums of money on get-rich-quick schemes. If family members or friends try to stop them, they are likely to become irritable, hostile, enraged, or even dangerous; they may even harm themselves as van Gogh did. Quite often, patients must be hospitalized during manic episodes to protect them and others from the disastrous consequences of their poor judgment.

Van Gogh was hospitalized shortly after severing his ear. After his release from the hospital, and consistent with the modern-day diagnosis of bipolar disorder, his career was marked by intense bursts of creativity. In one 2-month period in 1889, he produced 60 paintings, some of which are regarded as his best works (Thomas & Bracken, 2001). Between these frantic periods of almost nonstop work, van Gogh experienced phases of deep despair, in which he could do no work at all. Tragically, he committed suicide at age 37.

Bipolar disorder is much less common than major depressive disorder, affecting about 1.2% of the U.S. population in any given year, and the lifetime prevalence rates are about the same for males and females (NIMH, 2001). Bipolar disorder tends to appear in late adolescence or early childhood. About 90% of those with the disorder have recurrences, and about 50% experience another episode within a year of recovering from a previous one. The good news is that 70–80% of the patients return to a state of emotional stability (American Psychiatric Association, 1994), even though mild cognitive deficits, such as difficulty with planning, persist in many patients following a manic episode (Chowdhury et al., 2003). Still, in many cases, individuals with bipolar disorder can manage their symptoms, and thereby live a normal life, with the help of drugs such as lithium and divalproex. Moreover, psychotherapy can help them cope with the stress of facing life with a potentially disabling mental illness (Hollon et al., 2002).

■ **bipolar disorder**
A mood disorder in which manic episodes alternate with periods of depression, usually with relatively normal periods in between.

■ **manic episode**
(MAN-ik) A period of excessive euphoria, inflated self-esteem, wild optimism, and hyperactivity, often accompanied by delusions of grandeur and by hostility if activity is blocked.

Causes of Mood Disorders

What are some suggested causes of mood disorders?

Biological factors such as heredity and abnormal brain chemistry play a major role in bipolar disorder and major depressive disorder. PET scans have revealed abnormal patterns of brain activity in patients with both disorders (George et al., 1993). Drevets and others (1997) located a brain area that may trigger both the sadness of major depression and the mania of bipolar disorder. A small, thimble-size patch of brain tissue in the lower prefrontal cortex (about 2–3 inches behind the bridge of the nose) is a striking 40–50% smaller in people with major depression. Earlier research established that this area of the brain plays a key role in the control of emotions.

Moreover, the personality trait called *Neuroticism* is associated with both depression and abnormalities in the brain's serotonin levels (Fanous et al., 2002; Lesch, 2003). Research has shown that abnormal levels of serotonin are strongly linked to depression and to suicidal thoughts (Oquendo et al., 2003). Thus, individuals who are at the neurotic end of the Big Five personality dimension of Neuroticism may be predisposed to develop depression and to have suicidal thoughts.

Researchers have also found that the production, transport, and reuptake patterns for dopamine, GABA, and norepinephrine in people suffering from mood disorders differ from those in normal individuals (Kalidini & McGuffin, 2003). Neurotransmitter abnormalities may reflect genetic variations, thus helping to explain the significant heritability rates for mood disorders. Based on a study of 1,721 identical and fraternal female twins, Kendler, Neale, Kessler, and others (1993) estimated the heritability of major depressive disorder to be 70% and the contribution of environment to be 30%.

Evidence for a genetic basis for bipolar disorder is also strong. In one twin study, researchers found that 50% of the identical twins of bipolar sufferers had also been diagnosed with a mood disorder, compared to only 7% of fraternal twins (Kalidini & McGuffin, 2003). Mounting evidence indicates that the genetic and neurological bases of bipolar disorder are more like those of schizophrenia than those of major depressive disorder (Molnar et al., 2003). These findings may explain why biological relatives of bipolar disorder sufferers are at increased risk of developing a number of mental disorders, while those of major depressive disorder sufferers display an increased risk only for that disorder (Kalidini & McGuffin, 2003).

Of course, genetics isn't the whole story, especially with regard to depression. Depressed individuals view themselves, their world, and their future all in negative ways (Beck, 1967, 1991). They see their interactions with the world as a series of burdens and obstacles that usually end in failure. Depressed persons believe they are deficient, unworthy, and inadequate, and they attribute their perceived failures to their own physical, mental, or moral inadequacies. Depressed patients may think: "Everything always turns out wrong." "I never win." "Things will never get better." "It's no use."

Life stresses are also associated with depression. The vast majority of first episodes of depression strike after major life stress (Brown et al., 1994; Frank et al., 1994; Tennant, 2002). A longitudinal study of Harvard graduates that continued for over 40 years found that negative life events as well as family history played significant roles in the development of mood disorders (Cui & Vaillant, 1996). This seems particularly true of women, who are more likely to have experienced a severe negative life event just prior to the onset of depression (Spangler et al., 1996). Yet, recurrences of depression, at least in people who are biologically predisposed, often occur without significant life stress (Brown et al., 1994).

Suicide and Race, Gender, and Age

What are some of the risk factors for suicide?

Some depressed people commit the ultimate act of desperation—suicide. Mood disorders and schizophrenia, along with substance abuse, are major risk factors for suicide in all age groups (Mościcki, 1995; Pinikahana et al., 2003; Shaffer et al., 1996). Suicide risk also increases when people are exposed to particularly troubling life stressors, such as the violent death of a child (Murphy et al., 2003). There is also evidence that suicidal behavior runs in families (Brent et al., 1996; 2002). Even among people who have severe mood disturbances, such as bipolar disorder, those with a family history of suicide attempts are far more likely to kill themselves than are those without such history (Tsai et al., 2002).

Between 30,000 and 31,000 suicides are reported annually in the United States. Figure 15.5 shows the differences in U.S. suicide rates according to race, gender, and age (NCHS, 2001a, 2002a). As you can see, White Americans are more likely than African Americans to commit suicide. Native American suicide rates are similar to those of White Americans; rates for Hispanic Americans are similar to those of

FIGURE 15.5 Differences in Suicide Rates According to Race, Gender, and Age

In every age group, the suicide rate is highest for White American males and second-highest for African American males. The general conclusion is that males are more likely to commit suicide than females, and that White Americans are more likely to do so than are African Americans. Suicide rates indicated by asterisks (*) are too low to be statistically reliable.

Source: Data from NCHS (2001a, 2002a).

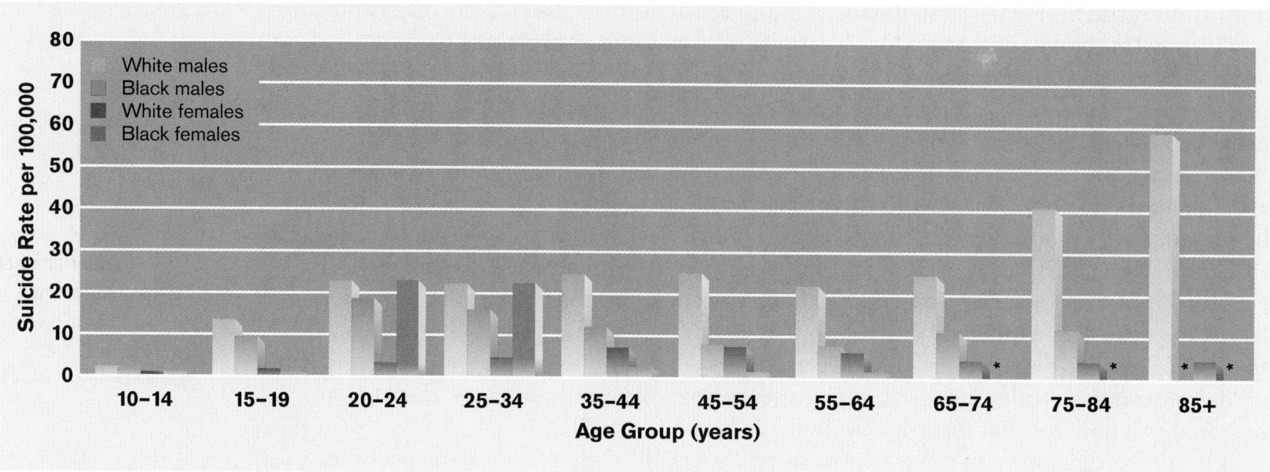

Evidence suggests that suicidal behavior tends to run in families. Les Franklin founded the Shaka Franklin Foundation for Youth, a suicide prevention organization, in memory of his son Shaka, who had killed himself. Ten years later, Franklin's other son, Jamon, also committed suicide.

African Americans (NCHS, 2001b). Asian Americans have the lowest suicide rates of all ethnic groups in the United States (NCHS, 2002a).

You will also note in the Figure 15.5 that suicide rates are far lower for both White and African American women than for men. However, studies show that women are four times more likely than men to attempt suicide (Anderson, 2002). The higher rate of completed suicides in males is due to the methods men and women use. Emergency room records show that the rate of firearms use by suicide attempters and completers is 10 times higher in males than in females, while the rates of poisoning and drug overdose are higher in females (CDC, 2002). Consequently, a higher proportion of male suicide attempters succeed in killing themselves.

Although suicide rates among teens and young adults have increased in the past few decades, older Americans are at far greater risk for suicide than younger people. White males aged 85 and over have the highest recorded suicide rate, with over 75 suicides for every 100,000 people in that age group, about five times the average national suicide rate of 15.2 per 100,000 (U.S. Census Bureau, 1999). Poor general health, serious illness, loneliness (often due to the death of a spouse), and decline in social and economic status are conditions that may push many older Americans, especially those aged 75 and over, to commit suicide.

About 90% of individuals who commit suicide leave clues (Shneidman, 1994). They may communicate verbally: "You won't be seeing me again." They may provide behavioral clues, such as giving away their most valued possessions; withdrawing from friends, family, and associates; taking unnecessary risks; showing personality changes; acting and looking depressed; and losing interest in favorite activities. These warning signs should always be taken seriously. If you suspect you are dealing with a suicidal person, the best thing you can do is to encourage the person to get professional help. There are 24-hour suicide hotlines all over the country. A call might save a life.

Remember It 15.3

1. Jamal has periods in which he is so depressed that he becomes suicidal. At other times, he is energetic and euphoric. He would probably receive the diagnosis of __________ disorder.
2. Some episodes of depression follow exposure to major __________ .
3. For ethnic groups in the United States, suicide is least frequent among __________ .

ANSWERS: 1. bipolar; 2. life stresses; 3. Asian Americans

Schizophrenia

Schizophrenia is a serious psychological disorder characterized by loss of contact with reality (a condition often referred to as **psychosis**), hallucinations, delusions, inappropriate or flat affect, some disturbance in thinking, social withdrawal, and/or other bizarre behavior.

■ schizophrenia
(SKIT-soh-FREE-nee-ah) A severe psychological disorder characterized by loss of contact with reality, hallucinations, delusions, inappropriate or flat affect, some disturbance in thinking, social withdrawal, and/or other bizarre behavior.

Positive Symptoms of Schizophrenia

What are the major positive symptoms of schizophrenia?

The *positive symptoms* of schizophrenia are the abnormal behaviors that are present in people with the disorder. One of the clearest positive symptoms of schizophrenia is the presence of **hallucinations,** or imaginary sensations. Schizophrenic patients may see, hear, feel, taste, or smell strange things in the absence of any stimulus in the environment, but hearing voices is the most common type of hallucination. Most often, the voices accuse or curse the patients or engage in a running commentary on their behavior. Visual hallucinations, less common than auditory hallucinations, are usually in black and white and commonly take the form of friends, relatives, God, Jesus, or the devil. Schizophrenics also may experience exceedingly frightening and painful bodily sensations and feel that they are being beaten, burned, or sexually violated.

Having **delusions**, or false beliefs not generally shared by others in the culture, is another positive symptom of schizophrenia. Schizophrenics with **delusions of grandeur** may believe they are a famous person (the president or Moses, for example) or a powerful or important person who possesses some great knowledge, ability, or authority. Those with **delusions of persecution** have the false notion that some person or agency is trying to harass, cheat, spy on, conspire against, injure, kill, or in some other way harm them.

Another positive symptom is the loosening of associations, or *derailment*, that is evident when a schizophrenic does not follow one line of thought to completion but, on the basis of vague connections, shifts from one subject to another in conversation or writing. A schizophrenic's *grossly disorganized behavior*, another positive symptom, can include such things as childlike silliness, inappropriate sexual behavior (masturbating in public), disheveled appearance, and peculiar dress. There may also be unpredictable agitation, including shouting and swearing, and unusual or inappropriate motor behavior, including strange gestures, facial expressions, or postures. Schizophrenics may also display *inappropriate affect*; that is, their facial expressions, tone of voice, and gestures may not reflect the emotion that would be expected under the circumstances. A person might cry when watching a TV comedy and laugh when watching a news story showing bloody bodies at the scene of a fatal automobile accident.

■ psychosis
(sy-CO-sis) A condition characterized by loss of contact with reality.

■ hallucination
An imaginary sensation.

■ delusion
A false belief, not generally shared by others in the culture.

■ delusion of grandeur
A false belief that one is a famous person or a powerful or important person who has some great knowledge, ability, or authority.

■ delusion of persecution
A false belief that some person or agency is trying in some way to harm one.

Negative Symptoms of Schizophrenia

What normal functions are reduced or absent in schizophrenics?

A *negative symptom* of schizophrenia is a loss of or deficiency in thoughts and behaviors that are characteristic of normal functioning. Negative symptoms include social withdrawal, apathy, loss of motivation, lack of goal-directed activity, very limited speech, slowed movements, poor hygiene and grooming, poor problem-solving abilities, and a distorted sense of time (Davalos et al., 2002; Hatashita-Wong et al., 2002; Skrabalo, 2000). Some who suffer from schizophrenia have *flat affect*, showing practically no emotional response at all, even though they often report feeling the emotion. These patients may speak in a monotone, have blank and emotionless facial expressions, and act and move more like robots than humans.

Not all schizophrenics have negative symptoms. Those who do seem to have the poorest outcomes (Fenton & McGlashan, 1994). Negative symptoms are predictors of impaired overall social and vocational functioning. Schizophrenics tend to withdraw from normal social contacts and retreat into their own world. They have difficulty relating to people, and often their functioning is too impaired for them to hold a job or even to care for themselves.

Brain Abnormalities in Schizophrenics

What does research indicate about the neurological functioning of schizophrenics?

Several abnormalities in brain structure and function have been found in schizophrenic patients, such as low levels of neural activity in the frontal lobes (Glantz & Lewis, 2000; Kim et al., 2000). Many schizophrenics have defects in the neural circuitry of the cerebral cortex and the limbic system (Benes, 2000; MacDonald et al., 2003; McGlashan & Hoffman, 2000). There is also evidence of reduced volume in the hippocampus, amygdala, thalamus, and frontal lobes (Gur et al., 2000; Sanfilippo et al., 2000; Staal et al., 2000). Further, schizophrenics display abnormal lateralization of brain functions and slow communication between left and right hemispheres (Florio et al., 2002).

Abnormal dopamine activity in the brain is observed in many schizophrenics. Such altered dopamine activity sometimes results from cocaine abuse, which can pose an increased risk for schizophrenia (Benes, 2000; Tzschentke, 2001). Much of the brain's dopamine activity occurs in the limbic system, which is involved in human emotions. Drugs that are effective in reducing the symptoms of schizophrenia block dopamine action, although about one-third of the patients who take these drugs do not show improvement.

Types of Schizophrenia

What are the four types of schizophrenia?

Even though various symptoms are commonly shared by schizophrenics, certain features distinguish one type of schizophrenia from another. For example, people with **paranoid schizophrenia** usually suffer from delusions of grandeur or persecution. They may be convinced that they have an identity other than their own—that they are the president, the Virgin Mary, or God—or that they possess great ability or talent. They may feel that they are in charge of the hospital or on a secret assignment for the government. Paranoid schizophrenics often show exaggerated anger and suspiciousness. If they have delusions of persecution and feel that they are being harassed or threatened, they may become violent in an attempt to defend themselves against their imagined persecutors. Usually, the behavior of a patient with paranoid schizophrenia is not so obviously disturbed as that of one with the catatonic or disorganized type, and the chance for recovery is better.

■ **paranoid schizophrenia** (PAIR-uh-noid) A type of schizophrenia characterized by delusions of grandeur or persecution.

Disorganized schizophrenia, the most serious type, tends to occur at an earlier age than the other types and is marked by extreme social withdrawal, hallucinations, delusions, silliness, inappropriate laughter, grimaces, grotesque mannerisms, and other bizarre behavior. These patients show flat or inappropriate affect and are frequently incoherent. They often exhibit obscene behavior, may masturbate openly, and may swallow almost any kind of object or material. Disorganized schizophrenia results in the most severe disintegration of the personality, and its victims have the poorest chance of recovery (Fenton & McGlashan, 1991).

Persons with **catatonic schizophrenia** may display complete stillness and stupor or great excitement and agitation. Frequently, they alternate rapidly between the two. They may become frozen in a strange posture or position and remain there for hours without moving. **Undifferentiated schizophrenia** is the general term used when schizophrenic symptoms either do not conform to the criteria of any one type of schizophrenia or conform to more than one type.

A person with catatonic schizophrenia may become frozen in an unusual position, like a statue, for hours at a time.

■ **disorganized schizophrenia**
The most serious type of schizophrenia, marked by extreme social withdrawal, hallucinations, delusions, silliness, inappropriate laughter, grotesque mannerisms, and other bizarre behavior.

■ **catatonic schizophrenia**
(KAT-uh-TAHN-ik) A type of schizophrenia characterized by complete stillness or stupor or great excitement and agitation; patients may assume an unusual posture and remain in it for long periods of time.

■ **undifferentiated schizophrenia**
A catchall term used when schizophrenic symptoms either do not conform to the criteria of any one type of schizophrenia or conform to more than one type.

Risk Factors in Schizophrenia

What factors increase the risk of developing schizophrenia?

Genetic factors appear to play a major role in the development of schizophrenia (Cannon et al., 1998; Gottesman, 1991; Kendler & Diehl, 1993; Owen & O'Donovan, 2003). Figure 15.6 shows how the chance of developing schizophrenia varies with the degree of relationship to a schizophrenic person. However, genes are not destiny; schizophrenia develops when there is both a genetic predisposition toward the disorder and more stress than a person can

FIGURE 15.6 Genetic Similarity and Probability of Developing Schizophrenia

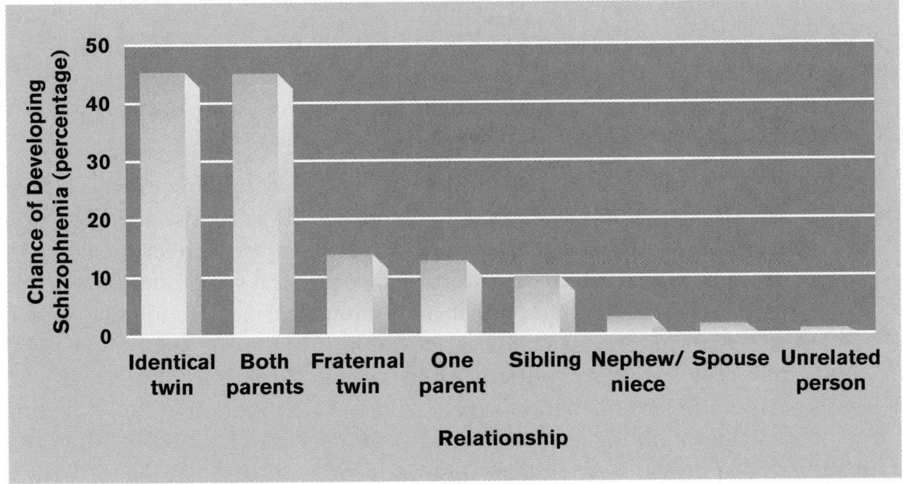

Research strongly indicates a genetic factor associated with schizophrenia. Identical twins have identical genes, and if one twin develops schizophrenia, the other twin has a 46% chance of also developing it. In fraternal twins, the chance is only 14%. A person with one schizophrenic parent has a 13% chance of developing schizophrenia, but a 46% chance if both parents are schizophrenic.
Source: Data from Nicol & Gottesman (1983).

handle. Any environmental factor—birth trauma, a virus, malnutrition, head injury, and so on—that can interfere with normal brain development brings an increased risk for schizophrenia (McDonald & Murray, 2000; McNeill et al., 2000).

Schizophrenia is more likely to strike men than women. Men also tend to develop the disorder at an earlier age (Takahashi et al., 2000), they do not respond as well to treatment, they spend more time in mental hospitals, and they are more likely to relapse. The earlier age of onset of the disorder among males appears to be independent of culture and socioeconomic variables. Studies of male and female schizophrenics conducted in Japan more than 40 years apart (in the 1950s and the 1990s) revealed that the Japanese males had an earlier onset of the disorder than the Japanese females did and that the average age of onset did not change over the 40-year period. Thus, the age of onset was not influenced by the dramatic cultural and socioeconomic changes in Japan during the postwar period (Takahashi et al., 2000).

Remember It 15.4

1. Match each symptom of schizophrenia with the appropriate example.

____ (1) delusions of grandeur
____ (2) hallucinations
____ (3) inappropriate affect
____ (4) delusions of persecution

a. Bill believes he is Moses.
b. Christina thinks her family is poisoning her food.
c. Sal hears voices cursing him.
d. Ophelia laughs at tragedies and cries when she hears a joke.

2. Match each subtype of schizophrenia with the appropriate example.

____ (1) paranoid schizophrenia
____ (2) disorganized schizophrenia
____ (3) catatonic schizophrenia
____ (4) undifferentiated schizophrenia

a. Katy stands for hours in the same strange position.
b. Vu believes that aliens are trying to kidnap him.
c. Ethan makes silly faces, laughs a lot, and masturbates openly.
d. Pam has symptoms of schizophrenia but does not fit any one type.

ANSWERS: 1. (1) a, (2) c, (3) d, (4) b; 2. (1) b, (2) c, (3) a, (4) d

Somatoform and Dissociative Disorders

Somatoform Disorders

What are two somatoform disorders, and what symptoms do they share?

Have you heard the word *psychosomatic* applied to a symptom or illness? Laypersons usually use this term to refer to physical disorders of psychological origin. The DSM-IV-TR uses the term *somatoform disorder* to refer to such conditions. The **somatoform disorders** involve physical symptoms that are due to psychological causes rather than any known medical condition. Although their symptoms are psychological in origin, patients are sincerely convinced that they spring from real physical disorders. People with somatoform disorders are not consciously faking illness to avoid work or other activities.

People with **hypochondriasis** are overly concerned about their health and fear that their bodily symptoms are a sign of some serious disease. A person with this somatoform disorder "might notice a mole and think of skin cancer or read about Lyme disease and decide it might be the cause of that tired feeling" (Barsky, 1993, p. 8). Yet, the symptoms are not usually consistent with known physical disorders, and even when a medical examination reveals no physical problem, people with hypochondriasis are not convinced. They may "doctor shop," going from one physician to another, seeking confirmation of their worst fears. Unfortunately, hypochondriasis is not easily treated, and there is usually a poor chance for recovery.

A person is diagnosed with a **conversion disorder** when there is a loss of motor or sensory functioning in some part of the body, which is not due to a physical cause but which solves a psychological problem. A person may become blind, deaf, or unable to speak or may develop a paralysis in some part of the body. Many of Freud's patients suffered from conversion disorder, and he believed that they unconsciously developed a physical disability to help resolve an unconscious sexual or aggressive conflict.

Today, psychologists think that conversion disorder can act as an unconscious defense against any intolerable anxiety situation that the person cannot otherwise escape. For example, a soldier who desperately fears going into battle might escape the anxiety by developing a paralysis or some other physically disabling symptom. One reason for this hypothesis is that those with conversion disorder exhibit a calm and cool indifference to their symptoms, called "la belle indifference." Furthermore, many seem to enjoy the attention, sympathy, and concern their disability brings them.

■ **somatoform disorders**
(so-MAT-uh-form) Disorders in which physical symptoms are present that are due to psychological causes rather than any known medical condition.

■ **hypochondriasis**
(HI-poh-kahn-DRY-uh-sis) A somatoform disorder in which persons are preoccupied with their health and fear that their physical symptoms are a sign of some serious disease, despite reassurance from doctors to the contrary.

■ **conversion disorder**
A somatoform disorder in which a person suffers a loss of motor or sensory functioning in some part of the body; the loss has no physical cause but solves some psychological problem.

Dissociative Disorders

How do the various dissociative disorders affect behavior?

Imagine how disconcerting it would be if you were unable to recognize your own leg. In his book *A Leg to Stand On*, neurologist Oliver Sacks (1984) described the case of a hospitalized man who could not feel or even recognize his own leg. This patient insisted that the leg wasn't even connected to his body, and his attempts to throw the leg out of his bed resulted in numerous falls. This unfortunate man was suffering from a profound disintegration of his physical and psychological self. Mental health professionals refer to this process as *dissociation*—the loss of one's ability to integrate all the components of self into a coherent representation of one's identity. In this case, the patient's dissociation was the result of an underlying physical illness. In many other instances, dissociation has a psychological rather than a physical cause.

In response to unbearable stress, some people develop a **dissociative disorder,** in which they lose the ability to consciously integrate their identities. Their consciousness becomes dissociated from their identity or their memories of important personal events, or both. For example, **dissociative amnesia** is a complete or partial loss of the ability to recall personal information or identify past experiences that cannot be attributed to ordinary forgetfulness or substance use. It is often caused by a traumatic experience—a psychological blow, so to speak—or a situation that creates unbearable anxiety causing the person to escape by "forgetting."

Several people previously thought to have been killed in the terrorist attacks on the World Trade Center on September 11, 2001, were discovered in mental hospitals many months later with diagnoses of dissociative amnesia (*Daily Hampshire Gazette*, 2002). They had been brought to hospitals on the day of the tragedy but were carrying no identification and were unable to remember their names or other identifying information. Extensive investigative work, including DNA testing in some cases, was required before they were identified. The fact that some were homeless people with schizophrenia who lived on the streets or in the subway stations near the World Trade Center made the task of identifying them all the more difficult. Such cases illustrate a puzzle concerning dissociative amnesia: Sufferers forget items of personal reference, such as their name, age, and address, and may fail to recognize their parents, other relatives, and friends, but they do not forget how to carry out routine tasks or how to read and write or solve problems, and their basic personality structure remains intact.

■ **dissociative disorders**
Disorders in which, under unbearable stress, consciousness becomes dissociated from a person's identity or her or his memories of important personal events, or both.

■ **dissociative amnesia**
A dissociative disorder in which there is a complete or partial loss of the ability to recall personal information or identify past experiences.

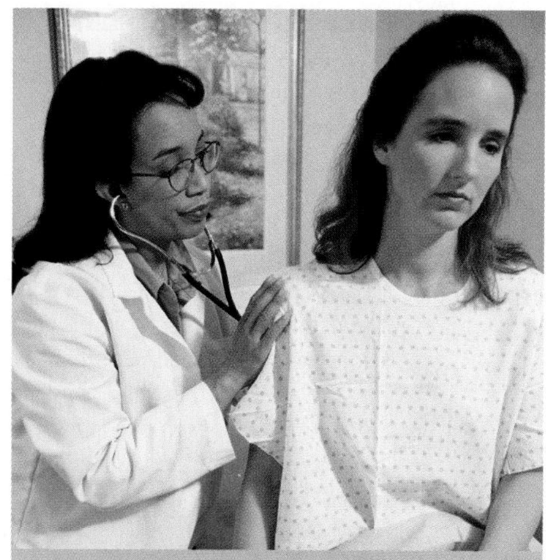

A person who continually complains of various symptoms and seeks medical treatment for them, even though doctors can discover nothing wrong, may be suffering from a somatoform disorder.

Even more puzzling than dissociative amnesia is **dissociative fugue**. In a fugue state, people not only forget their identity, they also travel away from home. Some take on a new identity that is usually more outgoing and uninhibited than their former identity. The fugue state may last for hours, days, or even months. The fugue is usually a reaction to some severe psychological stress, such as a natural disaster, a serious family quarrel, a deep personal rejection, or military service in wartime. Fortunately for most people, recovery from dissociative fugue is rapid, although they may have no memory of the initial stressor that brought on the fugue state. When people recover from the fugue, they often have no memory of events that occurred during the episode.

In **dissociative identity disorder (DID)**, two or more distinct, unique personalities exist in the same individual, and there is severe memory disruption concerning personal information about the other personalities. In 50% of the cases, there are more than 10 different personalities. The change from one personality to another often occurs suddenly and usually during stress. The personality in control of the body the largest percentage of time is known as the *host personality* (Kluft, 1984). The alternate personalities, or *alter personalities*, may differ radically in intelligence, speech, accent, vocabulary, posture, body language, hairstyle, taste in clothes, manners, and even handwriting and sexual orientation. In 80% of the cases of dissociative identity disorder, the host personality does not know of the alter personalities, but the alters have varying levels of awareness of each other (Putnam, 1989). The host and alter personalities commonly show amnesia for certain periods of time or for important life events such as a graduation or wedding. A common complaint is of "lost time"—periods for which a given personality has no memory because he or she was not in control of the body.

Dissociative identity disorder usually begins in early childhood but is rarely diagnosed before adolescence (Vincent & Pickering, 1988). About 90% of the treated cases have been women (Ross et al., 1989), and more than 95% of the patients reveal early histories of severe physical and/or sexual abuse (Coons, 1994; Putnam, 1992). The splitting off of separate personalities is apparently a way of coping with intolerable abuse. Researchers have found evidence to confirm the severe trauma and abuse suffered by many patients with DID (Gleaves, 1996). Dissociative identity disorder can be treated, often by psychotherapy, and some evidence indicates that DID patients respond well to treatment (Ellason & Ross, 1997).

■ **dissociative fugue**
(FEWG) A dissociative disorder in which one has a complete loss of memory of one's entire identity, travels away from home, and may assume a new identity.

■ **dissociative identity disorder (DID)**
A dissociative disorder in which two or more distinct, unique personalities occur in the same person, and there is severe memory disruption concerning personal information about the other personalities.

Remember It 15.5

1. Match each psychological disorder with the appropriate example.

____ (1) dissociative identity disorder	a. Tyra is convinced she has some serious disease, although her doctors can find nothing physically wrong.
____ (2) dissociative fugue	b. David is found far away from his hometown, calling himself by another name and having no memory of his past.
____ (3) dissociative amnesia	c. Theresa suddenly loses her sight, but doctors can find no physical reason for the problem.
____ (4) hypochondriasis	d. Manuel has no memory of being in the boat with other family members on the day that his older brother drowned.
____ (5) conversion disorder	e. Nadia has no memory of blocks of time in her life and often finds clothing in her closet that she cannot remember buying.

2. __________ disorders involve physical symptoms that have psychological causes.

ANSWERS: 1. (1) e, (2) b, (3) d, (4) a, (5) c; 2. Somatoform

Other Psychological Disorders

Sexual Disorders

What are the main characteristics of the various sexual disorders?

Most psychologists define **sexual disorders** as behavior patterns that are related to sexuality or sexual functioning and are destructive, guilt- or anxiety-producing, compulsive, or a cause of discomfort or harm to one or both parties involved. Table 15.2 lists several types of sexual disorders.

Perhaps the most common of all of the sexual disorders are the *sexual dysfunctions*—persistent, recurrent, and distressing problems involving sexual desire, sexual arousal, or the pleasure associated with sex or orgasm (see Chapter 12). Drug treatments for sexual dysfunctions have been successful for both men and women. For men, the drug *sildenafil citrate (Viagra)* has been proven effective in restoring erectile function. And orgasmic disorders and other sexual dysfunctions in women are increasingly being treated with hormones such as *dehydroepiandrosterone (DHEA)* (Munarriz et al., 2002). However, experts in sexual dysfunction point out that while biochemical treatments may restore or enhance physiological functions, other interventions, including individual and couples therapy, are required to improve sufferers' intimate relationships (Besharat, 2001; Heiman, 2002; Lieblum, 2002).

Another important aspect of treatment concerns the link between depression and sexual dysfunction in both men and women (Seidman, 2002). Depression is both a cause and an effect of sexual dysfunctions. Consequently, researchers advise health professionals to question patients who complain of sexual difficulties about factors

■ **sexual disorders**
Disorders with a sexual basis that are destructive, guilt- or anxiety-producing, compulsive, or a cause of discomfort or harm to one or both parties involved.

TABLE 15.2 DSM-IV Categories of Sexual Disorders

TYPE OF DISORDER	SYMPTOMS
Sexual dysfunctions	Persistent, recurrent, and distressing problems with sexual desire, sexual arousal, or the pleasure associated with sex or orgasm
Paraphilias	Recurrent sexual urges, fantasies, and behavior involving nonhuman objects, children, other nonconsenting persons, or the suffering or humiliation of the individual or his/her partner
Fetishism	Sexual urges, fantasies, and behavior involving an inanimate object, such as women's undergarments or shoes
Pedophilia	Sexual urges, fantasies, and behavior involving sexual activity with a prepubescent child or children
Exhibitionism	Sexual urges, fantasies, and behavior involving exposing one's genitals to an unsuspecting stranger
Voyeurism	Sexual urges, fantasies, and behavior involving watching unsuspecting people naked, undressing, or engaging in sexual activity
Sexual masochism	Sexual urges, fantasies, and behavior involving being beaten, humiliated, bound, or otherwise made to suffer
Sexual sadism	Sexual urges, fantasies, and behavior involving inflicting physical or psychological pain and suffering on another
Other paraphilias	Sexual urges, fantasies, and behavior involving, among other things, animals, feces, urine, corpses, filth, or enemas
Gender identity disorder	Problem accepting one's identity as male or female

Source: Based on DSM-IV (American Psychiatric Association, 1994).

■ paraphilias
Sexual disorders in which recurrent sexual urges, fantasies, or behavior involve nonhuman objects, children, other nonconsenting persons, or the suffering or humiliation of the individual or his or her partner.

■ gender identity disorder
Sexual disorder characterized by a problem accepting one's identity as male or female.

that may indicate the presence of depression. However, antidepressant drugs often increase the incidence of sexual difficulties (Coleman et al., 2001). Thus, experts advocate combined biochemical and psychological interventions that address both mood and sexual functioning for depressed patients (Montejo et al., 2001).

Paraphilias are disorders in which a person experiences recurrent sexual urges, fantasies, or behaviors involving children, other nonconsenting persons, nonhuman objects, or the suffering or humiliation of the individual or his or her partner. To be diagnosed as having a paraphilia, the person must experience considerable psychological distress or an impairment in functioning in an important area of his or her life.

Gender identity disorder is characterized by a problem accepting one's identity as male or female; children either express a desire to be or insist that they are the other gender. They show a strong preference for the clothes, games, pastimes, and playmates of the opposite sex. Twin studies suggest that genes strongly influence the development of gender identity disorder (Coolidge et al., 2002). The cross-sex preferences of individuals with this disorder go far beyond the cross-gender play behaviors of other children. In fact, these children often express the desire to *be* the other sex, not just engage in the activities associated with it. In adulthood, an individual may feel so strongly that she or he is psychologically of the other gender that *sex-reassignment surgery* is undergone.

Personality Disorders

What behaviors are associated with personality disorders in clusters A, B, and C?

Do you know someone who is impossible to get along with and who always blames others for his or her problems? Such a person may have a **personality disorder**—a long-standing, inflexible, maladaptive pattern of behaving and relating to others, which usually begins early in childhood or adolescence.

Characteristics of Personality Disorders Personality disorders are among the most common of mental disorders; the DSM-IV-TR indicates that 10–15% of North Americans have one or more personality disorders. People who suffer from other disorders, especially mood disorders, are often diagnosed with personality disorders as well (Brieger et al., 2003; Joyce et al., 2003). In most cases, the causes of personality disorders have yet to be identified.

People with personality disorders are extremely difficult to get along with. As a result, most have unstable work and social histories. Some sufferers know that their behavior causes problems, yet they seem unable to change. But more commonly, they blame other people or situations for their problems. Thus, because medications have not proved to be very useful in the treatment of personality disorders, treatment options are few. After all, to seek and benefit from therapy, a person must realize that he or she has a problem and be somewhat cooperative with the therapist. Most individuals with personality disorders seek treatment only when forced to by legal authorities or family members and, once in therapy, seldom engage in the kind of self-reflection that is essential to successful psychotherapy.

Types of Personality Disorders There are several different types of personality disorders, and the criteria used to differentiate among them overlap considerably. Thus, the DSM-IV-TR groups personality disorders into *clusters*, as shown in Table 15.3. The individual disorders within each cluster have similarities. For example, all the personality disorders in Cluster A are characterized by odd behavior. Those who suffer from *paranoid personality disorder* display extreme suspiciousness, while those with *schizoid personality disorder* isolate themselves from others and appear to be unable to form emotional bonds. Individuals with *schizotypal personality disorder* are often mistakenly diagnosed as schizophrenic because their odd appearance, unusual thought patterns, and lack of social skills are also symptoms of schizophrenia.

■ personality disorder
A long-standing, inflexible, maladaptive pattern of behaving and relating to others, which usually begins in early childhood or adolescence.

Cluster B disorders are characterized by erratic, overly dramatic behavior, such as complaining loudly in a store about being slighted or insulted by a clerk. These disorders are associated with an increased risk of suicide (Lambert, 2003). A pervasive

TABLE 15.3 Types of Personality Disorders

PERSONALITY DISORDER	SYMPTOMS
Cluster A: Odd behavior	
Paranoid	Individual is highly suspicious, untrusting, guarded, hypersensitive, easily slighted, lacking in emotion; holds grudges.
Schizoid	Individual isolates self from others; appears unable to form emotional attachments; behavior may resemble that of autistic children.
Schizotypal	Individual dresses in extremely unusual ways; lacks social skills; may have odd ideas resembling the delusions of schizophrenia.
Cluster B: Erratic, overly dramatic behavior	
Narcissistic	Individual has exaggerated sense of self-importance and entitlement; is self-centered, arrogant, demanding, exploitive, envious; craves admiration and attention; lacks empathy.
Histrionic	Individual seeks attention and approval; is overly dramatic, self-centered, shallow, demanding, manipulative, easily bored, suggestible; craves excitement; often, is attractive and sexually seductive.
Borderline	Individual is unstable in mood, behavior, self-image, and social relationships; has intense fear of abandonment; exhibits impulsive and reckless behavior and inappropriate anger; makes suicidal gestures and performs self-mutilating acts.
Antisocial	Individual disregards rights and feelings of others; is manipulative, impulsive, selfish, aggressive, irresponsible, reckless, and willing to break the law, lie, cheat, and exploit others for personal gain, without remorse; fails to hold jobs.
Cluster C: Anxious, fearful behavior	
Obsessive-compulsive	Individual is concerned with doing things the "right" way and is generally a perfectionist; relationships are emotionally shallow.
Avoidant	Individual fears criticism and rejection; avoids social situations in order to prevent being judged by others.
Dependent	Person overly dependent on others for advice and approval; may cling to lovers and friends, fearing abandonment.

desire to be the center of others' attention is characteristic of both *narcissistic personality disorder* and *histrionic personality disorder*, as is a lack of concern for others.

A more serious Cluster B disorder is *borderline personality disorder*, whose sufferers are highly unstable. Fear of abandonment is the primary theme of their social relationships. Consequently, they tend to cling to those for whom they feel affection. Once a relationship ends, however, the individual with borderline personality disorder views the former lover or friend as a mortal enemy. For the most part, though, people with this disorder direct their negative emotions toward themselves. They often harm themselves in bizarre ways, such as pulling out their hair or making tiny cuts in their forearms.

A significant proportion of patients with borderline personality disorder have histories of childhood abuse or disturbances in attachment relationships (Trull et al., 2003). Moreover, many of these patients suffer from mood disorders as well (Brieger et al., 2003). Thus, suicidal thoughts and behaviors are a major concern of therapists working with these patients. However, research indicates that antidepressant medication, combined with psychotherapy, can be effective in treating this disorder (Trull et al., 2003).

People who suffer from another Cluster B disorder, *antisocial personality disorder*, have a "pervasive pattern of disregard for, and violation of, the rights of others that begins in childhood or early adolescence and continues into adulthood" (American

Psychiatric Association, 1994, p. 645). As children they lie, steal, vandalize, initiate fights, skip school, run away from home, and may be physically cruel to others and to animals (Arehart-Treichel, 2002). By early adolescence, they usually drink excessively, use drugs, and engage in promiscuous sex. In adulthood, they cannot keep a job, act as a responsible parent, honor financial commitments, or obey the law.

Brain-imaging studies suggest that people with antisocial personality disorder do not comprehend the emotional significance of words and images (Hare, 1995). They show the same level of brain arousal, measured by EEG recordings, whether they are confronting neutral stimuli (words such as *chair*, *table*, and *stone*) or emotionally charged stimuli (words such as *cancer*, *rape*, and *murder*). Such findings suggest that there is a neurophysiological basis for the lack of normal empathic responses shown by most individuals with this disorder (Habel et al., 2002). Some experts estimate that as many as 20% of people who are in prisons in the United States suffer from antisocial personality disorder.

Finally, Cluster C personality disorders are associated with fearful or anxious behavior. Individuals diagnosed with *obsessive-compulsive personality disorder* fear falling short of perfectionistic standards. Most have shallow emotional relationships because of their tendency to hold others to equally unrealistic standards of behavior. Order is important to them, but they do not experience the kinds of irrational obsessions and compulsions that dominate the lives of those who suffer from obsessive-compulsive disorder.

Two other Cluster C disorders, *avoidant personality disorder* and *dependent personality disorder*, represent opposite approaches to social relationships. A person with avoidant personality disorder shuns relationships because of excessive sensitivity to criticism and rejection. By contrast, someone with dependent personality disorder relies on others to an inappropriate degree. Such people can't make everyday decisions, such as what to have for dinner, without seeking others' advice and approval. Because of their dependency on others, they fear abandonment and tend to be "clingy" in social relationships.

Because the characteristics involved in personality disorders are quite similar to normal variations in personality, it is especially important when thinking about them to remember the criteria for abnormality discussed at the beginning of this chapter. For example, if a friend suspects a neighbor of poisoning his cat, and you think this an unreasonable suspicion, don't jump to the conclusion that your friend has paranoid personality disorder. This tendency toward suspiciousness is likely to be simply a personality trait your friend possesses.

Remember It 15.6

1. ___________ are disorders in which sexual urges, fantasies, and behaviors involve children, other nonconsenting persons, or nonhuman objects.

2. ___________ disorders typically cause problems in sufferers' social relationships and at work.

3. Match each cluster of personality disorders with its chief characteristic.

____ (1) Cluster A	a. odd behavior
____ (2) Cluster B	b. anxious, fearful behavior
____ (3) Cluster C	c. overly dramatic behavior

4. Classify each of the following personality disorders as part of Cluster A, B, or C.

____ (1) narcissistic personality disorder
____ (2) obsessive-compulsive personality disorder
____ (3) histrionic personality disorder
____ (4) schizotypal personality disorder
____ (5) schizoid personality disorder
____ (6) paranoid personality disorder
____ (7) antisocial personality disorder
____ (8) dependent personality disorder
____ (9) avoidant personality disorder
____ (10) borderline personality disorder

ANSWERS: 1. Paraphilias; 2. Personality; 3. (1) a, (2) c, (3) b; 4. (1) B, (2) C, (3) B, (4) A, (5) A, (6) A, (7) B, (8) C, (9) C, (10) B

Apply It

Overcoming the Fear of Public Speaking

Do you break out in a cold sweat and start trembling when you have to speak in public? If so, cheer up; you're in good company: Fear of public speaking is the number one fear reported by American adults in surveys. More people fear public speaking than flying, sickness, or even death (*CBS News*, July 31, 2002)!

What Causes It?

Fear of public speaking is a form of performance anxiety, a common type of social phobia. Much of the fear of public speaking stems from fear of being embarrassed or of being judged negatively by others. Some people cope with this fear by trying to avoid situations in which they may be required to speak in public. A more practical approach is to examine the incorrect beliefs that can cause the fear of public speaking and then take specific steps to overcome it. Here are some incorrect beliefs associated with public speaking (Orman, 1996):

- To succeed, a speaker has to perform perfectly. (Not true; no audience expects perfection.)
- A good speaker presents as many facts and details about the subject as possible. (Not true; all you need is two or three main points.)
- If some members of the audience aren't paying attention, the speaker needs to do something about it. (Not true; you can't please everyone, and it's a waste of time to try to do so.)

What Can You Do?

Some of the steps you can take to manage fear of public speaking deal with how you present yourself to your audience; others focus on what's going on inside you. Here are some of the many suggestions offered by experts at Toastmasters International (2003), an organization devoted to helping people improve their public speaking skills:

- *Know your material well.* Practice aloud, and revise your speech, if necessary.
- *Visualize your speech.* Imagine yourself giving your speech in a confident, clear manner.
- *Relax.* Reduce your tension by doing deep breathing or relaxation exercises.
- *Be familiar with the place where you will speak.* Arrive early, and practice using the microphone and any other equipment you plan to use.
- *Connect with the audience.* Greet some members of the audience as they arrive; then, when you give your speech, speak to the audience as though they were a group of your friends.
- *Project confidence through your posture.* Stand or sit in a self-assured manner, smile, and make eye contact with the audience.
- *Focus on your message, not on yourself.* Turn your attention away from your nervousness and focus on the purpose of your speech, which is to transmit information to your audience.
- *Remember that the audience doesn't expect you to be perfect.* Don't apologize for any problems you think you have with your speech. Just be yourself.

By applying these few simple tips, you can overcome nervousness and speak confidently on any topic—even on the spur of the moment.

Summary *and* Review

What Is Abnormal? p. 505

What criteria can be used to determine whether behavior is abnormal? p. 505

Behavior might be considered abnormal if it differs radically from what is considered normal in the person's own culture, if it leads to personal distress or impaired functioning, or if it results in the person's being a danger to self and/or others.

How prevalent are psychological disorders? p. 506

Psychological disorders are more common than many physical diseases. About 22% of Americans are diagnosed with a psychological disorder each year. The lifetime risk of developing such a disorder is 50% in the United States.

What are the theoretical approaches that attempt to explain the causes of psychological disorders? p. 506

Five theoretical perspectives on the causes of psychological disorders are the biological perspective, the biopsychosocial perspective, the psychodynamic perspective, the learning perspective, and the cognitive perspective.

Anxiety Disorders p. 509

How is generalized anxiety disorder manifested? p. 510

Generalized anxiety disorder is characterized by chronic, excessive worry that is so severe that it interferes with daily functioning.

How does panic disorder affect the lives of those who suffer from it? p. 511

Panic disorder is marked by recurrent, unpredictable panic attacks—episodes of overwhelming anxiety, fear, or terror, during which people experience a pounding heart, uncontrollable trembling or shaking, choking or smothering sensations, and the feeling that they are going to die or lose their sanity. Those who suffer from panic disorder must also cope wth anxiety about the occurrence and consequences of further attacks.

What are the characteristics of the three categories of phobias? p. 511

The three categories of phobias are (1) agoraphobia, an intense fear of being in situations where immediate escape is impossible or help is not available in case of incapacitating anxiety; (2) social phobia, an intense fear of social or performance situations where one might be embarrassed or humiliated by appearing clumsy, foolish, or incompetent; and (3) specific phobia, a marked fear of a specific object or situation (any phobia other than agoraphobia or social phobia).

What thought and behavior patterns are associated with obsessive-compulsive disorder? p. 513

Obsessive-compulsive disorder is characterized by recurrent obsessions (persistent, involuntary thoughts, images, or impulses that cause great distress) and/or compulsions (persistent, irresistible, irrational urges to perform an act or ritual repeatedly).

Mood Disorders p. 514

What are the symptoms of major depressive disorder? p. 514

Major depressive disorder is characterized by feelings of great sadness, despair, and hopelessness, as well as a loss of the ability to feel pleasure. Other symptoms include psychomotor disturbance and, possibly, psychotic depression.

How are culture, gender, and depression related? p. 515

Lifetime rates of depression vary widely from one culture to another. However, worldwide, women are more likely to suffer from depression than men.

What are the extremes of mood suffered by those with bipolar disorder? p. 516

Bipolar disorder is a mood disorder in which a person suffers from manic episodes (periods of wild optimism, inflated self-esteem, excessive euphoria, and hyperactivity) that alternate with periods of major depression.

What are some suggested causes of mood disorders? p. 516

Some of the proposed causes of mood disorders are (1) a genetic predisposition, (2) disturbances in the brain's serotonin levels, (3) abnormal patterns in the neurotransmitters dopamine, GABA, and norepinephrine, (4) distorted and negative views of oneself, the world, and the future, and (5) major life stress.

What are some of the risk factors for suicide? p. 517

Depression, mood disorders, schizophrenia, and substance abuse are major risk factors for suicide. Other risk factors include particularly troubling life stressors and a genetic tendency to suicidal behavior. Elderly, White males commit suicide more often than members of other race or age groups, perhaps due to poor health or loneliness. Research shows that women are more likely to attempt suicide, but men are more likely to be successful.

Schizophrenia p. 519

What are the major positive symptoms of schizophrenia? p. 519

The positive symptoms of schizophrenia are abnormal behaviors and characteristics, including hallucinations, delusions, derailment, grossly disorganized behavior, and inappropriate affect.

What normal functions are reduced or absent in schizophrenics? p. 520

The negative symptoms of schizophrenia represent loss of or deficiencies in thoughts and behavior that are characteristic of normal functioning. They include social withdrawal, apathy, loss of motivation, lack of goal-directed activity, very limited speech, slowed movements, flat affect, poor problem-solving abilities, a distorted sense of time, and poor hygiene and grooming.

What does research indicate about the neurological functioning of schizophrenics? p. 520

Schizophrenics exhibit low levels of neural activity in the frontal lobes. Many also have defects in the neural circuitry of the cerebral cortex and limbic system, as well as abnormalities in the hippocampus, amygdala, thalamus, and frontal lobes. They display abnormal lateralization of brain functions and slow communication between left and right hemispheres. Dopamine activity is also abnormal in many schizophrenics.

What are the four types of schizophrenia? p. 520

The four types of schizophrenia are paranoid, disorganized, catatonic, and undifferentiated schizophrenia.

What factors increase the risk of developing schizophrenia? p. 521

Some risk factors for schizophrenia are a genetic predisposition, more stress than a particular individual can handle, any environmental factor that can interfere with normal brain development, and excessive dopamine activity in the brain. Men are more likely than women to develop schizophrenia.

Somatoform and Dissociative Disorders p. 522

What are two somatoform disorders, and what symptoms do they share? p. 522

Somatoform disorders involve physical symptoms that cannot be identified as any of the known medical conditions. Hypochondriasis involves a persistent fear that bodily symptoms are the sign of some serious disease, and conversion disorder involves a loss of motor or sensory functioning in some part of the body, which has no physical cause but does solve a psychological problem.

How do the various dissociative disorders affect behavior? p. 523

People with dissociative amnesia have a complete or partial loss of memory of important personal events and/or their entire personal identity. In dissociative fugue, people forget their entire identity, travel away from home, and may assume a new identity somewhere else. In dissociative identity disorder, two or more distinct, unique personalities exist in the same person, and there is severe memory disruption concerning personal information about the other personalities.

Other Psychological Disorders p. 525

What are the main characteristics of the various sexual disorders? p. 525

Sexual disorders are behavior patterns that are related to sexuality or sexual functioning and are destructive, guilt- or anxiety-producing, compulsive, or a cause of discomfort or harm to one or both parties involved. A sexual dysfunction is a problem with sexual desire, sexual arousal, or the pleasure associated with sex or orgasm. Paraphilias are disorders in which sufferers have recurrent sexual urges, fantasies, and behaviors that involve children, other nonconsenting persons, nonhuman objects, or the suffering and humiliation of the individual or his or her partner. People who feel that their psychological gender identity is different from that typically associated with their biological sex may suffer from gender identity disorder.

What behaviors are associated with personality disorders in Clusters A, B, and C? p. 526

People with personality disorders have long-standing, inflexible, maladaptive patterns of behavior that cause problems in their social relationships and at work and often cause personal distress. Such people seem unable to change and blame others for their problems. Cluster A disorders are characterized by odd behavior. The disorders in Cluster B involve erratic, overly dramatic behavior. Cluster C includes disorders that are associated with fearful and anxious behaviors.

Key Terms

agoraphobia, p. 511
anxiety disorders, p. 509
bipolar disorder, p. 516
catatonic schizophrenia, p. 521
compulsion, p. 513
conversion disorder, p. 523
delusion, p. 519
delusions of grandeur, p. 519
delusions of persecution, p. 519
disorganized schizophrenia, p. 521
dissociative amnesia, p. 523
dissociative disorders, p. 523
dissociative fugue, p. 524
dissociative identity disorder (DID), p. 524
DSM-IV, p. 507
gender identity disorder, p. 526
generalized anxiety disorder, p. 510
hallucination, p. 519
hypochondriasis, p. 522
major depressive disorder, p. 514
manic episode, p. 516
mood disorders, p. 514
obsession, p. 513
obsessive-compulsive disorder (OCD), p. 513
panic attack, p. 511
panic disorder, p. 511
paranoid schizophrenia, p. 520
paraphilias, p. 526
personality disorder, p. 526
phobia, p. 511
psychological disorders, p. 504
psychosis, p. 519
schizophrenia, p. 519
sexual disorders, p. 525
social phobia, p. 512
somatoform disorders, p. 522
specific phobia, p. 512
undifferentiated schizophrenia, p. 521

chapter 16

Therapies

Insight Therapies

- *What are the basic techniques of psychoanalysis, and how are they used to help patients?*
- *What are the role and the goal of the therapist in person-centered therapy?*
- *What is the major emphasis of Gestalt therapy?*

Relationship Therapies

- *What problems commonly associated with major depression does interpersonal therapy focus on?*
- *What is the goal of family therapy?*
- *What are some advantages of group therapy?*

Behavior Therapies

- *How do behavior therapists modify clients' problematic behavior?*
- *What behavior therapies are based on classical conditioning?*
- *How does participant modeling help people overcome their fears?*

Cognitive Therapies

- *What is the aim of rational-emotive therapy?*
- *How does Beck's cognitive therapy help people overcome depression and panic disorder?*

Biological Therapies

- *What are the advantages and disadvantages of using drugs to treat psychological disorders?*
- *What is electroconvulsive therapy (ECT) used for?*
- *What is psychosurgery, and for what problems is it used?*

Evaluating the Therapies

- *What therapy, if any, is most effective in treating psychological disorders?*

Culturally Sensitive and Gender-Sensitive Therapy

- *What characterizes culturally sensitive and gender-sensitive therapy?*

What would you do to try to overcome a phobia?

"If you fall off a horse, the best thing to do is to get back on immediately. Otherwise, you might develop a fear of riding." The core assumption of this advice is that exposing yourself to something of which you are, or might be, afraid can cure or prevent that fear. Do psychotherapists agree? Consider the following situation:

Bill, a 21-year-old college student, suffered from a debilitating phobia, an intense fear of any kind of sudden loud noise. He had become so anxious about possible exposure to noises that he had almost no social life. Balloons were especially frightening (they might pop!), so he avoided birthday parties, weddings, and other events where balloons might be present. Bill's girlfriend insisted that he get help.

On the first day of his therapy, two people led Bill into a small room filled with 100 large balloons. One person stood close to Bill, while the other person explained that he was going to begin popping the balloons. While some 50 balloons were popped with a pin, Bill shook uncontrollably, tears streaming down his face. Bill had to endure the popping of another 50 balloons before he was allowed to leave. And he returned on the next 2 days for still more balloon popping.

During the course of the 3 days, Bill became progressively less fearful and was eventually even able to join in stepping on hundreds of balloons and popping them. In a 1-year follow-up, Bill reported that he experienced no distress in the presence of balloons and no longer avoided situations where he might encounter them. Neither was he ill at ease when he sat relatively near a fireworks display on the Fourth of July. (Adapted from Houlihan et al., 1993.)

Bill's therapists were using a rapid treatment technique known as *flooding*, a form of behavior therapy in which the patient agrees to be instantly and totally immersed in the feared situation or surrounded by the feared object. (Notice the similarity between flooding and the advice given earlier.) When applied systematically and carefully, flooding is known to be effective in treating various types of phobias (Coles & Heinberg, 2000). But flooding is only one of the many effective therapies you will learn about in this chapter.

Psychotherapy uses psychological rather than biological means to treat emotional and behavioral disorders. The practice of psychotherapy has grown and changed enormously since its beginnings more than 100 years ago, when Freud and his colleagues began using it.

■ **psychotherapy** Any type of treatment for emotional and behavioral disorders that uses psychological rather than biological means.

■ **insight therapies** Approaches to psychotherapy based on the notion that psychological well-being depends on self-understanding.

■ **psychodynamic therapies** Psychotherapies that attempt to uncover childhood experiences that are thought to explain a patient's current difficulties.

■ **psychoanalysis** (SY-ko-uh-NAL-ul-sis) The first psychodynamic therapy, which was developed by Freud and uses free association, dream analysis, and transference.

Insight Therapies

Do you recall a form of learning called *insight* that you read about in Chapter 5? Such learning is the foundation of several approaches to psychotherapy. These approaches, fittingly enough, are collectively referred to as **insight therapies** because their assumption is that psychological well-being depends on self-understanding—understanding of one's own thoughts, emotions, motives, behavior, and coping mechanisms.

Psychodynamic Therapies

What are the basic techniques of psychoanalysis, and how are they used to help patients?

Psychodynamic therapies attempt to uncover childhood experiences that are thought to explain a patient's current difficulties. The techniques associated with the first such therapy—Freud's **psychoanalysis**—are still used by psychodynamic therapists today (Epstein et al., 2001). One such technique is **free association**, in which the patient is asked to reveal whatever thoughts, feelings, or images come to mind, no matter how trivial, embarrassing, or terrible they might seem. The analyst then pieces together the free-flowing associations, explains their meanings, and helps patients gain insight into the thoughts and behaviors that are troubling them. But some patients avoid revealing certain painful or embarrassing thoughts while engaging in free association, a phenomenon Freud called *resistance*. Resistance may take the form of halting speech during free association, "forgetting" appointments with the analyst, or arriving late.

■ **free association** A psychoanalytic technique used to explore the unconscious by having patients reveal whatever thoughts, feelings, or images come to mind.

Dream analysis is another technique used by psychoanalysts. Freud believed that areas of emotional concern repressed in waking life are sometimes expressed in sym-

Freud's famous couch was used by his patients during psychoanalysis.

Carl Rogers (at upper right) facilitates discussion in a therapy group.

bolic form in dreams. He claimed that patient behavior may have a symbolic quality as well. At some point during psychoanalysis, Freud said, the patient reacts to the analyst with the same feelings that were present in another significant relationship—usually with the mother or father. This reaction of the patient is called **transference**. Freud believed that encouraging patients to achieve transference was a essential part of psychotherapy. He claimed that transference allows the patient to relive troubling experiences from the past with the analyst as a parent substitute, thereby resolving any hidden conflicts.

Many therapists today practice brief psychodynamic therapy, in which the therapist and patient decide on the issues to explore at the outset rather than waiting for them to emerge in the course of treatment. The therapist assumes a more active role and places more emphasis on the present than in traditional psychoanalysis. Brief psychodynamic therapy may require only one or two visits per week for as few as 12 to 20 weeks. In a meta-analysis of 11 well-controlled studies, Crits-Christoph (1992) found brief psychodynamic therapy to be as effective as other psychotherapies. More recent research has also shown brief psychodynamic therapy to be comparable to other forms of psychotherapy in terms of successful outcomes (Hager et al., 2000).

■ **transference**
An emotional reaction that occurs during psychoanalysis, in which the patient displays feelings and attitudes toward the analyst that were present in another significant relationship.

■ **humanistic therapies**
Psychotherapies that assume that people have the ability and freedom to lead rational lives and make rational choices.

■ **person-centered therapy**
A nondirective, humanistic therapy developed by Carl Rogers, in which the therapist creates an accepting climate and shows empathy, freeing clients to be themselves and releasing their natural tendency toward self-actualization.

Humanistic Therapies

Humanistic therapies assume that people have the ability and freedom to lead rational lives and make rational choices. **Person-centered therapy**, developed by Carl Rogers (1951), is one of the most frequently used humanistic therapies. According to this view, people are innately good and if allowed to develop naturally, they will grow toward *self-actualization*—the realization of their inner potential. The humanistic perspective suggests that psychological disorders result when a person's natural tendency toward self-actualization is blocked either by himself or by others. In the 1940s and 1950s, person-centered therapy enjoyed a strong following among psychologists.

What are the role and the goal of the therapist in person-centered therapy?

The person-centered therapist attempts to create an accepting climate, based on *unconditional positive regard* for the client. The therapist also empathizes with the client's concerns and emotions. When the client speaks, the therapist responds by restating or reflecting back her or his ideas and feelings. Using these techniques, the therapist allows the direction of the therapy sessions to be controlled by the client. Rogers rejected all forms of therapy that cast the therapist in the role of expert and clients in the role of patients who expect the therapist to prescribe something that "cures" their problem. Thus, person-centered therapy is called a **nondirective therapy**.

■ **nondirective therapy**
Any type of psychotherapy in which the therapist allows the direction of the therapy sessions to be controlled by the client; an example is person-centered therapy.

Gestalt Therapy

What is the major emphasis of Gestalt therapy?

■ **Gestalt therapy**
A therapy that was originated by Fritz Perls and that emphasizes the importance of clients' fully experiencing, in the present moment, their feelings, thoughts, and actions and then taking responsibility for them.

■ **directive therapy**
Any type of psychotherapy in which the therapist takes an active role in determining the course of therapy sessions and provides answers and suggestions to the patient; an example is Gestalt therapy.

Gestalt therapy, developed by Fritz Perls (1969), emphasizes the importance of clients' fully experiencing, in the present moment, their feelings, thoughts, and actions and then taking responsibility for them. The goal of Gestalt therapy is to help clients achieve a more integrated self and become more authentic and self-accepting. In addition, they learn to assume personal responsibility for their behavior rather than blaming society, past experiences, parents, or others.

Gestalt therapy is a **directive therapy**, one in which the therapist takes an active role in determining the course of therapy sessions and provides answers and suggestions to the client. The well-known phrase "getting in touch with your feelings" is a major objective of Gestalt therapy. Perls suggested that those of us who are in need of therapy carry around a heavy load of unfinished business, which may be in the form of resentment toward or conflicts with parents, siblings, lovers, employers, or others. If not resolved, these conflicts are carried forward into our present relationships. One method for dealing with unfinished business is the "empty chair" technique (Paivio & Greenberg, 1995). The client sits facing an empty chair and imagines, for example, that a wife, husband, father, or mother sits there. The client proceeds to tell the chair what he or she truly feels about that person. Then, the client moves to the empty chair and role-plays what the imagined person's response would be to what was said.

Remember It 16.1

1. In psychoanalysis, the technique whereby a patient reveals every thought, idea, or image that comes to mind is called ___________; the patient's attempt to avoid revealing certain thoughts is called ___________.
2. Attempting to uncover childhood experiences that may explain a patient's current problems is the goal of ___________ therapies.
3. ___________ therapy is the nondirective psychotherapy developed by Carl Rogers.
4. ___________ therapy is a directive psychotherapy that emphasizes the importance of the client's fully experiencing, in the present moment, his or her thoughts, feelings, and actions.

ANSWERS: 1. free association, resistance; 2. psychodynamic; 3. Person-centered; 4. Gestalt

■ **relationship therapies**
Therapies that attempt to improve patients' interpersonal relationships or create new relationships to support patients' efforts to address psychological problems.

Relationship Therapies

Insight therapies focus on the self, which is not always the most appropriate approach to a psychological problem. **Relationship therapies** look not only at the individual's internal struggles but also at his or her interpersonal relationships. Some deliberately create new relationships for people that can support them in their efforts to address their problems.

What problems commonly associated with major depression does interpersonal therapy focus on?

Interpersonal Therapy

Interpersonal therapy (IPT) is a brief psychotherapy that has proven very effective in the treatment of depression (Elkin et al., 1989, 1995; Klerman et al., 1984). IPT is designed specifically to help patients understand and cope with four types of interpersonal problems commonly associated with major depression:

1. *Unusual or severe responses to the death of a loved one.* The therapist and patient discuss the patient's relationship with the deceased person and feelings (such as guilt) that may be associated with the death.
2. *Interpersonal role disputes.* The therapist helps the patient to understand others' points of view and to explore options for bringing about change.
3. *Difficulty in adjusting to role transitions, such as divorce, career change, and retirement.* Patients are helped to see the change not as a threat but as a challenge that they can master and an opportunity for growth.
4. *Deficits in interpersonal skills.* Through role-playing and analysis of the patient's communication style, the therapist tries to help the patient develop the interpersonal skills necessary to initiate and sustain relationships.

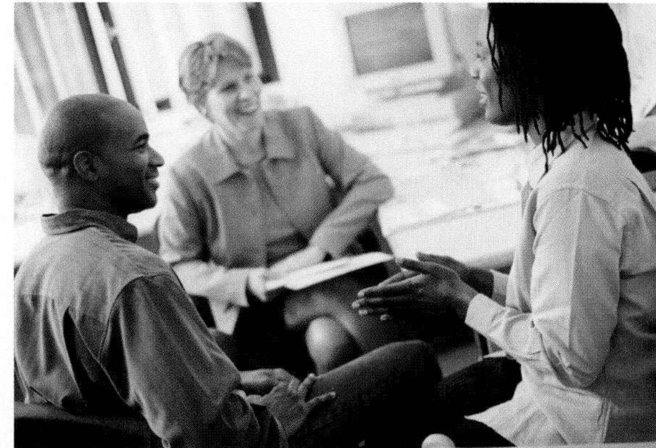

Therapists working with couples pay attention to the dynamics between the two people—how they communicate, act toward each other, and view each other.

Interpersonal therapy is relatively brief, consisting of 12 to 16 weekly sessions. A large study conducted by the National Institute of Mental Health found IPT to be an effective treatment even for severe depression and to have a low dropout rate (Elkin et al., 1989, 1995). Research also indicates that patients who recover from major depression can enjoy a longer period without relapse when they continue with monthly sessions of IPT (Frank et al., 1991).

■ **interpersonal therapy (IPT)**
A brief psychotherapy designed to help depressed people better understand and cope with problems relating to their interpersonal relationships.

Family Therapy and Couples Therapy

What is the goal of family therapy?

Some therapists work with couples to help them resolve their difficulties. Others specialize in treating troubled families. In **family therapy**, parents and children enter therapy as a group. The therapist pays attention to the dynamics of the family unit—how family members communicate, how they act toward one another, and how they view each other. The goal of the therapist is to help family members reach agreement on certain changes that will help heal the wounds of the family unit, improve communication patterns, and create more understanding and harmony within the group (Hawley & Weisz, 2003).

Couples therapy and family therapy appear to have positive effects in treating a number of disorders and clinical problems (Lebow & Gurman, 1995). Couples therapy can be helpful in the treatment of sexual dysfunctions (Gehring, 2003). And, when it accompanies medication, family therapy can be beneficial in the treatment of schizophrenia and can reduce relapse rates (Carpenter, 1996). Schizophrenic patients are more likely to relapse if their family members express emotions, attitudes, and behaviors that involve criticism, hostility, or emotional overinvolvement (Linszen et al., 1997); this pattern is labeled *high in expressed emotion*, or *high EE* (Falloon, 1988; Jenkins & Karno, 1992). Family therapy can help other family members modify their behavior toward the patient. Family therapy also seems to be the most favorable setting for treating adolescent drug abuse (Lebow & Gurman, 1995).

■ **family therapy**
Therapy involving an entire family, with the goal of helping family members reach agreement on changes that will help heal the family unit, improve communication problems, and create more understanding and harmony within the group.

■ **group therapy**
A form of therapy in which several clients (usually 7 to 10) meet regularly with one or more therapists to resolve personal problems.

Group Therapy

What are some advantages of group therapy?

Group therapy is a form of therapy in which several clients (usually 7 to 10) meet regularly with one or more therapists to resolve personal problems. Besides being less expensive than individual therapy, group therapy gives the individual a sense of belonging and opportunities to express feelings, to get feedback from other members, and to give and receive help and emotional support. Learning that others also share their problems helps people feel less alone and ashamed. A meta-analysis of studies comparing prisoners who

Group therapy can give individuals a sense of belonging and an opportunity to give and receive emotional support.

participated in group therapy to those who did not found that group participation was helpful for a variety of problems, including anxiety, depression, and low self-esteem (Morgan & Flora, 2002).

A variant of group therapy is the *self-help group*. About 12 million people in the United States participate in roughly 500,000 self-help groups, most of which focus on a single problem such as substance abuse or depression. Self-help groups usually are not led by professional therapists. They are simply groups of people who share a common problem and meet to give and receive support.

One of the oldest and best-known self-help groups is Alcoholics Anonymous, which claims 1.5 million members worldwide. Other self-help groups patterned after Alcoholics Anonymous have been formed to help individuals overcome many other addictive behaviors, from overeating (Overeaters Anonymous) to gambling (Gamblers Anonymous). One study indicated that people suffering from anxiety-based problems were helped by participating in groups that used a multimedia self-help program called Attacking Anxiety. Of the 176 individuals who participated in the study, 62 were reported to have achieved significant improvement, and another 40 reported some improvement (Finch et al., 2000).

Remember It 16.2

1. A depressed person who would be *least* likely to benefit from interpersonal therapy (IPT) is one who

a. is unable to accept the death of a loved one.

b. has been depressed since his or her retirement.

c. was sexually abused by a parent.

d. feels isolated and alone because of difficulty making friends.

2. Match each description with the appropriate type(s) of therapy.

____ (1) led by professional therapists

____ (2) effective for supporting individuals recovering from alcoholism

____ (3) provides members with a sense of belonging

____ (4) less expensive than individual therapy but still provides contact with trained therapists

a. group therapy

b. self-help groups

c. both group therapy and self-help groups

3. In family therapy, the therapist pays attention to the __________ of the family unit.

ANSWERS: 1. c; 2. (1) a, (2) b, (3) c, (4) a; 3. dynamics

Behavior Therapies

Sometimes, individuals seek help from a mental health professional because they want to rid themselves of a troublesome habit, or they want to develop a better way to respond to specific situations in their lives. In such cases, psychotherapists may employ a behavioral approach.

A **behavior therapy** is a treatment approach consistent with the learning perspective on psychological disorders—that abnormal behavior is learned. Instead of viewing maladaptive behavior as a symptom of some underlying disorder, the behavior therapist sees the behavior itself as the disorder. If a person comes to a therapist with a fear of flying, that fear of flying is seen as the problem. Behavior therapies use learning principles to eliminate inappropriate or maladaptive behaviors and replace them with more adaptive responses—an approach referred to as **behavior modification**. The goal is to change the troublesome behavior, not to change the individual's personality structure or to search for the origin of the problem behavior.

behavior therapy
A treatment approach that is based on the idea that abnormal behavior is learned and that applies the principles of operant conditioning, classical conditioning, and/or observational learning to eliminate inappropriate or maladaptive behaviors and replace them with more adaptive responses.

behavior modification
An approach to therapy that uses learning principles to eliminate inappropriate or maladaptive behaviors and replace them with more adaptive responses.

Behavior Modification Techniques Based on Operant Conditioning

Behavior modification techniques based on operant conditioning seek to control the consequences of behavior. Extinction of an undesirable behavior is accomplished by terminating, or withholding, the reinforcement that is maintaining that behavior (Lerman & Iwata, 1996). Behavior therapists also seek to reinforce desirable behavior in order to increase its frequency. Institutional settings such as hospitals, prisons, and school classrooms are well suited to behavior modification techniques, because they provide a restricted environment where the consequences of behavior can be strictly controlled.

How do behavior therapists modify clients' problematic behavior?

Some institutions use **token economies** that reward appropriate behavior with tokens such as poker chips, play money, gold stars, or the like. These tokens can later be exchanged for desired goods (candy, gum, cigarettes) and/or privileges (weekend passes, free time, participation in desirable activities). Sometimes, individuals are fined a certain number of tokens for undesirable behavior. Mental hospitals have successfully used token economies with chronic schizophrenics for decades to improve their self-care skills and social interactions (Ayllon & Azrin, 1965, 1968).

Other behavior therapies based on operant conditioning have been effective in modifying some behaviors of seriously disturbed people. Although these techniques do not cure schizophrenia, autism, or mental retardation, they can increase the frequency of desirable behaviors and decrease the frequency of undesirable behaviors. For example, a large proportion of people who suffer from schizophrenia smoke cigarettes. Among this group, monetary reinforcement has been found to be as effective as nicotine patches for the reduction of smoking (Tidey et al., 2002). Sometimes, modifying such behaviors enables the family members of people with schizophrenia to accept and care for them more easily.

Another effective method used to eliminate undesirable behavior, especially in children and adolescents, is **time out** (Kazdin & Benjet, 2003). Children are told in advance that if they engage in certain undesirable behaviors, they will be removed from the situation and will have to pass a period of time (usually no more than 15 minutes) in a place containing no reinforcers (no television, books, toys, friends, and so on). Theoretically, the undesirable behavior will stop if it is no longer followed by attention or any other positive reinforcers.

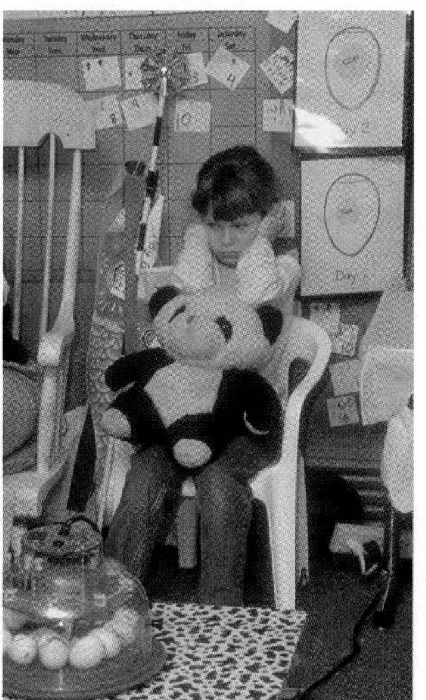

A time out is effective because it prevents a child from receiving reinforcers for undesirable behaviors. The child learns that once the behavior is under control, he or she will again have access to reinforcers. Similar behavioral techniques, such as token economies, are useful with adults in mental hospitals and other institutions.

token economy
A behavior modification technique that rewards appropriate behavior with tokens that can be exchanged later for desired goods and/or privileges.

time out
A behavior modification technique used to eliminate undesirable behavior, especially in children and adolescents, by withdrawing all reinforcers for a period of time.

Behavior modification techniques can also be used by people who want to break bad habits such as smoking and overeating or to develop good habits such as a regular exercise regime. If you want to modify any of your behaviors, devise a reward system for desirable behaviors, and remember the principles of shaping. Reward gradual changes in the direction of your ultimate goal. If you are trying to develop better eating habits, don't try to change a lifetime of bad habits all at once. Begin with a small step, such as substituting frozen yogurt for ice cream. Set realistic weekly goals that you are likely to be able to achieve.

Behavior Therapies Based on Classical Conditioning

What behavior therapies are based on classical conditioning?

Behavior therapies based on classical conditioning can be used to rid people of fears and other undesirable behaviors. These therapies include systematic desensitization, flooding, exposure and response prevention, and aversion therapy.

Systematic Desensitization One of the pioneers in the application of classical conditioning techniques to therapy, psychiatrist Joseph Wolpe (1958, 1973), reasoned that if he could get people to relax and stay relaxed while they thought about a feared object, person, place, or situation, they could conquer their fear. In Wolpe's therapy, known as **systematic desensitization**, clients are trained in deep muscle relaxation. Then, they confront a hierarchy of fears—a graduated series of anxiety-producing situations—either *in vivo* (in real life) or in their imagination, until they can remain relaxed even in the presence of the most feared situation. The technique can be used for everything from fear of animals to claustrophobia, social phobia, and other situational fears.

■ **systematic desensitization** A behavior therapy that is based on classical conditioning and used to treat fears by training clients in deep muscle relaxation and then having them confront a graduated series of anxiety-producing situations (real or imagined) until they can remain relaxed while confronting even the most feared situation.

Many experiments, demonstrations, and case reports confirm that systematic desensitization is a highly successful treatment for eliminating fears and phobias in a relatively short time (Kalish, 1981; Rachman & Wilson, 1980). It has proved effective for specific problems such as test anxiety, stage fright, and anxiety related to sexual disorders.

Flooding **Flooding**, a behavior therapy used in the treatment of phobias, was the type of therapy used to help Bill in this chapter's opening story. It involves exposing clients to the feared object or event (or asking them to imagine it vividly) for an extended period, until their anxiety decreases. The person is exposed to the fear all at once, not gradually as in systematic desensitization. An individual with a fear of heights, for example, might have to go onto the roof of a tall building and remain there until the fear subsided.

■ **flooding** A behavior therapy based on classical conditioning and used to treat phobias by exposing clients to the feared object or event (or asking them to imagine it vividly) for an extended period, until their anxiety decreases.

Flooding can be a useful treatment for phobias, such as fear of dogs.

Flooding sessions typically last from 30 minutes to 2 hours and should not be terminated until patients are markedly less afraid than they were at the beginning of the session. Additional sessions are required until the fear response is extinguished or reduced to an acceptable level. It is rare for a patient to need more than six treatment sessions (Marshall & Segal, 1988). *In vivo* flooding, the real-life experience, works faster and is more effective than simply imagining the feared object (Chambless & Goldstein, 1979; Marks, 1972). Thus, a person who fears flying would benefit more from taking an actual plane trip than from just thinking about one.

Exposure and Response Prevention **Exposure and response prevention** has been successful in treating obsessive-compulsive disorder (Baer, 1996; Foa, 1995; Rhéaume & Ladouceur, 2000). The first component of this technique involves *exposure*—exposing patients to objects or situations they have been avoiding because they trigger obsessions and compulsive rituals. The second component is *response prevention*, in which patients agree to resist performing their compulsive rituals for progressively longer periods of time.

Initially, the therapist identifies the thoughts, objects, or situations that trigger the compulsive ritual. For example, touching a doorknob, a piece of unwashed fruit, or a garbage bin might send people with a fear of contamination to the nearest bathroom to wash their hands. Patients are gradually exposed to stimuli that they find more and more distasteful and anxiety-provoking. They must agree not to perform the normal ritual (hand washing, bathing, or the like) for a specified period of time after each exposure. A typical treatment course—about 10 sessions over a period of 3 to 7 weeks—can bring about considerable improvement in 60–70% of patients (Jenike, 1990). And patients treated with exposure and response prevention are less likely to relapse after treatment than those treated with drugs alone (Greist, 1992). Exposure and response prevention has also proved useful in the treatment of posttraumatic stress disorder (Cloitre et al., 2002).

Aversion Therapy **Aversion therapy** is used to stop a harmful or socially undesirable behavior by pairing it with a painful, sickening, or otherwise aversive stimulus. Electric shock, emetics (which cause nausea and vomiting), or other unpleasant stimuli are paired with the undesirable behavior time after time until a strong negative association is formed and the person comes to avoid that behavior. Treatment continues until the bad behavior loses its appeal and becomes associated with pain or discomfort.

Alcoholics are sometimes given a nausea-producing substance such as Antibes, which reacts violently with alcohol and causes a person to retch and vomit until the stomach is empty. But for most problems, aversion therapy need not be so intense as to make a person physically ill. A controlled comparison of treatments for chronic nail biting revealed that mild aversion therapy—painting a bitter-tasting substance on the fingernails—yielded significant improvement (Allen, 1996).

Participant Modeling

How does participant modeling help people overcome their fears?

Therapies derived from Albert Bandura's work on observational learning are based on the belief that people can overcome fears and acquire social skills through modeling. The most effective type of therapy based on observational learning theory is called **participant modeling** (Bandura, 1977a; Bandura et al., 1975, 1977). In this therapy, not only does the model demonstrate the appropriate response in graduated steps, but the client attempts to imitate the model step by step, while the therapist gives encouragement and support. Most specific phobias can be extinguished in only 3 or 4 hours of client participation in modeling therapy. For instance, participant modeling could be used to help someone overcome a fear of dogs. A session would begin with the client watching others petting and playing with a dog. As the client becomes more comfortable, he or she would be encouraged to join in. Alternatively, a client would be shown a video of people playing with a dog and then would be encouraged to play with a live dog.

exposure and response prevention
A behavior therapy that exposes patients with obsessive-compulsive disorder to stimuli that trigger obsessions and compulsive rituals, while patients resist performing the compulsive rituals for progressively longer periods of time.

aversion therapy
A behavior therapy in which an aversive stimulus is paired with a harmful or socially undesirable behavior until the behavior becomes associated with pain or discomfort.

participant modeling
A behavior therapy in which an appropriate response to a feared stimulus is modeled in graduated steps and the client attempts to imitate the model step by step, encouraged and supported by the therapist.

Remember It 16.3

1. Behavior therapies based on __________ conditioning are used to change behavior by reinforcing desirable behavior and removing reinforcers for undesirable behavior.
2. Behavior therapies based on __________ conditioning are sometimes used to rid people of fears and undesirable behaviors or habits.
3. Exposure and response prevention is a treatment for people with __________ disorder.
4. Match each therapy with the appropriate description.

____ (1) flooding	a. practicing deep muscle relaxation during gradual exposure to feared object
____ (2) aversion therapy	b. associating a painful or sickening stimuli with undesirable behavior
____ (3) systematic desensitization	c. being exposed directly to a feared object until the fear response is reduced or eliminated
____ (4) participant modeling	d. imitating a model who is responding appropriately in a feared situation

ANSWERS: 1. operant; 2. classical; 3. obsessive-compulsive; 4. (1) c, (2) b, (3) a, (4) d

Cognitive Therapies

Remember from earlier chapters that behavioral theories have often been criticized for ignoring internal variables such as thinking and emotion. As you might predict, behavior therapies are often criticized for the same reason. Cognitive psychologists argue that behaviors cannot be changed in isolation from the thoughts that produce them. Accordingly, they have developed cognitively based therapeutic approaches.

Cognitive therapies, based on the cognitive perspective, assume that maladaptive behavior can result from irrational thoughts, beliefs, and ideas, which the therapist tries to change. Cognitive therapies are also often referred to as *cognitive-behavioral approaches* because they combine the insights into behavior provided by cognitive psychology with the methodological approaches of behaviorism (Carson et al., 2000). That is, cognitive therapists seek to change the way clients think (cognitive), and they determine the effectiveness of their interventions by assessing changes in clients' behavior (behavioral).

cognitive therapies Therapies that assume maladaptive behavior can result from irrational thoughts, beliefs, and ideas.

Rational-Emotive Therapy

What is the aim of rational-emotive therapy?

Clinical psychologist Albert Ellis (1961, 1977, 1993) developed **rational-emotive therapy** in the 1950s. This type of therapy is based on Ellis's *ABC theory.* The A refers to the activating event, the B to the person's belief about the event, and the C to the emotional consequence that follows. Ellis claims that it is not the event itself that causes the emotional consequence, but rather the person's belief about the event. In other words, A does not cause C; B causes C. If the belief is irrational, then the emotional consequence can be extreme distress, as illustrated in Figure 16.1.

rational-emotive therapy A directive form of psychotherapy, developed by Albert Ellis and designed to challenge clients' irrational beliefs about themselves and others.

Rational-emotive therapy is a directive form of psychotherapy designed to challenge clients' irrational beliefs about themselves and others. Most clients in rational-emotive therapy see a therapist individually, once a week, for 5 to 50 sessions. In Ellis's view, clients do not benefit from warm, supportive therapeutic approaches that help them feel better but do not address the irrational thoughts that underlie their problems.

FIGURE 16.1 The ABCs of Rational-Emotive Therapy

Rational-emotive therapy teaches clients that it is not the activating event (A) that causes the upsetting consequences (C). Rather, it is the client's beliefs (B) about the activating event. According to Albert Ellis, irrational beliefs cause emotional distress. Rational-emotive therapists help clients identify their irrational beliefs and replace them with rational ones.

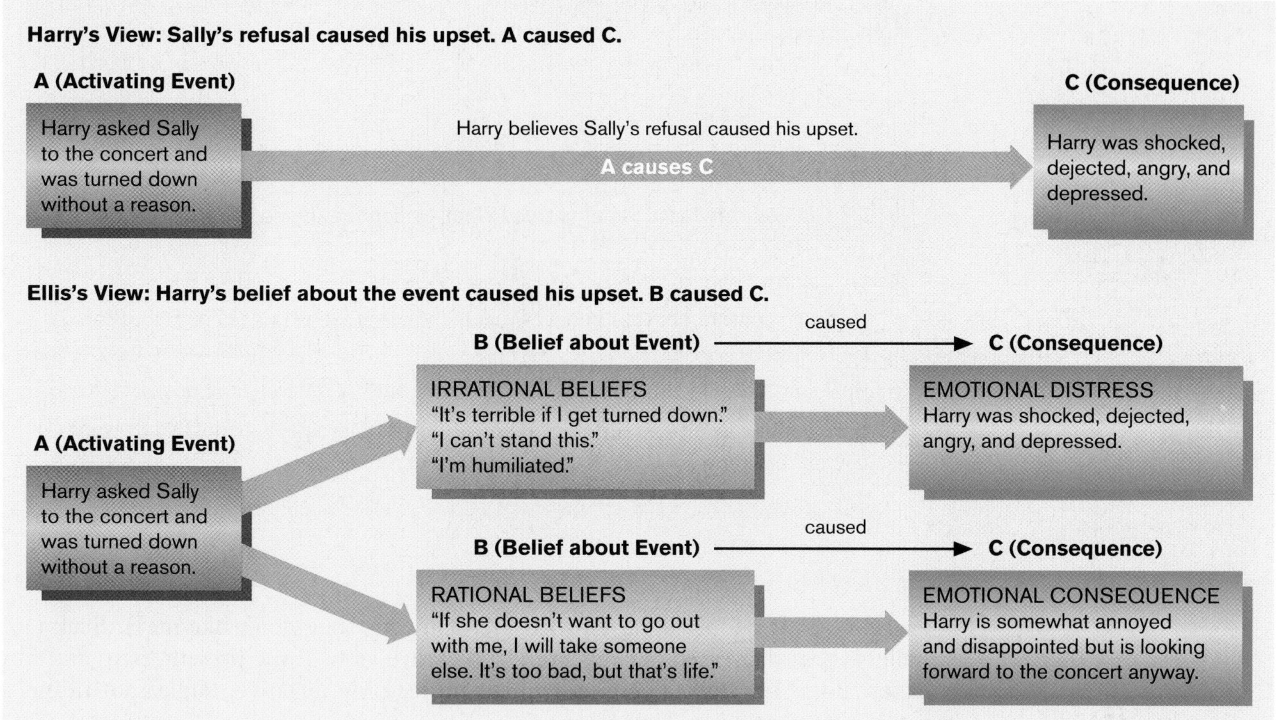

Instead, he argues that as clients begin to replace irrational beliefs with rational ones, their emotional reactions become more appropriate, less distressing, and more likely to lead to constructive behavior. For example, a client might tell a therapist that he is feeling anxious and depressed because of his supervisor's unreasonable demands. Using Ellis's rational-emotive therapeutic model, the therapist would help the client distinguish between the supervisor's demands and the client's emotional reactions to them. The goal would be to help the client understand that his reactions to his supervisor's demands are the source of his anxiety and depression, not the demands themselves. Ultimately, the rational-emotive therapist would lead the client to the conclusion that while he may not be able to control his supervisor's demands, he is capable of controlling his emotional reactions to them. Once the client changes his thinking about the problem, the rational-emotive therapist helps him learn behavioral strategies, such as relaxation techniques, that can help him control his emotional reactions.

One meta-analysis of 28 studies showed that individuals receiving rational-emotive therapy did better than those receiving no treatment or a placebo, and about the same as those receiving systematic desensitization (Engels et al., 1993). Take a moment to apply Ellis's ideas to your own irrational thoughts in *Try It 16.1* (on page 546).

How does Beck's cognitive therapy help people overcome depression and panic disorder?

Beck's Cognitive Therapy

Psychiatrist Aaron T. Beck (1976) claims that much of the misery endured by a depressed and anxious person can be traced to *automatic thoughts*—unreasonable but unquestioned ideas that rule the person's life ("To be happy, I must be liked by

Try It 16.1 Dealing with Irrational Beliefs

Use what you have learned about Albert Ellis's rational-emotive therapy to identify—and perhaps even eliminate—an irrational belief that you hold about yourself.

First, identify an irrational belief, preferably one that causes some stress in your life. For example, maybe you feel that you must earn all A's in order to think of yourself as a good person.

Ask yourself the following questions, and write down your answers in as much detail as possible.

- Where does this belief come from? Can you identify the time in your life when it began?
- Why do you think this belief is true? What evidence can you think of that "proves" your belief?
- Can you think of any evidence to suggest that this belief is false? What evidence contradicts your belief? Do you know anyone who does not cling to this belief?
- How does holding this belief affect your life, both negatively and positively?
- How would your life be different if you stopped holding this belief? What would you do differently?

everyone"; "If people disagree with me, it means they don't like me"). Beck (1991) believes that depressed persons hold "a negative view of the present, past, and future experiences" (p. 369). These individuals notice only negative, unpleasant things and jump to upsetting conclusions.

The goal of Beck's **cognitive therapy** is to help clients stop their negative thoughts as they occur and replace them with more objective thoughts. After identifying and challenging client's irrational thoughts, the therapist sets up a plan and guides the client so that her or his personal experience can provide actual evidence in the real world to refute the false beliefs. Clients are given homework assignments, such as keeping track of automatic thoughts and the feelings evoked by them and then substituting more rational thoughts.

Cognitive therapy is brief, usually lasting only 10 to 20 sessions (Beck, 1976). This therapy has been researched extensively and is reported to be highly successful in the treatment of mild to moderately depressed individuals (Holloa et al., 2002; Thase et al., 1991). There is some evidence that depressed people who have received cognitive therapy are less likely to relapse than those who have been treated with antidepressant drugs (Evans et al., 1992; Scott, 1996).

Cognitive therapy has also been shown to be effective for treating panic disorder (Barlow, 1997; Power et al., 2000). By teaching clients to change the catastrophic interpretations of their symptoms, cognitive therapy helps prevent the symptoms from escalating into panic. Studies have shown that after 3 months of cognitive therapy, about 90% of individuals with panic disorder are panic-free (Robins & Hayes, 1993). Not only does cognitive therapy have a low dropout rate and a low relapse rate, but clients often continue to improve even after treatment is completed (Öst & Westling, 1995). And cognitive therapy has proved effective for generalized anxiety disorder (Beck, 1993; Wetherell et al., 2003), OCD (Abramowitz, 1997), cocaine addiction (Carroll et al., 1994), insomnia (Quesnel et al., 2003), and bulimia (Agras et al., 2000). Some research even indicates that cognitive therapy is effective in treating both negative and positive symptoms of schizophrenia (Bach & Hayes, 2002; Lecomte & Lecomte, 2002; Sensky et al., 2000).

■ cognitive therapy
A therapy designed by Aaron Beck to help patients stop their negative thoughts as they occur and replace them with more objective thoughts.

Remember It 16.4

1. Cognitive therapists believe that, for the most part, maladaptive behavior results from __________ beliefs and ideas.
2. __________ therapists challenge clients' beliefs.
3. The goal of cognitive therapy is to help clients replace __________ thoughts with more __________ thoughts.
4. Cognitive therapy has proved very successful in the treatment of __________ and __________.

ANSWERS: 1. irrational; 2. Rational-emotive; 3. negative, objective; 4. panic disorder, depression

Biological Therapies

Do you know someone who takes or has taken a drug prescribed by a physician or psychiatrist as a means of overcoming a psychological problem? Chances are good that you do, because millions of people the world over are now taking various medications for just such reasons. Treatment with drugs is a cornerstone of the biological approach to therapy. Predictably, professionals who favor the biological perspective—the view that psychological disorders are symptoms of underlying physical problems—usually favor a **biological therapy**. The three main biological therapies are drug therapy, electroconvulsive therapy (ECT), and psychosurgery.

■ **biological therapy** A therapy (drug therapy, electroconvulsive therapy, or psychosurgery) that is based on the assumption that psychological disorders are symptoms of underlying physical problems.

What are the advantages and disadvantages of using drugs to treat psychological disorders?

Drug Therapy

The most frequently used biological treatment is drug therapy. Breakthroughs in drug therapy, coupled with the federal government's effort to reduce involuntary hospitalization of mental patients, lowered the mental hospital patient population in the United States from about 560,000 in 1955, when the drugs were introduced, to about 100,000 by 1990 (see Figure 16.2); this figure continued to

FIGURE 16.2 Decrease in Patient Populations in State and County Mental Hospitals (1950–2000)

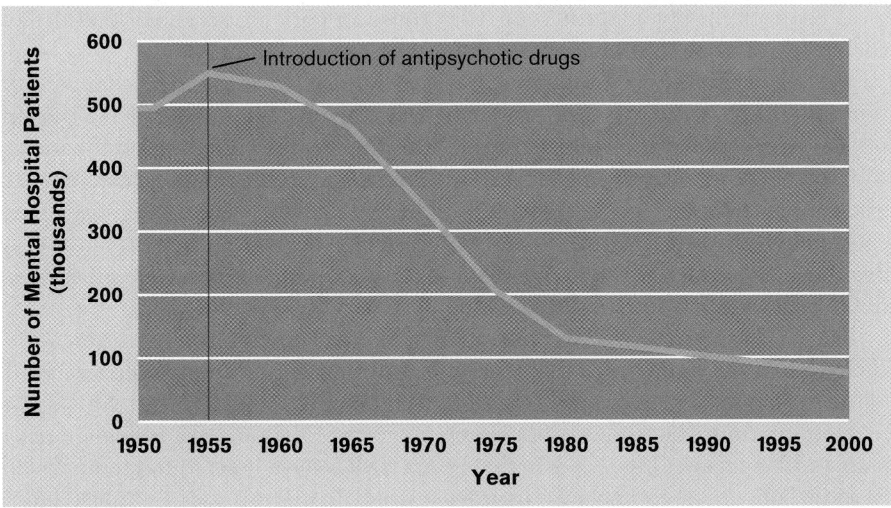

State and county mental hospital patient populations peaked at approximately 560,000 in 1955, the same year that antipsychotic drugs were introduced. These drugs, coupled with the federal government's efforts to reduce involuntary hospitalization of mental patients, resulted in a dramatic decrease in the patient population to fewer than 100,000 in 2000.
Source: Data from Mandersheid & Henderson (2001).

drop throughout the 1990s. Furthermore, the average stay of patients who do require hospitalization is now usually a matter of days.

Antipsychotics **Antipsychotic drugs** known as *neuroleptics* are prescribed primarily for schizophrenia. You may have heard of these drugs by their brand names—Thorazine, Stelazine, Compazine, and Mellaril. Their purpose is to control hallucinations, delusions, disorganized speech, and disorganized behavior (Andreasen et al., 1995). The neuroleptics work primarily by inhibiting the activity of the neurotransmitter dopamine. About 50% of patients have a good response to the standard antipsychotics (Kane, 1996). But many patients, particularly those with an early onset of schizophrenia, are not helped by them (Meltzer et al., 1997), and others show only slight or modest improvement in symptoms. The long-term use of typical antipsychotic drugs carries a high risk of a severe side effect, *tardive dyskinesia*—almost continual twitching and jerking movements of the face and tongue, and squirming movements of the hands and trunk (Glazer et al., 1993).

Newer antipsychotic drugs called *atypical neuroleptics* (clozapine, risperidone, olanzipine) can treat not only the positive symptoms of schizophrenia but the negative symptoms as well, leading to marked improvement in patients' quality of life (Worrel et al., 2000). Atypical neuroleptics target both dopamine and seratonin receptors (Kawanishi et al., 2000). About 10% of patients who take clozapine find the results so dramatic that they almost feel as though they have been reborn. Clozapine produces fewer side effects than standard neuroleptics, and patients taking it are less likely to develop tardive dyskinesia (Casey, 1996). It may also be more effective at suicide prevention than other antipsychotic drugs (Meltzer et al., 2003). However, clozapine is extremely expensive, and without careful monitoring, it can cause a fatal blood defect in 1–2% of patients who take it. Risperidone appears to be effective and safe and also has fewer side effects than standard neuroleptics (Marder, 1996a; Tamminga, 1996). Another advantage of risperidone is that it is much more effective than other neuroleptics in treating the negative symptoms of schizophrenia (Marder, 1996a).

Antidepressants **Antidepressant drugs** act as mood elevators for people who are severely depressed (Elkin et al., 1995) and are also helpful in the treatment of certain anxiety disorders. About 65–75% of patients who take antidepressants find themselves significantly improved, and 40–50% of those are essentially completely recovered (Frazer, 1997). It is important to note, though, that most antidepressant research involves severely depressed patients—those who are most likely to show a significant change after treatment (Zimmerman et al., 2002). Thus, these studies may not apply to mildly depressed individuals. Moreover, research has shown that participants respond almost as frequently to placebo treatments as to real drugs (Walsh et al., 2002). In fact, EEG studies of patients who receive placebos have documented neurological changes that, while different from those in patients receiving real drugs, are associated with improvements in mood (Leuchter et al., 2002)

The first-generation antidepressants are known as the *tricyclics* (amitriptyline, imipramine) (Nutt, 2000). The tricyclics work against depression by blocking the reuptake of norepinephrine and serotonin into the axon terminals, thus enhancing the action of these neurotransmitters in the synapses. But tricyclics can have some unpleasant side effects, including sedation, dizziness, nervousness, fatigue, dry mouth, forgetfulness, and weight gain (Frazer, 1997). Progressive weight gain (an average of more than 20 pounds) is the main reason people stop taking tricyclics, in spite of the relief these drugs provide from distressing psychological symptoms.

The second-generation antidepressants, the *selective serotonin reuptake inhibitors (SSRIs)*, block the reuptake of the neurotransmitter serotonin, increasing its availability at the synapses in the brain (Nutt, 2000; Vetulani & Nalepa, 2000). SSRIs (fluoxetine, clomipramine) have fewer side effects (Nelson, 1997) and are safer than tricyclics if an overdose occurs (Thase & Kupfer, 1996). SSRIs have been found to be promising in treating obsessive-compulsive disorder (Goodwin, 1996), social phobia (Jefferson,

■ **antipsychotic drugs**
Drugs used to control severe psychotic symptoms, such as delusions, hallucinations, disorganized speech, and disorganized behavior, by inhibiting dopamine activity; also known as neuroleptics.

■ **antidepressant drugs**
Drugs that act as mood elevators for severely depressed people and are also prescribed to treat some anxiety disorders.

1995), panic disorder (Coplan et al., 1997; Jefferson, 1997), and binge eating (Hudson et al., 1996). However, SSRIs can cause sexual dysfunction, although normal sexual functioning returns when the drug is discontinued. Reports indicating that SSRIs, especially fluoxetine (Prozac), increase the risk of suicide have not been substantiated (Warshaw & Keller, 1996).

Another line of treatment for depression is the use of *monoamine oxidase (MAO) inhibitors* (sold under the names Marplan, Nardil, and Parnate). By blocking the action of an enzyme that breaks down norepinephrine and serotonin in the synapses, MAO inhibitors increase the availability of these neurotransmitters. MAO inhibitors are usually prescribed for depressed patients who do not respond to other antidepressants (Thase et al., 1992). They are also effective in treating panic disorder (Sheehan & Raj, 1988) and social phobia (Marshall et al., 1994). But MAO inhibitors have many of the same unpleasant side effects as tricyclic antidepressants, and patients taking MAO inhibitors must avoid certain foods or run the risk of stroke.

Lithium and Anticonvulsant Drugs **Lithium**, a naturally occurring salt, is considered a wonder drug for 40–50% of patients suffering from bipolar disorder (Thase & Kupfer, 1996). It is said to begin to quiet the manic state within 5 to 10 days. This is an amazing accomplishment, because the average episode, if untreated, lasts about 3 to 4 months. A proper maintenance dose of lithium reduces depressive episodes as well as manic ones. Published reports over a period of three decades show that the clinical effectiveness of lithium for treating depression and bipolar disorder is unmatched (Ross et al., 2000). But 40–60% of those who take a maintenance dose will experience a recurrence (Thase & Kupfer, 1996). Also, monitoring of the level of lithium in the patient's blood every 2 to 6 months is necessary to guard against lithium poisoning and permanent damage to the nervous system (Schou, 1997).

Recent research suggests that *anticonvulsant drugs*, such as Depakote (divalproex), may be just as effective for managing bipolar symptoms as lithium, with fewer side effects (Kowatch et al., 2000). Moreover, many bipolar patients, especially those whose manic states include symptoms of psychosis, benefit from taking antipsychotic drugs along with the anticonvulsants (Bowden et al., 2000; Sachs et al., 2002). Furthermore, a growing body of research suggests that long-term treatment with antispsychotic drugs may prevent recurrences of mania (Vieta, 2003).

Tranquilizers The family of minor tranquilizers called *benzodiazepines* includes, among others, the well-known drugs sold as Valium and Librium and the newer high-potency drug Xanax (pronounced "ZAN-ax"). Used primarily to treat anxiety, benzodiazepines are prescribed more often than any other class of psychoactive drugs (Medina et al., 1993). They have been found to be an effective in treating panic disorder (Davidson, 1997; Noyes et al., 1996) and generalized anxiety disorder (Lydiard et al., 1996).

Xanax, the largest selling psychiatric drug (Famighetti, 1997), appears to be particularly effective in relieving anxiety and depression. When used to treat panic disorder (Noyes et al., 1996), Xanax works faster and has fewer side effects than antidepressants (Ballenger et al., 1993; Jonas & Cohon, 1993). However, if patients discontinue treatment, relapse is likely (Rickels, Schweizer et al., 1993). There is a downside to Xanax. Many patients, once they no longer experience panic attacks, find themselves unable to discontinue the drug because they experience moderate to intense withdrawal symptoms, including intense anxiety (Otto et al., 1993). Valium seems to be just as effective as Xanax for treating panic disorder, and withdrawal is easier. Although withdrawal is a problem with benzodiazepines, the abuse and addiction potential of these drugs is fairly low (Romach et al., 1995).

Disadvantages of Drug Therapy Beyond the drugs' unpleasant or dangerous side effects, another disadvantage in using drug therapy is the difficulty in establishing the proper dosages. Also, it's important to note that drugs do not cure psychological disorders,

■ **lithium**
A drug used to treat bipolar disorder, which at proper maintenance dosage reduces both manic and depressive episodes.

so patients usually experience a relapse if they stop taking the drugs when their symptoms lift. Maintenance doses of antidepressants following a major depressive episode reduce the probability of recurrence (Prien & Kocsis, 1995). Maintenance doses are usually required with anxiety disorders as well, or symptoms are likely to return (Rasmussen et al., 1993). Further, some studies suggest that the trend away from involuntary hospitalization brought about by the availability of antipsychotic and other psychiatric drugs has led to an increase in homelessness among people who suffer from chronic mental illnesses such as schizophrenia (Carson et al., 2000). Unfortunately, after being discharged from mental hospitals because they have shown favorable responses to antipsychotic drugs, many schizophrenic patients do not get adequate follow-up care. As a result, some stop taking their medications, relapse into psychotic states, and are unable to support themselves.

Electroconvulsive Therapy

What is electroconvulsive therapy (ECT) used for?

electroconvulsive therapy (ECT) A biological therapy in which an electric current is passed through the right hemisphere of the brain; usually reserved for severely depressed patients who are suicidal.

Antidepressant drugs are relatively slow-acting. A severely depressed patient needs at least 2 to 6 weeks to obtain relief, and 30% of these patients don't respond at all. This situation can be too risky for suicidal patients. **Electroconvulsive therapy (ECT)** is sometimes used with such patients. ECT has a bad reputation because it was misused and overused in the 1940s and 1950s. Nevertheless, when used appropriately, ECT is a highly effective treatment for major depression (Folkerts, 2000; Little et al., 2002). And depressed patients who are 75 and older tolerate the procedure as well as younger patients do and reap comparable therapeutic benefits (Tew et al., 1999).

For many years, ECT was performed by passing an electric current through both cerebral hemispheres, a procedure known as *bilateral ECT*. Today, electric current is administered to the right hemisphere only, and the procedure is called *unilateral ECT*. Research suggests that unilateral ECT is as effective as the more intense bilateral form while producing milder cognitive effects (Sackeim et al., 2000). Also, a patient undergoing ECT today is given anesthesia, controlled oxygenation, and a muscle relaxant.

Experts think that ECT changes the biochemical balance in the brain, resulting in a lifting of depression. When ECT is effective, cerebral blood flow in the prefrontal cortex is reduced, and delta waves (usually associated with slow-wave sleep) appear (Sackeim et al., 1996). Some psychiatrists and neurologists have spoken out against the use of ECT, claiming that it causes pervasive brain damage and memory loss. But advocates of ECT say that claims of brain damage are based on animal studies in which dosages of ECT were much higher than those now used in human patients. No structural brain damage from ECT has been revealed by studies comparing MRI or CT scans before and after a series of treatments (Devanand et al., 1994).

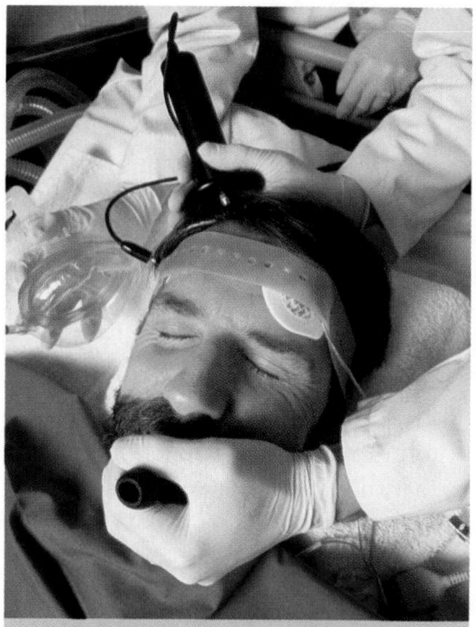

In electroconvulsive therapy, a mild electric current is passed through the right hemisphere of the brain for 1 to 2 seconds, causing a brief seizure.

Toward the end of the 20th century, a new brain-stimulation therapy known as *rapid transcranial magnetic stimulation (rTMS)* was developed. This magnetic therapy is not invasive in any way. Performed on patients who are not sedated, it causes no seizures, no memory loss, and has no known side effects. Its therapeutic value is similar to that of ECT, and it is much more acceptable to the public (Vetulani & Nalepa, 2000). This therapy has been used effectively in conjunction with SSRIs in treating depressed patients (Conca et al., 2000).

Psychosurgery

What is psychosurgery, and for what problems is it used?

An even more drastic procedure than ECT is **psychosurgery**—brain surgery performed to alleviate serious psychological disorders, such as severe depression, severe anxiety, or obsessions, or to provide relief from unbearable chronic pain. The first experimental brain surgery for human patients, the *lobotomy*, was developed by Portuguese neurologist Egas Moniz in 1935 to treat severe phobias, anxiety, and obsessions. Surgeons performing a lobotomy would sever the neural connections between the frontal lobes and the deeper brain centers involved in emotion. But no brain tissue was removed. At first, the procedure was considered a tremendous contribution, and Moniz won for the Nobel Prize in medicine in 1949. Eventually, however, it became apparent that this treatment left patients in a severely deteriorated condition.

Modern psychosurgery procedures result in less intellectual impairment because, rather than using conventional surgery, surgeons deliver electric currents through electrodes to destroy a much smaller, more localized area of brain tissue. In one procedure, called a *cingulotomy*, electrodes are used to destroy the *cingulum*, a small bundle of nerves connecting the cortex to the emotional centers of the brain. Several procedures, including cingulotomy, have been helpful for some extreme cases of obsessive-compulsive disorder (Baer et al., 1995; Trivedi, 1996). But the results of psychosurgery are still not predictable, and the consequences—whether positive or negative—are irreversible. For these reasons, the treatment is considered experimental and absolutely a last resort.

■ **psychosurgery**
Brain surgery performed to alleviate serious psychological disorders or unbearable chronic pain.

Remember It 16.5

1. For the most part, advocates of biological therapies assume that psychological disorders have __________ causes.
2. Match each disorder with the type of drug most often used for its treatment.

____ (1) panic disorder	a. lithium
____ (2) schizophrenia	b. antipsychotic drug
____ (3) bipolar disorder	c. antidepressant drug
____ (4) major depression	
____ (5) obsessive-compulsive disorder	

3. Medication that relieves the symptoms of schizophrenia is thought to work by blocking the action of __________.
4. The disorder for which ECT is typically used is __________.
5. Psychosurgery may be helpful in the treatment of extreme cases of __________ disorder.

ANSWERS: 1. physical; 2. (1) c, (2) b, (3) a, (4) c, (5) c; 3. dopamine; 4. severe depression; 5. obsessive-compulsive

Evaluating the Therapies

What therapy, if any, is most effective in treating psychological disorders?

How effective are the various therapies summarized in *Review and Reflect 16.1* (on page 552)? Research results are mixed. In a classic study of therapeutic effectiveness, Smith and his colleagues (1980) analyzed the results of 475 studies, which involved 25,000 patients. Their findings revealed that psychotherapy

REVIEW *and* REFLECT 16.1

Summary and Comparison of the Therapies

TYPE OF THERAPY	PERCEIVED CAUSE OF DISORDER	GOALS OF THERAPY	METHODS USED	PRIMARY DISORDERS OR SYMPTOMS TREATED
Psychoanalysis	Unconscious sexual and aggressive urges or conflicts; fixations; weak ego	Help patient bring disturbing, repressed material to consciousness and work through unconscious conflicts; strengthen ego functions	Psychoanalyst analyzes and interprets dreams, free associations, resistance, and transference.	General feelings of unhappiness; unresolved problems from childhood
Person-centered therapy	Blocking of normal tendency toward self-actualization; incongruence between real and desired self; overdependence on positive regard of others	Increase self-acceptance and self-understanding; help patient become more inner-directed; increase congruence between real and desired self; enhance personal growth	Therapist shows empathy, unconditional positive regard, and genuineness, and reflects client's expressed feelings back to client.	General feelings of unhappiness; interpersonal problems
Interpersonal therapy	Difficulty with relationships and/or life transitions, as well as possible biological causes	Adjust to bereavement; overcome interpersonal role disputes; improve interpersonal skills; adjust to role transitions such as divorce, career change, and retirement	Therapist helps patient (1) release the past, (2) understand others' points of view and explore options for change, (3) view change as a challenge rather than a threat, and/or (4) improve interpersonal skills, using techniques such as role-playing.	Depression
Family therapy and couples therapy	Problems caused by faulty communication patterns, unreasonable role expectations, drug and/or alcohol abuse, and so on	Create more understanding and harmony within the relationships; improve communication patterns; heal wounds of family unit	Therapist sees clients individually or several family members at a time and explores such things as communication patterns, power struggles, and unreasonable demands and expectations.	Family problems such as marriage or relationship problems, troubled or troublesome teenagers, abusive relationships, drug or alcohol problems, schizophrenic family member
Behavior therapy	Learning of maladaptive behaviors or failure to learn appropriate behaviors	Extinguish maladaptive behaviors and replace with more adaptive ones; help patient acquire needed social skills	Therapist uses methods based on classical and operant conditioning and modeling, which include systematic desensitization, flooding, exposure and response prevention, and aversion therapy.	Fears, phobias, panic disorder, obsessive-compulsive disorder, bad habits
Cognitive therapy	Irrational and negative assumptions and ideas about self and others	Change faulty, irrational, and/or negative thinking	Therapist helps client identify irrational and negative thinking and substitute rational thinking.	Depression, anxiety, panic disorder, general feelings of unhappiness
Biological therapies	Underlying physical disorder caused by structural or biochemical abnormality in the brain; genetic inheritance	Eliminate or control biological cause of abnormal behavior; restore balance of neurotransmitters	Physician prescribes drugs such as antipsychotics, antidepressants, lithium, or tranquilizers; uses ECT or psychosurgery.	Schizophrenia, depression, bipolar disorder, anxiety disorders

Want to be sure you've fully absorbed the material in this chapter? Visit **www.ablongman.com/wood5e** for access to free practice tests, flashcards, interactive activities, and links developed specifically to help you succeed in psychology.

was better than no treatment, but that no one type of psychotherapy was more effective than another. A subsequent reanalysis of the same data by Hans Eysenck (1994), however, showed a slight advantage for behavior therapies over other types. A study by Holloa and others (2002) found that cognitive and interpersonal therapies had an advantage over psychodynamic approaches for depressed patients.

But how do the patients themselves rate the therapies? To answer this question, *Consumer Reports* (1995) conducted the largest survey to date on patient attitudes toward psychotherapy. Martin Seligman (1995, 1996), a consultant for the study, summarized its findings:

- Overall, patients believed that they benefited substantially from psychotherapy.
- Patients seemed equally satisfied with their therapy, whether it was provided by a psychologist, a psychiatrist, or a social worker.
- Patients who were in therapy for more than 6 months did considerably better than the rest; generally, the longer patients stayed in therapy, the more they improved.
- Patients who took a drug such as Prozac or Xanax believed it helped them, but overall, psychotherapy alone seemed to work about as well as psychotherapy plus drugs.

Choosing a therapist with the type of training best suited to your problem can be crucial to how helpful the therapy turns out to be. Table 16.1 lists the various types of mental health professionals. One important difference among professionals, about which many people are confused, is that a **psychologist** has an advanced degree, usually at the doctoral level, in psychology, while a **psychiatrist** is a medical doctor. Historically,

■ **psychologist**
A mental health professional who possesses a doctoral degree in psychology.

■ **psychiatrist**
A mental health professional who is a medical doctor.

TABLE 16.1 Mental Health Professionals

PROFESSIONAL TITLE	TRAINING	SERVICES PROVIDED
Psychiatrist	Medical degree (M.D. or O.D.); residency in psychiatry	Psychotherapy; drug therapy; hospitalization for serious psychological disorders
Psychoanalyst	M.D., Ph.D., or Psy.D.; additional training in psychoanalysis	Psychodynamic therapy
Clinical psychologist	Ph.D. or Psy.D.; internship in clinical psychology	Diagnosis and treatment of psychological disorders; can prescribe drugs in some settings after additional training; psychological testing
Counseling psychologist	Ph.D. or Ed.D.; internship in counseling psychology	Assessment and therapy for normal problems of life (e.g., divorce); psychological testing
School psychologist	Ph.D., Ed.D., or master's degree; internship in school psychology	Assessment and treatment of school problems in children and adolescents; psychological testing
Clinical or psychiatric social worker (M.S.W.)	Master's degree; internship in psychiatric social work	Diagnosis and treatment of psychological disorders; identification of supportive community services
Licensed professional counselor (L.P.C.)	Master's degree; internship in counseling	Assessment and therapy for normal problems of life; some psychological testing
Licensed marriage and family therapist (L.M.F.T.)	Master's degree; internship in couples therapy and family therapy	Assessment and therapy for relationship problems
Licensed chemical dependency counselor (L.C.D.C.)	Educational requirements vary from one state to another; often former addicts themselves	Treatment and education for substance abuse problems

drug therapy has been available only from psychiatrists. At present, however, there is a movement that is gaining momentum in the United States to allow psychologists with special training in psychopharmacology to prescribe drugs. Only the U.S. military and a couple of states have authorized prescribing privileges for psychologists so far.

Regardless of training or theoretical orientation, all therapists are bound by ethical standards established by professional organizations and, in most cases, codified in state laws. Each profession (e.g., psychologists, social workers) has its own ethical standards, but certain features are common to all of them and are exemplified by the ethics code of the American Psychological Association (2002). One important standard is the requirement for *informed consent*. Therapists must inform clients of the cost and expected duration of therapy prior to beginning any intervention. Moreover, clients must be informed of the legal limits of confidentiality. For example, if a client reveals that she or he has committed a crime, in most cases the therapist is obligated to report the confession to the appropriate authorities. In addition, some insurance companies require that therapists' notes be available for review without regard to clients' confidentiality.

The nature of the therapeutic relationship is also governed by ethical standards. Therapists are forbidden to engage in any kind of intimate relationship with a client or with anyone close to the client. They are also prohibited from providing therapeutic services to former intimate partners. When ending a therapeutic relationship, a therapist must counsel a client about the reason for terminating therapy and provide him or her with alternatives.

With regard to testing, therapists are ethically obligated to use tests that are reliable and valid. Moreover, they must have appropriate training for administering, scoring, and evaluating each test they use. They are also required to explain the purpose of testing to clients and to provide them with test results in a timely and confidential manner.

Remember It 16.6

1. Match each problem or disorder with the most appropriate therapy.

____ (1) debilitating fears

____ (2) schizophrenia

____ (3) general unhappiness, interpersonal problems

____ (4) severe depression

a. behavior therapy

b. insight therapy

c. drug therapy

2. The main difference between a psychologist and a psychiatrist is that the latter has a ____________ degree.

ANSWERS: 1. (1) a, (2) c, (3) b, (4) c; 2. medical

Culturally Sensitive and Gender-Sensitive Therapy

What characterizes culturally sensitive and gender-sensitive therapy?

Think for a moment about the role played by culture and gender in our social relationships. Do you think it's possible that these variables could affect relationships between therapists and their clients?

Among most psychotherapists, there is a growing awareness of the need to consider cultural variables in diagnosing and treating psychological disorders (Bernal & Castro, 1994). In fact, the American Psychological Association recently published guidelines to help psychologists be more sensitive to cultural issues (APA, 2003). Similarly, many psychologists have expressed concern about the need for awareness of gender differences when practicing psychotherapy (Addis & Mahalik, 2003; Gehart & Lyle, 2001).

culturally sensitive therapy
An approach to therapy in which knowledge of clients' cultural backgrounds guides the choice of therapeutic interventions.

Culturally Sensitive Therapy

According to Kleinman and Cohen (1997), people experience and suffer from psychological disorders within a cultural context that may dramatically affect the meaning of symptoms, outcomes, and responses to therapy. And cultural differences between therapist and client may undermine the *therapeutic alliance*, the bond between therapist and client that is known to be a factor in the effectiveness of psychotherapy (Blatt et al., 1996). Thus, many experts advocate an approach called **culturally sensitive psychotherapy** in which knowledge of clients' cultural backgrounds guides the choice of therapeutic interventions (Kumpfer et al., 2002).

Culturally sensitive therapists recognize that language differences between therapists and patients can pose problems (Santiago-Rivera & Altarriba, 2002). For example, a patient who speaks both Spanish and English but is more fluent in Spanish may exhibit hesitations, back-tracking, and delayed responses to questions when being interviewed in English. As a result, the therapist may erroneously conclude that this patient is suffering from the kind of disordered thinking that is often displayed by people with schizophrenia (Martinez, 1986). Such language differences may also affect patients' results on standardized tests used by clinicians. In one frequently cited study, researchers found that when a group of Puerto Rican patients took the Thematic Apperception Test (TAT) in English, their pauses and their choices of words were incorrectly interpreted as indications of psychological problems (Suarez, 1983). Thus, culturally sensitive therapists become familiar with patients' general fluency in the language in which they will be assessed prior to interviewing and testing them.

When working with recent immigrants to the United States, culturally sensitive therapists take into account the impact of the immigration experience on patients' thoughts and emotions (Lijtmaer, 2001; Smolar, 1999). Some researchers who have studied the responses of recent Asian immigrants to psychotherapy recommend that, prior to initiating diagnosis and treatment, therapists encourage patients who are immigrants to talk about the feelings of sadness they have experienced as a result of leaving their native culture, as well as their anxieties about adapting to life in a new society. Using this strategy, therapists may be able to separate depression and anxiety related to the immigration experience from true psychopathology.

Some advocates of culturally sensitive therapy point out that sometimes cultural practices can be used as models for therapeutic interventions. Traditional Native American *healing circles*, for example, are being used by many mental health practitioners who serve Native Americans (Garrett et al., 2001). Members of a healing circle are committed to promoting the physical, mental, emotional, and spiritual well-being of one another. Healing circle participants typically engage in member-led activities such as discussion, meditation, and prayer. However, some more structured healing circles include a recognized Native American healer who leads the group in traditional healing ceremonies.

When therapist and client have the same racial or ethnic background, they are more likely to share cultural values and communication styles, which can facilitate the therapeutic process.

Culturally sensitive therapists also attempt to address group differences that can affect the results of therapy. For example, many studies have found that African Americans with mental disorders are less likely than White Americans with the same diagnoses to follow their doctor's or therapist's instruction about taking medications. (Fleck et al., 2002; Hazlett-Stevens et al., 2002). A culturally sensitive approach to this problem might be based on a therapist's

■ gender-sensitive therapy An approach to therapy that takes into account the effects of gender on both the therapist's and the client's behavior.

understanding of the importance of kinship networks and community relationships in African American culture. A therapist might increase African American patients' compliance level by having the patient participate in a support group with other African Americans suffering from the same illness and taking the same medications (Muller, 2002). In addition, researchers and experienced therapists recommend that non–African American therapists and African American patients openly discuss their differing racial perspectives prior to beginning therapy (Bean et al., 2002).

Gender-Sensitive Therapy

Many psychotherapists note the need for **gender-sensitive therapy**, a therapeutic approach that takes into the account the effects of gender on both the therapist's and the client's behavior (Gehart & Lyle, 2001). To implement gender-sensitive therapy, therapists must examine their own gender-based prejudices. They may assume men to be more analytical, and women to be more emotional, for example. These stereotypical beliefs may be based on a therapist's socialization background or knowledge of research findings on gender differences.

Advocates of gender-sensitive therapy point out that knowledge of real differences between the sexes is important to the practice of gender-sensitive therapy. For instance, because of men's gender role socialization, interventions focused on emotional expression may be less effective for them than for women. Moreover, men may view seeking therapy as a sign of weakness or as a threat to their sense of masculinity (Addis & Mahalik, 2003). As a result, researchers advise therapists to try to avoid creating defensiveness in their male clients. Nevertheless, therapists must guard against using research findings as a basis for stereotyping either male or female clients. They have to keep in mind that there is more variation within each gender than across genders, and thus each man or women must be considered as an individual.

Some therapists who are motivated by a sincere desire to be sensitive to gender issues may place too much emphasis on gender issues and misinterpret clients' problems (Addis & Mahalik, 2003). For example, in one study, researchers found that therapists expect people who are working in nontraditional fields—female engineers and male nurses, for instance—to have more psychological problems (Rubinstein, 2001). As a result, therapists may assume that such clients' difficulties arise from gender role conflicts, when, in reality, their problems have completely different origins.

Remember It 16.7

1. __________ variables can influence the results of standardized tests used by psychologists.
2. Culturally sensitive therapy involves all of the following except:
   a. incorporation of cultural practices into therapeutic interventions.
   b. assessment of a client's language skills.
   c. avoidance of discussions of race and culture with clients.
   d. sensitivity to the emotions associated with living in a new culture.
3. Gender-sensitive therapy requires that therapists examine their own __________.

ANSWERS: 1. Cultural; 2. c; 3. gender biases

Apply It

Is E-therapy Right for You?

If you were trying to overcome a substance abuse problem or needed help getting through a period of bereavement, would you turn to an online support group? Many people do. For example, researchers Taylor and Luce (2003) reported that, when Senator Edward Kennedy mentioned a Web site for a particular support group on a nationally televised program, the site received more than 400,000 e-mail inquiries over the next few days. But what about psychotherapy? Can online sessions with a trained therapist be just as effective as face-to-face therapy?

Thousands of people all over the world are turning to *e-therapy*—ongoing online interaction with a trained therapist (Alleman, 2002; Taylor & Luce, 2003). This form of therapy typically involves the exchange of e-mail messages over a period of hours or days but can also include video-conferencing and telephone sessions (Day & Schneider, 2002).

Advantages of E-therapy

E-therapy enables clients to be much less inhibited than they might be in a face-to-face situation. It is also less expensive than traditional therapy (Roan, 2000). Another advantage is that the therapist and the client do not have to be in the same place at the same time. The client can write to the therapist whenever he or she feels like it and can keep records of "sessions" (e-mail correspondence) to refer to later (Ainsworth, 2000; Stubbs, 2000). A therapist can also keep accurate records of communications with clients and can answer their questions at times of day when telephone calls are inconvenient, thus making his or her therapy practice more efficient (Andrews & Erskine, 2003).

Ainsworth (2000) and Walker (2000) have found that e-therapy can be an especially helpful alternative to psychotherapy for people with any of several characteristics:

- They are often away from home or have full schedules.
- They cannot afford traditional therapy.
- They live in rural areas and do not have access to mental health care.
- They have disabilities.
- They are too timid or embarrassed to make an appointment with a therapist.
- They are good at expressing their thoughts and feelings in writing.

Disadvantages of E-therapy

Because of the anonymity of Internet interactions, it is easy for imposters to pose as therapists. So far, there is no system for regulating or licensing e-therapists. In addition, e-therapy poses some potential ethical problems, such as the possibility of breaches of confidentiality. But like all reputable therapists, the best e-therapists do everything they can to protect clients' privacy and confidentiality—except when it is necessary to protect them or someone else from immediate harm (Ainsworth, 2000). Perhaps the most serious drawback of e-therapy is the fact that the therapist cannot see the client and therefore cannot use visual and auditory cues to determine when the person is becoming anxious or upset. This reduces the effectiveness of treatment (Roan, 2000; Walker, 2000).

Another important limitation of e-therapy is that it is not appropriate for diagnosing and treating serious psychological disorders, such as schizophrenia or bipolar disorder (Manhal-Baugus, 2001). In addition, e-therapy is not appropriate for someone who is in the midst of a serious crisis. There are better ways to get immediate help, such as suicide hotlines.

Finding an E-therapist

If you wish to locate an e-therapist, the best place to start is http://www.metanoia.org. The site lists online therapists whose credentials have been checked by Mental Health Net. It provides information about the location of the therapist, the services offered, payment method, and so forth (Roan, 2000). When choosing a therapist, be sure to do the following (Ainsworth, 2000):

- Make sure the person's credentials have been verified by a third party.
- Get real-world contact information.
- Verify that you'll receive a personal reply to your messages.
- Find out in advance how much the therapist charges.

If you decide to contact an e-therapist, bear this in mind: While e-therapy may be a good way to get started, if you have persistent problems, it would be wise in the long run to obtain traditional psychotherapy (Roan, 2000).

Summary *and* Review

Insight Therapies p. 536

What are the basic techniques of psychoanalysis, and how are they used to help patients? p. 536

The techniques associated with psychoanalysis are free association, dream analysis, and transference. They are used to uncover the repressed memories, impulses, and conflicts presumed to be the cause of the patient's problems.

What are the role and the goal of the therapist in person-centered therapy? p. 537

Person-centered therapy is a nondirective therapy in which the therapist provides empathy and a climate of unconditional positive regard. The goal is to allow the client to determine the direction of the therapy sessions and to move toward self-actualization.

What is the major emphasis of Gestalt therapy? p. 538

Gestalt therapy emphasizes the importance of clients' fully experiencing, in the present moment, their feelings, thoughts, and actions and taking personal responsibility for their behavior.

Relationship Therapies p. 538

What problems commonly associated with major depression does interpersonal therapy focus on? p. 538

Interpersonal therapy (IPT) is designed to help depressed patients cope with unusual or severe responses to the death of a loved one, interpersonal role disputes, difficulty in adjusting to role transitions, and deficits in interpersonal skills.

What is the goal of family therapy? p. 539

The goal of family therapy is to help family members heal their wounds, improve communication patterns, and create more interpersonal understanding and harmony.

What are some advantages of group therapy? p. 539

Group therapy is less expensive than individual therapy, and it gives people opportunities to express their feelings, to get feedback from other group members, and to give and receive help and emotional support.

Behavior Therapies p. 540

How do behavior therapists modify clients' problematic behavior? p. 541

Behavior therapists use operant conditioning techniques such as the use of reinforcement to shape or increase the frequency of desirable behaviors (token economies) and the withholding of reinforcement to eliminate undesirable behaviors (time out).

What behavior therapies are based on classical conditioning? p. 542

Behavior therapies based on classical conditioning are systematic desensitization, flooding, exposure and response prevention, and aversion therapy.

How does participant modeling help people overcome their fears? p. 543

In participant modeling, an appropriate response to a feared stimulus is modeled in graduated steps, and the client is asked to imitate each step with the encouragement and support of the therapist. This process extinguishes the client's fear response.

Cognitive Therapies p. 544

What is the aim of rational-emotive therapy? p. 544

Rational-emotive therapy is a directive form of therapy whose aim is to challenge and modify a client's irrational beliefs, which are believed to be the cause of personal distress.

How does Beck's cognitive therapy help people overcome depression and panic disorder? p. 545

Beck's cognitive therapy helps people overcome depression and panic disorder by pointing out the irrational thoughts causing them misery and by helping them learn other, more realistic ways of looking at themselves and their experiences.

The Biological Therapies p. 547

What are the advantages and disadvantages of using drugs to treat psychological disorders? p. 547

The use of drug therapy has reduced the number of patients in mental hospitals. Antipsychotic drugs control the major symptoms of schizophrenia by inhibiting the activity of dopamine. Antidepressants are helpful in the treatment of severe depression and certain anxiety disorders. Lithium and anticonvulsant drugs can control symptoms of manic episodes and can even out the mood swings in bipolar disorder. Some problems with the use of drugs are unpleasant or dangerous side effects, the difficulty in establishing the proper dosages, and the fact that relapse is likely if the drug therapy is discontinued. Also, the movement away from hospitalization has led to an increase in the number of homeless people with mental disorders.

What is electroconvulsive therapy (ECT) used for? p. 550

The unilateral form of ECT is used to treat people with severe depression, especially those who are in imminent danger of committing suicide.

What is psychosurgery, and for what problems is it used? p. 551

Psychosurgery is brain surgery performed to relieve some severe, persistent, and debilitating psychological disorders or unbearable chronic pain. A highly controversial technique, psychosurgery is considered experimental and a last resort.

Evaluating the Therapies p. 551

What therapy, if any, is most effective in treating psychological disorders? p. 551

Although no one therapeutic approach has proved generally superior overall, specific therapies have proven to be most effective for treating particular disorders. For example, cognitive and interpersonal therapies are preferred for depressed patients.

Culturally Sensitive and Gender-Sensitive Therapy p. 554

What characterizes culturally sensitive and gender-sensitive therapy? p. 554

These approaches to therapy help mental health professionals be more aware of cultural variables and gender differences that may influence patients' responses to the therapy and the therapist as well as therapists' responses to patients. Patients' cultural backgrounds and practices may be useful in guiding the choice of therapeutic interventions.

Key Terms

antidepressant drugs, p. 548
antipsychotic drugs, p. 548
aversion therapy, p. 543
behavior modification, p. 541
behavior therapy, p. 541
biological therapy, p. 547
cognitive therapies, p. 544
cognitive therapy, p. 546
culturally sensitive therapy, p. 555
directive therapy, p. 538
electroconvulsive therapy (ECT), p. 550
exposure and response prevention, p. 543
family therapy, p. 539
flooding, p. 542
free association, p. 536
gender-sensitive therapy, p. 556
Gestalt therapy, p. 538
group therapy, p. 539
humanistic therapies, p. 537
insight therapies, p. 536
interpersonal therapy (IPT), p. 538
lithium, p. 549
nondirective therapy, p. 537
participant modeling, p. 543
person-centered therapy, p. 537
psychiatrist, p. 553
psychoanalysis, p. 536
psychodynamic therapies, p. 536
psychologist, p. 553
psychosurgery, p. 551
psychotherapy, p. 536
rational-emotive therapy, p. 544
relationship therapies, p. 538
systematic desensitization, p. 542
time out, p. 541
token economy, p. 541
transference, p. 537

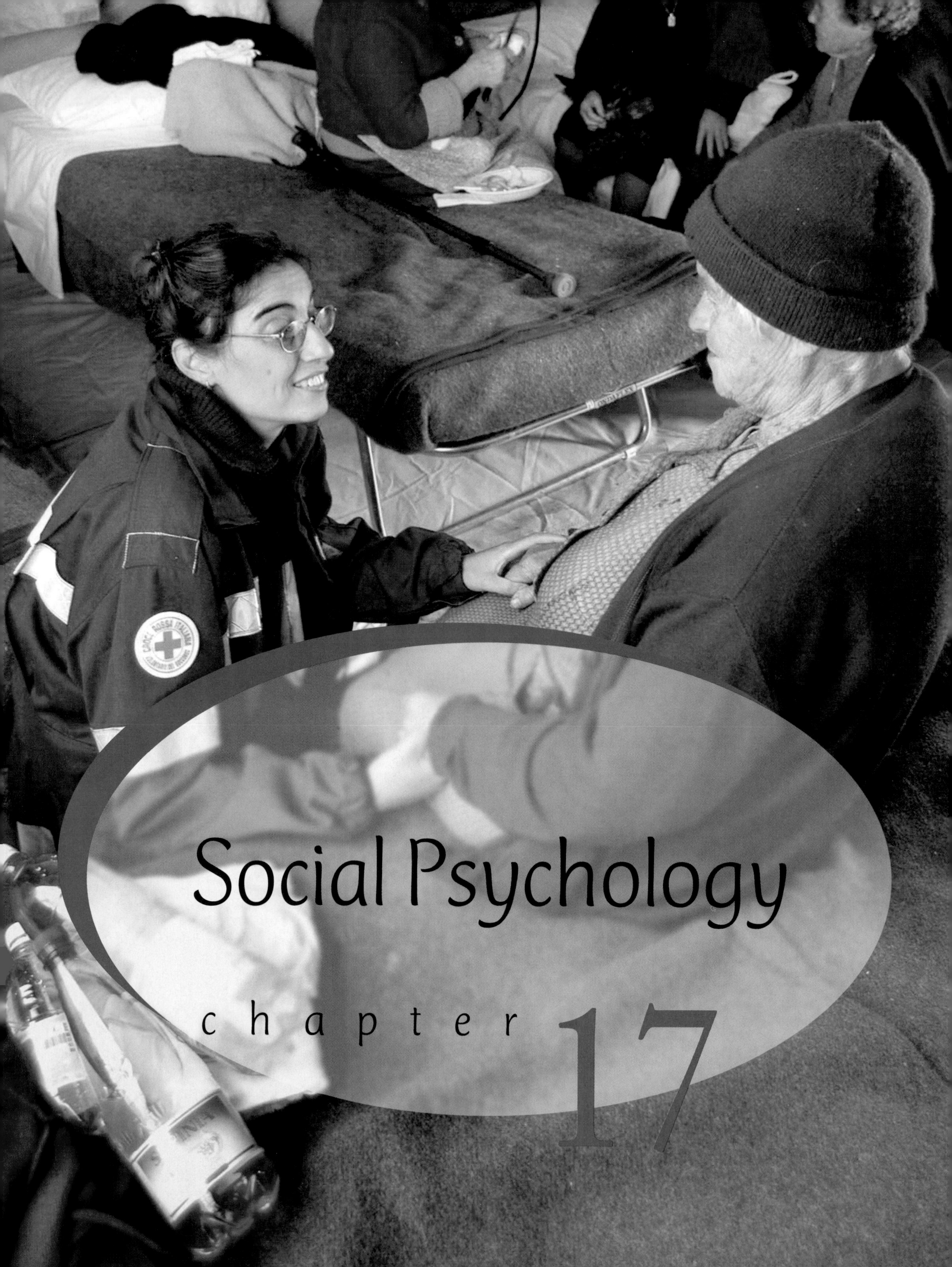

Social Psychology

chapter 17

Social Perception
- *Why are first impressions so important?*
- *What is the difference between a situational attribution and a dispositional attribution?*

Attraction
- *What factors contribute to attraction?*
- *How important is physical attractiveness to attraction?*
- *How do psychologists explain romantic attraction and mating?*

Conformity, Obedience, and Compliance
- *What did Asch find in his famous experiment on conformity?*
- *What did researchers find when they varied the circumstances of Milgram's classic study of obedience?*
- *What are three techniques used to gain compliance?*

Group Influence
- *How does social facilitation affect performance?*
- *What is social loafing, and what factors reduce it?*
- *What are group polarization and groupthink?*
- *How do social roles influence individual behavior?*

Attitudes and Attitude Change
- *What are the three components of an attitude?*
- *What is cognitive dissonance, and how can it be reduced?*
- *What are the elements of persuasion?*

Prosocial Behavior
- *What motivates one person to help another?*
- *What is the bystander effect, and why does it occur?*

Aggression
- *What biological factors are thought to be related to aggression?*
- *What other factors contribute to aggression?*
- *According to social learning theory, what causes aggressive behavior?*

Prejudice and Discrimination
- *What factors contribute to the development of prejudice and discrimination?*
- *What evidence suggests that prejudice and discrimination are decreasing?*

Are there any circumstances under which you could be persuaded to deliberately harm another person?

Many people think they could never be persuaded to do such a thing. But a classic study suggests otherwise.

In the 1960s, an advertisement appeared in newspapers in New Haven, Connecticut, and other communities near Yale University. It read: "Wanted: Volunteers to serve as subjects in a study of memory and learning at Yale University." Many people responded to the ad, and 40 male participants between the ages of 20 and 50 were selected. Yet, instead of a memory experiment, a staged drama was planned. The cast of characters was as follows:

- The Experimenter: A 31-year-old high school biology teacher, dressed in a gray laboratory coat, who assumed a stern and serious manner
- The Learner: A middle-aged man (an actor and accomplice of the experimenter)
- The Teacher: One of the volunteers

The experimenter led the teacher and the learner into one room, where the learner was strapped into an electric-chair apparatus. The teacher was delivered a sample shock of 45 volts, supposedly for the purpose of testing the equipment and showing the teacher what the learner would feel. Next, the script called for the learner to complain of a heart condition and say that he hoped the electric shocks will not be too painful. The experimenter admitted that the stronger shocks would hurt but hastened to add, "Although the shocks can be extremely painful, they cause no permanent tissue damage" (Milgram, 1963, p. 373).

Then, the experimenter took the teacher to an adjoining room and seated him in front of an instrument panel with 30 lever switches arranged horizontally across the front. The first switch on the left, he was told, delivered only 15 volts, but each successive switch was 15 volts stronger than the previous one, up to the last switch, which carried 450 volts. The switches on the instrument panel were labeled with designations ranging from "Slight Shock" to "Danger: Severe Shock." The experimenter instructed the teacher to read a list of word pairs to the learner and then test his memory. When the learner made the right choice, the teacher was supposed to go on to the next pair. If the learner missed a question, the teacher was told to flip a switch and shock him, moving one switch to the right—delivering 15 additional volts—each time the learner missed a question.

The learner performed well at first but then began missing about three out of every four questions. The teacher began flipping the switches. When he hesitated, the experimenter urged him to continue. If he still hesitated, the experimenter said, "The experiment requires that you continue," or more strongly, "You have no other choice, you must go on" (Milgram, 1963, p. 374). At the 20th switch, 300 volts, the script required the learner to pound on the wall and scream, "Let me out of here, let me out, my heart's bothering me, let me out!" (Meyer, 1972, p. 461). From this point on, the learner answered no more questions. If the teacher expressed concern or a desire to discontinue the experiment, the experimenter answered, "Whether the learner likes it or not, you must go on" (Milgram, 1963, p. 374). At the flip of the next switch—315 volts—the teacher heard only groans from the learner. Again, if the teacher expressed reluctance to go on, the experimenter said, "You have no other choice, you must go on" (Milgram, 1963, p. 374). If the teacher insisted on stopping at this point, the experimenter allowed him to do so.

How many of the 40 participants in the Milgram study do you think obeyed the experimenter to the end—450 volts? Not a single participant stopped before the 20th switch, at supposedly 300 volts, when the learner began pounding the wall. Amazingly, 26 participants—65% of the sample—obeyed the experimenter to the bitter end. But this experiment took a terrible toll on the participants. They "were observed to sweat, tremble, stutter, bite their lips, groan, and dig their fingernails into their flesh. These were characteristic rather than exceptional responses to the experiment" (Milgram, 1963, p. 375).

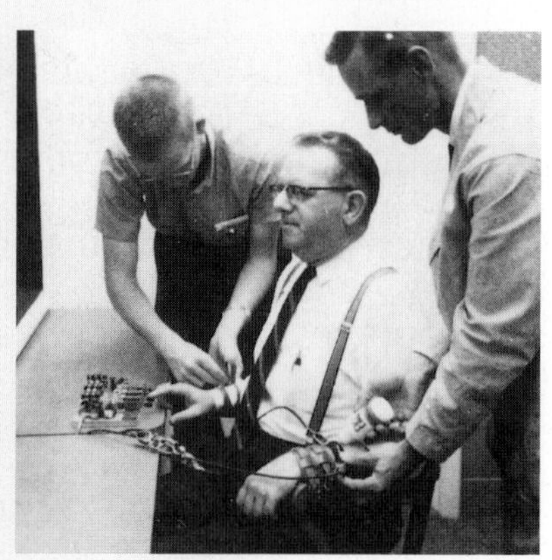

You have just read a description of a classic experiment in **social psychology**, the subfield that attempts to explain how the actual, imagined, or implied presence of others influences the thoughts, feelings, and behavior of individuals. A study like Milgram's could not be performed today because it would violate the American Psychological Association's code of ethics for researchers. Still, deception has traditionally been a part of social psychologists' research. To accomplish this deception, a researcher often must use one or more **confederates**—people who pose as participants in a psychology experiment but who are actually assisting the researcher, like the learner in the Milgram experiment. A **naive subject**—like the teacher in Milgram's study—is a person who has agreed to participate in an experiment but is not aware that deception is being used to conceal its real purpose. You will continue to see why it is often necessary to conceal the purpose of an experiment as you read about other classic studies in social psychology.

■ **social psychology**
The subfield that attempts to explain how the actual, imagined, or implied presence of others influences the thoughts, feelings, and behavior of individuals.

■ **confederate**
A person who poses as a participant in an experiment but is actually assisting the experimenter.

■ **naive subject**
A person who has agreed to participate in an experiment but is not aware that deception is being used to conceal its real purpose.

Social Perception

What are the strategies we use to assess and make judgments of other people? Our ability to understand others is important because we live in a social world. The process we use to obtain critically important social information about others is known as *social perception* (Allison et al., 2000).

Impression Formation

Why are first impressions so important?

When we meet people for the first time, we begin forming impressions about them right away, and, of course, they are busily forming impressions of us. Naturally, we notice the obvious attributes first—gender, race, age, dress, and how physically attractive or unattractive someone appears (Shaw & Steers, 2001). Such attributes, combined with people's verbal and nonverbal behavior, play a part in establishing first impressions. Research shows that a firm handshake still makes a powerful first impression (Chaplin et al., 2000). It conveys that a person is positive, confident, and outgoing, not shy or weak-willed. Moods also play a part. When we are happy, our impressions of others are usually more positive than when we are unhappy.

A number of studies reveal that an overall impression or judgment of another person is influenced more by the first information that is received about that person than by information that comes later (Luchins, 1957). This phenomenon is called the **primacy effect**. It seems that we attend to initial information more carefully, and once an impression is formed, it provides the framework through which we interpret later information (Gawronski et al., 2002). Any information that is consistent with the first impression is likely to be accepted, thus strengthening the impression. Information that does not fit with the earlier information is more likely to be disregarded. Remember, any time you list your personal traits or qualities, always list your most positive qualities first. It pays to put your best foot forward—first.

What is your first impression of the person shown here?

■ **primacy effect**
The tendency for an overall impression of another to be influenced more by the first information that is received about that person than by information that comes later.

Attribution

What is the difference between a situational attribution and a dispositional attribution?

Why do people do the things they do? To answer this question, we make **attributions**—that is, we assign or attribute causes to explain the behavior of others or of ourselves. One kind of attribution is called a **situational attribution** (an external attribution), in which we attribute a person's behavior to some external cause or factor operating within the situation. After failing an exam, you might say, "The test was unfair" or "The professor didn't give us enough time." Or you might make a **dispositional attribution** (an internal attribution) and attribute the behavior to some internal cause, such as a personal trait, motive, or attitude. For example, you might attribute a poor grade to lack of ability or to a poor memory.

We tend to use situational attributions to explain our own failures, because we are aware of factors in the situation that influenced us to act as we did (Jones, 1976, 1990; Jones & Nisbett, 1971). When we explain others' failures, we focus more on personal factors than on the factors operating within the situation (Gilbert & Malone, 1995; Leyens et al., 1996; van Boven et al., 2003). The tendency to attribute our own shortcomings primarily to external, or situational, factors and those of others to internal, or dispositional, factors is known as the **actor-observer effect**. Members of both Catholic and Protestant activist groups in Northern Ireland are subject to the actor-observer effect. Each group attributes the violence of the other group to dispositional characteristics (they are murderers, they have evil intentions, etc.), and each group attempts to justify its own violence by attributing it to situational causes (we were just protecting ourselves, we were only retaliating, etc.) (Hunter et al., 2000).

There is one striking inconsistency in the way we view our own behavior: the **self-serving bias**. We use the self-serving bias when we attribute our successes to dispositional causes and blame our failures on situational causes (Baumgardner et al., 1986; Brown & Rogers, 1991; Pansu & Gilibert, 2002). For example, if you interview for a job and get it, you tell yourself it is because you have the right qualifications; if someone else gets the job, it is probably because he or she knew the right people. The self-serving bias allows us to take credit for our successes and shift the blame for our failures to the situation. Research examining the attributions of professional athletes, for example, has shown that they attribute victories to internal traits, such as ability and effort, and losses to situational factors, poor officiating and the like (Roesch & Amirkhan, 1997). Interestingly, managers prefer job applicants who make dispositional attributions during interviews, especially when the attributions focus on effort rather than natural ability (Pansu & Gilibert, 2002).

Culture apparently contributes to attributional biases as well. In a series of studies, researchers compared Koreans' and Americans' situational and dispositional attributions for both desirable and undesirable behaviors (Choi et al., 2003). They found that Koreans, on average, made more situational attributions than Americans did, no matter what kind of behavior participants were asked to explain. The reason for the difference, according to the researchers, was that the Koreans took into account more information than the Americans did before making attributions.

■ **attribution**
An assignment of a cause to explain one's own or another's behavior.

■ **situational attribution**
Attributing a behavior to some external cause or factor operating within the situation; an external attribution.

■ **dispositional attribution**
Attributing a behavior to some internal cause, such as a personal trait, motive, or attitude; an internal attribution.

■ **actor-observer effect**
The tendency to attribute one's own behavior primarily to situational factors and the behavior of others primarily to dispositional factors.

■ **self-serving bias**
The tendency to attribute one's successes to dispositional causes and one's failures to situational causes.

Remember It 17.1

1. Because of the __________, people pay closer attention to early information they receive about a person than to later information.
2. People tend to make __________ attributions to explain their own behavior and __________ attributions to explain the behavior of others. This tendency is called the __________.
3. Attributing a person's good grades to her intellectual ability is a __________ attribution.

ANSWERS: 1. primacy effect; 2. situational, dispositional, self-serving bias; 3. dispositional

Attraction

Think for a moment about your friends. What makes you like, or even fall in love with, one person and ignore or react negatively to someone else?

Factors Influencing Attraction

What factors contribute to attraction?

Several factors influence attraction. One is **proximity**, or physical or geographic closeness. Obviously, it is much easier to make friends with people who are close at hand. One reason proximity matters is the **mere-exposure effect**, the tendency to feel more positively toward a stimulus as a result of repeated exposure to it. People, food, songs, and clothing styles become more acceptable the more we are exposed to them. Advertisers rely on the positive effects of repeated exposure to increase people's liking for products and even for political candidates.

Our own moods and emotions, whether positive or negative, can influence how much we are attracted to people we meet. We may develop positive or negative feelings toward others simply because they are present when very good or very bad things happen to us. Further, we tend to like the people who also like us—or who we *believe* like us—a phenomenon called *reciprocity* or *reciprocal liking*.

Beginning in elementary school and continuing through life, people are also more likely to pick friends of the same age, gender, race, and socioeconomic class. We tend to choose friends and lovers who have similar views on most things that are important to us. Similar interests and attitudes toward leisure-time activities make it more likely that time spent together is rewarding.

■ **proximity** Physical or geographic closeness; a major influence on attraction.

■ **mere-exposure effect** The tendency to feel more positively toward a stimulus as a result of repeated exposure to it.

Physical Attractiveness

How important is physical attractiveness to attraction?

Perhaps no other factor influences attraction more than physical attractiveness. People of all ages have a strong tendency to prefer physically attractive people (Langlois et al., 2000). Even 6-month-old infants, when given the chance to look at a photograph of an attractive or an unattractive woman, man, or infant, will spend more time looking at the attractive face. How people behave, especially the simple act of smiling, influences our perceptions of their attractiveness (Reis et al., 1990). But physical appearance matters as well.

Based on studies using computer-generated faces, researchers Langlois and Roggman (1990) reported that perceptions of attractiveness are based on features that are approximately the mathematical average of the features in a general population. In addition, Perrett and others (1994) found that averaging faces tends to make them more symmetrical. Symmetrical faces and bodies, are seen as more attractive and sexually appealing (Singh, 1995b; Thornhill & Gangestad, 1994).

In a review of 11 meta-analyses of cross-cultural studies of attractiveness, Langlois and others (2000) found that males and females across many cultures have similar ideas about the physical attractiveness of members of the opposite sex. When native Asian, Hispanic American, and White American male students rated photographs of Asian, Hispanic, African American, and White females on attractiveness, Cunningham and others (1995) reported a very high mean correlation (.93) among the groups in attractiveness ratings. When African American and White American men rated photos of African American women, their agreement on facial features was also very high—a correlation of .94. Evolutionary psychologists suggest that this cross-cultural similarity is because of a

The halo effect—the attribution of other favorable qualities to those who are attractive—helps explain why physical attractiveness is so important.

halo effect The tendency to assume that a person has generally positive or negative traits as a result of observing one major positive or negative trait.

tendency, shaped by natural selection, to look for indicators of health in potential mates (Fink & Penton-Voak, 2002).

Why does physical attractiveness matter? When people have one trait that we either admire or dislike very much, we often assume that they also have other positive or negative traits—a phenomenon known as the **halo effect** (Nisbett & Wilson, 1977). Dion and others (1972) found that people generally attribute additional favorable qualities to those who are attractive. Attractive people are seen as more exciting, personable, interesting, and socially desirable than unattractive people. As a result, job interviewers are more likely to recommend highly attractive people (Dipboye et al., 1975).

Does this mean that unattractive people don't have a chance? Fortunately not. Eagly and her colleagues (1991) suggest that the impact of physical attractiveness is strongest in the perception of strangers. But once we get to know people, other qualities assume more importance. In fact, as we come to like people, they begin to look more attractive to us, while people with undesirable personal qualities begin to look less attractive.

Romantic Attraction and Mating

How do psychologists explain romantic attraction and mating?

You probably have heard that opposites attract, but is this really true? The **matching hypothesis** suggests that we are likely to end up with a partner similar to ourselves in physical attractiveness and other assets (Berscheid et al., 1971; Feingold, 1988; Walster & Walster, 1969). Furthermore, couples mismatched in attractiveness are more likely to end the relationship (Cash & Janda, 1984). It has been suggested that we estimate our social assets and realistically expect to attract someone with approximately equal assets. In terms of physical attractiveness, some people might consider a movie star or supermodel to be the ideal man or woman, but they do not seriously consider their ideal to be a realistic, attainable possibility. Fear of rejection keeps many people from pursuing those who are much more attractive than they are. But instead of marrying an extremely handsome man, a very beautiful woman may opt for money and social status. Extremely handsome men have been known to make similar "sacrifices." The matching hypothesis is generally applicable to friendships as well (Cash & Derlega, 1978), although it is more true of males than of females (Feingold, 1988).

matching hypothesis The notion that people tend to have lovers or spouses who are similar to themselves in physical attractiveness and other assets.

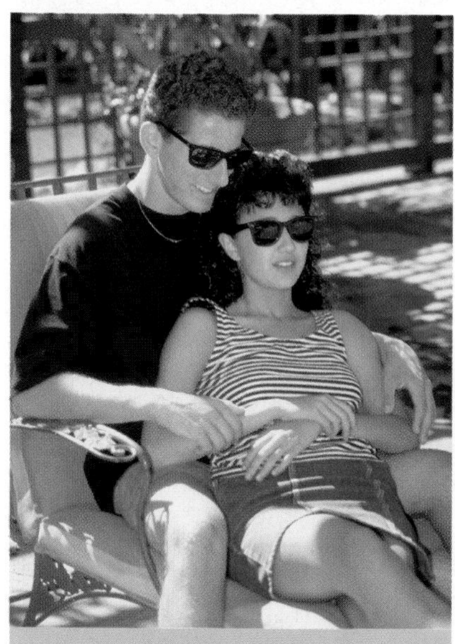

You are more likely to be attracted to someone who is similar to you than to someone who is your opposite.

But is a virtual clone of oneself the most desirable life partner? Not necessarily. Robert Winch (1958) proposes that men and women tend to choose mates with needs and personalities that are complementary rather than similar to their own. Winch sees complementary needs not necessarily as opposite, but as needs that supply what the partner lacks. A talkative person may seek a quiet mate who prefers to listen. There is some support for this view (Dryer & Horowitz, 1997).

Most research, however, indicates that similarity in needs is mainly what attracts (Buss, 1984; Phillips et al., 1988). Similarities in personality, physical traits, intellectual ability, education, religion, ethnicity, socioeconomic status, and attitudes are also related to partner choice (O'Leary & Smith, 1991). And similarities in needs and in personality appear to be related to marital success as well as to marital choice (O'Leary & Smith, 1991). Similarities wear well. If you were to select a marriage partner, what qualities would attract you? Complete *Try It 17.1* to evaluate your own preferences.

Compare your rankings from the *Try It* to those of men and women from 33 countries and 5 major islands around the world. Generally, men and women across those cultures rate these four qualities as most important in mate selection: (1) mutual attraction/love, (2) dependable character, (3) emotional stability and maturity, and (4) pleasing disposition (Buss et al., 1990). Aside from these first four choices, however, women and men differ somewhat in the attributes they prefer. According to the controversial views of evolution-

Try It 17.1 Choosing a Mate

In your choice of a mate, which qualities are most and least important to you? Rank these 18 qualities of a potential mate from most important (1) to least important (18) to you.

____ Ambition and industriousness
____ Chastity (no previous sexual intercourse)
____ Desire for home and children
____ Education and intelligence
____ Emotional stability and maturity
____ Favorable social status or rating
____ Good cooking and housekeeping skills
____ Similar political background
____ Similar religious background
____ Good health
____ Good looks
____ Similar education
____ Pleasing disposition
____ Refinement/neatness
____ Sociability
____ Good financial prospects
____ Dependable character
____ Mutual attraction/love

ary psychologist David Buss (1994), "Men prefer to mate with beautiful young women, whereas women prefer to mate with men who have resources and social status" (p. 239). These preferences, he claims, have been adaptive in human evolutionary history. To a male, beauty and youth suggest health and fertility—the best opportunity to send his genes into the next generation. To a female, resources and social status provide security for her and her children (Buss, 2000b). As was noted in Chapter 12, social role theorists maintain that gender differences in mate preferences are influenced by economic and social forces as well as evolutionary forces (Eagly & Wood, 1999).

Remember It 17.2

1. Match each situation with the appropriate term.

____ (1) Manny sees Susan at the library often and begins to like her.

____ (2) Letitia assumes that because Carter is handsome, he must be popular and sociable.

____ (3) Travis and Faith are going together and are both very attractive.

a. matching hypothesis

b. halo effect

c. mere-exposure effect

2. People are usually drawn to others who are ____________ themselves.

3. Which attribute(s) do men and women across cultures view as most important in a prospective mate?

a. mutual attraction/love

b. dependable character

c. emotional stability and maturity

d. pleasing disposition

e. all of the above

ANSWERS: 1. (1) c, (2) b, (3) a; 2. similar to; 3. e

■ conformity
Changing or adopting a behavior or an attitude in order to be consistent with the social norms of a group or the expectations of other people.

Conformity, Obedience, and Compliance

Conformity

What did Asch find in his famous experiment on conformity?

Do you like to think of yourself as a nonconformist? Many people do, but research suggests that everyone is subject to social influence in some way. **Conformity** is changing or adopting a behavior or an attitude in order to be consistent with the social norms of a group or the expectations of other people.

FIGURE 17.1 Asch's Classic Study of Conformity

If you were one of eight participants in the Asch experiment who were asked to pick the line (1, 2, or 3) that matched the standard line shown above them, which line would you choose? If the other participants all chose line 3, would you conform and answer line 3?

Source: Based on Asch (1955).

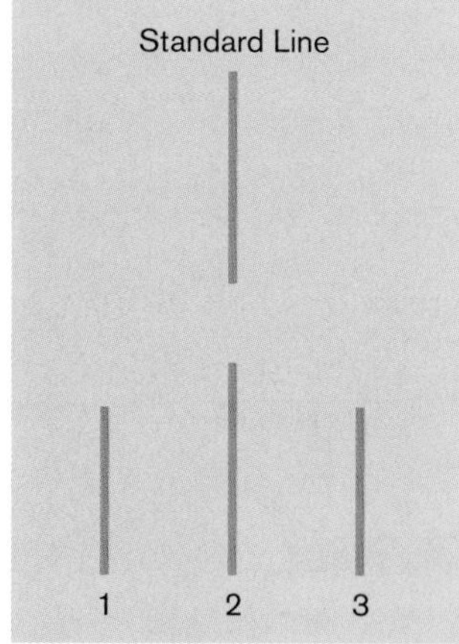

■ **social norms**
The attitudes and standards of behavior expected of members of a particular group.

In this scene from Asch's experiment on conformity, all but one of the "subjects" were really confederates of the experimenter. They deliberately chose the wrong line to try to influence the naive subject (second from right) to go along with the majority.

Social norms are the standards of behavior and the attitudes that are expected of members of a particular group. Some conformity is necessary if we are to have a society at all. We cannot drive on the other side of the road anytime we please. And we conform to other people's expectations in order to have their esteem or approval, their friendship or love, or even their company. In fact, researchers have found that teenagers who attend schools where the majority of students are opposed to smoking, drinking, and drug use are less likely to use these substances than are peers who attend school where the majority approves of these behaviors (Kumar et al., 2002).

The best-known experiment on conformity was conducted by Solomon Asch (1951, 1955), who designed the simple test shown in Figure 17.1. Eight male participants were seated around a large table and were asked, one by one, to tell the experimenter which of the three lines matched the standard line. But only one of the eight was an actual participant; the others were confederates assisting the experimenter. There were 18 trials—18 different lines to be matched. During 12 of these trials, the confederates all gave the same wrong answer, which of course puzzled the naive participant. Remarkably, Asch found that 5% of the subjects conformed to the incorrect, unanimous majority all of the time, 70% conformed some of the time, but 25% remained completely independent and were never swayed by the group.

Varying the experiment with groups of various sizes, Asch found that the tendency to go along with the majority opinion remained in full force even when there was a unanimous majority of only 3 confederates. Surprisingly, unanimous majorities of 15 confederates produced no higher conformity rate than did those of 3. Asch also discovered that if just one other person voices a dissenting opinion, the tendency to conform is not as strong. When just one confederate in the group disagreed with the incorrect majority, the naive subjects' errors dropped drastically, from 32% to 10.4%.

Other research on conformity and the Big Five personality dimensions reveals that people who are low in Neuroticism but high in Agreeableness and Conscientiousness are more likely to conform than those who score oppositely on those dimensions (DeYoung et al., 2002). But, contrary to conventional wisdom, women are no more likely to conform than men (Eagly & Carli, 1981). And an individual's conformity is greater if the sources of influence are perceived as belonging to that person's own group (Abrams et al., 1990). Even so, those who hold minority opinions on an issue have more influence in changing a majority view if they present a well-organized, clearly stated argument and if they are especially consistent in advocating their views (Wood et al., 1994).

What did researchers find when they varied the circumstances of Milgram's classic study of obedience?

Obedience

Can you imagine a world where each person always did exactly what he or she wanted, without regard for rules or respect for authority? We would stop at red lights only when we felt like it or weren't in a hurry. Someone might decide that he likes your car better than his own and take it. Or worse, someone might kill you because of an interest in your intimate partner.

Clearly, most people must obey most rules and respect those in authority most of the time if society is to survive and function. However, unquestioned obedience can cause humans to commit unbelievably horrible acts. One of the darkest chapters in human history arose from the obedience of officials in Nazi Germany, who carried out Adolph Hitler's orders to exterminate Jews and other "undesirables."

The study you read about at the beginning of this chapter demonstrated how far ordinary citizens would go to obey orders; remember, more than 60% of Milgram's participants delivered the "maximum" voltage, despite the pleading and eventual collapse of the "learner." Another researcher repeated the experiment in a three-room office suite in a run-down building rather than at prestigious Yale University. Even there, 48% of the participants administered the maximum shock (Meyer, 1972).

Milgram (1965) conducted a variation of the original experiment: Each trial involved three teachers, two of whom were confederates and the other, a naive participant. One confederate was instructed to refuse to continue after 150 volts, and the other confederate after 210 volts. In this situation, 36 out of 40 naive participants (90%) defied the experimenter before the maximum shock could be given, compared with only 14 out of 40 participants in the original experiment (Milgram, 1965). In Milgram's experiment, as in Asch's conformity study, the presence of another person who refused to go along gave many of the participants the courage to defy authority.

Compliance

What are three techniques used to gain compliance?

How often do you do what others want you to do? There are many times when people act, not out of conformity or obedience, but in accordance with the wishes, suggestions, or direct requests of others. This type of action is called **compliance**. One strategy people use to gain the compliance of others, the **foot-in-the-door technique**, is designed to gain a favorable response to a small request first. The intent is to make the person more likely to agree later to a larger request (the result desired from the beginning).

In a classic study of the foot-in-the-door technique, a researcher claiming to represent a consumers' group called a number of homes and asked whether the people answering the phone would mind responding to a few questions about the soap products they used. Then, a few days later, the same person called those who had agreed to the first request and asked if he could send five or six of his assistants to conduct an inventory of the products in their home. The researcher told the people that the inventory would take about 2 hours and that the inventory team would have to search all drawers, cabinets, and closets in the house. Nearly 53% of those asked preliminary questions agreed to the larger request, compared to 22% of a control group who were contacted only once with the larger request (Freedman & Fraser, 1966).

With the **door-in-the-face technique**, a large, unreasonable request is made first. The expectation is that the person will refuse but will then be more likely to respond favorably to a smaller request later (the result desired from the beginning). In one of the best-known studies on the door-in-the-face technique, college students were approached on campus. They were asked to agree to serve without pay as counselors to juvenile delinquents for 2 hours each week for a minimum of 2 years. As you would imagine, not a single person agreed (Cialdini et al., 1975). Then, the experimenters presented a much smaller request, asking if the students would agree to take a group of juveniles on a 2-hour trip to the zoo. Half the students agreed, a fairly high compliance rate. The researchers used another group of college students as controls, asking them to respond only to the smaller request, for the zoo trip. Only 17% agreed when the smaller request was presented alone.

Another method used to gain compliance is the **low-ball technique**. A very attractive initial offer is made to get people to commit themselves to an action, and then the terms are made less favorable. In a frequently cited study of this technique, college students were asked to enroll in an experimental course for which they would receive credit. After the students had agreed to participate, they were informed that the class would meet at 7:00 a.m. Control group participants were told about the class meeting time when first asked to enroll. More than 50% of the low-balled group agreed to participate, but only 25% of control participants did so (Cialdini et al., 1978).

■ **compliance**
Acting in accordance with the wishes, suggestions, or direct requests of other people.

■ **foot-in-the-door technique**
A strategy designed to gain a favorable response to a small request at first, with the intent of making the person more likely to agree later to a larger request.

■ **door-in-the-face technique**
A strategy in which someone makes a large, unreasonable request with the expectation that the person will refuse but will then be more likely to respond favorably to a smaller request later.

■ **low-ball technique**
A strategy in which someone makes a very attractive initial offer to get a person to commit to an action and then makes the terms less favorable.

Remember It 17.3

1. Match each example with the appropriate technique.

____ (1) Chantal agrees to sign a letter supporting an increase in taxes to fund construction of new schools. Later, she agrees to make 100 phone calls urging people to vote for the measure.

____ (2) Bart refuses a phone request for a $20 donation but agrees to give $5.

____ (3) Hue agrees to babysit for her next-door neighbors and is then informed that their three nephews will be there, too.

a. door-in-the-face technique
b. low-ball technique
c. foot-in-the-door technique

2. What percentage of the participants in the original Asch study never conformed to the majority's unanimous incorrect response?

3. What percentage of the participants in Milgram's original obedience experiment administered what they thought was the maximum 450-volt shock?

ANSWERS: 1. (1) c, (2) a, (3) b; 2. 25%; 3. 65%

Group Influence

■ **social facilitation** Any positive or negative effect on performance that can be attributed to the presence of others, either as an audience or as co-actors.

Have you ever done something you really didn't want to do just to maintain harmony with a friend or friends? You may have seen a movie in which you really weren't interested or gone to the beach when you would have preferred to stay home. Being part of a group often means giving up a bit of individuality, but the reward is the support and camaraderie of the group. Clearly, we behave differently in a variety of ways when we are part of a group, small or large. What happens when the group of which we are a part is made up of strangers? Do such groups influence our behavior as well?

Social Facilitation

How does social facilitation affect performance?

In certain cases, individual performance can be either helped or hindered by the mere physical presence of others. The term **social facilitation** refers to any effect on performance, whether positive or negative, that can be attributed to the presence of others. Research on this phenomenon has focused on two types of effects: (1) **audience effects,** the impact of passive spectators on performance, and (2) **co-action effects**, the impact on performance caused by the presence of other people engaged in the same task.

In one of the first studies in social psychology, Norman Triplett (1898) looked at co-action effects. He had observed in official records that bicycle racers pedaled faster when they were pedaling against other racers than when they were racing against the clock. Was this pattern of performance peculiar to competitive bicycling? Or was it part of a more general phenomenon whereby people would work faster and harder in the presence of others than when performing alone? Triplett set up a study in which he told 40 children to wind fishing reels as quickly as possible under one of two conditions: (1) alone, or (2) in the presence of other children performing the same task. He found that children worked faster when other reel turners were present. But later studies on social facilitation found that, in the presence of

■ **audience effects** The impact of passive spectators on performance.

■ **co-action effects** The impact on performance of the presence of other people engaged in the same task.

FIGURE 17.2 Social Facilitation: Performing in the Presence of Others

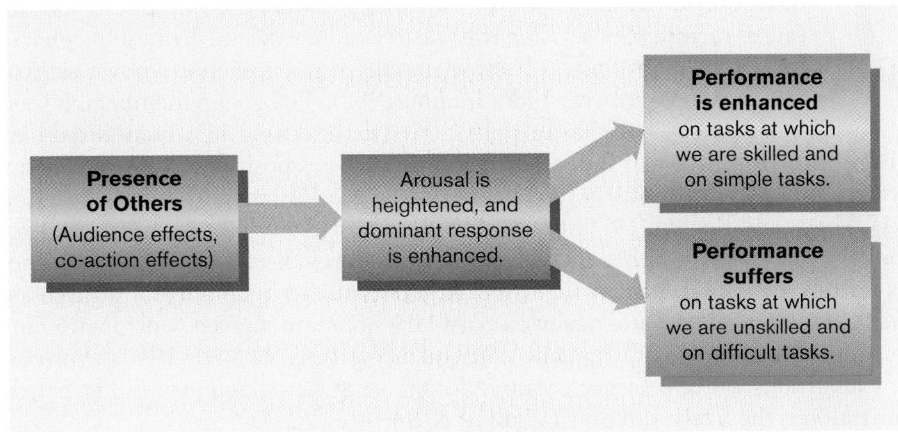

The presence of others (either as an audience or as co-actors engaged in the same task) may have opposite effects, either helping or hindering an individual's performance. Why? First, the presence of others heightens arousal, and, second, heightened arousal leads to better performance on tasks the individual is good at and worse performance on tasks that are difficult for him or her.

Source: Based on Zajonc & Sales (1966).

others, people's performance improves on easy tasks but suffers on difficult tasks (Michaels et al., 1982). See Figure 17.2.

Social Loafing

What is social loafing, and what factors reduce it?

Have you ever been assigned by a teacher or professor to work in a group and, at the end of the project, felt that you had carried more than your fair share of the workload? Such feelings are not uncommon. Researcher Bibb Latané used the term **social loafing** to refer to people's tendency to put forth less effort when working with others on a common task than they do when they are working alone (Latané et al., 1979). Social loafing occurs in situations where no one person's contribution to the group can be identified and individuals are neither praised for a good performance nor blamed for a poor one (Williams et al., 1981). Social loafing is a problem in many workplaces, especially where employees have unlimited access to the Internet (Lim, 2002). Employees tend to justify "cyberloafing" in terms of perceived injustices committed by their supervisors.

social loafing The tendency to put forth less effort when working with others on a common task than when working alone.

In one experiment, Latané and others (1979) asked male students to shout and clap as loudly as possible, first alone and then in groups. In groups of two, individuals made only 71% of the noise they had made alone; in groups of four, each person put forth 51% of his solo effort; and with six persons, each made only a 40% effort. But Harkins and Jackson (1985) found that social loafing disappeared when participants in a group were led to believe that each person's output could be monitored and his or her performance evaluated. Even the possibility that the group performance may be evaluated against some standard can be sufficient to eliminate social loafing (Harkins & Szymanski, 1989).

Studying in a group could lead to social loafing through a diffusion of responsibility effect.

Some 80 experimental studies have been conducted on social loafing in diverse cultures, including those of Taiwan, Japan, Thailand, India, China, and the United States. Social loafing on a variety of tasks was evident to some degree in all of the cultures studied. But it appears to be more common in individualistic Western cultures such as the United States (Karau & Williams, 1993).

Group Polarization and Groupthink

What are group polarization and groupthink?

■ **group polarization** The tendency of members of a group, after group discussion, to shift toward a more extreme position in whatever direction the group was leaning initially.

■ **groupthink** The tendency for members of a tightly knit group to be more concerned with preserving group solidarity and uniformity than with objectively evaluating all alternatives in decision making.

■ **social roles** Socially defined behaviors considered appropriate for individuals occupying certain positions within a given group.

It is commonly believed that groups tend to make more moderate decisions than individuals do. However, research shows that group discussion often causes members of a group to shift to a more extreme position in whatever direction the group was leaning initially, a phenomenon known as **group polarization** (Isenberg, 1986; Lamm, 1988). The group members, it seems, will decide to take a greater risk if they were leaning in a risky direction to begin with, but they will shift toward a more cautious position if they were, on the average, somewhat cautious at the beginning of the discussion (Myers & Lamm, 1975). Myers and Bishop (1970) found that group polarization can lead group discussions of racial issues to either increase or decrease prejudice. However, group members do not always all lean in the same direction at the beginning of a discussion. When evidence both for and against a particular stand on a given topic is presented, group polarization is an infrequent consequence (Kuhn & Lao, 1996). Moreover, when subgroups within a larger group hold opposing views, compromise rather than polarization is the likely outcome (Vinokur & Burnstein, 1978).

Groupthink is the term social psychologist Irving Janis (1982) applies to the decision-making approach often seen in tightly knit groups. When a tightly knit group is more concerned with preserving group solidarity and uniformity than with objectively evaluating all possible alternatives in decision making, individual members may hesitate to voice any dissent. The group may also discredit opposing views from outsiders and begin to believe it is incapable of making mistakes. To guard against groupthink, Janis suggests that it is necessary to encourage open discussion of alternative views and the expression of any objections and doubts. He further recommends that outside experts sit in and challenge the views of the group. At least one group member should take the role of devil's advocate whenever a policy alternative is evaluated. Finally, to avoid groupthink in workplace situations, managers should withhold their own opinions when problem-solving and decision-making strategies are being considered (Bazan, 1998).

How do social roles influence individual behavior?

Social Roles

Social roles are socially defined behaviors that are considered appropriate for individuals occupying certain positions within a given group. These roles can shape our behavior, sometimes quickly and dramatically. Consider a classic experiment in which psychologist Philip Zimbardo (1972) simulated a prison experience. College student volunteers were randomly assigned to be either guards or prisoners. The guards, wearing uniforms and carrying small clubs, strictly enforced harsh rules. The prisoners were stripped naked, searched, and deloused. Then, they were given prison uniforms, assigned numbers, and locked away in small, bare cells. The guards quickly adapted to their new role, some even to the point of becoming heartless and sadistic. One guard remembered forcing prisoners to clean toilets with their bare hands. And the prisoners began to act debased and subservient. The role playing became all too real—so much so that the experiment had to be ended in only 6 days.

Of course, social roles have positive effects on behavior as well. In classic research examining adolescents with learning disabilities, Palinscar and Brown (1984) reported that students' learning behaviors were powerfully affected by their being assigned to play either the "teacher" or the "student" role in group study sessions. Participants summarized reading assignments more effectively, and as a result learned more from them, when functioning as a teacher than when functioning as a student.

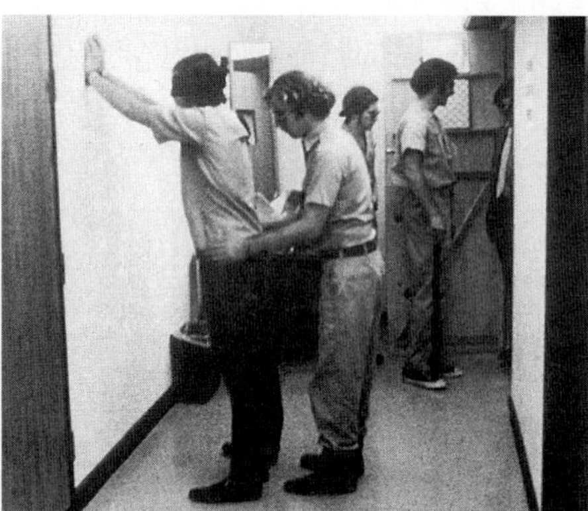

Zimbardo's experiment simulated the prison environment by randomly assigning participants to the social roles of prison guards or inmates. The social roles influenced the participants' behavior: The prisoners began acting like real prisoners, and the prison guards, like real prison guards.

Remember It 17.4

1. __________ leads to improved performance on easy tasks and poorer performance on more difficult tasks.
2. Social loafing most likely to occur when __________ cannot be identified.
3. __________ can lead group members to take greater risks than they would on their own, provided they are already leaning in a risky direction.
4. When members of a group are more concerned with preserving group solidarity than with evaluating all possible alternatives in making a decision, __________ occurs.

ANSWERS: 1. Social facilitation; 2. individual output; 3. Group polarization; 4. groupthink

Attitudes and Attitude Change

Attitudes

What are the three components of an attitude?

We use the word *attitude* frequently in everyday speech. We say that someone has a "bad attitude," for instance. But what is an attitude?

Essentially, **attitudes** are relatively stable evaluations of persons, objects, situations, or issues, along a continuum ranging from positive to negative (Petty et al., 1997). Most attitudes have three components: (1) a cognitive component, consisting of thoughts and beliefs about the attitudinal object; (2) an emotional component, made up of feelings toward the attitudinal object; and (3) a behavioral component, composed of predispositions concerning actions toward the object (Breckler, 1984). See Figure 17.3. Attitudes enable us to appraise people, objects, and situations, and provide structure and consistency in the social environment (Fazio, 1989). Attitudes also help us process social information (Pratkanis, 1989), guide our

■ **attitude**
A relatively stable evaluation of a person, object, situation, or issue, along a continuum ranging from positive to negative.

FIGURE 17.3 The Three Components of an Attitude

An attitude is a relatively stable evaluation of a person, object, situation, or issue. Most of our attitudes have (1) a cognitive component, (2) an emotional component, and (3) a behavioral component.

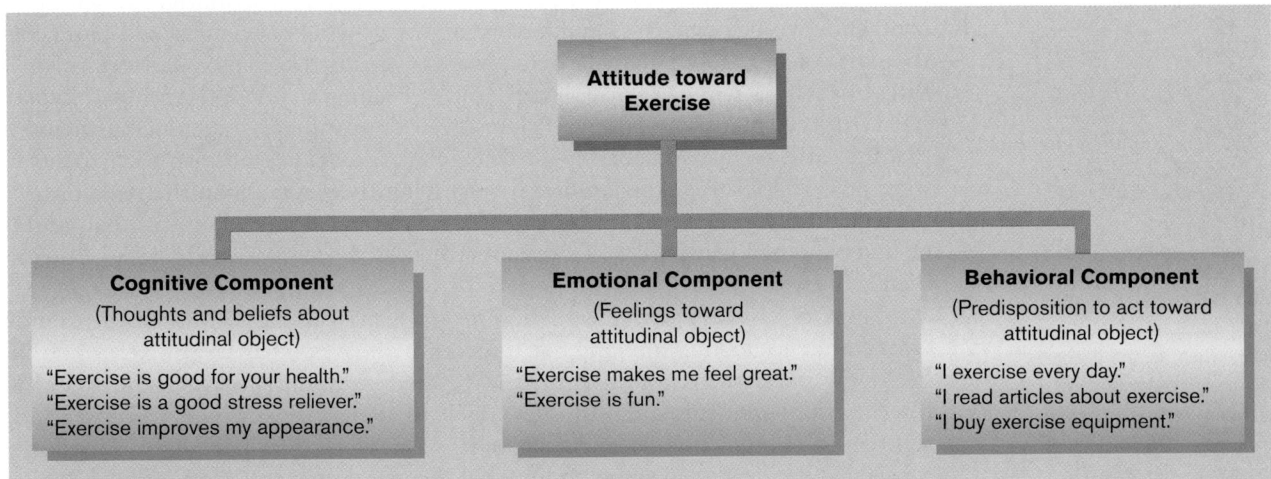
Attitude toward Exercise
Cognitive Component
(Thoughts and beliefs about attitudinal object)
"Exercise is good for your health."
"Exercise is a good stress reliever."
"Exercise improves my appearance."
Emotional Component
(Feelings toward attitudinal object)
"Exercise makes me feel great."
"Exercise is fun."
Behavioral Component
(Predisposition to act toward attitudinal object)
"I exercise every day."
"I read articles about exercise."
"I buy exercise equipment."

behavior (Sanbonmatsu & Fazio, 1990), and influence our social judgments and decisions (Jamieson & Zanna, 1989).

Some attitudes are acquired through firsthand experiences with people, objects, situations, and issues. Others are acquired when children hear parents, family, friends, and teachers express positive or negative attitudes toward certain issues or people. The mass media, including advertising, influence people's attitudes and reap billions of dollars annually for their efforts. As you might expect, however, the attitudes that people form through their own direct experience are stronger than those they acquire vicariously and are also more resistant to change (Wu & Shaffer, 1987). Despite ageist stereotypes, many studies have found that older adults are more likely to change their attitudes than are middle-aged adults (Visser & Krosnick, 1998).

We often hear that attitude change is the key to behavior change. However, a number of studies in the mid-20th century showed that attitudes predict behavior only about 10% of the time (Wicker, 1969). People, for example, may express strong attitudes in favor of protecting the environment and conserving natural resources, yet not take their aluminum cans to a recycling center or join a carpool. However, attitudes are better predictors of behavior if they are strongly held, are readily accessible in memory (Bassili, 1995; Fazio & Williams, 1986; Kraus, 1995), and vitally affect the holder's interests (Sivacek & Crano, 1982).

Cognitive Dissonance

What is cognitive dissonance, and how can it be reduced?

What happens when attitudes contradict one another, or when attitudes and behaviors are inconsistent? According to psychologist Leon Festinger (1957), if people discover that some of their attitudes are in conflict or that their attitudes are not consistent with their behavior, they are likely to experience an unpleasant state called **cognitive dissonance**. Psychologists believe that cognitive dissonance results from a desire to maintain self-esteem (Stone, 2003). Moreover, individuals can experience such dissonance when observing conflicts in the attitudes and/or behaviors of others—this is *vicarious cognitive dissonance* (Norton et al., 2003). People usually try to reduce the dissonance by changing the behavior or the attitude or by somehow explaining away the inconsistency or minimizing its importance (Aronson, 1976; Festinger, 1957). By changing the attitude, individuals retain their self-esteem and reduce the discomfort caused by dissonance (Elliot & Devine, 1994).

In classic research, Festinger and Carlsmith (1959) placed research participants alone in a room to play a boring game. Upon completing the game, participants were instructed to tell the next participants that the game was fun. Participants were randomly assigned to two experimental groups. One group was paid $1 for following instructions, while the other was paid $20. Festinger and Carlsmith assumed that the conflict between participants' self-esteem and their lying behavior would cause cognitive dissonance. How could participants resolve this dissonance and get rid of the threat to self-esteem caused by lying? Just as Festinger and Carlsmith had hypothesized, participants who were paid $1 resolved the conflict by convincing themselves that the game really had been fun—a change in attitude. By contrast, participants who were paid $20 resolved the conflict by justifying their actions on the basis of having been paid a fairly large sum of money relative to the amount of effort it had required to lie to the next participant. Consequently, they did not view the lie as a threat to their self-esteem.

■ **cognitive dissonance** The unpleasant state that can occur when people become aware of inconsistencies between their attitudes or between their attitudes and their behavior.

Smoking creates a perfect situation for cognitive dissonance. Faced with a mountain of evidence linking smoking to a number of diseases, what are smokers to do? The healthiest, but perhaps not the easiest, way to reduce cognitive dissonance is to change the behavior—quit smoking. Another way is to change the attitude, to convince oneself that smoking is not as dangerous as it is said to be. Smokers may also tell themselves that they will stop smoking long before any permanent damage is done, or that

FIGURE 17.4 Methods of Reducing Cognitive Dissonance

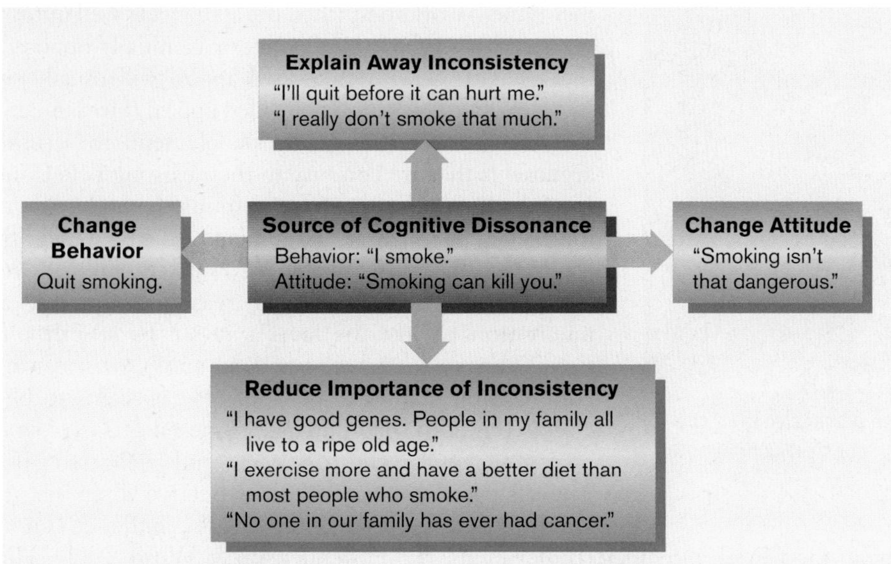
Explain Away Inconsistency
"I'll quit before it can hurt me."
"I really don't smoke that much."
Change Behavior
Quit smoking.
Source of Cognitive Dissonance
Behavior: "I smoke."
Attitude: "Smoking can kill you."
Change Attitude
"Smoking isn't that dangerous."
Reduce Importance of Inconsistency
"I have good genes. People in my family all live to a ripe old age."
"I exercise more and have a better diet than most people who smoke."
"No one in our family has ever had cancer."

Cognitive dissonance can occur when people become aware of inconsistencies in their attitudes or between their attitudes and their behavior. People try to reduce dissonance by (1) changing their behavior, (2) changing their attitude, (3) explaining away the inconsistency, or (4) reducing its importance. Here are examples of how a smoker might use these methods to reduce the cognitive dissonance created by his or her habit.

medical science is advancing so rapidly that a cure for cancer or emphysema is just around the corner. Figure 17.4 illustrates the methods a smoker may use to reduce cognitive dissonance.

Expanding the applicability of cognitive dissonance theory, Aronson and Mills (1959) argued that the more people have to sacrifice, give up, or suffer to become a member of an organization—say, a fraternity or sorority—the more positive their attitudes are likely to become toward the group, in order to justify their sacrifice. Members of cults are often required to endure hardships and make great sacrifices, such as severing ties with their families and friends and turning over their property and possessions to the group. Such extreme sacrifice can then be justified only by a strong and radical defense of the cult, its goals, and its leaders.

Persuasion

What are the elements of persuasion?

Have you ever tried to convince another person to agree with your political opinions or to do something you wanted them to do? **Persuasion** is a deliberate attempt to influence the attitudes and/or the behavior of another person. Attempts at persuasion are pervasive parts of work experience, social experience, and even family life. Researchers have identified four elements of persuasion: (1) the source of the communication (who is doing the persuading), (2) the audience (who is being persuaded), (3) the message (what is being said), and (4) the medium (the means by which the message is transmitted).

Some factors that make the source (the communicator) more persuasive are credibility, attractiveness, and likability. A credible communicator is one who has expertise (knowledge of the topic at hand) and trustworthiness (truthfulness and integrity). Other characteristics of the source—including physical attractiveness, celebrity status, and similarity to the audience—also contribute to our responses to the sources of persuasive messages.

Audience characteristics influence responses to persuasion as well. In general, people with low IQs are easier to persuade than those with high IQs (Rhodes & Wood, 1992). Evidence suggests that a one-sided message is usually most persuasive if

■ **persuasion**
A deliberate attempt to influence the attitudes and/or behavior of another person.

Celebrity status can make someone more persuasive than she or he would otherwise be, a key factor in political campaigning.

the audience is not well informed on the issue, is not highly intelligent, or already agrees with the point of view. A two-sided message (where both sides of an issue are mentioned) works best when the audience is well informed on the issue, is fairly intelligent, or is initially opposed to the point of view. A two-sided appeal will usually sway more people than will a one-sided appeal (Hovland et al., 1949; McGuire, 1985). And people tend to scrutinize arguments that are contrary to their existing beliefs more carefully and exert more effort refuting them; they are also more likely to judge such arguments as being weaker than those that support their beliefs (Edwards & Smith, 1996).

A message can be well reasoned, logical, and unemotional ("just the facts"); it can be strictly emotional ("make their hair stand on end"); or it can be a combination of the two. Arousing fear seems to be an effective method for persuading people to quit smoking, get regular chest X rays, and wear seat belts. Appeals based on fear are most effective when the presentation outlines definite actions the audience can take to avoid the feared outcomes (Buller et al., 2000; Stephenson & Witte, 1998). However, nutritional messages are more effective when framed in terms of the benefits of dietary change rather than the harmful effects of a poor diet (van Assema et al., 2002).

Another important factor in persuasion is repetition. The more often a product or a point of view is presented, the more people will be persuaded to buy it or embrace it. Advertisers apparently believe in the mere-exposure effect, for they repeat their messages over and over (Bornstein, 1989). But messages are likely to be less persuasive if they include vivid elements (colorful language, striking examples) that hinder the reception of the content (Frey & Eagly, 1993).

Remember It 17.5

1. The three components of an attitude are __________, __________, and __________.
2. Changing an attitude can reduce cognitive __________.
3. Credibility relates most directly to a communicator's __________ and __________.
4. With a well-informed audience, __________ messages are more persuasive than __________ messages.
5. Appeals based on __________ are most effective if they provide definite actions that people can take to avoid dreaded outcomes.

ANSWERS: 1. cognitive, emotional, behavioral; 2. dissonance; 3. expertise, trustworthiness; 4. two-sided, one-sided; 5. fear

Prosocial Behavior

According to the Association of Fundraising Professionals, Americans contributed nearly $250 billion to various causes in 2002 ("Charity holds its own," 2000). This giving supports our belief in the basic goodness of human beings. But what does it mean when people ignore others in need? In a now-famous case from 1964, New York City resident Kitty Genovese was murdered while her neighbors looked on, apparently indifferent to her plight. More recently, in early 2003, several people were caught on videotape doing nothing as a man who had just been shot lay dying in a gas station driveway (CNN.com, February 16, 2003). One person even stared at the victim for a few minutes and then calmly returned to the task of filling a can with kerosene. What causes such extreme variations in helping behavior?

■ prosocial behavior
Behavior that benefits others, such as helping, cooperation, and sympathy.

Reasons for Helping

What motivates one person to help another?

There are many kinds of **prosocial behavior**—behavior that benefits others, such as helping, cooperation, and sympathy. Such impulses arise early in life. Researchers agree that young children respond sympathetically to companions in distress, usually before their second birthday (Hay, 1994; Kochanska, 1993). The term **altruism** is usually reserved for behavior that is aimed at helping others, requires some self-sacrifice, and is not performed for personal gain. Batson and colleagues (1989) believe that we help out of *empathy*—the ability to take the perspective of others, to put ourselves in their place.

■ altruism
Behavior that is aimed at helping another, requires some self-sacrifice, and is not performed for personal gain.

■ bystander effect
A social factor that affects prosocial behavior: As the number of bystanders at an emergency increases, the probability that the victim will receive help decreases, and the help, if given, is likely to be delayed.

Commitment is another factor influencing altruism. We are more likely to behave in an altruistic fashion in the context of relationships to which we are deeply committed (Powell & Van Vugt, 2003). The influence of commitment is strongest when the cost of an altruistic act is high. For instance, you would probably be more likely to volunteer to donate a kidney, let's say, to a family member than to a stranger.

The degree to which society values altruism is another variable that can influence individual decisions about altruistic behavior. Cultures vary in their norms for helping others—that is, their *social responsibility norms*. According to Miller and others (1990), people in the United States tend to feel an obligation to help family members, friends, and even strangers in life-threatening circumstances, but only family members in moderately serious situations. In contrast, in India the social responsibility norm extends to strangers whose needs are only moderately serious or even minor.

Whatever the motive for altruism, people who regularly engage in behavior that helps others reap significant benefits (Seenoo & Takagi, 2003). One interesting benefit is that, the more people help, the more altruistic they become. In other words, behaving altruistically generates or enhances an individual's altruistic attitudes. Along with this attitude change comes an increased appreciation for life. Thus, the costs of altruistic behavior are balanced by its benefits, both for those who are helped and for the helpers themselves.

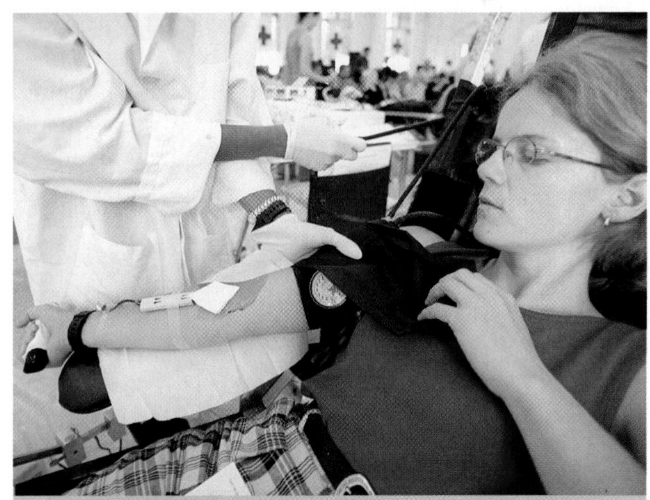
Altruistic acts, such as donating blood, may be motivated by social responsibility norms.

The Bystander Effect

What is the bystander effect, and why does it occur?

A variety of social circumstances contribute to the decision to help another person. One example is the **bystander effect**: As the number of bystanders at an emergency increases, the probability that the victim will receive help from them decreases, and the help, if given, is likely to be delayed. Psychologists have suggested that the bystander effect explains the failure of Kitty Genovese's neighbors to help her.

In now-classic research, Darley and Latané (1968a) placed a series of research participants alone in a small room and told them that they would be participating in a discussion group by means of an intercom system. Some participants were told that they would be communicating with only one other participant, some believed that two other participants would be

FIGURE 17.5 The Bystander Effect

In their intercom experiment, Darley and Latané showed that the more people a participant believed were present during an emergency, the longer it took the participant to respond and help a person in distress.

Source: Data from Darley & Latané (1968a).

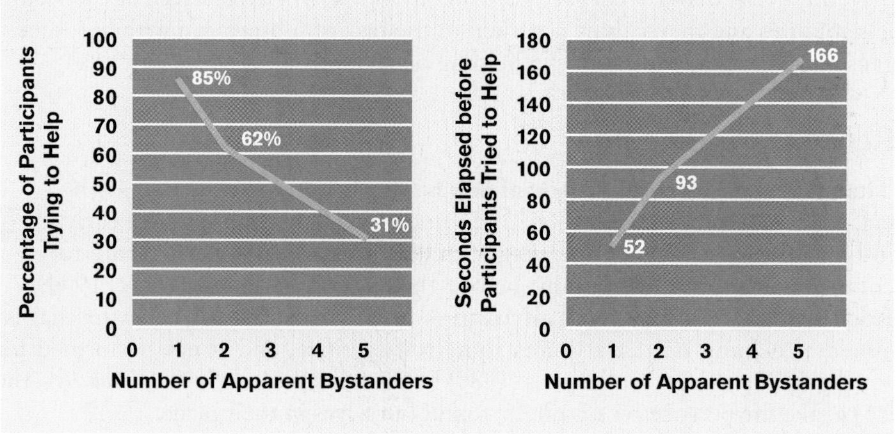

involved; and some were told that five other people would participate. There really were no other participants in the study—only the prerecorded voices of confederates assisting the experimenter. Shortly after the discussion began, the voice of one confederate was heard over the intercom calling for help, indicating that he was having an epileptic seizure. Of the participants who believed that they alone were hearing the victim, 85% went for help before the end of the seizure. When participants believed that one other person heard the seizure, 62% sought help. But when they believed that four other people were aware of the emergency, only 31% tried to get help before the end of the seizure. Figure 17.5 shows how the number of bystanders affects both the number of people who try to help and the speed of response.

diffusion of responsibility The feeling among bystanders at an emergency that the responsibility for helping is shared by the group, making each person feel less compelled to act than if he or she alone bore the total responsibility.

Darley and Latané (1968a) suggest that, when bystanders are present in an emergency, they generally feel that the responsibility for helping is shared by the group, a phenomenon known as **diffusion of responsibility**. Consequently, each person feels less compelled to act than if she or he were alone and felt the total responsibility; each bystander thinks, "Somebody else must be doing something." Another reason for the bystander effect is the influence of other bystanders who appear calm. When others seem calm, we may conclude that nothing is really wrong and that no intervention is necessary (Darley & Latané, 1968b).

Ironically, though, with regard to catastrophes, such as the events of September 11, 2001, the bystander effect is greatly reduced. In fact, people are likely to put forth extraordinary effort to help others in such situations. This phenomenon was seen in the countless individual acts of altruism that occurred in New York City, Pennsylvania, and Washington, DC, immediately after the attacks. Those who couldn't help directly contributed millions of dollars to the families of victims within hours after the events. Research on public responses to large-scale disasters would predict just such a level of response (Shepperd, 2001).

Why do people ignore someone who is unconscious on the sidewalk? Diffusion of responsibility is one possible explanation.

Remember It 17.6

1. __________ involves making a sacrifice to help another person without expectation of reward.
2. As the number of bystanders at an emergency increases, the probability that the victim will receive help __________.
3. Cultural standards for helping others are called __________.

ANSWERS: 1. Altruism; 2. decreases; 3. social responsibility norms

Aggression

One of the enduring themes of research in social psychology for many years has been the study of aggression. **Aggression** is the intentional infliction of physical or psychological harm on others. Aggression has many forms and takes places in a variety of locations—at home, at work, and even among drivers on the road. Acts of aggression against persons or property take place very frequently in the United States, as shown in Figure 17.6. But why does one person intentionally harm another?

aggression
The intentional infliction of physical or psychological harm on others.

FIGURE 17.6 The Crime Clock

This clock shows the frequency at which certain crimes occur in the United States.
Source: Federal Bureau of Investigation (1999).

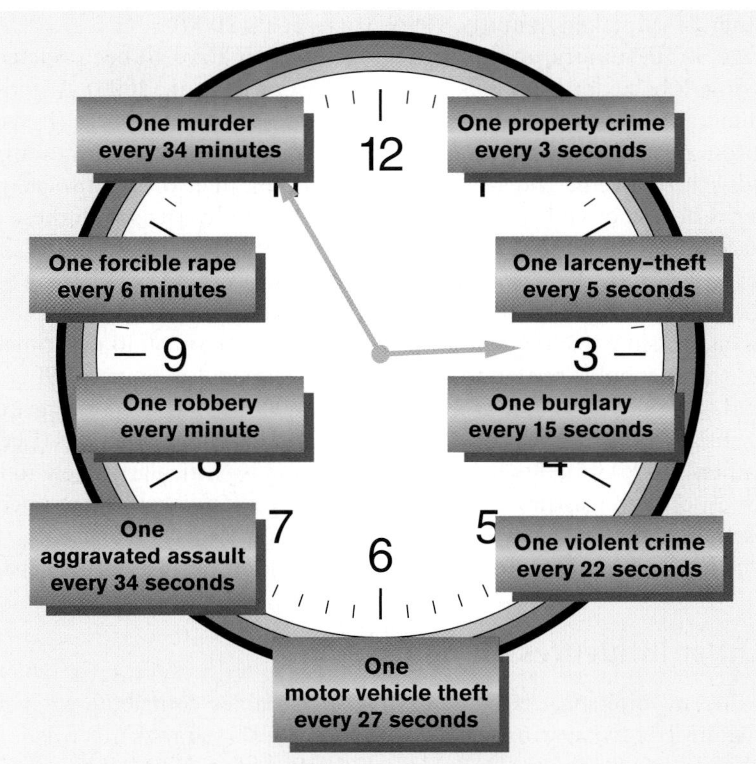
One murder every 34 minutes
One property crime every 3 seconds
One forcible rape every 6 minutes
One larceny-theft every 5 seconds
One robbery every minute
One burglary every 15 seconds
One aggravated assault every 34 seconds
One violent crime every 22 seconds
One motor vehicle theft every 27 seconds

Biological Factors in Aggression

What biological factors are thought to be related to aggression?

Sigmund Freud believed that humans have an aggressive instinct that can be turned inward as self-destruction or outward as aggression or violence toward others. While rejecting this view, many psychologists do concede that biological factors are involved. A meta-analysis of 24 twin and adoption studies of several personality measures of aggression revealed a heritability estimate of about .50 for aggression (Miles & Carey, 1997). Twin and adoption studies have also revealed a genetic link for criminal behavior (DiLalla & Gottesman, 1991). Cloninger and others (1982) found that adoptees with a criminal biological parent were four times as likely as members of the general population to commit crimes, while adoptees with a criminal adoptive parent were at twice the risk of committing a crime. But adoptees with both a criminal biological and a criminal adoptive parent were 14 times as likely to commit crimes, indicating the power of the combined influences of nature and nurture. Thus, many researchers believe that genes that predispose individuals to aggressive behavior may cause them to be more sensitive to models of aggressiveness in the environment (Rowe, 2003).

One biological factor that seems very closely related to aggression is a low arousal level of the autonomic nervous system (Raine, 1996). Low arousal level (low heart rate and lower reactivity) has been linked to antisocial and violent behavior (Brennan et al., 1997). People with a low arousal level tend to seek stimulation and excitement and often exhibit fearlessness, even in the face of danger.

Men are more physically aggressive than women (Green et al., 1996), and a correlation between high testosterone levels and aggressive behavior has been found in males (Archer, 1991; Dabbs & Morris, 1990). In fact, the primary biological variable related to domestic violence (both verbal and physical abuse) appears to be high testosterone levels, which are highly heritable (Soler et al., 2000). Harris and others (1996) found testosterone levels in male and female college students to be positively correlated with aggression and negatively correlated with prosocial behavior. Furthermore, violent behavior has been associated with low levels of the neurotransmitter serotonin (Gartner & Whitaker-Azimitia, 1996; Mitsis et al., 2000).

Brain damage, brain tumors, and temporal lobe epilepsy have all been related to aggressive and violent behavior (Mednick et al., 1988; van Elst et al., 2000). A study of 15 death row inmates revealed that all had histories of severe head injuries (Lewis et al., 1986). According to Eronen and others (1996), homicide rates are 8 times higher among men with schizophrenia and 10 times higher among men with antisocial personality disorder. The risk of violence is even greater when individuals with these disorders abuse alcohol (Hodgins et al., 1996; Tiihonen et al., 1997). In children, high levels of lead exposure (Needleman et al., 1996) and low IQ and problems paying attention (Loeber & Hay, 1997) are related to aggressive behavior and delinquency.

Alcohol and aggression are frequent partners. A meta-analysis of 30 experimental studies indicated that alcohol is related to aggression (Bushman & Cooper, 1990). The use of alcohol and other drugs that affect the brain's frontal lobes may lead to aggressive behavior in humans and other animals by disrupting normal executive functions (Lyvers, 2000). Ito and others (1996) found that alcohol intoxication is particularly likely to lead to aggression in response to frustration. People who are intoxicated commit the majority of murders, spouse beatings, stabbings, and instances of physical child abuse.

Review and Reflect 17.1 summarizes the possible biological causes of aggression.

Other Influences on Aggression

What other factors contribute to aggression?

Beyond biological factors, what other variables contribute to aggression? The **frustration-aggression hypothesis** suggests that frustration produces aggression (Dollard et al., 1939; Miller, 1941). If a traffic jam caused you to be late for an appointment and you were frustrated, would

REVIEW *and* REFLECT 17.1

Possible Biological Causes of Aggression

CAUSE	EVIDENCE
Heredity	If one identical twin is aggressive, there is a 50% chance that the other twin is aggressive as well. Adopted children's aggressive tendencies are more like those of their biological parents than their adopted parents.
Low arousal level	People with low levels of arousal seek stimulation and excitement to increase arousal.
High testosterone level	High levels of testosterone have been found to be correlated with some forms of aggression, such as intimate partner abuse, in both men and women.
Neurological disorders	Brain tumors and other neurological diseases have been linked to aggressive behavior.
Alcohol abuse	People who are intoxicated commit the majority of murders and most other violent crimes.

Want to be sure you've fully absorbed the material in this chapter? Visit **www.ablongman.com/wood5e** for access to free practice tests, flashcards, interactive activities, and links developed specifically to help you succeed in psychology.

you lean on your horn, shout obscenities out of your window, or just sit patiently and wait? Frustration doesn't always cause aggression, but it is especially likely to do so if it is intense and seems to be unjustified (Doob & Sears, 1939; Pastore, 1950). Berkowitz (1988) points out that even if frustration is justified and not aimed specifically at an individual, it can cause aggression if it arouses negative emotions.

Aggression in response to frustration is not always focused on the actual cause of the frustration. If the preferred target is too threatening or not available, the aggression may be displaced. For example, children who are angry with their parents may take out their frustration on a younger sibling. Sometimes, members of minority groups or other innocent targets who are not responsible for a frustrating situation become targets of displaced aggression, a practice known as **scapegoating** (Koltz, 1983).

People often become aggressive when they are in pain (Berkowitz, 1983) or are exposed to loud noise or foul odors (Rotton et al., 1979). Extreme heat has also been linked to aggression in several studies (Anderson & Anderson, 1996; Rotton & Cohn, 2000). These and other studies lend support to the *cognitive-neoassociationistic model* proposed by Berkowitz (1990). He has suggested that anger and aggression result from aversive events and from unpleasant emotional states, such as sadness, grief, and depression. The cognitive component of Berkowitz's model occurs when the angered person appraises the aversive situation and makes attributions about the motives of the people involved. As a result of the cognitive appraisal, the initial reaction of anger can be intensified, reduced, or suppressed. This process makes the person either more or less likely to act on his or her aggressive tendency.

Personal space is an area surrounding each individual, much like an invisible bubble, that the person considers part of himself or herself and uses to regulate the closeness of interactions with others. Personal space serves to protect privacy and to regulate the level of intimacy with others. The size of personal space varies according to the person or persons with whom an individual is interacting and the nature of the interaction. When personal space is reduced, aggression can result.

Crowding—the subjective judgment that there are too many people in a confined space—often leads to higher physiological arousal, and males typically experience its effects more negatively than females do. The effects of crowding also vary across cultures and situations. Researchers have studied its effects on such diverse populations as male heads of households in India and middle-class male and female college students

■ **frustration-aggression hypothesis**
The hypothesis that frustration produces aggression.

■ **scapegoating**
Displacing aggression onto members of minority groups or other innocent targets not responsible for the frustrating situation.

■ **personal space**
An area surrounding each person, much like an invisible bubble, that the person considers part of himself or herself and uses to regulate the level of intimacy with others.

■ **crowding**
The subjective judgment that there are too many people in a confined space.

Crowding may or may not be stressful, depending on the situation—waiting in a crowded airport terminal is more likely to be perceived as stressful than being part of a large crowd at a rally on Martin Luther King, Jr., Day.

in the United States (Evans & Lepore, 1993). In both of these studies, psychological distress was linked to household crowding. Furthermore, studies in prisons have shown that the more inmates per cell, the greater the number of violent incidents (Paulus et al., 1988). However, keep in mind that a prison is an atypical environment with a population whose members have been confined precisely because they tend to be aggressive.

Finally, researchers Roy and Judy Eidelson have identified several beliefs that may lead members of a group of people to act aggressively toward outsiders (Eidelson & Eidelson, 2003). One such belief is a group's conviction that its members are superior to others, together with a sense of "chosenness" for a particular task. The view that one's own group has a legitimate grievance against outsiders can also spark aggression. Group members who believe themselves to be vulnerable may justify aggression as a form of defense. Similarly, those who are convinced that promises made by outsiders to respect the rights of group members cannot be trusted may act aggressively. Finally, group members who believe that aggression is the only strategy available to them for addressing grievances or protecting themselves may resort to violence. Group leaders play an important role in either encouraging or discouraging these beliefs among group members. So, positive leadership may be able to prevent intergroup aggression.

The Social Learning Theory of Aggression

According to social learning theory, what causes aggressive behavior?

The *social learning theory of aggression* holds that people learn to behave aggressively by observing aggressive models and by having their aggressive responses reinforced (Bandura, 1973). It is well known that aggression is higher in groups and subcultures that condone violent behavior and accord high status to aggressive members. A leading advocate of the social learning theory of aggression, Albert Bandura (1976), claims that aggressive models in the subculture, the family, and the media all play a part in increasing the level of aggression in society.

Abused children certainly experience aggression and see it modeled day after day. And the rate of physical abuse is seven times greater in families where there is a stepparent (Daly & Wilson, 1996). "One of the most commonly held beliefs in both the scholarly and popular literature is that adults who were abused as children are more likely to abuse their own children" (Widom, 1989, p. 6). There is some truth to this belief. On the basis of original research and an analysis of 60 other studies, Oliver (1993) concludes that one-third of people who are abused go on to become abusers, one-third do not, and the final one-third may become abusers if their lives are highly stressful. Further, individuals who were sexually abused as children are more likely than others to become child sexual abusers as adults (Burton, 2003).

Most abusive parents, however, were not abused as children (Widom, 1989). Although abused and neglected children are at higher risk of becoming delinquent, criminal, or violent, the majority do not become abusive themselves (Widom & Maxfield, 1996). Several researchers suggest that the higher risk for aggression may not be due solely to an abusive family environment but may be partly influenced by the genes (DiLalla & Gottesman, 1991). Some abused children become withdrawn and isolated rather than aggressive and abusive (Dodge et al., 1990).

The research evidence overwhelmingly supports a relationship between TV violence and viewer aggression (Huesmann & Moise, 1996; Singer et al., 1999). And the negative effects of TV violence are even worse for individuals who are, by nature, highly aggressive (Bushman, 1995). According to Eron (1987, p. 438), "One of the best predictors of how aggressive a young man would be at age 19 was the violence of the TV programs he preferred when he was 8 years old." A longitudinal study conducted in Finland also found that the viewing of TV violence was related to criminality in young adulthood (Viemerö, 1996). Moreover, a review of 28 studies of the effects of media violence on children and adolescents revealed that "media violence enhances children's and adolescents' aggression in interactions with strangers, classmates, and friends" (Wood et al., 1991, p. 380). It may stimulate physiological arousal, lower inhibitions, cause unpleasant feelings, and decrease sensitivity to violence and make it more acceptable to people.

Researchers have also found a correlation between playing violent video games and aggression (Anderson & Dill, 2000). Moreover, aggressiveness increases as more time is spent playing such games (Colwell & Payne, 2000). However, researchers in the Netherlands found that boys who choose aggressive video games tend to be more aggressive, less intelligent, and less prosocial in their behavior (Weigman & van Schie, 1998). So, the link between aggression and video games may be due to the tendency of aggressive individuals to prefer entertainment media that feature aggression.

Remember It 17.7

1. Biological influences on aggression include ________, ________, and ________.
2. The ________ theory of aggression claims that aggressive behavior is learned from models.
3. The kind of aggression that might occur after a person has been stuck in a traffic jam for several hours is best explained by the ________ hypothesis.
4. If a child who is angry at his parents responds by acting aggressively toward a younger sibling, ________ has occurred.
5. Males are more likely than females to respond aggressively to ________.

ANSWERS: 1. heredity, low arousal level, high testosterone level; 2. social learning; 3. frustration-aggression; 4. scapegoating; 5. crowding

Prejudice and Discrimination

prejudice Attitudes (usually negative) toward others based on their gender, religion, race, or membership in a particular group.

discrimination Behavior (usually negative) directed toward others based on their gender, religion, race, or membership in a particular group.

Do you know the difference between *prejudice* and *discrimination?* **Prejudice** consists of attitudes (usually negative) toward others based on their gender, religion, race, or membership in a particular group. Prejudice involves beliefs and emotions (not actions) that can escalate into hatred. **Discrimination** consists of behavior—actions (usually negative) toward others based on their gender, religion, race, or membership in a particular group. Many Americans have experienced prejudice and discrimination—minority racial groups (racism), women (sexism), the elderly (ageism), the handicapped, homosexuals, religious groups, and others. What are the roots of prejudice and discrimination?

What factors contribute to the development of prejudice and discrimination?

The Roots of Prejudice and Discrimination

Social psychologists have proposed several theories to explain the psychological bases for prejudice and discrimination. Moreover, a number of studies have provided insight into their origins.

realistic conflict theory The view that as competition increases among social groups for scarce resources, so do prejudice, discrimination, and hatred.

in-group A social group with a strong sense of togetherness, from which others are excluded.

out-group A social group made up of individuals specifically identified by the in-group as not belonging.

Realistic Conflict Theory One of the oldest explanations as to how prejudice arose cites competition among various social groups that must struggle against each other for scarce resources—good jobs, homes, schools, and so on. Commonly called the **realistic conflict theory**, this view suggests that as competition increases, so do prejudice, discrimination, and hatred among the competing groups. Some historical evidence supports the realistic conflict theory. Prejudice and hatred were high between the American settlers and the Native Americans, who struggled over land during the westward expansion. The multitudes of Irish and German immigrants who came to the United States in the 1830s and 1840s felt the sting of prejudice and hatred from other Americans who were facing economic scarcity. But prejudice and discrimination are attitudes and actions too complex to be explained solely by economic conflict and competition.

In-Groups and Out-Groups Prejudice can also spring from the distinct social categories into which people divide the world, employing an "us-versus-them" mentality (Turner et al., 1987). An **in-group** is a social group with a strong sense of togetherness, from which others are excluded. Members of college fraternities and sororities often exhibit strong in-group feelings. The **out-group** consists of individuals specifically identified by the in-group as not belonging. Us-versus-them thinking can lead to excessive competition, hostility, prejudice, discrimination, and even war. Prejudiced individuals are reluctant to admit outsiders to their racial in-group if there is the slightest doubt about the outsiders' racial purity (Blascovich et al., 1997).

A famous study by Sherif and Sherif (1967) shows how in-group/out-group conflict can escalate into prejudice and hostility rather quickly, even between groups that are very much alike. The researchers set up their experiment at the Robber's Cave summer camp. Their subjects were 22 bright, well-adjusted, 11- and 12-year-old White middle-class boys from Oklahoma City. Divided into two groups and housed in separate cabins, the boys were kept apart for all their daily activities and games. During the first week, in-group solidarity, friendship, and cooperation developed within each of the groups. One group called itself the "Rattlers"; the other group took the name "Eagles."

During the second week of the study, competitive events were purposely scheduled so that the goals of one group could be achieved "only at the expense of the other group" (Sherif, 1958, p. 353). The groups were happy to battle each other, and intergroup conflict quickly emerged. Name-calling began, fights broke out, and accusations were hurled back and forth. During the third week of the experiment, the researchers tried to put an end to the hostility and to turn rivalry into cooperation. They simply brought the groups together for pleasant activities, such as eating meals and watching movies. "But far from reducing conflict, these situations only served as opportunities for the rival groups to berate and attack each other. . . . They threw paper, food and vile names at each other at the tables" (Sherif, 1956, pp. 57–58).

Finally, experimenters manufactured a series of crises that could be resolved only if all the boys combined their efforts and resources and cooperated. The water supply, sabotaged by the experimenters, could be restored only if all the boys worked together. After a week of several activities requiring cooperation, cut-throat competition gave way to cooperative exchanges. Friendships developed between groups, and before the end of the experiment, peace was declared. Working together toward shared goals had turned hostility into friendship.

Social-Cognitive Theory According to *social-cognitive theory*, people learn attitudes of prejudice and hatred the same way they learn other attitudes. If children hear their parents, teachers, peers, and others openly express prejudices toward different racial, ethnic, or cultural groups, they may be quick to learn such attitudes. And if parents, peers, and others reward children with smiles and approval for parroting their own prejudices (operant conditioning), children may learn these prejudices even more quickly. Phillips and Ziller (1997) suggest that people learn to be nonprejudiced in the same way.

Can you perceive differences among the young girls shown here? Research shows that people typically perceive more variability among members of groups to which they belong and more similarity among members of groups with which they are unfamiliar.

Social cognition refers to the ways in which people typically process social information—the mental processes used to notice, interpret, and remember information about the social world. The very processes we use to simplify, categorize, and order the social world are the same processes that distort our views of it. So, prejudice may arise not only from heated negative emotions and hatred toward other social groups, but also from cooler cognitive processes that govern how we think and process social information (Kunda & Oleson, 1995).

One way people simplify, categorize, and order the world is by using stereotypes. **Stereotypes** are widely shared beliefs about the characteristic traits, attitudes, and behaviors of members of various social groups (racial, ethnic, or religious), including the assumption that "they" are usually all alike. Once a stereotype is in place, people tend to pay more attention to information that confirms their beliefs than to information that challenges them (Wigboldus et al., 2003).

Macrae and colleagues (1994) suggest that people apply stereotypes in their interactions with others because doing so requires less mental energy than trying to understand others as individuals. Stereotyping allows people to make quick, automatic (thoughtless) judgments about others and apply their mental resources to other activities (Forgas & Fiedler, 1996). Research by Anderson and others (1990) showed that participants could process information more efficiently and answer questions faster when they were using stereotypes.

Some research has revealed that people tend to perceive more diversity or more variability within the groups to which they belong (in-groups), but they see more similarity among members of other groups (out-groups) (Ostrom et al., 1993). For example, White Americans see more diversity among themselves but more sameness within groups of African Americans or Asian Americans. This tendency in thinking can also be based on gender, age, or any other characteristic. One study showed that a group of 100 young college students believed there was much more variability or diversity in their group than in a group of 100 elderly Americans, whom the students perceived to be much the same (Linville et al., 1989). And a study involving elderly adults showed that they perceived more variability within their own age group than among college students. Age stereotypes can be even more pronounced and negative than gender stereotypes (Kite et al., 1991).

Some research indicates that prejudice and stereotyping (whether conscious or not) may be a means of bolstering one's self-image by disparaging others (Fein & Spencer, 1997). Moreover, some minority group members may protect their self-esteem by attempting to minimize discrimination or by denying its significance (Ruggiero & Taylor, 1997).

■ **social cognition**
The mental processes that people use to notice, interpret, and remember information about the social world.

■ **stereotypes**
Widely shared beliefs about the characteristic traits, attitudes, and behaviors of members of various social groups (racial, ethnic, or religious), including the assumption that the members of such groups are usually all alike.

Is Prejudice Decreasing?

What evidence suggests that prejudice and discrimination are decreasing?

Few people will readily admit to being prejudiced. Gordon Allport (1954), a pioneer in research on prejudice, said, "Defeated intellectually, prejudice lingers emotionally" (p. 328). Even those who are sincerely intellectually opposed to prejudice may still harbor some prejudiced feelings (Devine, 1989). However, most people feel guilty when they catch themselves having prejudiced thoughts or engaging in discriminatory behavior (Volis et al., 2002).

Is there any evidence that prejudice is decreasing in U.S. society? Gallup polls have revealed that White Americans became more racially tolerant over the final decades of the 20th century (Gallup & Hugick, 1990). When White Americans were

FIGURE 17.7 **Perceptions of Racism in the United States**

African Americans and Hispanic Americans are more likely than White Americans to say that racism is a major problem in various areas of life.
Source: Data from Princeton Survey Research/Kaiser Family Foundation (1999).

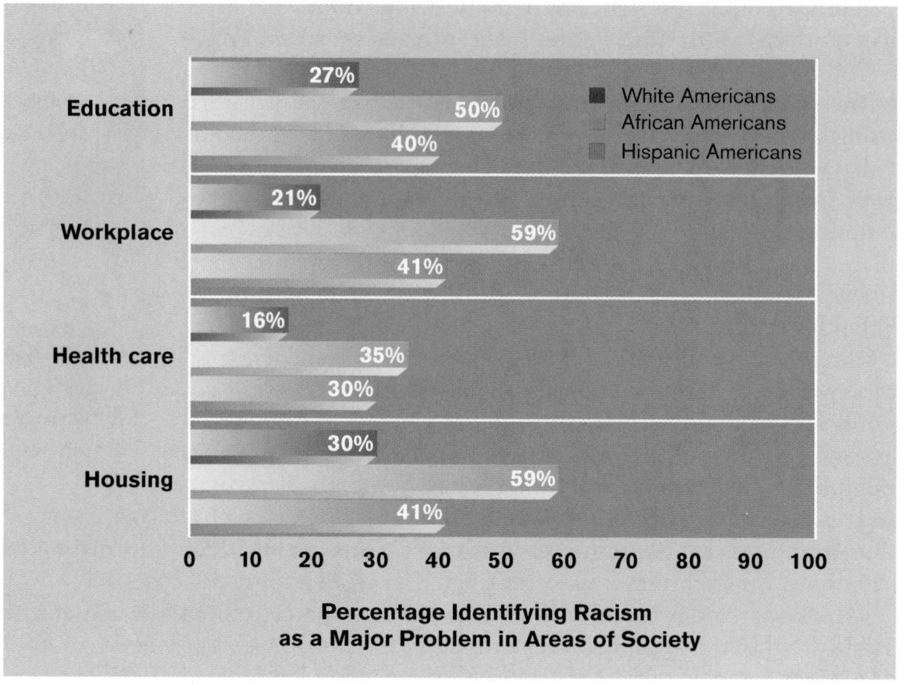

asked in 1990 whether they would move if African Americans were to move next door to them, 93% said no, compared with 65% in 1965. Even if African Americans were to move into their neighborhood in great numbers, 68% of White Americans still said they would not move. Moreover, both White and African Americans overwhelmingly agree that conditions have improved for minorities in the United States over the past several decades (Public Agenda Online, 2002). However, there are still marked differences of opinion among ethnic groups as to whether racism continues to be a problem in the United States, as you can see in Figure 17.7.

Recall, too, that attitudes do not always predict behavior. In a recent study, researchers asked participants to judge whether a fictitious woman was qualified to be the president of a parent-teacher organization (Lott & Saxon, 2002). Participants were provided with information about the woman's occupation and education. In addition, they were told, based on random assignment, that the woman was Hispanic, Anglo-Saxon, or Jewish in ethnic origin. The experimenters found that participants who believed the woman to be Hispanic were more likely to say that she was not qualified for the position than those who thought her to be Anglo-Saxon or Jewish. Moreover, researchers have learned that teachers are more likely to attribute White children's behavior problems to situational factors and those of minority children to dispositional factors (Jackson, 2002).

Such studies suggest that racial stereotyping is still evident in the United States. But there are many things we can do to combat prejudice and discrimination, as you will learn from reading the *Apply It*.

Remember It 17.8

1. Match each situation with the appropriate term.

____ (1) Darlene thinks all Whites are racists.

____ (2) Betty's salary is $5,000 less than that of her male counterparts.

____ (3) Bill doesn't like police officers.

a. stereotypic thinking
b. discrimination
c. prejudice

2. Members of an in-group usually dislike people in a(n) ____________.

3. The social-cognitive theory suggests that prejudice develops and is maintained through ____________ and ____________.

4. Prejudice and ____________ may be means of bolstering one's self-image by disparaging others.

ANSWERS: 1. (1) a, (2) b, (3) c; 2. out-group; 3. modeling, reinforcement; 4. discrimination

Apply It

"Unlearning" Prejudice

Today's college population is more diverse than ever before. In the United States, members of minority groups are attending college in higher numbers. And people from cultures all over the world come to the United States to further their educations. Consequently, for many young people, campus life represents a unique opportunity to interact with others of different racial, ethnic, or cultural groups. How can students make the most of this opportunity to "unlearn" the prejudices they may bring with them to college?

Intergroup Contact

As you learned from the Robber's Cave experiment (Sherif & Sherif, 1967), intergroup contact can sometimes lead to increased stereotyping. Under the right conditions, though, intergroup contact can reduce prejudice. College can provide a context in which students from diverse backgrounds study together, endure the same trials (midterms and finals), develop a shared sense of school spirit, join clubs in which members from different backgrounds share common goals, and so on.

The Jigsaw Technique

Methods such as the *jigsaw technique,* a strategy that works well in college classrooms and as a game in less formal interactions, represent a more direct approach. Each participant in a jigsaw group is given a small amount of information and asked to teach it to other participants. The group must use all the individual pieces of information to solve a problem. This approach increases interaction among participants and helps them develop empathy for members of other ethnic and racial groups (Aronson, 1988; Aronson et al., 1978; Singh, 1991; Walker & Crogan, 1998). A side benefit is that it is an effective way of learning a new solution to a problem.

Diversity Education

Many colleges offer students and faculty opportunities to participate in seminars and workshops designed to combat racism. In such settings, participants learn about racial and cultural perspectives that may differ from their own. They also learn to identify behaviors that may be construed as racist by others, even when that may not be what they intend. Researchers have found that such programs help to reduce automatic stereotyping among participants (Hill & Augoustinos, 2001; Rudman et al., 2001).

Open Discussions of Prejudice and Discrimination

Perhaps the greatest potential of the college campus for reducing prejudice and discrimination lies in the nature of its intellectual climate. Traditionally, college classes, as well as club meetings, gatherings at restaurants, all-night study sessions in coffee shops, and late-night debates in dorm rooms, often feature lively discussions of a variety of topics. And when we hear others speak passionately about racism, sexism, and other types of injustice, we are likely to adopt more tolerant attitudes ourselves.

So, the next time you hear someone make a statement you feel is racist or sexist or prejudiced in any way, speak up! You never know how influential your voice might be.

Summary *and* Review

Social Perception p. 563

Why are first impressions so important? p. 563

First impressions are important because (1) people attend more carefully to the first information they receive about another person, and (2) once formed, an impression acts as a framework through which later information is interpreted.

What is the difference between a situational attribution and a dispositional attribution? p. 564

An attribution is an inference about the cause of one's own or another's behavior. In making a situational attribution, people attribute the cause of the behavior to some factor operating within the situation. With a dispositional attribution, the inferred cause is internal, such as some personal trait, motive, or attitude. People tend to attribute their own shortcomings primarily to situational factors and those of others primarily to dispositional factors, a tendency known as the actor-observer effect.

Attraction p. 565

What factors contribute to attraction? p. 565

Proximity contributes to attraction because it is easier to develop relationships with people close at hand. Proximity also increases the likelihood that there will be repeated contacts, and there is a tendency to feel more positively toward a stimulus as a result of repeated exposure to it (the mere-exposure effect). Our moods and emotions influence how much we are attracted to those we meet. We also tend to like people who like us (reciprocity). Other factors that contribute to attraction are similarities in age, gender, race, and socioeconomic class and similar views and interests.

How important is physical attractiveness to attraction? p. 565

Physical attractiveness is a major factor in attraction for people of all ages. People attribute positive qualities to those who are physically attractive, a phenomenon called the halo effect.

How do psychologists explain romantic attraction and mating? p. 566

Psychologists have proposed the matching hypothesis to explain the finding that people are often attracted to others who are similar to themselves. Others argue that individuals choose mates whose characteristics complement their own. Evolutionary psychologists argue that men and women are attracted to one another on the basis of what each can contribute to the creation and support of a family.

Conformity, Obedience, and Compliance p. 567

What did Asch find in his famous experiment on conformity? p. 567

In Asch's classic study on conformity, 5% of the participants went along with the incorrect, unanimous majority all the time; 70% went along some of the time; and 25% remained completely independent.

What did researchers find when they varied the circumstances of Milgram's classic study of obedience? p. 568

Participants were almost as likely to obey experimenters when the study was repeated at a shabby office building rather than at Yale University. However, when participants were paired with confederates who refused to obey the experimenter, they were less likely to obey.

What are three techniques used to gain compliance? p. 569

Three techniques often used to gain compliance are the foot-in-the-door technique, the door-in-the-face technique, and the low-ball technique.

Group Influence p. 570

How does social facilitation affect performance? p. 570

When others are present, either as an audience or as co-actors, people's performance on easy tasks is usually improved through social facilitation. However, performance on difficult tasks is usually impaired.

What is social loafing, and what factors reduce it? p. 571

Social loafing is people's tendency to put forth less effort when they are working with others on a common task than when working alone. It is less likely to occur when individual output can be monitored or when people have a personal stake in the outcome.

What are group polarization and groupthink? p. 572

Following group discussions, group decisions usually shift to a more extreme position in whatever direction the members were leaning toward initially—a phenomenon known as group polarization. Groupthink occurs when individuals in a tightly knit group hesitate to voice a dissenting opinion because group solidarity and uniformity are more highly valued than objectivity.

How do social roles influence individual behavior? p. 572

Individual behavior can be guided by the expectations associated with certain social roles. The effects of such roles can be either negative or positive.

Attitudes and Attitude Change p. 573

What are the three components of an attitude? p. 573

An attitude usually has a cognitive, an emotional, and a behavioral component.

What is cognitive dissonance, and how can it be reduced? p. 574

Cognitive dissonance is an unpleasant state that can occur when people become aware of inconsistencies among their attitudes or between their attitudes and their behavior. People can reduce cognitive dissonance by changing the behavior or the attitude or by explaining away the inconsistency or minimizing its importance.

What are the elements of persuasion? p. 575

The four elements of persuasion are the source of the communication, the audience, the message, and the medium.

Prosocial Behavior p. 576

What motivates one person to help another? p. 577

Some prosocial behavior is motivated by altruism. In other cases, cultural norms influence helping behavior. We are more likely to help those in need if we are in a committed relationship with them or we perceive them to be similar to us.

What is the bystander effect, and why does it occur? p. 577

The bystander effect is a social factor that affects prosocial behavior: As the number of bystanders at an emergency increases, the probability that the victim will receive help decreases, and the help, if given, is likely to be delayed. The bystander effect may be due in part to diffusion of responsibility or the influence of other bystanders who seem calm.

Aggression p. 579

What biological factors are thought to be related to aggression? p. 580

Biological factors thought to be related to aggression are a genetic link in criminal behavior, low arousal levels, high testosterone levels, low levels of serotonin, and brain damage or certain brain disorders.

What other factors contribute to aggression? p. 580

The frustration-aggression hypothesis holds that frustration produces aggression and that this aggression may be directed at the person causing the frustration or displaced onto another target, as in scapegoating. Aggression has been associated with aversive conditions such as pain, heat, loud noise, and foul odors and with unpleasant emotional states such as sadness, grief, and depression. Invasions of privacy and crowding may also contribute to aggression. Finally, belief in the superiority of one's own group may lead to aggression toward outsiders.

According to social learning theory, what causes aggressive behavior? p. 582

According to social learning theory, people acquire aggressive responses by observing aggressive models, in the family, the subculture, and the media, and by having aggressive responses reinforced.

Prejudice and Discrimination p. 583

What factors contribute to the development of prejudice and discrimination? p. 583

Prejudice consists of attitudes (usually negative) toward others based on their gender, religion, race, or membership in a particular group. Discrimination consists of actions (usually negative) against others based on the same factors. Prejudice can arise out of competition for scarce resources or from people's tendency to divide the world into distinct social categories—in-groups and out-groups. According to social-cognitive theory, prejudice is learned in the same way that other attitudes are—through modeling and reinforcement.

What evidence suggests that prejudice and discrimination are decreasing? p. 585

White Americans are less likely to object to living in racially mixed neighborhoods than in the past. But ethnic groups still have varying views of the degree to which prejudice and discrimination continue to be problematic in the United States.

Key Terms

actor-observer effect, p. 564
aggression, p. 579
altruism, p. 577
attitude, p. 573
attribution, p. 564
audience effects, p. 570
bystander effect, p. 577
co-action effects, p. 570
cognitive dissonance, p. 574
compliance, p. 569
confederate, p. 563
conformity, p. 567
crowding, p. 581
diffusion of responsibility, p. 578
discrimination, p. 583
dispositional attribution, p. 564
door-in-the-face technique, p. 569
foot-in-the-door technique, p. 569
frustration-aggression hypothesis, p. 580
group polarization, p. 572
groupthink, p. 572
halo effect, p. 566
in-group, p. 584
low-ball technique, p. 569
matching hypothesis, p. 566
mere-exposure effect, p. 565
naive subject, p. 563
out-group, p. 584
personal space, p. 581
persuasion, p. 575
prejudice, p. 583
primacy effect, p. 563
prosocial behavior, p. 577
proximity, p. 565
realistic conflict theory, p. 584
scapegoating, p. 581
self-serving bias, p. 564
situational attribution, p. 564
social cognition, p. 585
social facilitation, p. 570
social loafing, p. 571
social norms, p. 568
social psychology, p. 563
social roles, p. 572
stereotypes, p. 585

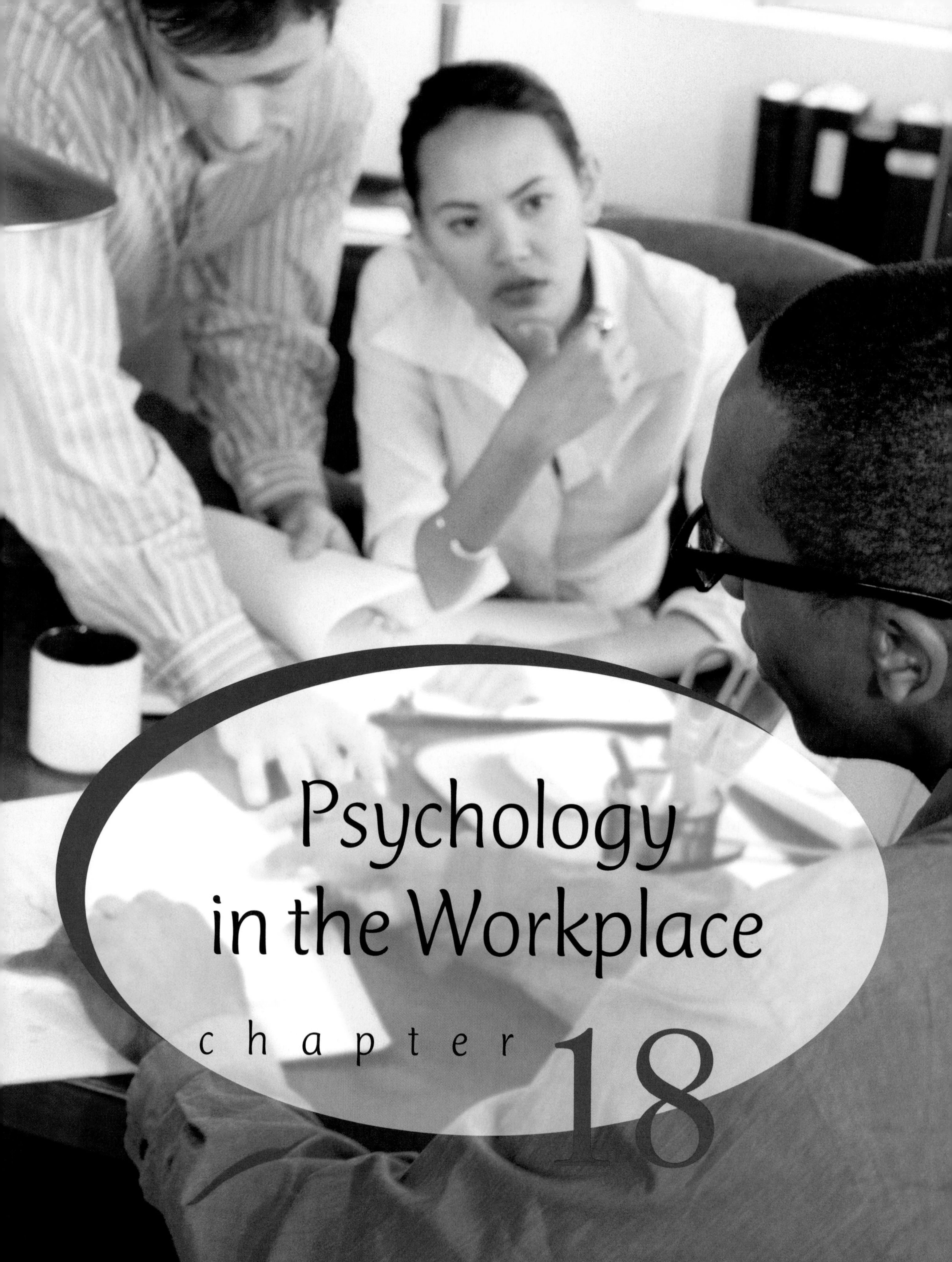

Psychology in the Workplace

chapter 18

Personnel Psychology

- *What strategies do personnel psychologists use to hire the best workers?*
- *How do organizations train employees in job-related and interpersonal skills?*
- *What are some approaches used to evaluate workers?*

Organizational Psychology

- *What is the difference between Theory X and Theory Y management approaches?*
- *What are several types of effective leaders, and how do psychologists explain effective leadership?*
- *What is the relationship between organizational culture and organizational climate?*
- *What are some key perspectives on workplace ethics?*

Human Factors Psychology

- *What are key aspects of workplace design?*
- *What are some of the innovations associated with the quality of work life movement?*
- *What are the causes of desk rage?*

Gender Issues at Work

- *In what ways do women's work patterns differ from men's?*
- *How do men's and women's responses to job-related stress differ?*
- *What evidence is there to suggest that women are breaking the glass ceiling?*
- *What are the two categories of sexual harassment complaints?*

Human Diversity in the Workplace

- *What is ethnocentrism, and how does it affect the workplace?*
- *What are some factors that have led to increased cultural diversity in the workplace?*
- *What are some common misconceptions about older workers?*
- *How does the Americans with Disabilities Act benefit workers with disabilities?*
- *Why have some gay and lesbian workers been reluctant to reveal their sexual orientation to co-workers?*
- *What steps can organizations take to build a more diverse workforce?*

Pursuing a Career

- *What factors influence career choice and development?*
- *What variables are associated with job satisfaction?*

Where do you want to be in 5, 10, or even 15 years?

If you're like many college students, you may not have settled on an answer to this question yet. Sometimes, we can benefit from others' experiences when we approach important life decisions.

Approximately 30 years ago, a young single mother named Christine King was where you are today, contemplating the "where do you want to be" question while taking college courses. She decided that a career in teaching would be the best route to freeing herself and her young son from dependence on welfare. However,

King's life took a different turn when, without giving the matter too much thought, she took a few elective courses in engineering. She quickly learned that she had a natural talent for this subject and, upon completing her 2-year degree, was hired as a technician at the IBM laboratory in East Fishkill, New York. Over the next 4 years, King worked diligently to complete a bachelor's degree in engineering, while maintaining her full-time job at IBM and raising her son.

The intelligence and creativity King brought to the computer industry, along with her personal work ethic, enabled her to steadily advance through the ranks at IBM. When she left IBM in 2001 after 23 years of service with the company, she held the position of vice president for semiconductor products. King accepted the position of CEO (chief executive officer) at AMI Semiconductor in Pocatello, Idaho. When she took over the reins at AMIS, she became the world's first female CEO of a semiconductor company.

Predictably, King's track record at AMIS has been studded with successes that have benefited both the company and its employees. Moreover, King has become a powerful spokesperson for her new hometown and hopes to help the area become one of the top technology corridors in the United States. Christine King's story shows that goals are important, but remaining open to new experiences can also be critical to success.

industrial/organizational (I/O) psychologists Psychologists who apply psychological principles and research results in the workplace.

personnel psychology The branch of industrial/organizational psychology that deals with the design of appropriate and effective strategies for hiring, training, and evaluating employees.

In this chapter, we examine how the principles of psychology can be applied in the workplace. Psychologists who apply psychological principles and research results in the workplace are known as **industrial/organizational (I/O) psychologists**. Industrial/organizational psychologists may be found in all kinds of organizations—factories, retail stores, transportation companies, hospitals, the military, government and nonprofit agencies, and volunteer organizations. I/O psychology has three broad subfields: personnel psychology, organizational psychology, and human factors psychology. We'll look at each of these in some detail. Then, we'll consider gender issues and human diversity in today's workplace.

Personnel Psychology

Personnel psychology is the subfield of industrial/organizational psychology that deals with the design of appropriate and effective strategies for hiring, training, and evaluating employees.

Hiring Workers

What strategies do personnel psychologists use to hire the best workers?

If you owned a business and wanted to hire some help, where would you begin? Wouldn't it be best to start by thinking about exactly how many employees you need and what you need each of those employees to do for you?

Job Analysis Personnel psychologists typically begin the hiring process with a **job analysis,** in which they determine the work that needs to be done and the skills required to do it. Think of a company that manufactures men's shirts, for example. Workers are needed to cut the various fabric pieces that will be sewn together and to do the stitching. But is it most efficient to have workers who both cut and sew, or is it better to have workers who cut and others who sew? A thorough job analysis can determine whether the cutting and sewing tasks should be assigned to different categories of workers or to the same category. The end result of a job analysis is a **job description**, an outline of the responsibilities associated with a given job category. An appropriate job description, based on a thorough job analysis, is a key ingredient in finding and hiring the best workers (Bowen, 2003).

Recruitment, Selection, and Testing **Recruitment** involves the identification of appropriate candidates for a particular position. For example, a common recruitment strategy used by employers who want to hire new college graduates is participation in career fairs on college campuses. Employers may also use employment agencies, which screen and prequalify potential employees before the interview process.

Selection is the process of matching applicants to jobs. To facilitate the process, personnel psychologists develop appropriate assessment tools. One of these tools is the employment application itself. Personnel psychologists are often responsible for designing job applications that allow employers to obtain information about a candidate's prior work experience, educational background, and additional skills that are relevant to a position.

In some cases, personnel psychologists use psychological or other tests to aid in the selection process. These tests may measure general ability, a specific aptitude (e.g., mechanical ability), a physical skill (e.g., typing speed), or personality. Personnel psychologists are responsible for ensuring that the tests used by an organization and the procedures used to administer them are reliable and valid. Researchers have found that the validity of personality self-ratings, for example, can be enhanced by asking applicants to use the tests to describe themselves at work rather than in general (Hunthausen et al., 2003).

A new approach to pre-employment testing used by large corporations involves an **assessment center**, a facility devoted to testing job applicants, where work simulations and other comprehensive assessment tools can be used. At assessment centers, tests can be administered to large numbers of job applicants at once. These centers usually offer comfortable settings for comprehensive interviews, in which applicants interact with personnel psychologists, other human resource professionals, and individuals with whom they will work if hired. For example, in the assessment center of one major airline, pilot applicants are assessed by both personnel professionals and senior pilots (Damitz et al., 2003).

Assessment centers usually provide environments in which applicants can be tested in simulated work situations. One such simulation that has been used for more than 30 years is the **in-basket test** (Frederickson, 1962). In this test, applicants for managerial positions are given a stack of memos, reports, and other kinds of papers they might be expected to deal with on the job. They are expected to generate decisions based on the contents of this in-basket in a limited amount of time. Evaluation of an applicant's performance is based on both the quality of his or her decisions and the efficiency with which he or she uses the time allowed.

Because assessment centers incorporate work simulations into the selection process, they may yield more valid evaluations than those based solely on interviews and tests (Arthur et al., 2003). Moreover, when compared to conventional pre-employment procedures, assessment center evaluations better predict applicants' subsequent job performance. However, these centers are expensive to set up and maintain. Thus, organizations

■ job analysis
An assessment by a personnel psychologist of a job category to determine the work that needs to be done and the skills required to do it.

■ job description
An outline of the responsibilities associated with a given job category; the end result of a job analysis.

■ recruitment
The identification of appropriate candidates for a particular position.

■ selection
The process of matching applicants to jobs.

■ assessment center
A facility devoted to testing job applicants using work simulations and other comprehensive assessment tools.

■ in-basket test
A work simulation test in which applicants for managerial positions are given a stack of memos, reports, and other kinds of papers and expected to generate decisions based on their contents in a limited amount of time.

Many companies participate in career fairs at colleges and universities. Students who attend these events can learn about job opportunities that may be available to them after graduation and perhaps practice their interviewing skills.

need to balance the cost of an assessment center against any gains it may offer in the selection process (Harel et al., 2003).

Interviews Another important function of personnel psychologists is to design **structured interviews**, which consist of standardized interview questions and procedures that are used with all applicants for a position. Structured interviews are most useful when they are based on a sound job analysis, include questions that ask about specific job-related skills and experience, and involve more than one interviewer. Standardized questions help employers compare applicants fairly, by reviewing how they responded to the same questions. Once an interview has been completed, multiple interviewers can discuss points of agreement and disagreement about an applicant's responses.

structured interviews Standardized interview questions and procedures that are used with all applicants for a position.

Employee Training and Development

How do organizations train employees in job-related and interpersonal skills?

Many organizations provide formal training programs designed by personnel psychologists for their employees. One way of teaching job skills is through **on-the-job training**, an approach in which workers receive instruction while actually performing the job. A variation on on-the-job training is the **apprenticeship**, in which a novice employee is teamed with a more experienced one. Typically, the more experienced employee guides the novice toward gradual assumption of full responsibility for the work involved. In another approach, **off-the-job training**, employees watch videos or demonstrations and are expected to implement what they learn when back on the job.

Management training often involves **job rotation**. In this kind of training, employees spend relatively short periods of time performing the various jobs in an organization. A restaurant management trainee, for example, might spend a few weeks learning how to clear tables and wash dishes, then move on to working as a food server. Next, he might learn kitchen operations by working as a food preparer. From there, he might move on to beverage management, then to accounting procedures. The idea is that, when the job rotation process is finished, the potential manager will know how to perform every job in the restaurant.

Whatever the approach used, studies show that employees who are provided with training beyond that which is necessary to learn minimal job functions are more satisfied with their jobs and less likely to be absent than are employees who receive only minimal training (Landstad et al., 2001). Training in human relations can be especially helpful. Thus, a growing number of organizations are providing employees, especially those who will be placed in supervisory positions, with formal training in **conflict resolution**, a process of evaluating a conflict and identifying a strategy for resolving it (Lawrence et al., 2002). The following strategies are typical of those offered in conflict resolution training programs:

- *Avoidance.* Manager remains neutral and delegates responsibility for conflict resolution to the parties in conflict.
- *Accommodation.* Manager urges conflicting parties to minimize differences and highlight similarities.
- *Compromise.* Manager sees to it that all parties give up something of value to the other parties involved.
- *Authoritative command.* Manager asserts authority and reminds parties in conflict of their subordinate status.
- *Collaboration.* Manager and conflicting parties work together to gather information relevant to the conflict and to find a solution that is beneficial to everyone.

Complete *Try It 18.1* to get an idea of how these strategies can be applied to different kinds of workplace conflicts. (By the way, these conflict resolution strategies can also be applied effectively in relationships and settings outside the workplace.)

on-the-job training An approach to training in which employees receive instruction while actually performing the job.

apprenticeship An approach to training in which a novice employee is teamed with a more experienced one.

off-the-job training An approach to training in which employees watch videos or demonstrations and are expected to implement what they learn when on the job.

job rotation An approach to training in which employees spend relatively short periods of time performing the various jobs in an organization.

conflict resolution A process in which a conflict is evaluated and an appropriate strategy for resolving it is identified.

Try It 18.1 Resolving Conflicts

How might a manager or supervisor implement the suggested conflict resolution strategy for each situation?

1. *Avoidance:* Two workers in a manufacturing facility disagree about where a trash can should be placed.
2. *Accommodation:* A new employee irritates co-workers by criticizing their actions and routines with the comment, "That's not the way we did it where I worked before."
3. *Compromise:* Cashiers in a busy retail store can't agree on which one of them should get to go on break first.
4. *Authoritative command:* An office employee is distressed because he is often asked to cover for a co-worker who is habitually tardy.
5. *Collaboration:* Teachers disagree about how to discipline disruptive students.

Evaluating Workers

What are some approaches used to evaluate workers?

Most organizations use a formal process to determine how well each employee is functioning in his or her job. This process is known as **performance appraisal.** In some cases, identifying an appropriate evaluation strategy is fairly straightforward. For example, an individual who is hired to sew shirts might be expected to produce a given number of shirts each day. If he produces fewer, he is judged as performing below expectations. If his production rate exceeds the target, he is judged as performing above expectations.

However, most jobs include performance expectations that are far less tangible than the number of shirts produced per day. To ensure that employee evaluations are as objective as possible, many organizations use **behavioral observation scales.** These instruments require respondents—the employee, co-workers, and/or the supervisor—to rate an employee's performance on observable behaviors. For instance, a supervisor might rate an employee on participation in meetings, which might be broken down into the behaviors of regular attendance and constructive responses.

Another approach to evaluation is known as **management by objectives (MBO).** With this strategy, subordinates and supervisors set performance goals together. In addition, they agree on how goal attainment will be measured and how much time will be allowed to reach each goal. Periodically, progress toward the goals is assessed. Employees' raises, bonuses, and promotions are often tied to this progress.

A relatively new evaluation strategy is **360-degree evaluation,** which combines worker performance ratings from supervisors, co-workers, subordinates, customers, and the workers themselves. Many people regard this approach as fairer and more meaningful than evaluations conducted exclusively by supervisors. However, research suggests that 360-degree evaluations have limited reliability and validity (Brett & Atwater, 2001; Hoffman et al., 2001; LeBreton et al., 2003). These limitations are largely due to discrepancies among ratings from various sources (Valle & Bozeman, 2002); self-ratings and supervisor ratings, for example, often vary considerably.

Who do you think is a better evaluator of a worker's performance—the worker or the supervisor? In one study that addressed this question, researchers collected job performance ratings from workers and from their supervisors, co-workers in similar positions, and subordinates (Atkins & Wood, 2002). These ratings were used to predict how well the workers would perform in a work-simulation test. They found that the most accurate predictions came from supervisors and subordinates. Workers tended to overestimate their own abilities and those of their co-workers. In fact, some of the poorest performers on the work-simulation test received the highest self- and peer-rating scores.

■ **performance appraisal**
A formal process used to determine how well an employee is functioning in his or her job.

■ **behavioral observation scales**
Instruments for employee evaluation that require respondents to rate an employee's performance on observable behaviors.

■ **management by objectives (MBO)**
An evaluation approach in which subordinates and supervisors set performance goals together and agree on how goal attainment will be measured and how much time will be allotted to reach each goal.

■ **360-degree evaluation**
An evaluation strategy that combines worker performance ratings from supervisors, peers, subordinates, customers, and the workers themselves.

Nevertheless, some studies show that employees are better able to identify their strengths and weaknesses after receiving feedback on their work performance from several different sources (B. Green, 2002). Moreover, participating in 360-degree evaluations fosters positive attitudes among workers (Maurer et al., 2002). Thus, many experts argue that, despite its limitations, 360-degree evaluation can be useful for performance appraisal.

Remember It 18.1

1. When employers set up booths at college career fairs, they are engaging in the process of ___________.
2. The process of ___________ often involves the use of psychological tests and structured interviews.
3. Match each of the following approaches to training with the appropriate description.

   ____ (1) off-the-job training
   ____ (2) apprenticeship
   ____ (3) on-the-job training

   a. Employees receive instruction while actually performing the job.
   b. A novice employee is teamed with a more experienced one.
   c. Employees watch videos or demonstrations and implement what they learn afterward.
4. An evaluation technique in which workers receive feedback from multiple sources is known as the ___________.

ANSWERS: 1. recruitment; 2. selection; 3. (1) c, (2) b, (3) a; 4. 360-degree evaluation

organizational psychology The study of individuals and groups in formal organizations.

Organizational Psychology

Experts define **organizational psychology** as the study of individuals and groups in formal organizations. We'll begin our discussion of organizational psychology with a brief look at the kinds of strategies managers use to get subordinates to do their work efficiently and effectively.

What is the difference between Theory X and Theory Y management approaches?

Approaches to Management

If you were hired as a manager in an organization, one of your key responsibilities would almost certainly be to ensure that your subordinates were doing their work. Determining the best way to get employees to complete their assigned tasks is the subject of a great deal of debate among I/O psychologists.

scientific management An approach to management that assumes that workers and their supervisors operate more effectively and efficiently when job requirements are based on empirical data.

The assumption underlying **scientific management**, an approach developed by psychologist Frederick Taylor, is that workers and their supervisors work best when job requirements are based on empirical data. In the early 20th century, Taylor conducted **time-motion studies,** in which he examined the exact physical motions that were required to perform a given manufacturing function in the least amount of time. Once Taylor had completed a time-motion study of a particular task, he trained all workers who performed that task to do it in exactly the same way. Employers found that Taylor's approach resulted in significant gains in productivity among factory workers.

Today, scientific management is often referred to as **Theory X** (McGregor, 1960). This type of approach to management focuses on *work efficiency*, that is, on how well an employee performs specific job tasks. Critics of the Theory X approach claim that work efficiency may depend on *psychological efficiency*, or the degree to which a job has a positive psychological impact on an employee. A theory of management that emphasizes psychological efficiency is often called **Theory Y**.

One frequent goal of Theory Y managers is **job simplication**, the process of standardizing the tasks associated with a particular job. For example, if you go to the kitchen area of a fast-food restaurant, you will probably see large posters showing exactly how various food items are to be assembled. Advocates of this kind of job simplification claim that workers experience less job-related stress because of the clarity provided by the posters.

To lessen workers' boredom, managers may use another Theory Y strategy. **Job enrichment** is the process of changing a job so that it will be more intrinsically motivating, often by adding responsibilities that are normally assigned only to managers. For example, employees may be asked to evaluate the tasks they perform and to make suggestions as to how they could be done more efficiently. Job enrichment may also involve allowing employees greater freedom in determining how and when their work is performed. This flexibility results in higher levels of job satisfaction among workers (Culpan & Wright, 2002; Niehoff et al., 2001).

Another Theory Y strategy is **participative management**, in which managers involve subordinates in the decision-making process. A related technique is the organization of workers into **self-managed teams**, which have complete responsibility for planning, carrying out, and evaluating their work. All workers on a team are on the same level and are collectively accountable for achieving, or failing to achieve, specified goals. Organizing workers into self-managed teams can increase productivity (Glassop, 2002). However, research indicates that productivity increases are most likely under the following circumstances:

- Supervisors must allow the teams to manage themselves and resist the temptation to "micromanage" (Douglas, 2002).
- Team members must be committed to continuous learning and improvement (Bunderson & Sutcliffe, 2003; Druskat & Pescosolido, 2002).
- Team members must respect one another and share responsibility for leadership (Pearce & Sims, 2002).

Similar to a self-managed team is a **quality circle**, a group of employees who meet regularly to search for ways to increase a company's productivity, improve the quality of its products, or reduce its costs. Members may represent various departments in an organization or may be from the same department. Typically, quality circles are led by individuals who have received special training in team building and leadership. However, such leaders are not "supervisors" in the traditional sense of the term. Instead, they serve as facilitators, whose goal is to maximize participation by all members of the quality circle.

time-motion studies
Research examining the exact physical motions required to perform a given manufacturing function in the least amount of time.

Theory X
An approach to management that focuses on work efficiency, or how well an employee performs specific job tasks.

Theory Y
An approach to management that emphasizes psychological efficiency, or the degree to which a job has a positive psychological impact on an employee.

job simplification
The process of standardizing the tasks associated with a particular job.

job enrichment
The process of changing a job so that it will be more intrinsically motivating.

participative management
A management technique in which managers involve subordinates in the decision-making process.

self-managed teams
A group of workers who have complete responsibility for planning, executing, and evaluating their work.

quality circle
A group of employees who meet regularly to search for ways to increase a company's productivity, improve the quality of its products, or reduce its costs.

leadership
The ability to get individuals or groups to do what the leader wants done.

Leadership

What are several types of effective leaders, and how do psychologists explain effective leadership?

Every organization has managers, but managers are not always effective leaders. **Leadership** is defined as the ability to get individuals or groups to do what a leader wants done. What makes a good leader? To answer this question, psychologists have devised numerous classification systems identifying different kinds of leaders. The three types of leaders that we will discuss here are charismatic leaders, transactional leaders, and transformational leaders.

Quality circles often involve members from many departments who meet together regularly to devise ways of improving the quality of the organization's products or services.

Charismatic Leaders **Charismatic leaders** are those who lead by the sheer force of their personalities. In many cases, charismatic leaders have a great need for power and extraordinary confidence in their ability to lead. They usually also believe passionately in the superiority of their goals over those of others and will pursue their goals even if it involves personal self-sacrifice (De Cremer, 2002). Charismatic leaders are typically highly persuasive and lead by convincing followers to share their passionate commitment to their goals. Cult leaders, as well as many of the darker figures in human history such as Adolf Hitler, are often of this type. But other charismatic leaders such as Martin Luther King, Jr., and Robert F. Kennedy have been positive forces. Moreover, leadership experts classify Franklin D. Roosevelt and Ronald Reagan, two U.S. presidents with very different political philosophies, as charismatic leaders (Deluga, 1998).

■ **charismatic leaders**
Leaders who rely on the sheer force of their personalities.

■ **transactional leaders**
Leaders who focus on motivating followers to accomplish routine, agreed-on goals.

■ **transformational leaders**
Leaders who encourage followers to achieve excellence in the accomplishment of routine goals and to pursue goals that go beyond the status quo.

Transactional and Transformational Leadership Much of the current research on leadership focuses on differences between transactional and transformational leaders. **Transactional leaders** are those who focus on motivating followers to accomplish routine, agreed-on goals. By contrast, **transformational leaders** encourage followers to achieve excellence in the accomplishment of routine goals and to pursue goals that go beyond the status quo. Generally, good organizational leaders are those who can combine transactional and transformational leadership to effectively manage an organization or a team (Al-Dmour & Al-Awamleh, 2002; Bass et al., 2003; Dvir et al., 2002; Kark et al., 2003).

The notion of transformational leadership has been most fully developed by organizational psychology researcher Bernard Bass. In general, Bass (1998) asserts that transformational leadership has four dimensions: The first dimension is *charisma*. The transformational leader's personality attracts followers and gives them a sense of pride in being part of the leader's organization. A good example of a transformational leader with charisma is Herb Kelleher, the founder of Southwest Airlines. Kelleher came on the airline scene in the 1970s with the idea that air travel should be as common as travel by city bus. Thus, it had to be inexpensive and reliable. Employees of the fledgling airline were won over by his confidence in the workability of his dream and believed themselves to be participants in an industry revolution. Southwest Airlines became and continues to be one of the most successful companies in its industry.

Charismatic leaders can motivate people to make significant changes. One such leader, Martin Luther King, Jr. (1927–1968), is often credited with being the driving force—through his personality, character, commitment, and example—behind the civil rights movement of the 1950s and 1960s in the United States.

The second dimension of transformational leadership is *inspiration*, which involves the use of symbols to make organizational goals clear. For example, you may have seen United Parcel Service's TV commercial that suggests that its distinctive brown delivery trucks participate in stock car races. Linking the company's symbol, its trucks, with the concept of a race symbolizes that the company's goal is to deliver customers' packages as rapidly as possible.

The third dimension of transformational leadership is *intellectual stimulation*, which focuses on rational problem solving. Followers are encouraged to base decisions on data and logic rather than on emotion. For example, suppose two professors in a psychology department want to teach a course in I/O psychology, but there are only enough interested students to fill one section each semester. The logical solution, suggested by a transformational leader, would be that the professors teach the course in alternate semesters.

Finally, transformational leaders treat each follower as an individual, a leadership dimension called *individualized consideration*. They believe that the

REVIEW and REFLECT 18.1

Three Types of Leaders

TYPE	CHARACTERISTIC
Charismatic	Lead by sheer force of personality
Transactional	Motivate followers to accomplish agreed-on goals
Transformational	Encourage followers to go beyond the status quo

Want to be sure you've fully absorbed the material in this chapter? Visit **www.ablongman.com/wood5e** for access to free practice tests, flashcards, interactive activities, and links developed specifically to help you succeed in psychology.

group or organization is best served by encouraging individual expression and personal growth. Business leaders exhibit individual consideration when they devise compensation schemes that allow all employees to share in a company's profits, based on their individual efforts.

Review and Reflect 18.1 summarizes the three types of leaders we've discussed.

Explaining Differences in Leaders' Effectiveness What makes leaders effective? One possible explanation, the **trait approach**, is that leaders possess intrinsic characteristics that help them influence others. In other words, the trait approach holds that some people are natural-born leaders. Cross-cultural studies showing that leaders in different societies demonstrate similar characteristics, such as problem-solving ability, support this view (Robie et al., 2001).

A different view of leadership is proposed by the **situational approach**. From this perspective, the effectiveness of a leader depends on the match between the leader's characteristics and the situations in which she or he is called upon to lead. For example, leadership researchers believe that the way in which U.S. President Franklin D. Roosevelt responded to the historical challenges that arose during his terms of office (the Great Depression and World War II) continue to shape positive perceptions of his leadership abilities. Similarly, prior to the terrorist attacks of September 11, 2001, many observers were critical of President George W. Bush's bluntness and rather direct way of expressing ideas. However, after the attacks, even his harshest critics acknowledged that these characteristics were assets that helped him build political support for changes in a variety of government policies.

But can leadership be taught? The **behavioral approach** to explaining leadership effectiveness holds that it can be taught and is, in fact, the result of specific behaviors exhibited by leaders. Many researchers classify leadership behaviors under two broad categories: consideration and initiating structure. *Consideration* includes behaviors that communicate the leader's interest in followers as individuals. By contrast, *initiating structure* encompasses behaviors that focus on a task and the means employed to accomplish it. To be most effective, a leader must know when and how to demonstrate both kinds of behaviors (Schermerhorn et al., 2000).

Effective leadership behaviors can be acquired through formal training (Tjosvold et al., 2003). However, some studies show that personality traits determine how well leaders do at learning both consideration and

■ **trait approach**
A perspective on leadership that holds that leaders possess intrinsic characteristics that help them influence others.

■ **situational approach**
A perspective that explains the effectiveness of leadership as depending on the match between a leader's characteristics and the situations in which she or he is called upon to lead.

■ **behavioral approach**
A perspective that holds that leadership effectiveness can be taught and is the result of specific behaviors exhibited by leaders.

The situational approach to explaining differences in leadership claims that circumstances shape leaders' behavior and the perceptions their followers have of them. For example, even many of President George W. Bush's critics noted that he exhibited effective leadership behaviors after the terrorist attacks of September 11, 2001.

leader-member exchange (LMX) theory A behavioral perspective on leadership that assumes that leaders and followers exert mutual influences on one another and takes into account the emotional aspects of leader-follower relationships.

initiating structure behaviors (Wang & Chen, 2002). Thus, training can help, but pre-existing characteristics appear to impose some limits on who can or cannot become an effective leader via formal training.

A recent variation on the behavioral approach to leadership is **leader-member exchange (LMX) theory,** which is based on the assumption that leaders and followers exert mutual influences on one another. Furthermore, LMX theory takes into account the emotional aspects of leader-follower relationships (Dasborough & Ashkanasy, 2002). According to advocates of LMX theory, leaders act differently toward individuals to whom they are closest (their in-group) than toward individuals with whom they do not have close relationships (their out-group).

But are leaders' exchanges with in-groups and out-groups really all that different? Research shows that leaders tend to assign more interesting tasks to in-group members. Moreover, in-group members often have more influence on a leader's decisions than do out-group members. Conversations between leaders and in-group members often include more personal statements than do conversations between leaders and out-group members. Further, as you may know from your own work experience, out-group members often resent in-group members and may even quit their jobs to escape unpleasant feelings of exclusion. Not surprisingly, in-group members experience higher levels of job satisfaction and get more raises and promotions than out-group members do.

Organizational Culture and Climate

What is the relationship between organizational culture and organizational climate?

The term *culture* usually applies to a country or an ethnic group. An **organizational culture** is defined as a system of shared values, beliefs, and practices that evolves within an organization and influences the behavior of its members.

Surveys show that managers and their subordinates often think of organizational culture as involving purely physical aspects, such as who reports to whom and the physical layout of the workplace (Lurie & Riccucci, 2003). These are certainly elements of organizational culture. However, researchers point out that organizational culture has many of the same, sometimes hidden, elements that are found in larger cultures. For instance, *stories* are part of an organizational culture. These are stories about the founding and development of the organization as well as about how individuals in the organization attained their positions.

Researchers also say that, just as individuals are *socialized* into their respective cultures as children, new employees experience a parallel process of integration into an organizational culture. Familiarizing new employees with the stories of the organizational culture is an important part of a socialization process that occurs formally and informally. When you start a new job, for example, you may receive a booklet or view a video detailing the company's history. Obviously, this is a kind of formal socialization. If a fellow employee takes you aside to give you the inside scoop on how others in the organization got to their current positions, you are experiencing informal socialization.

Organizational cultures also have both formal and informal *rites*, recurring events that carry specific meanings. For example, many organizations have annual ceremonies in which employees are recognized for their length of service or outstanding achievements. Formal recognition of this kind is associated with positive attitudes among employees (Markham et al., 2002). Less formal rites may characterize subgroups within an organization. For instance, a subgroup may have a habit of going to a particular restaurant for lunch every Friday. If a member of the subgroup invites a new employee to attend, the new employee may become part of that subgroup.

organizational culture The system of shared values, beliefs, and practices that evolves within an organization and influences the behavior of its members.

In addition to stories and rights, organizational cultures also have *symbols*, objects that transmit meaning to both insiders and outsiders. For instance, the distinctive vehicles of the U.S. Postal Service communicate to outsiders that the drivers are associated with the service. Moreover, the vehicles have significance for postal service employees because a letter carrier must complete training before being authorized to drive one and is then set apart from co-workers.

Finally, an organization's culture is often characterized by a management philosophy that employees believe sets the organization apart from others. *A management philosophy* is a broad statement of an organization's goals and the means that are used to attain them. For example, a retail electronics store may have a management philosophy that goes something like this: "We're going to be the best electronics store in town by putting customer service ahead of profits." This statement may be implemented in a policy of matching any other store's advertised price for an item the store sells. Employees' sense of belonging to an organization may be enhanced when they carry out such philosophically inspired policies.

The various components of an organization's culture work together to shape its organizational climate. **Organizational climate** refers to how employees perceive and respond emotionally to the culture of an organization. An emotionally positive organizational climate is associated with low employee turnover and high employee commitment to the organization's goals. One factor associated with organizational climate is the degree to which employees believe that the procedures used to evaluate them and to resolve their conflicts are fair (Brockner et al., 2003; De Cremer & van Knippenberg, 2003; Simons & Roberson, 2003). Another such factor is the confidence employees have in their managers' abilities (Goris et al., 2003).

■ organizational climate Employees' perceptions and emotional responses to the culture of an organization.

Ethics in the Workplace

What are some key perspectives on workplace ethics?

Have you ever taken a pen or a notepad home from your workplace? Have you ever used your employer's telephone to make personal long distance calls? It might surprise you to learn that such actions by employees, though they may seem inconsequential, cost U.S. employers millions of dollars each year. For this reason, a growing number of organizations are promoting the concept of *workplace ethics*. But, as you'll see, ethical rules can be applied to the behavior of organizations as well to that of their employees.

Workplace ethics does not imply any single set of rules. Instead, there are guidelines that apply to different behaviors and issues. For example, with regard to individual behavior, the **moral-rights perspective** suggests that individuals within an organization should be guided by the same respect for basic rights endorsed by the larger culture. For example, most people agree that stealing is wrong. Further, you wouldn't take a pencil from your neighbor or use her phone to make toll calls, because you respect her property rights. Thus, say advocates of this perspective, you shouldn't do so at work either.

However, organizations often face decisions that are far more ethically complex. For example, how does a corporation decide whether to close an unprofitable manufacturing plant? What carries greater weight—the impact on workers if the plant is closed, or the impact on shareholders and workers in other locations if an unprofitable plant continues to operate? One approach to such dilemmas, called the **utilitarian perspective**, defines ethical behavior in terms of the greatest good for the greatest number of people. If a plant's closing will harm several hundred workers but will benefit thousands of shareholders and employees in other locations, the utilitarian approach says that it is ethical to close the plant and unethical to keep it open.

But, obviously, there is more to such decisions than just numbers. Consequently, the utilitarian perspective is often tempered by a sense of **organizational social responsibility**, a perspective based on the idea that an organization's policies should take into consideration the interests of the larger society of which it is a part. Thus, from this perspective, laying off several hundred workers provides a financial benefit to an organization, but it will also place a burden on taxpayers who will have to provide assistance to the displaced employees. When layoffs are unavoidable, however, socially responsible organizations try to minimize their impact both on the individuals involved and on society. For example, a company might provide job training, severance pay, and placement services for laid-off employees.

■ moral-rights perspective An approach to organizational ethics that suggests that individual behavior within an organization should be guided by the same respect for basic rights that is endorsed by the larger culture.

■ utilitarian perspective An approach to organizational ethics that defines ethical behavior in terms of the greatest good for the greatest number of people.

■ organizational social responsibility A perspective based on the idea that an organization's policies should take into consideration the interests of the larger society of which it is a part.

Remember It 18.2

1. Worker satisfaction is more important in the __________ management approach than in the __________ management approach.
2. Barbara says that her boss is a great leader because he is so intelligent. Her assessment of her boss is consistent with the __________ approach to leadership effectiveness.
3. The degree to which employees perceive their company as fair to employees is a component of __________.
4. Proponents of __________ suggest that businesses should take into consideration the interests of the larger society.

ANSWERS: 1. Theory Y, Theory X; 2. trait; 3. organizational climate; 4. organizational social responsibility

Human Factors Psychology

■ **human factors psychology** The subfield of industrial/organizational psychology that deals with the ways in which workers interact with the characteristics of a workplace.

■ **ergonomics** Human factors psychology.

In the comic strip *Dilbert*, the hero works in an office in which each worker is assigned to a cubicle. Such a layout has become very common. How do you think office designers decide how large each cubicle should be and how high the partitions between them should be? Such decisions are the subject matter of **human factors psychology**, often called **ergonomics**. One of the most important functions of human factors psychologists is to study and enhance the ways in which workers interact with the physical and social characteristics of a workplace.

Workplace Design

What are key aspects of workplace design?

Open Designs Many workplaces today are arranged according to what human factors psychologists call an *open design*. In an open design, a large number of workers are placed in a very large space. Sometimes, there are partitions or other kinds of barriers between workers. Such designs allow organizations to use large spaces flexibly by rearranging individual workspaces as needed. Further, open designs are less expensive to construct because they have few walls and doors.

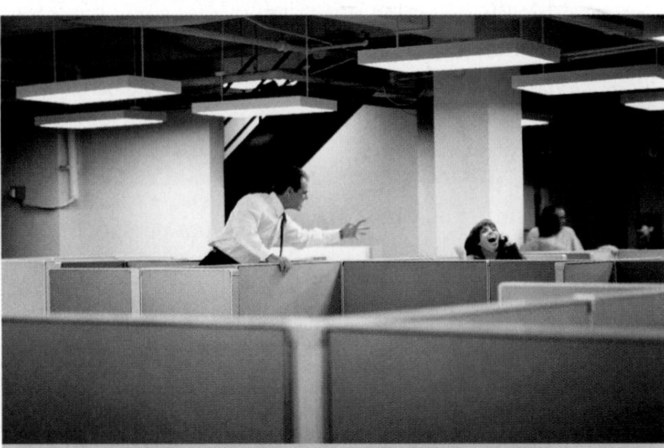

Cubicles and other features of an organization's physical layout are often designed by human factors psychologists. Using cubicles to define workers' spaces in large, open offices can add flexibility and save on construction costs. However, some workers complain about noise and a lack of privacy.

However, many workers do not like open designs. For one thing, these workplaces are noisier than those with individual workspaces, and workers sometimes complain about interruptions and lack of privacy (Ettorre, 1995). Moreover, a private office is perceived as a status symbol, so employees in management positions expect to have rooms with doors. They argue that they need privacy to meet with their subordinates and to discuss decisions with their peers and superiors. Consequently, most open designs include at least a few private spaces, usually managers' offices and conference rooms.

The Workspace Envelope **Workspace envelope** refers to the three-dimensional space in which an individual worker performs the tasks that comprise his or her job. Some workspace envelopes are more comfortable than others. What makes the difference?

One factor to consider in the design of a workspace envelope is physical size. One of the most important contributions of human factors psychologists to workplace comfort is adjustable furniture. In many of today's workplaces, chairs, desks, and other features of the workspace envelope can be adjusted to fit about 95% of the population, men and women ranging from about 63 to 74 inches in height.

Many of the workspace envelope innovations introduced by human factors psychologists in recent years address aspects of computer use. Poor computer workstation designs are responsible for a growing number of workplace injuries such as chronic neck, shoulder, and wrist pain, as well as eyestrain and frequent headaches (Sarkis, 2000). As a result, some general guidelines for setting up a computer workstation have been developed. For example, human factors experts suggest placing the monitor directly behind the keyboard. However, some studies suggest that allowing each worker to adjust the placement of all the physical elements of her or his workstation to suit personal preferences is a better way of reducing computer-use injuries (Krumm, 2001). Moreover, programming employees' computers with software that reminds them to take breaks and to practice exercises that reduce muscle and eyestrain can be an effective means of reducing such injuries (Krasowska, 1996).

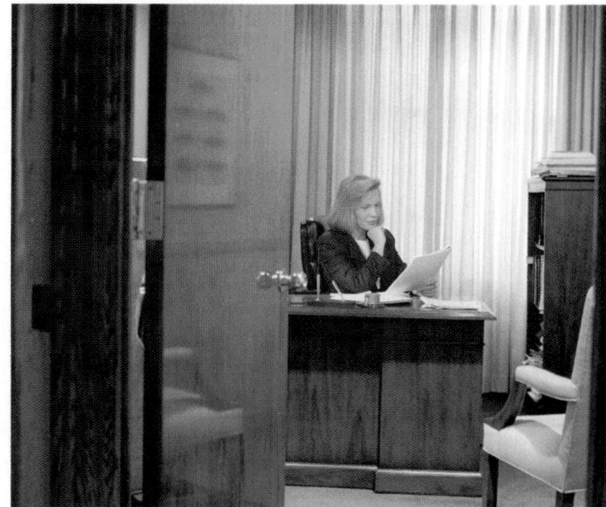

Artifactual communication is the process of using human-made objects to send messages to others. What kind of message does this woman's office convey?

Artifactual Communication One important aspect of workplace design is **artifactual communication**, which is the use of objects to communicate nonverbal messages. (*Artifactual* means "made by human hands.") The location of an individual's office and its architectural and decorative features are one source of such messages. For example, large offices with windows are usually reserved for employees who hold managerial positions.

The size and architectural features of an office are part of its formal design and reflect an individual's relationship to the organization. However, the arrangement and condition of an individual's workspace can send messages as well. For instance, furniture placement and wall decorations can convey a feeling of welcome or coldness: "Come in; sit down and relax" or "Stand there and be intimidated; I'm too important to spend time with you." An office in which there are piles of paper everywhere, office supplies are strewn about, and the trash can is overflowing with soda cans and styrofoam cups may say, "I have more work to do than I can handle." By contrast, one in which papers are arranged in an organized way, office supplies are neatly stored in compartments or drawers, and there is little or no trash may say, "I'm in control."

■ **workspace envelope**
The three-dimensional space in which an individual worker performs the tasks that comprise his or her job.

■ **artifactual communication**
The use of objects to communicate nonverbal messages.

■ **quality of work life (QWL) movement**
An approach to reducing work-related stress by basing job and workplace design on analyses of the quality of employee experiences in an organization.

The Quality of Work Life Movement

What are some of the innovations associated with the quality of work life movement?

As you learned in Chapter 13, jobs can be highly stressful. Human factors psychologists have developed one approach to reducing employees' work-related stress—the **quality of work life (QWL) movement**. Advocates of the QWL movement emphasize job and workplace designs based on analyses of the quality of employees' experiences in an organization. The idea is that, when people are happier at work, they will be more productive. For example, the on-site child-care center is one innovation that has come about because of concern for the quality of work life. Even though providing on-site child-care can be expensive, QWL advocates argue that it will pay for itself in terms of reduced absences and lower stress levels among employees who are parents.

Another QWL innovation is **telecommuting**. Telecommuters work in their homes and are connected to their workplaces by computer, fax machine, and telephone. Some

■ **telecommuting**
An arrangement in which employees work in their homes and are connected to their workplaces by computer, fax machine, and telephone.

telecommuters work at home every day; others do so only one or two days each week. Allowing workers to telecommute accomplishes several organizational goals. For example, telecommuting reduces the number of workers who drive to work, thereby reducing pollution and the number of parking spaces the organization must provide. Further, telecommuting gives workers a great deal of flexibility and autonomy. They can choose whether to prepare written reports, for example, during normal working hours or in the middle of the night. This kind of flexibility can increase job satisfaction (Wilde, 2000). Moreover, telecommuting helps employees balance work and family responsibilities. It can also be helpful to employees with disabilities that make it difficult for them to get around.

When you think of telecommuters, do you imagine them spending a lot of time watching television or playing video games or engaging in other kinds of personal activities rather than working? If so, you might be surprised to learn that several studies have shown telecommuters to be just as productive as employees in conventional work settings (Greengard, 1994). In fact, many telecommuters say that the lack of interruptions at home helps them get their work done more efficiently (Flynn, 1995).

Two other innovations associated with the QWL movement are flextime and job sharing. *Flextime* involves allowing employees to create their own work schedules. Most organizations that use flextime have certain times (usually called "core hours") when all employees must be present. At other times, though, employees are free to come and go as long as their work is done and they put in the required number of hours. Many employees take advantage of the flextime option to reduce work-family conflicts (Sharpe et al., 2002). Others use this option to enhance their job performance by coming to the workplace at times when they believe they can be most productive. Further, flextime workers report that they experience less transportation-related stress—that is, they don't worry as much about rush-hour traffic jams and late trains or buses as they would if working a conventional schedule (Lucas & Heady, 2002). Researchers have found that flextime helps to build employee loyalty, thereby reducing turnover (Roehling et al., 2001).

Job sharing is a QWL innovation in which a full-time job is shared by two or more employees. For example, a receptionist's position might be filled by one person on Monday, Wednesday, and Friday and by another on Tuesday and Thursday. In fact, it's theoretically possible that the job could be filled by a different individual each day of the week. Employers have found job sharing to be a particularly effective way to help employees gradually return to full-time work after a leave of absence for reasons such as illness or pregnancy (Krumm, 2001).

Aggression and Violence in the Workplace

What are the causes of desk rage?

Have you heard or used the phrase "going postal" in reference to an angry tirade by a fellow employee? The phrase came from a very small number of well-publicized events in the 1990s involving shooting sprees carried out by employees of the U.S. Postal Service. Fortunately, most aggressive acts in the workplace don't reach such a level. Nevertheless, rude, hostile, and aggressive behavior in work settings, often called **desk rage** in the mass media, has become more common in recent years. In one survey of 1,500 adults, about half reported that they had witnessed desk rage incidents (Daw, 2001). Moreover, many respondents indicated that such behavior exhibited by co-workers caused them to feel stressed, to miss work, and even to look for new jobs.

Like aggressive and violent behavior outside the workplace, desk rage is often exhibited by individuals who mistakenly perceive another's actions as hostile (Homant & Kennedy, 2003). For example, suppose a supervisor asks an employee who has had a private office to begin sharing a space with another worker because of limited office availability. A change of this sort may lead to a desk rage incident if the employee believes that the supervisor's request is motivated by personal dislike or hostility.

desk rage
Rude, hostile, and aggressive behavior in work settings.

Job-related stress is another factor that contributes to desk rage. Noise in the work setting seems to increase the amount of such behavior (Daw, 2001). Unresolved interpersonal conflicts may be another source of stress that sets the stage for desk rage incidents. Thus, to decrease the likelihood of desk rage incidents, human factors psychologists recommend that organizations identify sources of stress and make efforts to reduce them.

Remember It 18.3

1. The height of a computer worker's desk is one component of her __________ .
2. The __________ movement supports innovations such as telecommuting and job sharing.
3. A worker who believes he has been treated unfairly by his employer or supervisor is more likely than one who feels satisfied with his job to exhibit __________ .

ANSWERS: 1. workspace envelope; 2. quality of work life (QWL); 3. desk rage

Gender Issues at Work

One of the most profound changes in employment patterns has been the tremendous increase in the number of women in the workplace. By the end of the 20th century, women made up 47% of the civilian labor force in the United States (U.S. Census Bureau, 2001). However, there are important differences in the working lives of men and women.

Women's Work Patterns

In what ways do women's work patterns differ from men's?

Women's work patterns are less likely than those of men to be continuous. Most women move in and out of the workforce at least once, usually to spend time rearing children (Drobnic et al., 1999). Further, women are more likely than men to choose lower-paying careers, such as teaching, in which this discontinuous work pattern has less negative impact than it does in corporate management (Blanchard & Lichtenberg, 2003). Thus, this pattern, usually referred to as the **mommy track**, can adversely influence the earnings of women who follow it (Hattiangadi & Habib, 2000). However, some research suggests that the current cohort of young women expect both to be continuously employed and to have a family in adulthood (Davey, 1998). Thus, the number of women on the mommy track may diminish in the future.

■ **mommy track** A work pattern in which women move in and out of the workforce, usually to spend time rearing children.

Gender Differences in On-the-Job Coping Styles

How do men's and women's responses to job-related stress differ?

Like patterns of employment, patterns of job satisfaction among women are often more complex than those of men (Schieman & Taylor, 2001). This may be because men and women respond differently to work-related stress (Perho & Korhonen, 1999). Both sexes complain about the same stress factors: time pressure, getting along with co-workers, boring tasks, and fear of losing one's job. However, men typically address such problems directly by negotiating with supervisors and co-workers to bring about changes. In Chapter 13, you learned that this approach is known as *problem-focused coping*. By contrast, women tend to use *emotion-focused coping*. So, instead of confronting co-workers and supervisors directly, they often discuss job-related stressors with female co-workers. They may also adopt the kinds of defense mechanisms (e.g., repression) you learned about in Chapter 14.

At first glance, you might judge men's problem-focused coping strategies to be more effective than women's emotion-focused coping strategies. However, research has shown that the emotion-focused coping adopted by many female workers enables them to balance their dissatisfactions against their areas of contentment more effectively than their male co-workers do. For example, the statement "I don't enjoy working with spreadsheets all day long, but the 4-day work week in this company fits my needs" is more likely to come from a woman than a man. Thus, men may be more likely to improve their job satisfaction in situations where change is possible, but women probably cope more effectively when work stressors are difficult or impossible to change (Hattar-Pollara et al., 2003). Moreover, some research indicates that women are better able than men to assess the degree to which their skills and personality traits fit particular jobs, thus avoiding the stress associated with selecting an inappropriate career (Liff & Ward, 2001).

Gender Discrimination

What evidence is there to suggest that women are breaking the glass ceiling?

At the beginning of the 21st century, women reportedly held 53% of the more than 20 million professional jobs in the United States. However, the majority of those jobs—such as public school teaching and nursing—pay only moderately well. Women hold only slightly over 28% of the more than 8 million higher-paying professional jobs in the United States. Figure 18.1 charts the percentages of women who were holding various jobs through the end of the 20th century and shows women's earnings as a percentage of men's earnings for each job (Doyle, 2000).

In the late 1980s, the term **glass ceiling** was introduced into the American vocabulary by management consultant Ann Morrison and her colleagues (Morrison et al.,

FIGURE 18.1 Representation of Women in Various Jobs and Professions in the United States, 1950–2000

Women steadily increased their representation in all sectors of the U.S. workforce over the last five decades of the 20th century.

Source: Doyle (2000).

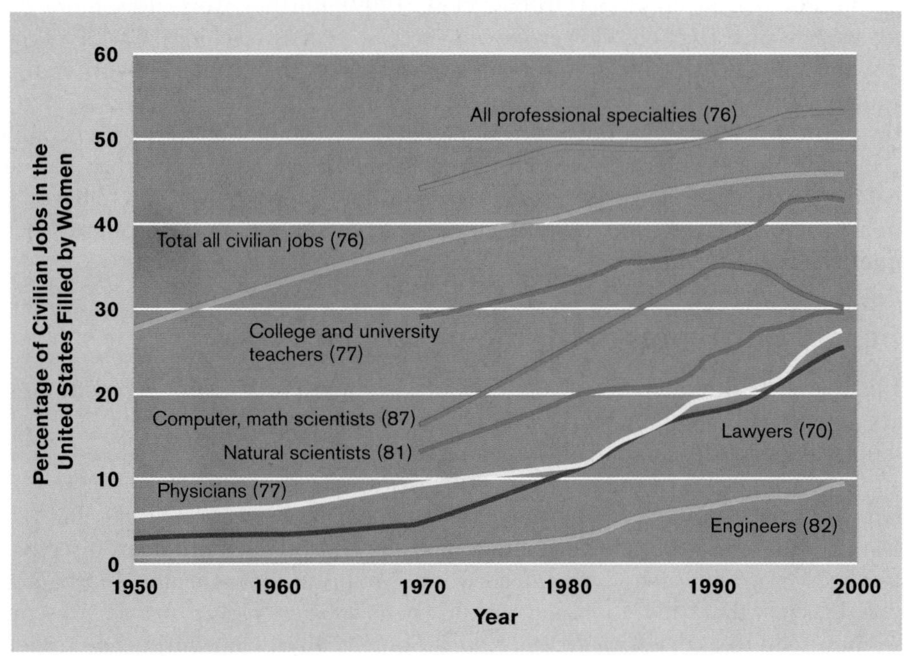

1987). Their book, *Breaking the Glass Ceiling*, claimed that women had entered the previously male-dominated world of business management but were unable to reach the highest executive positions because of institutional barriers such as sexism and the so-called good-old-boy network. At that time, there were only a handful of women serving as corporate CEOs in the United States.

Recent research has looked at the glass ceiling differently. Researchers at the Glass Ceiling Institute report that, when Morrison's book was published, there were very few highly educated, middle-aged women in the workforce (Adler, 2001a, 2001b). This fact is critical, they say, to understanding female representation in corporate America. Their research, based on decades of accumulated data from large corporations, shows that the requirements for attaining a CEO position include a master of business administration (MBA) degree and at least 25 years of experience. Further, the average age at which business professionals attain CEO positions is 52. In the late 1980s, they argue, there were very few middle-aged women in the American workforce who possessed these characteristics.

By contrast, 33% of today's MBAs are women, and female representation in top corporate management positions has increased as women have accumulated work experience (Adler, 2001a). At present, about 18% of upper-level managers in U.S. corporations are women, and more women are attaining CEO positions every year. You read about one such woman, Christine King of AMI Semiconductor, at the beginning of this chapter. Another is Carly Fiorina, CEO of Hewlett Packard, one of the world's largest corporations. Indeed, research shows that well-qualified women are now two to four times as likely as men with equal qualifications to be promoted to top executive positions. Researchers at the Glass Ceiling Institute claim that the preference for female executives arises from both corporations' greater interest in diversity and women's records as top managers. Their research shows that corporations headed by women and those that have "women-friendly" policies, such as on-site child care, are more profitable than more traditional businesses (Adler, 2001b).

Since the 1980s, the number of women serving as CEOs of large corporations has increased. One of today's most successful female CEOs is Carly Fiorina, who has headed Hewlett Packard since 1999.

Similar advances have been documented in women's attainment of leadership positions in educational institutions and government agencies (Addi-Raccah & Ayalon, 2002; Baker et al., 2002). Moreover, the number of female collegiate athletic directors rose dramatically during the 1990s (Whisenant et al., 2002). More women are found among the authors of studies in psychology today than in the past (McSweeney & Parks, 2002). Further, many women have avoided the glass ceiling by starting their own businesses in every area of the U.S. economy (Weiler & Bernasek, 2001).

Despite these advances, gender stereotypes often taint evaluations of women's job performance (Penny, 2001). And there are still a number of areas in which women have made few inroads. For example, even though more women now publish articles in psychology journals, women are still poorly represented among journal editors (McSweeney & Parks, 2002). Moreover, studies show that women are less likely than men to actively seek promotions to upper-level management positions because of potential conflicts between their work and family roles (Sarrio et al., 2002; van Vianen & Fischer, 2002). Thus, breaking the glass ceiling may ultimately require changes in attitudes about women's roles both at work and at home.

■ **glass ceiling**
An invisible, institutional barrier that prevents women from reaching the highest executive positions in organizations.

■ **sexual harassment**
Any kind of unwanted or offensive sexual expression in the workplace.

Sexual Harassment

What are the two categories of sexual harassment complaints?

As female representation in the workforce has increased, discussions about the appropriateness of various forms of sexual expression in the workplace have become more common. Specifically, concerns about sexual harassment have increased. **Sexual harassment** is a very broad term encompassing any kind of unwanted or offensive sexual expression in the workplace. Generally, sexual harassment complaints fall into two categories (Lovoy, 2001): In *quid pro quo* complaints, workers claim to have been offered something in exchange for sexual favors. *Hostile work environment* complaints involve inappropriate

TABLE 18.1 Types of Sexual Harassment

TYPE	EXAMPLE
Sexual bribery (quid pro quo)	A supervisor promises a raise to a subordinate in exchange for sexual intercourse.
Sexual coercion (quid pro quo)	A supervisor threatens to fire a subordinate who refuses to have intercourse with him.
Gender harassment (hostile work environment)	A female day-care worker belittles a male co-worker because she believes men are incapable of caring for children.
Seductive behavior (hostile work environment)	An employee sends e-mail messages to a co-worker in which he describes in detail sexual fantasies involving both of them.
Sexual imposition (hostile work environment)	An employee displays pornographic pictures and refuses to remove them when asked to do so by co-workers.

behavior of a sexual nature that creates an intolerable level of discomfort for the complainant. Table 18.1 presents types of sexual harassment that give rise to these complaints.

Often, sexual harassment involves a supervisor and a subordinate, but it can also involve workers at the same level. Furthermore, although the stereotype associated with sexual harassment is that of a male worker harassing a female worker, sexual harassment can be male-to-female, female-to-male, male-to-male, or female-to-female. Further, in today's high-tech workplaces, the incidence of computer-based harassment is increasing dramatically (Cooper et al., 2002). "Cyber-harassers" use an organization's e-mail system to send sexually explicit messages or even pornographic materials to co-workers. They may target individuals or send such items to everyone in the organization's e-mail directory. Cyber-harassers often believe that their actions will be viewed as humorous rather than as harassing.

Research shows that sexual harassment has detrimental effects on employees' job satisfaction and may lead to higher turnover rates, increased absenteeism, and even higher levels of alcohol and drug abuse (Piotrkowski, 1998; Wislar et al., 2002). Sexual harassment is especially distressing when it is accompanied by aggressive or threatening behavior (Kinney, 2003). Most victims of sexual harassment cope with the stresses involved by using a combination of problem- and emotion-focused strategies (Magley, 2002). And, although sexual harassment affects victims in all racial and cultural groups in similar ways, a strong sense of ethnic identity helps minority men and women cope when they are victimized (Bergman & Drasgow, 2003; Shupe et al., 2002).

But what about sexual behaviors that may be regarded by most people as annoying, but don't quite rise to the level of illegality? Researchers have found that inappropriate sexual behaviors by co-workers are often cited as a major source of job stress, especially for women (Lyons, 2002). Moreover, women regard the climate of an organization more positively when leaders actively work to prevent inappropriate behavior of this kind and take action to stop it when it does occur (Offerman & Malamut, 2002).

To decrease the likelihood of sexual harassment, many organizations provide supervisors and workers with training in recognizing and combating it. Moreover, in the United States, federal labor laws require employers to take certain actions with regard to sexual harassment (Krumm, 2001). Employers must have written sexual harassment policies and distribute copies of them to employees. These policies must include a formal procedure for filing and reviewing sexual harassment complaints, which must be investigated and resolved in a timely manner.

Remember It 18.4

1. Women's work patterns are less likely to be ___________ than those of men.
2. Men are less likely than women to use ___________ coping strategies to address workplace stressors.
3. The ___________ is often used to refer to the invisible barrier women face in advancing to top management positions.
4. Jane's boss offers to give her a raise if she will go out on a date with him. Jane might be justified in making a ___________ complaint of sexual harassment.

ANSWERS: 1. continuous; 2. emotion-focused; 3. glass ceiling; 4. quid pro quo

Human Diversity in the Workplace

In addition to training employees to recognize and combat sexual harassment, many organizations are providing employees with **diversity training** to help them acquire the human relations skills they need to function effectively in a diverse workplace. Before examining the content and effectiveness of diversity training, let's look at some of the factors that underlie diversity in today's society.

Race and Ethnicity in the Workplace

What is ethnocentrism, and how does it affect the workplace?

Often the terms *race* and *ethnicity* are used interchangeably. Although the distinctions between the two concepts are somewhat fuzzy, social scientists typically use *race* to refer to shared biological characteristics (e.g., skin color) and *ethnicity* to refer to shared social characteristics (e.g., language and customs). Thus, two people might be of the same race, but differ in ethnicity. For example, Germans and Italians are the same race but not the same ethnicity. Similarly, two individuals may share ethnicity but differ in race. In Latin America, for example, many people are descended from African slaves and, thus, have the same racial heritage as African Americans in the United States. But such individuals are ethnically Hispanic because they share the Spanish language and Spanish-based customs with Latin Americans who are of European and Native American descent.

Changing Demographics As the overall population of the United States has changed, so has the workforce. Figure 18.2 (on page 612) shows that, from 1990 to 2000, the proportions of individuals who identified themselves as belonging in most of the racial categories used by the U.S. Census Bureau remained constant, while the proportion who classified themselves as Asian American increased a bit. At the same time, the proportion of individuals of Hispanic origin increased from 9% in 1990 to 13% in 2000. (Remember, Hispanic Americans are of varied races.) Even though the proportion of African Americans in the overall U.S. population hasn't changed, African Americans are in the workforce in greater numbers than ever before. Some experts estimate that almost half of new entrants into the U.S. workforce are members of minority groups (Society for Industrial/Organizational Psychology [SIOP], 2002).

Minority groups are increasing their numbers not only among employees, but also among employers. More minority group members own businesses today than in the past (U.S. Census Bureau, 2003).

■ **diversity training** Formal training aimed at equipping workers with the human relations skills they need to function effectively in a diverse workplace.

FIGURE 18.2 Demographics of Minority Groups in the U.S. Population

The proportions of Asian Americans and Hispanic Americans increased from 1990 to 2000, while other minority groups either remained constant or declined.
Source: U.S. Census Bureau (2001).

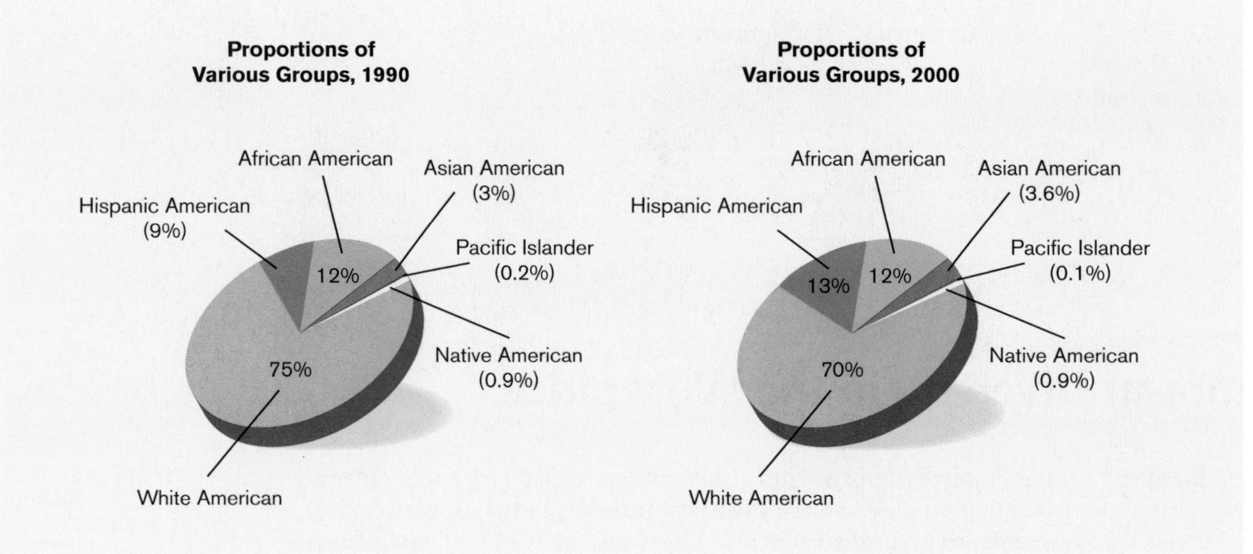

Why Race and Ethnicity Matter in the Workplace According to most surveys, Americans of all races and ethnicities believe that intergroup relations are better today than at any time in U.S. history (Public Agenda, 2003a). But most say that there is still room for improvement. Researchers and diversity trainers agree that ethnocentrism can be an obstacle to improving race relations (Ensari, 2001; Hansen, 2003). **Ethnocentrism** is the tendency to look at situations from one's own racial or cultural perspective.

■ **ethnocentrism**
The tendency to look at situations from one's own racial or cultural perspective.

As you might suspect, most individuals are surprised to learn how great an influence ethnocentrism has on their everyday thinking and behavior (Danto, 2000). For instance, what do you expect to see when you open a box of "flesh-colored" adhesive bandages? If you are White, you will probably not perceive anything incongruous about the color of the bandages. It usually doesn't occur to most Whites that these common, everyday items are actually not flesh-colored for most of the world's population. Diversity training facilitators use such examples to illustrate how ethnocentrism affects everyday life.

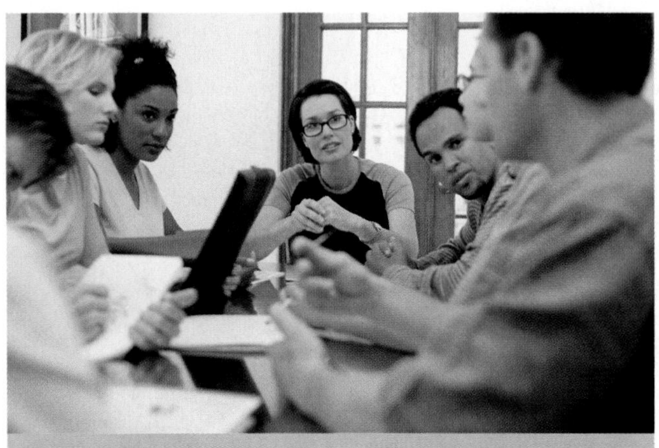
Employees of all races and ethnic groups may interpret interracial interactions ethnocentrically.

Ethnocentrism may prevent us from realizing that workers from backgrounds different from our own may view workplace interactions quite differently. For example, researchers have found that African Americans are more likely than White Americans to perceive negative encounters between supervisors and subordinates of different races as being racial in nature (Johnson et al., 2003). To further complicate matters, members of each group believe their opinion is right and the other opinion is wrong. However, diversity trainers help workers understand that such differences are not a matter of right versus wrong. African Americans' views are shaped by real associations among career success variables, such as income, unemployment, and race, as indicated in Figure 18.3. Similarly, the perspective of many White Americans derives from their belief that racism is no longer a significant problem in the United States (look back at Figure 17.7 on page 586; Kaiser Family Foundation, 1999). Thus, the differing views of African and White Americans are derived from looking at interpersonal interactions through different lenses, so to speak. And to think of either perspective as right or wrong is to oversimplify the rational and emotional processes that contribute to its development.

FIGURE 18.3 Income by Educational Level and Unemployment Rates among White Americans, African Americans, and Hispanic Americans

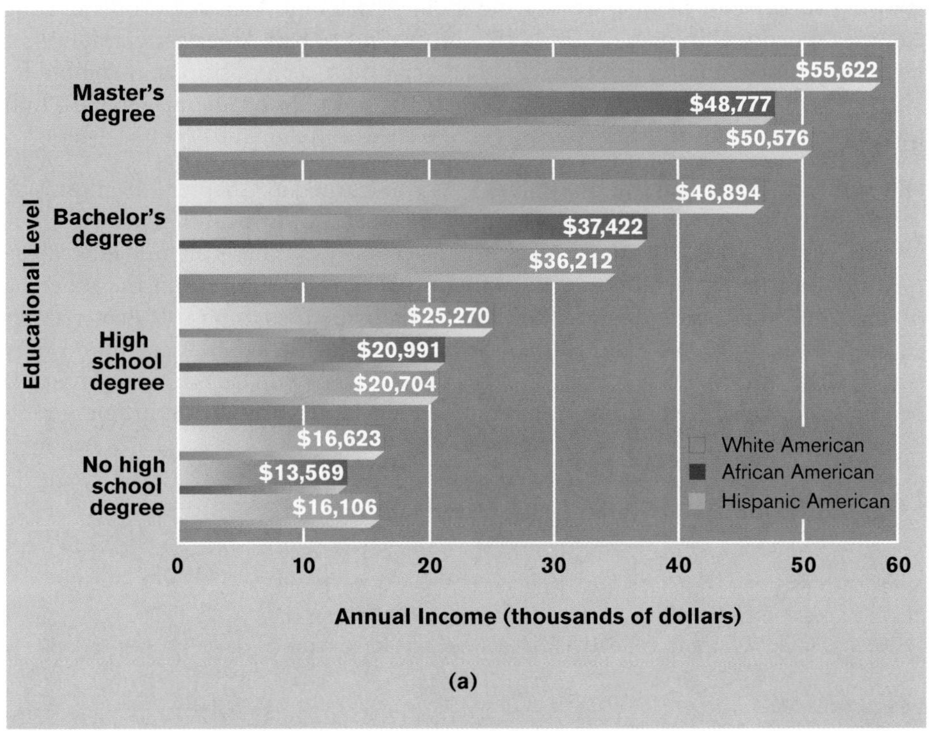

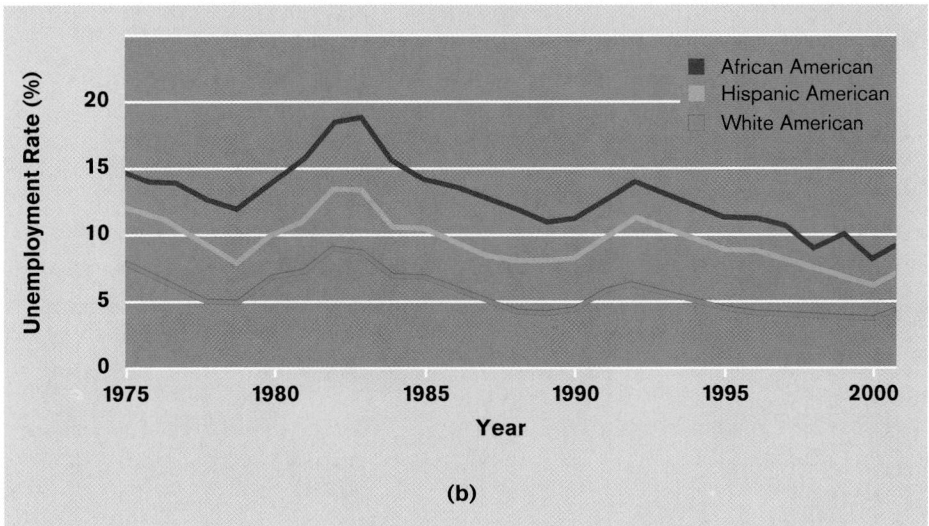

(a) There is considerable disparity in the average incomes of White Americans, African Americans, and Hispanic Americans at all educational levels. (b) The same economic factors contribute to unemployment among members of all groups. So, in the recession years of the early 1980s, unemployment rates were high for everyone. Similarly, in the boom years of the 1990s, rates declined to historic lows. Still, differences in unemployment rates across minority groups have remained fairly constant. No matter how good or bad the economy, more African Americans and Hispanic Americans than White Americans were out of work during any given period.

Source: U.S. Census Bureau (2001).

Cultural Diversity in the Workplace

What are some factors that have led to increased cultural diversity in the workplace?

Today's workforce is more culturally diverse than in the past. What factors have contributed to this change?

Globalization One source of greater workplace diversity is **globalization**, the process through which workers all over the world have been brought into more frequent contact with one another as a result of advances in transportation and communications technology. Such advances mean that individuals whose workplaces are thousands of miles apart may communicate frequently with one another. It is no longer unusual for an employee of a firm in the United States to have daily interactions with suppliers in Japan, or customers in Poland, or fellow employees of the same firm who are based in Kenya.

Immigration Immigration is another force behind increasing cultural diversity. A growing number of people are moving from Africa and Asia to Europe and North America seeking employment. In both Europe and North America, immigrants may be found in jobs ranging from unskilled labor to high-tech positions in computer science and engineering. Currently, more than 10% of U.S. residents, about 30 million people, were born in another country (U.S. Census Bureau, 2001).

Why Culture Matters in the Workplace As you learned in Chapter 14, cultures differ with regard to the *individualism/collectivism dimension*, and this difference affects individuals' personalities. Individualist cultures place more emphasis on individual achievement than on group achievement. People in collectivist cultures, on the other hand, often define themselves in terms of their group membership. You may recall that American and European cultures tend to be individualist, while those found in Asia, Africa, and Latin America are often more collectivist. As you can see from Figure 18.4, people from collectivist cultures represented a far larger proportion of immigrants to

■ **globalization**
The process through which workers all over the world have been brought into more frequent contact with one another as a result of advances in transportation and communications technology.

FIGURE 18.4 Place of Origin of Immigrants to the United States, 1965 and 2001

Individuals from collectivist cultures such as those in Asia, Africa, and Latin America represent a far larger proportion of immigrants who come to the United States today than they did in the 1960s. Consequently, conflicts between individualist and collectivist ideals have become more common in the workplace.

Source: Immigration and Naturalization Service (2002).

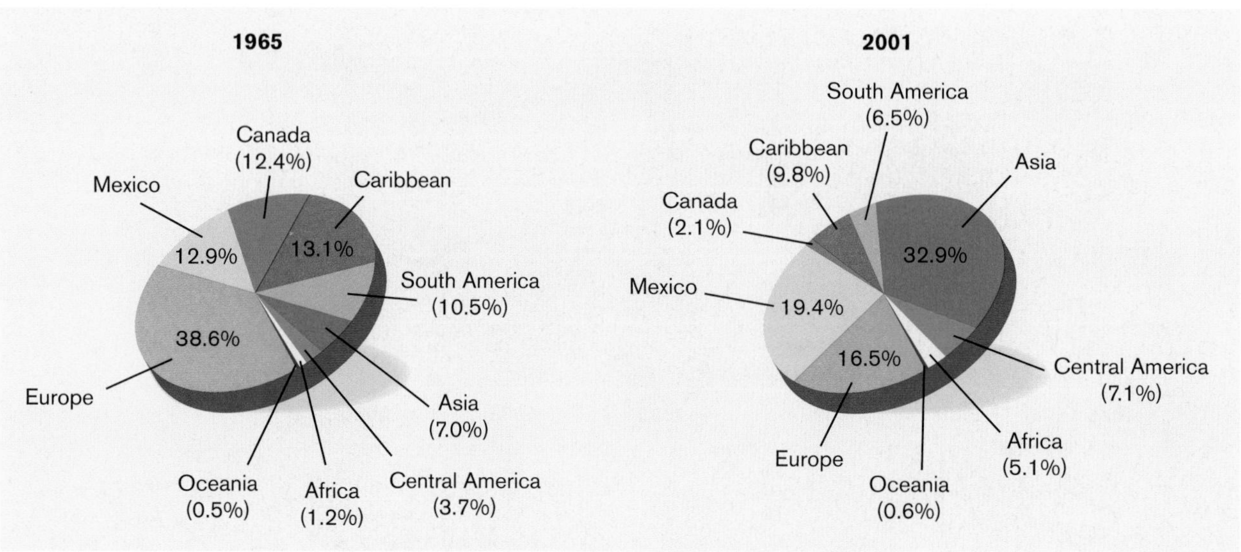

the United States in 2001 than they did in the 1960s. Consequently, individualist versus collectivist conflicts are more likely to arise today than they were in the past.

One situation in which differences in individualism/collectivism become evident occurs when organizations attempt to implement in individualist cultures practices that have been successful in collectivist cultures, or vice versa. For example, *lean production* is a manufacturing management model that emphasizes cost control over all other considerations. This approach has been highly successful in Japan, but its implementation in North America and Europe has met with disappointing results. Why?

Researchers point to cultural differences between Japan and the West (Rafferty & Tapsell, 2001). They say that in the lean production model each worker is viewed as a component of a large system, a cog in a gigantic machine, so to speak. The individualist cultures of the West socialize people to value autonomy, so Western workers find the lean production approach to be psychologically stifling. Indeed, many critics who argue that the lean production model represents a return to a Theory X management approach are not surprised that this model has met with limited success in Western organizations (S. D. Green, 2002).

Differences in cultural values may cause management strategies that are successful in one culture to be less so in another.

In response, lean production advocates argue that a clearly stated organizational goal can encourage workers to make meaningful contributions. In practice, though, organizations that implement the lean production model often become highly centralized, and upper-level managers receive credit for most of the organization's achievements. Western cultures tend to value individual recognition, while Asian cultures socialize individuals to associate their individual identities with those of the groups to which they belong (Matsumo, 2000). Thus, if a Japanese manufacturing plant becomes more cost-efficient, the Japanese worker takes pride in his employer's achievement. In contrast, the North American or European worker who makes a suggestion that leads to a reduction in costs wants to be personally recognized for her idea.

The Older Worker

What are some common misconceptions about older workers?

Would you be surprised to learn that, by 2015, more than 20% of the U.S. workforce will be over the age of 55 (American Association of Retired Persons [AARP], 2003)? Because people are living longer and staying healthier, older workers are making up a larger proportion of the workforce. This "graying" of the workforce presents some challenges, both for older workers and for the organizations that employ them.

Changing Age Norms Combating **ageism**, the belief that aging is inevitably associated with a loss of competence (Palmore, 1990), is one of the main challenges facing older workers. Since our perceptions of different age groups are influenced by culturally based *age norms*, we tend to associate certain unwritten, and often unspoken, social rules with normal life experiences. These norms cover the "right" age for marriage and child-bearing, as well as for retirement. One way of combating ageism is to educate workers and employers that yesterday's age norms are no longer appropriate. For one thing, a significant number of adults now continue working past the stereotypical retirement age of 65. About 47% of men and 37% of women over age 65 are employed in the United States (FIFARS, 2000).

Of course, these findings come from studies of individuals who are already elderly. What does the next cohort of older adults, the "baby boomers," expect to do in their "golden" years? Surveys indicate that these adults plan to retire in their early 60s (Monroy, 2000). However, they expect to live at least 20 years past retirement. Many

ageism
The belief that aging is inevitably associated with a loss of competence.

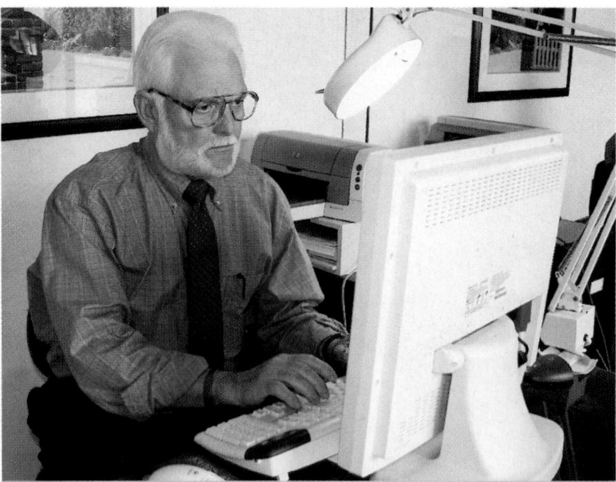
Ageism may lead employers to believe that older workers are incapable of learning the skills necessary in today's high-tech workplace. However, research shows that older workers can outperform younger ones.

see their later years as a time during which they can pursue a second career, one they may have viewed as impractical when they were younger. Such findings suggest that age norms are likely to continue to change in the future.

Job Skills and Performance Do you believe the old adage "You can't teach an old dog new tricks"? Unfortunately, many people have the idea that older people can't learn new job skills. In fact, surveys show that many potential employers express concerns about older adults' ability to learn new job skills (Forte & Hansvick, 1999). However, studies of age differences in job skill learning demonstrate that the learning process itself does not change with age. The same factors—interest, anxiety, motivation, quality of instruction, self-efficacy, and so on—predict skill learning in both older and younger adults (Chasseigne et al., 1999; Gardiner et al., 1997; Mead & Fisk, 1998; Plaud et al., 1999; Truluck & Courtneay, 1999).

Not only are older workers able to learn new job skills, they are often just as productive, or even more so, than the younger adults with whom they work. One productivity study found that computer workers over the age of 60 worked more slowly but made fewer mistakes than their younger co-workers did (Czaja et al., 1998). Further, many supervisors regard older employees as more reliable than younger ones and rate the quality of their work more favorably (Forte & Hansvick, 1999; Rao & Rao, 1997).

How does the Americans with Disabilities Act benefit workers with disabilities?

Workers with Disabilities

What would it be like to search for a job if you were blind or confined to a wheelchair? You would probably worry about the extent to which your disability might affect your chances of being hired. And what if your disability was a hidden one, such as diabetes or bipolar disorder? You might be concerned that revealing the disability to a potential employer would negatively affect the probability of getting a job (Bishop & Allen, 2001; Dalgin & Gilbride, 2003; Olney & Brockelman, 2003; Weber et al., 2002).

Fortunately, the **Americans with Disabilities Act (ADA)**, enacted in 1990, made it illegal to discriminate against applicants and employees on the basis of a physical or mental disability. This law also recognizes the individual's right to keep his or her disability private during the application and interview process. It further specifies that, once individuals with disabilities are hired, employers must make necessary, *reasonable accommodations* for them and that benefits such as health insurance must be equal for workers with and without disabilities.

Surveys indicate that most people in the United States have heard of the ADA but know very little about it (Hernandez et al., 2003). For example, just exactly what is a disability? The law, as interpreted by numerous administrative rulings and court decisions, defines a **disability** as a physical or mental condition that limits major life activities such as seeing, hearing, speaking, walking, breathing, working with one's hands, taking care of one's personal needs, learning, reproduction, child rearing, and working. This definition can apply to many conditions besides obvious physical disabilities such as blindness; for example, it covers obesity, psychiatric disorders, chronic health conditions such as diabetes, and HIV/AIDS.

The Americans with Disabilities Act, passed in 1990, requires employers to make accommodations for workers' disabilities.

Furthermore, the ADA's protection against discrimination and its requirement for reasonable accommodations apply equally to workers who are currently disabled and to those who have a history of disability. For this reason, recovering alcoholics and drug abusers who can document their participation in a formal rehabilitation program are protected by the ADA to the same extent as workers who are blind or deaf or suffer from other physical disabilities (Westreich, 2002). However, the ADA does not protect recovering substance abusers from being disciplined by an employer for violations of the organization's alcohol and drug use policies (Krumm, 2001).

How do workers with disabilities function on the job? Most research indicates that, with appropriate accommodations, their performance equals or exceeds that of workers without disabilities (Krumm, 2001). In fact, one unanticipated benefit of the ADA has been that personnel managers have generally developed better job descriptions since the law came into effect. For example, a job description specifying that a worker must possess a driver's license might lead to discrimination against applicants with visual or physical impairments. Consequently, human resource managers are required to carefully scrutinize the actual work performed by those who fill the position. In so doing, they may find that the position requires driving only once a month. Thus, when necessary, driving responsibilities could be assigned to another worker in order to make the job accessible to a worker with a disability. For this and other reasons, many managers believe that the ADA has helped them tap into a previously underutilized worker pool (Callahan, 1994). At the same time, the ADA has allowed many employees without disabilities to learn more about the perspectives of those who are differently abled.

Americans with Disabilities Act (ADA) A law enacted in the United States in 1990 making it illegal to discriminate against job applicants and employees on the basis of physical or mental disability.

disability A physical or mental condition that limits major life activities.

Sexual Orientation in the Workplace

Why have some gay and lesbian workers been reluctant to reveal their sexual orientation to co-workers?

Recent surveys have found that about two-thirds of Americans under age 60 say that they personally know someone who is gay or lesbian (Public Agenda, 2003b). Despite increasing awareness and acceptance of homosexuality, some gays and lesbians are reluctant to reveal their sexual orientation in work situations because they fear discrimination (Ragins et al., 2003). However, surveys also show that about two-thirds of Americans believe that homosexuals should be legally protected against discrimination in employment or for promotion (Public Agenda, 2003b). Many states, counties, and cities have adopted laws that provide such protections.

According to researchers, the main type of discrimination based on sexual orientation is not loss of employment or promotion opportunities but rather takes more subtle forms, such as ostracism or jokes about sexual orientation. Some researchers have found that 50% or more of gay and lesbian Americans have experienced such treatment by their co-workers (American Psychological Association, 1998). In response to concerns expressed by gay and lesbian workers, more than 90% of employers in the United States have adopted formal policies prohibiting employees from discriminating against gay and lesbian workers in any way (Christensen, 2002). However, an employer's stated policies and the actual behavior of its workers and managers may be quite different (Hirschman, 2001). Thus, because many gay and lesbian workers have experienced discrimination, even in organizations that prohibit it, helping workers learn to be more tolerant of differences in sexual orientation is another goal of diversity training.

Promoting Diversity

What steps can organizations take to build a more diverse workforce?

There are many reasons for promoting diversity in an organization's workforce. One practical reason is that organizations can provide better services when they hire employees with racial and cultural backgrounds similar to those of their customers (Cioffi, 2003). Another, perhaps more important, reason for seeking diversity is that it promotes a sense of fairness, one component of a positive organizational climate (Foley et al., 2002; Krysan & Farley, 2002). What's the best approach to achieving a diverse workforce?

■ **affirmative action** A process through which organizations actively seek to build an employee pool that includes members of as many racial and cultural groups as possible.

Affirmative Action One way that organizations can promote diversity is to actively seek to build an employee pool that includes members of as many racial and cultural groups as possible. This process is known as **affirmative action**. Many people view affirmative action as synonymous with fixed racial quotas (Arriola & Cole, 2001). However, true affirmative action programs focus on opening up the recruitment, selection, and promotion processes in ways that enable women and minorities to gain access to positions in which they have been historically underrepresented. One component of such a program, for example, might involve sponsoring career fairs at historically Black colleges. Another would be to provide female and minority employees with special training opportunities to help them acquire leadership skills.

One key to accomplishing affirmative action goals involves keeping minority candidates involved in the job selection process. Researchers have found that minority applicants are more likely than White applicants to withdraw from the process (Ployhart et al., 2002), possibly because they are more likely to be anxious about preemployment testing and to perceive the tests as invalid (Chan, 1997). Thus, organizations may be able to keep more minority group members in the applicant pool by providing them with data showing that the tests they will be required to take predict job performance equally well for Whites and minorities.

Training managers to avoid stereotypic thinking during interviews is also critical to building and maintaining a diverse workforce. This process, sometimes called *distortion management*, involves learning to recognize aspects of social information processing, such as stereotyping, when they happen and making conscious efforts to minimize their effects. Moreover, interviewers are legally forbidden to ask applicants about some topics, such as disability or marital status. For this reason, interviewers have to learn how to intentionally forget such information if interviewees mention it (Oien & Goernert, 2003).

Diversity Training Once an organization has a diverse workforce, how can it help employees work together harmoniously? *Diversity training* is one approach. To be effective, diversity training must include information that can increase workers' awareness of ethnocentrism and the perspectives of different groups.

Once the goal of awareness has been achieved, diversity trainers often focus on the development of interaction skills. One common activity used for this purpose is called the *international meeting* (SIOP, 2002). Trainers divide participants into "cultures" and instruct them to adopt behaviors representing four categories of cultural norms: greetings, personal space, eye contact, and individualism/collectivism. For example, participants in one culture might greet others with handshakes, maintain a 6-inch personal space in conversations, avoid eye contact during social interactions, and display a collectivist orientation by always referring to themselves as group members rather than as individuals. By contrast, participants in another culture might greet others with a nod of the head, maintain a 2-foot personal distance, stare at people while talking to them, and demonstrate an individualist orientation by talking about themselves as individuals rather than as group members. After practicing the assigned norms, each participant is paired with a person from another culture. Each partner must introduce himself or herself to the other in a way consistent with the norms and find out one fact about that person. Afterward, participants discuss how they responded emotionally to the varying norms and how each of the behaviors influenced their views of others. As a result of this activity, participants become more aware of their own culture-based social behaviors and how they might be perceived by people from different cultural backgrounds.

Does diversity training really help? One study found that the effects of the training were dependent on trainees' personalities; those who were more open to new experiences benefited most (Lievens et al., 2003). Other research has suggested that men may be initially less open to diversity training than women are, but they derive similar benefits from it (Lin & Rancer, 2003). Still, most studies show that, at the very least, diversity training helps workers who deal with culturally diverse suppliers, co-workers, or customers to feel more positively about their interactions with them (Cioffi, 2003). Moreover, learning to recognize ethnocentrism in their reactions to American ways of doing things appears to help immigrants to the United States cope with the stresses associated with working and living in an unfamiliar culture (Caruana & Chircop, 2001).

Remember It 18.5

1. The tendency to assess a situation from one's own cultural perspective is known as __________.
2. __________ and __________ are two factors that have led to increased diversity in the workplace.
3. The belief that getting older inevitably means becoming less competent is known as __________.
4. The Americans with Disabilities Act (ADA) requires employers to make __________ accommodations for workers with disabilities.
5. Subtle forms of discrimination against gay and lesbian Americans in the workplace include __________ and __________.
6. Employers can increase workplace diversity by adjusting their __________ and __________ procedures.

ANSWERS: 1. ethnocentrism; 2. Globalization, immigration; 3. ageism; 4. reasonable; 5. ostracism, jokes about sexual orientation; 6. recruitment, selection

Pursuing a Career

Let's return to the question posed at the beginning of this chapter: Where do you want to be in 5 years, 10 years, 15 years? How can you begin to form a personally meaningful answer to a question about your long-term goals? A good place to start is by looking at what research reveals about careers and job satisfaction.

Career Choice and Development

What factors influence career choice and development?

Perhaps the most important factor in career choice is personality. The work of John Holland has been very influential in shaping psychologists' ideas about personality and career. Holland (1973, 1992) proposes six basic personality types: realistic, investigative, artistic, social, enterprising, and conventional (see Table 18.2, on page 620).

Studies in several nations, as well as research involving African Americans, Hispanic Americans, Native Americans, and White Americans, have supported Holland's theory (Kahn et al., 1990; Lent et al., 2003; Leong et al., 1998; Tett & Burnett, 2003; Tokar et al., 1998; Tracey & Rounds, 1993; Upperman & Church, 1995). Ministers, for example, generally score higher on the social scale than on other dimensions. And car salespersons attain their highest scores on the enterprising scale. Further, as Holland's theory predicts, people whose personality matches their job are also more likely to be satisfied with their work. Thus, a personality assessment may help you make an appropriate occupational choice for yourself and give you confidence about the decision (Francis-Smythe & Smith, 1997).

Once you've chosen a career compatible with your personality, you'll probably start thinking about moving up the *career ladder*—the sequence typically followed to

TABLE 18.2 **Holland's Personality Types and Work Preferences**

TYPE	PERSONALITY TRAITS	WORK PREFERENCES
Realistic	Aggressive, masculine, physically strong, often with low verbal or interpersonal skills	Mechanical activities and tool use; often chooses a job such as mechanic, electrician, or surveyor
Investigative	Oriented toward thinking (particularly abstract thinking), organizing, and planning; low in social skills	Ambiguous, challenging tasks; often a scientist or engineer
Artistic	Asocial	Unstructured, highly individual activity; often an artist
Social	Extraverted; people-oriented, sociable, and needing attention; avoids intellectual activity and dislikes highly ordered activity	Working with people in service jobs like nursing and education
Enterprising	Highly verbal and dominating; enjoys organizing and directing others; persuasive and a strong leader	Often chooses a career in sales
Conventional	Prefers structured activities and subordinate roles; likes clear guidelines; accurate and precise	May choose an occupation such as bookkeeping or filing

Source: Holland (1973, 1992).

reach the higher-level positions in a field. For example, people who teach at universities must progress through the ranks of assistant and associate professor before becoming eligible for consideration for a full professorship. However, movement from lower to higher positions is only one aspect of a much larger process psychologists call career development. *Career development* includes not only advancement in a career but also the psychological and social changes that occur over the course of people's working lives. For instance, as individuals progress in their careers, they acquire new skills and meet new people. Thus, a person's self-concept and self-esteem may also change as he or she pursues a career.

Psychologist Donald Super proposed that career development happens in stages that begin in infancy (Super, 1971, 1986). First comes the *growth stage* (from birth to 14 years), in which you learn about your abilities and interests. Next is the *exploratory stage* (roughly from age 15 to 24), in which there is a lot of trial and error, so job changes happen frequently. The *establishment stage* (from about age 25 to 44) follows. This stage begins with learning about various aspects of your career and the culture of your organization and progresses up the lower rungs of the career ladder. Sometimes, additional formal training is required during this stage. Mentoring by an experienced co-worker will often help you negotiate this stage successfully. Once an individual has become well established in a career, she or he enters the *maintenance phase* (age 45 through retirement), in which the goal is to protect and maintain the gains made in earlier years. Of course, in today's rapidly changing economy, people are often required to change careers. Thus, an individual may re-enter the exploratory stage at any time. As with most stage theories, the ages associated with Super's stages of career development are less important than the sequence of the stages.

Job Satisfaction

What variables are associated with job satisfaction?

The career you choose may suit your personality perfectly, but does that mean you will always be happy in your work? Not necessarily. How positively we feel about our work situations is a variable psychologists call **job satisfaction**. It predicts not only how happy and productive we are on the job, but also how positively we feel about other aspects of our lives, including romantic relationships and family life (Sonnentag, 2003). The happier we are with our jobs, the healthier our bodies are as well (Cass et al., 2003).

■ job satisfaction The degree to which an individual feels positively about his or her job.

What makes us happy in our work? Personality is one important factor. People who are generally optimistic are more satisfied with their jobs (Diener et al., 2002). Workplace variables also influence job satisfaction. For example, the degree to which a work setting encourages or discourages employees' efforts makes a difference (Blustein et al., 1997). Age is also linked to job satisfaction. Many studies show that job satisfaction is at its lowest in early adulthood and rises steadily until retirement (Glenn & Weaver, 1985).

Why does job satisfaction increase with age? Interestingly, the most important reason isn't career advancement or money. Instead, a classic cross-sectional study involving men of all ages suggests that job satisfaction increases with age because, as people get older, work becomes less central to their lives (Tamir, 1982). Thus, finding the right balance between work and other pursuits in life may be the key ingredient in job satisfaction.

A Final Word

You don't have to wait until middle or late adulthood to integrate your career objectives with your other interests and goals. You may be able to avoid the job-related dissatisfactions experienced by many young adults if you spend some time right now developing your own definition of success. Is it wealth? A happy family? Social prestige? All of these? Whatever your goals, thinking about them now and setting priorities may pay off in reduced stress in the future. But remember the experience of Christine King, whose story you read at the beginning of the chapter. Even if you've decided on a career, be open to all the opportunities for new experiences that college can offer. You might end up building a life and attaining goals that, right now, you can't even imagine.

Remember It 18.6

1. Psychologist John Holland is known for his research examining the relationships between ________ and career choice.
2. Many college students are in Donald Super's ________ stage of career development.
3. People who have the personality trait of ________ are more likely than others to be satisfied with their jobs.
4. (Younger/Older) adults are more likely to be satisfied with their jobs than are (younger/older) adults.

ANSWERS: 1. personality; 2. exploratory; 3. optimism; 4. Older, younger

Apply It

Tips for Successful Interviewing

Do your skills and background look great on paper, but your job interviews usually go badly? Following several steps can help improve your chances of landing that elusive job.

Impression Management

Think of the interview as an opportunity to make a particular impression on a potential employer. Psychologists use the term *impression management* to refer to the process of deliberately controlling your behavior in ways that will create the impression you desire. For instance, dressing appropriately and using polite language are components of impression management. Researchers have found that interviewees who display these kinds of impression management behaviors are viewed more positively by interviewers (Bolino & Turnley, 2003). However, you should refrain from using strategies such as exaggerating your qualifications or experience. Experienced interviewers are skilled at recognizing such exaggerations and tend to look unfavorably upon interviewees who use them (Paulhus et al., 2003).

Educate Yourself

One of the most often overlooked keys to successful interviewing is learning about the job you're applying for. You should learn as much as you can about the business or industry you want to work in and about the particular firm to which you are applying. Many major corporations and organizations host Web sites that provide extensive information on their history, mission statement, products, employees, and job listings. These sites can be a great place to start researching potential employers. Study the job qualifications, both required and preferred, if they're available, and get a good idea of how your qualifications match up.

Prepare an Effective Resume

Even if the job you're applying for doesn't require a resume, it's a good idea to prepare one and take it—along with some extra copies—with you to the interview. For one thing, preparing a resume will provide an opportunity for you to rehearse your knowledge about your work history, job skills, and other qualifications. As a result, you'll be able to retrieve the information from your memory more rapidly when the interviewer questions you. A good resume is a quick source of information for the interviewer, who needs to know about your entire work history to create questions based on it. This preparation will leave more time for you to discuss more substantive issues with the interviewer. Most colleges and universities have career centers that provide advice on resume preparation and related services.

Practice

Practice answering interview questions with a friend. Many college career centers have lists of frequently asked interview questions, and you should always create your own list of questions that you think the interviewer might ask. Try to avoid saying negative things about yourself, even when answering such questions as "What are your strengths and weaknesses?" Remember, too, that consistent eye contact will show the interviewer that you have confidence.

Dress Professionally

When you are interviewing for a job, your clothing, visible adornments on your body (e.g., tattoos, jewelry), how well-groomed you are, and even the way you smell can be forms of artifactual communication (discussed earlier in this chapter). Thus, details are important. Male interviewees should consider the research finding that both male and female interviewers respond more positively to clean-shaven applicants (de Souza et al., 2003).

Ideally, your appearance should communicate to the interviewer that you understand the environment in which you hope to be working. For example, if you are interviewing for a position as a construction worker, jeans and a t-shirt, along with a pair of sturdy shoes, are appropriate. When interviewing for an office job, a suit and dress shoes would be better choices. Keep in mind, too, that your appearance influences your own self-confidence. Researchers have found that the more formal interviewees' clothing is, the more positive are the remarks they make about themselves during the interview (Hannover & Kuehnen, 2002).

Be Punctual

Do you feel frustrated when others keep you waiting? Interviewers respond emotionally to tardiness, just as you do. Consequently, it's best to arrive early. And if you are unavoidably delayed, call and reschedule.

Greet the Interviewer Appropriately

Your greeting plays an important role in the interview process as well. In the United States, it's best to look your interviewer directly in the eyes, shake hands firmly, pronounce her or his name correctly, and have good posture.

Follow Up

After the interview, it's a good idea to send a thank-you note. If you met with more than one interviewer, send a note to each of them, mentioning some specific aspect of the discussion that you found interesting. This will indicate that you were fully engaged in the conversation, listening intently, and interested in the interviewer's knowledge about the open position and the organization. The note should also express your appreciation for the interviewer's time and your interest in the position.

Summary *and* Review

Personnel Psychology p. 594

What strategies do personnel psychologists use to hire the best workers? p. 594

Personnel psychologists use job analysis, recruitment and selection, preemployment testing, and interviewing to hire the best workers.

How do organizations train employees in job-related and interpersonal skills? p. 596

Organizations train employees through on-the-job training, apprenticeship, and off-the-job training. Management training often involves job rotation. Conflict resolution training is also useful for helping supervisors and employees get along in the workplace.

What are some approaches used to evaluate workers? p. 597

Performance appraisal, behavioral observation scales, management by objectives (MBO), and 360-degree evaluation are some approaches used for evaluating workers.

Organizational Psychology p. 598

What is the difference between Theory X and Theory Y management approaches? p. 598

The Theory X approach focuses on work efficiency, or how well an employee performs specific job tasks. The Theory Y approach focuses on psychological efficiency, or the degree to which a job has a positive psychological impact on a worker.

What are several types of effective leaders, and how do psychologists explain effective leadership? p. 599

Effective leaders may be charismatic, transactional, or transformational. The trait approach holds that effective leaders possess intrinsic characteristics that help them influence others. Advocates of the situational approach say that effective leadership depends on the match between a leader's characteristics and the situations in which she or he is called upon to lead. According to the behavioral approach, leadership can be taught and is the result of specific behaviors exhibited by leaders. Leader-member exchange (LMX) theory focuses on leaders' relationships with favored and nonfavored followers.

What is the relationship between organizational culture and organizational climate? p. 602

Organizational culture is the system of shared values, beliefs, and practices that evolves within an organization and influences the behavior of its members. Organizational climate refers to how employees perceive and respond emotionally to the culture of an organization.

What are some key perspectives on workplace ethics? p. 603

The moral-rights perspective suggests that individual behavior within an organization should be guided by the same respect for basic rights that is endorsed by the larger culture. The utilitarian perspective defines ethical behavior in terms of the greatest good for the greatest number of people. Organizational social responsibility is the idea that businesses and other organizations have an obligation to behave in ways that take into consideration the interests of the larger society of which they are a part.

Human Factors Psychology p. 604

What are key aspects of workplace design? p. 604

In an open design, a large number of workers are placed in a very large space. The workspace envelope is the three-dimensional space in which an individual worker performs the tasks that comprise his or her job. Office location and size convey information about an employee's status.

What are some of the innovations associated with the quality of work life movement? p. 605

On-site child-care centers are one innovation that has arisen out of concern for the quality of work life. Telecommuters are able to work in their homes and are connected to their workplaces by computer, fax machine, and telephone. Flextime involves allowing employees to create their own work schedules. Job sharing is an innovation in which a full-time job is divided between two or more employees.

What are the causes of desk rage? p. 606

Like aggressive and violent behavior outside the workplace, desk rage incidents often involve individuals who mistakenly perceive others' actions as hostile. Job-related stress, especially that arising from noise and unresolved interpersonal conflicts, is another factor that contributes to desk rage.

Gender Issues at Work p. 607

In what ways do women's work patterns differ from men's? p. 607

Women's work patterns are less likely than those of men to be continuous, as many women move in and out of the workforce to bear and raise children.

How do men's and women's responses to job-related stress differ? p. 607

Men are more likely to use problem-focused coping to respond to job-related stress, while women typically rely on emotion-focused coping. As a result, men deal more effectively than women with job stressors that can be changed. By contrast, women are better able to cope with work situations in which change is impossible.

What evidence is there to suggest that women are breaking the glass ceiling? p. 608

One indication that the glass ceiling is breaking is that 33% of today's MBAs are women, and female representation in top corporate management positions has increased as women have accumulated work experience. About 18% of upper-level managers in U.S. corporations are women, and more women are attaining CEO positions every year. Research shows that well-qualified women are now two to four times as likely as men with equal qualifications to be promoted to top executive positions.

What are the two categories of sexual harassment complaints? p. 609

In *quid pro quo* complaints, workers claim to have been offered something in exchange for sexual favors. Hostile work environment complaints concern inappropriate behavior of a sexual nature that creates an intolerable level of discomfort for the complainant.

Human Diversity in the Workplace p. 611

What is ethnocentrism, and how does it affect the workplace? p. 611

Ethnocentrism is the tendency to look at situations from one's own racial or cultural perspective. Ethnocentrism may prevent workers from realizing that individuals from backgrounds different from theirs may view workplace interactions quite differently.

What are some factors that have led to increased cultural diversity in the workplace? p. 614

Globalization and immigration have increased cultural diversity in the workplace.

What are some common misconceptions about older workers? p. 615

Age norms can lead to ageism, the belief that aging is inevitably associated with a loss of competence. Many people believe that older adults can't learn new job skills and should retire at a particular age. Studies of age differences in job skill learning demonstrate that the learning process itself does not change with age. And older workers are often as productive as younger ones.

How does the Americans with Disabilities Act benefit workers with disabilities? p. 616

The Americans with Disabilities Act (ADA) made it illegal to discriminate against a job applicant or employee on the basis of a physical or mental disability. This law also recognizes the individual's right to keep his or her disability private during the application and interview process. Further, once individuals with disabilities are hired, employers must make necessary, reasonable accommodations for them, and benefits such as health insurance must be equal for workers with and without disabilities. Personnel managers have developed better job descriptions as a result of the ADA. Also, employees without disabilities are now able to learn more about the perspectives of those who are differently abled.

Why have some gay and lesbian workers been reluctant to reveal their sexual orientation to co-workers? p. 617

Some researchers have found that 50% or more of gay and lesbian Americans have experienced forms of discrimination, such as ostracism, by their co-workers. More than 90% of U.S. employers have adopted formal policies prohibiting any discrimination based on sexual orientation.

What steps can organizations take to build a more diverse workforce? p. 617

Organizations can promote diversity by actively seeking to build an employee pool that includes members of as many racial and cultural groups as possible. Such an approach is known as affirmative action. Training managers to avoid stereotypic thinking during interviews is also critical to building and maintaining a diverse workforce.

Pursuing a Career p. 619

What factors influence career choice and development? p. 619

Personality is an important factor in career choice. Career development is affected by the psychological and social changes that occur during a person's working life. Psychologist Donald Super suggested that career development takes place in a sequence of stages.

What variables are associated with job satisfaction? p. 621

Psychological research suggests that personality traits, characteristics of the workplace, and age are some of the variables that affect job satisfaction. Job satisfaction appears to increase with age because, as people get older, they may do a better job of balancing work and other pursuits.

Key Terms

affirmative action, p. 618
ageism, p. 615
Americans with Disabilities Act (ADA), p. 616
apprenticeship, p. 596
artifactual communication, p. 605
assessment center, p. 595
behavioral approach, p. 601
behavioral observation scales, p. 597
charismatic leaders, p. 600
conflict resolution, p. 596
desk rage, p. 606
disability, p. 616
diversity training, p. 611
ergonomics, p. 604
ethnocentrism, p. 612
glass ceiling, p. 608
globalization, p. 614
human factors psychology, p. 604
in-basket test, p. 595
industrial/organizational (I/O) psychologists, p. 594
job analysis, p. 594
job description, p. 595
job enrichment, p. 599
job rotation, p. 596
job satisfaction, p. 621
job simplification, p. 599
leader-member exchange (LMX) theory, p. 602
leadership, p. 599
management by objectives (MBO), p. 597
mommy track, p. 607
moral-rights perspective, p. 603
off-the-job training, p. 596
on-the-job training, p. 596
organizational climate, p. 603
organizational culture, p. 602
organizational psychology, p. 598
organizational social responsibility, p. 603
participative management, p. 599
performance appraisal, p. 597
personnel psychology, p. 594
quality circles, p. 599
quality of work life (QWL) movement, p. 605
recruitment, p. 595
scientific management, p. 598
selection, p. 595
self-managed teams, p. 599
sexual harassment, p. 609
situational approach, p. 601
structured interviews, p. 596
telecommuting, p. 605
Theory X, p. 599
Theory Y, p. 599
360-degree evaluation, p. 597
time-motion studies, p. 598
trait approach, p. 601
transactional leaders, p. 600
transformational leaders, p. 600
utilitarian perspective, p. 603
workspace envelope, p. 604

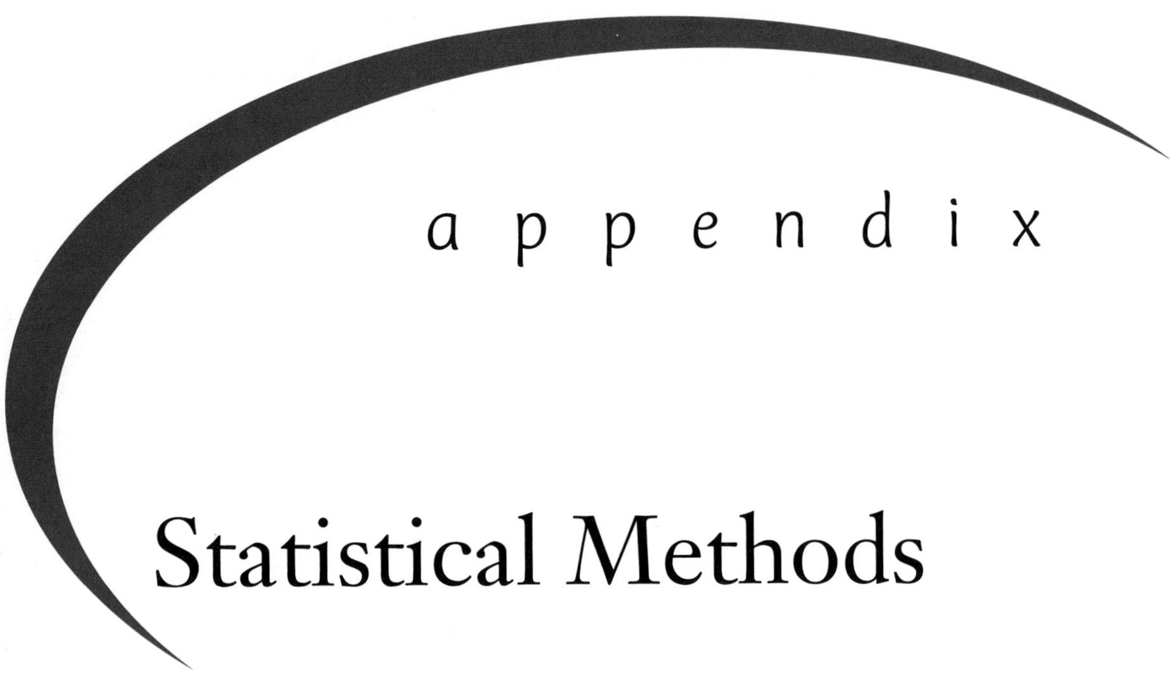

appendix

Statistical Methods

Statistics, a branch of mathematics, enables psychologists and other scientists to organize, describe, and draw conclusions about the quantitative results of their studies. We will explore the two basic types of statistics that psychologists use—descriptive statistics and inferential statistics.

■ **descriptive statistics** Statistics used to organize, summarize, and describe data.

■ **measure of central tendency** A measure or score that describes the center, or middle, of a distribution of scores (example: mean, median, or mode).

■ **mean** The arithmetic average of a group of scores; calculated by adding all the single scores and dividing the sum by the number of scores.

Descriptive Statistics

Descriptive statistics are statistics used to organize, summarize, and describe data. Descriptive statistics include measures of central tendency, variability, and relationship.

Measures of Central Tendency

A **measure of central tendency** is a measure or score that describes the center, or middle, of a distribution of scores. The most widely used and most familiar measure of central tendency is the **mean,** the arithmetic average of a group of scores. The mean is computed by adding all the single scores and dividing the sum by the number of scores.

Carl sometimes studies and does well in his classes, but he occasionally procrastinates and fails a test. Table A.1 shows how Carl performed on the seven tests in his psychology class last semester. Carl computes his mean score by adding up all his test scores and dividing the sum by the number of tests. Carl's mean, or average, score is 80.

TABLE A.1 Carl's Psychology Test Scores

Test 1	98
Test 2	74
Test 3	86
Test 4	92
Test 5	56
Test 6	68
Test 7	86
Sum:	560
Mean: 560 ÷ 7 = 80	

The mean is an important and widely used statistical measure of central tendency, but it can be misleading when a group of scores contains one or several extreme scores. Table A.2 (on page A-2) lists the annual incomes of ten people in rank order. When an income of $1 million is averaged with several more modest incomes, the mean does not provide a true picture of the group. Therefore, when one or a few individuals score far above or below the middle range of a group, a

TABLE A.2 **Annual Income for Ten People**

SUBJECT	ANNUAL INCOME	
1	$1,000,000	
2	$50,000	
3	$43,000	
4	$30,000	
5	$28,000	$27,000 = Median
6	$26,000	
7	$22,000	Mode
8	$22,000	
9	$16,000	
10	$10,000	
Sum:	$1,247,000	

Mean: $1,247,000 ÷ 10 = $124,700

Median: $27,000

Mode: $22,000

different measure of central tendency should be used. The **median** is the middle score or value when a group of scores are arranged from highest to lowest. When there are an odd number of scores, the score in the middle is the median. When there are an even number of scores, the median is the average of the two middle scores. For the ten incomes arranged from highest to lowest in Table A.2, the median is $27,000, which is the average of the middle incomes, $28,000 and $26,000. The $27,000 median income is a truer reflection of the comparative income of the group than is the $124,700 mean.

Another measure of central tendency is the **mode.** The mode is easy to find because it is the score that occurs most frequently in a group of scores. The mode of the annual-income group in Table A.2 is $22,000.

median
The middle score or value when a group of scores are arranged from highest to lowest.

mode
The score that occurs most frequently in a group of scores.

frequency distribution
An arrangement showing the numbers of scores that fall within equal-sized class intervals.

histogram
A bar graph that depicts the number of scores within each class interval in a frequency distribution.

frequency polygon
A line graph that depicts the frequency, or number, of scores within each class interval in a frequency distribution.

Describing Data with Tables and Graphs

A researcher tested 100 students for recall of 20 new vocabulary words 24 hours after they had memorized the list. The researcher organized the scores in a **frequency distribution**—an arrangement showing the numbers of scores that fall within equal-sized class intervals. To organize the 100 test scores, the researcher decided to use intervals of 2 points each. Next, the researcher tallied the frequency (number of scores) within each 2-point interval. Table A.3 presents the resulting frequency distribution.

The researcher then made a **histogram,** a bar graph that depicts the number of scores within each class interval in the frequency distribution. The intervals are plotted along the horizontal axis, and the frequency of scores in each interval is plotted along the vertical axis. Figure A.1 shows the histogram for the 100 test scores.

Another common method of representing frequency data is the **frequency polygon.** As in a histogram, the class intervals are plotted along the horizontal axis and the frequencies are plotted along the vertical axis. However, in a frequency polygon, each class interval is represented by a graph point that is placed at the middle (midpoint) of

TABLE A.3 Frequency Distribution of 100 Vocabulary Test Scores

CLASS INTERVAL	TALLY OF SCORES IN EACH CLASS INTERVAL	NUMBER OF SCORES IN EACH CLASS INTERVAL (FREQUENCY)
1–2	|	1
3–4	||	2
5–6	卌 |	6
7–8	卌 卌 卌 |||	18
9–10	卌 卌 卌 卌 |||	23
11–12	卌 卌 卌 卌 |||	23
13–14	卌 卌 卌 ||	17
15–16	卌 |||	8
17–18	|	1
19–20	|	1

the class interval so that its vertical distance above the horizontal axis shows the frequency of that interval. Lines are drawn to connect the points, as shown in Figure A.2 (on page A-4). The histogram and the frequency polygon are simply two different ways of presenting data.

Measures of Variability

In addition to a measure of central tendency, researchers also need a measure of the **variability** of a set of scores—how much the scores spread out, away from the mean. Both groups in Table A.4 (on page A-4) have a mean and a median of 80. However, the scores in Group II cluster tightly around the mean, while the scores in Group I vary widely from the mean.

The simplest measure of variability is the **range**—the difference between the highest and lowest scores in a distribution of scores. Table A.4 reveals that Group I has

■ **variability**
How much the scores in a distribution spread out, away from the mean.

■ **range**
The difference between the highest score and the lowest score in a distribution of scores.

FIGURE A.1 A Frequency Histogram

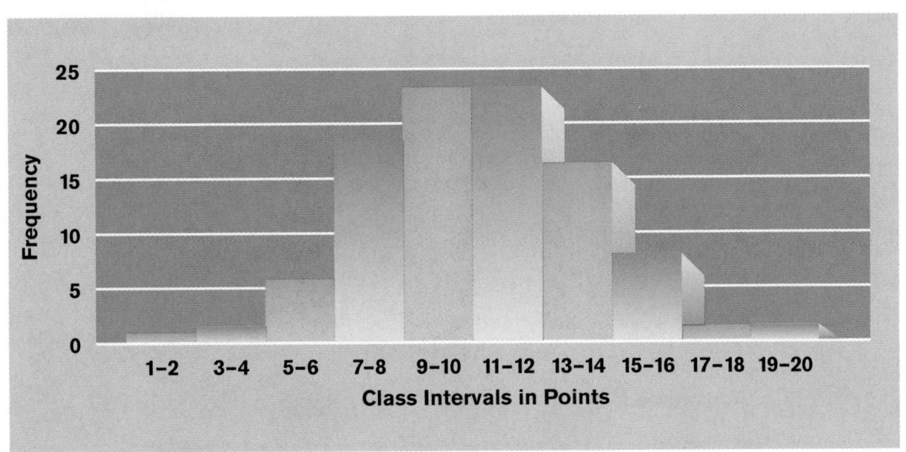

Vocabulary test scores from the frequency distribution in Table A.3 are plotted here in the form of a histogram. Class intervals of 2 points each appear on the horizontal axis. Frequencies of the scores in each class interval are plotted on the vertical axis.

FIGURE A.2 A Frequency Polygon

Vocabulary test scores from the frequency distribution in Table A.3 are plotted here in the form of a frequency polygon. Class intervals of 2 points each appear on the horizontal axis. Frequencies of the scores in each class interval are plotted on the vertical axis.

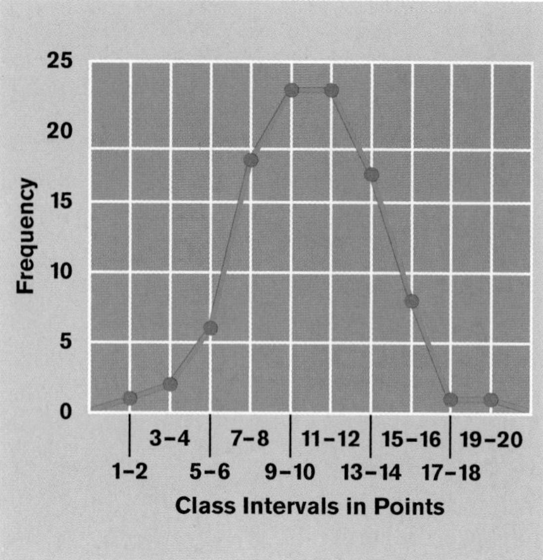

a range of 47, indicating high variability, while Group II has a range of only 7, showing low variability. Unfortunately, the range reveals only the difference between the lowest score and the highest score; it tells nothing about the scores in between.

The **standard deviation** is a descriptive statistic reflecting the average amount that scores in a distribution deviate, or vary, from their mean. The larger the standard deviation, the greater the variability in a distribution of scores. Refer to Table A.4 and note the standard deviations for the two distributions of test scores. In Group I, the relatively large standard deviation of 18.1 reflects the wide variability in that distribution. By contrast, the small standard deviation of 2.14 in Group II indicates that the variability is low, and you can see that the scores cluster tightly around the mean.

The Normal Curve

Psychologists and other scientists often use descriptive statistics in connection with an important type of frequency distribution known as the **normal curve,** pictured in Figure A.3. If a large number of people are measured on any of a wide variety of traits (such as height or IQ score), the great majority of values will cluster in the middle, with fewer and fewer individuals measuring extremely low or high on these variables. Note that slightly over 68% of the scores in a normal distribution fall within 1 standard deviation of the mean (34.13% within 1 standard deviation above the mean, and

TABLE A.4 Comparison of Range and Standard Deviation for Two Small Groups of Scores Having Identical Means and Medians

GROUP I			GROUP II		
TEST	SCORE		TEST	SCORE	
1	99		1	83	
2	99		2	82	
3	98		3	81	
4	80	Median	4	80	Median
5	72		5	79	
6	60		6	79	
7	52		7	76	
Sum:	560		Sum:	560	
Mean: 560 ÷ 7 = 80			Mean: 560 ÷ 7 = 80		
Median: 80			Median: 80		
Range: 99 − 52 = 47			Range: 83 − 76 = 7		
Standard deviation: 18.1			Standard deviation: 2.14		

■ standard deviation
A descriptive statistic reflecting the average amount that scores in a distribution deviate, or vary, from their mean.

■ normal curve
A symmetrical, bell-shaped frequency distribution that represents how scores are normally distributed in a population; most scores fall near the mean, and fewer and fewer scores occur in the extremes either above or below the mean.

FIGURE A.3 The Normal Curve

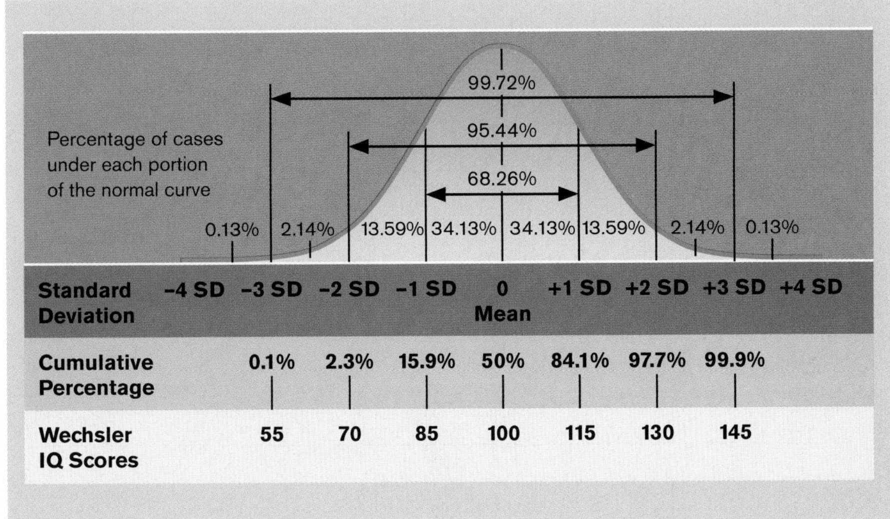

The normal curve is a symmetrical, bell-shaped curve that represents how scores are normally distributed in a population. Slightly over 68% of the scores in a normal distribution fall within 1 standard deviation above and below the mean. Almost 95.5% of the scores lie between 2 standard deviations above and below the mean, and about 99.75% fall between 3 standard deviations above and below the mean.

34.13% within 1 standard deviation below the mean). Almost 95.5% of the scores in a normal distribution lie between 2 standard deviations above and below the mean. And the vast majority of scores in a normal distribution—99.72%—fall between 3 standard deviations above and below the mean.

Using the properties of the normal curve and knowing the mean and the standard deviation of a normal distribution, we can find where any score stands (how high or low) in relation to all the other scores in the distribution. For example, on the Wechsler intelligence scales, the mean IQ is 100 and the standard deviation is 15. Thus, 99.72% of the population has an IQ score within 3 standard deviations above and below the mean, ranging from an IQ of 55 to an IQ of 145.

The Correlation Coefficient

A **correlation coefficient** is a number that indicates the degree and direction of relationship between two variables. Correlation coefficients can range from +1.00 (a perfect positive correlation) to .00 (no correlation) to −1.00 (a perfect negative correlation), as illustrated in Figure A.4 (on page A-6). A **positive correlation** indicates that two variables vary in the same direction. An increase in one variable is associated with an increase in the other variable, or a decrease in one variable is associated with a decrease in the other. There is a positive correlation between the number of hours college students spend studying and their grades. The more hours they study, the higher their grades are likely to be. A **negative correlation** means that an increase in one variable is associated with a decrease in the other variable. There may be a negative correlation between the number of hours students spend watching television and studying. The more hours they spend watching TV, the fewer hours they may spend studying, and vice versa.

The sign (+ or −) in a correlation coefficient merely tells whether the two variables vary in the same or opposite directions. (If no sign appears, the correlation is assumed to be positive.) The number in a correlation coefficient indicates the relative strength of the relationship between the two variables—the higher the number, the stronger the relationship. For example, a correlation of −.70 is higher than a correlation of +.56; a correlation of −.85 is just as strong as one of +.85. A correlation of .00 indicates that no relationship exists between the variables. IQ and shoe size are examples of two variables that are not correlated.

■ **correlation coefficient**
A numerical value indicating the strength and direction of relationship between two variables, which ranges from +1.00 (a perfect positive correlation) to −1.00 (a perfect negative correlation).

■ **positive correlation**
A relationship between two variables in which both vary in the same direction.

■ **negative correlation**
A relationship between two variables in which an increase in one variable is associated with a decrease in the other variable.

FIGURE A.4 Understanding Correlation Coefficients

Correlation coefficients can range from −1.00 (a perfect negative correlation) through .00 (no correlation) to +1.00 (a perfect positive correlation). As the arrows indicate, a negative correlation exists when an increase in one variable is associated with a decrease in the other variable, and vice versa. A positive correlation exists when both variables tend to either increase or decrease together.

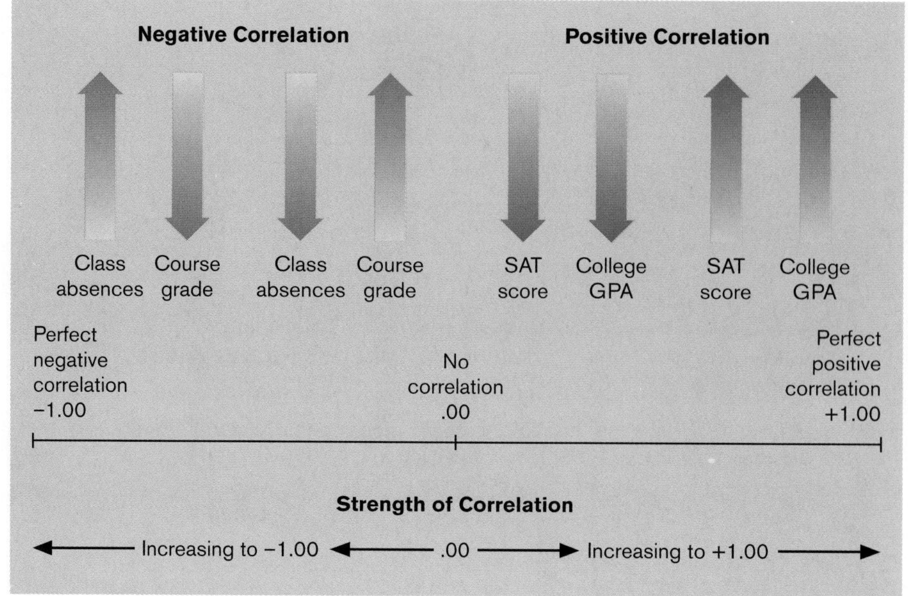

Table A.5 shows the measurements of two variables—high school GPA and college GPA for 11 college students. Looking at the data, we can see that 6 of the 11 students had a higher GPA in high school, while 5 of the students had a higher GPA in college. A clearer picture of the actual relationship is shown by the *scatterplot* in Figure A.5. High school GPA (variable X) is plotted on the horizontal axis, and college GPA (variable Y) is plotted on the vertical axis.

TABLE A.5 High School and College GPAs for 11 Students

STUDENT	HIGH SCHOOL GPA (VARIABLE X)	COLLEGE GPA (VARIABLE Y)
1	2.0	1.8
2	2.2	2.5
3	2.3	2.5
4	2.5	3.1
5	2.8	3.2
6	3.0	2.2
7	3.0	2.8
8	3.2	3.3
9	3.3	2.9
10	3.5	3.2
11	3.8	3.5

One dot is plotted for each of the 11 students at the point where high school GPA, variable X, and college GPA, variable Y, intersect. For example, the first student is represented by a dot at the point where her high school GPA of 2.0 on the horizontal (x) axis and college GPA of 1.8 on the vertical (y) axis intersect. The scatterplot in Figure A.5 reveals a relatively high correlation between high school and college GPAs, because the dots cluster near the diagonal line. It also shows that the correlation is positive, because the dots run diagonally upward from left to right. The correlation coefficient for the high school and college GPAs of these 11 students is .71. If the correlation were perfect (1.00), all the dots would fall exactly on the diagonal line.

A scatterplot shows whether a correlation is low, moderate, or high and whether it is positive or negative. Scatterplots that run diagonally up from left to right reveal positive correlations. Scatterplots that run diagonally down from left to right indicate negative correlations. The closer the dots are to the diagonal line, the higher the correlation. The scatterplots in Figure A.6 (on page A-8) depict a variety of correlations. It is important to remember that correlation does not demonstrate cause and effect. Even a perfect correlation (+1.00 or −1.00) does not mean that one variable causes or is caused by the other. Correlation shows only that two variables are related.

Not all relationships between variables are positive or negative. The relationships between some variables are said to be *curvilinear.* A curvilinear relationship exists when two variables correlate positively (or negatively) up to a certain point and then change direction. For example, there is a positive correlation between physical strength and age up to about 40 or 45 years of age. As age increases from childhood to middle age, so does the strength of handgrip pressure. But beyond middle adulthood, the relationship becomes negative, and increasing age is associated with decreasing handgrip strength. Figure A.6(d) shows a scatterplot of this curvilinear relationship.

FIGURE A.5 A Scatterplot

A scatterplot reveals a relatively high positive correlation between the high school and college GPAs of the 11 students listed in Table A.5. One dot is plotted for each of the 11 students at the point where high school GPA (plotted on the horizontal axis) and college GPA (plotted on the vertical axis) intersect.

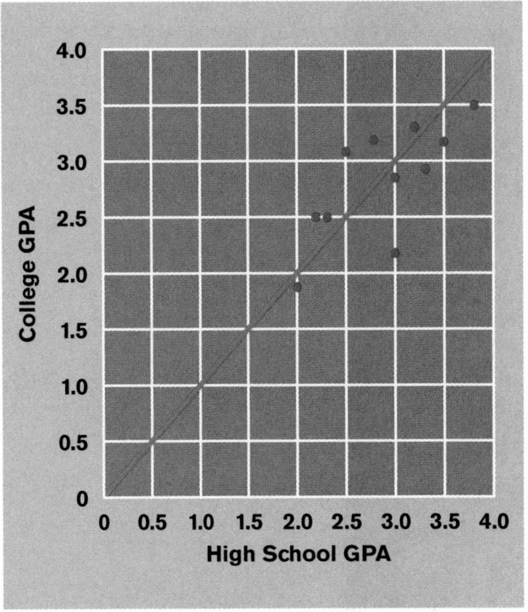

Inferential Statistics

Inferential statistics allow researchers (1) to make inferences about the characteristics of the larger population from their observations and measurements of a sample and (2) to derive estimates of how much faith or confidence can be placed in those inferences. In statistical theory, a **population** is the entire group that is of interest to researchers—the group to which they wish to apply their findings. For example, a population could be all the registered voters in the United States. Usually, researchers cannot directly measure and study the entire population of interest. Consequently, they make inferences about a population from a relatively small **sample** selected from that population. For researchers to draw conclusions about the larger population, the sample must be representative—that is, its characteristics must mirror those of the larger population. (See Chapter 1 for more information about representative samples.)

■ inferential statistics
Statistical procedures that allow researchers to make inferences about the characteristics of the larger population from observations and measurements of a sample and to derive estimates of how much confidence can be placed in those inferences.

■ population
The entire group of interest to researchers and to which they wish to generalize their findings; the group from which a sample is selected.

■ sample
The portion of any population that is selected for study and from which generalizations are made about the entire population.

Statistical Significance

Suppose 200 students are randomly assigned either to an experimental group that will be taught psychology with innovative materials or to a control group that will receive traditional instruction. At the end of the semester, researchers find that the mean test

FIGURE A.6 A Variety of Scatterplots

A scatterplot moving diagonally up from left to right, as in (a), indicates a positive correlation. A scatterplot moving diagonally down from left to right, as in (c), indicates a negative correlation. The more closely the dots cluster around a diagonal line, the higher the correlation. Scatterplot (b) indicates no correlation. Scatterplot (d) shows a curvilinear relationship that is positive up to a point and then becomes negative. Age and strength of handgrip have a curvilinear relationship: Handgrip increases in strength up to about age 40 and then decreases with continued aging.

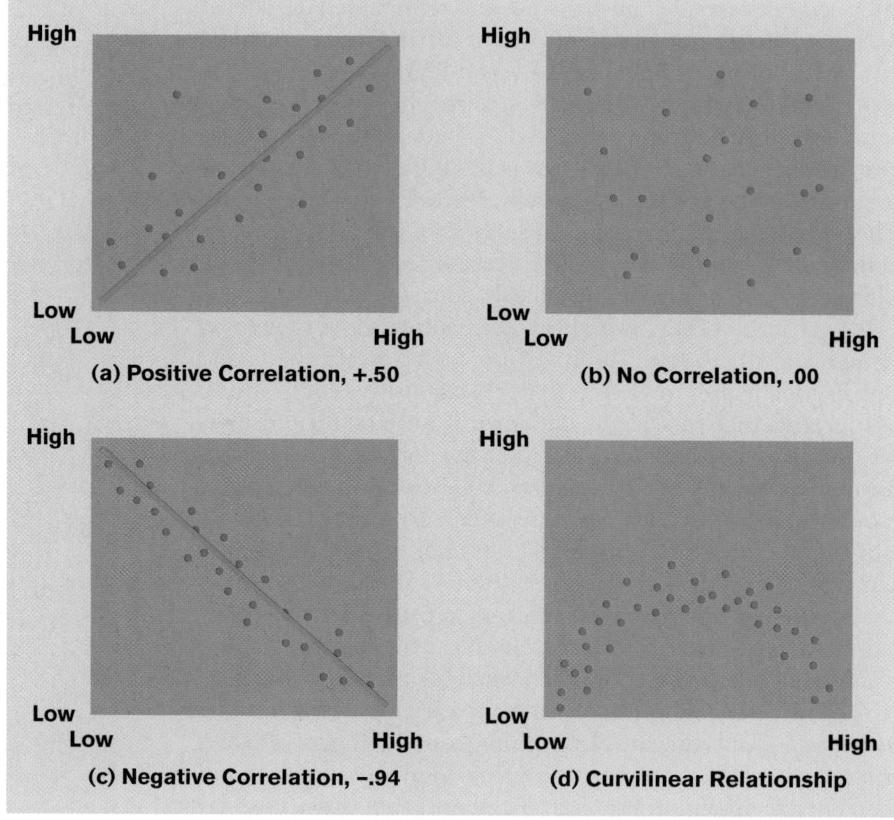

scores of the experimental group are considerably higher than those of the control group. To conclude that the instructional methods caused the difference, the researchers must use **tests of statistical significance** to estimate how often the experimental results could have occurred by chance alone. The estimates derived from tests of statistical significance are stated as probabilities. A probability of .05 means that the experimental results would be expected to occur by chance no more than 5 times out of 100. The .05 level of significance is usually required as a minimum for researchers to conclude that their findings are statistically significant. Often the level of significance reached is even more impressive, such as the .01 level. The .01 level means that the probability is no more than 1 in 100 that the results occurred by chance.

■ **tests of statistical significance**
Statistical tests that estimate the probability that a particular research result could have occurred by chance.

The inferences researchers make are not absolute. They are based on probability, and there is always a possibility, however small, that experimental results could occur by chance. For this reason, replication of research studies is recommended.

References

Abbot, N. C., Stead, L. F., White, A. R., Barnes, J., & Ernst, E. (2000). Hypnotherapy for smoking cessation. *Cochrane Database System Review, 2*, CD001008. [4]

Abe, M., Herzog, E., Yamazaki, S., Straume, M., Tei, H., Sakaki, Y., & Menaker, M. (2002). Circadian rhythms in isolated brain regions. *Journal of Neuroscience, 22*, 350–356. [4]

Abraham, H., & Duffy, F. (2001). EEG coherence in post-LSD visual hallucinations. *Psychiatry Research: Neuroimaging, 107*, 151–163. [4]

Abramowitz, J. S. (1997). Effectiveness of psychological and pharmacological treatments for obsessive-compulsive disorder: A quantitative review. *Journal of Consulting and Clinical Psychology, 65*, 44–52. [16]

Abrams, D., Wetherell, M., Cochrane, S., Hogg, M. A., & Turner, J. C. (1990). Knowing what to think by knowing who you are: Self-categorization and the nature of norm formation, conformity and group polarization. *British Journal of Social Psychology, 29*(Pt. 2), 97–119. [17]

Accardo, P., Tomazic, T., Fete, T., Heaney, M., Lindsay, R., & Whitman, B. (1997). Maternally reported fetal activity levels and developmental diagnoses. *Clinical Pediatrics, 36*, 279–283. [9]

Ackerman, M. D., & Carey, M. P. (1995). Psychology's role in the assessment of erectile dysfunction: Historical precedents, current knowledge, and methods. *Journal of Consulting and Clinical Psychology, 63*, 862–876. [12]

Ackerman, S., Zuroff, D. C., & Moskowitz, D. S. (2000). Generativity in midlife and young adults: Links to agency, communion and subjective well-being. *International Journal of Aging and Human Development, 50*, 17–41. [10]

Adams, J. H., Graham, D. I., & Jennett, B. (2000). The neuropathology of the vegetative state after an acute brain insult. *Brain, 123*, 1327–1338. [2]

Adams, M., & Henry, M. (1997). Myths and realities about words and literacy. *School Psychology Review, 26*, 425–436. [9]

Addi-Raccah, Q., & Ayalon, H. (2002). Gender inequality in leadership positions of teachers. *British Journal of Sociology of Education, 23*, 157–177. [18]

Addis, M., & Mahalik, J. (2003). Men, masculinity, and the contexts of help seeking. *American Psychologist, 58*, 5–14. [13, 16]

Ader, D. N., & Johnson, S. B. (1994). Sample description, reporting, and analysis of sex in psychological research: A look at APA and APA division journals in 1990. *American Psychologist, 49*, 216–218. [1]

Ader, R. (1985). CNS immune systems interactions: Conditioning phenomena. *Behavioral and Brain Sciences, 9*, 760–763. [5]

Ader, R. (2000). On the development of psychoneuroimmunology. *European Journal of Pharmacology, 405*, 167–176. [13]

Ader, R., & Cohen, N. (1982). Behaviorally conditioned immunosuppression and murine systemic *Lupus erythematosus. Science, 215*, 1534–1536. [5]

Adesman, A. (1996). Fragile X syndrome. In A. Capute & P. Accardo (Eds.). *Developmental disabilities in infancy and childhood* (2nd ed., Vol. 2, pp. 255–269). Baltimore: Brookes. [2]

Adler, A. (1927). *Understanding human nature.* New York: Greenberg. [14]

Adler, A. (1956). In H. L. Ansbacher & R. R. Ansbacher (Eds.), *The individual psychology of Alfred Adler: A systematic presentation in selections from his writings.* New York: Harper & Row. [14]

Adler, J. (1997, Spring/Summer). It's a wise father who knows. . . . *Newsweek* [Special Edition], p. 73. [9]

Adler, R. (2001a). *Glass ceiling basics.* Malibu, CA: Glass Ceiling Research Institute. Retrieved January 22, 2003, from http://www.glass-ceiling.com/ArticlesFolder/GlassCeilingBasicsPage1.html [18]

Adler, R. (2001b). *Women in the executive suite correlate to high profits.* Malibu, CA: Glass Ceiling Research Institute. Retrieved January 22, 2003, from http://www.glass-ceiling.com/InTheNewsFolder/HBRArticlePage1.html [18]

Agras, W. S., Rossiter, E. M., Arnow, B., Telch, C. F., Raeburn, S. D., Bruce, B., & Koran, L. M. (1994). One-year follow-up of psychosocial and pharmacologic treatments for bulimia nervosa. *Journal of Clinical Psychiatry, 55*, 179–183. [11]

Agras, W. S., Walsh, T., Fairburn, C. G., Wilson, T., & Kraemer, H. C. (2000). A multicenter comparison of cognitive-behavioral therapy and interpersonal psychotherapy for bulimia nervosa. *Archives of General Psychiatry, 57*, 459–466. [16]

Ahmad, S. (1994, November). *Culturally sensitive caregiving for the Pakistani woman.* Lecture presented at the Medical College of Virginia Hospitals, Richmond, VA. [3]

Aiken, L. R. (1997). *Psychological testing and assessment* (9th ed.). Boston: Allyn & Bacon. [8]

Ainsworth, M. (2000). ABCs of "internet therapy." *Metanoia* [Electronic version]. Retrieved from www.metanoia.org [16]

Ainsworth, M. D. S. (1973). The development of infant-mother attachment. In B. Caldwell & H. Ricciuti (Eds.), *Review of child development research* (Vol. 3). Chicago: University of Chicago Press. [9]

Ainsworth, M. D. S. (1979). Infant-mother attachment. *American Psychologist, 34*, 932–937. [9]

Ainsworth, M. D. S., Blehar, M. C., Walters, E., & Wall, S. (1978). *Patterns of attachment.* Hillsdale, NJ: Erlbaum. [9]

Åkerstedt, T. (1990). Psychological and psychophysiological effects of shift work. *Scandinavian Journal of Work and Environmental Health, 16*, 67–73. [4]

Al'absi, M., Hugdahl, K., & Lovallo, W. (2002). Adrenocortical stress responses and altered working memory performance. *Psychophysiology, 39*, 95–99. [6]

Albeck, S., & Kaydar, D. (2002). Divorced mothers: Their network of friends pre- and post-divorce. *Journal of Divorce & Remarriage, 36*, 111–138. [10]

Albert, M. L., & Helm-Estabrooks, N. (1988). Diagnosis and treatment of aphasia: Part II. *Journal of the American Medical Association, 259,* 1205–1210. [2]

Albrecht, K. (1979). *Stress and the manager: Making it work for you.* Englewood Cliffs, NJ: Prentice-Hall. [13]

Aldhous, P. (1992). The promise and pitfalls of molecular genetics. *Science, 257,* 164–165. [14]

Al-Dmour, H., & Al-Awamleh, R. (2002). Effects of transactional and transformational leadership styles of sales managers on job satisfaction and self-perceived performance of sales people: A study of Jordanian manufacturing public shareholding companies. *Dirasat: Administrative Sciences, 29,* 247–261. [18]

Alexander, G. E., Furey, M. L., Grady, C. L., Pietrini, P., Brady, D. R., Mentis, M. J., & Schapiro, M. B. (1997). Association of premorbid intellectual function with cerebral metabolism in Alzheimer's disease: Implications for the cognitive reserve hypotheses. *American Journal of Psychiatry, 154,* 165–172. [10]

Alleman, J. (2002). Online counseling: The Internet and mental health treatment. *Psychotherapy: Theory, Research, Practice, Training, 39,* 199–209. [16]

Allen, B. P. (1997). *Personality theories: Development, growth, and diversity* (2nd ed.). Boston: Allyn & Bacon. [14]

Allen, G., Buxton, R. B., Wong, E. C., & Courchesne, E. (1997). Attentional activation of the cerebellum independent of motor involvement. *Science, 275,* 1940–1943. [2]

Allen, J., McElhaney, K., Land, D., Kupermine, G., Moore, C., O'Beirne-Kelly, H., & Kilmer, S. (2003). A secure base in adolescence: Markers of attachment security in the mother-adolescent relationship. *Child Development, 74,* 292–307. [10]

Allen, K. W. (1996). Chronic nailbiting: A controlled comparison of competing response and mild aversion treatments. *Behaviour Research and Therapy, 34,* 269–272. [16]

Allison, T., Puce, A., & McCarthy, G. (2000). Social perception from visual cues: Role of the STS region. *Trends in Cognitive Sciences, 4,* 267–278. [17]

Allport, G. W. (1954). *The nature of prejudice.* Reading, MA: Addison-Wesley. [17]

Allport, G. W. (1961). *Pattern and growth in personality.* New York: Holt, Rinehart & Winston. [14]

Allport, G. W., & Odbert, J. S. (1936). Trait names: A psycholexical study. *Psychological Monographs, 47*(1, Whole No. 211), 1–171. [14]

Alpert, B., Field, T., Goldstein, S., & Perry, S. (1990). Aerobics enhances cardiovascular fitness and agility in preschoolers. *Health Psychology, 9,* 48–56. [13]

Alsaker, F. D. (1995). Timing of puberty and reactions to pubertal changes. In M. Rutter (Ed.), *Psychosocial disturbances in young people* (pp. 37–82). New York: Cambridge University Press. [10]

Altermatt, E., & Pomerantz, E. (2003). The development of competence-related and motivational beliefs: An investigation of similarity and influence among friends. *Journal of Educational Psychology, 95,* 111–123. [8, 10]

Amabile, T. M. (1983). *The social psychology of creativity.* New York: Springer-Verlag. [8]

Amabile, T. M. (1990). Within you, without you: The social psychology of creativity, and beyond. In M. A. Runco & R. S. Albert (Eds.), *Theories of creativity.* Newbury Park, CA: Sage. [8]

Amato, S. (1998). Human genetics and dysmorphy. In R. Behrman & R. Kliegman (Eds.), *Nelson essentials of pediatrics* (3rd ed., pp. 167–225). Philadelphia: W. B. Saunders. [9]

American Association of Retired Persons. (2002). *Evaluating health information on the Internet: How good are your sources?* Retrieved November 1, 2002, from http://www.aarp.org/confacts/health/wwwhealth.html [13]

American Association of Retired Persons (AARP). (2003, June 10). *AARP outlines what 45+ workers seek from employers.* Retrieved December 16, 2003, from: http://www.aarp.org [18]

American Cancer Society. (2002). *Cancer facts & figures/2002.* Retrieved November 10, 2002, from http://www.cancer.org/downloads/STT/CancerFacts&Figures2002TM [15]

American Medical Association. (1994). *Report of the Council on Scientific Affairs: Memories of childhood abuse.* CSA Report 5-A–94. [6]

American Psychiatric Association. (1993). *Statement approved by the Board of Trustees, December 12, 1993.* Washington, DC: Author. [6]

American Psychiatric Association. (1993a). Practice guideline for eating disorders. *American Journal of Psychiatry, 150,* 212–228. [11]

American Psychiatric Association. (1994). *Diagnostic and statistical manual of mental disorders* (4th ed.). Washington DC: Author. [4, 11, 12, 15]

American Psychiatric Association. (1997). Practice guideline for the treatment of patients with Alzheimer's disease and other dementias of late life. *American Journal of Psychiatry, 154,* 1–39. [10]

American Psychiatric Association. (2000). *The Diagnostic and Statistical Manual of Mental Disorders* (4th ed., Text Revision). Washington, DC: Author. [15]

American Psychological Association. (1994). *Interim report of the APA Working Group on Investigation of Memories of Childhood Abuse.* Washington, DC: Author. [6]

American Psychological Association. (1995). Psychology: Scientific problem-solvers—Careers for the 21st century. Retrieved March 7, 2002, from http://www.apa.org/students/brochure/outlook.html#bachelors [1]

American Psychological Association (APA). (1998). Hate crimes today: An age-old foe in modern dress. Retrieved June 20, 2003, from http://www.apa.org [18]

American Psychological Association. (2000). Psychologists in the red [Online factsheet]. Retrieved March 7, 2002, from http://www.apa.org/ppo/issues/ebsinthered.html [1]

American Psychological Association. (2002). Ethical principles of psychologists and code of conduct. *American Psychologist, 57,* 1060–1073. [1]

American Psychological Association (APA). (2002). Ethnical principles of psychologists and code of conduct. *American Psychologist, 57,* 1060–1073. [16]

American Psychological Association (APA). (2003). Guidelines on multicultural education, training, research, practice, and organizational change for psychologists. *American Psychologist, 58,* 377–402. [16]

Anagnostaras, S. B., Josselyn, S. A., Frankland, P. W., & Silva, A. J. (2000). Computer-assisted behavioral assessment of Pavlovian fear conditioning in mice. *Learning & Memory, 7,* 48–57. [5]

Anand, B. K., & Brobeck, J. R. (1951). Hypothalamic control of food intake in rats and cats. *Yale Journal of Biological Medicine, 24,* 123–140. [11]

Andersen, B. L., & Cyranowski, J. M. (1995). Women's sexuality: Behaviors, responses, and individual differences. *Journal of Consulting and Clinical Psychology, 63,* 891–906. [12]

Anderson, C., & Bushman, B. (2001). Effects of violent video games on aggressive behavior, aggressive cognition, aggressive affect, physiological arousal, and prosocial behavior: A meta-analytic review of the scientific literature. *Psychological Science, 12,* 353–359. [5]

Anderson, C. A., & Anderson, K. B. (1996). Violent crime rate studies in philosophical context: A destructive testing approach to heat and southern culture of violence effects. *Journal of Personality and Social Psychology, 70,* 740–756. [17]

Anderson, C. A., & Dill, K. E. (2000). Video games and aggressive thoughts, feelings, and behavior in the laboratory and in life. *Journal of Personality & Social Psychology, 78*, 772–790. [17]

Anderson, R. (2002). Deaths: Leading causes for 2000. *National Vital Statistics Reports, 50* (16), 1–86. [15]

Anderson, S. M., Klatzky, R. L., & Murray, J. (1990). Traits and social stereotypes: Efficiency differences in social information processing. *Journal of Personality and Social Psychology, 59*, 192–201. [17]

Andreasen, N. C., Arndt, S., Alliger, R., Miller, D., & Flaum, M. (1995). Symptoms of schizophrenia: Methods, meanings, and mechanisms. *Archives of General Psychiatry, 52*, 341–351. [15, 16]

Andreasen, N. C., & Black, D. W. (1991). *Introductory textbook of psychiatry*. Washington, DC: American Psychiatric Press. [4]

Andreasen, N. C., Cohen, G., Harris, G., Cizaldlo, T., Parkkinen, J., Rezai, K., & Swayze, V. W. (1992). Image processing for the study of brain structure and function: Problems and programs. *Journal of Neuropsychiatry and Clinical Neurosciences, 4*, 125–133. [2]

Andreasen, N. C., Flaum, M., Swayze, V., O'Leary, D. S., Alliger, R., Cohen, G., Ehrhardt, J., & Yuh, W. T. C. (1993). Intelligence and brain structure in normal individuals. *American Journal of Psychiatry, 150*, 130–134. [2]

Andrews, G., & Erskine, A. (2003). Reducing the burden of anxiety and depressive disorders: The role of computerized clinician assistance. *Current Opinion in Psychiatry, 16*, 41–44. [16]

Angeleri, F., Angeleri, V. A., Foschi, N., Giaquinto, S., Nolfe, G., Saginario, A., & Signorino, M. (1997). Depression after stroke: An investigation through catamnesis. *Journal of Clinical Psychiatry, 58*, 261–265. [2]

Anokhin, A., Vedeniapin, A., Sitevaag, E., Bauer, L., O'Connor, S., Kuperman, S., Porjesz, B., Reich, T., Begleiter, H., Polich, J., & Rohrbaugh, J. (2000). The P300 brain potential is reduced in smokers. *Psychopharmacology, 149*, 409–413. [4, 13]

Anstey, K., Stankov, L., & Lord, S. (1993). Primary aging, secondary aging, and intelligence. *Psychology and Aging, 8*, 562–570. [10]

Apuzzio, J. J. (1990, February). A patient guide: Genital herpes. *Medical Aspects of Human Sexuality, 24*, 15–16. [12]

Arai, M., Wanca-Thibault, M., & Shockley-Zalabak, P. (2001). Communication theory and training approaches for multiculturally diverse organizations. *Public Personnel Management, 30*, 445–455. [18]

Aram, D., & Levitt, I. (2002). Mother-child joint writing and storybook reading: Relations with literacy among low SES kindergarteners. *Merrill-Palmer Quarterly, 48*, 202–224. [9]

Archer, J. (1991). The influence of testosterone on human aggression. *British Journal of Social Psychology, 82*(Pt. 1), 1–28. [17]

Archer, J. (1996). Sex differences in social behavior: Are the social role and evolutionary explanations compatible? *American Psychologist, 51*, 909–917. [1]

Arehart-Treichel, J. (2002). Researchers explore link between animal cruelty, personality disorders. *Psychiatric News, 37*, 22. [15]

Armstrong, M., & Shikani, A. (1996). Nasal septal necrosis mimicking Wegener's granulomatosis in a cocaine abuser. *Ear Nose Throat Journal, 75*, 623–626. [4]

Arnett, J. J. (1999). Adolescent storm and stress, reconsidered. *American Psychologist, 54*, 317–326. [10]

Aronson, E. (1976). Dissonance theory: Progress and problems. In E. P. Hollander & R. C. Hunt (Eds.), *Current perspectives in social psychology* (4th ed., pp. 316–328). New York: Oxford University Press. [17]

Aronson, E. (1988). *The social animal* (3rd ed.). San Francisco: W. H. Freeman. [17]

Aronson, E., & Mills, J. (1959). The effect of severity of initiation on liking for a group. *Journal of Abnormal and Social Psychology, 59*, 177–181. [17]

Aronson, E., Stephan, W., Sikes, J., Blaney, N., & Snapp, M. (1978). *Cooperation in the classroom*. Beverly Hills, CA: Sage. [17]

Arriola, K., & Cole, E. (2001). Framing the affirmative-action debate: Attitudes toward out-group members and White identity. *Journal of Applied Social Psychology, 31*, 2462–2483. [18]

Arseneault, R., Tremblay, R., Boulerice, B., & Saucier, J. (2002). Obstetrical complications and violent delinquency: Testing two developmental pathways. *Child Development, 73*, 496–508. [9]

Arthur, W., Day, E., McNelly, T., & Edens, P. (2003). A meta-analysis of the criterion-related validity of assessment center dimensions. *Personnel Psychology, 56*, 125–154. [18]

Asch, S. E. (1951). Effects of group pressure upon the modification and distortion of judgments. In H. Guetzkow (Ed.), *Groups, leadership, and men*. Pittsburgh, PA: Carnegie Press. [17]

Asch, S. E. (1955). Opinions and social pressure. *Scientific American, 193*, 31–35. [17]

Asher, S., & Paquette, J. (2003). Loneliness and peer relations in childhood. *Current Directions in Psychological Science, 12*, 75–78. [9]

Aspendorf, J. B., Warkentink, V., & Baudonniere, P. M. (1996). Self-awareness and other-awareness II: Mirror self-recognition, social contingency awareness, and synchronic imitation. *Developmental Psychology, 32*, 313–321. [9]

Aspinwall, L. G., & Taylor, S. E. (1997). A stitch in time: Self-regulation and proactive coping. *Psychological Bulletin, 121*, 417–436. [13]

Assefi, S., & Garry, M. (2003). Absolut memory distortions: Alcohol placebos influence the misinformation effect. *Psychological Science, 14*, 77–80. [4]

Astington, J., & Jenkins, J. (1999). A longitudinal study of the relation between language and theory-of-mind development. *Developmental Psychology, 35*, 1311–1320. [9]

Atkins, P., & Wood, R. (2002). Self- versus others' ratings as predictors of assessment center ratings: Validation evidence for 360-degree feedback programs. *Personnel Psychology, 55*, 871–904. [18]

Atkinson, R. C., & Shiffrin, R. M. (1968). Human memory: A proposed system and its controlled processes. In K. W. Spence & J. T. Spence (Eds.), *The psychology of learning and motivation* (Vol. 2, pp. 89–195). New York: Academic. [6]

Atwood, J., & Donnelly, J. (2002). The children's war: Their reactions to devastating events. *Family Journal: Counseling & Therapy for Couples & Families, 10*, 11–18. [9]

Au, J. G., & Donaldson, S. I. (2000). Social influences as explanations for substance use differences among Asian-American and European-American adolescents. *Journal of Psychoactive Drugs, 32*, 15–23. [4]

Aubé, J., & Koestner, R. (1992). Gender characteristics and adjustment: A longitudinal study. *Journal of Personality and Social Psychology, 63*, 485–493. [12]

Augestad, L. B. (2000). Prevalence and gender differences in eating attitudes and physical activity among Norwegians. *Eating and Weight Disorders: Studies on Anorexia, Bulimia, and Obesity, 5*, 62–72. [11]

Ault, R. L. (1983). *Children's cognitive development* (2nd ed.). Oxford: Oxford University Press. [10]

Aunola, K., Stattin, H., & Nurmi, J. E. (2000). Parenting styles and adolescents' achievement strategies. *Journal of Adolescence, 23*, 2205–2222. [9, 10]

Axel, R. (1995, October). The molecular logic of smell. *Scientific American, 273,* 154–159. [3]

Axelsson, A., & Jerson, T. (1985). Noisy toys: A possible source of sensorineural hearing loss. *Pediatrics, 76,* 574–578. [3]

Ayllon, T., & Azrin, N. (1965). The measurement and reinforcement of behavior of psychotics. *Journal of the Experimental Analysis of Behavior, 8,* 357–383. [5, 16]

Ayllon, T., & Azrin, N. (1968). *The token economy: A motivational system for therapy and rehabilitation.* New York: Appleton-Century-Crofts. [5, 16]

Azar, B. (2000). A web of research. *Monitor on Psychology, 31* [Online version]. Retrieved March 13, 2002, from http://www.apa.org/monitor/ [1]

Azrin, N. H., & Holz, W. C. (1966). Punishment. In W. K. Honig (Ed.), *Operant behavior: Areas of research and application.* New York: Appleton-Century-Crofts. [5]

Bach, M., & Hoffman, M. B. (2000). Visual motion detection in man is governed by non-retinal mechanisms. *Vision Research, 40,* 2379–2385. [3]

Bach, P., & Hayes, S. (2002). The use of acceptance and commitment therapy to prevent the rehospitalization of psychotic patients: A randomized controlled trial. *Journal of Consulting and Clinical Psychology, 70,* 1129–1139. [16]

Bäckman, L., Almkvist, O., Nyberg, L., & Anderson, J. (2000). Functional changes in brain activity during priming in Alzheimer's disease. *Journal of Cognitive Neuroscience, 12,* 134–141. [10]

Baddeley, A. D. (1990). *Human memory.* Boston, MA: Allyn & Bacon. [6]

Baddeley, A. D. (1992). Working memory. *Science, 255,* 556–559. [6]

Baddeley, A. D. (1995) Working memory. In M. S. Gazzaniga (Ed.), *The cognitive neurosciences.* Cambridge, MA: MIT Press.

Baer, J. (1996). The effects of task-specific divergent-thinking training. *Journal of Creative Behavior, 30,* 183–187. [8]

Baer, J. (1998). The case for domain specificity of creativity. *Creativity Research Journal, 11,* 173–177. [8]

Baer, L. (1996). Behavior theory: Endogenous serotonin therapy? *Journal of Clinical Psychiatry, 57*(6, Suppl.), 33–35. [16]

Baer, L., Rauch, S. L., Ballantine, T., Jr., Martuza, R., Cosgrove, R., Cassem, E., Giriunas, I., Manzo, P. A., Dimino, C., & Jenike, M. A. (1995). Cingulotomy for intractable obsessive-compulsive disorder. *Archives of General Psychiatry, 52,* 384–392. [16]

Bagby, R. M., Rogers, R., & Buis, T. (1994). Detecting malingered and defensive responding on the MMPI-2 in a forensic inpatient sample. *Journal of Personality Assessment, 62,* 191–203. [14]

Bahrick, H. P., Bahrick, P. O., & Wittlinger, R. P. (1975). Fifty years of memory for names and faces: A cross-sectional approach. *Journal of Experimental Psychology: General, 104,* 54–75. [6]

Bahrick, H. P., Hall, L. K., & Berger, S. A. (1996). Accuracy and distortion in memory for high school grades. *Psychological Science, 7,* 265–271. [6]

Bailey, J. M., & Benishay, D. S. (1993). Familial aggregation of female sexual orientation. *American Journal of Psychiatry, 150,* 272–277. [12]

Bailey, J. M., Nothnagel, J., & Wolfe, M. (1995). Retrospectively measured individual differences in childhood sex-typed behavior among gay men: Correspondence between self- and maternal reports. *Archives of Sexual Behavior, 24,* 613–622. [12]

Bailey, J. M., & Pillard, R. C. (1991). A genetic study of male sexual orientation. *Archives of General Psychiatry, 48,* 1089–1096. [12]

Bailey, J. M., & Pillard, R. C. (1994). The innateness of homosexuality. *Harvard Mental Health Letter, 10*(7), 4–6. [12]

Bailey, J. M., Pillard, R. C., Neale, M. C., & Agyei, Y. (1993). Heritable factors influence sexual orientation in women. *Archives of General Psychiatry, 50,* 217–223. [12]

Bailey, J. M., & Zucker, K. J. (1995). Childhood sex-typed behavior and sexual orientation: A conceptual analysis and quantitative review. *Developmental Psychology, 31,* 43–55. [12]

Baillargeon, R., & DeVos, J. (1991). Object permanence in young infants: Further evidence. *Child Development, 62,* 1227–1246. [9]

Baker, B., Wendt, A., & Slonaker, W. (2002). An analysis of gender equity in the federal labor relations career field. *Public Personnel Management, 31,* 559–567. [18]

Baldwin, J. D., & Baldwin, J. I. (1997). Gender differences in sexual interest. *Archives of Sexual Behavior, 26,* 181–210. [12]

Ball, S. G., Baer, L., & Otto, M. W. (1996). Symptom subtypes of obsessive-compulsive disorder in behavioral treatment studies: A quantitative review. *Behaviour Research and Therapy, 34,* 47–51. [15]

Ballenger, J. C., Pecknold, J., Rickels, K., & Sellers, E. M. (1993). Medication discontinuation in panic disorder. *Journal of Clinical Psychiatry, 54*(10, Suppl.), 15–21. [16]

Ballor, D. L., Tommerup, L. J., Thomas, D. P., Smith, D. B., & Keesey, R. E. (1990). Exercise training attenuates diet-induced reduction in metabolic rate. *Journal of Applied Physiology: Respiratory, Environmental, and Exercise Physiology, 68,* 2612–2617. [11]

Balon, R. (1996). Antidepressants in the treatment of premature ejaculation. *Journal of Sex and Marital Therapy, 22,* 85–96. [12]

Baltes, P. B., Reese, H. W., & Lipsitt, L. P. (1980). Life-span developmental psychology. *Annual Review of Psychology, 31,* 65–110. [10]

Baltimore, D. (2000). Our genome unveiled. *Nature, 409,* 814–816. [9]

Band, G. P., & Kok, A. (2000). Age effects on response monitoring in a mental-rotation task. *Biological Psychology, 51,* 201–221. [7]

Bandura, A. (1969). *Principles of behavior modification.* New York: Holt, Rinehart & Winston. [5]

Bandura, A. (1973). *Aggression: A social learning analysis.* Englewood Cliffs, NJ: Prentice-Hall. [17]

Bandura, A. (1976). On social learning and aggression. In E. P. Hollander & R. C. Hunt (Eds.), *Current perspectives in social psychology* (4th ed., pp. 116–128). New York: Oxford University Press. [17]

Bandura, A. (1977a). *Social learning theory.* Englewood Cliffs, NJ: Prentice-Hall. [5, 9, 14, 16]

Bandura, A. (1977b). Self-efficacy: Toward a unifying theory of behavioral change. *Psychological Review, 84,* 191–215. [14]

Bandura, A. (1986). *Social functions of thought and action: A social-cognitive theory.* Englewood Cliffs, NJ: Prentice-Hall. [5, 14]

Bandura, A. (1989). Social cognitive theory. *Annals of Child Development, 6,* 1–60. [14]

Bandura, A. (1997a, March). Self-efficacy. *Harvard Mental Health Letter, 13*(9), 4–6. [14]

Bandura, A. (1997b). *Self-efficacy: The exercise of control.* New York: Freeman. [14]

Bandura, A., Adams, N. E., & Beyer, J. (1977). Cognitive processes mediating behavioral change. *Journal of Personality and Social Psychology, 35,* 125–139. [16]

Bandura, A., Jeffery, R. W., & Gajdos, E. (1975). Generalizing change through participant modeling with self-directed mastery. *Behaviour Research and Therapy, 13,* 141–152. [16]

Bandura, A., Ross, D., & Ross, S. A. (1961). Transmission of aggression through imitation of aggressive models. *Journal of Abnormal and Social Psychology, 63,* 575–582. [5]

Bandura, A., Ross, D., & Ross, S. A. (1963). Imitation of film-mediated aggressive models. *Journal of Abnormal and Social Psychology, 66,* 3–11. [5]

Bard, P. (1934). The neurohumoral basis of emotional reactions. In C. A. Murchison (Ed.), *Handbook of general experimental psychology.* Worcester, MA: Clark University Press. [11]

Bargmann, C. (1996). From the nose to the brain. *Nature, 384,* 512–513. [3]

Barinaga, M. (1997). How jet-lag hormone does double duty in the brain. *Science, 277,* 480. [4]

Barlow, D. H. (1997). Cognitive-behavioral therapy for panic disorder: Current status. *Journal of Clinical Psychiatry, 58*(6, Suppl.), 32–36. [16]

Barsh, G. S., Farooqi, I. S., & O'Rahilly, S. (2000). Genetics of body-weight regulation. *Nature, 404,* 644–651. [11]

Barsky, A. J. (1993, August). How does hypochondriasis differ from normal concerns about health? *Harvard Mental Health Letter, 10*(3), 8. [15]

Bartlett, A. (2002). Current perspectives on the goals of psychoanalysis. *Journal of the American Psychoanalytic Association, 50,* 629–638. [14]

Bartlett, F. C. (1932). *Remembering: A study in experimental and social psychology.* London: Cambridge University Press. [6]

Bartoshuk, L. M., & Beauchamp, G. K. (1994). Chemical senses. *Annual Review of Psychology, 45,* 419–449. [3, 9]

Bartoshuk, L. M., Fast, K., Karrer, T. A., Marino, S., Price, R. A., & Reed, D. A. (1992). PROP supertasters and the perception of sweetness and bitterness. *Chemical Senses, 17,* 594 (Abstract). [3]

Basic Behavioral Science Task Force of the National Advisory Mental Health Council. (1996). Basic behavioral science research for mental health: Perception, attention, learning, and memory. *American Psychologist, 51,* 133–142. [5, 6]

Basile, K. (2002). Prevalence of wife rape and other intimate partner sexual coercion in a nationally representative sample of women. *Violence & Victims, 17,* 511–524. [12]

Bass, B. (1998). *Transformational leadership: Industrial, military and educational impact.* Mahwah, NJ: Lawrence Erlbaum. [18]

Bass, B., Avolio, B., Jung, D., & Berson, Y. (2003). Predicting unit performance by assessing transformational and transactional leadership. *Journal of Applied Psychology, 88,* 207–218. [18]

Bass, E., & Davis, L. (1988). *The courage to heal.* New York: Harper & Row. [6]

Bassili, J. N. (1995). Response latency and the accessibility of voting intentions: What contributes to accessibility and how it affects vote choice. *Personality and Social Psychology Bulletin, 21,* 686–695. [17]

Bates, M., Labouvie, D., & Voelbel, G. (2002). Individual differences in latent neuropsychological abilities at addictions treatment entry. *Psychology of Addictive Behaviors, 16,* 35–46. [4]

Bateson, G. (1982). Totemic knowledge in New Guinea. In U. Neisser (Ed.), *Memory observed: Remembering in natural contexts.* San Francisco: W. H. Freeman. [6]

Batson, C. D., Batson, J. G., Griffitt, C. A., Barrientos, S., Brandt, J. R., Sprengelmeyer, P., & Bayly, M. J. (1989). Negative-state relief and the empathy-altruism hypothesis. *Journal of Personality and Social Psychology, 56,* 922–933. [17]

Baumgardner, A. H., Heppner, P. P., & Arkin, R. M. (1986). Role of causal attribution in personal problem solving. *Journal of Personality and Social Psychology, 50,* 636–643. [17]

Baumrind, D. (1967). Child care practices anteceding three patterns of preschool behavior. *Genetic Psychology Monographs, 75,* 43–88. [9]

Baumrind, D. (1971). Current patterns of parental authority. *Developmental Psychology Monographs, 4*(1, Pt. 2). [9]

Baumrind, D. (1980). New directions in socialization research. *American Psychologist, 35,* 639–652. [9]

Baumrind, D. (1991). The influence of parenting style on adolescent competence and substance use. *Journal of Early Adolescence, 11,* 56–95. [9, 10]

Bavelier, D., Tomann, A., Hutton, C., Mitchell, T., Corina, D., Liu, G., & Neville, H. (2000). Visual attention to the periphery is enhanced in congenitally deaf individuals. *Journal of Neuroscience, 20,* 1–6. [3]

Bazan, S. (1998). Enhancing decision-making effectiveness in problem-solving teams. *Clinical Laboratory Management Review, 12,* 272–276. [17]

Bean, R., Perry, B., & Bedell, T. (2002). Developing culturally competent marriage and family therapists: Treatment guidelines for non-African American therapists working with African American families. *Journal of Marital & Family Therapy, 28,* 153–164. [16]

Bechara, A., Damasio, H., & Damasio, A. R. (2000). Emotion, decision making and the orbitofrontal cortex. *Cerebral Cortex, 10,* 295–307. [4]

Beck, A. T. (1967). *Depression: Causes and treatment.* Philadelphia: University of Pennsylvania Press. [15]

Beck, A. T. (1976). *Cognitive therapy and the emotional disorders.* New York: New American Library. [16]

Beck, A. T. (1991). Cognitive therapy: A 30-year retrospective. *American Psychologist, 46,* 368–375. [15, 16]

Beck, A. T. (1993). Cognitive therapy: Past, present, and future. *Journal of Consulting and Clinical Psychology, 61,* 194–198. [16]

Beck, J. G. (1995). Hypoactive sexual desire disorder: An overview. *Journal of Consulting and Clinical Psychology, 63,* 919–927. [12]

Bee, H. & Boyd, D. (2003). *The developing child* (10th ed.). Boston, MA: Allyn & Bacon. [9]

Beebe, D. W., Pfiffner, L. J., & McBurnett, K. (2000). Evaluation of the validity of the Wechsler Intelligence Scale for Children—Third Edition comprehension and picture arrangement subtests as measures of social intelligence. *Psychological Assessment, 12,* 197–201. [8]

Beilin, H., & Fireman, G. (1999). The foundation of Piaget's theories: Mental and physical action. *Advances in Child Development and Behavior, 27,* 221–246. [9]

Beirut, L., Dinwiddie, S., Begleiter, H., Crowe, R., Hesselbrock, V., Nurnberger, J., Porjesz, B., Schuckit, M., & Reich, T. (1998). Familial transmission of substance dependence: Alcohol, marijuana, cocaine, and habitual smoking: A report from the collaborative study on the genetics of alcoholism. *Archives of General Psychiatry, 55,* 982–988. [4, 13]

Békésy, G. von. (1957). The ear. *Scientific American, 197,* 66–78. [3]

Bekker, M. H. J. (1996). Agoraphobia and gender: A review. *Clinical Psychology Review, 16,* 129–146. [15]

Belcourt-Dittloff, A., & Stewart, J. (2000). Historical racism: Implications for Native Americans. *American Psychologist, 55,* 1164–1165. [13]

Bell, A. P., Weinberg, M. S., & Hammersmith, S. K. (1981). *Sexual preference: Its development in men and women.* Bloomington: Indiana University Press. [12]

Bell, M. A., & Fox, N. A. (1992). The relationship between frontal brain electrical activity and cognitive development during infancy. *Child Development, 63,* 1142–1163. [9]

Bellis, M., Cook, P., Clark, P., Syed, Q., & Hoskins, A. (2002). Re-emerging syphilis in gay men: A case-control study of behavioural risk factors and HIV status. *Journal of Epidemiology & Community Health, 56,* 235–236. [12]

Belsky, J., & Fearon, R. (2002). Infant-mother attachment security, contextual risk, and early development: A moderational analysis. *Development & Psychopathology, 14,* 293–310. [9]

Belsky, J., Rovine, M., & Fish, M. (1989). The developing family system. In M. Gunnar (Ed.), *Minnesota symposium on child psychology: Vol. 22. Systems and development.* Hillsdale, NJ: Erlbaum. [10]

Bem, S. L. (1974). The measurement of psychological androgyny. *Journal of Consulting and Clinical Psychology, 42,* 155–162. [12]

Bem, S. L. (1975). Sex role adaptability: One consequence of psychological androgyny. *Journal of Personality and Social Psychology, 31,* 634–643. [12]

Bem, S. L. (1977). On the utility of alternative procedures for assessing psychological androgyny. *Journal of Consulting and Clinical Psychology, 45,* 196–205. [12]

Bem, S. L. (1981). Gender schema theory: A cognitive account of sex typing. *Psychological Review, 88,* 354–364. [12]

Bem, S. L. (1985). Androgyny and gender schema theory: A conceptual and empirical integration. In T. B. Sonderegger (Ed.), *Nebraska symposium on motivation: Psychology of gender* (Vol. 32, pp. 179–226). Lincoln: University of Nebraska Press. [12]

Benazzi, F. (2000). Late-life atypical major depressive episode: A 358-case study in outpatients. *American Journal of Geriatric Psychiatry, 8,* 117–122. [10]

Benes, F. M. (2000). Emerging principles of altered neural circuitry in schizophrenia. *Brain Research Reviews, 31,* 251–269. [15]

Bengtson, V., Rosenthal, C., & Burton, L. (1990). Families and aging: Diversity and heterogeneity. In R. H. Binstock & L. K. George (Eds.), *Handbook of aging and the social sciences* (3rd ed., pp. 263–287). San Diego: Academic. [10]

Benjafield, J. G. (1996). *A history of psychology.* Boston: Allyn & Bacon. [1]

Benjamin, L., & Crouse, E. (2002). The American Psychological Association's response to *Brown v. Board of Education*: The case of Kenneth B. Clark. *American Psychologist, 57,* 38–50. [1]

Benjamin, L. T. (2000). The psychology laboratory at the turn of the 20th century. *American Psychologist, 55,* 318–321. [1]

Bennett, M. R. (2000). The concept of long-term potentiation of transmission at synapses. *Progress in Neurobiology, 60,* 109–137. [6]

Bennett, M. V. L. (2000). Seeing is relieving: Electrical synapses between visualized neurons. *Nature Neuroscience, 3,* 7–9. [2]

Bennett, S. K. (1994). The American Indian: A psychological overview. In W. J. Lonner & R. Malpass (Eds.), *Psychology and culture* (pp. 35–39). Boston: Allyn & Bacon. [14]

Bennett, W. I. (1990, November). Boom and doom. *Harvard Health Letter, 16,* 1–4. [3]

Ben-Porath, Y. S., & Butcher, J. N. (1989). The comparability of MMPI and MMPI–2 scales and profiles. *Psychological Assessment: A Journal of Consulting and Clinical Psychology, 1,* 345–347. [14]

Benson, E. (2003, February). Intelligent intelligence testing. *APA Monitor on Psychology, 34,* 48. [8]

Berenbaum, S. A., Korman, K., & Leveroni, C. (1995). Early hormones and sex differences in cognitive abilities. *Learning and Individual Differences,* 7, 303–321. [12]

Berenbaum, S. A., & Snyder, E. (1995). Early hormonal influences on childhood sex-typed activity and playmate preferences: Implications for the development of sexual orientation. *Developmental Psychology, 31,* 31–42. [12]

Bergem, A. L. M., Engedal, K., & Kringlen, E. (1997). The role of heredity in late-onset Alzheimer's disease and vascular dementia. *Archives of General Psychiatry, 54,* 264–270. [10]

Bergman, M., & Drasgow, F. (2003). Race as a moderator in a model of sexual harassment: An empirical test. *Journal of Occupational Health Psychology, 8,* 131–145. [18]

Berk, L. E. (1994a). *Child development* (3rd ed.). Boston: Allyn & Bacon. [9]

Berk, L. E. (1997). *Child development* (4th ed.). Boston: Allyn & Bacon. [10]

Berkman, L. F., & Syme, S. L. (1979). Social networks, host resistance, and mortality: A nine-year followup study of Alameda County residents. *American Journal of Epidemiology, 109,* 184–204. [13]

Berkowitz, L. (1983). Aversively stimulated aggression: Some parallels and differences in research with animals and humans. *American Psychologist, 38,* 1135–1144. [17]

Berkowitz, L. (1988). Frustrations, appraisals, and aversively stimulated aggression. *Aggressive Behavior, 14,* 3–11. [17]

Berkowitz, L. (1990). On the formation and regulation of anger and aggression: A cognitive-neoassociationistic analysis. *American Psychologist, 45,* 494–503. [17]

Berlin, B., & Kay, P. (1969). *Basic color terms: Their universality and evolution.* Berkeley: University of California Press. [7]

Berlyne, D. E. (1960). *Conflict, arousal, and curiosity.* New York: McGraw-Hill. [11]

Bernal, M. E., & Castro, F. G. (1994). Are clinical psychologists prepared for service and research with ethnic minorities? Report of a decade of progress. *American Psychologist, 49,* 797–805. [16]

Bernardi, L., Sleight, P., Bandinelli, G., Cencetti, S., Fattorini, L., Wdowczyc-Szulc, J., & Lagi, A. (2001). Effect of rosary prayer and yoga mantras on autonomic cardiovascular rhythms: Comparative study. *BMJ: British Medical Journal, 323,* 1446–1449. [4]

Berndt, E. R., Koran, L. M., Finkelstein, S. N., Gelenberg, A. J., Kornstein, S. G., Miller, I. M., Thase, M. E., Trapp, G. A., & Keller, M. B. (2000). Lost human capital from early-onset chronic depression. *American Journal of Psychiatry, 157,* 940–947. [15]

Berndt, T. J. (1992). Friendship and friends' influence in adolescence. *Current Directions in Psychological Science, 1,* 156–159. [10]

Berndt, T. J., Cheung, P. C., Lau, S., Hau, K. T., & Lew, W. J. F. (1993). Perceptions of parenting in mainland China, Taiwan, and Hong Kong: Sex differences and societal differences. *Developmental Psychology, 29,* 156–164. [9]

Bernstein, I. L. (1985). Learned food aversions in the progression of cancer and its treatment. *Annals of the New York Academy of Sciences, 443,* 365–380. [5]

Bernstein, I. L., Webster, M. M., & Bernstein, I. D. (1982). Food aversions in children receiving chemotherapy for cancer. *Cancer, 50,* 2961–2963. [5]

Berquier, A., & Aston, R. (1992). Characteristics of the frequent nightmare sufferer. *Journal of Abnormal Psychology,* 101, 246–250. [4]

Berscheid, E., Dion, K., Walster, E., & Walster, G. W. (1971). Physical attractiveness and dating choice: A test of the matching hypothesis. *Journal of Experimental Social Psychology,* 7, 173–189. [17]

Besharat, M. (2001). Management strategies of sexual dysfunctions. *Journal of Contemporary Psychotherapy, 31*, 161–180. [15]

Bexton, W. H., Herron, W., & Scott, T. H. (1954). Effects of decreased variation in the sensory environment. *Canadian Journal of Psychology, 8*, 70–76. [11]

Bialystok, E., Shenfield, T., & Codd, J. (2000). Languages, scripts, and the environment: Factors in developing concepts of print. *Developmental Psychology, 36*, 66–76. [7]

Billiard, M., Pasquiré-Magnetto, V., Heckman, M., Carlander, B., Besset, A., Zachariev, Z., Eliaou, J. F., & Malafosse, A. (1994). Family studies in narcolepsy. *Sleep, 17*, S54–S59. [4]

Binet, A. (1905). New methods for the diagnosis of the intellectual level of subnormals. *L'annee psychologique, 12*, 191–244. Retrieved July 1, 2002, from http://psychclassics.yorku.ca/Binet/binet1.htm [8]

Binson, D., Michaels, S., Stall, R., Coates, T. J., Gagnon, J. H., & Catania, J. A. (1995). Prevalence and social distribution of men who have sex with men: United States and its urban centers. *Journal of Sex Research, 32*, 245–254. [12]

Biondi, M., & Picardi, A. (2003). Increased probability of remaining in remission from panic disorder with agoraphobia after drug treatment in patients who received concurrent cognitive-behavioural therapy: A follow-up study. *Psychotherapy & Psychosomatics, 72*, 34–42. [15]

Birch, D. (1998). The adolescent parent: A fifteen-year longitudinal study of school-age mothers and their children. *Internal Journal of Adolescent Medicine & Health, 19*, 141–153. [10]

Bird, T. (2001). *Alzheimer overview* [Online brochure]. Retrieved March 25, 2002, from http://www.geneclincis.org [2]

Birren, J. E., & Fisher, L. M. (1995). Aging and speed of behavior: Possible consequences for psychological functioning. *Annual Review of Psychology, 46*, 329–353. [10]

Bishop, J., & Lane, R. C. (2000). Father absence and the attitude of entitlement. *Journal of Contemporary Psychotherapy, 30*, 105–117. [9, 10]

Bishop, M., & Allen, C. (2001). Employment concerns of people with epilepsy and the question of disclosure: Report of a survey of the epilepsy foundation. *Epilepsy & Behavior, 2*, 490–495. [18]

Bisiach, E. (1996). Unilateral neglect and the structure of space representation. *Current Directions in Psychological Science, 5*, 62–65. [2]

Bjork, D. W. (1993). *B. F. Skinner: A life.* New York: Basic Books. [5]

Bjorklund, D. F., Cassel, W. S., Bjorklund, B. R., Brown, R. D., Park, C. L., Ernst, K., & Owen, F. A. (2000). Social demand characteristics in children's and adults' memory and suggestibility: The effect of different interviewers on free recall and recognition. *Applied Cognitive Psychology, 14*, 421–433. [6]

Bjorklund, D. F., & Coyle, T. R. (1995). Utilization deficiencies in the development of memory strategies. In F. E. Weinert & W. Schneider (Eds.), *Research on memory development: State of the art and future directions.* Hillsdale, NJ: Erlbaum. [9]

Björkqvist, K., Lagerspetz, K. M. J., & Kaukiainen, A. (1992). Do girls manipulate and boys fight? Developmental trends in regard to direct and indirect aggression. *Aggressive Behavior, 18*, 117–127. [12]

Blagrove, M., & Hartnell, S. (2000). Lucid dreaming: Associations with internal locus of control, need for cognition and creativity. *Personality & Individual Differences, 28*, 41–47. [4]

Blanchard, C., & Lichtenberg, J. (2003). Compromise in career decision making: A test of Gottfredson's theory. *Journal of Vocational Behavior, 62*, 250–271. [18]

Blascovich, J., Wyer, N. A., Swart, L. A., & Kibler, J. L. (1997). Racism and racial categorization. *Journal of Personality and Social Psychology, 72*, 1364–1372. [17]

Blatt, S. J., Sanislow, C. A., III, Zuroff, D. C., & Pilkonis, P. A. (1996). Characteristics of effective therapists: Further analyses of data from the National Institute of Mental Health Treatment of Depression Collaborative Research Program. *Journal of Consulting and Clinical Psychology, 64*, 1276–1284. [16]

Bliese, P. D., & Castro, C. A. (2000). Role clarity, work overload and organizational support: Multilevel evidence of the importance of support. *Work & Stress, 14*, 65–73. [13]

Bliss, T. V., & Lomo, T. (2000). Plasticity in a monosynaptic cortical pathway. *Journal of Physiology, 207*, 61. [6]

Bloom, B. S. (Ed.). (1985). *Developing talent in young people.* New York: Ballantine. [8]

Bloomer, C. M. (1976). *Principles of visual perception.* New York: Van Nostrand Reinhold. [3]

Blumer, D. (2002). The illness of Vincent van Gogh. *American Journal of Psychiatry, 159*, 519–526. [15]

Blustein, D., Phillips, S., Jobin-Davis, K., & Finkelberg, S. (1997). A theory-building investigation of the school-to-work transition. *Counseling Psychology, 25*, 364–402. [8]

Blyth, D. A., Simmons, R. G., Bulcroft, R., Felt, D., VanCleave, E. F., & Bush, D. M. (1981). The effects of physical development on self-image and satisfaction with body-image for early adolescent males. In R. G. Simmons (Ed.), *Research in community and mental health* (Vol. 2). Greenwich, CT: JAI. [10]

Bochner, S. (1994). Cross-cultural differences in the self concept: A test of Hofstede's individualism/collectivism distinction. *Journal of Cross-Cultural Psychology, 25*, 273–283. [11, 14]

Bogen, J. E., & Vogel, P. J. (1963). Treatment of generalized seizures by cerebral commissurotomy. *Surgical Forum, 14*, 431. [2]

Bohannon, J. N., III. (1988). Flashbulb memories for the Space Shuttle disaster: A tale of two theories. *Cognition, 29*, 179–196. [6]

Boivin, D. B., Czeisler, C. A., Dijk, D-J., Duffy, J. F., Folkard, S., Minors, D. S., Totterdell, P., & Waterhouse, J. M. (1997). Complex interaction of the sleep-wake cycle and circadian phase modulates mood in healthy subjects. *Archives of General Psychiatry, 54*, 145–152. [4]

Bolino, M., & Turnley, W. (2003). More than one way to make an impression: Exploring profiles of impression management. *Journal of Management, 29*, 141–160. [18]

Bonanno, G. A., Keltner, D., Holen, A., & Horowitz, M. J. (1995). When avoiding unpleasant emotions might not be such a bad thing: Verbal-autonomic response dissociation and midlife conjugal bereavement. *Journal of Personality and Social Psychology, 69*, 975–989. [10]

Bonnel, A., Mottron, L., Peretz, I., Tudel, M., Gallun, E., & Bonnel, A. (2003). Enhanced pitch sensitivity in individuals with autism: A signal detection analysis. *Journal of Cognitive Neuroscience, 15*, 226–235. [8]

Bonnet, M. H., & Arand, D. L. (1995). We are chronically sleep deprived. *Sleep, 18*, 908–911. [4]

Bonson, K., Grant, S., Contoreggi, C., Links, J., Metcalfe, J., Weyl, H., Kurian, V., Ernst, M., & London, E. (2002). Neural systems and cue-induced cocaine craving. *Neuropsychopharmacology, 26*, 376–386. [4]

Borbely, A. A. (1984). Sleep regulation: Outline of a model and its implications for depression. In A. A. Borbely & J. L. Valatx (Eds.), *Sleep mechanisms.* Berlin: Springer-Verlag. [4]

Borbely, A. A., Achermann, P., Trachsel, L., & Tobler, I. (1989). Sleep initiation and initial sleep intensity: Interactions of homeostatic and circadian mechanisms. *Journal of Biological Rhythms, 4*, 149–160. [4]

Bornstein, M. H., & Marks, L. E. (1982, January). Color revisionism. *Psychology Today*, pp. 64–73. [9]

Bornstein, R. F. (1989). Exposure and affect: Overview and meta-analysis of research, 1968–1987. *Psychological Bulletin, 106*, 265–289. [17]

Borrelli, B., Niaura, R., Keuthen, N. J., Goldstein, M. G., DePue, J. D., Murphy, C., & Abrams, D. B. (1996). Development of major depressive disorder during smoking-cessation treatment. *Journal of Clinical Psychiatry, 57*, 534–538. [13]

Bosse, R., Aldwin, C. M., Levenson, M. R., & Workman-Daniels, K. (1991). How stressful is retirement? *Journal of Gerontology, 46*, 9–14. [10]

Bouchard, T. J., Jr. (1994). Genes, environment, and personality. *Science, 264*, 1700–1701. [14]

Bouchard, T. J., Jr. (1997, September/October). Whenever the twain shall meet. *The Sciences, 37*, 52–57. [8, 9, 14]

Bouchard, T. J., Jr. (1998, May 13). Personal communication. [8]

Bouchard, T. J., Jr., Lykken, D. T., McGue, M., Segal, N. L., & Tellegen, A. (1990). Sources of human psychological differences: The Minnesota study of twins reared apart. *Science, 250*, 223–228. [8, 14]

Bouchard, T. J., Jr., & McGue, M. (1981). Familial studies of intelligence: A review. *Science, 212*, 1055–1058. [8]

Bourassa, D., McManus, I., & Bryden, M. (1996). Handedness and eye-dominance: A meta-analysis of their relationship. *Laterality, 1*, 5–34. [2]

Bourassa, M., & Vaugeois, P. (2001). Effects of marijuana use on divergent thinking. *Creativity Research Journal, 13*, 411–416. [4]

Bouton, M. E. (1993). Context, time, and memory retrieval in the interference paradigms of Pavlovian learning. *Psychological Bulletin, 114*, 80–89. [5]

Bouton, M. E., & Ricker, S. T. (1994) Renewal of extinguished responding in a second context. *Animal Learning and Behavior, 22*, 317–324. [5]

Bovbjerg, D. H., Redd, W. H., Maier, L. A., Holland, J. C., Lesko, L. M., Niedzwiecki, D., Rubin, S. C., & Hakes, T. B. (1990). Anticipatory immune suppression and nausea in women receiving cyclic chemotherapy for ovarian cancer. *Journal of Consulting and Clinical Psychology, 58*, 153–157. [5]

Bowden, C., Lecrubier, Y., Bauer, M., Goodwin, G., Greil, W., Sachs, G., & von Knorring, L. (2000). Maintenance therapies for classic and other forms of bipolar disorder. *Journal of Affective Disorders, 59*(1), S57–S67. [16]

Bowen, C. (2003). A case study of job analysis. *Journal of Psychological Practice, 8*, 46–55. [18]

Bowen-Reid, T., & Harrell, J. (2002). Racist experiences and health outcomes: An examination of spirituality as a buffer. *Journal of Black Psychology, 28*, 18–36. [13]

Bower, G. H. (1973, October). How to . . . uh . . . remember! *Psychology Today*, 63–70. [6]

Bower, G. H., Thompson-Schill, S., & Tulving, E. (1994). Reducing retroactive interference: An interference analysis. *Journal of Experimental Psychology: Learning, Memory, and Cognition, 20*, 51–66. [6]

Bowers, K. S. (1992). Imagination and dissociative control in hypnotic responding. *International Journal of Clinical and Experimental Hypnosis, 40*, 253–275. [4]

Bowers, K. S., & Farvolden, P. (1996). Revisiting a century-old Freudian slip—from suggestion disavowed to the truth repressed. *Psychological Bulletin, 119*, 355–380. [6]

Bowers, K. S., & Woody, E. Z. (1996). Hypnotic amnesia and the paradox of intentional forgetting. *Journal of Abnormal Psychology, 105*, 381–390. [4]

Bowlby, J. (1969). *Attachment and loss* (Vol. 1). New York: Basic Books. [9]

Brain imaging and psychiatry—Part I. (1997, January). *Harvard Mental Health Letter, 13*(7), 1–4. [2]

Bramblett, D. A. (1997, October). Personal communication. [3]

Braten, L., & Olaussen, B. (1998). The learning and study strategies of Norwegian first-year college students. *Learning & Individual Differences, 10*, 309–327. [10]

Braun, A., Balkin, T., Wesensten, N., Gwadry, F., Carson, R., Varga, M., Baldwin, P., Belenky, G., & Herscovitch, P. (1998). Dissociated pattern of activity in visual cortices and their projections during human rapid eye movement sleep. *Science, 279*, 91–95. [4]

Brawman-Mintzer, O., & Lydiard, R. B. (1996). Generalized anxiety disorder: Issues in epidemiology. *Journal of Clinical Psychiatry, 57*(7, Suppl.), 3–8. [15]

Brawman-Mintzer, O., & Lydiard, R. B. (1997). Biological basis of generalized anxiety disorder. *Journal of Clinical Psychiatry, 58*(3, Suppl.), 16–25. [15]

Bray, G. A. (1991). Weight homeostasis. *Annual Review of Medicine, 42*, 205–216. [11]

Bray, G. A., & Tartaglia, L. A. (2000). Medicinal strategies in the treatment of obesity. *Nature, 404*, 672–677. [11]

Breckler, S. J. (1984). Empirical validation of affect, behavior, and cognition as distinct attitude components. *Journal of Personality and Social Psychology, 47*, 1191–1205. [17]

Breedlove, S. M. (1994). Sexual differentiation of the human nervous system. *Annual Review of Psychology, 45*, 389–418. [12]

Breland, K., & Breland, M. (1961). The misbehavior of organisms. *American Psychologist, 16*, 681–684. [5]

Brennan, P. A., Raine, A., Schulsinger, F., Kirkegaard-Sorensen, L., Knop, J., Hutchings, B., Rosenberg, R., & Mednick, S. A. (1997). Psychophysiological protective factors for male subjects at high risk for criminal behavior. *American Journal of Psychiatry, 154*, 853–855. [17]

Brent, D. A., Bridge, J., Johnson, B. A., & Connolly, J. (1996). Suicidal behavior runs in families: A controlled family study of adolescent suicide victims. *Archives of General Psychiatry, 53*, 1145–1152. [15]

Brent, D., Oquendo, M., Birmaher, B., Greenhill, L., Kolko, D., Stanley, B., Zelazny, J., Brodsky, B., Bridge, J., Ellis, S., Salazar, J., & Mann, J. (2002). Familial pathways to early-onset suicide attempt. *Archives of General Psychiatry, 59*, 801. [15]

Breslau, N., Davis, G. C., Peterson, E. L., & Schultz, L. (1997). Psychiatric sequelae of posttraumatic stress disorder in women. *Archives of General Psychiatry, 54*, 81–87. [13]

Breslau, N., Kilbey, M. N., & Andreski, P. (1993). Nicotine dependence and major depression: New evidence from a prospective investigation. *Archives of General Psychiatry, 50*, 31–35. [13]

Bretherton, I. (1992). The origins of attachment theory: John Bowlby and Mary Ainsworth. *Developmental Psychology, 28*, 759–775. [9]

Brett, J., & Atwater, L. (2001). 360-degree feedback: Accuracy, reactions, and perceptions of usefulness. *Journal of Applied Psychology, 86*, 930–942. [18]

Bridges, K. M. B. (1932). Emotional development in early infancy. *Child Development, 3*, 324–341. [11]

Brieger, P., Ehrt, U., & Marneros, A. (2003). Frequency of comorbid personality disorders in bipolar and unipolar affective disorders. *Comprehensive Psychiatry, 44*, 28–34. [15]

Brienza, R., Stein, M., & Fagan, M. (2002). Delay in obtaining conventional healthcare by female internal medicine patients who use herbal therapies. *Journal of Women's Health & Gender-Based Medicine, 11*, 79–87. [4]

Broadbent, D. E. (1958). *Perception and communication.* New York: Pergamon Press. [6]

Brockner, J., Heuer, L., Magner, N., Folger, R., Umphress, E., van den Box, K., Vermunt, R., Magner, M., & Siegel, P. (2003). High procedural fairness heightens the effect of outcome favorability on self-evaluations: An attributional analysis. *Organizational Behavior & Human Decision Processes, 91,* 51–68. [18]

Brody, A., Saxena, S., Fairbanks, L., Alborzian, S., Demaree, H., Maidment, K., & Baxter, L. (2000). Personality changes in adult subjects with major depressive disorder or obsessive-compulsive disorder treated with paroxetine. *Journal of Clinical Psychiatry, 61,* 349–355. [14]

Brody, E. M., Johnson, P. T., & Fulcomer, M. C. (1984). What should adult children do for elderly parents? Opinions and preferences of three generations of women. *Journal of Gerontology, 39,* 736–746. [10]

Brody, E. M., Litvin, S. J., Hoffman, C., & Kleban, M. H. (1992). Differential effects of daughters' marital status on their parent care experiences. *The Gerontologist, 32,* 58–67. [10]

Brody, J. A., Grant, M. D., Frateschi, L. J., Miller, S. C., & Zhang, H. (2000). Reproductive longevity and increased life expectancy. *Age and Ageing, 29,* 75–78. [10]

Brody, J. E. (1995, August 30). Hormone replacement therapy for men: When does it help? *The New York Times,* p. C8. [12]

Brody, L. R. (1985). Gender differences in emotional development: A review of theories and research. *Journal of Personality, 53,* 102–149. [11]

Brody, N. (1992). *Intelligence* (2nd ed.). San Diego, CA: Academic. [8]

Bronfenbrenner, U. (1979). *The ecology of human development.* Cambridge, MA: Harvard University Press. [9]

Bronfenbrenner, U. (1989). Ecological systems theory. *Annals of Child Development, 6,* 187–249. [9]

Bronfenbrenner, U. (1993). The ecology of cognitive development: Research methods and fugitive findings. In R. Wozniak and K. Fischer (Eds.), *Development in context: Acting and thinking in specific environments.* Hillsdale, NJ: Erlbaum. [9]

Brooks-Gunn, J. (2003). Do you believe in magic? What we can expect from early childhood intervention programs. *Social Policy Report, 17,* 3–14. [8]

Brooks-Gunn, J., & Furstenberg, F. F. (1989). Adolescent sexual behavior. *American Psychologist, 44,* 249–257. [10]

Brotman, A. W. (1994). What works in the treatment of anorexia nervosa? *Harvard Mental Health Letter, 10*(7), 8. [11]

Broughton, R. J., & Shimizu, T. (1995). Sleep-related violence: A medical and forensic challenge. *Sleep, 18,* 727–730. [4]

Broughton, W. A., & Broughton, R. J. (1994). Psychosocial impact of narcolepsy. *Sleep, 17,* S45–S49. [4]

Brown, A. (1996, Winter). Mood disorders in children and adolescents. *NARSAD Research Newsletter,* pp. 11–14. [15]

Brown, A., & Day, J. (1983). Macrorules for summarizing text: The development of expertise. *Journal of Verbal Learning and Verbal Behavior, 22,* 1–14. [10]

Brown, A. M. (1990). Development of visual sensitivity to light and color vision in human infants: A critical review. *Vision Research, 30,* 1159–1188. [8]

Brown, G. W., Harris, T. O., & Hepworth, C. (1994). Life events and endogenous depression: A puzzle reexamined. *Archives of General Psychiatry, 51,* 525–534. [15]

Brown, J. D., & Rogers, R. J. (1991). Self-serving attributions: The role of physiological arousal. *Personality and Social Psychology Bulletin, 17,* 501–506. [17]

Brown, R. (1973). *A first language: The early stages.* Cambridge, MA: Harvard University Press. [9]

Brown, R., Cazden, C., & Bellugi, U. (1968). The child's grammar from I to III. In J. P. Hill (Ed.), *Minnesota symposium on child psychology* (Vol. 2, pp. 28–73). Minneapolis: University of Minnesota Press. [9]

Brown, R., & Kulik, J. (1977). Flashbulb memories. *Cognition, 5,* 73–99. [6]

Brown, R., & McNeil, D. (1966). The "tip of the tongue" phenomenon. *Journal of Verbal Learning and Verbal Behavior, 5,* 325–337. [6]

Brown, R. J., & Donderi, D. C. (1986). Dream content and self-reported well-being among recurrent dreamers, past-recurrent dreamers, and nonrecurrent dreamers. *Journal of Personality and Social Psychology, 50,* 612–623. [4]

Brown, W., O'Connell, A., & Fillit, H. (2002). New developments in pharmacotherapy for Alzheimer disease. *Drug Benefit Trends, 14,* 34–44. [10]

Brown, W. A. (1998, January). The placebo effect. *Scientific American, 278,* 90–95. [3]

Brownell, K. D., & Wadden, T. A. (1992). Etiology and treatment of obesity: Understanding a serious, prevalent, and refractory disorder. *Journal of Consulting and Clinical Psychology, 60,* 505–517. [11]

Brownlee, S., & Schrof, J. M. (1997, March 17). The quality of mercy. *U.S. News & World Report,* pp. 54–67. [3]

Bruch, M., Fallon, M., & Heimberg, R. (2003). Social phobia and difficulties in occupational adjustment. *Journal of Counseling Psychology, 50,* 109–117. [15]

Brunetti, A., Carta, P., Cossu, G., Ganadu, M., Golosio, B., Mura, G., & Pirastru, M. (2002). A real-time classification system of thalassemic pathologies based on artificial neural networks. *Medical Decision Making, 22,* 18–26. [7]

Brunila, T., Lincoln, N., Lindell, A., Tenovuo, O., & Haemelaeinen, H. (2002). Experiences of combined visual training and arm activation in the rehabilitation of unilateral visual neglect: A clinical study. *Neuropsychological Rehabilitation, 12,* 27–40. [2]

Buck, L. B. (1996). Information coding in the vertebrate olfactory system. *Annual Review of Neuroscience, 19,* 517–544. [3]

Buckingham, H. W., Jr., & Kertesz, A. (1974). A linguistic analysis of fluent aphasics. *Brain and Language, 1,* 29–42. [2]

Buhusi, C., & Meck, W. (2002). Differential effects of methamphetamine and haloperidol on the control of an internal clock. *Behavioral Neuroscience, 116,* 291–297. [4]

Buis, J. M., & Thompson, D. N. (1989). Imaginary audience and personal fable: A brief review. *Adolescence, 24,* 773–781. [10]

Buller, D. B., Burgoon, M., Hall, J. R., Levine, N., Taylor, A. M., Beach, B. H., Melcher, C., Buller, M. K., Bowen, S. L., Hunsaker, F. G., & Bergen, A. (2000). Using language intensity to increase the success of a family intervention to protect children from ultraviolet radiation: Predictions from language expectancy theory. *Preventive Medicine, 30,* 103–113. [17]

Bunderson, J., & Sutcliffe, K., (2003). Management team learning orientation and business unit performance. *Journal of Applied Psychology, 88,* 552–560. [18]

Buonomano, D. V., & Merzenich, M. M. (1995). Temporal information transformed into a spatial code by a neural network with realistic properties. *Science, 267,* 1028–1030. [7]

Burchinal, M., Campbell, F., Bryant, D., Wasik, B., & Ramey, C. (1997). Early intervention and mediating processes in cognitive performance of children of low-income African American families. *Child Development, 68,* 935–954. [8]

Burke, A., Heuer, F., & Reisberg, D. (1992). Remembering emotional events. *Memory and Cognition, 20,* 277–290. [6]

Burns, J., & Swerdlow, R. (2003). Right orbitofrontal tumor with pedophilia symptom and constructional apraxia sign. *Archives of Neurology, 60*, 437–440. [12]

Burt, D. B., Zembar, M. J., & Niederehe, G. (1995). Depression and memory impairment: A meta-analysis of the association, its pattern, and specificity. *Psychological Bulletin, 117*, 285–305. [6]

Burton, D. (2003). Male adolescents: Sexual victimization and subsequent sexual abuse. *Child & Adolescent Social Work Journal, 20*, 277–296. [17]

Busch, C. M., Zonderman, A. B., & Costa, P. T. (1994). Menopausal transition and psychological distress in a nationally representative sample: Is menopause associated with psychological distress? *Journal of Aging and Health, 6*, 209–228. [10]

Bushman, B. (2002). Does venting anger feed or extinguish the flame? Catharsis rumination, distraction, anger and aggressive responding. *Personality & Social Psychology Bulletin*, 28, 724–731. [11]

Bushman, B., & Cantor, J. (2003). Media ratings for violence and sex: Implications for policymakers and parents. *American Psychologist, 58*, 130–141. [5, 9]

Bushman, B. J. (1995). Moderating role of trait aggressiveness in the effects of violent media on aggression. *Journal of Personality and Social Psychology, 69*, 950–960. [17]

Bushman, B. J., & Cooper, H. M. (1990). Effects of alcohol on human aggression: An integrative research review. *Psychological Bulletin, 107*, 341–354. [17]

Buss, D. M. (1984). Marital assortment for personality dispositions: Assessment with three different data sources. *Behavioral Genetics, 14*, 111–123. [17]

Buss, D. M. (1994). The strategies of human mating. *American Scientist, 82*, 238–249. [12, 17]

Buss, D. M. (1999). *Evolutionary psychology: The new science of the mind.* Boston: Allyn & Bacon. [1, 5, 12, 17]

Buss, D. M. (2000a). *The dangerous passion: Why jealousy is as necessary as sex and love.* New York: Free Press. [1, 5]

Buss, D. M. (2000b). Desires in human mating. *Annals of the New York Academy of Sciences, 907*, 39–49. [1, 11, 12, 17]

Buss, D. M., Abbott, M., Angleitner, A., Asherian, A., Biaggio, A., Blanco-Villasenor, A., Bruchon-Schweitzer, M., et al. (1990). International preferences in selecting mates: A study of 37 cultures. *Journal of Cross-Cultural Psychology, 21*, 5–47. [1, 17]

Buss, D. M., Larson, R., Westen, D., & Semmelroth, J. (1992). Sex differences in jealousy: Evolution, physiology, and psychology. *Psychological Science, 3*, 251–255. [1]

Buss, D., Shackelford, T., Kirkpatrick, L., & Larsen, R. (2001). A half century of mate preferences: The cultural evolution of values. *Journal of Marriage and the Family, 63*, 491–503. [1]

Bussey, K., & Bandura, A. (1999). Social cognitive theory of gender development and differentiation. *Psychological Review, 106*, 676–713. [12]

Butcher, J. N. (1992, October). International developments with the MMPI–2. *MMPI–2 News & Profiles, 3*, 4. [14]

Butcher, J. N., Dahlstrom, W. G., Graham, J. R., Tellegen, A., & Kaemmer, B. (1989). *Manual for the restandardized Minnesota Multiphasic Personality Inventory: MMPI–2. An administrative and interpretive guide.* Minneapolis: University of Minnesota Press. [14]

Butcher, J. N., & Graham, J. R. (1989). *Topics in MMPI–2 interpretation.* Minneapolis: Department of Psychology, University of Minnesota. [14]

Butcher, J. N., Graham, J. R., & Ben-Porath, Y. S. (1995). Methodological problems and issues in MMPI, MMPI-2, and MMPI-A research. *Psychological Assessment*, 7, 320–329. [14]

Butcher, J. N., & Rouse, S. V. (1996). Personality: Individual differences and clinical assessment. *Annual Review of Psychology, 47*, 89–111. [14]

Butler, R., & Lewis, M. (1982). *Aging and mental health* (3rd ed.). St. Louis: Mosby. [10]

Butterworth, G., Franco, F., McKenzie, B., Graupner, L., & Todd, B. (2002). Dynamic aspects of visual event perception and the production of pointing by human infants. *British Journal of Developmental Psychology, 20*, 1–24. [2]

Buunk, B. P., Angleitner, A., Oubaid, V., & Buss, D. M. (1996). Sex differences in jealousy in evolutionary and cultural perspective: Tests from the Netherlands, Germany and the United States. *Psychological Science*, 7, 359–363. [1]

Byne, W. (1993a). Human sexual orientation: The biologic theories reappraised. *Archives of General Psychiatry, 50*, 228–239. [12]

Byne, W. (1993b). Sexual orientation and brain structure: Adding up the evidence. Paper presented at the annual meeting of the International Academy of Sex Research. Pacific Grove, CA. [12]

Byne, W. (1994). The biological evidence challenged. *Scientific American, 270*, 50–55. [12]

Byne, W., & Parsons, B. (1993). Human sexual orientation: The biologic theories reappraised. *Archives of General Psychiatry, 50*, 228–239. [12]

Byne, W., & Parsons, B. (1994). Biology and human sexual orientation. *Harvard Mental Health Letter, 10*(8), 5–7. [12]

Cahill, L., Babinsky, R., Markowitsch, H. J., & McGaugh, J. L. (1995). The amygdala and emotional memory. *Nature, 377*, 295–296. [2, 6]

Cahill, L., & McGaugh, J. (1995). A novel demonstration of enhanced memory associated with emotional arousal. *Consciousness & Cognition, 4*, 410–421. [6]

Callahan, J. (1997, May–June). Hypnosis: Trick or treatment? You'd be amazed at what modern doctors are tackling with an 18th century gimmick. *Health, 11*, 52–54. [4]

Camp, D. S., Raymond, G. A., & Church, R. M. (1967). Temporal relationship between response and punishment. *Journal of Experimental Psychology, 74*, 114–123. [5]

Campbell, F., Pungello, E., Miller-Johnson, S., Burchinal, M., & Ramey, C. (2001). The development of cognitive and academic abilities: Growth curves from an early childhood educational experiment. *Developmental Psychology, 37*, 231–242. [8]

Campbell, F., & Ramey, C. (1994). Effects of early intervention on intellectual and academic achievement: A follow-up study of children from low-income families. *Child Development, 65*, 684–698. [8]

Campbell, F., Ramey, D., Pungello, E., Spurling, J., & Miller-Johnson, S. (2002). Early childhood education: Young adult outcomes from the Abecedarian Project. *Applied Developmental Science, 6*, 42–57. [8]

Campbell, P., & Dhand, R. (2000). Obesity. *Nature, 404*, 631. [11]

Campbell, R., & Brody, E. M. (1985). Women's changing roles and help to the elderly: Attitudes of women in the United States and Japan. *The Gerontologist, 25*, 584–592. [10]

Campbell, S. S. (1985). Spontaneous termination of ad libitum sleep episodes with special reference to REM sleep. *Electroencephalography & Clinical Neurophysiology, 60*, 237–242. [4]

Campbell, S. S. (1995). Effects of timed bright-light exposure on shift-work adaptation in middle-aged subjects. *Sleep, 18*, 408–416. [4]

Campbell, S. S., & Murphy, P. J. (1998). Extraocular circadian phototransduction in humans. *Science, 279*, 396–399. [4]

Campos, J. J., Langer, A., & Krowitz, A. (1970). Cardiac responses on the visual cliff in prelocomotor human infants. *Science, 170,* 196–197. [9]

Camras, L., Meng, Z., Ujiie, T., Dharamsi, S., Miyake, K., Oster, H., Wang, L., Cruz, J., Murdoch, A., & Campos, J. (2002). Observing emotion in infants: Facial expression, body behavior, and rater judgments of responses to an expectancy-violating event. *Emotion, 2,* 179–193. [11]

Cañizares, S., Boget, T., Salamero, M., Rumià, J., Elices, E., & Arroyo, S. (2000). Reliability and clinical usefulness of the short forms of the Wechsler memory scale (revised) in patients with epilepsy. *Epilepsy Research, 41,* 97–106. [8]

Cannon, T. D., Kaprio, J., Lönnqvist, J., Huttunen, M., & Koskenvuo, M. (1998). The genetic epidemiology of schizophrenia in a Finnish twin cohort: A population-based modeling study. *Archives of General Psychiatry, 55,* 67–74. [15]

Cannon, W. B. (1927). The James-Lange theory of emotions: A critical examination as an alternative theory. *American Journal of Psychology, 39,* 106–112. [11]

Cannon, W. B. (1929). *Bodily changes in pain, hunger, fear and rage* (2nd ed.). New York: Appleton. [2]

Cannon, W. B. (1935). Stresses and strains of homeostasis. *American Journal of Public Health, 189,* 1–14. [2]

Capel, B. (2000). The battle of the sexes. *Mechanisms of Development, 92,* 89–103. [9, 12]

Cardena, E. (2000). Hypnosis in the treatment of trauma: A promising, but not fully supported, efficacious intervention. *International Journal of Clinical Experimental Hypnosis, 48,* 225–238. [4]

Cardoso, S. H., de Mello, L. C., & Sabbatini, R. M. E. (2000). How nerve cells work. Retrieved from http://www.epub.org.br/cm/n09/fundamentos/transmissao/voo_i.htm [2]

Carlat, D. J., Camargo, C. A., Jr., & Herzog, D. B. (1997). Eating disorders in males: A report on 135 patients. *American Journal of Psychiatry, 154,* 1127–1132. [11]

Carlson, N. R. (1998). *Foundations of physiological psychology* (4th ed.). Boston: Allyn & Bacon. [4]

Carlsson, I., Wendt, P. E., & Risberg, J. (2000). On the neurobiology of creativity. Differences in frontal activity between high and low creative subjects. *Neuropsychologia, 38,* 873–885. [8]

Carpenter, S. (2001). Sights unseen. *Monitor on Psychology, 32* [Electronic version]. Retrieved May 13, 2003, from http://www.apa.org/monitor/apr01/blindness.html [3]

Carpenter, W. T., Jr. (1996). Maintenance therapy of persons with schizophrenia. *Journal of Clinical Psychiatry, 57*(9, Suppl.), 10–18. [16]

Carrier, J. (1980). Homosexual behavior in cross-cultural perspective. In J. Marmor (Ed.), *Homosexual behavior* (pp. 100–122). New York: Basic Books. [12]

Carroll, K. M., Rounsaville, B. J., Nich, C., Gordon, L. T., Wirtz, P. W., & Gawin, F. (1994). One-year follow-up of psychotherapy and pharmacotherapy for cocaine dependence: Delayed emergence of psychotherapy effects. *Archives of General Psychiatry, 51,* 989–997. [16]

Carskadon, M. A., & Dement, W. C. (1989). Normal human sleep: An overview. In M. H. Kryger, T. Roth, & W. C. Dement (Eds.), *Principles and practice of sleep medicine* (pp. 3–13). Philadelphia: W. B. Saunders. [4]

Carskadon, M. A., & Rechtschaffen, A. (1989). Monitoring and staging human sleep. In M. H. Kryger, T. Roth, & W. C. Dement (Eds.), *Principles and practice of sleep medicine* (pp. 665–683). Philadelphia: W. B. Saunders. [4]

Carskadon, M., Wolfson, A., Acebo, D., Tzischinsky, O., & Seifer, R. (1998). Adolescent sleep patterns, circadian timing, and sleepiness at a transition to early school days. *Sleep: Journal of Sleep Research & Sleep Medicine, 21,* 871–881. [4]

Carson, R., Butcher, J., & Mineka, S. (2000). *Abnormal psychology and modern life* (11th ed.). Boston: Allyn & Bacon. [16]

Carson, R. C. (1989). Personality. *Annual Review of Psychology, 40,* 227–248. [14]

Caruana, A., & Chircop, S. (2001). The dark side of globalization and liberalization: Helpfulness, alienation and ethnocentrism among small business owners and managers. *Journal of Nonprofit & Public Sector Marketing, 9,* 63–73. [18]

Caruso, J. C., & Cliff, N. (2000). Increasing the reliability of Wechsler Intelligence Scale for Children—Third Edition difference scores with reliable component analysis. *Psychological Assessment, 12,* 189–196. [8]

Carver, C. S., Pozo, C., Harris, S. D., Noriega, V., Scheier, M. F., Robinson, D. S., Ketcham, A. S., Moffat, F. L., Jr., & Clark, K. C. (1993). How coping mediates the effect of optimism on distress: A study of women with early stage breast cancer. *Journal of Personality and Social Psychology, 65,* 375–390. [13]

Carver, C. S., & Scheier, M. F. (1996). *Perspectives on personality* (3rd ed.). Boston: Allyn & Bacon. [14]

Case, R. (Ed.). (1992). *The mind's staircase: Exploring the conceptual underpinnings of children's thought and knowledge.* Hillsdale, NJ: Erlbaum. [9]

Casey, D. E. (1996). Side effect profiles of new antipsychotic agents. *Journal of Clinical Psychiatry, 57*(11, Suppl.), 40–45. [16]

Cash, T. F., & Derlega, V. J. (1978). The matching hypothesis: Physical attractiveness among same-sexed friends. *Personality and Social Psychology Bulletin, 4,* 240–243. [17]

Cash, T. F., & Janda, L. H. (1984, December). The eye of the beholder. *Psychology Today,* pp. 46–52. [17]

Caspi, A. (2000). The child is father of the man: Personality continuities from childhood to adulthood. *Journal of Personality & Social Psychology, 78,* 158–172. [9, 14]

Caspi, A., Lynam, D., Moffitt, T. E., & Silva, P. A. (1993). Unraveling girls' delinquency: Biological, dispositional, and contextual contributions to adolescent misbehavior. *Developmental Psychology, 29,* 19–30. [10]

Caspi, A., & Silva, P. A. (1995). Temperamental qualities at age three predict personality traits in young adulthood: Longitudinal evidence from a birth cohort. *Child Development, 66,* 486–498. [9]

Cass, M., Siu, O., Faragher, E., & Cooper, C. (2003). A meta-analysis of the relationship between job satisfaction and employee health in Hong Kong. *Stress & Health: Journal of the International Society for the Investigation of Stress, 19,* 79–95. [18]

Cassidy, J., Ziv, Y., Mehta, T., & Feeney, B. (2003). Feedback seeking in children and adolescents: Associations with self-perceptions, attachment representations, and depression. *Child Development, 74,* 612–628. [10]

Catala, E., Reig, E., Artes, M., Aliaga, L., Lopez, J., & Segu, J. (2002). Prevalence of pain in the Spanish population: Telephone survey in 5000 homes. *European Journal of Pain, 6,* 133–140. [3]

Cattell, R. B. (1950). *Personality: A systematic, theoretical, and factual study.* New York: McGraw-Hill. [14]

Cattell, R. B., Eber, H. W., & Tatsuoka, M. M. (1977). *Handbook for the 16 personality factor questionnaire.* Champaign, IL: Institute of Personality and Ability Testing. [14]

Cattell, R. B., Saunders, D. R., & Stice, G. F. (1950). *The 16 personality factor questionnaire.* Champaign, IL: Institute of Personality and Ability Testing. [14]

CBS News. (July 31, 2002). Fear of public speaking. Retrieved February 14, 2003, from http://www.cbsnews.com/stories/2002/07/30 [15]

Ceci, S., & Bronfenbrenner, U. (1985). "Don't forget to take the cupcakes out of the oven": Prospective memory, strategic time-monitoring, and context. *Child Development, 56,* 152–164. [10]

Centers for Disease Control and Prevention (CDC). (1999). Physical activity and health. Retrieved January 29, 2003, from http://www.cdc.gov/needphp/sgr/ataglan.htm [13]

Centers for Disease Control and Prevention (CDC). (2000). Tracking the hidden epidemics: Trends in STDs in the United States 2000. Retrieved November 11, 2003, from http://www.cdc.gov/nchstp/dstd/Stats_Trends/Trends2000.pdf [12]

Centers for Disease Control and Prevention (CDC). (2000). Youth risk behavior surveillance—United States, 1999. *Morbidity and Mortality Weekly Report, 49,* 1–96. [10]

Centers for Disease Control and Prevention (CDC). (2001a). STD surveillance 2000. Retrieved January 16, 2003, from http://www.cdc.gov/std/stats00/2000NatOverview.htm [12]

Centers for Disease Control and Prevention (CDC). (2001b). Genital herpes. Retrieved January 27, 2003, from http://www. cdc.gov/nchstp/dst/Fact_Sheets_facts_Gnital_Herpes.htm [12]

Centers for Disease Control and Prevention (CDC). (2001c). HIV/AIDS update: A glance at the HIV epidemic. Retrieved January 24, 2003, from http://www.cdc.gov/nchstp/od/news/At-a-Glance.pdf [12]

Centers for Disease Control and Prevention. (2002). Nonfatal self-inflicted injuries treated in hospital emergency departments—United States, 2000. *Morbidity & Mortality Weekly Report, 51,* 436–438. [15]

Centers for Disease Control and Prevention (CDC). (2003). About minority health. Retrieved August 8, 2003, from http://www.cdc.gov/omh/AMH/AMH.htm [13]

Centers for Disease Control and Prevention (CDC). (2003). *Hearing Loss* [Online factsheet]. Retrieved May 13, 2003, from http://www.cdc.gov/ncbddd/dd/ddhi.htm [3]

Challis, B. H. (1996). Implicit memory research in 1996: Introductory remarks. *Canadian Journal of Experimental Psychology, 50,* 1–4. [6]

Chambless, D. L., & Goldstein, A. J. (1979). Behavioral psychotherapy. In R. J. Corsini (Ed.), *Current psychotherapies* (2nd ed., pp. 230–272). Itasca, IL: F. E. Peacock. [16]

Chan, D. (1997). Racial subgroup differences in predictive validity perceptions on personality and cognitive ability tests. *Journal of Applied Psychology, 82,* 311–320. [18]

Chang, E., & Merzenich, M. (2003). Environmental noise retards auditory cortical development. *Science, 300,* 498–502. [2]

Chao, R. (2001). Extending research on the consequences of parenting style for Chinese Americans and European Americans. *Child Development,* 72, 1832–1843. [9]

Chaplin, W. F., Philips, J. B., Brown, J. D., Clanton, N. R., & Stein, J. L. (2000). Handshaking, gender, personality, and first impressions. *Journal of Personality and Social Psychology, 19,* 110–117. [17]

Chapman, R. S. (2000). Children's language learning: An interactionist perspective. *Journal of Child Psychology & Psychiatry, 41,* 133–154. [9]

"Charity holds its own in tough times." (2003). Press release. Retrieved November 25, 2003, from http://www.aafrc.org/press_releases/trustreleases/charityholds.html [17]

Charles, S., Mather, M., & Carstensen, L. (2003). Aging and emotional memory: The forgettable nature of negative images for older adults. *Journal of Experimental Psychology, 132,* 310–324. [10]

Chase, M. H., & Morales, F. R. (1990). The atonia and myoclonia of active (REM) sleep. *Annual Review of Psychology, 41,* 557–584. [4]

Chassin, L., Presson, C., Sherman, S., & Kim, K. (2003). Historical changes in cigarette smoking and smoking-related beliefs after 2 decades in a midwestern community. *Health Psychology, 22,* 347–353. [13]

Chavez, M., & Spitzer, M. (2002). Herbals and other dietary supplements for premenstrual syndrome and menopause. *Psychiatric Annals, 32,* 61–71. [4]

Chen, J. C., Borson, S., & Scanlan, J. M. (2000). Stage-specific prevalence of behavioral symptoms in Alzheimer's disease in a multi-ethnic community sample. *American Journal of Geriatric Psychiatry, 8,* 123–133. [10]

Chen, X., Chang, L., & He, Y. (2003). The peer group as a context: Mediating and moderating effects on relations between academic achievement and social functioning in Chinese children. *Child Development, 74,* 710–727. [9]

Cheng, D., Knight, D., Smith, C., Stein, E., & Helmstetter, F. (2003). Functional MRI of human amygdala activity during Pavlovian fear conditioning: Stimulus processing versus response expression. *Behavioral Neuroscience, 117,* 3–10. [5]

Chen-Sea, M.-J. (2000). Validating the Draw-A-Man Test as a personal neglect test. *American Journal of Occupational Therapy, 54,* 391–397. [2]

Chickering, A., & Reisser, L. (1993). *Education and identity* (2nd ed.). San Francisco: Jossey-Bass. [10]

Chilosi, A., Cipriani, P., Bertuccelli, B., Pfanner, L., & Cioni, G. (2001). Early cognitive and communication development in children with focal brain lesions. *Journal of Child Neurology, 16,* 309–316. [2]

Chipuer, H. M., Plomin, R., Pedersen, M. L., McClearn, G. E., & Nesselroade, J. R. (1993). Genetic influence on family environment: The role of personality. *Developmental Psychology, 29,* 110–118. [14]

Cho, K. (2001). Chronic "jet lag" produces temporal lobe atrophy and spatial cognitive deficits. *Nature Neuroscience, 4,* 567–568. [4]

Cho, K., Ennaceur, A., Cole, J., & Kook Suh, C. (2000). Chronic jet lag produces cognitive deficits. *Journal of Neuroscience, 20,* RC66. [4]

Choi, I., Dalal, R., Kim-Prieto, C., & Park, H. (2003). Culture and judgment of causal relevance. *Journal of Personality & Social Psychology, 84,* 46–59. [17]

Choi, J., & Silverman, I. (2002). The relationship between testosterone and route-learning strategies in humans. *Brain & Cognition, 50,* 116–120. [12]

Chollar, S. (1989). Conversation with the dolphins. *Psychology Today, 23,* 52–57. [7]

Chomsky, N. (1968). *Language and mind.* New York: Harcourt, Brace & World. [9]

Chomsky, N. (1986). *Knowledge of language: Its nature, origin, and use.* New York: Praeger. [7]

Chomsky, N. (1990). On the nature, use and acquisition of language. In W. G. Lycan (Ed.), *Mind and cognition* (pp. 627–646). Oxford, England: Blackwell. [7]

Chowdhury, R., Ferrier, I., & Thompson, J. (2003). Cognitive dysfunction in bipolar disorder. *Current Opinion in Psychiatry, 16,* 7–12. [15]

Christensen, J. (2002). *Corporate America is gay-friendly.* Retrieved June 30, 2003, from http://www.gay.com [18]

Christensen, L. B. (1997). *Experimental methodology* (7th ed.). Boston: Allyn & Bacon. [1]

Christensen, L. B. (2001). *Experimental methodology* (8th ed.). Boston: Allyn & Bacon. [1]

Christianson, S-Å. (1992). Emotional stress and eyewitness memory: A critical review. *Psychological Bulletin, 112*, 284–309. [6]

Chronicle of Higher Education. (1997, August 29). Almanac: Facts about the U.S., each of the 50 states, and D.C. Washington, DC: Author. [10]

Chu, S., & Downes, J. J. (2000). Long live Proust: The odour-cued autobiographical memory bump. *Cognition, 75*, B41–B50. [3]

Chumlea, W. C. (1982). Physical growth in adolescence. In B. B. Wolman (Ed.), *Handbook of developmental psychology.* Englewood Cliffs, NJ: Prentice-Hall. [10]

Church R. M. (1963). The varied effects of punishment on behavior. *Psychological Review, 70*, 369–402. [5]

Church, R. M. (1989). Theories of timing behavior. In S. P. Klein & R. Mowrer (Eds.), *Contemporary learning theories: Instrumental conditioning theory and the impact of biological constraints on learning.* Hillsdale, NJ: Erlbaum. [5]

Cialdini, R. B., Cacioppo, J. T., Basset, R., & Miller, J. A. (1978). Low-ball procedure for producing compliance: Commitment then cost. *Journal of Personality and Social Psychology, 36*, 463–476. [17]

Cialdini, R. B., Vincent, J. E., Lewis, S. K., Catalan, J., Wheeler, D., & Darby, B. L. (1975). Reciprocal concessions procedure for inducing compliance: The door-in-the-fact technique. *Journal of Personality and Social Psychology, 31*, 206–215. [17]

Cioffi, R. (2003). Communicating with culturally and linguistically diverse patients in an acute care setting: Nurses; experiences. *International Journal of Nursing Studies, 40*, 299–306. [18]

Clark, D. M., & Teasdale, J. D. (1982). Diurnal variation in clinical depression and accessibility of memories of positive and negative experiences. *Journal of Abnormal Psychology, 91*, 87–95. [6]

Classen, J., Liepert, J., Wise, S., Hallett, M., & Cohen, L. (1998). Rapid plasticity of human cortical movement representation induced by practice. *Journal of Neurophysiology, 79*, 1117–1123. [2]

Clay, R. (2002). An indigenized psychology. *APA Monitor on Psychology, 33*, 58–59. [4]

Clay, R. (2002). Research on 9/11: What psychologists have learned so far. *APA Monitor on Psychology, 33*, 28–30. [13]

Clay, R., Daw, J., & Dittman, M. (2002). More research on America's response. *APA Monitor on Psychology, 33*, 31. [13]

Clayton, K. N. (1964). T-maze choice learning as a joint function of the reward magnitudes for the alternatives. *Journal of Comparative and Physiological Psychology, 58*, 333–338. [5]

Clayton, N. S. (1998). Memory and the hippocampus in food-storing birds: A comparative approach. *Neuropharmacology, 37*, 441–452. [6]

Clément, K., Vaisse, C., Lahlou, N., Cabrol, S., Pelloux, V., Cassuto, D., Gourmelen, M., Dina, C., Chambaz, J., Lacorte, J-M., Basdevant, A., Bougnères, P., Lubouc, Y., Froguel, P., & Guy-Grand, B. (1998). A mutation in the human leptin receptor gene causes obesity and pituitary dysfunction. *Nature, 392*, 398–401. [11]

Cleveland, H., & Wiebe, R. (2003). The moderation of adolescent-to-peer similarity in tobacco and alcohol use by school levels of substance use. *Child Development, 74*, 279–291. [10]

Clifford, E. (2000). Neural plasticity: Merzenich, Taub, and Greenough. *Harvard Brain* [Special Issue], *6*, 16–20. [2]

Cloitre, M., Koenen, K., Cohen, L., & Han, H. (2002). Skills training in affective and interpersonal regulation followed by exposure: A phase-based treatment for PTSD related to childhood abuse. *Journal of Consulting and Clinical Psychology, 70*, 1067–1074. [16]

Cloninger, C. R., Sigvardsson, S., Bohman, M., & von Knorring, A. L. (1982). Predispositions to petty criminality in Swedish adoptees, II. Cross-fostering analysis of gene-environment interaction. *Archives of General Psychiatry, 39*, 1242–1249. [17]

CNN.com. (February 16, 2003). Fatal shooting caught on tape. Retrieved February 17, 2003, from http://www.cnn.com/2003/US/South/02/16/gas.shooting.ap/index.html [17]

Coffey, C., Saxton, J., Ratcliff, G., Bryan, R., & Lucke, J. (1999). Relation of education to brain size in normal aging: Implications for the reserve hypothesis. *Neurology, 53*, 189–196. [2]

Cohan, C., & Kleinbaum, S. (2002). Toward a greater understanding of the cohabitation effect: Premarital cohabitation and marital communication. *Journal of Marriage & Family, 64*, 180–192. [10]

Cohen, L. L., & Shotland, R. L. (1996). Timing of first sexual intercourse in a relationship: Expectations, experiences, and perceptions of others. *Journal of Sex Research, 33*, 291–299. [9]

Cohen, S. (1988). Psychosocial models of the role of social support in the etiology of physical disease. *Health Psychology, 7*, 269–297. [13]

Cohen, S. (1996). Psychological stress, immunity, and upper respiratory infections. *Current Directions in Psychological Science, 5*, 86–89. [13]

Cohen, S., Doyle, W. J., Skoner, D. P., Rabin, B. S., & Gwaltney, J. M., Jr. (1997). Social ties and susceptibility to the common cold. *Journal of the American Medical Association, 277*, 1940–1944. [13]

Cohen, S., & Herbert, T. B. (1996). Health psychology: Psychological factors and physical disease from the perspective of human psychoneuroimmunology. *Annual Review of Psychology, 47*, 113–142. [13]

Cohen, S., & Williamson, G. M. (1991). Stress and infectious disease in humans. *Psychological Bulletin, 109*, 5–54. [13]

Colby, A., Kohlberg, L., Gibbs, J., & Lieberman, M. (1983). A longitudinal study of moral judgment. *Monographs of the Society for Research in Child Development, 48*(1–2, Serial No. 200). [10]

Colcombe, S., & Kramer, A. (2003). Fitness effects on the cognitive function of older adults: A meta-analytic study. *Psychological Science, 14*, 125–130. [10]

Cole, P. M. (1986). Children's spontaneous control of facial expression. *Child Development, 57*, 1309–1321. [11]

Cole, R., Smith, J., Alcala, Y., Elliott, J., & Kripke, D. (2002). Bright-light mask treatment of delayed sleep phase syndrome. *Journal of Biological Rhythms, 17*, 89–101. [4]

Coleman, C., King, B., Bolden-Watson, C., Book, M., Segraves, R., Richard, N., Ascher, J., Batey, S., Jamerson, B., & Metz, A. (2001). A placebo-controlled comparison of the effects on sexual functioning of bupropion sustained release and fluoxetine. *Clinical Therapeutics: The International Peer-Reviewed Journal of Drug Therapy, 23*, 1040–1058. [12, 15]

Coles, M. E., & Heinberg, R. G. (2000). Patterns of anxious arousal during exposure to feared situations in individuals with social phobia. *Behaviour Research & Therapy, 38*, 405–424. [16]

Collaer, M. L., & Hines, M. (1995). Human behavioral sex differences: A role for gonadal hormones during early development. *Psychological Bulletin, 118*, 55–107. [12]

Collier, A. C., Coombs, R. W., Schoenfeld, D. A., Bassett, R. L., Timpone, J., Baruch, A., Jones, M., Facey, K., Whitacre, C., McAuliffe, V. J., Friedman, H. M., Merigan, T. C., Reichman, R. C., Hooper, C., & Corey, L. (1996). Treatment of human immunodeficiency virus infection with saquinavir, zidovudine, and zalcitabine. *New England Journal of Medicine, 334*, 1011–1017. [12]

Collins, N. L. (1996). Working models of attachment: Implications for explanation, emotion, and behavior. *Journal of Personality and Social Psychology, 71,* 810–832. [9]

Collins, V., Halliday, J., Kahler, S., & Williamson, R. (2001). Parents' experiences with genetic counseling after the birth of a baby with a genetic disorder: An exploratory study. *Journal of Genetic Counseling, 10,* 53–72. [2]

Collins, W. A., & Gunnar, M. R. (1990). Social and personality development. *Annual Review of Psychology, 41,* 387–416. [9, 11]

Colombo, M., & Broadbent, N. (2000). Is the avian hippocampus a functional homologue of the mammalian hippocampus? *Neuroscience and Biobehavioral Reviews, 24,* 465–484. [6]

Colwell, J., & Payne, J. (2000). Negative correlates of computer game play in adolescents. *British Journal of Psychology, 91*(Pt. 3), 295–310. [17]

Conca, A., Swoboda, E., König, P., Koppi, S., Beraus, W., Künz, A., et al. (2000). Clinical impacts of single transcranial magnetic stimulation (sTMS) as an add-on therapy in severely depressed patients under SSRI treatment. *Human Psychopharmacology: Clinical and Experimental, 15,* 429–438. [16]

Coney, J., & Fitzgerald, J. (2000). Gender differences in the recognition of laterally presented affective nouns. *Cognition and Emotion, 14,* 325–339. [11]

Conroy, D., Poczwardowski, A., & Henschen, K. (2001). Evaluative criteria and consequences associated with failure and success for elite athletes and performing artists. *Journal of Applied Sport Psychology, 13,* 300–322. [11]

Consumer Reports. (1995, November) Mental health: Does therapy help? pp. 734–739. [16]

Conway, M. A., Cohen, G., & Stanhope, N. (1991). On the very long-term retention of knowledge acquired through formal education: Twelve years of cognitive psychology. *Journal of Experimental Psychology: General, 120,* 395–409. [6]

Conway, M. A., Collins, A. F., Gathercole, S. E., & Anderson, S. J. (1996). Recollections of true and false autobiographical memories. *Journal of Experimental Psychology: General, 125,* 69–95. [6]

Cooke, P. (1992, December/January). TV or not TV. *Health,* pp. 33–43. [9]

Coolidge, F., Thede, L., & Young, S. (2002). The heritability of gender identity disorder in a child and adolescent twin sample. *Behavior Genetics, 32,* 251–257. [15]

Coons, P. M. (1994). Confirmation of childhood abuse in child and adolescent cases of multiple personality disorder and dissociative disorder not otherwise specified. *Journal of Nervous and Mental Disease, 182,* 461–464. [15]

Cooper, A., Golden, G., & Kent-Ferraro, J. (2002). Online sexual behaviors in the workplace: How can human resource departments and employee assistance programs respond effectively? *Sexual Addiction & Compulsivity, 9,* 149–165. [18]

Cooper, L. A., & Shepard, R. N. (1984). Turning something over in the mind. *Scientific American, 251,* 106–114. [7]

Cooper, R. (1994). Normal sleep. In R. Cooper (Ed.), *Sleep.* New York: Chapman & Hall. [4]

Coplan, J. D., Papp, L. A., Pine, D., Marinez, J., Cooper, T., Rosenblum, L. A., Klein, D. F., & Gorman, J. M. (1997). Clinical improvement with fluoxetine therapy and noradrenergic function in patients with panic disorder. *Archives of General Psychiatry, 54,* 643–648. [16]

Corballis, M. C. (1989). Laterality and human evolution. *Psychological Review, 96,* 492–509. [2]

Coren, S. (1993). *The left-hander syndrome: The causes and consequences of left-handedness.* New York: Vintage Books. [2]

Coren, S. (1996a). Accidental death and the shift to daylight savings time. *Perceptual and Motor Skills, 83,* 921–922. [4]

Coren, S. (1996b). Daylight savings time and traffic accidents. *New England Journal of Medicine, 334,* 924. [4]

Cork, L. C., Clarkson, T. B., Jacoby, R. O., Gaertner, D. J., Leary, S. L., Linn, J. M., Pakes, S. P., Ringler, D. H., Strandberg, J. D., & Swindle, M. M. (1997). The costs of animal research: Origins and options. *Science, 276,* 758–759. [1]

Cornelius, M. D., Leech, S. L., Goldschmidt, L., & Day, N. L. (2000). Prenatal tobacco exposure: Is it a risk factor for early tobacco experimentation? *Nicotine & Tobacco Research, 2,* 45–52. [9, 13]

Cosmides, L., & Tooby, J. (2000). Evolutionary psychology and the emotions. In M. Lewis, Jr., & J. M. Haviland-Jones (Eds.), *Handbook of emotions* (2nd ed.). New York: Guilford. [1]

Costa, P. T., Jr., & McCrae, R. R. (1985). *The NEO Personality Inventory.* Odessa, FL: Psychological Assessment Resources. [14]

Costa, P. T., Jr., & McCrae, R. R. (1992). *NEO-PI-R: Revised NEO Personality Inventory (NEO-PI-R).* Odessa, FL: Psychological Assessment Resources. [14]

Costa, P. T., Jr., & McCrae, R. R. (1997). Stability and change in personality assessment: The Revised NEO Personality Inventory in the year 2000. *Journal of Personality Assessment, 68,* 8694. [14]

Costa E Silva, J. A., Chase, M., Sartorius, N., & Roth, T. (1996). Special report from a symposium held by the World Health Organization and the World Federation of Sleep Research Societies: An overview of insomnias and related disorders—recognition, epidemiology, and rational management. *Sleep, 19,* 412–416. [4]

Costanzo, P. R., & Schiffman, S. S. (1989). Thinness—not obesity—has a genetic component. *Neuroscience and Biobehavioral Reviews, 13,* 55–58. [11]

Cotman, C. W., & Lynch, G. S. (1989). The neurobiology of learning and memory. *Cognition, 33,* 201–241. [6]

Council on Ethical and Judicial Affairs, American Medical Association. (1991). Gender disparities in clinical decision making. *Journal of the American Medical Association, 266,* 559–562. [13]

Courage, M. L., & Adams, R. J. (1990). Visual acuity assessment from birth to three years using the acuity card procedures: Cross-sectional and longitudinal samples. *Optometry and Vision Science, 67,* 713–718. [9]

Courtney, S. M., Ungerleider, L. G., Keil, K., & Haxby, J. V. (1997). Transient and sustained activity in a distributed neural system for human working memory. *Nature, 386,* 608–611. [6]

Covey, E. (2000). Neural population coding and auditory temporal pattern analysis. *Physiology and Behavior, 69,* 211–220. [3]

Cowan, C. P., & Cowan, P. A. (1992, July/August). Is there love after baby? *Psychology Today,* 58–63. [10]

Cowan, N. (1988). Evolving conceptions of memory storage, selective attention, and their mutual constraints within the human information-processing system. *Psychological Bulletin, 104,* 163–191. [6]

Cowan, R., O'Connor, N., & Samella, K. (2003). The skills and methods of calendrical savants. *Intelligence, 31,* 51–65. [8]

Coyle, J., & Draper, E. S. (1996). What is the significance of glutamate for mental health? *Harvard Mental Health Letter, 13*(6), 8. [2]

Craik, F. I. M., & Lockhart, R. S. (1972). Levels of processing: A framework for memory research. *Journal of Verbal Learning and Verbal Behavior, 11,* 671–684. [6]

Craik, F. I. M., & Tulving, E. (1975). Depth of processing and the retention of words in episodic memory. *Journal of Experimental Psychology: General, 104,* 268–294. [6]

Crasilneck, H. B. (1992). The use of hypnosis in the treatment of impotence. *Psychiatric Medicine, 10,* 67–75. [4]

Cravens, H. (1992). A scientific project locked in time: The Terman genetic studies of genius, 1920s–1950s. *American Psychologist, 47,* 183–189. [8]

Crick, F., & Mitchison, G. (1983). The function of dream sleep. *Nature, 304,* 408–416. [4]

Crick, F., & Mitchison, G. (1995). REM sleep and neural nets. *Behavioural Brain Research, 69,* 147–155. [4]

Criglington, A. (1998). Do professionals get jet lag? A commentary on jet lag. *Aviation, Space, & Environmental Medicine, 69,* 810. [4]

Crits-Christoph, P. (1992). The efficacy of brief dynamic psychotherapy: A meta-analysis. *American Journal of Psychiatry, 149,* 151–158. [16]

Cromie, W. (2001, May 10). Getting into the rhythms of Alzheimer's disease. *Harvard University Gazette* [Electronic version]. Retrieved October 17, 2003, from http://www.news.harvard.edu/gazette/2001/05.10/01-alzheimers.html [4]

Crowder, R. G. (1992) Sensory memory. In L. R. Squire (Ed.), *Encyclopedia of learning and memory.* New York: Macmillan. [6]

Crowe, L. C., & George, W. H. (1989). Alcohol and human sexuality: Review and integration. *Psychological Bulletin, 105,* 374–386. [4]

Crowther, J., Kichler, J., Shewood, N., & Kuhnert, M. (2002). The role of familial factors in bulimia nervosa. *Eating Disorders: The Journal of Treatment & Prevention, 10,* 141–151. [11]

Crystal, D. S., Chen, C., Fulligni, A. J., Stevenson, H. W., Hsu, C-C., Ko, H-J., Kitamura, S., & Kimura, S. (1994). Psychological maladjustment and academic achievement: A cross-cultural study of Japanese, Chinese, and American high school students. *Child Development, 65,* 738–753. [8]

Csikszentmihalyi, M. (1990). *Flow: The psychology of optimal experience.* Cambridge, England: Cambridge University Press. [11]

Csikszentmihalyi, M. (1996, July/August). The creative personality. *Psychology Today, 29,* 36–40. [8]

Cui, X-J., & Vaillant, G. E. (1996). Antecedents and consequences of negative life events in adulthood: A longitudinal study. *American Journal of Psychiatry, 153,* 21–26. [15]

Culbertson, F. M. (1997). Depression and gender: An international review. *American Psychologist, 52,* 25–31. [15]

Cull, W. L. (2000). Untangling the benefits of multiple study opportunities and repeated testing for cued recall. *Applied Cognitive Psychology, 14,* 215–235. [6]

Culpan, O., & Wright, G. (2002). Women abroad: Getting the best results from women managers. *International Journal of Human Resource Management, 13,* 784–801. [18]

Cunningham, M. R., Roberts, A. R., Barbee, A. P., Druen, P. B., & Wu, C-H. (1995). "Their ideas of beauty are, on the whole, the same as ours": Consistency and variability in the cross-cultural perception of female physical attractiveness. *Journal of Personality and Social Psychology, 68,* 261–279. [17]

Cupach, W. R., & Canary, D. J. (1995). Managing conflict and anger: Investigating the sex stereotype hypothesis. In P. J. Kalbfleisch & M. J. Cody (Eds.), *Gender, power, and communication in human relationships.* Hillsdale, NJ: Erlbaum. [11]

Curci, A., Luminet, O., Finkenauer, C., & Gisler, L. (2002). Flashbulb memories in social groups: A comparative test-retest study of the memory of French president Mitterrand's death in a French and a Belgian group. *Memory, 9,* 81–101. [6]

Curran, P. J., Stice, E., & Chassin, L. (1997). The relation between adolescent alcohol use and peer alcohol use: A longitudinal random coefficients model. *Journal of Consulting and Clinical Psychology, 65,* 130–140. [4]

Cyranowski, J. M., Frand, E., Young, E., & Shear, M. K. (2000). Adolescent onset of the gender difference in lifetime rates of major depression. *Archives of General Psychiatry, 57,* 21–27. [15]

Dabbs, J. M., Jr., & Morris, R. (1990). Testosterone, social class, and antisocial behavior in a sample of 4,462 men. *Psychological Science, 1,* 209–211. [17]

Dahloef, P., Norlin-Bagge, E., Hedner, J., Ejnell, H., Hetta, J., & Haellstroem, T. (2002). Improvement in neuropsychological performance following surgical treatment for obstructive sleep apnea syndrome. *Acta Oto-Laryngologica, 122,* 86–91. [4]

Daily Hampshire Gazette [Electronic version]. (September 7, 2002). Two missing after 9/11 found. Retrieved November 8, 2002, from http://www.gazettenet.com [15]

Dakof, G. A. (2000). Understanding gender differences in adolescent drug abuse: Issues of comorbidity and family functioning. *Journal of Psychoactive Drugs, 32,* 25–32. [4]

Dale, N., & Kandel, E. R. (1990). Facilitatory and inhibitory transmitters modulate spontaneous transmitter release at cultured Aplysia sensorimotor synapses. *Journal of Physiology, 421,* 203–222. [6]

Daley, T., Whaley, S., Sigman, M., Espinosa, M., & Neumann, C. (2003). IQ on the rise: The Flynn Effect in rural Kenyan children. *Psychological Science, 14,* 215–219. [8]

Dalgin, R., & Gilbride, D. (2003). Perspectives of people with psychiatric disabilities on employment disclosure. *Psychiatric Rehabilitation Journal, 26,* 306–310. [18]

Dallard, I., Cathebras, P., & Sauron, C. (2001). Is cocoa a psychotropic drug? Psychopathological study of self-labeled "chocolate addicts." *Encephale, 27,* 181–186. [4]

Dallas, C., Wilson, T., & Salgado, V. (2000). Gender differences in teen parents' perceptions of parental responsibilities. *Public Health Nursing, 17,* 423–433. [10]

Dallery, J., Silverman, K., Chutuape, M., Bigelow, G., & Stitzer, M. (2001). Voucher-based reinforcement of opiate plus cocaine abstinence in treatment-resistant methadone patients: Effects of reinforcer magnitude. *Experimental & Clinical Psychopharmacology, 9,* 317–325. [5]

Daly, M., & Wilson, M. I. (1996). Violence against stepchildren. *Current Directions in Psychological Science, 5,* 77–81. [17]

Damasio, A. R. (1994). *Descartes' error: Emotion, reason, and the human brain.* New York: Lyons Press. [11]

Damasio, A. R. (1999). *The feeling of what happens: Body and emotion in the making of consciousness.* New York: Harcourt. [11]

Damitz, M., Manzey, D., Kleinmann, M., & Severin, K. (2003). Assessment center for pilot selection: Construct and criterion validity and the impact of assessor type. *Applied Psychology: An International Review, 52,* 193–212. [18]

Danto, E. (2000). Conflict vs. cohesion: EAP-based diversity training in small groups. *Employee Assistance Quarterly, 15,* 1–14. [18]

Dantzker, M., & Eisenman, R. (2003). Sexual attitudes among Hispanic college students: Differences between males and females. *International Journal of Adolescence & Youth, 11,* 79–89. [12]

Darley, J. M., & Latané, B. (1968a). Bystander intervention in emergencies: Diffusion of responsibility. *Journal of Personality and Social Psychology, 8,* 377–383. [17]

Darley, J. M., & Latané, B. (1968b, December). When will people help in a crisis? *Psychology Today,* pp. 54–57, 70–71. [17]

Darwin, C. (1872/1965). *The expression of emotion in man and animals.* Chicago: University of Chicago Press. (Original work published 1872). [11]

Dasborough, M., & Ashkanasy, N. (2002). Emotion and attribution of intentionality in leader-member relationships. *Leadership Quarterly, 13*, 615–634. [18]

Dasen, P. R. (1994). Culture and cognitive development from a Piagetian perspective. In W. J. Lonner & R. Malpass (Eds.), *Psychology and culture* (pp. 145–149). Boston: Allyn & Bacon. [9]

Dashiell, J. F. (1925). A quantitative demonstration of animal drive. *Journal of Comparative Psychology, 5*, 205–208. [11]

Davalos, D., Kisley, M., & Ross, R. (2002). Deficits in auditory and visual temporal perception in schizophrenia. *Cognitive Neuropsychiatry, 7*, 273–282. [15]

Davey, F. (1998). Young women's expected and preferred patterns of employment and child care. *Sex Roles, 38*, 95–102. [18]

Davidson, J. R. T. (1997). Use of benzodiazepines in panic disorder. *Journal of Clinical Psychiatry, 58*(2, Suppl.), 26–28. [16]

Davies, L., McKinnon, M., & Rains, P. (2001). Creating a family: Perspectives from teen mothers. *Journal of Progressive Human Services, 12*, 83–100. [10]

Davis, S., Butcher, S. P., & Morris, R. G. M. (1992). The NMDA receptor antagonist D-2-amino-5-phosphonopentanoate (D-AP5) impairs spatial learning and LTP in vivo at intracerebral concentrations comparable to those that block LTP in vitro. *Journal of Neuroscience, 12*, 21–34. [6]

Davis, T. L. (1995). Gender differences in masking negative emotions: Ability or motivation? *Developmental Psychology, 31*, 660–667. [11]

Daw, J. (2001, July/August). Road rage, air rage, now "desk rage." *Monitor on Psychology*. Retrieved November 29, 2003, from www.apa.org/monitor [18]

Dawkins, B. J. (1990). Genital herpes simplex infections. *Primary Care: Clinics in Office Practice, 17*, 95–113. [12]

Day, S., & Schneider, P. (2002). Psychotherapy using distance technology: A comparison of face-to-face, video, and audio treatment. *Journal of Counseling Psychology, 49*, 499–503. [16]

D'Azevedo, W. A. (1982). Tribal history in Liberia. In U. Neisser (Ed.), *Memory observed: Remembering in natural contexts.* San Francisco: W. H. Freeman. [6]

de Castro, J. M., & de Castro, E. S. (1989). Spontaneous meal patterns of humans: Influence of the presence of other people. *Journal of Clinical Nutrition, 50*, 237–247. [11]

De Cremer, D. (2002). Charismatic leadership and cooperation in social dilemmas: A matter of transforming motives? *Journal of Applied Social Psychology, 32*, 997–1016. [18]

De Cremer, D., & van Knippenberg, D. (2003). Cooperation with leaders in social dilemmas: On the effects of procedural fairness and outcome favorability in structural cooperation. *Organizational Behavior & Human Decision Processes, 91*, 1–11. [18]

de Jong, P., & vander Leij, A. (2002). Effects of phonological abilities and linguistic comprehension on the development of reading. *Scientific Studies of Reading, 6*, 51–77. [9]

de Lacoste, M., Horvath, D., & Woodward, J. (1991). Possible sex differences in the developing human fetal brain. *Journal of Clinical and Experimental Neuropsychology, 13*, 831. [2]

de Leon, M. J., Convit, A., George, A. E., Golomb, J., de Santi, S., Tarshish, C., Rusinek, H., Bobinski, M., Ince, C., Miller, D., & Wisniewski, H. (1996). *In vivo* structural studies of the hippocampus in normal aging and in incipient Alzheimer's disease. *Annals of the New York Academy of Sciences, 777*, 1–13. [10]

De Raad, B., & Kokkonen, M. (2000). Traits and emotions: A review of their structure and management. *European Journal of Personality, 14*, 477–496. [14]

De Souza, A., Baiao, V., & Otta, E. (2003). Perception of men's personal qualities and prospect of employment as a function of facial hair. *Psychological Reports, 92*, 201–208. [18]

De Vos, S. (1990). Extended family living among older people in six Latin American countries. *Journal of Gerontology: Social Sciences, 45*, S87–S94. [10]

Deak, G., Ray, S., & Brenneman, K. (2003). Children's perseverative appearance-reality errors are related to emerging language skills. *Child Development, 74*, 944–964. [9]

Deary, I. J., & Stough, C. (1996). Intelligence and inspection time: Achievements, prospects, and problems. *American Psychologist, 51*, 599–608. [8]

DeBortoli, M., Tifner, S., & Zanin, L. (2001). The effect of the human androsterone pheromone on mood in men. *Revista intercontinental de psicologia y educacion, 3*, 23–28. [3]

DeCasper, A. J., & Fifer, W. P. (1980). Of human bonding: Newborns prefer their mothers' voices. *Science, 208*, 1174–1176. [9]

DeCasper, A. J., & Spence, M. J. (1986). Prenatal maternal speech influences newborns' perception of speech sounds. *Infant Behavior and Development, 9*, 133–150. [9]

Deci, E. L., Koestner, R., & Ryan, R. M. (1999). A meta-analytic review of experiments examining the effects of extrinsic rewards on intrinsic motivation. *Psychological Bulletin, 125*, 627–668. [5]

Deese, J. (1959). On the prediction of occurrence of particular verbal intrusions in immediate recall. *Journal of Experimental Psychology, 58*, 17–22. [6]

Deinzer, R., Kleineidam, C., Stiller-Winkler, R., Idel, H., & Bachg, D. (2000). Prolonged reduction of salivary immunoglobulin (sIgA) after a major academic exam. *International Journal of Psychophysiology, 37*, 219–232. [13]

Dekovic, M., & Janssens, J. M. A. M. (1992). Parents' child-rearing style and child's sociometric status. *Developmental Psychology, 28*, 925–932. [9]

Delgado, J. M. R., & Anand, B. K. (1953). Increased food intake induced by electrical stimulation of the lateral hypothalamus. *American Journal of Physiology, 172*, 162–168. [11]

DeLongis, A., Folkman, S., & Lazarus, R. S. (1988). The impact of daily stress on health and mood: Psychological and social resources as mediators. *Journal of Personality and Social Psychology, 54*, 486–495. [13]

Deluga, R. (1998). American presidential proactivity, charismatic leadership, and rated performance. *Leadership Quarterly, 9*, 265–291. [18]

Demb, J., Boynton, G., & Heeger, D. (1998). Functional magnetic resonance imaging of early visual pathways in dyslexia. *Journal of Neuroscience, 18*, 6939–6951. [3]

Dement, W. C. (1974). *Some must watch while some must sleep.* San Francisco: W. H. Freeman. [4]

Dement, W., & Kleitman, N. (1957). The relation of eye movements during sleep to dream activity: An objective method for the study of dreaming. *Journal of Experimental Psychology, 53*, 339–346. [4]

Denham, S. A., Workman, E., Cole, P. M., Weissbrod, C., Kendziora, K. T., & Zahn-Waxler, C. (2000). Prediction of externalizing behavior problems from early to middle childhood: The role of parental socialization and emotion expression. *Developmental Psychopathology, 12*, 123–145. [9]

Dennis, W. (1968). Creative productivity between the ages of 20 and 80. In B. L. Neugarten (Ed.), *Middle age and aging* (pp. 106–114). Chicago: University of Chicago Press. [10]

Deovell, L. Y., Bentin, S., & Soroker, N. (2000). Electrophysiological evidence for an early (pre-attentive) information processing deficit in patients with right hemisphere damage and unilateral neglect. *Brain, 123*, 353–365. [2]

DePietro, J., Bornstein, M., Costigan, K., Pressman, E., Hahn, C., Painter, K., Smith, B., & Yi, L. (2002). What does fetal movement predict about behavior during the first two years of life? *Developmental Psychology*, *40*, 358–371. [9]

Devanand, D. P., Dwork, A. J., Hutchinson, M. S. E., Bolwig, T. G., & Sackeim, H. A. (1994). Does ECT alter brain structure? *American Journal of Psychiatry*, *151*, 957–970. [16]

Devine, P. G. (1989). Stereotypes and prejudice: Their automatic and controlled components. *Journal of Personality and Social Psychology*, *56*, 5–18. [17]

Dewsbury, D. A. (2000). Introduction: Snapshots of psychology circa 1900. *American Psychologist*, *55*, 255–259. [1]

DeYoung, C., Peterson, J., & Higgins, D. (2002). Higher-order factors of the Big Five predict conformity: Are there neuroses of health? *Personality & Individual Differences*, *33*, 533–552. [17]

Dickens, W., & Flynn, R. (2001). Heritability estimates versus large environmental effects: The IQ paradox resolved. *Psychological Review*, *108*, 346–369. [8]

Diener, E., & Diener, C. (1996). Most people are happy. *Psychological Science*, *7*, 181–185. [10]

Diener, E., Nickerson, C., Lucas, R., & Sandvik, E. (2002). Dispositional affect and job outcomes. *Social Indicators Research*, *59*, 229–259. [18]

Dietz, W. H. (1989). Obesity. *Journal of the American College of Nutrition*, *8*(Suppl.), 139–219. [11]

Dijksterhuis, A., & Aarts, H. (2003). On wildebeests and humans: The preferential detection of negative stimuli. *Psychological Science*, *14*, 14–18. [11]

DiLalla, D. L., Carey, G., Gottesman, I. J., & Bouchard, T. J., Jr. (1996). Heritability of MMPI personality indicators of psychopathology in twins reared apart. *Journal of Abnormal Psychology*, *105*, 491–499. [14]

DiLalla, L. F., & Gottesman, I. I. (1991). Biological and genetic contributors to violence—Widom's untold tale. *Psychological Bulletin*, *109*, 125–129. [17]

Dindia, K., & Allen, M. (1992). Sex differences in self-disclosure: A meta-analysis. *Psychological Bulletin*, *112*, 106–124. [12]

Dion, K., Berscheid, E., & Walster, E. (1972). What is beautiful is good. *Journal of Personality and Social Psychology*, *24*, 285–290. [17]

Dipboye, R. L., Fromkin, H. L., & Wilback, K. (1975). Relative importance of applicant sex, attractiveness, and scholastic standing in evaluation of job applicant resumes. *Journal of Applied Psychology*, *60*, 39–43. [17]

DiPietro, J., Hodgson, D., Costigan, K., & Johnson, T. (1996a). Fetal antecedents of infant temperament. *Child Development*, *67*, 2568–2583. [9]

DiPietro, J., Hodgson, D., Costigan, K., Hilton, S., & Johnson, T. (1996b). Fetal neurobehavioral development. *Child Development*, *67*, 2553–2567. [9]

Dittman, M. (2003). Fighting ageism. *APA Monitor on Psychology*, *34*, 50–52. [10]

Dodge, K. A., Bates, J. E., & Pettit, G. S. (1990). Mechanisms in the cycle of violence. *Science*, *250*, 1678–1683. [17]

Dodge, K. A., Cole, J. D., Pettit, G. S., & Price, J. M. (1990). Peer status and aggression in boys' groups: Developmental and contextual analyses. *Child Development*, *61*, 1289–1309. [9]

Dodson, C. S., Koutstaal, W., & Schacter, D. L. (2000). Escape from illusion: Reducing false memories. *Trends in Cognitive Sciences*, *4*, 391–397. [6]

Dogil, G., Ackermann, H., Grodd, W., Haider, H., Kamp, H., Mayer, J., Riecker, A., & Wildgruber, D. (2002). The speaking brain: A tutorial introduction to fMRI experiments in the production of speech, prosody, and syntax. *Journal of Neurolinguistics*, *15*, 59–90. [7]

Dohanich, G. (2003). Ovarian steroids and cognitive function. *Current Directions in Psychological Science*, *12*, 57–61. [6]

Dollard, J., Doob, L. W., Miller, N., Mowrer, O. H., & Sears, R. R. (1939). *Frustration and aggression*. New Haven: Yale University Press. [17]

Domino, G. (1984). California Psychological Inventory. In D. J. Keyser & R. C. Sweetland (Eds.), *Test Critiques* (Vol. 1, pp. 146–157). Kansas City: Test Corporation of America. [14]

Domjan, M, & Purdy, J. E. (1995). Animal research in psychology: More than meets the eye of the general psychology student. *American Psychologist*, *50*, 496–503. [1]

Doniger, A., Adams, E., Utter, C., & Riley, J. (2001). Impact evaluation of the "Not Me, Not Now" abstinence-oriented, adolescent pregnancy prevention communication program, Monroe County, New York. *Journal of Health Communication*, *6*, 45–60. [10]

Donnerstein, E., Slaby, R. G., & Eron, L. D. (1994). The mass media and youth aggression. In L. D. Eron, J. H. Gentry, & P. Schlegel (Eds.), *Reason to hope: A psychosocial perspective on violence and youth* (pp. 219–250). Washington, DC: American Psychological Association. [9]

Doob, L. W., & Sears, R. R. (1939). Factors determining substitute behavior and the overt expression of aggression. *Journal of Abnormal and Social Psychology*, 34, 293–313. [17]

Dorz, S., Lazzarini, L., Cattelan, A., Meneghetti, F., Novara, C., Concia, E., Sica, C., & Sanavio, E. (2003). Evaluation of adherence to antiretroviral therapy in Italian HIV patients. *AIDS Patient Care & STDs*, *17*, 33–41. [12]

Douglas, C. (2002). The effects of managerial influence behavior on the transition to self-directed work teams (SDWTs). *Journal of Managerial Psychology*, *17*, 628–635. [18]

Downing, P., Jiang, Y., Shuman, M., & Kanwisher, N. (2001). A cortical area selective for visual processing of the human body. *Science*, *293*, 2470–2473. [3]

Doyle, R. (2000). Women and the professions. *Scientific American*, *282*, 30. [12]

Dreikurs, R. (1953). *Fundamentals of Adlerian psychology*. Chicago: Alfred Adler Institute. [14]

Drevets, W. C., Price, J. L., Simpson, J. R., Jr., Todd, R. D., Reich, T., Vannier, M., & Raichle, M. E. (1997). Subgenual prefrontal cortex abnormalities in mood disorders. *Nature*, *386*, 824–827. [2, 15]

Druckman, D., & Bjork, R. A. (Eds.) (1994). *Learning, remembering, believing: Enhancing human performance*. Washington, DC: National Academy Press. [4]

Drug Enforcement Administration. National Drug Intelligence Center. (2003). *National Drug Threat Assessment/2003* [Online report]. Retrieved October 22, 2003, from http://www.usdoj.gov/ndic/pubs3/3300/pharm.htm [4]

Drug Free Workplace. (2002, September). Designer Drugs. *National Medical Report* [Electronic version]. Retrieved May 25, 2003, from http://www.drugfreeworkplace.com/drugsofabuse/designer.htm [4]

Drummond, S. P. A., Brown, G. G., Gillin, J. C., Stricker, J. L., Wong, E. C., & Buxton, R. B. (2000). Altered brain response to verbal learning following sleep deprivation. *Nature*, *403*, 655–657. [4]

Druskat, V., & Pescosolido, A. (2002). The content of effective teamwork mental models in self-managing teams: Ownership, learning and heedful interrelating. *Human Relations*, *55*, 283–314. [18]

Dryer, D. C., & Horowitz, L. M. (1997). When do opposites attract? Interpersonal complementarity versus similarity. *Journal of Personality and Social Psychology, 72*, 592–603. [17]

Duck, S. (1983). *Friends for life: The psychology of close relationships.* New York: St. Martin's Press. [10]

Duggan, J. P., & Booth, D. A. (1986). Obesity, overeating, and rapid gastric emptying in rats with ventromedial hypothalamic lesions. *Science, 231*, 609–611. [11]

Duncan, J., Seitz, R. J., Kolodny, J., Bor, D., Herzog, H., Ahmed, A., Newell, F. N., & Emslie, H. (2000). A neural basis for general intelligence. *Science, 289*, 457–460. [8]

Dunkel-Schetter, C., Feinstein, L. G., Taylor, S. E., & Falke, R. L. (1992). Patterns of coping with cancer. *Health Psychology, 11*, 79–87. [13]

Dunn, J., Cutting, A., & Fisher, N. (2002). Old friends, new friends: Predictors of children's perspective on their friends at school. *Child Development, 73*, 621–635. [9]

Durex Global Sex Survey. (2002). Retrieved January 20, 2003, from http://www.durex.com/uk/sexsurvey/globalsexsurvey2002/global_sex2002_freqb.htm [12]

Duyme, M. (1988). School success and social class: An adoption study. *Developmental Psychology, 24*, 203–209. [8]

Dvir, T., Eden, D., Avolio, B., & Shamir, B. (2002). Impact of transformational leadership on follower development and performance: A field experiment. *Academy of Management Journal, 45*, 735–744. [18]

Dywan, J., & Bowers, K. (1983). The use of hypnosis to enhance recall. *Science, 222*, 184–185. [4, 6]

Eagly, A. H., Ashmore, R. D., Makhijani, M. G., & Longo, L. C. (1991). What is beautiful is good . . . : A meta-analytic review of research on the physical attractiveness stereotype. *Psychological Bulletin, 110*, 109–128. [17]

Eagly, A. H., & Carli, L. (1981). Sex of researchers and sex-typed communications as determinants of sex differences in influence-ability: A meta-analysis of social influence studies. *Psychological Bulletin, 90*, 1–20. [17]

Eagly, A. H., & Wood, W. (1999). The origins of sex differences in human behavior: Evolved dispositions versus social roles. *American Psychologist, 54*, 408–423. [12, 17]

Easton, C. J., Swann, S., & Sinha, R. (2000). Prevalence of family violence in clients entering substance abuse treatment. *Journal of Substance Abuse Treatment, 18*, 23–28. [4]

Eating disorders—part II. (1997, November). *Harvard Mental Health Letter, 14*(5), 1–5. [11]

Ebbinghaus, H. (1913). *Memory* (H. Ruyer & C. E. Bussenius, Trans.). New York: Teacher's College Press. (Original work published 1885) [6]

Ebbinghaus, H. E. (1885/1964). *Memory: A contribution to experimental psychology* (H. A. Ruger & C. E. Bussenius, Trans.). New York: Dover. (Original work published 1885). [6]

Ebstein, R., Benjamin, J., & Belmaker, R. (2003). Behavioral genetics, genomics, and personality. In R. Plomin, J. DeFries, I. Craig, & P. McGuffin (Eds.), *Behavioral genetics in the postgenomic era* (pp. 365–388). Washington, DC: American Psychological Association. [14]

Edwards, B., Atkinson, G., Waterhouse, J., Reilly, T., Godfrey, R., & Budgett, R. (2000). Use of melatonin in recovery from jet-lag following an eastward flight across 10 time-zones. *Ergonomics, 43*, 1501–1513. [4]

Edwards, K., & Smith, E. E. (1996). A disconfirmation bias in the evaluation of arguments. *Journal of Personality and Social Psychology, 71*, 5–24. [17]

Egeth, H. E. (1993). What do we not know about eyewitness identification? *American Psychologist, 48*, 577–580. [6]

Ehrhardt, A. A., Evers, K., & Money, J. (1968). Influence of androgen and some aspects of sexual dimorphic behavior in women with the late-treated adrenogenital syndrome. *Johns Hopkins Medical Journal, 123*, 115–122. [12]

Eibl-Eibesfeldt, I. (1973). The expressive behavior of the deaf-and-blind-born. In M. von Cranach & I. Vine (Eds.), *Social communication and movement.* New York: Academic Press. [11]

Eich, J. E. (1980). The cue dependent nature of state-dependent retrieval. *Memory and Cognition, 8*, 157–173. [6]

Eichenbaum, H. (1997). Declarative memory: Insights from cognitive neurobiology. *Annual Review of Psychology, 48*, 547–572. [2, 6]

Eichenbaum, H., & Fortin, N. (2003). Episodic memory and the hippocampus: It's about time. *Current Directions in Psychological Science, 12*, 53–57. [6]

Eichenbaum, H., & Otto, T. (1993). LTP and memory: Can we enhance the connection? *Trends in Neurosciences, 16*, 163. [6]

Eidelson, R., & Eidelson, J. (2003). Dangerous ideas. *American Psychologist, 58*, 182–192. [17]

Ekman, P. (1972). Universals and cultural differences in facial expression of emotion. In J. Cole (Ed.), *Nebraska symposium on motivation* (Vol. 19). Lincoln: University of Nebraska Press. [11]

Ekman, P. (1993). Facial expression and emotion. *American Psychologist, 48*, 384–392. [11]

Ekman, P., & Friesen, W. V. (1975). *Unmasking the face: A guide to recognizing emotions from facial clues.* Englewood Cliffs, NJ: Prentice-Hall. [11]

Ekman, P., Levenson, R. W., & Friesen, W. V. (1983). Autonomic nervous system activity distinguishes among emotions. *Science, 221*, 1208–1210. [11]

Elal, G., Altug, A., Slade, P., & Tekcan, A. (2000). Factor structure of the Eating Attitudes Test (EAT) in a Turkish university sample. *Eating and Weight Disorders: Studies on Anorexia, Bulimia, and Obesity, 5*, 46–50. [11]

Elbert, T., Pantev, C., Wienbruch, C., Rockstroh, B., & Taub, E. (1995). Increased cortical representation of the fingers of the left hand in string players. *Science, 270*, 305–307. [2]

Elkin, I., Gibbons, R. D., Shea, M. T., Sotsky, S. M., Watkins, J. T., Pikonis, P. A., & Hedeker, D. (1995). Initial severity and differential treatment outcome in the National Institute of Mental Health Treatment of Depression Collaborative Research Program. *Journal of Consulting and Clinical Psychology, 63*, 841–847. [16]

Elkin, I., Shea, M. T., Watkins, J. T., et al. (1989). National Institute of Mental Health Treatment of Depression Collaborative Research Program: General effectiveness of treatments. *Archives of General Psychology, 46*, 971–982. [16]

Elkind, D. (1967). Egocentrism in adolescence. *Child Development, 38*, 1025–1034. [10]

Ellason, J. W., & Ross, C. A. (1997). Two-year follow–up of inpatients with dissociative identity disorder. *American Journal of Psychiatry, 154*, 832–839. [15]

Elliot, A. J., & Devine, P. G. (1994). On the motivational nature of cognitive dissonance: Dissonance as psychological discomfort. *Journal of Personality and Social Psychology, 67*, 382–394. [17]

Elliott, R., Friston, K. J., & Dolan, R. J. (2000). Dissociable neural responses in human reward systems. *Journal of Neuroscience, 20*, 6159–6165. [5]

Ellis, A. (1961). *A guide to rational living.* Englewood Cliffs, NJ: Prentice-Hall. [16]

Ellis, A. (1977). The basic clinical theory of rational-emotive therapy. In A. Ellis & R. Grieger (Eds.), *Handbook of rational-emotive therapy* (pp. 3–33). New York: Springer. [16]

Ellis, A. (1993). Reflections on rational-emotive therapy. *Journal of Consulting and Clinical Psychology*, *61*, 199–201. [16]

Ellis, B., Bates, J., Dodge, K., Fergusson, D., Horwood, J., Pettit, G., & Woodward, L. (2003). Does father absence place daughters at special risk for early sexual activity and teenage pregnancy? *Child Development*, *74*, 801–821. [9, 10]

Ellis, R. (2001). A theoretical model of the role of the cerebellum in cognition, attention and consciousness. *Consciousness & Emotion*, *2*, 300–309. [2]

Embick, D., Marantz, A., Miyashita, Y., O'Neil, W., & Sakai, K. L. (2000). A syntactic specialization for Broca's area. *Proceedings of the National Academy of Science*, *97*, 6150–6154. [2]

Engel, G. L. (1977). The need for a new medical model: A challenge for biomedicine. *Science*, *196*, 126–129. [13]

Engel, G. L. (1980). The clinical application of the biopsychosocial model. *American Journal of Psychiatry*, *137*, 535–544. [13]

Engels, G. I., Garnefski, N., & Diekstra, R. F. W. (1993). Efficacy of rational-emotive therapy: A quantitative analysis. *Journal of Consulting and Clinical Psychology*, *61*, 1083–1090. [16]

Engen, T. (1982). *The perception of odors.* New York: Academic Press. [3]

Ensari, N. (2001). How can managers reduce intergroup conflict in the workplace? Social psychological approaches to addressing prejudice in organizations. *Psychologist-Manager Journal*, *5*, 83–93. [18]

Epstein, J. (1983). Examining theories of adolescent friendships. In J. Epstein & N. Karweit (Eds.), *Friends in school.* New York: Academic Press. [10]

Epstein, J., Stern, E., & Silbersweig, D. (2001). Neuropsychiatry at the millennium: The potential for mind/brain integration through emerging interdisciplinary research strategies. *Clinical Neuroscience Research*, *1*, 10–18. [16]

Erel, O., & Burman, B. (1995). Interrelatedness of marital relations and parent-child relations: A meta-analytic review. *Psychological Bulletin*, *118*, 108–132. [10]

Erez, A., Lepine, J., & Elms, H. (2002). Effects of rotated leadership and peer evaluation on the functioning and effectiveness of self-managed teams: A quasi-experiment. *Personnel Psychology*, *55*, 929–948. [18]

Ericsson, K. A., & Charness, N. (1994). Expert performance: Its structure and acquisition. *American Psychologist*, *49*, 725–747. [8, 17]

Erikson, E. H. (1980). *Identity and the life cycle.* New York: Norton. [10]

Erlenmeyer-Kimling, L., & Jarvik, L. F. (1963). Genetics and intelligence: A review. *Science*, *142*, 1477–1479. [8]

Eron, L. D. (1987). The development of aggressive behavior from the perspective of a developing behaviorism. *American Psychologist*, *42*, 435–442. [17]

Eronen, M., Hakola, P., & Tiihonen, J. (1996). Mental disorders and homicidal behavior in Finland. *Journal of Personality and Social Psychology*, *53*, 497–501. [17]

Escher, M., Desmeules, J., Giostra, E., & Mentha, G. (2001). Hepatitis associated with kava, a herbal remedy for anxiety. *BMJ: British Medical Journal*, *322*, 139. [4]

Escorihuela, R., Tobena, A., & Fernandez-Terual, A. (1994). Environmental enrichment reverses the detrimental action of early inconsistent stimulation and increases the beneficial effects of postnatal handling on shuttlebox learning in adult rats. *Behavioral Brain Research*, *61*, 169–173. [2]

Espelage, D., Holt, M., & Henkel, R. (2003). Examination of peer-group contextual effects on aggression during early adolescence. *Child Development*, *74*, 205–220. [10]

Estes, W. K. (1994). *Classification and cognition.* New York: Oxford University Press. [7]

Etcoff, N., Ekman, P., Magee, J., & Frank, M. (2000). Lie detection and language comprehension. *Nature*, *405*, 139. [2]

Ettore, B. (1995, November). When the walls come tumbling down. *Management Review*, *84*, 33–37. [18]

Evans, D., & Zarate, O. (2000). *Introducing evolutionary psychology.* New York: Totem Books. [1]

Evans, G. W., & Lepore, S. J. (1993). Household crowding and social support: A quasiexperimental analysis. *Journal of Personality and Social Psychology*, *65*, 308–316. [17]

Evans, M. D., Hollon, S. D., DeRubeis, R. J., Piasecki, J. M., Grove, W. M., Garvey, M. J., & Tuason, V. B. (1992). Differential relapse following cognitive therapy and pharmacotherapy for depression. *Archives of General Psychiatry*, *49*, 802–808. [16]

Everson, S. A., Goldberg, D. E., Kaplan, G. A., Cohen, R. D., Pukkala, E., Tuomilehto, J., & Salonen, J. T. (1996). Hopelessness and risk of mortality and incidence of myocardial infarction and cancer. *Psychosomatic Medicine*, *58*, 113–121. [13]

Ewin, D. M. (1992). Hypnotherapy for warts (*Verruca vulgaris*): 41 consecutive cases with 33 cures. *American Journal of Clinical Hypnosis*, *35*, 1–10. [4]

Exner, J. E. (1993). *The Rorschach: A comprehensive system: Vol. 1. Basic foundations* (3rd ed.). New York: Wiley. [14]

Exton, M. S., von Auer, A. K., Buske-Kirschbaum, A., Stockhorst, U., Göbel, U., & Schedlowski, M. (2000). Pavlovian conditioning of immune function: Animal investigation and the challenge of human application. *Behavioural Brain Research*, *110*, 129–141. [5]

Eyeferth, K. (1961). Leistungen verschiedener Gruppen von Besatzungskindern in Hamburg-Wechsler Intelligenztest für Kinder (HAWIK). *Archir für die Gesamte Psychologie*, *113*, 224–241. [8]

Eysenbach, G., Powell, J., Kuss, O., & Sa, E. (2002). Empirical studies of health information for consumers on the World Wide Web: A systematic review. *JAMA: Journal of the American Medical Association*, *287*, 2691–2700. [13]

Eysenck, H. J. (1990). Genetic and environmental contributions to individual differences: The three major dimensions of personality. *Journal of Personality*, *58*, 245–261. [14]

Eysenck, H. J. (1994). The outcome problem in psychotherapy: What have we learned? *Behaviour Research and Therapy*, *32*, 477–495. [16]

Fackelmann, K. (1997). Marijuana on trial: Is marijuana a dangerous drug or a valuable medicine? *Science News*, *151*, 178–179, 183. [4]

Fagiolini, M., & Hensch, T. K. (2000). Inhibitory threshold for critical-period activation in primary visual cortex. *Nature*, *404*, 183–186. [3]

Fagot, B. (1995). Observations of parent reactions to sex-stereotyped behavior: Age and sex effects. *Child Development*, *62*, 617–628. [8]

Fairburn, C. G., Welch, S. L., Doll, H. A., Davies, B. A., & O'Connor, M. E. (1997). Risk factors for bulimia nervosa: A community-based case-control study. *Archives of General Psychiatry*, *54*, 509–517. [11]

Falbo, T., & Polit, D. F. (1986). Quantitative review of the only child literature: Research evidence and theory development. *Psychological Bulletin*, *100*, 176–189. [11]

Falloon, I. R. H. (1988). Expressed emotion: Current status. *Psychological Medicine*, *18*, 269–274. [16]

Famighetti, R. (Ed.). (1997). *The world almanac and book of facts 1998.* Mahwah, NJ: World Almanac Books. [11, 16]

Fang, C., & Myers, H. (2001). The effects of racial stressors and hostility on cardiovascular reactivity in African American and Caucasian men. *Health Psychology, 20,* 64–70. [13]

Fanous, A., Gardner, C., Prescott, C., Cancro, R., & Kendler, K. (2002). Neuroticism, major depression and gender: A population-based twin study. *Psychological Medicine, 32,* 719–728. [15]

Fantz, R. L. (1961). The origin of form perception. *Scientific American, 204,* 66–72. [9]

Farah, M. J. (1995). The neural bases of mental imagery. In M. S. Gazzaniga (Ed.), *The cognitive neurosciences.* Cambridge, MA: MIT Press. [7]

Farde, L. (1996). The advantage of using positron emission tomography in drug research. *Trends in Neurosciences, 19,* 211–214. [2]

Faryna, E., & Morales, E. (2000). Self-efficacy and HIV-related risk behaviors among multiethnic adolescents. *Cultural Diversity and Ethnic Minority Psychology, 6,* 42–56. [4]

Fauerbach, J., Lawrence, J., Haythornthwaite, J., & Richter, L. (2002). Coping with the stress of a painful medical procedure. *Behaviour Research & Therapy, 40,* 1003–1015. [14]

Faunce, G. (2002). Eating disorders and attentional bias: A review. *Eating Disorders: The Journal of Treatment & Prevention, 10,* 125–139. [11]

Fazio, R. H. (1989). On the power and functionality of attitudes: The role of attitude accessibility. In A. R. Pratkanis, S. J. Breckler, & A. G. Greenwald (Eds.), *Attitude structure and function* (pp. 153–179). Hillsdale, NJ: Erlbaum. [17]

Fazio, R. H., & Williams, C. J. (1986). Attitude accessibility as a moderator of the attitude perception and attitude-behavior relations: An investigation of the 1984 presidential election. *Journal of Personality and Social Psychology, 51,* 505–514. [17]

Federal Bureau of Investigation. (1999). United States crime rates 1960–1998. Retrieved from http://www.disastercenter.com/crime/uscrime.htm [17]

Federal Interagency Forum on Aging—Related Statistics (FIFARS). (2000). *Older Americans 2000: Key indicators of well–being.* Retrieved July 30, 2003, from http://www. agingstats.gov [10]

Federal Interagency Forum on Child and Family Statistics (FIFCFS). (2000). *America's children: Key national indicators of well-being 2000.* Washington, DC: Author. [10]

Fein, S., & Spencer, S. J. (1997). Prejudice as self-image maintenance: Affirming the self through derogating others. *Journal of Personality and Social Psychology, 73,* 31–44. [17]

Feingold, A. (1988). Matching for attractiveness in romantic partners and same-sex friends: A meta-analysis and theoretical critique. *Psychological Bulletin, 104,* 226–235. [17]

Feldman, H. A., Goldstein, I., Hatzichristou, D. G., Krane, R. J., & McKinlay, J. B. (1994). Impotence and its medical and psychosocial correlates: Results of the Massachusetts male aging study. *Journal of Urology, 151,* 54–61. [12]

Fenn, K., Nusbaum, H., & Margoliash, D. (2003). Consolidaiton during sleep of perceptual learning of spoken language. *Nature, 425,* 614–616. [4]

Fenton, W. S., & McGlashan, T. H. (1991). Natural history of schizophrenia subtypes: I. Longitudinal study of paranoid, hebephrenic, and undifferentiated schizophrenia. *Archives of General Psychiatry, 48,* 969–977. [15]

Fenton, W. S., & McGlashan, T. H. (1994). Antecedents, symptom progression, and long-term outcome of the deficit syndrome in schizophrenia. *American Journal of Psychiatry, 151,* 351–356. [15]

Fernald, A. (1993). Approval and disapproval: Infant responsiveness to vocal affect in familiar and unfamiliar languages. *Child Development, 64,* 637–656. [9]

Fernandez, Y., & Marshall, W. (2003). Victim empathy, social self-esteem, and psychopathy in rapists. *Sexual Abuse: Journal of Research & Treatment, 15,* 11–26. [12]

Fernández-Dols, J.-M., & Ruiz-Belda, M.-A. (1995). Are smiles a sign of happiness? Gold medal winners at the Olympic games. *Journal of Personality and Social Psychology, 69,* 1113–1119. [11]

Festinger, L. (1957). *A theory of cognitive dissonance.* Evanston, IL: Row, Peterson. [17]

Festinger, L., & Carlsmith, J. M. (1959). Cognitive consequences of forced compliance. *Journal of Abnormal and Social Psychology, 58,* 203–210. [17]

Fiatarone, M. A., Morley, J. E., Bloom, E. T., Benton, D., Makinodan, T., & Solomon, G. F. (1988). Endogenous opioids and the exercise-induced augmentation of natural killer cell activity. *Journal of Laboratory and Clinical Medicine, 112,* 544–552. [13]

Field, M., & Duka, T. (2002). Cues paired with a low dose of alcohol acquire conditioned incentive properties in social drinkers. *Psychopharmacology, 159,* 325–334. [5]

Field, T., Schanberg, S. M., Scfidi, F., Bauer, C. R., Vega-Lahr, N., Garcia, R., Nystrom, J., & Kuhn, C. (1986, May). Tactile/kinesthetic stimulation effects on preterm neonates. *Pediatrics, 77,* 654–658. [3]

Fields, J., Walton, K., & Schneider, R. (2002). Effect of a multimodality natural medicine program on carotid atherosclerosis in older subjects: A pilot trial of Maharishi Verdic Medicine. *American Journal of Cardiology, 89,* 952–958. [4]

Fiez, J. A. (1996). Cerebellar contributions to cognition. *Neuron, 16,* 13–15. [2]

Finch, A. E., Lambert, M. J., & Brown, G. (2000). Attacking anxiety: A naturalistic study of a multimedia self-help program. *Journal of Clinical Psychology, 56,* 11–21. [16]

Fincham, F. (2003). Marital conflict: Correlates, structure, and context. *Current Directions in Psychological Science, 12,* 23–27. [10]

Fink, B., & Penton-Voak, I. (2002). Evolutionary psychology of facial attractiveness. *Current Directions in Psychological Science, 11,* 154–158. [17]

Finkel, D., & McGue, M. (1997). Sex differences and nonadditivity in heritability of the Multidimensional Personality Questionnaire scales. *Journal of Personality and Social Psychology, 72,* 929–938. [14]

Fischbach, G. D. (1992). Mind and brain. *Scientific American, 267,* 48–56. [6]

Fischer, K., & Rose, S. (1994). Dynamic development of coordination of components in brain and behavior: A framework for theory and research. In K. Fischer & G. Dawson (Eds.), *Human Behavior and the Developing Brain* (pp. 3–66). New York: Guilford Press. [2]

Fixx, J. F. (1978). *Solve It! A perplexing profusion of puzzles.* New York: Doubleday. [7]

Flavell, J. H. (1992). Cognitive development: Past, present, and future. *Developmental Psychology, 28,* 998–1005. [9, 10]

Flavell, J. H. (1996). Piaget's legacy. *Psychological Science, 7,* 200–203. [9]

Flavell, J. H., Green, F. L., & Flavell, E. R. (1995). Young children's knowledge about thinking. *Monographs of the Society for Research in Child Development, 60*(1, Serial No. 243). [9]

Fleck, D., Hendricks, W., DelBellow, M., & Strakowski, S. (2002). Differential prescription of maintenance antipsychotics to African American and White patients with new-onset bipolar disorder. *Journal of Clinical Psychiatry, 63,* 658–664. [16]

Fleming, J. D. (1974, July). Field report: The state of the apes. *Psychology Today,* pp. 31–46. [7]

Fletcher, J. M., Page, B., Francis, D. J., Copeland, K., Naus, M. J., Davis, C. M., Morris, R., Krauskopf, D., & Satz, P. (1996). Cognitive correlates of long-term cannabis use in Costa Rican men. *Archives of General Psychiatry, 53*, 1051–1057. [4]

Flint, A. J., & Rifat, S. L. (2000). Maintenance treatment for recurrent depression in late life: A four-year outcome study. *American Journal of Geriatric Psychiatry, 8*, 112–116. [10]

Flood, J. F., Silver, A. J., & Morley, J. E. (1990). Do peptide-induced changes in feeding occur because of changes in motivation to eat? *Peptides, 11*, 265–270. [11]

Florian, V., Mikulincer, M., & Taubman, O. (1995). Does hardiness contribute to mental health during a stressful real-life situation? The roles of appraisal and coping. *Journal of Personality and Social Psychology, 68*, 687–695. [13]

Florida Institute for Neurologic Rehabilitation, Inc. (2002). V.D.2. Case study [Online report]. Retrieved May 25, 2003, from http://www.floridainstitute.com [4]

Florio, V., Fossella, S., Maravita, A., Miniussi, C., & Marzi, C. (2002). Interhemispheric transfer and laterality effects in simple visual reaction time in schizophrenics. *Cognitive Neuropsychiatry, 7*, 97–111. [15]

Flowers, L. (2002). The impact of college racial composition on African American students' academic and social gains: Additional evidence. *Journal of College Student Development, 43*, 403–410. [10]

Flowers, L., & Pascarella, E. (1999). Cognitive effects of college racial composition on African American students after 3 years of college. *Journal of College Student Development, 40*, 669–677. [10]

Flynn, G. (1995, November). Telecommuters report higher productivity—and better home lives. *Personnel Journal, 74*, 23. [18]

Flynn, J. (1999). Searching for justice: The discovery of IQ gains over time. *American Psychologist, 54*, 5–20. [8]

Flynn, J. (2003). Movies about intelligence: The limitations of *g*. *Current Directions in Psychological Science, 12*, 95–99. [8]

Flynn, J. R. (1987). Race and IQ: Jensen's case refuted. In S. Modgil, & C. Modgil (Eds.), *Arthur Jensen: Consensus and controversy.* New York: Palmer Press. [8]

Foa, E. B. (1995). How do treatments for obsessive-compulsive disorder compare? *Harvard Mental Health Letter, 12*(1), 8. [16]

Foa, E. B., & Meadows, E. A. (1997). Psychosocial treatments for posttraumatic stress disorder: A critical review. *Annual Review of Psychology, 48*, 449–480. [13]

Fogel, J., Albert, S., Schnabel, F., Ditkoff, B., & Neugut, A. (2002). Internet use and social support in women with breast cancer. *Health Psychology, 21*, 398–404. [13]

Foley, D. J., Monjan, A. A., Brown, S. L., Simonsick, E. M., Wallace, R. B., & Blazer, D. G. (1995). Sleep complaints among elderly persons: An epidemiologic study of three communities. *Sleep, 18*, 425–432. [4]

Foley, S., Kidder, D., & Powell, G. (2002). The perceived glass ceiling and justice perceptions: An investigation of Hispanic law associates. *Journal of Management, 28*, 471–496. [18]

Folkard, S. (1990). Circadian performance rhythms: Some practical and theoretical implications. *Philosophical Transactions of the Royal Society of London. Series B: Biological Sciences, 327*, 543–553. [4]

Folkerts, H. (2000). Electroconvulsive therapy of depressive disorders. *Ther. Umsch, 57*, 290–294. [16]

Folkman, S. (1984). Personal control and stress and coping processes: A theoretical analysis. *Journal of Personality and Social Psychology, 46*, 839–852. [13]

Folkman, S., Chesney, M., Collette, L., Boccellari, A., & Cooke, M. (1996). Postbereavement depressive mood and its prebereavement predictors in HIV$^+$ and HIV$^-$ gay men. *Journal of Personality and Social Psychology, 70*, 336–348. [10]

Folkman, S., & Lazarus, R. S. (1980). An analysis of coping in a middle-aged community sample. *Journal of Health and Social Behavior, 21*, 219–239. [13]

Ford, C. S., & Beach, F. A. (1951). *Patterns of sexual behavior.* New York: Harper & Row. [12]

Forey, J. P., Walker, S., Poston, C., II, & Goodrick, G. K. (1996). Future directions in obesity and eating disorders. *Addictive Behaviors, 21*, 767–778. [11]

Forgas, J. P., & Fiedler, K. (1996). Us and them: Mood effects on intergroup discrimination. *Journal of Personality and Social Psychology, 70*, 28–40. [17]

Foulkes, D. (1996). Sleep and dreams: Dream research: 1953–1993. *Sleep, 19*, 609–624. [4]

Fox, E., Lester, V., Russo, R., Bowles, R. J., Pichler, A., & Dutton, K. (2000b). Facial expressions of emotion: Are angry faces detected more efficiently? *Cognition and Emotion, 14*, 61–92. [11]

Fox, M. (2002). *Lucky man: A memoir.* New York: Hyperion Press. [13]

Fox, N. A., & Bell, M. A. (1990). Electrophysiological indices of frontal lobe development: Relations to cognitive and affective behavior in human infants over the first year of life. *Annals of the New York Academy of Sciences, 608*, 677–698. [9]

Francis-Smythe, J., & Smith, P. (1997). The psychological impact of assessment in a development center. *Human Relations, 50*, 149–167. [18]

Frank, E., Anderson, B., Reynolds, C. F., III, Ritenour, A., & Kupfer, D. J. (1994). Life events and the research diagnostic criteria endogenous subtype. *Archives of General Psychiatry, 51*, 519–524. [15]

Frank, E., Kupfer, D. J., Wagner, E. F., McEachran, A. B., & Cornes, C. (1991). Efficacy of interpersonal psychotherapy as a maintenance treatment of recurrent depression: Contributing factors. *Archives of General Psychiatry, 48*, 1053–1059. [16]

Frank, M., Formaker, B., & Hettinger, T. (2003). Taste response to mixtures: Analytic processing of quality. *Behavioral Neuroscience, 117*, 228–235. [3]

Frankenburg, W. K., Dodds, J. B., Archer, P., et al. (1992). *Denver II training manual.* Denver: Denver Developmental Materials. [9]

Franklin, B., Majault, Roy, L., Sallin, Bailly, J., D'Arcet, B., Guillotin, J., & Lavoisier, A. (1784/2002). Report of the commissioners charged by the King with the examination of animal magnetism. *International Journal of Clinical & Experimental Hypnosis, 50*, 332–363. [4]

Frantz, K., Hansson, K., Stouffer, D., & Parsons, L. (2002). 5-HT-sub-6 receptor antagonism potentiates the behavioral and neurochemical effects of amphetamine but not cocaine. *Neuropharmacology, 42*, 170–180. [4]

Franz, C. E., McClelland, D. C., & Weinberger, J. (1991). Childhood antecedents of conventional social accomplishment in midlife adults: A 36-year prospective study. *Journal of Personality and Social Psychology, 60*, 586–595. [9]

Fraser, A. M., Brockert, J. E., & Ward, R. H. (1995). Association of young maternal age with adverse reproductive outcomes. *New England Journal of Medicine, 332*, 1113–1117. [9, 10]

Frazer, A. (1997). Antidepressants. *Journal of Clinical Psychiatry, 58*(6, Suppl.), 9–25. [16]

Frazer, N., Larkin, K., & Goodie, J. (2002). Do behavioral responses mediate or moderate the relation between cardiovascular reactivity to stress and parental history of hypertension? *Health Psychology, 21*, 244–253. [13]

Frederickson, N. (1962). Factors in in-basket performance. *Psychological Monographs, 76*. [18]

Fredricks, J., & Eccles, J. (2002). Children's competence and value beliefs from childhood through adolescence growth trajectories in two male-sex-typed domains. *Developmental Psychology, 38*, 519–533. [12]

Fredrikson, M., Annas, P., Fischer, H., & Wik, G. (1996). Gender and age differences in the prevalence of specific fears and phobias. *Behaviour Research and Therapy, 34*, 33–39. [15]

Freedman, J. L., & Fraser, S. C. (1966). Compliance without pressure: The foot-in-the-door technique. *Journal of Personality and Social Psychology, 4*, 195–202. [17]

Freeman, W. J. (1991). The physiology of perception. *Scientific American, 264*, 78–85. [3]

French, S., Jeffery, R., & Murray, D. (1999). Is dieting good for you? Prevalence, duration and associated weight and behaviour changes for specific weight loss strategies over four years in US adults. *International Journal of Obesity Related Metabolic Disorders, 23*, 320–327. [11]

Freud, A. (1958). *Adolescence: Psychoanalytic study of the child* (Vol. 13). New York: Academic Press. [10]

Freud, S. (1900/1953a). The interpretation of dreams. In J. Strachey (Ed. and Trans.), *The standard edition of the complete psychological works of Sigmund Freud* (Vols. 4 and 5). London: Hogarth Press. (Original work published 1900). [4]

Freud, S. (1905/1953b). Three essays on the theory of sexuality. In J. Strachey (Ed. and Trans.), *The standard edition of the complete psychological works of Sigmund Freud* (Vol. 7). London: Hogarth Press. (Original work published 1905). [14]

Freud, S. (1920/1963b). *A general introduction to psycho-analysis* (J. Riviere, Trans.). New York: Simon & Schuster. (Original work published 1920). [14, 16]

Freud, S. (1922). *Beyond the pleasure principle.* London: International Psychoanalytic Press. [6]

Freud, S. (1925/1963a). *An autobiographical study* (J. Strachey, Trans.). New York: W.W. Norton. (Original work published 1925). [14, 16]

Freud, S. (1930/1962). *Civilization and its discontents* (J. Strachey, Trans.). New York: W. W. Norton. (Original work published 1930). [14]

Freud, S. (1933/1965). *New introductory lectures on psychoanalysis* (J. Strachey, Trans.). New York: W. W. Norton. (Original work published 1933). [14]

Frey, K. P., & Eagly, A. H. (1993). Vividness can undermine the persuasiveness of messages. *Journal of Personality and Social Psychology, 65*, 32–44. [17]

Friedland, N., Keinan, G., & Regev, Y. (1992). Controlling the uncontrollable: Effects of stress on illusory perceptions of controllability. *Journal of Personality and Social Psychology, 63*, 923–931. [13]

Friedman, J. M. (1997). The alphabet of weight control. *Nature, 385*, 119–120. [11]

Friedman, J. M. (2000). Obesity in the new millennium. *Nature, 404*, 632–634. [11]

Friedman, M., & Rosenman, R. H. (1974). *Type A behavior and your heart.* New York: Fawcett. [13]

Friedman, M. I., Tordoff, M. G., & Ramirez, I. (1986). Integrated metabolic control of food intake. *Brain Research Bulletin, 17*, 855–859. [11]

Fry, A. F., & Hale, S. (1996). Processing speed, working memory, and fluid intelligence. *Psychological Science, 7*, 237–241. [8]

Fujita, F., Diener, E., & Sandvik, E. (1991). Gender differences in negative affect and well-being: The case for emotional intensity. *Journal of Personality and Social Psychology, 61*, 427–434. [11]

Fuligni, A. J., & Stevenson, H. W. (1995). Time use and mathematics achievement among American, Chinese, and Japanese high school students. *Child Development, 66*, 830–842. [8]

Furstenberg, F., & Weiss, C. (2000). Intergenerational transmission of fathering roles in at-risk families. *Marriage & Family Review, 29*, 181–201. [10]

Fyer, A. J. (1993). Heritability of social anxiety: A brief review. *Journal of Clinical Psychiatry, 54*(12, Suppl.), 10–12. [15]

Gabrieli, J. D. E., Desmond, J. E., Demb, J. B., Wagner, A. D., Stone, M. V., Viadya, C. J., & Glover, G. H. (1996). Functional magnetic resonance imaging of semantic memory processes in the frontal lobes. *Psychological Science, 7*, 278–283. [6]

Galambos, N., Barker, E., & Almeida, D. (2003). Parents do matter: Trajectories of change in externalizing and internalizing problems in early adolescence. *Child Development, 74*, 578–594. [10]

Gallistel, C. R., & Gibbon, J. (2000). Time, rate, and conditioning. *Psychological Review, 107*, 289–344. [5]

Gallo, L., Troxel, W., Matthews, K., Jansen-McWilliams, L., Kuller, L., & Suton-Tyrrell, K. (2003). Occupation and subclinical carotid artery disease: Are clerical workers at greater risk? *Health Psychology, 22*, 19–29. [13]

Gallup, G., Jr., & Hugick, L. (1990). Racial tolerance grows, progress on racial equality less evident. *Gallup Poll Monthly*, No. 297, 23–32. [17]

Galton, F. (1874). *English men of science: Their nature and nurture.* London: Macmillan. [8]

Gana, K., Allouche, J., & Beaugrand, C. (2001). The effect of sex-role orientation on the participation of married men in household tasks. *Revue internationale de psychologie sociale, 14*, 151–164. [12]

Ganellen, R. J. (1996). Comparing the diagnostic efficiency of the MMPI, MCMI-II, and Rorschach: A review. *Journal of Personality Assessment, 67*, 219–243. [14]

Gao, J-H., Parsons, L. M., Bower, J. M., Xiong, J., Li, J., & Fox, P. T. (1996). Cerebellum implicated in sensory acquisition and discrimination rather than motor control. *Science, 272*, 545–547. [2]

Garavan, H., Morgan, R. E., Levitsky, D. A., Hermer-Vasquez, L., & Strupp, B. J. (2000). Enduring effects of early lead exposure: Evidence for a specific deficit in associative ability. *Neurotoxicology and Teratology, 22*, 151–164. [8]

Garbarino, S., Beelke, M., Costa, G., Violani, C., Lucidi, F., & Ferrillo, F. (2002). Brain function and effects of shift work: Implications for clinical neuropharmacology. *Neuro-psychobiology, 45*, 50–56. [4]

Garcia, J., & Koelling, A. (1966). Relation of cue to consequence in avoidance learning. *Psychonomic Science, 4*, 123–124. [5]

Gardner, H. (1983). *Frames of mind: The theory of multiple intelligences.* New York: Basic Books. [8]

Gardner, H., & Hatch, T. (1989). Multiple intelligences go to school: Educational implication of the theory of multiple intelligences. *Educational Researcher, 18*(8), 6. [8]

Gardner, R. A., & Gardner, B. T. (1969). Teaching sign language to a chimpanzee. *Science, 165*, 664–672. [7]

Garfield, C. (1986). *Peak performers: The new heroes of American business.* New York: Morrow. [7]

Garma, L., & Marchand, F. (1994). Non-pharmacological approaches to the treatment of narcolepsy. *Sleep, 17*, S97–S102. [4]

Garmon, L. C., Basinger, K. S., Gregg, V. R., & Gibbs, J. C. (1996). Gender differences in stage and expression of moral judgment. *Merrill-Palmer Quarterly, 42*, 418–437. [10]

Garrett, M., Garrett, J., & Brotherton, D. (2001). Inner circle/outer circle: A group technique based on Native American healing circles. *Journal for Specialists in Group Work, 26*, 17–30. [16]

Garry, M., & Loftus, E. F. (1994). Pseudomemories without hypnosis. *International Journal of Clinical and Experimental Hypnosis, 42*, 363–373. [6]

Gartner, J., & Whitaker-Azimitia, P. M. (1996). Developmental factors influencing aggression: Animal models and clinical correlates. *Annals of the New York Academy of Sciences, 794*, 113–120. [17]

Gastil, J. (1990). Generic pronouns and sexist language: The oxymoronic character of masculine generics. *Sex Roles, 23*, 629–643. [7]

Gates, A. I. (1917). Recitation as a factor in memorizing. *Archives of Psychology, 40.* [6]

Gawin, F. H. (1991). Cocaine addiction: Psychology and neurophysiology. *Science, 251*, 1580–1586. [4]

Gawronski, B., Alshut, E., Grafe, J., Nespethal, J., Ruhmland, A., & Schulz, L. (2002). Processes of judging known and unknown persons. *Zeitschrift fuer Sozialpsychologie, 33*, 25–34. [17]

Gazelle, H., & Ladd, G. (2003). Anxious solitude and peer exclusion: A diathesis-stress model of internalizing trajectories in childhood. *Child Development, 74*, 257–278. [9]

Gazzaniga, M. S. (1983). Right hemisphere language following brain bisection: A 20-year perspective. *American Psychologist, 38*, 525–537. [2]

Ge, X., Brody, G., Conger, R., Simons, R., & Murry, V. (2002). Contextual amplification of pubertal transition effects on deviant peer affiliation and externalizing behavior among African American children. *Developmental Psychology, 38*, 42–54. [10]

Geary, D., Lin, F., Chen, G., & Saults, S. (1999). Contributions of computational fluency to cross-national differences in arithmetical reasoning abilities. *Journal of Educational Psychology, 91*, 716–719. [8]

Geary, D. C. (1996). Sexual selection and sex differences in mathematical abilties. *Behavioral and Brain Sciences, 19*, 229–284. [12]

Geen, R. G. (1984). Human motivation: New perspectives on old problems. In A. M. Rogers & C. J. Scheier (Eds.), *The G. Stanley Hall lecture series* (Vol. 4). Washington, DC: American Psychological Association. [11]

Geer, K., Ropka, M., Cohn, W., Jones, S., & Miesfeldt, S. (2001). Factors influencing patients' decisions to decline cancer genetic counseling services. *Journal of Genetic Counseling, 10*, 25–40. [2]

Gehart, D., & Lyle, R. (2001). Client experience of gender in therapeutic relationships: An interpretive ethnography. *Family Process, 40*, 443–458. [16]

Gehring, D. (2003). Couple therapy for low sexual desire: A systematic approach. *Journal of Sex & Marital Therapy, 29*, 25–38. [16]

Geiselman, R. E., Schroppel, T., Tubridy, A., Konishi, T., & Rodriguez, V. (2000). Objectivity bias in eye witness performance. *Applied Cognitive Psychology, 14*, 323–332. [6]

George, M. S., Ketter, T. A., & Post, R. M. (1993). SPECT and PET imaging in mood disorders. *Journal of Clinical Psychiatry, 54*(11, Suppl.), 6–13. [15]

Gerbner, G., & Signorielli, N. (1990). *Violence profile, 1967 through 1988–1989. Enduring patterns.* Unpublished manuscript, Annenberg School of Communication, University of Pennsylvania, Philadelphia. [9]

Gergen, K. J., Gulerce, A., Lock, A., & Misra, G. (1996). Psychological science in cultural context. *American Psychologist, 51*, 496–503. [1]

Gerrits, M., Petromilli, P., Westenberg, H., Di Chiara, G., & van Ree, J. (2002). Decrease in basal dopamine levels in the nucleus accumbens shell during daily drug-seeking behavior in rats. *Brain Research, 924*, 141–150. [4]

Gerull, F., & Rapee, R. (2002). Mother knows best: The effects of maternal modelling on the acquisition of fear and avoidance behaviour in toddlers. *Behaviour Research & Therapy, 40*, 279–287. [5]

Gevins, A., Leong, H., Smith, M. E., Le, J., & Du, R. (1995). Mapping cognitive brain function with modern high-resolution electroencephalography. *Trends in Neurosciences, 18*, 429–436. [2]

Gibbons, A. (1991). Déjà vu all over again: Chimp-language wars. *Science, 251*, 1561–1562. [7]

Gibson, E., & Walk, R. D. (1960). The "visual cliff." *Scientific American, 202*, 64–71. [9]

Giedd, J. N., Rapoport, J. L., Garvey, M. A., Perlmutter, S., & Swedo, S. E. (2000). MRI assessment of children with obsessive-compulsive disorder or tics associated with streptococcal infection. *American Journal of Psychiatry, 157*, 2281–2283. [15]

Gilbert, D. T., & Malone, P. S. (1995). The correspondence bias. *Psychological Bulletin, 117*, 21–38. [17]

Gilligan, C. (1982). *In a different voice: Psychological theory and women's development.* Cambridge, MA: Harvard University Press. [10]

Gillon, G., & Young, A. (2002). The phonological awareness skills of children who are blind. *Journal of Visual Impairment & Blindness, 96*, 38–49. [9]

Ginsberg, G., & Bronstein, P. (1993). Family factors related to children's intrinsic/extrinsic motivational orientation and academic performance. *Child Development, 64*, 1461–1474. [11]

Ginty, D. D., Kornhauser, J. M., Thompson, M. A., Bading, H., Mayo, K. E., Takahashi, J. S., & Greenberg, M. E. (1993). Regulation of CREB phosphorylation in the suprachiasmatic nucleus by light and a circadian clock. *Science, 260*, 238–241. [4]

Ginzburg, K., Solomon, Z., & Bleich, A. (2002). Repressive coping style, acute stress disorder, and post-traumatic stress disorder after mycardial infarction. *Journal of the American Psychosomatic Society, 64*, 748–757. [13]

Giraud, A., Price, C., Graham, J., & Frackowisk, R. (2001). *Neuropsychopharmacology, 124*, 1307–1316. [2]

Girolamo, G., & Bassi, M. (2003). Community surveys of mental disorders: Recent achievements and works in progress. *Current Opinion in Psychiatry, 16*, 403–411. [15]

Gladue, B., & Delaney, H. (1990). Gender differences in perception of attractiveness of men and women in bars. *Personality and Social Psychology Bulletin, 16*, 378–391. [12]

Glantz, L. A., & Lewis, D. A. (2000). Decreased dendritic spine density on prefrontal cortical pyramidal neurons in schizophrenia. *Archives of General Psychiatry, 57*, 65–73. [15]

Glass, D. C., & Singer, J. E. (1972). *Urban stress: Experiments in noise and social stressors.* New York: Academic Press. [13]

Glassman, A. H. (1993). What is the relationship between depression and cigarette smoking? *Harvard Mental Health Letter, 10*(4), 8. [13]

Glassop, L. (2002). The organizational benefits of teams. *Human Relations, 55*, 225–249. [18]

Glazer, W. M., Morgenstern, H., & Doucette, J. T. (1993). Predicting the long-term risk of tardive dyskinesia in outpatients maintained on neuroleptic medications. *Journal of Clinical Psychiatry, 54*, 133–139. [16]

Gleaves, D. J. (1996). The sociocognitive model of dissociative identity disorder: A reexamination of the evidence. *Psychological Bulletin, 120*, 42–59. [15]

Glover, J. A., & Corkill, A. J. (1987). Influence of paraphrased repetitions on the spacing effect. *Journal of Educational Psychology, 79*, 198–199. [6]

Gluck, M. A., & Myers, C. E. (1997). Psychobiological models of hippocampal function in learning and memory. *Annual Review of Psychology, 48*, 481–514. [2, 6]

Godden, D. R., & Baddeley, A. D. (1975). Context-dependent memory in two natural environments: On land and underwater. *British Journal of Psychology, 66*, 325–331. [6]

Goh, V. H., Tong, T. Y., & Lee, L. K. (2000). Sleep/wake cycle and circadian disturbances in shift work: Strategies for their management—a review. *Annals of the Academy of Medicine Singapore, 29*, 90–96. [4]

Gohm, C. (2003). Mood regulation and emotional intelligence: Individual differences. *Journal of Personality & Social Psychology, 84*, 594–607. [8]

Gökcebay, N., Cooper, R., Williams, R. L., Hirshkowitz, M., & Moore, C. A. (1994). Function of sleep. In R. Cooper (Ed.), *Sleep*. New York: Chapman & Hall. [4]

Goldenberg, R. L., & Klerman, L. V. (1995). Adolescent pregnancy—another look. *New England Journal of Medicine, 332*, 1161–1162. [10]

Goldvarg, Y., & Johnson-Laird, P. N. (2000). Illusions in modal reasoning. *Memory and Cognition, 28*, 282–294. [7]

Goleman, D. (1995). *Emotional intelligence*. New York: Bantam. [8]

Goleman, D., Kaufman, P., & Ray, M. (1992). *The creative spirit*. New York: Dutton. [8]

Gollan, T., & Silverberg, N. (2001). Tip-of-the-tongue states in Hebrew-English bilinguals. *Bilingualism: Language and Cognition, 4*, 63–83. [7]

Gonzalez, R., Ellsworth, P. C., & Pembroke, M. (1993). Response biases in lineups and showups. *Journal of Personality and Social Psychology, 64*, 525–537. [6]

Goodglass, H. (1993). *Understanding aphasia*. San Diego, CA: Academic Press. [2]

Goodwin, G. M. (1996). How do antidepressants affect serotonin receptors? The role of serotonin receptors in the therapeutic and side effect profile of the SSRIs. *Journal of Clinical Psychiatry, 57*(4, Suppl.), 9–13. [16]

Goodwin, R., & Fitzgibbon, M. (2002). Social anxiety as a barrier to treatment for eating disorders. *International Journal of Eating Disorders, 32*, 103–106. [11]

Goodwin, R., & Stein, M. (2003). Peptic ulcer disease and neuroticism in the United States adult population. *Psychotherapy & Psychosomatics, 72*, 10–15. [14]

Goodyear, R., Newcomb, M., & Allison, R. (2000). Predictors of Latino men's paternity in teen pregnancy: Test of a mediational model of childhood experiences, gender role attitudes, and behaviors. *Journal of Counseling Psychology, 47*, 116–128. [10]

Goodyear, R., Newcomb, M., & Locke, T. (2002). Pregnant Latina teenagers: Psychosocial and developmental determinants of how they select and perceive the men who father their children. *Journal of Counseling Psychology, 49*, 187–201. [10]

Gordon, H. (2002). Early environmental stress and biological vulnerability to drug abuse. *Psychoneuroendocrinology, 27*, 115–126. [4]

Goris, J., Vaught, B., & Petit, J. (2003). Effects of trust in superiors and influence of superiors on the association between individual-job congruence and job performance/satisfaction. *Journal of Business & Psychology, 17*, 327–343. [18]

Gorman, C. (1996, Fall). Damage control. *Time* [Special Issue], 31–35. [2]

Gormezano, I. (1984). The study of associative learning with CS-CR paradigms. In D. L. Alkon & J. Farley (Eds.), *Primary neural substrates of learning and behavioral change* (pp. 5–24). New York: Cambridge University Press. [5]

Gosling, S., Ko, S., Mannarelli, T., & Morris, M. (2002). A room with a cue: Personality judgments based on offices and bedrooms. *Journal of Personality & Social Psychology, 82*, 379–398. [14]

Gossett, B., Cuyjet, M., & Cockriel, I. (1998). African Americans' perception of marginality in the campus culture. *College Student Journal, 32*, 22–32. [10]

Gottesman, I. I. (1991). *Schizophrenia genesis: The origins of madness*. New York: W. H. Freeman. [15]

Gottesmann, C. (2000). Hypothesis for the neurophysiology of dreaming. *Sleep Research Online, 3*, 1–4. [4]

Gottfried, A. E., Fleming, J. S., & Gottfried, A. W. (1994). Role of parental motivational practices in children's academic intrinsic motivation and achievement. *Journal of Educational Psychology, 86*, 104–113. [11]

Gottman, J. (with Silver, N.). (1994). *Why marriages succeed or fail and how you can make yours last*. New York: Simon & Schuster. [10, 11]

Gough, H. (1987). *California Psychological Inventory: Administrator's Guide*. Palo Alto: Consulting Psychologists Press. [14]

Gould, E. R., Reeves, A. J., Graziano, M. S. A., & Gross, C. (1999). Neurogenesis in the neocortex of adult primates. *Science, 286*, 548. [2]

Graham, K. S., Simons, J. S., Pratt, K. H., Patterson, K., & Hodges, J. R. (2000). Insights from semantic dementia on the relationship between episodic and semantic memory. *Neuropsychologia, 38*, 313–324. [6]

Graham, S. (1992). "Most of the subjects were white and middle class": Trends in published research on African Americans in selected APA journals, 1970–1989. *American Psychologist, 47*, 629–639. [1]

Grant, B. F., & Dawson, D. A. (1998). Age at onset of alcohol use and its association with *DSM-IV* alcohol abuse and dependence: Results from the National Longitudinal Alcohol Epidemiologic Survey. *Journal of Substance Abuse, 9*, 103–110. [13]

Grant, B. F., Harford, T. C., Chou, P., Pickering, M. S., Dawson, D. A., Stinson, F. S., & Noble, J. (1991). Prevalence of DSM-III-R alcohol abuse and dependence: United States, 1988. *Alcohol Health & Research World, 15*, 91–96. [13]

Greden, J. F. (1994). Introduction Part III. New agents for the treatment of depression. *Journal of Clinical Psychiatry, 55*(2, Suppl.), 32–33. [2, 15]

Greeff, A., & Malherbe, H. (2001). Intimacy and marital satisfaction in spouses. *Journal of Sex & Marital Therapy, 27*, 247–257. [12]

Green, A. R., & Goodwin, G. M. (1996). Ecstasy and neurodegeneration: Ecstasy's long term effects are potentially more damaging than its acute toxicity. *British Medical Journal, 312*, 1493–1494. [4]

Green, B. (2002). Listening to leaders: Feedback on 360-degree feedback one year later. *Organization Development Journal, 20*, 8–16. [18]

Green, B. L., Lindy, J. D., & Grace, M. C. (1985). Post-traumatic stress disorder: Toward DSM-IV. *Journal of Nervous and Mental Disorders, 173*, 406–411. [13]

Green, J., & Shellenberger, R. (1990). *The dynamics of health and wellness: A biopsychosocial approach*. Fort Worth: Holt, Rinehart & Winston. [13]

Green, J. P., & Lynn, S. J. (2000). Hypnosis and suggestion-based approaches to smoking cessation: An examination of the evidence. *International Journal of Clinical Experimental Hypnosis, 48*, 195–224. [4]

Green, J. T., & Woodruff-Pak, D. S. (2000). Eyeblink classical conditioning: Hippocampal formation is for neutral stimulus associations as cerebellum is for association-response. *Psychological Bulletin, 126*, 138–158. [5]

Green, L. R., Richardson, D. R., & Lago, T. (1996). How do friendship, indirect, and direct aggression relate? *Aggressive Behavior, 22*, 81–86. [17]

Green, S. D. (2002). The human resource implications of lean construction: Critical perspectives and conceptual chasms. *Journal of Construction Research, 3*, 147–166. [18]

Greenberg, H. (2001). "Kids and fires are no match": Fire and trauma prevention for teen parents. *Child & Adolescent Social Work Journal, 18*, 223–232. [10]

Greengard, S. (1994, September). Workers go virtual. *Personnel Journal, 73*, 71. [18]

Gregory, R. J. (1996). *Psychological testing: History, principles, and applications* (2nd ed.). Boston: Allyn & Bacon. [8, 14]

Greist, J. H. (1992). An integrated approach to treatment of obsessive compulsive disorder. *Journal of Clinical Psychiatry, 53*(4, Suppl.), 38–41. [16]

Greist, J. H. (1995). The diagnosis of social phobia. *Journal of Clinical Psychiatry, 56*(5, Suppl.), 5–12. [15]

Griffin, M., Patterson, M., & West, M. (2001). Job satisfaction and teamwork: The role of supervisor support. *Journal of Organizational Behavior, 22*, 537–550. [18]

Griffith, R. M., Miyago, O., & Tago, A. (1958). The universality of typical dreams: Japanese vs. Americans. *American Anthropologist, 60*, 1173–1179. [4]

Grigorenko, E. (2003). Epistasis and the genetics of complex traits. In R. Plomin, J. DeFries, I. Craig, & P. McGuffin (Eds.), *Behavioral genetics in the postgenomic era*. (pp. 247–266). Washington, DC: American Psychological Association. [11]

Grigorenko, E., Jarvin, L., & Sternberg, R. (2002). School-based tests of the triarchic theory of intelligence: Three settings, three samples, three syllabi. *Contemporary Educational Psychology, 27*, 167–208. [8]

Grinker, J. A. (1982). Physiological and behavioral basis for human obesity. In D. W. Pfaff (Ed.), *The physiological mechanisms of motivation*. New York: Springer-Verlag. [11]

Grochowicz, P., Schedlowski, M., Husband, A., King, M., Hibberd, A., & Bowen, K. (1991). Behavioral conditioning prolongs heart allograft survival in rats. *Brain, Behavior, and Immunity, 5*, 349–356. [5]

Gron, G., Wunderlich, A. P., Spitzer, M., Tomczrak, R., & Riepe, M. W. (2000). Brain activation during human navigation: Gender-different neural networks as substrate of performance. *Nature Neuroscience, 3*, 404–408. [2]

Gronfier, C., Luthringer, R., Follenius, M., Schaltenbrand, N., Macher, J. P., Muzet, A., & Brandenberger, G. (1996). A quantitative evaluation of the relationships between growth hormone secretion and delta wave electroencephalographic activity during normal sleep and after enrichment in delta waves. *Sleep, 19*, 817–824. [4]

Groome, L., Mooney, D., Holland, S., Smith, L., Atterbury, J., & Dykman, R. (1999). Behavioral state affects heart rate response to low-intensity sound in human fetuses. *Early Human Development, 54*, 39–54. [9]

Gross, J. (2002). Emotion regulation: Affective, cognitive, and social consequences. *Psychophysiology, 39*, 281–291. [11]

Grossman, H. J. (Ed.). (1983). *Manual on terminology and classification in mental retardation*. Washington, DC: American Association on Mental Deficiency. [8]

Grossman, M., & Wood, W. (1993). Sex differences in intensity of emotional experience: A social role interpretation. *Journal of Personality and Social Psychology, 65*, 1010–1022. [11]

Grouios, G., Sakadami, N., Poderi, A., & Alevriadou, A. (1999). Excess of non-right handedness among individuals with intellectual disability: Experimental evidence and possible explanations. *Journal of Intellectual Disability Research, 43*, 306–313. [2]

Guagliardo, M., Huang, A., & D'Angelo, L. (1999). Fathering pregnancies: Marking health-risk behaviors in urban adolescents. *Journal of Adolescent Health, 24*, 10–15. [10]

Guilford, J. P. (1967). *The nature of human intelligence*. New York: McGraw-Hill. [7, 8]

Guilleminault, C. (1993). 1. Amphetamines and narcolepsy: Use of the Stanford database. *Sleep, 16*, 199–201. [4]

Gunn, R. A., Montes, J. M., Toomey, K. E., Rolfs, R. T., Greenspan, J. R., Spitters, C. E., & Waterman, S. H. (1995). Syphilis in San Diego county 1983–1992: Crack cocaine, prostitution, and the limitations of partner notification. *Sexually Transmitted Diseases, 22*, 60–66. [12]

Gupta, D., & Vishwakarma, M. S. (1989). Toy weapons and firecrackers: A source of hearing loss. *Laryngoscope, 99*, 330–334. [3]

Gur, R. E., Cowell, P. E., Latshaw, A., Turetsky, B. I., Grossman, R. I., Amold, S. E., Bilker, W. B., & Gur, R. C. (2000). Reduced dorsal and orbital prefrontal gray matter volumes in schizophrenia. *Archives of General Psychiatry, 57*, 761–768. [15]

Gurin, J. (1989, June). Leaner, not lighter. *Psychology Today*, pp. 32–36. [11]

Gustavson, C. R., Garcia, J., Hankins, W. G., & Rusiniak, K. W. (1974). Coyote predation control by aversive conditioning. *Science, 184*, 581–583. [5]

Guthrie, J. P., Ash, R. A., & Bendapudi, V. (1995). Additional validity evidence for a measure of morningness. *Journal of Applied Psychology, 80*, 186–190. [4]

Guthrie, R. V. (1998). *Even the rat was white* (2nd ed.). Boston: Allyn & Bacon. [1]

Haag, L., & Stern E. (2003). In search of the benefits of learning Latin. *Journal of Educational Psychology, 95*, 174–178. [7]

Habel, U., Kuehn, E., Salloum, J., Devos, H., & Schneider, F. (2002). Emotional processing in psychopathic personality. *Aggressive Behavior, 28*, 394–400. [15]

Haber, R. N. (1980). How we perceive depth from flat pictures. *American Scientist, 68*, 370–380. [6]

Haberlandt, D. (1997). *Cognitive psychology* (2nd ed.). Boston: Allyn & Bacon. [1, 7, 8]

Hackel, L. S., & Ruble, D. N. (1992). Changes in the marital relationship after the first baby is born: Predicting the impact of expectancy disconfirmation. *Journal of Personality and Social Psychology, 62*, 944–957. [10]

Hackman, J., & Oldham, G. (1980). *Work redesign*. Reading, MA: Addison-Wesley. [18]

Hada, M., Porjesz, B., Begleiter, H., & Polich, J. (2000). Auditory P3a assessment of male alcoholics. *Biological Psychiatry, 48*, 276–286. [4, 13]

Hada, M., Porjesz, B., Chorlian, D., Begleiter, H., & Polich, J. (2001). Auditory P3a deficits in male subjects at high risk for alcoholism. *Biological Psychiatry, 49*, 726–738. [4, 13]

Hagberg, M., Hagberg, B., & Saveman, B. (2002). The significance of personality factors for various dimensions of life quality among older people. *Aging & Mental Health, 6*, 178–185. [10]

Hager, W., Leichsenring, F., & Schiffler, A. (2000). When does a study of different therapies allow comparisons of their relative efficacy? *Psychother. Psychosom. Med. Psychol., 50*, 251–262. [16]

Häkkänen, H., & Summala, H. (1999). Sleepiness at work among commercial truck drivers. *Sleep, 23*, 49–57. [4]

Hakuta, K., Bialystok, E., & Wiley, E. (2003). Critical evidence: A test of the critical-period hypothesis for second-language acquisition. *Psychological Science, 14*, 31–38. [7]

Halaas, J. L., Gajiwala, K. S., Maffei, M., Cohen, S. L., Chait, B. T., Rabinowitz, D., Lallone, R. L., Burley, S. K., & Friedman, J. M. (1995). Weight-reducing effects of the plasma protein encoded by the obese gene. *Science, 269*, 543–546. [11]

Halemaskel, B., Dutta, A., & Wutoh, A. (2001). Adverse reactions and interactions among herbal users. *Issues in Interdisciplinary Care, 3*, 297–300. [4]

Halford, G. S. (1989). Reflections on 25 years of Piagetian cognitive developmental psychology, 1963–1988. *Human Development, 32*, 325–327. [9]

Halligan, P. W., & Marshall, J. C. (1994). Toward a principled explanation of unilateral neglect. *Cognitive Neuropsychology, 11*, 167–206. [2]

Halmi, K. A. (1996). Eating disorder research in the past decade. *Annals of the New York Academy of Sciences, 789*, 67–77. [11]

Halpern, C. T., Joyner, K., Udry, J. R., & Suchindran, C. (2000). Smart teens don't have sex (or kiss much either). *Journal of Adolescent Health, 26*, 3213–3225. [8]

Hamann, S., Monarch, E., & Goldstein, F. (2002). Impaired fear conditioning in Alzheimer's disease. *Neuropsychologia, 40*, 1187–1195. [10]

Hamer, D. H., Hu, S., Magnuson, V. L., Hu, N., & Pattatucci, A. M. L. (1993). A linkage between DNA markers on the X chromosome and male sexual orientation. *Science, 261*, 321–327. [12]

Hamilton, C. S., & Swedo, S. E. (2001). Autoimmune-mediated, childhood onset obsessive-compulsive disorder and tics: A review. *Clinical Neuroscience Research, 1*, 61–68. [15]

Hamilton, M. C. (1988). Using masculine generics: Does generic "he" increase male bias in the user's imagery? *Sex Roles, 19*, 785–789. [7]

Hamm, J. V. (2000). Do birds of a feather flock together? The variable bases for African American, Asian American, and European American adolescents' selection of similar friends. *Developmental Psychology, 36*, 209–219. [10]

Hammond, D. C. (1992). Hypnosis with sexual disorders. *American Journal of Preventive Psychiatry & Neurology, 3*, 37–41. [4]

Hanley, N. A., Hagan, D. M., Clement-Jones, M., Ball, S. G., Strachan, T., Salas-Cortés, L., McElreavey, K., Lindsay, S., Robson, S., Bullen, P., Ostre, H., & Wilson, D. I. (2000). *SRY, SOX9*, and *DAX1* expression patterns during human sex determination and gonadal development. *Mechanisms of Development, 91*, 403–407. [12]

Hanley, S., & Abell, S. (2002). Maslow and relatedness: Creating an interpersonal model of self-actualization. *Journal of Humanistic Psychology, 42*, 37–56. [14]

Hannover, B., & Kuehnen, U. (2002). "The clothing makes the self" via knowledge activation. *Journal of Applied Social Psychology, 32*, 2513–2525. [18]

Hansen, C. (2003). Cultural myths in stories about human resource development: Analyzing the cross-cultural transfer of American models to Germany and the Cote d'Ivoire. *International Journal of Training & Development*, 7, 16–30. [18]

Hansenne, M., Pinto, E., Pitchot, W., Reggers, J., Scantamburlo, G., Moor, M., & Ansseau, M. (2002). Further evidence on the relationship between dopamine and novelty seeking: A neuroendocrine study. *Personality & Individual Differences, 33*, 967–977. [14]

Hare, R. D. (1995, September). Psychopaths: New trends in research. *Harvard Mental Health Letter, 12*(3), 4–5. [15]

Harel, G., Arditi-Vogel, A., & Janz, T. (2003). Comparing the validity and utility of behavior description interview versus assessment center ratings. *Journal of Managerial Psychology, 18*, 94–104. [18]

Hargadon, R., Bowers, K. S., & Woody, E. Z. (1995). Does counterpain imagery mediate hypnotic analgesia? *Journal of Abnormal Psychology, 104*, 508–516. [4]

Hariri, A., Mattay, V., Tessitore, A., Kolachana, B., Fera, F., Goldman, D., Egan, M., & Weinberger, D. (2002). Serotonin transporter genetic variation and the response of the human amygdala. *Science, 297*, 400–403. [14]

Harkins, S. G., & Jackson, J. M. (1985). The role of evaluation in eliminating social loafing. *Personality and Social Psychology Bulletin, 11*, 456–465. [17]

Harkins, S. G., & Szymanski, K. (1989). Social loafing and group evaluation. *Journal of Personality and Social Psychology, 56*, 941–943. [17]

Harlow, H. F. (1950). Learning and satiation of response in intrinsically motivated complex puzzle performance by monkeys. *Journal of Comparative and Physiological Psychology, 43*, 289–294. [11]

Harlow, H. F., & Harlow, M. K. (1962). Social deprivation in monkeys. *Scientific American, 207*, 137–146. [9]

Harlow, H. F., Harlow, M. K., and Suomi, S. J. (1971). From thought to therapy: Lessons from a primate laboratory. *American Scientist, 59*, 538–549. [9]

Harlow, J. M. (1848). Passage of an iron rod through the head. *Boston Medical and Surgical Journal, 39*, 389–393. [2]

Harlow, R. E., & Cantor, N. (1996). Still participating after all these years: A study of life task participation in later life. *Journal of Personality and Social Psychology, 71*, 1235–1249. [10]

Harper, D., Stopa, E., McKee, A., Satlin, A., Harlan, P., Goldstein, R., & Volicer, L. (2001). Differential circadian rhythm disturbances in men with Alzheimer disease and frontotemporal degeneration. *Archives of General Psychiatry, 58*, 353–360. [4]

Harris, J. (1998). *The nurture assumption.* New York: Free Press. [10]

Harris, J. A., Rushton, J. P., Hampson, E., & Jackson, D. N. (1996). Salivary testosterone and self-report aggressive and pro-social personality characteristics in men and women. *Aggressive Behavior, 22*, 321–331. [14]

Harris, L. J., & Blaiser, M. J. (1997). Effects of a mnemonic peg system on the recall of daily tasks. *Perceptual and Motor Skills, 84*, 721–722. [6]

Harris, R. A., Brodie, M. S., & Dunwiddie, T. V. (1992). Possible substrates of ethanol reinforcement: GABA and dopamine. *Annals of the New York Academy of Sciences, 654*, 61–69. [4]

Harrison, Y., & Horne, J. A. (2000). Sleep loss and temporal memory. *Journal of Experimental Psychology, 53*, 271–279. [4]

Hart, D., Hofmann, V., Edelstein, W., & Keller, M. (1997). The relation of childhood personality types to adolescent behavior and development: A longitudinal study of Icelandic children. *Developmental Psychology, 33*, 195–205. [9]

Harter, S. (1990). Processes underlying adolescent self-concept formation. In R. Montemayor, G. R. Adams, & T. P. Gullotta (Eds.), *From childhood to adolescence: A transitional period?* (pp. 205–239). Newbury Park, CA: Sage. [14]

Hatashita-Wong, M., Smith, T., Silverstein, S., Hull, J., & Willson, D. (2002). Cognitive functioning and social problem-solving skills in schizophrenia. *Cognitive Neuropsychiatry, 7*, 81–95. [15]

Hattar-Pollara, M., Meleis, A., & Nagib, H. (2003). Multiple role stress and patterns of coping of Egyptian women in clerical jobs. *Journal of Transcultural Nursing, 14*, 125–133. [18]

Hattiangadi, A., & Habib, A. (2000). A closer look at comparable worth. Washington, DC: Employment Policy Foundation. [12, 18]

Hauser, M. D. (1993). Right hemisphere dominance for the production of facial expression in monkeys. *Science, 261*, 475–477. [2]

Hawley, K., & Weisz, J. (2003). Child, parent and therapist (dis)agreement on target problems in outpatient therapy: The therapist's dilemma and its implications. *Journal of Consulting & Clinical Psychology, 71*, 62–70. [16]

Haxby, J., Gobbini, M., Furey, M., Ishai, A., Schouten, J., & Pietrini, P. (2001). Distributed and overlapping representations of faces and objects in ventral temporal cortex. *Science, 293*, 2425–2430. [3]

Haxby, J., Hoffman, E., & Gobbini, M. (2002). Human neural systems for face recognition and social communication. *Biological Psychiatry, 51*, 59–67. [3]

Hay, D. F. (1994). Prosocial development. *Journal of Child Psychology and Psychiatry, 35*, 29–71. [17]

Hayley, W. E., Roth, D. L., Coleton, M. I., Ford, G. R., West, C. A. C., Collins, R. P., & Isobe, T. L. (1996). Appraisal, coping, and social support as mediators of well-being in Black and White family caregivers of patients with Alzheimer's disease. *Journal of Consulting and Clinical Psychology, 64*, 121–129. [10]

Hazlett-Stevens, H., Craske, M., Roy-Byrne, P., Sherbourne, C., Stein, M., & Bystritsky, A. (2002). Predictors of willingness to consider medication and psychosocial treatment for panic disorder in primary care patients. *General Hospital Psychology, 24*, 316–321. [16]

HCF Nutrition Foundation. (2003). *The benefits of fiber*. Retrieved January 29, 2003 from http://www.hcf-nutrition.org/fiber/fiberben_article.html [13]

Heaton, T. (2002). Factors contributing to increasing marital stability in the U.S. *Journal of Family Issues, 23*, 392–409. [10]

Hebb, D. O. (1949). *The organization of behavior.* New York: John Wiley & Sons. [6]

Hecht, S., Shlaer, S., & Pirenne, M. H. (1942). *Journal of General Physiology, 25*, 819. [3]

Hedges, L. B., & Nowell, A. (1995). Sex differences in mental test scores, variability, and numbers of high-scoring individuals. *Science, 269*, 41–45. [12]

Hedley, L. M., Hoffart, A., Dammen, T., Ekeberg, O., & Friis, S. (2000). The relationship between cognitions and panic attack intensity. *Acta Psychiatrica Scandinavica, 102*, 300–302. [15]

Heiman, J. (2002). Psychologic treatments for female sexual dysfunction: Are they effective and do we need them? *Archives of Sexual Behavior, 31*, 445–450. [15]

Held, R. (1993). What can rates of development tell us about underlying mechanisms? In C. E. Granrud (Ed.), *Visual perception and cognition in infancy* (pp. 75–89). Hillsdale, NJ: Erlbaum. [9]

Hellige, J. B. (1990). Hemispheric asymmetry. *Annual Review of Psychology, 41*, 55–80. [2]

Hellige, J. B. (1993). *Hemispheric asymmetry: What's right and what's left.* Cambridge, MA: Harvard University Press. [2]

Hellige, J. B., Bloch, M. I., Cowin, E. L., Eng, T. L., Eviatar, Z., & Sergent, V. (1994). Individual variation in hemispheric asymmetry: Multitask study of effects related to handedness and sex. *Journal of Experimental Psychology: General, 123*, 235–256. [2]

Hendin, H., & Haas, A. P. (1991). Suicide and guilt as manifestations of PTSD in Vietnam combat veterans. *American Journal of Psychiatry, 148*, 586–591. [13]

Hendler, J. (1994). High-performance artificial intelligence. *Science, 265*, 891–892. [7]

Henkel, L. A., Franklin, N., & Johnson, M. K. (2000). Cross-modal source monitoring confusions between perceived and imagined events. *Journal of Experimental Psychology: Learning, Memory, and Cognition, 26*, 321–335. [6]

Henley, N. M. (1989). Molehill or mountain? What we know and don't know about sex bias in language. In M. Crawford & M. Gentry (Eds.), *Gender and thought: Psychological perspectives.* New York: Springer-Verlag. [7]

Hennevin, E., Hars, B., Maho, C., & Bloch, V. (1995). Processing of learned information in paradoxical sleep: Relevance for memory. *Behavioural Brain Research, 69*, 125–135. [4]

Henningfield, J. E., & Ator, N. A. (1986). *Barbiturates: Sleeping potion or intoxicant?* New York: Chelsea House. [4]

Henson, R., Shallice, T., Gorno-Tempini, M., & Dolan, R. (2002). Face repetition effects in implicit and explicit memory as measured by fMRI. *Cerebral Cortex, 12*, 178–186. [6]

Hepper, P. G., Shahidullah, S., & White, R. (1990). Origins of fetal handedness. *Nature, 347*, 431. [2]

Herbert, T. B., & Cohen, S. (1993). Depression and immunity: A meta-analytic review. *Psychological Bulletin, 113*, 472–486. [13]

Herek, G. (2002). Gender gaps in public opinion about lesbians and gay men. *Public Opinion Quarterly, 66*, 40–66. [12]

Herkenham, M. (1992). Cannabinoid receptor localization in brain: Relationship to motor and reward systems. *Annals of the New York Academy of Sciences, 654*, 19–32. [4]

Herman, L. (1981). Cognitive characteristics of dolphins. In L. Herman (Ed.), *Cetacean behavior.* New York: Wiley. [7]

Hernandez, B., Keys, C., & Balcazar, F. (2003). The Americans with Disabilities Act knowledge survey: Strong psychometrics and weak knowledge. *Rehabilitation Psychology, 48*, 93–99. [18]

Hernandez, L., & Hoebel, B. G. (1989). Food intake and lateral hypothalamic self-stimulation covary after medial hypothalamic lesions or ventral midbrain 6-hydroxydopamine injections that cause obesity. *Behavioral Neuroscience, 103*, 412–422. [11]

Hernandez, S., Camacho-Rosales, J., Nieto, A., & Barroso, J. (1997). Cerebral asymmetry and reading performance: Effect of language lateralization and hand preference. *Child Neuropsychology, 3*, 206–225. [2]

Herness, S. (2000). Coding in taste receptor cells: The early years of intracellular recordings. *Physiology and Behavior, 69*, 17–27. [3]

Herrnstein, R. J., & Murray, C. (1994). *The bell curve: Intelligence and class structure in American life.* New York: Free Press. [8]

Hertzog, C. (1991). Aging, information processing speed, and intelligence. In K. W. Schaie & M. P. Lawton (Eds.), *Annual Review of Gerontology and Geriatrics* (Vol. 11, pp. 55–79). [10]

Hetherington, A. W., & Ranson, S. W. (1940). Hypothalamic lesions and adiposity in the rat. *Anatomical Record, 78*, 149–172. [11]

Hetherington, E. M., Stanley-Hagan, M., & Anderson, E. R. (1989). Marital transitions: A child's perspective. *American Psychologist, 44*, 303–312. [10]

Heyman, G., Gee, C., & Giles, J. (2003). Preschool children's reasoning about ability. *Child Development, 74*, 516–534. [8]

Hicks, D., & Gwynne, M. (1966). *Cultural Anthropology.* Boston: Allyn & Bacon. [2]

Higbee, K. L. (1977). *Your memory: How it works and how to improve it.* Englewood Cliffs, NJ: Prentice-Hall. [6]

Higdon, H. (1975). *The crime of the century.* New York: G. P. Putnam's Sons. [14]

Higgins, A. (1995). Educating for justice and community: Lawrence Kohlberg's vision of moral education. In W. M. Kurtines & J. L. Gerwirtz (Eds.), *Moral development: An introduction* (pp. 49–81). Boston: Allyn & Bacon. [10]

Hilgard, E. R. (1975). Hypnosis. *Annual Review of Psychology, 26,* 19–44. [4]

Hilgard, E. R. (1986). *Divided consciousness: Multiple controls in human thought and action.* New York: Wiley. [4]

Hilgard, E. R. (1992). Dissociation and theories of hypnosis. In E. Fromm & M. R. Nash (Eds.), *Contemporary hypnosis research.* New York: Guilford. [4]

Hill, M., & Augoustinos, M. (2001). Stereotype change and prejudice reduction: Short- and long-term evaluation of a cross-cultural awareness programme. *Journal of Community & Applied Social Psychology, 11,* 243–262. [17]

Hillebrand, J. (2000). New perspectives on the manipulation of opiate urges and the assessment of cognitive effort associated with opiate urges. *Addictive Behaviors, 25,* 139–143. [4]

Hindman, J., & Peters, J. (2001). Polygraph testing leads to better understanding of adult and juvenile sex offenders. *Federal Probation, 65,* 8–15. [11]

Hinton, G. E., Dayan, P., Frey, B. J., & Neal, R. M. (1995). The "wake-sleep" algorithm for unsupervised neural networks. *Science, 268,* 1158–1161. [7]

Hipwell, A. E., Goossens, F. A., Melhuish, E. C., & Kumar, R. (2000). Severe maternal psychopathology and infant–mother attachment. *Developmental Psychopathology, 12,* 2157–2175. [9]

Hirsch, J. (1997). Some heat but not enough light. *Nature, 387,* 27–28. [11]

Hirschfeld, M. A. (1995). The impact of health care reform on social phobia. *Journal of Clinical Psychiatry, 56*(5, Suppl.), 13–17. [15]

Hirschman, A. (2001). Lesbian executive: Lucent harassment forced me out. Retrieved June 30, 2003, from http://www.gfn.com [18]

Hittner, J., & Daniels, J. (2002). Gender-role orientation, creative accomplishments, and cognitive styles. *Journal of Creative Behavior, 36,* 62–75. [12]

Hobson, C., & Delunas, L., (2001). National norms and life-event frequencies for the revised Social Readjustment Rating Scale. *International Journal of Stress Management, 8,* 299–314. [13]

Hobson, J. A. (1988). *The dreaming brain.* New York: Basic Books. [4]

Hobson, J. A. (1989). *Sleep.* New York: Scientific American Library. [4]

Hobson, J. A., & McCarley, R. W. (1977). The brain as a dream state generator: An activation-synthesis hypothesis of the dream process. *American Journal of Psychiatry, 134,* 1335–1348. [4]

Hocevar, D., & Bachelor, P. (1989). A taxonomy and critique of measurements used in the study of creativity. In J. A. Glover, R. R. Ronning, & C. R. Reynolds (Eds.), *Handbook of creativity.* New York: Plenum. [8]

Hodges, J. R., Graham, N., & Patterson, K. (1995). Charting the progression in semantic dementia: Implications for the organisation of semantic memory. *Memory, 3,* 463–495. [6]

Hodgins, S., Mednick, S. A., Brennan, P. A., Schulsinger, F., & Engberg, M. (1996). Mental disorder and crime: Evidence from a Danish birth cohort. *Journal of Personality and Social Psychology, 53,* 489–496. [17]

Hoebel, B. G., & Teitelbaum, P. (1966). Weight regulation in normal and hypothalamic hyperphagic rats. *Journal of Comparative and Physiological Psychology, 61,* 189–193. [11]

Hoffman, C., Olson, D., & Haase, S. (2001). Contrasting a 360-degree feedback measure with behaviorally-based assessment tools: An application of generalizability theory. *Psychologist-Manager Journal, 5,* 59–72. [18]

Hofstede, G. (1980). *Culture's consequences: International differences in work-related values.* Beverly Hills, CA: Sage. [14]

Hofstede, G. (1983). Dimensions of national cultures in fifty countries and three regions. In J. Deregowski, S. Dzuirawiec, and R. Annis (Eds.), *Explications in cross-cultural psychology.* Lisse: Swets and Zeitlinger. [14]

Holden, C. (1996). Sex and olfaction. *Science, 273,* 313. [3]

Holland, J. G., & Skinner, B. F. (1961). *The analysis of behavior.* New York: McGraw-Hill. [5]

Holland, J. L. (1973). *Making vocational choices: A theory of careers.* Englewood Cliffs, NJ: Prentice Hall. [18]

Holland, J. L. (1992). *Making vocational choices: A theory of vocational personalities and work environments* (2nd ed.). Odessa, FL: Psychological Assessment Resources. [18]

Holloa, S., These, M., & Marches, J. (2002). Treatment and prevention of depression. *Psychological Science in the Public Interest, 3,* 39–77. [16]

Hollon, S., Thase, M., & Markowitz, J. (2002). Treatment and prevention of depression. *Psychological Science in the Public Interest, 3,* 39–77. [15]

Holmes, T. H., & Masuda, M. (1974). Life change and illness susceptibility. In B. S. Dohrenwend & B. P. Dohrenwend (Eds.), *Stressful life events: Their nature and effects.* New York: Wiley. [13]

Holmes, T. H., & Rahe, R. H. (1967). The social readjustment rating scale. *Journal of Psychosomatic Research, 11,* 213–218. [13]

Holt-Lunstad, J., Uchino, B., Smith, T., Olson-Cerny, C., & Nealey-Moore, J. (2003). Social relationships and ambulatory blood pressure: Structural and qualitative predictors of cardiovascular function during everyday social interactions. *Health Psychology, 22,* 388–397. [13]

Homant, R., & Kennedy, D. (2003). Hostile attribution in perceived justification of workplace aggression. *Psychological Reports, 92,* 185–194. [18]

Hoosain, Z., & Roopnarine, J. L. (1994). African-American fathers' involvement with infants: Relationship to their functioning style, support, education, and income. *Infant Behavior and Development, 17,* 175–184. [9]

Hopkins, W., Dahl, J., & Pilcher, D. (2001). Genetic influence on the expression of hand preferences in chimpanzees (*Pan troglodytes*): Evidence in support of the right-shift theory and developmental instability. *Psychological Science, 12,* 299–303. [2]

Horgan, J. (1995, November). Gay genes, revisited. *Scientific American, 273,* 26. [12]

Horn, J. L. (1982). The theory of fluid and crystallized intelligence in relation to concepts of cognitive psychology and aging in adulthood. In F. I. M. Craik & S. Trehub (Eds.), *Aging and cognitive processes* (pp. 201–238). New York: Plenum Press. [10]

Horn, L. J., & Zahn, L. (2001). From bachelor's degree to work: Major field of study and employment outcomes of 1992–93 bachelor's degree recipients who did not enroll in graduate education by 1997 (NCES 2001–165). Retrieved March 7, 2002, from http://nces.ed.gov/pubs2001/quarterly/spring/q5_2.html [1]

Horne, J. (1992). Annotation: Sleep and its disorders in children. *Journal of Child Psychology and Psychiatry, 33,* 473–487. [4]

Horney, K. (1937). *The neurotic personality of our time.* New York: W. W. Norton. [14]

Horney, K. (1939). *New ways in psychoanalysis.* New York: W. W. Norton. [14]

Horney, K. (1945). *Our inner conflicts.* New York: W. W. Norton. [14]

Horney, K. (1950). *Neurosis and human growth.* New York: W. W. Norton. [14, 15]

Horstmann, G. (2003). What do facial expressions convey: Feeling states, behavioral intentions, or action requests? *Emotion, 3,* 150–166. [11]

Horwath, E., Lish, J. D., Johnson, J., Hornig, C. D., & Weissman, M. M. (1993). Agoraphobia without panic: Clinical reappraisal of an epidemiologic finding. *American Journal of Psychiatry, 150,* 1496–1501. [15]

Horwitz, L. A. (1998). Aromachologists nose out the secret powers of smell. *Insight on the News, 13,* pp. 36–37. [3]

Houlihan, D., Schwartz, C., Miltenberger, R., & Heuton, D. (1993). The rapid treatment of a young man's balloon (noise) phobia using in vivo flooding. *Journal of Behavior Therapy and Experimental Psychiatry, 24,* 233–240. [16]

Hovland, C. I., Lumsdaine, A. A., & Sheffield, F. D. (1949). *Experiments on mass communication.* Princeton, NJ: Princeton University Press. [17]

Howard, A. D., Feighner, S. D., Cully, D. F., Arena, J. P., Liberator, P. A., Rosenblum, C. I., et al. (1996). A receptor in pituitary and hypothalamus that functions in growth hormone release. *Science, 273,* 974–977. [2]

Howard, M. (2002). When does semantic similarity help episodic retrieval? *Journal of Memory & Language, 46,* 85–98. [6]

Hoyenga, K. B., & Hoyenga, K. T. (1993). *Gender-related differences: Origins and outcomes.* Boston: Allyn & Bacon. [12]

Hrushesky, W. J. M. (1994, July/August). Timing is everything. *The Sciences,* pp. 32–37. [4]

Hubel, D. H. (1963). The visual cortex of the brain. *Scientific American, 209,* 54–62. [3]

Hubel, D. H. (1995). *Eye, brain, and vision.* New York: Scientific American Library. [3]

Hubel, D. H., & Wiesel, T. N. (1959). Receptive fields of single neurons in the cat's striate cortex. *Journal of Physiology, 148,* 547–591. [3]

Hubel, D. H., & Wiesel, T. N. (1979). Brain mechanisms of vision. *Scientific American, 241,* 130–144. [3]

Hudson, J. I., Carter, W. P., & Pope, H. G., Jr. (1996). Antidepressant treatment of binge-eating disorder: Research findings and clinical guidelines. *Journal of Clinical Psychiatry, 57*(8, Suppl.), 73–79. [16]

Huesman, L., Moise-Titus, J., Podolski, C., & Eron, L. (2003). Longitudinal relations between children's exposure to television violence and their aggressive and violent behavior in young adulthood. *Developmental Psychology, 39,* 201–221. [5]

Huesmann, L. R., & Moise, J. (1996, June). Media violence: A demonstrated public health threat to children. *Harvard Mental Health Letter, 12*(12), 5–7. [17]

Huff, C. R. (1995). *Convicted but innocent.* Thousand Oaks, CA: Sage. [6]

Hughes, J. R. (1992). Tobacco withdrawal in self-quitters. *Journal of Consulting and Clinical Psychology, 60,* 689–697. [13]

Hugick, L. (1992). Public opinion divided on gay rights. *Gallup Poll Monthly,* No. 321, 2–6. [12]

Hull, C. L. (1943). *Principles of behavior.* New York: Appleton-Century-Crofts. [11]

Hull, M., Fiebich, B. L., Schumann, G., Lieb, K., & Bauer, J. (1999). Anti-inflammatory substances—a new therapeutic option in Alzheimer's disease. *Drug Discovery Today, 4,* 275–282. [10]

Hummer, R. A., Rogers, R. G., Nam, C. B., & Ellison, C. G. (1999). Religious involvement and U.S. adult mortality. *Demography, 36,* 273–285. [13]

Hund-Georgiadis, M., & von Cramon, D. Y. (1999). Motor-learning-related changes in piano players and non-musicians revealed by functional magnetic-resonance sounds. *Experimental Brain Research, 125,* 417–425. [7]

Hunter, J. A., Reid, J. M., Stokell, N. M., & Platow, M. J. (2000). Social attribution, self-esteem, and social identity. *Current Research in Social Psychology, 5,* 97–125. [17]

Hunthausen, J., Truxillo, D., Bauer, T., & Hammer, L. (2003). A field study of frame-of-reference effects on personality test validity. *Journal of Applied Psychology, 88,* 545–551. [18]

Hurvich, L. M., & Jameson, D. (1957). An opponent-process theory of color vision. *Psychological Review, 64,* 384–404. [3]

Huttenlocher, P. (1994). Synaptogenesis, synapse elimination, and neural plasticity in human cerebral cortex. In C. Nelson (Ed.), *The Minnesota symposia on child psychology* (Vol. 27, pp. 35–54). Hillsdale, NJ: Erlbaum.

Hyman, I. E., Jr., Husband, T. H., & Billings, E. J. (1995). False memories of childhood. *Applied Cognitive Psychology, 9,* 181–197. [6]

Hyman, I. E., Jr., & Pentland, J. (1996). The role of mental imagery in the creation of false childhood memories. *Journal of Memory and Language, 35,* 101–117. [6]

Immigration and Naturalization Service. (2002). *2001 statistical yearbook.* Washington DC: Author. [18]

Inglehart, R. (1990). *Culture shift in advanced industrial society.* Princeton, NJ: Princeton University Press. [10]

Insel, T. R. (1990). Phenomenology of obsessive compulsive disorder. *Journal of Clinical Psychiatry, 51*(2, Suppl.), 4–8. [12]

International Food Information Council (IFIC). (1998). *Everything you need to know about caffeine* [Online brochure]. Retrieved October 17, 2003, from http://www.ific.org/publications/brochures/caffeinebroch.cfm [4]

Intons-Peterson, M. J., & Fournier, J. (1986). External and internal memory aids: When and how often do we use them? *Journal of Experimental Psychology: General, 115,* 267–280. [6]

Intons-Peterson, M., & Roskos-Ewoldsen, B. (1989). Sensory-perceptual qualities of images. *Journal of Experimental Psychology: Learning, Memory, and Cognition, 15,* 188–199. [7]

Irwin, M., Mascovich, A., Gillin, C., Willoughby, R., Pike, J., & Smith, T. L. (1994). Partial sleep deprivation reduces natural killer cell activity in humans. *Psychosomatic Medicine, 56,* 493–498. [4]

Isay, R. A. (1989). *Being homosexual: Gay men and their development.* New York: Farrar, Straus, & Giroux. [12]

Isenberg, D. J. (1986). Group polarization: A critical review and meta-analysis. *Journal of Personality and Social Psychology, 50,* 1141–1151. [17]

Ishii, K., Reyes, J., & Kitayama, S. (2003). Spontaneous attention to word content versus emotional tone: Differences among three cultures. *Psychological Science, 14,* 39–46. [11]

Ito, T. A., Miller, N., & Pollock, V. E. (1996). Alcohol and aggression: A meta-analysis on the moderating effects of inhibitory cues, triggering events, and self-focused attention. *Psychological Bulletin, 120,* 60–82. [17]

Izard, C. E. (1971). *The face of emotion.* New York: Appleton-Century-Crofts. [11]

Izard, C. E. (1977). *Human emotions.* New York: Plenum Press. [11]

Izard, C. E. (1990). Facial expressions and the regulation of emotions. *Journal of Personality and Social Psychology, 58,* 487–498. [11]

Izard, C. E. (1992). Basic emotions, relations among emotions, and emotion-cognition relations. *Psychological Review, 99,* 561–565. [11]

Izard, C. E. (1993). Four systems for emotion activation: Cognitive and noncognitive processes. *Psychological Review, 100,* 68–90. [11]

Jacklin, C. N. (1989). Female and male: Issues of gender. *American Psychologist, 44*, 127–133. [12]

Jackson, S. (2002). A study of teachers' perceptions of youth problems. *Journal of Youth Studies, 5*, 313–322. [17]

Jaffee, S., Moffitt, T., Caspi, A., & Taylor, A. (2003). Life with (or without) father: The benefits of living with two biological parents depend on the father's antisocial behavior. *Child Development, 74*, 109–126. [9]

James, W. (1884). What is an emotion? *Mind, 9*, 188–205. [11]

James, W. (1890). *Principles of psychology.* New York: Holt. [1, 11]

Jamieson, D. W., & Zanna, M. P. (1989). Need for structure in attitude formation and expression. In A. R. Pratkanis, S. J. Breckler, & A. G. Greenwald (Eds.), *Attitude structure and function* (pp. 383–406). Hillsdale, NJ: Erlbaum. [17]

Janis, I. L. (1982). *Groupthink: Psychological studies of policy decisions and fiascoes* (2nd ed.). Boston: Houghton Mifflin. [17]

Janssen, T., & Carton, J. (1999). The effects of locus of control and task difficulty on procrastination. *Journal of Genetic Psychology, 160*, 436–442. [14]

Jarrold, C., Butler, D. W., Cottington, E. M., & Jimenez, F. (2000). Linking theory of mind and central coherence bias in autism and in the general population. *Developmental Psychology, 36*, 1126–1138. [9]

Jefferson, J. W. (1995). Social phobia: A pharmacologic treatment overview. *Journal of Clinical Psychiatry, 56*(5, Suppl.), 18–24. [16]

Jefferson, J. W. (1996). Social phobia: Everyone's disorder? *Journal of Clinical Psychiatry, 57*(6, Suppl.), 28–32. [15]

Jefferson, J. W. (1997). Antidepressants in panic disorder. *Journal of Clinical Psychiatry, 58*(2, Suppl.), 20–24. [16]

Jelicic, M., & Bonke, B. (2001). Memory impairments following chronic stress? A critical review. *European Journal of Psychiatry, 15*, 225–232. [6]

Jellinek, E. M. (1960). *The disease concept of alcoholism.* New Brunswick, NJ: Hillhouse Press. [13]

Jenike, M. A. (1990, April). Obsessive-compulsive disorder. *Harvard Medical School Health Letter, 15*, 4–8. [16]

Jenkins, J. H., & Karno, M. (1992). The meaning of expressed emotion: Theoretical issues raised by cross-cultural research. *American Journal of Psychiatry, 149*, 9–21. [16]

Jenkins, J. J., Jimenez-Pabon, E., Shaw, R. E., & Sefer, J. W. (1975). *Schuell's aphasia in adults: Diagnosis, prognosis, and treatment* (2nd ed.). Hagerstown, MD: Harper & Row. [2]

Jensen, A. (1969). How much can we boost IQ and scholastic achievement? *Harvard Educational Review, 39*, 1–123. [8]

Jernigan, T. L., Butters, N., DiTraglia, G., Schafer, K., Smith, T., Irwin, M., Grant, I., Schuckit, M., & Cermak, L. S. (1991). Reduced cerebral grey matter observed in alcoholics using magnetic resonance imaging. *Alcoholism: Clinical and Experimental Research, 15*, 418–427. [13]

Jockin, V., McGue, M., & Lykken, D. T. (1996). Personality and divorce: A genetic analysis. *Journal of Personality and Social Psychology, 71*, 288–299. [14]

Johnson, M. P., Duffy, J. F., Dijk, D-J., Ronda, J. M., Dyal, C. M., & Czeisler, C. A. (1992). Short-term memory, alertness and performance: A reappraisal of their relationship to body temperature. *Journal of Sleep Research, 1*, 24–29. [4]

Johnson, S., Bremner, G., Slater, A., Mason, U., Foster, K., & Cheshire, A. (2003). Infants' perception of object trajectories. *Child Development, 74*, 94–108. [9]

Johnson, S. C. (2000). The recognition of mentalistic agents in infancy. *Trends in Cognitive Sciences, 4*, 22–28. [9]

Johnson, W. G., Tsoh, J. Y., & Varnado, P. J. (1996). Eating disorders: Efficacy of pharmacological and psychological interventions. *Clinical Psychology Review, 16*, 457–478. [11]

Johnson-Laird, P. (2001). Mental models and deduction. *Trends in Cognitive Sciences, 5*, 434–442. [7]

Johnston, L. E., O'Malley, P. M., & Bachman, J. G. (1997). *National survey results on drug use from the Monitoring the Future Study, 1975–1996/97: Vol. 1. Secondary school students.* The University of Michigan Institute for Social Research; National Institute on Drug Abuse, 5600 Fishers Lane, Rockville, MD 20857; USDHHS, Public Health Service, National Institutes of Health. [4]

Johnston, L. E., O'Malley, P. M., & Bachman, J. G. (2001). *Monitoring the Future national results on adolescent drug use: Overview of key findings, 2000* (NIH Publication No. 01-4923). Rockville MD: National Institute on Drug Abuse. [1, 4]

Johnston, L. E., O'Malley, P. M., & Bachman, J. G. (2002). *Monitoring the Future national survey results on drug use, 1975–2001. Volume I: Secondary school students* (NIH Publication No. 02–5106). Bethesda, MD: National Institute on Drug Abuse. [4]

Jolicoeur, D., Richter, K., Ahgluwalia, J., Mosier, M., & Resnicow, K. (2003). Smoking cessation, smoking reduction, and delayed quitting among smokers given nicotine patches and a self-help pamphlet. *Substance Abuse, 24*, 101–106. [4]

Jonas, J. M., & Cohon, M. S. (1993). A comparison of the safety and efficacy of alprazolam versus other agents in the treatment of anxiety, panic, and depression: A review of the literature. *Journal of Clinical Psychiatry, 54* (10, Suppl.), 25–45. [16]

Jones, E. E. (1976). How do people perceive the causes of behavior? *American Scientist, 64*, 300–305. [17]

Jones, E. E. (1990). *Interpersonal perception.* New York: Freeman. [17]

Jones, E. E., & Nisbett, R. E. (1971). *The actor and the observer: Divergent perceptions of the causes of behavior.* New York: General Learning. [17]

Jones, H. E., Herning, R. I., Cadet, J. L., & Griffiths, R. R. (2000). Caffeine withdrawal increases cerebral blood flow velocity and alters quantitative electroencephalography (EEG) activity. *Psychopharmacology, 147*, 371–377. [4]

Jones, M. C. (1924). A laboratory study of fear: The case of Peter. *Pedagogical Seminary, 31*, 308–315. [5]

Jorgensen, M., & Keiding, N. (1991). Estimation of spermarche from longitudinal spermaturia data. *Biometrics, 47*, 177–193. [10]

Joseph, R. (2000). Fetal brain behavior and cognitive development. *Developmental Review, 20*, 81–98. [9]

Josephs, R., Newman, M., Brown, R., & Beer, J. (2003). Status, testosterone, and human intellectual performance. *Psychological Science, 14*, 158–163. [12]

Joyce, P., Mulder, R., Luty, S., McKenzie, J., Sullivan, P., & Cloninger, R. (2003). Borderline personality disorder in major depression: Symptomatology, temperament, character, differential drug response, and 6-month outcome. *Comprehensive Psychiatry, 44*, 35–43. [15]

Judd, L. L., Akiskal, H. S., Zeller, P. J., Paulus, M., Leon, A. C., Maser, J. D., Endicott, J., Coryell, W., Kunovac, J. L., Mueller, T. I., Rice, J. P., & Keller, M. B. (2000). Psychosocial disability during the long-term course of unipolar major depressive disorder. *Archives of General Psychiatry, 57*, 375–380. [15]

Juengling, F., Schmahl, C., Heblinger, B., Ebert, D., Bremner, J., Gostomzyk, J., Bohus, M., & Lieb, K. (2003). Positron emission tomography in female patients with borderline personality disorder. *Journal of Psychiatric Research, 37*, 109–115. [2]

Juliano, S. L. (1998). Mapping the sensory mosaic. *Science, 279*, 1653–1654. [2]

Julien, R. M. (1995). *A primer of drug action* (7th ed.). New York: W.H. Freeman. [4]

Jung, C. G. (1933). *Modern man in search of a soul.* New York: Harcourt Brace Jovanovich. [14]

Jung, C. G. (1953). *The psychology of the unconscious* (R. F. C. Hull, Trans.), *Collected works* (Vol. 7). Princeton, NJ: Princeton University Press. (Original work published 1917). [14]

Jung, C. G. (1961). *Memories, dreams, reflections* (R. Winston & C. Winston, Trans.). New York: Random House. [14]

Jung, C. G. (1966). *Two essays on analytical psychology* (R. F. C. Hull, Trans.). Princeton, NJ: Princeton University Press. [14]

Kagan, J. (2003). Foreward: A behavioral science perspective. In R. Plomin, J. DeFries, I. Craig, & P. McGuffin (Eds.), *Behavioral genetics in the postgenomic era* (pp. xvii–xxiii). Washington, DC: American Psychological Association. [14]

Kagitcibasi, C. (1992). A critical appraisal of individualism-collectivism: Toward a new formulation. In U. Kim, H. C. Triandis, and G. Yoon (Eds.), *Individualism and collectivism: Theoretical and methodological issues.* Newbury Park, CA: Sage. [14]

Kahn, S., Alvi, S., Shaukat, N., Hussain, M., & Baig, T. (1990). A study of the validity of Holland's theory in a non-Western culture. *Journal of Vocational Behavior, 36*, 132–146. [18]

Kahneman, D., & Tversky, A. (1984). Choices, values, and frames. *American Psychologist, 39*, 341–350. [7]

Kail, R. (2000). Speed of information processing: Developmental change and links to intelligence. *Journal of School Psychology, 38*, 51–61. [9]

Kail, R., & Hall, L. (1999). Sources of developmental change in children's word-problem performance. *Journal of Educational Psychology, 91*, 660–668. [8]

Kaiser Family Foundation. (1999, October). Race, ethnicity, & medical care: A survey of public perceptions and experiences. Retrieved November 26, 2003, from http://www.kff.org/content/1999/19901014a/chartpack.pdf [17]

Kalb, C. (1997, August 25). Our embattled ears: Hearing loss once seemed a normal part of aging, but experts now agree that much of it is preventable. How to protect yourself. *Newsweek, 130*, 75–76. [3]

Kalichman, S., Benotsch, E., Weinhardt, L., Austin, J., Webster, L., & Chauncey, C. (2003). Health-related Interent use, coping, social support, and health indicators in people living with HIV/AIDS: Preliminary results from a community survey. *Health Psychology*, *22*, 111–116. [13]

Kalidini, S., & McGuffin, P. (2003). The genetics of affective disorders: Present and future. In R. Plomin, J. Defries, I. Craig, & P. McGuffin (Eds.), *Behavioral genetics in the postgenomic era* (pp. 481–502). Washington, DC: American Psychological Association. [15]

Kalish, H. I. (1981). *From behavioral science to behavior modification.* New York: McGraw-Hill. [5, 16]

Kaltiala-Heino, R., Rimpelae, M., Rissanen, A., & Rantanen, P. (2001). Early puberty and early sexual activity are associated with bulimic-type eating pathology in middle adolescence. *Journal of Adolescent Health, 28*, 346–352. [10]

Kamin, L. J. (1995). Behind the curve [Review of *The Bell Curve: Intelligence and class structure in American life*]. *Scientific American*, *272*, 99–103. [8]

Kampman, M., Keijsers, G., Hoogduin, C., & Hendriks, G. (2002). A randomized, double-blind, placebo-controlled study of the effects of adjunctive paroxetine in panic disorder patients unsuccessfully treated with cognitive-behavioral therapy alone. *Journal of Clinical Psychiatry*, *63*, 772–777. [15]

Kanaya, Y., Nakamura, C., and Miyake, D. (1989). Cross-cultural study of expressive behavior of mothers in response to their five-month-old infants' different emotion expression. *Research and Clinical Center for Child Development Annual Report*, *11*, 25–31. [11]

Kandel, D. B., & Davies, M. (1996). High school students who use crack and other drugs. *Archives of General Psychiatry, 53*, 71–80. [4]

Kane, H., & Oakland, T. (2000). Secular declines in Spearman's *g*: Some evidence from the United States. *Journal of Genetic Psychology*, *161*, 337–345. [8]

Kane, J. M. (1996). Treatment-resistant schizophrenic patients. *Journal of Clinical Psychiatry*, *57*(9, Suppl.), 35–40. [16]

Kanner, A. D., Coyne, J. C., Schaefer, C., & Lazarus, R. S. (1981). Comparison of two modes of stress measurement: Daily hassles and uplifts versus major life events. *Journal of Behavioral Medicine*, *4*, 1–39. [13]

Kaplan, G. A., Wilson, T. W., Cohen, R. D., Kauhanen, J., Wu, M., & Salomen, J. T. (1994). Social functioning and overall mortality: Prospective evidence from the Kuopio Ischemic Heart Disease Risk Factor Study. *Epidemiology, 5*, 495–500. [13]

Kaplan, H. S. (1974). *The new sex therapy: Active treatment of sexual dysfunction.* New York: Brunner/Mazel. [12]

Karacan, I. (1988). Parasomnias. In R. L. Williams, I. Karacan, & C. A. Moore (Eds.), *Sleep disorders: Diagnosis and treatment* (pp. 131–144). New York: John Wiley. [4]

Karau, S. J., & Williams, K. D. (1993). Social loafing; a meta-analytic review and theoretical integration. *Journal of Personality and Social Psychology, 65*, 681–706. [17]

Kark, R., Shamir, B., & Chen, G. (2003). The two faces of transformational leadership: Empowerment and dependency. *Journal of Applied Psychology, 88*, 246–255. [18]

Karni, A., Tanne, D., Rubenstein, B. S., Askenasy, J. J. M., & Sagi, D. (1994). Dependence on REM sleep of overnight improvement of a perceptual skill. *Science, 265*, 679–682. [4]

Kasch, F. W., Boyer, J. L., Schmidt, P. K., Wells, R. H., Wallace, J. P., Verity, L. S., Guy, H., & Schneider, D. (1999). Ageing of the cardiovascular system during 33 years of aerobic exercise. *Age and Ageing, 28*, 531–536. [10]

Kashihara, K., Takahashi, K., & Shohmori, T. (1999). Circadian rhythm sleep disorder associated with pontine lesion. *European Journal of Neurology, 6*, 99–102. [4]

Kastenbaum, R. (1992). *The psychology of death.* New York: Springer-Verlag. [10]

Katon, W. (1996). Panic disorder: Relationship to high medical utilization, unexplained physical symptoms, and medical costs. *Journal of Clinical Psychiatry, 57*(10, Suppl.), 11–18. [15]

Katz, E., Robles-Sotelo, E., Correia, C., Silverman, K., Stitzer, M., & Bigelow, G. (2002). The brief abstinence test: Effects of continued incentive availability on cocaine abstinence. *Experimental & Clinical Psychopharmacology, 10*, 10–17. [5]

Katz, G., Durst, R., & Knobler, H. (2001). Exogenous melatonin, jet lag, and psychosis: Preliminary case results. *Journal of Clinical Psychopharmacology, 21*, 349–351. [4]

Katz, G., Knobler, H., Laibel, Z., Strauss, Z., & Durst, R. (2002). Time zone change and major psychiatric morbidity: The results of a 6-year study in Jerusalem. *Comprehensive Psychiatry, 43*, 37–40. [4]

Katzell, R. A., & Thompson, D. E. (1990). Work motivation: Theory and practice. *American Psychologist, 45*, 144–153. [11]

Katzenberg, D., Young, T., Finn, L., Lin, L., King, D. P., Takahishi, J. S., & Mignot, E. (1998). A CLOCK polymorphism associated with human diurnal preference. *Sleep, 21*, 569. [4]

Kaut, K., Bunsey, M., & Riccio, D. (2003). Olfactory learning and memory impairments following lesions to the hippocampus and perirhinal-entorhinal cortex. *Behavioral Neuroscience, 117*, 304–319. [3]

Kawachi, I., Colditz, G. A., Speizer, F. E., Manson, J. E., Stampfer, M. J., Willett, W. C., & Hennekens, C. H. (1997). A prospective study of passive smoking and coronary heart disease. *Circulation, 95,* 2374–2379. [13]

Kawanishi, Y., Tachikawa, H., & Suzuki, T. (2000). Pharmacogenomics and schizophrenia. *European Journal of Pharmacology, 410,* 227–241. [16]

Kay, S. A. (1997). PAS, present, and future: Clues to the origins of circadian clocks. *Science, 276,* 753–754. [4]

Kazdin, A., & Benjet, C. (2003). Spanking children: Evidence and issues. *Current Directions in Psychological Science, 12,* 99–103. [16]

Keating, C. R. (1994). World without words: Messages from face and body. In W. J. Lonner & R. Malpass (Eds.), *Psychology and culture* (pp. 175–182). Boston: Allyn & Bacon. [11]

Keefauver, S. P., & Guilleminault, C. (1994). Sleep terrors and sleepwalking. In M. Kryger, T. Roth, & W. C. Dement (Eds.), *Principles and practice of sleep medicine* (pp. 567–573). Philadelphia: W.B. Saunders. [4]

Keesey, R. E. (1988). The body-weight set point. What can you tell your patients? *Postgraduate Medicine, 83,* 114–118, 121–122, 127. [11]

Keesey, R. E., & Powley, T. L. (1986). The regulation of body weight. *Annual Review of Psychology, 37,* 109–133. [11]

Keitner, G. I., Ryan, C. E., Miller, I. W., & Norman, W. H. (1992). Recovery and major depression: Factors associated with twelve-month outcome. *American Journal of Psychiatry, 149,* 93–99. [15]

Keller, H., Schlomerich, A., & Eibl-Eibesfeldt, I. (1988). Communication patterns in adult-infant interactions in western and non-western cultures. *Journal of Cross-Cultural Psychology, 19,* 427–445. [11]

Kelly, J. J., Davis, P. G., & Henschke, P. N. (2000). The drug epidemic: Effects on newborn infants and health resource consumption at a tertiary perinatal centre. *Journal of Paediatric Child Health, 36,* 262–264. [9]

Kelner, K. L. (1997). Seeing the synapse. *Science, 276,* 547. [2]

Kendall-Tackett, K. A., Williams, L. M., & Finkehor, D. (1993). Impact of sexual abuse on children: A review and synthesis of recent empirical studies. *Psychological Bulletin, 113,* 164–180. [12]

Kendler, K. S., & Diehl, S. R. (1993). The genetics of schizophrenia: A current genetic-epidemiologic perspective. *Schizophrenia Bulletin, 19,* 261–285. [15]

Kendler, K. S., Gardner, C. O., & Prescott, C. A. (1997). Religion, psychopathology, and substance use and abuse: A multimeasure, genetic-epidemiologic study. *American Journal of Psychiatry, 154,* 322–329. [4]

Kendler, K. S., MacLean, C., Neale, M., Kessler, R., Heath, A., & Eaves, L. (1991). The genetic epidemiology of bulimia nervosa. *American Journal of Psychiatry, 148,* 1627–1637. [11]

Kendler, K. S., Neale, M. C., Kessler, R. C., Heath, A. C., & Eaves, L. J. (1992). The genetic epidemiology of phobias in women. *Archives of General Psychiatry, 49,* 273–281. [15]

Kendler, K. S., Neale, M. C., Kessler, R. C., Heath, A. C., & Eaves, L. J. (1993). The lifetime history of major depression in women: Reliability of diagnosis and heritability. *Archives of General Psychiatry, 50,* 863–870. [15]

Kennedy, C. (2002). Effects of REM sleep deprivation on a multiple schedule of appetitive reinforcement. *Behavioural Brain Research, 128,* 205–214. [4]

Kensinger, E., Brierley, B., Medford, N., Growdon, J., & Corkin, S. (2002). Effects of normal aging and Alzheimer's disease on emotional memory. *Emotion, 2,* 118–134. [10]

Kessler, R. C., McGonagle, K. A., Zhao, S., Nelson, C. B., Hughes, M., Eshleman, S., Wittchen, H-U., & Kendler, K. S. (1994). Lifetime and 12-month prevalence of *DSM-III-R* psychiatric disorders in the United States: Results from the National Comorbidity Survey. *American Journal of Psychiatry, 51,* 8–19. [15]

Kessler, R. C., Stein, M. B., & Berglund, P. (1998). Social phobia subtypes in the National Comorbidity Survey. *American Journal of Psychiatry, 155,* 613–619. [15]

Kickul, J., Lester, S., & Finkl, J. (2002). Promise breaking during radical organizational change. *Journal of Organizational Behavior, 23,* 469–488. [11]

Kiecolt-Glaser, J. K., Fisher, L. D., Ogrocki, P., Stout, J., Speicher, C. E., & Glaser, R. (1987). Marital quality, marital disruption, and immune function. *Psychosomatic Medicine, 49,* 13–34. [13]

Kiecolt-Glaser, J. K., Glaser, R., Gravenstein, S., Malarkey, W. B., & Sheridan, J. (1996). Chronic stress alters the immune response to influenza virus vaccine in older adults. *Proceedings of the National Academy of Science, 93,* 3043–3047. [13]

Kiecolt-Glaser, J., McGuire, L., Robles, T., & Glaser, R. (2002). Psychoneuroimmunology: Psychological influences on immune function and health. *Journal of Consulting and Clinical Psychology, 70* , 537–547. [13]

Kihlstrom, J. F. (1985). Hypnosis. *Annual Review of Psychology, 26,* 557–591. [4]

Kihlstrom, J. F. (1986). Strong inferences about hypnosis. *Behavioral and Brain Sciences, 9,* 474–475. [4]

Kihlstrom, J. F. (1995). The trauma-memory argument. *Consciousness and Cognition, 4,* 65–67. [6]

Kihlstrom, J. F., & Barnhardt, T. M. (1993). The self-regulation of memory: For better and for worse, with and without hypnosis. In D. M. Wegner & J. W. Pennebaker (Eds.), *Handbook of mental control.* Englewood Cliffs, NJ: Prentice Hall. [4]

Kilbride, J. E., & Kilbride, P. L. (1975). Sitting and smiling behavior of Baganda infants. *Journal of Cross-Cultural Psychology, 6,* 88–107. [9]

Kilpatrick, D., Ruggiero, K., Acierno, R., Saunders, B., Resnick, H., & Best, C. (2003). Violence and risk of PTSD, major depression, substance abuse/dependence, and comorbidity: Results from the National Survey of Adolescents. *Journal of Consulting and Clinical Psychology, 71,* 692–700. [13]

Kim, J. J., Mohamed, S., Andreasen, N. C., O'Leary, D. S., Watkins, L., Ponto, L. L. B., & Hichwa, R. D. (2000). Regional neural dysfunctions in chronic schizophrenia studied with positron emission tomography. *American Journal of Psychiatry, 157,* 542–548. [15]

Kim, K. H. S., Relkin, N. R., Lee, K-M., & Hirsch, J. (1997). Distinct cortical areas associated with native and second languages. *Nature, 388,* 171–174. [7]

Kim, S-G., Ugurbil, K., & Strick, P. L. (1994). Activation of a cerebellar output nucleus during cognitive processing. *Science, 265,* 949–951. [2]

Kimura, D. (1992). Sex differences in the brain. *Scientific American, 267,* 118–125. [12]

Kimura, D. (2000). *Sex and cognition.* Cambridge, MA: MIT Press. [12]

King, L. A., Walker, L. M., & Broyles, S. J. (1996). Creativity and the five-factor model. *Journal of Research on Personality, 30,* 189–203. [14]

Kingsbury, S. J. (1993). Brief hypnotic treatment of repetitive nightmares. *American Journal of Clinical Hypnosis, 35,* 161–169. [4]

Kington, R. S., & Smith, J. P. (1997). Socioeconomic status and racial and ethnic differences in functional status associated with chronic diseases. *American Journal of Public Health, 87,* 805–810. [13]

Kinney, A., Croyle, R., Bailey, C., Pelias, M., & Neuhausen, S. (2001). Knowledge, attitudes, and interest in breast-ovarian cancer gene testing: A survey of a large African American kindred with a BRCA1 mutation. *Journal of Genetic Counseling, 10,* 41–51. [2]

Kinney, T. (2003). Themes and perceptions of written sexually harassing messages and their link to distress. *Journal of Language & Social Psychology, 22,* 8–28. [18]

Kinnunen, T., Zamansky, H. S., & Block, M. L. (1994). Is the hypnotized subject lying? *Journal of Abnormal Psychology, 103,* 184–191. [4]

Kinomura, S., Larsson, J., Gulyás, B., & Roland, P. E. (1996). Activation by attention of the human reticular formation and thalamic intralaminar nuclei. *Science, 271,* 512–515. [2]

Kinsey, A. C., Pomeroy, W. B., & Martin, C. E. (1948). *Sexual behavior in the human male.* Philadelphia: W. B. Saunders. [12]

Kinsey, A. C., Pomeroy, W. B., Martin, C. E., & Gebhard, P. H. (1953). *Sexual behavior in the human female.* Philadelphia: W. B. Saunders. [12]

Kirchner, T., & Sayette, M. (2003). Effects of alcohol on controlled and automatic memory processes. *Experimental & Clinical Psychopharmacology, 11,* 167–175. [4]

Kirkcaldy, B., Shephard, R., & Furnham, A. (2002). The influence of Type A behavior and locus of control upon job satisfaction and occupational health. *Personality & Individual Differences, 33,* 1361–1371. [14]

Kirsch, I., & Lynn, S. J. (1995). The altered state of hypnosis: Changes in the theoretical landscape. *American Psychologist, 50,* 846–858. [4]

Kirveskari, E., Partinen, M., & Santavuouri, P. (2001). Sleep and its disturbance in a variant form of late infantile neuronal ceroid lipofuscinosis (CLN5). *Journal of Child Neurology, 16,* 707–713. [4]

Kisilevsky, B., Hains, S., Lee, K., Xie, X., Huang, H., Ye, H., Zhang, K., & Wang, A. (2003). Effects of experience on fetal voice recognition. *Psychological Science, 14,* 220–224. [9]

Kitayama, S., & Markus, H. R. (2000). The pursuit of happiness and the realization of sympathy: Cultural patterns of self, social relations, and well-being. In E. Diener & E. M. Suh (Eds.), *Subjective well-being across cultures.* Cambridge, MA: MIT Press. [14]

Kite, M. E., Deaux, K., & Miele, M. (1991). Stereotypes of young and old: Does age outweigh gender? *Psychology and Aging, 6,* 19–27. [17]

Kiyatkin, E., & Wise, R. (2002). Brain and body hyperthermia associated with heroin self-administration in rats. *Journal of Neuroscience, 22,* 1072–1080. [4]

Klaczynski, P., Fauth, J., & Swanger, A. (1998). Adolescent identity: Rational vs. experiential processing, formal operations, and critical thinking beliefs. *Journal of Youth & Adolescence, 27,* 185–207. [10]

Klahr, D. (1992). Information-processing approaches to cognitive development. In M. H. Bornstein & M. E. Lamb (Eds.), *Developmental psychology: An advanced textbook,* 3rd ed. (pp. 273–335). Hillsdale, NJ: Erlbaum. [9]

Klatzky, R. L. (1980). *Human memory: Structures and processes* (2nd ed.). New York: W. H. Freeman. [6]

Klatzky, R. L. (1984). *Memory and awareness: An information-processing perspective.* New York: W. H. Freeman. [6]

Kleinman, A., & Cohen, A. (1997, March). Psychiatry's global challenge. *Scientific American, 276,* 86–89. [16]

Kleinmuntz, B., & Szucko, J. J. (1984). A field study of the fallibility of polygraph lie detection. *Nature, 308,* 449–450. [11]

Klerman, G. L., Weissman, M. N., Rounsaville, B. J., & Chevron, E. S. (1984). *Interpersonal therapy of depression.* New York: Academic Press. [16]

Kliegman, R. (1998). Fetal and neonatal medicine. In R. Behrman & R. Kliegman (Eds.), *Nelson essentials of pediatrics* (3rd ed., pp. 167–225). Philadelphia: W. B. Saunders. [9]

Klinnert, M. D., Campos, J. J., Sorce, J. F., Emde, R. N., & Suejda, M. (1983). Emotions as behavior regulators: Social referencing in infancy. In R. Plutchik & H. Kellerman (Eds.), *Emotions in early development:* Vol. 2: *The emotions* (pp. 57–86). New York: Academic Press. [11]

Kluft, R. P. (1984). An introduction to multiple personality disorder. *Psychiatric Annals, 14,* 19–24. [15]

Kluft, R. P. (1992). Hypnosis with multiple personality disorder. *American Journal of Preventative Psychiatry & Neurology, 3,* 19–27. [4]

Knight, R. T. (1996). Contribution of human hippocampal region to novelty detection. *Nature, 383,* 256–259. [2]

Knisely, J. S., Barker, S. B., Ingersoll, K. S., & Dawson, K. S. (2000). Psychopathology in substance abusing women reporting childhood sexual abuse. *Journal of Addictive Diseases, 19,* 31–44. [4]

Knowles, E. S., & Condon, C. A. (2000). Does the rose still smell as sweet? Item variability across test forms and revisions. *Psychological Assessment, 12,* 245–252. [8]

Kobasa, S. (1979). Stressful life events, personality, and health: An inquiry into hardiness. *Journal of Personality and Social Psychology, 37,* 1–11. [13]

Kobasa, S. C., Maddi, S. R., & Kahn, S. (1982). Hardiness and health: A prospective study. *Journal of Personality and Social Psychology, 42,* 168–177. [13]

Kochanska, G. (1993). Toward a synthesis of parental socialization and child temperament in early development of conscience. *Child Development, 64,* 325–347. [17]

Kochavi, D., Davis, J., & Smith, G. (2001). Corticotropin-releasing factor decreases meal size by decreasing cluster number in Koletsky (LA/N) rats with and without a null mutation of the leptin receptor. *Physiology & Behavior, 74,* 645–651. [11]

Koehler, T., Tiede, G., & Thoens, M. (2002). Long and short-term forgetting of word associations: An experimental study of the Freudian concepts of resistance and repression. *Zeitschrift fuer Klinische Psychologie, Psychiatrie und Psychotherapie, 50,* 328–333. [14]

Koenig, J. A., & Leger, K. F. (1997). A comparison of retest performance and test-preparation methods for MCAT examinees grouped by gender and race-ethnicity. *Academic Medicine, 72,* S100–S102. [8]

Kohlberg, L. (1966). A cognitive-developmental analysis of children's sex-role concepts and attitudes. In E. E. Maccoby (Ed.), *The development of sex differences* (pp. 82–173). Stanford, CA: Stanford University Press. [12]

Kohlberg, L. (1968, September). The child as a moral philosopher. *Psychology Today,* pp. 24–30. [10]

Kohlberg, L. (1969). *Stages in the development of moral thought and action.* New York: Holt, Rinehart & Winston. [10]

Kohlberg, L. (1981). *Essays on moral development,* Vol. 1. *The philosophy of moral development.* New York: Harper & Row. [10]

Kohlberg, L. (1984). *Essays on moral development,* Vol. 2. *The psychology of moral development.* San Francisco: Harper & Row. [10]

Kohlberg, L. (1985). *The psychology of moral development.* San Francisco: Harper & Row. [10]

Kohlberg, L., & Ullian, D. Z. (1974). In R. C. Friedman, R. M. Richart, & R. L. Vande Wiele (Eds.), *Sex differences in behavior* (pp. 209–222). New York: Wiley. [12]

Köhler, W. (1925). *The mentality of apes* (E. Winter, Trans.). New York: Harcourt Brace Jovanovich. [5]

Koivisto, M., & Revensuo, A. (2000). Semantic priming by pictures and words in the cerebral hemispheres. *Cognitive Brain Research, 10,* 91–98. [6]

Koltz, C. (1983, December). Scapegoating. *Psychology Today,* pp. 68–69. [17]

Kon, M. A., & Plaskota, L. (2000). Information complexity of neural networks. *Neural Networks, 13,* 365–375. [6]

König, P., & Verschure, F. (2002). Neurons in action. *Science, 296,* 1817–1818. [7]

Konishi, M. (1993). Listening with two ears. *Scientific American, 268,* 66–73. [3]

Kopinska, A., & Harris, L. (2003). Spatial representation in body coordinates: Evidence from errors in remembering positions of visual and auditory targets after active eye, head, and body movements. *Canadian Journal of Experimental Psychology, 57,* 23–37. [3]

Kopp, C. P., & Kaler, S. R. (1989). Risk in infancy: Origins and implications. *American Psychologist, 44,* 224–230. [9]

Kosslyn, S. M. (1975). Information representation in visual images. *Cognitive Psychology,* 7, 341–370. [7]

Kosslyn, S. M. (1988). Aspects of a cognitive neuroscience of mental imagery. *Science, 240,* 1621–1626. [7]

Kosslyn, S. M., Alpert, N. M., Thompson, W. L., Malijkovic, V., Weise, S. B., Chabris, C. F., Hamilton, S. E., Rauch, S. L., & Buoanno, F. S. (1993). Visual mental imagery activates topographically organized visual cortex: PET investigations. *Journal of Cognitive Neuroscience, 5,* 263–287. [7]

Kosslyn, S. M., & Sussman, A. L. (1995). Roles of imagery in perception: Or, there is no such thing as immaculate perception. In M. S. Gazzaniga (Ed.), *The cognitive neurosciences.* Cambridge, MA: MIT Press. [7]

Koutsky, L. A., et al. (1992). A cohort study of the risk of cervical intraepithelial neoplasia Grade 2 or 3 in relation to papillomavirus infection. *New England Journal of Medicine, 327,* 1272. [12]

Kovacs, D., Mahon, J., & Palmer, R. (2002). Chewing and spitting out food among eating-disordered patients. *International Journal of Eating Disorders, 32,* 112–115. [11]

Kowatch, R., Suppes, T., Carmody, T., Bucci, J., Hume, J., Kromelis, M., Emslie, G., Weinberg, W., & Rush, A. (2000). Effect size of lithium, divalproex sodium, and carbamazepine in children and adolescents with bipolar disorder. *Journal of the American Academy of Child & Adolescent Psychiatry, 39,* 713–720. [16]

Kozak, M. J., Foa, E. B., & McCarthy, P. R. (1988). Obsessive-compulsive disorder. In C. G. Last & M. Herson (Eds.), *Handbook of anxiety disorders* (pp. 87–108). New York: Pergamon Press. [15]

Krantz, D. S., Grunberg, N. E., & Baum, A. (1985). Health psychology. *Annual Review of Psychology, 36,* 349–383. [13]

Krantz, M. (1987). Physical attractiveness and popularity: A predictive study. *Psychological Reports, 60,* 723–726. [9]

Kranzler, H. R. (1996). Evaluation and treatment of anxiety symptoms and disorders in alcoholics. *Journal of Clinical Psychiatry, 57*(6, Suppl.). [15]

Krasowska, F. (1996, February). Software, sites can subdue strain. *Occupational Health and Safety, 65,* 20. [18]

Kraus, S. J. (1995). Attitudes and the prediction of behavior: A meta-analysis of the empirical literature. *Personality and Social Psychology Bulletin, 21,* 58–75. [17]

Krcmar, M., & Cooke, M. (2001). Children's moral reasoning and their perceptions of television violence. *Journal of Communication, 51,* 300–316. [5]

Kripke, D., Garfinkel, L., Wingard, D., Klauber, M., & Marler, M. (2002). Mortality associated with sleep duration. *Archives of General Psychiatry, 59,* 131–136. [4]

Kroll, N. E. A., Ogawa, K. H., & Nieters, J. E. (1988). Eyewitness memory and the importance of sequential information. *Bulletin of the Psychonomic Society, 26,* 395–398. [6]

Kropyvnytskyy, I., Saunders, F., Pols, M., & Sarowski, C. (2001). Circadian rhythm of temperature in head injury. *Brain Injury, 15,* 511–518. [4]

Krosigk, M. von. (1993). Cellular mechanisms of a synchronized oscillation in the thalamus. *Science, 261,* 361–364. [2]

Krueger, J. M., & Takahashi, S. (1997). Thermoregulation and sleep: Closely linked but separable. *Annals of the New York Academy of Sciences, 813,* 281–286. [4]

Krueger, W. C. F. (1929). The effect of overlearning on retention. *Journal of Experimental Psychology, 12,* 71–81. [6]

Krumm, D. (2001). *Psychology at work: An introduction to industrial/organizational psychology.* New York: Worth. [18]

Krysan, M., & Farley, R. (2002). The residential preferences of blacks: Do they explain persistent segregation? *Social Forces, 80,* 937–980. [18]

Kübler-Ross, E. (1969). *On death and dying.* New York: Macmillan. [10]

Kucharska-Pietura, K., & Klimkowski, M. (2002). Perception of facial affect in chronic schizophrenia and right brain damage. *Acta Neurobiologiae Experimentalis, 62,* 33–43. [2]

Kuhn, D. (1992). Thinking as argument. *Harvard Educational Review, 62,* 155–178. [9]

Kuhn, D., & Lao, J. (1996). Effects of evidence on attitudes: Is polarization the norm? *Psychological Science,* 7, 115–120. [17]

Kukla, A. (1972). Foundations of an attributional theory of performance. *Psychological Review, 79,* 454–470. [11]

Kumar, R., O'Malley, P., Johnston, L., Schulenberg, J., & Bachman, J. (2002). Effects of school-level norms on student substance abuse. *Prevention Science, 3,* 105–124. [17]

Kummervold, P., Gammon, D., Bergvik, S., Johnsen, J., Hasvold, T., & Rosenvinge, J. (2002). Social support in a wired world: Use of online mental health forums in Norway. *Nordic Journal of Psychiatry, 56,* 59–65. [13]

Kumpfer, K., Alvarado, R., Smith, P., & Ballamy, N. (2002). Cultural sensitivity and adaptation in family-based prevention interventions. *Prevention Science, 3,* 241–246. [16]

Kunda, Z., & Oleson, K. C. (1995). Maintaining stereotypes in the face of disconfirmation: Construction grounds for subtyping deviants. *Journal of Personality and Social Psychology, 68,* 565–579. [17]

Kunz, D., & Herrmann, W. M. (2000). Sleep-wake cycle, sleep-related disturbances, and sleep disorders: A chronobiological approach. *Comparative Psychology, 41*(2, Suppl. 1), 104–105. [4]

Kupersmidt, J. B., & Coie, J. D. (1990). Preadolescent peer status, aggression, and school adjustment as predictors of externalizing problems in adolescence. *Child Development, 61,* 1350–1362. [9]

Kupersmidt, J. B., Coie, J. D., & Dodge, K. A. (1990). Predicting disorder from peer social problems. In S. R. Asher & J. D. Coie (Eds.), *Peer rejection in childhood.* New York: Cambridge University Press. [9]

Kuroda, K. (2002). An image retrieval system by impression words and specific object names-IRIS. *Neurocomputing: An International Journal, 43,* 259–276. [7]

Kurup, R., & Kurup, P. (2002). Detection of endogenous lithium in neuropsychiatric disorders. *Human Psychopharmacology Clinical & Experimental, 17,* 29–33. [1, 2]

Lack, S., Kumar, V., & Arevalo, S. (2003). Fantasy proneness, creative capacity, and styles of creativity. *Perceptual & Motor Skills, 96,* 19–24. [8]

Lafuente, M., Grifol, R., Segarra, J., Soriano, J., Gorba, M., & Montesinos, A. (1997). Effects of the Firstart method of prenatal stimulation on psychomotor development: The first six months. *Pre- & Peri-Natal Psychology Journal, 13,* 317–326. [9]

Laird, R., Pettit, G., Bates, J., & Dodge, K. (2003). Parents' monitoring-relevant knowledge and adolescents' delinquent behavior: Evidence of correlated developmental changes and reciprocal influences. *Child Development, 74,* 752–768. [10]

Lal, S. (2002). Giving children security: Mamie Phipps Clark and the racialization of child psychology. *American Psychologist, 57,* 20–28. [1]

Lalonde, R., & Botez, M. I. (1990). The cerebellum and learning processes in animals. *Brain Research Reviews, 15,* 325–332. [2]

Lam, L., & Kirby, S. (2002). Is emotional intelligence an advantage? An exploration of the impact of emotional and general intelligence on individual performance. *Journal of Social Psychology, 142,* 133–143. [8]

Lambe, E. K., Katzman, D. K., Mikulis, D. J., Kennedy, S. H., & Zipursky, R. B. (1997). Cerebral gray matter volume deficits after weight recovery from anorexia nervosa. *Archives of General Psychiatry, 54,* 537–542. [11]

Lamberg, L. (1996). Narcolepsy researchers barking up the right tree. *Journal of the American Medical Association, 276,* 265–266. [4]

Lambert, M. (2003). Suicide risk assessment and management: Focus on personality disorders. *Current Opinion in Psychiatry, 16,* 71–76. [15]

Lamborn, S. D., Mounts, N. S., Steinberg, L., & Dornbusch, S. M. (1991). Patterns of competence and adjustment among adolescents from authoritative, authoritarian, indulgent, and neglectful families. *Child Development, 62,* 1049–1065. [9, 10]

Lamm, H. (1988). A review of our research on group polarization: Eleven experiments on the effects of group discussion on risk acceptance, probability estimation, and negotiation positions. *Psychological Reports, 62,* 807–813. [17]

Landis, C. A., Savage, M. V., Lentz, M. J., & Brengelmann, G. L. (1998). Sleep deprivation alters body temperature dynamics to mild cooling and heating, not sweating threshold in women. *Sleep, 21,* 101–108. [4]

Landry, D. W. (1997, February). Immunotherapy for cocaine addiction. *Scientific American, 276,* 42–45. [4]

Landstad, B., Vinberg, S., Ivergard, T., Gelin, G., & Ekholm, J. (2001). Change in pattern of absenteeism as a result of workplace intervention for personnel support. *Ergonomics, 44,* 63–81. [18]

Lang, A., Craske, M., Brown, M., & Ghaneian, A. (2001). Fear-related state dependent memory. *Cognition & Emotion, 15,* 695–703. [6]

Lang, A. R., Goeckner, D. J., Adesso, V. J., & Marlatt, G. A. (1975). Effects of alcohol on aggression in male social drinkers. *Journal of Abnormal Psychology, 84,* 508–518. [1]

Lange, C. G., & James, W. (1922). *The emotions* (I. A. Haupt, Trans.). Baltimore: Williams and Wilkins. [11]

Langer, E. J., & Rodin, J. (1976). The effects of choice and enhanced personal responsibility for the aged: A field experiment in an institutional setting. *Journal of Personality and Social Psychology, 34,* 191–198. [13]

Langevin, B., Sukkar, F., Léger, P., Guez, A., & Robert, D. (1992). Sleep apnea syndromes (SAS) of specific etiology: Review and incidence from a sleep laboratory. *Sleep, 15,* S25–S32. [4]

Langlois, J. H. (1985). From the eye of the beholder to behavioral reality: The development of social behaviors and social relations as a function of physical attractiveness. In C. P. Herman (Ed.), *Physical appearance, stigma, and social behavior.* Hillsdale, NJ: Erlbaum. [9]

Langlois, J. H., Kalakanis, L., Rubenstein, A. J., Larson, A., Hallam, M., & Smoot, M. (2000). Maxims or myths of beauty? A meta-analytic and theoretical review. *Psychological Bulletin, 126,* 390–423. [17]

Langlois, J. H., & Roggman, L. A. (1990). Attractive faces are only average. *Psychological Science, 1,* 115–121. [17]

Lanza, S., & Collins, L. (2002). Pubertal timing and the onset of substance use in females during early adolescence. *Prevention Science, 3,* 69–82. [10]

Lara, M. E., Leader, J., & Klein, D. N. (1997). The association between social support and course of depression: Is it confounded with personality? *Journal of Abnormal Psychology, 106,* 478–482. [13]

Larson, R., & Verma, S. (1999). How children and adolescents spend time across the world: Work, play, and developmental opportunities. *Psychological Bulletin, 125,* 701–736. [8]

Latané, B., Williams, K., & Harkins, S. (1979). Many hands make light the work: The causes and consequences of social loafing. *Journal of Personality and Social Psychology, 37,* 822–832. [17]

Lattal, K. A., & Neef, N. A. (1996). Recent reinforcement-schedule research and applied behavior analysis. *Journal of Applied Behavior Analysis, 29,* 213–230. [5]

Laumann, E. O., Gagnon, J. H., Michael, R. T., & Michaels, S. (1994). *The social organization of sexuality.* Chicago: University of Chicago Press. [12]

Laurent, J., Swerdik, M., & Ryburn, M. (1992). Review of validity research on the Stanford-Binet Intelligence Scale: Fourth Edition. *Psychological Assessment, 4,* 102–112. [8]

Lavie, P., Herer, P., Peled, R., Berger, I., Yoffe, N., Zomer, J., & Rubin, A-H. (1995). Mortality in sleep apnea patients: A multivariate analysis of risk factors. *Sleep, 18,* 149–157. [4]

Lawrence, J., Boxer, P., & Tarakeshwar, N. (2002). Determining demand for EAP services. *Employee Assistance Quarterly, 18,* 1–15. [18]

Layton, L., Deeny, K., Tall, G., & Upton, G. (1996). Researching and promoting phonological awareness in the nursery class. *Journal of Research in Reading, 19,* 1–13. [9]

Lazar, T. A. (2000). Sexual differentiation of the brain. Akira Matsumoto (Ed.). *Trends in Neurosciences, 23,* 507. [12]

Lazarus, R. S. (1966). *Psychological stress and the coping process.* New York: McGraw-Hill. [13]

Lazarus, R. S. (1984). On the primacy of cognition. *American Psychologist, 39,* 124–129. [11]

Lazarus, R. S. (1991a). Cognition and motivation in emotion. *American Psychologist, 46,* 352–367. [11]

Lazarus, R. S. (1991b). Progress on a cognitive-motivational-relational theory of emotion. *American Psychologist, 46,* 819–834. [11]

Lazarus, R. S. (1995). Vexing research problems inherent in cognitive-mediational theories of emotion—and some solutions. *Psychological Inquiry, 6,* 183–187. [11]

Lazarus, R. S., & DeLongis, A. (1983). Psychological stress and coping in aging. *American Psychologist, 38,* 245–253. [13]

Lazarus, R. S., & Folkman, S. (1984). *Stress, appraisal, and coping.* New York: Springer. [13]

Lebow, J. L., & Gurman, A. S. (1995). Research assessing couple and family therapy. *Annual Review of Psychology, 46,* 27–57. [16]

LeBreton, J., Burgess, J., Kaiser, R., Atchley, E., & James, L. (2003). The restriction of variance hypothesis and interrater reliability and agreement: Are ratings from multiple sources really dissimilar? *Organizational Research Methods, 6,* 80–128. [18]

Lecomte, T., & Lecomte, C. (2002). Toward uncovering robust principles of change inherent to cognitive-behavioral therapy for psychosis. *American Journal of Orthopsychiatry, 72,* 50–57. [16]

LeDoux, J. E. (1994). Emotion, memory, and the brain. *Scientific American, 270,* 50–57. [2]

LeDoux, J. E. (1995). Emotion: clues from the brain. *Annual Review of Psychology, 46,* 209–235. [2]

LeDoux, J. E. (1996). *The emotional brain: The mysterious underpinnings of emotional life.* New York: Simon & Schuster. [11]

LeDoux, J. E. (2000). Emotion circuits in the brain. *Annual Review of Neuroscience, 23,* 155–184. [2, 11]

Lee, I., & Kesner, R. (2002). Differential contribution of NMDA receptors in hippocampal subregions to spatial working memory. *Nature Neuroscience, 5,* 162–168. [6]

Lehman, D., & Nisbett, R. (1990). A longitudinal study of the effects of undergraduate training on reasoning. *Developmental Psychology, 26,* 952–960. [10]

Leichtman, M. D., & Ceci, S. J. (1995). The effects of stereotypes and suggestions on preschoolers' reports. *Developmental Psychology, 31,* 568–578. [6]

Leigh, B. C., & Stall, R. (1993). Substance use and risky sexual behavior for exposure to HIV: Issues in methodology, interpretation, and prevention. *American Psychologist, 48,* 1035–1045. [12]

Leitenberg, H., & Henning, K. (1995). Sexual fantasy. *Psychological Bulletin, 117,* 469–496. [4, 9]

Leland, J. (1997, Spring/Summer). The magnetic tube. *Newsweek* [Special Edition], pp. 89–90. [9]

Lenneberg, E. (1967). *Biological foundations of language.* New York: Wiley. [9]

Lent, R., Brown, S., Nota, L., & Soresi, S. (2003). Testing social cognitive interest and choice hypotheses across Holland types in Italian high school students. *Journal of Vocational Behavior, 62,* 101–118. [18]

Leon, M. (1992). The neurobiology of filial learning. *Annual Review of Psychology, 43,* 337–398. [9]

Leong, F., Austin, J., Sekaran, U., & Komarraju, M. (1998). An evaluation of the cross-cultural validity of Holland's theory: Career choices by workers in India. *Journal of Vocational Behavior, 52,* 441–455. [18]

Lerman, D. C., & Iwata, B. A. (1996). Developing a technology for the use of operant extinction in clinical settings: An examination of basic and applied research. *Journal of Applied Behavior Analysis, 29,* 345–382. [16]

Lerman, D. C., Iwata, B. A., Shore, B. A., & Kahng, S. W. (1996). Responding maintained by intermittent reinforcement: Implications for the use of extinction with problem behavior in clinical settings. *Journal of Applied Behavior Analysis, 29,* 153–171. [5]

Lerner, J., Gonzalez, R., Small, D., & Fischoff, B. (2003). Effects of fear and anger on perceived risks of terrorism: A national field experiment. *Psychological Science, 14,* 144–150. [11]

Lesch, K. (2003). Neuroticism and serotonin: A developmental genetic perspective. In R. Plomin, J. DeFries, I. Craig, & P. McGuffin (Eds.), *Behavioral genetics in the postgenomic era* (pp. 389–423). Washington, DC: American Psychological Association. [14, 15]

Leshowitz, B., Eignor DiCerbo, K., & Okun, M. (2002). Effects of instruction in methodological reasoning on information evaluation. *Teaching of Psychology, 29,* 5–10. [7]

Leuchter, A., Cook, I., Witte, E., Morgan, M., & Abrams, M. (2002). Changes in brain function of depressed subjects during treatment with placebo. *American Journal of Psychiatry, 159,* 122–129. [16]

Leung, F. (2002). Behind the high achievement of East Asian students. *Educational Research & Evaluation, 8,* 87–108. [8]

Levandowski, D. (2001). Adolescent fatherhood: Reviewing the international literature. *Estudos de Psicologia, 6,* 195–209. [10]

LeVay, S. (1991). A difference in hypothalamic structure between heterosexual and homosexual men. *Science, 253,* 1034–1037. [12]

LeVay, S. (1993). *The sexual brain.* Cambridge, MA: MIT Press. [12]

LeVay, S., & Hamer, D. H. (1994). Evidence for a biological influence in male homosexuality. *Scientific American, 270,* 44–49. [12]

Levenson, R. W. (1992). Autonomic nervous system differences among emotions. *Psychological Science, 3,* 23–27. [11]

Levenson, R. W., Ekman, P., & Friesen, W. (1990). Voluntary facial action generates emotion-specific autonomic nervous system activity. *Psychophysiology, 27,* 363–385. [11]

Leventhal, T., & Brooks-Gunn, J. (2003). Children and youth in neighborhood contexts. *Current Directions in Psychological Science, 12,* 27–31. [8]

Levine, W. C., Berg, A. O., Johnson, R. E., Rolfs, R. T., Stone, K. M., Hook, E. W., III, Handsfield, H. H., Holmes, K. K., Islam, M. Q., Piot, P., Brady, W. E., Schmid, G. P., and STD Treatment Guidelines Project Team and consultants. (1994). Development of sexually transmitted diseases treatment guidelines, 1993: New methods, recommendations, and research priorities. *Sexually Transmitted Diseases, 21*(2, Suppl.), S96–S101. [12]

Levitt, E. E., & Duckworth, J. C. (1984). Minnesota Multiphasic Personality Inventory. In D. J. Keyser & R. C. Sweetland (Eds.), *Test critiques* (Vol. 1, pp. 466–472). Kansas City: Test Corporation of America. [14]

Levy, J. (1985, May). Right brain, left brain: Fact and fiction. *Psychology Today,* pp. 38–44. [2]

Levy-Shiff, R., Lerman, M., Har-Even, D., & Hod, M. (2002). Maternal adjustment and infant outcome in medically defined high-risk pregnancy. *Developmental Psychology, 38,* 93–103. [8]

Lewin, C., & Herlitz, A. (2002). Sex differences in face recognition: Women's faces make the difference. *Brain & Cognition, 50,* 121–128. [12]

Lewinsohn, P. M., & Rosenbaum, M. (1987). Recall of parental behavior by acute depressives, remitted depressives, and nondepressives. *Journal of Personality and Social Psychology, 52,* 611–619. [6]

Lewis, A., & Sherman, S. (2003). Hiring you makes me look bad: Social-identity based reversals of the ingroup favoritism effect. *Organizational Behavior & Human Decision Processes, 90,* 262–276. [18]

Lewis, D. O., Pincus, J. H., Feldman, M., Jackson, L., & Bard, B. (1986). Psychiatric, neurological, and psychoeducational characteristics of 15 death row inmates in the United States. *American Journal of Psychiatry, 143,* 838–845. [17]

Lewis, M. (1995, January/February). Self-conscious emotions. *American Scientist, 83,* 68–78. [11]

Leyens, J-P., Yzerbyt, V., & Olivier, C. (1996). The role of applicability in the emergence of the overattribution bias. *Journal of Personality and Social Psychology, 70,* 219–229. [17]

Li, J. (2003). U.S. and Chinese cultural beliefs about learning. *Journal of Educational Psychology, 95,* 258–267. [8]

Lidz, C., & Macrine, S. (2001). An alternative approach to the identification of gifted culturally and linguistically diverse learners: The contribution of dynamic assessment. *School Psychology International, 22,* 74–96. [8]

Lieblum, S. (2002). After sildenafil: Bridging the gap between pharmacologic treatment and satisfying sexual relationships. *Journal of Clinical Psychiatry, 63,* 17–22. [15]

Liepert, J., Terborg, C., & Weiller, C. (1999). Motor plasticity induced by synchronized thumb and foot movements. *Experimental Brain Research, 125,* 435–439. [2]

Lievens, F., Harris, M., Van Keer, E., & Bisqueret, C. (2003). Predicting cross-cultural training performance: The validity of personality, cognitive ability, and dimensions measured by an assessment center and a behavioral description interview. *Journal of Applied Psychology, 88*, 476–489. [18]

Liff, S., & Ward, K. (2001). Distorted views through the glass ceiling: The construction of women's understandings of promotion and senior management positions. *Gender, Work & Organization, 8*, 19–36. [18]

Lijtmaer, R. (2001). Splitting and nostalgia in recent immigrants: Psychodynamic considerations. *Journal of the American Academy of Psychoanalysis, 29*, 427–438. [16]

Lim, V. (2002). The IT way of loafing on the job: Cyberloafing, neutralizing and organizational justice. *Journal of Organizational Behavior, 23*, 675–694. [17]

Lindenberger, U., Mayr, U., & Kliegl, R. (1993). Speed and intelligence in old age. *Psychology and Aging, 8*, 207–220. [10]

Linn, R. L. (1982). Ability testing: Individual differences, prediction, and differential prediction. In A. K. Wigdor & W. R. Garner (Eds.), *Ability testing: Uses, consequences, and controversies* (Part II). Washington, DC: National Academy Press. [8]

Linszen, D. H., Dingemans, P. M., Nugter, M. A., Van der Does, J. W., Scholte, W. F., & Lenior, M. A. (1997). Patient attributes and expressed emotion as risk factors for psychotic relapse. *Schizophrenia Bulletin, 23*, 119–130. [16]

Linton, M. (1979, July). I remember it well. *Psychology Today*, pp. 80–86. [6]

Linville, P. W., Fischer, G. W., & Salovey, P. (1989). Perceived distributions of the characteristics of in-group and out-group members: Empirical evidence and a computer simulation. *Journal of Personality and Social Psychology, 57*, 165–188. [17]

Lipsitt, L. P. (1990). Learning processes in the human newborn: Sensitization, habituation, and classical conditioning. *Annals of the New York Academy of Sciences, 608*, 113–123. [9]

Lishman, W. A. (1990). Alcohol and the brain. *British Journal of Psychiatry, 156*, 635–644. [13]

Little, J., McFarlane, J., & Ducharme, H. (2002). ECT use delayed in the presence of comorbid mental retardation: A review of clinical and ethical issues. *Journal of ECT, 18*, 218–222. [16]

Lizza, E. F., & Cricco-Lizza, R. (1990, October). Impotence—Finding the cause. *Medical Aspects of Human Sexuality, 24*, 30–40. [12]

Locke, E. A., & Latham, G. P. (1990). *A theory of goal setting and task performance.* Englewood Cliffs, NJ: Prentice-Hall. [11]

Loeber, R., & Hay, D. (1997). Key issues in the development of aggression and violence from childhood to early adulthood. *Annual Review of Psychology, 48*, 371–410. [17]

Loehlin, J. C. (1992). *The limits of family influence: Genes, experience, and behavior.* New York: Guilford. [14]

Loehlin, J. C., Horn, J. M., & Willerman, L. (1990). Heredity, environment, and personality change: Evidence from the Texas Adoption Project. *Journal of Personality, 58*, 221–243. [14]

Loehlin, J. C., Lindzey, G., & Spuhler, J. N. (1975). *Race differences in intelligence.* San Francisco: Freeman. [8]

Loehlin, J. C., Vandenberg, S., & Osborne, R. (1973). Blood group genes and Negro-White ability differences. *Behavior Genetics, 3*, 263–270. [8]

Loehlin, J. C., Willerman, L., & Horn, J. M. (1987). Personality resemblance in adoptive families: A 10-year follow-up. *Journal of Personality and Social Psychology, 53*, 961–969. [14]

Loehlin, J. C., Willerman, L., & Horn, J. M. (1988). Human behavior genetics. *Annual Review of Psychology, 39*, 101–133. [8, 14, 15]

Loftus, E. F. (1979). *Eyewitness testimony*. Cambridge, MA: Harvard University Press. [6]

Loftus, E. F. (1984, February). Eyewitnesses: Essential but unreliable. *Psychology Today*, pp. 22–27. [6]

Loftus, E. F. (1993a). Psychologists in the eyewitness world. *American Psychologist, 48*, 550–552. [6]

Loftus, E. F. (1993b). The reality of repressed memories. *American Psychologist, 48*, 518–537. [6]

Loftus, E. F. (1997). Creating false memories. *Scientific American, 277*, 71–75. [6]

Loftus, E. F., & Hoffman, H. G. (1989). Misinformation and memory: The creation of new memories. *Journal of Experimental Psychology: General, 118*, 100–104. [6]

Loftus, E. F., & Loftus, G. R. (1980). On the permanence of stored information in the human brain. *American Psychologist, 35*, 409–420. [6]

Loftus, E. F., & Pickrell, J. (1995). The formation of false memories. *Psychiatric Annals, 25*, 720–725. [6]

London, E. D., Ernst, M., Grant, S., Bonson, K., & Weinstein, A. (2000). Orbitofrontal cortex and human drug abuse: Functional imaging. *Cerebral Cortex, 10*, 334–342. [4, 5]

Long, D., & Baynes, K. (2002). Discourse representation in the two cerebral hemispheres. *Journal of Cognitive Neuroscience, 14*, 228–242. [2]

Long, G. M., & Crambert, R. F. (1990). The nature and basis of age-related changes in dynamic visual acuity. *Psychology and Aging, 5*, 138–143. [10]

Lott, B., & Saxon, S. (2002). The influence of ethnicity, social class and context on judgments about U.S. women. *Journal of Social Psychology, 142*, 481–499. [17]

Lotze, M., Montoya, P., Erb, M., Hulsmann, E., Flor, H., Klose, U., Birbaumer, N., & Grodd, W. (1999). Activation of cortical and cerebellar motor areas during executed and imagined hand movements: An fMRI study. *Journal of Cognitive Neuroscience, 11*, 491–501. [7]

Louderback, L. A., & Whitley, B. E., Jr. (1997). Perceived erotic value of homosexuality and sex-role attitudes as mediators of sex differences in heterosexual college students' attitudes toward lesbians and gay men. *Journal of Sex Research, 34*, 175–182. [12]

Lovett, S. B., & Flavell, J. H. (1990). Understanding and remembering: Children's knowledge about the differential effects of strategy and task variables on comprehension and memorization. *Child Development, 61*, 1842–1858. [9]

Lovoy, L. (2001). A historical survey of the glass ceiling and the double bind faced by women in the workplace: Options for avoidance. *Law & Psychology Review, 25*, 179–203. [18]

Lowell, B. B., & Spiegelman, B. M. (2000). Towards a molecular understanding of adaptive thermogenesis. *Nature, 404*, 652–660. [11]

Lubart, T. (2003). In search of creative intelligence. In R. Sternberg, J. Lautrey, & T. Lubart (Eds.), *Models of intelligence: International perspective* (pp. 279–292). Washington, DC: American Psychological Association. [8]

Lubman, D. I., Peters, L. A., Mogg, K., Bradley, B. P., & Deakin, J. F. (2000). Attentional bias for drug cues in opiate dependence. *Psychological Medicine, 30*, 169–175. [4]

Lucas, J., & Heady, R. (2002). Flextime commuters and their driver stress, feelings of time urgency, and commute satisfaction. *Journal of Business & Psychology, 16*, 565–572. [18]

Luchins, A. S. (1957). Experimental attempts to minimize the impact of first impressions. In C. I. Hovland (Ed.), *Yale studies in attitude and communication: Vol. 1. The order of presentation in persuasion* (pp. 62–75). New Haven, CT: Yale University Press. [17]

Luciano, M., Wright, M., Smith, G., Geffen, G., Geffen, L., & Margin, N. (2001). Genetic covariance among measures of information processing speed, working memory, and IQ. *Behavior Genetics, 31*, 581–592. [8]

Luciano, M., Wright, M., Smith, G., Geffen, G., Geffen, L., & Martin, N. (2003). Genetic covariance between processing speed and IQ. In R. Plomin, J. DeFries, I. Craig, & P. McGuffin (Eds.), *Behavioral genetics in the postgenomic era* (pp. 163–182). Washington, DC: American Psychological Association. [8]

Lucio, E., Reyes-Lagunes, I., & Scott, R. L. (1994). MMPI-2 for Mexico: Translation and adaptation. *Journal of Personality Assessment, 63*, 105–116. [14]

Lundgren, C. B. (1986, August 20). Cocaine addiction: A revolutionary new treatment. *St. Louis Jewish Light*, p. 7. [4]

Lundy, J. (2002). Age and language skills of deaf children in relation to theory of mind development. *Journal of Deaf Studies & Deaf Education*, 7, 41–56. [9]

Lurie, I., & Riccucci, N. (2003). Changing the "culture" welfare offices: From vision to the front lines. *Administration & Society, 34*, 653–677. [18]

Lustig, C., & Hasher, L. (2002). Working memory span: The effect of prior learning. *American Journal of Psychology, 115*, 89–101. [6]

Lutchmaya, S., Baron-Cohen, S., & Raggatt, P. (2002). Foetal testosterone and vocabulary size in 18- and 24-month-old infants. *Infant Behavior & Development, 24*, 418–424. [12]

Lydiard, R. B., Brawman-Mintzer, O., & Ballenger, J. C. (1996). Recent developments in the psychopharmacology of anxiety disorders. *Journal of Consulting and Clinical Psychology, 64*, 660–668. [16]

Lykken, D. T. (1981). *A tremor in the blood: Uses and abuses of the lie detector.* New York: McGraw-Hill. [11]

Lykken, D. T. (1985). The probity of the polygraph. In S. M. Kassin & L. S. Wrightsman (Eds.), *The psychology of evidence and trial procedure.* Beverly Hills, CA: Sage. [11]

Lykken, D. T., Bouchard, T. J., Jr., McGue, M., & Tellegen, A. (1993). Heritability of interests: A twin study. *Journal of Applied Psychology, 78*, 649–661. [14, 17]

Lykken, D., & Tellegen, A. (1996). Happiness is a stochastic phenomenon. *Psychological Science*, 7, 186–189. [14]

Lynch, E. B., Coley, J. D., & Medin, D. L. (2000). Tall is typical: Central tendency, ideal dimensions, and graded category structure among tree experts and novices. *Memory and Cognition, 28*, 41–50. [7]

Lynn, S. J., Kirsch, I., Barabasz, A., Cardena, E., & Patterson, D. (2000). Hypnosis as an empirically supported clinical intervention: The state of the evidence and a look to the future. *International Journal of Clinical Experimental Hypnosis, 48*, 239–259. [4]

Lynn, S. J., & Nash, M. R. (1994). Truth in memory: Ramifications for psychotherapy and hypnotherapy. *American Journal of Clinical Hypnosis, 36*, 194–208. [4]

Lyon, M., Cline, J., Totosy de Zepetnek, J., Jie Shan, J., Pang, P., & Benishin, C. (2001). Effect of the herbal extract combination *Panax quinquefolium* and *Ginko biloba* on attention-deficit hyperactivity disorder: A pilot study. *Journal of Psychiatry & Neuroscience. 26*, 221–228. [4]

Lyons, E. (2002). Psychosocial factors related to job stress and women in management. *Work: Journal of Prevention, Assessment & Rehabilitation, 18*, 89–93. [18]

Lyvers, M. (2000). "Loss of control" in alcoholism and drug addiction: A neuroscientific interpretation. *Experimental and Clinical Psychopharmacology, 8*, 225–245. [4]

Lyvers, M. (2000). Cognition, emotion, and the alcohol–aggression relationship: Comment on Giancola. *Experimental Clinical Psychopharmacology, 8*, 612–617. [17]

Maccoby, E. E. (1992). The role of parents in the socialization of children: An historical overview. *Developmental Psychology, 28*, 1006–1017. [9]

Maccoby, E. E., & Martin, J. A. (1983). Socialization in the context of the family: Parent-child interaction. In P. H. Mussen (Ed.), *Handbook of child psychology* (4th ed., Vol. 4). New York: John Wiley. [9]

MacDonald, A., Pogue-Geile, M., Johnson, M., & Carter, C. (2003). A specific deficit in context processing in the unaffected siblings of patients with schizophrenia. *Archives of General Psychiatry, 60*, 57–65. [15]

Macey, P., Henderson, L., Macey, K., Alger, J., Frysinger, R., Woo, M., Harper, R., Yan-Go, F., & Harper, R. (2002). Brain morphology associated with obstructive sleep apnea. *American Journal of Respiratory and Critical Care Medicine, 166*, 1382–1387. [4]

Mack, A., & Rock, I. (1998). *Inattentional blindness.* Cambridge, MA: MIT Press. [3]

Macrae, C. N., Milne, A. B., & Bodenhausen, G. V. (1994). Stereotypes as energy-saving devices: A peek inside the cognitive toolbox. *Journal of Personality and Social Psychology, 66*, 37–47. [17]

Madey, S., Simo, M., Dillworth, D., Kemper, D., Toczynski, A., & Perella, A. (1996). They do get more attractive at closing time, but only when you are not in a relationship. *Basic & Applied Social Psychology, 18*, 387–393. [12]

Magee, J. C., & Johnston, D. (1997). A synaptically controlled, associative signal for Hebbian plasticity in hippocampal neurons. *Science, 275*, 209–213. [2]

Maguire, E. A., Gadian, D. G., Johnsrude, I. S., Good, C. D., Ashburner, J., Frackowiak, R. S. J., & Frith, C. D. (2000). Navigation-related structural change in the hippocampi of taxi drivers. *Proceedings of the National Academy of Science, 97*, 4398–4403. [2, 6]

Mahler, H., Kulik, J., Gibbons, F., Gerrard, M., & Harrell, J. (2003). Effects of appearance-based intervention on sun protection intentions and self-reported behaviors. *Health Psychology, 22*, 199–209. [13]

Maiden, R., Peterson, S., Caya, M., & Hayslip, B. (2003). Personality changes in the old-old: A longitudinal study. *Journal of Adult Development, 10*, 31–39. [14]

Maier, S. F., & Laudenslager, M. (1985, August). Stress and health: Exploring the links. *Psychology Today*, pp. 44–49. [13]

Main, M., & Solomon, J. (1990). Procedures for identifying infants as disorganized/disoriented during the Ainsworth Strange Situation. In M. Greenberg, D. Cicchetti, & M. Cummings (Eds.), *Attachment in the preschool years: Theory, research, and intervention* (pp. 121–160). Chicago: University of Chicago Press. [9]

Maitra, S., & Schensul, S. (2002). Reflecting diversity and complexity in marital sexual relationships in a low-income community in Mumbai. *Culture, Health & Sexuality, 4*, 133–151. [12]

Maj, M. (1990). Psychiatric aspects of HIV–1 infection and AIDS. *Psychological Medicine, 20*, 547–563. [12]

Malkoff, S. B., Muldoon, M. F., Zeigler, Z. R., & Manuck, S. B. (1993). Blood platelet responsivity to acute mental stress. *Psychosomatic Medicine, 55*, 477–482. [13]

Maltz, W. (1991). *The sexual healing journey: A guide for survivors of sexual abuse.* New York: HarperCollins. [6]

Mancini, J., Lethel, V., Hugonenq, C., & Chabrol, B. (2001). Brain injuries in early foetal life: Consequences for brain development. *Developmental Medicine & Child Neurology, 43,* 52–60. [2]

Manderscheid, R., & Henderson, M. (2001). *Mental health, United States, 2000.* Rockville, MD: Center for Mental Health Services. Retrieved January 14, 2003, from http://www.mentalhealth.org/publications/allpubs/SMA01-3537/ [13]

Manhal-Baugus, M. (2001). E-therapy: Practical, ethical, and legal issues. *CyberPsychology and Behavior, 4,* 551–563. [16]

Manly, T., Lewis, G., Robertson, I., Watson, P., & Datta, A. (2002). Coffee in the cornflakes: Time-of-day as a modulator of executive response control. *Neuropsychologia, 40,* 1–6. [4]

Manton, K. G., Siegler, I. C., & Woodbury, M. A. (1986). Patterns of intellectual development in later life. *Journal of Gerontology, 41,* 486–499. [10]

Manzardo, A., Stein, L., & Belluzi, J. (2002). Rats prefer cocaine over nicotine in a two-level self-administration choice test. *Brain Research, 924,* 10–19. [4]

Maratsos, M., & Matheny, L. (1994). Language specificity and elasticity: Brain and clinical syndrome studies. *Annual Review of Psychology, 45,* 487–516. [2]

Marcia, J. (1980). Identity in adolescence. In J. Adelson (Ed.), *Handbook of adolescent psychology* (pp. 159–187). New York: Wiley. [10]

Marder, S. R. (1996a). Clinical experience with risperidone. *Journal of Clinical Psychiatry, 57*(9, Suppl.), 57–61. [16]

Mareschal, D. (2000). Object knowledge in infancy: Current controversies and approaches. *Trends in Cognitive Sciences, 4,* 408–416. [9]

Marín, G. (1994). The experience of being a Hispanic in the United States. In W. J. Lonner & R. Malpass (Eds.), *Psychology and culture* (pp. 23–27). Boston: Allyn & Bacon. [14]

Markham, S., Scott, K., & McKee, G. (2002). Recognizing good attendance: A longitudinal, quasi-experimental field study. *Personnel Psychology, 55,* 639–660. [18]

Markovic, B. M., Dimitrijevic, M., & Jankovic, B. D. (1993). Immunomodulation by conditioning: Recent developments. *International Journal of Neuroscience, 71,* 231–249. [5]

Marks, G. A., Shatfery, J. P., Oksenberg, A., Speciale, S. G, & Roff-warg, H. P. (1995). A functional role for REM sleep in brain maturation. *Behavioral Brain Research, 69,* 1–11. [4]

Marks, I. (1987). The development of normal fear: A review. *Journal of Child Psychology and Psychiatry, 28,* 667–697. [9]

Marks, I. M. (1972). Flooding (implosion) and allied treatments. In W. S. Agras (Ed.), *Behavior modification.* New York: Little, Brown. [16]

Marlatt, G. A., & Rohsenow, D. J. (1981, December). The think-drink effect. *Psychology Today,* pp. 60–69, 93. [1]

Marsh, A., Elfenbein, H., & Ambady, N. (2003). Nonverbal "accents": Cultural differences in facial expressions of emotion. *Psychological Science, 14,* 373–376. [11]

Marshall, G. D., & Zimbardo, P. G. (1979). Affective consequences of inadequately explained physiological arousal. *Journal of Personality and Social Psychology, 37,* 970–988. [11]

Marshall, J. R. (1997a). Alcohol and substance abuse in panic disorder. *Journal of Clinical Psychiatry, 58*(2, Suppl.), 46–49. [15]

Marshall, R. D., Schneier, F. R., Fallon, B. A., Feerick, J., & Liebowitz, M. R. (1994). Medication therapy for social phobia. *Journal of Clinical Psychiatry, 56*(6, Suppl.), 33–37. [16]

Marshall, W. L., & Segal, Z. (1988). Behavior therapy. In C. G. Last & M. Hersen (Eds.), *Handbook of anxiety disorders* (pp. 338–361). New York: Pergamon. [16]

Martikainen, P., & Valkonen, R. (1996). Mortality after the death of a spouse: Rates and causes of death in a large Finnish cohort. *American Journal of Public Health, 86,* 1087–1093. [10]

Martin, C. L., & Little, J. K. (1990). The relation of gender understanding to children's sex-typed preferences and gender stereotypes. *Child Development, 61,* 1427–1439. [12]

Martin, J. T. (2000). Sexual dimorphism in immune function: The role of prenatal exposure to androgens and estrogens. *European Journal of Pharmacology, 405,* 251–261. [12]

Martin, S. K., & Eastman, C. I. (1998). Medium-intensity light produces circadian rhythm adaptation to simulated night-shift work. *Sleep, 21,* 154–165. [4]

Martinez, C. (1986). Hispanics: Psychiatric issues. In C. B. Wilkinson (Ed.), *Ethnic psychiatry* (pp. 61–88). New York: Plenum. [16]

Martinez, J. L., Jr., & Derrick, B. E. (1996). Long-term potentiation and learning. *Annual Review of Psychology, 47,* 173–203. [6]

Martorano, S. C. (1977). A developmental analysis of performance on Piaget's formal operations tasks. *Developmental Psychology, 13,* 666–672. [10]

Masataka, N. (1996). Perception of motherese in a signed language by 6-month-old deaf infants. *Developmental Psychology, 32,* 874–879. [9]

Masland, R. H. (1996). Unscrambling color vision. *Science, 271,* 616–617. [3]

Masten, A. (2001). Ordinary magic: Resilience processes in development. *American Psychologist, 56,* 227–238. [9]

Masten, A., Hubbard, J., Gest, S., Tellegen, A., Garmezy, N., & Ramirez, M. (1999). Competence in the context of adversity: Pathways to resilience and maladaptation from childhood to late adolescence. *Development & Psychopathology, 11,* 143–169. [9]

Masters, W. H., & Johnson, V. E. (1966). *Human sexual response.* Boston: Little, Brown [10, 12]

Masters, W. H., & Johnson, V. E. (1975). *The pleasure bond: A new look at sexuality and commitment.* Boston: Little, Brown. [12]

Mathew, R. J., & Wilson, W. H. (1991). Substance abuse and cerebral blood flow. *American Journal of Psychiatry, 148,* 292–305. [4]

Mathy, R. (2002). Suicidality and sexual orientation in five continents: Asia, Australia, Europe, North America, and South America. *International Journal of Sexuality & Gender Studies, 7,* 215–225. [1]

Matlin, M. W. (1989). *Cognition* (2nd ed.). New York: Holt, Rinehart & Winston. [6, 7]

Matlin, M. W., & Foley, H. J. (1997). *Sensation and perception* (4th ed.). Boston: Allyn & Bacon. [3]

Matsuda, L., Lolait, S. J., Brownstein, M. J., Young, A. C., & Bonner, T. I. (1990). Structure of a cannabinoid receptor and functional expression of the cloned CDNA. *Nature, 346,* 561–564. [4]

Matsumo, D. (2000). *Culture and psychology: People around the world* (2nd ed.). Belmont, CA: Wadsworth. [18]

Matsunami, H., Montmayeur, J-P., & Buck, L. B. (2000). A family of candidate taste receptors in human and mouse. *Nature, 404,* 601–604. [3]

Matthews, K. A. (1992). Myths and realities of the menopause. *Psychosomatic Medicine, 54,* 1–9. [10]

Matthews, K. A., Shumaker, S. A., Bowen, D. J., Langer, R. D., Hunt, J. R., Kaplan, R. M., Klesges, R. C., & Ritenbaugh, C. (1997). Women's health initiative: Why now? What is it? What's new? *American Psychologist, 52,* 101–116. [13]

Maurer, T., Mitchell, D., & Barbeite, F. (2002). Predictors of attitudes toward a 360-degree feedback system and involvement in post-feedback management development activity. *Journal of Occupational & Organizational Psychology, 75,* 87–107. [18]

Mayo Clinic. (1997, July). Coffee: What's the scoop on its health effects? *Mayo Clinic Health Letter.* [4]

Mazur, J. E. (1993). Predicting the strength of a conditioned reinforcer: Effects of delay and uncertainty. *Current Directions in Psychological Science, 2*(3), 70–74. [5]

Mazzoni, G., & Memon, A. (2003). Imagination can create false autobiographical memories. *Psychological Science, 14*, 186–188. [6]

McAdams, D. P. (1992). The five-factor model in personality: A critical appraisal. *Journal of Personality, 60*, 329–361. [14]

McAnulty, R. D., & Burnette, M. M. (2001). *Exploring human sexuality: Making healthy decisions* (pp. 144-150). Boston: Allyn & Bacon. [9]

McBride-Chang, C., & Treiman, R. (2003). Hong Kong Chinese kindergarteners learn to read English analytically. *Psychological Science, 14*, 138–143. [9]

McCall, R. B. (1994). Academic underachievers. *Current Directions in Psychological Science, 3*, 15–19. [11]

McCarthy, P. (1989, March). Ageless sex. *Psychology Today*, p. 62. [10]

McCartney, K., Harris, M. J., & Bernieri, F. (1990). Growing up and growing apart: A developmental meta-analysis of twin studies. *Psychological Bulletin, 107*, 226–237. [8]

McClearn, G. E., Johansson, B., Berg, S., Pedersen, N. L., Ahern, F., Petrill, S. A., & Plomin, R. (1997). Substantial genetic influence on cognitive abilities in twins 80 or more years old. *Science, 276*, 1560–1563. [8]

McClelland, D. C. (1958). Methods of measuring human motivation. In J. W. Atkinson (Ed.), *Motives in fantasy, action and society: A method of assessment and study.* Princeton, NJ: Van Nostrand. [11]

McClelland, D. C. (1961). *The achieving society.* Princeton, NJ: Van Nostrand. [11]

McClelland, D. C. (1985). *Human motivation.* New York: Cambridge University Press. [11]

McClelland, D. C., & Pilon, D. A. (1983). Sources of adult motives in patterns of parent behavior in early childhood. *Journal of Personality and Social Psychology, 44*, 564–574. [11]

McClelland, D. C., Atkinson, J. W., Clark, R. W., & Lowell, E. L. (1953). *The achievement motive.* New York: Appleton-Century-Crofts. [11]

McClelland, J. L., McNaughton, B. L., & O'Reilly, R. C. (1995). Why there are complementary learning systems in the hippocampus and neocortex: Insights from the successes and failures of connectionist models of learning and memory. *Psychological Bulletin, 102*, 419–457. [6]

McCormack, L., & Mellor, D. (2002). The role of personality in leadership: An application of the five-factor model in the Australian military. *Military Psychology, 14*, 179–197. [14]

McCormick, C. B., & Kennedy, J. H. (2000). Father–child separation, retrospective and current views of attachment relationship with father and self-esteem in late adolescence. *Psychological Reports, 86*, 827–834. [9]

McCourt, W. F., Gurrera, R. J., & Cutter, H. S. G. (1993). Sensation seeking and novelty seeking: Are they the same? *Journal of Nervous and Mental Disease, 181*, 309–312. [11]

McCrae, R. (1984). Situational determinants of coping responses: Loss, threat, and challenge. *Journal of Personality and Social Psychology, 46*, 919–928. [13]

McCrae, R. (2002). The maturation of personality psychology: Adult personality development and psychological well-being. *Journal of Research in Personality, 36*, 307–317. [14]

McCrae, R. R. (1987). Creativity, divergent thinking, and openness to experience. *Journal of Personality and Social Psychology, 52*, 1258–1265. [8]

McCrae, R. R. (1993). Moderated analyses of longitudinal personality stability. *Journal of Personality and Social Psychology, 65*, 577–583. [14]

McCrae, R. R. (1996). Social consequences of experiential openness. *Psychological Bulletin, 120*, 323–337. [14]

McCrae, R. R., & Costa, P. T., Jr. (1987). Validation of the five-factor model of personality across instruments and observers. *Journal of Personality and Social Psychology, 52*, 81–90. [14]

McCrae, R. R., & Costa, P. T., Jr. (1990). *Personality in adulthood.* New York: Guilford. [10, 14]

McCrae, R. R., Costa, P. T., Jr., Ostendorf, F., Angleitner, A., Hrebickova, M., Avia, S. J., Sanchez-Bernardos, M. L., Kusdil, M. E., Woodfield, R., Saunders, P. R., & Smith, P. B. (2000). Nature over nurture: Temperament, personality, and life span development. *Journal of Personality & Social Psychology, 78*, 173–186. [14]

McCue, J. M., Link, K. L., Eaton, S. S., & Freed, B. M. (2000). Exposure to cigarette tar inhibits ribonucleotide reductase and blocks lymphocyte proliferation. *Journal of Immunology, 165*, 6771–6775. [13]

McCullough, M. E., Hoyt, W. T., Larson, D. B., Koenig, H. G., & Thoresen, C. (2000). Religious involvement and mortality: A meta-analytic review. *Health Psychology, 19*, 211–222. [13]

McDonald, C., & Murray, R. M. (2000). Early and late environmental risk factors for schizophrenia. *Brain Research Reviews, 31*, 130–137. [15]

McDonald, J. L. (1997). Language acquisition: The acquisition of linguistic structure in normal and special populations. *Annual Review of Psychology, 48*, 215–241. [7]

McDowell, C., & Acklin, M. W. (1996). Standardizing procedures for calculating Rorschach interrater reliability: Conceptual and empirical foundations. *Journal of Personality Assessment, 66*, 308–320. [14]

McElree, B., Jia, G., & Litvak, A. (2000). The time course of conceptual processing in three bilingual populations. *Journal of Memory & Language, 42*, 229–254. [7]

McFadden, D. (2002). Masculinization effects in the auditory system. *Archives of Sexual Behavior, 31*, 99–111. [12]

McGlashan, T. H., & Hoffman, R. E. (2000). Schizophrenia as a disorder of developmentally reduced synaptic connectivity. *Archives of General Psychiatry, 57*, 637–648. [15]

McGregor, D. (1960). *The human side of enterprise.* New York: McGraw-Hill. [18]

McGue, M., Bouchard, T. J., Jr., Iacono, W. G., & Lykken, D. T. (1993). Behavioral genetics of cognitive ability: A life-span perspective. In R. Plomin & G. E. McClearn (Eds.), *Nature, nurture and psychology* (pp. 59–76). Washington, DC: American Psychological Association. [8]

McGuinness, D. (1993). Gender differences in cognitive style: Implications for mathematics performance and achievement. In I. A. Penner, G. M. Batsche, H. M. Knoff, & D. L. Nelson (Eds.), *The challenge of mathematics and science education: Psychology's response.* Washington, DC: American Psychological Association. [12]

McGuire, W. J. (1985). Attitudes and attitude change. In G. Lindzey & E. Aronson (Ed.), *Handbook of social psychology* (Vol. 2, 3rd ed.). New York: Random House. [17]

McInerney, F. (2000). "Requested death": A new social movement. *Social Science and Medicine, 50*, 137–154. [10]

McKay, H., Glasgow, R., Feil, E., Boles, S., & Barrera, M. (2002). Internet-based diabetes self-management and support: Initial outcomes from the Diabetes Network Project. *Rehabilitation Psychology, 47*, 31–48. [13]

McMellon, C., & Schiffman, L. (2002). Cybersenior empowerment: How some older individuals are taking control of their lives. *Journal of Applied Gerontology, 21*, 157–175. [13]

McNally, R. (2003). Recovering memories of trauma: A view from the laboratory. *Current Directions in Psychological Science, 12*, 32–35. [6]

McNeil, T. F., Cantor-Graae, E., & Weinberger, D. R. (2000). Relationship of obstetric complications and differences in size of brain structures in monozygotic twin pairs discordant for schizophrenia. *American Journal of Psychiatry, 157*, 203–212. [15]

McReynolds, P. (1989). Diagnosis and clinical assessment: Current status and major issues. *Annual Review of Psychology, 40*, 83–108. [14]

McSweeney, F., & Parks, C. (2002). Participation by women in developmental, social, cognitive, and general psychology: A context for interpreting trends in behavior analysis. *Behavior Analyst, 25*, 37–44. [18]

Medina, J. H., Paladini, A. C., & Izquierdo, I. (1993). Naturally occurring benzodiazepines and benzodiazepine-like molecules in brain. *Behavioural Brain Research, 58*, 1–8. [16]

Mednick, S. A., Brennan, P., & Kandel, E. (1988). Predisposition to violence. *Aggressive Behavior, 14*, 25–33. [17]

Mednick, S. A., & Mednick, M. T. (1967). *Examiner's manual, Remote Associates Test.* Boston: Houghton-Mifflin. [8]

Medzerian, G. (1991). *Crack: Treating cocaine addiction.* Blue Ridge Summit, PA: Tab Books. [4, 5]

Mehagnoul-Schipper, D., van der Kallen, B., Colier, W., van der Sluijs, M., van Erning, L., Thijssen, H., Oeseburg, B., Hoefnagel, W., & Jansen, R. (2002). Simultaneous measurement of cerebral oxygenation changes during brain activation by near-infrared spectroscopy and functional magnetic resonance imaging in healthy young and elderly subjects. *Human Brain Mapping, 16*, 14–23. [10]

Meier, R. P. (1991). Language acquisition by deaf children. *American Scientist, 79*(1), 60–70. [9]

Mellet, E., Tzourio-Mazoyer, N., Bricogne, S., Mazoyer, B., Dennis, M., & Kosslyn, S. M. (2000). Functional anatomy of high-resolution visual mental imagery. *Journal of Cognitive Neuroscience, 12*, 98–109. [7]

Meltzer, H. (1930). Individual differences in forgetting pleasant and unpleasant experiences. *Journal of Educational Psychology, 21*, 399–409. [6]

Meltzer, H., Alphs, L., Green, A., Altamura, A., Anand, R., Bertoldi, A., Bourgeois, M., Chouinard, G., Islam, Z., Kane, J., Krishnan, R., Lindenmayer, J., & Potkin, S. (2003). Clozapine treatment for suicidality in schizophrenia: International suicide prevention trial. *Archives of General Psychiatry, 60*, 82–91. [16]

Meltzer, H. Y., Rabinowitz, J., Lee, M. A., Cola, P. A., Ranjan, R., Findling, R. L., & Thompson, P. A. (1997). Age at onset and gender of schizophrenic patients in relation to neuroleptic resistance. *American Journal of Psychiatry, 154*, 475–482. [16]

Meltzoff, A. N. (1988a). Imitation of televised models by infants. *Child Development, 59*, 1221–1229. [9]

Melzack, R., & Wall, P. D. (1965). Pain mechanisms: A new theory. *Science, 150*, 971–979. [3]

Melzack, R., & Wall, P. D. (1983). *The challenge of pain.* New York: Basic Books. [3]

Mendez, M. F., Chow, T., Ringman, J., Twitchell, G., & Hinkin, C. H. (2000). Pedophilia and temporal lobe disturbances. *Journal of Neuropsychiatry & Clinical Neurosciences, 12*, 171–176. [12]

Mertens, T. E., & Low-Beer, D. (1996). HIV and AIDS: Where is the epidemic going? *WHO Bulletin OMS, 74*, 121–128. [12]

Meschyan, G., & Hernandez, A. (2002). Is native-language decoding skill related to second-language learning? *Journal of Educational Psychology, 94*, 14–22. [7]

Metter, E. J. (1991). Brain-behavior relationships in aphasia studied by positron emission tomography. *Annals of the New York Academy of Sciences, 620*, 153–164. [2]

Meyer, A. (1997, March/April). Patching up testosterone. *Psychology Today, 30*, 54–57, 66–70. [12]

Meyer, G. & Wuerger, S. (2001). Cross-modal integration of auditory and visual motion signals. *Neuroreport: For Rapid Communication of Neuroscience Research, 12*, 2557–2560. [3]

Meyer, P. (1972). If Hitler asked you to electrocute a stranger, would you? In R. Greenbaum & H. A. Tilker (Eds.), *The challenge of psychology* (pp. 456–465). Englewood Cliffs, NJ: Prentice-Hall. [17]

Meyer-Bahlburg, H. F. L., Ehrhardt, A. A., Rosen, L. R., & Gruen, R. S. (1995). Prenatal estrogens and the development of homosexual orientation. *Developmental Psychology, 31*, 12–21. [12]

Michaels, J. W., Bloomel, J. M., Brocato, R. M., Linkous, R. A., & Rowe, J. S. (1982). Social facilitation and inhibition in a natural setting. *Replications in Social Psychology, 2*, 21–24. [17]

Middlebrooks, J. C., & Green, D. M. (1991). Sound localization by human listeners. *Annual Review of Psychology, 42*, 135–159. [3]

Miles, D. R., & Carey, G. (1997). Genetic and environmental architecture of human aggression. *Journal of Personality and Social Psychology*, 72, 207–217. [14, 17]

Miles, R. (1999). A homeostatic switch. *Nature, 397*, 215–216. [2]

Milgram, S. (1963). Behavioral study of obedience. *Journal of Abnormal and Social Psychology, 67*, 371–378. [17]

Milgram, S. (1965). Liberating effects of group pressure. *Journal of Personality and Social Psychology, 1*, 127–134. [17]

Miller, E. M. (2000). Homosexuality, birth order, and evolution: Toward an equilibrium reproductive economics of homosexuality. *Archives of Sexual Behavior, 29*, 11–34. [12]

Miller, G., Cohen, S., & Ritchey, A. (2002). Chronic psychological stress and the regulation of pro-inflammatory cytokines: A glucocorticoid-resistance model. *Health Psychology, 21*, 531–541. [13]

Miller, G. A. (1956). The magical number seven, plus or minus two: Some limits on our capacity for processing information. *Psychological Review, 63*, 81–97. [6]

Miller, G. A., & Gildea, P. M. (1987). How children learn words. *Scientific American, 257*, 94–99. [9]

Miller, J. G., & Bersoff, D. M. (1992). Culture and moral judgment: How are conflicts between justice and interpersonal responsibilities resolved? *Journal of Personality and Social Psychology, 62*, 541–554. [10]

Miller, J. G., Bersoff, D. M., & Harwood, R. L. (1990). Perceptions of social responsibilities in India and in the United States: Moral imperatives or personal decisions? *Journal of Personality and Social Psychology, 58*, 33–47. [17]

Miller, L. (1988, February). The emotional brain. *Psychology Today*, pp. 34–42. [2]

Miller, L. (1989, November). What biofeedback does (and doesn't) do. *Psychology Today*, pp. 22–23. [5]

Miller, N. E. (1941). The frustration-aggression hypothesis. *Psychological Review, 48*, 337–342. [17]

Miller, N. E. (1985, February). Rx: Biofeedback. *Psychology Today*, pp. 54–59. [5]

Miller, N. S., & Gold, M. S. (1994). LSD and Ecstasy: Pharmacology, phenomenology, and treatment. *Psychiatric Annals, 24*, 131–133. [4]

Miller, S. A. (2000). Children's understanding of preexisting differences in knowledge and belief. *Developmental Review, 20*, 227–282. [9]

Miller, T. Q., Smith, T. W., Turner, C. W., Guijarro, M. L., & Hallet, A. J. (1996). A meta-analytic review of research on hostility and physical health. *Psychological Bulletin, 119,* 322–348. [13]

Miller, T. Q., Turner, C. W., Tindale, R. S., Posavac, E. J., & Dugoni, B. L. (1991). Reasons for the trend toward null findings in research on Type A behavior. *Psychological Bulletin, 110,* 469–485. [13]

Miller, W., & Thoresen, C. (2003). Spirituality, religion, and health: An emerging research field. *American Psychologist, 58,* 24–35. [13]

Millman, R. B., & Beeder, A. B. (1994). The new psychedelic culture: LSD, Ecstasy, "rave" parties and The Grateful Dead. *Psychiatric Annals, 24,* 148–150. [4]

Milner, B. (1966). Amnesia following operation on the temporal lobes. In C. W. M. Whitty & O. L. Zangwill (Eds.), *Amnesia* (pp. 109–133). London: Butterworth. [6]

Milner, B. (1970). Memory and the medial temporal regions of the brain. In K. H. Pribram & D. E. Broadbent (Eds.), *Biology of memory.* New York: Academic Press. [6]

Milner, B., Corkin, S., & Teuber, H. L. (1968). Further analysis of the hippocampal amnesic syndrome: 14-year follow-up study of H. M. *Neuropsychologia, 6,* 215–234. [6]

Milos, G., Spindler, A., Ruggiero, G., Klaghofer, R., & Schnyder, U. (2002). Comorbidity of obsessive-compulsive disorders and duration of eating disorders. *International Journal of Eating Disorders, 31,* 284–289. [11]

Mischel, W. (1966). A social-learning view of sex differences in behavior. In E. E. Maccoby (Ed.), *The development of sex differences* (pp. 56–81). Stanford, CA: Stanford University Press. [12]

Mischel, W. (1968). *Personality and assessment.* New York: Wiley. [14]

Mischel, W. (1973). Toward a cognitive social learning reconceptualization of personality. *Psychological Review, 80,* 252–283. [14]

Mischel, W. (1977). The interaction of person and situation. In D. Magnusson & N. S. Endler (Eds.), *Personality at the crossroads: Current issues in interactional psychology.* Hillsdale, NJ: Lawrence Erlbaum. [14]

Mischoulon, D. (2002). The herbal anxiolytics kava and valerian for anxiety and insomnia. *Psychiatric Annals, 32,* 55–60. [4]

Mishra, R. (1997). Cognition and cognitive development. In J. Berry, P. Dasen, & T. Sarswthi (Eds.), *Handbook of cross-cultural psychology* (Vol. 2). Boston, MA: Allyn & Bacon. [9]

Mishra, R., & Singh, T. (1992). Memories of Asur children for locations and pairs of pictures. *Psychological Studies, 37,* 38–46. [6]

Mistry, J., & Rogoff, B. (1994). Remembering in cultural context. In W. J. Lonner & R. Malpass (Eds.), *Psychology and culture* (pp. 139–144). Boston: Allyn & Bacon. [6]

Mitchell, S. (2002). Psychodynamics, homosexuality, and the question of pathology. *Studies in Gender & Sexuality, 3,* 3–21. [12]

Mitler, M. M., Aldrich, M. S., Koob, G. F., & Zarcone, V. P. (1994). Narcolepsy and its treatment with stimulants. *Sleep, 17,* 352–371. [4]

Mitsis, E. M., Halperin, J. M., & Newcorn, J. H. (2000). Serotonin and aggression in children. *Current Psychiatry Reports, 2,* 95–101. [17]

Moeller-Leimkuehler, A., Schwarz, R., Burtscheidt, W., & Gaebel, W. (2002). Alcohol dependence and gender-role orientation. *European Psychiatry, 17,* 1–8. [12]

Mohanty, A., & Perregaux, C. (1997). Language acquisition and bilingualism. In J. Berry, P. Dasen, & T. Saraswathi (Eds.), *Handbook of cross-cultural psychology* (pp. 217–254). Boston: Allyn & Bacon. [7]

Mohr, D., Goodkin, D., Nelson, S., Cox, D., & Weiner, M. (2002). Moderating effects of coping on the relationship between stress and the development of new brain lesions in multiple sclerosis. *Psychosomatic Medicine, 64,* 803–809. [13]

Moldofsky, H., Gilbert, R., Lue, F. A., & MacLean, A. W. (1995). Sleep-related violence. *Sleep, 18,* 731–739. [4]

Molnar, M., Potkin, S., Bunney, W., & Jones, E. (2003). MRNA expression patterns and distribution of white matter neurons in dorsolateral prefrontal cortex of depressed patients differ from those in schizophrenia patients. *Biological Psychiatry, 53,* 39–47. [15]

Money, J., & Schwartz, M. (1977). Dating, romantic and nonromantic friendships, and sexuality in 17 early-treated adrenogenital females, aged 16–25. In P. A. Lee et al. (Eds.), *Congenital adrenal hyperplasia.* Baltimore: University Park Press. [12]

Monk, T. H. (1989). Circadian rhythms in subjective activation, mood, and performance efficiency. In M. H. Kryger, T. Roth, & W. C. Dement (Eds.), *Principles and practice of sleep medicine* (pp. 163–172). Philadelphia: W. B. Saunders. [4]

Monroy, T. (2000, March 15). Boomers alter economics. *Interactive Week.* Retrieved March 21, 2000, from www.ZDNet. com [18]

Montejo, A., Llorca, G., Izquierdo, J., & Rico-Villademoros, F. (2001). Incidence of sexual dysfunction associated with antidepressant agents: A prospective multicenter study of 1022 outpatients. *Journal of Clinical Psychiatry, 62,* 10–21. [12, 15]

Montgomery, G. (2003). Color blindness: More prevalent among males. *Seeing, Hearing, and Smelling the World.* Retrieved May 13, 2003, from http://www.hhmi.org/senses/b130.html [3]

Montgomery, G., Weltz, C., Seltz, M., & Bovbjerg, D. (2002). Brief presurgery hypnosis reduces distress and pain in excisional breast biopsy patients. *International Journal of Clinical & Experimental Hypnosis, 50,* 17–32. [4]

Montgomery, G. H., DuHamel, K. N., & Redd, W. H. (2000). A meta-analysis of hypnotically induced analgesia: How effective is hypnosis? *International Journal of Clinical Experimental Hypnosis, 48,* 138–153. [4]

Moore, D. W. (1993). Public polarized on gay issue. *Gallup Poll Monthly,* No. 331, 30–34. [12]

Moore, R., Vadeyar, S., Fulford, J., Tyler, D., Gribben, C., Baker, P., James, D., & Gowland, P. (2001). Antenatal determination of fetal brain activity in response to an acoustic stimulus using functional magnetic resonance imaging. *Human Brain Mapping, 12,* 94–99. [9]

Moore-Ede, M. (1993). *The twenty-four hour society.* Reading, MA: Addison-Wesley. [4]

Moraglia, G. (1994). C. G. Jung and the psychology of adult development. *Journal of Analytical Psychology, 39,* 55–75. [14]

Moran, M. G., & Stoudemire, A. (1992). Sleep disorders in the medically ill patient. *Journal of Clinical Psychiatry, 53*(6, Suppl.), 29–36. [4]

Morgan, C., Chapar, G. N., & Fisher, M. (1995). Psychosocial variables associated with teenage pregnancy. *Adolescence, 118,* 277–289. [10]

Morgan, C. D., & Murray, H. A. (1935). A method for investigating fantasies: The Thematic Apperception Test. *Archives of Neurology and Psychiatry, 34,* 289–306. [14]

Morgan, C. D., & Murray, H. A. (1962). Thematic Apperception Test. In H. A. Murray et al. (Eds.), *Explorations in personality: A clinical and experimental study of fifty men of college age* (pp. 530–545). New York: Science Editions. [14]

Morgan, C. L. (1996). Odors as cues for the recall of words unrelated to odor. *Perceptual and Motor Skills, 83,* 1227–1234. [6]

Morgan, R., & Flora, D. (2002). Group psychotherapy with incarcerated offenders: A research synthesis. *Group Dynamics: Theory, Research, and Practice, 6,* 203–218. [16]

Morgan, R. E., Levitsky, D. A., & Strupp, B. J. (2000). Effects of chronic lead exposure on learning and reaction time in a visual discrimination task. *Neurotoxicology and Teratology, 22,* 337–345. [8]

Morin, C. M., & Wooten, V. (1996). Psychological and pharmacological approaches to treating insomnia: Critical issues in assessing their separate and combined effects. *Clinical Psychology Review, 16,* 521–542. [4]

Morley, J. E., & van den Berg, L. (Eds.). (2000). *Contemporary endocrinology* (No. 20). Totowa, NJ: Humana Press. [10]

Morofushi, M., Shinohara, K., Funabashi, T., & Kimura, F. (2000). Positive relationship between menstrual synchrony and ability to smell 5alpha-androst-16-en-3alpha-ol. *Chemical Senses, 25,* 407–411. [3]

Morofushi, M., Shinohara, K., & Kimura, F. (2001). Menstrual and circadian variations in time perceptions in healthy women and women with premenstrual syndrome. *Neuroscience Research, 41,* 339–344. [4]

Morris, J. S., Frith, C. D., Perrett, D. I., Rowland, D., Young, A. W., Calder, A. J., & Dolan, R. J. (1996). A differential neural response in the human amygdala to fearful and happy facial expressions. *Nature, 383,* 812–815. [2]

Morris, P., Bloom, D., Kemple, J., & Hendra, R. (2003). The effects of a time-limited welfare program on children: The moderating role of parents' risk of welfare dependency. *Child Development, 74,* 851–874. [10]

Morrison, P., Allardyce, J., & McKane, J. (2002). Fear knot: Neurobiological disruption of long-term memory. *British Journal of Psychiatry, 180,* 195–197. [6]

Morrow, B. A., Roth, R. H., & Elsworth, J. D. (2000). TMT, a predator odor, elevates mesoprefrontal dopamine metabolic activity and disrupts short-term working memory in the rat. *Brain Research Bulletin, 52,* 519–523. [6]

Mościcki, E. K. (1995). Epidemiology of suicidal behavior. *Suicide and Life-Threatening Behavior, 25,* 22–31. [15]

Most, S., Simons, D., Scholl, B., Jimenez, R., Clifford, E., & Chabris, C. (2001). How not to be seen: The contribution of similarity and selective ignoring to sustained inattentional blindness. *Psychological Science, 12,* 9–17. [3]

Moulin, D., Clark, A., Speechley, M., & Morley-Forster, P. (2002). Chronic pain in Canada: Prevalence, treatment, impact and the role of opioid analgesia. *Pain Research & Management, 7,* 179–184. [3]

Mourtazaev, M. S., Kemp, B., Zwinderman, A. H., & Kamphuisen, H. A. C. (1995). Age and gender affect different characteristics of slow waves in the sleep EEG. *Sleep, 18,* 557–564. [4]

Mui, A. C. (1992). Caregiver strain among black and white daughter caregivers: A role theory perspective. *The Gerontologist, 32,* 203–212. [10]

Mukerjee, M. (1997). Trends in animal research. *Scientific American, 276,* 86–93. [1]

Muller, L. (2002). Group counseling for African American males: When all you have are European American counselors. *Journal for Specialists in Group Work, 27,* 299–313. [16]

Mumme, D., & Fernald, A. (2003). The infant as onlooker: Learning from emotional reactions observed in a television scenario. *Child Development, 74,* 221–237. [9]

Mumtaz, S., & Humphreys, G. (2002). The effect of Urdu vocabulary size on the acquisition of single word reading in English. *Educational Psychology, 22,* 165–190. [9]

Munarriz, R., Talakoub, L., Flaherty, E., Gioia, M., Hoag, L., Kim, N., Traish, A., Goldstein, I., Guay, A., & Spark, R. (2002). Androgen replacement therapy with dehydroepiandrosterone for androgen insufficiency and female sexual dysfunction: Androgen and questionnaire results. *Journal of Sex & Marital Therapy, 28,* 165–173. [15]

Munroe, R. H., Shimmin, H. S., & Munroe, R. L. (1984). Gender role understanding and sex role preference in four cultures. *Developmental Psychology, 20,* 673–682. [12]

Munzar, P., Li, H., Nicholson, K., Wiley, J., & Balster, R. (2002). Enhancement of the discriminative stimulus effects of phencyclidine by the tetracycline antibiotics doxycycline and minocycline in rats. *Psychopharmacology, 160,* 331–336. [4]

Murnen, S., Wright, C., & Kaluzny, G. (2002). If "boys will be boys," then girls will be victims? A meta-analytic review of the research that relates masculine ideology to sexual aggression. *Sex Roles, 46,* 359–375. [12]

Murphy, E. (2003). Being born female is dangerous to your health. *American Psychologist, 58,* 205–210. [12]

Murphy, S., Tapper, V., Johnson, L., & Lohan, J. (2003). Suicide ideation among parents bereaved by the violent deaths of their children. *Issues in Mental Health Nursing, 24,* 5–25. [15]

Murray, B. (1998, June). Dipping math scores heat up debate over math teaching. *APA Monitor on Psychology, 29,* 34–35. [8]

Murray, B. (2002). Finding the peace within us. *APA Monitor on Psychology, 33,* 56–57. [4]

Murray, D. W. (1995, July/August). Toward a science of desire. *The Sciences, 35,* 244–249. [2]

Murray, H. (1938). *Explorations in personality.* New York: Oxford University Press. [11, 14]

Murray, H. A. (1965). Uses of the Thematic Apperception Test. In B. I. Murstein (Ed.), *Handbook of projective techniques* (pp. 425–432). New York: Basic Books. [14]

Murray, K., & Abeles, N. (2002). Nicotine's effect on neural and cognitive functioning in an aging population. *Aging & Mental Health, 6,* 129–138. [10]

Murray, S. L., Holmes, J. G., & Griffin, D. W. (1996a). The benefits of positive illusions: Idealization and the construction of satisfaction in close relationships. *Journal of Personality and Social Psychology, 70*(1), 79–98. [10]

Murray, S. L., Holmes, J. G., & Griffin, D. W. (1996b). The self-fulfilling nature of positive illusions in romantic relationships: Love is not blind, but prescient. *Journal of Personality and Social Psychology 71*(6), 1155–1180. [10]

Myers, D. A. (1992). *The pursuit of happiness: Discovering the pathway to fulfillment, well-being, and enduring personal joy.* New York: Avon. [11, 14]

Myers, D. G., & Bishop, G. D. (1970). Discussion effects on racial attitudes. *Science, 169,* 778–779. [17]

Myers, D. G., & Lamm, H. (1975). The polarizing effect of group discussion. *American Scientist, 63,* 297–303. [17]

Nader, K. 2003. Re-recording human memories. *Nature, 425,* 571–572. [4]

Nader, K., Schafe, G. E., & Le Doux, J. E. (2000). Fear memories require protein synthesis in the amygdala for reconsolidation after retrieval. *Nature, 406,* 722–726. [6]

Nadon, R., Hoyt, I. P., Register, P. A., & Kilstrom, J. F. (1991). Absorption and hypnotizability: Context effects reexamined. *Journal of Personality and Social Psychology, 60,* 144–153. [4]

Naglieri, J. A., & Ronning, M. E. (2000). Comparison of White, African American, Hispanic, and Asian children on the Naglieri Nonverbal Ability Test. *Psychological Assessment, 12,* 328–334. [8]

Nash, J. M. (1997, March 24). Gift of love. *Time,* pp. 80–82. [10]

Nash, M. (1987). What, if anything, is regressed about hypnotic age regression? A review of the empirical literature. *Psychological Bulletin, 102,* 42–52. [4]

Nash, M., & Baker, E. (1984, February). Trance encounters: Susceptibility to hypnosis. *Psychology Today,* pp. 18, 72–73. [4]

Nash, M. R. (1991). Hypnosis as a special case of psychological regression. In S. J. Lynn & J. W. Rhue (Eds.), *Theories of hypnosis: Current models and perspectives* (pp. 171–194). New York: Guilford. [4]

National Cancer Institute. (2000). *Questions and answers about smoking cessation*. Retrieved January 29, 2003, from http://cis.nci.nih.gov/fact/ 8_13.htm [13]

National Center for Educational Statistics (NCES). (1997). *Non-traditional undergraduates*. Washington, DC: Author. [10]

National Center for Educational Statistics (NCES). (2000). *Trends in international mathematics and science study: TIMSS results*. Retrieved July 12, 2003, from http://nces.ed.gov/timss/results.asp [8]

National Center for Educational Statistics (NCES). (2003). *Highlights from the TIMSS 1999 video study of eighth-grade mathematics teaching* (NCES Publication No. 2003011). Washington, DC: Author. [8]

National Center for Health Statistics. (2000). *Health, United States, 2000 with adolescent health chartbook*. Retrieved from http://www.cdc.gov/nchs/products/pubs/pubd/hus/hestatus.htm [13]

National Center for Health Statistics. (2000, June 23). Gonorrhea—United States, 1998. *MMWR Weekly*, *49*, 538–542. [12]

National Center for Health Statistics. (2001a). Death rates for 358 selected causes, by 10-year age groups, race, and sex: United States, 1999–2000. *National Vital Statistics Report*, *49*, (8). [Electronic version]. Retrieved November 10, 2002, from http://www.cdc.gov/nchs/data/dvs/VS00100.WTABLE 12.pdf [15]

National Center for Health Statistics. (2001b). Deaths from each cause, by 5-year age groups, Hispanic origin, race for non-Hispanic population, and sex: United States, 1999–2000. *National Vital Statistics Report*, *49*, (11). [Electronic version]. Retrieved November 10, 2002, from http://www.cdc.gov/nchs/fastats/pdf/nvsr49_11tb2.pdf [15]

National Center for Health Statistics. (2002a). Deaths, percent of total deaths, and death rates for the 15 leading causes of death in 5-year age groups, by race and sex: United States, 1999–2000. *National Vital Statistics Report*, *50*, (16). [Electronic version]. Retrieved November 10, 2002, from http://www.cdc.gov/nchs/data/dvs/LCWK1_2000.pdf [15]

National Center for Health Statistics (NCHS). (2002b). *Fast stats A to Z: Mental health*. [Online fact sheet]. Retrieved November 9, 2002, from http://www.cdc.gov/nchs/fastats/mental. htm [15]

National Center for Injury Prevention and Control (NCIPC). (2000). Rape fact sheet. Retrieved January 21, 2003, from http://www.cdc.gov/ncipc/factsheets/rape.htm [12]

National Center for Injury Prevention and Control (NCIPC). (2002). Injury fact book 2001–2002. Retrieved January 20, 2003, from http://www.cdc.gov/ncipc/fact_book/12_Child_Maltreatment.htm [12]

National Institute of Mental Health. (1999a). Does this sound like you? Retrieved from http://www.nimh.nih.gov/soundlikeyou.htm [15]

National Institute of Mental Health. (1999c). The invisible disease—depression Retrieved from http://www.nimh.nih.gov/publicat/ invisible.cfm [15]

National Institute of Mental Health (NIMH). (2001). *The numbers count: Mental disorders in America* (NIMH Report No. 01–4584). Washington, DC: Author. [15]

National Institute of Neurological Disorders and Stroke rt-PA Stroke Study Group. (1995). Tissue plasminogen activator for acute ischemic stroke. *New England Journal of Medicine*, *333*, 1581–1587. [2]

National Institute on Drug Abuse (NIDA). (2001). Ecstasy: What we know and don't know about MDMA: A scientific review [Online report]. Retrieved October 17, 2003, from http://www.nida.nih.gov/Meetings/MDMA/MDMAExSummary.html [4]

National Institutes of Health (NIH). (2002). HIV vaccine research is "best hope" for controlling AIDS pandemic. Retrieved January 16, 2003, from http://nih.gov/news/pr/may2002/niaid-16.htm [12]

National Institutes of Health (NIH). (2003). HIV/AIDS statistics. Retrieved November 11, 2003 from http://www.niaid.nih.gov/factsheets/aidsstat.htm [12]

National Safety Council. (1997). Accident facts. Chicago: Author. [13]

National Science Foundation (NSF). (2000). Women, minorities, and persons with disabilities in science and engineering: Annual report to the U.S. Congress. Washington, DC: Author. [1]

National Science Foundation (NSF). (2002). *Science and engineering: Indicators 2002*. Retrieved January 29, 2003, from http://www.nsf.gov/sbc/srs/seind02/toc.htm [13]

Needleman, H. L., Riess, J. A., Tobin, M. J., Biesecker, G. E., & Greenhouse, J. B. (1996). Bone lead levels and delinquent behavior. *Journal of the American Medical Association*, *275*, 363–369. [17]

Neimark, J., Conway, C., & Doskoch, P. (1994, September/October). Back from the drink. *Psychology Today*, pp. 46–53. [13]

Neisser, U. (1967). *Cognitive psychology*. New York: Appleton-Century-Crofts. [6]

Neisser, U., Boodoo, G., Bouchard, T. J., Jr., Boykin, A. W., Brody, N., Ceci, S. J., Halpern, D. F., Loehlin, J. C., Perloff, R., Sternberg, R. J., & Urbina, S. (1996). Intelligence: Knowns and unknowns. *American Psychologist*, *51*, 77–101. [8]

Neisser, U., & Harsch, N. (1992). Phantom flashbulbs: False recollections of hearing the news about Challenger. In E. Winograd & U. Neisser (Eds.), *Affect and accuracy in recall: Studies of "flashbulb" memories* (pp. 9–31). New York: Cambridge University Press. [6]

Neitz, J., Neitz, M., & Kainz, M. (1996). Visual pigment gene structure and the severity of color vision defects. *Science*, *274*, 801–804. [3]

Neitz, M., & Neitz, J. (1995). Numbers and ratios of visual pigment genes for normal red-green color vision. *Science*, *267*, 1013–1016. [3]

Nelson, J. C. (1997). Safety and tolerability of the new antidepressants. *Journal of Clinical Psychiatry*, *58*(6, Suppl.), 26–31. [16]

Nelson, T. (1996). Consciousness and metacognition. *American Psychologist*, *51*, 102–116. [4]

Nelson, W. L., Hughes, H. M., Katz, B., & Searight, H. R. (1999). Anorexic eating attitudes and behaviors of male and female college students. *Adolescence*, *34*, 621–633. [11]

Nestadt, G., Samuels, J., Riddle, M., Bienvenu, J., Liang, K., LaBuda, M., Walkup, J., Grados, M., & Hoehn-Saric, R. (2000). A family study of obsessive-compulsive disorder. *Archives of General Psychiatry*, *57*, 358–363. [12]

Nestor, P., Graham, K., Bozeat, S., Simons, J., & Hodges, J. (2002). Memory consolidation and the hippocampus: Further evidence from studies of autobiographical memory in semantic dementia and frontal variant frontotemporal dementia. *Neuropsychologia*, *40*, 633–654. [6]

Neugarten, B. L. (1982). Must everything be a midlife crisis? In T. H. Carr & H. E. Fitzgerald (Eds.), *Human development 82/83* (pp. 162–163). (Reprinted from *Prime Time*, February 1980, 45–48). Guilford, CT: Dushkin. [10]

Neumann, Y., Finaly, E., & Reichel, A. (1988). Achievement motivation factors and students' college outcomes. *Psychological Reports*, *62*, 555–560. [11]

Neville, H. J., Bavelier, D., Corina, D., Rauschecker, J., Karni, A., Lalwani, A., Braun, A., Clark, V., Jezzard, P., & Turner, R.

(1998). Cerebral organization for language in deaf and hearing subjects: Biological constraints and effects of experience. *Proceedings of the National Academy of Sciences, 95,* 922–929. [2]

Newberg, A., Alavi, A. Baime, M., Pourdehnad, M., Santanna, J. d'Aquili, E. (2001). The measurement of cerebral blood flow during the complex cognitive task of meditation: A preliminary SPECT study. *Psychiatry Research: Neuroimaging, 106,* 113–122. [4]

Newberry, H., Duncan, S., McGuire, M., & Hillers, V. (2001). Use of nonvitamin, nonmineral dietary supplements among college students. *Journal of American College Health, 50,* 123–129. [4]

Newcomb, A. F., Bukowski, W. M., & Pattee, L. (1993). Children's peer relations: A meta-analytic review of popular, rejected, neglected, controversial, and average sociometric status. *Psychological Bulletin, 113,* 99–128. [9]

Newcomb, M. D. (1997). Psychosocial predictors and consequences of drug use: A developmental perspective within a prospective study. *Journal of Addictive Diseases, 16,* 51–89. [4]

Newell, A., & Simon, H. A. (1972). *Human problem solving.* Englewood Cliffs, NJ: Prentice-Hall. [7]

Newell, P., & Cartwright, R. (2000). Affect and cognition in dreams: A critique of the cognitive role in adaptive dream functioning and support for associative models. *Psychiatry: Interpersonal & Biological Processes, 63,* 34–44. [4]

Ng K., Tsui, S., & Chan, W. (2002). Prevalence of common chronic pain in Hong Kong adults. *Clinical Journal of Pain, 18,* 275–281. [3]

Ng, S. H. (1990). Androcentric coding of *man* and *his* in memory by language users. *Journal of Experimental Social Psychology, 26,* 455–464. [7]

Nguyen, P. V., Abel, T., & Kandel, E. R. (1994). Requirement of a critical period of transcription for induction of a late phase of LTP. *Science, 265,* 1104–1107. [6]

Ni, W., Constable, R. T., Menci, W. E., Pugh, K. R., Fulbright, R. K., & Shaywitz, S. E. (2000). An event-related neuroimaging study distinguishing form and content in sentence processing. *Journal of Cognitive Neuroscience, 12,* 120–133. [7]

NICHD Early Child Care Research Network. (1997). The effects of infant child care on infant–mother attachment security. *Child Development, 68,* 860–879. [10]

Nicholl, C. S., & Russell, R. M. (1990). Analysis of animal rights literature reveals the underlying motives of the movement: Ammunition for counter offensive by scientists. *Endocrinology, 127,* 985–989. [1]

Nicholls, M., Clode, D., Lindell, A., & Wood, A. (2002). Which cheek to turn? The effect of gender and emotional expressivity on posing behavior. *Brain & Cognition, 48,* 480–484. [11]

Nickerson, R. S., & Adams, M. J. (1979). Long-term memory for a common object. *Cognitive Psychology, 11,* 287–307. [6]

Nicol, S. E., & Gottesman, I. I. (1983). Clues to the genetics and neurobiology of schizophrenia. *American Scientist, 71,* 398–404. [15]

Niehoff, B., Moorman, R., Blakely, G., & Fuller, J. (2001). The influence of empowerment and job enrichment on employee loyalty in a downsizing environment. *Group & Organization Management, 26,* 93–113. [18]

Nisbett, R. E., & Wilson, T. D. (1977). The halo effect: Evidence for unconscious alteration of judgments. *Journal of Personality and Social Psychology, 35,* 250–256. [17]

Nishimura, H., Hashikawa, K., Doi, K., Iwaki, T., Watanabe, Y., Kusuoka, H., Nishimura, T., & Kubo, T. (1999). Sign language "heard" in the auditory cortex. *Nature, 397,* 116. [2]

Niskar, A. S., Kieszak, S. M., Holmes, A., Esteban, E., Rubin, C., & Brody, D. J. (1998). Prevalence of hearing loss among children 6 to 19 years of age: The Third National Health and Nutrition Examination Survey. *Journal of the American Medical Association, 279,* 1071–1075. [3]

Nogrady, H., McConkey, K. M., & Perry, C. (1985). Enhancing visual memory: Trying hypnosis, trying imagination, and trying again. *Journal of Abnormal Psychology, 94,* 195–204. [4, 6]

Noise Pollution Council. (2003). Comparing standards for safe noise exposure. Retrieved May 16, 2003, from http://www.nonoise.org/hearing/exposure/standardschart.htm [3]

Norris, F. H., & Kaniasty, K. (1996). Received and perceived social support in times of stress: A test of the social support deterioration deterrence model. *Journal of Personality and Social Psychology, 71,* 498–511. [13]

Norris, J. E., & Tindale, J. A. (1994). *Among generations: The cycle of adult relationships.* New York: Freeman. [10]

Norton, M., Moniu, B., Cooper, J., & Hogg, M. (2003). Vicarious dissonance: Attitude change from the inconsistency of others. *Journal of Personality & Social Psychology, 85,* 47–62. [17]

Novello, A. C. (1990). The Surgeon General's 1990 report on the health benefits of smoking cessation: Executive summary. *Morbidity and Mortality Weekly Report, 39* (No. RR–12). [4, 13]

Nowak, M. A., & McMichael, A. J. (1995). How HIV defeats the immune system. *Scientific American, 273,* 58–65. [12]

Noyes, R., Jr., Burrows, G. D., Reich, J. H., Judd, F. K., Garvey, M. J., Norman, T. R., Cook, B. L., & Marriott, P. (1996). Diazepam versus alprazolam for the treatment of panic disorder. *Journal of Clinical Psychiatry, 57,* 344–355. [16]

Nutt, D. (2000). Treatment of depression and concomitant anxiety. *European Neuropsychopharmacology, 10* (Suppl. 4), S433–S437. [16]

O'Brien, C. P. (1996). Recent developments in the pharmacotherapy of substance abuse. *Journal of Consulting and Clinical Psychology, 64,* 677–686. [4]

Ochs, R. (1994, January 11). Cervical cancer comeback. *New York Newsday,* pp. 55, 57. [12]

Offerman, L., & Malamut, A. (2002). When leaders harass: The impact of target perceptions of organizational leadership and climate on harassment reporting and outcomes. *Journal of Applied Psychology, 87,* 885–893. [18]

Ohman, A., & Mineka, S. (2003). The malicious serpent: Snakes as a prototypical stimulus for an evolved module of fear. *Current Directions in Psychological Science, 12,* 5–8. [5]

Ohring, R., Graber, J., & Brooks-Gunn, J. (2002). Girls' recurrent and concurrent body dissatisfaction: Correlates and consequences over 8 years. *International Journal of Eating Disorders, 31,* 404–415. [10]

Oien, K., & Goernert, P. (2003). The role of intentional forgetting in employee selection. *Journal of General Psychology, 13,* 97–110. [18]

Okazaki, S., & Sue, S. (2000). Implications of test revisions for assessment with Asian Americans. *Psychological Assessment, 12,* 272–280. [8]

O'Leary, K. D., & Smith, D. A. (1991). Marital interactions. *Annual Review of Psychology, 42,* 191–212. [17]

Oliver, J. E. (1993). Intergenerational transmission of child abuse: Rates, research, and clinical implications. *American Journal of Psychiatry, 150,* 1315–1324. [17]

Olney, M., & Brockelman, K. (2003). Out of the disablity closet: Strategic use of perception management by select university students with disabilities. *Disability & Society, 18,* 35–50. [18]

Olson, H., Cummings, H., & Wigmore, J. (1924). The Loeb-Leopold murder of Franks in Chicago, May 21, 1924. *Journal of Criminal Law & Criminology*, *15*, 347–405. [14]

O'Neil, H. (2000, September 28). A perfect witness. *St. Louis Post-Dispatch*, p. A8. [6]

Ono, H. (2003). Women's economic standing, marriage timing and cross-national contexts of gender. *Journal of Marriage & Family*, *65*, 275–286. [12]

Oquendo, M., Placidi, G., Malone, K., Campbell, C., Kelp, J., Brodsky, B., Cagoules, L., Cooper, T., Parsey, R., Van Heertum, R., & Mann, J. (2003). Positron emission tomography of regional brain metabolic responses to a serotonergic challenge and lethality of suicide attempts in major depression. *Archives of General Psychiatry*, *60*, 14–22. [15]

Orman, M. (1996). How to conquer public speaking fear. Retrieved February 15, 2003, from http://www.stresscure.com/jobstress/speak.html [15]

Orne, M. (1983, December 12). Hypnosis "useful in medicine, dangerous in court." *U.S. News & World Report*, pp. 67–68. [4]

Öst, L-G., & Westling, B. E. (1995). Applied relaxation vs. cognitive behavior therapy in the treatment of panic disorder. *Behavior Research and Therapy*, *33*, 145–158. [16]

Ostrom, T. M., Carpenter, S. L., Sedikides, C., & Li, F. (1993). Differential processing of in-group and out-group information. *Journal of Personality and Social Psychology*, *64*, 21–34. [17]

Otto, M. W., Pollack, M. H., Sachs, G. S., Reiter, S. R., Meltzer-Brody, S., & Rosenbaum, J. F. (1993). Discontinuation of benzodiazepine treatment: Efficacy of cognitive-behavioral therapy for patients with panic disorder. *American Journal of Psychiatry*, *150*, 1485–1490. [16]

Overmeier, J. B., & Seligman, M. E. P. (1967). Effects of inescapable shock upon subsequent escape and avoidance responding. *Journal of Comparative and Physiological Psychology*, *67*, 28–33. [5]

Owen, M., & O'Donovan, M. (2003). Schizophrenia and genetics. In R. Plomin, J. Defries, I. Craig, & P. McGuffin (Eds.), *Behavioral genetics in the postgenomic era* (pp. 463–480). Washington, DC: American Psychological Association. [15]

Owens, J., Maxim, R., McGuinn, M., Nobile, C., Msall, M., & Alario, A. (2000). Television-viewing habits and sleep disturbance in school children. *Pediatrics*, *104*(3), 27. [9]

Oyewumi, L. (1998). Jet lag and relapse of schizoaffective psychosis despite maintenance clozapine treatment. *British Journal of Psychiatry*, *173*, 268. [4]

Paivio, S. C., & Greenberg, L. S. (1995). Resolving "unfinished business": Efficacy of experiential therapy using empty-chair dialogue. *Journal of Consulting and Clinical Psychology*, *63*, 419–425. [16]

Palinscar, A. S., & Brown, A. L. (1984). Reciprocal teaching of comprehension-fostering and comprehension-monitoring activities. *Cognition and Instruction*, *1*, 117–175. [17]

Palmore, E. (1990). *Ageism: Negative and positive*. New York: Springer. [18]

Pansu, P., & Gilibert, D. (2002). Effect of causal explanations on work-related judgments. *Applied Psychology: An International Review*, *51*, 505–526. [17]

Papousek, I., & Schulter, G. (2002). Covariations of EEG asymmetries and emotional states indicate that activity at frontopolar locations is particularly affected by state factors. *Psychophysiology*, *39*, 350–360. [11]

Papper, B., & Gerhard, M. (2002). Radio-Television News Directors Association & Foundation and Ball State University annual survey on women and minorities. *Communicator*, July/August. Retrieved May 26, 2003, from http://www.rtndf.org [5]

Paraherakis, A., Charney, D., & Gill, K. (2001). Neuropsychological functioning in substance-dependent patients. *Substance Use & Misuse*, *36*, 257–271. [4]

Park, K. A., & Waters, E. (1989). Security of attachment and preschool friendships. *Child Development*, *60*, 1076–1081. [9]

Parke, R. D. (1977). Some effects of punishment on children's behavior–revisited. In E. M. Hetherington, E. M. Ross, & R. D. Parke (Eds.), *Contemporary readings in child psychology*. New York: McGraw-Hill. [5]

Parker, J. G., & Asher, S. R. (1987). Peer relations and later personal adjustment: Are low-accepted children at risk? *Psychological Bulletin*, *102*, 357–389. [9]

Parkes, K. (2002). Age, smoking, and negative affectivity as predictors of sleep patterns among shift workers in two environments. *Journal of Occupational Health Psychology*, 7, 156–173. [4]

Parkinson, W. L., & Weingarten, H. P. (1990). Dissociative analysis of ventromedial hypothalamic obesity syndrome. *American Journal of Physiology*, *259*, 829–835. [11]

Partinen, M. (1994). Epidemiology of sleep disorders. In M. Kryger, T. Roth, & W. C. Dement (Eds.), *Principles and practice of sleep medicine* (pp. 437–453). Philadelphia: W.B. Saunders. [4]

Partinen, M., Hublin, C., Kaprio, J., Koskenvuo, M., & Guilleminault, C. (1994). Twin studies in narcolepsy. *Sleep*, *17*, S13–S16. [4]

Parvizi, J., & Damasio, A. (2001). Consciousness and the brainstem. *Cognition*, *79*, 135–159. [4]

Pascarella, E. (1999). The development of critical thinking: Does college make a difference? *Journal of College Student Development*, *40*, 562–569. [10]

Pascarella, E., & Terenzi, P. (1991). *How college affects students: Findings and insights from twenty years of research*, San Francisco: Jossey-Bass. [10]

Pascual-Leone, A., Dhuna, A., Altafullah, I., & Anderson, D. C. (1990). Cocaine-induced seizures. *Neurology*, *40*, 404–407. [4]

Pastore, N. (1950). The role of arbitrariness in the frustration-aggression hypothesis. *Journal of Abnormal and Social Psychology*, *47*, 728–731. [17]

Patricelli, G., Uy, J., Walsh, G., & Borgia, G. (2002). Male displays adjusted to female's response. *Nature*, *415*, 279–280. [7]

Patterson, C. J. (1995). Sexual orientation and human development: An overview. *Developmental Psychology*, *31*, 3–11. [12]

Patterson, D. R., & Ptacek, J. T. (1997). Baseline pain as a moderator of hypnotic analgesia for burn injury treatment. *Journal of Consulting and Clinical Psychology*, *65*, 60–67. [4]

Patterson, G. R., Crosby, L., & Vuchinich, S. (1992). *Journal of Quantitative Criminology*, *8*, 335–355. [9]

Paul, T., Schroeter, K., Dahme, B., & Nutzinger, D. (2002). Self-injurious behavior in women with eating disorders. *American Journal of Psychiatry*, *159*, 408–411. [11]

Paul, W. E. (1993). Infectious diseases and the immune system. *Scientific American*, *269*, 90–99. [13]

Paulesu, E., McCrory, E., Fazio, L., Menoncello, N., Brunswick, N., Cappa, S. F., et al. (2000). A cultural effect on brain function. *Nature Neuroscience*, *3*, 91–96. [7]

Paulhus, D., Harms, P., Bruce, M., & Lysy, D. (2003). The overclaiming technique: Measuring self-enhancement independent of ability. *Journal of Personality & Social Psychology*, *84*, 890–904. [18]

Paulus, P. B., Cox, V. C., & McCain, G. (1988). *Prison crowding: A psychological perspective*. New York: Springer-Verlag. [17]

Paunonen, S. V., Keinonen, M., Trzebinski, J., Forsterling, F., Grishenko-Roze, N., Kouznetsova, L., & Chan, D. W.

(1996). The structure of personality in six cultures. *Journal of Cross-Cultural Psychology, 27,* 339–353. [14]

Pause, B. M., & Krauel, K. (2000). Chemosensory event-related potentials (CSERP) as a key to the psychology of odors. *International Journal of Psychophysiology, 36,* 105–122. [3]

Pavlidis, I., Eberhardt, N., & Levine, J. (2002). Seeing through the face of deception. *Nature, 415,* 35. [11]

Pavlov, I. P. (1927/1960). *Conditioned reflexes: An investigation of the physiological activity of the cerebral cortex* (G. V. Anrep, Trans.). New York: Dover. (Original translation published 1927). [5]

Pearce, C., & Sims, H. (2002). Vertical versus shared leadership as predictors of the effectiveness of change management teams: An examination of aversive, directive, transactional, transformational, and empowering leader behaviors. *Group Dynamics, 6,* 172–197. [18]

Pearsall, N., Skipper, J., & Mintzes, J. (1997). Knowledge restructuring in the life sciences: A longitudinal study of conceptual change in biology. *Science Education, 81,* 193–215. [10]

Pedersen, D. M., & Wheeler, J. (1983). The Müller-Lyer illusion among Navajos. *Journal of Social Psychology, 121,* 3–6. [3]

Pelletier, L. G., & Vallerand, R. J. (1996). Supervisors' beliefs and subordinates' intrinsic motivation: A behavioral confirmation analysis. *Journal of Personality and Social Psychology, 71,* 231–240. [11]

Penfield, W. (1969). Consciousness, memory, and man's conditioned reflexes. In K. Pribram (Ed.), *On the biology of learning* (pp. 129–168). New York: Harcourt Brace Jovanovich. [6]

Penfield, W. (1975). *The mystery of the mind: A critical study of consciousness and the human brain.* Princeton, NJ: Princeton University Press. [6]

Pennebaker, J., Dyer, M., Caulkins, R., Litowitz, D., Ackreman, P., Anderson, D., & McGraw, K. (1979). Don't the girls get prettier at closing time: A country and western application to psychology. *Personality & Social Psychology Bulletin, 5,* 123–125. [12]

Pennebaker, J., & Seagal, J. (1999). Forming a story: The health benefits of narrative. *Journal of Clinical Psychology, 55,* 1243–1254. [13]

Pennisi, E. (1997). Tracing molecules that make the brain-body connection. *Science, 275,* 930–931. [13]

Penny, J. (2001). Differential item functioning in an international 360-degree assessment: Evidence of gender stereotype, environmental complexity, and organizational contingency. *European Journal of Work & Organizational Psychology, 10,* 245–271. [18]

Peplau, L. (2003). Human sexuality: How do men and women differ? *Current Directions in Psychological Science, 12,* 37–40. [12]

Pepperberg, I. M. (1991, Spring). Referential communication with an African grey parrot. *Harvard Graduate Society Newsletter,* 1–4. [7]

Pepperberg, I. M. (1994a). Numerical competence in an African grey parrot (*Psittacus erithacus*). *Journal of Comparative Psychology, 108,* 36–44. [7]

Pepperberg, I. M. (1994b). Vocal learning in grey parrots (*Psittacus erithacus*): Effects of social interaction, reference, and context. *The Auk, 111,* 300–314 . [7]

Perls, F. S. (1969). *Gestalt therapy verbatim.* Lafayette, CA: Real People Press. [16]

Perls, T. T. (1995). The oldest old. *Scientific American, 272,* 70–75. [10]

Perrett, D. I., May, K. A., & Yoshikawa, S. (1994). Facial shape and judgements of female attractiveness. *Nature, 368,* 239–242. [17]

Perry, R. & Zeki, S. (2000). The neurology of saccades and covert shifts in spatial attention: An event-related fMRI study. *Brain, 123,* 2273–2288. [3]

Pert, C. B., Snowman, A. M., & Snyder, S. H. (1974). Localization of opiate receptor binding in presynaptic membranes of rat brain. *Brain Research, 70,* 184–188. [2]

Perusse, L., Chagnon, Y. C., Weisnagel, J., & Bouchard, C. (1999). The human obesity gene map: The 1998 update. *Obesity Research, 7,* 111–129. [11]

Peskind, E. R. (1996). Neurobiology of Alzheimer's disease. *Journal of Clinical Psychiatry, 57*(14, Suppl.), 5–8. [10]

Pesonen, A., Raeikkoenen, K., Keskivaara, P., & Keltikangas-Jaervinen, L. (2003). Difficult temperament in childhood and adulthood: Continuity from maternal perceptions to self-ratings over 17 years. *Personality & Individual Differences, 34,* 19–31. [14]

Peters, A., Leahu, D., Moss, M. B., & McNally, J. (1994). The effects of aging on area 46 of the frontal cortex of the rhesus monkey. *Cerebral Cortex, 6,* 621–635. [10]

Peterson, A. C. (1987, September). Those gangly years. *Psychology Today,* pp. 28–34. [10]

Peterson, B. (2002). Longitudinal analysis of midlife generativity, intergenerational roles, and caregiving. *Psychology & Aging, 17,* 161–168. [10]

Peterson, I. (1993). Speech for export: Automating the translation of spoken words. *Science News,* 144, 254–255 [7]

Peterson, L. R., & Peterson, M. J. (1959). Short-term retention of individual verbal items. *Journal of Experimental Psychology, 58,* 193–198. [6]

Petitto, L. A., & Marentette, P. R. (1991). Babbling in the manual mode: Evidence for the ontogeny of language. *Science, 251,* 1493–1496. [9]

Petri, H. L. (1996). *Motivation: Theory, research, and applications* (4th ed.). Pacific Grove, CA: Brooks/Cole. [11]

Petrill, S. (2003). The development of intelligence: Behavioral genetic approaches. In R. Sternberg, J. Lautrey, & T. Lubart (Eds.), *Models of intelligence: International perspective* (pp. 81–90). Washington, DC: American Psychological Association. [8]

Petty, R. E., Wegener, D. T., & Fabrigar, L. R. (1997). Attitudes and attitude change. *Annual Review of Psychology, 48,* 609–647. [17]

Phillips, G. P., & Over, R. (1995). Differences between heterosexual, bisexual, and lesbian women in recalled childhood experiences. *Archives of Sexual Behavior, 24,* 1–20. [12]

Phillips, K., Fulker, D. W., Carey, G., & Nagoshi, C. T. (1988). Direct marital assortment for cognitive and personality variables. *Behavioral Genetics, 18,* 347–356. [17]

Phillips, S. T., & Ziller, R. C. (1997). Toward a theory and measure of the nature of nonprejudice. *Journal of Personality and Social Psychology,* 72, 420–434. [17]

Piaget, J. (1963). *Psychology of intelligence.* Patterson, NJ: Littlefield, Adams. [9]

Piaget, J. (1964). *Judgment and reasoning in the child.* Patterson, NJ: Littlefield, Adams. [9]

Piaget, J., & Inhelder, B. (1969). *The psychology of the child.* New York: Basic Books. [9, 10]

Pich, E. M., Pagliusi, S. R., Tessari, M., Talabot-Ayer, D., van Huijsduijnen, R. H., & Chiamulera, C. (1997). Common neural substrates for the addictive properties of nicotine and cocaine. *Science, 275,* 83–86. [4]

Pierrehumbert, B., Miljkovitch, R., Plancherel, B., Halfon, O., & Ansermet, F. (2000). Attachment and temperament in early childhood: Implications for later behavior problems. *Infant and Child Development, 9,* 17–32. [9]

Pietrzak, R., Laird, J., Stevens, D., & Thompson, N. (2002). Sex differences in human jealousy: A coordinated study of forced-choice, continuous rating scale, and physiological responses on the same subjects. *Evolution & Human Behavior, 23,* 83–94. [11]

Pigott, T. A. (1996). OCD: Where the serotonin selectivity story begins. *Journal of Clinical Psychiatry, 57*(6, Suppl.), 11–20. [15]

Pihl, R. O., Lau, M. L., & Assaad, J-M. (1997). Aggressive disposition, alcohol, and aggression. *Aggressive Behavior, 23,* 11–18. [4]

Pilcher, J. J., & Huffcutt, A. I. (1996). Effects of sleep deprivation on performance: A meta-analysis. *Sleep, 19,* 318–326. [4]

Pilcher, J. J., Lambert, B. J., & Huffcutt, A. I. (2000). Differential effects of permanent and rotating shifts on self-report sleep length: A meta-analytic review. *Sleep, 23,* 155–163. [4]

Pillemer, D. B. (1990). Clarifying the flashbulb memory concept: Comment on McCloskey, Wible, and Cohen (1988). *Journal of Experimental Psychology: General, 119,* 92–96. [6]

Pillow, D. R., Zautra, A. J., & Sandler, I. (1996). Major life events and minor stressors: Identifying mediational links in the stress process. *Journal of Personality and Social Psychology, 70,* 381–394. [13]

Pilowsky, T., Yirmiya, N., Arbelle, S., & Mozes, T. (2000). Theory of mind abilities of children with schizophrenia, children with autism, and normally developing children. *Schizophrenia Research, 42,* 2145–2155. [9]

Pinel, J. P. L. (2000). *Biopsychology* (4th ed.). Boston: Allyn & Bacon. [2]

Pinikahana, J., Happell, B., & Keks, N. (2003). Suicide and schizophrenia: A review of literature for the decade (1990–1999) and implications for mental health nursing. *Issues in Mental Health Nursing, 24,* 27–43. [15]

Pinker, S. (1994). *The language instinct: How the mind creates language.* New York: Morrow. [7]

Pinquart, M., & Sörensen, S. (2000). Influences of socioeconomic status, social network, and competence on subjective well-being in later life: A meta-analysis. *Psychology and Aging, 15,* 187–224. [10]

Piotrkowski, C. (1998). Gender harassment, job satisfaction, and distress among employed white and minority women. *Journal of Occupational Health Psychology, 3,* 33–43. [18]

Pittenger, D. J. (1993). The utility of the Myers-Briggs Type Indicator. *Review of Educational Research, 63,* 467–488. [14]

Pittman, L., & Chase-Lansdale, P. (2001). African American adolescent girls in impoverished communities: Parenting style and adolescent outcomes. *Journal of Research on Adolescence, 11,* 199–224. [9]

Pitz, G. F., & Sachs, N. J. (1984). Judgment and decision: Theory and application. *Annual Review of Psychology, 35,* 139–163. [7]

Plomin, R. (1989). Environment and genes: Determinants of behavior. *American Psychologist, 44,* 105–111. [8, 14]

Plomin, R. (1999). Genetics and general cognitive ability. *Nature, 402*(Suppl.), C25–C29. [8]

Plomin, R. (2001). Genetics and behavior. *Psychologist, 14,* 134–139. [9]

Plomin, R., & Dale, P. S. (2000). Genetics and early language development: A UK study of twins. In D. V. M. Bishop & L. B. Leonard (Eds.), *Speech and language impairment in children: Causes, characteristics, intervention and outcome.* Oxford: Oxford University Press. [8]

Plomin, R., & Daniels, D. (1987). Why are children in the same family so different from one another? *Behavioral and Brain Sciences, 10,* 1–60. [14]

Plomin, R., Defries, J., Craig, I., & McGuffin, P. (2003). *Behavioral genetics in the postgenomic era.* Washington, DC: American Psychological Association. [1]

Plomin, R., DeFries, J. C., & Fulker, D. W. (1988). *Nature and nurture during infancy and early childhood.* New York: Cambridge University Press. [8]

Plomin, R., DeFries, J. C., McClearn, G. E., & Rutter, M. (1997). *Behavioral genetics* (3rd ed.). New York: Freeman. [8]

Plomin, R., Owen, M. J., & McGuffin, P. (1994). The genetic basis of complex human behaviors. *Science, 264,* 1733–1739. [8, 9, 14]

Plomin, R., & Rende, R. (1991). Human behavioral genetics. *Annual Review of Psychology, 42,* 161–190. [8, 14]

Plous, S. (1996). Attitudes toward the use of animals in psychological research and education: Results from a national survey of psychologists. *American Psychologist, 51,* 1167–1180. [1]

Ployhart, R., McFarland, L., & Ryan, A. (2002). Examining applicants' attributions for withdrawal from a selection procedure. *Journal of Applied Social Psychology, 32,* 2228–2252. [18]

Plummer, D. L., & Slane S. (1996). Patterns of coping in racially stressful situations. *Journal of Black Psychology, 22,* 302–315. [13]

Pollack, R. H. (1970). Müller-Lyer illusion: Effect of age, lightness contrast and hue. *Science, 179,* 93–94. [3]

Pontieri, F. C., Tanda, G., Orzi, F., & Di Chiara, G. (1996). Effects of nicotine on the nucleus accumbens and similarity to those of addictive drugs. *Nature, 382,* 255–257. [2, 4]

Poponoe, D., & Whitehead, B. D. (2000). Sex without strings, relationships without rings: Today's young singles talk about mating and dating. In National Marriage Project, "The State of Our Unions, 2000." Retrieved from http://marriage.rutgers.edu/ 2000.htm [10]

Porac, C., & Friesen, I. (2000). Hand preference side and its relation to hand preference switch history among old and oldest-old adults. *Developmental Neuropsychology, 17,* 222–239. [2]

Porjesz, B., Begleiter, H., Reich, T., Van Eerdewegh, P., Edenberg, H., Foroud, T., Goate, A., Litke, A., Chorlian, D., Stimus, A., Rice, J., Blangero, J., Almasy, L., Sorbell, J., Bauer, L., Kuperman, S., O'Connor, S., & Rohrbaugh, J. (1998). Amplitude of visual P3 event-related potential as a phenotypic marker for a predisposition to alcoholism: Preliminary results from the COGA project. *Alcoholism: Clinical & Experimental Research, 22,* 1317–1323. [4, 13]

Porrino, L. J., & Lyons, D. (2000). Orbital and medial prefrontal cortex and psychostimulant abuse: Studies in animal models. *Cerebral Cortex, 10,* 326–333. [4, 5]

Porte, H. S., & Hobson, J. A. (1996). Physical motion in dreams: One measure of three theories. *Sleep, 105,* 3329–3335. [4]

Porter, F. L., Porges, S. W., & Marshall, R. E. (1988). Newborn pain cries and vagal tone: Parallel changes in response to circumcision. *Child Development, 59,* 495–505. [9]

Posada, G., Jacobs, A., Richmond, M., Carbonell, O., Alzate, G., Bustamante, M., & Quiceno, J. (2002). Maternal caregiving and infant security in two cultures. *Developmental Psychology, 38,* 67–78. [9]

Posner, M. I. (1996, September). Attention and psychopathology. *Harvard Mental Health Letter, 13*(3), 5–6. [2]

Posner, M. I., & Raichle, M. E. (1995). Précis of *Images of Mind. Behavioral and Brain Sciences, 18,* 327–383. [7]

Postman, L., & Phillips, L. W. (1965). Short-term temporal changes in free recall. *Quarterly Journal of Experimental Psychology, 17,* 132–138. [6]

Potts, N. L. S., Davidson, J. R. T., & Krishman, K. R. R. (1993). The role of nuclear magnetic resonance imaging in psychiatric research. *Journal of Clinical Psychiatry, 54*(12, Suppl.), 13–18. [2]

Powell, C., & Van Vugt, M. (2003). Genuine giving or selfish sacrifice? The role of commitment and cost level upon willingness to sacrifice. *European Journal of Social Psychology, 33,* 403–412. [17]

Powell, L., Shahabi, L., & Thoresen, C. (2003). Religion and spirituality: Linkages to physical health. *American Psychologist, 58*, 36–52. [13]

Power, F. C., Higgins, A., & Kohlberg, L. (1989). *Lawrence Kohlberg's approach to moral education.* New York: Columbia University Press. [10]

Power, K. G., Sharp, D. M., Swanson, V., & Simpson, R. J. (2000). Therapist contact in cognitive behaviour therapy for panic disorder and agoraphobia in primary care. *Clinical Psychology & Psychotherapy*, 7, 37–46. [16]

Powers, D., & Rock, D. (1999). Effects of coaching on SAT I: Reasoning test scores. *Journal of Educational Measurement, 36*, 93–118. [8]

Powlishta, K. K. (1995). Intergroup processes in childhood: Social categorization and sex role development. *Developmental Psychology, 31*, 781–788. [12]

Prabhu, V., Porjesz, B., Chorlian, D., Wang, K., Stimus, A., & Begleiter, H. (2001). Visual P3 in female alcoholics. *Alcoholism: Clinical & Experimental Research, 25*, 531–539. [4, 13]

Pratkanis, A. R. (1989). The cognitive representation of attitudes. In A. R. Pratkanis, S. J. Breckler, & A. G. Greenwald (Eds.), *Attitude structure and function* (pp. 71–93). Hillsdale, NJ: Erlbaum. [17]

Pratt, M., Danso, H., Arnold, M., Norris, J., & Filyer, R. (2001). Adult generativity and the socialization of adolescents: Relations to mothers' and fathers' parenting beliefs, styles, and practices. *Journal of Personality, 69*, 89–120. [10]

Premack, D. (1971). Language in chimpanzees. *Science, 172*, 808–822. [7]

Premack, D., & Premack, A. J. (1983). *The mind of an ape.* New York: Norton. [7]

Pressley, M., & Wharton-McDonald, R. (1997). Skilled comprehension and its development through instruction. *School Psychology Review, 26*, 448–466. [9]

Price, R., Choi, J., & Vinokur, A. (2002). Links in the chain of adversity following job loss: How financial strain and loss of personal control lead to depression, impaired functioning, and poor health. *Journal of Occupational Health Psychology*, 7, 302–312. [10, 13]

Prien, R. F., & Kocsis, J. H. (1995). Long-term treatment of mood disorders. In F. E. Bloom & D. J. Kupfer (Eds.), *Psychopharmacology: The fourth generation of progress* (pp. 1067–1079). New York: Raven. [16]

Prigerson, H. G., Bierhals, A. J., Kasl, S. V., Reynolds, C. F., III, Shear, M. K., Day, N., Beery, L. C., Newsom, J. T., & Jacobs, S. (1997). Traumatic grief as a risk factor for mental and physical mortality. *American Journal of Psychiatry, 154*, 616–623. [13]

Pring, L., & Hermelin, B. (2002). Numbers and letters: Exploring an autistic savant's unpractised ability. *Neurocase, 8*, 330–337. [8]

Prinz, P. N., Vitiello, M. V., Raskind, M. A., & Thorpy, M. J. (1990). Geriatrics: Sleep disorders and aging. *New England Journal of Medicine, 323*, 520–526. [4]

Provine, R. R. (1996, January/February). Laughter. *American Scientist, 84*, 38–45. [11]

Pryke, S., Lindsay, R. C. L., & Pozzulo, J. D. (2000). Sorting mug shots: Methodological issues. *Applied Cognitive Psychology, 14*, 81–96. [6]

Psychologists' pigeons score 90 pct. picking Picasso. (1995, May 7). *St. Louis Post-Dispatch*, p. 2A. [5]

Public Agenda. (2003a). *Race relations: A nation divided?* Retrieved June 25, 2003, from http://www.publicagenda.org [18]

Public Agenda. (2003b). *Gay rights: A nation divided?* Retrieved June 25, 2003 from http://www.publicagenda.org [18]

Public Agenda Online. (2002). *The issues: Race*. Retrieved November 13, 2002 from http://www.publicagenda.com/issues/overview.dfm?issue_type=race [17]

Public Health Service. (1991). *Healthy people 2000: National health promotion and disease prevention objectives* [Summary]. (DHHS Publication No. PHS 91-50213). Washington, DC: U.S. Department of Health and Human Services. [13]

Pulvermüller, F., Mohr, B., Schleichert, H., & Veit, R. (2000). Operant conditioning of left-hemispheric slow cortical potentials and its effect on word processing. *Biological Psychology, 53*, 177–215. [5]

Purnine, D., & Carey, M. (1998) Age and gender differences in sexual behavior preferences: A follow-up report. *Journal of Sex & Marital Therapy, 24*, 93–102. [10]

Putnam, F. (2003). Ten-year research update review: Child sexual abuse. *Journal of the American Academy of Child & Adolescent Psychiatry, 42*, 269–278. [12]

Putnam, F. W. (1989). *Diagnosis and treatment of multiple personality disorder.* New York: Guilford Press. [15]

Putnam, F. W. (1992). Altered states: Peeling away the layers of a multiple personality. *The Sciences, 32*, 30–36. [15]

Putzke, J., Rickert, E., Duke, L., Marson, D., & Harrell, L. (2000). Differential automatic processing deficits in early stage Alzheimer's disease. *Aging, Neuropsychology, and Cognition*, 7, 112–118. [10]

Pyevich, D., & Bogenschultz. M. (2001). Herbal diuretics and lithium toxicity. *American Journal of Psychiatry, 158*, 1329. [4]

Quadrel, M. J., Fischhoff, B., & Davis, W. (1993). Adolescent (in)vulnerability. *American Psychologist, 48*, 102–116. [10]

Quaid, K., Aschen, S., Smiley, C., Nurnberger, J. (2001). Perceived genetic risks for bipolar disorder in patient population: An exploratory study. *Journal of Genetic Counseling, 10*, 41–51. [2]

Querido, J., Warner, T., & Eyberg, S. (2002). Parenting styles and child behavior in African American families of preschool children. *Journal of Clinical Child & Adolescent Psychology, 31*, 272–277. [9]

Quesnel, C., Savard, J., Simard, S., Ivers, H., & Morin, C. (2003). Efficacy of cognitive-behavioral therapy for insomnia in women treated for nonmetastatic breast cancer. *Journal of Consulting & Clinical Psychology, 71*, 189–200. [16]

Quiroga, T., Lemos-Britton, Z., Mostafapour, E., Abbott, R., & Berninger, V. (2002). Phonological awareness and beginning reading in Spanish-speaking ESL first graders: Research into practice. *Journal of School Psychology, 40*, 85–111. [9]

Rachman, S. (1997). The conditioning theory of fear acquisition: A critical examination. *Behavior Research and Therapy, 15*, 375–387. [15]

Rachman, S. J., & Wilson, G. T. (1980). *The effects of psychological therapy* (2nd ed.). New York: Pergamon. [16]

Raeikkoenen, K., Matthews, K., & Salomon, K. (2003). Hostility predicts metabolic syndrome risk factors in children and adolescents. *Health Psychology, 22*, 279–286. [13]

Rafferty, J., & Tapsell, J. (2001). Self-managed work teams and manufacturing strategies: Cultural influences in the search for team effectiveness and competitive advantage. *Human Factors & Ergonomics in Manufacturing, 11*, 19–34. [18]

Ragins, B., Cornwell, J., & Miller, J. (2003). Heterosexism in the workplace: Do race and gender matter? *Group & Organization Management, 28*, 45–74. [18]

Ragozzino, M., Detrick, S., & Kesner, R. (2002). The effects of prelimbic and infralimbic lesions on working memory for visual objects in rats. *Neurobiology of Learning & Memory*, 77, 29–43. [6]

Rahe, R. J., Meyer, M., Smith, M., Kjaer, G., & Holmes, T. H. (1964). Social stress and illness onset. *Journal of Psychosomatic Research, 8*, 35–44. [13]

Rahman, Q., & Wilson, G. (2003). Born gay? The psychobiology of human sexual orientation. *Personality & Individual Differences, 34*, 1337–1382. [12]

Raine, A. (1996). Autonomic nervous system factors underlying disinhibited, antisocial, and violent behavior: Biosocial perspectives and treatment implications. *Annals of the New York Academy of Sciences, 794*, 46–59. [17]

Ralph, M. R. (1989, November/December). The rhythm maker: Pinpointing the master clock in mammals. *The Sciences, 29*, 40–45. [4]

Ramey, C. (1993). A rejoinder to Spitz's critique of the Abecedarian experiment. *Intelligence, 17*, 25–30. [8]

Ramey, C., & Campbell, F. (1987). The Carolina Abecedarian project. An educational experiment concerning human malleability. In J. J. Gallagher & C. T. Ramey (Eds.), *The malleability of children*, (pp. 127–140). Baltimore: Brookes. [8]

Ramsay, D. S., & Woods, S. C. (1997). Biological consequences of drug administration: Implications for acute and chronic tolerance. *Psychological Review, 104*, 170–193. [4]

Randel, B., Stevenson, H., & Witruk, E. (2000). Attitudes, beliefs, and mathematics achievement of German and Japanese high school students. *International Journal of Behavioral Development, 24*, 190–198. [8]

Rao, S. C., Rainer, G., & Miller, E. K. (1997). Integration of what and where in the primate prefrontal cortex. *Science, 276*, 821–824. [6]

Rapp, S., Espeland, M., Shumaker, S., Henderson, V., Brunner, R., Manson, J., Gass, M., Stefanick, M., Lane, D., Hays, J., Johnson, K., Coker, L., Dailey, M., & Bowen, D. (2003). Effect of estrogen plus progestin on global cognitive function in postmenopausal women: The Women's Health Initiative Memory Study: A randomized controlled trial. *Journal of the American Medical Association (JAMA), 289*, 2663–2672. [6]

Rasmussen, S. A., & Eisen, J. L. (1990). Epidemiology of obsessive compulsive disorder. *Journal of Clinical Psychiatry, 51*(2, Suppl.), 10–13. [15]

Rasmussen, S. A., Eisen, J. L., & Pato, M. T. (1993). Current issues in the pharmacologic management of obsessive compulsive disorder. *Journal of Clinical Psychiatry, 54*(6, Suppl.), 4–9. [15, 16]

Rate of births for teen-agers drops again. (1995, September 22). *The New York Times*, p. A18. [10]

Rathus, S. A., Nevid, J. S., & Fichner-Rathus, L. (2000). *Human sexuality in a world of diversity* (4th ed., pp. 216–217). Boston: Allyn & Bacon. [12]

Ratty, H., Vaenskae, J., Kasanen, K., & Kaerkkaeinen, R. (2002). Parents' explanations of their child's performance in mathematics and reading: A replication and extension of Yee and Eccles. *Sex Roles, 46*, 121–128. [12]

Raz, A., Deouell, L., & Bentin, S. (2001). Is pre-attentive processing compromised by prolonged wakefulness? Effects of total sleep deprivation on the mismatch negativity. *Psychophysiology, 38*, 787–795. [4]

Razoumnikova, O. M. (2000). Functional organization of different brain areas during convergent and divergent thinking: An EEG investigation. *Cognitive Brain Research, 10*, 11–18. [8]

Rebs, S., & Park, S. (2001). Gender differences in high-achieving students in math and science. *Journal for the Education of the Gifted, 25*, 52–73. [12]

Reinke, B. J., Ellicott, A. M., Harris, R. L., & Hancock, E. (1985). Timing of psychosocial changes in women's lives. *Human Development, 28*, 259–280. [10]

Reis, H. T., Wilson, I. M., Monestere, C., Bernstein, S., Clark, K., Seidl, E., Franco, M., Gioioso, E., Freeman, L., & Radoane, K. (1990). What is smiling is beautiful and good. *European Journal of Social Psychology, 20*, 259–267. [17]

Reite, M., Buysse, D., Reynolds, C., & Mendelson, W. (1995). The use of polysomnography in the evaluation of insomnia. *Sleep, 18*, 58–70. [4]

Reneman, L., Booij, J., Schmand, B., van den Brink, W., & Gunning, B. (2000). Memory disturbances in "Ecstasy" users are correlated with an altered brain serotonin neurotransmission. *Psychopharmacology, 148*, 322–324. [4]

Rentfrow, P., & Gosling, S. (2003). The do re mi's of everyday life: The structure and personality correlates of music preferences. *Journal of Personality & Social Psychology, 84*, 1236–1256. [14]

Rescorla, R. A. (1967). Pavlovian conditioning and its proper control procedures. *Psychological Review, 74*, 71–80. [5]

Rescorla, R. A. (1968). Probability of shock in the presence and absence of CS in fear conditioning. *Journal of Comparative and Physiological Psychology, 66*, 1–5. [5]

Rescorla, R. A. (1988). Pavlovian conditioning: It's not what you think it is. *American Psychologist, 43*, 151–160. [5]

Rescorla, R. A., & Wagner, A. R. (1972). A theory of Pavlovian conditioning: Variations in the effectiveness of reinforcement and nonreinforcement. In A. Black & W. F. Prokasy (Eds.), *Classical conditioning: II. Current research and theory.* New York: Appleton. [5]

Restak, R. (1988). *The mind.* Toronto: Bantam. [7]

Restak, R. (1993, September/October). Brain by design. *The Sciences*, pp. 27–33. [2]

Revensuo, A. (2000). The reinterpretation of dreams: An evolutionary hypothesis of the function of dreaming. *Behavioral & Brain Science, 23*. [4]

Reyner, A., & Horne, J. A. (1995). Gender- and age-related differences in sleep determined by home-recorded sleep logs and actimetry from 400 adults. *Sleep, 18*, 127–134. [4]

Reyner, L. A., & Horne, J. A. (1998). Evaluation of "in-car" countermeasures to sleepiness: Cold air and radio. *Sleep, 21*, 46–50. [4]

Reynolds, E. (2002). Benefits and risks of folic acid to the nervous system. *Journal of Neurology*, 72, 567–571. [10]

Rhéaume, J., & Ladouceur, R. (2000). Cognitive and behavioural treatments of checking behaviours: An examination of individual cognitive change. *Clinical Psychology & Psychotherapy*, 7, 118–127. [16]

Rhodes, N., & Wood, W. (1992). Self-esteem and intelligence affect influenceability: The medicating role of message reception. *Psychological Bulletin, 111*, 156–171. [17]

Rice, M. L. (1989). Children's language acquisition. *American Psychologist, 44*, 149–156. [9]

Rice, M. L., Huston, A. C., Truglio, R., & Wright, J. (1990). Words from "Sesame Street": Learning vocabulary while viewing. *Developmental Psychology, 26*, 421–428. [9]

Richter, W., Somorjai, R., Summers, R., Jarmasz, M., Ravi, S., Menon, J. S., et al. (2000). Motor area activity during mental rotation studied by time-resolved single-trial fMRI. *Journal of Cognitive Neuroscience, 12*, 310–320. [7]

Rickels, K., Schweizer, E., Weiss, S., & Zavodnick, S. (1993). Maintenance drug treatment for panic disorder II. Short- and long-term outcome after drug taper. *Archives of General Psychiatry, 50*, 61–68. [16]

Riedel, G. (1996). Function of metabotropic glutamate receptors in learning and memory. *Trends in Neurosciences, 19,* 219–224. [2, 6]

Righetti, P. (1996). The emotional experience of the fetus: A preliminary report. *Pre- & Peri-Natal Psychology Journal, 11,* 55–65. [9]

Riley, K., Snowdon, D., & Markesbery, W. (2002). Alzheimer's neurofibrillary pathology and the spectrum of cognitive function: Findings from the Nun study. *Annals of Neurology, 51,* 567–577. [10]

Rimland, B. (1978). Inside the mind of the autistic savant. *Psychology Today, 12,* 69–80. [8]

Riva, D., & Giorgi, C. (2000). The cerebellum contributes to higher functions during development. *Brain, 123,* 1051–1061. [2]

Rivas-Vasquez, R. (2001). St. John's Wort (Hypericum Perforatum): Practical considerations based on the evidence. *Professional Psychology: Research and Practice, 32,* 329–332. [4]

Roan, S. (2000, March 6). Cyber analysis. *L.A. Times.* [16]

Roberts, B. W., & DelVecchio, W. F. (2000). The rank-order consistency of personality traits from childhood to old age: A quantitative review of longitudinal studies. *Psychological Bulletin, 126,* 3–25. [14]

Roberts, J., & Bell, M. (2000). Sex differences on a mental rotation task: Variations in electroencephalogram hemispheric activation between children and college students. *Developmental Neuropsychology, 17,* 199–223. [2]

Roberts, P., & Moseley, B. (1996, May/June). Fathers' time. *Psychology Today, 29,* 48–55, 81. [9]

Robertson, G. L. (1983). Thirst and vasopressin function in normal and disordered states of water balance. *Journal of Laboratory and Clinical Medicine, 101,* 351–371. [11]

Robertson, I. H., & Murre, J. M. J. (1999). Rehabilitation of brain damage: Brain plasticity and principles of guided recovery. *Psychological Bulletin, 125,* 544–575. [2]

Robie, C., Johnson, K., Nilsen, D., & Hazucha, J. (2001). The right stuff: Understanding cultural differences in leadership performance. *Journal of Management Development, 20,* 639–650. [18]

Robins, C. J., & Hayes, A. M. (1993). An appraisal of cognitive therapy. *Journal of Consulting and Clinical Psychology, 61,* 205–214. [16]

Robins, R. W., Gosling, S. D., & Craik, K. H. (1999). An empirical analysis of trends in psychology. *American Psychologist, 54,* 117–128. [1]

Robinson, D., Phillips, P. Budygin, E., Trafton, B., Garris, P., & Wightman, R. (2001). Sub-second changes in accumbal dopamine during sexual behavior in male rats. *Neuroreport: For Rapid Communication of Neuroscience Research, 12,* 2549–2552. [4]

Rock, I., & Palmer, S. (1990). The legacy of Gestalt psychology. *Scientific American, 263,* 84–90. [5]

Rodin, J. (1985). Insulin levels, hunger, and food intake: An example of feedback loops in body weight regulation. *Health Psychology, 4,* 1–24. [11]

Rodin, J., & Ickovics, J. R. (1990). Women's health: Review and research agenda as we approach the 21st century. *American Psychologist, 45,* 1018–1034. [13]

Rodin, J., & Salovey, P. (1989). Health psychology. *Annual Review of Psychology, 40,* 533–579. [13]

Rodin, J., & Wing, R. R. (1988). Behavioral factors in obesity. *Diabetes/Metabolism Reviews, 4,* 701–725. [11]

Rodin, J., Wack, J., Ferrannini, E., & DeFronzo, R. A. (1985). Effect of insulin and glucose on feeding behavior. *Metabolism, 34,* 826–831. [11]

Roediger, H. L., III. (1980). The effectiveness of four mnemonics in ordering recall. *Journal of Experimental Psychology: Human Learning and Memory, 6,* 558–567. [6]

Roediger, H. L., III, & McDermott, K. B. (1995). Creating false memories: Remembering words not presented in lists. *Journal of Experimental Psychology: Learning, Memory, and Cognition, 21,* 803–814. [6]

Roehling, P., Roehling, M., & Moen, P. (2001). The relationship between work-life policies and practices and employee loyalty: A life course perspective. *Journal of Family & Economic Issues, 22,* 141–170. [18]

Roehrich, L., & Kinder, B. N. (1991). Alcohol expectancies and male sexuality: Review and implications for sex therapy. *Journal of Sex and Marital Therapy, 17,* 45–54. [4]

Roesch, S. C., & Amirkhan, J. H. (1997). Boundary condition for self-serving attributions: Another look at the sports pages. *Journal of Applied Social Psychology, 27,* 245–261. [17]

Rogers, C. R. (1951). *Client-centered therapy: Its current practice, implications, and theory.* Boston: Houghton Mifflin. [14, 16]

Rogoff, B., & Mistry, J. (1985). Memory development in cultural context. In M. Pressley & C. Brainerd (Eds.), *The cognitive side of memory development.* New York: Springer-Verlag. [6]

Romach, M., Busto, U., Somer, G., et al. (1995). Clinical aspects of chronic use of alprazolam and lorazepam. *American Journal of Psychiatry, 152,* 1161–1167. [16]

Roorda, A., & Williams, D. R. (1999). The arrangement of the three cone classes in the living human eye. *Nature, 397,* 520–521. [3]

Rosch, E. H. (1973). Natural categories. *Cognitive Psychology, 4,* 328–350. [7]

Rosch, E. H. (1987). Linguistic relativity. *Et Cetera, 44,* 254–279. [7]

Rose, R. J., Koskenvuo, M., Kaprio, J., Sarna, S., & Langinvainio, H. (1988). Shared genes, shared experiences, and similarity of personality: Data from 14,288 adult Finnish co-twins. *Journal of Personality and Social Psychology, 54,* 161–171. [14]

Rosekind, M. R. (1992). The epidemiology and occurrence of insomnia. *Journal of Clinical Psychiatry, 53*(6, Suppl.), 4–6. [4]

Rosen, R. C. (1996). Erectile dysfunction: The medicalization of male sexuality. *Clinical Psychology Review, 16,* 497–519. [12]

Rosen, R. C., & Leiblum, S. R. (1995). Treatment of sexual disorders in the 1990s: An integrated approach. *Journal of Consulting and Clinical Psychology, 63,* 877–896. [12]

Rosenbluth, R., Grossman, E. S., & Kaitz, M. (2000). Performance of early-blind and sighted children on olfactory tasks. *Perception, 29,* 101–110. [3]

Rosenfeld, J. P. (1995). Alternative views of Bashore and Rapp's (1993) alternatives to traditional polygraphy: A critique. *Psychological Bulletin, 117,* 159–166. [11]

Rosengren, A., Tibblin, G., & Wilhelmsen, L. (1991). Self-perceived psychological stress and incidence of coronary artery disease in middle-aged men. *American Journal of Cardiology, 68,* 1171–1175. [13]

Rosenhan, D. L. (1973). On being sane in insane places. *Science, 179,* 250–258. [3]

Rosenstein, R., & Glickman, A. (1994). Type size and performance of the elderly on the Wonderlic Personnel Test. *Journal of Applied Gerontology, 13,* 185–192. [18]

Rosenvinge, J. H., Matinussen, M., & Ostensen, E. (2000). The comorbidity of eating disorders and personality disorders: A meta-analytic review of studies published between 1983 and 1998. *Eating and Weight Disorders: Studies on Anorexia, Bulimia, and Obesity, 5,* 52–61. [11]

Rosenzweig, M. R. (1961). Auditory localization. *Scientific American, 205,* 132–142. [3]

Ross, C. A., Norton, G. R., & Wozney, K. (1989). Multiple personality disorder: An analysis of 236 cases. *Canadian Journal of Psychiatry, 34,* 413–418. [15]

Ross, J., Baldessarini, R. J., & Tondo, L. (2000). Does lithium treatment still work? Evidence of stable responses over three decades. *Archives of General Psychiatry, 57*, 187–190. [16]

Rosser, R. (1994). *Cognitive development: Psychological and biological perspectives.* Boston, MA: Allyn & Bacon. [9]

Rossow, I., & Amundsen, A. (1997). Alcohol abuse and mortality: a 40-year prospective study of Norwegian conscripts. *Social Science & Medicine, 44*, 261–267. [10, 13]

Roth, T. (1996b). Social and economic consequences of sleep disorders. *Sleep, 19*, S46–S47. [4]

Rotter, J. B. (1966). Generalized expectancies for internal versus external control of reinforcement. *Psychological Monographs, 80*(1, Whole No. 609). [14]

Rotter, J. B. (1971, June). External control and internal control. *Psychology Today*, pp. 37–42, 58–59. [14]

Rotter, J. B. (1990). Internal versus external control of reinforcement: A case history of a variable. *American Psychologist, 45*, 489–493. [14]

Rotton, J., & Cohn, E. G. (2000). Violence is a curvilinear function of temperature in Dallas: A replication. *Journal of Personality & Social Psychology, 78*, 1074–1082. [17]

Rotton, J., Frey, J., Barry, T., Milligan, M., & Fitzpatrick, M. (1979). The air pollution experience and physical aggression. *Journal of Applied Social Psychology, 9*, 397–412. [17]

Rovee-Collier, C. (1990). The "memory system" of prelinguistic infants. *Annals of the New York Academy of Sciences, 608*, 517–576. [9]

Rowe, D. (1994). *The limits of family influence: Genes, experience, and behavior.* New York: Guilford. [14]

Rowe, D. (2003). Assessing genotype-environment interactions and correlations in the postgenomic era. In R. Plomin, J. DeFries, I. Craig, & P. McGuffin (Eds.), *Behavioral genetics in the postgenomic era* (pp. 71–86). Washington, DC: American Psychological Association. [17]

Rowe, D. C. (1987). Resolving the person-situation debate: Invitation to an interdisciplinary dialogue. *American Psychologist, 42*, 218–227. [14]

Rowe, J., & Kahn, R. (1998). *Successful aging.* New York: Pantheon. [10]

Rowland, D., & Tai, W. (2003). A review of plant-derived and herbal approaches to the treatment of sexual dysfunctions. *Journal of Sex & Marital Therapy, 29*, 185–205. [12]

Rowland, D., Tai, W., & Slob, A. (2003). An exploration of emotional response to erotic stimulation in men with premature ejaculation: Effects of treatment with clomipramine. *Archives of Sexual Behavior, 32*, 145–153. [12]

Rowley, S. (2000). Profiles of African American college students' educational utility and performance: A cluster analysis. *Journal of Black Psychology, 26*, 3–26. [10]

Royall, D., Chiodo, L., Polk, M., & Jaramillo, C. (2002). Severe dysosmia is specifically associated with Alzheimer-like memory deficits in nondemented elderly retirees. *Neuroepidemiology, 21*, 68–73. [3]

Rozell, E., Pettijohn, C., & Parker, R. (2002). An empirical evaluation of emotional intelligence: The impact on management development. *Journal of Management Development, 21*, 272–289. [8]

Rozin, P., & Zellner, D. (1985). The role of Pavlovian conditioning in the acquisition of food likes and dislikes. *Annals of the New York Academy of Sciences, 443*, 189–202. [5]

Rubin, K., Burgess, K., & Hastings, P. (2002). Stability and social-behavioral consequences of toddlers' inhibited temperament and parenting behaviors. *Child Development, 73*, 483–495. [9]

Rubinstein, G. (2001). Sex-role reversal and clinical judgment of mental health. *Journal of Sex & Marital Therapy, 27*, 9–19. [16]

Ruby, N., Dark, J., Burns, D., Heller, H., & Zucker, I. (2002). The suprachiasmatic nucleus is essential for circadian body temperature rhythms in hibernating ground squirrels. *Journal of Neuroscience, 22*, 357–364. [4]

Rudman, L., Ashmore, R., & Gary, M. (2001). "Unlearning" automatic biases: The malleability of implicit prejudice and stereotypes. *Journal of Personality & Social Psychology, 81*, 856–868. [17]

Rugg, M. D., Allan, K., & Birch, C. S. (2000). Electrophysiological evidence for the modulation of retrieval orientation by depth of study processing. *Journal of Cognitive Neuroscience, 12*, 664–678. [6]

Ruggero, M. A. (1992). Responses to sound of the basilar membrane of the mammalian cochlea. *Current Opinion in Neurobiology, 2*, 449–456. [3]

Ruggiero, K. M., & Taylor, D. M. (1997). Why minority group members perceive or do not perceive the discrimination that confronts them: The role of self-esteem and perceived control. *Journal of Personality and Social Psychology, 72*, 373–389. [17]

Rushton, J. P., Fulker, D. W., Neale, M. C., Nias, D. K. B., & Eysenck, H. J. (1986). Altruism and aggression: The heritability of individual differences. *Journal of Personality and Social Psychology, 50*, 1192–1198. [14, 17]

Rushton, J., & Jensen, A. (2003). African-White IQ differences from Zimbabwe on the Wechsler Intelligence Scale for Children-Revised are mainly on the *g* factor. *Personality & Individual Differences, 34*, 177–183. [8]

Russell, J. A. (1995). Facial expressions of emotion: What lies beyond minimal universality? *Psychological Bulletin, 118*, 379–391. [11]

Ryan, R., Kim, Y., & Kaplan, U. (2003). Differentiating autonomy from individualism and independence: A self-determination theory perspective on internalization of cultural orientations and well-being. *Journal of Personality and Social Psychology, 84*, 97–110. [14]

Sachs, G., Grossman, F., Ghaemi, S., Okamoto, A., & Bosden, C. (2002). Combination of a mood stabilizer with risperidone or haloperidol for treatment of acute mania: A double-blind, placebo-controlled comparison of efficacy and safety. *American Journal of Psychiatry, 159*, 1146–1154. [16]

Sackeim, H. A., Luber, B., Katzman, G. P., Moeller, J. R., Prudic, J., Devanand, D. P., & Nobler, M. S. (1996). The effects of electroconvulsive therapy on quantitative electroencephalograms. *Archives of General Psychiatry, 53*, 814–824. [16]

Sackeim, H. A., Prudic, J., Devanand, D. P., Nobler, M. S., Lisanby, S. H., Peyser, S., Fitzsimons, L., Moody, B. J., & Clark, J. (2000). A prospective, randomized, double-blind comparison of bilateral and right unilateral electroconvulsive therapy at different stimulus intensities. *Archives of General Psychiatry, 57*, 425–434. [16]

Sacks, O. (1984). *A leg to stand on.* New York: Harper & Row. [15]

Saczynski, J., Willis, S., & Schaie, K. W. (2002). Strategy use in reasoning training with older adults. *Aging, Neuropsychology, & Cognition, 9*, 48–60. [10]

Sadeh, A., Gruber, R., & Raviv, A. (2003). The effect of sleep restriction and extension on school-age children: What a difference an hour makes. *Child Development, 74*, 444–455. [4]

Sadker, D., & Sadker, M. (1994). *Failing at fairness: How America's schools cheat girls.* New York: Scribner's. [12]

Salisch, M. (2001). Children's emotional development: Challenges in their relationships to parents, peers, and friends. *International Journal of Behavioural Development, 25*, 310–319. [11]

Salmon, J., Owen, N., Crawford, D., Bauman, A., & Sallis, J. (2003). Physical activity and sedentary behavior: A population-based study of barriers, enjoyment, and preference. *Health Psychology, 22*, 178–188. [13]

Salo, J., Niemelae, A., Joukamaa, M., & Koivukangas, J. (2002). Effect of brain tumour laterality on patients' perceived quaity of life. *Journal of Neurology, Neurosurgery, & Psychiatry, 72*, 373–377. [2]

Salovey, P., & Pizarro, D. (2003). The value of emotional intelligence. In R. Sternberg, J. Lautrey, & T. Lubart (Eds.), *Models of intelligence: International perspective* (pp. 263–278). Washington, DC: American Psychological Association. [8]

Salthouse, T. A. (1996). The processing-speed theory of adult age differences in cognition. *Psychological Review, 103*, 403–428. [10]

Salzinger, S., Feldman, R. S., Hammer, M., & Rosario, M. (1993). The effects of physical abuse on children's social relationships. *Child Development, 64*, 169–187. [9]

Sanbonmatsu, D. M., & Fazio, R. H. (1990). The role of attitudes in memory-based decision making. *Journal of Personality and Social Psychology, 59*, 614–622. [17]

Sandfur, G. D., Rindfuss, R. R., & Cohen, B. (Eds.). (1996). *American Indian demography and public health*. Washington, DC: National Academy Press. [13]

Sanes, J. N., & Donoghue, J. P. (2000). Plasticity and primary motor cortex. *Annual Review of Neuroscience, 23*, 393–415. [2]

Sanes, J. N., Donoghue, J. P., Thangaraj, V., Edelman, R. R., & Warach, S. (1995). Shared neural substrates controlling hand movements in human motor cortex. *Science, 268*, 1775. [2]

Sanfilippo, M., Lafargue, T., Rusinek, H., Arena, L., Loneragan, C., Lautin, A., Feiner, D., Rotrosen, J., & Wolkin, A. (2000). Volumetric measure of the frontal and temporal lobe regions in schizophrenia. *Archives of General Psychiatry, 57*, 471–480. [15]

Sano, M., Ernesto, C., Thomas, R. G., Kauber, M. R., Schafer, K., Grundman, M., Woodbury, P., Growdon, J., Cotman, C. W., Pfeiffer, E., Schneider, L. S., & Thal, L. J. (1997). A controlled trial of selegiline, alpha-tocopherol, or both as treatment for Alzheimer's disease. *New England Journal of Medicine, 336*, 1216–1222. [10]

Santiago-Rivera, A., & Altarriba, J. (2002). The role of language in therapy with the Spanish-English bilingual client. *Professional Psychology: Research & Practice, 33*, 30–38. [16]

Sarfati, Y. (2000). Deficit of the theory-of-mind in schizophrenia: Clinical concept and review of experimental arguments. *Canadian Journal of Psychiatry, 45*, 4363–4368. [9]

Sarkis, K. (2000, May). Computer workers at risk for stress injuries. *Occupational Hazards, 62*, 33. [18]

Sarrio, M., Barbera, E., Ramos, A., & Candela, C. (2002). The glass ceiling in the professional promotion of women. *Revista de Psicologia Social, 17*, 167–182. [18]

Sass, H., Soyha, M., Mann, K., & Zieglgänsberger, W. (1996). Relapse prevention by acamprosate: Results from a placebo-controlled study on alcohol dependence. *Archives of General Psychiatry, 53*, 673–680. [13]

Sastry, R., Lee, D., & Har-El, G. (1997). Palate perforation from cocaine abuse. *Otolaryngol Head Neck Surgery, 116*, 565–566. [4]

Sateia, M. J., Doghramji, K., Hauri, P. J., & Morin, C. M. (2000). Evaluation of chronic insomnia. An American Academy of Sleep Medicine review. *Sleep, 23*, 243–308. [4]

Savage-Rumbaugh, E. S. (1986). *Ape language*. New York: Columbia University Press. [7]

Savage-Rumbaugh, E. S. (1990). Language acquisition in a nonhuman species: Implications for the innateness debate. *Developmental Psychology, 26*, 599–620. [7]

Savage-Rumbaugh, E. S. (1993). Language learnability in man, ape, and dolphin. In H. L. Roitblat, L. M. Herman, & P. E. Nachtigall (Eds.), *Language and communication: Comparative perspectives. Comparative cognition and neuroscience* (pp. 457–484). Hillsdale, NJ: Erlbaum. [7]

Savage-Rumbaugh, E. S., Sevcik, R. A., Brakke, K. E., & Rumbaugh, D. M. (1992). Symbols: Their communicative use, communication, and combination by bonobos (*Pan paniscus*). In L. P. Lipsitt & C. Rovee-Collier (Eds.). *Advances in infancy research* (Vol. 7, pp. 221–278). Norwood, NJ: Ablex. [7]

Scarr, S., Pakstis, A., Katz, S., & Barker, W. (1977). Absence of a relationship between degree of White ancestry and intellectual skills within a Black population. *Human Genetics, 39*, 69–86. [8]

Scarr, S., & Weinberg, R. (1976). The influence of "family background" on intellectual attainment. *American Sociological Review, 43*, 674–692. [8]

Schaal, B., Marlier, L., & Soussignan, R. (1998). Olfactory function in the human fetus: Evidence from selective neonatal responsiveness to the odor of amniotic fluid. *Behavioral Neuroscience, 112*, 1438–1449. [9]

Schab, F. R. (1990). Odors and the remembrance of things past. *Journal of Experimental Psychology: Learning, Memory, and Cognition, 16*, 648–655. [6]

Schachter, S., & Singer, J. E. (1962). Cognitive, social, and physiological determinants of emotional state. *Psychological Review, 69*, 379–399. [11]

Schaie, K. W. (1990). Late life potential and cohort differences in mental abilities. In M. Perlmutter (Ed.), *Late life potential* (pp. 43–61). Washington, DC: Gerontological Society. [10]

Schaie, K. W. (1993). Ageist language in psychological research. *American Psychologist, 48*, 49–51. [1]

Schaie, K. W. (1994). The course of adult intellectual development. *American Psychologist, 49*, 304–313. [10]

Schaie, K. W. (1995). *Intellectual development in adulthood: The Seattle Longitudinal Study*. New York: Cambridge University Press. [10]

Schaie, K. W., & Willis, S. L. (1996). *Adult development and aging* (4th ed.). New York: HarperCollins. [10]

Schenck, C. H., & Mahowald, M. W. (1995). A polysomnographically documented case of adult somnambulism with long-distance automobile driving and frequent nocturnal violence: Parasomnia with continuing danger as a noninsane automatism? *Sleep, 18*, 765–772. [4]

Schenck, C. H., & Mahowald, M. W. (2000). Parasomnias. Managing bizarre sleep-related behavior disorders. *Postgraduate Medicine, 107*, 145–156. [4]

Scherer, K. R., & Wallbott, H. G. (1994). Evidence for universality and cultural variation of differential emotion response patterning. *Journal of Personality and Social Psychology, 66*, 310–328. [11]

Scherer, K. R., Wallbott, H. G., & Summerfield, A. B. (1986). *Experiencing emotion: A cross-cultural study*. Cambridge, England: Cambridge University Press. [11]

Schermerhorn, J., Hunt, J., & Osborn, R. (2000). *Organizational Behavior* (7th ed.). New York: John Wiley & Sons. [18]

Scheuffgen, K., Happé, F., Anderson, M., & Frith, U. (2000). High "intelligence," low "IQ"? Speed of processing and measured IQ in children with autism. *Developmental Psychopathology, 12*, 183–190. [8]

Scheuneman, J., Camara, W., Cascallar, A., Wendler, C., & Lawrence, I. (2002). Calculator access, use, and type in relation to performance on the SAT I: Reasoning in mathematics. *Applied Measurement in Education, 15*, 95–112. [8]

Schieber, M. H., & Hibbard, L. S. (1993). How somatotopic is the motor cortex hand area? *Science, 261*, 489–492. [2]

Schieman, S., & Taylor, J. (2001). Statuses, roles, and the sense of mattering. *Sociological Perspectives, 44*, 469–484. [18]

Schiff, M., & Lewontin, R. (1986). *Education and class: The irrelevance of IQ genetic studies.* Oxford, England: Clarendon. [8]

Schiller, F. (1993). *Paul Broca: Explorer of the brain.* Oxford: Oxford University Press. [2]

Schlenger, W., Caddell, J., Ebert, L., Jordan, B., Rourke, K., Wilson, D., Thalji, L., Dennis, J., Fairbank, J., & Kulka, R. (2002). Psychological reactions to terrorist attacks: Findings from the National Study of Americans' Reactions to September 11. *JAMA: Journal of the American Medical Association, 288*, 581–588. [13]

Schmidt, S., Oliveira, R., Rocha, F., & Abreu-Villaca, Y. (2000). Influence of handedness and gender on the grooved pegboard task. *Brain & Cognition, 44*, 445–454. [2]

Schneider, W., & Pressley, M. (1989). *Memory development between 2 and 20.* New York: Springer-Verlag. [9]

Schofield, J. W., & Francis, W. D. (1982). An observational study of peer interaction in racially mixed "accelerated" classrooms. *Journal of Educational Psychology, 74*, 722–732. [9]

Scholl, T. O., Heidiger, M. L., & Belsky, D. H. (1996). Prenatal care and maternal health during adolescent pregnancy: A review and meta-analysis. *Journal of Adolescent Health, 15*, 444–456. [10]

Scholz, U., Dona, B., Sud, S., & Schwarzer, R. (2002). Is general self-efficacy a universal construct? Psychometric findings from 25 countries. *European Journal of Psychological Assessment, 18*, 242–251. [14]

Schou, M. (1997). Forty years of lithium treatment. *Archives of General Psychiatry, 54*, 9–13. [16]

Schuckit, M., Edenberg, H., Kalmijn, J., Flury, L., Smith, T., Reich, T., Beirut, L., Goate, A., & Foroud, T. (2001). A genome-wide search for gens that relate to a low level of response to alcohol. *Alcoholism: Clinical & Experimental Research, 25*, 323–329. [4]

Schuckit, M. A., Tipp, J. E., Bergman, M., Reich, W., Hesselbrock, V. M., & Smith, T. L. (1997). Comparison of induced and independent major depressive disorders in 2,945 alcoholics. *American Journal of Psychiatry, 154*, 948–957. [13]

Schultz, D. (1975). *A history of modern psychology* (2nd ed.). New York: Academic Press. [5]

Schulz, R., & Heckhausen, J. (1996). A life span model of successful aging. *American Psychologist, 51*, 702–714. [10]

Schupp, H., Junghöfer, M., Weike, A., & Hamm, A. (2003). Emotional facilitation of sensory processing in the visual cortex. *Psychological Science, 14*, 7–13. [11]

Schwartz, D. L. (2000). Physical imagery: Kinematic versus dynamic models. *Cognitive Psychology, 38*, 433–464. [7]

Schwartz, G. E. (1982). Testing the biopsychosocial model: The ultimate challenge facing behavioral medicine? *Journal of Consulting and Clinical Psychology, 50*, 1040–1052. [13]

Schwartz, N. (1999). Self-reports: How the questions shape the answers. *American Psychologist, 54*, 93–105. [1]

Schwartz, R. H., & Miller, N. S. (1997). MDMA (Ecstasy) and the rave: A review. *Pediatrics, 100*, 705–708. [4]

Schwartz, S., & Maquet, P. (2002). Sleep imaging and the neuropsychological assessment of dreams. *Trends in Cognitive Sciences, 6*, 23–30. [4]

Schwebke, J. R. (1991a, March). Gonorrhea in the '90s. *Medical Aspects of Human Sexuality, 24*, 42–46. [12]

Schwebke, J. R. (1991b, April). Syphilis in the '90s. *Medical Aspects of Human Sexuality, 25*, 44–49. [12]

Schwitzer, A., Griffin, O., Ancie, J., & Thomas, C. (1999). Social adjustment experiences of African American college students. *Journal of Counseling & Development, 77*, 189–197. [10]

Scott, J. (1996). Cognitive therapy of affective disorders: A review. *Journal of Affective Disorders, 37*, 1–11. [16]

Scott, S. K., Young, A. W., Calder, A. J., Hellawell, D. J., Aggleton, J. P., & Johnson, M. (1997). Impaired auditory recognition of fear and anger following bilateral amygdala lesions. *Nature, 385*, 254–257. [2]

Scully, J., Tosi, H., & Banning, K. (2000). Life event checklists: Revisiting the Social Readjustment Rating Scale after 30 years. *Educational & Psychological Measurement, 60*, 864–876. [13]

Sedikides, C., Gaertner, L., & Toguchi, Y. (2003). Pancultural self-enhancement. *Journal of Personality & Social Psychology, 84*, 60–79. [14]

Seeman, M., & Seeman, A. Z. (1992). Life strains, alienation, and drinking behavior. *Alcoholism: Clinical and Experimental Research, 16*, 199–205. [13]

Seeman, T., Dubin, L., & Seeman, M. (2003). Religiosity/spirituality and health. *American Psychologist, 58*, 53–63. [4, 13]

Seenoo, K., & Takagi, O. (2003). The effect of helping behaviors on helper: A case study of volunteer work for local resident welfare. *Japanese Journal of Social Psychology, 18*, 106–118. [17]

Segal, S. J., & Fusella, V. (1970). Influence of imaged pictures and sounds on detection of visual and auditory signals. *Journal of Experimental Psychology, 83*, 458–464. [7]

Segal, Z., Williams, M., & Teasdale, J. (2001). *Mindfulness-based cognitive therapy for depression.* New York: Guilford Press. [4]

Segall, M. H. (1994). A cross-cultural research contribution to unraveling the nativist/empiricist controversy. In J. Lonner & R. Malpass (Eds.), *Psychology and culture* (pp. 135–138). Boston: Allyn & Bacon. [3]

Segall, M. H., Campbell, D. T., & Herskovitz, M. J. (1966). *The influence of culture on visual perception.* Indianapolis: Bobbs-Merrill. [3]

Seger, C. A., Desmond, J. E., Glover, G. H., & Gabrieli, J. D. E. (2000). Functional magnetic resonance imaging evidence for right-hemisphere involvement in processing unusual semantic relationships. *Neuropsychology, 14*, 361–369. [2]

Seidman, S. (2002). Exploring the relationship between depression and erectile dysfunction in aging men. *Journal of Clinical Psychiatry, 63*, 5–12. [15]

Sejnowski, T. J. (1997). The year of the dendrite. *Science, 275*, 178–179. [2]

Seligman, M. E. P. (1970). On the generality of the laws of learning. *Psychological Review, 77*, 406–418. [5]

Seligman, M. E. P. (1972). Phobias and preparedness. In M. E. P. Seligman & J. L. Hager (Eds.), *Biological boundaries of learning.* Englewood Cliffs, NJ: Prentice Hall.

Seligman, M. E. P. (1975). *Helplessness: On depression, development and death.* San Francisco: Freeman. [5]

Seligman, M. E. P. (1990). *Learned optimism: How to change your mind and your life.* New York: Simon & Schuster. [8, 13, 14]

Seligman, M. E. P. (1991). *Learned optimism.* New York: Knopf. [5]

Seligman, M. E. P. (1995). The effectiveness of psychotherapy: The *Consumer Reports* Study. *American Psychologist, 50*, 965–974. [16]

Seligman, M. E. P. (1996). Science as an ally of practice. *American Psychologist, 51*, 1072–1079. [16]

Selkoe, D. J. (1997). Alzheimer's disease: Genotypes, phenotype, and treatments. *Science, 275*, 630–631. [10]

Sell, R. L., Wells, J. A., and Wypij, D. (1995). The prevalence of homosexual behavior and attraction in the United States, the United Kingdom and France: Results of national population-based samples. *Archives of Sexual Behavior, 24*, 235–248. [12]

Selye, H. (1956). *The stress of life.* New York: McGraw-Hill. [13]

Senchak, M., Leonard, K., & Greene, B. (1998). Alcohol use among college students as a function of their typical social drinking context. *Psychology of Addictive Behaviors, 12*, 62–70. [10]

Sensky, T., Turkington, D., Kingdon, D., Scott, J. L., Scott, J., Siddle, R., O'Carroll, M., & Barnes, T. R. E. (2000). A randomized controlled trial of cognitive-behavioral therapy for persistent symptoms in schizophrenia resistant to medication. *Archives of General Psychiatry, 57*, 165–172. [16]

Serdula, M. K., Collins, M. E., Williamson, D. F., Anda, R. F., Pamuk, E. P., & Byers, T. E. (1993). Weight control practices of U.S. adolescents and adults. *Annals of Internal Medicine, 119*, 667–671. [11]

Serpell R., & Hatano, G. (1997). Education, schooling, and literacy. In J. Berry, P. Dasen, & T. Sarswthi (Eds.), *Handbook of cross-cultural psychology* (Vol. 2). Boston, MA: Allyn & Bacon. [9]

Shackelford, T., Buss, D., & Bennett, K. (2002). Forgiveness or breakup: Sex differences in responses to a partner's infidelity. *Cognition & Emotion, 16*, 299–307. [1]

Shaffer, D., Gould, M. S., Fisher, P., Trautman, P., Moreau, D., Kleinman, M., & Flory, M. (1996). Psychiatric diagnosis in child and adolescent suicide. *Archives of General Psychiatry, 53*, 339–348. [15]

Shapiro, J. P., & Schrof, J. M. (1995, February 27). Honor thy children. *U.S. News & World Report*, pp. 38–49. [9]

Sharpe, D., Hermsen, J., & Billings, J. (2002). Gender differences in use of alternative full-time work arrangements by married workers. *Family & Consumer Sciences Research Journal, 31*, 78–111. [18]

Sharpe, P. (2002). Preparing for primary school in Singapore: Aspects of adjustment to the more formal demands of the primary one mathematics syllabus. *Early Child Development & Care, 172*, 329–335. [8]

Shaw, J. I., & Steers, W. N. (2001). Gathering information to form an impression: Attribute categories and information valence. *Current Research in Social Psychology, 6*, 1–21. [14]

Shaw, J. S., III. (1996). Increases in eyewitness confidence resulting from postevent questioning. *Journal of Experimental Psychology: Applied, 2*, 126–146. [6]

Shaw, V. N., Hser, Y.-I., Anglin, M. D., & Boyle, K. (1999). Sequences of powder cocaine and crack use among arrestees in Los Angeles County. *American Journal of Drug and Alcohol Abuse, 25*, 47–66. [4]

Shears, J., Robinson, J., & Emde, R. (2002). Fathering relationships and their associations with juvenile delinquency. *Infant Mental Health Journal, 23*, 79–87. [9]

Sheehan, D. V., & Raj, A. B. (1988). Monoamine oxidase inhibitors. In C. G. Last & M. Hersen (Eds.), *Handbook of anxiety disorders* (pp. 478–506). New York: Pergamon. [16]

Shepard, R. J. (1986). Exercise in coronary heart disease. *Sports Medicine, 3*, 26–49. [13]

Shepard, R. N., & Metzler, J. (1971). Mental rotation of three-dimensional objects. *Science, 171*, 701–703. [7]

Shepperd, J. (2001). The desire to help and behavior in social dilemmas: Exploring responses to catastrophes. *Group Dynamics, 5*, 304–314. [17]

Shepperd, J. A. (1993). Productivity loss in performance groups: A motivation analysis. *Psychological Bulletin, 113*, 67–81. [11]

Sher, A. E., Schechtman, K. B., & Piccirillo, J. F. (1996). The efficacy of surgical modifications of the upper airway in adults with obstructive sleep apnea syndrome. *Sleep, 19*, 156–177. [4]

Sherbourne, C. D., Wells, K. B., & Judd, L. L. (1996). Functioning and well-being of patients with panic disorder. *American Journal of Psychiatry, 153*, 213–218. [15]

Sherif, M. (1956). Experiments in group conflict. *Scientific American, 195*, 53–58. [17]

Sherif, M. (1958). Superordinate goals in the reduction of intergroup conflict. *American Journal of Sociology, 63*, 349–358. [17]

Sherif, M., & Sherif, C. W. (1967). The Robbers' Cave study. In J. F. Perez, R. C. Sprinthall, G. S. Grosser, & P. J. Anastasiou, *General psychology: Selected readings* (pp. 411–421). Princeton, NJ: D. Van Nostrand. [17]

Sherman, C. (1994, September/October). Kicking butts. *Psychology Today*, 41–45. [4, 13]

Shimamura, A. P., Berry, J. M., Mangela, J. A., Rusting, C. L., & Jurica, P. J. (1995). Memory and cognitive abilities in university professors: Evidence for successful aging. *Psychological Science, 6*, 271–277. [10]

Shneidman, E. (1989). The Indian summer of life: A preliminary study of septuagenarians. *American Psychologist, 44*, 684–694. [8]

Shneidman, E. S. (1994). Clues to suicide, reconsidered. *Suicide and Life-Threatening Behavior, 24*, 395–397. [15]

Shoda, Y., Mischel, W., & Peake, P. K. (1990). Predicting adolescent cognitive and self-regulatory competencies from preschool delay of gratification. *Developmental Psychology, 26*, 978–986. [8]

Shu, H., Anderson, R., & Wu, N. (2000). Phonetic awareness: Knowledge of orthography-phonology relationships in the character acquisition of Chinese children. *Journal of Educational Psychology, 92*, 56–62. [9]

Shumaker, S., Legault, C., Rapp, S., Thal, L., Wallace, R., Ockene, J., Hendrix, S., Jones, B., Assaf, A., Jackson, R., Kotchen, J., Wassertheil-Smoller, S., & Wactawski-Wende, J. (2003). Estrogen plus progestin and the incidence of dementia and mild cognitive impairment in postmenopausal women: The Women's Health Initiative Memory Study: A randomized controlled trial. *Journal of the American Medical Association (JAMA), 289*, 2651–2662. [6]

Shupe, E., Cortina, L., Ramos, A., Fitzgerald, L., & Salisbury, J. (2002). The incidence and outcomes of sexual harassment among Hispanic and non-Hispanic white women: A comparison across levels of cultural affiliation. *Psychology of Women Quarterly, 26*, 298–308. [18]

Siegrist, J., Peter, R., Junge, A., Cremer, P., & Seidel, D. (1990). Low status control, high effort at work and ischemic heart disease: Prospective evidence from blue-collar men. *Social Science and Medicine, 31*, 1127–1134. [13]

Silva, C. E., & Kirsch, I. (1992). Interpretive sets, expectancy, fantasy proneness, and dissociation as predictors of hypnotic response. *Journal of Personality and Social Psychology, 63*, 847–856. [4]

Silver, R., Holman, E., McIntosh, D., Poulin, M., & Gil-Rivas, V. (2002). Nationwide longitudinal study of psychological responses to September 11. *JAMA: Journal of the American Medical Association, 288*, 1235–1244. [13]

Simon, H. A. (1995). The information-processing theory of mind. *American Psychologist, 50*, 507–508. [7]

Simon, H. B. (1988, June). Running and rheumatism. *Harvard Medical School Health Letter, 13*, 2–4. [13]

Simons, D. & Chabris, C. (1999). Gorillas in our midst: Sustained inattentional blindness for dynamic events. *Perception, 28*, 1059–1074. [3]

Simons, D., Wurtele, S., & Heil, P. (2002). Childhood victimization and lack of empathy as predictors of sexual offending against women and children. *Journal of Interpersonal Violence, 17*, 1291–1307. [12]

Simons, J., & Carey, K. (2002). Risk and vulnerability for marijuana use problems. *Psychology of Addictive Behaviors, 16*, 72–75. [4, 11]

Simons, T., & Roberson, Q. (2003). Why managers should care about fairness: The effects of aggregate justice perceptions on organizational outcomes. *Journal of Applied Psychology, 88*, 432–443. [18]

Singer, J. L., & Singer, D. G. (1979, March). Come back, Mister Rogers, come back. *Psychology Today*, pp. 56–60. [9]

Singer, M. I., Miller, D. B., Guo, S., Flannery, D. J., Frierson, T., & Slovak, K. (1999). Contributors to violent behavior among elementary and middle school children. *Pediatrics, 104*(Pt. 1), 878–884. [17]

Singh, B. (1991). Teaching methods for reducing prejudice and enhancing academic achievement for all children. *Educational Studies, 17*, 157–171. [17]

Singh, D. (1995b). Female health, attractiveness, and desirability for relationships: Role of breast asymmetry and waist-hip ratio. *Ethology and Sociobiology, 16*, 445–481. [17]

Sivacek, J., & Crano, W. D. (1982). Vested interest as a moderator of attitude-behavior consistency. *Journal of Personality and Social Psychology, 43*, 210–221. [17]

Skinner, B. F. (1938). *The behavior of organisms.* New York: Appleton-Century-Crofts. [5]

Skinner, B. F. (1948a). "Superstition" in the pigeon. *Journal of Experimental Psychology, 38*, 168–172. [5]

Skinner, B. F. (1948b). *Walden two.* New York: Macmillan. [5]

Skinner, B. F. (1953). *Science and human behavior.* New York: Macmillan. [5, 14]

Skinner, B. F. (1957). *Verbal behavior.* New York: Appleton Century. [9]

Skinner, B. F. (1971). *Beyond freedom and dignity.* New York: Knopf. [5]

Skrabalo, A. (2000). Negative symptoms in schizophrenia(s): The conceptual basis. *Harvard Brain, 7*, 7–10. [15]

Skuy, M., Taylor, M., O'Carroll, S., Fridjhon, P., & Rosenthal, L. (2000). Performance of black and white South African children on the Wechsler Intelligence Scale for Children—Revised and the Kaufman Assessment Battery. *Psychological Reports, 86*, 1727–1737. [8]

Slaby, R. G., Roedell, W. C., Arezzo, D., & Hendrix, K. (1995). *Early violence prevention.* Washington, DC: National Association for the Education of Young Children. [9]

Slawinski, E. B., Hartel, D. M., & Kline, D. W. (1993). Self-reported hearing problems in daily life throughout adulthood. *Psychology and Aging, 8*, 552–561. [10]

Smith, B., Elliott, A., Chambers, W., Smith, W., Hannaford, P., & Penny, K. (2001). The impact of chronic pain in the community. *Family Practice, 18*, 292–299. [3]

Smith, C. (1995). Sleep states and memory processes. *Behavioural Brain Research, 69*, 137–145. [4]

Smith, L. (2003). Learning to recognize objects. *Psychological Science, 14*, 244–250. [7]

Smith, M. L., Glass, G. V., & Miller, T. I. (1980). *The benefits of psychotherapy.* Baltimore, MD: Johns Hopkins University Press. [16]

Smith, P. K. (1979). The ontogeny of fear in children. In W. Sluckin (Ed.), *Fears in animals and man* (pp. 164–168). London: Von Nostrand Reinhold. [9]

Smith, S. M., Glenberg, A., & Bjork, R. A. (1978). Environmental context and human memory. *Memory & Cognition, 6*, 342–353. [6]

Smith, T., & Ruiz, J. (2002). Psychosocial influences on the development and course of coronary heart disease: Current status and implications for research and practice. *Journal of Consulting and Clinical Psychology, 70* , 548–568. [13]

Smolar, A. (1999). Bridging the gap: Technical aspects of the analysis of an Asian immigrant. *Journal of Clinical Psychoanalysis, 8*, 567–594. [16]

Snarey, J. R. (1985). Cross-cultural universality of social-moral development: A critical review of Kohlbergian research. *Psychological Bulletin, 97*, 202–232. [10]

Snarey, J. R. (1995). In communitarian voice: The sociological expansion of Kohlbergian theory, research, and practice. In W. M. Kurtines & J. L. Gerwirtz (Eds.), *Moral development: An introduction* (pp. 109–134). Boston: Allyn & Bacon. [10]

Snow, C. E. (1993). Bilingualism and second language acquisition. In J. B. Gleason & N. B. Ratner (Eds.), *Psycholinguistics.* Fort Worth, TX: Harcourt. [7, 8]

Snowden, J. S., Griffiths, H. L., & Neary, D. (1996). Semantic-episodic memory interactions in semantic dementia: Implications for retrograde memory function. *Cognitive Neuropsychology, 13*, 1101–1137. [6]

Sobin, C., & Sackeim, H. A. (1997). Psychomotor symptoms of depression. *American Journal of Psychiatry, 154*, 4–17. [15]

Society for Industrial and Organizational Psychology, Inc. (SIOP). (2002). An instructor's guide for introducing industrial-organizational psychology. Retrieved June 10, 2003, from http://www.siop.org [18]

Söderfeldt, B., Rönnberg, J., & Risberg, J. (1994). Regional cerebral blood flow in sign language users. *Brain and Language, 46*, 59–68. [2]

Sokolov, E. N. (2000). Perception and the conditioning reflex: Vector encoding. *International Journal of Psychophysiology, 35*, 197–217. [3]

Solano, L., Donati, V., Pecci, F., Perischetti, S., & Colaci, A. (2003). Postoperative course after papilloma resection: Effects of written disclosure of the experience in subjects with different alexithymia levels. *Psychosomatic Medicine, 65*, 477–484. [13]

Soler, H., Vinayak, P., & Quadagno, D. (2000). Biosocial aspects of domestic violence. *Psychoneuroendocrinology, 25*, 721–739. [17]

Solms, M. (2000). Dreaming and REM sleep are controlled by different brain mechanisms. *Behavioral and Brain Sciences, 23*(6). [4]

Solso, R. (1991). *Cognitive psychology* (3rd ed.). Boston: Allyn & Bacon. [7]

Sonnentag, S. (2003). Recovery, work engagement, and practice behavior: A new look at the interface between nonwork and work. *Journal of Applied Psychology, 88*, 518–528. [18]

Soyka, M., Preuss, U., Koller, G., Zill, P., & Bondy, B. (2002). Dopamine D4 receptor gene polymorphism and extraversion revisited: Results from the Munich Gene Bank Project for Alcoholism. *Journal of Psychiatric Research, 36*, 429–435. [14]

Spangler, D. L., Simons, A. D., Monroe, S. M., & Thase, M. E. (1996). Gender differences in cognitive diathesis-stress domain match: Implications for differential pathways to depression. *Journal of Abnormal Psychology, 105*, 653–657. [15]

Spanos, N. P. (1986). Hypnotic behavior: A social-psychological interpretation of amnesia, analgesia, and "trance logic." *Behavioral and Brain Sciences, 9*, 499–502. [4]

Spanos, N. P. (1991). A sociocognitive approach to hypnosis. In S. J. Lynn & J. W. Rhue (Eds.), *Theories of hypnosis: Current models and perspectives* (pp. 324–361). New York: Guilford. [4]

Spanos, N. P. (1994). Multiple identity enactments and multiple personality disorder: A sociocognitive perspective. *Psychological Bulletin, 116*, 143–165. [4, 15]

Spearman, C. (1927). *The abilities of man.* New York: Macmillan. [8]

Spencer, R., Zelaznik, H., Diedrichsen, J., & Ivry, R. (2003). Disrupted timing of discontinuous but not continuous movements by cerebellar lesions. *Science, 300*, 1437–1439. [2]

Sperling, G. (1960). The information available in brief visual presentations. *Psychological Monographs: General and Applied 74* (Whole No. 498), 1–29. [6]

Sperry, R. W. (1964). The great cerebral commissure. *Scientific American, 210*, 42–52. [2]

Sperry, R. W. (1968). Hemisphere deconnection and unity in conscious experience. *American Psychologist, 23,* 723–733. [2]

Spetch, M. L., Wilkie, D. M., & Pinel, J. P. J. (1981). Backward conditioning: A reevaluation of the empirical evidence. *Psychological Bulletin, 89,* 163–175. [5]

Spiers, H., Maguire, E., & Burgess, N. (2001). Hippocampal amnesia. *Neurocase, 7,* 357–382. [6]

Spirito, A., Jelalian, E., Rasile, D., Rohrbeck, C., & Vinnick, L. (2000). Adolescent risk taking and self-reported injuries associated with substance use. *American Journal of Drug and Alcohol Abuse, 26,* 113–123. [4]

Spitzer, M. W., & Semple, M. N. (1991). Interaural phase coding in auditory midbrain: Influence of dynamic stimulus features. *Science, 254,* 721–724. [3]

Spooner, A., & Kellogg, W. N. (1947). The backward conditioning curve. *American Journal of Psychology, 60,* 321–334. [5]

Sporer, S. L., Penrod, S., Read, D., & Cutler, B. (1995). Choosing, confidence, and accuracy: A meta-analysis of the confidence-accuracy relation in eyewitness identification studies. *Psychological Bulletin, 118,* 315–327. [6]

Sprecher, S., & Hatfield, E. (1996). Premarital sexual standards among U.S. college students: Comparison with Russian and Japanese students. *Archives of Sexual Behavior, 25,* 261–288. [12]

Spreen, O., Risser, A., & Edgell, D. (1995). *Developmental Neuropsychology.* New York: Oxford University Press. [1, 2]

Squire, L. R. (1992). Memory and the hippocampus: A synthesis from findings with rats, monkeys, and humans. *Psychological Review, 99,* 195–231. [2, 6]

Squire, L. R., Knowlton, B., & Musen, G. (1993). The structure and organization of memory. *Annual Review of Psychology, 44,* 453–495. [6]

Srivastava, S., John, O., Gosling, S., & Potter, J. (2003). Development of personality in early and middle adulthood: Set like plaster or persistent change? *Journal of Personality & Social Psychology, 84,* 1041–1053. [14]

St. Louis County Department of Health. (2003). Chlamydia. Retrieved August 5, 2003, from http://www.co.stlouis.mo.us/doh/ancilary/cdc/STD_site/chlamydia.html [12]

Staal, W. G., Pol, H. E. H., Schnack, H. G., Hoogendoorn, M. L. C., Jellema, K., & Kahn, R. S. (2000). Structural brain abnormalities in patients with schizophrenia and their healthy siblings. *American Journal of Psychiatry, 157,* 416–421. [15]

Stafford, J., & Lynn, S. (2002). Cultural scripts, memories of childhood abuse, and multiple identities: A study of role-played enactments. *International Journal of Clinical & Experimental Hypnosis, 50,* 67–85. [6]

Stage, K. B., Glassman, A. H., & Covey, L. S. (1996). Depression after smoking cessation: Case reports. *Journal of Clinical Psychiatry, 57,* 467–469. [13]

Standage, M., Duda, J., & Ntoumanis, N. (2003). A model of contextual motivation in physical education: Using constructs from self-determination and achievement goal theories to predict physical activity intentions. *Journal of Educational Psychology, 95,* 97–110. [11]

Stanislov, R., & Nikolova, V. (2003). Treatment of erectile dysfunction with pycnogenol and L-arginine. *Journal of Sex & Marital Therapy, 29,* 207–213. [12]

Stattin, H., & Magnusson, D. (1990). *Pubertal maturation in female development.* Hillsdale, NJ: Erlbaum. [10]

Stea, R. A., & Apkarian, A. V. (1992). Pain and somatosensory activation. *Trends in Neurosciences, 15,* 250–251. [2]

Steblay, N. M. (1992). A meta-analytic review of the weapon focus effect. *Law and Human Behavior, 16,* 413–424. [6]

Steele, J., & Mayes, S. (1995). Handedness and directional asymmetry in the long bones of the human upper limb. *International Journal of Osteoarchaeology, 5,* 39–49. [2]

Steeves, R. (2002). The rhythms of bereavement. *Family & Community Health, 25,* 1–10. [10]

Steffens, A. B., Scheurink, A. J., & Luiten, P. G. (1988). Hypothalamic food intake regulating areas are involved in the homeostasis of blood glucose and plasma FFA levels. *Physiology and Behavior, 44,* 581–589. [11]

Steffensen, M., & Calker, L. (1982). Intercultural misunderstandings about health care: Recall of descriptions of illness and treatments. *Social Science and Medicine, 16,* 1949–1954. [6]

Stein, A. H., & Friedrich, L. K. (1975). Impact of television on children and youth. In E. M. Hetherington (Ed.), *Review of child development research* (Vol. 5, pp. 183–256). Chicago: University of Chicago Press. [9]

Stein, M. B., & Kean, Y. M. (2000). Disability and quality of life in social phobia: Epidemiologic findings. *American Journal of Psychiatry, 157,* 1606–1613. [15]

Stein, M. B., Walker, J. R., & Forde, D. R. (1996). Public-speaking fears in a community sample: Prevalence, impact on functioning, and diagnostic classification. *Archives of General Psychiatry, 53,* 169–174. [15]

Stein-Behrens, B., Mattson, M. P., Chang, I., Yeh, M., & Sapolsky, R. (1994). Stress exacerbates neuron loss and cytoskeletal pathology in the hippocampus. *Journal of Neuroscience, 14,* 5373–5380. [13]

Steinberg, L. (1992). Ethnic differences in adolescent achievement: An ecological perspective. *American Psychologist, 47,* 723–729. [10]

Steinberg, L., & Dornbusch, S. (1991). Negative correlates of part-time employment during adolescence: Replication and elaboration. *Developmental Psychology, 27,* 304–313. [8]

Steinberg, L., Elman, J. D., & Mounts, N. S. (1989). Authoritative parenting, psychosocial maturity, and academic success among adolescents. *Child Development, 60,* 1424–1436. [9, 10]

Steinberg, L., Lamborn, S. D., Darling, N., Mounts, N. S., & Dornbusch, S. M. (1994). Over-time changes in adjustment and competence among adolescents from authoritative, authoritarian, indulgent, and neglectful families. *Child Development, 65,* 754–770. [10]

Steinman, L. (1993). Autoimmune disease. *Scientific American, 269,* 106–114. [13]

Steinmetz, J. E. (2000). Brain substrates of classical eyeblink conditioning: A highly localized but also distributed system. *Behavioural Brain Research, 110,* 13–24. [5]

Stemberger, R. T., Turner, S. M., Beidel, D. C., & Calhoun, K. S. (1995). Social phobia: An analysis of possible developmental factors. *Journal of Abnormal Psychology, 104,* 526–531. [15]

Stephan, K. M., Fink, G. R., Passingham, R. E., Silbersweig, D., Ceballos-Baumann, A. O., Frith, C. D., & Frackowiak, R. S. J. (1995). Functional anatomy of the mental representation of upper extremity movements in healthy subjects. *Journal of Neurophysiology, 73,* 373–386. [7]

Stephenson, M. T., & Witte, K. (1998). Fear, threat, and perceptions of efficiency from frightening skin cancer messages. *Public Health Review, 26,* 147–174. [17]

Steptoe, A. (2000). Stress, social support and cardiovascular activity over the working day. *International Journal of Psychophysiology, 37,* 299–308. [11, 13]

Steriade, M. (1996). Arousal: Revisiting the reticular activating system. *Science, 272,* 225–226. [2]

Stern, W. (1914). *The psychological methods of testing intelligence.* Baltimore: Warwick and York. [8]

Sternberg, R., Castejon, J., Prieto, M., Hautamacki, J., & Grigorenko, E. (2001). Confirmatory factor analysis of the Sternberg Triarchic Abilities Test in three international samples: An empirical test of the triarchic theory of intelligence. *European Journal of Psychological Assessment, 17*, 1–16. [7, 13]

Sternberg, R. J. (1985a). *Beyond IQ: A triarchic theory of human intelligence.* New York: Cambridge University Press. [8]

Sternberg, R. J. (1985b). Human intelligence: The model is the message. *Science, 230*, 1111–1118. [8]

Sternberg, R. J. (1986a). *Intelligence applied: Understanding and increasing your intellectual skills.* San Diego: Harcourt Brace Jovanovich. [8]

Sternberg, R. J. (1986b). A triangular theory of love. *Psychological Review, 93*, 119–135. [11]

Sternberg, R. J. (1987). Liking versus loving: A comparative evaluation of theories. *Psychological Bulletin, 102*, 331–345. [11]

Sternberg, R. J. (2000). The holey grail of general intelligence. *Science, 289*, 399–401. [8]

Sternberg, R. J., Wagner, R. K., Williams, W. M., & Horvath, J. A. (1995). Testing common sense. *American Psychologist, 50*, 912–927. [8]

Stevens, M., Golombok, S., & Beveridge, M. (2002). Does father absence influence children's gender development? Findings from a general population study of preschool children. *Parenting: Science & Practice, 2*, 47–60. [12]

Stevenson, H. W. (1992). Learning from Asian schools. *Scientific American, 267*, 70–76. [8]

Stevenson, H. W., Chen, C., & Lee, S. Y. (1993). Mathematics achievement of Chinese, Japanese, and American children: Ten years later. *Science, 259*, 53–58. [8]

Stevenson, H. W., Lee, S. Y., & Stigler, J. W. (1986). Mathematics achievement of Chinese, Japanese, and American children. *Science, 231*, 693–699. [8]

Stevenson, H. W., Lee, S. Y., Chen, C., Stigler, J. W., Hsu, C. C., & Kitamura, S. (1990). Contexts of achievement. *Monographs of the Society for Research in Child Development, 55*(1–2, Serial No. 221). [8]

Stewart, V. M. (1973). Tests of the "carpentered world" hypothesis by race and environment in America and Zambia. *International Journal of Psychology, 8*, 83–94. [3]

Stigler, J., & Stevenson, H. (1991). How Asian teachers polish each lesson to perfection. *American Educator*, 12–20, 43–47. [8]

Still, C. (2001). Health benefits of modest weight loss. Retrieved January 29, 2003, from http://abcnews.go.com/sections/living/ Healthology/weightloss_benefits011221.html [13]

Stilwell, N., Wallick, M., Thal, S., & Burleson, J. (2000). Myers-Briggs type and medical specialty choice: A new look at an old question. *Teaching & Learning in Medicine, 12*, 14–20. [14]

Stone, J. (2003). Self-consistency for low self-esteem in dissonance processes: The role of self-standards. *Personality & Social Psychology Bulletin, 29*, 846–858. [17]

Stone, K., Karem, K., Sternberg, M., McQuillan, G., Poon, A., Unger, E., & Reeves, W. (2002). Seroprevalence of human papillomavirus type 16 infection in the United States. *Journal of Infectious Diseases, 186*, 1396–1402. [12]

Stovall, K. C., & Dozier, M. (2000). The development of attachment in new relationships: Single subject analyses for 10 foster infants. *Developmental Psychopathology, 12*, 2133–2156. [9]

Strack, F., Martin, L. L., & Stepper, S. (1988). Inhibiting and facilitating conditions of facial expressions: A nonobtrusive test of the facial feedback hypothesis. *Journal of Personality and Social Psychology, 54*, 768–777. [11]

Strauss, E., Spreen, O., & Hunter, M. (2000). Implications of test revisions for research. *Psychological Assessment, 12*, 237–244. [8]

Strawbridge, W. J., Cohen, R. D., Shema, S. J., & Kaplan, G. A. (1997). Frequent attendance at religious services and mortality over 28 years. *American Journal of Public Health, 87*, 957–961. [13]

Strayer, D., Drews, F., & Johnston, W. (2003). Cell phone-induced failures of visual attention during simulated driving. *Journal of Experimental Psychology: Applied, 9*, 23–32. [3]

Strickland, B. R. (1995). Research on sexual orientation and human development: A commentary. *Developmental Psychology, 31*, 137–140. [12]

Stroebe, M., & Schut, H. (1999). The dual process model of coping with bereavement: Rationale and description. *Death Studies, 23*, 197–224. [10]

Strohmetz, D., Rind, B., Fisher, R., & Lynn, M. (2002). *Journal of Applied Social Psychology, 32*, 300–309. [4]

Stromeyer, C. F., III. (1970, November). Eidetikers. *Psychology Today*, pp. 76–80. [6]

Stubbs, P. (2000). *Mental health care online.* [16]

Stuss, D. T., Gow, C. A., & Hetherington, C. R. (1992). "No longer Gage": Frontal lobe dysfunction and emotional changes. *Journal of Consulting and Clinical Psychology, 60*, 349–359. [2]

Styron, W. (1990). *Darkness visible: A memoir of madness.* New York: Vintage Books. [15]

Suarez, M. G. (1983). Implications of Spanish-English bilingualism in the TAT stories. Unpublished doctoral dissertation, University of Connecticut. [16]

Sullivan, A., Maerz, J., & Madison, D. (2002). Anti-predator response of red-backed salamanders (Plethodon cinereus) to chemical cues from garter snakes (Thamnophis sirtalis): Laboratory and field experiments. *Behavioral Ecology & Sociobiology, 51*, 227–233. [3]

Sullivan, A. D., Hedberg, K., & Fleming, D. W. (2000). Legalized physician-assisted suicide in Oregon—The second year. *New England Journal of Medicine, 342*, 598–604. [10]

Sullivan, E., Fama, R., Rosenbloom, M., & Pfefferbaum, A. (2002). A profile of neuropsychological deficits in alcoholic women. *Neuropsychology, 16*, 74–83. [13]

Sullivan, M. J. L., Bishop, S. R., & Pivik, J. (1995). The pain catastrophizing scale: Development and validation. *Psychological Assessment, 7*, 524–532. [3]

Sung, K-T. (1992). Motivations for parent care: The case of filial children in Korea. *International Journal of Aging and Human Development, 34*, 109–124. [10]

Super, C. W. (1981). Behavioral development in infancy. In R. H. Munroe, R. L. Munroe, & B. B. Whiting (Eds.), *Handbook of cross-cultural human development* (pp. 181–269). Chicago: Garland. [9]

Sussman, S., & Dent, C. W. (2000). One-year prospective prediction of drug use from stress-related variables. *Substance Use & Misuse, 35*, 717–735. [4]

Sutherland, T. (2002, December 3). Remember when people were not so conscious of their weight?—about 50 years ago! *Senior Journal* [Online version]. Retrieved November 20, 2003, from http://www.seniorjournal.com/NEWS/Fitness/2-12-03GallupLoseWeight.htm [11]

Swaab, D. E., & Hofman, M. A. (1995). Sexual differentiation in the human hypothalamus in relation to gender and sexual orientation. *Trends in Neurosciences, 18*, 264–270. [12]

Swaffer, T., Hollin, C., Beech, A., Beckett, R., & Fisher, D. (2000). An exploration of child sexual abusers' sexual fantasies before and after treatment. *Sexual Abuse: A Journal of Research and Treatment, 2*, 61–68. [12]

Swain, I. U., Zelazo, P. R., & Clifton, R. K. (1993). Newborn infants' memory for speech sounds retained over 24 hours. *Developmental Psychology, 29*, 312–323. [9]

Swan, G., & Carmelli, D. (2002). Impaired olfaction predicts cognitive decline in nondemented older adults. *Neuroepidemiology, 21*, 58–67. [3]

Swanson, L. W. (1995). Mapping the human brain: past, present, and future. *Trends in Neurosciences, 18,* 471–474. [2]

Swanson, N. G. (2000). Working women and stress. *Journal of the American Medical Womens Association, 55,* 276–279. [13]

Sweatt, J. D., & Kandel, E. R. (1989). Persistent and transcriptionally dependent increase in protein phosphorylation in long-term facilitation of Aplysia sensory neurons. *Nature, 339,* 51–54. [6]

Sweller, J., & Levine, M. (1982). Effects of goal specificity on means-end analysis and learning. *Journal of Experimental Psychology: Learning, Memory, and Cognition, 8,* 463–474. [7]

Symister, P., & Friend, R. (2003). The influence of social support and problematic support on optimism and depression in chronic illness: A prospective study evaluating self-esteem as a mediator. *Health Psychology, 22,* 123–129. [13]

Szymura, B., & Wodniecka, Z. (2003). What really bothers neurotics? In search for factors impairing attentional performance. *Personality & Individual Differences, 34,* 109–126. [14]

Tabb, K., Davey, N., Adams, R., & George, S. (2002). The recognition and analysis of animate objects using neural networks and active countour models. *Neurocomputing: An International Journal, 43,* 145–172. [7]

Takahashi, S., Matsuura, M., Tanabe, E., Yara, K., Nonaka, K., Fukura, Y., Kikuchi, M., & Kojima, T. (2000). Age at onset of schizophrenia: Gender differences and influence of temporal socioeconomic change. *Psychiatry and Clinical Neurosciences, 54,* 153–156. [15]

Takanishi, R. (1993). The opportunities of adolescence—research, interventions, and policy: Introduction to the special issue. *American Psychologist, 48,* 85–87. [10]

Tamminga, C. A. (1996, Winter). The new generation of antipsychotic drugs. *NARSAD Research Newsletter,* pp. 4–6. [16]

Tamminga, C. A., & Conley, R. R. (1997). The application of neuroimaging techniques to drug development. *Journal of Clinical Psychiatry, 58*(10, Suppl.), 3–6. [2]

Tanda, G., Pontieri, F. E., & Di Chiara, G. (1997). Cannabinoid and heroin activation of mesolimbic dopamine transmission by a common μ1 opioid receptor mechanism. *Science, 276,* 2048–2050. [4]

Tanner, J. (1990). *Fetus into man: Physical growth from conception to maturity.* Cambridge, MA: Harvard University Press. [2]

Tanner, J. M. (1990). *Fetus into man* (2nd ed.). Cambridge MA: Harvard University Press. [10]

Tan-Niam, C., Wood, D., & O'Malley, C. (1998). A cross-cultural perspective on children's theories of mind and social interaction. *Early Child Development & Care, 144,* 55–67. [9]

Tate, D., Paul, R., Flanigan, T., Tashima, K., Nash, J., Adair, C., Boland, R., & Cohen, R. (2003). The impact of apathy and depression on quality of life in patients infected with HIV. *AIDS Patient Care & STDs, 17,* 117–120. [12]

Taub, G., Hayes, B., Cunningham, W., & Sivo, S. (2001). Relative roles of cognitive ability and practical intelligence in the prediction of success. *Psychological Reports, 88,* 931–942. [8]

Taylor, C., & Luce, K. (2003). Computer- and Internet-based psychotherapy interventions. *Current Directions in Psychological Science, 12,* 18–22. [7, 16]

Taylor, D., Helms Tillery, S., & Schwartz, A. (2002). Direct cortical control of 3D neuroprosthetic devices. *Science, 296,* 1829–1832. [7]

Taylor, S. E. (1991). *Health psychology* (2nd ed.). New York: McGraw-Hill. [13]

Taylor, S. E., & Repetti, R. L. (1997). Health psychology: What is an unhealthy environment and how does it get under the skin? *Annual Review of Psychology, 48,* 411–447. [13]

Tchanturia, K., Serpell, L., Troop, N., & Treasure, J. (2001). Perceptual illusions in eating disorders: Rigid and fluctuating styles. *Journal of Behavior Therapy & Experimental Psychiatry, 32,* 107–115. [11]

Tellegen, A., Lykken, D. T., Bouchard, T. J., Jr., Wilcox, K. J., Segal, N. L., & Rich, S. (1988). Personality similarity in twins reared apart and together. *Journal of Personality and Social Psychology, 54,* 1031–1039. [14]

Temmerman, M. (1994). Sexually transmitted diseases and reproductive health. *Sexually Transmitted Diseases, 21*(2, Suppl.), S55–S58. [12]

Teng, E., Stefanacci, L., Squire, L. R., & Zola, S. M. (2000). Contrasting effects on discrimination learning after hippocampal lesions and conjoint hippocampal-caudate lesions in monkeys. *Journal of Neuroscience, 20,* 3853–3863. [6]

Tennant, C. (2002). Life events, stress and depression: A review of the findings. *Australian & New Zealand Journal of Psychiatry, 36,* 173–182. [15]

Tepper, B., & Ullrich, N. (2002). Influence of genetic taste sensitivity to 6-n-propylthiouracil (PROP), dietary restraint and disinhibition on body mass index in middle-aged women. *Physiology & Behavior, 75,* 305–312. [3]

Tercyak, K., Johnson, S., Roberts, S., & Cruz, A. (2001). Psychological response to prenatal genetic counseling and amniocentesis. *Patient Education & Counseling, 43,* 73–84. [2]

Terman, L. M. (1925). *Genetic studies of genius, Vol. 1: Mental and physical traits of a thousand gifted children.* Stanford, CA: Stanford University Press. [8]

Terman, L. M., & Oden, M. H. (1947). *Genetic studies of genius, Vol. 4: The gifted child grows up.* Stanford, CA: Stanford University Press. [8]

Terman, L. M., & Oden, M. H. (1959). *Genetic studies of genius, Vol. 5: The gifted group at mid-life.* Stanford, CA: Stanford University Press. [8]

Termine, N. T., & Izard, C. E. (1988). Infants' responses to their mother's expressions of joy and sadness. *Developmental Psychology, 24,* 223–229. [11]

Terrace, H. S. (1981). A report to an academy. *Annals of the New York Academy of Sciences, 364,* 115–129. [7]

Terrace, H. S. (1985). In the beginning was the "name." *American Psychologist, 40,* 1011–1028. [7]

Terrace, H. S. (1986). *Nim: A chimpanzee who learned sign language.* New York: Columbia University Press. [7]

Tett, R., & Burnett, D. (2003). A personality trait-based interactionist model of job performance. *Journal of Applied Psychology, 88,* 500–517. [18]

Tew, J. D., Mulsant, B. H., Haskett, R. F., Prudic, J., Thase, M. E., Crowe, R. R., Dolata, D., Begley, A. E., Reynolds, C. F., III, & Sackeim, H. A. (1999). Acute efficacy of ECT in the treatment of major depression in the old-old. *American Journal of Psychiatry, 156,* 1865–1870. [16]

Tham, K., Borell, L., & Gustavsson, A. (2000). The discovery of disability: A phenomenological study of unilateral neglect. *American Journal of Occupational Therapy, 54,* 398–406. [2]

Thase, M. E., Frank, E., Mallinger, A. G., Hammer, T., & Kupfer, D. J. (1992). Treatment of imipramine-resistant recurrent depression, III: Efficacy of monoamine oxidise inhibitors. *Journal of Clinical Psychiatry, 53*(1, Suppl.), 5–11. [16]

Thase, M. E., & Kupfer, D. J. (1996). Recent developments in the pharmacotherapy of mood disorders. *Journal of Consulting and Clinical Psychology, 64,* 646–659. [16]

Thase, M. E., Simons, A. D., Cahalane, J. F., & McGeary, J. (1991). Cognitive behavior therapy of endogenous depression: Part 1: An outpatient clinical replication series. *Behavior Therapy, 22,* 457–467. [16]

Thaxton, L., & Myers, M. (2002). Sleep disturbances and their management in patients with brain injury. *Journal of Head Trauma Rehabilitation, 17*, 335–348. [4]

Thomas, A., Chess, S., & Birch, H. G. (1970). The origin of personality. *Scientific American, 223*, 102–109. [9]

Thomas, P., & Bracken, P. (2001). Vincent's bandage: The art of selling a drug for bipolar disorder. *British Medical Journal, 323*, 1434. [15]

Thompson, R. A. (2000). The legacy of early attachments. *Child Development, 71*, 145–152. [9]

Thompson, R. F., Swain, R., Clark, R., & Shinkman, P. (2000). Intracerebellar conditioning—Brogden and Gantt revisited. *Behavioural Brain Research, 110*, 2–11. [5]

Thompson, S. C., Sobolew-Shubin, A., Galbraith, M. E., Schwankovsky, L., & Cruzen, D. (1993). Maintaining perceptions of control: Finding perceived control in low-control circumstances. *Journal of Personality and Social Psychology, 64*, 293–304. [13]

Thornberry, T., Wei, E., Stouthamer-Loeber, M., & Van Dyke, J. (2000). Teenage fatherhood and delinquent behavior. *Juvenile Justice Bulletin* [Electronic version]. Retrieved August 1, 2002, from http://www.ncjrs.org/html/ojjdp/jjbul2000_1/contents.html [10]

Thorndike, E. (1898). Some experiments on animal intelligence. *Science*, 7(181), 818–824. [5]

Thorndike, E. L. (1911/1970). *Animal intelligence: Experimental studies.* New York: Macmillan. (Original work published 1911). [5]

Thornhill, R., & Gangestad, G. W. (1994). Human fluctuating asymmetry and sexual behavior. *Psychological Science, 5*, 297–302. [17]

Thorpe, M., Pittenger, D., & Reed, B. (1999). Cheating the researcher: A study of the relation between personality measures and self-reported cheating. *College Student Journal, 33*, 49–59. [10]

Thurstone, L. L. (1938). *Primary mental abilities.* Chicago: University of Chicago Press. [8]

Tideman, E., Nilsson, A., Smith, G., & Stjernqvist, K. (2002). Longitudinal follow-up of children born preterm: The mother-child relationship in a 19-year perspective. *Journal of Reproductive & Infant Psychology, 20*, 43–56. [9]

Tidey, J., O'Neill, S., & Higgins, S. (2002). Contingent monetary reinforcement of smoking reductions, with and without transferal nicotine, in outpatients with schizophrenia. *Experimental and Clinical Psychopharmacology, 10*, 241–247. [16]

Tiedemann, J. (2000). Parents' gender stereotypes and teachers' beliefs as predictors of children's concept of their mathematical ability in elementary school. *Journal of Educational Psychology, 92*, 144–151. [12]

Tiihonen, J., Isohanni, M., Räsänen, P., Koiranen, M., & Moring, J. (1997). Specific major mental disorders and criminality: A 26-year prospective study of the 1966 northern Finland birth cohort. *American Journal of Psychiatry, 154*, 840–845. [17]

Tinkle, M. B. (1990). Genital human papillomavirus infection: A growing health risk. *Journal of Obstetric, Gynecologic, & Neonatal Nursing, 19*, 501–507. [12]

Tjosvold, D., Coleman, P., & Sun, H. (2003). Effects of organizational values on leaders' use of informational power to affect performance in China. *Group Dynamics*, 7, 152–166. [18]

Toastmasters International. (2003). Ten tips for successful public speaking. Retrieved November 25, 2003, from http://www.toastmasters.org/pdfs/top10.pdf [15]

Tokar, D., Fischer, A., & Subich, L. (1998). Personality and vocational behavior: A selective review of the literature, 1993–1997. *Journal of Vocational Behavior, 53*, 115–153. [18]

Tolman, E. C. (1932). *Purposive behavior in animals and men.* New York: Appleton-Century-Crofts. [5]

Tolman, E. C., & Honzik, C. H. (1930). Introduction and removal of reward, and maze performance in rats. *University of California Publications in Psychology, 4*, 257–275. [5]

Tomasello, M. (2000). The item-based nature of children's early syntactic development. *Trends in Cognitive Sciences, 4*, 156–163. [9]

Tomkins, S. (1962). *Affect, imagery, and consciousness: The positive effects* (Vol. 1). New York: Springer. [11]

Tomkins, S. (1963). *Affect, imagery, and consciousness: The negative effects* (Vol. 2). New York: Springer. [11]

Tori, C., & Bilmes, M. (2002). Multiculturalism and psychoanalytic psychology: The validation of a defense mechanism's measure in an Asian population. *Psychoanalytic Psychology, 19*, 701–721. [14]

Torrey, E., (1992). *Freudian fraud: The malignant effect of Freud's theory on American thought and culture.* New York: Harper Collins. [14]

Tourangeau, R., Smith, T. W., & Rasinski, K. A. (1997). Motivation to report sensitive behaviors on surveys: Evidence from a bogus pipeline experiment. *Journal of Applied Social Psychology, 27*, 209–222. [1]

Tracey, T., & Rounds, J. (1993). Evaluating Holland's and Gati's vocational-interest models: A structural meta-analysis. *Psychological Bulletin, 113*, 229–246. [18]

Trautner, H., Gervai, J., & Nemeth, R. (2003). Appearance-reality distinction and development of gender constancy understanding in children. *International Journal of Behavioral Development, 27*, 275–283. [12]

Traverso, A., Ravera, G., Lagattolla, V., Testa, S., & Adami, G. F. (2000). Weight loss after dieting with behavioral modification for obesity: The predicting efficiency of some psychometric data. *Eating and Weight Disorders: Studies on Anorexia, Bulimia, and Obesity, 5*, 102–107. [11]

Travis, J. (1996). Brains in space. *Science News, 149*, 28–29. [2]

Trevitt, J., Carolson, B., Correa, M., Keene, A., Morales, M., & Salamone, J. (2002). Interactions between dopamine D1 receptors and gamma-aminobutyric acid mechanisms in substantia nigra pars reticulata of the rat: Neurochemical and behavioral studies. *Psychopharmacology, 159*, 229–237. [2]

Triandis, H. C. (1994). *Culture and social behavior.* New York: McGraw-Hill. [11]

Triandis, H. C., McCusker, C., Betancourt, H., Iwao, S., Leung, K., Salazar, J. M., Setiadi, B., Sinha, J. B. P., Touzard, H., & Zaleski, Z. (1993). An etic-emic analysis of individualism and collectivism. *Journal of Cross-Cultural Psychology, 24*, 366–383. [14]

Triplett, N. (1898). The dynamogenic factors in pacemaking and competition. *American Journal of Psychology, 9*, 507–533. [17]

Trivedi, M. J. (1996). Functional neuroanatomy of obsessive-compulsive disorder. *Journal of Clinical Psychiatry, 57*(8, Suppl.), 26–36. [15, 16]

Troxel, W., Matthews, K., Bromberger, J., & Sutton-Tyrrell, K. (2003). Chronic stress burden, discrimination, and subclinical carotid artery disease in African American and Caucasian women. *Health Psychology, 22*, 300–309. [13]

Trull, T., Stepp, S., & Durrett, C. (2003). Research on borderline personality disorder: An update. *Current Opinion in Psychiatry, 16*, 77–82. [15]

Trzesniewski, K., Donnellan, M., & Robins, R. (2003). Stability of self-esteem across the life span. *Journal of Personality and Social Psychology, 84*, 205–220. [14]

Tsai, S., Kuo, C., Chen, C., & Lee, H. (2002). Risk factors for completed suicide in bipolar disorder. *Journal of Clinical Psychiatry, 63*, 469–476. [15]

Tubbs, M. E., Boehne, D., & Dahl, J. G. (1993). Expectancy, valence, and motivational force functions in goal-setting research: An empirical test. *Journal of Applied Psychology, 78,* 361–373. [11]

Tueth, M. J. (2000). Exposing financial exploitation of impaired elderly persons. *American Journal of Geriatric Psychiatry, 8,* 104–111. [10]

Tulving, E. (1974). Cue-dependent forgetting. *American Scientist, 62,* 74–82. [6]

Tulving, E. (1989). Remembering and knowing the past. *American Scientist, 77,* 361–367. [6]

Tulving, E. (1995). Organization of memory: Quo vadis? In M. S. Gazzaniga (Ed.), *The cognitive neurosciences.* Cambridge, MA: MIT Press. [6]

Tulving, E. (2002). Episodic memory: From mind to brain. *Annual Review of Psychology, 53,* 1–25. [6]

Tulving, E., & Thompson, D. M. (1973). Encoding specificity and retrieval processes in episodic memory. *Psychological Review, 80,* 352–373. [6]

Tuncer, A. M., & Yalcin, S. S. (2000). Multimedia and children in Turkey. *Turkish Journal of Pediatrics, 41*(Suppl.), 27–34. [9]

Turley, R. (2003). Are children of young mothers disadvantaged because of their mother's age or family background? *Child Development, 74,* 465–474. [10]

Turner, C. F., Danella, R. D., & Rogers, S. M. (1995). Sexual behavior in the United States, 1930–1990: Trends and methodological problems. *Sexually Transmitted Diseases, 22,* 173–190. [12]

Turner, J. C., Hogg, M. A., Oakes, P. J., Reicher, S. D., & Wetherell, M. S. (1987). *Rediscovering the social group: A self-categorization theory.* Oxford, England: Blackwell. [17]

Tversky, A. (1972). Elimination by aspects: A theory of choice. *Psychological Review, 79,* 281–299. [7]

Tweed, R., & Lehman, D. (2002). Learning considered within a cultural context: Confucian and Socratic approaches. *American Psychologist, 57,* 89–99. [1]

Tzschentke, T. M. (2001). Pharmacology and behavioral pharmacology of mesocortical dopamine system. *Progress in Neurobiology, 63,* 241–320. [15]

Uchino, B. N., Cacioppo, J. T., & Kiecolt-Glaser, J. K. (1996). The relationship between social support and physiological processes: A review with emphasis on underlying mechanisms and implications for health. *Psychological Bulletin, 119,* 488–531. [13]

Underwood, B. J. (1957). Interference and forgetting. *Psychological Review, 64,* 49–60. [6]

Underwood, B. J. (1964). Forgetting. *Scientific American, 210,* 91–99. [6]

Ungerleider, S. (1992, July/August). Visions of victory. *Psychology Today,* pp. 46–53, 83. [7]

Upperman, P., & Church, A. (1995). Investigating Holland's typological theory with army occupational specialties. *Journal of Vocational Behavior, 47,* 61–75. [18]

U.S. Bureau of the Census. (2001). *Statistical abstract of the United States.* Washington, DC: U.S. Government Printing Office. [8, 12]

U.S. Census Bureau. (1994). *Statistical abstract of the United States 1994* (114th ed.). Washington, DC: U.S. Government Printing Office. [10, 15]

U.S. Census Bureau. (1997). *Statistical abstracts of the United States 1997* (117th ed.). Washington, DC: U.S. Government Printing Office. [10, 12, 14]

U.S. Census Bureau. (1999). *Projections of the Resident Population by Age, Sex, Race, and Hispanic Origin: 1999 to 2100.* Retrieved July 30, 2003, from http://www.census.gov/ population/projections/nation/detail/d2041_50.pdf [10]

U.S. Census Bureau. (1999). *Statistical abstracts of the United States 1999* (119th ed.). Washington DC: U.S. Government Printing Office. [15]

U.S. Census Bureau. (2000). Native resident population estimates of the United States by sex, race, and Hispanic origin. Population Estimates Program, Population Division. Retrieved from http://www.census.gov/populationestimates/nation/nativity/nbtab003.txt [1, 13]

U.S. Census Bureau. (2001). *Statistical abstract of the United States.* Washington, DC: Author. [7, 10, 15, 18]

U.S. Census Bureau. (2003a). *1997 surveys of minority- and women-owned business enterprises.* Retrieved June 17, 2003, from http://www.census.gov/csd/mwb [18]

U.S. Census Bureau. (2003b). *TM-P031. Percent of persons who are foreign born: 2000.* Retrieved June 22, 2003, from http://factfinder.census.gov/servlet/ThematicMapDrawServlet?geo [18]

U.S. Department of Health and Human Services. (2000). *Reducing tobacco use: A report of the Surgeon General—executive summary.* Atlanta: Department of Health and Human Services, Centers for Disease Control and Prevention, National Center for Chronic Disease Prevention and Health Promotion, Office on Smoking and Health. [13]

U.S. Department of Health and Human Services. (2001). Ecstasy: Teens speak out [Online factsheet]. Retrieved October 22, 2003, from http://www.health.org/govpubs/prevalert/v4/8.aspx [4]

Utsey, S., Chae, M., Brown, C., & Kelly, D. (2002). Effect of ethnic group membership on ethnic identity, race-related stress and quality of life. *Cultural Diversity & Ethnic Minority Psychology, 8,* 367–378. [13]

Vaccarino, V., Abramson, J., Veledar, E., & Weintraub, W. (2002). Sex differences in hospital mortality after coronary artery bypass surgery: Evidence for a higher mortality in younger women. *Circulation, 105,* 1176. [13]

Valle, M., & Bozeman, D. (2002). Interrater agreement on employees' job performance: Review and directions. *Psychological Reports, 90,* 975–985. [18]

Van Assema, P., Martens, M., Ruiter, A., & Brug, J. (2002). Framing of nutrition education messages in persuading consumers of the advantages of a healthy diet. *Journal of Human Nutrition & Dietetics, 14,* 435–442. [17]

Van Boven, L., White, K., Kamada, A., & Gilovich, T. (2003). Intuitions about situational correction in self and others. *Journal of Personality & Social Psychology, 85,* 249–258. [17]

Van Cauter, E. (2000). Slow-wave sleep and release of growth hormone. *Journal of the American Medical Association, 284,* 2717–2718. [4]

van den Hout, M., & Merckelbach, H. (1991). Classical conditioning: Still going strong. *Behavioural Psychotherapy, 19,* 59–79. [5]

Van der Zee, K., Thijs, M., & Schakel, L. (2002). The relationship of emotional intelligence with academic intelligence and the Big Five. *European Journal of Personality, 16,* 103–125. [8]

Van Eerde, W., & Thierry, H. (1996). Vroom's expectancy models and work-related criteria: A meta-analysis. *Journal of Applied Psychology, 81,* 575–586. [11]

van Elst, L. T., Woermann, F. G., Lemieux, L., Thompson, P. J., & Trimble, M. R. (2000). Affective aggression in patients with temporal lobe epilepsy. *Brain, 123,* 234–243. [17]

van IJzendoorn, M. (1995). Adult attachment representations, parental responsiveness, and infant attachment: A meta-analysis on the predictive validity of the Adult Attachment Interview. *Psychological Bulletin, 117,* 387–403. [8]

Van Lancker, D. (1987, November). Old familiar voices. *Psychology Today*, pp. 12–13. [2]

van Vianen, A., & Fischer, A. (2002). Illuminating the glass ceiling: The role of organizational culture preferences. *Journal of Occupational & Organizational Psychology*, *75*, 315–337. [18]

Vandell, D. L., & Mueller, E. C. (1980). Peer play and friendships during the first two years. In H. C. Foot, A. J. Chapman, & J. R. Smith (Eds.), *Friendship and social relations in children*. New York: Wiley. [9]

Vander Meer, R., & Alonso, L. (2002). Queen primer pheromone affects conspecific fire ant (Solenopsis invicta) aggression. *Behavioral Ecology & Sociobiology*, *51*, 122–130. [3]

Vargha-Khadem, F., Gadian, D. G., Watkins, D. E., Connelly, A., Van Paesschen, W., & Mishkin, M. (1997). Differential effects of early hippocampal pathology on episodic and semantic memory. *Science*, *277*, 376–380. [2, 6]

Vasterling, J., Duke, L., Brailey, K., Constans, J., Allain, A., & Sutker, P. (2002). Attention, learning, and memory performances and intellectual resources in Vietnam veterans: PTSD and no disorder comparisons. *Neuropsychology*, *16*, 5–14. [13]

Vetulani, J., & Nalepa, I. (2000). Antidepressants: Past, present and future. *European Journal of Pharmacology*, *405*, 351–363. [16]

Viemerö, V. (1996). Factors in childhood that predict later criminal behavior. *Aggressive Behavior*, *22*, 87–97. [17]

Vieta, E. (2003). Atypical antipsychotics in the treatment of mood disorders. *Current Opinion in Psychiatry*, *16*, 23–27. [16]

Villani, S. (2001). Impact of media on children and adolescents: A 10-year review of the research. *Journal of the American Academy of Child & Adolescent Psychiatry*, *40*, 392–401. [5]

Vincent, K. R. (1991). Black/white IQ differences: Does age make the difference? *Journal of Clinical Psychology*, *47*, 266–270. [8]

Vincent, K. R. (1993, Fall). On the perfectibility of the human species: Evidence using fixed reference groups. *TCA Journal*, pp. 60–63. [8]

Vincent, M., & Pickering, M. R. (1988). Multiple personality disorder in childhood. *Canadian Journal of Psychiatry*, *33*, 524–529. [15]

Vinokur, A., & Burnstein, E. (1978). Depolarization of attitudes in groups. *Journal of Personality and Social Psychology*, *36*, 872–885. [17]

Visser, P. S., & Krosnick, J. A. (1998). Development of attitude strength over the life cycle: Surge and decline. *Journal of Personality & Social Psychology*, *75*, 1389–1410. [17]

Vitousek, K., & Manke, F. (1994). Personality variables and disorders in anorexia nervosa and bulimia nervosa. *Journal of Abnormal Psychology*, *103*, 137–147. [11]

Volicer, L., Harper, D., Manning, B., Goldstein, R., & Satlin, A. (2001). Sundowning and circadian rhythms in Alzheimer's disease. *American Journal of Psychiatry*, *158*, 704–711. [4]

Volis, C., Ashburn-Nardo, L., & Monteith, M. (2002). Evidence of prejudice-related conflict and associated affect beyond the college setting. *Group Processes & Intergroup Relations*, *5*, 19–33. [17]

Volkow, N. D., & Fowler, J. S. (2000). Addiction, a disease of compulsion and drive: Involvement of the orbitofrontal cortex. *Cerebral Cortex*, *10*, 318–325. [4, 5]

Volkow, N. D., Wang, G-J., Fowler, J. S., Hitzemann, R., Angrist, B., Gatley, S. J., et al. (1999). Association of methylphenidate-induced craving with changes in right straito-orbitofrontal metabolism in cocaine abusers: Implications in addiction. *American Journal of Psychiatry*, *156*, 19–26. [4]

Von Dras, D. D., & Siegler, I. C. (1997). Stability in extraversion and aspects of social support at midlife. *Journal of Personality and Social Psychology*, *72*, 233–241. [13]

Votruba, S., Horvitz, M., & Schoeller, D. (2000). The role of exercise in the treatment of obesity. *Nutrition*, *16*, 179–188. [13]

Voyer, D., & Rodgers, M. (2002). Reliability of laterality effects in a dichotic listening task with nonverbal material. *Brain & Cognition*, *48*, 602–606. [9]

Vroomen, J., Driver, J., & deGelder, B. (2001). Is cross-modal integration of emotional expressions independent of attentional resources? *Cognitive, Affective & Behavioral Neuroscience*, *1*, 382–387. [3]

Vygotsky, L. S. (1936/1986). *Thought and language* (A. Kozulin, Trans.). Cambridge, MA: MIT Press. (Original work published 1936). [9]

Wadden, T. A. (1993). Treatment of obesity by moderate and severe caloric restriction: Results of clinical research trials. *Annals of Internal Medicine*, *119*, 688–693. [11]

Waid, W. M., Orne, E. C., & Orne, M. T. (1981). Selective memory for social information, alertness, and physiological arousal in the detection of deception. *Journal of Applied Psychology*, *66*, 224–232. [11]

Waite, L., & Joyner, K. (2001). Emotional satisfaction and physical pleasure in sexual unions: Time horizon, sexual behavior, and sexual exclusivity. *Journal of Marriage & the Family*, *63*, 247–264. [12]

Wald, G. (1964). The receptors of human color vision. *Science*, *145*, 1007–1017. [3]

Wald, G., Brown, P. K., & Smith, P. H. (1954). Iodopsin. *Journal of General Physiology*, *38*, 623–681. [3]

Walker, D. (2000). Online therapy? Not yet. *CBS News*. New York: CBS. [16]

Walker, I., & Crogan, M. (1998). Academic performance, prejudice and the jigsaw classroom: New pieces to the puzzle. *Journal of Community & Applied Social Psychology*, *8*, 381–393. [17]

Walker, L. (1989). A longitudinal study of moral reasoning. *Child Development*, *60*, 157–166. [10]

Walker, M., Brakefield, T., Hobson, J., & Stickgold, R. (2003). Dissociable stages of human memory consolidation and reconsolidation. *Nature*, *425*, 616–620. [4]

Walsh, B., Seidman, S., Sysko, R., & Gould, M. (2002). Placebo response in studies of major depression: Variable, substantial, and growing. *JAMA: Journal of the American Medical Association*, *287*, 1840–1847. [16]

Walster, E., & Walster, G. W. (1969). The matching hypothesis. *Journal of Personality and Social Psychology*, *6*, 248–253. [17]

Walters, C. C., & Grusec, J. E. (1977). *Punishment*. San Francisco: Freeman. [5]

Wang, Z., & Chen, M. (2002). Managerial competency modeling: A structural equation testing. *Psychological Science (China)*, *25*, 513–516. [18]

Ward, C. (1994). Culture and altered states of consciousness. In W. J. Lonner & R. Malpass (Eds.), *Psychology and culture* (pp. 59–64). Boston: Allyn & Bacon. [4]

Wark, G. R., & Krebs, D. L. (1996). Gender and dilemma differences in real-life moral judgment. *Developmental Psychology*, *32*, 220–230. [10]

Warshaw, M. G., & Keller, M. B. (1996). The relationship between fluoxetine use and suicidal behavior in 654 subjects with anxiety disorders. *Journal of Clinical Psychiatry*, *57*, 158–166. [16]

Washington University School of Medicine. (2003). *Epilepsy surgery* [Online factsheet]. Retreived September 29, 2003, from http://neurosurgery.wustl.edu/clinprog/epilepsysurg.htm [2]

Wasserman, E. A., & Miller, R. R. (1997). What's elementary about associative learning? *Annual Review of Psychology*, *48*, 573–607. [5]

Waterman, A. (1985). Identity in the context of adolescent psychology. *Child Development*, *30*, 5–24. [10]

Watkins, L., Connor, K., & Davidson, J. (2001). Effect of kava on vagal cardiac control in generalized anxiety disorder: Preliminary findings. *Journal of Pyschopharmacology*, *15*, 283–286. [4]

Watson, D. (2001). Dissociations of the night: Individual differences in sleep-related experiences and their relation to dissociation and schizotypy. *Journal of Abnormal Psychology*, *110*, 526–535. [4]

Watson, D. (2002). Predicting psychiatric symptomatology with the Defense Style Questionnaire-40. *International Journal of Stress Management*, *9*, 275–287. [14]

Watson, J. B., & Rayner, R. (1920). Conditioned emotional reactions. *Journal of Experimental Psychology*, *3*, 1–14. [5]

Wayment, H. A., & Peplau, L. A. (1995). Social support and well-being among lesbian and heterosexual women: A structural modeling approach. *Personality and Social Psychology Bulletin*, *21*, 1189–1199. [10]

Webb, R., Lubinski, D., & Benbow, C. (2002). Mathematically facile adolescents with math-science aspirations: New perspectives on their educational and vocational development. *Journal of Educational Psychology*, *94*, 785–794. [12]

Webb, W. (1995). The cost of sleep-related accidents: A reanalysis. *Sleep*, *18*, 276–280. [4]

Webb, W. B. (1975). *Sleep: The gentle tyrant.* Englewood Cliffs, NJ: Prentice-Hall. [4]

Webb, W. B., & Campbell, S. S. (1983). Relationships in sleep characteristics of identical and fraternal twins. *Archives of General Psychiatry*, *40*, 1093–1095. [4]

Weber, P., Davis, E., & Sebastian, R. (2002). Mental health and the ADA: A focus group discussion with human resource practitioners. *Employee Responsibilities & Rights Journal*, *14*, 45–55. [18]

Weber, S. E. (1996). Cultural aspects of pain in childbearing women. *Journal of Obstetric, Gynecologic & Neonatal Nursing*, *25*, 67–72. [3]

Weekes, J. R., Lynn, S. J., Green, J. P., & Brentar, J. T. (1992). Pseudomemory in hypnotized and task-motivated subjects. *Journal of Abnormal Psychology*, *101*, 356–360. [4]

Weeks, D. L., & Anderson, L. P. (2000). The interaction of observational learning with overt practice: Effects on motor skill learning. *Acta Psychologia*, *104*, 259–271. [5]

Weigman, O., & van Schie, E. G. (1998). Video game playing and its relations with aggressive and prosocial behaviour. *British Journal of Social Psychology*, *37*(Pt. 3), 367–378. [17]

Weiler, S., & Bernasek, A. (2001). Dodging the glass ceiling? Networks and the new wave of women entrepreneurs. *Social Science Journal*, *38*, 85–103. [18]

Weiner, B. (Ed.). (1974). *Achievement motivation and attribution theory.* Norristown, NJ: General Learning Press. [11]

Weiner, I. B. (1996). Some observations on the validity of the Rorschach Inkblot Method. *Psychological Assessment*, *8*, 206–213. [14]

Weiner, I. B. (1997). Current status of the Rorschach Inkblot Method. *Journal of Personality Assessment*, *68*, 5–19. [14]

Weinfield, N., Ogawa, J., & Sroufe, L. (1997). Early attachment as a pathway to adolescent peer competence. *Journal of Research on Adolescence*, *7*, 241–265. [9]

Weingartner, H., Adefris, W., Eich, J. E., & Murphy, D. L. (1976). Encoding-imagery specificity in alcohol state-dependent learning. *Journal of Experimental Psychology: Human Learning and Memory*, *2*, 83–87. [6]

Weiss, J. M. (1972). Psychological factors in stress and disease. *Scientific American*, *226*, 104–113. [13]

Weissman, M. M., Bland, R. C., Canino, G. J., Faravelli, C., Greenwald, S., Hwu, H-G., Joyce, P. R., Karam, E. G., Lee, C-K., Lellouch, J., Lepine, J-P., Newman, S. C., Rubio-Stepic, M., Wells, J. E., Wickramaratne, P. J., Wittchen, H-U., & Yeh, E-K. (1996). Cross-national epidemiology of major depression and bipolar disorder. *Journal of the American Medical Association*, *276*, 293–299. [15]

Weissman, M. M., Bland, R. C., Canino, G. J., Greenwald, S., Hwu, H-G., Lee, C. K., Newman, S. C., Oakley-Browne, M. A., Rubio-Stipec, M., Wickramaratne, P. J., Wittchen, H-U., & Yeh, E-K. (1994). The cross national epidemiology of obsessive compulsive disorder. *Journal of Clinical Psychiatry*, *55*(3, Suppl.), 5–10. [15]

Wells, D. L., & Hepper, P. G. (2000). The discrimination of dog odours by humans. *Perception*, *29*, 111–115. [3]

Wells, G. L. (1993). What do we know about eyewitness identification? *American Psychologist*, *48*, 553–571. [6]

Wells, G. L., Malpass, R. S., Lindsay, R. C., Fisher, R. P., Turtle, J. W., & Fulero, S. M. (2000). From the lab to the police station. A successful application of eyewitness research. *American Psychologist*, *55*, 6581–6598. [6]

Werker, J., & Desjardins, R. (1995). Listening to speech in the first year of life: Experiential influences on phoneme perception. *Current Directions in Psychological Science*, *4*, 76–81. [9]

Wertheimer, M. (1912). Experimental studies of the perception of movement. *Zeitschrift fur Psychologie*, *61*, 161–265. [3]

Wertz, K., & Hermann, B. G. (2000). Large-scale screen for genes involved in gonad development. *Mechanisms of Development*, *98*, 51–70. [12]

Wesensten, N., Balenky, G., Kautz, M., Thorne, D., Reichardt, R., & Balkin, T. (2002). Maintaining alertness and performance during sleep deprivation: Modafinil versus caffeine. *Psychopharmacology*, *159*, 238–247. [4]

West, M. J., Coleman, P. D., Flood, D. G., & Troncoso, J. C. (1994). Differences in the pattern of hippocampal neuronal loss in normal ageing and Alzheimer's disease. *Lancet*, *344*, 769–772. [2, 10]

West, R., Courts, S., Beharry, S., May, S., & Hajek, P. (1999). Acute effect of glucose tablets on desire to smoke. *Psychopharmacology*, *147*, 319–321. [4]

Westergaard, G., & Lussier, I. (1999). Left-handedness and longevity in primates. *International Journal of Neuroscience*, *99*, 79–87. [2]

Westreich, L. (2002). Addiction and the Americans with Disabilities Act. *Journal of the American Academy of Psychiatry & the Law*, *30*, 355–363. [18]

Weström, L. V. (1994). Sexually transmitted diseases and infertility. *Sexually Transmitted Diseases*, *21*(2, Suppl.), S32–S37. [12]

Wetherell, J., Gatz, M., & Craske, M. (2003). Treatment of generalized anxiety disorder in older adults. *Journal of Consulting & Clinical Psychology*, *71*, 31–40. [16]

Wetter, M. W., Baer, R. A., Berry, T. R., Robison, L. H., & Sumpter, J. (1993). MMPI-2 profiles of motivated fakers given specific symptom information: A comparison to matched patients. *Psychological Assessment*, *5*, 317–323. [14]

Wheatley, D. (2001). Stress-induced insomnia treated with kava and valerian. Singly and in combination. *Human Psychopharmacology Clinical & Experimental*, *16*, 353–356. [4]

Wheeler, M., & McMillan, C. (2001). Focal retrograde amnesia and the episodic-semantic distinction. *Cognitive, Affective & Behavioral Neuroscience*, *1*, 22–36. [6]

Wheeler, M. A., Stuss, D. T., & Tulving, E. (1997). Toward a theory of episodic memory: The frontal lobes and autonoetic consciousness. *Psychological Bulletin*, *121*, 331–354. [6]

Whisenant, W., Pedersen, P. & Obenour, B. (2002). Success and gender: Determining the rate of advancement for intercollegiate athletic directors. *Sex Roles, 47,* 485–491. [18]

Whisenhunt, B. L., Williamson, D. A., Netemeyer, R. G., & Womble, L. G. (2000). Reliability and validity of the Psychosocial Risk Factors Questionnaire (PRFQ). *Eating and Weight Disorders: Studies on Anorexia, Bulimia, and Obesity, 5,* 1–6. [11]

Whitam, F. L., Diamond, M., & Martin, J. (1993). Homosexual orientation in twins: A report on 61 pairs and three triplet sets. *Archives of Sexual Behavior, 22,* 187–296. [12]

White, D. P. (1989). Central sleep apnea. In M. H. Kryger, T. Roth, & W. C. Dement (Eds.), *Principles and practice of sleep medicine* (pp. 513–524). Philadelphia: W. B. Saunders. [4]

White, G. L., & Mullen, P. E. (1989). *Jealousy: Theory, research, and clinical strategies.* New York: Guilford. [11]

White, S. D., & DeBlassie, R. R. (1992). Adolescent sexual behavior. *Adolescence, 27,* 183–191. [10]

Whitehouse, D. (2000). Rats control robot arm with brain power alone. Retrieved from http://www.robotbooks.com/robotrats.htm [7]

Whitmore, D., Foulkes, N. S., & Sassone-Corsi, P. (2000). Light acts directly on organs and cells in culture to set the vertebrate circadian clock. *Nature, 404,* 87–91. [4]

Whorf, B. L. (1956). Science and linguistics. In J. B. Carroll (Ed.), *Language, thought, and reality: Selected writings of Benjamin Lee Whorf.* Cambridge, MA: MIT Press. [7]

Wickelgren, I. (1996). For the cortex, neuron loss may be less than thought. *Science, 273,* 48–50. [8]

Wicker, A. W. (1969). Attitudes versus action: The relationship of verbal and overt behavioral responses to attitude objects. *Journal of Social Issues, 25,* 41–78. [17]

Widom, C. S. (1989). Does violence beget violence? A critical examination of the literature. *Psychological Bulletin, 106,* 3–28. [5, 17]

Widom, C. S., & Maxfield, M. G. (1996). A prospective examination of risk for violence among abused and neglected children. *Annals of the New York Academy of Sciences, 794,* 224–237. [17]

Widom, C. S., & Morris, S. (1997). Accuracy of adult recollections of childhood victimization: Part 2. Childhood sexual abuse. *Psychological Bulletin, 9,* 34–46. [6]

Wigboldus, D., Dijksterhuis, A., & Van Knippenberg, A. (2003). When stereotypes get in the way: Stereotypes obstruct stereotype-inconsistent trait inferences. *Journal of Personality & Social Psychology, 84,* 470–484. [17]

Wiggins, J. S. (Ed.). (1996). *The five-factor model of personality: Theoretical perspectives.* New York: Guilford. [14]

Wilde, C. (2000, April 10). The new workplace: Telework programs are on the rise. *Information Week, 781,* 189. [18]

Wilken, J. A., Smith, B. D., Tola, K., & Mann, M. (2000). Trait anxiety and prior exposure to non-stressful stimuli: Effects on psychophysiological arousal and anxiety. *International Journal of Psychophysiology, 37,* 233–242. [11]

Wilkins, A., & Lewis, E. (1999). Coloured overlays, text, and texture, *Perception, 28,* 641–650. [3]

Willems, P. J. (2000). Genetic causes of hearing loss. *New England Journal of Medicine, 342,* 1101–1109. [3]

Williams, K., Harkins, S. G., & Latané, B. (1981). Identifiability as a deterrent to social loafing: Two cheering experiments. *Journal of Personality and Social Psychology, 40,* 303–311. [17]

Williams, L. M. (1994). Recall of childhood trauma: A prospective study of women's memories of child sexual abuse. *Journal of Consulting and Clinical Psychology, 62,* 1167–1176. [6]

Williams, R. (1993). *Anger kills.* New York: Times Books. [13]

Willoughby, J. C., & Glidden, L. M. (1995). Fathers helping out: Shared child care and marital satisfaction of parents of children with disabilities. *American Journal on Mental Retardation, 99,* 399–406. [9]

Willoughby, T., Wood, E., McDermott, C., & McLaren, J. (2000). Enhancing learning through strategy instruction and group interaction: Is active generation of elaborations critical? *Applied Cognitive Psychology, 14,* 19–30. [6]

Wills, T. A., & Cleary, S. D. (1996). How are social support effects mediated? A test with parental support and adolescent substance use. *Journal of Personality and Social Psychology, 71,* 937–952. [4]

Wills, T. A., McNamara, G., Vaccaro, D., & Hirky, A. E. (1996). Escalated substance use: A longitudinal grouping analysis from early to middle adolescence. *Journal of Abnormal Psychology, 105,* 166–180. [4]

Wilson, F. R. (1998). *The hand: How its use shapes the brain, language, and human culture.* New York: Pantheon. [2]

Wilson, M. A., & McNaughton, B. L. (1993). Dynamics of the hippocampal ensemble code for space. *Science, 261,* 1055–1058. [2]

Wilson, R., & Bennett, D. (2003). Cognitive activity and risk of Alzheimer's disease. *Current Directions in Psychological Science, 12,* 87–91. [10]

Wilson, W., Mathew, R., Turkington, T., Hawk, T., Coleman, R. E., & Provenzale, J. (2000). Brain morphological changes and early marijuana use: A magnetic resonance and positron emission tomography study. *Journal of Addictive Diseases, 19,* 1–22. [4]

Winch, R. F. (1958). *Mate selection: A study of complementary needs.* New York: Harper & Row. [17]

Wink, P., & Helson, R. (1993). Personality change in women and their partners. *Journal of Personality and Social Psychology, 65,* 597–605. [10]

Winograd, E. (1988). Some observations on prospective remembering. In M. M. Gruneberg, P. E. Morris, & R. N. Sykes (Eds.), *Practical aspects of memory: Current research and issues: Vol. 1* (pp. 348–353). Chichester, England: John Wiley & Sons. [6]

Winokur, G., Coryell, W., Keller, M., Endicott, J., & Akiskal, H. S. (1993). A prospective follow-up of patients with bipolar and primary unipolar affective disorder. *Archives of General Psychiatry,* 50, 457–465. [15]

Winsler, A., & Naglieri, J. (2003). Overt and covert verbal problem-solving strategies: Developmental trends in use, awareness, and relations with task performance in children aged 5 to 17. *Child Development, 74,* 659–678. [10]

Winson, J. (1990). The meaning of dreams. *Scientific American, 263,* 86–96. [4]

Wintre, M., & Yaffe, M. (2000). First-year students' adjustment to university life as a function of relationships with parents. *Journal of Adolescent Research, 15,* 9–37. [10]

Wislar, J., Richman, J., Fendrich, M., & Flaherty, J. (2002). Sexual harassment, generalized workplace abuse and drinking outcomes: The role of personality vulnerability. *Journal of Drug Issues, 32,* 1071–1088. [18]

Witelson, S. F. (1985). The brain connection: The corpus callosum is larger in left-handers. *Science, 229,* 665–668. [2]

Wolford, G., Miller, M. B., & Gazzaniga, M. (2000). The left hemisphere's role in hypothesis formation. *Journal of Neuroscience, 20,* 1–4. [8]

Wolpe, J. (1958). *Psychotherapy by reciprocal inhibition.* Stanford, CA: Stanford University Press. [16]

Wolpe, J. (1973). *The practice of behavior therapy* (2nd ed.). New York: Pergamon. [16]

Wolters, C. (2003). Understanding procrastination from a self-regulated learning perspective. *Journal of Educational Psychology, 95*, 179–187. [5]

Wood, J. M., Nezworski, M. T., & Stejskal, W. J. (1996). The Comprehensive System for the Rorschach: A critical examination. *Psychological Science, 7*, 3–10. [14]

Wood, W., Lundgren, S., Ovellette, J. A., Busceme, S., & Blackstone, T. (1994). Minority influence: A meta-analytic review of social influence processes. *Psychological Bulletin, 115*, 323–345. [17]

Wood, W., Rhodes, N., & Whelan, M. (1989). Sex differences in positive well-being: A consideration of emotional style and marital status. *Psychological Bulletin, 106*, 249–264. [10, 11]

Wood, W., Wong, F. Y., & Chachere, J. G. (1991). Effects of media violence on viewers' aggression in unconstrained social interaction. *Psychological Bulletin, 109*, 371–383. [5, 17]

Woodman, G., & Luck, S. (2003). Serial deployment of attention during visual search. *Journal of Experimental Psychology: Human Perception and Performance, 29*, 121–138. [3]

Woodruff-Pak, D. (2001). Eyeblink classical conditioning differentiates normal aging from Alzheimer's disease. *Integrative Physiological & Behavioral Science, 36*, 87–108. [5]

Woods, S. C., & Gibbs, J. (1989). The regulation of food intake by peptides. *Annals of the New York Academy of Sciences, 575*, 236–243. [11]

Woody, E. Z., & Bowers, K. S. (1994). A frontal assault on dissociated control. In S. J. Lynn & J. W. Rhue (Eds.), *Dissociation: Clinical, theoretical and research perspectives* (pp. 52–79). New York: Guilford. [4]

Woolley, J., & Boerger, E. (2002). Development of beliefs about the origins and controllability of dreams. *Development Psychology, 38*, 24–41. [4]

Word, C. O., Zanna, M. P., & Cooper, J. (1974). The nonverbal mediation of self-fulfilling prophecies in interracial interaction. *Journal of Experimental Social Psychology, 10*, 109–120. [17]

World Health Organization (WHO). (1996). Sexually transmitted diseases. Retrieved November 11, 2003, from http://www.who.int/inf-fs/en/fact110.html [12]

World Health Organization (WHO). (2002a). Sexual violence factsheet. Retrieved January 21, 2003, from http://www.who.int/violence_injury_prevention [12]

World Health Organization (WHO). (2002b). Violence against women: Rape and sexual assault. Retrieved January 20, 2003, from http://www.who.int/gender/violence/v6.pdf [12]

Worrel, J. A., Marken, P. A., Beckman, S. E., & Ruehter, V. L. (2000). Atypical antipsychotic agents: A critical review. *American Journal of Health System Pharmacology, 57*, 238–255. [16]

Worthen, J., & Wood, V. (2001). Memory discrimination for self-performed and imagined acts: Bizarreness effects in false recognition. *Quarterly Journal of Experimental Psychology, 54A*, 49–67. [6]

Wright, J. C., & Huston, A. C. (1983). A matter of form: Potentials of television for young viewers. *American Psychologist, 38*, 835–843. [9]

Wright, J. C., & Mischel, W. (1987). A conditional approach to dispositional constructs: The local predictability of social behavior. *Journal of Personality and Social Psychology, 53*, 1159–1177. [14]

Wu, C., & Shaffer, D. R. (1987). Susceptibility to persuasive appeals as a function of source credibility and prior experience with the attitude object. *Journal of Personality and Social Psychology, 52*, 677–688. [17]

Xie, H., Cairns, B., & Cairns, R. (2001). Predicting teen motherhood and teen fatherhood: Individual characteristics and peer affiliations. *Social Development, 10*, 488–511. [10]

Yackinous, C., & Guinard, J. (2002). Relation between PROP (6-n-propylthiouracil) taster status, taste anatomy and dietary intake measures for young men and women. *Appetite, 38*, 201–209. [3]

Yale-New Haven Hospital. (2003). Making the right choice: Speak up about complementary and alternative therapies. Retrieved August 6, 2003, from http://www.ynhh.org/choice/cam.html [13]

Yanagita, T. (1973). An experimental framework for evaluation of dependence liability in various types of drugs in monkeys. *Bulletin of Narcotics, 25*, 57–64. [4]

Yang, C., & Spielman, A. (2001). The effect of a delayed weekend sleep pattern on sleep and morning functioning. *Psychology & Health, 16*, 715–725. [4]

Yapko, M. D. (1994). Suggestibility and repressed memories of abuse: A survey of psychotherapists' beliefs. *American Journal of Clinical Hypnosis, 36*, 163–171. [4]

Yoo, S., & Lee, D. (2001). Human brain mapping of auditory imagery: Event-related functional MRI study. *Neuroreport: For Rapid Communication of Neuroscience Research, 12*, 3045–3049. [7]

Yousef, D. (2002). Job satisfaction as a mediator of the relationship between job stressors and affective, continuance, and normative commitment: A path analytical approach. *International Journal of Stress Management, 9*, 99–112. [11]

Zajonc, R. B. (1980). Feeling and thinking: Preferences need no inferences. *American Psychologist, 35*, 151–175. [11]

Zajonc, R. B. (1984). On the primacy of affect. *American Psychologist, 39*, 117–123. [11]

Zajonc, R. B., & Mullally, P. R. (1997). Birth order: Reconciling conflicting effects. *American Psychologist, 52*, 685–699. [8]

Zajonc, R. B., & Sales, S. M. (1966). Social facilitation of dominant and subordinate responses. *Journal of Experimental Social Psychology, 2*, 160–168. [17]

Zald, D. H., & Pardo, J. V. (2000). Functional neuroimaging of the olfactory system in humans. *International Journal of Psychophysiology, 36*, 165–181. [3]

Zaragoza, M. S., & Mitchell, K. J. (1996). Repeated exposure to suggestion and the creation of false memories. *Psychological Science, 7*, 294–300. [6]

Zatorre, R., Belin, P., & Penhune, V. (2002). Structure and function of the auditory cortex: Music and speech. *Trends in Cognitive Sciences, 6*, 37–46. [2]

Zborowski, M. (1952). Cultural components in response to pain. *Journal of Social Issues, 8*, 16–30. [3]

Zea, M., Reisen, C., Bell, C., & Caplan, R. (1997). Predicting intention to remain in college among ethnic minority and nonminority students. *Journal of Social Psychology, 137*, 149–160. [10]

Zhang, D., Li, Z., Chen, X., Wang, Z., Zhang, X., Meng, X., He, S., & Hu, X. (2003). Functional comparison of primacy, middle and recency retrieval in human auditory short-term memory: An event-related fMRI study. *Cognitive Brain Research, 16*, 91–98. [2]

Zhang, X., Cohen, H., Porjesz, B., & Begleiter, H. (2001). Mismatch negativity in subjects at high risk for alcoholism. *Alcoholism: Clinical & Experimental Research, 25*, 330–337. [4, 10]

Zimbardo, P. G. (1972). Pathology of imprisonment. *Society, 9*, 4–8. [17]

Zimmerman, M., Posternak, K., & Chelminski, I. (2002). Symptom severity and exclusion from antidepressant efficacy trials. *Journal of Clinical Psychopharmacology*, *22*, 610–614. [16]

Zinkernagel, C., Naef, M., Bucher, H., Ladewig, D., Gyr, N., & Battegay, M. (2001). Onset and pattern of substance use in intravenous drug users of an opiate maintenance program. *Drug & Alcohol Dependence*, *64*, 105–109. [4]

Zisapel, N. (2001). Circadian rhythm sleep disorders: Pathophysiology and potential approaches to management. *CNS Drugs*, *15*, 311–328. [4]

Zola, S. M., Squire, L. R., Teng, E., Stenfanacci, L., Buffalo, E. A., & Clark, R. E. (2000). Impaired recognition memory in monkeys after damage limited to the hippocampal region. *Journal of Neuroscience*, *20*, 451–463. [6]

Zucker, A., Ostrove, J., & Stewart A. (2002). College-educated women's personality development in adulthood: Perceptions and age differences. *Psychology & Aging*, *17*, 236–244. [10]

Zuckerman, M. (1979). *Sensation seeking: Beyond the optimal level of arousal.* Hillsdale, NJ: Erlbaum. [11]

Glossary

absolute threshold The minimum amount of sensory stimulation that can be detected 50% of the time.

accommodation In vision, the flattening and bulging action of the lens as it focuses images of objects on the retina. In learning, the mental process of modifying existing schemes and creating new ones in order to incorporate new objects, events, experiences, and information.

acetylcholine (ah-SEET-ul-KOH-leen) A neurotransmitter that plays a role in learning new information, causes the skeletal muscle fibers to contract, and keeps the heart from beating too rapidly.

acquired immune deficiency syndrome (AIDS) A devastating and incurable illness that is caused by HIV and progressively weakens the body's immune system, leaving the person vulnerable to opportunistic infections that usually cause death.

action potential The sudden reversal of the resting potential, which initiates the firing of a neuron.

activation-synthesis hypothesis of dreaming The hypothesis that dreams are the brain's attempt to make sense of the random firing of brain cells during REM sleep.

actor-observer effect The tendency to attribute one's own behavior primarily to situational factors and the behavior of others primarily to dispositional factors.

additive strategy A decision-making approach in which each alternative is rated on each important factor affecting the decision, and the alternative rated highest overall is chosen.

adolescence The developmental stage that begins at puberty and encompasses the period from the end of childhood to the beginning of adulthood.

adoption study method A method researchers use to assess the relative effects of heredity and environment by studying children who were adopted very early in life.

adrenal glands (ah-DREE-nal) A pair of endocrine glands that release hormones that prepare the body for emergencies and stressful situations and also release corticoids and small amounts of the sex hormones.

aerobic exercise (ah-RO-bik) Exercise that uses the large muscle groups in continuous, repetitive action and increases oxygen intake and breathing and heart rates.

affirmative action A process through which organizations actively seek to build an employee pool that includes members of as many racial and cultural groups as possible.

afterimage A visual sensation that remains after a stimulus is withdrawn.

ageism The belief that aging is inevitably associated with a loss of competence.

aggression The intentional infliction of physical or psychological harm on others.

agoraphobia (AG-or-uh-FO-bee-ah) An intense fear of being in a situation from which escape is not possible or in which help would not be available if one experienced overwhelming anxiety or a panic attack.

alarm stage The first stage of the general adaptation syndrome, in which the person experiences a burst of energy that aids in dealing with the stressful situation.

algorithm A systematic, step-by-step procedure that guarantees a solution to a problem of a certain type if the algorithm is executed properly.

alpha wave The brain-wave pattern associated with deep relaxation.

altered state of consciousness Changes in awareness produced by sleep, meditation, hypnosis, and drugs.

alternative medicine Any treatment or therapy that has not been scientifically demonstrated to be effective.

altruism Behavior that is aimed at helping another, requires some self-sacrifice, and is not performed for personal gain.

Alzheimer's disease A progressive and incurable disorder that involves widespread degeneration and disruption of brain cells, resulting in dementia.

Americans with Disabilities Act (ADA) A law enacted in the United States in 1990 making it illegal to discriminate against job applicants and employees on the basis of physical or mental disability.

amnesia A partial or complete loss of memory due to loss of consciousness, brain damage, or some psychological cause.

amplitude The measure of the loudness of a sound; expressed in the unit called the decibel.

amygdala (ah-MIG-da-la) A structure in the limbic system that plays an important role in emotion, particularly in response to unpleasant or punishing stimuli.

analogy heuristic A heuristic strategy that applies a solution used for a past problem to a current problem that shares many similar features.

androgens Male sex hormones.

androgyny (an-DROJ-uh-nee) A combination of desirable masculine and feminine characteristics in one person.

anorexia nervosa An eating disorder characterized by an overwhelming, irrational fear of gaining weight or becoming fat, compulsive dieting to the point of self-starvation, and excessive weight loss.

anterograde amnesia The inability to form long-term memories of events occurring after a brain injury or brain surgery, although memories formed before the trauma are usually intact and short-term memory is unaffected.

antidepressant drugs Drugs that act as mood elevators for severely depressed people and are also prescribed to treat some anxiety disorders.

antipsychotic drugs Drugs used to control severe psychotic symptoms, such as delusions, hallucinations, disorganized speech, and disorganized behavior by inhibiting dopamine activity; also known as neuroleptics.

anxiety disorders Psychological disorders characterized by frequent fearful thoughts about what might happen in the future.

aphasia (uh-FAY-zyah) A loss or impairment of the ability to use or understand language, resulting from damage to the brain.

apparent motion Perceptions of motion that seem to be psychologically constructed in response to various kinds of stimuli.

applied research Research conducted specifically to solve practical problems and improve the quality of life.

apprenticeship An approach to training in which a novice employee is teamed with a more experienced one.

approach-approach conflict A conflict arising from having to choose between equally desirable alternatives.

approach-avoidance conflict A conflict arising when the same choice has both desirable and undesirable features.

aptitude test A test designed to predict a person's achievement or performance at some future time.

archetype (AR-ka-type) Existing in the collective unconscious, an inherited tendency to respond to universal human situations in particular ways.

arousal A state of alertness and mental and physical activation.

arousal theory A theory of motivation suggesting that people are motivated to maintain an optimal level of alertness and physical and mental activation.

artifactual communication The use of objects to communicate nonverbal messages.

artificial intelligence (AI) Programming of computer systems to simulate human thinking in solving problems and in making judgments and decisions.

artificial neural networks (ANNs) Computer systems that are intended to mimic the human brain.

assessment center A facility devoted to testing job applicants using work simulations and other comprehensive assessment tools.

assimilation The mental process by which new objects, events, experiences, and information are incorporated into existing schemes.

association areas Areas of the cerebral cortex that house memories and are involved in thought, perception, and language.

attachment The early, close relationship formed between infant and caregiver.

attitude A relatively stable evaluation of a person, object, situation, or issue, along a continuum ranging from positive to negative.

attribution An assignment of a cause to explain one's own or another's behavior.

audience effects The impact of passive spectators on performance.

audition The sensation and process of hearing.

authoritarian parents Parents who make arbitrary rules, expect unquestioned obedience from their children, punish misbehavior, and value obedience to authority.

authoritative parents Parents who set high but realistic and reasonable standards, enforce limits, and encourage open communication and independence.

autokinetic illusion Apparent motion caused by the movement of the eyes rather than the movement of the objects being viewed.

availability heuristic A cognitive rule of thumb that bases the probability of an event or the importance assigned to it on its availability in memory.

aversion therapy A behavior therapy in which an aversive stimulus is paired with a harmful or socially undesirable behavior until the behavior becomes associated with pain or discomfort.

avoidance learning Learning to avoid events or conditions associated with aversive consequences or phobias.

avoidance-avoidance conflict A conflict arising from having to choose between undesirable alternatives.

axon (AK-sahn) The slender, tail-like extension of the neuron that transmits signals to the dendrites or cell body of other neurons and to muscles, glands, and other parts of the body.

babbling Vocalization of the basic units of sound (phonemes).

basic emotions Emotions that are unlearned and universal, that are reflected in the same facial expressions across cultures, and that emerge in children according to their biological timetable of development; fear, anger, disgust, surprise, happiness, and sadness are usually considered basic emotions.

basic research Research conducted to seek new knowledge and to explore and advance general scientific understanding.

behavior modification A method of changing behavior through a systematic program based on the learning principles of classical conditioning, operant conditioning, or observational learning; also called behavior therapy.

behavior therapy A treatment approach that is based on the idea that abnormal behavior is learned and that applies the principles of operant conditioning, classical conditioning, and/or observational learning to eliminate inappropriate or maladaptive behaviors and replace them with more adaptive responses.

behavioral approach A perspective that holds that leadership effectiveness can be taught and is the result of specific behaviors exhibited by leaders.

behavioral genetics A field of research that uses twin studies and adoption studies to investigate the relative effects of heredity and environment on behavior.

behavioral observation scales Instruments for employee evaluation that require respondents to rate an employee's performance on observable behaviors.

behaviorism The school of psychology founded by John B. Watson that views observable, measurable behavior as the appropriate subject matter for psychology and emphasizes the key role of environment as a determinant of behavior.

beta wave (BAY-tuh) The brain-wave pattern associated with mental or physical activity.

binocular depth cues Depth cues that depend on both eyes working together.

biofeedback The use of sensitive equipment to give people precise feedback about internal physiological processes so that they can learn, with practice, to exercise control over them.

biological psychology The school of psychology that looks for links between specific behaviors and equally specific biological processes that often help explain individual differences.

biological sex Physiological status as male or female.

biological therapy A therapy (drug therapy, electroconvulsive therapy, or psychosurgery) that is based on the assumption that psychological disorders are symptoms of underlying physical problems.

biomedical model A perspective that explains illness solely in terms of biological factors.

biopsychosocial model A perspective that focuses on health as well as illness and holds that both are determined by a combination of biological, psychological, and social factors.

bipolar disorder A mood disorder in which manic episodes alternate with periods of depression, usually with relatively normal periods in between.

blind spot The point in each retina where there are no rods or cones because the cable of ganglion cells is extending through the retinal wall.

bottom-up processing Information processing in which individual components of a stimulus are combined in the brain and prior knowledge is used to make inferences about these patterns.

brainstem The structure that begins at the point where the spinal cord enlarges as it enters the brain and handles functions critical to physical survival. It includes the medulla, the pons, and the reticular formation.

brightness The intensity of the light energy that is perceived as a color.

Broca's aphasia (BRO-kuz uh-FAY-zyah) An impairment in the physical ability to produce speech sounds or, in extreme cases, an inability to speak at all; caused by damage to Broca's area.

Broca's area (BRO-kuz) The area in the frontal lobe, usually in the left hemisphere, that controls the production of speech sounds.

bulimia nervosa An eating disorder characterized by repeated and uncontrolled (and often secretive) episodes of binge eating.

bystander effect A social factor that affects prosocial behavior: As the number of bystanders at an emergency increases, the probability that the victim will receive help decreases, and the help, if given, is likely to be delayed.

California Personality Inventory (CPI) A highly regarded personality test developed especially for normal individuals aged 13 and older.

Cannon-Bard theory of emotion The theory that an emotion-provoking stimulus is transmitted simultaneously to the cerebral cortex, providing the conscious mental experience of the emotion, and to the sympathetic nervous system, causing the physiological arousal.

case study A descriptive research method in which a single individual or a small number of persons are studied in great depth, usually over an extended period of time.

catatonic schizophrenia (KAT-uh-TAHN-ik) A type of schizophrenia characterized by complete stillness or stupor or great excitement and agitation; patients may assume an unusual posture and remain in it for long periods of time.

cell body The part of a neuron that contains the nucleus and carries out the metabolic functions of the neuron.

central nervous system (CNS) The part of the nervous system comprising the brain and the spinal cord.

centration A preoperational child's tendency to focus on only one dimension of a stimulus.

cerebellum (sehr-uh-BELL-um) The brain structure that helps the body execute smooth, skilled movements and regulates muscle tone and posture.

cerebral cortex (seh-REE-brul KOR-tex) The gray, convoluted covering of the cerebral hemispheres that is responsible for the higher mental processes of language, memory, and thinking.

cerebral hemispheres (seh-REE-brul) The right and left halves of the cerebrum, covered by the cerebral cortex and connected by the corpus callosum; they control movement and feeling on the opposing sides of the body.

cerebrum (seh-REE-brum) The largest structure of the human brain, consisting of the two cerebral hemispheres connected by the corpus callosum and covered by the cerebral cortex.

charismatic leaders Leaders who rely on the sheer force of their personalities.

chlamydia (klah-MIH-dee-uh) A highly infectious bacterial STD that is found in both sexes and can cause infertility in females.

chromosomes Rod-shaped structures in the nuclei of body cells, which contain all the genes and carry all the genetic information necessary to make a human being.

chunking A memory strategy that involves grouping or organizing bits of information into larger units, which are easier to remember.

circadian rhythm (sur-KAY-dee-un) Within each 24-hour period, the regular fluctuation from high to low points of certain bodily functions and behaviors.

circadian theory of sleep The theory that sleep evolved to keep humans out of harm's way during the night; also known as the evolutionary theory.

classical conditioning A type of learning through which an organism learns to associate one stimulus with another.

co-action effects The impact on performance of the presence of other people engaged in the same task.

cochlea (KOK-lee-uh) The fluid-filled, snail-shaped, bony chamber in the inner ear that contains the basilar membrane and its hair cells (the sound receptors).

cognition The mental processes that are involved in acquiring, storing, retrieving, and using information and that include sensation, perception, memory, imagery, concept formation, reasoning, decision making, problem solving, and language.

cognitive dissonance (COG-nuh-tiv) The unpleasant state that can occur when people become aware of inconsistencies between their attitudes or between their attitudes and their behavior.

cognitive map A mental representation of a spatial arrangement such as a maze.

cognitive processes Mental processes such as thinking, knowing, problem solving, remembering, and forming mental representations.

cognitive psychology The school of psychology that sees humans as active participants in their environment; studies mental processes such as memory, problem solving, decision making, perception, language, and other forms of cognition.

cognitive therapies Therapies that assume maladaptive behavior can result from irrational thoughts, beliefs, and ideas.

cognitive therapy A therapy designed by Aaron Beck to help patients stop their negative thoughts as they occur and replace them with more objective thoughts.

coitus (KOY-tus) Penile-vaginal intercourse.

collective unconscious In Jung's theory, the most inaccessible layer of the unconscious, which contains the universal experiences of humankind throughout evolution.

color blindness The inability to distinguish certain colors from one another.

compliance Acting in accordance with the wishes, suggestions, or direct requests of other people.

compulsion A persistent, irresistible, and irrational urge to perform an act or ritual repeatedly.

concept A mental category used to represent a class or group of objects, people, organizations, events, situations, or relations that share common characteristics or attributes.

concrete operations stage Piaget's third stage of cognitive development (ages 6 to 11 or 12 years), during which a child acquires the concepts of reversibility and conservation and is able to attend to two or more dimensions of a stimulus at the same time.

conditioned reflex A learned involuntary response.

conditioned response (CR) The learned response that comes to be elicited by a conditioned stimulus as a result of its repeated pairing with an unconditioned stimulus.

conditioned stimulus (CS) A neutral stimulus that, after repeated pairing with an unconditioned stimulus, becomes associated with it and elicits a conditioned response.

conditions of worth Conditions on which the positive regard of others rests.

cones The light-sensitive receptor cells in the retina that enable humans to see color and fine detail in adequate light but do not function in very dim light.

confederate A person who poses as a participant in an experiment but is actually assisting the experimenter.

conflict resolution A process in which a conflict is evaluated and an appropriate strategy for resolving it is identified.

conformity Changing or adopting a behavior or an attitude in order to be consistent with the social norms of a group or the expectations of other people.

confounding variables Factors or conditions other than the independent variable(s) that are not equivalent across groups and could cause differences among the groups with respect to the dependent variable.

conscious (KON-shus) The thoughts, feelings, sensations, or memories of which a person is aware at any given moment.

consciousness Everything of which we are aware at any given time—our thoughts, feelings, sensations, and external environment.

conservation The understanding that a given quantity of matter remains the same if it is rearranged or changed in its appearance, as long as nothing is added or taken away.

consolidation A physiological change in the brain that allows encoded information to be stored in memory.

consolidation failure Any disruption in the consolidation process that prevents a long-term memory from forming.

consummate love According to Sternberg's theory, the most complete form of love, consisting of all three components—intimacy, passion, and commitment.

contexts of development Bronfenbrenner's term for the interrelated and layered settings (family, neighborhood, culture, etc.) in which a child grows up.

continuous reinforcement Reinforcement that is administered after every desired or correct response; the most effective method of conditioning a new response.

control group In an experiment, a group similar to the experimental group that is exposed to the same experimental environment but is not given the treatment; used for purposes of comparison.

conventional level Kohlberg's second level of moral reasoning, in which the individual has internalized the standards of others and judges right and wrong in terms of those standards.

conversion disorder A somatoform disorder in which a person suffers a loss of motor or sensory functioning in some part of the body; the loss has no physical cause but solves some psychological problem.

coping Efforts through action and thought to deal with demands that are perceived as taxing or overwhelming.

cornea (KOR-nee-uh) The tough, transparent, protective layer that covers the front of the eye and bends light rays inward through the pupil.

corpus callosum (KOR-pus kah-LO-sum) The thick band of nerve fibers that connects the two cerebral hemispheres and makes possible the transfer of information and the synchronization of activity between the hemispheres.

correlation coefficient A numerical value that indicates the strength and direction of the relationship between two variables; ranges from +1.00 (a perfect positive correlation) to -1.00 (a perfect negative correlation).

correlational method A research method used to establish the degree of relationship (correlation) between two characteristics, events, or behaviors.

creativity The ability to produce original, appropriate, and valuable ideas and/or solutions to problems.

critical period A period during the embryonic stage when certain body structures are developing and can be harmed by negative influences in the prenatal environment.

critical thinking The process of objectively evaluating claims, propositions, and conclusions to determine whether they follow logically from the evidence presented.

cross-sectional study A type of developmental study in which researchers compare groups of participants of different ages on various characteristics to determine age-related differences.

crowding The subjective judgment that there are too many people in a confined space.

crystallized intelligence A type of intelligence comprising verbal ability and accumulated knowledge, which tend to increase over the lifespan.

CT scan (computerized axial tomography) A brain-scanning technique that uses a rotating, computerized X-ray tube to produce cross-sectional images of the structures of the brain.

culturally sensitive therapy An approach to therapy in which knowledge of clients' cultural backgrounds guides the choice of therapeutic interventions.

culture-fair intelligence test An intelligence test that uses questions that will not penalize those whose cultural background and/or language differs from that of the White middle and upper classes.

decay theory The oldest theory of forgetting, which holds that memories, if not used, fade with time and ultimately disappear altogether.

decibel (dB) (DES-ih-bel) A unit of measurement for the loudness of sounds.

decision making The process of considering alternatives and choosing among them.

declarative memory The subsystem within long-term memory that stores facts, information, and personal life events that can be brought to mind verbally or in the form of images and then declared or stated; also called explicit memory.

deductive reasoning Reasoning from the general to the specific, or drawing particular conclusions from general principles.

deep structure The underlying meaning of a sentence.

defense mechanism A means used by the ego to defend against anxiety and to maintain self-esteem.

delta wave The slowest brain-wave pattern; associated with deep sleep (Stage 3 and Stage 4 NREM sleep).

delusion A false belief, not generally shared by others in the culture.

delusion of grandeur A false belief that one is a famous person or a powerful or important person who has some great knowledge, ability, or authority.

delusion of persecution A false belief that some person or agency is trying in some way to harm one.

dementias A group of neurological disorders in which problems with memory and thinking affect an individual's emotional, social, and physical functioning; caused by physical deterioration of the brain.

dendrites (DEN-drytes) In a neuron, the branchlike extensions of the cell body that receive signals from other neurons.

denial A defense mechanism in which one refuses to acknowledge consciously the existence of danger or a threatening condition.

dependent variable The factor or condition that is measured at the end of an experiment and is presumed to vary as a result of the manipulations of the independent variable(s).

depressants A category of drugs that decrease activity in the central nervous system, slow down bodily functions, and reduce sensitivity to outside stimulation; also called "downers."

depth perception The ability to perceive the visual world in three dimensions and to judge distances accurately.

descriptive research methods Research methods that yield descriptions of behavior.

desk rage Rude, hostile, and aggressive behavior in work settings.

developmental psychology The study of how humans grow, develop, and change throughout the life span.

deviation score An IQ test score calculated by comparing an individual's score with the scores of others of the same age.

difference threshold A measure of the smallest increase or decrease in a physical stimulus that is required to produce a difference in sensation that is noticeable 50% of the time.

diffusion of responsibility The feeling among bystanders at an emergency that the responsibility for helping is shared by the group, making each person feel less compelled to act than if he or she alone bore the total responsibility.

directive therapy Any type of psychotherapy in which the therapist takes an active role in determining the course of therapy sessions and provides answers and suggestions to the patient; an example is Gestalt therapy.

disability A physical or mental condition that limits major life activities.

discrimination In classical conditioning, the learned ability to distinguish between similar stimuli so that the conditioned response occurs only to the original conditioned stimulus but not to similar stimuli. In social psychology, behavior (usually negative) directed toward others based on their gender, religion, race, or membership in a particular group.

discriminative stimulus A stimulus that signals whether a certain response or behavior is likely to be rewarded, ignored, or punished.

disinhibitory effect Displaying a previously suppressed behavior because a model does so without receiving punishment.

disorganized schizophrenia The most serious type of schizophrenia, marked by extreme social withdrawal, hallucinations, delusions, silliness, inappropriate laughter, grotesque mannerisms, and other bizarre behavior.

displacement With regard to memory, the event that occurs when short-term memory is filled to capacity and each new, incoming item pushes out an existing item, which is then forgotten. With regard to behavior, a defense mechanism in which one substitutes a less threatening object or person for the original object of a sexual or aggressive impulse.

display rules Cultural rules that dictate how emotions should generally be expressed and when and where their expression is appropriate.

dispositional attribution Attributing a behavior to some internal cause, such as a personal trait, motive, or attitude; an internal attribution.

dissociative amnesia A dissociative disorder in which there is a complete or partial loss of the ability to recall personal information or identify past experiences.

dissociative disorders Disorders in which, under unbearable stress, consciousness becomes dissociated from a person's identity or her or his memories of important personal events, or both.

dissociative fugue (FEWG) A dissociative disorder in which one has a complete loss of memory of one's entire identity, travels away from home, and may assume a new identity.

dissociative identity disorder (DID) A dissociative disorder in which two or more distinct, unique personalities occur in the same person, and there is severe memory disruption concerning personal information about the other personalities.

divergent thinking The ability to produce multiple ideas, answers, or solutions to a problem for which there is no agreed-on solution.

diversity training Formal training aimed at equipping workers with the human relations skills they need to function effectively in a diverse workplace.

dominant-recessive pattern A set of inheritance rules in which the presence of a single dominant gene causes a trait to be expressed but two genes must be present for the expression of a recessive trait.

door-in-the-face technique A strategy in which someone makes a large, unreasonable request with the expectation that the person will refuse but will then be more likely to respond favorably to a smaller request later.

dopamine (DOE-pah-meen) A neurotransmitter that plays a role in learning, attention, movement, and reinforcement; neurons in the brains of those with Parkinson's disease and schizophrenia are less sensitive to its effects.

double-blind technique A procedure in which neither the participants nor the experimenter knows who is in the experimental and control groups until after the data have been gathered; a control for experimenter bias.

drive An internal state of tension or arousal that is brought about by an underlying need and that an organism is motivated to reduce.

drive-reduction theory A theory of motivation suggesting that biological needs create internal states of tension or arousal called drives, which organisms are motivated to reduce.

drug tolerance A condition in which the user becomes progressively less affected by the drug and must take larger and larger doses to maintain the same effect or high.

DSM-IV The *Diagnostic and Statistical Manual of Mental Disorders*, 4th Edition, a manual published by the American Psychiatric Association, which describes the criteria used to classify and diagnose mental disorders.

dyspareunia (dis-PAH-roo-nee-yah) A sexual pain disorder marked by genital pain associated with sexual intercourse; more common in females than in males.

ego (EE-go) In Freud's theory, the logical, rational, largely conscious system of personality, which operates according to the reality principle.

eidetic imagery (eye-DET-ik) The ability to retain the image of a visual stimulus for several minutes after it has been removed from view and to use this retained image to answer questions about the visual stimulus.

elaborative rehearsal A memory strategy that involves relating new information to something that is already known.

electroconvulsive therapy (ECT) A biological therapy in which an electric current is passed through the right hemisphere of the brain; usually reserved for severely depressed patients who are suicidal.

electroencephalogram (EEG) (ee-lek-tro-en-SEFF-uh-lo-gram) A record of brain-wave activity made by a machine called the electroencephalograph.

elicitation effect Exhibiting a behavior similar to that shown by a model in an unfamiliar situation.

elimination by aspects A decision-making approach in which alternatives are eliminated if they do not satisfy a set of factors that have been ordered from most to least important.

embryo The developing human organism during the period from week 3 through week 8, when the major systems, organs, and structures of the body develop.

emotion An identifiable feeling state involving physiological arousal, a cognitive appraisal of the situation or stimulus causing that internal body state, and an outward behavior expressing the state.

emotional intelligence The ability to apply knowledge about emotions to everyday life; this type of intelligence involves an awareness of and an ability to manage one's own emotions, self-motivation, empathy, and the ability to handle relationships.

emotion-focused coping A response involving reappraisal of a stressor to reduce its emotional impact.

encoding The process of transforming information into a form that can be stored in memory.

encoding failure A cause of forgetting that occurs when information was never put into long-term memory.

endocrine system (EN-duh-krin) A system of ductless glands in various parts of the body that manufacture hormones and secrete them into the bloodstream, thus affecting cells in other parts of the body.

endorphins (en-DOR-fins) Chemicals produced naturally by the brain that reduce pain and the stress of vigorous exercise and positively affect mood.

epinephrine (EP-ih-NEF-rin) A neurotransmitter that affects the metabolism of glucose and nutrient energy stored in muscles to be released during strenuous exercise.

episodic memory (ep-ih-SOD-ik) The type of declarative memory that records events as they have been subjectively experienced.

equilibration The mental process that motivates humans to keep schemes in balance with the real environment.

ergonomics Human factors psychology.

estrogen (ES-truh-jen) A female sex hormone that promotes the secondary sex characteristics in females and controls the menstrual cycle.

ethnocentrism The tendency to look at situations from one's own racial or cultural perspective.

evolutionary psychology The school of psychology that studies how humans have adapted the behaviors required for survival in the face of environmental pressures over the long course of evolution. It focuses on traits that exist in every member of a species.

excitement phase The first stage of the sexual response cycle, characterized by an erection in males and a swelling of the clitoris and vaginal lubrication in females.

exemplars The individual instances, or examples, of a concept that are stored in memory from personal experience.

exhaustion stage The third stage of the general adaptation syndrome, which occurs if the organism fails in its efforts to resist the stressor.

experimental group In an experiment, the group that is exposed to an independent variable.

experimental method The only research method that can be used to identify cause-effect relationships between two or more conditions or variables.

experimenter bias A phenomenon that occurs when a researcher's preconceived notions or expectations in some way influence participants' behavior and/or the researcher's interpretation of experimental results.

expert systems Computer programs designed to carry out highly specific functions within a limited domain.

exposure and response prevention A behavior therapy that exposes patients with obsessive-compulsive disorder to stimuli that trigger obsessions and compulsive rituals, while patients resist performing the compulsive rituals for progressively longer periods of time.

extinction In classical conditioning, the weakening and eventual disappearance of the conditioned response as a result of repeated presentation of the conditioned stimulus without the unconditioned stimulus. In operant conditioning, the weakening and eventual disappearance of the conditioned response as a result of the withholding of reinforcement.

extrinsic motivation The desire to behave in a certain way in order to gain some external reward or to avoid some undesirable consequence.

facial-feedback hypothesis The idea that the muscular movements involved in certain facial expressions produce the corresponding emotions (for example, smiling makes one feel happy).

family therapy Therapy involving an entire family, with the goal of helping family members reach agreement on changes that will help heal the family unit, improve communication problems, and create more understanding and harmony within the group.

fat cells Cells (also called adipose cells) that serve as storehouses for liquefied fat in the body; their number is determined by both genes and eating habits, and they decrease in size but not in number with weight loss.

feature detectors Neurons in the brain that respond only to specific visual patterns (for example, to lines or angles).

female orgasmic disorder A sexual dysfunction in which a woman is persistently unable to reach orgasm or delays in reaching orgasm, despite adequate sexual stimulation.

female sexual arousal disorder A sexual dysfunction in which a woman may not feel sexually aroused in response to sexual stimulation or may be unable to achieve or sustain an adequate lubrication-swelling response to sexual excitement.

fetal alcohol syndrome A condition that is caused by maternal alcohol intake early in prenatal development and that leads to facial deformities as well as mental retardation.

fetus The developing human organism during the period from week 9 until birth, when rapid growth and further development of the structures, organs, and systems of the body occur.

fight-or-flight response A response to stress in which the parasympathetic nervous system triggers the release of hormones that prepare the body to fight or flee.

five-factor theory A trait theory that attempts to explain personality using five broad dimensions, each of which is composed of a constellation of personality traits.

fixation Arrested development at a psychosexual stage occurring because of excessive gratification or frustration at that stage.

fixed-interval schedule A schedule in which a reinforcer is given following the first correct response after a specific period of time has elapsed.

fixed-ratio schedule A schedule in which a reinforcer is given after a fixed number of correct, nonreinforced responses.

flashbulb memory An extremely vivid memory of the conditions surrounding one's first hearing the news of a surprising, shocking, or highly emotional event.

flooding A behavior therapy based on classical conditioning and used to treat phobias by exposing clients to the feared object or event (or asking them to imagine it vividly) for an extended period, until their anxiety decreases.

fluid intelligence A type of intelligence comprising abstract reasoning and mental flexibility, which peak in the early 20s and decline slowly as people age.

foot-in-the-door technique A strategy designed to gain a favorable response to a small request at first, with the intent of making the person more likely to agree later to a larger request.

formal concept A concept that is clearly defined by a set of rules, a formal definition, or a classification system.

formal operations stage Piaget's fourth and final stage of cognitive development (ages 11 or 12 years and beyond), which is characterized by the ability to apply logical thinking to abstract problems and hypothetical situations.

fovea (FO-vee-uh) A small area at the center of the retina that provides the clearest and sharpest vision because it has the largest concentration of cones.

framing The way information is presented so as to emphasize either a potential gain or a potential loss as the outcome of a decision based on that information.

free association A psychoanalytic technique used to explore the unconscious by having patients reveal whatever thoughts, feelings, or images come to mind.

frequency The number of cycles completed by a sound wave in one second, determining the pitch of the sound; measured in the unit called the hertz.

frequency theory The theory of hearing that holds that hair cell receptors vibrate the same number of times per second as the sounds that reach them.

frontal lobes The largest of the brain's lobes, which contain the motor cortex, Broca's area, and the frontal association areas.

frustration-aggression hypothesis The hypothesis that frustration produces aggression.

functional fixedness The failure to use familiar objects in novel ways to solve problems because of a tendency to view objects only in terms of their customary functions.

functional MRI (fMRI) A brain-imaging technique that reveals both brain structure and brain activity more precisely and rapidly than PET.

functionalism An early school of psychology that was concerned with how humans and animals use mental processes in adapting to their environment.

***g* factor** Spearman's term for a general ability that underlies all intellectual functions.

GABA Primary inhibitory neurotransmitter in the brain.

gender (JEN-der) The psychological and sociocultural definition of masculinity or femininity, based on the expected behaviors for males and females.

gender constancy The understanding that activities and clothes do not affect gender stability; acquired between ages 6 and 8.

gender identity The sense of being male or female; acquired between ages 2 and 3.

gender identity disorder Sexual disorder characterized by a problem accepting one's identity as male or female.

gender roles Cultural expectations about the behaviors appropriate to each gender.

gender schema theory A theory suggesting that young children are motivated to attend to and behave in ways consistent with gender-based standards and stereotypes of their culture.

gender stability The awareness that gender is a permanent characteristic; acquired between ages 4 and 5.

gender typing The process by which individuals acquire the traits, behaviors, attitudes, preferences, and interests that the culture considers appropriate for their biological sex.

gender-sensitive therapy An approach to therapy that takes into account the effects of gender on both the therapist's and the client's behavior.

general adaptation syndrome (GAS) The predictable sequence of reactions (alarm, resistance, and exhaustion stages) that organisms show in response to stressors.

generalization In classical conditioning, the tendency to make a conditioned response to a stimulus that is similar to the original conditioned stimulus. In operant conditioning, the tendency to make the learned response to a stimulus similar to that for which the response was originally reinforced.

generalized anxiety disorder An anxiety disorder in which people experience chronic, excessive worry for 6 months or more.

genes The segments of DNA that are located on the chromosomes and are the basic units for the transmission of all hereditary traits.

genital herpes An STD that is caused by the herpes simplex virus and results in painful blisters on the genitals; presently incurable, the infection usually recurs and is highly contagious during outbreaks.

genital warts Growths on the genitals that are caused by the human papillomavirus (HPV).

genitals (JEN-uh-tulz) The internal and external reproductive organs of males or females.

Gestalt (geh-SHTALT) A German word that roughly refers to the whole form, pattern, or configuration that a person perceives.

Gestalt psychology The school of psychology that emphasizes that individuals perceive objects and patterns as whole units and that the perceived whole is more than the sum of its parts.

Gestalt therapy A therapy that was originated by Fritz Perls and that emphasizes the importance of clients' fully experiencing, in the present moment, their feelings, thoughts, and actions and then taking responsibility for them.

glass ceiling An invisible, institutional barrier that prevents women from reaching the highest executive positions in organizations.

glial cells (GLEE-ul) Specialized cells in the brain and spinal cord that hold neurons together, remove waste products such as dead neurons, and perform other manufacturing, nourishing, and cleanup tasks.

globalization The process through which workers all over the world have been brought into more frequent contact with one another as a result of advances in transportation and communications technology.

glutamate (GLOO-tah-mate) Primary excitatory neurotransmitter in the brain.

gonads The sex glands; the ovaries in females and the testes in males.

gonorrhea (gahn-ah-REE-ah) A bacterial STD that, in males, causes a puslike discharge from the penis and painful urination; if untreated, females can develop pelvic inflammatory disease and possibly infertility.

group polarization The tendency of members of a group, after group discussion, to shift toward a more extreme position in whatever direction the group was leaning initially.

group therapy A form of therapy in which several clients (usually 7 to 10) meet regularly with one or more therapists to resolve personal problems.

groupthink The tendency for members of a tightly knit group to be more concerned with preserving group solidarity and uniformity than with objectively evaluating all alternatives in decision making.

gustation The sense of taste.

habituation A decrease in response or attention to a stimulus as an infant becomes accustomed to it.

hair cells Sensory receptors for hearing that are attached to the basilar membrane in the cochlea.

hallucination An imaginary sensation.

hallucinogens (hal-LU-sin-o-jenz) A category of drugs that can alter and distort perceptions of time and space, alter mood, produce feelings of unreality, and cause hallucinations; also called psychedelics.

halo effect The tendency to assume that a person has generally positive or negative traits as a result of observing one major positive or negative trait.

hardiness A combination of three psychological qualities—commitment, control, and challenge—shared by people who can handle high levels of stress and remain healthy.

hassles Little stressors, including the irritating demands that can occur daily, that may cause more stress than major life changes do.

health psychology The subfield within psychology that is concerned with the psychological factors that contribute to health, illness, and recovery.

heritability A measure of the degree to which a characteristic is estimated to be influenced by heredity.

heuristic (yur-RIS-tik) A rule of thumb that is derived from experience and used in decision making and problem solving, although there is no guarantee of its accuracy or usefulness.

higher-order conditioning Conditioning that occurs when conditioned stimuli are linked together to form a series of signals.

hippocampal region A part of the limbic system, which includes the hippocampus itself and the underlying cortical areas, involved in the formation of semantic memories.

hippocampus (hip-po-CAM-pus) A structure in the limbic system that plays a central role in the storing of new memories, the response to new or unexpected stimuli, and navigational ability.

homeostasis The natural tendency of the body to maintain a balanced internal state in order to ensure physical survival.

homophobia An intense, irrational hostility toward or fear of homosexuals.

hormone A chemical substance that is manufactured and released in one part of the body and affects other parts of the body.

hue The dimension of light that refers to the specific color perceived.

human factors psychology The subfield of industrial/organizational psychology that deals with the ways in which workers interact with the characteristics of a workplace.

human immunodeficiency virus (HIV) The virus that causes AIDS.

human papillomavirus (HPV) A virus that causes genital warts; also believed to contribute to cervical cancer.

humanistic psychology The school of psychology that focuses on the uniqueness of human beings and their capacity for choice, growth, and psychological health.

humanistic therapies Psychotherapies that assume that people have the ability and freedom to lead rational lives and make rational choices.

hypnosis A procedure through which one person, the hypnotist, uses the power of suggestion to induce changes in thoughts, feelings, sensations, perceptions, or behavior in another person, the subject.

hypoactive sexual desire disorder A sexual dysfunction marked by low or nonexistent sexual desire or interest in sexual activity.

hypochondriasis (HI-poh-kahn-DRY-uh-sis) A somatoform disorder in which persons are preoccupied with their health and fear that their physical symptoms are a sign of some serious disease, despite reassurance from doctors to the contrary.

hypothalamus (HY-po-THAL-uh-mus) A small but influential brain structure that regulates hunger, thirst, sexual behavior, internal body temperature, other body functions, and a wide variety of emotional behaviors.

hypothesis A prediction about a cause-effect relationship between two or more variables.

id (ID) The unconscious system of the personality, which contains the life and death instincts and operates on the pleasure principle; source of the libido.

identity crisis The emotional turmoil a teenager experiences when trying to establish a sense of personal identity.

illusion A false perception or a misperception of an actual stimulus in the environment.

imagery The representation in the mind of a sensory experience—visual, auditory, gustatory, motor, olfactory, or tactile.

inattentional blindness The phenomenon in which we shift our focus from one object to another and, in the process, fail to notice changes in objects to which we are not directly paying attention.

in-basket test A work simulation test in which applicants for managerial positions are given a stack of memos, reports, and other kinds of papers and expected to generate decisions based on their contents in a limited amount of time.

incentive An external stimulus that motivates behavior (for example, money or fame).

inclusion Educating mentally retarded students in regular schools by placing them in classes with nonhandicapped students for part of the day or in special classrooms in regular schools; also known as mainstreaming.

independent variable In an experiment, a factor or condition that is deliberately manipulated in order to determine whether it causes any change in another behavior or condition.

individualism/collectivism dimension A measure of a culture's emphasis on either individual achievement or social relationships.

inductive reasoning Reasoning in which general conclusions are drawn from particular facts or individual cases.

industrial/organizational (I/O) psychologists Psychologists who apply psychological principles and research results in the workplace and are especially interested in work motivation and job performance.

infantile amnesia The relative inability of older children and adults to recall events from the first few years of life.

information-processing theory An approach to the study of mental structures and processes that uses the computer as a model for human thinking.

in-group A social group with a strong sense of togetherness, from which others are excluded.

inhibitory effect Suppressing a behavior because a model is punished for displaying the behavior.

inner ear The innermost portion of the ear, containing the cochlea, the vestibular sacs, and the semicircular canals.

insight The sudden realization of the relationship between elements in a problem situation, which makes the solution apparent.

insight therapies Approaches to psychotherapy based on the notion that psychological well-being depends on self-understanding.

insomnia A sleep disorder characterized by difficulty falling or staying asleep, by waking too early, or by sleep that is light, restless, or of poor quality.

instinct theory A theory of motivation suggesting that human behavior is motivated by certain inborn, unlearned tendencies, or instincts, that are shared by all individuals.

intelligence An individual's ability to understand complex ideas, to adapt effectively to the environment, to learn from experience, to engage in various forms of reasoning, and to overcome obstacles through mental effort.

intelligence quotient (IQ) An index of intelligence originally derived by dividing mental age by chronological age and then multiplying by 100; now derived by comparing an individual's score with the scores of others of the same age.

interference A cause of forgetting that occurs because information or associations stored either before or after a given memory hinder the ability to remember it.

interpersonal therapy (IPT) A brief psychotherapy designed to help depressed people better understand and cope with problems relating to their interpersonal relationships.

intrinsic motivation The desire to behave in a certain way because it is enjoyable or satisfying in and of itself.

inventory A paper-and-pencil test with questions about a person's thoughts, feelings, and behaviors, which measures several dimensions of personality and can be scored according to a standard procedure.

James-Lange theory of emotion The theory that emotional feelings result when an individual becomes aware of a physiological response to an emotion-provoking stimulus (for example, feeling fear because of trembling).

job analysis An assessment by a personnel psychologist of a job category to determine the work that needs to be done and the skills required to do it.

job description An outline of the responsibilities associated with a given job category; the end result of a job analysis.

job enrichment The process of changing a job so that it will be more intrinsically motivating.

job rotation An approach to training in which employees spend relatively short periods of time performing the various jobs in an organization.

job satisfaction The degree to which an individual feels positively about his or her job.

job simplification The process of standardizing the tasks associated with a particular job.

just noticeable difference (JND) The smallest change in sensation that a person is able to detect 50% of the time.

kinesthetic sense The sense providing information about the position of body parts in relation to each other and the movement of the entire body or its parts.

laboratory observation A descriptive research method in which behavior is studied in a laboratory setting, where researchers can exert more control and use more precise equipment to measure responses.

language A means of communicating thoughts and feelings, using a system of socially shared but arbitrary symbols (sounds, signs, or written symbols) arranged according to rules of grammar.

latent content Freud's term for the underlying meaning of a dream.

latent learning Learning that occurs without apparent reinforcement and is not demonstrated until the organism is motivated to do so.

lateral hypothalamus (LH) The part of the hypothalamus that acts as a feeding center to incite eating.

lateralization The specialization of one of the cerebral hemispheres to handle a particular function.

law of effect One of Thorndike's laws of learning, which states that the consequence, or effect, of a response will determine whether the tendency to respond in the same way in the future will be strengthened or weakened.

Lazarus theory of emotion The theory that a cognitive appraisal is the first step in an emotional response and all other aspects of an emotion, including physiological arousal, depend on it.

leader-member exchange (LMX) theory A behavioral perspective on leadership that assumes that leaders and followers exert mutual influences on one another and takes into account the emotional aspects of leader-follower relationships.

leadership The ability to get individuals or groups to do what the leader wants done.

learned helplessness A passive resignation to aversive conditions that is learned through repeated exposure to inescapable or unavoidable aversive events.

learning A relatively permanent change in behavior, knowledge, capability, or attitude that is acquired through experience and cannot be attributed to illness, injury, or maturation.

left hemisphere The hemisphere that controls the right side of the body, coordinates complex movements, and, in most people, handles most of the language functions.

lens The transparent disc-shaped structure behind the iris and the pupil that changes shape as it focuses on objects at varying distances.

levels-of-processing model A model of memory that holds that retention depends on how deeply information is processed.

lifespan perspective The view that developmental changes happen throughout the human lifespan and that interdisciplinary research is required to fully understand human development.

limbic system A group of structures in the midbrain, including the amygdala and hippocampus, that are collectively involved in emotional expression, memory, and motivation.

linguistic relativity hypothesis The notion proposed by Whorf that the language a person speaks largely determines the nature of that person's thoughts.

lithium A drug used to treat bipolar disorder, which at proper maintenance dosage, reduces both manic and depressive episodes.

locus of control Rotter's concept of a cognitive factor that explains how people account for what happens in their lives—either seeing themselves as primarily in control of their behavior and its consequences (internal locus of control) or perceiving what happens to them to be in the hands of fate, luck, or chance (external locus of control).

longitudinal study A type of developmental study in which the same group of participants is followed and measured at different ages.

long-term memory (LTM) The memory system with a virtually unlimited capacity that contains vast stores of a person's permanent or relatively permanent memories.

long-term potentiation (LTP) An increase in the efficiency of neural transmission at the synapses that lasts for hours or longer.

low birth weight A weight at birth of less than 5.5 pounds.

low-ball technique A strategy in which someone makes a very attractive initial offer to get a person to commit to an action and then makes the terms less favorable.

lucid dream A dream that an individual is aware of dreaming and whose content the individual is often able to influence while the dream is in progress.

lymphocytes The white blood cells—including B cells and T cells—that are the key components of the immune system.

major depressive disorder A mood disorder marked by feelings of great sadness, despair, and hopelessness as well as the loss of the ability to experience pleasure.

male erectile disorder A sexual dysfunction in which a man experiences the repeated inability to have or sustain an erection firm enough for coitus; also known as erectile dysfunction or impotence.

male orgasmic disorder A sexual dysfunction in which a man experiences the absence of ejaculation, or ejaculation occurs only after strenuous effort over a prolonged period.

management by objectives (MBO) An evaluation approach in which subordinates and supervisors set performance goals together and agree on how goal attainment will be measured and how much time will be allotted to reach each goal.

manic episode (MAN-ik) A period of excessive euphoria, inflated self-esteem, wild optimism, and hyperactivity, often accompanied by delusions of grandeur and by hostility if activity is blocked.

manifest content Freud's term for the content of a dream as recalled by the dreamer.

massed practice Learning in one long practice session without rest periods.

matching hypothesis The notion that people tend to have lovers or spouses who are similar to themselves in physical attractiveness and other assets.

maturation Each infant's own genetically determined, biological pattern of development.

means-end analysis A heuristic strategy in which the current position is compared with a desired goal, and a series of steps is formulated and then taken to close the gap between the two.

meditation (concentrative) A group of techniques that involve focusing attention on an object, a word, one's breathing, or one's body movements in order to block out all distractions, to enhance well-being, and to achieve an altered state of consciousness.

medulla (muh-DUL-uh) The part of the brainstem that controls heartbeat, blood pressure, breathing, coughing, and swallowing.

menopause The cessation of menstruation, which usually occurs between ages 45 and 55 and marks the end of reproductive capacity.

mental retardation Subnormal intelligence reflected by an IQ below 70 and by adaptive functioning that is severely deficient for one's age.

mental set The tendency to apply a familiar strategy to solve a problem even though another approach might be better.

mere-exposure effect The tendency to feel more positively toward a stimulus as a result of repeated exposure to it.

metabolic rate (meh-tuh-BALL-ik) The rate at which the body burns calories to produce energy.

metamemory The ability to think about and control one's own memory processes.

microelectrode A small wire used to monitor the electrical activity of or stimulate activity within a single neuron.

microsleep A brief lapse (2 to 3 seconds long) from wakefulness into sleep, usually occurring when a person has been sleep-deprived.

middle ear The portion of the ear containing the ossicles, which connect the eardrum to the oval window and amplify sound waves.

Minnesota Multiphasic Personality Inventory (MMPI) The most extensively researched and widely used personality test, which is used to screen for and diagnose psychiatric problems and disorders; revised as MMPI-2.

model The individual who demonstrates a behavior or whose behavior is imitated.

modeling Another name for observational learning.

modeling effect Learning a new behavior from a model through the acquisition of new responses.

mommy track A work pattern in which women move in and out of the workforce, usually to spend time rearing children.

monocular depth cues (mah-NOK-yu-ler) Depth cues that can be perceived by one eye alone.

mood disorders Disorders characterized by extreme and unwarranted disturbances in emotion or mood.

moral-rights perspective An approach to organizational ethics that suggests that individual behavior within an organization should be guided by the same respect for basic rights that is endorsed by the larger culture.

morphemes The smallest units of meaning in a language.

motivated forgetting Forgetting through suppression or repression in order to protect oneself from material that is painful, frightening, or otherwise unpleasant.

motivation All the processes that initiate, direct, and sustain behavior.

motives Needs or desires that energize and direct behavior toward a goal.

motor cortex The strip of tissue at the rear of the frontal lobes that controls voluntary body movement and participates in learning and cognitive events.

MRI (magnetic resonance imagery) A diagnostic scanning technique that produces high-resolution images of the structures of the brain.

multifactorial inheritance A pattern of inheritance in which a trait is influenced by both genes and environmental factors.

myelin sheath (MY-uh-lin) The white, fatty coating wrapped around some axons that acts as insulation and enables impulses to travel much faster.

Myers-Briggs Type Indicator (MBTI) A personality inventory useful for measuring normal individual differences; based on Jung's theory of personality.

naive subject A person who has agreed to participate in an experiment but is not aware that deception is being used to conceal its real purpose.

narcolepsy An incurable sleep disorder characterized by excessive daytime sleepiness and uncontrollable attacks of REM sleep.

narcotics A class of depressant drugs derived from the opium poppy that produce both pain-relieving and calming effects.

natural concept A concept acquired not from a definition but through everyday perceptions and experiences.

naturalistic observation A descriptive research method in which researchers observe and record behavior in its natural setting, without attempting to influence or control it.

nature-nurture controversy The debate over whether intelligence (or another trait) is primarily the result of heredity (nature) or the environment (nurture).

need for achievement (*n* Ach) The need to accomplish something difficult and to perform at a high standard of excellence.

negative reinforcement The termination of an unpleasant condition after a response, which increases the probability that the response will be repeated.

neglecting parents Parents who are permissive and are not involved in their children's lives.

neodissociation theory of hypnosis A theory proposing that hypnosis induces a split, or dissociation, between two aspects of the control of consciousness: the planning function and the monitoring function.

neonate A newborn infant up to 1 month old.

neuron (NEW-ron) A specialized cell that conducts impulses through the nervous system and contains three major parts—a cell body, dendrites, and an axon.

neuroscience An interdisciplinary field that combines the work of psychologists, biologists, biochemists, medical researchers, and others in the study of the structure and function of the nervous system.

neurotransmitter (NEW-ro-TRANS-mit-er) A chemical substance that is released into the synaptic cleft from the axon terminal of a sending neuron, crosses a synapse, and binds to appropriate receptor sites on the dendrites or cell body of a receiving neuron, influencing the cell either to fire or not to fire.

nightmares Frightening dreams that occur during REM sleep and are likely to be remembered in vivid detail.

nondeclarative memory The subsystem within long-term memory that stores motor skills, habits, and simple classically conditioned responses; also called implicit memory.

nondirective therapy Any type of psychotherapy in which the therapist allows the direction of the therapy sessions to be controlled by the client; an example is person-centered therapy.

nonsense syllable A consonant-vowel-consonant combination that does not spell a word and is used in memory research.

norepinephrine (nor-EP-ih-NEF-rin) A neurotransmitter affecting eating, alertness, and sleep.

norms Standards based on the test scores of a large number of individuals and used as bases of comparison for other test takers.

NREM dream A type of dream occurring during NREM sleep that is typically less frequent and memorable than REM dreams are.

NREM sleep Non-rapid eye movement sleep, which consists of four sleep stages and is characterized by slow, regular respiration and heart rate, little body movement, an absence of rapid eye movements, and blood pressure and brain activity that are at their 24-hour low points.

object permanence The realization that objects continue to exist even when they are out of sight.

observational learning Learning by observing the behavior of others and the consequences of that behavior; learning by imitation.

obsession A persistent, involuntary thought, image, or impulse that invades consciousness and causes great distress.

obsessive-compulsive disorder (OCD) An anxiety disorder in which a person suffers from recurrent obsessions and/or compulsions.

occipital lobes (ahk-SIP-uh-tul) The lobes that are involved in the reception and interpretation of visual information; they contain the primary visual cortex.

Oedipus complex (ED-uh-pus) Occurring in the phallic stage, a conflict in which the child is sexually attracted to the opposite-sex parent and feels hostility toward the same-sex parent.

off-the-job training An approach to training in which employees watch videos or demonstrations and are expected to implement what they learn when on the job.

olfaction (ol-FAK-shun) The sense of smell.

olfactory bulbs Two matchstick-sized structures above the nasal cavities, where smell sensations first register in the brain.

olfactory epithelium Two 1-square-inch patches of tissue, one at the top of each nasal cavity, which together contain about 10 million olfactory neurons, the receptors for smell.

on-the-job training An approach to training in which employees receive instruction while actually performing the job.

operant conditioning A type of learning in which the consequences of behavior are manipulated in order to increase or decrease the frequency of an existing response or to shape an entirely new response.

opponent-process theory The theory of color vision suggesting that three kinds of cells respond by increasing or decreasing their rate of firing when different colors are present.

optic nerve The nerve that carries visual information from each retina to both sides of the brain.

organization Piaget's term for a mental process that uses specific experiences to make inferences that can be generalized to new experiences.

organizational climate Employees' perceptions and emotional responses to the culture of an organization.

organizational culture The system of shared values, beliefs, and practices that evolves within an organization and influences the behavior of its members.

organizational psychology The study of individuals and groups in formal organizations.

organizational social responsibility A perspective based on the idea that an organization's policies should take into consideration the interests of the larger society of which it is a part.

orgasm The third stage of the sexual response cycle, marked by a sudden discharge of accumulated sexual tension and involuntary muscle contractions.

outer ear The visible part of the ear, consisting of the pinna and the auditory canal.

out-group A social group made up of individuals specifically identified by the in-group as not belonging.

overextension The application of a word, on the basis of some shared feature, to a broader range of objects than is appropriate.

overlearning Practicing or studying material beyond the point where it can be repeated once without error.

overregularization The act of inappropriately applying the grammatical rules for forming plurals and past tenses to irregular nouns and verbs.

panic attack An episode of overwhelming anxiety, fear, or terror.

panic disorder An anxiety disorder in which a person experiences recurring, unpredictable episodes of overwhelming anxiety, fear, or terror.

paranoid schizophrenia (PAIR-uh-noid) A type of schizophrenia characterized by delusions of grandeur or persecution.

paraphilias Sexual disorders in which recurrent sexual urges, fantasies, or behavior involve nonhuman objects, children, other nonconsenting persons, or the suffering or humiliation of the individual or his or her partner.

parasomnias Sleep disturbances in which behaviors and physiological states that normally take place only in the waking state occur while a person is sleeping.

parasympathetic nervous system The division of the autonomic nervous system that brings the heightened bodily responses back to normal following an emergency.

parental investment A term used by evolutionary psychologists to denote the amount of time and effort men or women must devote to parenthood.

parietal lobes (puh-RY-uh-tul) The lobes that contain the somatosensory cortex (where touch, pressure, temperature, and pain register) and other areas that are responsible for body awareness and spatial orientation.

partial reinforcement A pattern of reinforcement in which some but not all correct responses are reinforced.

partial-reinforcement effect The greater resistance to extinction that occurs when a portion, rather than all, of the correct responses are reinforced.

participant modeling A behavior therapy in which an appropriate response to a feared stimulus is modeled in graduated steps and the client attempts to imitate the model step by step, encouraged and supported by the therapist.

participative management A management technique in which managers involve subordinates in the decision-making process.

pelvic inflammatory disease (PID) An infection in the female pelvic organs, which can result from untreated chlamydia or gonorrhea and can cause pain, scarring of tissue, and even infertility or an ectopic pregnancy.

perception The process by which sensory information is actively organized and interpreted by the brain.

perceptual constancy The phenomenon that allows us to perceive objects as maintaining stable properties, such as size, shape, and brightness, despite differences in distance, viewing angle, and lighting.

perceptual set An expectation of what will be perceived, which can affect what actually is perceived.

performance appraisal A formal process used to determine how well an employee is functioning in his or her job.

peripheral nervous system (PNS) (peh-RIF-er-ul) The nerves connecting the central nervous system to the rest of the body.

permeability (perm-ee-uh-BIL-uh-tee) The capability of being penetrated or passed through.

permissive parents Parents who make few rules or demands and usually do not enforce those that are made; they allow children to make their own decisions and control their own behavior.

personal space An area surrounding each person, much like an invisible bubble, that the person considers part of himself or herself and uses to regulate the level of intimacy with others.

personal unconscious In Jung's theory, the layer of the unconscious that contains all of the thoughts, perceptions, and experiences accessible to the conscious, as well as repressed memories, wishes, and impulses.

personality A person's characteristic patterns of behaving, thinking, and feeling.

personality disorder A long-standing, inflexible, maladaptive pattern of behaving and relating to others, which usually begins in early childhood or adolescence.

person-centered therapy A nondirective, humanistic therapy developed by Carl Rogers, in which the therapist creates an accepting climate and shows empathy, freeing clients to be themselves and releasing their natural tendency toward self-actualization.

personnel psychology The branch of industrial/organizational psychology that deals with the design of appropriate and effective strategies for hiring, training, and evaluating employees.

persuasion A deliberate attempt to influence the attitudes and/or behavior of another person.

PET scan (positron-emission tomography) A brain-imaging technique that reveals activity in various parts of the brain, based on patterns of blood flow, oxygen use, and glucose consumption.

pheromones Chemicals excreted by humans and other animals that can have a powerful effect on the behavior of other members of the same species.

phi phenomenon Apparent motion that occurs when several stationary lights in a dark room are flashed on and off in sequence, causing the perception that a single light is moving from one spot to the next.

phobia (FO-bee-ah) A persistent, irrational fear of some specific object, situation, or activity that poses little or no real danger.

phonemes The smallest units of sound in a spoken language.

phonological awareness Sensitivity to the sound patterns of a language and how they are represented as letters.

physical drug dependence A compulsive pattern of drug use in which the user develops a drug tolerance coupled with unpleasant withdrawal symptoms when the drug use is discontinued.

pituitary gland The endocrine gland located in the brain that releases hormones that activate other endocrine glands as well as growth hormone; often called the "master gland."

place theory The theory of hearing that holds that each individual pitch a person hears is determined by the particular location along the basilar membrane of the cochlea that vibrates the most.

placebo (pluh-SEE-bo) An inert or harmless substance given to the control group in an experiment as a control for the placebo effect.

placebo effect The phenomenon that occurs in an experiment when a participant's response to a treatment is due to his or her expectations about the treatment rather than to the treatment itself.

plasticity The capacity of the brain to adapt to changes such as brain damage.

plateau phase The second stage of the sexual response cycle, during which muscle tension and blood flow to the genitals increase in preparation for orgasm.

polygraph A device designed to detect the changes in heart rate, blood pressure, respiration rate, and skin conductance response that typically accompany arousal.

population The entire group of interest to researchers, to which they wish to generalize their findings; the group from which a sample is selected.

positive reinforcement Any pleasant or desirable consequence that follows a response and increases the probability that the response will be repeated.

postconventional level Kohlberg's highest level of moral reasoning, in which moral reasoning involves weighing moral alternatives and realizing that laws may conflict with basic human rights.

posttraumatic stress disorder (PTSD) A prolonged and severe stress reaction to a catastrophic event or to severe, chronic stress.

pragmatics The characteristics of spoken language, such as intonation and gestures, that indicate the social meaning of utterances.

preconscious The thoughts, feelings, and memories that a person is not consciously aware of at the moment but that may be easily brought to consciousness.

preconventional level Kohlberg's first level of moral reasoning, in which moral reasoning is governed by the standards of others rather than the person's own internalized standards of right and wrong; acts are judged as good or bad based on their physical consequences.

prejudice Attitudes (usually negative) toward others based on their gender, religion, race, or membership in a particular group.

premature ejaculation A chronic or recurring orgasmic disorder in which orgasm and ejaculation occur with little stimulation, before, during, or shortly after penetration and before the man wishes; the most common sexual dysfunction in males.

prenatal development Development that occurs between conception and birth and consists of three stages (germinal, embryonic, and fetal).

preoperational stage Piaget's second stage of cognitive development (ages 2 to 6 years), which is characterized by the development and refinement of schemes for symbolic representation.

presbyopia (prez-bee-O-pee-uh) A condition, developing in the mid- to late 40s, in which the lenses of the eyes no longer accommodate adequately for near vision, and reading glasses or bifocals are required for reading.

primacy effect In memory, the tendency to recall the first items in a sequence more readily than the middle items. In social psychology, the tendency for an overall impression of another to be influenced more by the first information that is received about that person than by information that comes later.

primary appraisal A cognitive evaluation of a potentially stressful event to determine whether its effect is positive, irrelevant, or negative.

primary auditory cortex The part of each temporal lobe where hearing registers in the cerebral cortex.

primary drive A state of tension or arousal that arises from a biological need and is unlearned.

primary mental abilities According to Thurstone, seven relatively distinct abilities that, singly or in combination, are involved in all intellectual activities.

primary reinforcer A reinforcer that fulfills a basic physical need for survival and does not depend on learning.

primary sex characteristics The internal and external reproductive organs; the genitals.

primary visual cortex The area at the rear of the occipital lobes where vision registers in the cerebral cortex.

priming The phenomenon by which an earlier encounter with a stimulus (such as a word or a picture) increases the speed or accuracy of naming that stimulus or a related stimulus at a later time.

proactive coping Active measures taken in advance of a potentially stressful situation in order to prevent its occurrence or to minimize its consequences.

problem solving Using thoughts and actions to achieve a desired goal that is not readily attainable.

problem-focused coping A direct response aimed at reducing, modifying, or eliminating a source of stress.

progesterone (pro-JES-tah-rone) A female sex hormone that plays a role in the regulation of the menstrual cycle and prepares the lining of the uterus for pregnancy.

projection A defense mechanism in which one attributes one's own undesirable thoughts, impulses, personality traits, or behavior to others or minimizes the undesirable in oneself and exaggerates it in others.

projective test A personality test in which people respond to inkblots, drawings of ambiguous human situations, or incomplete sentences by projecting their inner thoughts, feelings, fears, or conflicts onto the test materials.

prosocial behavior Behavior that benefits others, such as helping, cooperation, and sympathy.

prospective forgetting Not remembering to carry out some intended action.

prototype An example that embodies the most common and typical features of a concept.

proximity Physical or geographic closeness; a major influence on attraction.

pruning The process through which the developing brain eliminates unnecessary or redundant synapses.

psychiatrist A mental health professional who is a medical doctor.

psychoactive drug Any substance that alters mood, perception, or thought; called a controlled substance if approved for medical use.

psychoanalysis (SY-ko-ah-NAL-ih-sis) The term Freud used for both his theory of personality and his therapy for the treatment of psychological disorders; the unconscious is the primary focus of psychoanalytic theory, and the therapy uses free association, dream analysis, and transference.

psychodynamic therapies Psychotherapies that attempt to uncover childhood experiences that are thought to explain a patient's current difficulties.

psycholinguistics The study of how language is acquired, produced, and used, and how the sounds and symbols of language are translated into meaning.

psychological disorders Mental processes and/or behavior patterns that cause emotional distress and/or substantial impairment in functioning.

psychological drug dependence A craving or irresistible urge for a drug's pleasurable effects.

psychological perspectives General points of view used for explaining people's behavior and thinking, whether normal or abnormal.

psychologist A mental health professional who possesses a doctoral degree in psychology.

psychology The scientific study of behavior and mental processes.

psychoneuroimmunology (sye-ko-NEW-ro-IM-you-NOLL-oh-gee) A field in which psychologists, biologists, and medical researchers combine their expertise to study the effects of psychological factors on the immune system.

psychosexual stages A series of stages through which the sexual instinct develops; each stage is defined by an erogenous zone around which conflict arises.

psychosis (sy-CO-sis) A condition characterized by loss of contact with reality.

psychosocial stages Erikson's eight developmental stages through which individuals progress during their lifespan; each stage is defined by a conflict involving the individual's relationship with the social environment, which must be resolved satisfactorily in order for healthy development to occur.

psychosurgery Brain surgery performed to alleviate serious psychological disorders or unbearable chronic pain.

psychotherapy Any type of treatment for emotional and behavioral disorders that uses psychological rather than biological means.

puberty A period of several years in which rapid physical growth and physiological changes occur, culminating in sexual maturity.

punishment The removal of a pleasant stimulus or the application of an unpleasant stimulus, thereby lowering the probability of a response.

quality circle A group of employees who meet regularly to search for ways to increase a company's productivity, improve the quality of its products, or reduce its costs.

quality of work life (QWL) movement An approach to reducing work-related stress by basing job and workplace design on analyses of the quality of employee experiences in an organization.

random assignment The process of selecting participants for experimental and control groups by using a chance procedure to guarantee that each participant has an equal probability of being assigned to any of the groups; a control for selection bias.

rational-emotive therapy A directive form of psychotherapy, developed by Albert Ellis and designed to challenge clients' irrational beliefs about themselves and others.

rationalization A defense mechanism in which one supplies a logical, rational, or socially acceptable reason rather than the real reason for an action or event.

reaction formation A defense mechanism in which one expresses exaggerated ideas and emotions that are the opposite of one's disturbing unconscious impulses and desires.

real motion Perceptions of motion tied to movements of real objects through space.

realistic conflict theory The view that as competition increases among social groups for scarce resources, so do prejudice, discrimination, and hatred.

reasoning A form of thinking in which conclusions are drawn from a set of facts.

recall A memory task in which a person must produce required information by searching memory.

recency effect The tendency to recall the last items in a sequence more readily than those in the middle.

receptors Protein molecules on the surfaces of dendrites and cell bodies that have distinctive shapes and will interact only with specific neurotransmitters.

reciprocal determinism Bandura's concept of a mutual influential relationship among behavior, cognitive factors, and environment.

recognition A memory task in which a person must simply identify material as familiar or as having been encountered before.

reconstruction An account of an event that has been pieced together from a few highlights, using information that may or may not be accurate.

recruitment The identification of appropriate candidates for a particular position.

reflex An inborn, unlearned, automatic response (such as blinking, sucking, and grasping) to a particular environmental stimulus.

regression A defense mechanism in which one reverts to a behavior that might have reduced anxiety at an earlier stage of development.

rehearsal The act of purposely repeating information to maintain it in short-term memory.

reinforcement Any event that follows a response and strengthens or increases the probability that the response will be repeated.

reinforcer Anything that follows a response and strengthens it or increases the probability that it will occur.

relationship therapies Therapies that attempt to improve patients' interpersonal relationships or create new relationships to support patients' efforts to address psychological problems.

relearning method A measure of memory in which retention is expressed as the percentage of time saved when material is relearned compared with the time required to learn the material originally.

reliability The ability of a test to yield nearly the same score when the same people are tested and then retested on the same test or an alternative form of the test.

REM dream A type of dream occurring almost continuously during each REM period and having a storylike quality; typically more vivid, visual, and emotional than NREM dreams.

REM rebound The increased amount of REM sleep that occurs after REM deprivation; often associated with unpleasant dreams or nightmares.

REM sleep A type of sleep characterized by rapid eye movements, paralysis of large muscles, fast and irregular heart and respiration rates, increased brain-wave activity, and vivid dreams.

replication The process of repeating a study with different participants and preferably a different investigator to verify research findings.

representative sample A sample that mirrors the population of interest; it includes important subgroups in the same proportions as they are found in that population.

representativeness heuristic A thinking strategy based on how closely a new object or situation is judged to resemble or match an existing prototype of that object or situation.

repression A defense mechanism in which one involuntarily removes painful or threatening memories, thoughts, or perceptions from consciousness, so that one is no longer aware that a painful event occurred, or prevents unconscious sexual and aggressive impulses from breaking into consciousness.

resistance stage The second stage of the general adaptation syndrome, when there are intense physiological efforts to either resist or adapt to the stressor.

resolution phase The final stage of the sexual response cycle, during which the body returns to an unaroused state.

resting potential The slight negative electrical potential of the axon membrane of a neuron at rest, about -70 millivolts.

restorative theory of sleep The theory that the function of sleep is to restore body and mind.

reticular formation A structure in the brainstem that plays a crucial role in arousal and attention and that screens sensory messages entering the brain.

retina The layer of tissue that is located on the inner surface of the eyeball and contains the sensory receptors for vision.

retrieval The process of bringing to mind information that has been stored in memory.

retrieval cue Any stimulus or bit of information that aids in retrieving particular information from long-term memory.

retrograde amnesia (RET-ro-grade) A loss of memory for experiences that occurred shortly before a loss of consciousness.

reuptake The process by which neurotransmitters are taken from the synaptic cleft back into the axon terminal for later use, thus terminating their excitatory or inhibitory effect on the receiving neuron.

reversibility The fact that when only the appearance of a substance has been changed, it can be returned to its original state.

right hemisphere The hemisphere that controls the left side of the body and, in most people, is specialized for visual-spatial perception.

robotics The science of automating human and animal functions.

rods The light-sensitive receptor cells in the retina that look like slender cylinders and allow the eye to respond to as few as five photons of light.

Rorschach Inkblot Method (ROR-shok) A projective test composed of 10 inkblots that the test taker is asked to describe; used to assess personality, make differential diagnoses, plan and evaluate treatment, and predict behavior.

sample A part of population that is studied in order to reach conclusions about the entire population.

saturation The purity of a color, or the degree to which the light waves producing it are of the same wavelength.

savant syndrome A condition that allows an individual whose level of general intelligence is very low to perform highly creative or difficult mental feats.

savings score The percentage of time saved when relearning material compared with the amount of time required for the original learning.

scapegoating Displacing aggression onto members of minority groups or other innocent targets not responsible for the frustrating situation.

Schachter-Singer theory of emotion A two-factor theory stating that for an emotion to occur, there must be (1) physiological arousal and (2) a cognitive interpretation or explanation of the arousal, allowing it to be labeled as a specific emotion.

schedule of reinforcement A systematic process for administering partial reinforcement that produces a distinct rate and pattern of responses and degree of resistance to extinction.

schemas The integrated frameworks of knowledge and assumptions a person has about people, objects, and events, which affect how the person encodes and recalls information.

scheme A plan of action, based on previous experiences, to be used in similar circumstances.

schizophrenia (SKIT-soh-FREE-nee-ah) A severe psychological disorder characterized by loss of contact with reality, hallucinations, delusions, inappropriate or flat affect, some disturbance in thinking, social withdrawal, and/or other bizarre behavior.

scientific management An approach to management that assumes that workers and their supervisors operate more effectively and efficiently when job requirements are based on empirical data.

scientific method The orderly, systematic procedures that researchers follow as they identify a research problem, design a study to investigate the problem, collect and analyze data, draw conclusions, and communicate their findings.

secondary appraisal A cognitive evaluation of available resources and options prior to deciding how to deal with a stressor.

secondary reinforcer A reinforcer that is acquired or learned through association with other reinforcers.

secondary sex characteristics Those physical characteristics that are not directly involved in reproduction but that appear at puberty and distinguish the mature male from the mature female.

selection The process of matching applicants to jobs.

selection bias The assignment of participants to experimental or control groups in such a way that systematic differences among the groups are present at the beginning of the experiment.

self-actualization Developing to one's fullest potential.

self-efficacy The perception a person has of his or her ability to perform competently whatever is attempted.

self-managed teams A group of workers who have complete responsibility for planning, executing, and evaluating their work.

self-serving bias The tendency to attribute one's successes to dispositional causes and one's failures to situational causes.

semantic memory The type of declarative memory that stores general knowledge, or objective facts and information.

semantics The meaning derived from morphemes, words, and sentences.

semicircular canals Three fluid-filled tubular canals in the inner ear that sense the rotation of the head.

sensation The process through which the senses pick up visual, auditory, and other sensory stimuli and transmit them to the brain.

sensorimotor stage Piaget's first stage of cognitive development (ages birth to 2 years), in which infants gain an understanding of their world through their senses and their motor activities; culminates with the development of object permanence and the beginning of representational thought.

sensory adaptation The process in which sensory receptors grow accustomed to constant, unchanging levels of stimuli over time.

sensory deprivation A condition in which sensory stimulation is reduced to a minimum or eliminated.

sensory memory The memory system that holds information from the senses for a period of time ranging from only a fraction of a second to about 2 seconds.

sensory receptors Highly specialized cells in the sense organs that detect and respond to one type of sensory stimuli—light, sound, or odor, for example—and transduce (convert) the stimuli into neural impulses.

separation anxiety The fear and distress shown by infants and toddlers when the parent leaves, occurring from 8 to 24 months and reaching a peak between 12 and 18 months.

serial position effect The finding that, for information learned in a sequence, recall is better for the beginning and ending items than for the middle items in the sequence.

serotonin (ser-oh-TOE-nin) A neurotransmitter that plays an important role in regulating mood, sleep, impulsivity, aggression, and appetite.

set point The weight the body normally maintains when one is trying neither to gain nor to lose weight.

sex chromosomes The pair of chromosomes that determines the biological sex of a person (XX in females and XY in males).

sexual aversion disorder A sexual dysfunction characterized by an aversion to and active avoidance of genital contact with a sexual partner.

sexual disorders Disorders with a sexual basis that are destructive, guilt- or anxiety-producing, compulsive, or a cause of discomfort or harm to one or both parties involved.

sexual dysfunction A persistent or recurrent problem that causes marked distress and interpersonal difficulty and that may involve some combination of the following: sexual desire, sexual arousal or the pleasure associated with sex, or orgasm.

sexual harassment Any kind of unwanted or offensive sexual expression in the workplace.

sexual orientation The direction of one's sexual preference, erotic feelings, and sexual activity—toward members of the opposite sex (heterosexuality), toward one's own sex (homosexuality), or toward both sexes (bisexuality).

sexual response cycle According to Masters and Johnson, the typical pattern of the human sexual response in both males and females, consisting of four phases: excitement, plateau, orgasm, and resolution.

sexual violence Any kind of sexual contact in which one or more participants are either unable to give consent or are forced into participation.

sexually transmitted diseases (STDs) Infections that are spread primarily through intimate sexual contact.

shaping An operant conditioning technique that consists of gradually molding a desired behavior (response) by reinforcing any movement in the direction of the desired response, thereby gradually guiding the responses toward the ultimate goal.

short-term memory (STM) The memory system that codes information according to sound and holds about seven (from five to nine) items for less than 30 seconds without rehearsal; also called working memory.

situational approach A perspective that explains the effectiveness of leadership as depending on the match between a leader's characteristics and the situations in which she or he is called upon to lead.

situational attribution Attributing a behavior to some external cause or factor operating within the situation; an external attribution.

Skinner box A soundproof chamber with a device for delivering food to an animal subject; used in operant conditioning experiments.

sleep apnea A sleep disorder characterized by periods during sleep when breathing stops and the individual must awaken briefly in order to breathe.

sleep cycle A period of sleep lasting about 90 minutes and including one or more stages of NREM sleep, followed by REM sleep.

sleep terrors A sleep disturbance that occurs during partial arousal from Stage 4 sleep, in which the sleeper springs up in a state of panic.

slow-wave sleep Deep sleep; associated with Stage 3 and Stage 4 sleep.

social cognition The mental processes that people use to notice, interpret, and remember information about the social world.

social facilitation Any positive or negative effect on performance that can be attributed to the presence of others, either as an audience or as co-actors.

social loafing The tendency to put forth less effort when working with others on a common task than when working alone.

social motives Motives (such as the needs for affiliation and achievement) that are acquired through experience and interaction with others.

social norms The attitudes and standards of behavior expected of members of a particular group.

social phobia An irrational fear and avoidance of any social or performance situation in which one might embarrass or humiliate oneself in front of others by appearing clumsy, foolish, or incompetent.

social psychology The subfield that attempts to explain how the actual, imagined, or implied presence of others influences the thoughts, feelings, and behavior of individuals.

Social Readjustment Rating Scale (SRRS) Holmes and Rahe's measure of stress, which ranks 43 life events from most to least stressful and assigns a point value to each.

social roles Socially defined behaviors considered appropriate for individuals occupying certain positions within a given group.

social support Tangible and/or emotional support provided in time of need by family members, friends, and others; the feeling of being loved, valued, and cared for by those toward whom we feel a similar obligation.

socialization The process of learning socially acceptable behaviors, attitudes, and values.

sociocognitive theory of hypnosis A theory suggesting that the behavior of a hypnotized person is a function of that person's expectations about how subjects behave under hypnosis.

sociocultural approach The view that social and cultural factors may be just as powerful as evolutionary and physiological factors in affecting behavior and mental processing and that these factors must be understood when interpreting the behavior of others.

somatoform disorders (so-MAT-uh-form) Disorders in which physical symptoms are present that are due to psychological causes rather than any known medical condition.

somatosensory cortex (so-MAT-oh-SENS-or-ee) The strip of tissue at the front of the parietal lobes where touch, pressure, temperature, and pain register in the cerebral cortex.

somnambulism Sleepwalking; a parasomnia that occurs during partial arousal from Stage 4 sleep.

somniloquy Sleeptalking; a parasomnia that can occur during any sleep stage.

specific phobia A marked fear of a specific object or situation; a general label for any phobia other than agoraphobia and social phobia.

spinal cord An extension of the brain, from the base of the brain through the neck and spinal column, that transmits messages between the brain and the peripheral nervous system.

split-brain operation A surgical procedure, performed to treat severe cases of epilepsy, in which the corpus callosum is cut, separating the cerebral hemispheres.

spontaneous recovery The reappearance of an extinguished response (in a weaker form) when an organism is exposed to the original conditioned stimulus following a rest period.

SQ3R method A study method involving the following five steps: (1) survey, (2) question, (3) read, (4) recite, and (5) review.

Stage 4 sleep The deepest stage of NREM sleep, characterized by an EEG pattern of more than 50% delta waves.

standardization The process of establishing both norms for interpreting scores on a test and standard procedures for administering the test.

Stanford-Binet Intelligence Scale An individually administered IQ test for those aged 2 to 23; Terman's revision of the Binet-Simon scale.

state-dependent memory effect The tendency to recall information better if one is in the same pharmacological or psychological state as when the information was encoded.

stereotypes Widely shared beliefs about the characteristic traits, attitudes, and behaviors of members of various social groups (racial, ethnic, or religious), including the assumption that the members of such groups are usually all alike.

stimulants A category of drugs that speed up activity in the central nervous system, suppress appetite, and can cause a person to feel more awake, alert, and energetic; also called "uppers."

stimulus (STIM-yu-lus) Any event or object in the environment to which an organism responds; plural is stimuli.

stimulus motives Motives that cause humans and other animals to increase stimulation when the level of arousal is too low (examples are curiosity and the motive to explore).

storage The process of keeping or maintaining information in memory.

stranger anxiety A fear of strangers common in infants at about 6 or 7 months of age, which increases in intensity until about 12½ months and then declines.

stress The physiological and psychological response to a condition that threatens or challenges a person and requires some form of adaptation or adjustment.

stressor Any stimulus or event capable of producing physical or emotional stress.

stroke The most common cause of damage to adult brains, arising when blockage of an artery cuts off the blood supply to a particular area of the brain or when a blood vessel bursts.

structuralism The first formal school of thought in psychology, aimed at analyzing the basic elements, or structure, of conscious mental experience.

structured interviews Standardized interview questions and procedures that are used with all applicants for a position.

subjective night The time during a 24-hour period when the biological clock is telling a person to go to sleep.

sublimation A defense mechanism in which one rechannels sexual or aggressive energy into pursuits or accomplishments that society considers acceptable or admirable.

substantia nigra (sub-STAN-sha NI-gra) The structure in the midbrain that controls unconscious motor movements.

successive approximations A series of gradual steps, each of which is more similar to the final desired response.

superego (sue-per-EE-go) The moral system of the personality, which consists of the conscience and the ego ideal.

suprachiasmatic nucleus (SCN) A pair of tiny structures in the brain's hypothalamus that control the timing of circadian rhythms; the biological clock.

surface structure The literal words of a sentence that are spoken or written (or signed).

survey A descriptive research method in which researchers use interviews and/or questionnaires to gather information about the attitudes, beliefs, experiences, or behaviors of a group of people.

syllogism A scheme for logical reasoning in which two statements known as premises are followed by a valid conclusion.

sympathetic nervous system The division of the autonomic nervous system that mobilizes the body's resources during stress and emergencies, preparing the body for action.

synapse (SIN-aps) The junction where the axon terminal of a sending neuron communicates with a receiving neuron across the synaptic cleft.

syntax The aspect of grammar that specifies the rules for arranging and combining words to form phrases and sentences.

syphilis A bacterial STD that progresses through three predictable stages; if untreated, it can eventually be fatal.

systematic desensitization A behavior therapy that is based on classical conditioning and used to treat fears by training clients in deep muscle relaxation and then having them confront a graduated series of anxiety-producing situations (real or imagined) until they can remain relaxed while confronting even the most feared situation.

tactile Pertaining to the sense of touch.

taste aversion The intense dislike and/or avoidance of a particular food that has been associated with nausea or discomfort.

taste buds Structures in many of the tongue's papillae that are composed of 60 to 100 receptor cells for taste.

telecommuting An arrangement in which employees work in their homes and are connected to their workplaces by computer, fax machine, and telephone.

telegraphic speech Short sentences that follow a rigid word order and contain only three or so essential content words.

temperament A person's behavioral style or characteristic way of responding to the environment.

temporal lobes The lobes that are involved in the reception and interpretation of auditory information; they contain the primary auditory cortex, Wernicke's area, and the temporal association areas.

teratogens Viruses and other harmful agents that can have a negative impact on prenatal development.

testosterone (tes-TOS-tah-rone) The most important androgen, which influences the development and maintenance of male sex characteristics and sexual motivation and, in small amounts, maintains sexual interest and responsiveness in females.

thalamus (THAL-uh-mus) The structure, located above the brainstem, that acts as a relay station for information flowing into or out of the forebrain.

Thematic Apperception Test (TAT) A projective test consisting of drawings of ambiguous human situations, which the test taker describes; thought to reveal inner feelings, conflicts, and motives, which are projected onto the test materials.

theory A general principle or set of principles proposed to explain how a number of separate facts are related.

theory of dissociated control The theory that hypnosis is an authentic altered state of consciousness in which the control the executive function exerts over other subsystems of consciousness is weakened.

Theory X An approach to management that focuses on work efficiency, or how well an employee performs specific job tasks.

Theory Y An approach to management that emphasizes psychological efficiency, or the degree to which a job has a positive psychological impact on an employee.

360-degree evaluation An evaluation strategy that combines worker performance ratings from supervisors, peers, subordinates, customers, and the workers themselves.

timbre (TAM-burr) The distinctive quality of a sound that distinguishes it from other sounds of the same pitch and loudness.

time-motion studies Research examining the exact physical motions required to perform a given manufacturing function in the least amount of time.

time out A behavior modification technique used to eliminate undesirable behavior, especially in children and adolescents, by withdrawing all reinforcers for a period of time.

token economy A behavior modification technique that rewards appropriate behavior with tokens that can be exchanged later for desired items or privileges.

top-down processing Information processing in which previous experience and conceptual knowledge are applied in order to recognize the nature of a "whole" and then logically deduce the individual components of that whole.

trait A personal quality or characteristic, which is stable across situations, that is used to describe or explain personality.

trait approach A perspective on leadership that holds that leaders possess intrinsic characteristics that help them influence others.

transactional leaders Leaders who focus on motivating followers to accomplish routine, agreed-on goals.

transduction The process through which sensory receptors convert the sensory stimulation into neural impulses.

transference An emotional reaction that occurs during psychoanalysis, in which the patient displays feelings and attitudes toward the analyst that were present in another significant relationship.

transformational leaders Leaders who encourage followers to achieve excellence in the accomplishment of routine goals and to pursue goals that go beyond the status quo.

trial and error An approach to problem solving in which one solution after another is tried in no particular order until an answer is found.

trial-and-error learning Learning that occurs when a response is associated with a successful solution to a problem after a number of unsuccessful responses.

triangular theory of love Sternberg's theory that three components—intimacy, passion, and commitment—singly and in various combinations, produce seven different kinds of love.

triarchic theory of intelligence Sternberg's theory that there are three types of intelligence—componential (analytical), experiential (creative), and contextual (practical).

trichomatic theory The theory of color vision suggesting that there are three types of cones in the retina that make a maximal chemical response to one of three colors—red, green, or blue.

Type A behavior pattern A behavior pattern marked by a sense of time urgency, impatience, excessive competitiveness, hostility, and anger; considered a risk factor in coronary heart disease.

Type B behavior pattern A behavior pattern marked by a relaxed, easygoing approach to life, without the time urgency, impatience, and hostility of the Type A pattern.

unconditional positive regard Unqualified caring and nonjudgmental acceptance of another.

unconditioned response (UR) A response that is elicited by an unconditioned stimulus without prior learning.

unconditioned stimulus (US) A stimulus that elicits a specific unconditioned response without prior learning.

unconscious (un-KON-shus) For Freud, the primary motivating force of human behavior, containing repressed memories as well as instincts, wishes, and desires that have never been conscious.

underextension The restriction of a word to only a few, rather than to all, members of a class of objects.

undifferentiated schizophrenia A catchall term used when schizophrenic symptoms either do not conform to the criteria of any one type of schizophrenia or conform to more than one type.

uplifts The positive experiences in life, which may neutralize the effects of many hassles.

utilitarian perspective An approach to organizational ethics that defines ethical behavior in terms of the greatest good for the greatest number of people.

vaginismus (VAJ-ah-NIZ-mus) A sexual pain disorder in which involuntary muscle contractions tighten and even close the vagina, making intercourse painful or impossible.

validity The ability of a test to measure what it is intended to measure.

variable-interval schedule A schedule in which a reinforcer is given after the first correct response that follows a varying time of nonreinforcement, based on an average time.

variable-ratio schedule A schedule in which a reinforcer is given after a varying number of nonreinforced responses, based on an average ratio.

ventromedial hypothalamus (VMH) The part of the hypothalamus that acts as a satiety (fullness) center to inhibit eating.

vestibular sense (ves-TIB-yu-ler) The sense that detects movement and provides information about the body's orientation in space.

visible spectrum The narrow band of electromagnetic waves that are visible to the human eye.

visual cliff An apparatus used to measure infants' ability to perceive depth.

Weber's law The law stating that the just noticeable difference (JND) for all the senses depends on a proportion or percentage of change in a stimulus rather than on a fixed amount of change.

Wechsler Adult Intelligence Scale (WAIS-III) An individual intelligence test for adults that yields separate verbal and performance (nonverbal) IQ scores as well as an overall IQ score.

Wernicke's aphasia (VUR-nih-keys) Aphasia that results from damage to Wernicke's area and in which the person's speech is fluent and clearly articulated but does not make sense to listeners.

Wernicke's area The language area in the left temporal lobe involved in comprehending the spoken word and in formulating of coherent speech and written language.

withdrawal symptoms The physical and psychological symptoms (usually the exact opposite of the effects produced by the drug) that occur when a regularly used drug is discontinued and that terminate when the drug is taken again.

work motivation The conditions and processes responsible for the arousal, direction, magnitude, and maintenance of effort of workers on the job.

working backwards A heuristic strategy in which a person discovers the steps needed to solve a problem by starting with the solution and working back through the problem.

workspace envelope The three-dimensional space in which an individual worker performs the tasks that comprise his or her job.

Yerkes-Dodson law The principle that performance on tasks is best when the arousal level is appropriate to the difficulty of the task: higher arousal for simple tasks, moderate arousal for tasks of moderate difficulty, and lower arousal for complex tasks.

zygote The single cell that forms when a sperm and egg unite.

Name Index

Subject Index

(cont.)

Credits

Photos

CHAPTER 1, p. 2: © Brian Bailey/Getty Images/Stone; **7:** © Ron Chapple; **8:** © Carlos Lopez-Barillas/Getty Images; **9:** AP/Wide World Photos; **10:** © Howard Huang/Getty Images/The Image Bank; **11:** © Pictor International/Pictor International Ltd./PictureQuest; **17:** © Steve Skjold/PhotoEdit; **20:** © Steve Winter/Black Star; **21:** © David Young-Wolff/PhotoEdit; **26:** © Lon C. Deihl/PhotoEdit; **28:** © Sonda Dawes/The Image Works; **30 left:** © James Strachan/Getty Images/Stone; **30 right:** © Leland Bobbe/Getty Images/Stone; **33:** © Jeff Greenberg/PhotoEdit.

CHAPTER 2, p. 38: © Gandee Vasan/Getty Images/The Image Bank; **41:** © BioPhoto/Photo Researchers, Inc.; **42:** Biophoto/PhotoResearchers, Inc.; **45:** © Bill Aron/PhotoEdit; **52:** © A. Glauberman/Photo Researchers, Inc.; **55:** Reprinted with permission from Damasio H, Grabowski T, Frank R, Galaburda AM, Damasio AR: The return of Phineas Gage: Clues about the brain from a famous patient. *Science*, 264:1102–1105. © 1994 American Association for the Advancement of Science. Photo courtesy of H. Damasio, Human Neuroanatomy and Neuroimaging Laboratory, Department of Neurology, University of Iowa; **61:** AP/Wide World Photos; **63 left:** © Alexander Tsiaras/Photo Researchers, Inc.; **63 middle:** © Berwyn MRI Center/Getty Images/Stone; **63 right:** Dr. Michael Phelps and Dr. John Mazziotta; **64:** © Peter Menzel/Material World; **65:** © Tony Freeman/PhotoEdit; **73:** © Robin Nelson/PhotoEdit.

CHAPTER 3, p. 78: © Marin Barraud/Getty Images/Stone; **80:** Library of Congress; **82:** © Philip Condit II/Getty Images/Stone; **84:** © Carolina Biological Supply Company/Phototake; **89 left:** © Robert Harbison; **89 right:** © Robert Harbison; **91:** AP/Wide World Photos; **93:** © Martin Rogers/Stock Boston, LLC; **96:** © Spencer Grant/PhotoEdit; **98:** © Omikron/Photo Researchers, Inc.; **102:** © Gerard Vandeystadt/Photo Researchers, Inc.; **106:** Courtesy of Geotyme Enterprises; **107 top left:** © Kent Meireis/The Image Works; **107 top middle left:** © James Randklev/Getty Images/The Image Bank; **107 top middle right:** © Bernd Euler/plus 49/The Image Works; **107 top right:** © Mike Yamashita/Woodfin Camp & Associates; **107 bottom left:** © David Muench/CORBIS; **107 bottom middle:** © Randi Anglin/Syracuse Newspaper The Image Works; **107 bottom right:** © Pete Turner/Getty Images/The Image Bank; **110:** © Richard Lord Ente/The Image Works; **112:** Simons, D. J., & Chabris, C. F. (1999). Gorillas in our midst: Sustained inattentional blindness for dynamic events. *Perception*, *28*, 1059–1074; **114:** © Larry Williams/CORBIS.

CHAPTER 4, p. 118: © Chip Simons/Getty Images/The Image Bank; **122:** © Firefly Productions/CORBIS; **123:** © Reza Estakhrian/Getty Images/Stone; **128:** © Kent Meireis/The Image Works; **133:** MATRIX RELOADED, Keanu Reeves, Lung Yun Chao, 2003, © Warner Brothers/Courtesy Everett Collection; **134:** © Louis Psihoyos; **137:** © Michael Newman/PhotoEdit; **138:** © Robert Frerck/Getty Images/Stone; **145:** © Tony Freeman/PhotoEdit; **146:** © Ghislian & Marie David de Lossy/Getty Images/The Image Bank; **148:** © Michael Richards/PhotoEdit; **151:** © Michael Newman/PhotoEdit.

CHAPTER 5, p. 156: © James D. Wilson/Woodfin Camp & Associates; **158:** AP/Wide World Photos; **160:** © Bettmann/CORBIS; **163:** © Yellow Dog Productions/Getty Images/The Image Bank; **165:** Archives of the History of American Psychology—University of Akron; **167:** © Kevin Laubacher/Getty Images/Taxi; **168:** Courtesy of the National Fluid Milk Processor Promotion Board; **172:** © Nina Leen/Time Life Pictures/Getty Images; **174:** © Arthur Tilley/Getty Images/Taxi; **176:** © Christoph Wilhelm/Getty Images/Taxi; **180:** © Jeff Greenberg/The Image Works; **182:** © Rachel Epstein/PhotoEdit; **188 all:** Courtesy of Dr. Albert Bandura, Stanford University; **189:** © 2003 Laura Dwight.

CHAPTER 6, p. 194: © Bill Bachmann/The Image Works; **196:** AP/Wide World Photos; **198:** © Kent Wood/Photo Researchers, Inc.; **200:** © Chris Trotman/CORBIS; **203:** Royalty-Free/CORBIS; **205:** © Grantpix/Photo Researchers, Inc.; **207:** © James Shaffer/PhotoEdit; **209:** AP/Wide World Photos; **210:** © M & E Bernheim/Woodfin Camp & Associates; **217:** © Michael Newman/PhotoEdit.

CHAPTER 7, p. 230: © Andy Sacks/Getty Images/Stone; **234:** AP/Wide World Photos; **235 left:** © Jim Simncen/Getty Images/Stone; **235 right:** © Art Wolfe/Getty Images/Stone; **240:** © Jeff Greenberg/PhotoEdit; **244:** © Topham Picture Point/The Image Works; **245:** AP/Wide World Photos; **247:** © Geoff Tompkinson/Science Photo Library/Photo Researchers, Inc.; **250:** © Owen Franken/CORBIS; **253:** Royalty-Free/CORBIS.

CHAPTER 8, p. 260: © David Young-Wolff/PhotoEdit; **262:** AP/Wide World Photos; **264:** © Jim Cummins/Getty Images/Taxi; **265 left:** © Bernard Wolf; **265 middle:** © Rafael Macia/Photo Researchers, Inc.; **265 right:** © B&C Alexander/Photo Researchers, Inc.; **270:** © Lew Merim/Photo Researchers, Inc.; **275:** © Lon C. Diehl/PhotoEdit; **278:** © Portfield/Chickering/Photo Researchers, Inc.; **279:** © 1995 Syracuse Newspapers/Peter Chen/The Image Works; **284:** © Charles Gupton/Getty Images/Stone; **287:** © Jim Craigmyle/CORBIS; **288:** © Arlene Collins; **292:** © Kirk McCoy/Material World.

CHAPTER 9, p. 298: © Jose Carillo/PhotoEdit; **300:** © Derek Hudson/CORBIS; **302:** © David Young-Wolff/PhotoEdit; **304 left:** © Francis Leroy/Science Photo Library/Photo Researchers, Inc.; **304 middle:** © Lennart Nilsson, A Child Is Born/Bonniers; **304 right:** © Lennart Nilsson, A Child Is Born/Bonniers; **306:** © George Steinmetz; **310:** © Mark Richards/PhotoEdit; **313:** © Martin Rogers/Stock Boston, LLC; **315:** © Laura Dwight/PhotoEdit; **317 both:** © Doug Goodman/Photo Researchers, Inc.; **324:** © Frank Siteman/PhotoEdit; **328 top:** © Robert E. Daemmrich/Getty Images/Stone; **328 bottom:** © Bob Daemmrich/The Image Works; **332:** AP/Wide World Photos; **334:** © Ariel Skelley/CORBIS.

CHAPTER 10, p. 338: © Jon Riley/Index Stock; **340 middle:** AP/Wide World Photos; **340 bottom:** © Bill Bachman/The Image Works; **343:** © George Shelley/CORBIS; **344:** © David Young-Wolff/PhotoEdit; **350:** © Paul Barton/CORBIS; **353:** © Steve Skjold/PhotoEdit; **361 top:** © Will and Demi McIntyre/Photo Researchers, Inc.; **361 bottom:** © Paul Barton/CORBIS; **363:** © Jim Craigmyle/CORBIS; **364:** © David Young-Wolff/PhotoEdit; **365 both:** © Howard J. Radzyner/Phototake; **367 left:** © Ariel Skelley/CORBIS; **367 right:** © David Young-Wolff/PhotoEdit; **369:** © HIRB/Index Stock.

CHAPTER 11, p. 372: © Stu Forster/Allsport/Getty Images; **377:** © Anthony Neste; **378:** © Don Mason/CORBIS; **381:** Prentice Hall, Inc.; **382:** © Bruce Forster/Getty Images/Stone; **383 both:** © Gregory Pace/CORBIS; **385:** AP/Wide World Photos; **388:** © REUTERS/Robert Galbraith/CORBIS; **395:** © Myrleen Ferguson Cate/PhotoEdit; **396 all:** Reprinted by permission of the Human Interaction Laboratory/© Paul Ekman 1975; **397:** © Wally McNamee/CORBIS; **403:** © Spencer Grant/PhotoEdit.

CHAPTER 12, p. 408: © Myrleen Ferguson Cate/PhotoEdit; **410:** © Bettmann/CORBIS; **412 top:** © Peter Cade/Getty Images/Stone; **412 bottom:** © Arnold Gold/New Haven Register/The Image Works; **417 left:** © Richard Hutchings/Photo Researchers, Inc.; **417 right:** © Carl Glassman/The Image Works; **422:** © 1998 Tom & DeAnn McCarthy/CORBIS; **425:** © Jeff Christensen/REUTERS/CORBIS; **427:** © Bob Daemmrich/Stock Boston, LLC; **434:** AP/Wide World Photos; **436:** © Lori Adamski Peek/Getty Images/Stone.

CHAPTER 13, p. 440: © Ryan McVay/Getty Images/PhotoDisc Green; **442:** © David McNew/Getty Images; **443:** © Michael Greenlar/The Image Works; **446:** © Spencer Grant/PhotoEdit; **447:** © M. Granitsas/The Image Works; **449:** © Ariel Skelley/CORBIS; **454:** © Jose Luis Pelaez, Inc./CORBIS; **455:** © Paul S. Howell/Liaison Agency; **458:** © Ronnie Kaufman/CORBIS; **463:** © Sonda Dawes/The Image Works.

CHAPTER 14, p. 468: © FujiPhotos/The Image Works; **470:** © Bettmann/CORBIS; **472:** © Hulton-Deutsch Collection/CORBIS; **476:** © Tom Prettyman/PhotoEdit; **478:** © Bettmann/CORBIS;

480: © Zefa Visual Media—Germany/Index Stock; **482:** © Bettmann/CORBIS; **486:** AP/Wide World Photos; **487:** © Ariel Skelley/CORBIS; **490:** © Chris Arend/Getty Images/Stone.

CHAPTER 15, p. 502: © Dion Ogust/The Image Works; **504:** AP/Wide World Photos; **505 left:** © Robert Harbison; **505 right:** © Dean Conger/CORBIS; **513:** © Spencer Grant/PhotoEdit; **518:** AP/Wide World Photos; **521:** © Will Hart; **524:** PhotoDisc/Getty Images; **529:** © Jose Pelaez/CORBIS.

CHAPTER 16, p. 534: © Bob Daemmrich/The Image Works; **537 left:** AP/Wide World Photos; **537 right:** © Michael Rougier/Time Life Pictures/Getty Images; **539:** © CORBIS; **540:** © Bruce Ayers/Getty Images/Stone; **541:** © David Young-Wolff/PhotoEdit; **542:** © Geri Engberg/The Image Works; **550:** © W & D McIntyre/Photo Researchers, Inc.; **555:** © Michael Newman/PhotoEdit; **557:** © Jose Pelaez/CORBIS.

CHAPTER 17, p. 560: © Roby Bettolini/Granata/The Image Works; **562:** From the film *Obedience*, copyright 1965 by Stanley Milgram and distributed by Penn State Media Sales; **563:** © C. Gatewood/The Image Works; **565:** © J. Christopher Briscoe/Photo Researchers, Inc.; **566:** © Tony Freeman/PhotoEdit; **568:** William Vandivert/Scientific American; **571:** © Mark Richards/PhotoEdit; **572:** Philip G. Zimbardo, Inc.; **576:** AP/Wide World Photos; **577:** © AFP Photo/Manny Ceneta/CORBIS; **578:** © Robert Brenner/PhotoEdit; **582:** © Paul Gish; **585:** © Gary A. Conner/PhotoEdit.

CHAPTER 18, p. 592: © Farmhouse Productions/Getty Images/The Image Bank; **595:** © Steven Rubin/The Image Works; **600 top:** © Walter Hodges/Getty Images/Stone; **600 bottom:** AP/Wide World Photos; **601:** AP/Wide World Photos; **604:** © Franco Vogt/CORBIS; **605:** © Jose Luis Pelaez, Inc./CORBIS; **609:** AP/Wide World Photos; **612:** © RNT Productions/CORBIS; **615:** © Adamsmith Productions/CORBIS; **616 top:** © Tom Prettyman/PhotoEdit; **616 bottom:** PhotoDisc Green/Getty Images; **622:** PhotoDisc Red/Getty Images.

Text and Art

CHAPTER 1

Figure 1.3, p. 29: Buunk, B. P., Angleitner, A., Oubaid, V., & Buss, D. M. (1996), "Sex differences in jealousy in evolutionary and cultural perspectives: Tests from the Netherlands, Germany, and the United States," *Psychological Science*, 1996, 7, pp. 359–363.

CHAPTER 3

Figure 3.8, p. 95: From John P. J. Pinel, *Biopsychology*, Fourth Edition. Copyright © 1999 by Allyn and Bacon. Reprinted with permission.

Figure 3.9(b), p. 98: From John P. J. Pinel, *Biopsychology*, Fourth Edition. Copyright © 1999 by Allyn and Bacon. Reprinted with permission.

Figure 3.10, p. 99: Reprinted from *Proceedings of the National Academy of Sciences*, Vol. 90, p. 3594, April 1993. Copyright 1993 National Academy of Sciences, U.S.A.

CHAPTER 4

Figure 4.3, p. 143: http://monitoringthefuture.org/data/99data/fig99_1.gif

CHAPTER 5

Figure 5.4, p. 164: Pavlov, I. P. (1927). *Conditional Reflexes* (G. V. Anrep, Trans.). London: Oxford University Press.

Figure 5.6, p. 175: Margaret Gladback for Dan Todd, *Scientific American*, November, 1961, p. 96.

Figure 5.8, p. 185: From "Introduction and Removal of Reward and Maze Performance in Rats" by E. Tolman & C. H. Honzik, *University of California Publications in Psychology, 4*, 1930. Reprinted by permission of University of California Press.

CHAPTER 6

Opening vignette, pp. 195–196: *St. Louis Post Dispatch*, Thursday, Sept. 28, 2000, page A8, by Helen O'Neill. Reprinted with permission of The Associated Press.

Figure 6.3, p. 198: From "Short-Term Retention of Individual Verbal Items" by L.R. Peterson & M. J. Peterson, *Journal of Experimental Psychology*, Vol. 58, 1959.

Figure 6.6, p. 210: From R. N. Haber, "Eidetic Images Are Not Just Imaginary," *Psychology Today*, Vol. 14, 1980, p. 74. Copyright © 1980 (Sussex Publishers, Inc.)

Figure 6.8, p. 215: From E. A. Maguire, D. G. Gadian, I. S. Johnsrude, C. D. Good, J. Ashburner, R. S. J. Franowaik, and C. D. Frick (2000), *Proceedings of the National Academy of Sciences, 97*, pp. 4398–4403.

Try It 6.2, p. 219: Drawing based on R. S. Nickerson & M. J. Adams, "Long-Term Memory for a Common Object," *Cognitive Psychology*, Vol. 11, p. 297, copyright © 1979 by Academic Press, reproduced by permission of the publisher.

Figure 6.13, p. 240: Adapted from G. H. Bower, "How to, uh, Remember," *Psychology Today*, 1973, pp. 63–70.

CHAPTER 7

Figure 7.1, p. 233: Reprinted with permission from R. N. Shepard & J. Metzler, "Mental Rotation of Three-Dimensional Objects," *Science*, Vol. 171 (2/19/71), p. 701+. Copyright 1971 by the American Association for the Advancement of Science.

Figure 7.2, p. 236: From Linda B. Smith (2003), "Learning to Recognize Objects," *Psychological Science, 14*, pp. 244–250.

Try It 7.1, p. 243: From *Solve It! A Perplexing Profusion of Puzzles* by James F. Fixx. Copyright © 1978 by James F. Fixx. Used by permission of Doubleday, a division of Random House, Inc.

Figure 7.3, p. 251: From David Premack, "Language in Chimanzees?" *Science*, Vol. 172, pp. 808–822. Copyright 1971 by the AAAS.

Figure 7.5, p. 255: From Kenji Hakuta, Ellen Bialystock, and Edward Wiley (2003), "Critical Evidence: A Test of the Critical-Period Hypothesis for Second Language Acquisition," *Psychological Science*, 14, pp. 31–38.

CHAPTER 8

Figure 8.4, p. 275: From Ian J. Deary and Con Stough, "Intelligence and Inspection Time: Achievements, Prospects and Problems," *American Psychologist*, June 1996, Vol. 51, No. 6, pp. 599–601, Fig. 1. Copyright © 1996 by the American Psychological Association. Reprinted with permission.

Figure 8.7, p. 282: From F. A. Campbell and C. T. Ramey (1994), "Effects of Achievement: A Follow-up Study of Children from Low-Income Families," Fig. 1, p. 690, *Child Development, 65*, pp. 684–698.

Try It 8.1, p. 287: From *Emotional Intelligence* by Daniel Goleman, Copyright © 1995 by Daniel Goleman. Used by permission of Bantam Books, a division of Random House, Inc.

Figure 8.8, p. 290: Reprinted from *Neuropsychologia*, Volume 38, Issue 6: Ingegerd Carlsson, Peter E. Wend, and Jarl Risberg, " On the Neurobiology of Creative Differences in Frontal Activity Between High and Low Creative Subjects," June 2000, with permission from Elsevier Science.

CHAPTER 9

Figure 9.2, p. 309: Taken in part from *Denver II Training Manual* by W. K. Frankenburg, J. Dodds, P. Archer, et al., 1992. Published by Denver Developmental materials, Inc. Denver, CO. Reprinted by permission of W. K. Frankenburg.

Figure 9.4, p. 320: From Laura E. Berk, *Child Development*, Third Edition. Copyright © 1994 by Allyn and Bacon. Reprinted with permission.

CHAPTER 10

Figure 10.2, p. 348: From A. Colby, L. Kohlberg, J. Gibbs, and M. Lieberman (1983), "A Longitudinal Study of Moral Judgment," *Monographs of the Society for Research in Child Development, 48*(1–2, Serial No. 2000), Fig. 1, p. 46. Reprinted with permission.

CHAPTER 12

Figure 12.1, p. 416: Illustrations by Jared Schneidman from "Sex Differences in the Brain" by Doreen Kimura, *Scientific American*, September 1992, pp. 120, 121. Reprinted by permission of the artist.

Try It 12.1, p. 431: www.unspeakable.com

Try It 12.2, p. 433: http://onhealth.webmd.com/home/interactives/conditions/188_02asp

Apply It, p. 436: From Spencer A. Rathus, Jeffrey S. Nevid, & Lois Fichner-Rathus, *Human Sexuality in a World of Diversity*, Fourth Edition. Copyright © 2000 by Allyn and Bacon. Reprinted by permission.

CHAPTER 13

Table 13.1, p. 445: from Allen D. Kanner, James C. Coyne, C. Schaefer, and R. S. Lazarus, "Comparison of Two Modes of Stress Management: Daily Hassles and Uplifts Versus Major Life Events," *Journal of Behavioral Medicine, 4*, 1981, pp. 1–39.

Figure 13.4, p. 451: From "Personal Control and Stress and Coping Process: A Theoretical Analysis" by Susan K. Folkman, *Journal of Personality and Social Psychology, 46*, 1984, pp. 839–852. Copyright 1984 by the American Psychological Association. Adapted by permission of the publisher and author.

Figure 13.5, p. 453: From Judith Green and Robert D. Schellenberger, *The Dynamics of Health and Wellness: A Biopsychosocial Approach*, Fig. 1.3. Copyright © 1991 by Holt, Rinhart and Winston, Inc.

CHAPTER 14

Figure 14.1, p. 471: Freud, S. *New Introductory Lectures on Psychoanalysis*. New York: Norton, 1965. Page 111. Found in David G. Myers, *Psychology*, Sixth Editon, Worth Publications.

Figure 14.4, p. 485: Adapted from Cattell's *16PF® Fifth Edition Profile Sheet*. Copyright © 1993 by the Institute for Personality and Ability Testing, Inc., P.O. Box 1188, Champaign, IL, U.S.A. 61824-1188. Used with permission.

CHAPTER 15

Figure 15.4, p. 515: "Cross-national epidemiology of major depression and bipolar disorder." Weissman, M. M., Bland, R. C., Canino, G. J., Faravelli, C., Greenwald, S., Hwu, H. G., Joyce, P. R., Karam, E. G., Lee, C. K., Lellouch, J., Lepine, J. P., Wittchen, H., and Yeh, E. K. *Journal of the American Medical Association*, 1996, July 24–31, 276: 4293–9.

CHAPTER 17

Figure 17.6, p. 579: From "Crime in the United States," Federal Bureau of Investigation, 1999.